THE DISPUTE OF THE NEW WORLD

THE
DISPUTE
OF THE
NEW WORLD

The History of a Polemic, 1750-1900

BY

ANTONELLO GERBI

REVISED AND ENLARGED EDITION
TRANSLATED BY

JEREMY MOYLE

UNIVERSITY OF PITTSBURGH PRESS

Originally published in Italy, 1955, as *La disputa del Nuovo Mondo: Storia di una polemica, 1750–1900* by Riccardo Ricciardi Editore, Milano–Napoli. All rights reserved.

Library of Congress Catalog Card Number 70–181396
ISBN 0–8229–3250–4
Translation copyright © 1973, Jeremy Moyle
All rights reserved
Media Directions Inc., London
Manufactured in the United States of America

Contents

Translator's Preface

THIS English edition of Antonello Gerbi's masterpiece is the delayed sequel to suggestions that began to be heard as soon as the original version of the work was published in Italy in 1955. Reviewers and readers on both sides of the Atlantic expressed the hope that a work dealing with such a fundamental aspect of American civilization might someday become available in English. When I was asked to prepare such a translation I was delighted and flattered, and my subsequent experience confirmed my initial feeling that it was indeed a rare privilege. Not the least of the pleasures it afforded me was the chance to meet the author and spend some time in his company. From the beginning Dr. Gerbi has followed the preparation of the English edition of his work with lively interest and has been unstinting in his advice and help. The result has been a close and entirely harmonious collaboration, which has contributed more than any other factor, I feel, to the successful completion of the project. I am happy to have this chance to thank Dr. Gerbi for his hospitality, courtesy, and patience throughout this period.

Every task of translation has its problems, large and small. The most important of these, in my opinion, is the translator's need to recognize that his work must of necessity fall short of perfection. Each language is a unique and separate entity and the very process of translation is in itself a change in expression, quite apart from any alterations in connotative value that may, or seemingly must, result from the translation. The degree of imperfection, the "imprecision factor," varies with the nature of the text. In a scientific text it may be minimal; in a text where the author's style is an issue it must, regrettably, be somewhat greater. Dr. Gerbi is above all a fine stylist, as more than one reviewer has pointed out. His lightness of touch in dealing with the most abstruse subjects is something quite literally inimitable. In such a case the translator must recognize the limitations inherent in the nature of his undertaking, and attempt the possible; he must endeavor to do justice to each single allusion, suggestion, and innuendo, to say no more than the author says, and no less; and to say it in the way the author says it. This then is what

I have tried to do, and if in so doing I have caught even a respectable proportion of the wit and individuality of the original, I am more than satisfied.

Certain other problems are of a more practical nature, but may perhaps be briefly mentioned, if only to satisfy the reader moved to some curiosity about the rationale behind the solutions adopted. The work includes extensive citations from languages other than English or Italian, most notably Spanish, German, and French. The purist or polyglot would perhaps have liked to see these quotations transcribed in their original form; but this did not seem to me necessary, or even desirable, since with rare exceptions (e.g., Goethe) the passages quoted do not contain, or are not considered for, any literary value, but for their cargo of ideas. The interest is more in what is said than in how it is said. Thus all such citations have been put into English (the translations being my own, unless otherwise indicated).

The other more practical problems relate to questions of style, and particularly to italicizing and capitalization. Here the curious reader's demand for a rationale is less easily satisfied, since there is in fact no "reason" why one chooses to put a capital here and italics there. The only guide is custom, an elusive and ephemeral mentor at best. Who can say at what point the *philosophe* is sufficiently accepted into English to become a philosophe, or the *indios* linguistically integrated enough to become plain indios? The decisions are subjective, and one can only hope they do not conflict too radically with the reader's. In capitalization the same holds true. It is agreed that it is sometimes acceptable or proper to capitalize terms when they are conceptualized or personified; but who is there to tell one whether a notion is sufficiently specialized for capitals to be required? An open mind is the first essential, and nowhere more so than in the discussions that form the subject of the present work. Every historian or philosopher has met and manipulated the concepts of Progress and Reason, Beauty and Truth, Nature and Society; but he must not now be surprised that a Beard, a Moose, and a Giant can become concepts too; they can and do, and indeed without such concepts there would be no Dispute of the New World.

J.M.

Preface

THE author's preface, according to the most authoritative manuals of style, should begin by stating his reasons for undertaking the work. I once had such reasons, of course, but in the subsequent research and the actual process of drafting the work they were so superseded and absorbed that I have some doubt as to whether they are worth mentioning.

When I moved to Peru at the end of 1938, to carry out a study in economic geography, hardly a day passed without my ears being assailed by the eulogy and slander, the panegyric and vituperation of the New World, and, by reaction, the Old. Repeated on every side with disarming candor and unhesitating conviction, these confused expressions of passionate sentiment — consisting for the most part, obviously, of love and hate, apology and polemic — increased by no small amount the already considerable difficulty of delving into the problems raised by the vicissitudes and natural environment of the American continent: problems that are already apparent in Columbus's diary and letters, and that rapidly attain a high level of scientific seriousness in Oviedo's history.

In essence the basic theme of so many diatribes was, quite simply, the notion of the presumed inferiority of the nature of America, and especially its fauna, including man, in comparison with the Old World's, and the resulting unavoidable decadence and corruption to which the whole Western Hemisphere found itself condemned: a rudimentary theme, clearly, but one that bred prolifically, producing innumerable variations and reverberating with multiple echoes, in philosophy, in anthropology, in the satire of society, in the natural sciences, obviously, and, most surprisingly, in poetry.

The pernicious fecundity of the theme should not, however, induce us to extend it too far. This is not a history of the relationships between the two worlds, nor of the many literary, political, scientific, and aesthetic judgments passed by one world on the other. It is the narrative of a particularly successful "heresy" and its various manifestations in the most diverse authors.

The underlying motif was not completely new to me: in my first book,

xi

published in 1928, I had commented on the savage verdict on the American natives pronounced by de Pauw, one of the instigators of the dispute, and some of the responses it provoked. In other works I had touched on the theme of the innocence or innate wickedness of the savage and mentioned Hegel's flatly negative judgment on the whole American continent. But it was only at the end of 1943 that I published in Lima a first summary version of this study under the title *Viejas polémicas sobre el Nuevo Mundo.* The third edition (Lima, 1946) came to some three hundred pages. When I returned to Europe in 1948, I reworked all the material and in 1955 published in Milan *La disputa del Nuovo Mondo: Storia di una polemica,* a volume of almost eight hundred pages.

Μέγα βίβλιον, μέγα κακόν, "the bigger the book, the bigger the mischief." I was so conscious of this, so convinced that I could expect to bring down on my head a storm of criticism, or that I would be accused of heaven-knows-what omissions and lacunae, that almost as a challenge, and half jokingly, I added at the end a "negative bibliography"—a list of books I believed might have some relevance to the topic, but that I had not been able to see for one reason or another. In so doing I was hoping in a way to goad my critics and annihilators and to facilitate their work of denigration.

But not even with this device did I achieve what I had hoped for. And the "negative bibliography," included again in the Spanish edition (Mexico, 1960), has been more aptly retitled, in the present English edition, "Suggestions for Further Research," though the reiterated invitation for its use in rectifying errors or filling in insufficiencies of information or opinion remains unchanged.

This is, in fact, a typical "concertina" work, expandable (or contractible) at the author's whim. In the most unexpected writers one can find still further diatribes, albeit only implicit, on the "inferiority of the Americas." The theme runs underground from Buffon and de Pauw to our own times, but breaks the surface in the most unlikely places and leaves its mark on the most varied opinions, theories, and sophisms. In each separate writer it appears, perforce, in a different guise. But unless I am much mistaken it betrays itself in every one through the same utterly simple and fragile paradox.

The list of acknowledgments that custom requires would be too long for inclusion in this preface. For almost thirty years I have been a grateful recipient of stimulating suggestions and useful information. Perhaps I may be permitted to epitomize all my thanks by mentioning two names only, at the opposite extremities of my research. My gratitude, which may seem naïve, is extended first to that part of the world that gave rise to my awareness of the problem, and kept my interest in it alive, so that an episode in the history of ideas was transformed into a search for myself, myself as a European marooned in the Americas, anxious to reach a better understanding and a more critical awareness of the ideal relationship between two worlds (hence the at times "autobiographical" tone and resulting regrettable unevennesses of style and form). The second name, all too obviously, is that of Dr. Jeremy Moyle, who has translated the book with loving care and untiring patience, rendering every expression and every nuance with admirable precision.

A.G.

Prologue

THERE are several places in Hegel's works where he describes the Americas as an immature or impotent continent, or one that is in some other way "inferior" to the Old World. In expounding these passages the exegetes, even someone like Croce, even Ortega y Gasset, have looked on them as a typical aberration of Hegel's mind, a bizarre relic of his determination to enclose the infinite variety of the world within his scheme of triads. But in fact the thesis was adopted, not invented, by Hegel. And in its brief life-span it has reflected so many tendencies that it is perhaps not altogether idle to inquire into its varying fortunes. The pages that follow attempt to give a first broad outline of such an inquiry.

Their beginning with Buffon results not so much from a desire to plunge the reader *in medias res* as from the fact that in his writings certain observations and judgments and prejudices that up until then had been expressed as curious revelations of distant lands in the descriptions of the early travelers and naturalists in the New World, or as polemic paradoxes and fables in the reports of the missionaries, in the utopias and myths of the noble or evil savage, for the first time assume coherent and scientific form; and particularly because only from Buffon onward does the thesis of the inferiority of the Americas have an uninterrupted history, a precise trajectory passing through de Pauw, touching its vertex with Hegel[1] and then proceeding on a long decline into the mutual recriminations and childish boasts, the brusque condemnations and confused panegyrics so common still in our own times.

The ancient chroniclers of American nature, and in particular the greatest of them, Gonzalo Fernandez de Oviedo (1526, 1535), had already commented carefully and perspicaciously on the many physical peculiarities of the New World and the many differences between the animals of America and those of Europe. But even when they noted certain relatively weak aspects, certain specific deficiencies in the

---

1. Edmundo O'Gorman, "Trayectoria de América," in *Fundamentos de la historia de América* (Mexico, 1942), pp. 85–134, indicated in Buffon and de Pauw the sources of the Hegelian thesis, but without going into detail, and in fact indulging rather in apologetic considerations.

Americas, as did Father Acosta (1590), Antonio de Herrera (1601–15), and Father Cobo (1653), among others, they never reached the point of coordinating their observations in a general thesis of the inferiority of American nature (which in fact they admired and illustrated with loving devotion); nor even less did they conceive theories endowing it with a supposed "immaturity" or "degeneration," using concepts that suggested a development cut short when barely begun, or an exhaustion through old age.

This Buffon did. And under the stimulus of this all-powerful fourfold influence—the strength of Buffon's authority; the formulation of such a dynamic and historicizing concept of nature; the merging of other time-hallowed theories and pseudoscientific tendencies with this new evaluation of the men, the animals, the plants, and the very climate of America; and the maturing of a loftier and clearer self-awareness on the part of Europe simultaneously with the birth of an American patriotism and native pride—the polemic of America flared up on various levels, to burn on unquenched for several decades on both sides of the Atlantic.

Its threads are mingled and twisted together and are of diverse hue, of varied thickness and length. There are some that go all the way back to Aristotle, and even beyond. But unravel them we must, if we are not to find ourselves caught once again in their tangled skein.

From a more general point of view the history of this error has another claim on our interest. The facts on which the theories of the New World's inferiority were based were in many cases real. It is geologically true that America's mountain chains seem relatively recent and not yet completely mature. It is true that an unhealthy humidity prevails in many areas. It is true that the continent hosts a profusion of harmful insects, while lacking not only the great carnivores but many other larger animals. It is true that many of its peoples are beardless, others relatively weak, and yet others apparently incapable of civil progress. And it is true that certain species of animals were never successfully acclimatized there or else became sterile in the second generation. It is also very true that all these debates, however ill founded they were, contributed to the advancement of the science of nature, refining its methods, prying it painfully away from old errors, and enriching its material.

Why then, when we turn our attention back to it again today, do we call the thesis of the inferiority of the Americas an "error"? For one substantial reason and (if we may be a little pedantic) for three formal reasons. *Substantialiter,* because the above-mentioned elements of fact lose their validity when they are utilized in support of a thesis. *Formaliter,* because very often, too often, the single example was generalized into a universal rule, and the weakness of a native, the marshiness of a valley, the unusual appearance of a mountain chain were passed on, as if through the effect of some kind of paralyzing contagion, to all the races and valleys and mountains of the continent.

In other cases, moreover, and indeed often in the same cases, those objectively solid facts were hypostatized into value judgments, and to the improper generalization was thus added an improper pejorative qualification, with the assumption, sometimes implicit, sometimes explicit, that the beardless man is inferior to the bearded man, the swamp is worse than the desert, the lack of wild animals or deep geological strata is a stigma of telluric impotence, and the "giraffe" is "good" and the "cockroach," "bad."

And lastly, in the great majority of cases, factual data, particulars of information, and details of geography, zoology, and botany were illegitimately polarized, items that were and still are true in themselves, but are neither true nor false when placed in opposition to other data, elements, and details. The very basic antithesis between Old World and New World, the root of all those other single antitheses, has no existence outside the schemes of an impassioned and systematizing abstract and polemic mentality, directed now against the Old World, now against the New. The tiger, the savage, the marsh, and the beard — empirical realities and not concepts — were conceptualized in opposition to other individual phenomena, from which they were certainly distinct: an error born from an abuse of formal logic, and anticipating that corruption of the dialectic that in Hegel himself was to achieve the fatuous splendor of an immaterial architecture, the symphonic glory of the *chimaera bombinans in vacuo.*

Corruptio optimi pessima. I am afraid the pages that follow will offer more than enough to convince us of this sad fact. As viaticum and critical memento I have nothing better to offer than the ambiguous smile of Father Acosta, great eulogizer of the Indies, historiographer of a robust, mature, and fruitful America, who notes that the plants taken from the new lands to Spain "are few, and do not take well," while those "that have come from Spain are many, and thrive," and adds with gentle sarcasm: "I do not know if we can say that this is brought about by the goodness of the plants, so as to give the glory to this continent, or if we must say that it is the effect of the soil, and thus the glory of that other continent."[2]

The glory of one hemisphere or the other, glory of the seed or the sod? Father Acosta's skeptical alternative had already been answered by the sound good sense of Oviedo. The true reason why good vines do not grow

2. Joseph de Acosta, *Historia natural y moral de las Indias,* 1590, IV, 31; ed. Madrid, 1608, pp. 270–71; cf. ibid., IV, 18; ed. cit., pp. 242–43.

in Santo Domingo "is not to be found in the plant, nor in the earth . . .
but in human industry and in the laziness of the men."[3] It is the device
of the slothful to excuse themselves by accusing nature. Nature is not
better on this side or that side of the Atlantic. She has no absolute
preferences or antipathies, pays no heed to the vaunted claims of the
furrow or the grain, and does not stoop to flatter those poor vain hopes
of a supremacy whatsoever, the *idola tribus* and *idola fori,* puffed up
with the eternal boastful arrogance of nations and worlds.

3. Fernández de Oviedo, *Historia general y natural de las Indias.* VIII, 24, ed. Amador de los Rios
(Madrid, 1851–55), I, 310a.

THE DISPUTE OF THE NEW WORLD

Buffon and the Inferiority of the Animal Species of America

I. THE ABSENCE OF LARGE WILD ANIMALS

THE origins of the thesis of the "weakness" or "immaturity" of the Americas—if one discounts the occasional image in the Elizabethan poets, Donne's "that unripe side of earth,"[1] or Samuel Daniel's "yet unformed Occident"[2]—can be traced back to Buffon in the middle of the eighteenth century.

It was one of Buffon's most important discoveries, and one of which he himself was particularly proud,[3] that the animal species of the Old World *differed* from those of South America. And not only were those of the New World different, but in many cases inferior, weaker. When he is describing the American lion, or puma, he perceives with a sudden flash of intuition that this so-called lion is not a lion at all, but some other beast, peculiar to America, and in no way to be identified with the king of the beasts of the Old World. For a start, it has no mane, and then "it is also much smaller, weaker, and more cowardly than the real lion."[4] But

1. "That unripe side of earth" produces men naked like Adam before he ate the apple ("To the Countesse of Huntingdon," 1597, in *Complete Poetry and Selected Prose* [London–New York, 1939], p. 149).
2. In *Musophilos; containing a Generall Defence of Learning* (1599); the phrase is quoted frequently, for example, by C. Sumner in *Prophetic Voices Concerning America* (Boston, 1874), p. 7; and in *The Oxford Companion to English Literature*, ed. P. Harvey (Oxford, 1936), s.v. *Musophilos*. There is of course no lack of comment, particularly in the seventeenth century, on the scarcity or low quality of the animal and vegetable species: see Gustav H. Blanke, *Amerika im englischen Schrifttum des 16. und 17. Jahrhunderts* (Bochum-Langendreer, 1962), p. 117.
3. See chap. 9, sec. 1, "The Originality of Buffon."
4. *Oeuvres de Buffon* (ed. in quarto, ed., la Imprimerie Royale), IX, 13, quoted by P. Flourens, *Histoire des travaux et des idées de Buffon*, 2d ed. (Paris, 1850), pp. 133, 275. In the discourse on "Les Animaux de l'Ancien Continent," which prefaces the description of the individual species, Buffon says: "We shall see in discussing the lion that this animal did not exist at all in America, and that the puma of Peru is an animal of a different species" (*Oeuvres complètes*, ed. Richard [Paris: Delangle, 1824–28], XV, 404).

the sudden insight that had dawned on him when comparing the puma and the lion is extended in the same breath to cover the whole series of larger mammals. The animals file past him one after another as though they were just coming forth from Noah's ark. One by one the naturalist looks them over, and each in turn is refused American citizenship, *jure sanguinis et jure soli*.

"Elephants belong to the Old Continent and are not found in the New . . . one cannot even find there any animal that can be compared to the elephant for size or shape."[5] The only animal that bears a remote similarity is the tapir of Brazil, but this creature, America's largest, "this elephant of the New World," writes Buffon, with heavy irony (as if to say "this ridiculous little miniature elephant of the Americas"), "is the size of a six-month-old calf, or a very small mule."[6] It is a newborn calf, a baby mule, a pocket pachyderm.

There are no rhinoceroses. Nor hippopotamuses. Camels, dromedaries, giraffes are completely unknown. "There are no real monkeys in America."[7] The type of camel known as a llama is an even more wretched creature than the tapir. It looks big "on account of its extended neck and the length of its legs." But even if it stands on stilts and cranes its neck, it remains a small animal: "The *pacos* is much smaller still."[8] The comparisons could be continued. But they all confirm that the biggest American animals are "four, six, eight, and ten times" smaller than those of the Old Continent.

At the same time the species of quadrupeds are much less numerous in the New World than in the Old. Buffon counts one hundred and thirty in the Old and less than seventy in the New. The latter has therefore a more limited selection of species, and those which it has are generally more puny. The immediate conclusion is unavoidable: "Living nature is thus much less active there, much less varied, and we may even say, less strong."[9]

5. *Oeuvres complètes*, XV, 402.
6. Ibid., pp. 429–30. And elsewhere, with even more evident contempt: "This tapir, this elephant of the New World, has neither trunk nor defenses and is scarce bigger than a donkey!" ("Des époques de la Nature," in *Oeuvres complètes*, V, 224).
7. Cf., *contra*, Fr. Acosta: "There are innumerable monkeys" (*Historia natural y moral*, IV, 39; ed. cit., p. 333). The passage is quoted also by Garcilaso, *Comentarios reales de los Incas* (ed. Rosenblat, Buenos Aires, 1943), VIII, 18.
8. *Oeuvres complètes*, XV, 402–04, 429–30, 435. On the morphological relations between the giraffe, the camel, and the llama, see also XIX, 46. Cf. below, chap. 7, n. 311: the llama, "a fine diminutive" of the camel.
9. *Oeuvres complètes*, XV, 429. This summary verdict is quoted in a footnote by Marmontel, *Les Incas* (Paris, 1777), p. 22, and paraphrased by Flourens, op. cit., p. 145. As the examples show and, moreover, as he himself sometimes cautions, Buffon nearly always had in mind only South America. In North America there are a few Old World species (the wolf, the reindeer, the fallow deer, certain fur animals)—a fact which causes him serious embarrassment (see H. Daudin, *De Linné à Jussieu* [Paris, 1926], p. 142; also below, n. 103 and chap. 5, n. 434). Even today the problems of the South American

II. THE DETERIORATION OF THE DOMESTIC ANIMALS

This weakness of nature is confirmed by the fate of such domestic animals as were introduced into America by the Europeans. It is one long story of failure. In the new continent all of them dwindled, shrank, became reduced to dwarves, caricatures in miniature of their prototypes:

The horses, donkeys, oxen, sheep, goats, pigs, dogs, all these animals, I say, became smaller there; and . . . those which were not transported there, and which went there of their own accord, those, in short, common to both worlds, such as wolves, foxes, deer, roebuck, and moose, are likewise considerably smaller in America than in Europe, and *that without exception*.[10]

Sheep and goats were successfully acclimatized in America, but "they are generally thinner." The rams "in general are of less tender and less succulent flesh than in Europe." And to sum up — but always "in general" — one may say that "of all the domestic animals transported from Europe to America the pig is the one which has had the best and most general success."[11]

III. THE HOSTILITY OF NATURE

The argument can thus take a step forward. Indigenous animals are few and small. Imported animals have become smaller and less appetizing (with the exception of the pig). Thus the environment or nature of America is hostile to the development of animals. The purely geographical comparison is succeeded by a genetic criterion, and in this direction Buffon forges fearlessly ahead to extend his observations on quadrupeds to all "living nature":

There is thus, in the combination of the elements and other physical causes, something antagonistic to the increase of living nature in this new world: there are obstacles to the development and perhaps even to the formation of the great seeds; those very seeds which have received their fullest form, their most complete extension, under the beneficial influence of another climate, are here reduced, shrunken beneath this ungenerous sky and in this empty land, where man, scarce in number, was thinly spread, a wanderer, where far from making himself master of this territory as his own domain, he ruled over nothing; where having never subjugated either animals or the elements, nor tamed the waters, nor governed the rivers, nor worked the earth, he was himself no more than an animal

fauna remain largely unsolved; see the provocative observations of H. Krieg, "Tiergeographische und ökologische Beobachtungen und Probleme in Südamerika," in *Tier und Umwelt in Südamerika* (Hamburg, 1940), pp. 1–34.

10. *Oeuvres complètes*, XV, 444. Cf. J. Roger, *Les sciences de la vie dans la pensée française du XVIIIᵉ siècle* (Paris, 1963), pp. 574–75. There may be an element of truth in this thesis. In America the art of stockbreeding remained for a long time in arrears of the more advanced European techniques (cf. Daniel J. Boorstin, *The Americans: The Colonial Experience* [New York, 1966], p. 261). And the natural pastures of America were inferior in nutritive value to those of the Old World (Franklin J. Jameson, *The American Revolution Considered as a Social Movement* [Princeton, 1940], pp. 50–51).

11. *Oeuvres complètes*, XV, 412, 414.

of the first order, existing within nature as a creature without significance, a sort of helpless automaton, powerless to change nature or assist her. And she, Nature, had treated him less as mother than as stepmother, withholding from him the sentiment of love or the strong desire to multiply. For although the savage of the New World is of almost the same stature as the men of our world, that does not suffice for him to be an exception to the general rule of the reduction of living nature in the whole continent. The savage is feeble and small in his organs of generation; he has neither body hair nor beard, and no ardor for the female of his kind. Although lighter than the European, on account of his habit of running more, he is nevertheless much less strong in body: he is also much less sensitive, and yet more fearful and more cowardly; he lacks vivacity, and is lifeless in his soul; the activity of his body is less an exercise or voluntary movement than an automatic reaction to his needs; take from him hunger and thirst, and you will destroy at the same time the active cause of all his movements; he will remain either standing there stupidly or recumbent for days at a time.[12]

IV. THE IMPOTENCE OF THE SAVAGE

The passage is important above all for the function that it assigns to man. Being few in number and weak, the men of the New World were unable to tame a hostile nature, to conquer and subjugate her virgin power and turn it to their own profit. Instead of collaborating in the development of the animal species and the improvement of domestic types, man himself remained subject to the "control" of nature, a passive element in nature, an animal like the rest—hardly *primus inter pares*. Unwittingly Buffon lets himself be drawn on by the thread of his own argument and extends his negative verdict on the quadrupeds to the American savage. Man is no exception. In fact, he is rather worse off than the other animals on account of this sexual frigidity of his: "Nature, refusing him the powers of love, has maltreated and belittled him more than any other animal."[13]

The particular connection between the impotence of the savage and the absence of large wild beasts—an idea typical of that subtly scabrous eroticism of the eighteenth century—seems to suggest to Buffon another great step forward in his argument. The savage is cold. The snake is cold. Cold-blooded animals are cold. In America reptiles and insects abound

12. Ibid., pp. 443–46; cf. Roger, op. cit., p. 562. The loss of stature as a sign of degeneration, as well as the explanation of this by means of the obstacles to the *grands germes*, can be traced back to Pliny, who saw the human race "in the future becoming less rich in seed on account of its progressive drying-out through use" (*Naturalis Historia*, VII, 15, quoted by A. Lovejoy and G. Boas, *Primitivism and Related Ideas in Antiquity* [Baltimore, 1935], pp. 101–02). The absence of hair, which was to give rise to so much discussion, can be traced back, among modern authors, to de Maillet, who had noted in the *Telliamed* (1748), in words identical to those of Buffon, that "the Americans . . . have neither body hair nor beard" (*Telliamed, ou entretiens d'un philosophe indien . . .* , 2d ed. [Paris, 1755], II, 215; but already the editor of this "new edition" noted that "Telliamed is mistaken" because the savages remove the hair they have by plucking it and use depilatories!).

13. *Oeuvres complètes*, XV, 446–47; and L. Bertin et al., *Buffon* (collection Les Grands Naturalistes Français [Paris, 1952]), p. 80. On the other hand Rousseau (*Discours sur l'inégalité* [Paris, 1839], pp. 549–50) naturally praised the erotic moderation of the savage as proof of his placid obedience to natural instinct, being excited neither by murky fantasies, nor female wiles, nor absurd jealousies.

and often in gigantic size. There is no part of the world where the insects are so large as in America. "Toads, frogs, and other beasts of this kind are also very sizable in America."[14] Half the animal kingdom swells, while the other half shrinks. What is required is *one* explanation that can account for the *two* phenomena:

Let us now see why there are found in this new world such large reptiles, such big insects, such small quadrupeds, and such cold men. This is accounted for by the quality of the earth, the condition of the sky, the degree of warmth and humidity, the situation, the elevation of the mountains, the quantity of running or stagnant waters, the extent of the forests, and above all the crude state in which nature is found.[15]

Et voilà pourquoi votre fille est malade!

V. THE COLD AND HUMIDITY OF THE AMERICAN ENVIRONMENT

But this confused compendium of causes brings to the fore two very relevant features: the crude state of nature and the marshy aspect of the country. Oviedo had already repeated almost to the point of excess that "these Indies are a very wet land," that "this land is very wet," etc.,[16] and Father Acosta had gone so far as to say (1590) that in fact "the greater part of America, on account of this excess of water, is not fit for habitation."[17] And the reason? The great strength of the sun which draws up the vapors of the ocean and in the cool of the afternoon brings about their condensation into rain[18] — an incomplete meteorological explanation, but more rational than that of a flood or an imperfect drying out.

Buffon in his turn portrays the miry continent with all the magic of his descriptive style, giving us a profuse foretaste of Victor Hugo's poetic land "still soft and sodden from the flood" where man makes the disturbing discovery of the giants' footprints (*Booz endormi*), and of that unformed Brazil where "the land has still the softness of the earliest times."[19] The naturalist describes in vivid colors the warm soft climate, with its moist unhealthy vapors which promote the dense growth of a suffocating vegetation, and he concludes:

In this state of abandon, everything languishes, decays, stifles. The air and the earth, weighed down by the moist and poisonous vapors, cannot purify themselves nor profit from the influence of the star of life. The sun vainly pours down its liveliest rays on this cold mass, which is incapable of responding to its warmth;

---

14. *Oeuvres complètes*, XV, 447–48. On the hyperbolic dimensions attributed to American frogs, see P. G. Adams, *Travelers and Travel Liars, 1660–1800* (Berkeley, Calif., 1962), p. 233, and see below, p. 300.

15. *Oeuvres completès*, XV, 448.

16. *Historia general y natural*, I, 268b, 289b, 383a, 457b, etc.

17. *Historia natural y moral*, II, 6; ed. cit., p. 103.

18. Ibid., II, 7; ed. cit., p. 107.

19. C. Lévi-Strauss, *Tristes tropiques* (Paris, 1955), p. 178.

it will never produce anything but humid creatures, plants, reptiles, and insects; and cold men and feeble animals are all that it will ever nurture.[20]

So we come back to the point of departure, according to which nature in America is weak because man has not tamed it, and man has not tamed it because he in his turn is cold in love and more similar to the cold-blooded animals, closer to the watery putrescent character of the continent. And the erotic-hydraulic explanation of the singularity of American nature goes round and round in this same vicious circle:

It is thus principally because there were few men in America and because the majority of these men, leading an animal-like existence, left nature in its wild state and neglected the earth, that it has remained cold, incapable of producing active principles, developing the seeds of the great quadrupeds, for whose growth and multiplication there are required all the warmth and activity that the sun can give to a loving earth; and it is for the contrary reason that the insects and reptiles, and all the species of animal that crawl in the mud, whose blood is water, and who flourish in putrescence, are more numerous and larger in the low wet marshy lands of this new continent.[21]

The "loving earth" on the one hand and these animals that have water instead of blood in their veins on the other sum up in two vivid images the very nucleus of Buffon's theory.

VI. PUTRESCENCE AND GENERATION — WATER AND LIFE

But what is the origin of this theory linking the humidity of the surroundings with the abundance of insects and snakes? Everything points to its being a leftover of the protracted seventeenth-century debate on the spontaneous generation of worms and vipers from putrefying bodies or sodden earth. Father Kircher was satirized by Redi for his claims to have known snakes to be burned, crumbled to pieces, buried in earth sprinkled with rainwater, and then after eight days to produce "little worms" which when fed on milk and water became "perfectly shaped snakes."[22] Buffon's cold animals "which abound in putrescence" are descended from these "snakes breeding from putrescent matter" against which Redi argued.

20. *Oeuvres complètes*, XV, 452. See also the famous description of the "savannahs of South America . . . peopled with unspeakable animals . . . the cesspools of nature . . . impassable regions, still unformed." swarming with an "impure race" of reptiles and insects "swollen by the humid heat" (in *Morceaux choisis de Buffon* [Paris. 1829], p. 83).

21. *Oeuvres complètes*, XV, 452–54. On the connection Buffon makes between cold and humidity, on the one hand, and weakness, sterility, and death on the other, see Lesley Hanks, *Buffon avant l' "Histoire naturelle"* (Paris, 1966), pp. 173–74, 191. The example used is precisely that of the American forests, although by Buffon's time climatologists had already refuted that ancient theory. Cf. also Bertin, op. cit., p. 71.

22. *Esperienze intorno alla generazione degli insetti* (1668; ed. Florence. 1688), pp. 63–64. Father Kircher also maintained that Noah did not need to take reptiles and insects into the ark, because these animals are born spontaneously from putrefaction (see D. C. Allen, *The Legend of Noah* [Urbana, Ill.,

But in searching for the antecedents of the thesis of spontaneous generation from putrescent matter, one can go all the way back to Aristotle, for whom it explained the appearance of flies and mosquitoes (in accordance with his general theory of the four elements, in which the corruption of one is the generation of the next). It was reaffirmed specifically for snakes by Pliny, and taken up in modern times as an antiascetic motif by Le Roy (1579), by Vanini (1616),[23] in an apologetic and Catholic function by Tasso (1607),[24] and only defeated and demolished by Pasteur's famous experiments on fermentation. And not even then definitively: in his last treatise Claude Bernard discusses (and does not actually reject) the thesis that "life is a putrefaction . . . life is no more than decay"[25]—a statement with a peculiarly preexistentialist flavor about it.

Buffon, in order to avoid the dogmas of creationism and the theories of preformation, had adopted an expanded theory of "spontaneous generation," based on the incorrect observations (1745–48) of his friend Needham, the microscopist, who had observed swarms of infusorians pullulating in the warm broth of his faultily sealed test tubes.[26] Buffon then was convinced by the idea of inferior forms of life springing from humidity and decayed matter. The decayed, the wet, the newborn thus came to be for him related aspects of a single reality—which helps to explain how his ideas on American nature wavered between "immaturity" and "decadence," between a world in embryo and a world already rotting.

Perhaps Buffon also had in mind the widespread popular belief that toads are born from water or sodden earth. St. Augustine had already mentioned, for example, that "frogs are born from the earth."[27] Father Bartoli repeated that frogs "are formed instantaneously when in summer a

23. For Le Roy, see D. C. Allen, "The Degeneration of Man and Renaissance Pessimism," *Studies in Philology*, 35, no. 2 (April 1938), pp. 225–26. For Vanini, who apparently elaborated the ancient atomistic hypothesis of Epicurus, see G. Spini, *Ricerca dei libertini* (Rome, 1950), p. 130.

24. Monsters and birds of the air that "her extinct body produced from putrid limbs; or seedless and fatherless the ancient mother still produces and bears from her warmed and humid womb" (*Il mondo creato*, VI, 1244–47, ed. Petrocchi [Florence, 1951], p. 251).

25. *Leçons sur les phénomènes de la vie communs aux animaux et aux végétaux* (Paris, 1878), pp. 156, 176–77. For the history of this thesis, see E. Guyénot, *Les sciences de la vie aux XVIIe et XVIIIe siècles* (Paris, 1941), pp. 209 ff. The connection between decay and life was also theorized in reverse (i.e., by making the former an effect of the latter) by certain seventeenth-century theologians who, going beyond the fearful Augustinian doctrine of the *massa damnata*, insisted on seeing in every generation an element or principle of corruption, a step which widened irrevocably the distance from the original perfection of Adam *ante peccatum*; see V. Harris, *All Coherence Gone* (Chicago, 1949), pp. 187–88.

26. On Needham, see, for example, Delisle de Sales, *De la philosophie de la Nature* (Amsterdam, 1770–74), IV, 114–20, 241–42n.; and more recently, E. Nordenskiöld, *The History of Biology* (New York, 1936), pp. 225–26, 430; Guyénot, op. cit., pp. 194–95, 220–26; T. Monod, "En relisant Monsieur de Buffon," in *L'hippopotame et le philosophe* (Paris, 1946), p. 424; Paul Hazard, *La pensée européenne au XVIIIe siècle* (Paris, 1946), I, 183–84, 192; Roger, op. cit., pp. 494–520. On Buffon, see E. Genet-Varcin, "La génération des êtres vivants d'après Buffon," in Bertin, op. cit., pp. 149–50.

27. *De Civitate Dei*, XVI, 7. But see even earlier Genesis 1:20: "Producant aquae reptile animae viventis," and St. Basil, *Hexaemeron*, VII, followed by Tasso: "Let the waters now bring forth . . .

drop of water falls from the clouds into the dry dust."[28] And the great Vico records it as a well-known fact that "frogs are born from the earth, with the summer rains."[29] Juan and Ulloa, actually referring to the American Portobello, had said that "the great number that there are of them [toads], and the fact that they all appear after a cloudburst, has led some people to believe that each drop of water is converted into a toad."[30]

Buffon must, no doubt, have taken these abundant rainy embryologies as particular instances providing just the confirmation he wanted for what he himself had arrived at by intuition: a notion of awe-inspiring pessimism, a truly tragic viewpoint, according to which the meanest, most abject, most minuscule species are at the same time those which multiply with the most terrifying fertility. It is this morbid fecundity of the lower forms which assures their survival, while in the superior species, the larger, more beautiful and powerful animals, it is their noble courage and serene strength which enables them to protect themselves.[31] The elephant and the lion hold sway over the shapeless rabble of the unnumbered insects. Their trumpetings and roarings drown the feeble croaking of the myriads of batrachians. America, the moist, prolific mother of these minute and evil little animals, devoid of the great wild beasts, must have seemed to Buffon's eyes to be marked with the indelible stigma of some repugnant organic weakness.

Some years later Oliver Goldsmith was quick to accept Buffon's thesis that "the smallest animals multiply the fastest,"[32] an idea that turned upside down the apologetic pleadings of the theologians, who had shown themselves quite willing to defend the usefulness of the insects, their lawful worthiness, their value as instruments of divine justice, and even the meager fecundity of their more harmful species![33]

Over the years the idea of prolificity as a passive defense of the lower

---

28. *La ricreazione del savio*, 1659, in Ezio Raimondi, ed., *Trattatisti e narratori del Seicento* (Milan-Naples, 1960), p. 520.

29. *Scienza nuova*, ed. F. Nicolini (Bari, 1911–16), p. 279; cf. F. Nicolini, *Commento storico alla seconda Scienza nuova* (Rome, 1949–50), I, 39, 115–16, 233–34; II, 234.

30. *Relación histórica*, II, 5, ed. Madrid, 1748, I, 137; cf. earlier F. Carletti, *Ragionamenti* (1594; ed. Milan, 1926), pp. 26–27.

31. See the passages quoted and discussed by W. Lynskey, "Goldsmith and the Chain of Being," *Journal of the History of Ideas*, 6 (1945), pp. 366–67; and Bertin, op. cit., p. 73. Already Tasso, still following St. Basil, had stressed the meager fecundity of the "savage and untamed beasts" in contrast with the providential fertility of the tame and domesticated animals, which otherwise would have been devoured by the wild ones and made extinct (*Mondo creato*, IV, 738–40; ed. cit., pp. 137–38; and VI, 989–1015; ed. cit., p. 244).

32. *A History of the Earth and Animated Nature*, pt. II, bk. II, chap. 15 (London-Edinburgh ed., Fullarton and Co., n.d., I, 265); cf. J. H. Pitman, *Goldsmith's "Animated Nature"* (New Haven, 1924), p. 130.

33. F. C. Lesser, *Theologie des insectes, ou Démonstration des perfections de Dieu dans tout ce qui concerne les insectes* (trans. from the German with remarks by P. Lyonnet [the Hague, 1742]), I, 122–23; II, 256–59; cf. P. Hazard, op. cit., I, 125.

species had an eventful history: it was supported by Bonnet too (1764);[34] revived by de Pauw;[35] justified by Herder as an instrument of providence for the evolution of the nobler and less numerous species, with man as the peak of this "pyramid of creatures";[36] twisted by Brissot into the theory of the continuous and providential extermination of the overproductive species, whether useful or harmful;[37] welcomed by Father Molina;[38] rediscovered by the naïvely surprised Leopardi;[39] and in time endowed with almost proverbial standing.[40] But its ultimate destiny was to be taken over by representatives of the opposite extreme, so to speak, by much later biologists and ecologists with their idea of the "pyramid of numbers": "Every animal feeding on another species that is lower in the food chain must select a species that is much more numerous and usually one that is smaller"[41] — a theory as close to the banality of the big eating the little as it is removed from the inspired and impassioned visions of both Buffon and Bonnet.

Buffon's "application" of these ideas to the New World is too facile. But already a century and a half earlier (1616) Goodman, in his efforts to demonstrate the universal decadence and corruption of the cosmos, had ascribed this same feebleness and misfortune in maternal capacity to the whole earth: "Not able to produce couragious Lions, brave Unicornes, fierce Tigers, stout Elephants, shee makes it her taske and imployment to be the mother, the midwife of wormes, of gnats, and of butterflies."[42] And in the following century a poet who had read Buffon (see below, p. 375) was to come back, half in jest and half in desperation, to the theory of multiplication of insects as a sign of the imminent end of the world:

34. C. Bonnet: "The fruitfulness of the species is always proportional to the dangers which menace the individuals" (quoted by Daudin, op. cit., p. 175n.).

35. "Nature . . . has, as one knows, increased the degree of fecundity in proportion to the smallness of the animals" (*Défense des Recherches philosophiques sur les Américains* [Berlin, 1771], p. 97).

36. *Ideen*, X, 2; *Idées sur la philosophie de l'histoire de l'humanité*, trans. E. Quinet (Paris, 1827–28), II, 221–25; cf. *Forerunners of Darwin: 1745–1859*, ed. B. Glass, D. Temkin, W. C. Strauss, Jr. (Baltimore, 1959), p. 209.

37. *Recherches philosophiques sur le droit de propriété et sur le vol* (Paris, 1782), pp. 312 ff.; W. Stark, *America: Ideal and Reality* (London, 1947), pp. 84–85.

38. G. I. Molina, *Memorie di storia naturale* (Bologna, 1821), II, 49: "The species of bigger [animals] . . . are less abundant in individuals."

39. "I believe that the absolute multitude of each species of animals is in direct relation to their smallness . . . look up the naturalists and see if any of them have made this observation" (*Zibaldone*, ed. Flora [Milan, 1938], I, 102).

40. For example: "Like all the lower organisms, poor books multiply prodigiously, though the total number is kept down by a corresponding mortality" (Samuel M. Crothers, "The Hundred Best Books," in *Among Friends* [Boston–New York, 1910], p. 69).

41. W. Vogt, *The Road to Survival* (New York, 1948), p. 91.

42. Godfrey Goodman, *The Fall of Man, or the Corruption of Nature* (London, 1616), pp. 16, 19, quoted by Harris, op. cit., p. 44. His ideas also influenced some of the earliest writers investigating the raw state of nature in Australia: Bernard Smith, *European Vision and the South Pacific, 1768–1850* (Oxford, 1960), p. 172.

The scientists say that our planet is growing old, and it is therefore quite possible that the multiplication of insects, more and more noticeable with each passing year, is a festering symptom of the approaching death of the world. O tragic end to the world—to be consumed by lice! *Phthiriasis universalis,* one enormous swarm of lice! Ugh![43]

But already in the eighteenth century, for that matter, the earliest students of the population problem had been pointing with either dismay or satisfaction to the sterility of the aristocracy and the unbridled fertility of the poorer classes, and the theory of extreme productivity among the lowest orders of humanity was taken up again after Malthus and Humboldt[44] by a whole host of philosophizing sociologists and racist demographers; particularly popular at that time were the speculations about a possible "fecundity differential" in the human race, an idea persisting here and there even today. According to this notion the socially and anthropologically "inferior" elements, such as the peasants in the south of Italy, the proletariat of the city slums, or the simple country people of India and China, multiply more rapidly than the "superior" classes: a theory that paves the way for Fra Melitone's grotesque and horror-struck pronouncement: "But such beggars are of a truly terrifying fecundity."[45] Thus these misguided statisticians took what had been originally a hypothetical consequence of Original Sin and succeeded in extracting from it a corollary demonstrating the scientific necessity of poverty.[46]

43. N. Lenau, in a letter of 17 May 1844, in *Sämtliche Werke,* ed. Castle (Leipzig, 1913), V, 184. Lenau's anxiety is repeated in the contemporary scientists who have expressed their fear of the ruinous consequences that may result from the indiscriminate use of insecticides and pesticides. Insects are not only prolific and have a rapid reproductive cycle, but mithridatize themselves and become immune to chemical poisons. This is not the case with the higher animals—birds and mammals—whose species are much less numerous and whose reproductive cycles are slower. An unchecked use of insecticides over vast areas of the globe "might well result in the final extinction of many species of song-birds and innumerable other kinds of life which we value, leaving a population of insects which is completely resistant!" (W. H. Thorpe, Professor of Zoology at Cambridge, in a review of Rachel Carson's *Silent Spring,* in the *Observer,* 17 February 1963); cf. also Kenneth Mellanby, *Pesticides and Pollution* (London, 1967), reviewed in the *Times Literary Supplement,* 9 November 1967.

44. Charles Minguet, *Alexandre de Humboldt, historien et géographe de l'Amérique espagnole, 1799–1804* (Paris, 1969), p. 511.

45. F. M. Piave, *La forza del destino* (1861), act 4, sc. 2: "Ma tai pezzenti sono di una fecondità / Davvero spaventosa."

46. See D. E. C. Eversley, *Social Theories of Fertility and the Malthusian Debate* (Oxford, 1959), passim, but especially pp. 51–58 ("poverty breeds men"), 116, 123, 135, 151 (illiteracy and fertility), 159, 166, 169, 172 (hunger and fertility), 178, 187 (fecundity of the lower animals and of the poorer people), 189, 195. Cf. also *The Determinants and Consequences of Population Trends* (United Nations Population Studies, no. 17), pp. 74, 80–81, etc. One of the most recent students of the problem, Colin Clark, finds that the thesis of the fecundity of the lowest classes, as expounded in the 1930s, was approximately true in the nineteenth century, but is no longer so in the twentieth: "the larger families, so said the writers of those days (and some do still, in spite of the evidence to the contrary), are to be found among rural rather than urban population, among uneducated rather than educated, among poor rather than rich; and so, as a country becomes urbanized, better educated, wealthier, its productivity is bound to decline. These generalizations were on the whole true in the nineteenth century; but this was only a transitory phase": in the most recent decades in France, England, Sweden, and the United States, it is the wealthier, better-educated, and urbanized families that have shown themselves more prolific (C. Clark, "Do Population and Freedom Grow Together?," *Fortune,* 62, no. 6 [December 1960], pp. 137–38; cf. Eversley, op. cit., pp. 267–58).

But Buffon, with his distinctions and comparisons, had already removed the discussion from the level of tired and wilting theology to a plane that was at least embryonically scientific. His objective was not the contrition of the faithful but a better understanding of how our world is made.

Later on Hegel, arguing against the idea that nature lives and develops in time, be it centuries or millennia (and thus moving away from the beginnings of historicism already at work in Buffon), was to pour out his scorn on the "nebulous" fantasies of animals and plants being born from water.[47] But if we try to place these beliefs in the context of the remote past to which they belong, we are forced to recognize that the derivation of life from water is perhaps the most ancient of the scientific explanations, and one of humanity's remotest myths. In historical times one can go back at least as far as the first Greek philosopher, Thales of Miletus, who—in Vico's satirical words—"began from too insipid a principle, water; perhaps because he had seen pumpkins grow with water." As for prehistoric times, Frazer has conjured up pictures of spring storms whose torrential rains revive the animal and vegetable life, and the Wizard Kings whose magic can release the cataracts of the heavens. The Bible teaches us in its very first lines that God created the water before the land and the animals and the plants.[48] And the lively imagination of the Middle Ages associated life with water in the legends of the fountain of youth and the immortal "Rhine maidens."

To even the dullest mind, water suggests the unceasing flow of life— fresh, agile, fugitive. "Water, that is life begun anew."[49] Even the learned Florentines who gathered in academy in 1540 called themselves *gli Umidi*, "the wet ones," hoping thus for "strength and sustenance, just as created things grow and are maintained with the assistance of humidity."[50] But a knowledgeable and inquisitive naturalist like Buffon was certainly aware of the bold conjectures of de Maillet (1735, 1748) for whom life derived from the ocean, and all animals and man himself were descended from corresponding marine species, when the sea slowly withdrew from the mountaintops, leaving the valleys and the plains dry.[51] And he must certainly have been familiar with that "well-known" fact, that without water the greater organisms die once and for all, "while for the smaller, lesser organisms the withdrawal of water only suspends life," and that

47. *Enzyklopädie*, sec. 249. Cf. below, pp. 420–21.
48. Genesis, 1:2; see F. E. Jacobi, *Sulla dottrina dello Spinoza* (Bari, 1914), pp. 163–64, following G. Bruno, "De la Causa, Principio ed Uno," in *Dialoghi metafisici* (Bari, 1925), p. 242.
49. J. Michelet, *La Montagne* (Paris, 1868), p. 44.
50. J. Rilli, *Notizie . . . dell'Accademia Fiorentina* (Venice, 1700); quoted by Croce in a note (*Critica*, XL, 232) in which the "dry" is reciprocally characterized as "the death of all physical and spiritual life."
51. B. de Maillet, op. cit., see especially the sixth *Entretien*, which concludes ritually with the section: "The conformity of this system with Genesis." On de Maillet see among others, Roger, op. cit., pp. 520–26.

one only has to sprinkle with fresh moisture the dried-out tissues of rotifers, tardigrades, or maggots taken from blighted corn to see these miniscule and almost always harmful little animals revive and begin to move.[52] The life that lies latent within them can be reawakened with a few drops of the nearest available dew. The dampness of the New World meant that it was predisposed if not predestined to succor an unending swarm of insects, snakes, and amphibians. In fact, it was easier for Redi in the seventeenth century to laugh at Father Kircher's "blessed little handmade serpents" than for Buffon in the eighteenth century to free himself from the recent and ancient mental association of the liquid with the living.

VII. AMERICA AS A NEW CONTINENT

Another noteworthy fact in the last passage quoted from Buffon is the reemergence of a genetic explanation, at first on the physical level, and immediately afterward in reference to the humanity of America, much like the ideas we have just been admiring. Physically America is a new world, or at least considerably newer than the old, a world that remained a longer time beneath the waters of the sea, that in fact only recently emerged and is not yet properly dried out. On the human level, America is a continent still intact, as yet unpossessed by man and therefore unhealthy for civilized peoples or superior animals. After recalling how recent the historical records of the Mexican and Peruvian dynasties are, how little of the past is penetrated by the chronicles of the Americas, Buffon leaps from history to prehistory:

Everything then seems to indicate that the Americans were new men, or, to be more accurate, men who had left their homeland so long ago as to have lost all notion of it, all idea of the world from which they had issued.[53] All the evidence seems to point toward the greater part of the American continent being a new land, still untouched by men, in which nature had not had time to carry out all her plans, to develop herself to the full; the men are cold and the animals small, because the ardor of the men and the size of the animals are dependent on the healthiness and the warmth of the air; in several centuries, when the earth has been tilled, the forests cut down, the rivers controlled and the waters contained, this same land will become the most fruitful, healthy, and rich of all, as it is seen to be already in the parts that man has cultivated.[54]

---

52. C. Bernard, *Introduction à l'étude de la médecine expérimentale* (Paris, 1865), p. 207. The knowledge of these phenomena at the time of Buffon is evident from Littré's examples alone. In 1701 Leeuwenhoek made experiments on tardigrades and saw them pullulate as soon as he wet them and "these facts have had a great reverberation" (C. Bernard, *Leçons sur les phénomènes de la vie*, p. 85).

53. An incidental reaffirmation of the Buffonian thesis of the unity of the human race.

54. *Oeuvres complètes*, XV, 455–56. Cf. Bertin, op. cit., pp. 81–82 (giving examples of rapid improvement of animal and vegetable species), and below, p. 91.

In his enthusiasm for man's battle to overcome the physical world[55] Buffon does not quite go so far as to prophesy that the human race will one day succeed in making America teem with wild beasts. Nor will it be able to bring about any increase in the stature of these shrunken local species: the tapir will never be as big as an elephant or a hippopotamus. But "at least the animals transported there will not decrease in size." That's some comfort, anyway.

VIII. THE LARGER SPECIES MORE PERFECT AND MORE STABLE THAN THE SMALL

Implicit in all these comparisons and conjectures is an assumption that is not stated, but is nevertheless clear, and surprising. Buffon always starts out from the principle that the large is "better" than the small, the bulkier beasts superior to those of less volume, that physical strength is an attribute of the more perfect species. It would be too easy to reply with La Fontaine's boastful little mouse:

> Comme si d'occuper ou plus ou moins de place
> nous rendait, disait-il, plus ou moins importants! . . .
> Nous ne nous prisons pas, tout petits que nous sommes,
> d'un grain moins que les Elephants.[56]

It would be too easy to counter with some of the very recent theories according to which the inferior animals are essential in the economy of nature, while the earth could well do without the superior animals: "[It is] a kind of paradox . . . [that] many of the lower forms of animal life [protozoa, insects, invertebrates, and vertebrates down to the smallest mammals] play an essential part in the economy of nature. On the other hand, it is far from easy to prove that some of the higher orders or families of mammals ['large mammals,' such as the ungulates and carnivores, apart from the primates] are necessary to the life scheme of the earth."[57] And it would be too easy to remind him in this respect of those primitive species, massive and hugely powerful, that have completely disappeared from the face of the earth: the dinosaurs and the *Baluchitheria,* in comparison with which the pachyderms and hippopotamuses dear to Buffon would make an even meaner showing than the tapir compared with the

55. On Buffon's lofty concept of man, understood in the Renaissance sense as a force opposed to nature, see, for example, G. Lanson, *Histoire de la littérature française,* 3rd ed. (Paris, 1895), p. 742; E. Faguet, *Dix-huitième siècle* (Paris, 1894), pp. 444–48. For Buffon, as already stated, the human race is one, and therefore, unlike the animals, is not bound to climate or geographic zones: "Man, white in Europe, black in Africa, yellow in Asia, and red in America, is only the same man tinted with the color of the climate" (*Oeuvres de Buffon,* IX, 2, quoted by Flourens, op. cit., p. 154).

56. *Fables,* bk. 8, fable 15: "As if occupying more or less space should make us, said he, more or less important! . . . Small as we may be, we don't esteem ourselves one jot less than the elephant."

57. Fairfield Osborn, *Our Plundered Planet* (London, 1948), pp. 64–65.

elephant, or the llama craning his neck as he strives to compete with the giraffe.

When at a later stage in the development of his ideas he has to recognize that the mammoth is extinct, one detects a strange admiration, a Bossuet-like note of heartfelt sorrow in his funeral oration for the enormous beast: "The prodigious mammoth no longer exists anywhere. This species was certainly the first, the largest, the strongest of all quadrupeds; since this species has disappeared, how many others, smaller, weaker, and less noteworthy, must have perished without having left us evidence or information on their past existence."[58]

Thus for Buffon the mammoth assumes symbolic value, just as the great men of the world did for Bossuet, those whose deaths furnished an exemplary warning to we other "less noteworthy" and duly awestruck mortals. The *oraison funèbre* has a different subject, but the same tone.

Buffon has somewhat vague ideas on the state of the fauna before the flood, but he is not the man to shrink from any problem that presents itself to him. The problem of the relationship between the size and the evolutionary state of an animal is squarely faced and discussed in his essay bearing the significant title *Concerning the Degeneration of Animals* (1766): "The size of the body, which appears to be only a relative quantity, does in fact have positive attributes and real significance in the ordering of nature: the larger animal is as fixed in this ordering as the smaller is variable."[59] It is the advantage of the great over the small to be fixed and invariable. Or, if we break up this law into its component elements: the large is superior to the small; the fixed is superior to the changeable; the large is more fixed than the small.

All these relationships seem at first to be somewhat arbitrary. Let us consider them one by one.

IX. BUFFON'S AVERSION FOR MINUTIAE AND SMALL ANIMALS

The probable source of Buffon's preference for large animals, or at least a point of some significance in his psychological makeup, was the fact that he himself was a man of commanding physical presence. Buffon was a strong, well-built person and proud of it. Hume found that he

58. Passage quoted by E. Perrier, *La philosophie zoologique avant Darwin* (Paris, 1884), p. 64. It was precisely the huge animal fossils that induced Darwin to undertake a critical revision of Buffon's theory; see below, p. 454.
59. *Oeuvres complètes*, XIX, 21, repeated by Goldsmith, op. cit., I, 260. Cf. Glass, op. cit., p. 103. It seems possible to find a somewhat sounder logical foundation for another of Buffon's theses, clearly related to this one: namely that short-lived animals have undergone more changes or are more variable (from the prototypes) than long-lived ones, because, in an equal span of time, they have passed through a considerably greater number of generations (cf. Glass, p. 100). And one could draw direct corollaries concerning the cold and humid continent (America) from the related Buffonian theory that the larger animals are also those with more heat, which degenerate when heat is lost (or do they degenerate through loss of heat on the part of the environment?) (Glass, p. 236).

had more the build and manner of a marshal of France than a scientist.[60] "He was very fond of taking objects and creatures in order of size," and he began his history of the birds with the ostrich "which is as it were the elephant of the genus."[61] In fact, "it seemed as though the greater stature with which he himself had been endowed by nature made it difficult for him to lower himself to study the smaller things. He would willingly consider the cedar of Lebanon, but the hyssop seemed too small to warrant his interest."[62] The fly, he once curiously stated, must occupy no more space in the naturalist's mind than it does in nature.[63]

Such disdain was completely anachronistic at a point in time when a good century and a half had passed since Father Acosta first warned his readers that "from the very meanest and smallest animals one may derive much important study and profitable philosophy" (*Al lector*). It was no less long ago that Galileo's defense of his "little" satellites of Jupiter had included an eloquent and highly original plea for the virtue of tiny things, of minuscule animals and organs of restricted volume, concluding with a hymn of praise to Nature for deriving and producing "the most marvelous operations . . . from the most tenuous means."[64] Giannone (and after him Costantino) had insisted in his unpublished *L'ape ingegnosa* on "the perfection of very small animals like the ants and the bees";[65] Aldovrandi, following in the footsteps of the author of a 1564 treatise on painting, had exalted the beauty of the insects: "Thus the wisdom of God shines forth in these minuscule little animals";[66] Torquato Tasso had exalted "the great power of the great Lord, revealed in the tiniest things";[67] and the revolution brought about in biology by the Dutch microscopists was already nearly a hundred years old. One of the earliest English microscopists, Henry Power (1632–68), a disciple of Thomas Browne, had written in 1663 that the ancients, since they did not possess that miraculous instrument, described the very smallest animals "perfunctorily . . . as the disregarded pieces and hustlement of the Creation. In these pretty

60. C. A. Sainte-Beuve, *Causeries du lundi* (Paris, n.d., but 1924–28), II, 79; XIV, 330.

61. Ibid., X, 61.

62. Ibid., IV, 357.

63. Ibid., X, 61. For similar contempt for the oyster, etc., see Daudin, op. cit., pp. 155–56. "The passage from the small to the large often occupied Buffon's attention, which is not surprising really, considering his two predominant interests: comparisons and great dimensions" (Hanks, op. cit., p. 205; cf. pp. 209, 213, 226).

64. Letter of 21 May 1611, to Mons. P. Dini, in *Epistolario* (Leghorn, 1872), I, 121–22. From the telescope to the microscope: in 1624 Galilei took with him to Rome the *occhialino* that enabled him "to see the smallest things from close to" and with which he had "contemplated many tiny creatures with infinite admiration" (quoted in G. de Santillana, *Processo a Galileo* [Milan, 1960], p. 316).

65. G. Ricuperati, "Alle origini del *Triregno:* la *Philosophia Adamito-noetica* di A. Costantino," *Rivista Storica Italiana*, 77, no. 3 (1965), p. 662.

66. E. Battisti, *L'antirinascimento* (Milan, 1962), p. 271; and in *Le soleil à la Renaissance* (Brussels, 1965), p. 175.

67. *Mondo creato*, V, 596–97; ed. cit., p. 176.

Engines are lodged all the perfections of the largest animals. . . . Ruder heads stand amazed at prodigious and Colossean pieces of Nature, but in these narrow Engines there is a more curious Mathematicks."[68] The style is elegant, but the accusation leveled at the ancients not altogether justified. One can find almost the same words in the greatest naturalist of classic times. It was Pliny who pointed out at the beginning of his description of the insects (including the fly) that nowhere else does nature display such artifice; and that the vulgar masses (and Buffon!) were wrong to admire the elephants, bulls, lions, and tigers "when nature can only be seen in its entirety in the most miniature creatures."[69]

Take Buffon's contemporaries too; a couple of years before his *Histoire naturelle* began to appear, La Mettrie published his *L'homme machine* (1747), with its eulogies of the proteiform character of matter and the omnipotence of Nature: "No, . . . Nature knows no limitations to her workmanship. . . . Her power shines forth equally in the creation of the meanest insect or the proudest man."[70]

But all in vain. Buffon remained as indifferent to the ancient Pliny's reverent regard for the whole universe and the enthusiasm of the doctor, his contemporary, for the physical world as he did to the coupled lenses of the latest optical devices. His disdain for the most diminutive creatures was reinforced by another particular physiological characteristic of his,

68. Quoted in "The New World of Robert Hooke," *Times Literary Supplement*, 5 January 1946. Hooke himself, in his *Micrographia* (1665), had celebrated the grace, beauty, and strength of the smallest insects. Even the authoritative American, Cotton Mather, after seeing some tiny little worms under a microscope, perorated in one of his sermons (1689): "How Exquisite, how Stupendous must the Structure of them be." Huge whales, floating islands whose length can exceed a hundred feet, are less worthy of admiration than those minutest of fish (quoted by W. M. Smallwood, *Natural History and the American Mind* [New York, 1941], pp. 197–98). And the sermonizing American Emerson was to repeat: "The microscope cannot find the animalcule which is less perfect for being little" ("Compensation," in *Selected Essays*, ed. Nelson, p. 44).

69. *Naturalis Historia*, XI, 1. Pliny's words are echoed in Oviedo, who finds ants more wonderful than elephants, and are exactly repeated by Linnaeus: "Nature is never more complete than in the smallest creatures" (quoted by Daudin, op. cit., p. 157n.).

70. J. Offroy de La Mettrie, *L'homme machine*, ed. M. Solovine (Paris, 1921), p. 139. Similar expressions from Lesser, op. cit., I, 2–10, 113–14; II, 100–02, 122–26, and passim, and Henry Baker, *The Microscope Made Easy*, 2d ed. (London, 1743), are quoted by A. Vartamian, "Trembley's Polyp, La Mettrie, and XVIII Century French Materialism," *Journal of the History of Ideas*, 11 (1950), p. 268. The Jesuit Daniello Bartoli, in his *Ricreazione del Savio* (1659), had already taken up Tertullian's and Augustine's thesis that God is "greatest of all in his smallest creations" and expatiated with pleasure on the magnificence of "contemptible" little animals, such as snails, which even he had observed, by the thousands, under a microscope (in E. Raimondi, op. cit., pp. 517–31). In his *Amusement philosophique sur le language des bêtes* (1739), the Jesuit Father G. H. Bougeant had pronounced that "ignorance alone, and false prejudice, can induce us to make some distinction of preference amongst the animals based on their greatness or smallness" (op. cit., ed. Petin [Paris, 1783], p. 78). See also the quotations in Roger, op. cit., pp. 233–39, 448; Bonnet's observations on nature which "works in miniature" (quoted by E. L. Tuveson, *Millennium and Utopia* [Los Angeles, 1949], p. 182); the admiration of Delisle de Sales for "the prodigious magnificence of nature in the infinitely small beings" (*Philosophie de la Nature*, II, 286; cf. ibid., IV, 10–15); that of Father Clavigero for the "smallest animals, in which the power and wisdom of the Creator shines forth most" (*Storia antica del Messico* [Cesena, 1780], I, 105); and the analogous words of Pope Pius XII, according to whom "even the most humble creatures, like the microbes, reflect the Creator's perfection" (*Il Mondo*, 29 September 1953).

namely his shortsightedness, so serious as to prevent him from even using the microscope; and further buttressed by a psychological trait, once again negative, namely his unwillingness to involve himself in details or minutiae. This characteristic, a reflection of his faith in his own genius (although it was Buffon himself who coined the phrase "genius is merely an infinite capacity for taking pains"), comes out clearly in the way he refers to the "courage" it takes to "busy oneself continually with little objects, the examination of which requires the coldest patience and makes no demands on true talent."[71] It is obvious again in the celebrated reply to the chemist who wanted to carry out an experiment to check one of Buffon's intuitions: "The best crucible is the mind";[72] and once again when he expresses his boredom with the thousands and thousands of species of birds: "I have no desire to do any more work on feathers."[73] It is visible again in the curious statement he made, which earned him the ridicule of the students of games and probability calculations, that a "small" probability, less than one in ten thousand, is a "negligible quantity" that can safely be ignored;[74] in his complaint that in order to classify a plant according to Linnaeus's system "one must go microscope in hand" to observe not the stem, the shape, or the leaves, but just "the stamens, and if one cannot see the stamens, one knows nothing, one has seen nothing";[75] and finally in the contemptuous comments he makes after stating some facts about the intestines of birds of prey: "I leave the exact verification of this fact to those people who busy themselves with anatomy,"[76] and his haughty refusal to be called a "naturalist" or even a "great

71. *Histoire des animaux,* quoted in *Correspondance inédite de Buffon,* ed. H. Nadault de Buffon (Paris, 1860), II, 335–36, and in C. Sainte-Beuve, *Causeries du lundi,* X, 350.

72. C. Sainte-Beuve, *Causeries du lundi,* IV, 350; D. Mornet, *Les sciences de la nature en France au XVIIIᵉ siècle* (Paris, 1911), p. 114. For him, chemistry was a sort of culinary art, to be practiced in the kitchen and not in a laboratory: "Speaking one day with Monsieur de Buffon on the present ardor of chemical enquiry, he affected to consider chemistry but as cookery, and to place the toils of the laboratory on a footing with those of the kitchen" (letter of Thomas Jefferson to James Madison, 19 July 1788, *Papers,* ed. Julian P. Boyd [Princeton, 1950–], XIII, 381).

73. Quoted by Franck Bourdier, "Principaux aspects de la vie et de l'oeuvre de Buffon," in Bertin, op. cit., p. 35.

74. Karl Georg Zinn, "Buffons Beitrag zur Sozialwissenschaft – Die Entdeckung der messbaren Psyche im 18. Jahrhundert und die wertsubjektivistische Konsequenz," *Jahrbücher für Nationalökonomie und Statistik,* 181, no. 4 (March 1968), p. 346.

75. 1749, quoted by Daudin, op. cit., p. 126n.; on the danger of "falling into too many little details," cf. also ibid., p. 154n. Mornet (op. cit., p. 114) records another of his aphorisms: "The mind's eye is enough to perceive the real existence of all these little beings, without the microscope."

76. C. Sainte-Beuve, *Causeries du lundi,* X, 62. "Buffon is right; there are a thousand things that one must leave to laborers, otherwise one would be crushed, and one would never reach one's object" (Hérault de Séchelles, *Voyage à Montbard,* ed. Jouaust, 1890, p. 46). These words seem to echo Maupertuis, who described as "the philosophers' laborers" those "indefatigable observers" who waste time examining the auricular apparatus of certain fish or measuring how far a flea can jump, "not to mention so many other miserable undertakings"; minute details "are the sign of the limited genius of those who give themselves up thereto" (quoted by Roger, op. cit., p. 466). See also P. Hazard, op. cit., I, 192, and Hanks, op. cit., p. 181 (antipathy for repeating experiments). Contemporary examples of impatience in the study of natural minutiae: B. Smith, op. cit., pp. 33, 63.

naturalist": "Naturalists, linkboys, dentists, etc. . . . people who live by their work; a thing ill suited to a gentleman," whereas he himself insists on his native and inalienable claim to gentility: "I am a gentleman amusing myself with natural history."[77]

Buffon always says simply, "I had a rabbit [or a dog] opened up," never "I opened up," which has been explained, perhaps too superficially, as the reluctance of the gentleman to dirty his own hands with work he considered more becoming to the butcher.[78] But was the plebean and systematic Linnaeus in fact very different, when he asked his correspondents to attempt some dissection (of branchiostegals) and then happily carried on without using the precise data furnished by the anatomists and the voluminous detail (on infusorians) contained in the "micrographers' books"?[79] And did not Vico, another great man who trusted a little too much in his own unarguable genius, write at the beginning of his *Scienza nuova:* "Diligence must be set aside when one is working on subjects that have a greatness about them, because it is a small virtue, and being small likewise slow"?[80] Diderot, too, warned scientists in one of his writings inspired by Buffon that "one fails humanity in observing everything indistinctly." Posterity demands that great men spend their time better. "What would posterity think of us if all we had to hand down to it was a complete insectology, some immense history of microscopic creatures. Great minds must tackle great themes; the smaller things belong to lesser minds." After all, if these lesser minds did not have these minutiae to keep them busy, they would not produce anything at all.[81] *De minimis non curat praetor.*

And lastly even the greatest disciple and follower of Buffon, the half-blind Lamarck, disliked having to come down to earth from his lofty observatory where he would remain entranced with the vision of the metamorphoses of living creatures; and in his lectures — so we are told by an unexpected listener — "he would show himself a mortal enemy of the chemists, the analysts and experimenters in miniature, as he would call them."[82]

77. Victor Jacquemont, *Correspondance inédite avec sa famille et ses amis, 1824–32* (Paris, 1867), I, 134.
78. Pitman, op. cit., p. 39. Buffon has also been reproached for having spent too much time on polishing his sentences and consequently not enough on detailed and patient experiments (Mornet, op. cit., pp. 207–08).
79. Daudin, op. cit., pp. 75–76.
80. *Scienza nuova,* ed. cit., pp. 11–12; the maxim is taken from Longinus and used elsewhere too by Vico (B. Croce, *Il carattere della filosofia moderna* [Bari, 1941], p. 56; and *Quaderni della Critica,* nn. 17–18, p. 99); cf. F. Nicolini, *La giovinezza di G. B. Vico* (Bari, 1932), pp. 62 ff.
81. Diderot, *Pensées sur l'interprétation de la nature* (n.p., 1754), pp. 79–80.
82. Amaury, in C. Sainte-Beuve's *Volupté,* chap. XI (ed. Paris, 1881), p. 136.

X. QUANTITATIVE CRITERIA AND LITERARY SCRUPLES

The particular interest of these various comments lies in the fact that they reveal in Buffon a psychological attitude not unlike Hegel's in his outbursts of sarcasm and impatience with Master Krug,[83] and seem to foreshadow to some extent the naturalist's high-handed arbitrariness with the facts and data of the world, including the Americas. Buffon tells the scientist he cannot afford to waste time on the fly. Hegel was to write that science has other things to do than deduce a rose, a dog, a cat, or even Master Krug's pen. In a celebrated passage from the *Philosophy of History* he throws out the whole discussion about the future of America, which, he says "doesn't interest us," since it belongs neither to history nor philosophy, "which already give us enough to do."[84] This same impatience with lesser matters receives even more striking and comprehensive expression when he expounds his theory that history should concern itself only with the "great" occurrences, and ignore or leave to the writers of romances the "micrology" of the minor details, the little individual events.[85] But unfortunately the introduction of the notions of large and small is highly dangerous for the understanding of reality. *Qui incipit metiri, incipit errare* — "he who begins to measure begins to err." Diderot knew this so well that he once wittily put forward plans for a "great work" destined to confute the "mathematicians": the *Treatise on the Aberration of Measurement*.[86]

In Buffon, however, the insistence on quantitative characteristics is not merely psychological in origin, but has a literary motivation too. In every page of his writings one is struck by his enthusiasm, his flowing oratory. For every species lovingly described he tries to bring out some particular feature of excellence which allows him to linger over and enhance the portrait of that species, turning its instinctive reactions into human qualities. An almost inevitable result of this tendency is the making of comparisons of less and more, of better and worse, leading on to a desire to discover the fundamental reasons for such distinctions. The animals are no longer considered for themselves, but in respect to each other, the puma as weaker than the lion, the elephant as larger than the tapir. As early as 1770, Mme d'Epinay's plain common sense had noted

---

83. See the essay of the Jena period: *Wie der gemeine Menschenverstand die Philosophie nehme*, in *Werke* (Berlin, 1834), XVI, 56–58, *Phänomenologie des Geistes*, ed. Lasson (Leipzig, 1921), p. 69; *Enzyklopädie*, sec. 250; and Croce, *Saggio sullo Hegel* (Bari, 1913), p. 116. The target of Buffon's impatience, however, is minutiae; that of Hegel's, the pretense of deducing empirical realities logically, be they large or small.
84. Ed. Brunstäd (Leipzig, n.d., but ca. 1907), p. 134.
85. See Croce, *Saggio*, pp. 100–01.
86. *Pensées sur l'interprétation de la nature*, p. 3.

the weak point in Buffon's argument. "Why does he insist on pronouncing these eulogies or funeral orations over every species he names? *One is what one is.* One should set forth the chain of creatures, it seems to me, and not have them trespass upon each other's territory."[87]

This was in fact just the period when the theory of the chain of being was revived and temporalized by Robinet (1761–68), and also particularly Bonnet (1770). But Buffon, consistent in his opposition to any sort of rigid systemization, always refused to be enticed by the attractions of this splendid metaphysical structure. Nor was the naturalist at all impressed with the evolutionary theories that were slowly emerging with these ideas of a chain or scale or column of species and prototypes; Buffon at first (1749) expressed his doubts over the validity of the whole concept of species, and finally only accepted species as entities independent of time, invariable units, the real "constants" of creation.[88] For Buffon, we must remember, it is the privilege of the "large" animal to be fixed and not subject to variation.

XI. THE STABLE SUPERIOR TO THE CHANGEABLE: ARISTOTLE

What strikes one particularly in this basic subthesis is not the logical connection made between large and stable, but the tacit assumption that the stable, the fixed, the invariable has some special virtue setting it off from the variable; that the unchanging species are by nature superior to the changing ones. To alter means to drop in rank. The varieties of a species all are explained as degenerations from a prototype. Leaving aside some major species, such as man, the elephant, the rhinoceros, the hippopotamus, the tiger and lion, which hold a proud place apart, "the privilege of being an isolated species depends less on shape than on size" — the other species mingle with their neighbors and form "deteriorated affinity groups," types that have degenerated *ab immemorabili.*[89]

87. Letter of 6 November 1770, in *La signora d'Epinay e l'abate Galiani, Lettere inedite (1769–1772)*, ed. F. Nicolini (Bari, 1929), p. 114, my italics. In the version published by Perey and Maugras (*Correspondance de l'abbé Galiani* [Paris, 1881], I, 288–89), the concept of the "chain of being" is developed and other variants are noted.

88. A. O. Lovejoy, *The Great Chain of Being* (Cambridge, Mass., 1942), p. 230. Robinet (*De la Nature,* 1761–68) amended the old idea of the continuity of all natural forms, of the infinite chain which included every possible phenomenon and variety, asserting that the differences were merely quantitative. Through his reduction of specific differences from the qualitative to the quantitative, Robinet approaches the Buffonian theory of American fauna: "All the differences in nature must be differences of degree. Her most extreme productions must be recognized as mere exaggerations of something normal" (summarized by A. G. F. Gode-von Aesch, *Natural Science in German Romanticism* [New York, 1941], p. 143; cf. Lovejoy, op. cit., pp. 275–76). W. Lynskey ("Chain of Being," esp. pp. 367–68) has pointed out curious traces of the chain idea in Buffon. But in reality Buffon (like Robinet) always insists emphatically, even in the passages quoted by Lynskey, on the continuity of the real, on the imperceptible gradations of the physical world, or, in fact, on the critical principle *Natura non facit saltus,* much more than on the Platonic metaphysical architecture. For him nature is not a monumental staircase soaring up to the heavens, but an ever so gently inclined plane.

89. Daudin, op. cit., pp. 138, 140; Guyénot, op. cit., pp. 397–99.

One immediate result of this belief in the superiority of the fixed over the variable is that any tendency toward historicism in Buffon remains stifled and without issue. The theory owes its origins to Scholasticism, or rather to Aristotle. Buffon himself recounts how one day after considerable labor he thought he had discovered "a very clever system on generation"; but, he adds, "I open Aristotle, and what do I find but all my ideas in this wretched Aristotle. In fact, it's the best thing Aristotle did, for heaven's sake!"[90]

It is in fact well known that for the Stagyrite invariability is an attribute of perfection, just as immobility is an attribute of the Prime Mover; this is the way he translates into the realm of strict logic and incorporates in a system that superiority of the eternal incorruptible Ideas which Plato and even certain pre-Socratics had arrived at intuitively. Matter, mere Potentiality, is that which is moved and altered without itself moving or altering. Between God (the Pure Act) and nature (mere Potentiality) comes the whole range of natural phenomena, from the fixed stars, ethereal, immutable, close to God's presence, right down to the changeable and chaotic terrestrial world.[91] The more stable a thing is the more it is divine and happy to remain similar to itself ($\dot{\alpha}\dot{\iota}\delta\iota o\nu$); the more variable it is the further it is separated from God, and subject to corruption. In the world of nature, every natural substance is corruptible ($\varphi\theta\alpha\rho\tau\acute{o}\nu$), but the species are eternal ($\dot{\alpha}\dot{\iota}\delta\iota o\nu$). The species does not change for Aristotle; and if it does so for Buffon, it is wrong.[92] In earlier times the alchemists had venerated the fixity or unalterability of gold, in which they saw proof of its incorruptible perfection, and medieval science had been dismayed by the Copernican revolution and certain other advances in astronomy, such as the discovery of transient comets and sunspots, which

90. Hérault de Séchelles, op. cit., p. 28.
91. Cf. Dante, *Paradiso*, VII, 124 ff.
92. In times much closer to our own, Lovejoy has characterized the "classic" point of view as a yearning for uniformity with certain canons of excellence supposedly invariable and conforming to a postulated static constancy of nature (A. O. Lovejoy, "Optimism and Romanticism," *PMLA;* 42 [1927], pp. 942–43, quoted in H. M. Jones, *Ideas in America* [Cambridge, Mass., 1944], pp. 257–58), and John Dewey sees the fundamental error of the ethic of the philosophers and of modern societies in the transference to the moral world of that putative superiority of the eternal, the identical and the invariable which did exist for ancient science but which modern science has by now completely abandoned: "Changes of kind or species in plants and animals were observable only when monstruosities appeared" (by which every alteration seemed a degeneration; cf. also R. G. Collingwood, *The Idea of Nature* [Oxford, 1945], pp. 133–34; and Maupertuis, according to whom "most mutant forms are deleterious and at a disadvantage in comparison with the normal and wild types" and "all the varieties . . . tend to become extinguished; they are the deviations of nature"; see Glass, op. cit., p. 76). "Belief in the eternal uniformity of human nature is thus the surviving remnant of a belief once universally held about the heavens and about the living creatures" ("Challenge to Liberal Thought," *Fortune* [August 1944], p. 180). On this point one might observe that ethical values are, by definition, universal categories, while concepts of species or the laws of nature are typical abstractions. The legitimate criticism of the supposed absolute validity of these abstractions cannot be extended to the very principles of knowledge and to the basic criteria of every possible judgment as if they were particular instances of these abstractions. The constancy of human nature, in a broad sense, is an a priori, not an object of science.

meant that not even the fixed stars were exempt from change and corruption.[93] Following the very same path Buffon now takes up the lingering relics of Scholasticism to develop the thesis that the "large" is stable while the "small" is variable, and arrives at the point where he can attribute an objective superiority to the large over the small, and in point of fact sets up a classification of living beings in which they are ranked by volume.

Medieval natural science, influenced by the same canons and principles, had insisted on quantitative categorization; in this it had followed Pliny, who often describes the animals in order of size; this is the attitude which comes to be summed up poetically in Dante's "Greater health the greater body has"[94] and in the mythologizing of the great beasts like the whale and the elephant.[95] But Dante himself, rejoicing that Nature had

93. Abundant information, although limited to English literary history, in G. Williamson, "Mutability, Decay and XVII-Century Melancholy," *ELH: A Journal of English Literary History,* 2, no. 2 (September 1935), pp. 121–50; in D. C. Allen, "The Degeneration of Man" ("pessimism, developing from the mutation of things," p. 219); in Harris, op. cit., p. 2 and passim; and in Frank N. Egerton, "The Longevity of the Patriarchs: A Topic in the History of Demography," *Journal of the History of Ideas,* 27, no. 4 (October–December 1966), p. 578. Gordon L. Davies, "The Concept of Denudation in Seventeenth Century England," *Journal of the History of Ideas,* 27, no. 2 (April–June 1966), pp. 278–84, complains that the kernel of truth contained in those theories, namely the importance of erosion and "denudation" of the earth, was lost as eighteenth-century optimism prevailed. Davies quotes Hakewill, Goodman, and concludes by recalling the renewal of these "degenerative" (but only in a telluric, not a zoological, sense) theories on the part of Buffon. Cf. in particular the theories of the "pessimist" Goodman on "privation" as an agent, almost antidialectic, so to speak, of the changes and hence of the "corruption" of nature (Harris, op. cit., pp. 29–30, 187); and, in opposition, the reply of the "progressive" Hakewill, who cautions against confusing "changeableness" with "decadence" (pp. 55–56, 62, 79–80), and still leans desperately on the incorruptibility of the heavens as a guarantee of the constancy of nature (pp. 63–64). On Hakewill, see Perry Miller, *Errand into the Wilderness* (Cambridge, Mass., 1956), p. 220. The "decadentist" thesis was taken up again by Pierre du Moulin (Harris, op. cit., p. 117) and by William Drummond of Hawthornden (Harris, pp. 139–40), while the other was espoused by Tasso, who reaffirms the perpetuity and constancy of the species; no species whether through catastrophe, plague, or slaughter "was ever left extinct or deficient" (*Mondo creato,* V, 1618–19; ed. cit., p. 209); by John Donne in his youthful eulogy of inconstancy (Harris, op. cit., p. 124); by scientists in general after about 1635, who taught that one should see in changeability "a fluctuation rather than a degeneration" (Harris, p. 161); and naturally by the "moderns" in their battle against the "ancients" (Harris, p. 171). Thus the polemic over the decadence of nature ended by merging with the disputes which resulted in the elaboration of a new concept of Progress. And the accent shifted perceptibly from the physical to the human and historical world. But Buffon remained always on the plane of nature. The position of the great Newton had been similarly ambiguous (1706), for according to him the cosmos is a machine that runs down like a clock, ever less perfect and precise in its movements, tending, in short, toward dissolution, so that periodic adjustments are necessary on the part of the Creator, who intervenes from time to time by means of comets, until the salvation and regeneration of the world will be completed by the second coming of Christ on earth: thus decadentism and millenarianism join forces (David Kubrin, "Newton and the Cyclical Cosmos: Providence and the Mechanical Philosophy," *Journal of the History of Ideas,* 28, no. 3 [July–September 1967], pp. 325–46).

94. Dante, *Paradiso,* XXVIII, 68.

95. On the mythicizing of the elephant, see for example, *Physiologus; Gelli, Circe,* where it is the only animal that consents to return to being a man; and G. Boas, *The Happy Beast in French Thought of the Seventeenth Century* (Baltimore, 1923), pp. 28–35 (Gelli), 39 (Rorario), 44 (P. Gilles). Buffon's portrait of the elephant, "the most considerable creature of this world" (except for man) for its physical, moral, and intellectual virtues, loved and respected by all the animals, is particularly appealing. Chateaubriand, too, was to say that the elephants, "noble by nature," after the Fall stayed close to the cradle of the world, only leaving it to come and replace their companions who had died without issue in the service of man! (*Génie du christianisme,* pt. I, bk. V, chap. 9; ed. Paris, 1877, I, 117–18).

forgotten "the skill of creating suchlike animals," had expressed his horror of giants and had added that if Nature herself did not "repent of elephants and whales" this is because these great beasts are stupid, and therefore so much less dangerous than giants, who combined with "their evil will and strength . . . the power of the intellect."[96]

With this feeling of slight discomfort before such monstrous creatures, Dante seems to be reaffirming the classic taste for measure and fair proportion, and the subordination of nature to man. Even this "greater body" capable of greater "health" in fact refers to the heavens and is anyway immediately qualified: "provided it is equally well finished in all its parts."

XII. VOLUME AND PERFECTION IN MODERN ZOOLOGY

Some centuries were to elapse, however, before the criterion of size was definitively rejected. Bonnet was still asserting in 1764 that the larger animals are more intelligent and endowed with greater "bodily perfection" than the insects.[97] But with the dawning of the era of modern zoology, quantitative consideration of the animals was mentioned by Cuvier as the prime error that his new fundamental zoological classification would combat.[98] Nevertheless, before putting aside once and for all this ancient and ingenuous criterion, one should examine and be prepared to accept such factual truth as it does contain. Claude Bernard notes that "there are significant correlations between the size of an animal and the intensity of its vital phenomena. In general the vital phenomena are more intense in small animals than in large ones."[99] And a contemporary naturalist, J. B. S. Haldane, has lamented the fact that zoologists generally have paid very little attention to the differences in size between animals. Although he makes no specific reference to Buffon's work, Haldane follows the same line of approach and arrives at the notion of a structural superiority of the larger animals over the small: "The higher animals are not larger than the lower because they are more complicated. They are more complicated because they are larger." The most obvious advantage of size is the capacity it provides for maintaining body heat. And in fact "small" animals cannot live in the colder climates, nor even in the colder

---

96. *Inferno*, XXXI, 49–57, followed by Tasso in the *Mondo creato;* the earth obeys God, "although the ancients in their madness imagined it as Mother of savage monsters and giants" (III, 1099–1100; ed. cit., p. 97; cf. V, 553–57, p. 175).

97. Quoted in Daudin, op. cit., pp. 103–04, 109–10. Linnaeus attributed to natural instinct the expositive order beginning with man and ending with the smallest animals.

98. "If one considers the animal kingdom according to the principles just expounded, freeing oneself from the established prejudices on the divisions formerly admitted, and attending only to the organization and nature of the animals, *and not their size,* their usefulness, our greater or lesser knowledge of them, or all the other accessory circumstances, one will find . . ." (*Recherches sur les ossements fossiles des quadrupèdes* [1812], quoted in the *Encyclopedia Britannica*, 11th ed., s.v. "Zoology").

99. C. Bernard, *La médecine expérimentale*, p. 213.

seasons of temperate climates.[100] It is quite clear then that there was and is some solid foundation for Buffon's premise; that there exists at least a tenuous link between the volumetric displacement of animals and the immutability of the species in time.

XIII. THE INSTABILITY AND DECADENCE OF THE DOMESTIC SPECIES

Nature then, for Buffon, is not subject to the law of progress. It is at best immobility, at worst degeneration. And man himself brings about this degeneration of nature when he intervenes in nature seeking his own progress in defiance of nature. By the same token the wild beasts, not being subject to the actions of men, but closer to nature, are also less subject to change and degeneration: "Their nature seems to vary according to the different climates, but nowhere is it degenerate." Such a thesis was naturally bound to be attractive to the champions of nature in its pure state, uncorrupted by man's attentions. It revived the idea, once so staunchly held by Montaigne, that wild fruits are superior to cultivated ones: "It is the fruit that we have altered with our artifices and modified from the common order that we should really call wild. In natural fruits we can still find alive and active the true, useful, and natural virtues and properties, which we have adulterated in our cultivated fruit."[101] And it brought the added strength of scientific proof to ideas that were already familiar from Rousseau's impassioned intuition: "Nature treats with special favor all animals abandoned to her care." The wild horse, the wild cat, the wild bull, and even the wild donkey are stronger, more vigorous, and braver in the forest than when domesticated: "They lose half these advantages in becoming domestic, and one might say that the sole result of all our efforts is the bastardization of these types."[102]

The animal species in short are the more perfect the less they have varied, the more similar they have remained to their ideal prototypes. When they change they become weaker. And as they become weaker they leave themselves open to further changes and lose their racial stability. Smallness, changeability, and degeneracy are the alternating characteristics that form the links in the same pernicious chain.

---

100. "On Being the Right Size," in *Possible Worlds and Other Essays* (1927; ed. London, 1932), pp. 18–26.

101. *Essais* (Paris, 1937), I, 31, "Des cannibales," ed. Pléiade, p. 213.

102. J. J. Rousseau, *Discours sur l'inégalité* (1754; ed. F. C. Green, Cambridge, 1944), p. 32. Rousseau, in his turn, quotes Buffon on several occasions. The identical thesis is found in Maupertuis (cf. above, p. 23), and in the Buffonian *Animated Nature* of Goldsmith (Pitman, op. cit., pp. 119–20) and, later on, in Humboldt: wild animals are stable, while "modifications in bodily structure and color appear only in the domestic animals" (*Reise in die Aequinoctial-Gegenden des neuen Continents* [Stuttgart, 1859–60], II, 16, 54).

XIV. REFLECTIONS ON THE NEW WORLD

Let us get back to the Americas. With the sole exceptions of the fallow deer and roe deer, which are larger and stronger in Virginia and in temperate America than in Europe,[103] all the other animals are weaker and smaller than in the Old Continent: "This great decrease in size, whatever may be the cause of it, is a first kind of degeneration, which cannot have been brought about without considerably influencing the shape."[104]

But Buffon remains vague on the causes and phases of this "degeneration." In fact the existence of animals proper to the New World shows that their origin "cannot be attributed to simple degeneration." Other hypotheses are put forward. He suggests for instance that the two continents might once have been joined and that, when the ocean broke forth and submerged the lands which linked the two hemispheres, the species which preferred America found themselves in a differing environment from those which had made their home in Europe. This theory can be traced back substantially to the very earliest naturalists of the New World, to Oviedo and Father Acosta, and is still one of the most widely used by contemporary scientists.

It is true that man seems to be exempted from the general curse laid on the animals of America. Nature may have used a different scale in designing the New World, but "man is the only creature measured with the same yardstick."[105] It is true also that Buffon stresses man's radical difference from the animals: "Man is in all ways the handiwork of heaven; the animals are in many respects mere productions of the earth: those of one continent are not found in the other; those which are found are altered, shrunken, often changed almost to the point of being unrecognizable."[106] But in other passages, as we have already seen, the savage at least is subject to grievous limitations just like the other animals, and sometimes even more so.

One may say, in fact, that in this phase of his thought Buffon sees the American continent as immature, many of the animal species of its southern part imperfect because degenerate, and man afflicted with shortcomings which, although they do not prevent him from adapting himself to his surroundings, do make it extremely difficult for him to adapt these sur-

---

103. *Oeuvres complètes*, XIX, 22–23. The "skunks or evil-smelling animals of America" constitute another exception, because they exist there in four or five species, instead of the single European species, which is also of an "inferior or less exalted" nature than those of America (ibid., pp. 63–64). See above, n. 9.

104. Ibid., p. 56.

105. Ibid., XV, 415 (a passage quoted by Marmontel too, *Les Incas*, p. 22).

106. *Oeuvres complètes*, XV, 466; cf. Daudin, op. cit., p. 132, and below, p. 156.

roundings to himself, to tame or modify them, and thus to a certain extent cause him to share the sad fate of the higher animals.

XV. NOMENCLATURE AS THE CAUSE OF CONFUSION

The question we must ask ourselves now is this: What is the historical significance and the real value of Buffon's theory?

For a start, when he refuses the puma the noble title of "lion," and so forth, he is only really criticizing the age-old confusion resulting from the application of familiar European names to new species never before seen; from calling the jaguar quite simply a "tiger," and the alpaca a "sheep." "The names had confused the things," as Buffon himself put it.[107] And in another context, after listing various flagrant examples of mistakenly applied zoological labels, he concludes: "I have not attempted to indicate here all the errors in the nomenclature of the quadrupeds; I only want to show that there would be fewer of them if one had paid some attention to the differences of climate, if one had studied the history of the animals enough to recognize, as we did first, that the animals of the southern part of each continent are not found in both at the same time."[108]

From a formal point of view then, Buffon's thesis was the result of a need to find some way of overcoming the fact that the zoological types and concepts of the Old World could not be applied exactly as they stood to the natural phenomena of the New. A good two centuries before Buffon, Oviedo had been possibly the first to point out the mistakes in name-giving made by the earlier chroniclers and reporters in their anxiety to draw comparisons between the Old World and the New (the psychological explanation of such mistakes being the greater readiness with which one becomes aware of similarities rather than differences). And again at the end of the sixteenth century Father Acosta had complained that "to many of the things found in the Indies, the first Spaniards gave Spanish names taken from other things to which they bore some similarity, such as *piñas, pepinos, ciruelas* ['pineapples', 'cucumbers', 'plums'] when in fact they were quite different; nay, the differences between them and what are called by those names in Castile are greater than the similarities."[109]

The great philologist Justus Lipsius, a contemporary of Acosta, was another critic of these persistent lexical inaccuracies. Lipsius maintains

---

107. *Oeuvres complètes*, XV, 23, 421–22; cf. Flourens, op. cit., p. 134. Just as once the philosophers were cautioned against multiplying categories of Being, so "today one must say and repeat ceaselessly to the naturalists, do not multiply names needlessly" (quoted in Pitman, op. cit., p. 85).

108. *Oeuvres complètes*, XV, 462.

109. *Historia natural y moral*, VI, 19; ed. cit., p. 243. And on the banana, which the Spaniards called *plátano* because of "some similarity they found," cf. ibid., IV, 21; ed. cit., p. 248.

that every land has its own characteristic and unvarying fauna.[110] It is thus not permissible to apply to the animals of one region the names of the animals of another. There are no bears in Africa; "each animal evidently has its own proper area, according to its nature and characteristics," he goes on. But the Romans, being unfamiliar with the African lions, called them "bears," just as they called elephants "Lucanian cows," and ostriches "sparrows," etc.[111]

After Buffon both Father Molina and Jefferson[112] were to come back to the same point, with vehement criticisms of the muddled terminology. But the same thing occurred in physical geography, where its results are still apparent. One hears of mountain "knots" in the Andes, where there exist no such things, of "watersheds" or "divides" that do not divide, and of "passes" which are vast undulating plains disappearing out of sight. And extending the same criticism from the field of nature to that of society, Alfonso Reyes has justifiably lamented the confusion caused by the application of European political concepts to the American political scene.[113]

XVI. CONCLUSIONS

A. Buffon and Montesquieu. If at this point, having broken down Buffon's theory into its composite elements and defined its formal aspect, we turn our attention to its central idea, it is immediately revealed as a play of forces in a state of unstable equilibrium.

It contains first of all something found frequently in the eighteenth century, the tendency to interpret the organic link between the living and the natural, the creature and its environment, as a fixed, necessary, and causal relationship—just as Montesquieu established constant and determinate relationships between climates and institutions and customs, between "the nature of the earth" and "political laws." Montesquieu, as is well known, stressed the difficulty of setting up or maintaining free institutions in hot moist climates, which make the people lazy and servile. Buffon, in this respect showing more humanity than Montesquieu, found that man was, up to a certain point, exempt from this causal subjugation

---

110. Cf. *Physiologia stoicorum libri III* (Antwerp, 1640), bk. II, diss. XIX, pp. 125–26: "Once upon a time God created and produced the earth, the animals, and all you see therein. Certain different species can arise from the mingling of elements, but not absolutely from nothing. Whence comes this diversity then? Tell me, what causes it in Africa? What in furthest Asia? This Europe does not produce either lions or tigers or elephants, nor does it, as they say, nourish them. In the beginning God gave and assigned to each region its own diversity, according to its own particular climate and also its own peculiar nature." Cf. also D. C. Allen, *The Legend of Noah*, p. 130.
111. *Electorum liber II*, chap. 4, in *Opera omnia quae ad criticam propriam spectant* (Antwerp, 1600), pp. 461–62.
112. See below, pp. 213 ff. and 252 ff.
113. E. Romero, *Nuestra tierra* (Lima, 1941), p. 35; A. Reyes, *Ciencia social y deber social* (1941), in *Última Tule* (Mexico, 1942), p. 196.

to nature, and thus established his most important privilege. But as for the other animal varieties, he had no hesitation in "deducing" their qualities from the adverse factors of the soil, the humidity, and the climate. "I have stated principles, and I have seen particular cases adjust themselves thereto as if of their own volition": the famous statement from the preface to the *Esprit des lois* could equally well have been used as Buffon's epigraph.

In fact the naturalist liked to put his own ordered summary of the animal species almost on the same level as Montesquieu's analysis of political and civil laws (and Montesquieu, too, in his turn, made every effort to give his positive laws a scientific dignity equal to that of the laws of nature). Buffon was always happy to recall that his own first volumes and the *Esprit des lois* had come out simultaneously, and that he and Montesquieu had suffered together the torments of the Sorbonne and the assaults of the critics; though he himself managed considerably better than M. le Président to remain unruffled in the face of these attacks.[114] In any case Montesquieu was one of the five supreme authors recognized and revered by Buffon. "There are a bare five . . . ," he would say, "Newton, Bacon, Leibnitz, Montesquieu, and me."[115]

But it is none the less true that the application of Montesquieu's methods to the study of the natural world implied a very real scientific revolution. Such an approach took for granted first of all a considerable latitude in criticizing the work of the Maker, which no longer appeared to be perfect in each and every part, since it was now seen to include creatures some more and some less successful, more and less well formed, and even some that were actually enfeebled or corrupt. Buffon is always extremely careful in his choice of words, but this cannot disguise the fact that his attitude is radically different from that of the ancient naturalists, who held it to be their duty to sing the praises of the magnificence of all creation; or even, like Father Acosta, to threaten with the pains of hell whoever aspired to "improve the works which our Maker with highest wisdom and providence ordained in the construction of the universe."[116] Already in 1745–52, Maupertuis had demanded of the natural sciences not a mere description or classification, but the explanation of the processes by which the species have changed and animals have altered and diversified. Nature as it appears to our eyes is no more than a ruin, a

---

114. Hérault de Séchelles, op. cit., pp. 26–27.
115. Ibid., p. 37; see also pp. 44–48, for the plan outlined by Buffon for a treatise on universal legislation ("to take the spirit of all the laws existing in the universe"). "A comparison between Buffon and Montesquieu would be fruitful," wrote Sainte-Beuve, and he provided a rough outline of it himself (*Causeries du lundi*, IV, 366–67).
116. Referring in fact to the projected cutting of the Isthmus of Panama, but a statement which clearly presupposes a reverent adoration for every item of God's handiwork.

nobly proportioned building laid low by a thunderbolt.[117] And Diderot repeated (1754): "What we take to be the history of Nature is no more than the incomplete history of an instant," and safeguarding himself with a series of lofty professions of faith in the Bible, he goes on: "Just as in the animal and vegetable kingdoms an individual begins, so to speak, grows, endures a little, fades and passes on — could it not be the same for entire species?"[118] Clearly the created world was beginning to take its place in time and become if not actually historicized at least deprived of the attributes of an immobile perfection.

B. Zoological geography: Europe and America. Now examples representing these different levels of development in the natural kingdom were found to be present contemporaneously in the different parts of the globe. Reflection and deduction had decided that they were successive to each other, different stages of one and the same process. But observation revealed their simultaneous existence in this or that part of the globe. "Zoological geography" thus came into being as a provisory formulation of the theory of evolution — an early crystallization of historicist principles applied to the world of nature.

If it immediately showed signs of being affected by an anti-American bias, this was due both to the above-mentioned intrinsic tendencies and to the prevailing intellectual atmosphere of this period. In Buffon, too, one can detect the instinctive preference for the Old World and particularly its focal point, Europe. Although he stands in awe and admiration before the great carnivores, he is still at heart the instinctively superior European, accustomed to observe the strange creatures of other climes with an air of curious if benevolent condescension. Calling the American fauna immature amounted to calling the fauna of the Old World mature and perfect, worthy to serve as criterion and reference point for every other fauna in every corner of the globe. With Buffon "Europeocentrism" becomes firmly established in the new science of living nature. And it is no mere coincidence that this should have happened precisely when the idea of Europe was becoming more fully worked out, more tangible, more forceful;[119] nor is it insignificant that just as civil and political Europe was then defined by contradistinction to Asia and Africa, physical Europe should be closing ranks with the other continents of the Old World to present a bold and united front to the American world. The

117. A. O. Lovejoy, "Some Eighteenth-Century Evolutionists," *Popular Science Monthly*, 65 (1904), pp. 244–45, quoted by F. J. Teggart, *Theory and Processes of History* (Berkeley and Los Angeles, 1941), pp. 132–33; and Lovejoy, *The Great Chain of Being*, pp. 255, 268.

118. *L'interprétation de la nature*, ed. cit., pp. 91–92.

119. Cf. P. Hazard, op. cit., II, 221–35; F. Chabod, "L'idea di Europa," *Rassegna d'Italia*, 2, no. 4 (April 1947), pp. 3–17, and 2, no. 5 (May 1947), pp. 25–37, esp. pp. 30–31; C. Morandi, *L'idea dell' unità politica d'Europa nel XIX e XX secolo* (Milan, 1948), esp. pp. 41–44.

philosophers and publicists boasted of how Europe had shown the way to the rest of the world in the civil arts, in her discoveries in the technical field, and in her highly civilized social institutions; and it was actually the discovery of America that marked the date of the beginning of this new and unheard-of power and wealth on the part of the European continent.[120] Buffon follows just the same trend when he asserts that without doubt all the animals had been created in the Old World, from which some must have emigrated to the New, where in general they degenerated.[121]

Using this geographical distribution, and the hierarchy implicit in it, Buffon eluded the strict demands of the Linnaeus-style "systematizers," for whom he never showed anything but a mistrustful hostility; but he did satisfy their lesser requirements, for order, comparison, classification, and "system," which indeed he himself, in tune with them and with his age, felt to be necessary.[122] It may be true that to achieve this formal unity he made use of abstract antitheses, formed conceptual groupings of things and qualities quite plainly different from each other, and polarized into contrasted classes the "large" and the "small" animals, the Old World and the New.[123] But his method of classification and evaluation according to geographical position contained the seeds of an idea of temporal development, and this was enough to save his system from the fatal inflexibility of those other schemes.

C. *The new concept of species.*   The species vary from continent to continent, from the Old World to the New. And they are smaller or

120. "The effect of the discovery of America was to bind Asia and Africa to Europe" (Montesquieu, *L'esprit des lois,* XXI, 21), the first with American silver, the second with the traffic in slaves destined for the Americas.

121. 1766, passages quoted by Daudin, op. cit., p. 142.

122. As early as 1749, Malesherbes reproached him for not having understood Linnaeus and for having ignored the "systematizers" (Flourens, op. cit., pp. 8–9). Both were the object of lively attacks by Diderot, a great admirer of Buffon (*L'interprétation de la nature,* pp. 67–68); while Jefferson, the great adversary of Buffon, would call him "the great advocate of individualism, in opposition to classification" (letter of 22 February 1814, in *The Catalogue of the Library of Thomas Jefferson,* ed. E. M. Sowerby [Washington, D.C., 1952–59], I, 467). Today it is recognized that Buffon loathed schematic classifications of the Linnaeus type, but not classes and categories which were elements of an organic system; that his "descriptions" are the equivalent of the geometers' "definitions" (Perrier, op. cit., pp. 56–62; with reservations, Mornet, op. cit., pp. 113–16, 130–31, 151; Daudin, op. cit., pp. 39n., 166; E. Cassirer, *Goethe und die geschichtliche Welt* [Berlin, 1932], pp. 95–96; Nordenskiöld, op. cit., p. 222; Guyénot, op. cit., pp. 76–77; Glass, op. cit., p. 89; Roger, op. cit., pp. 468, 566–67; Hanks, op. cit., pp. 10, 65, 99–100; Bertin, op. cit., pp. 12, 60, 64); and that what displeased Buffon above all else in Linnaeus was the "awkward and unprepossessing appearance" he gave to natural history (Daudin, op. cit., p. 126; cf. ibid., pp. 128, 153). In general, the enemies of Linnaeus and systems will be found among the observers and lovers of nature (Adanson, 1757, quoted by Daudin, op. cit., p. 121; Rousseau, *Rêveries,* VII, ed. Garnier, p. 72; see also in *Faust,* Mephistopheles's sarcastic advice to the Scholar to "reduce and classify everything appropriately," and for other examples, Mornet, op. cit., pp. 98–104, 123–26).

123. Curious parallelisms and artificial contrasts between the two hemispheres in *Oeuvres complètes,* I, 284. It is also to be noted that Buffon, unlike almost all his friends, admirers, and disciples, looked on the rebellion of the North Americans against England with great coldness and deemed France unwise to have intervened on behalf of the United States (*Correspondance inédite,* ed. cit., II, 369).

weaker in the New World. Buffon's ideas on the weakness of the animals of America foreshadow the later theories of the variability of species — not those which see some sort of progress of the species from the imperfect to the perfect, from the inferior to the superior, but those that talk of species degenerating or possibly becoming weaker in unfavorable environments. Darwin himself was fully aware of the merits and shortcomings of Buffon's argument: "The *first* author who in modern times has treated it (species) in a scientific spirit was Buffon. But . . . his opinions fluctuated greatly at different times [see below, pp. 154–56] and . . . he does not enter on the causes or means of the transformation of species."[124] There can thus be no doubt that these barely developed intuitions of a real living history of nature, obviously related in Buffon's case to his awareness of the limitations of any schematic classification, form the major scientific result of his tortured inquiries into America's animals.

But if we look a little more deeply into Buffon's theory, we can see that it also contains implications of a logical problem that remains unsolved even today. Buffon never formulates the problem to himself with complete clarity, but instead wrestles with it blindly, with a brave but misguided recklessness. What was the basic problem implicit in Buffon's surprise and "discovery"? Clearly it was the conceivable existence of natural species that are *similar,* but distinct; the enigma of concepts in nature linked by undeniable affinities and yet separated by undeniable and irreducible individual traits. "None of the animals of South America resemble any of the animals of the south of our continent sufficiently for us to be able to regard them as being of the same species."[125] The puma is not a lion. But between the lion and the puma there are affinities that do not pertain between the fly and the elephant. What is the limit of the concept of species? Where shall we draw the line between the characteristics that seem to link two creatures as one concept, and the features that would make them into two different concepts? The whole logical foundation of the natural sciences is called into question as soon as one attempts to answer this question — even, implicitly, if one's system is built up on an *ad hoc* basis, classifying and defining as one goes along.[126]

124. C. Darwin, *The Origin of Species,* Introd., "An Historical Sketch," Modern Library ed. (New York, n.d.), p. 3; cf. Perrier, op. cit., p. 66; Daudin, op. cit., pp. 130–31, 219n., 231, 234; Lovejoy, *The Great Chain of Being,* pp. 229–30; F. Venturi, *Jeunesse de Diderot (de 1713 à 1753)* (Paris, 1939), pp. 303–08.

125. Only after a long examination can they be "suspected" of being *"the representatives* [sic] of some of those of our continent" (*Oeuvres complètes,* V, 224). Locke had already probed into some typical difficulties of the ambiguous concept of species (cf. *Essay Concerning Human Understanding,* III, chap. 6, secs. 33–39), inclining toward an absolute nominalism. On the acknowledgment of the diversity of species as an instinctive form of apprehending reality in its discontinuity, see the provocative observations of C. Lévi-Strauss, *La pensée sauvage* (Paris, 1962), pp. 180–81.

126. On his mistrust of the concept of species (only individuals exist in nature), see Glass, op. cit., pp. 90, 92–93, 96, 107.

Hard on the heels of this formidable problem came the no-less-difficult question of the existence of more or less perfect "species," with the implicit suggestion of teleological forces and evolutionary or degenerative factors. Buffon always remained faithful to a causalistic philosophy of nature, applying it enthusiastically to phenomena quite alien to the mechanism of causes — the concepts of animal species, their geographical instability, the slow varying of generations, in fact to the history, in the full sense of the word, of the world and its organisms. Such an approach revealed simultaneously his strength and his weakness; he demanded that the natural world in its entirety should be subject to his system, even if it meant charging half the known world with weakness, a quantitatively measurable weakness, to explain which he had to make alternative claims on the historicist and qualitative concepts of decadence and immaturity.[127]

127. On the interchangeability, and consequent insignificance, of the concepts of "primitive" and "decadent," see the acute observations of R. G. Collingwood, *The Idea of History* (Oxford, 1946), p. 327.

XᵉᴼXᵉᴼXᵉᴼXᵉᴼXᵉᴼXᵉᴼXᵉᴼ **2** ᵉᴼXᵉᴼXᵉᴼXᵉᴼXᵉᴼXᵉᴼXᵉᴼX

Some Figures
of the Enlightenment

I. HUME AND THE INFERIORITY OF THE INHABITANTS OF THE TROPICS

IT was unfortunate that out of the whole of Buffon's theory, so rich in motifs, so full of provocative suggestions and echoes of long-forgotten ideas, it should have been the very weakest part that his contemporaries chose to follow up, their appetite whetted by its facile moralizations, its verdicts of "better" and "worse." And while Buffon had left it as an implicit notion of secondary importance, the philosophers seized on it and lost no time in exploring all the possibilities of such a fruitful and colorful source of polemic and scandal.

Observing a certain caution in his choice of words, Hume in his famous essay *Of National Characters* (1748) had suggested that "there is some reason to think that all the nations which live beyond the polar circles or between the tropics, are inferior to the rest of the species." But he had immediately excluded geographico-naturalistic factors by adding that this could be explained by the "poverty" and "misery" of the inhabitants of the northern regions, and by the "indolence" of those of the south, "from their few necessities . . . without our having recourse to *physical* causes."[1] Hume is referring to the inhabitants of the Arctic and tropical zones, not to the Americans in particular; to men, not to zoological species; and to economic factors, although related to climate, not to a fixed and inescapable geographical determinism.

Hume, in fact, anticipating in this particular instance his own radical criticism of the principle of cause, reexamines and revises the age-old tradition of ethnopsychology and its attempts to pass from a mere description and typology of the characteristics of the various peoples to a causal and thus by definition emphatically naturalistic explanation for such characteristics.

1. D. Hume, *Essays* (World's Classics ed.), p. 213; his italics. Cf. on Hume's thesis A. J. Toynbee, *A Study of History* (London, 1935), I, 470 ff.; Teggart, op. cit., pp. 180–83.

35

The theory goes back to the time of man's earliest and most ambitious strivings after scientific knowledge. Hippocrates, the father of medicine and mythical great-grandson of Heracles and Asclepius, saw a connection between alteration in climate or sudden seasonal change and the varied temperaments and physiological qualities of men.[2] Socrates, in Plato's *Republic* (435e–436a), divides up the faculties of the soul among the various peoples, and assigns to the Thracians, to the Scythians, and in general to the northern races a strong passionality; to the Greeks the desire to learn, or philosophy; and to the Phoenicians and Egyptians the thirst for material profit.

Similarly Aristotle, in his *Politics* (VII, 1327b), says that the peoples "in the cold countries and in Europe are excessively impulsive," but rather unintelligent, and of limited organizational capacity; they are independent, but incapable of true government. The peoples of Asia are intelligent and resourceful "but morally weak and thus habitually live in submission and slavery." The Greeks, on the other hand, in a geographically intermediate region, are at the same time brave and intelligent, and live in liberty and with good government. Polybius and Strabo are in agreement in explaining the temperament of peoples by their climates, those who are subject to severe conditions being warlike, and those who inhabit regions where nature is gentle and benign being peaceable.[3]

Among the Latin writers, Titus Livy repeats of the Samnites that the people are similar to their environment. Cicero, in his *De Lege Agraria,* develops the idea that customs are shaped more by a people's surroundings and means of subsistence than by heredity. And in Lucan one reads that the peoples of the north are fierce and warlike, while those of the soft Levant are mild and peace-loving.[4] For the ancients the link between climate and spirit was almost a commonplace.

II. BODIN'S THEORY OF CLIMATES

But speculation along these lines had continued so feebly in the Middle Ages, stifled perhaps by the prevailing Christian doctrine of the universal equality of men (for which the sole remaining distinction was the

---

2. *Trattato delle Arie, Acque e Luoghi,* sec. 24, quoted by Teggart, op. cit., p. 174.

3. See quotations in Teggart, op. cit., pp. 174–75. For Polybius see also Bodin, below, sec. 2. But of Strabo, Hume writes that in the second book he "rejects, in a great measure, the influence of climates upon man. All is custom and education, says he" (*Essays,* ed. cit., p. 207n.).

4. *Pharsalia,* VIII, 363–68 (Lentulus's reply to Pompey, who had described the Orientals as gallant and brave in war: ibid., VIII, 295–97 and ff.). In a footnote (by either Hugo Grotius or T. Farnabius; Amsterdam ed., 1651) other authors are cited in support of the climatic thesis: Vegetius, I, 2; Aristotle; Herodotus; Vitruvius, bk. V; and the Italian R. Valturius (1405–75), in bk. VI of the *De re militari* (1460). Further quotations concerning the link between climate and ability can easily be collected from the writings of Plato (*Critias,* 109), Sallust, Plutarch, Tertullian, etc. Cf. also C. Curcio, *Europa — Storia di un'idea* (Florence, 1958), I, 58–78.

nongeographical one between the faithful and the unbelievers), that when such inquiries were revived in the Renaissance it was almost with a sense of new discovery. And even after Machiavelli and Guicciardini had made their incisive observations on the characters of the various peoples of Europe, Jean Bodin was convinced of his own originality in discussing the diverse forms of government suited or unsuited to each single people, "to the nature of the place . . . and to its natural laws." This was an extremely important subject, he declared, "and yet those who have written of the Republic have not discussed this topic at all."[5]

The classical writers had put forward a few conjectures on the subject. But they were so ignorant of the geography of the globe that they were not in a position to establish any scientific relationship or constant law linking the environment of each race with its civil and religious institutions. No, "obviously the ancient writers could leave us nothing of that kind." These questions are difficult and delicate and "no one has yet been able to cast any light on these obscure matters."[6]

Bodin is of course familiar with the fatalistic theories of Galen and Polybius, which see climate as an inflexible and inescapable influence on man, but he rejects these too. He appeals to Christian doctrine to help him refute and ridicule the astrological theories of Ptolemy and his followers right down to Jerome Cardan, for whom the destiny of all great states was governed by the tail of the Great Bear. Calling instead on nature and experience, Bodin describes zone by zone the temperament and customs of the northerners, the "midlanders," and the southerners—the first robust and warlike, the second versed in politics and letters, the last more inclined to philosophy and contemplation; or ringing the changes with other parallelisms and correspondences, he sees them as representing respectively youth, maturity, and old age; *ars, prudentia,* and *scientia;* the Phrygian, Doric, and Lydian modes; common sense, reason, and the intellect; democracy, magistracy, and pontificate; Mars, Jove, and Saturn; or the Moon, Mercury, and Venus.[7]

But enough of these intellectual relics and universal concordances,

5. *La République,* p. 661, quoted by P. Mesnard, *L'essor de la philosophie politique au XVIe siècle* (Paris, 1936), p. 531. According to E. Barker, in *National Character* (London, 1939), pp. 50–51, it was precisely the French theorists, beginning with Bodin, that made the idea of geographic determinism fashionable. On the theory of climate in Bodin, Botero, and Milton, see Zera S. Fink, *The Classical Republicans* (Evanston, Ill., 1945), pp. 91–94, 191–92; in Bodin, Nifo, etc., see Curcio, op. cit., I, 215, 220–22; and in Vasari, Bodin, and Proctor, see H. Weisinger, "Ideas of History during the Renaissance," *Journal of the History of Ideas,* 6 (1945), p. 426; as utilized in the verdicts on the Americas in particular, see R. Romeo, *Le scoperte americane nella coscienza italiana del Cinquecento* (Milan-Naples, 1954), pp. 120–24.

6. Jean Bodin, *La méthode de l'histoire (Methodus ad facilem historiarum cognitionem),* 1566; trans. P. Mesnard (Paris, 1941), pp. 68–69. On the ignorance of the ancients on the subject of astronomy too, cf. ibid., pp. 132, 226, 326.

7. *Méthode,* pp. 69–71, 94, 105, 108, 113, 131 ff., 224; Mesnard, op. cit., pp. 532–33; Romeo, op. cit., pp. 123–24.

which are as jarring in a realistic political thinker like Bodin as his theories of demonology or his cabalistic numerology. What *is* new and useful in Bodin in his idea of the globe, the whole globe, divided up from the poles to the equator in parallel bands that form so many relatively uniform climatic zones. He takes into account the altitude, the exposure to east or west, the winds, the fertility of the soil, the paths of communication and the national characteristics arising from all these factors and the history of each region. But latitude always remains the dominant factor, and all other factors are carefully referred back to that. The east has a great affinity with the south, and the west with the north. The westerners are thus as it were attenuated Nordics, the easterners pseudosoutherners. The plains stand in relation to the mountains as the warm south to the frigid north, and so on.[8]

The logical result of this reducing of every physical element, including longitude, to a question of parallels, is that there is no specific problem of the American continent. Every zone in America has the climate proper to the latitude to which it belongs, and to which certain zones of the Old World also belong. There is no opposition between the two hemispheres, but a parallelism in the strictest geographical sense. As Bodin shrewdly observes, one cannot even really say that the Americas are the Western world. Such an illusion arose perhaps from the antithesis between East and West Indies. Within our own hemisphere we can distinguish an Orient (the Moluccas or Spice Islands), from an Occident (the Canaries). Yet America is neither to the east or to the west, but separated from the Indies and Africa by immense distances; it is in fact "in the middle between Orient and Occident," and the influences acting on America are not those of either region.[9]

Thus Bodin's America eludes in advance the particular fate reserved for the west by later theories (see below, pp. 129 ff.), and remains intact, neither tainted with any special stigma nor crowned by any glowing halo. Nor has history stamped it with any particularly well-defined character; it is the *geographers* who tell us the histories of the Scythians, the Indians, the Ethiopians, *and the Americans,* while the historians of other countries consider themselves obliged to know and describe first the geography of these countries.[10] This is perhaps the earliest formulation of the notion that was to enjoy such popularity, of America as "geography" not "history," future not past, etc.; but in Bodin the idea has neither polemic acerbity nor any auspicious implication. Bodin is no admirer of primitive peoples. Referring to the mythical Golden Age, he writes sarcastically

8. *Méthode,* pp. 116–17, 122; Mesnard, op. cit., pp. 533–35; Teggart. op. cit., p. 175.
9. *Méthode,* pp. 70, 115.
10. Ibid., p. 11.

that in comparison with our own "it could well be an age of iron"; and he mocks as *laudatores temporis acti* the people who are always lamenting "that the human race never ceases to degenerate."[11] When Bodin hails America, then, it is not for the simple and uncorrupted customs of the natives—a monarchical society, he observes, and incapable of democracy and aristocracy even if they have never read Aristotle, a society that punishes incest without being acquainted either with Plato or the decrees of Pope Innocent, simply following what nature and experience usually require[12]—but instead, with lofty originality, for the plain fact of its existence being revealed and the resulting unification of the world; from that time on, commerce has increased and "all men have become brothers and share miraculously in the universal republic, as if they formed one same city."[13] The only point in which he seems to anticipate Buffon's theories is when he states that men and plants (and animals) degenerate slowly whenever they undergo a change of environment;[14] but this is only an incidental corollary to his basic thesis of a necessary and salutary harmony between the creature and his environment. And his influence on the later development of the debate on the nature of America only comes about indirectly when the theory of climate put forward in his *Methodus* (1566) and taken up again in his more famous work, the *Republic* (1576), began to be more generally known and in fact widely accepted.

III. THE THEORY OF CLIMATES FROM TASSO TO HUME

Tasso's *Gerusalemme liberata* appeared a few years later, in 1581. And at the very outset of the poem all Europe read and repeated how in that sweet land of Touraine, "the soft and smiling and happy earth produces inhabitants like unto itself."[15]

At the same time the theory of the relativity of human nature and its

11. Ibid., pp. 293–99.

12. Ibid., pp. 203, 206, 268.

13. Ibid., p. 198. La Popelinière repeated with equal admiration: "All the peoples of the world, formerly barbarians, savages, and enemies or completely unknown to each other, now know, frequent, love, and help one another, and even seem to converse ordinarily in this world as in one city" (1599; quoted by H. Hauser, *La modernité du XVI* siècle* [Paris, 1930], p. 55; on La Popelinière and the influence which the geographic discoveries had on his thought, see the study by Corrado Vivanti, "Alle origini dell'idea di civiltà. Le scoperte geografiche e gli scritti di Henri de la Popelinière," *Rivista Storica Italiana*, 74, no. 2 [June 1962], pp. 225–49). In the eighteenth century this function of America became a commonplace, and in the second half of the century the image of America as a market, as an outlet for European products, came to be more stressed than the traditional idea of America as a source of precious metals, spices, and tobacco (see examples from 1776 and 1792 in S. Zavala, *América en el espíritu francés del siglo XVIII* [Mexico, 1949], pp. 80, 82, 87, 254).

14. *Méthode*, pp. 71, 129; Buffon, however, would not have liked his argument that a large "state" is no more of a "state" than a small one, "any more than an elephant can be said to be any more of an animal than an ant" (ibid., p. 143).

15. *Gerusalemme liberata*, I, 62: "La terra molle e lieta e dilettosa / Simili a sé gli abitator produce." For other climatic theories of Tasso (dating from 1571), of possible derivation from Bodin, see L. Olschki, "La lettre du Tasse sur la France et les Français," *Romanic Review*, 34, no. 4 (December 1943), pp. 345, 348–49. Cf. Unánue, below, pp. 302 ff.

variability according to climate and latitude was being further confirmed and disseminated by Montaigne, and even more systematically by his disciple Charron; Botero and Campanella followed up Bodin's speculations on the physical environments of races; and with the voluminous data furnished by explorers, ethnographers, and missionaries continually adding to the knowledge of the anthropology and geography of all parts of the world, the problem of the link between climate, temperament, and customs was constantly rekindled and kept in the public eye. This mental association occurred so immediately and spontaneously that if we inquire into who was the first to criticize the climate of America and the temperament of its inhabitants we find ourselves taken right back to Columbus's patroness in person, Queen Isabella. When she first heard from the admiral that the trees in the Indies did not have deep roots, on account of the larger rainfall there and the resulting wetness of the earth, the sovereign displayed great distress and preoccupation, and commented that "this land, where the trees are not firmly rooted, must produce men of little truthfulness and less constancy."[16]

Oviedo, in relating the anecdote, expresses his admiration for Isabella's wisdom, adding on his own account that "these people of the Indies are very untruthful and of little firmness, like children of six or seven years old, or not even as reliable as them." But he adds that even "some Christians have been infected very much with the same disease," and thus provides us with one of the very earliest statements of the theory of America's "telluric inferiority" and the "tropicalization of the white man," part of which was of course bound to elicit the approval of de Pauw,[17] and did not escape Humboldt's attention either.[18]

Among the many scholars who looked into the effects of climate after Bodin, Voltaire mentions the traveler Chardin, who may have been acquainted with Ibn-Khaldun's climatic theories,[19] the ingenious Fontenelle, and the abbé Du Bos. Teggart adds to the list the names of Father Bouhours, Mme Dacier, and particularly that of Dr. John Arbuthnot,[20]

16. Oviedo, *Historia general y natural*, IV, 1 (ed. cit., I, 100–01). The idea has a curious parallel in Diderot, who likens intellectual notions without any base in nature "to these northern forests whose trees have no roots. It takes only a light gust of wind to blow down a whole forest of trees and ideas" (*L'interprétation de la nature*, VIII; ed. cit., p. 10).

17. *Recherches philosophiques sur les Américains ou Mémoires intéressants pour servir à histoire de l'espèce humaine* (Berlin, 1768–69), I, 9.

18. *Examen critique de l'histoire de la géographie du nouveau continent . . .* (Paris, 1835–39), III, 146n.

19. See Warren E. Gates, "The Spread of Ibn Khaldûn's Ideas on Climate and Culture," *Journal of the History of Ideas*, 37, no. 3 (July–September 1967), pp. 415–22.

20. *Essay concerning the Effects of Air on Human Bodies*, 1735 (French trans., 1742); cf. F. Meinecke, *Die Entstehung des Historismus* (Munich-Berlin, 1936), I, 150n., 185. De Pauw (*Défense*, 1771 ed., p. 183) mentions Charron, Chardin, Montesquieu, etc. On the transition between the abbé Du Bos and Montesquieu, with details on Arbuthnot and some minor authors, see R. Mercier, "La théorie des climats des *Réflexions critiques* à *l'Esprit des lois*," *Revue d'histoire littéraire de la France*, 53,

reputed to have inspired Montesquieu. Hume himself mentions Bacon and Berkeley, Cardinal Bentivoglio and Sir William Temple. In fact the subject was by this time becoming a commonplace, one of the topics of the day. And the various arguments and speculations received additional impetus from two other trends: firstly, from the desire to define the New World and its peoples and natural species, not generically, but in relation to Europe, and secondly, from the effort to explain in strict scientific terms the infinite and apparently useless variety of created beings; to clarify, and not just in terms of a simple relationship of cause and effect, the relationship between physical surroundings and living organisms, their evolving forms and, in the case of men, their capacity for progress and social institutions. In particular, "climate" seemed to bridge the logical gap between the thesis of the *physical* weakness of the American continent, and its *civil* and political inferiority. It was only one factor, but a crucial factor which made it possible to envisage a single explanation for an infinity of geographical and historical phenomena.

Thus when the subject of the Americas (and the exotic regions generally) came under the scrutiny of the great minds of the eighteenth century, the result was the appearance of a series of problems that were in some aspects quite new. And one notices this originality not only in regard to what the classical writers had to say about the "collective psychology" of peoples, but also in the bluntly positive or negative attitudes, the praises or slanders produced by almost all the early chroniclers and explorers. But to return to the starting point of this little digression, Hume's treatment of the problem is marked by its flexibility and elasticity; he rules out the play of mechanical "causes," and in every attempt at an equation he insists on the presence of an unknown quantity. At first sight, he admits, it would seem that the air, the food, and the climate have a decisive influence on living beings—the fierce bulldogs and fighting cocks of the English, the powerful Flemish horses, the nimble Spanish colts "when transplanted from one country to another will soon lose the qualities they gained from their native climate. Why, one must ask oneself, does the same thing not happen with men?"[21]

But after careful analysis Hume concludes "that physical causes have no discernible operation on the human mind,"[22] and that as for Europeans transplanted to other climes, "the Spanish, English, French, and Dutch

no. 1 (January–March 1953), pp. 17–37, and no. 2 (April–June 1953), pp. 159–74; on the transition between Du Bos and Herder, see M. Rouché, *La philosophie de l'histoire de Herder* (Paris, 1940), pp. 23 n. 2, 268.

21. Hume, *Essays*, ed. cit., p. 207; this is Bodin's thesis, see above, p. 00. On the links between food and national character, see G. Atkinson, *Les relations de voyages du XVIIe siècle* (Paris, 1924), pp. 169–70.

22. *Essays*, ed. cit., p. 209.

colonies are all distinguishable even between the tropics."[23] If the natives of the north have often conquered those of the south, this is not because the people of the north are more valorous or courageous, but because most of the conquests were made "by poverty and want upon plenty and riches."[24]

However, despite the drastic revision to which it had been subjected by Hume, even this ancient doctrine of the link between climate and character—duly modified to suit the new circumstances, drawing new life from the rationalists' urge for clear and precise relationships that do not vary in time but remain fixed like the laws of nature,[25] organized, self-evident, as simple and undeniable as hot and cold, drought and monsoon—this notion, too, in the end was made to concur in the summary verdict that Europe was about to pronounce on America. The continent which at the time of its discovery had raised so many problems for the philosophers and theologians, cosmographers and politicians, now after the eclipse of the baroque era once again became the focus of attention, as the practical and impassioned minds of the eighteenth century plunged into the polemic of Nature and Climate.

IV. VOLTAIRE: THE BEARDLESS INDIAN AND THE COWARDLY LION

One might think that Voltaire was taking Hume's geographico-political theories and applying them precisely to America when he comments: "There is one observation to be made on the nations of the New World that Father Lafitau did not make at all, namely that the peoples that live furthest away from the tropics have always been invincible, and those nearest to the tropics have almost always been submitted to monarchs."[26] But although Lafitau failed to make this observation, and Voltaire presents it as if it were his own discovery, it actually derives very clearly from the Baron de Montesquieu.[27]

23. Ibid., p. 210.

24. Ibid., p. 216. An exact precedent for this objection can be found in Boccalini: see Curcio, op. cit., I, 318–19, and a parallel in Turgot, ibid., pp. 392–93. Another Bodinian thesis: "The greatest empires have always spread to the south, almost never from south to north" (*Méthode*, p. 76). On the revival of the antithesis between "northern climate" and "southern climate" in romantic thought (Madame de Staël, Bonstetten, Leopardi, Melchiorre Gioia) see M. Petrocchi, *Miti e suggestioni nella storia europea* (Florence, 1950), pp. 51–58.

25. Croce has noted the vogue enjoyed by the concept of climate in the eighteenth century, "a refuge of ignorance serving to explain the varying characteristics of peoples and their histories, and naturalistically replacing the notion of development by intellectual and moral growth and inner dialectic" ("A proposito della filosofia italiana del Settecento," in *La letteratura del Settecento* [Bari, 1949], p. 219). A vigorous criticism of the climatic theories that postulate constant factors to explain the inconstant history of peoples is found in R. G. Collingwood, *The Idea of History*, p. 200; a denunciation of its racist tendencies appears in T. Simard, *Etude critique sur la formation de la doctrine des races au XVIII° siècle et son expansion au XIX° siècle* (Brussels, 1922), pp. 36–57 and passim.

26. "Discours préliminaire" to *Essai sur les moeurs* (1765; London ed., 1770–79), I, 37.

27. *L'esprit des lois*, bk. XVII. The peoples of warm climates are cowardly and enslaved, whereas those of cold climates are free: "This has been found to be true in America too: the despotic empires of Mexico and Peru were toward the equator, and almost all the free peoples were and still are toward the poles" (chap. II; see also ibid., chap. VII, n. 1).

Of course the liveliness of Voltaire's cosmopolitical interest—which also accounts for the best polemic element in his historiography, his reaction to Bossuet's "Europeocentrism"—suffices to save him from the temptation to condemn other peoples or continents out of hand. Voltaire does not believe anyway in the decisive influence of climate: "Climate has some power, government a hundred times more, and religion joined to government more still." And he refutes Montesquieu, whom he finds guilty of having exaggerated Bodin's system and the comments of Chardin, the abbé Du Bos, and Fontenelle, simply by reminding him of how much the characters of nations have changed over the centuries, while the climate has remained the same: "With time everything changes in the body and mind. Perhaps the day will come when the Americans will be teaching the arts to the peoples of Europe."[28]

Nor does Voltaire believe, like Buffon, in the common origin of the human race. Every continent is capable of producing its own animals. "If we are not surprised to find flies in America, it is absurd to be surprised to find men there."[29] There is no problem, Voltaire asserts, in the fact that certain species resemble each other, nor in the fact that others are partially or entirely different. And even less is there any reason to talk of superiority or inferiority. "America, like Africa and Asia, produces plants and animals that resemble those of Europe; and again like Africa and Asia, it produces many which have no possible similarity to those of the Old World."[30]

Up to this point Voltaire's position is unassailable, though strictly a defensive one. But his lively awareness of the infinite variety of the world induces him to pay too much attention, here as so often elsewhere, to the curious or surprising detail; he cannot resist a tendency to delight in whatever is strange, unexpected, paradoxical. Mme du Châtelet is to be amused. And M. de Voltaire has not read through these great tomes of Buffon without fishing out a few spicy little tales. So the historian in his flowing prose presents all the naturalist's brilliant new discoveries and explanations for them, but reduces them to the level of anecdote, little colorful sketches or witty observations.

28. *Dictionnaire philosophique* (1764) and *Questions sur l'Encyclopédie* (1770–72), s.v. "Climat" (in *Oeuvres* [London, 1770–79], XLII, 162–65). Religious precepts, Voltaire goes on, are often adapted to the climate and its hygienic demands, but dogmas depend "solely on opinion, that inconstant queen of the world" (ibid., pp. 166–67).

29. *Essai sur les moeurs* (1753–58), chap. 146, opening.

30. Ibid. Cf. "Discours préliminaire," ed. cit., I, 38–39: "The same Providence that produced the elephant, the rhinoceros, and the Negroes gave birth in another world to the *orignans* [or rather *orignacs* or *orignals*, i.e., "elks"], the *contours* [which are probably *kunturs* or "condors"], pigs with navels on their backs, and men of a character different from ours." In the Beuchot edition (XI, 26), the sentence about pigs is toned down to read "animals who were long believed to have navels on their backs"; but it comes directly from Oviedo: "These pigs . . . have the umbilicus in the middle of their spines" (*Sumario de la natural historia de las Indias* [1526; Madrid ed., 1858], I, 488–89; cf. *Historia general y natural*, 1535, bk. XII, chap. 20; ed. cit., I, 409).

Why is the continent half empty? There are few people, Voltaire summarizes, because America "is covered with marshes which make the air very unhealthy," because the earth of America produces "a prodigious number of poisons" (so that the arrows whose tips are envenomed with the juice squeezed from grass "make wounds that are always fatal"),[31] and also because its inhabitants were rather unindustrious and sometimes stupid too.

The cumulative result of these deficiencies is an extraordinary shortage of food, so that the animals are in general undernourished, the carnivores are almost extinct, and the men incapable of multiplying: "It is to be wondered at [Voltaire concludes] that in America there are more men than monkeys."[32] When Candide and his faithful Cacambo are captured by the Oreillons, and are about to be put into the cooking pot, the servant remarks to the savages that they have every right to eat them; to kill one's neighbor is a legitimate and common custom throughout the world. "If we do not avail ourselves of our right to eat our neighbors, this is because we can find elsewhere the wherewithal to make good cheer; but you do not have the same resources as us. . . ."[33]

The meagerness of nutrition in America formed part of the picture of the inhospitable continent, so mean toward its own progeny that they were forced into cannibalism, as poor in useful commodities as it was rich in deadly metals. This argument, supported as it was by plain and undeniable facts,[34] had the effect of making the continent of America seem more disturbingly alien and unattractive than ever.

But of all the observations on the physical aspect of America, "the most strange, perhaps," according to Voltaire, is that "there is only one race that have beards."[35] These hairless peoples were always easily overcome by the Europeans and made no attempts at rebellion[36] — and were thus endowed with spiritual qualities which harmonized perhaps with their ignominiously unadorned chins, but which for Voltaire, so little

31. In Oviedo *hierva* is used antonomastically to refer to the poisonous grass the *indios* use to make their arrows more lethal.

32. *Essai sur les moeurs*, chap. 146, conclusion.

33. *Candide*, XVI; Pléiade ed., 181 (and cf. below, p. 210). Another writer was to say (1787) that America did not have the means to nourish half the inhabitants said to have been massacred by the Europeans! (quoted by Zavala, *América*, p. 56).

34. Even today, in the non-grain-producing areas of South America, hunger is endemic; see, among more recent works, the eloquently titled book by Josué de Castro, *Geografia da fome: A fome no Brasil* (Rio de Janeiro, 1946). We shall come across "food shortage" again in de Pauw, of course; and the apologists of America, such as Clavigero, for example, will with great indignation deny this; cf. below, p. 211.

35. I.e., the Eskimos: "Discours préliminaire," I, 37–38; *Essai sur les moeurs*, chaps. 145, 146. But perhaps not even the Eskimos form an exception; see *Dictionnaire philosophique*, s.v. "Barbe," ed. Beuchot (Paris, 1878), XVII, 550; *Des singularités de la nature*, chap. 36, ed. cit., XXVII, 185.

36. *Essai sur les moeurs*, chap. 145. See also Jean David, "Voltaire et les Indiens d'Amérique," *Modern Language Quarterly*, 9, no. 1 (March 1948), pp. 90–101.

inclined to admire bloodthirsty heroes or a tumultuous populace, were in no way the marks of an incurable inferiority.

As for the fauna, Voltaire delights in stressing how it shows all the characteristics of a world turned upside down. America lacks both dogs and cats and many other very common domestic animals. There are oxen, but of a particularly monstrous and ferocious type—they seemed to be more like buffaloes or camels. And the pigs in Mexico—by some whim of nature that conjures up the image more of some sort of piggy bank—have their navels on their backs. The moral and physical characteristics of these animals of America are all topsy-turvy—the lambs are big and powerful, the lions "mean and cowardly."[37]

Voltaire enjoys himself at the expense of these poor cowardly lions with the same gusto he displays elsewhere in deflating other monarchs (not of the forest) and other (human) predators and bullies. "Mexico and Peru had lions, but small and without manes; and *what is even stranger,* the lion of these climates was a cowardly animal."[38] The men are beardless, the lions lack manes. *Sta senza chioma il fier leon*—"the proud lion is left shorn."[39] When Voltaire has done with this poor bald cringing feline, it almost becomes a sort of ancestor of the Reluctant Dragon or of that sentimental creature Ferdinand the Bull.

V. RAYNAL: AMERICA AS IMMATURE AND THE AMERICANS DECREPIT

Among Voltaire's followers, disciples, and popularizers, Buffon's theories become more heavily stressed. But it is always a question of verbal or rather rhetorical emphasis, never a matter of new speculative developments. Neither Raynal nor Marmontel, for instance, is the type to tackle such elevated and involved problems. For them the weakness of America serves as literary expedient—in Raynal's case because it provides the cue for a whole series of sensualistic themes, for Marmontel because it could be made to support his humanitarian theses.

In that lengthy and miscellaneous amalgam known as the *Histoire philosophique et politique des établissements et du commerce des Européens dans les deux Indes*—incidentally a typically inflated seventeenth-century title for a work that claims to be the embodiment of Reason in all its glory, but whose style, and method too, belong in fact to pre-Voltairian historiography—Raynal makes a number of distorted and

---

37. "Discours préliminaire," I, 38. Clavigero (*Storia antica del Messico,* ed. cit., I, 71–72) explains the origin of the error of the "early historians of America" concerning pigs with dorsal umbilici; "and even now," he adds, "there are people who still believe it. . . . That's how difficult it is to eradicate popular beliefs!"

38. *Essai sur les moeurs,* chap. 146: an almost exact echo of Buffon's words (see above, p. 3). On Voltaire's agreement with de Pauw, see below, p. 153. De Pauw, in the *Défense* (1771 ed., p. 17), quotes the entire passage from Voltaire given here on p. 44.

39. Lorenzo Mascheroni, *Invito a Lesbia Cidonia* (1793), line 413 (on the skeleton of a lion).

muddled references to the decadence of America. Such sheep as have been acclimatized in Mexico produce poor meat, milk, and wool.[40] The climate of Cartagena leads to degeneration.[41] The climate of Chile, however, is blessed by nature and does not bring degeneration but rather perfection of the species.[42] And if the European does not degenerate in America, this is because man has more "moral fiber."[43]

Only right at the end of the work (actually in the ninth volume of the edition we happen to have before us) does Raynal confront the fundamental problem of the new continent, or rather Buffon's version of it. Having regaled us with a number of brilliant symmetries and carefully contrived harmonies, "balances" and "correspondences" between the Old World and the New, the *philosophe* suddenly finds himself in a dilemma. He sees the Pacific Ocean so large and the Atlantic so small, the inexplicable way the southern extremities of the continents dwindle away to nothing, and this quirk of the Cordilleras by which they run from north to south instead of following the fundamental east-west direction like all the other

40. All the domestic animals taken to Mexico "degenerated very rapidly" through the inefficiency of the breeders (a non-Buffonian thesis: see above p. 5); but all, with the exception of the sheep, little by little made up the lost ground (an anti-Buffonian thesis). Only the milk, meat, and wool of the poor sheep remained "of inferior quality" (op. cit., III, 340).

41. Op. cit., IV, 79–80.

42. In Chile "none of the fruits of Europe degenerated. Several of its animals were perfected . . . [including the] horses. . . . Nature pushed her favors further": she gave the country copper and gold (op. cit., IV, 277). Father Acosta had already observed (1590): "Thus in the fruits of the earth, as in gifts of the mind, this land [Chile] is closer to the condition of Europe than any other in these Indies" (*Historia natural y moral*, II, 4; ed. cit., p. 90). "It is a land fertile and fresh of itself: it bears all sorts of Spanish fruits. There is bread and wine in abundance: it is plentiful in pasture and livestock; a healthy and temperate climate, not too cold or too hot. It has perfect summer and winter" (ibid., III, 24; ed. cit., p. 181). "In the kingdom of Chile one makes wine as in Spain, because it has the same climate" (ibid., IV, 32; ed. cit., p. 273). See Fr. Molina's defense, below, p. 213.

43. "The Europeans transplanted to the American islands should have degenerated there, like the animals that were taken there"; but instead they resisted "because of all creatures they are the ones with the most morale" (op. cit., VI, 167) — words which (if they were not contradicted by others on the bastardization of Europeans in America, and on the United States's lack of geniuses: see also Hans Wolpe, *Raynal et sa machine de guerre* [Paris, 1956], pp. 166–67, and below, pp. 262 ff., and if we forgot that Raynal describes de Pauw, without mentioning him by name however, as "an illustrious writer and one whom one must still admire even while disagreeing with him . . . a profound and enlightened philosopher": see A. Feugère, "Raynal, Diderot et quelques autres historiens des deux Indes," *Revue d'histoire littéraire de la France*, 22 [1915], pp. 409, 412) would make us doubt whether Raynal knew de Pauw's book, published just a few years before his own, in which the author insists on the contrary that both the natives and the Creoles degenerate (*Recherches philosophiques sur les Américains*, II, 68–69, 165). H. W. Church too ("Corneille de Pauw and the controversy over his *Recherches philosophiques sur les Américains*," *PMLA*, 51 [1936], pp. 192–93) remains doubtful about the relations between de Pauw and Raynal. For Wolpe, on the other hand, "one cannot deny . . . that . . . Raynal borrowed liberally from several works, and notably the *Recherches philosophiques sur les Américains* of Pauw [*sic*]" (Wolpe, op. cit., p. 13), which point had in any case been demonstrated with textual parallels by Feugère ("Raynal, Diderot . . . , *Revue d'histoire littéraire de la France* 20 [1913], pp. 343–78, and 22 [1915], pp. 409–13) who brings out other deformations and reversals of de Pauwian theses. In a violent attack on Raynal, Anacharsis Cloots, de Pauw's nephew, accused him directly of plagiarism: "My uncle de Pauw wrung his hands when he saw whole pages of his work on the Americans incorporated without quotation marks by the wily Raynal" (*Chronique de Paris* [1790–91], in G. Avenel, *A. Cloots* [Paris, 1865], I, 274). For the police persecution to which it was subjected, and the resulting increased success of Raynal's *Histoire*, see J. P. Belin, *Le mouvement philosophique de 1748 à 1789* (Paris, 1913), pp. 306–12.

mountains of Tartary and Europe.[44] Surveying such indiscipline and disorder, Raynal stops in his tracks, filled with vexation: "The mind halts and *is grieved* to see the crumbling of the plan of order and symmetry with which it had beautified its system of the earth. The observer is left still more unhappy with his dreams when he comes to consider the excessive height of the mountains of Peru. . . ." These immense peaks and the great rivers, the marshes and the absence of sands, and the rest "are so many marks of a world just coming to life."[45]

A world newborn, or just coming to life, a world poverty-stricken and half empty. At the mere mention of these words, as if at the pronouncing of some magic formula, all Buffon's theories come tumbling out — not textually quoted,[46] but clearly recognizable even in the way the sensualist Raynal deplores the scant erotic vigor of the Americans. "This hemisphere untilled and uninhabited can only signify a recent world," Raynal begins, "and does one not find besides in the Old World twice as many animal species as in the New; considerably larger animals within the same species; monsters more fierce and bloodthirsty, on account of a greater multiplication of men? [This seems to be one of Raynal's customary feeble oratorical sarcasms.] How Nature seems to have neglected the New World, on the other hand!" (Oh lazy, uncaring Nature, just like some slovenly servant girl!)[47]

The men there are less strong, less courageous, without beard or hair: degenerate in all the signs of manhood, feebly endowed with this lively and powerful sentiment, with this delicious love which is the source of all loves, the beginning of all attachments, the prime instinct, society's first bond, without which all other liaisons have neither depth nor durability.

44. The observation can be traced back to Buffon, from whom it was taken up by Kant (E. Adickes, *Kants Ansichten über Geschichte und Bau der Erde* [Tübingen, 1911], pp. 30–35), and also perhaps Herder, who after admiring the correct alignment of the mountains of Asia says with astonished candor: "How can one imagine, then, that in the other hemisphere they lie in the opposite direction, lengthways? And yet it is so!" (*Idées sur la philosophie de l'histoire de l'humanité*, I, 7; trans. Tandel [Paris, 1874], I, 61). See also the long and curious note by M. A. P. [Pictet?] in the French edition of the *Tableau de la situation actuelle des Etats Units, d'après Jedidiah Morse . . .* (Paris, 1795), I, 125–27, according to whom "the great mountain chains of the World were contemporary with the creation of our Planet, but before its rotation"! These are clearly residual traces of an ideal of nature as regularity, as just and tempered proportion. And yet the lucubrations over this striking singularity of the Western Hemisphere have still not been abandoned once and for all: see P. Deffontaine, "Meditaciones geográficas sobre América," *Estudios Americanos*, 3 (Seville, 1951), pp. 315–27 (summarized in *Revista de Historia de América*, 33 [Mexico, 1952], p. 264).

45. *Histoire philosophique*, IX, 20–21. Cf. Minguet, op. cit., pp. 366, 386.

46. The *Histoire philosophique* contains very few citations and no footnotes. But Raynal was certainly familiar with Buffon. On the possibility of acclimatizing the llama in the Alps, he writes: "This conjecture of Buffon, to whom we are indebted for so many useful and profound considerations on the animals, deserved the attention of the statesmen, who must be enlightened by philosophy in all their doings" (op. cit., IV, 161).

47. Nature is similarly reproached, though only in jest, by the moralist Emerson. Why is the American so hasty and immature? Simple: "Nature herself was in a hurry with these hasters and never finished one" (*Journal*, June 27, 1847; Boston–New York ed. [1913], VII, 294). But even at the end of the sixteenth century La Popelinière, whose vision encompassed the enlarged world and the expanded techniques, had written: "Nature is not so tired of working" (Hauser, op. cit., p. 54).

Raynal's tirade is not particularly relevant, but it does serve to give the reader pause and make him ponder a little on the disastrous conditions governing the love life of these poor American men. The women are of course still worse off. It is the laziness rather than the pleasure of the male to which they devote themselves.[48] They work for him. Raynal returns to the attack:

The indifference of the males toward that other sex to which Nature has entrusted the place of reproduction suggests an organic imperfection, a sort of infancy of the people of America similar to that of the individuals of our continent who have not reached the age of puberty. It is a deep-rooted failing of that other hemisphere, a sort of impotence that reveals clearly how new the continent is.[49]

America is immature. Not simply in its youth, but in its infancy. Nature forgot to make it grow.

In another context, leaving the physical environment of the continent and finding a new target for his anti-Americanism in the work of the Spanish colonists, he develops with even greater richness of scabrous detail the theme of the voluntary abstinence of the Indians, instead of their congenital impotence. The cruelties of the Spaniards put the Indians to flight, made them savage, and in fact "in some regions . . . the men resolved unanimously to have no commerce with their women." The desired end was what de Vigny's embittered Samson was to foresee when he spoke of the two sexes "exchanging distant angry looks, and perishing each on its own shore."

Now, Raynal goes on without a trace of irony, "this sad plot against Nature and against the sweetest of her pleasures, the unique example of such an occurrence that history records, seems to have been reserved for the age of the discovery of the New World, to characterize for all time the tyranny of the Spaniards. . . ." (Actually, one would hardly say unique; to illustrate the oppressed Jews' sufferings in Egypt, the traditional Haggadahs have naïve woodcuts which show with admirable clarity "the Israelites abstaining from cohabitation so that their children shall not be thrown into the Nile"; the Dalmatians of Trogir and Dubrovnik adopted the same extreme preventive measures so that their heirs might

48. This thesis has been given a new lease on life in the developments of Hahn and other ethnologists, who attribute to woman a progressive function, at least in the early stages of agriculture ("hoe-culture" as opposed to "plough-culture," characteristic of man). "Women invented work, for early man was an idler," summarizes R. H. Lowie (*The History of Ethnological Theory* [New York, 1937], p. 114). The tone of disapproval is lacking in the verdicts of the nineteenth-century men of science: the "idler" is simply the "otiose," not the "lazy" man referred to by Raynal. Absent likewise is the antithesis between pleasure and work as the proper object of the female. For the enlightened Raynal laziness was a vice but lasciviouness was not.

49. *Histoire philosophique*, IX, 23. Dillon, a belated disciple of Raynal, in his *Beautés de l'histoire du Méxique* (Paris, 1822) even manages to explain the fall of Montezuma's empire by the amatory coldness of Aztec males and the consequent preference of Doña Marina and other Mexican women for the hardy Spaniards! (quoted in Zavala, *América*, p. 271).

not suffer under the yoke of the foreigner, either Hapsburg or Napoleonic.)[50] And thus, Raynal continues, "the earth was soiled twice over, with the blood of the fathers and the seed of the sons"[51] (a somewhat forced antithesis — it could only in fact have been the "seed of the fathers").

But this land so defiled was already tainted of itself. Raynal continually comes back to the argument of America's disastrous physical nature. There is no catastrophe that America has been spared. Obviously the continent was once laid waste and has not yet recovered:

Everything points to some sickness from which the human race still suffers. The ruin of this world is still imprinted on the faces of its inhabitants; a race of men degraded or degenerate in their physical constitution, in their build, in their way of life, and in their minds which show so little aptitude for all the arts of civilization.[52]

Within the space of two pages, immaturity has become degeneracy, these overgrown children have become decrepit old men. And it is all, as usual, the fault of the humidity.

But humidity was the mark of a young world, not a world in decline. Raynal gets out of the contradiction by saying that America is not young, but "reborn"; or very young and very old, or rather dead, all at the same time: "The imperfection of Nature in America does not therefore prove the newness of this hemisphere, but its rebirth. It must without doubt have been populated as long ago as the old; but it could have been submerged later."[53] The peoples of America are ancient, certainly older than the three or four centuries of the Inca or Aztec dynasties, but not as ancient as the peoples of the Old World.[54]

After this Raynal takes off on one of his digressions, an extensive inquiry into who is happier, the savage or the civilized man, coming to an

50. Anthony R. Rhodes, *The Dalmatian Coast* (London, 1955), reviewed in the *Times Literary Supplement*, 21 October 1955.

51. *Histoire philosophique*, IV, 341. In 1530 the natives of Mexico apparently abstained from cohabitation so as not to bring into the world children who would be slaves (L. Hanke, *Aristotle and the American Indians — A Study in Race Prejudice in the Modern World* [London, 1959], p. 26; S. Zavala, "Nuño de Guzmán y la esclavitud de los Indios," *Historia Mexicana*, 1, no. 3 [1952], p. 413; Herrera, quoted by W. L. Sherman, "Indian Slavery and the Cerrato Reforms," *Hispanic American Historical Review*, 51, no. 1 [February 1971], p. 26); Raynal's source seems to be Gerolamo Benzoni, *La historia del Mondo Nuovo* (1565; Milan, 1965), pp. 61, 119. See also below, chap. 4, n. 129.

52. *Histoire philosophique*, IX, 25.

53. Ibid. The idea of a little flood peculiar to America goes back to Bacon (see below, p. 60). The "humidity" theory with the recent emersion of the continent and the weakness of the men is also summarized in X, 298. The superimposing of the thesis of "degeneration" on that of "impuberty" would seem to have been inspired by de Pauw (see below, pp. 53 ff.), and one seems to catch another echo of de Pauw in the pages in which, to the sound of the refrain "we must dismiss as fable," the vaunted splendors of the Incas are reduced to a few ruins at Cuzco, Quito, Pachacamac, and Las Capillas (ibid., IV, 44–48; cf. below, p. 57).

54. Ibid., IX, 26–27.

unexpected conclusion in favor of the savage,[55] the very same savage to whom he had just denied the supreme pleasure of love, the source of all other pleasures and delights.

VI. MARMONTEL AND THE DEFENSE OF THE WEAK
AND WRETCHED AMERICANS

Voltaire's disciple Marmontel, inclined to more positive statements and coherent arguments than Raynal, took upon himself the defense not of the free and happy savages but of those poor oppressed creatures, the *indios*. It is true "that in general [they] were feeble in mind and body, I admit,"[56] but they were not without a certain instinctive courage. He mentions Buffon in a footnote, but if one bears in mind that the latter had always concerned himself more with the inferiority of the animals than of the men of America, and referred, if at all, to the savages, not to the subjects of the Incas so dear to Marmontel, one cannot help suspecting that the comment is aimed more at de Pauw than at Buffon.

Marmontel's *The Incas* is a blend or rather a mélange of the most varied themes and attitudes: an exaltation of the ideal of tolerance, a moving apologia of the primitive, a relish for the exotic, a tear-filled eulogy of the conquered and enslaved peoples, and a dramatic trans- figuration of the Hero, that noble and generous warrior Pizarro who was scandalized, horror-struck, "filled with terror and compassion," when he chanced to witness an *auto-da-fè*. The work was published only in 1777, but had been begun ten years earlier,[57] and seems to have been completed by 1770.[58] De Pauw himself knew while writing his *Recherches* that Mar- montel was preparing "a work on the cruelty of the Spaniards,"[59] which allowed him to be brief on that subject.

We in our turn, having once mentioned Marmontel's "romance," need not linger over the copious literature on the same subject. Even if these works take an occasional lead from the polemic of America, their con- cern for the cruel political destiny of the natives and their indictment of the barbaric ferocity of the Spaniards are themes that belong more ac- curately to the major polemic currents of the day; springing from Rous- seau when they insist on the lost happiness of the aborigine (*locus classi- cus:* the *Nouvelle Héloise,* IV, 3), from the encyclopedists when they

55. Ibid., IX, 34. For Raynal's opinions on the Americans see also L. Villard, *La France et les Etats- Unis: Echanges et rencontres (1524–1800)* (Lyon, 1952), pp. 320–23.
56. Marmontel, *Les Incas,* ed. cit., pp. 17–18. On Marmontel cf. Berveiller, *Mirages et visages du Pérou* (Paris, 1959), pp. 308–10.
57. Marmontel, *Mémoires,* ed. Tourneux (Paris, 1891), II, 289, 295.
58. Ibid., II, 340.
59. *Recherches philosophiques sur les Américains,* ed. cit., II, 271–72.

denounce the fanaticism of their conquerors (*locus classicus:* the dedication of this same work *The Incas,* or Condorcet, *Esquisse,* VIII). They cannot necessarily be linked with de Pauw's infamous *Recherches,* in which all Americans and only the Americans are judged, in Marmontel's words, extremely "weak in mind and body."

De Pauw and
the Inferiority of
the Men of America

I. FAITH IN PROGRESS AND SOCIETY

SOON after Buffon, these slanders on the whole of American nature reached a definitive climax with the appearance of the *Recherches philosophiques sur les Américains ou Mémoires intéressants pour servir à l'histoire de l'espèce humaine* by Mr. de P. (the abbé Cornelius de Pauw).[1] The work is dated Berlin, 1768, the date and location of encyclopedism at its most glorious and triumphant. The contents of the work live up to the promise of the title page. De Pauw reveals himself a typical encyclopedist; he not only makes frequent attacks on religion and the Jesuits,[2] and exhibits a complete lack of modesty in his minutely detailed, almost Freudian, examination and description of sexual aberrations and peculiarities, but also provides a quite typical example of that combination of a firm and unquestioning faith in Progress with a complete lack of faith in the natural goodness of man.

If he believed in the goodness of Nature he would be a Rousseauian and à la Marmontel would have little trouble in adapting Buffon's thesis to the Americans, finding the men like the animals to be imperfectly

---

1. Cited hereafter simply as *Recherches*. (De Pauw's subsequent works dealing with [a] the Egyptians and Chinese and [b] the Greeks will be cited as *Recherches sur les Egyptiens* and *Recherches sur les Grecs* respectively; for further details, see the Bibliography of Works Cited and the index entries.) De Pauw's genealogy is discussed and his meager biography summarized by Gisbert Beyerhaus, "Abbé de Pauw und Friedrich der Grosse, eine Abrechnung mit Voltaire," *Historische Zeitschrift,* 134 (1926), pp. 465–93, and Church, op. cit., pp. 178–206. Denina gives Amsterdam as his birthplace (*La Prusse littéraire sous Frédéric II* [Berlin, 1790–91], III, 143), but Delisles de Sales (*Histoire philosophique du monde primitif* [Paris, 1795], VI, 20–22) calls him "Alsatian," in fact a "Strasburger"; on 26 August 1792 he was awarded honorary French citizenship, as were Bentham, Klopstock, Schiller, and the Founding Fathers of the United States (A. Mathiez, *La Révolution et les étrangers* [Paris, 1918], pp. 75–76); and in 1811 Napoleon had an obelisk erected to him at Xanten (Beyerhaus, op. cit., p. 469).
2. "The Jesuits, ever untrustworthy" (*Recherches*, I, 61); "their complete expulsion . . . regarded, in Peru, as a stroke of providence" (*Recherches*, II, 356); cf. *Défense* (1771 ed.), p. 36.

formed and relatively weak, yet lovable and "interesting" for this very weakness of theirs. But unlike Rousseau (whom he mentions only once in passing and then merely to criticize him),[3] de Pauw believes that man reaches perfection only in society, and that a man living alone in the state of nature can only be a brute, incapable of progress. Talking of Alexander Selkirk, the inspirer of *Robinson Crusoe* and eighteenth-century proto-type of man in a state of solitude, de Pauw asserts:

Man is thus nothing by himself; he owes what he is to society; the greatest Meta-physician, the greatest philosopher, if he were abandoned for ten years on the Isle of Fernandez, would come back transformed into a brute, dumb and imbecile, and would know nothing in the whole of nature.[4]

II. THE AMERICANS AS DEGENERATE

It is not difficult to anticipate de Pauw's attitude toward the American savages: they are animals, or little more than animals, "holding in abhor-rence the laws of society and the hindrances of education," living each one for himself, without a helping thought for his neighbor, in a state of indolence, inertia, complete dejection. The savage does not know that he must sacrifice a part of his freedom in order to cultivate his spirit, and yet "without this cultivation he is nothing."[5]

It is obvious that de Pauw is much more radical than Buffon. It was only a couple of years earlier that Buffon had published the fourteenth volume of the *Histoire naturelle* with its provocative essay "On the De-generation of the Animals," whose explosive potential was clearly not lost on him; referring to it in a letter to Brosses he wrote: "One can slip ideas into a quarto volume which would cause a public outcry if they ap-peared in a pamphlet."[6] Buffon, however, had sought to exclude man from his theory and had made him at worst a cold and sluggish brute, newly appeared and inexperienced. But for de Pauw the American is neither an immature animal nor an overgrown child: he is a degenerate. Nature in the Western Hemisphere is not imperfect; it is decayed and decaying further. Buffon is the only naturalist, writes de Pauw, "ever to maintain that mat-

3. *Recherches*, II, 63–64, on the subject of the orangutan. L. Baudin (*L'empire socialiste des Incas* [Paris, 1928], p. 19) sees de Pauw as Rousseau's complete antithesis, but considers him a mere para-doxist: de Pauw, "a philosopher priest, admired by Voltaire, amuses himself . . . taking the opposite position to Rousseau in systematically denigrating the Americans."

4. *Recherches*, I, 302. Thus Defoe bungled his theme: he could have derived therefrom "a more fin-ished production" (ibid., I, 303). On de Pauw's historiographical premises, in relation to the ideas of Montesquieu, Voltaire, Rousseau, etc., see Beyerhaus, op. cit., pp. 470–73.

5. *Recherches*, II, 207. And again: "He is alone in the world, and is unaware that it is possible to be beneficent, charitable, and generous."

6. F. Bourdier, "Principaux aspects de la vie et de l'oeuvre de Buffon," in Bertin, op. cit., p. 30. Buffon's argument was to be taken up ironically by P. L. Courier, *Pamphlet des pamphlets* (1824; Pléiade ed., Paris, 1940), p. 211.

ter has only recently been organized in the New World, and that its organization there is not yet by any means complete in our own day."[7]

If Buffon had extended this "strange hypothesis" of his beyond the plants and animals so as to include man too (which he does not do, since he considers that man is not autochthonous and therefore not immature either), then little Dr. Matthew Maty, de Pauw observes ironically, would have had some reason to attack him as he does, basing himself on the asserted existence of giants in Patagonia ("several hundred of them have been observed and *handled*"), and concluding allusively: "The soil of America can thus produce giants, and its generative power is not in its infancy at all."[8]

But in fact they are both mistaken. It has never been suggested that the men of America are smaller than those of learned Europe. But they are not giants either. Rather, like so many other indigenous species, they have degenerated in a climate that is so hostile to society and the human race: "The whole human race was indubitably weakened and rendered degenerate in the new continent." Buffon is an extremely able naturalist — "and sometimes more able than Nature herself."[9] How can one agree with him when he tries to persuade us that in Europe we are old, and that in America on the other hand the human race is fresh, recent, still unripe?

The difference between the two hemispheres is, admittedly, "total, as great as it could be, or as one could imagine it to be." And it is also a fact that it is difficult to explain "such an astonishing disparity between the two constituent parts of the same globe." "Nothing is more surprising." But to suggest that in the New World even the human race is "modern" is an "untenable supposition." Why should America have remained deserted from the moment of creation until a few centuries ago? "Could Nature have been so *powerless* as to be incapable of finishing her work?"[10]

The "impotence of nature" is here put forward as an argument by *demonstratio ad absurdum* against the thesis of the *immaturity* of the continent. Hegel was eventually to adopt it as the valid explanation.[11]

7. *Recherches*, I, 307. And the rebuke of "the modern Naturalists for having shown too great a predilection for the pompous style and manner" also catches Buffon fairly and squarely.

8. Ibid. Maty, of Provençal Huguenot descent, was born in Holland in 1718 and was for several years (1750–57) publisher of the *Journal britannique,* mentioned by de Pauw (ibid., I, 306), and later librarian of the British Museum, a post he held until his death in 1776. His smallness of stature was proverbial. Dr. Johnson, who detested him, called him a "little black dog," and would have liked to have thrown him in the Thames. Maty's paradoxical belief in giants was based on the account of Commodore Byron's voyage to the Tierra del Fuego (published in London, 1766: see copious details in P. G. Adams, op. cit., pp. 19–43, and on Maty in particular, pp. 29–30, 34–36; J. F. Smith too relies on Byron: *Voyage dans les Etats Unis* [Paris, 1791], I, 186). And Diderot, in his *Supplément au voyage de Bougainville* (1771), which contains other de Pauwian echoes (Pléiade ed., pp. 756–57), satirizes Maty and his famous Patagonians, denying that they were taller than five feet five or six inches. Maty is highly praised, on the other hand, in Brissot's *Mémoires* (Brussels, 1830), III, 58–61.

9. *Recherches*, I, 307; and ibid., p. 197.

10. Ibid., pp. 95–96; *Défense* (1771 ed.), p. 64.

11. See chap. 9, sec. 4, "The Impotence of Nature."

In the whole of de Pauw's book, implicitly and explicitly a polemic against the reports of the missionaries and the admirers of the Noble Savage, we find repeated *ad nauseam* the assertion that nature in America is weak and corrupt, weak because corrupt, inferior because degenerate. Only the insects, snakes, and harmful animals have prospered and become larger and fatter, more fearsome and more numerous than in the old continent. But all the quadrupeds — those few that are found there — are smaller — to be precise "smaller by a sixth than their analogues in the old continent," and have such an inelegant and "ill-formed" shape that the first people who tried to draw them found themselves in some difficulty (somewhat like a portrait painter faced with a rather homely subject). Even the large reptiles were enfeebled and debased: "The American crocodiles and alligators have neither the impetuosity nor the fury of those of Africa."[12]

If there were less proclivity for argumentativeness and scandal and a more solemn melancholy in this picture of senility and decay, one might justifiably recall Lucretius: *"Iamque adeo fracta est aetas, effetaque tellus / vix animalia parva creat quae cuncta creavit / saecla deditque ferarum ingentia corpora partu."*[13]

But de Pauw does not grieve over it. He surveys the poor animals of America with the haughty disdain of the lion tamer, the untouchable complacency of the Prussian *abbé-philosophe.* Those facts which so surprised Buffon and stimulated his scientific interest have here become a mere excuse for a slanderous and murderous assault on the whole of American humanity.

These men are in fact worse off than the animals. They are so weak that "in a fight the weakest European could crush them with ease."[14] They have less sensibility, less humanity, less taste and less instinct, less heart and less intelligence, less everything in fact. They are like idiot children, incurably lazy and incapable of any mental progress whatsoever.[15]

But this did not give the Europeans any right to maltreat them, as they have done and continue to do. The superiority of the European is not in question. But they have abused this superiority: "The distant peoples already have more than enough to complain of with regard to Europe." Let the Europeans then cease to plan new conquests and organize scien-

12. De Pauw, *Recherches,* I, 4–12 and passim. Cf., for the opposite view, Paolo Frisi: "The crocodiles of Egypt and America resemble one another" (*Illuministi italiani,* III, *Riformatori lombardi, piemontesi e toscani,* ed. Franco Venturi [Milan-Naples, 1958], p. 309).

13. *De rerum natura,* II, 1150–52. An echo of Lucretius's thesis is heard in Pliny, who according to St. Augustine (*De Civitate Dei,* XV, 9) "attests that with the gradual passing of the centuries nature produces smaller creatures." See above, pp. 24–25. De Pauw was of course familiar with Pliny and St. Augustine; and the epigraph of the *Recherches* ("*studio disposta fideli*") is taken from Lucretius.

14. De Pauw, ibid., I, 35.

15. Ibid., I, 35, 221; II, 102, 153–54 and passim.

tific expeditions in lands that have the good fortune to be still unknown: "Let us not massacre the Papuans just so as to be able to measure the climate of New Guinea on Réaumur's Thermometer."[16]

The development of his thesis thus presents at this point a strange mingling of arguments: on the one hand those of de Pauw the encyclopedist, the enthusiastic disciple of Progress and enemy of the primitives; on the other those of the same de Pauw but this time the humanitarian, with his horror of war, laying bare the hypocritical excuses put forward for waging it. The two approaches did not harmonize at all; nor was there any way of reconciling them within the limits of the philosophy of the Enlightenment. But in de Pauw they combined to crush the impotent and browbeaten Americans beneath the conjoined malediction of Nature and History.

III. EXAGGERATIONS IN THE ANTI-AMERICAN THESIS

In the vehemence of his anti-Americanism, de Pauw not only sometimes gets confused and (as we saw above) refers to the Americans as "children" rather than "dotards" (children who will never grow up however, or precocious dotards); but he is also subject to wild flights of fancy, much as the chroniclers and recounters of prodigies and marvels had previously been in their praises of America and as the tender admirers of the Noble Savage still were.

In point of fact, it should not be forgotten that de Pauw's biting scorn was in many ways a legitimate polemical retort to the fantastic reasoning and reporting of the defenders of the New World, both ancient and contemporary. To take just one example: the Englishman John Hawkins had affirmed the existence of lions in Florida with the following prime example of mythologico-heraldic ratiocination: the Floridians wear necklaces made from the horns of unicorns, thus there are certainly many unicorns in Florida, and thus there must be lions and tigers, "lions especially, if it is true what is said of enmity between them and unicorns, for there is no beast but hath his enemy . . . insomuch that whereas the one is the other cannot be missing."[17] *Quod erat demonstrandum.*

But the impetuous de Pauw gets carried away by his rebuttal, generalizing unashamedly and maintaining seriously that in the American climate many animals lose their tails, dogs lose their bark, the meat of the

---

16. Ibid., "Discours préliminaire." The echoes of Voltaire are unmistakable. The Americans' religious superstitions prove "that despite the diversity of climate the imbecility of the human spirit has been constant and immutable." Even the advice addressed to the European "to leave the *Terres Australes* alone and to devote more care to their own" echoes the concluding moral of *Candide:* to forget adventuring and metaphysics in order to *"cultiver notre jardin."*

17. *The Elizabethans' America*, ed. Louis B. Wright (London, 1965), p. 43.

ox becomes tough, and the genitals of the camel cease to function.[18] He explains that the Peruvians are like the camels, and this is why they are hairless ("it is a characteristic of their degeneration as in Eunuchs").[19] He tells of savages with pyramidal or conical craniums, and of Americans of the Marañon valley with "square or cubic heads"[20] — which may well be "the height of human extravagance," but is nonetheless a feature of a certain school of painting of the twentieth century that is as Parisian as one could wish; and is in any case a fairly wide-spread custom and well known to the anthropologists.[21] When he comes to grips with Garcilaso, he denies everything said by that author about the Incas, and instead describes the city of Cuzco as "a heap of little huts, which have neither fanlights nor windows," and which were of course completely demolished by the Spaniards, so that "there actually remains standing only *one* solitary stretch of wall."[22] In one of the "little huts" at Cuzco there was a sort of university (the *amautas,* the "sages") "where certain titled ignoramuses who could neither read nor write taught philosophy to other ignoramuses who could not speak."[23] Even iron, what little there is there,

18. *Recherches,* I, 12–13: camels were taken to Peru; but "the cold *deranged* their organs of reproduction." De Pauw's source is perhaps Fr. Acosta, who mentions having seen in Peru some camels that had been taken there from the Canaries, which had "multiplied there *but not for long*" (*Historia natural y moral,* IV, 33; ed. cit., p. 277) or the Inca Garcilaso, *Comentarios reales,* IX, 18 (ed. Rosenblat, II, 257). But Fr. Cobo, who was unknown to de Pauw (he was published only at the end of the nineteenth century), gives a more precise account of the matter: "The first Camels that arrived there produced offspring and multiplied *considerably,*" but later they were neglected; and when it was decided to take steps to avoid their extinction and an effort was made to collect together all surviving specimens, only two were to be found, and those two were both females. The last of these unhappy camelesses died in Lima in 1615 "which marked the end of the Camels in this kingdom, where they had lasted more than sixty years" (Father Bernabé Cobo, *Historia del Nuevo Mundo* [1653; Seville, 1890–93], II, 442–43). On the camels taken to Peru, see also J. F. de Caldas, *Semanario de la Nueva Granada* (Paris, 1849), p. 539n.; Robert Ricard's "Note on the Camel in Peru," *Journal de la Société des Américanistes,* n.s. 26 (1934), pp. 314–15; the texts cited by Hanke, *Aristotle and the Indians,* pp. 127–28; and C. A. Romero, "El camello en el Perú," *Revista Histórica* (Lima), 10 (1936), pp. 364–72. A camel also figures in a Brazilian landscape on a Gobelins tapestry of 1740–41. The failure to acclimatize camels in America at any time after the Conquest is also lamented by Humboldt, *Essai politique sur le royaume de la Nouvelle-Espagne* (Paris, 1811), IV, 344–57; idem, *Reise,* II, 308–10; cf. Minguet, op. cit., pp. 130–31.

19. *Recherches,* I, 144–45, but this particular misfortune seems to be accounted for by the "barbarous" oppression of the Spaniards: "Their tyranny even influenced the physical temperament of the Slaves" (an echo of Raynal?).

20. Ibid., 146–47. Delisle de Sales too condemns those American tribes that deform the skulls of the newborn children to give them "the bizarre shape of a cylinder" (*Philosophie de la Nature,* ed. cit., IV, xxx–xxxi; VI, 60–64); and Forster, who had read de Pauw, mentions that "on the continent of America there are many instances of nations who disfigure their heads to make them resemble the sun, the moon, or some other object" (*A Voyage Round the World* [London, 1777], II, 229).

21. A Red Indian of the Columbia River valley, when asked the reason for such "aberrations," replied: "And why do your women give themselves wasp waists?" (H. Wish, *Society and Thought in Early America* [New York, 1950], pp. 362–63). On cranial deformations in seventeenth-century Paris, see Reginald Reynolds, *Beds* (London, 1952), p. 46.

22. *Recherches,* II, 178–79.

23. Ibid., II, 185. This impassioned partiality, shared, as we have seen (above, p. 49), by Raynal, provoked reaction from a number of people, including Buffon: "I shall not take the trouble to cite anything here except the monuments of the Mexicans and Peruvians, whose existence he (M. P.) denies, and whose traces still remain however, and show the greatness and the genius of these peoples, whom he

loses its strength in America: it is "infinitely inferior to the iron of our continent, so that one could not even make nails out of it."[24]

When he reaches his conclusion he no doubt feels that he has inspired in us a due sense of consternation, though in fact one can only really be wryly amused as one agrees with him that "it is without doubt a great and terrible spectacle to see half the globe so thoroughly maltreated by Nature that everything in it was either degenerate or monstrous."[25]

IV. THE CAUSES OF THE CATASTROPHE

But how did things get into this mess? De Pauw is ambiguous. Sometimes he refers to climate, or permanent natural factors, though with a certain caution and reserve (for example, II, 84–85), and much more often he falls back on catastrophes or floods or other unwonted calamities. The hypothesis of a flood seems to him to provide a better explanation of "the majority of causes which have there [in America] vitiated and depraved the temperament of the inhabitants" than "the hypothesis of M. de Buffon, who supposes that Nature, still in its adolescence in America, had only recently organized and brought to life the creatures of that region."[26] And elsewhere he throws out dark hints about "physical catastrophes," "terrible earthquakes," "considerable floods."[27] "a general conflagration and terrifying vicissitudes,"[28] which constitute "the greatest difficulties and at the same time the most interesting points in the physical nature of the globe and the history of its creatures."[29]

One seems to catch an echo of some of the philosophical conjecturings of his contemporary Bonnet[30] and at the same time certain precocious suggestions of hypotheses that were to be developed later—like Cuvier's

---

treats as stupid creatures, degenerated forms of the human race, both in their bodies and their understanding" (*Oeuvres complètes*, ed. cit., XII, 436; see also below, pp. 155–56).

24. *Recherches*, II, 182; cf. below, p. 322. It was Father Acosta again who had said that as a result of certain corrosive winds (or, more likely, rust) the iron "shredded into little pieces, as if it were hay or dry straw" (*Historia natural y moral*, III, 9; ed. cit., p. 141). The natives had no iron weapons, whether offensive or defensive, which seemed to suggest they were not acquainted with the metal (see L. B. Wright, *The Elizabethans' America*, pp. 111, 128–29; but *contra*, ibid., pp. 57, 120, 220).

25. *Recherches*, "Discours préliminaire," not paginated (first page).

26. *Recherches*, I, 23.

27. Ibid., I, 101–02, 105–06.

28. Ibid., II, 177.

29. Ibid., I, 312, 317. In his other *Recherches* too, the *Recherches philosophiques sur les Egyptiens et les Chinois* (Amsterdam-Leyden, 1773), de Pauw writes mysteriously: "I believe, and I can even half see, that our globe has been subject to some extremely strange events, of which we do not have and shall never have any certain knowledge, because the thread of tradition is broken" (I, xiv).

30. Bonnet, in his *Palingénésie philosophique, ou Idées sur l'état passé et sur l'état futur des êtres vivants* (Amsterdam, 1769–70), maintained that the earth had passed "through a long series of epochs, each terminated by a 'revolution', i.e., a cataclysm, in which all the then existing organic structures were destroyed" (op. cit., I, 236 ff., cited in Lovejoy, *The Great Chain of Being*, p. 284; cf. Nordenskiöld, op. cit., p. 246). But Berossus of Babylon (third century B.C.) had already put forth the notion of an alternating cycle of cosmic floods and conflagrations (J. Baillie, *The Belief in Progress* [Oxford, 1950], p. 45). On the link between the diluvial theories and those suggesting a telluric decadence (see above, chap. 1, n. 93), see Kubrin, op. cit., p. 343.

"catastrophes" or perhaps De Vries's "sudden mutations" — which protect the impassioned de Pauw from ridicule and endow him instead with the weighty authority of these learned men. One can even find a few illustrious predecessors for this theory of his postulating a specifically American flood, which historicizes, so to speak, Buffon's version of a sodden continent.

It is hardly necessary to mention Boulanger too. True, de Pauw had read with close attention his *Recherches sur le despotisme oriental* (1761) and even his major work, *L'antiquité devoilée* (1766), which sees the origin of religious beliefs in man's fearful memory of the Flood.[31] Boulanger describes that catastrophe grandiosely as a "revolution of nature," a complete upheaval of sky, sea, and earth, a terrifying disease of all creation. And in the savages in general he recognizes the descendants of the hordes who had escaped the Flood, who were so shaken by it as to fall into a melancholic apathy, incapable of all progress; and the American savages in particular he depicts as oppressed by want and superstition, imprisoned within an insipid "Golden Age."[32]

But Boulanger's flood is biblical and universal; it submerged the whole world, not only the Americas. It is quite possible that de Pauw received certain ideas from him (perhaps even through Buffon, who was accused of having plagiarized Boulanger)[33] but his influence is distinctly secondary. It is rather more significant to notice that this attempt to explain the physical degradation of the Americas by means of a (second?) flood, affecting them alone, even if from one point of view it can be linked to the disquisitions of the church fathers and later commentators struggling with the difficulties presented by the biblical story of a "universal" flood,[34] in substance is merely an outstanding example of the general tendency of the "denigrators" of the New World to concentrate on these lands the maledictions and legends of catastrophe that had been thought up over

31. Op. cit., II, 230–34, refuting the hypothesis on the *couvade*, but always with great respect for "the memory of this learned man," for this "illustrious author," whom he opposes because only "the faults of great men are worth refuting"; cf. also the *Défense* (1771 ed.), p. 183.

32. F. Venturi, *L'antichità svelata e l'idea del Progresso in N. A. Boulanger* (Bari, 1947). On the Flood: pp. 13, 65, 119. On the savages: pp. 39–40, 51. Boulanger's ideas on the Egyptians and Chinese too (ibid., pp. 49–50) have points of contact with those that de Pauw was to put forward in 1773 (see below, pp. 150 ff.).

33. Sainte-Beuve, *Causeries du lundi*, ed. cit., XIV, 326.

34. See D. C. Allen, *The Legend of Noah*, pp. 74–75, 84–89; on the "second" flood, see de Pauw's *Défense* (1771 ed.), pp. 18–19; *Recherches sur les Egyptiens*, I, 213. Corresponding (and sometimes coinciding) with the theories hypothesizing a multiplicity of floods are the theses suggesting multiple, reiterated creations — both tendencies deriving ultimately from the same desire to reconcile Genesis with modern Science. The Maker remains as divine cause, but fractured, repeated, separated into pieces and adapted to the circumstances, as necessity demands. Still around 1830 the geologists, faced with the evidence of fossil strata, had to postulate a number of separate Creations in place of the single one affirmed by the Bible (see Glass, op. cit., pp. 364–65 and passim). The orthodox thesis, believable fideistically for its miraculous unitariness, thus loses all logical coherence and even the most limited plausibility, and becomes enveloped in inextricable contradictions.

the years for the universal world. (In just the same way it was suggested more than once by the "defenders" of America that it had been spared the Flood!)[35] The telluric inferiority of America is justified by the same arguments and depicted in the same terms as had once served to illustrate the sad condition of the *whole* earth after the Fall and after the second curse of the Flood: the degeneration of the fauna (cf. chapter 1, pp. 11, 24), the enfeeblement of nature, which in those far-off times, "in the prime of its vitality would daily conceive gigantic children,"[36] the instability that would in time bring about the decadence of the human race, the various signs giving forewarning of the end of the world, and finally the Flood itself, among whose effects Luther had already listed the uprooting of all good trees, the formation of deserts of barren sand, and the increase of harmful beasts and plants[37] — all typical marks of the Buffon-de Pauwian America. Still in 1625–29 there were those who would accuse the universal flood of having maimed the earth for all time, shortened human life, corroded the mountains, destroyed the forests, and broken into islands the world that was once whole and perfect.[38]

But at that time the hypothesis of a flood, or rather of a half flood, affecting America alone, had already been advanced by Francis Bacon — that very same "illustrious Chancellor Bacon" whom de Pauw quotes and criticizes concerning the origin of syphilis and whose fame was then reaching its peak[39] — and not just in one but in two of his most famous works, the *New Atlantis* and the last of his *Civil and Moral Essays*.

V. BACON: AMERICA A SODDEN CONTINENT

The Reverend Governor of the House of Strangers recounts how the great Atlantis, or America ("the great Atlantis, that you call America"),[40] "was utterly lost and destroyed: not by a great earthquake . . . for that whole tract is little subject to earthquake, but by a particular deluge or inundation: these countries having, at this day, far greater rivers, and far

---

35. E.g., Giacomo Costantino Beltrami, *Alle sorgenti del Mississippi*, ed. Luciano Gallina (Novara, 1965), p. 99.

36. Baudelaire, *Les fleurs du mal*. XIX, "La Géante."

37. Harris, op. cit., p. 90; cf. 110n. Reciprocally with the coming of the Messiah the earth will become more fertile, the pastures more lush and the moon will shine like the sun (Isaiah 30:23–26). This millenaristic motif was taken up again by the Calvinist preachers. One of them, John Edwards, insists (1699) in particular on the greater abundance and tastier meat of the edible animals in the millennium (Tuveson, op. cit., p. 133; cf. ibid., p. 144) — a feature that contrasts with the supposed toughness of the beef in America (see above, p. 57). De Pauw's stunted and leathery fauna seems almost an inverted echo of that appetizing beefsteak eschatology.

38. Harris, op. cit., pp. 141–42. Other examples, coeval and later: ibid., pp. 156–58, 182–83. See also D. C. Allen, *The Legend of Noah*, pp. 95 (Kircher), 153–54 (Milton), 191 (Kircher); and Tuveson, op. cit., p. 51 (lesser stature, lesser strength, and lesser longevity of man, according to John Dove, 1594).

39. *Recherches*, I, 228 ff.; Mornet, op. cit., p. 86.

40. F. Bacon, *Works* (London, 1902), p. 188. On "Atlantis (otherwise called America)" already in a map of 1580, see Blanke, op. cit., p. 40; cf. ibid., p. 88.

higher mountains, to pour down waters, than any part of the old world" (the superiority of inanimate nature in the American continent and its tendency to humidity). The flood "was not deep"; in many places "not past forty foot . . . from the ground"; but "that inundation, though it were shallow, had a long continuance" (more hints at the marshy nature of the country).

Men and beasts perished therefore, either drowned or starved. But the birds and "some few wild inhabitants of the woods" fled to the lofty frozen mountains (an embryonic explanation of the Andean civilizations). This is why there are so few people in America, and those few are barbarous and uncultured: "So as marvel you not at the *thin* population of America [even the Governor forgets the 'great Atlantis' and speaks like us of 'America'], nor at the *rudeness* and *ignorance* of the people; for you must account your inhabitants of America as a *young* people" (the New World is the young world), a thousand years younger than the rest of the world, because a thousand years passed "between the universal flood and their particular inundation."[41]

Then, with the slow passing of time, this "poor remnant of human seed . . . peopled the country again slowly, by little and little." But, "being *simple* and *savage* people, not like Noah and his sons, which was the chief family of the earth, they were not able to leave letters, arts and civility to their posterity."[42] And when they came down from the icy mountains to the torrid valleys they assumed of necessity this foul habit of theirs of going about naked. If they decorate themselves with the feathers of birds, it is in imitation of "those their ancestors of the mountains, who were invited unto it by the infinite flights of birds, that came up to the high grounds, while the waters stood below." With this grandiose and picturesque fantasy Bacon provides a simultaneous explanation for the youthfulness of the continent and the small number and the backward state of its inhabitants, a cosmic catastrophe and the savages' feather headdresses.

In essay LVIII, *Of Vicissitudes of Things*, the same story is told more succinctly:

If you consider well of the people of the West Indies, it is very probable that they are a newer or a younger people than the people of the old world; and it is much more likely, that the destruction that hath heretofore been there, was not by earthquakes . . . but rather, that it was desolated by a particular deluge; for earthquakes are seldom in those parts; but on the other side, they have such pouring rivers, as the rivers of Asia, and Africa, and Europe, are but brooks to

---

41. *Works*, ed. cit., p. 190.
42. On the lesser vigor and longevity of men after the flood—another age-old misconception contributing to the pronouncement of the wet continent as "degenerate"—see Augustine, *De Civitate Dei*, XV, 9, and above, p. 60.

them. Their Andes, likewise, or mountains, are far higher than those with us; whereby it seems, that the remnants of generations of men were in such a particular deluge saved.[43]

Here again Bacon (apparently recalling Plato's *Laws* [bk. III, 677–79] but developing in particular an ancient American legend recounted by Gómara [1584] and paraphrased by Montaigne[44]) emphasizes the youth and humidity of the continent (two characteristics whose cumulative effect would be summed up in the suggestion of its still not being properly drained and dried out), the immensity of its rivers, and the height of its mountains, all general signs of a primitive and threatening nature. The inhabitants are here mentioned only in passing; and it is clear in the first passage quoted that he sees them as almost impotent, certainly ("as for masculine love, they have no touch of it," and their people "is the virgin of the world"),[45] but much closer to the simple and noble savage than to de Pauw's degenerate and enfeebled Americans. De Pauw on the other hand is much closer to Bacon when he indicates the physical cause of America's present condition: he too plumps for the Flood, although he is still willing to accept the possibility of almost any other sort of calamity.

In short, we can credit the Prussian *philosophe* with a sharp and salutary reaction to those overindulgent portrayals of the savages and primitive peoples, and with a few acute observations, or moments of semiscientific insight. But his most significant achievement was to have presented the problem of the Americas in the crudest and at the same time the most explicit and provocative terms. Buffon had limited himself to the fauna and had discussed it as part of the fauna of the whole world.

43. *Works,* ed. cit., pp. 143–44. Both passages use the term "remnant," implying a notion of the Americans as "the few survivors."
44. *Essais,* II, 12; Pléiade ed., p. 556: "for in days gone by they were submerged by the flood of the heavenly waters; only a few families were saved, who fled to the high mountain hollows . . . and when they saw the rain cease . . . came down and repeopled the world, which they found to be filled with nothing but snakes." The Peruvian legend of the flood was well known to Grotius too, and to less eminent authors of the seventeenth and eighteenth centuries (cf. D. C. Allen, *The Legend of Noah,* pp. 86, 92; on a flood myth among the Canadian Indians in the seventeenth century, see S. Marion, *Relations des voyageurs français en Nouvelle France au XVII*[e] *siècle* [Paris, 1923], p. 259). But like so many other semifantastic truths, or inspired hypotheses, the Baconian myth has been taken up in quite recent times (a) in the pseudophilosophical excogitations of Keyserling, according to whom the *indios* took refuge on the Bolivian plateau "as in the West and East fastnesses and giant islands sank into the Ocean" (*Südamerikanische Meditationen* [Stuttgart-Berlin, 1933], p. 16); and (b) in the cosmological theories of the Viennese Hoerbiger, according to which a prelunar satellite supposedly provoked an immense tide around the tropics, "so that the waters left only certain 'island-refuges', Andinia being one," theories which in their turn were used by Bellamy for his proposed explanation of the archaeological enigmas of Tiahuanaco (H. S. Bellamy, *Built Before the Flood: The Problem of the Tiahuanaco Ruins* [London, 1943; 2d ed., 1947]; *idem* and P. Allen, *The Calendar of Tiahuanaco* [London, 1956]). Bellamy, having collected the unbelievable figure of six hundred different "flood myths," asked (in the *Times Literary Supplement* of 2 October 1959) to be informed of others, whether published or unpublished: an insatiability one could only find in the unpunished sorcerer's apprentice! A further development of his theories, with mention of degeneration of the savages (pp. 35, 37), can be found in Denis Saurat, *L'Atlantide et le règne des géants* (Paris, 1954).
45. *New Atlantis,* in *Works,* ed. cit., pp. 200, 202.

De Pauw puts the *people* of America at the center of his inquiry and thus focuses public attention and the angry retorts and reactions on his argument and himself. Although greatly inferior to the naturalist in scientific skill, in seriousness of purpose, and in literary talent, he still manages with his two slim volumes of the *Recherches* to obtain a result that the *Histoire naturelle* did not even aspire to, and which it could certainly never have achieved: the unleashing of a violent polemic, the explosive irruption into the question of the nature and destiny of America of a barrage of age-old arguments, a whole series of diatribes, traditional apologies, and stale prejudices, a complete arsenal, in fact, of assorted ancient formulas and growing political pruriences.

It sometimes takes a writer of lower rank to deconsecrate and breathe new life into a theme of far-reaching significance. Take Beverland: a Dutch freethinker (like de Pauw), he did not have a fraction of the intelligence of the theologians who had worked their way painfully through huge tomes on the dogma of Original Sin, but he wrote a scurrilous pamphlet in which he gave the most heretical and popular interpretation of it. Everyone was upset, scandalized, provoked into producing replies and confutations, which frequently did not even mention him (the same was to happen to de Pauw); but his lively and malicious mockery spread abroad the sacrilegious "hypothesis" until its effect was brought to bear on minds and in circles quite closed to the disquisitions of the church fathers or quite oblivious of those tremendous hermeneutical doubts. In the same way it fell to de Pauw to revive, in popular form, problems that had been subjected to scientific scrutiny and treated with almost mystical reverence from the time of Columbus and Oviedo right up until Buffon.

All in all, then, the very Americans so humiliated by him should have felt a reluctant but ardent gratitude toward him. Even the Creole might have forgiven the ferocious injustice of many of his criticisms in recognition of his clearly stated prophecy that the prospering colonists would one day tire of the Spanish yoke: "They will want to burst out of their tutelage, and when they want to do so, they will certainly have the means to do so and to affirm their liberty."[46]

VI. THE INDIAN AS ANIMAL AND THE INDIAN AS WEAKLING

As for those concerned with defending the cause of the natives, they too may feel inclined to be more indulgent toward the eighteenth-century

---

46. *Recherches*, I, 91. Cf. Raynal, similarly: "When these colonies have reached the degree of culture, enlightenment, and population which is proper to them, will they not detach themselves from a country which had built its splendor on their prosperity? When will the age of this revolution be? We do not know, but it must surely come to pass" (op. cit., X, 450; cf. on the question of the example given and the pressure exercised by the United States, ibid., IV, 394). After the American Revolution, in fact, the prophecies of the coming independence of the Spanish colonies became more frequent. See examples in Sumner, op. cit., and for Raynal, ibid., pp. 71–76.

publicist if they consider how long a history the denigration of the Indian had already had. While it is true that in general the missionaries had tended to idealize the native, their descriptions had sometimes been harshly critical.

The Jesuits, whom de Pauw scorned, undoubtedly did more than any other order to give a lively, sympathetic, and human portrait of the North American Indian, with their annual *Relations* (1632–74) and with summary accounts (Lafitau, Charlevoix, etc.) which were likewise addressed to the general public. They were motivated in this both by a sincere sympathy for their converts and by the need to encourage the generosity of their European benefactors and to persuade them that their money was well spent, that their converts really were converted and worth converting. Even when the Jesuits mentioned negative aspects of the savage's character, these aspects were the ones that best revealed the resolute patience and spirit of sacrifice of the good fathers, namely, the natives' deplorable tendencies toward cannibalism, their horrible mutilations, and their insatiable greed and drunkenness.

But physically what splendid specimens of humanity they were! In 1760 the painter Benjamin West compared a Mohawk warrior to the Apollo Belvedere, no less! A missionary found them "not in the least effeminate," and their heads were like sculptures of Roman emperors, Julius Caesar, Pompey, Augustus, Otto, profiles of such majesty as he had never really believed existed when he had seen them represented on ancient medallions or cut in copper plates. When gathered in assembly, another chronicler related, the redskins displayed a wisdom and eloquence that would not have shamed the Athenian Areopagus or the Roman Senate in their finest times. Their speeches could have come straight from Titus Livy.[47]

One should of course make some allowance for the Jesuits' propensity for classical comparison, an invariable feature of their scholastic method, and for the allusive and cloying obsequiousness of their propagandistic technique. But it is still not difficult to understand the reaction of someone like de Pauw.

And de Pauw, in any case, could find remote precursors for the thesis of the inferiority of the American natives in certain theologians like the

47. Examples taken from pp. 106, 138, and 167 of J. H. Kennedy, *Jesuit and Savage in New France* (New Haven, Conn., 1950), which gives a considerable number of passages from the writings of the missionaries, arranged according to subject, and contains a summary account of their activities in America and their relationships with France. But see also G. Atkinson, *Relations de voyages*, passim, esp. pp. 71, 119, 168n.; Marion, op. cit., pp. 89–90 and passim; Albert K. Weinberg, *Manifest Destiny* (Chicago, 1963), pp. 85–86; Edmund Wilson, *Apologies to the Iroquois* (London, 1960), p. 282 ("I have heard some fine Bernard Shaw speeches delivered by eloquent Indians"); Paul R. Baker, *The Fortunate Pilgrims: Americans in Italy, 1800–1860* (Cambridge, Mass., 1964), p. 14; and Romeo, op. cit., pp. 75–83.

Scotsman John Major (ca. 1510),[48] and further in such Dominicans as the *licenciado* Gregorio (1512), Fra Tomás Ortiz (1525), and Domingo de Betanzos (1528–38), and later the jurist Gregorio López de Tovar, who denied the Indian all the Thomistic attributes of humanity: "Never did God create a people more experienced in vices and bestiality, without mixture of goodness . . . or civility."[49] In the famous polemic preceding the appearance of the *New Laws,* Sepúlveda had given as the second reason justifying the war against the natives "the crudity of their minds, for they are by nature a servile and barbarous people and therefore subservient to more elegant minds, such as those of the Spaniards"; and Vitoria claimed that they were "naturally timid and moreover simple and lacking in judgment."[50]

De Pauw quotes Sepúlveda, but not (as far as I know) Vitoria. Nor does he mention Bayle, who in the famous *Dictionary,* under Cieza de León, had already summarized what that writer had to say about the innate "depravation" and "corruption" of the peoples of Peru, in overt polemic with those who "claim that it was the Christians that taught the peoples of America to be evil."

The natural wickedness and corruption of the Americans was thus a standard argument of the defenders, both sincere and hypocritical, of religion (according to which every man is simply a fallen Adam); while the Americans' instinctive goodness and morality was an argument of the rationalists (for whom man is endowed with his own goodness, and thus *Deus sibi ipsi,* "a God in himself"), and of the anticlericalists and their reluctant allies such as certain missionaries and followers of Las Casas. De Pauw, a rationalist turning against rationalism and its mythicizing of the savage, makes these humanitarian missionaries the target of his violent assault, thus preparing the ground for the Catholic reactionaries of the romantic period. De Maistre, who is, as we shall see, in a certain sense a successor of de Pauw, incorporating his ideas into a theological system, admits with a sigh: "There was but too much truth in that first

---

48. On whom see Pedro Leturia, "Maior y Vitoria ante la conquista de América," *Estudios Eclesiásticos* (Madrid), 11, no. 1 (January 1932), pp. 44–82.

49. P. Martire, *Décadas del Nuevo Mundo,* VII, 4; Buenos Aires ed., 1944, p. 519, quoting the words of Ortiz. A similar quotation, from Herrera, is noted by Silvio A. Zavala, *Las instituciones jurídicas en la conquista de América* (Madrid, 1935), p. 47; J. H. Parry, *The Spanish Theory of Empire in the XVI Century* (Cambridge, 1940), pp. 58–59. Betanzos's retraction from having said "that they were animals" (the *indios*) is mentioned and discussed by L. Hanke, "Pope Paul III and the American Indians," *The Harvard Theological Review,* 30 (1937), pp. 96–98, 101–02 (and in *Bartolomé de las Casas, pensador político, historiador, antropólogo* [Havana, 1949], pp. 14–15). See also the testimony of the laity collected by Romeo, op. cit., p. 34; and on Ortiz, ibid., p. 39.

50. Zavala, *Instituciones jurídicas,* pp. 107, 109, but cf. limitations mentioned in J. Höffner, *Christentum und Menschenwürde: Das Anliegen der spanischen Kolonialethik im goldenen Zeitalter* (Trier, 1947), pp. 226–28.

reaction of the Europeans who in Columbus's time refused to recognize their fellows in those degraded men dwelling in the New World."[51]

And there were contemporaries of de Maistre in North America who were just as convinced of the necessity of the redskins' disappearance to make way for Civilization and Progress as they were free of the religious sanctimony and legalistic scruples of the legitimist count. They had no hesitation in describing the Indians as beasts: "the animals, vulgarly called Indians."[52]

No less interesting than the history of the notion of the "noble savage," which now has a considerable bibliography, would be the history of the notion, or caricature, of the "ignoble savage," the savage as ill formed and evil.[53] This notion in its turn is closely linked to the thesis of the weakness of the native, another theme to which de Pauw returns. But while the spiritual or moral inferiority of the Indian, his "savagery," is a thesis typical of the enemies of the naked American, his physical inferiority, his bodily weakness, is one of the standard arguments of his friends and protectors, one of the arguments most frequently put forward to prove his full humanity and his right to liberty. The impetuous de Pauw rides roughshod over the subtle distinctions of the doctors and jurists, and condemns the natives as both immoral and flaccid, lazy and thus weak and debilitated.[54] This feebleness, however, had been one of the points most repeatedly stressed by their great protector, the Apostle of the Indies, Bartolomé de Las Casas: "They are the most delicate of peoples, frail and tender in constitution, the people least capable of withstanding hard labor, and who succumb most easily to any infirmity whatsoever." Las Casas added further decorative touches to this weakness of theirs with the assurance "that not even sons of princes or gentlemen, brought up in a life of deli-

---

51. *Soirées de Saint-Pétersbourg,* 2d ed. (Paris, n.d.), I, 79.

52. H. H. Brackenridge, 1782, cited in R. H. Pearce, *The Savages of America* (Baltimore, 1953), pp. 54, 181; cf. also Weinberg, op. cit., p. 77 and R. H. Pearce, "The Significance of the Captivity Narrative," *American Literature,* 19, no. 1 (March 1947), p. 18, with other curious examples.

53. Garasse (1624) vituperated the idealized Scythians (following Tertullian) and the savages of Virginia and Canada (G. Boas, op. cit., pp. 69–70). See S. Zavala, *Servidumbre natural y libertad cristiana* (Buenos Aires, 1944); and, with caution, E. O'Gorman, "Sobre la naturaleza bestial del indio americano," *Filosofia y Letras* (Mexico), nos 1 and 2 (1941), pp. 141–58, 305–15; and also Pearce, *The Savages,* pp. 5–6, 11–35. According to R. T. Clark, Jr., "Herder, Cesarotti and Vico," *Studies in Philology,* 44 (October 1947), p. 662, who seems to base himself on J. Thyssen, *Geschichte der Geschichtsphilosophie* (Berlin, 1936), "typical[?] philosophies of history of the eighteenth century regarded savages as *degenerates* from an earlier natural religion, or some other condition characteristic of the Golden Age." For the eighteenth century, cf. also H. N. Fairchild, *The Noble Savage* (New York, 1928), chap. 9, "Enemies of the Noble Savage"; and Eugene E. Reed, "The Ignoble Savage" (in Germany, between 1730 and 1780), *The Modern Language Review,* 59 (January 1964), pp. 53–64, which examines particularly the *Grosses, vollständiges Universal-Lexicon aller Wissenschaften und Künste* (Halle-Leipzig, 1732–49), the *Encyclopédie* of Diderot and d'Alembert, the reviews directed by Nicolai (all antiprimitivistic), the less rigid *Teutscher Merkur* of Wieland and the writings of de Pauw and Herder.

54. "The Savages [are] less strong than the civilized peoples, because these Savages never work, and one knows how much work strengthens the nerves" (*Défense* [1771 ed.], p. 12).

cacy and luxury, are more delicate than these people, even those among them who come of working families."[55]

These rude and wretched Indian peasants have the same delicate constitutions as the most effeminate Spanish nobles. Las Casas uses their "weakness" not to humiliate the poor Indians, but to raise them up to dizzy heights. It is a title of privilege which almost seems to suggest that they should be relieved of "manual offices," as if they were so many *hidalgos*. It is iniquitous, in fact, the good bishop continues in the eighth of his twenty arguments against the *encomiendas,* that this whole burden of services and obligations should be imposed "on men, and on such weak, delicate, and naked men"; it is "violent, unnatural, tyrannical and contrary to all reason and nature," and "against all justice and charity and human reason."[56] Again in his last known work, the petition to Pius V, Las Casas returns to the feeble "naturales" of the Indies, "who suffering under fearsome travails and cruelties (more than one can believe) carry *on their fragile shoulders,* against all divine and natural law, a crushing yoke and insupportable burden."[57]

VII. THE INDIAN A SLAVE BY NATURE: ARISTOTLE, LAS CASAS, AND SEPÚLVEDA

When Las Casas insists so much it begins to look as though the weakness of the Indians is for him not so much an empirically established "fact" or ethnographic notion as an article of faith, a passionately sustained theological axiom. In point of fact Las Casas uses the Americans' puny muscles not only as a means to bring out by contrast the cowardliness and bullying nature of the stronger conquerors, but mainly as the basic argument in the polemic that occupied his whole life, his opposition to the theory of natural slavery, or the legitimacy of native enslavement.

Here again, as previously for Buffon, we find ourselves taken back to "the master of those who know." At the very beginning of his *Politics,* Aristotle endeavors to demonstrate the existence of slaves by nature. The passage and its arguments were and are very well known. The soul is the natural ruler of the body, as man is of the animal: "Thus all those men who are as distant from their fellows as the body from the soul and the animal from man (and in such a condition are found all those who are *only good for the use of their physical strength,* and *this is their greatest advantage*) are slaves by nature."[58] From this first thesis, logically de-

---

55. "Brevísima relación de la destrucción de las Indias Occidentales, introducción," in Las Casas, *Doctrina* (Mexico, 1941), p. 4.
56. "Tratato," known as "El octavo remedio," included in *Doctrina,* p. 62.
57. Ibid., p. 162.
58. Aristotle, *Politics,* bk. 1, 1254b.

duced and almost by way of being a definition—slaves by nature are those who are *only* strong—Aristotle goes on to a second and even less acceptable thesis, in which he tries to produce an experimental confirmation of his first assertion: "Nature seems to want to make some distinction between the bodies of free men and the bodies of slaves: the latter vigorous for the purpose of rough work, the former on the other hand straight and elegant, unsuited to such labor but useful for the civil life."[59] Robustness thus becomes a sign of predisposition to slavery, and a weak constitution the mark of a native right to liberty.

His fretus—"on these fine foundations," as Manzoni once ironically translated it—Las Casas proves, or thinks he proves, against any possible theological or legal argument, the Indians' native right to liberty, since he shows them to be feeble, weak, incapable of any effort, and in short totally lacking the physical requirements to be slaves.

The good friar was made even more resolute in his position by the comments of his old enemy Oviedo, who had said of the Indians, in a single humorous observation that summed up both the positive (physical) qualities and the negative (mental) qualities defining the slave, that their heads were so hard that the Spaniards should take care in doing battle with them not to strike them on the skull because their swords would shatter; and there was further provocation in the writing of the authoritative theologian John Major, who perhaps first of anybody (1509) had justified the Conquest by referring to the natives' animal or rather ferine nature; "since they are slaves by nature" just as "the philosopher says in the first, third, and fourth of the *Politics.*"[60] But Las Casas's supreme motivation was the need to refute his great adversary, the jurist Sepúlveda, who in his efforts to justify the enslavement of the Indians had taken over wholesale the Aristotelian theories of natural servitude, transferring, stretch-

---

59. Ibid. Aristotle realizes the danger of the natural law thus formulated and hastens to add: "On the other hand the opposite often occurs, that the ones have only the bodies of free men, the others only the soul"—which comment deprives the law of any strict determinism and reduces it to what it was in the beginning, a mere metaphor. The lord commands the slave as the soul, the body. On the uncertainty in the Aristotelian theory, Hanke (*Las Casas, pensador político*, p. 92, and *Aristotle and the Indians*, pp. 56–57) refers to R. O. Schlaifer, "Greek Theories of Slavery from Homer to Aristotle," *Harvard Studies in Classical Philology*, 47 (1936), pp. 165–204. See also William L. Westermann, *The Slave Systems of Greek and Roman Antiquity* (Philadelphia, 1955), esp. pp. 26–27, 156; and Victoria Cuffel, "The Classical Greek Concept of Slavery," *Journal of the History of Ideas*, 27, no. 3 (1966), esp. p. 327; and M. I. Finley, ed., *Slavery in Classical Antiquity: Views and Controversies* (Cambridge, 1960). An ingenious defense of Aristotle against the accusation of having absolutely denied the common humanity of the free man and the slave has been attempted by Lester H. Rifkin, "Aristotle on Equality: A Criticism of A. J. Carlyle's Theory," *Journal of the History of Ideas*, 14, no. 2 (August 1953), pp. 276–83. See also Vittorio Tranquilli, "Il concetto di lavoro in Aristotele," *La rivista trimestrale* (Turin), 1, no. 1 (March 1962), pp. 27–62, esp. 53–60, with good observations, but without reference to our polemic.

60. See Leturia, op. cit., pp. 66, 68–69 (Spanish text), 81 (Latin text). Major's treatise had a first edition in 1510, a second in 1519 (ibid., p. 45). Major had used the discovery of America, a region unknown to Ptolemy, Pliny, and all the past cosmographers, as an argument for not believing the ancients in any matter whatsoever: "Why then should it not happen the same in other cases?" (ibid., p. 55).

ing, extending, and amplifying the relationship of Greek to barbarian in order to apply it to Spaniard and Indian, and treating the involved political and theological problem "with all the crudity of pure Aristotelianism" (Menéndez y Pelayo). His words sometimes sound like a straightforward transcription of the Philosopher: "Those who excel in wisdom and intelligence, *but not in physical prowess,* such are *lords* by nature; those on the other hand who are slow and dull of mind, but *powerful of body* so as to be capable of fulfilling their necessary tasks, these are *slaves* by nature . . . as is seen to be sanctified by Divine Law too."[61] Sepúlveda does not discuss whether the Indians are strong or weak, but in describing them as slaves by nature he suggests implicitly that they are "strong in body." He insists instead on their mental barbarism, their condition as subhumans (*homunculi*), their cowardice and foul vices and somber superstitions, with which he contrasts the valor, prudence, wisdom, and piety of the Spaniards.

Earlier, when Father Gregorio had been among the very first to invoke Aristotle and St. Thomas to justify the harsh slavery of those "speaking animals," the natives of the West Indies,[62] Las Casas had simply rejected and derided Aristotle as an authority, referring to him as a pagan already roasting in hell (1519). Now however he comes over to Aristotle's side, and admits the possibility of the existence, albeit rare, of slaves by nature; but he denies even more energetically that the natives of America can be considered as such, since there have now been found among them such civilized and organized nations as the Peruvians and the

---

61. Juan Ginés de Sepúlveda, *Democrates alter,* or *Tratado sobre las justas causas de la guerra contra los indios* (1547; 1st ed. 1892; Mexico ed., 1941), p. 84. See also the *Advertencia preliminar* of M. Menendez y Pelayo, p. viii, and the introduction by Manuel Garcia Pelayo, who compares the texts of Aristotle and Sepúlveda in parallel columns (pp. 21–22). In the same work there are other traces of the Aristotelian thesis on pp. 152, 176; for Aristotle as the supreme teacher, whose rules have absolute value, p. 68. There is perhaps an allusion to this part of the *Politics* and its implicit suggestion of a harsh government for the natives (slaves) in a passage from one of the notorious Bishop Vicente de Valverde's letters to the emperor (20 March 1539), written from Cuzco: "Of the quality of this land and of the sorts of peoples and races . . . I shall write very shortly . . . now I will only say that if one had paid more attention to Aristotle's *Politics,* in the founding of the Christian settlements, one would have lost nothing" (quoted in M. Jiménez de la Espada, *Relaciones geográficas de Indias,* I [Madrid, 1881], "Antecedentes," p. xlii). A defense of Sepúlveda, on the grounds that he was a supporter of feudal "serfdom" but not of the "slavery" of the natives, occurs in R. E. Quirk, "Some Notes on a Controversial Controversy: Juan Ginés de Sepúlveda and Natural Servitude," *Hispanic American Historical Review,* 34 (August 1954), pp. 357–64. Chaunu too, *L'Amérique et les Amériques* (Paris, 1965), p. 102, sees in the *Nuevas Leyes* the victory "of Christian scholastic meditation over pagan-Renaissance humanism, over the convenience offered by the Helleno-Aristotelian category applied to the Indians *servi a natura.*" On the appeal of the Aristotelian-Sepúlvedan theory, that permitted the warrior *hidalgos* to saddle the "slaves" with the hard work they themselves did not fancy, whether in Spain or in India, see Hanke, *Aristotle and the Indians,* pp. 13–14.

62. Höffner, op. cit., p. 176; on Bernardo de Mesa (1512), Juan de Quevedo (1519), and other supporters of the "Aristotelian" slavery of the *indios,* ibid., pp. 177–82, 226. On José de Sigüenza and Juan de Solórzano, see Hanke, *Aristotle and the Indians,* p. 92. Still in the nineteenth century there were those who reexhumed Aristotle's theory of "natural" slavery to defend the slavery of the Negroes (ibid., p. 102).

Mexicans. But since he can still hardly exalt their intellectual gifts and political virtues above those of his Christian compatriots (although he did make a strenuous attempt even at that, in his *Apologética historia,* 1527-50), he gives up the idea of assaulting Sepúlveda's argument head-on and instead goes for his flanks, so to speak; denying on the one hand that the Indians are strong enough to be slaves, and on the other that the Spaniards are pious and just enough to be masters—thus bringing down the entire structure of the argument put forward by Aristotle and renewed by the apologist of the just war against the Indians. The aim of his polemic is clear in the whole of *Apologética historia,*[63] and even more so in a passage of the *Historia de las Indias.* Las Casas recalls the Stagyrite's distinctions and producing in his turn what is almost a translation, outlines "the characteristics possessed by natural slaves," namely "that nature gave them robust, coarse, and ugly bodies," and "the signs by which one can know those who are masters," namely that they are endowed by nature with "delicate bodies and pleasing faces."[64] In our more sporting era one can only smile at this theory of delicacy as an attribute of lordship and solid muscle as a stigma of servility. But Mandeville echoes the same idea precisely—"robustness is the least thing required in an officer"[65]—and Parini's Nobleman, too, supported the thesis with haughty candor: "Away with you to the commoner," he said to the Poet, "and there you will find that trivial bodily strength of which you speak. To people of my rank there belongs a much frailer and more delicate constitution than you think."[66]

Now, like Parini's "commoners," Aristotle's slaves were men too.

---

63. In which he struggles at length to show that the *indios* have all the characteristics for being recognized as free *secundum Stagiritam:* see Hanke, *Las Casas, pensador político,* pp. 79–84, 93–97; idem., "Bartolomé de las Casas: An Essay in Hagiography and Historiography," *Hispanic American Historical Review,* 33, no. 1 (February 1953), pp. 144–47; and A. Pincherle, "La dignità dell'uomo e l'indigeno americano," *Atti del Congresso Internazionale di Studi Umanistici* (Rome, 1952), pp. 121–31, which shrewdly emphasizes Las Casas's humanistic (and not merely Christian) motives and his wide experience.

64. *Historia de las Indias,* bk. 3, chap. 150, quoted by S. Zavala, "Las Casas ante la doctrina de la servidumbre natural," *Revista de la Universidad de Buenos Aires,* 3rd ser., yr. II, no. 1 (1944), p. 49, which gives a careful picture of other alterations suffered by the Aristotelian doctrine at the hands of the two ardent polemicists, Las Casas and Sepúlveda. O'Gorman is substantially in agreement, though less precise, in his review of Hanke's *The Spanish Struggle for Justice in the Conquest of America,* contained in the *Hispanic American Historical Review,* 29 (1949), esp. pp. 567–68. For the relationship between these doctrines and the philosophy and publicistics of the time, see the works of the Dominican V. D. Carro, *La teologia y los teólogos-juristas españoles ante la conquista de América* (Madrid, 1944) and the previously mentioned theologian Höffner, as well as the texts cited by Hanke in *Aristotle and the Indians,* p. 129 n. 8 (Major, Vitoria, Palacios Rubios; on Major in particular, ibid., pp. 14, 64, 80, and Leturia, op. cit.).

65. Bernard Mandeville, *The Fable of the Bees* (1705-14; ed. F. B. Kaye, Oxford, 1924), I, 123 (remark L).

66. G. Parini, *Della Nobiltà,* in *Versi e prose* (Florence, 1860), p. 316. There is no reference to this passage in the recent study by Calogero Colicchi, *Il "Dialogo sopra la Nobiltà" e la polemica sociale di G. Parini* ([Florence, 1965]; in the critical text in the appendix the passage docs not even appear); nor in Luigi Poma, *Stile e società nella formazione del Parini* (Pisa, 1967), pp. 61–82; see also the text of the dialogue, pp. 95–129, in which the passage figures in version B, secs. 40–41, where it is said ambiguously that "the nobleman can number . . . no other merit" like physical force (p. 71).

And for the Christian all men are free and equal, all sons of God. Thus in order to justify the enslavement of the Indian the Christian was obliged to begin by denying that he was a man. This explains all the efforts to call him less than man, or almost an animal. (Acosta again was to say of some Mexicans that "they lived like animals," and that "one must teach them first to be men, and then to be Christians.")[67] But in following this line of argument they were getting away from Aristotle, for whom slaves help *like* animals, but remain indubitably men. If the Indians were really animals, they would not for the Stagyrite be men, nor therefore slaves. If they are men, no subtlety of theological argument can make them natural slaves.

In short, the Aristotelian antithesis "free man-slave" did not coincide with the Christian antithesis "man-animal." The attempt to reconcile them, to apply Aristotelian theories to a radically new problem, to a situation and a terminology completely transformed by Christianity, led to the appearance in this field too of some strange and complex anomalies.

Aristotle's rapid anthropological sketch had been expressed in cautious terms, with its qualifying "it would seem" and his swiftness to admit of possible exceptions to his theory (although at the same time it was implicitly reinforced by the scorn he invariably displayed toward primitive peoples and savages).[68] But for Las Casas it became an absolute criterion of discrimination. Seeing his enemies brandishing Aristotle's theory as a weapon in the polemic, he resolves to make it his own, grasps it without bothering to examine it closely, and obstinately tries to turn it against them. Impetuous and imprudent as ever, the more he tries to defend the natives' legal right to liberty, the more he succeeds in heaping insult and contempt on their physical powers.

The good Las Casas could hardly have expected that his ardent defense of the wretched, weak, languid, and innocent Indian would within two centuries be turned into a *proof* of the corrupt and degenerate nature of the Americans. He could hardly have imagined that Voltaire, for example, his successor in the campaign for humanitarianism, would so completely misunderstand its logical basis that he could write that the philanthropic friar represented the Americans "as a gentle and timid people, whose weak temperament makes them naturally slaves."[69] Nor could he

---

67. *Historia natural y moral,* VII, 2; ed. cit., p. 453. Acosta rejects the Aristotelian theory of natural slavery (L. Hanke, *Aristotle and the Indians,* p. 89).

68. See the passages quoted in Lovejoy and Boas, op. cit., pp. 177–80.

69. *Essai sur les moeurs,* chap. 148. One seems to catch an echo of these words of Voltaire in the observation of the émigré Baudry des Lozières (ca. 1800), a harsh critic of the savages and unrelenting apologist of slavery: "The word slave, in the colonies, means only the pauper class, *which nature seems to have created more particularly for labor*" (quoted by F. Baldensperger, *Le mouvement des idées dans l'émigration française* [Paris, 1924], I, 107; my italics). It may be no more than a verbal echo, but it has a profound and bitter significance: after a lapse of two and a half centuries the aristocratic "reactionary" comes back to the argument of the apologist of Indian enslavement, Sepúlveda.

have anticipated on the other hand that a later defender of the Americans, Father Clavigero, would insist with pride and satisfaction on their robustness as porters (see below, p. 204). In fact in the hands of his apologists the Indian, like every other object of impassioned praise or defense,[70] is made to vary in his physical characteristics, change his nature, and lose and regain his strength according to the demands of the polemic.

It should also be remembered that the simple word "savage" was not, at the beginning of the sixteenth century, a neutral label. It was already charged with negative spiritual attributes and positive physical characteristics. The "savage men," the *Naturmenschen*, who appear so frequently in the legends, drama, and literature of the Middle Ages, especially in northern Europe, and whose image recurs so regularly in the margins of manuscripts, sculpted on capitals, carved on jewel boxes and embroidered in a thousand colors in the glories of the tapestries, these were wild creatures, robust and hairy, lustful and salacious, dwellers in the depths of the forest or in echoing caves, subhuman certainly, but quite distinct from the monkeys and other animals.

Many of their characteristics reappear in the conventional portrait of the "savages" discovered in the New World. About the middle of the sixteenth century there are several cases of genuine aborigines from the forests of America figuring in festivals, processions, masques, and mystery plays, just as in the previous century it was required that such occasions always featured characters dressed up as "savage men."[71] And the highest poetic representation of one of these libidinous brutes, Caliban, brings together in one person features of both the medieval savage and the American native. "Do you put tricks upon 's," Stephano asks him, *"with savages and men of Ind?"*[72]

One is also tempted to wonder whether there might not be some sort of ritual mockery contained in the typical North American torture-punishment of "tarring and feathering" the victim, or stripping him, daubing him with pitch and covering him with feathers. The practice was known from about 1770 onward,[73] and could well represent a symbolic enrobing "as

70. The redskin too served equally for the propaganda of the Jesuits and the antireligious polemic of the rationalists (cf. Kennedy, op. cit., pp. 180, 182, 186).

71. See G. Chinard, *L'exotisme américain dans la littérature française au XVIᵉ siècle* (Paris, 1911), pp. 105–07; R. Bernheimer, *Wild Men in the Middle Ages* (Cambridge, Mass., 1952), pp. 69–71; Montaigne, *Essais*, I, xxxi (ed. cit., pp. 221–22); and the reference to "a strange pictorial treatment of 'Indians' in costumes and with accouterments suggesting a Renaissance carnival," in Josef Benzing, "Die Indianerbordüre und ihre Nachschnitte, 1518–1521," *Archiv für Geschichte des Buchwesens*, 2 (1960), pp. 742–48, cited in H. M. Jones, *O Strange New World—American Culture: The Formative Years* (New York, 1964), p. 401.

72. W. Shakespeare, *The Tempest*, act II, sc. II; my italics. See the whole of the above-mentioned interesting study by Bernheimer and esp. pp. 3, 5, 11, 20, 83, 107, 115; and Annemarie De Waal Malefijt, "Homo Monstrosus," *Scientific American* (October 1968), pp. 113–18, esp. 117.

73. See s.v., *Oxford English Dictionary*, and H. L. Mencken, *The American Language, Supplement One* (New York, 1945), pp. 204–05.

a savage."[74] Certainly in Poe's "Hop-Frog" (1846), based on the tragic *Bal des Ardents* (1392), which represented a masque of these savages (and which inspired in its turn the frenzied graphic masterpiece of James Ensor [1898]), after the king and his ministers had been "saturated with tar" there was someone who "suggested feathers."[75] And the "feathers" always remained in proverbial characteristic of the half-naked American savage. "Such of late / Columbus found th' American, so girt / with feathered cincture, naked else and wilde."[76] At the end of the eighteenth century that most melodious of savages, the timid, innocent, voracious, and robust Papageno, also appeared completely covered in multicolored feathers (*The Magic Flute,* 1791). And in our own day, in the neo-Gothic tapestries of Jean Lurçat, the "wild man" is shown with brilliant feathers rather than a shaggy coat.[77]

When one notes so many cases of the two symbolic figures becoming merged or confused, one realizes that there are other subtle doubts nagging at the mind.

Perhaps the writers who described the inhabitants of the Americas as "degenerate" remembered that those mythical creatures of the Middle Ages had "fallen" into that miserable state, and had *not* risen to it from an even more animal-like condition. And perhaps the constant astonishment at the hairlessness of these transatlantic savages also derived from the contrast between their actual appearance and the corpulent, hirsute, bearish image of the fantastic creatures made familiar through so many figurative and literary representations.[78]

It was an easy and almost necessary step from the absolute or relative lack of hair to the corollary that these glabrous Americans must also be weak and impotent. From the time of Samson onward the idea of physical vigor has been associated with the notion of hirsuteness, and particularly that specific capacity which is lacking in the smooth-skinned eunuchs and not supposed to show itself in the tonsured clerics.[79]

This may not be the place to relate the history of the beard, from the Emperor Julian's *Misopogon* to Fidel Castro, but it is a fact that facial hair has had a long and at least among the civilized Europeans close association with physical vigor, and particularly with virile potency (perhaps because the latter commences with puberty?). A belated successor to de Pauw, Professor Corrado Gini, commenting on his thesis that

74. Cf. Bernheimer, op. cit., p. 83.
75. *Works* (Philadelphia, 1895), III, 170.
76. Milton, *Paradise Lost,* IX, 1115–17.
77. See J. Roosval, in *Erasmus,* 7, nos. 7–8 (April 1957), p. 222, who also recalls that in Gérard David's *Majestas Domini* at the Louvre there are two angels, "on both sides of God the Father, one covered with soft hair, the other with small feathers."
78. Cf. Blanke, op. cit., p. 227.
79. See Bernheimer, op. cit., p. 10; G. R. Taylor, *Sex in History* (London, 1953), pp. 234, 255.

"America has been in a certain sense unfortunate" because "for a long time" her tribes "were thus, from the biological point of view, backward as compared to those of other continents," denies that hirsuteness has any indicative value: "The idea has remained that a hairy man is a strong man. This is what we are told in the Latin proverbs, and what is still impressed on the minds of the Asiatics. The Chinese—so it has been reported by a medical missionary who spent a long time among them and concerned himself with these questions—have an inferiority complex with regard to Europeans on account of that fact that their capillary system develops later. In point of fact there is no reason to believe that today's hairy men are stronger; the most successful athletes are not hairy men at all. This impression is very likely a throwback to the time when there existed hirsute hominoids or prehominoids like the abominable snowman, which were, and where they exist still are endowed, it seems, with extraordinary strength."[80] An unhairy "savage" was thus a living paradox; and especially since the women of these savage races in the New World displayed in fact that same aggressive lasciviousness that had characterized the wild women of medieval Europe.[81]

The labored intricacy of the intellectual constructions described above makes it abundantly clear just how difficult it was to define and qualify the ambiguous American native.

VIII. CLIMATE AND NATURAL SLAVERY

The discussion on the natural freedom or slavery of the Indian, originally more or less a theological problem, took a pseudoscientific turn with the introduction of the question of climatic influence; according to some writers this factor alone would have been enough to predispose the American native to slavery. Right up to the beginning of the nineteenth century, as we have seen, the use of the hygrometer and thermometer as criteria in the interpretation of history continued to be popular, bringing ingenious modifications to the thesis put forward by Montesquieu, which admitted a predisposition to natural slavery in warm countries and admired the flourishing of liberty wherever cold and frost prevailed (*L'esprit des lois*, XV, 7–8; XVII, 2). However this empirical concept had already been used as early as the sixteenth century to support the argument which denied to the Americans a priori the right to be free. The climate of the New World was in general warmer than that of Europe. The Indians were therefore condemned twice over to be slaves by nature: because they were strong, like Aristotle's born slaves, and because they

---

80. C. Gini, "Le migrazioni nella preistoria e nella storia e il popolamento del continente americano," *Rivista di politica economica*, 52, no. 11 (November 1962), pp. 1403–04. See below, p. 259.
81. Bernheimer, op. cit., p. 34.

dwelt in regions that had an enervating climate; in short, because they were robust and fierce and because they were weak and feeble.

This physical-climatic justification of slavery, which can once more be traced back to Ptolemy and Aristotle, was taken up again in medieval times by St. Thomas,[82] and most particularly in the *De Regimine Principum* which was attributed to Aquinas and in fact partly written by him.[83] Thus it comes as no surprise to see Dominican fathers digging it up once more and applying it to the indigenous population of America. Some of these have already been mentioned (above, p. 65), and another was Bernardo de Mesa who excused the state of semislavery of the inhabitants of the West Indies by pointing out that they were islanders and thus subject to the fickle influence of the Moon, Queen of the Waters. The climatic theory was embraced equally readily by the Aristotelians, like Sepúlveda, translator of the *Politics,* for whom the mere fact of being born in certain parts of the world was enough to condemn one to congenital and incurable slavery.[84]

This then was the form taken by the first radical criticisms leveled at the climate of the Americas, and their physical and geographical environment. The newly discovered lands seemed to be afflicted by some deep-seated inferiority, an intrinsic incapacity to generate free men. The European scholastics, in their anxiety to justify the bondage of the Indians by reference to authority, did not hesitate to condemn the earth that had bred them, the climate in which they had grown up, and even the inclement stars that watched over their nights. Just a century after Bernardo de Mesa, another Dominican father, Juan de la Puente, was maintaining (1612) that the Indians were easily attracted to idolatry because the sky of America "brings inconstancy, lasciviousness, and untruthfulness," not only in the Indian but also in Spaniards born under such unhappy constellations — a singular example of astrological slander which provoked the justified scorn of a learned Mexican Creole, and earned the Dominican a deserved reproof for having sullied in one stroke both the men and the skies of America.[85]

82. "Among these men there is a class . . . those . . . who are deficient in intellect, but are strong in body, and seem to have been designated to serve by nature" (*Summa contra Gentiles,* III, 81; Rome ed., 1894, p. 406, quoting Aristotle and Solomon); cf. Höffner, op. cit., pp. 63–64.

83. Egidio Romano's *De regimine principum* (1285) also follows the Aristotelian doctrine: "Those who are born and live in the warm countries . . . are deficient in boldness . . . cowards by nature" (*Li livres du gouvernement des rois,* ed. S. P. Molenaer [New York, 1899], p. 374). Egidio does not mention climate among the four reasons for natural slavery but allows the legal enslavement of the defeated and the weak to the victorious, the strong, and the brave (ibid., pp. 251–55). On Egidio and Albertus Magnus, cf. Curcio, op. cit., I, 143–45. St. Thomas and Egidio Romano were well known to the sixteenth-century Spanish jurists (see S. Zavala, *Servidumbre natural,* pp. 31, 37, 43, etc.).

84. S. Zavala, *La filosofía política en la conquista de América* (Mexico, 1947), pp. 49, 55, 59, 95. On Bernardo de Mesa, see also Zavala, *Servidumbre natural,* pp. 35–37; and F. Ortiz, "Prólogo" to Hanke, *Las Casas, pensador político,* pp. xxiii–xxiv.

85. Juan José de Eguiara y Eguren, *Prólogos a la Biblioteca mexicana* (1755; Mexico ed., 1944), pp. 219–21.

The notion of the weakness or inferiority of the continent thus has as one of its earliest sources the legalistic contrivances and sophisms of those who sought to uphold the natural right of the European newcomer to rule over the aborigine of the New Indies. It was an attempt to deny the natives their right to liberty with so-called geographical laws, to overcome stark reality with quotation and syllogism. It was in fact sham natural science, struggling to force the virgin liberty of this unexpected world into the historical vise of Politics and Authority.

One can now readily understand Las Casas's scorn and bitter anger. And one can comprehend more easily the full meaning of his attempts to demonstrate incontrovertibly the fragility of the native. From the Aristotelian point of view he was in so doing defending the Indians' birthright of liberty; from the Christian point of view, assuring him of God's benevolence; and from the worldly point of view, converting a stigma of biological inferiority into a claim to the king's protection.

IX. THE INEFFECTIVENESS OF THE LAWS FOR THE PROTECTION OF THE INDIANS

It has been pointed out more than once—a sadly ironic comment on this waste of good intentions—that the laws for the protection of the Indians did not even have the effect of relieving their immediate sufferings. Las Casas had established the basic notion of the Indian as frail and in need of protection, someone to be defended or put under guardianship, an idea which was incorporated into the *Nuevas leyes*. And it was said of another great apologist of the natives, the illustrious Palafox, that "like most of the Spanish thinkers who defended the Indians he created an unconscious image of their inferiority and timidity, their immaturity, their simplicity and incapacity to defend themselves alone, with the result that the Laws of the Indies were built on the notion of the weakness of the race."[86]

In fact, as a recent indiophile has sadly written, "The Indians were depicted with such characteristics of physical weakness and mental and moral limitations, that the notion did them more harm than the protective measures did them good."[87] The very best of intentions toward the natives only succeeded in confirming their inferiority and enslavement.

This bitterly disillusioned line of argument has a curious history too. It goes back substantially to the critics of the Indian like Domingo de

86. P. Gonzales Casanova, "Aspectos Políticos de Palafox y Mendoza," *Revista de Historia de América* (Mexico), 17 (1944), p. 47.

87. Genaro V. Vázquez, Procurador General de la República (Mexicana), *Doctrinas y realidades en la legislación para los Indios* (Mexico, 1940), p. 14. Similar expressions occur already in the Brazilian historian Francisco Adolfo de Varnhagen (1854), cited by Hanke, *Aristotle and the Indians*, p. 156, n. 46.

Betanzos, who prophesied with thoroughgoing pessimism that whatever was ordained for the benefit of the wretched Indians would in the end only be to their detriment. "As soon as you try to arrange anything for them [the Indians], a thousand difficulties arise. So that even if that which is arranged for them is good in itself and bestowed with the best intentions, when it is applied to its subject matter it finishes by being harmful and disordered and brings only the harm and diminution of those to whom we wish to do good."[88] Thus it was not worth the trouble of putting oneself out so greatly to help them or better them. Rather, said the Dominicans of Hispaniola, "far better let them go to hell by themselves, as before."[89] In Peru, the strong-minded viceroy, Garcia Hurtado de Mendoza, Marquis of Cañete (1587–96), observed sardonically that "the natives are so unfortunate that whatever one does or ordains in their favor seems to turn against them."[90] Nor should one imagine that this pessimism was confined to the Catholics. The Protestants in their turn were even less sanguine about their chances of saving these souls so ill disposed to Divine Grace. And in fact the Puritans made the same sort of discouraged observations on the redskins of North America.[91] Cotton Mather went so far as to say that the devil had probably decoyed these "miserable savages" to America "in hopes that the Gospel of the Lord Jesus Christ would never come here to destroy or disturb his Absolute Empire over them"![92] And Jonathan Edwards was to suppose that the devil, frightened by the progress of the true faith, withdrew bands of his followers into the deserts of America, in the time of Constantine, to subtract them from the fatal influence of the gospel![93]

Later on friars and archbishops, administrators and pious preachers were all to repeat that the case was hopeless, that the best one could do for the Indians was, usually, "let them be."[94] Solórzano himself, defending the Spaniards against the accusation of having maltreated the natives, states that the latter in many cases "gave sufficient reason to be warred upon and maltreated"; that their vices and the misfortunes which were sent by heaven to punish them were responsible, more than the maltreatment, for their destruction; and that their sad destiny seemed to be fated,

---

88. Unpublished and undated letter of Betanzos, quoted by Hanke, *Aristotle and the Indians*, p. 57, n. 55.

89. R. Ricard, *La "conquête spirituelle" du Mexique* (Paris, 1939), pp. 338–39.

90. Letter to the king, 17 May 1590, *Gobernantes del Perú*, vol. XII, quoted in J. Varallanos, *El derecho indiano* (Lima, 1946), p. 113, n, 58.

91. Their verdict was "that all Indians were victims beyond rescue of their low condition and that not much was to be gained by studying them" (Pearce, *The Savages*, p. 25). In fact, there too, as in Spanish America, "the frightening paradox was that the savage heathen was lowered, not raised, by this contact with the civilized Christian" (ibid., p. 30).

92. Quoted in M. Cunliffe, *The Literature of the United States* (London, 1954), p. 25.

93. Quoted in Blanke, op. cit., p. 208; cf. below, p. 134.

94. J. de Solórzano y Pereyra, *Política indiana* (1648), II, 28, secs. 3–5 (ed. cit., I, 418).

since "nothing is arranged, established or procured for their health, utility, and conservation, but it rebounds to their greater damage, detriment, and affliction."[95]

Up to this point, then, the ineffectiveness of the protective legislation was explained as a divine punishment, without anyone actually inquiring as to why exactly this power that aspired to do good always finished up by doing harm, the precise reverse of Goethe's Mephistopheles, "an offspring of that power which always desires what is evil and always brings about what is good."[96]

The explanation began to become apparent only with the maturing of a more humanitarian spirit and a more elevated concept of the dignity proper to every man and every race. While the well-intentioned Palafox, as we have seen, still considered the Indians weak and therefore in need of protection, Humboldt observed that by protecting them one humiliated and enfeebled them. One thought one was helping them, "treating them like minors, putting them under the guardianship of the whites for all time," but thus "they become a burden on themselves and on the state in which they live." In this connection he quotes a memorandum (ca. 1796) of the Bishop of Michoacán, Fr. A. De San Miguel, who reminded his readers that Solórzano and other Spanish jurists had asked themselves why on earth "the privileges accorded to the Indians produce effects consistently unfavorable to the caste,"[97] and concluded: "The philanthropists assure us that it is fortunate for the Indians that we do not concern ourselves with them in Europe because experience has sadly shown that most of the measures which have been taken to better their existence have produced an opposite effect."[98]

A thesis which so neatly, and with such subtle hypocrisy, rationalized and sanctioned the notion of the inferiority of the native was bound to reappear in our own time, among the crumbled remnants of colonialism and the recurrent regurgitations of racism. Enoch Powell, the English Conservative politician, in an extreme restatement of certain of Gunnar Myrdal's bitter observations, reaches the similar conclusion, worthy of Betanzos or Solórzano, that the first thing to do to help the wretched masses in Asia "is to cut off all foreign aid."[99] And the advice is repeated

---

95. Ibid., I, 12, secs. 31–32 (ed. cit., I, 126–27).
96. Goethe, *Faust*, I, "Studierzimmer."
97. On him see also V. A. Belaúnde, *Bolivar and the Political Thought of the Spanish American Revolution* (Baltimore, 1938), pp. 49–51; S. de Madariaga, *Cuadro histórico de las Indias* (Buenos Aires, 1950), pp. 671–72; and Ramón Ezquerra, "La crítica española sobre América en el siglo XVIII," *Revista de Indias*, 22 (1962). p. 261, who reminds us that "the laws for the protection of the *indios* still act against them."
98. A. von Humboldt, *La Nouvelle Espagne*. I, 433, 439, 447.
99. See Gunnar Myrdal, *Asian Drama: An Inquiry into the Poverty of Nations* (New York, 1968), I. 637 and passim; cf. *The Observer*. 25 August 1968.

word for word for the African Negroes: "Some theorists believe seriously that the best service the west could do Africa would be to clear out completely, cut all aid, and leave Africans to work out what they want, and how, in their own time."[100]

Thus when de Pauw revived and exacerbated the argument of the inferiority of the American it contained already, although he himself was largely unaware of it, a strange assortment of elements — strains of political theory and racial prejudice, humanitarian axioms and geogenic hypotheses, zoological laws and fragments of history: the dregs, in short, of three centuries of debate, all jumbled together with the leftovers of even older speculations picked up and swept along by this murky current to be finally deposited on the threshold of the new era.

100. John Ardagh, "Africa's Dilemma: Facing the Modern World," *The Times* (London), 27 March 1969.

European Reactions
to de Pauw

I. REACTIONS IMMEDIATE AND DELAYED

DE PAUW'S paradoxical and outrageous theories rapidly produced an angry swarm of replies and counterreplies; he was criticized in general and in detail, obliquely and directly. In Europe the Prussian abbé found himself facing the defenders of the Noble Savage and Virgin Nature, flanked on one side by the admirers of the ancient pre-Colombian civilizations and on the other by the paladins of the glory and humanity of Spain; bringing up the rear there was the odd geographer and naturalist armed with his eyewitness account, and finally a host of critics and believers willing to fight to the death to overcome such a pessimistic view of history. Providence, Nature, Progress, the civilizing mission of Christianity, and faith in the miracles of technology, trade, and good government—all were mobilized in one confused mass to beat back this corrosive slander threatening their dignity and prestige.

When this first violent reaction had subsided (ca. 1768–74), the *Recherches* continued its work but on a deeper level. And a decade after its publication—a decade which saw the arrival in Europe of the Jesuits ejected from Spanish America (1767) and the North American colonists' declaration of independence from England (1776)—the debate reopened, taking a rather loftier and more profitable turn with the contributions of Robertson, Clavigero, Carli, and Herder. While the other hemisphere was producing its first literary retorts, Europe was reaching that supreme stage of self-awareness in which even non-Europe, the rest of the world, was still somehow part and progeny of Europe; and as the romantic trend began to prevail the very foundations of the debate shifted, slipping from the realm of nature and ethnography into the domain of theology and history.

De Pauw's first opponents were men of somewhat limited horizons, more given to argument than to reflection; one was a Benedictine abbé,

Joseph Pernety; another, an obscure soldier and engineer, Zaccaria de Pazzi de Bonneville; and the others, the learned mathematician Paolo Frisi and the scientist Delisle de Sales,[1] seem to have become involved in the polemic almost accidentally. As for indirect or implied contradictions of de Pauw, one could well include all the apologies for the American native, beginning with Marmontel and his ideal Peruvians, Mexicans, and West Indians. But it took the poor Indians some time to recover from the blow de Pauw had dealt them. Although there was no lack of new and zealous defenders, the Indians were to suffer for some considerable time from the effects of de Pauw's degrading accusations. One need only observe how much more often after 1768 the savages are derided, denigrated, or ridiculed, even by authors who have really nothing to do with the polemic.[2]

It is also a great pity that the essay on the Americas written by that most dogmatic and almost demented assertor of man's innate and fundamental wickedness, the Marquis de Sade, should not have survived. The three volumes of the *Recherches* were among the few books he still had with him in his cell at the Bastille (ca. 1787), and one can presume that, in the apparent absence of other works on America in this prison library of his, it was de Pauw's work that inspired him to write his "philosophical essay on the New World," which according to the *Catalogue raisonné* of 1788 was to complete the first volume of the *Portefeuille d'un homme de lettres,* and according to the publicity announcement prepared by de Sade himself was to be a completely original work, a true product of his own genius.[3]

Be that as it may, the concealed effect of de Pauw's *Recherches* in undermining the idea of the Noble Savage — if only in furnishing ammunition to those who were already disciples of civilization and enemies of nature unadorned — was certainly greater than we can document in the present treatment of the subject. Dr. Johnson, for example, was certainly not the sort of man who needed a de Pauw to strengthen him in his convictions. In his *Rasselas, Prince of Abyssinia* (1759) he had already produced "the classical rebuttal of soft primitivism."[4] But one cannot help suspecting that he must have had at least some indirect contact with the *Recherches* (of 1768) when we find him replying (30 September 1769) to the ever-present Boswell, who had provoked him by expatiating on

1. Some other brief references to de Pauw are listed in Church, op. cit., p. 194, n. 33.
2. Silvio Zavala, in his *América,* mentions for example the verdicts of Hornot (1776; pp. 253, 260), Genty (1787; p. 63, but cf. p. 65), *Un citoyen* (1787; p. 50), Carle (1790; p. 75), Saint-Sauveur (1799; p. 142), Leblond (1813; p. 149), etc.
3. Gilbert Lely, *Vie du Marquis de Sade* (Paris, 1952–57), II, 253, 280, 283. The *Recherches* does not appear in the catalogue of his books drawn up in 1784, which would lead one to suppose that he obtained it between 1784 and 1787.
4. B. Smith, op. cit., p. 32.

the happiness of the savages: "Sir, there can be nothing more false. The savages have no bodily advantages beyond those of civilized men. They have not better health; and as to care or mental uneasiness, they are not above it, but below it, like bears."[5] And again four years later we find him demonstrating that a London shopkeeper has a better existence than a savage, and the latter is not braver than the former, just less intelligent.[6] Here again Johnson was quarreling with the "primitivist" Lord Monboddo.[7] He saw America as a land of incredibly and incurably ignorant barbarians; when in 1773 he went to visit Monboddo, who outdid even Rousseau with his defense of the simple goodness and quite human temperament of monkeys, the conversation came round to the subject of emigration. "To a man of mere animal life," suggested the doctor, "you can urge no argument against going to America. . . . But a man of any intellectual enjoyment will not easily go and immerse himself and his posterity for ages in barbarism."[8]

But let us get on to more solid examples.

II. PERNETY AND THE AMERICAN GIANTS

Pernety is a classic example of that extreme form of illuminism which pursued knowledge so enthusiastically and ingenuously that it finished up by becoming straightforward mysticism, and in some cases what can only be described as occultism. This passionate desire for enlightenment, if it was not held in check by some critical reserve, often ended in a search for the light amidst the thickest gloom; and all the accumulated knowledge, deprived of any solid religious or philosophical foundation, produced no more than mystification. The Benedictine Antoine Joseph Pernety (1716–1801), who as a young man had tried to interpret the Homeric poems as allegories of alchemy,[9] had been with Bougainville on his expedition to the Falkland Islands in 1763, as "almoner" or chaplain;[10]

5. James Boswell, *The Life of Samuel Johnson* (London, 1906), I, 358; the retort continues with an attack on Lord Monboddo and Rousseau; cf. ibid., I, 464. On Johnson's aversion for the Noble Savage, see Fairchild, op. cit., pp. 323–38; below, pp. 172–73; and B. Smith, op. cit., pp. 70–71, 91 n., 127. Delisle de Sales too denied (1770) that the Missouri savages, in having less needs, were any happier than the Europeans; see *Philosophie de la Nature*, II, 362–63.

6. James Boswell, *A Journal of a Tour to the Hebrides* (New York, 1936), pp. 56, 58 (though he adds that it would be just as easy to take the side of the savage!). Cf. also ibid., p. 210.

7. On "Monboddo and Rousseau," see A. O. Lovejoy, *Essays in the History of Ideas* (Baltimore, 1948), pp. 38–61; on Johnson, the Hill-Powell edition of Boswell's *Life*, II, 476–78, and the references (to America, Savages, Indian, Emigration) in the sixth volume (indexes).

8. James Boswell, *Tour to the Hebrides*, p. 54.

9. *Les fables égyptiennes et grecques dévoilées et réduites au même principe, avec une explication des hiéroglyphes* (Paris, 1758); Italian trans.: Bari, 1936. A. Viatte, *Les sources occultes du romantisme* (Paris, 1928), I, 92–103; II, 279–83, treats only Pernety the "illuminist."

10. The journey was described in a book, *Histoire d'un voyage aux Iles Malouines, fait en 1763-4, avec des observations sur le détroit de Magellan et sur les Patagons* (Paris, 1770), which was also translated into English, *The History of a Voyage to the Malouine (or Falkland) Islands, made in 1764, under the Command of M. de Bougainville, in order to form a settlement there; and of two voyages to*

on his return to Europe he and certain other members of his order had suggested a reform of the Benedictine rule, presumably aimed at "modernizing" it, adapting it to the new times. When the attempt failed, he threw off the cowl but soon after gained the protection of Frederick II, who made him his librarian and conferred on him the abbey of Bürgel in Thüringen. His rejection of religion had earned him the approval of the enlightened Voltairian despot, but as time passed his mystic and cabalistic tendencies gained the upper hand once again; he became a follower of Swedenborg and lost Frederick's favor. In 1783 he returned to France, but his reputation as a freethinker forced him to leave Paris and retire to the Midi, where he founded the illuminist sect at Avignon and died at the dawn of the new century.

De Pauw's book, with its tone of bitter sarcasm, must have offended Pernety both as a believer in the Noble Savage and Virgin Nature, and as a man of religious and humanitarian inclinations. As an eyewitness ("I had seen with my own eyes most of the things described therein") he believed himself well qualified to demolish it. Already on 7 September 1769 he had read a first rebuttal before the Berlin Academy, and the following year he published, once again in Berlin, a complete *Dissertation sur l'Amérique et les Américains, contre les Recherches philosophiques de Mr. de P * * *.* In the last few pages (132–33) of the dissertation he speaks as a Benedictine, or rather ex-Benedictine, defending his order against de Pauw's indiscriminate assaults. But in the whole of the rest of the book he speaks as a Rousseauian,[11] singing the praises of the goodness, wisdom, moderation, industry, and strength of the American natives. And most of all, speaking as someone who has actually been as far as the Tierra del Fuego, he flaunts before de Pauw that classic and extreme example of robustness, the Patagonian giant, the very model of a rich physical development, a living disproof of every sophism of American degeneration.[12] Denina writes that no sooner was the *Recherches* published than "Mr. Pernetty found things in them to object to; and he had remarks to make particularly on the subject of the Patagonians."[13]

The existence or nonexistence of giants was one of the oldest arguments in the discussion on the properties of the New World. Obviously

---

the *Streights of Magellan, with an account of the Patagonians* (London, 1771), and which received honorable mention again in Darwin's *Voyage of a Naturalist* (New York, 1871), I, 252–55; II, 174–75. See L. Hourcade, "Los primeros colonos de las Malvinas: El relato de Dom Pernetty," *Argentina Austral* (Buenos Aires), 31 (1960), n. 339, pp. 22–24.

11. Pernety too fails to make any explicit mention of Rousseau, who was not popular in Berlin. But on p. 113 he writes: "The primary intention of this union, or Social Contract, was to oblige all the contracting parties to lend each other mutual aid," etc.

12. Pp. 50 and ff.; for further details see Reed, op. cit., p. 62.

13. P. Denina, op. cit., III, 152.

creatures of such enormous bulk and such convincing muscles would have been the best proof of the power of nature in America, an almost overwhelming reply to the caviling European critics. And their existence had been stubbornly asserted from earliest times, once it had been established as a basically believable notion by biblical, classical, and medieval tradition.[14] Vespucci talks amusingly of American giants of both sexes, but it was actually through Pigafetta's journal (19 May 1520, etc.) that Europe first made the acquaintance of these Patagonians, who were to enjoy such success in literature and philosophy right up to Tasso[15] and Vico and indeed beyond. One of the earliest printed accounts of America says in reference to the Peruvians that "the Indians are strong and bold in matters of war . . . the people of the country are very large and wondrously like giants, and are very valiant in war."[16] And the existence of American giants is stoutly defended by Father Acosta: "One should not be amazed nor take it as fable that there are giants."[17]

These very same comments of Father Acosta were to provoke the scorn of the diminutive abbé Galiani two centuries later; in his unpublished treatise, "On Men of Extraordinary Stature and Giants" (1757–58), Galiani insinuated that the Jesuit had included them simply to please his beloved Americans, who would have been left "in tears" if they too had not had their giants, just like the Old World.[18] But at that time the existence of giants in America was still accepted by Maupertuis, who believed they had been pushed down to the south just as the tiny Lapps had been driven up north,[19] and somewhat more hesitantly by Rousseau ("there have been, and perhaps still are, nations of men of gigantic height");[20] and Buffon himself was even more firmly convinced of their

---

14. "The New World must have contained everything extraordinary that the ancient travelers had described," writes Enrique de Gandia, according to whom the legend was reinforced by the tradition of tall men having come from Australia and the discovery (mentioned and discussed by de Pauw too) of fossil remains and bones of prehistoric animals (*Historia crítica de los mitos de la conquista americana* [Madrid, 1929], p. 38). On the renewed belief in giants during the Renaissance, despite the adverse opinion of Augustine, see D. C. Allen, "Donne among the Giants," *Modern Language Notes*, 61 (April 1946), pp. 257–60. The existence or actual abundance of giants in ancient times and their rarity or absence in present times was one of the arguments frequently adduced by those who in the sixteenth and seventeenth centuries maintained that all nature was in decline and heading for ultimate ruin; see D. C. Allen, "The Degeneration of Man," pp. 219, 224, and Harris, op. cit., pp. 70–71, 96, 134, 161. On biblical giants as inspirers or legitimizers of the Patagonians, see P. G. Adams, op. cit., pp. 28, 36.

15. "On the shore they see the giant Patagonians, horrible and roaring" (*Gerusalemme liberata*, XV, 45), one of the stanzas rejected by the author; see *Scrittori d'Italia* edition, p. 519. See also Blanke, op. cit., pp. 227–28.

16. *Nouvelles certaines des Isles du Peru* (Lyon, 1534), reproduced in photogravure (tables 10 and 15) in R. Porras Barrenechea, *Las relaciones primitivas de la conquista del Perú* (Paris, 1937).

17. *Historia natural y moral*, VII, 3; ed. cit., p. 457, on the basis of the existence of enormous bones.

18. F. Nicolini, "G. B. Vico e F. Galiani," app. I, *Giornale storico della letteratura italiana*, 71 (1918), p. 200; and in *Bollettino dell'Archivio Storico del Banco di Napoli*, no. 4 (31 December 1951), pp. 49–123 (see pp. 114–21); Galiani, *Correspondance*, I, 317.

19. *Oeuvres* (Lyon, 1768), II, 99, 129–30, 387–88. Cf. Glass, *Forerunners of Darwin*, p. 77; P. G. Adams, op. cit., p. 234.

20. *Discours sur l'origine et les fondemens de l'inégalité parmi les hommes* (1754), note 10.

existence,[21] as was Voltaire, who was of the opinion that even allowing for exaggerations the Patagonians were "the tallest people on earth."[22]
By 1768, in fact, the very year which saw the appearance of the *Recherches,* "there had accumulated a . . . formidable body of evidence that
the natives of Patagonia were giants."[23] Within America itself, the evidence provided by Acosta (and others) was subtly used by the Mexican
Eguiara y Eguren (1755) to support his curious theory that bodily giants
had existed in America when it was ruled by the *indios,* and now under
the government of the Spaniards there were intellectual and cultural
giants.[24] The natural vitality of America apparently expressed itself first
in the physical and later in the spiritual domain! Another Mexican, Father
Clavigero, affirms unhesitatingly that there were giants (even if not whole
nations of giants) in New Spain and other parts of America, a fact rendered even more remarkable if one recalled that there were certainly neither hippopotamuses nor elephants there, nor any other such voluminous
quadrupeds![25] In America the animal man reaches greater dimensions
than any other zoological species.

On the other hand there were many who rejected the notion of American giants as sheer fantasy. Apart from de Pauw and Diderot,[26] and leaving aside Horace Walpole ("Oh, but we have discovered a race of
giants! Captain Byron has found a nation of Brobdignacs on the coast of
Patagonia"),[27] one might mention Wieland, who took exception (1769–
77) to the variously assembled evidence, including Byron's, and reduced
the towering Patagonians to mere six-footers,[28] and the abbé Raynal,

21. *Oeuvres complètes,* ed. cit., XII, 418–34; cf. Roger, op. cit., p. 538, n. 58.

22. *Essai sur les moeurs* (1753–58), chap. 146; London ed. (1770), IV, 376. Muratori too, taking the word of the Jesuit missionaries, believed (1743) the Patagonians to be "peoples of gigantic stature"; *Il cristianesimo felice nelle missioni de' Padri della Compagnia di Gesú nel Paraguai* (Venice, 1752), I, 28, and II, 112; and even G. Leopardi (*Saggio sopra gli errori popolari degli antichi,* 1815, Florence ed., 1859, pp. 250–51) quotes various authors from the end of the eighteenth century and is inclined to suspend judgment. Cf. also the ideas of the Jesuit Tomas Falkner, outlined in Guillermo Furlong's *Tomas Falkner y su "Acerca de los Patagones"* (Buenos Aires, 1954).

23. B. Smith, op. cit., pp. 20–22.

24. *Prólogos a la Biblioteca mexicana,* pp. 172–73, 186. In 1845 Sarmiento paid careful attention to two gigantic Patagonians that he saw in the theater at Santiago de Chile (Raul A. Orgaz, *Sarmiento y el naturalismo histórico* [Córdoba, Argentina, 1940], pp. 119–20). Even today the giants are not without their willing "supporters": see the follower of Bellamy (mentioned above, chap. 3, n. 44); Denis Saurat, *l'Atlantide et le règne des géants* (Paris, 1954; English trans.: London, 1957); and, in appendix to a new edition of Commodore Byron's *Journal* (London, 1964), the article "The Patagonian Giants" by Dr. Helen Wallis of the British Museum Map Room. "Dr. Wallis, after reviewing reports by travellers from Magellan's Pigafetta to Charles Darwin, inclines to agree that Patagonian Indians are somewhat above the average human height" (review by C. F. Nowell, in *Hispanic American Historical Review,* 45, no. 3 [August 1965], p. 484).

25. *Historia antigua de México,* ed. M. Cuevas (Mexico, 1958), I, 146–47, IV, 51.

26. De Pauw, *Recherches,* 1768, I, "Discours préliminaire," and I, 281–326; Diderot, *Supplément au voyage de Bougainville,* 1771, Pléiade ed., p. 757.

27. Letter to Horace Mann, 22 May 1766, quoted in P. G. Adams, op. cit., p. 38.

28. *Beyträge zur geheimen Geschichte der Menschheit,* in *Sämmtliche Werke,* XIV (Leipzig, 1796), pp. 138–39, 229–30.

who on the subject of the famous Patagonians observed coldly that "there are giants and dwarves in all countries."[29]

With the elimination of the giants—these men superior to all others—the way was clear for describing the Americans as inferior to the rest of the world. Once their powerful vanguard had been put to flight, the other inhabitants of the continent made a miserably easy target for the slanderers of America. But the defenders of America in their turn, having lost all hope of counting in their ranks such doughty champions, switched the basis of their defense from the men to the climate, from the peoples to the physical environment of the New World, and thus unintentionally strengthened yet further the notion of the absolute primacy of inanimate nature over the afflicted humanity of America.

III. PERNETY AGAINST BUFFON: THE COUNTERATTACK ON EUROPE

Through de Pauw, Pernety attacks Buffon too; he seems to be referring to Buffon when he criticizes de Pauw for defending unquestioningly "the opinion of an author which he had taken over for himself" (p. 6) slandering the New World and its creatures. But Pernety's reply, even when it is based on sound reasoning and common sense, never comes up to the speculative level of the naturalist's quest for a law to explain and justify the differences between the animals of the Old World and the New. He points out plausibly enough that the abundance of insects and reptiles in America, and their enormous size, is a proof that the "principle of life" in the New World is at least as active and fertile as in the Old (p. 42); and that these accursed and unhappy lands provide the "privileged" Europeans with their sugar, cocoa, coffee, cochineal, and precious woods; their Peruvian and West Indian spices; their gold, silver, and precious stones; and the skins and cotton that clothe them (p. 43). It is Europe rather that is poor, and America is the land that is "great and powerful, the rich magnet of the Europeans" who seek to use its riches to make up for the poverty and deficiencies of their own continent.[30] Another innovation by Pernety is his defense of the artistic work of the Americans, the Mexicans' feather weaving, the Incas' skill with gold, the fine embroideries of the Chileans, or the Caribbeans' wood carvings.[31] But too often he oversteps the mark and simply reverses de Pauw's thesis by slandering the European and idealizing the savage.

29. Op. cit., IV, 207. See below, p. 243: the final derivation of the polemics over the giants is the discussion of the stature of the North Americans.

30. In the later *Examen des Recherches* (Berlin, 1771), II, 457–58, Pernety wisely limits himself to the observation that one cannot compile two lists of "gifts" offered and received and thus makes a valid criticism of the "bookkeeping" theory of one continent's contributions to the other. But his argument has moral overtones: "There is something ungrateful about boasting of the benefits one has bestowed and concealing or remaining silent about those one has received."

31. *Dissertation*, pp. 107–11; see also *Examen*, II, 120–40, 305 ff.

All American men, says this strange specimen of a Benedictine, are handsome, strong, and well built (p. 112) "and better proportioned for the American women than the Europeans."[32] De Pauw was totally unjustified in extending Buffon's thesis on animals and plants (which was unacceptable anyway) to the men of America (p. 66). Europe had already robbed these poor Americans of all but their humanity: "Was it really necessary for Mr. de Pauw to have the final cruelty of trying to strip them of this too?" (p. 131). But the Americans are men, and what men! Nothing but the best! The Peruvians in the south and the Appalachians in the north (pp. 22 ff.) have shown themselves capable of building advanced civilizations. If the Peruvians of today are timid and few in number this is due to their cruel maltreatment and oppression at the hands of the Spaniards (p. 77). If the Americans show a complete disinterest in seeing other countries, their motives are patriotic and philosophical (p. 87). They are in fact true "rustic philosophers" (p. 80),[33] wisely abstaining from the preoccupations caused by knowledge and ambition (p. 94). And if sometimes they are vicious and violent, "is there anything more cruel than the European Soldier?" (p. 117).

In his counterblast against the Europeans, Pernety expresses equal disapproval of people who shave their moustaches and people who do not shave their beards (p. 121); he makes the somewhat indiscreet (for an abbé) discovery about the beautified ladies of Europe that "on close examination one finds the beauty of at least half of them to be quite spurious" (p. 123);[34] and finally he declares that the true vileness and

32. "Et mieux proportionnés pour les Américaines, que les Européans," *Dissertation*, p. 46. Pernety is obviously repeating Lahontan (the savage men of North America are "mieux proportionnez pour les Amériquaines, que pour les Européennes," *Dialogues curieux entre l'auteur et un sauvage de bon sens*, ed. G. Chinard [Paris, 1931], p. 93), but he gets hopelessly confused over the second term of the comparison.

33. An echo of the *Socrate rustique* (1762 and many reprints), the title given by the French translator, J. Frey des Landres, to Hirzel's *Die Wirtschaft eines philosophischen Bauers*, on which see Paul H. Johnstone, "The Rural Socrates," in *Journal of the History of Ideas*, 5 (April 1944), p. 151–75. Baron Lahontan had already (1703) called the redskins *philosophes rustiques* (op. cit., p. 99). See also Pernety, *Examen*, II, 510–11.

34. Already in the sixteenth century Jodelle had written of the savages: "ces barbares marchent tous nuds / Et nous nous marchons incognus, / Fardez, masquez" (quoted by A. A. de Mello Franco, *O indio Brasileiro e a Revuluçao Francesa* [Rio de Janeiro, 1937], p. 158, by John C. Lapp, "The New World in French Poetry of the Sixteenth Century," *Studies in Philology*, 45, no. 1 [April 1948], p. 154, who brings out the fact that these expressions anticipate Montaigne by twenty years, and by Elizabeth Armstrong, *Ronsard and the Age of Gold* [Cambridge, 1968], p. 138). The tirades against lipstick and skin creams are a regular part of the apologies of the savage: for one conspicuous example, see Delisle de Sales, op. cit., VI, 4–36; and, even closer to Pernety, Baron Lahontan, with his savage Adario, who mocks the gilded costumes beneath which it is impossible to distinguish *"les hanches et les fesses artificielles d'avec les naturelles"* (op. cit., p. 225). On the custom of wearing hairdos "like Congo birds' nests," rouge, etc., see C. F. D. Schubart (1777) in Ernst Fraenkel, *Amerika im Spiegel des deutschen politischen Denkens* (Cologne and Opladen, 1959), p. 50. De Pauw, of course, attaches no importance at all to the artificial European fashions, including that of having *"de gros ventres postiches et de gros culs postiches,"* as in the France of Francis II's time (*Défense*, Berlin ed., 1771, p. 221). But in his final *Recherches*, on the Greeks, he too takes issue with the frivolous and vulgar fashions adopted by the European women "over the last twenty years or so" (*Recherches philosophiques sur les Grecs* [Berlin, 1788], II, 346).

the real savagery is to be found "in the smoking rooms of England, Holland, or Flanders, or in the German, Danish, or Swedish music halls" (pp. 126–27).

Pernety devotes only a few pages to the defense of the animals of America. He has no desire to revive the whole polemic with Buffon, but he cannot resist mentioning in passing the enormous bears of North America, the savage creatures of the Brazilian forest, the tigers of Paraguay, which are even larger and more fearsome than those of Africa, and the real American lions, which should not be confused "with an animal of Peru and the frontiers of Chile" which the Peruvians incorrectly call a lion. As for domestic animals, there may be some that have degenerated, "but Mr. de P. is no less wrong to draw general conclusions from the particular.[35] I have seen in Brazil and on the banks of the River Plate, bulls as big and strong as the largest in France" (p. 129), and the same can be said of the goats, sheep, dogs, and horses.

IV. DE PAUW'S ANSWER TO PERNETY: DEGENERATION AND PROGRESS

De Pauw's reply to Pernety was swift. His *Défense des Recherches philosophiques sur les Américains* is dated 26 March 1770 and was published in Berlin that same year. It is almost double the length of Pernety's work, but actually more readable with its format of forty-four short chapters, and in content it marks a considerable advance on the position of the *Recherches*. There are still plenty of personal attacks,[36] but the polemic in general operates on a rather higher level. There is less propensity for scandal, almost none of those piquant and scabrous little details, and the overtones of miraculous and terrifying discovery are very much reduced. He is at pains to distinguish between different parts

35. There seems to be an echo of Pernety in the harshly critical review of the German edition of the *Recherches* (1769), published in the *Göttingische Anzeigen von Gelehrten Sachen,* 19 February 1770 (year 1770, pp. 177–82). The reviewer says he does not know de Pauw, but he dislikes his haughtiness of tone and the insults he habitually heaps upon his opponents, and in particular the defenders of the giants (p. 177: he is convinced that the Patagonians are at least an inch taller than the English). In defense of the intellectual gifts of the Americans, he recalls the great work of the Inca (Garcilaso?), the memory and eloquence of the redskins, the Peruvian roads, the Mexican calendar, etc. In short he would find it easy to show that all de Pauw's statements "are absolutely nothing more than general conclusions from special cases"; a criticism that almost repeats Pernety's words and which was to be repeated later by almost all de Pauw's adversaries.

36. To Pernety's boasts of his personal experience de Pauw replies that in his voyage to the Falkland Islands Pernety could not have seen any Americans, since the islands are uninhabited (p. 34; but Pernety also landed in Brazil, at Montevideo and by the Rio de la Plata); that he is a facile improviser, while he, de Pauw, worked nine years on the *Recherches* (pp. 6 and 152; on p. 98 de Pauw recalls that in 1762 he still thought the tapir was a sort of hippopotamus). He accuses Pernety of partiality as a Frenchman and Benedictine (p. 226) and is perhaps hoping to offend him when he refers disparagingly to Guedeville as "this defrocked monk" (p. 170). Other curious polemic expressions are de Pauw's apologies for the prosperity and civilization of Germany, although it took no part in the conquest of America (pp. 151, 224), while Pernety seems to suggest that it is still as barbarous as the American natives (p. 226).

of the continent, and one is even aware of some effort to reconcile the facts with the theory.

De Pauw becomes more tolerant toward the Spaniards too. Although he rivals Pernety's claims to philanthropy when he boasts of having rendered the memory of the marauding Spaniards more hateful than ever[37] and admits moreover that America could have been civilized "without massacring a single one of its stupid inhabitants" (p. 224), he denies that the depopulation of America can be blamed on the Spanish massacres and concludes lightheartedly as ever that "a greater number of Europeans came over to the West Indies than were natives destroyed there" (p. 25).

The natives are still however described as stupid, as we just saw, and extremely cowardly: "When they had to fight, the Peruvians exhibited no trace of courage, and more cowardly men have never been seen in the entire world" (pp. 45–46). And the women of America are all so ugly that "without certain marks" they could not be distinguished from the men: "Thus there is no fair sex there" (1771 ed., p. 16). Small wonder then that they were maltreated by their husbands and that in revenge they welcomed the Spanish like liberators and surrendered to them so freely (ibid., p. 43).

It is ridiculous to call savages philosophers when all they are doing is obeying their primal instincts (pp. 131, 218, 242). It is ridiculous to keep on asserting that there are giants in Patagonia (thirty pages refuting this!). And Pernety shows himself doubly ignorant in attacking de Pauw as if he had suggested that man was a recent arrival in America,[38] and in deluding himself that it will be easy to demolish Buffon's theory. What does he think he can set up against Buffon—facts? de Pauw blithely continues, little realizing that he is loosening the ground beneath his own feet (but unconsciously foreshadowing the statistical theories of natural laws)— facts? . . . But a hypothesis can only be contradicted by some other very strong probability "and not by facts; for when nature operates, she operates in silence, and, so to speak, without witnesses" (p. 204). At the beginning of his famous *Discours sur l'inégalité* (1754), Rousseau had written: "Let us begin by setting aside all the facts, for they are quite beside the point."[39] So the admirer and the slanderer of the savage find

37. *Défense*, p. 9. Elsewhere de Pauw denies that the Europeans in general can be blamed for "the infamous excesses of a few Spanish thieves" (p. 224).

38. Buffon's thesis, refuted by de Pauw (ibid., pp. 21–22, 201–02), who maintained not "recent organization" but "an ancient destruction." On the recent "organization of matter" in America see a long digression by Pernety, *Examen*, II, 408 ff.

39. Cf. Diderot's even earlier comment (1746): "A single demonstration impresses me more than fifty facts . . . I am more sure of my judgment than of my eyes" (*Pensées philosophiques*, sec. 50), and Montesquieu: "It is not impossible to attack a revealed religion, because it exists through particular facts, and facts, by their nature, can be subject to dispute" (letter to W. Warburton, 16 May 1754, in *Oeuvres diverses* [Paris, 1820], III, 324). These statements (and those of Raynal, below, p. 242) form

themselves for once in perfect agreement, in their mutual scorn of the humble facts.

Anyway, as regards the *facts* of the degeneration of animals in America, de Pauw simply refers back to Buffon (for example, pp. 76, 90, 93–94, etc.) or rather takes shelter behind the great man (1771 ed., pp. 90, 193), who on this particular point seems to support his thesis that life in America is not incipient and incomplete but already decayed and corrupt. He reminds the reader of the sterility of the first species that were transplanted to America and of the continuing necessity of having large quantities of smoked or salted meat sent over from Europe (pp. 79, 81). And moving on from the animal to the vegetable kingdom, he answers Pernety by pointing out that in America the sugar is not so sweet, nor the coffee so flavorful, nor the wood of the oak so strong as in the Old World (pp. 111, 114, 120). And as for mineral resources he has no trouble showing that gold and silver were as ruinous to Peru as they were to Spain (pp. 115–16).

But when he is not getting carried away by his urge to heap insults on the whole of America's nature and history,[40] de Pauw perceives the seriousness of the problem much more acutely than does Pernety; he realizes that Europe's ideas on geophysics at the time of the discovery "were totally inadequate to name and classify the new species found in America" (p. 97), and that even in his own time "nothing is more difficult for us to understand than the way in which Nature shared and distributed the animal species over the globe" (p. 94).

---

part of the polemic of Reason against tradition but have a particular significance when used against the testimonials of Revelation; on this aspect, see R. R. Palmer, *Catholics and Unbelievers in XVIII Century France* (Princeton, 1939), p. 78. For the sources on which Rousseau relies for almost all his "facts" (by far the most important being the *Histoire générale des voyages*), see G. Pire, "Jean-Jacques Rousseau et les relations de voyages," *Revue de l'histoire littéraire de France*, 56, no. 3 (July–September 1956), pp. 355–78.

40. And not only American. Anticipating the "slanders" on the Oriental races that he was to develop in his second *Recherches*, he says that the Chinese have neither astronomers, nor naturalists, nor sculptors, nor painters, and announces that he will publish a demonstration of the reasons that prevented the Orientals learning to paint, even in the areas not subjected to Mohammedanism "such as China and Japan, where still today they do not know how to draw correctly" (pp. 218–19n.). Although the accusation was immediately (1771) and vigorously rejected (*Examen*, II, 449–50) by Pernety, who invited de Pauw to visit the collections in Paris and Holland, the latter repeated it in the *Recherches philosophiques sur les Egyptiens et les Chinois*, 1773 (Paris ed., III, 1794–95, vols IV and V of the *Oeuvres philosophiques de Pauw*), which in fact give copious illustration of the "ridiculous drawing and frightful daubing of the Chinese" (I, 305), and conclude that "the arts have remained . . . in most of . . . the peoples of the East, in a sort of eternal infancy" (I, 312; on painting, see also I, 381–85). Some Japanese succeeded in painting flowers and animals tolerably well; but they too are "quite incapable . . . of touching the landscape or historical painting." Graded on the famous scale of Roger de Piles almost all the Orientals would receive zero in drawing, zero in composition, zero in expression, and zero in color (I, 333–34). See also Francesco Algarotti: "The mediocrity of the Chinese . . . is manifestly apparent in painting" ("Pensieri diversi," *Opere* [Livorno, 1764], VII, 194); Pierre-Joseph André Roubaud, *Histoire générale de l'Asie, de l'Afrique et de l'Amérique* (Paris, 1770–75), I, 213: the Japanese "were successful in color, but they had no knowledge of drawing, perspective, and the other learned parts," and cf. below, pp. 608–09.

However the most significant advance lies in the attempted reconciliation of the European doctrine of Progress with the thesis of the degeneration of America. Developing what had been merely hinted at in the *Recherches* (I, 25–26), de Pauw now claims that the Americans *were* degenerate at the moment of discovery, but under the cultural and artistic influence of Europe they have *progressed* in the three centuries elapsed and will progress further in the future. "After three hundred years America will as little resemble what it is today, as today it is unlike what it was at the time of the discovery."[41] Pernety refuses to recognize that the *Recherches* refers "almost always to the state in which the new continent was found" at the end of the fifteenth century and the beginning of the sixteenth, and *not* to contemporary America (1771 ed., pp. 63, 65, 101, 103, 109, 189, 211–12, 227).

Thus the degeneration of America is no longer seen as the result of some fatal curse laid on the whole continent, as it had been in the *Recherches;* now it becomes instead just one stage in its historical evolution. The lowest point of American decadence is pushed three centuries back into the past, and the new continent, from the time of entering within Europe's orbit, has begun, albeit slowly and hesitantly, to share in Europe's progress.

So the discovery of America really was "the greatest and most memorable event in history" (1771 ed., p. 141; an echo of Gómara's famous exordium?). Those abrupt causes of the age-old degeneration, the catastrophes, the floods, and volcanic eruptions, which were mentioned somewhat obscurely in the *Recherches* (and which are still admitted in the *Défense*), were not repeated. And the slow and constant causes, going under the inclusive title of *climate,* took a turn for the better.

So de Pauw comes back to another idea that had appealed to Buffon (see above, p. 14), an idea already sketched out by Oviedo and applied by Hume to the two Americas,[42] and one which contained an undeniable kernel of truth: namely that the work of man, his tilling of the soil and control of the rivers, his raising of cattle and reclaiming of the boggy marshes, can little by little bring about changes in the degree of healthiness and even the climate of a given area. Perhaps in two or three centuries they will even succeed in producing a wine in America like the wine of Burgundy! (1771 ed., p. 105). De Pauw still maintains that America's present climate weakens the Europeans (pp. 10–11; 1771 ed., p. 60), but he admits that one day the arts and sciences will flourish even

---

41. *Défense,* p. 108; cf. also Church, op. cit., p. 196. These two three-century periods call to mind the fact that three hundred years was precisely the period of time necessary, according to Goodman, for ascertaining a decadence or corruption of nature (see Harris, op. cit., p. 29).

42. *Of the Populousness of Ancient Nations,* in *Essays,* II, 11; ed. cit., pp. 441–42.

in America; and they will flourish earlier in the north than in the south, because the English colonists work "with an indescribable fervor to break up the terrain, purify the air, and drain away the marshy waters," while the Spanish and Portuguese, with the best provinces in America, have become as lazy as the natives among whom they live.[43]

De Pauw's new theses, with their alternating suggestions of decadence and civilization on the part of the Americans, bring to mind a curious dialogue written by Vauvenargues (1715–47) about thirty years earlier, but not actually published until 1857. In it the moralist presents an American criticizing, as usual, a European, in this particular case a Portuguese, for having taught the innocent natives the corrupt arts of civilization. But the Portuguese vigorously denies that civilization is a form of corruption or degeneration and proceeds to ask the American if he sees the mind of man as a great tree which with time has borne ripe fruit "but which later degenerated and lost its fertility and strength." The American agrees, saying that the metaphor supports his thesis that the Americans had reached the stage of perfected development, while the Europeans had gone beyond it into decadence. But the Portuguese breaks in triumphantly: "But who told you that you had reached this point of maturity in America? Who told you that having reached it, you didn't lose it?"[44] And poetic as always like a true Portuguese, he concludes by comparing the arts of Europe to the spring sun that revives the fields after the winter of barbarism.

The similarity between this and de Pauw's attitude in his reply to Pernety, though accidental of course, is quite clear. Vauvenargues's Portuguese is attempting to reconcile the old antithesis between nature and civilization by setting it in the context of history. De Pauw, without changing his qualification of America as a degenerate continent, now finds in it some capacity for progress.

In fact, while Pernety saw America as existing in a state of immobile and blessed perfection, in a golden "philosophical" state of nature, de Pauw—here at his most genuinely modern and enlightened—describes it

---

43. *Défense*, p. 13; on the modifications of climate, see also pp. 55, 57; the unhealthy climate of Panama, Cartagena, and Portobello is also resistant to improvement: ibid., p. 59. In the second *Recherches* there is reference (I, 80) to the Egyptians having "much corrected the climate of their country," and the influence of climate in general is very limited (I, 167, 180, 255). Among the many authors who took up and developed this thesis one might note the anti–de Pauwians Jefferson (together with certain of his followers; see Edwin T. Martin, *Thomas Jefferson: Scientist* [New York, 1952], pp. 139, 143, 204–09, 232) and Volney, in his *Tableau du climat et du sol des Etats-Unis*, 1803, in *Oeuvres complètes* (Paris, 1846), pp. 630–99, esp. 637, 685–86. The destruction of the forests in particular was discussed as a factor affecting the North American climate: see examples collected and commented on by G. Chinard, "La Forêt Américaine," in *L'homme contre la nature* (Paris, 1949), pp. 85–178; by H. N. Smith, *Virgin Land: The American West as Symbol and Myth* (Cambridge, Mass., 1950), pp. 179–83, and with reference to Buffon and John Evelyn (1664), Hanks, op. cit., p. 191. Cf. also Boorstin, *Colonial Experience*, p. 161.

44. L. Vauvenargues, *Oeuvres morales* (Paris, 1874), II, 325.

with the harsh realism of the economist as poor, exploited, and oppressed, because it must get all its manufactured goods from Europe, and because its population is too small. This makes America "politically speaking, the most wretched country in the world, because for this reason it is entirely at the mercy of foreigners." It has an infinitely greater need of Europe than Europe has of America. It is so enslaved to Europe by nature and politics "that its complete independence is something morally impossible; *but as time passes it will no longer be so*" (p. 124; 1771 ed., pp. 117–18). Already the northern colonies send foodstuffs to the south: "this is the first step toward independence from the mother countries" (1771 ed., p. 115n.). In fact industrialization and the capacity to be self-supporting will be the basis of America's future political independence — an idea one hardly expected to see formulated by the most classic slanderer and denigrator of the New World.

V. PERNETY'S SECOND OFFENSIVE: *REPETITA MINIME JUVANT*

Poor Pernety must have been shaken by de Pauw's rejoinder. He was thinking his authoritative eyewitness accounts had demolished the fantasies and exaggerations of the *Recherches* in one swift blow, and now here was de Pauw again, scornful and arrogant as ever, producing all sorts of new points and remaining completely unrepentant in his basic heresy.

His appeal before the Royal Academy of Berlin had failed, and de Pauw's reputation only increased. What higher court was there to hear his case? He had seen the pillars of his argument come tumbling down under the onslaught of de Pauw's sarcasms, but the patient little monk still did not lose heart; he set to work to build an even bigger and more solid edifice than the first. Gathering together a huge mass of authoritative testimony including that of Benjamin Franklin,[45] kneading it hastily into an American *summa apologetica,* he dished up in 1771 his *Examen des Recherches philosophiques sur l'Amérique et les Américains et de la Défense de cet ouvrage:* two volumes, of small format, true, but containing no less than nine hundred and sixty-two pages.

It is a blessing, for us anyway, that de Pauw produced no further reply. But in fact there was no reason to. Pernety presents no new points nor does he open any new perspectives on the problem. And although he was obviously enraged by de Pauw's response, and protests that he had never confused America of 1492 with eighteenth-century America,[46] he actually contents himself with one more display of long-winded erudition on the

---

45. *Examen,* II, 584, quoted by Durand Echeverria, *Mirage in the West: A History of the French Image of American Society to 1815* (Princeton, 1957), p. 30.
46. Op. cit. (Berlin, 1771; there apparently exists another edition of 1773), I, 28–30, 179; II, 69, etc.

subject of America. By and large, in fact, he treats his adversary with new respect: de Pauw has "conceived a hypothesis, and it takes intelligence to do that": the hypothesis may be completely mistaken, but it led him into new fields and produced some very original notions, and it may yet serve "to uncover new truths."[47] De Pauw's logical error is that he generalizes,[48] but at the root of this error is his perverse delight in argument for its own sake, the pleasure he finds in insulting his enemies, his haughty libertinism,[49] and his courtier's complacency. What a pity that this clever man should let himself be guided by a fantasy so lurid and bizarre that from its earliest infancy it sucks on putrid and foul-smelling waters, grows up amidst a filthy slime swarming with reptiles, snakes, and poisonous insects of monstrous proportions, and feeds insatiably on countless beetles, spiders, and gigantic toads. Its home is a dark and barren land of vertical precipices or marshes and forests, or immense deserts, inhabited only by a few families of animals with human features, idiotlike, dull, a blind prey to their instincts.[50] Turning his vengeful sarcasm from the defense of the natives to the defense of the ancient American civilizations, Pernety regrets that the valient Cortes could not count among his followers someone like de Pauw, who with a single stroke of the pen could have made whole fortified cities and armed multitudes disappear—even at the risk of making the great conquistador seem some sort of don Quixote doing battle with imaginary armies![51]

Apart from a few well-aimed barbs of this sort, Pernety's counterattack pursues a somewhat tedious strategy: against every statement by de Pauw he quotes extracts from chroniclers and travelers, sometimes pages long, saying the opposite; but at no time does he submit them to any sort of critical assessment, preferring to accept literally and quite indiscriminately anything nice they had to say about America. The rapt visions of Columbus, the calculated hyperboles of Cortes, the blithe romances of the pseudo-Vespucci, and the impassioned idealizations of Las Casas—all these are repeated by Pernety as if they had the same value as the carefully assembled information of Martire and Oviedo or the much later scientific reports of people like Condamine or Ulloa. Certainly he succeeds in casting doubt on some of de Pauw's more ex-

47. Op. cit., II, 116; see also ibid., I, xviii; II, v, 268, etc.
48. De Pauw proceeded like someone giving a picture of Europe based on the steppes of Lapland or the Italian *maremme* (op. cit., I, 103): cf. I, 276–77, 294; II, 157–58, 182, 195n., 203, 209, 286–87, 539, 543, 548–49, 598, and 599.
49. How does de Pauw, "a minister of the Christian religion," dare to call the priests of the European religions our "fakirs"? (ibid., II, 573). Cf. above, n. 35.
50. Ibid., I, 304–05; de Pauw's portrayal, Pernety continues, would only be acceptable, in part, for certain regions in Brazil: I, 311–12.
51. Ibid., I, 143–45, 305–06; de Pauw knew but deliberately ignored the reports of Cortes: I, 181.

treme suggestions; but the unbounded optimism of the overall picture is no more convincing than the gloominess of the portrait it is designed to replace.[52] In short, there is little to choose between them, unless one is already convinced of the superiority of Nature over civilized Society, or vice versa.

This then is the sole ideological basis of Pernety's *Examen* — an almost mystical primitivism with its customary accompaniment of moralistic prejudices against corrupt European society. It is this approach that allows Pernety to reconcile the two opposing theories that had seen America as either abundantly populated or completely deserted. De Pauw had "historicized" the problem, maintaining that America was thinly populated at the time of its discovery but had later grown in population as a result of the European migrations (see above, p. 191); Pernety reverses this idea and uses Las Casas's authority, which also happened to fit in with his own primitivism, to assert that America was swarming with people in 1492 ("the population of certain American countries might perhaps surpass that of Europe and equal that of Asia,"[53] no less); but then came the vile Europeans, and America was reduced to a desert by their slaughter and pillage. De Pauw almost comes out of it all a hispanophile, for having exonerated the conquerors of this awful crime![54]

Nature is prolific and civilization homicidal. Innocence is destined

---

52. Pernety writes for example that in Peru the mountains were covered with flocks of vicuña, "and the coca, that precious grass, grows abundantly there" (ibid., I, 282–83). The vicuña was always extremely rare, so that even the Incas protected it against extinction. The "coca" is a leaf, not a grass. Without having read the *Examen*, Carli judged its extreme philo-Americanism very accurately: "I am told that Pernety too replied to de Pauw with two well-argued volumes. *The spirit of America has invaded the Europeans*" (from Milan, 12 May 1778, in B. Ziliotto, *Trecentosessantasei lettere di Gian Rinaldo Carli capodistriano* [Trieste, 1909], p. 209).

53. *Examen*, I, 207–08; cf. also I, 24–25, 190 ff.

54. Ibid., I, 201. Father Nuix, for whom see below, p. 192, was to come back to this argument (1780) in his defense of the humanity of the Spaniards in the Indies. Already in that same year 1771, however, an obscure polygraph and enthusiastic follower of de Pauw had pointed out the contradiction between the New World's supposed lack of inhabitants and the alleged Spanish massacres (Jacques Vincent Delacroix, *Mémoires d'un Américain, avec une description de la Prusse et de l'Isle de Saint Domingue*, 2 vols. [Lausanne-Paris, 1771]). It was actually after his description of Santo Domingo (op. cit., II, 73–124) and the notes (II, 125–48) that Delacroix would have liked to insert a *Discours* describing the cruelty of the Spaniards, but "I was forestalled by a *philosophe* Author" (p. 149); and he then summarizes the de Pauwian theses on the noxious climate of America (p. 159), on the nonexistence of Patagonian giants (pp. 175–86), on the lasciviousness of the native women (p. 163) and the hairlessness of the men ("a sign of the feebleness of their constitution," p. 167), on the Eskimos, etc. He admits to some doubt about the Creoles degenerating within three generations (in Martinique and Santo Domingo the Creoles manage to "display much intelligence in their affairs," pp. 168–69), but the *Recherches* remains "the best [work] and the most philosophical of those that have appeared on America" (p. 169); of the others, he criticizes Prévost for being more elegant than truthful, Pernety as being overburdened with minor details and meager in philosophy, and La Condamine, who is among the few who have actually observed the natives (p. 170). J. M. Quérard, in *La France littéraire*, s.v., lists more than thirty works for Delacroix, including some notes on the translation of Adams's *Defence* (see below, p. 248) and a collection of European and American constitutions of which a copy was owned by Jefferson (*Catalogue of the Library*, III, 40–41).

for slaughter. If the natives had possessed less "humanity" and had massacred the invaders, de Pauw would not have found them stupid and brutalized at all but rather would have treated them with great respect. "My poor Mexicans, my poor Peruvians," the abbé concludes, why did you content yourselves with following the dictates of nature? "Why did you not go to school with our Machiavellis?"[55]

Pernety also uses "nature" to defend the Americans against these insidious accusations of scarce erotic inclination. If they are animals, as de Pauw would have it, their animal instincts must fill them with an ardent desire for their females. Indeed, whispers the dewy-eyed sentimentalist mystic, "if beauty's sway and this irresistible attraction which draws the sexes together is an institution of nature," who will be more bound and dedicated to it than those "who have nought but nature as their guide"?[56]

And furthermore the Indians are robust, bearded, and hirsute, and the women of these countries (attention, you women of Paris!) "are beautiful, intelligent, and of good conduct," and they cover their nakedness; there are some that are pale blonde, some ash-blonde, and some dark, and some that have fairer skins than the women of Europe.[57] If they do not particularly excite their men, this is because they go around naked, explains Pernety—all forgetful of having just vaunted their custom of modestly veiling themselves—and the men get accustomed to them like that, and *ab assuetis non fit passio.* A European would be quite aroused by them, but in America nakedness arouses men's passions less than the toilettes and coiffures and rouge do in Europe.[58] Poor Europeans, one feels like saying, disturbed as much by clothing as by lack of clothing. The Americans, on the other hand, may perhaps be unfamiliar with the passion of love, but they know tenderness and virtue: "Yes, the Indians of the new continent are men."[59] And they are not all syphilitic.[60]

True, they are inclined to laziness. And they do not get much exercise and so obviously could not lift weights like the Europeans. So what? "Not everyone is a porter."[61] Besides, if they were or are weak, this

55. *Examen,* I, 237–39.
56. Ibid., I, 262–63.
57. Ibid., II, 15–16.
58. Ibid., II, 90–92. An anonymous seventeenth-century traveler had already said of the women of Brazil that their nudity, far from provoking the men, "seems rather to make them less voluptuous" (quoted in G. Atkinson, *Relations de voyages,* p. 135). On the nudity of the native women, preferable to Europe's lascivious elegance, see also Blanke, op. cit., pp. 238–39.
59. *Examen,* II, 54, 93; and there are travelers and missionaries who have described these virtuous Americans as being addicted to lustful pleasures! Ibid., II, 99–102.
60. Ibid., II, 27–28.
61. Ibid., II, 81. And there is included, of course, the usual prolix (pp. 332–407) defense of the Patagonians and Giants of Magellan's Land! (for whom see also I, 47–48, and passim). Lahontan had written that the natives could not carry heavy loads, as the Europeans do, up to the age of thirty-five or forty; but after that (by dint of exercise?) they stay stronger than the Europeans up to the age of fifty-five or sixty (op. cit., p. 218).

shows that they were that much more intelligent and "spiritual" (Las Casas's theme, see above, p. 68); and if de Pauw calls them animals because they are not outstanding in the arts and sciences, what is to be said of the women of Europe? Are they too "a stupid brutalized race?"[62]

It should also be noted that the Creoles have already produced some very learned men, which is why the European governments have begun to be worried and have tried to suppress their talents with various restrictions, and why England is already sorry that it allowed them to develop. And the mestizos too have produced some excellent artists, like Miguel de Santiago, whose pictures have been admired in places as far away as Spain and even Rome.[63] And both Creole and mestizo are long-lived.[64] If some Creoles or some of the North American colonists have ruined their health, that's not the fault of the climate – their own "excessive debauchery" brought that about.[65]

What else? Pernety finds he has left himself one last task – to destroy whatever claims remained that Europe was in some way or other superior. De Pauw was "intoxicated with tenderness" toward his own hemisphere and its inhabitants,[66] But in fact it enjoys no special privilege, just as America has no exclusive right to misfortune. Nor is it true that Europe is the mother of the arts and sciences: "The arts and sciences were born in Africa and in Asia, whence they were brought to Europe." Europe fed them and raised them, true, but this only makes her their nurse, not their mother.[67] As for behavior, in the taverns and smoke shops of the north there are Europeans behaving worse than savages; and note this, gentlemen – half, yes, half at least of the women of Europe are disguised in whalebone corsets; and goiter, let de Pauw say what he will, disfigures the Tyrolese![68]

With de Pauw routed there still remained in the background the imposing figure of Buffon. Pernety treats Buffon with obsequious humility, noting particularly where the great naturalist differs from de Pauw and agrees with Rousseau (the virtuous savage, the vices of man in society), and quoting long extracts from his history of man; he sticks to man because on the subject of animals Buffon is, as we know, just as pessimistic as de Pauw. But undaunted and, alas, untiring, he comes back in the end to the lions and tigers, repeating on the strength of Martire's evidence

---

62. *Examen*, II, 79.
63. Ibid., II, 141–84; on Miguel de Santiago, see II, 170 and 306–07, where Ulloa's *Journal*, p. 229, is quoted. There are mentions of this painter, variously identified as mestizo or *indio*, in other apologists of America, up to Drouin de Bercy, *L'Europe et l'Amérique comparées* (Paris, 1818), II, 200.
64. *Examen*, II, 235 ff.
65. Ibid., II, 163, 245.
66. Ibid., I, vii, 73, etc.
67. Ibid., II, 440–48.
68. Ibid., II, 461–69, 479–90, 495–502. On goiter, see de Pauw, *Défense*, 1771 ed., p. 225.

that they do exist in America. If Mr. de Pauw is pleased to call them something else, let him by all means do so.[69] Even if it has no mane, and is of a rather ugly color and somewhat cowardly, the puma is still a lion; and the jaguar is still a tiger, even if not a real tiger![70] *Te baptizo carpam.* . . .

And if de Pauw is so worried about dimensions, what about the reptiles and insects in America? He can hardly deny that they at least are more perfect than their miniature, and therefore presumably degenerate, equivalents in Europe.[71] And if he insists that wild animals are the more perfect the fiercer they are, because this is the way Nature likes them, he is bound to conclude that a wild animal in its natural state is more perfect than a domestic one of the same species—an idea accepted by Buffon, but which does not quite fit in with the assertions of degeneration in the animal species of America. Nature, transmuted and adulterated in domestic animals, shines out pure and strong in the wild beasts.[72]

Nor is it true that all the animals which were already domesticated have degenerated in America; the pigs have improved (but Buffon had already conceded this); the quadrupeds in general are very prolific, and the horses—Pernety saw some at Montevideo—have excellent qualities. So they have become heavier? But this is because they were transferred from a dry terrain to a wet terrain; the same thing happens to the horses moved from the Limousin or Spain to the lowlands of Poitou or the lush fields of Normandy or the marshlands of Holland.[73] Europe's weaknesses —Pernety seems to be trying to say, as usual—are no less than America's.

VI. DE PAUW'S OPINION UNALTERED

Pernety's second offensive, with its ineffective ramblings diluted over nearly a thousand pages, was not the sort of thing to cause de Pauw any further worry. The same was true of Pernety's final contribution to the polemic, in which he withdrew still further from the extremism of his attempts to refute de Pauw, abandoning almost completely the fierce Patagonian giants (few, if any, and if Frezier and a number of other travelers are to be trusted) and depicting the native in quite unflattering

---

69. *Examen,* I, 68n.

70. Ibid., II, 214–26, correcting his former position, on which see above, p. 88. In the same way Pernety maintains that there is iron in Peru, although it is unserviceable: "This iron is so brittle that whatever was made with it was always extremely breakable" (ibid., II, 302); see above, pp. 57–58.

71. Ibid., II, 526: the argument was already present in the *Dissertation:* see above, p. 86.

72. *Examen,* II, 528–32; see above, p. 26.

73. Ibid., II, 191–92; and for the Yucatán, I, 102. Cf. Mazzei, below, p. 273. In one of the famous Tapestries of the Indians (Gobelins, 1687–88), two proud and noble horses in full harness and caparison stare down at a poor little curiously web-footed llama: superiority of the European fauna to the American? or proof of its successful acclimatization?

terms.[74] Anyway, de Pauw made no further attempt to defend himself against Pernety, nor in fact against any of his numerous other critics; nor did he write that "other work" that he had announced in the *Défense* (1771 ed., p. 20), which was to have shown that the savage is a "minor" in relation to civilized man; nor did he ever produce the new edition of the *Recherches,* which Pernety had fondly hoped would accept many of his criticisms.[75]

There is only one other work of his devoted to America, and in it he does little more than repeat the ideas of the *Recherches,* though somewhat less vigorously and pugnaciously. This was the long article he wrote for the *Supplément à l'Encyclopédie* and which was published in 1776.[76] In it the Americans are described as stupid, inert, indolent, physically weak, or at least not as robust as one might expect (partially the result of their laziness and inclination for strong drink); they are incapable of any civil progress whatever, few in number, scattered and unaware of each other's existence. The Creoles are pronounced inferior once again, with the inferiority ascribed in general to the climate, and thus considered a "misfortune" rather than something for which they should be blamed. But it is a misfortune striking all America impartially: in the *Recherches* he had cruelly derided the University of Lima, and now, perhaps because of the increased popularity in Europe of the North American colonists, he pours out his sarcasms on Harvard University too: "It is not apparent that the professors of the University of Cambridge, in New England, have formed any young Americans to the point where they are able to bring them out into the literary world."[77]

74. In the chapter "Des différences dans l'espèce humaine" contained (II, 316–24) in the treatise on physiognomy entitled *La connaissance de l'homme moral par celle de l'homme physique* (Berlin, 1776–77), where it is repeated (see above, n. 35) without naming de Pauw that certain "particular facts, on which one cannot judge the whole nation or a whole people," are not constant features of the Americans, but it is admitted that these people have a common origin, that they are lazy and idle, although not evil nor stupid, that they have bizarre and whimsical customs, etc. The defense of the native women remains unchanged: "The savage women are fat and very well built. . . ."

75. *Examen,* II, iv–v.

76. *Supplément à l'Encyclopédie, ou Dictionnaire raisonné des sciences, des arts et des métiers* (Amsterdam, 1776), I, 343–54: hereafter cited as "Amérique." (The second part of the article is by the geographer Samuel Engel: see Richard Switzer, "America in the Encyclopédie," in *Studies on Voltaire and the Eighteenth Century,* 58 [Transactions of the Second International Congress on the Enlightenment, IV], pp. 1481–99, esp. 1487–91.) Among the collaborators the preface lists de Pauw, who supposedly furnished "articles on *Antiquities, History,* and *Criticism* worthy of the reputation he has earned" (p. iii). But in the four folio volumes of the *Supplément* I have not been able to find a single article signed or initialed by de Pauw. The *Supplément,* as is well known, has nothing in common with the famous *Encyclopédie* beyond the names of two collaborators, D'Alembert and Marmontel; it was a commercial enterprise in which Diderot had no part whatsoever (L. S. Gaudin, *Les lettres anglaises dans l'Encyclopédie* [New York, 1942], p. i). Thus there seems to be no basis for the conclusions arrived at by certain scholars (Church, for example, op. cit., p. 194) regarding the favor de Pauw supposedly enjoyed among the "encyclopedists."

77. "Amérique," p. 351; cf. G. Chinard, "Eighteenth Century Theories on America as a Human Habitat," *Proceedings of the American Philosophical Society,* 91, no. 1 (1947), p. 36.

Thus the substance of his condemnation remains unchanged. But the tone is much less acrid and the frequent references to scabrous subjects have entirely disappeared. Most significantly of all, he abandons almost completely his claims to have discovered a system behind these "facts," and his attempts to produce a scientific (and fatalistic) explanation for them; and thus in turn a large part of his Europeistic complacency too. Some of these alterations are no doubt due to de Pauw himself, who as a sound man of letters knew the difference between a scandalmongering pamphlet and an encyclopedia article; other alterations may have been due to concern for his reputation as a historian, recently refreshed by the success of his second *Recherches* on the Egyptians and the Chinese, or even to the clamor of his critics; and yet others can perhaps be ascribed to the editors of the *Supplément*.[78]

The overall result is disconcerting; this last work of the once bold anti-American winds up pale, weak, and rambling. The inferiority of America is affirmed and reasserted emphatically, but there is no further talk of degeneration or immaturity. Several times he comes back to the indication of 1492 as the moment when this inferiority was most striking,[79] and he also recalls the hope that when the earth is tilled the climate will improve.[80] But the optimistic historical vision put forward in the *Défense* (see above, p. 91), of America's progress as a parabola in reverse, receives no further mention here. In fact, even the glittering prophecies of the economic and political independence of America (see above, p. 93), instead of drawing new strength from the revolt of the British colonies, fade into nothing with his final assessment: "Even today there does not exist in the whole New World an American tribe who are free or who think about instructing themselves in letters."[81]

His explanations for this all-embracing American inferiority turn out to be equally regressive in comparison to the *Défense*. There must have been volcanic eruptions, earthquakes, floods, and other cataclysms, but the true cause "is a secret of nature." All the adverse factors are still explained in terms of the "climate," but it is now said to be unhealthy only "in *certain* places," and the charge is made with some doubts and reservations: "there *could* exist in the climate of America particular *causes* which make *certain* animal species to be smaller than their counterparts living in our continent," and which bring about the degener-

---

78. Church, op. cit., p. 184, suspects there was some "censoring" from this source.
79. Columbus found a continent "where everything was in such a great state of desolation that one cannot reflect thereupon without astonishment" (p. 344a); "one can imagine . . . what an astonishing difference there was between the two hemispheres of our globe in the fifteenth century" (p. 346b); all the sciences were unknown in America, "so that the human spirit was there more than three thousand years behindhand" (p. 354a).
80. Ibid., p. 351b, referring to the new edition of the *Recherches philosophiques sur les Américains*.
81. "Amérique," p. 354a: the conclusion of the article.

ation, *in the extreme north,* of cattle brought over from Europe.[82] But is there any part of the globe about which one could not say something of the sort? De Pauw, unwilling to abandon his basic thesis, finds it impossible to extend his innate unshakable Europeistic optimism to the Americans (or to the whole human race); so that almost unawares he ends up doing precisely the opposite, applying to his precious Europeans some of those highly pessimistic judgments originally formulated to condemn the Americans. Arguing with the Spanish theologians, de Pauw reminds them that cannibals have been known in every climate, even in our own continent, "because when man is not enlightened by knowledge, when his head and his heart are not governed by laws, he falls everywhere into the same excesses."[83] And referring to the American Indians' intellectual capacities, whose existence he has just a while back categorically denied, he now observes that one could only demonstrate things for sure if one took them as newborn children and brought them up with all gentleness and philosophy; but the experiment would have to be carried out with a large number of children "since even in Europe out of so many children dedicated to study from their tenderest youth, one obtains such a small number of reasonable men, and an even smaller number of enlightened men."[84]

De Pauw, in short, persists in his condemnation of the Americans, but he had already turned his critical eye on some of the nations of the Old World, the Chinese and the Egyptians, and, after completing his examination of the most noble nations of Asia and Africa, was to conclude with the most illustrious people of Europe, the Greeks.

In these succeeding works de Pauw frequently mentions his first *Recherches,* quoting its theories as proven fact and occasionally enriching them with odd details. In the book on the Egyptians and the Chinese, he repeats, in passing, his attack on the brutality of the Europeans in America[85] and rather more frequently his slanders on the whole of American nature, from the laziness, stupidity, brutality, and misery of the savages, to the robber bands of escaped Negroes (the *Républiques de Voleurs* like the Brazilian Paulistas), and even to the precious stones of America, which are all "without exception" of inferior quality, soft and not solid, not even the diamonds, "which seems to be the result of the

---

82. Ibid., pp. 345b, 349–50. Other points on which the polemic is toned down a little: there *is* iron in America, but the Americans did not know how to forge it: p. 345b, the Americans are not as longeval as some would have it, but one cannot be sure of their age, and in the north at least they live as long as other men: p. 350b. The polemic against Spain, on the other hand, remains intact (Romulo D. Carbia, *Historia de la leyenda negra hispano-americana* [Buenos Aires, 1943], pp. 136–37).

83. "Amérique," p. 354a. Cf. de Maistre, below, p. 578.

84. "Amérique," p. 351a.

85. *Recherches sur les Egyptiens,* I, 143, 304; II, 227.

flood that the New World suffered in times subsequent to our own cataclysm."[86]

In his last *Recherches,* on the Greeks (1787), he mentions in the very first lines having published other "researches" on "savage and brutalized peoples, such as the Americans," and on nations condemned to eternal mediocrity, like the Egyptians and the Chinese (see also vol. I, p. 103). The passing years and his declining reputation have made him no less abrasive; and by now the polemic on the Americans had well and truly taken hold, thanks to his adversaries and thanks even more to Robertson, who in his famous *History of America* (1777) had appropriated some of de Pauw's findings: "Dr. Robertson [says de Pauw ambiguously] who has commented in English [*sic*] on my researches on the Americans. . . ."[87]

VII. THE PHILOSOPHER LA DOUCEUR AND THE NATIVES OF NORTH AMERICA

Meanwhile a little-known essayist had come forward to take upon himself the defense of the ex-Benedictine and to cut the Prussian philosopher down to size, which he does with relish. It is not known for sure who produced the monograph *Of America and the Americans, or Curious Observations of the Philosopher La Douceur, who traveled this Hemisphere during the last war, following the noble trade of killing men without eating them,*[88] but it is clear from the title that the author is or at least wishes to be thought an ex-soldier quite lacking in militaristic spirit but a mite sarcastic on the subject of the *philosophes*. Internal evidence (pp. 6–7) shows that the author cannot be Pernety himself; it was once customary to attribute the work to the physiocrat Pierre Poivre, author of the *Voyage d'un philosophe* (1768), but this too seems unlikely for a variety of reasons: in the first place because de Pauw quotes this work with great respect in his *Défense* (1771 ed., p. 183) and in his second *Recherches* (II, 6); and then also inasmuch as La Douceur's tirades against monarchs would hardly be fitting for someone like Poivre, a faithful servant of the crown, raised to the nobility and given a pension by the king of France; not to mention the fact that Poivre was never in America.[89] Nowadays

86. Ibid., I, 213; see also I, 19, 153, 166, 173; II, 4, 13, 153, 171, 254. The first *Recherches* is referred to on the usage of tobacco and the American savages' enamels: I, 170, 282.

87. *Recherches sur les Grecs*, II, 331–32. Cf., in fact, below, p. 166.

88. Berlin: Pitra, 1771; I have not seen the second edition (Berlin, 1772), which is apparently some thirty pages longer (referred to by Church, op. cit., p. 196, n. 34). The title recalls Vespucci's comment on the Brazilians, who marveled at we Europeans killing our enemies and then not eating them (A. von Humboldt, *Examen critique*, V, 26–27). Cf. below, p. 210.

89. Poivre, who was an excellent administrator in the French Islands of the Indian Ocean (see Lewis A. Maverick, "Pierre Poivre: Eighteenth Century Explorer of Southeast Asia," *The Pacific Historical Review*, 10 [1941], pp. 165–77), mentioned approvingly also by Adam Smith, *The Wealth of Nations* (Modern Library ed., bk. I, ch. XI, pt. I, p. 156), interests himself mainly, in his *Voyage*, in questions of agriculture and systems of fiscal imposition. It is curious however that Brissot de Warville too, who

the book is frequently attributed to Zaccaria de Pazzi de Bonneville, but this is not entirely convincing either. Bonneville is known to history as the eccentric inventor of a weapon called "the Lyonnaise," a sort of scythed war chariot that only needed two men to propel it and was "a thousand times more murderous than gunpowder," a machine he recommended for the preservation of the human race, the protection of sovereign states, and the achieving of perpetual peace. His only other claim to fame was as editor of the military writings of Maurice of Saxony. Neither of these activitities would seem to make him easily identifiable with an author who exhibits such limited respect for the noble profession of arms.[90]

But whoever the author is, the book is lively and good-humored, and the author's flashes of wit and easygoing attitude bring a new touch to the dry polemic. La Douceur—let us call him that—knows nothing at all of biological or cosmographic theories, nor has he read much of what the naturalists and travelers had to say; but he has been in America,[91] has made war and made love there, and so feels himself eminently qualified to plunge into the discussion and pronounce his opinion, which in fact he does on the very first page—Pernety is right and de Pauw wrong.

Admittedly de Pauw is an intelligent man, but it is possible to use one's intelligence wrongly and to be completely mistaken, particularly when one has not seen for oneself what one is writing about. Poor de Pauw has actually proved nothing; he has spent nine years toiling over a book three-quarters of seven-eighths of which (a strange mathematical hyperbole, corresponding to a mere 67.78125 percent) is mere regurgitation of discussions that have been gone over twenty times. And his *Défense* "is worth no more than the *Recherches;* it is a simple repetition thereof" —which, as we have seen, is far from being the case. When Pernety was

---

mentions having read with enthusiasm the *Voyage d'un philosophe* and visited its author, praises "his observations on the customs and arts of the peoples of America" (*Mémoires* [Brussels, 1830], II, 206–16).

90. It is to be noted however that Bonneville fought effectively against the English in America and wrote a work with the title *Esprit des lois de tactique* (1762), clearly inspired by Montesquieu, an author whom La Douceur praises as "the least fallible of men," (op. cit., p. 26; but Bonneville takes issue with him right at the very beginning of his *Lyonnaises*, written in 1764–69, published in Amsterdam, 1771, p. 6). Another possible indication: the demographic concerns, particularly in relation to the remedies for the slaughter of war, already present in the mind of the Maréchal de Saxe and his editor Bonneville (*Les rêveries, ou Mémoires sur l'art de la guerre* [La Haye, 1756], quarto ed., pp. 221–28, 16 mo. ed., II, 209–23, with notes by Bonneville, also against the idleness of the great; cf. also the *Lyonnaises*, throughout and below, p. 108, etc.). On the *Lyonnaises* of that "military patriot" Bonneville see the comment of Carlo Gastone della Torre di Rezzonico, *Ragionamento sulla filosofia del secolo XVIII* (1778), in *Raccolta di operette filosofiche e filologiche scritte nel secolo XVIII* (Milan, 1832), II, 79.

91. He has seen North America and part of South America, the Antilles, the coasts of Africa, a little of China ("but when one has seen one Chinese town and its inhabitants, one has seen all of them," p. 11), and a little of India and Persia, from which he traveled overland to Constantinople. Bonneville was also in China (*Lyonnaises*, p. 217).

attacking de Pauw he refrained from dealing with certain subjects, perhaps because they touched on matters "somewhat too spicy" for a Benedictine. La Douceur for his part feels no such compunction and will say whatever needs to be said to the arrogant de Pauw, with his shameless pretense of "pardoning" Dom Pernety, when it was in fact he himself who provoked him with his "unseeming tirade" against the worthy Benedictine. One can almost picture him, this gay globe-trotter, grasping his sword and waiting impatiently to pursue de Pauw through chapter after chapter of his book.

In the heat of the chase La Douceur almost forgets Pernety;[92] not because the friar, or ex-friar, could not keep up with the soldier, or ex-soldier, but more because Pernety had used his experiences in South America (the expedition to the Falkland Islands) to argue with de Pauw, and La Douceur on the other hand uses his knowledge of North America. So de Pauw's two opponents close in on him from either side. The *Recherches* had slandered all America impartially; now the twin paladins spring up side by side in its defense, one protecting its southern half and the other the northern. Later, as we shall see, every region of the New World and every republic that attained its independence would have its apologist against the slanders of Buffon and de Pauw. But even at the very outset of the polemic their campaign of vilification drew angry retorts on all sides.

La Douceur's basic point is that America is not degenerate. The New World really is "new" (p. 78) and thus generally speaking better than the Old. There is nothing decayed or putrefied about it at all. If he wanted to prove that there was, it would be up to de Pauw to show that the men, the plants, and the animals had at one time been larger, stronger, and more beautiful in America—which cannot possibly be proved. Besides, neither the lions nor the tigers can possibly have degenerated in America "because they simply don't exist there"; and the famous pumas "are no more lions than donkeys" (p. 74)—another exaggeration which he extends immediately afterward to jaguars and cougars as compared with tigers, but which actually succeeds merely in reinforcing the negative thesis of Buffon.

The wild oxen of America (bison?) are as big as the English oxen, and if the domestic cattle degenerated this was almost certainly the result of continual crossing of the same breed—just the same happens to horses and sheep in Spain. And so what if some European plants degenerated in America—even in the Old World vines degenerate when they are transplanted. And when the time comes that the whole of America is

92. He is mentioned on p. 74, when it is pointed out that he too was mistaken in believing in the existence of lions and tigers in America, on the basis of Zarate and other authors.

cultivated "one will find there, just as in Europe, areas favoring all sorts of production, even vines" (pp. 11–12, 24). But de Pauw had already said the same thing (see above, p. 91); and La Douceur, carried away by his thirst for revenge, goes on to weaken his own thesis yet further by picking a quarrel, heaven knows why, with the Egyptians—oldest of Old Worlds—whom he sees as completely degenerate: compared to what it once was the Egypt of today is a "sewer," and its inhabitants "such stupid, coarse, and evil creatures that I would be ashamed to compare them with the savagest savages of America" (p. 13).

The savages of America are not only not degenerate, they are not even fallen; like the Kalmucks and the Negroes, they are not descended from Adam and Eve, do not suffer the consequences of Original Sin, and so have not been redeemed by Christ (pp. 13–17, 77: echoes of the pre-adamites). Their condition is that of "Nature in its infancy," not its decrepitude. One has only to look at them; they are physically well made, and they are very wise to paint their bodies: "So they daub themselves?" The Italians would be obliged to do likewise if they went about naked, because Italy, that promised land of Europe, has as many insects as America (p. 35; see below, p. 213). The young men are gay, love dancing, and have a quite special liking for the French with their "light and playful sense of humor" so like their own. As for the old men, "nothing is more admirable than an elderly savage; he is another Epictetus or Carneades."

The intellectual gifts and capacities of the savages are more than adequate to their needs, and they are perfectly capable of mastering sciences and languages. That geometer-academician who spoke so ill of them saw only the mountains of Peru and the savages of Marañon.

Here our author is obviously referring[93] to the great geographer La Condamine, who had been in America with the scientific expedition sent to Quito (then Peru) to measure an arc of the meridian for the purpose of establishing the true shape of the earth, and who on his way back had crossed the whole of Amazonia. In his *Relation abrégée d'un voyage fait dans l'intérieur de l'Amérique méridionale, depuis la Côte de la Mer du Sud, jusques aux Côtes du Brésil et de la Guiane, en descendant la rivière des Amazones*,[94] his remarks on the savages are few but very much to the point. The natives differ greatly between one place and another, yet they all have "certain features of resemblance to each other . . . a same basic character."[95] They all have a fundamental brutishness about them that cannot be attributed to the degrading effect of slavery (as has

93. Op. cit., pp. 10, 76.

94. In *Histoire de l'Académie Royale des Sciences*, Année 1745 (Paris, 1749), pp. 391–492.

95. Ibid., pp. 418–19; cf. the same verdict of his companion on the expedition, Ulloa, below, pp. 216, 230, 285–86; Minguet, op. cit., p. 344.

been said of the modern Greeks) because it is equally apparent in the natives gathered within the missions; it shows "how *Man* abandoned to raw nature, lacking education and society, differs little from the Beast."[96] And as for the mestizo, he is "a type of man having only the vices of the nations of which he is a mixture."[97]

Such conclusions and his generally skeptical attitude in respect of the myths of the Amazons and the Eldorado[98] make La Condamine one of de Pauw's favorite authors. In point of fact, the serious and straight-forward scientist La Condamine did no more than establish an antithesis between civilization and nature in its crude state; it was Algarotti who went on from there to point out, with transparent allusion to La Condamine's judgment, "what miracles can be performed by legislature," transforming the torpid Peruvians into industrious subjects of the Incas.[99] But La Condamine never even mentions any harmful effects deriving from the physical environment nor does the thought of any organic de-generation ever enter his mind; and far from leveling charges at entire continents, he writes enthusiastically of American nature, both vegetable and animal, which latter boasts tigers as big and beautiful and fierce as those of Africa.[100] The puma, no, the puma is no lion even if that's the name they give it: "The male has no mane, and is much smaller than the African Lions. I haven't seen it alive, but only stuffed."[101] Despite all this, and even after La Douceur, La Condamine was frequently confused with Buffon's followers and the slanderers of America.[102]

It is true, La Douceur admits, that no native educated by the Spanish has yet made a name for himself, but then who among the Spanish them-selves ever made a name for himself, apart from Cervantes? All in all, there is no more brutalized, ignorant, savage, and barbarous people than the Spanish (pp. 55–61). Worse even than the Egyptians then, one feels like asking?

With the same self-confidence La Douceur takes up the challenge that Pernety had declined and comes down to de Pauw's level to discuss the

96. Op. cit., pp. 418–19 and 432; de Pauw was to say that the *indios* of the missions were "*esclaves fanatiques*" rather than men: "Amérique," p. 354.

97. *Journal du voyage fait par ordre du roi, à l'equateur* . . . (Paris, 1751–52), I, 52.

98. *Relation,* pp. 441–46, 452–54.

99. *Saggio sopra l'impero degli Incas,* in *Opere varie* (Venice, 1757), II, 123, and in *Opere* (Livorno, 1764), III, 188: an opinion taken over by Paolo Frisi in the preface to the Italian edition of the *Colombiade* of Mme du Boccage (Milan, 1771), p. xiii.

100. *Relation,* p. 468.

101. Ibid.; *Journal du voyage,* I, 153. For the birds, see below, p. 161.

102. See also Antonello Gerbi, *Viejas polémicas sobre el Nuevo Mundo* (Lima, 1946), pp. 263–64; Zavala, *América,* pp. 187–93; Berveiller, op. cit., pp. 306–07, and, without reference to our topic, Pierre M. Conlon, "La Condamine the Inquisitive," in *Studies on Voltaire and the Eighteenth Century,* 55 (Geneva, 1967; Transactions of the Second International Congress on the Enlightenment, I), pp. 361–93.

"somewhat coarse matters" such as the American's alleged sexual deviations and weaknesses. So they indulge in pederasty, "human nature's slip of the pen" (p. 40)? But pederasty is common among the most civilized people! The men are milk-bearing? But even in Europe there are many men who have milk; some of them of great erotic vigor. You want an example? The good La Douceur bursts out that he himself "I, who am no gelding nor woman, have had milk for a long time." One thought leads to another, and soon La Douceur finds the argument that will undermine de Pauw's accusations that the Indian women are extremely lascivious: "I recall with pleasure (begging the philosopher's pardon) the delightful moments spent with a native girl of Illinois, who far from being insatiable, as Mr. de Pauw would have it the women of America are, said softly to me: 'Oh my little warrior, you will do yourself harm, and you will not be any use at all for war any more'" (pp. 41–44).

After such a delightful touch of brazen honesty the customary counter-accusations of corruption among the Hispano-American women can only seem dull, and just as conventional are the defenses of the Indians' courage in war, the exaggerations on the pre-Colombian population (estimated at one hundred and eighty million),[103] the praises of the fine qualities of numerous American products, and the denial of the American origin of syphilis (caused, La Douceur says, by eating the meat of animals killed with poisoned arrows: pp. 45–46).

Somewhat more interesting, though by no means original after what Las Casas and Vico had written (below, pp. 577–78), is his explanation of cannibalism: "It is the savages' *Te Deum,* and each one in the ceremony often has no more than a half ounce of flesh for his share" (p. 47). But perhaps the most curious thing in La Douceur is the way he borrows the ancient myth of a primitive blessed equality to demolish the Europeans' claims to well-being. This well-being, so much vaunted by the philosophers, "is concentrated in a very small number of men who enjoy it at the expense of that of the majority." If these same philosophers were to take a look at America and then look again at how the peasants in our own hemisphere live, they would wish them "the happiness and the good cheer of the savages of America" (pp. 30–31). The kings, *pace* de Pauw, do their best: "I have no reason to love kings, they have never done me aught but evil"; but it is not at all easy to govern "so-called philosophers, who for the most part are no more than arguers," and a turbulent, illogical,

103. This was an indirect proof of both the fruitfulness of the earth and the generative capacity of the men: but elsewhere La Douceur accounts for the meager fecundity of the American savages in terms of the frequency of endotribal interbreeding and astutely explains the higher civilizations of Mexico and Peru by the harshness of the soil of these countries—a real Toynbee-type challenge victoriously overcome.

capricious people like the Europeans. Furthermore, he continues, all ills derive "from the too unequal distribution of riches" (pp. 68–69). The savages, to their great good fortune, are not "philosophers" and write no books nor pamphlets: this is why they can enjoy a happy life. "But that is a pig's life, someone will say." Yet why? "Three-quarters of our great lords live like that; the difference between them and the savages is only that instead of eating their prisoners they often eat their creditors" (p. 80). And with this final venomous thrust the philosopher La Douceur, who did not even eat the enemies he killed, brings to a close his humanitarian diatribe.

VIII. PAOLO FRISI CRITICIZES DE PAUW'S PHYSICOCLIMATIC THESIS

De Pauw had found little difficulty in producing answers to Pernety's agitated protests, to his impassioned defense of the Americans and counterattacks on the Europeans; and his thesis was if anything strengthened in the process. He would have found it even easier to parry the insolent efforts and ridicule the bizarre notions of the soldier La Douceur. But he would not have found it nearly so easy to defend himself against the few pages in which the Milanese naturalist and mathematician Paolo Frisi demolished the geophysical basis of the *Recherches* and invalidated simultaneously its anthropological conclusions, all of which he succeeded in doing without for once going into panegyrics over the Indians or lessening one whit the glories of the Europeans.

Frisi found the occasion for this brief but careful study in the preface he wrote for the translation into Italian blank verse of Mme du Boccage's *Colombiade* (Milan, 1771). The French poetess's work is singularly silly. Episodes from the *Aeneid* reappear translated into this more fashionable environment: demons weave love spells and angels overcome them, the pious hero is overwhelmed with love for a young savage and becomes in his turn the object of the desperate longing of a West Indian queen. In short, the whole Epic of the Faith Carried to America is colored by the conventional representation of an enchanted world full of naked and innocent young savages and elderly chieftains dripping wisdom and benevolence. The hillsides are richly laden, the forests perfumed, the fields productive without needing to be cultivated: "les animaux, les fruits, les arbres pleins d'encens / N'ont rien dans leur aspect qui ressemble a nos champs."[104] They are so superior that they cannot even be compared!

---

104. *La Colombiade*, I; in *Recueil des oeuvres de Mme du Boccage* (Lyon, 1770), II, 23; cf. ibid., II, 20, 21, 108–09, and passim. Buffon is mentioned in the ninth canto (ibid., II, 209). The most frequently cited source is Charlevoix; others: Garcilaso, Herrera, Solis, Frezier, Acosta, Ulloa.

Thus in presenting the poem to his Italian readers[105] Paolo Frisi could hardly refrain from mentioning de Pauw's recent and highly discordant description of America. So having assured his reader that the poem translated agrees with the most exact reports, he adds obliquely: "Therefore neither the constitution of the country, nor the character of its inhabitants is shown as being so wretched as the author of the recent Philosophical Researches on the Americans believed them to be" (p. vii). He may have written with "abundant erudition" and "great elegance," but (a) he generalized too easily and (b) he ignored certain laws and facts established concerning the physical nature of the globe.

America is a very large continent, and it differs from one part to another; it does contain marshlands but also vast regions where it never rains, such as Peru. Peru itself, Chile, and Mexico are very beautiful countries, with the people "very well organized," excellent climates, fertile soil, and splendid birds and plants. Among the peoples of America there are some stupid ones and some intelligent ones; one has only to read Garcilaso (who passes on the early legends of Peru just as Ossian once preserved the ancient tales of the Celts!) and the travelers, right up to the most recent times (Lahontan, Juan and Ulloa). Nor were the subjects of the Incas and Montezuma lacking in courage: they were easily conquered because they were divided and because their princes were irresolute.[106] The technical advances of the Americans are attested by all the historians and ethnographers. And in our own day, the learned Frisi

105. "Note that Mme de Boccage's poem was brought to Milan by abbé Frisi on his return from Paris, and that Verri and his other friends were thereby fired with the idea of translating it" (letter of 6 August 1803 of Anton Francesco Frisi, ms. Braidense AH.X.43, foglio 32; see also pp. 49–50 of the ms. of the *Elogio storico di P. Verri,* written by Father Isidoro Bianchi); the translation earned Frisi the deep gratitude of Mme du Boccage: see the letter of 7 February 1768, in E. and J. de Goncourt, *Portraits intimes du XVIII*ᵉ *siècle* (Paris, 1878), pp. 487–88; and those in F. K. Turgeon, "Unpublished Letters of Mme Du Boccage," *Modern Philology,* 27, no. 3 (February 1930), pp. 332–38, in which she refers to the "brute savages of the New World" and praises Frisi's "good preface" to her *Colombiade.* A few other details appear in G. Gill-Mark, *A. -M. Du Boccage* (Paris, 1927), pp. 90, 160–66. A letter of Louis (Auguste?) de Keralio to Paolo Frisi (27 April 1771) speaks of the translation he passed on to Mme Du Boccage, who is to reply shortly "to all your questions" (Silvana Tomani, *I manoscritti filosofici di Paolo Frisi* [Florence, 1968], p. 167).

106. As Algarotti showed "in his very fine essay on the Empire of the Incas" (p. x). In fact Algarotti says (*Saggio,* II, 117–37) that the Peruvians were overcome through surprise at the ships and firearms and through the hatefulness of Atahualpa (p. 137). The whole essay, which bears as epigraph Voltaire's line, "we alone are the Barbarians in these climes," is a defense of the political and educational systems of the Incas, "a quality of men between the missionaries and conquistadores," repeatedly compared to the ancient Romans, and put forward because we ignorant Europeans who hold them "at most fit to furnish material for our Novelists" (p. 121: a probable allusion to Mme de Graffigny's *Lettres d'une Péruvienne,* published with great success in 1747); but it is certainly no eulogy of the native capacities of the indigenous population: "Those that have lived in America and have been able to see for themselves how slow of mind the Peruvians are by nature, and mostly sluggish, are constrained to admit the miracles that legislature can work" (p. 133: a typical thesis of enlightened despotic reformism). Another evident sign of the Age of Enlightenment is the digression inquiring into whether the Incas did well or badly in preventing the spread of learning.

reminds us, "in Pennsylvania and at Philadelphia all the other glories of Europe have already been emulated, even to controlling the fires of heaven [Franklin's lighting conductor, 1753] and calculating the quantity of matter in comets [John Winthrop of Harvard? Andrew Oliver, Jr., of Massachusetts?]."

This positive judgment on the qualities of the American is even more significant when one remembers that as a young man the Barnabite Paolo Frisi had been of very much the same opinion as those Dominicans (see above, p. 65) who had reduced the native almost to the level of animal (it is perhaps indicative that the order of Barnabites came into being under the fervid inspiration of the Dominican Fra Battista da Crema): "For what more do they have than irrational animals [Frisi was asking himself rhetorically in his *Lectiones Ethicae* of 1756], those feeble and defenseless peoples who were driven into the interior by the ferocity of the ancient Spaniards?"[107]

But here already the Las Casian riposte against the ferocity of the Spaniards reveals a more humane touch, some tendency toward a more impartial view of the unfortunate natives—their bodily deformities and monstrosities are almost always artificial[108]—an attitude that ripens as his enlightened rationalism grows stronger (Frisi was always polemically anti-Jesuit and left the order in 1768) and which solidifies once and for all in the face of de Pauw's provocative slanders.

But de Pauw is particularly weak, Frisi goes on, in cosmography and meteorology. He is unaware of the studies on the variations of the ecliptic carried out by "a Milanese mathematician."[109] His hypotheses "on the former tendency of waters toward the poles and on their present return to the equator" are untenable, and his conjectures on volcanoes and his ideas concerning the heat of tropical countries are thus without foundation too (pp. xiv–xvi). As for heat and cold, America offers nothing to distinguish it from the old continent, although it is a fact that Peru "on account of the nearness of the sea and the mountains, and the elevation of the land, and for other *special causes* [one could almost think that Frisi had guessed at the current discovered by Humboldt], it is colder than other countries at the same latitude." Thus it is quite illegitimate to deduce skin color from degrees of latitude, as de Pauw does; "in the whole circle of the torrid zone" there are no Negroes except in Africa,

107. Tomani, op. cit., p. 131. On the human sacrifices and cannibalism of the Americans, deprived of Revelation, see the *Institutiones metaphysicae* of 1754–55, ibid., p. 100.

108. Tomani, op. cit., pp. 101–02.

109. Almost certainly Frisi himself, who treated the subject very originally in *De motu diurno terrae* (1758), and in the second book *De gravitate* (1768): see P. Verri, *Memorie appartenenti alla vita e agli studi del sr. d. Paolo Frisi* (Milan, 1787), pp. 35–36, 94.

"and they keep their dark color in any other climate to which they are transported."

Emboldened by his easy victory, Frisi has one last word to say in the defense of the giants: "Various travelers have been in agreement in telling us that the height of the Patagonians is greater than normal" (p. xix); but he does not insist on this point,[110] and leaving aside "so many other things" that could be said on the *Recherches* of de Pauw, he ends the digression and comes back to the subject of the *Colombiade*.

Frisi's contribution to the debate, although brief and incidental, is still significant, both because it shows how widespread de Pauw's notions were and because his attack on de Pauw is scientific in style and content. But for this very reason, perhaps, and also because Frisi never concerned himself with either the new problems of zoological geography or the heated discussions on the Indians and the notion of their perfection or degeneration, his work drew no immediate response, and in time fell into complete oblivion together with the translation which it introduced.[111]

IX. DELISLE DE SALES, DE PAUW'S ADMIRING ADVERSARY

Jean Baptiste Claude Isoard, better known by the name Delisle de Sales, that most prolific polygraph, is usually mentioned among the critics of the *Recherches*, and such indeed he is, but he is also one of de Pauw's most consistent admirers. There is no necessary contradiction between the two attitudes, because for de Sales "greatness of mind" is not incompatible with "paradoxes" nor erudition with unbridled fantasy; and because in any case all of the ideas he finds in de Pauw, the accurate with the quite erroneous, sink out of sight in the morass of de Sales's long-winded and conventional hodgepodge of ideas.

Delisle de Sales is basically a Voltairian. But in natural philosophy he often inclines to Robinet, and his idolization of Nature frequently brings him alongside Rousseau. He approves of Condillac, Helvétius, and with some hesitation of d'Holbach. As a convinced theist, however, he fulminates against the atheist La Mettrie; believing firmly in the immortality of the soul, he "demonstrates" it with the story of Richardson's Clarissa, and by way of further proof with a doleful tale of his own, "the pathetic history of Jenny Lille."[112]

110. In the *Institutiones metaphysicae* he had said cautiously of the Patagonian giants, "if however they are really to be thought of as being of that height, which several people maintain they have deduced, from the skulls that have been taken to England and to London" (Tomani, op. cit., p. 101).

111. Nor are they mentioned by P. Verri, *Memorie*, even in the bibliography of Frisi's writings. They are however referred to by G. R. Carli, *Delle lettere americane*, 2 vols. (Florence, 1780), I, 19, 105, and Drouin de Bercy, op. cit., II, 91.

112. *De la philosophie de la Nature* (Amsterdam, vols. I–III, 1770, vols. IV–VI, 1774), II, 317–57. The good Delisle is also the author of that *Mémoire en faveur de Dieu* (Paris, 1802) with which he hoped to combat atheism, but whose title caused it to be generally taken for a work of impious blasphemy! On

His major works, entitled *De la philosophie de la Nature* and *Histoire philosophique du monde primitif*—in six and seven volumes respectively —are confused cosmogonies and histories of the world in mythical and prehistoric times, which stop short, as is only right, at the beginning of "this collection of men's errors and crimes that one [i.e., Voltaire] calls history";[113] at which point they veer off the first into psychology, embryogeny, teratology, dissertations on suicide, and hymns in praise of modesty; the second into geology, physical geography, and profuse accounts of fantastic islands and famous voyages, and ancient heroes, demigods, and gods, even Almighty Jove himself—all neatly presented in alphabetical order "to relax the reader's mind."[114]

To such a naïvely cosmic spirit America could hardly present more than passing interest. The problem in question was of no great significance and presented no real difficulty; a simple formula was all that was needed to provide the answer. The age of a continent is in inverse proportion to the height of its mountains. The loftier they are, the less eroded and "degraded," the fresher and younger must those parts of the world be where these mountains rise. Now where are the most lofty peaks? Beginning with our own hemisphere, the best known: "We know of no mountain, either in Asia or in Africa, that is actually higher than Mont Blanc, and this fact [*sic*] followed naturally from our principles."[115] Europe is thus the youngest part of the Old World. But "America is infinitely newer than Europe, and if our theory has some justice we shall have to see the Alps themselves lower their proud peaks before the pinnacles of the Cordilleras." And in fact there are in the Andes higher peaks than Mont Blanc.

It only remains to be shown that Australia, which is still newer than America, has higher summits than Chimborazo. Unfortunately the navigators who discovered it have not yet penetrated into the interior. Thus it is not possible to substitute certain facts for conjecture; "but my

---

his leaning toward mysticism, for which he was derided by Grimm, see Palmer, op. cit., p. 211, and for his influence on Chateaubriand and Fabre d'Olivet, see respectively Léon Cellier, *Fabre d'Olivet* (Paris, 1953), p. 61, and below, chap. 7, n. 266. On the persecution suffered by the *Philosophie de la Nature*, Félix Rocquain, *L'esprit revolutionnaire avant la Révolution* (Paris, 1878), pp. 341–42, 363–64, and on Delisle's subsequent insane vanity, André Monglond, *Le préromantisme français* (Paris, 1966), II, 145–47.

113. *Philosophie de la Nature*, I, 320.

114. *Histoire philosophique du monde primitif* (Paris, 1780, def. ed., 1795), VII, 36. Montrol, publisher of the *Mémoires* of Brissot (to whom Delisle sent his *Histoire philosophique de la Grèce*, "twelve volumes, with atlas," as a gift) was to try in vain to rescue these treatises "from the disdain they arouse today" (1830! see Brissot's *Mémoires*, II, 142).

115. *Monde primitif*, IV, 129; cf. V, 30. The thesis seems to derive from de Maillet's *Telliamed*. Pernety, on the other hand, says that the oldest peoples must be those that are found on the highest mountains (*Examen*, II, 408 ff.); and Carli (see below, p. 234), analogously, that the oldest lands are the highest ones.

silence, proof of my frankness," Delisle de Sales boldly concludes, "does not cast the slightest shadow on my doctrine."[116]

This doctrine also falls in with Buffon's thesis on the Americas. For Delisle too the American continent is but recently emerged from the waters. A few centuries before its conquest it was still an archipelago formed by the crests of the Cordilleras and the Appalachians. The Old World empires described by history were already formed when America began to take shape as a continent "and added with this other hemisphere a counterweight to the balance of the globe."[117] When the Europeans arrived there it was still covered with stagnant waters and "Caspian Seas" (the Great Lakes, the Bay of Baffin, even the Gulf of Mexico), and "the fetid emanations from these remainders of the ocean caused epidemics there every year." Further proof of this very recent and still incomplete drying out is provided by the absence of great quadrupeds and the presence of a mere couple of civilized peoples.[118]

These theories and their corollaries, explicitly limited by Buffon to the plants and animals, took root in the fertile soil of de Pauw's imagination and in time produced all the clever paradoxes of the *Recherches*.[119] The author is always referred to as a man of great learning and intelligence; and he is quoted several times as a supporting authority for this or that point of geography or ethnography.[120] De Pauw, declares Delisle, is "one of the scholars that I most like to encounter in my travels, although our principles often tend to separate us,"[121] because his erudition is "the most vast and often the best digested."[122] So it comes about that Delisle, while inclining to the thesis so vigorously opposed by de Pauw in his second *Recherches*, of China as an Egyptian colony, and while still

116. *Monde primitif,* IV, 132; cf. ibid., IV, 139–40.
117. Ibid., V, 145 (a phrase that seems to anticipate Canning's famous statement: "I called the New World into existence to redress the balance of the Old," 12 December 1826); cf. ibid., V, 125, 280–81.
118. Ibid., IV, 302–06; V, 135, 147–48; VI, 26, 374; VII, 4, 31, lxix. Delisle sneers at the Mosaic tradition of the Flood (ibid., II, 206; V, 37, 235, 256–67) and, although he admires him, criticizes "the lugubrious Boulanger" (ibid., IV, 203–04; VI, 326). Note also the extraordinary compression of geological epochs into periods of a few centuries: a "telescopic" foreshortening which, at the end of the eighteenth century, is actually more surprising and more mythic than the six "days" of Moses' account.
119. *Philosophie de la Nature,* V, 231–32; *Monde primitif,* VII, vi.
120. The *Philosophie de la Nature* quotes the *Défense* (IV, 248n.) and the *Recherches* (V, 149n., 175–76, 280; VI, 60–61, 72–74, 82–83, 87, 88, 98, 238n., 276) of this "ingenious Author." In the *Monde primitif* de Pauw is also quoted on the subject of the slow drying up of the Baltic Sea (V, 78–79, xvi, quoting *Recherches* I, 103n.); on the American peoples "issuing from the mountainsides" (V, xxi–xxii, quoting *Recherches* I, 198); on the former link between the Caspian Sea and the Persian Gulf (V, 211–13, xliv, quoting *Recherches* II, 328–29); on the Tartars, first teachers of the human race (VI, 20–22, 28, and VII, ii, iii–vi, quoting *Recherches,* II, 295, 296–97, 303, 303–04, 319–20, 346, 347–48); on Greenland, on the Chinese, etc. (VII, xi–xii, xlviii, etc., quoting *Recherches,* I, 257, and *Recherches sur les Egyptiens,* I, 15–16), and also, with the complete works in seven volumes, in the final list of authors used.
121. *Monde primitif,* V, 78–79. Elsewhere de Pauw's authority is corroborated by reference to him as "a scholar who has traveled much [*sic*] in America, and who often strayed from his path" to enlighten us concerning other parts of the globe (ibid., V, 211).
122. Ibid., VI, 20–22.

remaining as enthusiastic as Voltaire in his admiration of the Chinese and Confucius, does not hesitate, at the very point where he is discussing the origin of the Chinese, to describe de Pauw, the bitter critic of these people, as "the scholar who explained best the antiquities of Asia."[123]

Thus when he finds he has no choice but to contradict de Pauw, he seems almost embarassed to do so and adopts a tone of great humility. One wonders whether he may not have been intimidated by the complacent arrogance of his opponent. It would seem so, because even as he girds himself up to demolish de Pauw's "paradox on the infancy of the peoples of the New World," he begins by describing the *Recherches* as "a singular work, but full of knowledge," which does not permit "an extended criticism, and even if it demanded it, my adversary being alive, my peace-loving pen would fear to undertake it." So he will limit himself to a few observations, a few respectful observations, "which I submit in advance to the scrutiny of the ingenious writer whom I am constrained to refute."[124]

The first of these observations, as one might expect from such an enthusiast for Nature, concerns the giants in general, and those of Patagonia in particular, whose existence is defended against the "Pyrrhonism" of the *Recherches*. The proofs of their existence, frequent in the sixteenth century, rare in the seventeenth century because the Patagonians, terrified by the Europeans, withdrew into the interior, "reappear in abundance in the eighteenth century"; and one can only be amused at the way in which de Pauw rejects under one pretext or another the evidence of all the explorers, from Pigafetta to Commodore Byron, who have seen and described the giants. The truth of the matter is that the giants would have brought down his whole thesis on the weakness of the nature of America, "and a writer does not willingly adopt a truth which would cost him the sacrifice of three volumes of paradoxes."[125]

The large bones found in America cannot be animal bones. It is well known that there are no giraffes nor hippopotamuses nor elephants nor rhinoceroses there: "Nature which maintained her vigor in the reptiles

123. Ibid., V, 295–96, 300; VI, xlviii, quoting *Recherches sur les Egyptiens*, I, 17 (1773 ed., I, 15–16). For Delisle's sinophilia, see *Philosophie de la Nature*, IV, xcix–ci; V, 44–45.

124. *Philosophie de la Nature*, V, 232. Delisle's peace-loving pen did not save him from frequent troubles with the censors: see ibid., VI, 371; *Monde primitif*, I, v; II, 206; IV, 209, the details s.v. in the *Biographie universelle* (Michaud) and the curious particulars gathered by J. -P. Belin, op. cit., pp. 301–06. The *Philosophie de la Nature* was burned in the Place de Grève on 14 December 1775, and its author imprisoned in the Châtelet in 1777. See also n. 112.

125. *Philosophie de la Nature*, V, 200–04; in his impetuosity Delisle accuses de Pauw of having said of Corneille de Maye that he "took giants . . . for rocks." De Pauw of course insinuates that, on the contrary, de Maye took a rock for a man (*Recherches*, I, 298–99): the same criticism occurs in *Monde primitif*, VI, 20–22. On the same subject of the Patagonian giants Delisle had already taken issue with de Pauw, an author who wanted to be "read" but not to "enlighten" the reader, in the "Discours préliminaire" inserted by him in the second edition (Paris, 1770, 2 vols.) of the *Journey to the Malvine Islands* written by de Pauw's first antagonist, Pernety.

is there totally degenerate in the quadrupeds." De Pauw would have it that these carcasses belong to animals that became extinct in that terrible catastrophe which maimed the whole continent. But why do we need these massive unknown beasts, "when one has beneath one's eyes [*sic!*] such large men, living since time immemorial in the lands of Magellan?"[126] Why, if not to support some malign fixation? In fact, de Pauw is a *slanderer*. He slandered the New World when he defined its one hundred and fifty million inhabitants as "children"—they are "children" who form societies, reproduce vigorously, and live to the age of a hundred and fifty![127]—and he slandered Nature in suggesting that the species degenerate in embryo.[128] Worst of all, he repeated the infamous slanders of the Spanish conquerors, who went so far as to cast doubt on the humanity of the American natives. They at least spread these slanders to justify their massacres and wrote history with a calculated treachery, a *noirceur réfléchie*.[129] But was there any good reason for de Pauw to repeat these slanders, "he who wielded a pen of fire in favor of tolerance"?[130]

The strong hints of moral criticism in the word "slander" cast an air of injured innocence over those "slandered," endowing them with the virginal purity of "children of nature." In describing the primitive peoples Vossius and Garcilaso "slandered the human race; the more savage these people were, the closer they were to Nature."[131] Mother Nature was thus the ultimate target of all this calumny. Yet this august progenitor is always right and makes no mistakes. It is Nature, for example, that makes man well; society makes him ill, and to the curse of disease adds the curse of doctors.[132] So in America nature has produced smooth-skinned men? All right, but these beardless youths are no less prolific than the Chinese or the most nobly bearded metaphysician.[133] It is true that these virile American men before the Conquest used to nurse their offspring. But why else would the male have mammae, if not to suckle children? Or would someone like to suggest that Nature acted without

126. *Philosophie de la Nature,* V, 212–13; cf. ibid., IV, 109.
127. Ibid., V, 232–37; VI, 276.
128. Nor does Delisle believe consistently in the degeneration of animals: "The tajacou is America's wild boar. Some naturalists have taken it for a degenerated version of our pig" (*Philosophie de la Nature,* I, 36n.); and *contra,* above, p. 49.
129. A frequently repeated argument: *Philosophie de la Nature,* I, 36n.; V, 94, 195, 237, 246–47; VI, 243–44. For Delisle, of course, "the most precise and judicious author perhaps that has written on the New World" is Las Casas; and naturally he repeats Thomas Gage's story of the American women who had abortions to save their offspring from enslavement to the Hispano-Catholics (ibid., II, 49–50; see above, p. 49).
130. Ibid., V, 237.
131. Ibid., I, 40n. Buffon too "slandered nature" with his theory of the epochs of the solar system (*Monde primitif,* II, 205).
132. *Philosophie de la Nature,* VI, 190–226, quoting Rousseau, of course.
133. Ibid., VI, 71, 238. Lahontan's savage (1703) was reluctant to become French for fear of growing "hairy and bearded like an animal" and having to shave every three days (op. cit., p. 208); but Lahontan always seems to have his tongue in his cheek. . . .

any aim in mind, or even that she erred, giving men this pseudoorgan? Once he sets out on these arguments, which might seem more at home in Manzoni's heroicomic Don Ferrante, "can you deny that there are stars? Or are you going to try and tell me that they are up there for no purpose whatsoever?" — Delisle de Sales almost reaches the point of lamenting that the massacres, the Inquisition[!], and the frequency of intermarriage have little by little led to the disappearance of this singular "original distinction" of the Americans; and he forgets to inform us whether their breasts were as perfect as those of the divine Aspasia who, he has assured us a little earlier, possessed breasts "shaped in the form of a pear, and not in the form of a half apple, as our little mistresses desire them"[134] — and as moreover one imagines the simple Alcibiades preferred them.

But let us get back to the native of the New World. Even with his role reduced to that of dry nurse, in his physique he is "the most adroit of creatures" and "relatively to the volume of his body the strongest of creatures."[135] As for moral and intellectual gifts, the inhabitants of Mexico and Peru have shown themselves amply endowed. Nor is it true that the Europeans degenerate in America: just look at La Condamine, or the learned proceedings of the Philadelphia Academy of Sciences, and the unfailing Benjamin Franklin, the "Descartes of Electricity."[136] "Nature then did not go astray in one entire hemisphere. The Americans are men." If the American is still a slave today, this is because he does not dare to think: "But if he thought today, tomorrow he would be free"[137] — a prophecy which echoes and enlarges on similar ones of Raynal and de Pauw himself (see above, p. 63).

What is de Pauw's error then? It is his "generalizing," his deducing of an absolute law from a single occurrence. This formal failing of the *Recherches* is well grasped by Delisle de Sales, who had a sort of instinctive horror of abstractions, systems (other people's), and general concepts; who admired the empiricist in Buffon as much as he distrusted the systematic in him; who could write of "species": "The word species is a technical term, which we have invented to compensate for our weakness of memory and understanding: Nature does not really make species at all, it makes only individuals";[138] who, while admitting the decisive influence of climate on the character of peoples, noted that climate itself could alter with time and natural disasters, with the creative and

---

134. *Philosophie de la Nature*, V, 51–52, 74–76, with echoes of Rousseau's defense of the milk-bearing capacities of the mothers (but not the fathers!).
135. Ibid., V, 4–7; VI, 260. See also the conversation (ibid., III, 27–39) between a Parisian and a Caribbean, who has simple tastes and well-developed senses.
136. Ibid., V, 245–46: same title for Franklin, ibid., IV, 52. Linnaeus is "this Descartes of botany" (V, 347n.).
137. Ibid., V, 245.
138. Ibid., IV, xcv n.; cf. IV, 40; V, 86, 138, 334.

destructive work of man;[139] and who finally, in vigorous opposition to the anti-Semites, defended the Jews' right to be adjudged men like all others.[140]

But as for the fundamental problems in the American polemic—the ideal and physical relationship pertaining between the two worlds, the concepts of progress and humanity, the values of primitivism and so-called civilization—Delisle de Sales, far from skirting round them, is hardly even aware of them. And for all his familiarity with a number of writers in the famous controversy—from Pernety, whose journey to the Falkland Islands he presented to the public in a new edition, and whose *Dissertation sur l'Amérique*[141] he quotes, to Raynal, Molina, and the much respected Carli (whose ideas on Atlantis he rejects however)[142]—he contributes nothing genuinely his own, nor does he go deeply into a single one of the problems.

X. THE ABBÉ ROUBAUD: AMERICA AND THE PHYSIOCRATS

The criticisms directed at de Pauw by another polygraph, the abbé Roubaud, are equally unoriginal and uninspired; but Roubaud differs from Delisle de Sales in approaching the subject with a heavy-footed methodicality that leads him to produce not just a few incidental comments on the *Recherches* but a formal rebuttal thereof covering some three hundred and fifty pages. It would however be a fruitless quest if one searched the catalogs for it under any title giving an idea of its contents; and consequently it remained completely unknown, despite its size, even to the numerous apologists and slanderers of America—a branch of the "dispute" that died without issue.

It is not in fact a work in itself but a digression, without even its own subheading, appearing in and disproportionately bloating the thirteenth of the fifteen volumes which comprise the prolific abbé's *Histoire générale de l'Asie, de l'Afrique et de l'Amérique*. As soon as it is glimpsed alongside the other volumes and since it is twice as fat, this thirteenth volume immediately betrays some abnormality: the polemical excursus, the only one in the whole *Histoire*, has grown up in it like a tumor, provoked by the prussic acid of de Pauw's writings; so we have yet another, and voluminous, confirmation of the strength of that powerful irritant.

The *Recherches* was still a recent novelty when Roubaud began the compilation of his history; his first volumes appeared in 1770, and the

---

139. Ibid., IV, lxv–lxviii and the whole *Discours préliminaire sur la morale de l'homme-physique.*
140. See the "Apologie des Juifs" in the *Philosophie de la Nature,* II, 63–122; III, xxiv.
141. See above, n. 10 and ff.; n. 125; *Philosophie de la Nature,* V, 201n.; VI, 267n.
142. On Molina, see *Monde primitif,* V, 8; on Carli, ibid., I, 28; V, xxvii, lxi, 318–20.

digression against de Pauw, published in 1775, was composed between December 1772 and March 1773.[143] It opens, as expected, with protests against the assertions of the American males' impuberty and lactiferous breasts and an ingenious explanation of the latter phenomenon: perhaps some European traveler came across a group of natives in the act of practicing the couvade, and being unaware that this same custom is fairly widespread in Europe too, and even in France (Béarn), he imagined that they were suckling their young.[144]

But once Roubaud has tasted his opponent's blood he is in no mind to let go and proceeds relentlessly to crush every thesis and every argument. A few years earlier he had used the same tactics against another very gifted dilettante, the abbé Galiani. Roubaud, who was an enthusiastic contributor to the physiocratically inspired economic reviews and who had also published (1769) the *Représentations aux magistrats sur le commerce des grains,* fell on Galiani's glittering "little dialogues" the moment they appeared, refuting them with a minutely detailed and implacable analysis. Strictly speaking, he says, such a task was not even necessary, since they were "completely refuted in advance" in his *Représentations;*[145] but he had felt like checking them over for errors, and when he satisfied his fancy he found "so many, many mistakes on every page, on every line! . . ." that when he has finished he seems to heave a great sigh of relief: he had completed "this terrible task, the task of clarifying and annotating your large Book page by page and almost sentence by sentence."[146]

The same technique is applied to de Pauw's *Recherches,* so that it would be well to limit ourselves to the basic points of his prolix argument. The Patagonians do exist, although their "giantism" is a matter of a mere foot above the average.[147] And the Old World is indeed infinitely

---

143. *Histoire,* XIII, 159, 347. The *Histoire* came out simultaneously in a quarto edition in five vols., which I have not seen; I have also been unable to find Roubaud's first work, with the suggestively Solorzanesque title *Le politique indien* (Paris, 1768).

144. *Histoire,* XIII, 10–11.

145. *Recréations economiques, ou Lettres de l'auteur des Représentations aux magistrats, à M. le chevalier Zanobi principal interlocuteur des Dialogues sur le commerce des bleds* (Amsterdam; but Paris, 1770), p. 96, etc.

146. Ibid., p. 220, 236. On Roubaud the physiocrat, see Léonce de Lavergne, *Les économistes français au XVIIIᵉ siècle* (Paris, 1870), pp. 174, 182; some brief comments can be found in the histories of economic thought. On the links between the physiocrats and America, via Franklin, see D. Echeverria, "Roubaud and the Theory of American Degeneration," *French-American Review,* 3 (1950), pp. 26, 31–32. On the polemic with Galiani, see Galiani, *Correspondance,* I, 210–13; *D'Epinay e Galiani,* pp. 74, 89–90, 109–10, 136, and the relevant footnotes; F. Nicolini, *Gli ultimi anni della signora d'Epinay: Lettere inedite all'abate Galiani, 1773–1782* (Bari, 1933), p. 185; and the correspondence of Grimm ("Roubaud, doctor of the school of the absurd . . . is tilting at windmills against the chevalier Zanobi," ed. cit., IX, 83–84).

147. *Histoire,* XIII, 50–74. Note that before being provoked by de Pauw, Roubaud had expressed doubts (ibid., I, xxiii–xxiv) about the Patagonian giants. It is from this very point that he takes his cue, after some preliminary skirmishing, for a summary exposition of the doctrines of M. de Paff (*sic,* p. 74), on the completion of which (pp. 75–101) he sets about their systematic destruction.

superior to the New; but why could de Pauw not be content with reas-
serting this obvious truth? Why did he feel he had to demonstrate the
universal degeneration of every creature and object of America? And
anyway, degeneration as compared to what pristine state or condition?. . .
De Pauw has made no attempt to show that in the past, before the discovery, America was in a more flourishing state than after; no more does
he suggest that the state of nature is "less unformed" than the state in
which the American natives were found.

Of the land itself, he does not say that it was barren, but quite the opposite, that its natural goodness, ungoverned and unexploited by man,
ran to waste and decay. The continent was thus quite simply unworked
because its peoples were savages, more concerned with hunting and
fishing than agriculture: "America was, so to speak, a new land,"[148] a
sparsely inhabited archipelago, but its inhabitants were not stupid; here
and there they tilled the soil, learned the nutritive properties of cereals
and roots, tubers and berries, and extracted minerals and precious
stones; and all this without a knowledge of iron: "Take iron from our continent and what would it become?"[149]

And what would Europe be without the products and techniques inherited from other continents? "America in the sixteenth century had
only what it had produced itself." The fine arts too, which in Europe
were developed over thousands of years by an infinite variety of peoples,
in Mexico and Peru "were the product of the particular genius of their
inhabitants, with only a few bare centuries of experience behind them."[150]
The progress of the North American colonists, skipped over so lightly
by de Pauw, makes it seem likely that "North America will one day be
the capital, if I may put it like that, of the human race."[151]

And let it not be said that the environment is unfavorable to such a
prodigious increase. If plants are carefully tended they can do well in
America too: "Soon perhaps America will be able to stand up to European competition in wines, as it can already in grain." Even the poisonous
plants can be domesticated and made edible, and the much-maligned
maize does not cause either constipation or scabies.[152] The animal species
in the New World may indeed be fewer in number, as Buffon would have
it, but each one is more numerous in itself, and in any case the surface
area of the New World is only two-fifths that of the Old. Nor are all its
animals tiny. There are fossil remains of gigantic beasts. How on earth

---

148. Ibid., XIII, 109, 136.
149. Ibid., p. 115.
150. Ibid., pp. 124–25.
151. Ibid., p. 130.
152. Ibid., pp. 131–39, quoting the passage from Buffon given above, p. 14.

did they become extinct? Roubaud forgoes any attempt at explanation. "That is something one would try in vain to discover."[153]

And as for man in America, he is a splendid specimen, vigorous, long-lived and prolific, whether native or shrewd and careful colonist. So the women give birth easily? A proof of their robust constitutions! And they keep their milk for years on end? They make generous wet nurses, and so much the better for the bairn! "The longer the childhood, the longer and later old age."[154] The American male is hairless? Maybe, but this does not mean he is weak: the Negroes are smooth skinned, but a Hottentot can fell a lion. Nor is the American cowardly and stupid. Roubaud rounds off his apology with disarming naïveté: "We shall bring this discussion to a close with a piece of irrefutable testimony; namely what the famous Mr. Franklin said of the Americans" in a letter of June 1772, which Roubaud has seen with his own eyes: "we ourselves have read this testimony";[155] and to back it up he quotes Mr. Dickinson, "the Demosthenes of the English colonies"; the Philadelphia Academy; the *Dissertations mêlées* of J. J. Rambach, Rector of the college of Quedlinburg; and Fathers Feijóo and Sarmiento, so frivolously derided by de Pauw.[156]

Of course none of this makes any difference to Europe's primacy, but it is a matter of "an accidental and acquired superiority, not a natural and *innate* superiority"[157] — a fair enough approximative characterization of the "historicity" of European civilization, and a perfectly valid excuse for evading the question of the naturalistic contrast between the two hemispheres. But this novel outlook does not last long with Roubaud, steeped as he is in the historiographical pessimism of his time and ruled by its philanthropic and anticolonial corollaries. When it comes to attacking the Spaniards, Roubaud is wholeheartedly in agreement with de Pauw: "The conquest of America is the most terrible calamity suffered by the human race at the hands of man."[158] And not only for the in-

153. Ibid., p. 142.
154. Ibid., p. 149. For the European colonists, Roubaud repeats Pernety's argument, on which see above, p. 97.
155. Ibid., p. 162. Franklin's letter has apparently been lost. Even Echeverria, "Roubaud," p. 29, has failed to find any trace of it.
156. *Histoire*, p. 166. Dickinson's *Lettres d'un fermier de Penslyvanie* had been translated by the physiocrat Du Bourg in 1769 at Franklin's suggestion, and it was Franklin that introduced his physiocrat friends to the Transactions of the Academy of Philadelphia (vol. I, 1771; see Echeverria, "Roubaud," p. 30).
157. *Histoire*, XIII, 167.
158. Ibid., p. 355. The passage is quoted *in extenso* in the physiocratic *Nouvelles ephémérides économiques* (1776), III, 48–76, directed by the abbé Baudeau, which had already given considerable attention to the second volume of Roubaud's *Histoire* (1771, VI, 249–60). In the preceding pages Roubaud rejects many particular points of early American history, including Mexican and especially Peruvian items, that de Pauw had maintained. This emphatic disapproval sometimes seems to carry an echo of the sermonizing Raynal (quoted fairly frequently: XIII, 40–47, 396–97, 449–50, 487, 535; XIV, 3, 146–48;

habitants of the New World. Roubaud's pessimism is displayed in an almost Blake-like apocalyptic vision: "The Old World has dragged the New into its vortex; but in the impact of these two great bodies the stronger could not crush the weaker without breaking asunder and being shattered itself."[159]

Hence there is nothing more illusory than the classic notion of an exchange of useful products between the two hemispheres: "There has been an appalling interchange of evils between Europe and America, and there has been no mutual exchange of benefits at all."[160] To support this lethal theory Roubaud vituperates one by one all the so-called gifts of America, with an arrogance worthy of de Pauw. The evil influence of American gold was by then a commonplace in political moralism and the budding science of economics. But in fact there is not a single item either American or just generally exotic that survives his blast: spices burn us, tea dries us up, drugs poison us, and the potato is a sad remedy for hunger; arctic furs are an effeminacy in our climate; tobacco, useless and dangerous in itself, has become an instrument of torture in the hands of the revenue authorities; coffee is a "pernicious drink"; cochineal and precious stones are costly and frivolous toys; and sugar—well, sugar could very easily be produced in our own hemisphere, without imposing oppressive monopolies on the other.

And here the physiocrat completely forgets the original purpose of his argument and looses the full thunder of his eloquence against trade in general and against colonial trade in particular. "Europe set its glory, its power, and its salvation in far-off, precarious, and useless possessions, purchased at great expense, exploited at great expense, maintained at great expense. The Empires left their bases and stooped down or reached out to lean on rushes."[161]

So has Columbus's discovery been nothing but a source of misfortune? Up till now, yes. But soon it will become a blessing. As soon as the North American colonies are independent, "all the rest of America will soon be free . . . then all these peoples will devote themselves to culture and

---

XV, 56, 127, 389, 397, 415, 487, 503, 517). Other noteworthy features are his philo-Quakerism, despite "the theological errors of these sectaries" (XV, 5–10, 537–38), and his hostility toward the greatest Spanish historian of the Indies, "the infamous Oviedo" (XIII, 387).

159. *Histoire,* XIII, 337.

160. Ibid., p. 336. Roubaud, then, is ready to agree at least once with de Pauw, who for the occasion earns the title of *"Philosophe hollandais,"* because he recognized the exchange of America's syphilis for Europe's plague as the most dismal trading of catastrophes in all history (ibid., pp. 465–66). In the rest of the volume de Pauw is occasionally attacked on the subjects of the enslavement of the Negroes (p. 442), Cortez's companions (pp. 554–55), the exploitation of the colonies (pp. 588–90), and Atahualpa's wives, who were violated, not prostituted to the conqueror (p. 603).

161. Ibid., p. 341–44 (and cf. pp. 589–90). A little further on Roubaud borrows Voltaire's famous statement: "The ownership of a few acres of snow in the depths of America will be enough to bring about a general conflagration. The loss of Canada has been a relief to France" (pp. 346–47).

commerce, to the most fruitful arts, all will prosper. . . . All Europe, freed of all expense, will trade profitably with all America, and with prosperity [sic]."[162]

Thus what was to have been the defense of a continent against the stigma of physical degeneration winds up as a theorem of political economy. And its author, rapt in these radiant visions, even forgets to trace the picture of the manners and customs of these natives without history that he had formally promised his readers.[163] But the poor fellow's forgetfulness and other faults have been more than expiated by the oblivion he suffered himself; he was forgotten as an opponent of Galiani,[164] forgotten as a critic (and one of the better ones) of de Pauw,[165] forgotten as a lexicographer, despite his important work on synonyms,[166] and so completely forgotten in his old age that when in 1795 the Convention awarded him a pension the abbé Pierre Roubaud had already four years earlier passed on to a better life.

XI. GALIANI: THE "ROUGHCAST" CONTINENT AND THE WORLD OF THE FUTURE

It should not be imagined that de Pauw was forgotten as soon as these immediate reactions to his work had calmed down. On the contrary, the frequent new editions and translations[167] of the book and even the chance references to it in the literature of the decade 1770–80 show how the work that had provoked such a clamor of opposition on its first appearance continued to be read and even thought about. Some of the most interesting observations and developments appear in fact in the correspondence of the period or in discussions not directly related to the polemic. The current of the debate is enriched by new themes borrowed from the most ancient sources. The whole polemic was to flare up again publicly toward the end of the decade, with Robertson, Carli, Clavigero, and then Jefferson. But one cannot gain a true perspective of this re-

---

162. Ibid., p. 350: can commerce help, then? . . . The final words of the long work echo with this prophecy: "Today or tomorrow the war will begin. . . . In the end English America will be free, and its liberty will soon be that of all America" (ibid., XV, 545).

163. Ibid., XIII, 167.

164. To Galiani's protests Mme d'Epinay replied that there was no point in venting his anger on "this strumpet of an abbé Roubaud . . . he is in oblivion . . . nobody in Paris is aware of his existence" etc. D'Epinay e Galiani, p. 89). And Grimm: "These recreations make up a pamphlet which has remained as obscure as the other feats of the economists" (Correspondence, IX, 83–84).

165. He was "rediscovered" by Durand Echeverria; see "Roubaud" and Mirage, pp. 30, 32.

166. The four volumes of his Nouveaux synonymes françaises (1785), which won an Academy prize, were several times reprinted and finally reshaped into a Dictionnaire des synonymes (1810) by various authors, and were still praised in Larousse (s.v.), and by Guizot (Dictionnaire universel des synonymes de la langue française [1864], iv–vii, xxxiv–xxxix, with some reservations about their etymologies: ix, xxxii–xxxiv).

167. Among the editions known are those of Berlin, 1770, 1771, 1772, 1774, and 1777; Cleves, 1772; London, 1771, and 1774; and the translation into German of 1769, and into Dutch of 1771–72. Later editions and translations will be mentioned below.

kindling of the dispute if one ignores the constant attention that de Pauw's theories received in the meanwhile. In 1773 the publication of his second *Recherches* was already reminding the public about his first. Pietro Verri found it to be "a book crammed with ideas and well written," and yet "at every turn" it made him laugh: "it seems [*sic*] to be by the same author as the work on the Americans."[168] These researches on the Americans in their turn did not perhaps move to laughter but did at least "tickle" the wizard of the north, Hamann, who refers to them and the second *Recherches* in a couple of pronouncements of truly Sibylline obscurity (1773, 1775);[169] and writing to his friend Kapellmeister Reichardt in Berlin, he asks after their author with mock solicitude: "Can't you give me any news of Canon Pauw? Where is he living now? May we expect his Philosophical researches on the Germans in the near future?"[170]

A rather more explicit reaction is seen on the other hand in the case of another Italian, the abbé Ferdinando Galiani, who followed somewhat more strictly in the Vicoan tradition than either Verri or Frisi. Galiani was always curious about the latest developments in the literary world, and as soon as the Baron D'Holbach wrote to him about the uproar provoked by de Pauw's book (3 June 1770) the good abbé replied begging for a copy to be sent to him in Naples. "I should very much like to see the *Recherches philosophiques sur les Américains*. You can quite safely send it to me. The books which come in here are not examined at all— they know that no one will read them."[171]

In fact he soon received a copy of the book through Dr. Angelo Gatti and delivered his judgment on it, with his usual sneer, in a letter to his beloved Mme d'Epinay: "I was delighted to see that there are still Saumaises, Casaubons, and Scaligers in our century, and that it is possible, in philosophy just as in the study of antiquity, to search endlessly and find nothing, to produce a whole string of erudite comments and leave them quite unconnected, to glimpse without perceiving, and to set out from no principle and arrive nowhere; that is called piling up stones and thinking you have built something."

The Neapolitan's criticism is something new. The book is condemned not for its basic idea but for its poor method: it is a conglomeration of

168. From Milan, 13 October 1773, in E. Greppi and A. Giulini, eds., *Carteggio di Pietro e di Alessandro Verri dal 1766 al 1797*, vol. VI (Milan, 1928), lett. CL (493), pp. 126–27.

169. *Schriften*, ed. F. Roth (Berlin, 1823–24), IV, 271–72 (*Hierophantische Briefe*, V, quoting both the *Recherches*); V, 36 (letter to Nicolai, 7 June 1773). Hamann had in his possession the *Recherches*, Pernety's first reply, and de Pauw's *Défense* (*Sämtliche Werke*, ed. J. Nadler [Vienna, 1949–57], V, 80), and refers disdainfully to Pernety's travels and works on alchemy and physiognomy (ibid., III, 329). In the same *Hierophantische Briefe*, III, is cited (ed. cit., IV, 246; cf. ibid., 245 n. 2, and VIIIa, 262) Voltaire's *Lettres chinoises*, for which see below, p. 153.

170. Letter of 16 December 1776, in *Briefwechsel*, ed. Ziesemer and Henkel, vol. III (Leipzig, 1957), p. 274.

171. G. Perey and G. Maugras, *Correspondance*, I, 203.

undigested erudition, barren and inconclusive. Still half serious and half joking the abbé goes on to promise that one day he will himself provide the real solution to the problem: "I shall show then that America is a *roughcast* Asia [*une Asie ébauchée*], because it is much more modern." It is a new land and there are always giants in a new land; but their race is declining and being replaced by a smooth-skinned race, which will give way in its turn "to the bearded race which is the most perfect of all."[172]

There are two points to note about this reply. The first is the criticism of the climatic theory, implicit in the way he stresses race, whether smooth skinned or hirsute. In another letter of this same year the abbé insists that everything depends on race and not on education, as Rousseau so mistakenly suggests.[173] And a few years later he was to write, while referring specifically to the Americans, that "everything that has been said about climate is sheer stupidity, a *non causa pro causa,* the simplest error of logic," and that "everything depends on race." And of all the various races, he was to repeat, the white and bearded race is the only one capable of progress. The native of California, as in general every creature not civilized by the bearded whites, is still really an animal, not even properly speaking a man, but "the sliest, shrewdest, and most mischievous of monkeys."[174]

When he says "race, not climate" Galiani really means "history, not geography," or "society, not nature." In putting forward such human and historicist criteria of interpretation Galiani had Vico to support him. Already in a work of his more youthful days, in other words of the time when the influence of the *Scienza nuova* was still fresh in his mind, Galiani had attempted to explain the ancient legends of mythology in terms of the similarities offered by the "stories of modern-day travelers . . . to the new lands." He sought confirmation for the fantasies of the Greeks in the existing natural environment of the Indies and America. "The sirens are those aquatic birds called penguins, which abound nowadays on Magel-

---

172. Letter of 7 December 1771, ibid., I, 487–89. In this passage Galiani seems to believe in the American giants (cf. above, p. 84). And his irony on the subject of de Pauw's smooth-skinned savages is obvious. One would say the abbé, in reaction to the *Recherches,* was inclined to a rehabilitation of the Americans, their stature and piliferous system. His letter crossed with one in which d'Holbach, who three months earlier had written to tell him that it was not so easy to find him the book (the *Recherches* "is very rare in this country"), adjudged it, like Galiani, a gross compilation "somewhat undiscriminating" and its basic error being to "treat as degeneration what in life is no more than lack of development" — an idea conforming to the rigid ideology of progress, that boiled down to substantially the same definition as Galiani's, of America as a "roughcast continent." D'Holbach was wrong, on the other hand, to say of de Pauw's reply to Pernety, with evident verbal embarrassment, that it "seemed" to him "in truth, a little too systematic" (F. Nicolini, *Amici e corrispondenti francesi dell'abate Galiani* [Naples, 1954], pp. 204, 212; letters of 25 August and 1 December 1771).
173. Letter of 19 January 1771, in *Correspondance,* I, 342.
174. Letter of 12 October 1776, in *Correspondance,* II, 473–74. Savages too, indeed even cats, can be educated and civilized, but it takes time. Cats must have taken forty or fifty thousand years to learn what they know now. In Asia civilization began twelve thousand years ago. It is therefore right that the Californians and Australians, "who are three or four thousand years old" should still be brute animals.

lan's coast, and which from afar resemble [*sic!*] naked women out of water." Somewhat more plausibly he suggested that the harpies would probably be the Guanays, "voracious aquatic birds which nest on deserted reefs in such great numbers as to make these places almost inaccessible to man."

Later he applied this same method of comparative interpretation to the history of the conquest of America, observing that the natives, if they had not learned writing from the Europeans, would certainly have transfigured Columbus and Cortes, Queen Isabel and Charles V, just as the unsophisticated ancient Greeks transformed their primitive warriors and monarchs into gods and heroes: Hercules, Mercury, and Saturn were for them what in twenty centuries the Catholic sovereigns might have become for the Americans.[175]

The fluidity of this viewpoint helps us to understand the second element observable in Galiani's response to de Pauw, which consists of his acceptance of the concept or at least the *image* of a "roughcast" continent, with its strong suggestions of a progressive evolution. America (he seems to say) has not yet achieved the maturity of the other continents. Will it one day achieve such maturity? Galiani moves on from physical considerations to political considerations and on two separate occasions replies strongly in the affirmative.

A few months after she had received Galiani's scornful judgment on de Pauw, Mme d'Epinay sent him another book on the subject of America, the famous *Histoire philosophique du commerce dans les Deux Indes* by the abbé Raynal, recommending it to him as an excellent book and "in better taste than . . . the Americans."[176]

But the critical little abbé was not so easily satisfied. Disregarding the panegyrics of his lady friend, Galiani replied that he was very happy about the success of the book, which he thought full of good intentions and elegant writing; but the author's cloying and sentimental humanitarianism he found quite repulsive. With his customary affectation of cynicism he wrote that in politics he could accept only "the purest Machiavellism, unadulterated, crude, in all its harshness and severity," and concluded: "My opinion is that we should continue our ravages in the Indies just as long as we are successful in so doing, save that we

---

175. *Dell'antichissima storia della navigazione nel Mediterraneo,* ca. 1746 (summarized in a note to the 2d ed., 1780, of *Della moneta:* see Bari ed., 1915, pp. 315–16); and letter to Mme d'Epinay, 24 April 1773 (*Correspondance,* II, 201–03). Cf. F. Nicolini, "Vico e Galiani," passim and esp. pp. 14–16. See also pp. 61–63 in the later version of this article.

176. Letter of 26 July 1772, in F. Nicolini, *D'Epinay e Galiani,* p. 273. Already on 22 March 1772 Mme d'Epinay had written to Galiani with glowing praises of Raynal's book (ibid., p. 256), which was simultaneously lauded by the Marchese Caracciolo (letter to Galiani of 24 March 1772), who however added the following annotation on the name of the presumed author, the abbé Raynal: "You know him: a tremendous bore, tiresome, contentious, arrogant, and insolent" (Nicolini, *Amici e corrispondenti,* p. 42).

should withdraw when we are beaten." The single truly desirable and profitable trade consists in the exchange of thrashings handed out for rupees gathered in.[177] Cruelty is eternal; in Peru the Spaniards *had* to be cruel, because they were few, greedy, and surrounded by enemies.[178]

Before many years passed the North Americans showed the English that they were no longer disposed to take beatings and pay taxes. The English withdrew, as Galiani had suggested; and Galiani, adhering faithfully to his political philosophy, rejoiced over the triumph of America. For although Galiani professed to know the English well, and hold them in respect, he had little liking for them.[179] Hume had written in 1769 that he could murder Galiani for all the evil he spoke of England.[180] When Spain ceded Florida to England Galiani had been worried because by this purchase and with Canada in the north "the English Empire in America . . . will become so solid, well-rounded, strong and compact that I cannot see any way of getting one's teeth into it and biting it. Thus this Empire alone will be enough to hold the rest of unwarlike America in subjection."[181] And in the years that followed he persisted in his belief that the center of gravity of English power was shifting toward the New World. England was becoming depopulated in favor of its American colonies: "A great quantity of English men and Manufactures have been poured into these colonies, whence they are already casting a baleful eye on their imprudent mother-country."[182]

177. Letter of 5 September 1772 (*Correspondance*, II, 114–15). Mme d'Epinay and Grimm reacted enthusiastically to Galiani's criticism and economic recipe (Nicolini, *D'Epinay e Galiani*, pp. 288, 359) — which hit at de Pauw's moralistic counsel too: see above, p. 55. One seems to catch belated echoes of the same advice both in the letter of the sceptical ex-minister Aranda, the Spanish ambassador in Paris, to the incumbent Floridablanca: "while we have it [Spanish America] let us make use of it and help ourselves to whatever nourishment we can get from it, because when the time comes for us to lose it we shall miss that good bit of bacon for our thick soup" (21 July 1785, quoted at second hand by J. R. Spell, *Rousseau in the Spanish World before 1833* [Austin, 1938, p. 217]), and in the dedication to the *Geschlossene Handelstaat* (1800) of Fichte, who after pointing out the enormous and unjust profit made by Europe in trading with the rest of the world, and the improbability of such exploitation lasting indefinitely, imagines that someone objects: "At least this state of affairs has lasted until now—there still lasts the subjection of the colonies to the mother countries, there is still the slave trade—and we shall not live to see the time when all this will cease. *Let us take advantage of it, as long as it lasts"*—to which he confesses himself unable to reply. But Galiani even later, when Secretary to the Tribunale del Commercio of the kingdom of Naples, expressed himself (1784) in very cold and almost diffident terms on the subject of commercial exchange between the newborn United States and Naples (see Furio Diaz, "L'abate Galiani consigliere di commercio estero del Regno di Napoli," *Rivista storica italiana*, 80, no. 4 [1968], pp. 881–84).

178. Letter of D'Alembert, 25 September 1773 (*Correspondance*, II, 267). Cortes and Pizarro were "two pirates, real buccaneers" (letter to Mme d'Epinay, 29 February 1772, ibid., II, 32). But Charles V was "a gentle despot, as his son was a harsh despot" (letter to d'Epinay, 29 June 1771, ibid., I, 412).

179. See the letter from London of 8 December 1767, in A. Bazzoni, ed., *Lettere di Ferdinando Galiani al Marchese Bernardo Tanucci* (Florence, 1880), p. 169, and now in *Dialogues sur le commerce des bleds*, Nicolini ed. (1959), pp. 328–29; *Dialogues sur le commerce des bleds* (1770), III, Venice ed., 1791, p. 96; Nicolini ed., pp. 63–64.

180. Letter to abbé Morellet, 10 July 1769, in J. Y. T. Greig, ed., *The Letters of D. Hume* (Oxford, 1932), II, 433.

181. Letter to Tanucci, 8 November 1762, op. cit., pp. 56–57.

182. *Dialogues*, VI, 218 (see below, n. 184). On the advantages and disadvantages of the acquisition of remote colonies, which "properly speaking is not increasing oneself but dismembering oneself," see

"Within a century," he wrote in 1771, "England will break off from Europe . . . she will join herself to America, of which she will possess the greater part, and control the commerce of the rest."[183] When relations between the colonies and the mother country began to deteriorate rapidly and England found herself with the growing difficulties that he had foreseen as early as 1764,[184] Galiani was filled with new optimism and fixed his hopeful gaze on the rebel colonies. He felt no deep attachment for the "American Quakers" (he calls them "the dregs"),[185] but he was uneasy over the glaring and outrageous vices eating away at the roots of

---

ibid., pp. 221–23. Hume, in his *History of England (Appendix to the Reign of James I)* had mentioned the fears of many Englishmen at the time of the establishment of the earliest colonies in America, that "after draining their mother country of inhabitants, they [the colonies] would soon shake off their yoke and erect an independent government in America," but only to reject these fears from the lesson of experience (quoted in Sumner, op. cit., pp. 129–30). The contrast between the lively and prosperous colonies of the ancients and the "passive" establishments in America is underlined by A. von Humboldt, *Reise,* I, 281–83. John Adams, on the other hand, the future second president of the United States, had based himself (1775) on the demographic progress of the colonies in looking forward to the time a century hence when the United States would have more inhabitants "than England itself," and "the great seat of empire" would pass from England to America (Sumner, op. cit., p. 52); and he was followed by a number of other observers who judged America's independence to be ripe or proximate: Benjamin Franklin, 1760; Dean Josiah Tucker, 1766 and 1776; minister Choiseul, 1767; John Cartwright, 1774; Adam Smith, 1776; Richard Price, 1776: see Sumner, op. cit., pp. 69–70, 84, 91, 108–09, 111–12; M. Curti, *The Roots of American Loyalty* (New York, 1946), p. 8, and Adam Smith, *The Wealth of Nations,* IV, 7, iii (Modern Library ed., p. 590), who also uses the expression "the seat of empire," which Gibbon had frequently adopted, and which was then current and remained popular in the United States; for an example from 1808, see H. Bernstein, *Origins of Inter-American Interest, 1700–1812* (Philadelphia, 1945), p. 86, and another from 1841, Curti, op. cit., p. 42. *Contra,* the Englishman Andrew Burnaby, who in his polemic with the Americans judged (1775) as "singular and chimerical" the idea that the seat of dominating nations might migrate toward the West (Bernard Fabian, *Alexis de Tocquevilles Amerikabild* [Heidelberg, 1957], p. 91).

183. Letter to Mme d'Epinay, 27 April 1771, in *Correspondance,* I, 338. In 1766 J. Tucker also discussed the idea that the "seat of empire" should pass to America, and Great Britain be governed by viceroys sent by the Court of Philadelphia or New York: see Sumner, op. cit, p. 86. Even the anglophile and loyalist David Leonard (for whom see V. L. Parrington, *Main Currents in American Thought* [New York, 1930], I, 207–13), foresees (1774–75) the time when the king will cross the ocean, and North America and its parliament will govern the British Empire (see H. Kohn, *The Idea of Nationalism* [New York, 1945], p. 282).

184. Letter to Tanucci, 13 August 1764, ed. cit., p. 129: "The English have committed a gross blunder in providing their American colonies with an *exit.* Within thirty years they will realize it." He is probably referring to the permission to trade with the Antilles, conceded for fiscal purposes in 1764. Cf. similar prophecies by the Marquis d'Argenson (1694–1757), who foresaw the English colonies raising themselves up as independent republics, prospering, growing in population and civilization and within a short time controlling all America, and especially the gold mines (in other words the Spanish dominions): see Sumner, op. cit., p. 37; and by Turgot, who compares the colonies in general, and the American ones in particular, to fruits which, once ripened, fall from the tree (*Discours sur les progrès successifs de l'esprit humain,* 1750, in appx. to E. Lerminier, *De l'influence de la philosophie du XVIIIe siècle,* etc. [Paris, 1833], p. 454; cf. ibid., p. 218, and for other comment from 1770 and 1778, Sumner, op. cit., pp. 42–43; B. Fay, *L'esprit révolutionnaire en France et aux Etats-Unis à la fin du XVIIIe siècle* [Paris, 1925], pp. 32, 49–51). The fear that the North American colonies, once independent and united, would swallow the whole continent, was fairly widespread in Europe about 1780 (see Sumner, op. cit., pp. 59–60), and reechoes in the abbé Grégoire, *De la littérature des nègres,* 1808, p. 283, quoted in Sumner, op. cit., p. 154.

185. Letter to Tanucci, of March or April 1769, ed. cit., p. 219. The Quakers were never much liked by the Italians: for Mazzei, see below, p. 272; for Genovesi, Castiglioni, etc., see D. Visconti, *Le origini degli Stati Uniti d'America e l'Italia* (Padua, 1940), pp. 46–48 and the unpublished thesis of A. Violo, *Relazioni tra l'Italia e gli Stati Uniti durante il Settecento* (Rome, 1950–51), pp. 67–70.

France and all Europe[186] and rejoiced to see the American colonies rising up and conquering. Almost on the eve of their Declaration of Independence he pronounced his solemn judgment: "The time has come of the total collapse of Europe and the transmigration to America. Here everything is falling into decay — religion, laws, arts and sciences; and everything will be rebuilt anew in America."[187] History's greatest revolution will be the one that decides whether America will dominate Europe or vice versa: "I would bet in favor of America, for the quite material reason that genius moves in the contrary fashion to our diurnal motion and has been going from East to West for the last five thousand years, without exception."[188] The future belongs to the New World.

Montaigne, at the end of the sixteenth century, had said something similar. But it hardly needs to be pointed out that the implications behind Montaigne's predictions are quite different. Montaigne sees in America the freshness of Nature, the "infancy" of the savage contrasting with the so-called wisdom of Europe. Galiani, a city and society man par excellence, has no such sentimental feeling about the Noble Savage, the good indigen, or the primitive purity of Nature. Galiani is the antithesis of Rousseau in politics, pedagogy, economics, everything.[189] When Bougainville had come back from the South Sea Islands and published his famous description of the idyllic state of nature there, in which even the *teterrima belli causa* was an instrument of peace, Galiani had written mockingly of "this Bougainville the Jew of the islands, selling old stuff for new, who says he has discovered Plato's republic in the south," and he suspected him of being one of Minister Choiseul's spies.[190]

Galiani's enthusiasm for America is in fact entirely on the civil and political plane; it is the enthusiasm of the disciple of Vico and Machiavelli for a young strong state in the midst of its sure and surging rise to future greatness.

---

186. Letter to Mme d'Epinay, 4 June 1774 (*Correspondance*, II, 317–18).

187. Letter to Mme d'Epinay, of 18 May 1776 (ibid., II, 443). A few years later Gibbon rejoiced in the thought that if Europe was submerged by an invasion of Tartars, it "would revive and flourish in the American world, which is already filled with her colonies and institutions" (*The Decline and Fall of the Roman Empire*, XXXVIII, conclusion, ed. J. B. Bury [London, 1896–1900], IV, 166). And Antonio Genovesi saw the (American) colonies becoming the metropolises and the former metropolises becoming colonies (quoted by A. Annoni, *L'Europa nel pensiero italiano del Settecento* [Milan, 1959], pp. 113–14).

188. Letter to Mme d'Epinay, 25 July 1778 (*Correspondance*, II, 553).

189. Cf. ibid., I, 342, 400–01; F. Nicolini, *Intorno a F. Galiani* (Turin, 1908), p. 30, and idem, *G. B. Vico e F. Galiani*, pp. 24–25.

190. Letter to Tanucci, of March or April 1769, *Correspondance*, pp. 218–19. (The Horatian expression was also used by Hume, *Essays*, XIV, ed. cit., p. 129; and by Kant, *Anthropologie*, Akad.-Ausgabe, XV, 667). Note the usual spontaneous outburst of political cynicism. Later Galiani requested Bougainville's *Voyage*, "*et d'autres voyages véridiques*," and read it with interest (letter of 1771, in *Correspondance*, I, 406, 412, 473–74). See also his savage criticism of Voltaire's *Alzire* (ibid., II, 31–32, 170–71).

XII. THE GLORIOUS FUTURE OF THE WEST

America is Europe's heir. Buffon and de Pauw had never in their wildest moments contributed to this notion or prophecy, nor had those who first set out to refute them. But such announcements and predictions of a new civilization that would flourish beyond the ocean represent an element that simply cannot be ignored in the whole history of the polemic. It is often this very notion which gives that impassioned tone to the apologists' pleadings or which works its way surreptitiously into the defenses of America's nature. Elsewhere, as with Galiani, it serves to straighten out some de Pauwian inaccuracy (the "roughcast" continent replaces the "rotted" continent), or, finally, asserts its absolute authority to correct the excesses of the polemic. Even abbé Raynal, who had such a low opinion of the Americans, once allowed himself to be seduced by this glowing prophecy: "If any happy revolution comes to the world, it will be through America. Although it was once laid waste this new world will flourish in its time, and *perhaps dominate the old;* it will be the sanctuary for our peoples suffering under political oppression, or driven out by wars: the savage inhabitants will become civilized, and persecuted foreigners will there find freedom."[191]

So even Raynal foresaw America ruling Asia and Europe, grasping the scepter of the world. But although the idea gained a new lease of life with the successful outcome of the American Revolution, its origins are considerably more ancient, going back in fact to the very conquest of the continent.

Right from the first decades after Columbus's landing, the Christianization of the New World had been seen as "compensation" for the conquests of Islam, and Europe's push toward the far West was understood as the consequence and continuation of the Muslims' thrust out of the East toward the West of Africa and Europe. It was Columbus himself, sailing westward in the hope of discovering in the Indies the means for the last crusade and the liberation of the Holy Sepulchre, who had given the first impulse to this almost symbolic idea, which hails the West Indies as the indemnity offered to Christianity for the injuries suffered at the hands of the nomads emerging from the deserts of Arabia. And Toynbee expresses the same idea in the terminology of today's sociological dialectic when he explains the Iberians' westward expansion as the result of the "Syriac pressure" exerted on the Peninsula by the Moors.[192]

There was another idea clearly related to this, already implicit in Alexander VI's bull *Inter coetera divinae* and readily accepted by the Spanish

---

191. *Histoire,* VI, 174; my italics. See also above, chap. 3, n. 46.
192. A. J. Toynbee, op. cit., II, 204–06, 363; Max Mittler, *Mission und Politik* (Zurich, 1951), pp. 17–18.

people, by publicists, pamphleteers, and poets, according to which the Indies were the *reward* falling to Spain for her eight centuries of fighting the Moors. Here then the Indies are no longer an indemnity for defeat but a trophy of victory. The distinction and the link between the two ideas comes out clearly in the way Levene interprets the pontifical bull, as implying not so much a *prize* as an *investiture,* or an invitation to continue overseas the struggle against the infidel, for which Spain was so well prepared by those very centuries of the Reconquest, and for which it thus offered the best assurance of Catholic purity and military valor.[193]

It was an obvious and very simple doctrine, but at the same time one so malleable that with a little subtlety the other nations of Europe could make it serve their own ends equally well. In 1545 Jacques Cartier pointed out that the holy faith had been born in Palestine, in the East; that from there it had passed into France; and that it was thus logical that from France it should be further propagated westward beyond the seas. Spain, he continued, had already carried the gospel to Central and South America. What was Francis I waiting for to bring the true religion to the savages of the north? And the king, who had already asked acidly if he could see Adam's will to find out whether Spain and Portugal were really the sole heirs of his estate in the Indies (1541), His Most Christian Majesty, convinced by this mixture of apostolic and political considerations, furnished him with men and money.[194]

Now with all these suggestions of a westward migration of Christian civilization and the awesome political and commercial expansion of Spain in the Western Hemisphere, the ground was prepared for a wholesale translation into geographical terms (a movement from East to West) of some of the world's oldest historiographical theories. These were the theories, found in the books of Daniel and Polybius and the poetry of Hesiod and Ovid, that had ordered human history according to the schemes of the four monarchies or six ages of the world, and which had provided a full and final explanation for the greatness and decadence and cyclical succession of Empires. Trogus Pompeus, who "combines the notion of *translatio imperii* with that of Theopompeian universal history and thus lays the foundations for the Christians' universal history . . . maintains that civilization is shifting Westward."[195]

A dazzling future was already being foretold for these new territories

---

193. R. Levene, *Introducción a la historia del derecho indiano* (Buenos Aires, 1924), p. 56. An even more hyperbolical and generous concatenation appears in the words of Mazzini, who sees Italy offering Europe a New World just as Europe was about to tear her to pieces and sink her (quoted in F. Chabod, *Storia della politica estera italiana dal 1870 al 1896,* I, *Le premesse* [Bari, 1951], p. 196, n. 5).
194. Kennedy, op. cit., pp. 15–16.
195. A. Momigliano, in *Rivista storica italiana,* 79, no. 1 (1967), p. 215. Other references to the fruitful antithesis of East and West in the classical world: Curcio, op. cit., I, 70–72, 75–76.

acquired for the Faith. Now in the fullness of time the hidden meaning of the words of the prophets, seers, and those absorbed historians of human affairs was becoming clear. Finally one could understand the rhythm they assigned to history, a rhythm of steadily increasing strength from kingdom to kingdom and age to age, culminating in the setting of a seal of inescapable glory on the extreme west.

St. Jerome[196] and St. Augustine[197] gave new strength and depth to these age-old geogonies and crude chronographies, and following their appearance in the universal histories of the two Spaniards, Paulus Orosius and Isidore of Seville, they became accepted and widely known notions throughout the centuries of the Middle Ages. Orosius's *Moesta Mundi* depicted the succession of the four monarchies, and the *Chronicon* of Isidore outlined the allegory of six epochs corresponding to the six days of the creation. Their fame was long lasting, and still in Dante's *Paradise* they figure in the garland of the twelve great theologians—"the bold spirit of Isidore" and Paulus Orosius, "the advocate of Christian times," in the incandescent ecstasy of the "glorious wheel" of supreme wisdom.[198] And following in the footsteps of Augustine and Orosius, Otto of Freising saw civilization and world monarchy marching from east to west.[199]

With the maturing of the Renaissance, the sacred texts and classics of the early Middle Ages lost their weight of authority, and the theories of

196. Who attempted to link Nebuchadnezzar's dream (in the Book of Daniel) with the Ptolemaic-Hellenistic conception of the four universal monarchies, thus guaranteeing the duration of the Roman Empire, identified with the "kingdom of iron," until the Day of Judgment—a thesis which of course nullified the importance of the advent of Christ, but which later proved useful to the supporters of the notion of the continuity of the Roman Empire in the German nation and found defenders even in the eighteenth century (H. Spangenberg, "Die Perioden der Weltgeschichte," *Historische Zeitschrift*, 127 [1923], pp. 7–8; M. Bloch, *Apologie pour l'histoire, ou Métier d'historien* [Paris, 1949], p. 90). On the probable Persian origin of the myth, see the lecture of Harald Fuchs, "Antike Lehren von der Abfolge der Weltreiche und Weltaltern," summarized in *Basler Nachrichten*, 23 November 1948; but cf. also J. Gwyn Griffiths, "Archaeology and Hesiod's Five Ages," *Journal of the History of Ideas*, 17, no. 1 (1956), pp. 109–19.

197. St. Augustine in fact already connects them with the movement of history toward the West: "After the illustrious kingdoms of the East flourished for some considerable time, God willed that one [the Roman] should arise in the West, later in time, but more illustrious for the extent and greatness of its dominion" (*De Civitate Dei*, V, 13); "Two empires rose to greater heights than all the others, first that of the Assyrians, then that of the Romans, coordinated and distinguished one from the other, regarding both time and place. In fact, as the former arose first, so the other arose later; the former in the East, the latter in the West; and the end of the former coincided with the immediate beginning of the latter" (ibid., XVIII, 2).

198. *Paradiso*, X, 119, 130–34, 145. Cf. G. Falco, *La polemica sul Medio Evo* (Turin, 1933), pp. 4, 35 and passim; Piero Treves, *Il mito di Alessandro e la Roma di Augusto* (Milan-Naples, 1953), p. 126, with important references.

199. Sverker Arnoldsson, *La leyenda negra, estudios sobre sus orígenes* (Gothenburg, 1960), pp. 46, 168, with reference to the theories of *translatio imperii*. For Orosius, with the fall of Babylon into the hands of Cyrus and the expulsion of the Tarquinians "then the Empire of the East fell and the Empire of the West arose," see J. Fischer, *Oriens-Occidens-Europa, Begriff und Gedanke "Europa" in der späten Antike und im frühen Mittelalter* (Wiesbaden, 1957), p. 26. On the analogy between the theory of the four empires and the ancient theory of the four ages of the world (Gold, Silver, Copper, and Iron) see Armstrong, op. cit., pp. 154–55.

the four monarchies and the ages of gold and silver crumbled under the onslaught of Bodin's arguments.[200] The proud conscience of the age of progress rejected these apologues of decadence, Nature rose up to challenge the Scriptures, and even the history of mankind patterned itself on the greatest phenomenon of the physical world, the succession of dawn and nightfall. Empires and their destinies took their course from the curving path of the sun. The peak of their power coincided with the mobile zenith of the great star.

This inspired notion was reinforced and enriched in its turn by an impressive array of fact, myth, and mental association. The Orient had always been connected or almost identified with the most remote antiquity. The Levant has an almost sacred quality in the visions of Isaiah (27:8; 41:2) and Ezekiel (43:1–4). The Redeemer himself announces to his disciples: "For as the lightning cometh out of the east, and shineth even unto the west; so shall also the coming of the Son of man be" (Matthew 24:27). *Ex Oriente lux.*[201] And all of ancient civilization followed in fact in its general course an east-west trajectory, a trajectory which for the Greeks was underlined by the distinctions they proudly observed between themselves and the "barbarians" to the East.[202]

When the Judeo-Christian tradition merged with the spiritual heritage of Greece the authority of the Bible confirmed that the east had been the source of Revelation and the laws for civilized existence, and of man himself and the Son of Man. For the European the east was represented by Eden and Mt. Sinai, Jerusalem and the land of Canaan. And when Rinaldo went off to the Crusades he was drawn on by "the trumpet heard in the East" (*Gerusalemme liberata,* 1, 59). Thus in Christian thought the antithesis between east and west slowly took on a new prophetic sense or symbolic value. Pope Nicholas I, in his efforts to assert the supremacy of the Roman pontiff over the Byzantine emperor, had recourse to the apostles Peter and Paul, who had come from the East to Italy, to Rome, so that "the west by their presence became the east."[203] Toward the year 1000 the monk and chronicler Radulphus Glaber saw in the crucifixion a presage of the solemn destiny of the west; it was the west that unfolded before the eyes of the martyred Christ, while he turned

200. *Méthode*, VII—followed by Hakewill, who mocks "that idle tale and vaine fancie forged by Poets, and taken up by some Historians, and believed by the vulgar of the foure ages of the world," but believes in the "passage of learning from East to West" (see G. Williamson, op. cit., pp. 132, 147).

201. Still further passages in Fischer, op. cit., pp. 60–61, with constant emphasis, however, on the thesis that the East is light, redemption, salvation, while the West is darkness, perdition, ruin, or at least passivity (ibid., p. 73).

202. See M. Rostovzeff, *A History of the Ancient World*, I, *The Orient and Greece* (Oxford, 1936), pp. 8, 333.

203. Fischer, op. cit., pp. 54–73.

his back on the savage peoples of the east.[204] It was a grandiose interpretation, its suggestiveness irresistible to those who recalled the division of the Roman Empire under Diocletian and the speculations over the *translatio imperii* "in the person of the great Charles from the Greeks . . . to the Germans,"[205] and its echoes were heard again, centuries later, on the eve of the discovery of America, in the jubilation over the resurrection in Italy and Europe of the civilization which had been extinguished in Byzantium.

Everything thus combined to impress on men the vision of the path of history moving from east to west, and so to facilitate the inclusion of the recently discovered Americas in this historiographical system. As early as 1512 the notion is becoming fatally interwoven with the ancient *topos* of the *naturae cursus,* to give a seal of approval, of metaphysical legitimacy, to the new lands discovered in the west.[206] But its success was even more surely guaranteed on the plane of earthly politics, being so perfectly suited to the needs of those who upheld the lawful rights of Spain — the extreme west of the Mediterranean world — who could claim that the indigenous monarchies in Mexico and Peru had already reached their maximum development, or even commenced their downward path, when the Spanish arrived to take up the succession.[207] It gave emphasis and meaning to the boast of Charles V (or the hyperbole of his courtiers) that his was a kingdom on which the sun never set. And it was taken up again in the praises of the Italian writers who hailed Spain as Rome's

204. "So even then the West stood before His [Christ's] eyes, waiting to be filled with the light of faith" (Radulphus Glaber, *Historiarum sui temporis libri V,* bk. I, chap. V, in Migne, *Patrologia Latina,* vol. 142, p. 626b). Glaber, an industrious pursuer of occult links and meanings, also explains how the faith spread more in the north than in the south because the Lord's right hand stretched out to the north: and, after a few centuries, the Normans became Christians. But he adds that the faith is catholic and welcomes everyone: only divine wisdom knows why some men are more and some less ready for salvation. Tasso comes back to the same image, and in the four arms of the cross sees a sign of the four parts of the world: *"L'Orto e l'Occaso, l'Aquilone e l'Austro"* (*Mondo creato,* II, 556–59; ed. cit., p. 48).

205. Decretal of Innocent III *Venerabilem fratrem,* 1202 (in Carl Mirbt, *Quellen zur Geschichte des Papsttums und des römischen Katholizismus* [Tübingen, 1924], p. 175). On the *translatio imperii,* see Werner Goez, *Translatio Imperii, Ein Beitrag zur Geschichte des Geschichtsdenken und der politischen Theorien im Mittelalter und in der frühen Neuzeit* (Tübingen, 1958), quoted in Arnoldsson, *La leyenda negra,* p. 168, n. 65, and for its influence on the "Gothic Renaissance" of the eighteenth and nineteenth centuries, Samuel Kliger, "The Gothic Revival and the German *translatio,*" *Modern Philology,* 45, no. 2 (November 1947), pp. 73–103. On the parallel *translatio studii* from Athens and Rome to Alcuin's Paris, and on the movement of civilization from East to West, see Jacques Le Goff, "Au Moyen Age: Temps de l'Eglise et temps du marchand," *Annales,* 15, no. 3 (May–June 1960), pp. 423–24, quoting E. Gilson, P. Renucci, and M.-D. Chenu.

206. Hans Galinsky, *"Naturae Cursus* — Der Weg einer antiken kosmologischen Metapher von der Alten in die Neue Welt — Ein Beitrag zu einer historischen Metaphorik der Weltliteratur," in *Arcadia* (Berlin), 2 (1967), p. 47.

207. See for example Acosta, *Historia natural y moral,* VII, 28 (the last chapter of the work) with explicit reference to the prophecy of Daniel (2:31–35) concerning the downfall of Nebuchadnezzar's golden reign, and the arrival of Christ's law "when the Monarchy of Rome had reached its peak." See also Curcio, op. cit., I, 262–81, 296–97, 438.

westward neighbor and her true heir and continuator;[208] and who in the prophecy of the seer Andronica watched the Spaniards, the New Argonauts, sailing away westward:

> E del sole imitando il cammin tondo
> Ritrovar nuove terre e nuovo mondo.[209]

Thus already by the end of the sixteenth century it was a commonplace to represent the parabola of universal history as arching over the Atlantic, from the shores of Spain to those of America. Justus Lipsius, ever faithful to Polybius, differed from his contemporary Montaigne in considering the American Indians barbarians. But he still believed, this time with Montaigne, or better with Galiani, that America would succeed Europe as empress of the world: "I see arising from the West the sun of some new and unknown Empire." "I know not by what decree of Providence, things and forces go from East . . . to West."[210]

America as the spiritual and religious heir of Christianity was also a favored notion, almost a commonplace, among the post-Reformation Catholic apologists, who took up the theme of the Indies as compensation for Islamic expansions, and rejoiced at the reparation found by the Roman faith in overseas territories for the losses suffered in northern Europe. Already in 1533 when the licentiate Spinoza was informing Charles V of the great tidings from Peru and of all her riches, he encouraged him to make use of this gift of Providence "so that with greater vigor and means he might prosecute the holy enterprise and war against the Turk and Lutheran and other enemies of the Faith."[211] And a few years later, in 1546, in a formal address to the Council of Trent, the Dominican Marco Lauri was exhorting the council fathers to tend the wounds of the church: "You see it lifted up and enlarged in the Indies, our antipodes; do not permit it to be ruined in Europe."[212] The Dominican

---

208. Suffice it to mention the opening lines of Campanella's *Monarchia di Spagna* (written 1600–01; 1st ed., 1620) "Proceeding on its way from East to West, the universal Monarchy . . . came in time into the hands of the Spanish" (D'Ancona, ed. [Turin, 1854], II, 85). Charles V, king of Spain, did in fact obtain the crown of the Holy Roman Empire (1519). But as early as 1509 Antonio de Nebrija gave his opinion that the "monarchy" in its march toward the West had arrived in Spain (Arnoldsson, *La leyenda negra*, p. 168). Bodin accuses the Germans of national arrogance in boasting of themselves as heirs of the Roman Empire; the king of Spain possesses considerably vaster and more populous dominions, including the Americas, which are three times the size of Europe; not to mention the Sultan of the Turks, the Prince of Ethiopia, or the Emperor of the Tartars, lord of innumerable and indomitable nations. Proud Germany, in comparison, looks like a fly beside an elephant! (*Méthode*, pp. 288–89).

209. L. Ariosto, *Orlando furioso*, XV, 22.

210. *De Constantia*, I, 16 (Antwerp ed., 1605, pp. 27–28); *Admiranda sive de magnitudine Romana*, I, 3 (Antwerp, 1605, p. 22). See also G. Williamson, op. cit., p. 133–34, and my study on "Diego de León Pinelo contra Justo Lipsio," in *Fénix*, Lima, nos. 2–3 (1945–46), and in extract, I, 18–20.

211. Document of the Archivio Segreto Vaticano, quoted by G. Galasso, "L'opera del Brandi e alcuni studi recenti su Carlo V," *Rivista Storica Italiana*, 74, no. 1 (March 1962), p. 114.

212. Fr. Mateos, S.J., "Ecos de América en Trento," *Revista de Indias* (Madrid), 22 (1945), p. 571. See also above, p. 77.

visionary Francisco de la Cruz, who was burned by the Inquisition of Lima in 1578, had envisaged a new church rising in America to replace the one brought to ruin in Europe by Luther and the Turks.[213] At the end of the sixteenth century Father Geronimo de Mendieta hails the conquest as having been willed by God, so that "the Catholic Church might be restored and recompensed, by the conversion of many souls, for the loss and great damage brought about by the accursed Luther in the same season and time in old Christendom."[214] And finally the illustrious college *De Propaganda Fide* had been founded in Rome in 1622 to make good the losses suffered by the true faith in Europe with the spiritual conquest of other continents.[215]

Again toward the end of the seventeenth century Gabriel Fernandez de Villalobos, Marquis of Varinas, found it very significant that Cortes had been born in the same year as Luther — clear proof that the Lord intended to make up in the New World for what he was about to lose in the Old.[216] A little later Father Feijóo repeated: "The Gospel gained much more land in this hemisphere than it lost in Europe — heaven gained more land in this continent than it lost in the other."[217] And Father Lafitau echoed his sentiments in 1733 as he wondered at the migrations of the true faith, which even as it languished and fell prey to heresy in Europe found a providential home in faraway lands, both barbarous and civilized, which fell adoring at its feet.[218]

It is true that as the Spanish monarchy declines these smug simplistic platitudes tend to fade into the background too; just as the sycophantic

213. See Marcel Bataillon, *Etudes sur Bartolomé de Las Casas* (Paris, 1965), pp. 264–67, 309–24, esp. 314–15, and L. Hanke, *Aristotle and the Indians*, pp. 20–21.

214. *Historia eclesiástica indiana,* 1596, cited by Sverker Arnoldsson, *La conquista española de América* . . . (Madrid, 1960), p. 17.

215. G. de Santillana, op. cit., p. 311.

216. *Mano de relox* (1687), IX, in *Colección de documentos inéditos relativos al descubrimiento, conquista y organización de las antiguas posesiones de Ultramar,* 2d ser., vol. XII (Madrid, 1899), p. 359, cited by de Madariaga, op. cit., p. 656.

217. *Glorias de España,* sec. XXIV, 1730, in *Obras escogidas,* by D. V. de la Fuente (Madrid, 1863), p. 209a; cf. E. O'Gorman, "Estudio preliminar" to his edition of Acosta (Mexico, 1940), p. xlvii, n. 51. The phrase is repeated almost word for word by Macaulay in his essay on Ranke (1840): *Essays and Lays of Ancient Rome* (London, 1902), p. 548. On the other hand with the rapid Christianization of the Americas, "Europe ceased to be the only Christian continent and thus lost one of its typical and exclusive characteristics" and "the term 'Christians' no longer defined merely the peoples of Europe" (C. Morandi, *L'unità politica,* pp. 16, 40). The ending of this European privilege (despite the later Novalisian identification) did however pave the way for the thesis of the westward movement of the higher values of history.

218. *Histoire des découvertes et conquêtes des Portugais dans le Nouveau-Monde* (Paris, 1733), quoted by Zavala, *América,* pp. 235–50, esp. 248. In the nineteenth century the theme was again taken up and developed by Fr. Joachim Ventura, who in his panegyric of the blessed Martin de Porres of Peru (read in Rome, 5 November 1836) referred to the evangelization of the Americas as the compensation bestowed by Providence to neutralize the damage of the Protestant heresy (*La Raison philosophique et la Raison catholique, Conférences* [Paris, 1864], IV, 445–534, esp. 451–52: Fr. Ventura quotes Las Casas and de Maistre and argues with the "Protestant" Robertson); while Giuseppe Ferrari, on the other hand, saw in Luther's protest an advantage for Germany "to oppose the world discovered by Christopher Columbus" (*La disfatta della Francia,* ed. Ugo Guanda [Modena, 1943], pp. 49–50).

prophecies addressed to the sovereign rulers of the West Indies had eventually spent themselves. But it is significant that the consolations and prophecies begin again in favor of new beneficiaries when other powers are established in America, importing their own religion to rival the Catholic, and their own laws and commerce. Of course there is no more talk about rewards and indemnities for the Lutheran heresy. But in 1589 the Protestant Edward Haie, captaining the flagship on Sir Humphrey Gilbert's last expedition, sees as certain "in this last age of the world" the evangelization of the Terranova (i.e., of all America, the "new land" par excellence) since God's word and religion "from the beginning hath moved from the East, toward, and at last unto the West, where it is like to end."[219] And the Puritans of New England, millenarists to a man, console themselves and rejoice in the belief that God, in this extremity of time, has decided to carry his gospel to the west—the gospel, "this great light of the World," which like the sun was born in the East and lit the east with its rays, and which today instead, as the world draws to the end of its day, comes to shine resplendent before nightfall on the last western shores.[220] Abraham Cowley, who had once considered emigrating to the colonies of the New World, announced from his retreat in Kent that although America had been ravaged by the Spaniards it still had its "liberty" and its natural products, which left it richer than the Spaniard with all his ill-gotten gains; and he saw the time approaching when Europe, "the world's most noble part," corrupted by American gold, would fall into anarchy and ruin, while the new nations of America, strong and virtuous like Republican Rome, would rise to the peak of their power:

> Meanwhile your rising glory you shall view,
> Wit, learning, virtue, discipline of war,
> Shall for protection to your world repair,
> And fix a long illustrious empire there.[221]

At about the same time (1692) Burnet, who did not however mention America, saw the course of history in terms of the nations taking turns to dominate, each for an instant imposing its will on the whole universe,

---

219. Galinsky, op. cit., II, 49–51, with precise references to the historiographical thesis of *translatio imperii* and citing Augustine. Gilbert's tragic voyage was in 1583, but Haie's account was published in 1589, in Hakluyt's *Principal Navigations*.

220. *New England's First Fruits*, cited in D. J. Boorstin, *The Genius of American Politics* (Chicago, 1953), p. 51, who comments: "Even the points of the compass took on a theological import." See also the curious examples collected by Blanke, op. cit., pp. 323–24.

221. *History of Plants*, V: pub. in Latin 1662–78, in English 1705, cited in Summer, op. cit., p. 13. Thomas Browne, on the other hand, in his pamphlet *A Prophecy concerning the Future State of Several Nations* (pub. 1684) holds a less moralistic and more practical economic opinion of America's gold; and imagines that the inhabitants of the New World, when they have reached a higher level of civilization and political organization, "will no longer suffer their treasure of gold and silver to be sent out to maintain the luxury of Europe and other parts," but will use it for themselves, and will maybe even attack the Europeans and wage war and piracy against them (Sumner, op. cit., pp. 14–16).

and then fading away again; and he added: "Learning, like the Sun, began to take its Course from the *East,* then turned *Westward,* where we have long rejoiced in its light. Who knows whether, leaving these Seats, it may not yet take a further Progress?" — or even perhaps spread equally over the whole globe?[222]

When the preacher John Edwards repeated Burnet's words some years later (1699),[223] the notion was no longer a possibility but a certainty, a certainty which became even more gloriously optimistic and emphatic when taken over by George Berkeley. At the beginning of the eighteenth century the future Bishop of Cloyne was suggesting that in America the Reformed Church could regain the territory lost in Europe: "In *Europe,* the Protestant Religion hath of late years considerably lost ground, and *America* seems the likeliest place, wherein to make up for what hath been lost in Europe."[224] And when he came back from the overseas colonies, although he had been disappointed in his apostolic projects he expressed in soaring verses his faith "on the prospect of planting Arts and Learning in America, . . . not such as Europe breeds in her decay: such as she bred when fresh and young." With religion restored and the arts and sciences growing apace, what else could be hoped for or promised? The prophecy of America's glorious future is crowned by the promise of political power.

> Westward the Course of Empire takes its way
> The four first Acts already past,
> A fifth shall close the Drama with the Day;
> Time's noblest offspring is the last.[225]

Berkeley's prophecy was to enjoy a most successful career. Its echoes are heard time and again in American literature of the eighteenth century[226] and the English writers of the early nineteenth. Around 1760–63 a Roman *improvvisatore* was paraphrasing it in honor of Benjamin

222. I have not been able to locate in the *Archaeologiae Philosophicae libri duo* (Amsterdam, 1699), the passage quoted by E. L. Tuveson, op. cit., p. 166, in the English translation. Toward the end of the eighteenth century Lord Monboddo was of the opinion "that not only all arts and sciences have come from the East, but even the race of man," and with prophetic insight suggested that the very languages we speak come from the East, from Sanskrit (letter of 20 June 1789, to Sir William Jones, the man who revealed Sanskrit to the Europeans, in W. Knight, *Lord Monboddo and Some of His Contemporaries* [London, 1900], pp. 268–69).

223. Cf. Tuveson, op. cit., p. 139.

224. *A Proposal for the Better Supplying of Churches in Our Foreign Plantations . . .* , 1725, in *A Miscellany . . . by the Bishop of Cloyne* (London, 1752), p. 203. Note how from Radulphus Glaber onward it is almost always the Faith that guides the destinies of the world toward the West.

225. *The Querist,* 1735, in *A Miscellany,* pp. 186–87. Cf. the acute comments of Galinsky, op. cit., II, 63–70; III, 139 ff.

226. See examples from ca. 1745, from 1760, 1763, 1771, 1773, 1774, 1775, 1782, 1784, in M. Kraus, *The Atlantic Civilization: Eighteenth-Century Origins* (Ithaca, N.Y., 1949), p. 73; Sumner, op. cit., pp. 25–27; Fr. Brie, "Die Anfänge des Amerikanismus," *Historisches Jahrbuch,* 59, nos. 3–4 (1939), p. 358; H. N. Smith, op. cit., pp. 3–12.

West,[227] and an 1812 travel guide repeats as a *locus communis* the fact that "Empire has hitherto rolled westwards."[228] In 1834 George Bancroft quoted Berkeley's auspicious words on the cover of the first of the ten volumes of his *History of the United States,*[229] and fifty-six years later, at the ripe age of ninety, he was busy refurbishing the ancient theory as a means of exalting the American West, and somehow extracting from it a prophecy that civilization, by the destiny of history, would find its center on America's Pacific Coast, "the terminal of the great Aryan march," as superior to the Atlantic Coast as America was superior to Europe.[230] In 1859 the march of empire to the west was allegorized, portrayed, and summed up in Berkeley's words at the head of the west stairway of the Capitol in Washington. And in 1866, in the Union's extreme west, at the Golden Gateway to the Pacific, the auspicious name of Berkeley was given to the city where there would one day rise the new and now world-famous university.[231]

We have already seen (above, p. 127) how as early as 1776 Adam Smith was predicting the passage of the "seat of empire" from England to the North American colonies. In the same year Taube in Germany considered it an accomplished fact: England is nothing without America; the colonies are the blood and sap of England's power.[232] But eleven years earlier even, in 1765, Ebeling, while still a student at Göttingen, had expressed his opinion on the likelihood of America surpassing Europe in political power and allowed a strong possibility of a transatlantic migration of the arts and letters too;[233] and Johannes von Müller many times gave voice to the same anxious prediction.[234]

In Italy one might mention the later and easier prophecies of the Neapolitan Filangieri (1780), the Genoese Ceronio (1780), and the Venetian ambassador in Paris, Dolfin (1783).[235] In 1791 the very shrewd De Giuliani too warns that industry, the sciences, and the fine arts may emigrate from the more prosperous regions of Europe, but the choice of

227. Van Wyck Brooks, *The Dream of Arcadia: American Writers and Artists in Italy, 1760–1915* (New York, 1958), p. 3.

228. J. C. Eustace, *A Classical Tour through Italy* (1812; IV ed. London, 1817), I, 23.

229. Marcus Cunliffe, *The Nation Takes Shape: 1789–1837* (Chicago, 1959), p. 195.

230. Quoted by Cushing Strout, *The American Image of the Old World* (New York, 1963), p. 142.

231. Galinsky, op. cit., III, 140. In the Capitol the line is modified to become: "Westward the *star* of Empire takes its way."

232. *Geschichte der englischen Handelschaft, Manufacturen, Kolonien und Schiffahrt* (Leipzig, 1776), pp. 110–11, quoted by E. E. Doll, "American History as Interpreted by German Historians from 1770 to 1815," *Transactions of the American Philosophical Society* (Philadelphia), n.s., vol. 38, pt. 5 (1948), p. 458.

233. Article in the *Hannoverisches Magazin,* cited by Doll, op. cit., pp. 437–38; cf. ibid., p. 449.

234. See passages quoted by H. S. King, *Echoes of the American Revolution in German Literature* (Berkeley, Calif., 1929), pp. 162–70.

235. See A. Pace, *Benjamin Franklin and Italy* (Philadelphia, 1958), pp. 113, 132, 155, 391. On the "heliodromic" ideas of Genovesi (1766) and Filangeri, cf. ibid., p. 125.

destination is left to them, whether they prefer to go to Russia, Austria, or the Kingdom of Naples, or "to cross the sea" to the New World, which will thus be "revenged of so many slaughters," and indemnified for the populations destroyed.[236] When the new century was still young, Luigi Ornato wrote that "Italy had three great eras of glory, under the Romans it was the strongest country in the world. . . . The genius of Rome is now gone to dwell in the lands of America."[237]

But we must get back to Berkeley. The philosopher, writing in prose, is hardly less emphatic than the prophet in verse. The prosperity and civilization of the English colonies show that a state can flourish even though it possess neither gold nor silver; while the political capacity of the natives is demonstrated by the ancient empires of Mexico and Peru, "in which there appeared a Reach of Politics, and a degree of Art and Politeness, which no European people were ever known to have arrived at without the use of Letters or of Iron, and which some perhaps have fallen short of with both these Advantages."[238] The Western Hemisphere is better endowed for politics than ours, Bishop Berkeley seems to say, anticipating abbé Galiani.

At the same time Vico was describing how the origins of civilized society could be traced back to the fierce bands of Polyphemes and *Patacones*, who had "vast bodies," "a very limited understanding, enormous fantasy, and violent passions"; ungainly creatures, maybe, but of "heroic" mind;[239] in other words our old friends the Patagonians, those giant paladins of the greatness of the New World. The eighteenth century's enthusiasm for Nature gave new breadth and power to these suggestions of an ideal history of the nations, transforming them eventually into romanticism's great theme of the primitive peoples with their spontaneous poetry and divine right to freedom. By the end of the century the radiant myth of young peoples crossed the ocean and set a seal of historical approval on the colonists' and Creoles' first tentative mo-

---

236. One more "compensation"! See Antonio de Giuliani, *La cagione riposta delle decadenze e delle rivoluzioni* (Bari, 1934), pp. 27, 101; cf. below, p. 173.

237. Letter of 2 May 1815 to Luigi Provana, in Leone Ottolenghi, *Vita, studii e lettere inedite di Luigi Ornato* (Turin, 1878), p. 201.

238. *The Querist*, nn. 251–53 (ed. cit., pp. 146–47) and n. 449 (ibid., p. 168), but the savages exist in squalid poverty: ibid., n. 358, p. 158; *A Proposal*, pp. 206–07. Cowley on the other hand had looked forward to America's having free and classical-type empires, not ones "like Montezuma's or Guanapaci's [Huayna Capac?] court" (loc. cit.).

239. *Scienza nuova*, ed. Nicolini, pp. 129, 181, 298, 643; in the final version Vico eliminated the reference to the necessary shrinking of the Patagonians when they became civilized: "They will come to our just statures and human customs" (ibid., p. 1031). On the reduction of man's stature, from the primitive giants to we pygmies ("we are dwarves compared with them," Sebastian Verro, 1581), see above, n. 14, and in general all the supporters of the idea of a decadence of the human race from the Edenic or primitive natural state: for example, Lord Monboddo, in an incomplete work on *The Degeneracy of Man in a State of Society*, has a long digression on his "favourite topic of the decreasing stature of man" (Knight, op. cit., p. 276).

tions toward independence. The prophecies of Berkeley and Galiani were lit up in the burning glow of revolution and romanticism.

The heliodromic theory may have been naïvely simplistic, but with the support of so much historical evidence, and with its pliability enabling it to embrace even a world so new, it represented a considerable advance, from the inherited parable of the four monarchies to this world vision of universal history; and it is equally clear how superior this dynamic and historicizing (albeit in mythic form) vision is to the static and naturalistic notions of climate and racial character. It dissolves their fixity, frees them to move with the centuries, and at the same time knits together into one single thread the various distinct characteristics of the nations; and finally it allows the reerection of the triumphal arch of universal history on the model of the arc of light traced each day in the skies.[240] One could also see in the idea of succession of empires from East to West a crude formulation of the need to bring together geography and history in a complete study of the life stories of the states, a need which has been recognized in our own day under the emphatic title of geopolitics.

It is remarkable then that this radical change in the old historiographical schemes, their actualization of the whole past, this unfolding of the centuries along the meridians and of empires along a terrestrial path, should have received so little attention from the scholars of the time. In this connection Fueter mentions only an obscure professor from Leyden, George Horn (1620–70), who "somewhat confusedly combined the partition according to the four empires with a geographical distribution of the material," but who was first to include the Americans in his historiographical scheme and among the first to define the Middle Ages as a distinct period in the history of the world.[241] Thus, as often happens, a lesser mind sketched out the first crude formulations of historical schemes and concepts that had been long ages in ripening and which were to be of revolutionary significance.

240. With this quality it has of so effectively undermining the schemes of immobility, the heliodromic theory can be compared with the Buffonian transformism which broke down the systems preaching an invariability of the animal species. Toward the end of his life even Huntington, the most authoritative modern supporter of the climatic theory, seems to have been moving in the direction of an attempted synthesis between his deterministic theories and the heliodromic notions: "He had come to believe in a migration of climates which had carried westward the optimal conditions for the development of civilization and power from Egypt . . . to the east of the United States." And he went on dauntlessly to conclude therefrom that it had been easy for Germany to conquer Czechoslovakia and Yugoslavia in 1938–41 "because these countries were situated to the southeast, or in a direction of more feeble climate" (Jean Gottmann, "Mer et terre – Esquisse de géographie politique," Annales, IV [1949], n. 1, pp. 20–21).

241. See E. Fueter, Geschichte der neueren Historiographie (Munich-Berlin, 1936), p. 188, and Falco, op. cit., pp. 86–89, with the reservations of W. K. Ferguson, The Renaissance in Historical Thought (Boston, 1948), p. 74. Some other examples are briefly mentioned by Blanke, op. cit., p. 316.

Horn repeats the theory of the four successive universal monarchies, laboriously entwining it with the story of Noah's three sons each inheriting a continent: Ham, Africa and Arabia; Shem, Asia; and Japhet, the rest.[242] But when he reaches the end of the ancient world he superimposes on this hybrid historicogeographical construction a division according to parts of the world, joining onto the old hemisphere of the East the new Western Hemisphere and the even newer Austral territories.[243] At this point however, since records of the past vicissitudes of the New World aborigines are lacking, he decides to fill the "vacuum of times and things" with a description of the customs of the Americans. The history of the world stops short; or rather the insipid chronicle of kingdoms, dynasties, and conquests gives way to a long chapter of highly colorful ethnography.[244]

The four monarchies still appear in allegorical form in the engraved frontispiece. But in the whole of the last part of the *Arca Noae*, Horn forgets the Bible and its interpreters and gives a minute and loving portrayal of the nations and tribes of America, from the savagest to the most civilized.[245]

It is a fact, however, that up until the middle of the nineteenth century the world's history was still often summed up and explained with a broad arrow sweeping across the globe from right to left.

The thesis of America's glowing future fell in very neatly with the theory which saw the rationality and unity of history in a movement and progress from east to west—indeed became almost a particular and particularly eloquent example of that theory, which was to entice some of the very greatest minds of the period. Hegel states bluntly that world history moves from east to west.[246] Humboldt refers on a number of occasions to a westward course of civilization.[247] The historians of the English "liberal Anglican" school see progress as a movement toward the West.[248] Byron, Shelley, and Mme de Staël contribute to the same

242. G. Horn, *Arca Noae* (Leida-Rotterdam, 1666), p. 35.

243. Ibid., p. 183.

244. Ibid., pp. 455–539, quoting Gómara, Acosta, Garcilaso, etc. On his ideas on the origins of the Americans, see D. C. Allen, *The Legend of Noah*, pp. 128–29, and various passages in the *Arca Noae*.

245. Jean Bodin too had criticized and mocked the scheme of the four monarchies (*Méthode*, pp. 287–93), and although he suggests a progressive movement of history from the peoples of the east to those of the Mediterranean and the north, his emphasis is always on the differences of climate, between warm and cold, in other words south and north, and not east and west. And furthermore, although according to him the south is all in all superior to the north (*Méthode*, p. 108), it is the north that usually conquers the south (ibid., p. 76; cf. above, p. 38). In our own time (1943) J. Huizinga (*Lo scempio del mondo* [Milan-Rome, 1948], p. 17) is once again surprised to note that the antithesis between north and south (cold and warmth: the basis of the climatic theories) is considerably less striking than that between east and west (dualism of civilization).

246. *Philosophie der Geschichte*, ed. Lasson, I, 232–33; and cf. below, p. 433.

247. *La Nouvelle-Espagne*, I, 184; IV, 115.

248. D. Forbes, *The Liberal Anglican Idea of History* (Cambridge, 1952), pp. 83–84.

historiographical myth.[249] The Saint-Simonian Michel Chevalier assures us that the march to the West is a "general law" of civilization, with the scepter passing on each time into hands more worthy to wield it;[250] and Tocqueville refers quite clearly to the movement of Europe toward America and the Americans toward the Pacific.[251]

The German poet Augustus von Platen, of liberal and therefore anti-czarist tendencies, has his Columbus tell the exiled and departing Napoleon: "Sail westward . . . for westward flies world history."[252] And the English poet Clough concludes his poem "Say not the struggle nought availeth" with the line "But Westward look the land is bright," a line quoted and immortalized in Winston Churchill's historic radio address to the English people on 27 April 1941. A similar image presented itself to Julius Froebel, who in 1849 saw Europe on the threshhold of twilight and darkness, "but in the West a new day dawns already."[253]

In the first half of the nineteenth century there were repeated prophecies from Germans, Tyrolese, and Danes on the coming supremacy of America,[254] while Miss Martineau in England and Alexandre Dumas and others in France foresaw the shifting of the center of civilization to North America.[255] In Italy, Aleardo Aleardi lifted his hymn of praise to man, the "immortal pilgrim," panting along beneath his burden of glory and grief:

> . . . e par che il suo governi
> Sul viaggio del Sol. In Oriente
> Nato, adulto risté sulle latine
> E le celtiche terre; e forse accenna
> Vecchio, sull'ala di fumanti prue
> Di valicare un giorno il mansueto

249. For the first two, see below, pp. 346–52. For Mme de Staël (1809, 1817), see G. Ticknor, *Life, Letters and Journals* (Boston, 1909), I, 133, and J. Christopher Herold, *Mistress to an Age: A Life of Madame de Staël* (Indianapolis–New York, 1958), pp. 384, 470.

250. *Lettres sur l'Amérique du Nord* (Paris, 1836), I, iii; II, 401–05; and again thirty years later, *Rapports du Jury International: Exposition Universelle de 1867 à Paris*, I, dxiv–dxvi, quoted in Sumner, op. cit., in epigraph.

251. On the exploitation of this geographico-historical "law" on the part of the North Americans to justify first the occupation of the West, and then the annexation of even more remote "western" territories, Hawaii, the Philippines (and today quite possibly the intervention in Vietnam), see Weinberg, op. cit., pp. 215–17, 260, 276. The wildest theoretician of this politico-solar myth was (1846) a misguided follower of Humboldt, William Gilpin (see Boorstin, *The National Experience*, pp. 232–33).

252. *Colombos Geist*, 1818, in *Platens Werke*, ed. G. W. Wolff and V. Schweizer (Leipzig-Vienna, n.d., but 1895), I, 13. Platen himself was thinking of emigrating to the United States at this time: ibid., I, xviii–xix.

253. Quoted by Curcio, op. cit., II, 711.

254. See the comments of H. Gollwitzer, *Europabild und Europagedanke* (Munich, 1951) on E. L. Posselt (1796), p. 81; on August Wilhelm Schlegel (1813), p. 191; on Gervinus (1853), p. 383; on Joseph Ennemoser (ca. 1850), pp. 356, 448, n. 19; and on C. F. von Schmidt-Phiseldeck (1820), pp. 242–44, who thereby earned the praise of the *American Quarterly Review* (1831) and the mockery of Mrs. Frances Trollope, *Domestic Manners of the Americans* (1832; New York ed., 1949), pp. 324–25. On Schmidt-Phiseldeck, see also Fabian, op. cit., pp. 94–96.

255. See René Remond, *Les Etats-Unis devant l'opinion française, 1815–52* (Paris, 1962), p. 822, n. 129.

Atlantico, e posar su le novelle
Care al tramonto piagge americane.[256]

In this same period Gioberti is found attempting to restore but in fact managing only to destroy the ancient thesis with his assertion that "the geographical law governing human civilization . . . consists in the inter-woven dialectics of two mutually opposed forces, one of which is a current from east to west and the other a countercurrent from the latter to the former, like the ebb and flow and the contrasting currents which carry the sea back and forth. We are the east for America, which is our west," and thus "a future Europe, greener and more fruitful than that which is past," which one day perhaps "continuing the westward course of the sun of civilization" will cross "the Chinese rampart and the unwelcoming shores of Japan," to bring "Christianity and Gentility to that great Asiatic world." Then Asia "will become a second Europe through young America."

This then is the "current," flowing constantly from east to west. But what of the "countercurrent"? Gioberti produces two examples: the first is "the countercurrent of European civilization toward the countries of the Levant," so that soon Asia "will have to give way to the uncon-trollable tide of two contrary currents from east and west"; the second, a much more interesting case for our purposes, "although less heeded, is the countercurrent of the New toward the Old World; so that one can truthfully say that just as America came out of Europe, so now modern Europe is growing closer to America." The most obvious aspect of this countercurrent is the flow of political ideas, which from America (i.e., the United States) spread to England, France, "and more or less to the other parts" of Europe, heading it irresistibly toward republican forms of government. Just as Franklin and Washington involuntarily promoted and "ratified" the Revolution of '89, so the '48 Revolution was helped along by the writings in praise of American democracy of two such conservatives as Botta and Tocqueville.[257]

Gioberti's attempts to dialectalize the heliodromic theory is interesting even though (or precisely because) it ends up, as we have already noted, by robbing it of all explicatory or organizational value, and in a certain sense both completes it and nullifies it. But the accent is always on the movement from east to west, on the "current" without which there could

256. ". . . and seems to govern his own steps in accordance with the path of the Sun. Born in the East, reaching adulthood in the Latin and Celtic lands, and in old age perhaps bidding fair to cross the meek Atlantic on the wings of smoking prows and alight on the new American shores beloved of the setting sun": *Le prime storie*, 1857, ed. Verona, 1858, p. 41. Could the "smoking prows" be steamships? But even for them the Atlantic could hardly be called "meek.". . .

257. V. Gioberti, *Del rinnovamento civile d'Italia* (1815; Bari ed., 1911), II, 248–51; III, 80. On the ideological link between the American Revolution and the French Revolution, cf. also ibid., II, 254; III, 64.

be no "countercurrent," on the "challenge" that allows the "response." The east is still "the land of origins,"[258] the "cradle of every art both learned and pleasant."[259] And America is almost forgotten when Gioberti fixes his gaze on the relations (still those of "current" and "countercurrent") between Europe and the east and pronounces that "in this mutual ebb and flow between two parts of our hemisphere [i.e., the Old World] there resides the progress of civilization from remotest times up to our own day."[260]

Gioberti's contemporary, Lasaulx, more simplistic in approach and perhaps for that reason more popular than the Italian, repeats that the tide of civilization moves from east to west, like the great tropical currents and like the apparent parabola of the sun, heading for the New World, for America, so that Asia's fate will one day fall to Europe.[261] And again in our own time, while an anthropologist is struck by humanity's "unconscious belief that the direction of the sun's movement is positive, and the opposite direction negative," and the westward path is the path of "accomplishment,"[262] the Mexican philosopher Antonio Caso sees in the heliodromic thesis (1922) an unfailing promise of a new and glorious Latin American civilization,[263] and a Latin American sociologist discovers (1947) in the timeworn theme the sole possibility of unifying world history.[264]

So the idea certainly bore fruit; but when the heliodromic theory was first formulated in the seventeenth century, and presented in political and utilitarian terms, its immediate barrenness led to its neglect in favor of other more grandiose and more traditional conceptions of the fate of

258. Ibid., III, 165.
259. Ibid., pp. 208–09.
260. Ibid.
261. Ernst von Lasaulx, *Neuer Versuch einer alten auf die Wahrheit der Tatsachen gegründeten Philosophie der Geschichte* (1856, rpt. Munich, 1952), pp. 109–10, 169. The mystically inclined Lasaulx, as is well known, mixes Hegel and Schelling with Görres (but cf. below, chap. 7, n. 407). For him, besides the authors quoted in the 1952 reprint, see Humboldt's letter to Varnhagen von Ense (7 February 1857) and Varnhagen's strongly critical reply (9 February 1857); R. Flint, *La philosophie de l'histoire en Allemagne* (Paris, 1878), pp. 375–88; Gollwitzer, op. cit., pp. 361–68; and Stephen J. Tonsor, "The Historical Morphology of Ernst von Lasaulx," *Journal of the History of Ideas*, 25, no. 3 (July–Sept. 1964), pp. 374–92, esp. 385, 390, with many bibliographical references. His considerable influence on Burckhardt is well known (see Ernst Schulin, *Die weltgeschichtliche Erfassung des Orients bei Hegel und Ranke* [Göttingen, 1958], p. 298), although Burckhardt rejects him as an empty philosophizer (*Weltgeschichtliche Betrachtungen* [1868–71; ed. R. Marx, Leipzig: 1935], pp. 6–7, 330–32).
262. C. Lévi-Strauss, *Tristes tropiques*, p. 102.
263. Juan Hernandez Luna, "Antonio Caso y el Porvenir de América Latina," *Cuadernos Americanos* (Mexico), 6 (1947), no. 3, pp. 123–30. See above, p. 142, and below, pp. 524–25.
264. V. Domingo Bouilly, "El Camino de Occidente — Proposición de un criterio sobre historia universal," *Cuadernos Americanos*, 6, no. 6 (1947), pp. 116–41. See also the editorial in the *Times Literary Supplement* of 28 November 1952, and the recent modification (in fact Giobertian trivilization) of the thesis at the hands of C. Northcote Parkinson, who sees in universal history "a cycle of alternating ascendancy between East and West" producing "a piston drive of decay and expansion" (*East and West* [New York, 1963]).

humanity. There is of course no trace of the westward course of empire in the theologian Bossuet. Up to the time of its transformation into the theory of the spirits of peoples, each in turn guiding the fate of humanity, this thesis of the solar course of history remained no more than an embryo — mere expedient oratory.

XIII. MLLE PHLIPON AND HER SCHOOLFRIEND

Not all of de Pauw's critics expressed their feelings in public, like Pernety and La Douceur. The comments of Mlle Phlipon were private and almost confidential, or certainly much more so than Galiani's letter to Mme d'Epinay, but they are of considerable interest, because they show us how de Pauw could arouse readers who were not even particularly concerned with the problem of the Americas and who were totally unqualified in the fields of zoology and geophysics.

Mlle Manon Phlipon was a young Parisienne, a gay and sensitive soul, pretty and pugnacious. She was to go down in history as Mme Roland, whose stormy political career culminated in heroically borne imprisonment and eventual execution. But she was only twenty-two when in 1776 she read the *Recherches sur les Américains,* and as was her custom wrote to her schoolfriend Mlle Henriette Cannet about it, giving a lengthy account of her impressions. These impressions were lively and at first mainly favorable. De Pauw is a "wise" man, cultured, industrious, erudite: "His reasoning seems sound, his conjectures likely,"[265] though his love of system may have led him to rather farfetched conclusions. To Manon, for example, it is not totally obvious "that the Americans are as degenerate and brutalized as he claims." But she agrees with him entirely in doubting the existence of giants in Patagonia. And one fact is certain — that the discovery of America revealed a continent "more savage and less inhabited" than all the others; "an unhealthy land, covered with woods and swamps; with enormous reptiles and small quadrupeds"; and but few people, scattered and lacking culture, except the usual Mexicans and Peruvians: "That is what one sees, that is what is shown and what constitutes the phenomenon that demands an explanation." But what explanation? Here too Mlle Manon accepts de Pauw's (or rather Buffon's) reply: "This land had undergone, at some time later than our own continent, a revolution caused by the waters."

So what is it that the shy young thing cannot agree with? Why, with de Pauw's suggestions of a physiological explanation of the Americans' degeneration, with this impotence and insensibility that he attributes to the natives of the New World. Not that Mlle Phlipon is shocked. She

---

265. Other eulogies in the letter of 16 July 1776, *Lettres de Madame Roland* (ed. Perroud, Paris, 1913–15), I, 440 (passage missing in the Dauban edition).

has read much worse than this and would be more likely to blush at being suspected of a lack of unquenchable curiosity or at having her bold and reckless logic doubted. Now, she says, does not de Pauw write that the American women used on their consorts "certain drugs whose effect was to remedy their natural indolence"?[266] Well then, Manon persists, this must mean that the women at least were not so frigid! But how can there possibly be such a difference between the sexes, if men and women live in the same climate? Mlle Phlipon wrinkles her nose with learned disapproval: "I find in this a contradiction which shocks me and makes me begin to doubt." De Pauw argued from the feebleness of the men, his genteel reader from the eroticism of the women. *Arcades ambo,* and tarred with the same brush.

But the Prussian *philosophe* can quote an impressive array of supporting authorities. Where will Manon find hers? Who will be *her* witnesses when she presents the case against her adversary? By a stroke of good luck — "imagine what joy" — a certain M. de Sainte-Lette was in Paris just then, who was a retired colonial administrator just returned from Pondicherry, but who had previously spent fourteen years in Louisiana and who furthermore was the good friend and mentor of de Pauw's aspiring critic. An atheist and humanitarian, a lover of reform and good literature, Sainte-Lette had acquired great influence over the young Mlle Phlipon.[267] And he had had close acquaintance with the savages, had dealt with them, and had had them accompany him in his travels. He was just the person she needed to gag de Pauw. And indeed he told her how the savages in general were good-looking, tall and well built; they were not completely smooth skinned (less hirsute than the Europeans, true, but this was because they removed the hair from their skin out of cleanliness);[268] they loved their wives and would not dream of offering them to travelers. The young girls, it is true, did what they wanted: the little

---

266. René Doumic (*Etudes sur la littérature française,* II [Paris, 1913], p. 81) is struck by the immodesty of these remarks and does not seem to recognize their origin in de Pauw. See below, chap. 5, n. 365. Baron Lahontan had already (1703) noted without any particular amazement that among the savages of North America "the men are as indifferent as the girls are passionate" (op. cit., pp. 115, 219, 223). But even before Mlle Phlipon made use of it the contrast had served as polemical argument for the abbé Roubaud: "Why would the American female be as ardent as M. de P. paints her, if the male were as cold as he imagines?" (*Histoire,* XIII, 153).

267. At that time she definitely preferred him to M. Roland. On Sainte-Lette, see the *Lettres . . . de Madame Roland (Mademoiselle Phlipon) aux demoiselles Cannet,* ed. C. A. Dauban (Paris, 1867), passim, and esp. I, 326–28, 346–48, 426–28, 431–33, 438, 442–43, or, better, the Perroud edition, I, 378–81, 383–85, etc. (see the index of names); *Mémoires de Mme Roland,* ed. Cl. Perroud (Paris, 1905), II, 4, 226–28, 237–38; M. Clemenceau-Jacquemarie, *Vie de Madame Roland* (Paris, 1929), I, 42, 44, 52–54; Edith Bernardin, *Les idées religieuses de Madame Roland* (Paris, 1933), pp. 41–42, 45–47, 61.

268. Here Mlle Phlipon wonders if this habit could over a long period have left them smooth skinned; and she concludes that it could not, because Jews and Arabs circumcise themselves "with the greatest assiduity," and yet continue to be born with prepuces (the argument and the reply were already present in de Pauw, *Recherches,* I, 40; II, 131–32). De Pauw's errors derive, she decides, "from having concluded from the particular to the general" (Dauban ed., I, 426; Perroud ed., I, 462).

female savages "enjoy the greatest liberty in the widest meaning of the term; they abandon themselves to whoever they please and this is called walking out" (somewhere beneath the outraged air one seems to detect a hint of envy, and it is quite clear that Sainte-Lette relishes being able to repeat these enormities to his young friend). But what was one to do? "The young men lead them off into the woods, and there they work things out together." Then "after a good walking out" they get married and become chaste and reserved. There is even a tribe, Manon repeats with an ambiguous shudder of horror, where adultery is punished by the law of talion, "which is to say that the woman is condemned to be married by all the men of the nation until death should ensue."[269] And then in the north there are other savages with such a refined sense of honor that they even punish people who gossip or make fun of others; furthermore they are so intelligent that they can draw topographical maps in charcoal in perfect scale![270]

In the days that followed (August 1776) the conversations continued, sometimes lasting hours at a time. Manon never tired of interrogating the friendly old skeptic who knew the Americans so well—and who like Othello with Desdemona was no doubt delighted to find such an ardent and responsive listener. The cumulative result of his information was the piecemeal destruction of de Pauw's entire picture. Are the American men degenerate? . . . On the contrary, M. de Sainte-Lette saw them and could only conclude that they were "the finest shoots that Nature has produced." Even the native women are fresh and handsome "except that their hips are too wide." They have pale peach complexions, and skin so soft and fine that it betrays the slightest blush. In short even a blind man would fall in love with them, and, Manon insinuates maliciously, "I do believe that M. de Sainte-Lette, with his excellent eyesight, found them very much to his liking."

Only the animals are left. It is true that the quadrupeds are smaller and the reptiles and insects enormous. But it is not true that European animals degenerate in the climate of America. Some of them, like the pigs and oxen, actually improve. Nor do dogs lose their bark in America; sometimes the wind makes them a little hoarse, but not for long. And the vigorous bark of the dogs of Santo Domingo still echoes in M. de

---

269. Dauban ed., I, 427; Perroud ed., I, 462. On the redskins' famous prematrimonial promiscuity, resulting in frequent abortions, and their conjugal chastity, see also J. F. Smith (op. cit., I, 94–95), of whom Jefferson wrote that he "saw every thing thro' the medium of strong prejudice" (letter of 16 August 1786, in *Papers*, X, 262–63). See also the travelers' accounts in Blanke, op. cit., pp. 267–68, and Forster, *Werke*, I, 207 ("an unmarried girl can favor many lovers . . . but as soon as they marry . . .").
270. Dauban ed., I, 423–28; Perroud ed., I, 460–63; map-making natives (1608) also occur in L. Wright, *The Elizabethans' America*, p. 185. On the soft and indolent life in the Antilles (slaves, idleness, ignorance, parties), see an earlier letter of 1773, Dauban ed., I, 129–30; Perroud ed., I, 141.

Sainte Lette's ears. As for the plants, the subject does not even bear discussion. Louisiana is an earthly paradise.[271]

So much for de Pauw, it seemed. But some authorities are more easily defeated than forgotten. Reminders of the *Recherches sur les Américains* bob up again in a piece Mlle Phlipon wrote that same year (1776) but which actually remained unpublished until 1933.[272] And when a few months later, in October, the young lady read the *Recherches sur les Egyptiens et les Chinois,* her brain began to "boil like molten wax" and the summary she made of it for her friends was so lengthy and wordy — she herself was aware of having "a chatterbox of a pen" — that not even her long-suffering correspondents read it, and the publishers of her letters have thought it best to leave it out completely.[273] But there was one unexpected result of her enthusiasm, in that the innocent Henriette in her turn immediately read the *Recherches sur les Américains* and forthwith confided to her friend that it left her grieved, saddened, and disheartened.

Manon seems to feel somewhat responsible for her friend's confusion. She writes to remind Henriette of her reservations and objections. She denies that the savage is necessarily unhappy. But she makes the very fair comment that if she herself still clung to the religious principles to which Henriette paid homage (instead of being, as she was, a total unbeliever) de Pauw's suggestion would have been a severe blow to her faith in the goodness of creation and the lofty destiny of man. One must grow "wise," and in so doing submit silently and serenely "to the irreversible laws of nature and necessity."

But the kindhearted young lady realizes at once how little these highflown sentiments will be likely to calm Henriette, and she goes on to protest that she has no intention of undermining anyone's faith, adding almost apologetically: "If I had directed your reading I would not have given you M. de Pauw nor anything like him." But now that the harm is done she is quick to offer the remedy. Bossuet, Fénelon? Not any more. Something else is needed: "Since you have reached this point, I invite you to read and meditate on the Discourse of Jean-Jacques Rousseau on the origins of inequality among men," the famous discourse which exalts the virtues of the savages. It is an antidote that cannot fail: "It is full of sinew and sap."[274]

---

271. Dauban ed., I, 431–33; Perroud ed., I, 381, 440, 456, 460–63. According to Bernardin, op. cit., pp. 73–83, the reading of de Pauw and other describers of exotic customs (Raynal, etc.) acted as a decisive anti-Christian influence on the moral and religious ideas of Mlle Phlipon.

272. Bernardin, op. cit., pp. 169, 171–72.

273. Dauban ed., I, 456, 463, 466; Perroud ed., I, xiv, n. 3, 515n., 522–23, 525 (and cf. Perroud, in a note to his edition of the *Mémoires,* II, 195). On the "chatterbox of a pen," see Dauban ed., I, 87; Perroud ed., I, 107.

274. Dauban ed., II, 163–64 (*"de feu et de nerf"*); Perroud ed., I, 473–74; cf. H. Buffenoir, *Le prestige de J. -J. Rousseau* (Paris, 1909), pp. 128–29.

This episode makes it clear that Manon did not find it easy to get de Pauw out of her mind. She read him again in 1781,[275] and this reading too must have left a deep impression on her, since there are references to it even in the *Mémoires* she wrote in prison.[276] But the most convincing proof of de Pauw's influence on her came a few months later, in January 1777. At that time she was preparing a paper, for the Academy of Besançon, on "How the education of women could contribute to making men better," and in it she included a sentence which was a straightforward summary of de Pauw. One of the most surprising spectacles of the New World, she says, has been "the misfortune and vices resulting from the brute and stupid indifference of the human race toward those [i.e., the women] who should sweeten it." There were savages who were "more degenerate than the others, . . . incapable of virtue because they could not be reached by the sentiment which makes it blossom,"[277] and these savages were fierce, cruel, and lazy. In her letters she had denied the frigidity of the savage, and now in her paper she uses it to throw more favorable light on the educative mission of woman.

Mme Roland was never too concerned with the internal coherence of her ideas; she was far too easily swayed by first impressions, too easily taken with some shocking paradox, some effective cliché or apparently penetrating objection. Thus she took no particular trouble to reconcile whatever she had borrowed from de Pauw with her unfailing enthusiasm for the North American revolutionaries. In this "new and active" America, she says, the seeds of the most stupendous revolutions are steadily ripening; man, climate, environment, and products offer a thousand "diverse and interesting" pictures.[278] In 1777 she looked forward to the liberty of America "as a just revenge of Natural law, which has so frequently been violated in this unhappy continent so little suited to such ravages,"[279] and again in 1788, when the United States was already victorious and free, she wrote enviously: "Let us bless America."[280]

275. Letter of 15 November 1781 to Roland, cited by Perroud in his edition of the *Mémoires*, II, 195n.

276. Where she writes that about 1776–77 she was reading the preachers, Bossuet, Fléchier, Bourdaloue, Massillon: "There was nothing more amusing than seeing them lined up there on my little bookshelves with de Paw, Raynal, and the *Système de la Nature*" (*Mémoires*, II, 195). Again in 1777 she looked forward with ambiguous de Pauwism to the triumph of the insurgents of America, "this unhappy continent so little made for being so" (letter of 4 October 1777, in *Lettres*, Perroud ed., II, 144). Cf. also Monglond, op. cit., II, 186–97.

277. I have made some small corrections in the obviously corrupt text given by Faugère in the appendix to his edition of the *Mémoires* (Paris, 1864, II, 345) and by Dauban in the appendix to the *Lettres* (II, 463). A little further on Mlle Phlipon derides the poets' Golden Age and the philosophers' "state of nature," which perhaps never existed (Faugère, II, 348; Dauban, II, 465)—but which she was using at precisely that time to try to console her friend Henriette. On this discourse see also *Lettres*, Dauban ed., II, 194, 301–02; Perroud ed., II, 13, 84, 97, 151, 183, 269.

278. 1 July 1777, in *Lettres*, Dauban ed., II, 126; Perroud ed., II, 92; cf. ibid., Dauban ed., II, 173–75, 232–33; Perroud ed., II, 132–33, 184.

279. Letter of 4 October 1777: Dauban ed., II, 187; Perroud ed., II, 144: more echoes of de Pauw?

280. Letter to Bosc, 1 October 1788, in *Lettres*, Dauban ed., II, 571.

And finally in 1790 she mentioned with a sigh that she and her husband would already have left for America a while back if he had not been so old; but at least they had less reason to grieve over the "promised land" now that they could hope for a real homeland in France.[281]

So de Pauw's acid has lost its bite. The "unhealthy land" has turned into a "promised land." The stately figure of George Washington overshadows the unmanned and cowardly savage. A radiant and star-spangled republic rises upon the infested marshlands.

XIV. VOLTAIRE, FREDERICK OF PRUSSIA, AND DE PAUW'S SECOND *RECHERCHES*

Voltaire's reaction to de Pauw was rather more superficial and personal, and therefore of somewhat less import than the replies of Machiavelli's drily witty disciple or the tender and irrepressible Mlle Phlipon.

At first Voltaire greeted de Pauw enthusiastically as a "true scholar," who thought with his head and was not too easily seduced by the moderns (for moderns read Rousseau) and who could hold his own against the missionaries and their followers like Pernety.[282] But when de Pauw began to criticize the Chinese he soon lost the sympathy of the unshakably sinophile patriarch.

The *Recherches philosophiques sur les Egyptiens et les Chinois* came out five years after the publication of the *Recherches sur les Américains*. The work is in two volumes, and its point of departure is the refutation of the thesis expounded by de Guignes[283] suggesting that the Chinese were a "colony" of the ancient Egyptians; however from there it goes on to show that there is no trace whatever of Egyptian influence on the arts, customs, religions, or institutions of China, that in fact one can find abso-

---

281. Letter to Brissot (early months of 1790) in C. A. de Sainte-Beuve, *Portraits de femmes* (Paris, 1882), p. 170. Thomas Paine's influence on Mme Roland's ideas is well known. For an analysis of the numerous North American inspirations of the principal Girondists, see Lucy M. Gidney, *L'influence des Etats-Unis d'Amérique sur Brissot, Condorcet et Mme Roland* (Paris, 1930: emphasis on Brissot). Three days before her execution Mme Roland was still thinking of going to America (see *Mémoires*, Faugère ed., II, 44).

282. *Fragment sur l'histoire générale* (1773), art. II, *De la Chine* (in *Oeuvres*, Beuchot ed., XXIX, 228–30). De Pauw is cited approvingly again a little further on, XXIX, 234.

283. Joseph de Guignes, *Mémoire dans lequel on prouve que les Chinois sont une colonie Egyptienne* (Paris, 1759–60). On the polemic it provoked, see Jurgis Baltrušaitis, *La quête d'Isis* (Paris, 1967), pp. 226–32. The thesis had been put forward first by Athanasius Kircher (1654), discussed and partially accepted by Horn (*Arca Noae*, 1666, pp. 53–54), and taken up again about 1700, despite the recurrent confutations, by Thomas Burnet (cf. Tuveson, op. cit., p. 163; a passage I have not been able to find in the Latin edition of the *Archaeologiae*) and then by the learned Daniel Huet (1716) and the academician Mairan (1759). It was discussed at length about 1760–70 (see the objections of Delisle de Sales, *Philosophie de la Nature*, I, 115–23n); accepted in substance by the abbé Roubaud (*Histoire*, I, 329–47); rejected as totally absurd by Forster (*Werke*, I, 595); fancifully elaborated by Giuseppe Ferrari, who found between Egypt and China a "correlation of contrasts" and a hostile "communication" through the medium of the wars with the peoples in between, the Arabs, Persians, and Tartars (!) (*La Chine et l'Europe* [Paris, 1867; 2d ed., 1868], see esp. pp. 195–203); and then periodically reexhumed at least up until 1905! (see H. Cordier, *Histoire générale de la Chine* [Paris, 1920], I, 11–25).

lutely no point of contact between the two civilizations. But in the course of this quite reasonable argument de Pauw never misses a chance to vent his sarcasm on both these peoples, and particularly the Chinese, so that in the end the work amounts to nothing less than the total demolition of the conventional image of the "virtuous mandarin," who in the political and literary conventions of the century was as cherished a figure as the "noble savage."[284]

The two works have much in common; they have the same stylistic tricks, they indulge in the same polemics against the missionaries and their overoptimistic reports, and they are further linked by the frequent references to the first in the second work. But what binds them most closely is the common attitude of scornful superiority toward exotic or primitive peoples and civilizations, and the pleasure de Pauw takes in stressing whatever will shock the honest and inexperienced reader. Thus it was inevitable that the Egyptians and Chinese too should be sucked into the polemic on the Americans, and that their defenders, all Europeans naturally (while the Americans soon found champions among the fellow citizens of Washington and the scholars of Spanish America), should avail themselves of arguments suited to the deeper demands of the new historiography.

The thesis of de Guignes which de Pauw attacked so furiously is doubtless critically untenable.[285] But when one remembers that the ancient

284. "No writer has ever yet spoken so badly of them [the Chinese] as the author of the *Recherches philosophiques sur les Egyptiens et les Chinois*. He is M. Pauw, to whom we are already indebted for an excellent work on the Americans" (Grimm, Diderot, etc., *Correspondance,* Tourneux ed. [Paris, 1877–82], X, 298). For the attacks on the sinophile Raynal, see Feugère, op. cit., XXII, 444.

285. Which no doubt earned de Pauw's second work, so much more learned and less amusing and scandalous than the first, a better acceptance among scholars: Jacobi devoted one of his earliest writings to it, a long review in three Hamann-like letters to the *Deutsche Merkur* (1773; see the *Werke,* ed. F. Roth [Leipzig, 1825], VI, 265–344). One can detect in the letters Jacobi's delight in seeing de Pauw demolish one of the idols of the *Aufklärung*. Jacobi praises his talents (270–71) and style (281–82), notes his agreement with Winckelmann (313–14) and declares that he will abstain from criticisms because they would take too much space, because some of them would be prohibited by the peace-loving *Merkur* (343–44), and because de Guignes has already produced some and will yet produce more. He, for his part, although he holds the heretical opinion that discord is the salt of the earth, sticks to the favorable judgment expressed in the first letter, which however occasionally became a "prophetic satire" (344; this last letter at least seemed to Jacobi worthy of preservation: *Werke,* ed. cit., VI, v). Kant himself read and recommended the second *Recherches* to one of his correspondents (12 August 1777; *Briefwechsel,* Akad.-Ausgabe, X, 210). Later on Herder, for whom see below, chap. 5, n. 560, and C. F. Dupuis, in his lengthy *Origine de tous les cultes* (1796) quote it frequently; Goethe admires it (see below, pp. 369–70); the penetrating and erudite A. H. L. Heeren, *Ideen ueber die Politik, den Verkehr und den Handel der vornehmsten Völker der alten Welt,* vol. V (Göttingen, 1826), pp. 139, 396, respectfully discusses two conjectures of this "recent writer" on the Egyptians. Even those such as Scherer who took up the task of refuting de Pauw and defending de Guignes describe him as an elegant writer, though insubstantial (Jean Benoit Scherer, *Recherches historiques et géographiques sur le Nouveau-Monde* [Paris, 1777], pp. xii and 218–65). And even on the obelisk that was erected to his memory at Xanten in 1811 (see above, chap. 3, n. 1), de Pauw is described as "Author of the Researches on the Egyptians, the Chinese and the Greeks" and only last of all "the Americans." On the relatively meager success of the work with the public, as shown by the small number of reprintings, see G. Beyerhaus, op. cit., pp. 478–87.

Greeks, beginning with Homer himself, had already been hailed as disciples of the Egyptians,[286] it should not seem too surprising that the Chinese too, these more recent models of perfect wisdom, were considered to be descended at least spiritually from the Nilotic civilization. And in fact the basic motivation of the thesis – the desire to ensure the continuity of world history and to maintain its Mediterranean center of gravity – was not really so unreasonable. By this system the Chinese took their place in the contemporary historical world of the Europeans. If one could succeed in establishing their descent from a civilization that meshed with the biblicoclassical system, then serious chronological difficulties could be avoided and the notion of the unity of the human race satisfied.[287]

The idea of "colonies" functioning as "graftings" of civilizations was a familiar one to the scholars and widely used in their attempted syntheses. One has only to think of Vico's coastal and overseas "heroic colonies," which he saw as the origin of the "transmigration of peoples." And had not Fénelon already stated that the peoples of Asia and Egypt were the most ancient and civilized of all peoples? "We have here as it were the source of colonies," he had written, and although he arrived at the final conclusion that China was a colony of the Babylonians, he had still candidly confessed: "The Chinese seem to me to be quite similar to the Egyptians."[288] Did de Pauw remember this? The opening and closing words of his book say precisely the opposite: "Never did two peoples have less in common than the Egyptians and the Chinese."[289]

It was about this same time, 1773–74, that Herder took over Fénelon's unitary approach in his campaign against the *Aufklärung*, going even so far as to repeat with an air of mystery its summarizing formula: "China is but Egypt's copy; just think about it and reach your own conclusions."[290] But he never went on to seek out the ancient links of colony and

286. Cf. Tuveson, op. cit., pp. 211–12. "The Athenians were also an Egyptian colony" in the opinion (20 June 1789) of Lord Monboddo, who in his major work, *The Origin and Progress of Language* (1773–92) maintained that all European culture derived from Egypt (Knight, op. cit., pp. 34, 270).

287. See in fact how de Guignes, op. cit., pp. 78–79, offers his theory in defense of the Pentateuch. On Chinese chronology, used in the eighteenth century in support of Egyptian chronology, and incompatible with the biblical version, cf. A. Momigliano, "La nuova storia romana di G. B. Vico," *Rivista storica italiana*, 77 (1965), no. 4, p. 780.

288. *Dialogues des Morts, Confucius et Socrate*, ed. Lutetia, pp. 170, 176–78. On the problems of colonies, see also above, n. 182, and Annoni, op. cit., pp. 80–94.

289. *Recherches sur les Egyptiens*, II, 320; cf. the opening: "never was there a more ill-founded supposition" than that of their contact (ibid., I, xiii).

290. *Werke*, ed. Suphan, V, 489 (quoted in A. Gerbi, *La politica del Romanticismo* [Bari, 1932], p. 127n.); see also below, p. 285. Hegel (*Philosophie der Geschichte*, ed. cit., I, 186, 203–04) later stresses the "Asiaticness" of Egypt, a great river valley like those of China and India, and different from every other part of Africa; but without the least reference to any transmission of civilization, in fact "history begins with the empire of China" (ibid., p. 275). For more recent Marxist-type parallels based on the "Oriental" features of modern Egypt and its social structure, see Pierre Vidal-Naquet, "Histoire et idéologie: Karl Wittfogel et le concept de 'Mode de production asiatique'," *Annales*, 19, no. 3 (May–June 1964), pp. 531–49, esp. 547–48.

influence, preferring instead to follow where his religiosity and innermost organic sense of history led him and to come down decisively on the side of the Near East of the patriarchs at the expense of the far-distant China.[291] The Egyptians were marginal to sacred history and thus worth little more than the Confucians. So de Pauw's objections fell on willing ears. Herder quotes the *Recherches sur les Egyptiens et les Chinois*[292] with interest and approval, and again in the *Ideen* of 1784 he dwells on the comparison between China and Egypt, generally at the expense of the former;[293] which does not however prevent him from criticizing and slandering the Egyptians too when in 1787 he reaches the third part of the work.[294]

Voltaire does not go quite so far. At first (1773) he had agreed with de Pauw's thesis, replying negatively to the question he had set himself of *Whether the Egyptians peopled China*.[295] But on 5 September 1774, he was writing huffily to the Count d'Argental that it was ridiculous to ascribe the *Lettres d'un théologien* "to a German called de Pauw, the author of certain rash conjectures on the Americans and the Chinese in an obscure and involved style."[296] And the following year he girded himself for the task of disproving de Pauw's theses on the Chinese, the Indians and the Egyptians, although he was (predictably) still willing enough to accept de Pauw's firm denial of any dependence of the first of these on the latter. In a letter to Frederick II he informed him that "I shall shortly be so bold as to place at your feet certain somewhat scientific, somewhat ridiculous letters, which I took the liberty of writing to M. Pauw about his Chinese, Egyptians, and Indians."[297] But he feels no animosity toward the king of Prussia's protégé and adds cautiously: "I do not know M. Pauw at all. My letters are from a little Benedictine [the *Lettres Chinoises, Indiennes et Tartares à M. de Pauw* are attributed by Voltaire to a Benedictine] quite different from M. Pernetti. I find M. Pauw a very capable man, full of wit and imagination; a little systematic, in truth, but someone capable of amusing and instructing one."[298]

The "little work of Saint Benedict," which Voltaire was hoping to complete in a month or two, actually came out early in 1776,[299] but con-

291. Rouché, op. cit., p. 43.

292. *Werke,* ed. Suphan, VI, xx, 368, 395, 525; XIV, 33; *Ideen,* XI, 5; trans. Tandel, II, 225.

293. See for example *Ideen,* XI, 1; XII, 5; ed. cit., II, 200–01, 283; cf. also Rouché, op. cit., pp. 276, 344–45, 432, 436–38.

294. Rouché, op. cit., pp. 408–11, 549.

295. *Fragment sur l'histoire générale,* art. IV (*Oeuvres complètes,* ed. Moland, XXIX, 234).

296. *Oeuvres,* ed. cit., XLIX, 74. The *Lettres* were by Condorcet, but Voltaire had let it be believed that he was the author (Beyerhaus, op. cit., p. 487).

297. Hamann too refers to these letters as being addressed "to Mr. Pow": *Hierophantische Briefe,* III, in *Sämtliche Werke,* ed. cit., III, 143.

298. Letter of 21 December 1775 in *Oeuvres,* ed. cit., XLIX, 458.

299. Ibid., XXIX, 451–98; cf. XLIX, 545, 559.

tains scarcely even a passing reference to de Pauw's writings on America.[300] On 7 April 1776 Frederick wrote to inform Voltaire that he had read his "curious letters," adding: "Abbé Pauw is quite proud of having the letters addressed to him." Indeed, the abbé believes he is basically in agreement with Voltaire, since he too admires the Chinese and would criticize only their barbarous custom of exposing their newborn children, their "inveterate roguery," and the atrocious tortures they practice.

But de Pauw cannot altogether overcome his belief in European superiority, and he goes on to say that there are worse abuses in China than in our own continent; and when a Mandarin arrives in Holland and turns out to be ignorant and stupid "abbé Pauw rejoices at the news." But Frederick shrewdly points out to him that Voltaire is only using the Chinese like Tacitus did the Germans, as models or examples to rebuke the corruptions of Europe: "Make mandarins of your encyclopedists, and you will be well governed."[301]

These anecdotic minutiae show how limited was Voltaire's real interest in the problem of America, and how both de Pauw and Buffon only attracted him for their usefulness in the furtherance of strictly European polemics.

XV. BUFFON'S NEW POSITION: AMERICA AS IMMATURE BUT THE AMERICAN STRONG AND HANDSOME

Buffon's case is very different. Feeling himself unable to accept de Pauw's slanders on the American continent and, above all, the extravagant conclusions he drew therefrom, Buffon modified his original position, which, as we have already described, oscillated between nature as immature and nature as degenerate. When he saw de Pauw's scandal-loving extremism describing all America as degenerate, Buffon abandoned his own timid suggestions of degeneracy and in the *Epoques de la nature* (1777) repeated emphatically that America was a young world and in many ways immature: "Nature, *far from being degenerate through old age there,* is on the contrary recently born and has never existed there with the same force, the same active power as in the northern countries."[302] The living species and above all the terrestrial animals

---

300. Ibid., XXIX, 460.

301. Letter of Frederick to Voltaire, in Voltaire, *Oeuvres*, ed. cit., XLIX, 577–78. "These supposed *literati* [the mandarins]," de Pauw had written (*Recherches sur les Egyptiens*, II, 166), "are persons of extreme ignorance." See also de Pauw's "Amérique," p. 344a. Cf. G. Chinard, *L'Amérique et le rêve exotique dans la littérature française au XVIIᵉ et au XVIIIᵉ siècle* (Paris, 1913), p. 371. Other details of the controversy can be found in the articles of Beyerhaus, op. cit., pp. 478–90, and in Church, op. cit., pp. 181–82.

302. *Oeuvres complètes*, V, 225. De Pauw had attacked Buffon on this point (see above, p. 53), and in the article "Amérique" had repeated (1776): "It is not possible . . . to admit a recent organization of matter in the hemisphere opposite to ours" (p. 347b).

were established there much later than in the north "and perhaps the difference in time is more than four or five thousand years."[303]

The continent is still so young that the waters prevail yet in large areas, like Amazonia, Guiana, and Canada: "In casting one's eyes over the map of this country one sees that the waters have spread there on all sides, that there are a great number of lakes and very large rivers, which shows that these lands are new."[304] The oldest parts are the mountainous areas, like Peru and Mexico; and in fact, Buffon adds, with a truly amazing compression of geological epochs into historical periods, these are the only regions where men formed societies.[305] But these same societies prove that the continent was only recently inhabited: because they were numerically small (America "was very sparsely and *consequently* very recently inhabited at the time of the arrival of the Spaniards");[306] because there are very few monuments remaining "of the so-called greatness of these peoples" (an involuntary echo of de Pauw's contempt?); and because the very traditions of these peoples confirm it: "The Peruvians counted only twelve kings, of which the first had begun to civilize them; thus it is a mere three hundred years or less since they ceased to be complete savages like the others."[307]

One might notice in passing that the exaggerations of Buffon's argument—a completely uncivilized pre-Inca Peru—are in precise opposition to de Pauw's equally farfetched suggestion, that of Peru of the Incas being absolutely uncultured and primitive. The two impassioned adversaries competed in their slanders of one or the other phase of Peru's past. This is not the only example of a country's reputation suffering through the impetuous rivalry of two zealous scholars. Peru has perhaps suffered more than any other country in the bitter and unceasing campaign of "defamation" by Spaniards against the *indios,* by *libertadores* against *godos,* by indigenists against Creoles, by everybody against everybody.

Before the Incas, then, the Peruvians were "savages," like all the other Americans. . . . Yes, savages, says Buffon, but neither weak nor degenerate. When de Pauw tries to tell us that the Americans were weak and buckled under the slightest weight, is he really unaware that the Caribs, the Iroquois, the Hurons, the Floridians, the Mexicans, the Tlascaltecans, and the Peruvians, etc., were men of nerve and muscle and very coura-

303. *Oeuvres complètes.* V, 224. The smallness of this figure is a better proof than any refutation of the fragility of the basis of Buffon's theory.
304. Ibid.. I, 285.
305. Ibid. Cf.: "Mexico and Peru can be regarded as the oldest lands of this continent, and the longest populated, since they are the highest, and the only ones where men have been found gathered in society" (ibid., XII, 337). Cf. above, n. 118.
306. *Histoire de l'homme, Variété de l'espèce humaine,* in *Oeuvres complètes,* XII, 333.
307. Ibid. Cf. above, n. 118.

geous despite the inferiority of their weapons? Is he really unaware that in South America, where all the animals are pygmies, there are men who are giants? "For it cannot be doubted that men have been encountered in South America in great numbers [in this "sparsely populated" continent are only the giants numerous?!] all taller, solider, broader, and stronger than all other men on earth."[308] Buffon's insistence on a clear distinction between man and the other animals also derives from and underlines his aversion for all classificatory systems; such systems, in fact, always ended up by setting man too close to the monkey.[309]

Nothing can stop Buffon once he gets started on his panegyric of the American male: neither the contradictions with his preceding thesis, nor de Pauw's complacency,[310] nor even certain unarguable facts which he now quickly relegates to the level of local accidents:

It is true that there are certain countries in South America, especially in the lower part of the continent, such as Guiana, the Amazon, the low countries on the isthmus, etc., where the natives of the country seem to be less robust than the Europeans, but this is due to local and particular causes.[311]

In all the rest of America the men, unlike the animals,[312] whatever de Pauw says, have no reason to envy the proud Europeans:

In general all the inhabitants of North America and those of the higher countries in South America, such as New Mexico, Peru, Chile, etc., were men perhaps less active but no less robust than the Europeans.[313]

Previous to de Pauw's onslaught the American native had been described by Buffon as impotent and feeble. He recovers his powers and his youth – at least his historical if not his physiological youth – only after de Pauw has roundly slandered him. And of his former condition all that remains is a certain contemplative laziness: he is . . . "less active."

308. *Oeuvres complètes,* V, 264; XII, 434. Earlier Buffon had written cautiously of the Patagonians: "If these giants exist, it is in small numbers" (quoted by Pernety, *Examen,* II, xvi). Is it in reaction to de Pauw that they multiply into a "great number"?

309. J. Piveteau, *La pensée religieuse de Buffon,* in L. Bertin, *Buffon,* p. 129.

310. "He (M. Pauw) claims that the Americans in general are degenerate men; that it is not easy to conceive that beings just created can be in a state of decrepitude or caducity, and that that is the state of the Americans" (*Oeuvres complètes,* XII, 436–37).

311. Ibid., p. 438; cf. B. Fay, *L'esprit,* p. 14. The previous year a German who had read and makes use of Buffon had asserted that the southern colonies were inhabited by a degenerate race, lacking energy and robustness (Christian Leiste, *Beschreibung des brittischen Amerika* [Wolfenbuttel, 1778], quoted by Doll, op. cit., p. 459). And still toward the end of the century this thesis was maintained by C. Meiners in the *Göttingisches historisches Magazin,* under the title "Ueber die Ausartung der Europäer in fremden Erdtheilen," with climatic arguments (ibid., pp. 469–70).

312. In this phase of his thought Buffon also returns to his favorite thesis that South America, "reduced to its own forces, gave birth only to animals feebler and smaller than those which came from the north to people our southern lands" (*Oeuvres complètes,* V, 222–23).

313. Ibid., XII, 439; cf. Villard, op. cit., pp. 334, 391–92, and Minguet, op. cit., pp. 374–75, n. 8, citing the *Additions à l'histoire de l'homme, Des Américains.*

The Second Phase
of the Dispute

I. THE POLEMIC EXPANDED AND UPLIFTED

WITH these refinements and modifications of Buffon's position the first phase of the polemic comes to a close. America and the Americans had found themselves sucked into a maelstrom of debate, trapped in the middle of its endless arguments on problems of zoological geography, ethnography, climatology, moral theology, and the philosophy of history; and with the coming of de Pauw they were thrust to the very depths of this vortex of doctrine and diatribe.

As Europe of the Enlightenment became fully aware of itself as a new civilization with its own distinct character and a universal, no longer quite simply Christian, mission, it realized too the necessity of finding a place in its schemes for the transoceanic world — this world that it had rescued from obscurity, on which it had already begun to set its mark, and which had almost no other connections apart from those with Europe; a world that had disappointed the hopes of its earliest panegyrists in the sixteenth century, but which now once more seemed to exemplify an ideal way of life, to give promise of a splendid future.

Such an optimistic vision seemed too good to be true, and this age of keen criticism and sharpened Europeistic self-esteem greeted it with doubt, denigration, and abuse. Crippling attacks were leveled at the entire physical nature of the new continent. But to stem the tide of insult, as it engulfed men and animals, the land, the flora, and the atmosphere, there arose from the depths of time the vision of history marching toward the west; and it was this that guaranteed the future of the New World and barred the way to the prophets of degeneration.

It was this same vision again which in its turn enriched the relationship between Europe and America by providing it with its own internal dialectic. America was Europe's offspring (as Asia and Africa obviously were not; as Oceania too would be, but on a so much smaller scale) — it

157

was both Europe and non-Europe—its geographical, physical, and soon even political antithesis. Thus, as Europe's heir, it could be entrusted with a mission that neither Asia nor Africa had ever been qualified to receive.

As the threads of the polemic are slowly disentangled one becomes aware then that its fundamental concern is a search for synthesis, a need to account for all parts of the world, both behind and beyond Europe, to bring within the reach of man's mind and understanding the entire world, and within that world to find Europe the most complete and richest part. Bodin had once given voice to his aspirations in rapt impatient jubilation; with the discovery of the Americas the world is complete: "All men are linked one to another and partake marvelously of the universal Republic, as if they formed but one same city";[1] now these very same ideas were reappearing, but this time as a critical notion, as a problem to be solved.

Yet it was an angrier and stormier historical climate in which they made their reappearance. The reborn and growing faith of the Europeans in their civilizing task came face to face with the burgeoning reputation of America, where the colonies were becoming restless for independence; and the reflected glow of this fiery political conflict lit up the scientific debate kindled by Buffon, giving it both an impassioned ardor and an interest of immediacy.[2] It was at this stage that the dispute began to attract the attention of men of superior intellect and culture, men with practical rather than merely cognitive interests. Never straying too far from its initial starting point, the debate then tackled the most heteroclite subjects, expanding as it passed from country to country and continent to continent, touching on all sorts of ancient and modern manias, provoking oblique objections and unexpected doubts, and occasionally lending its support to the most timeworn prejudices.

II. ROBERTSON AND THE VASTNESS AND POVERTY OF NATURE IN AMERICA

The work which made Buffon's and de Pauw's ideas known and indeed almost commonplace throughout Europe was William Robertson's highly successful *History of America* (1777). Fluent and elegant in its presentation, and published at a time when interest in America was at its height,[3] the book was immediately translated into a number of languages and was repeatedly reprinted right up into the middle of the nineteenth century. Even Humboldt considered it a classic, and in 1827 gave his encourage-

1. Bodin, op. cit., p. 298; cf. Zavala, *América*, p. 16.
2. See F. Chabod, "L'idea di Europa," pp. 31–32.
3. It was in 1776 that the United States declared its independence; and it was precisely the war following on that event that persuaded Robertson to publish his still incomplete work dealing with the discovery and the Spanish conquests (see preface).

ment to a new edition of it in French.[4] In that same year its harsh opinions on the redskins were still a subject of discussion in North America.[5] Many of the supporters and even more of the critics of the thesis of the telluric inferiority of America seem to know it only through the work of the Scottish historian.

Robertson was a thoroughgoing Voltairian in inspiration, solidly opposed to the Rousseauian thesis[6] and thus highly receptive to de Pauw's naturalistic pessimism. This then was the state of mind in which, having already described the birth of the European society of nations in his famous introduction to the *History of the Reign of Charles V,* he turned his attention to the overseas acquisitions of that same monarch. The discovery and conquest of the Americas, the character, customs, and institutions of its inhabitants, were arguments that could not be treated as a mere "episode" in the story of the emperor.[7] Thus the *History of America* came into being as a digression from the *History of Charles V,* but his recognition of the far-reaching importance and historical worthiness of these regions was already implicit in his decision to make them the subject of an entirely separate work.

The first characteristic of the American continent is its vastness, its immense extent, greater than that of Europe, of Africa, and even of Asia.[8] Nature there set a huge imprint on everything: "Nature seems here to have carried on her operations with a bolder hand, and to have distinguished the features of this country by a peculiar magnificence." The mountains there are a third higher than the peak of Teneriffe, the highest point (so it was believed) in the Old World. The rivers are like seas and the lakes like landlocked oceans — which makes communications very much easier.

However — and here his reservations begin — "what most distinguishes America from other parts of the earth, is the peculiar temperature of her climate . . . *cold predominates.*" America is the cold continent. The latitudes which in other countries produce grapes and figs are here under

4. See the dedication and foreword to the French edition (trans. Suard and Morellet) prepared by De La Roquette and several times reprinted (5th ed., Paris, 1848). This version is filled out with notes taken from Jefferson, Clavigero, Humboldt, etc., intended to correct Robertson's "errors" (mostly anti-American). For other editions — including one in Armenian, Trieste, 1784 — see Zavala, *América*, p. 233. On its popularity in Germany, see Harold von Hofe, "Jacobi, Wieland and the New World," *Monatshefte* (Madison, Wis.), 49, no. 4 (May 1957), p. 187. In the United States Robertson's history was even published in installments, like a popular novel, in one hundred and fifty issues of a Boston weekly (Bernstein, *Origins,* p. 63, n. 43).

5. Pearce, *The Savages,* pp. 89–91, who illustrates its derivation from the Scots school but does not go into its judgment on the North American savages.

6. See Fueter, op. cit., p. 368, and Meinecke, op. cit., pp. 255–61, and esp. p. 260, for an analysis of Robertson's attitude, completely unromantic in regard to primitive peoples and the infancy or youth of nations, but carefully attentive to the American Indians as examples of undeniable humanity.

7. See the preface to the *History of the Reign of the Emperor Charles V.*

8. *Sic,* in *The History of America* (London, 1777–78), I, 248; cf. below, n. 345.

snow for six months of the year. A perpetual frost grips the parallels corresponding to the most fertile regions of Europe. Even the tropics are lukewarm, because of cooling fogs and breezes.[9]

The "rude and indolent" inhabitants have done nothing to improve the land, which has thus become inhospitable and in fact almost everywhere unhealthy for the European, and strangely feeble in all that it produces:

The principle of life seems to have been less active and vigorous there, than in the ancient continent . . . the different species of animals peculiar to it are much fewer in proportion, than those of the other hemisphere. . . . Nature was not only less prolific in the New World, but she appears likewise to have been less vigorous in her productions. The animals originally belonging to this quarter of the globe appear to be of an inferior race, neither so robust, nor so fierce, as those of the other continent.

There are no wild beasts — the puma and the jaguar, Robertson assures us, are "inactive and timid animals" — and the animals that have come from Europe, the wolves, foxes, and deer, have become smaller or degenerated.[10]

These same climatic factors that proved hostile to the "nobler" animals have also favored the multiplication and monstrous development of reptiles and insects. The birds are a category apart. There are many of them, it is true, and some very large ones, like the condor, and some that are very beautiful with their brightly colored plumage, "but nature, satisfied with clothing them in this gay dress, has denied most of them that melody of sound, and variety of notes, which catch and delight the ear"[11] — almost like the producer of some musical comedy so happy with the beautiful costumes and other evident attractions of his chorus girls that he never stops to ask himself whether or not they can sing! The silence of the equatorial forest chills the traveler's heart.

9. Ibid., I, 252, 263 (and referring back to Buffon: I, 449 ff.). He is obviously ignorant of the climatic effects of the great sea currents, both Humboldt's and the Gulf Stream. Robertson explains America's coldness in terms of the absence of seas between the continent and the North Pole, and the east winds that are cooled as they cross the Atlantic and remain so over the forests, marshes, and Andes (ibid., I, 253–55). On the excellent climate and soil of Chile, ibid., II, 333–34.

10. Ibid., I, 259–61. The citations refer back to Buffon and some of the travelers who support his theory. A footnote admits that skeletons apparently belonging to elephants have been found in Ohio. And others in Siberia. But the elephant only lives in the tropics. So then? Robertson wriggles out of it à la de Pauw: "The more we contemplate the face of nature, and consider the variety of her productions, the more we must be satisfied that astonishing changes have been made in the terraqueous globe by convulsions and revolutions, of which no account is preserved in history" (n. xxxiv, ibid., I, 456–57). As for the degeneration of the domestic animals, in the South the cause must be climate, but in the northern colonies it seems more probably the result of a lack of proper care and sufficient forage (n. xxxv, ibid., I, 457–58).

11. Ibid., I, 262; for the reptiles, see also I, 325. On this contrast between "call" and "coloring" (which La Fontaine's crow should have remembered!), see John Robert Moore, "Goldsmith's Degenerate Song-birds: An Eighteenth-Century Fallacy in Ornithology," *Isis*, 96 (Spring 1943), vol. 34, pt. IV, p. 325. See also below, pp. 161 and 276.

III. GOLDSMITH'S SONGLESS BIRDS

Here again we have conflicting exaggerations. This exaggerated muteness was more or less the antithesis of what had been reported by Columbus, who thought he heard nightingales on Haiti,[12] and Vespucci, who had heard the forests of Brazil resound with whole choirs of brightly colored songsters. And there was even a Peruvian chronicler who had heard the feathered creatures intone their sweet melodies through the *via prepóstera*.[13] Hardly surprising that some people blocked up their ears whenever these birds gave forth.

The legend was carried on by the Jesuit missionaries. Again in the middle of the eighteenth century we find Muratori repeating that there exists in Paraguay "a tiny little bird . . . of tuneful song, not unlike the nightingale's."[14] And a few decades earlier the author of the *Relation des voyages de François Coréal aux Indes Occidentales* (1722) had written of the hummingbird "that its 'melodious song' is 'similar to that of a nightingale,'" when actually this little hummingbird's sound is produced by the whirring of its wings."[15]

Buffon had already remarked on this melodic deficiency on the part of the American avifauna and explained it as being the result of the cold wet climate, which was harmful to the sexual organs of the birds, and the harsh voices of the savages, which were all that the birds had to imitate, leaving them thus deprived of any more harmonious models and quite unaware of the possibilities of *bel canto*.[16] There is of course an element of truth in the whole thing, and it must have come as a shock to the European familiar with the nocturnal warblings of every little copse or the magic murmur of the Nibelung forest.[17] But at that time it was

12. See L. Olschki, *Storia letteraria delle scoperte geografiche* (Florence, 1937), pp. 11–21. And a recent art historian provides "ear-witness" confirmation: "The present writer heard the nightingale sing outside his window, in November, just as Columbus did" (E. W. Palm, *Los monumentos arquitectónicos de la Española* [Ciudad Trujillo, 1955], I, 11), while H. M. Jones (*Strange New World*, p. 14) flatly affirms that the nightingale "does not exist in the New World."

13. José Ignacio de Lecuanda, *Descripción geográfica de la ciudad y partido de Trujillo* (cited by R. Vargas Ugarte, *Historia del Peru—Fuentes* [Lima, 1945], p. 190, as *Descripción de los partidos de la intendencia de Trujillo;* see also Ventura Garcia Calderón, *Vale un Peru* (Brussels, 1939), p. 34.

14. *Il cristianesimo felice,* I, 21.

15. P. G. Adams, op. cit., p. 123; the origin of Lecuanda's fantasy?

16. For Buffon, see the passages quoted by J. Moore, op. cit., p. 326. Réaumur had made the same observation. Linnaeus had adopted vocal emissions as a criterion for the classification of the animals (Daudin, op. cit., p. 72n.)

17. We shall hear the laments of Chateaubriand, Lenau, and Leopardi (see below, pp. 352, 372, and 380). For Sheridan (1775) and Robert Graves (1941) see J. Moore, op. cit., p. 325. In his last novel, *Il secolo che muore* (written ca. 1871, pub. posthumously in 1885) F. D. Guerrazzi introduces a long episode in the United States, between Mississippi and Texas, abounding with birds "gorgeously arrayed in dazzling feathers; but cruel nature had denied them sweetness of song . . . and some mockingly imitated the human voice, whence the name mockingbird" (op. cit., Rome, 1885, IV, 260). Guerrazzi mentions Humboldt and Chateaubriand (ibid., II, 8, 353), treats American nature as "enormous, rather than great; fearful, not beautiful" (ibid., IV, 244) and refers also to "cowardly" leopards (ibid., IV, 318);

taken as a characteristic mark of the mournful and toneless quality of all American nature, as a poetic symbol of its expressive impotency. Where the lion lost its mane the very least that could happen to a nightingale was to become raucous and strident.

In 1743 the doctor and botanist Pierre Barrère lamented that the solemn quiet of the tropical night was broken solely by the shrieks of the wild beasts or the "displeasing noises" of the birds;[18] La Condamine found hardly a single bird that sang pleasantly in all America: "They are remarkable mainly for the brilliance and diversity of color of their plumage."[19] The abbé Charles César Robin states: "In these somber forests, I heard no more singing"; and of Virginia's so-called nightingale he says sadly: "Even if Nature has treated it better in the matter of plumage, she has not by any means given it such a melodious voice."[20] And Molina mentions that "travelers have generally conceded to the birds of America both beauty and splendor of raiment, but denied them grace and harmony of song. This opinion is commonly accepted by the naturalists," but it is denied by Clavigero for the torrid zone, and contrary to fact for the southern temperate zone.[21] Mme du Boccage too, though overflowing with enthusiasm for the Americas, admitted in 1756 that the splendid birds of those countries had raucous voices: "Their savage song has less flattering sounds / Than the sweet nightingale and the tender thrush."[22] Chateaubriand seems to recall these lines when he is arguing with the old explorers who had found the birds multicolored but mute, and writes that there are lots of little birds in America "whose *song* is as *sweet* as that of our *thrushes*."[23] And the strange American birds of Heine's *Vitzluputzli* (1851) are "glowing with color," but at the same time "taciturn."[24]

Even Thomas Jefferson, the most unshakable champion of a robust

---

but his opinions on the Americas are generically anti-Spanish (see II, 92–93) or anti-Catholic and anti-clerical (IV, 342), and he resorts to sarcasm to tell us that in the past America "was one of the scales of the balance of the universe" (an echo of Canning? see above, chap. 4, n. 117). And only recently a sober Swiss naturalist bewailed the fact that in Peru the natives rarely sang "and from the birds too one fails to hear any sweet voices" (A. Heim, *Wunderland Peru, Naturerlebnisse* [Berne, 1948], p. 172).

18. *Nouvelle relation de la France Equinoxiale* (Paris, 1743), quoted by Zavala, *América,* p. 187.

19. *Relation,* p. 472.

20. *Nouveau voyage dans l'Amérique septentrionale en l'année 1781* . . . (Philadelphia [Paris], 1782), pp. 51–52.

21. *Saggio sulla storia naturale del Chile* (Bologna, 1782; 2d ed., 1810), p. 214.

22. *La Colombiade,* canto I; ed. cit., II, 24, on the word of Charlevoix. Clavigero mentions, among the slanderers of the song of the American birds, "two modern Italians, the author of a certain meta-physico-political dissertation *on the proportion of talents, and of their use,* who committed many blunders on America, and the Author of some nice little Indian tales, in one of which he has an American bird discoursing with a nightingale": they reveal themselves to be "as learned in certain speculative matters as they are ignorant in the things of America" (*Storia antica del Messico,* ed. cit., IV, 135).

23. *Voyage en Amérique,* ed. Richard Switzer (Paris, 1964), p. 213.

24. Heinrich Heine, *Vitzliputzli,* Präludium, in *Sämtliche Werke,* ed. O. Walzel (Leipzig, 1911–15), III, 58–59.

American nature, surrendered to the attraction of the ambiguous analogy between the ornithological and lyrical mutism of the New World. Near Vaucluse — echoing with Petrarchan melodies — he hears a chorus of nightingales break out in rich and marvelous song; he finds their voices stronger and fuller than those on the banks of the Seine (in fact see below, n. 406) and though he has only just mentioned the famous mockingbirds he pauses in wistful reflection: "It explains to me another circumstance, why there never was a poet North of the Alps [Heavens! and Shakespeare?] and why there never will be one. A poet is as much the creature of climate as an orange or palm tree. What a bird the nightingale would be in the climates of America! We must colonize him thither," so that America too, he seems to be suggesting, might have poets to rival them![25] But it is one of these longed-for poets himself, Henry Wadsworth Longfellow, who regrets that "for Americans skylarks and nightingales 'only warble in books'."[26] And in our own day G. A. Borgese has deplored the fact that the nightingale has never been able to acclimatize itself in America and that its "earthbound brothers," the poets, are never really at home there.[27]

But the dumbness of American avian life is most abundantly illustrated and consequently most widely known, at least in English speaking countries, through the poetry and prose of the celebrated author of the *Vicar of Wakefield,* Oliver Goldsmith. In his well-known poem or versesermon, *The Deserted Village* (published in 1769), which describes the depopulation of the countryside and the scourge of luxury, Georgia is portrayed in somber de Pauwian shades: the land is parched and gloomy, infested with deadly scorpions, voiceless bats and rattlesnakes, with ferocious tigers waiting to pounce, and even more ferocious Indians. There is no glimmer of comfort for whosoever should wander into those dense forests, "those matted woods where birds forget to sing."

This singular lament is repeated here and there by Goldsmith in his vast *History of the Earth and Animated Nature* (eight volumes, 1774) which enjoyed such long-lasting and unlikely success.[28] In point of fact the good Goldsmith knew nothing about America; in another of his history books he was to include an imaginary battle between Montezuma and Alexander the Great and to amuse his readers with repetitions of the legends of Patagonian giants, preaching monkeys, and fluently talkative nightingales. But in this popular treatise on physical geography and

25. Letter to William Short, 21 May 1787; *Papers,* XI, 372. Cf. Martin, op. cit., p. 60.
26. Quoted in Strout, op. cit., p. 77.
27. "L'usignolo di Pereyra," *Corriere della Sera,* 26 February 1952.
28. Jefferson, who even admired Goldsmith's *History of Greece* (letter to P. Carr, 19 August 1785, in *Papers,* VIII, 407), possessed a copy of the 1795 ed. (*Catalogue of the Library,* I, 467); cf. below, chap. 8, nn. 285, 349.

descriptive zoology the honest Oliver remained punctiliously faithful to Buffon[29] and informed his reader in passing that "the birds of the torrid zone are very bright and vivid in their colors; but they have screaming voices, or are totally silent."[30] He attached no particular importance to this item and even less did he trouble himself to set up a general theory of the superiority of the Old World over the New. His concern is purely narrative; he points out some curious detail and passes on. On the same page, for instance, he mentions quite disinterestedly that according to some people the swallows migrate in winter, while according to others they take refuge like bats within hollow trees, "or even sink into the deepest lakes, and find security for the winter season by remaining there in clusters at the bottom."[31] Dr. Johnson had paradoxically preferred Goldsmith to Robertson but was still not far from the truth when he concluded with one of his savage witticisms: "He is now writing a Natural History, and will make it as entertaining as a Persian Tale."[32]

Further on Goldsmith relates the marvelous feats of the American mockingbird that can imitate any other creature of the forest from the wolf to the crow (creatures that are hardly celebrated for the melodiousness of their vocal products) and which as it settles on the chimneys of the American planters' houses continues to pour out throughout the night "the sweetest and most various notes of any bird whatsoever." If this be true, Goldsmith concludes impartially, one must admit that "the deficiency of most other song-birds in that country is made up by

29. Buffon's lasting influence on Goldsmith is well known: see for example Pitman, op. cit., esp. pp. 37, 44, 46; A. L. Sells, *Les sources françaises de Goldsmith* (Paris, 1924), p. 177–84; W. Lynskey, "The Scientific Sources of Goldsmith's *Animated Nature*," *Studies in Philology*, 40 (1943), pp. 33–57, esp. pp. 35–36, 44, 51–52; the latter, however, who shows Goldsmith's able use not only of other compilers and popularizers but also of first-class scientific sources, excludes from her examination the principal source, Buffon (see p. 35, n. 10). The Englishman utilized the *Histoire naturelle* as his prime source and derived therefrom, among other items, the thesis that the lesser dimensions of an animal imply its inferiority, at least in a relative sense. Unaware of the precedents, Lynskey defines the thesis (see above, pp. 15–22) as an "arbitrary . . . bold assumption" and notes with a certain wonder that "both Buffon and Goldsmith make it." Another derivation from Buffon is the very singular and privileged position that Goldsmith too concedes to man: see W. Lynskey, "Chain of Being," pp. 363–74, rectified by A. O. Lovejoy, "Goldsmith and the Chain of Being," *Journal of the History of Ideas*, 7 (1946), pp. 91–98.
30. Op. cit., pt. III, bk. I, chap. 2 (ed. Fullarton, London-Edinburgh, n.d., II, 12).
31. This curious theory, which can be traced back even to Aristotle, was first formulated explicitly by Olaus Magnus (1555), attracted William Harvey, Linnaeus, Pehr Kalm, and Gilbert White, was accepted even by the scornful Samuel Johnson (1768: *Life*, ed. cit., I, 347: cf. 1773, ibid. I, 478), echoes still in Joseph Priestley (1800) and the great Cuvier (1817), and is perpetuated in the popular belief in the winter lethargy of swallows: see Richard Garnett, "Defoe and the Swallows," *Times Literary Supplement*, 13 February 1969, pp. 161–62; cf. ibid., 20 February 1969, p. 186; 27 February 1969, p. 211; 6 March 1969, p. 242; 3 April 1969; Julian Jaynes, "The Problem of Animate Motion in the XIII Century," *Journal of the History of Ideas*, 31, no. 2 (1970), p. 222.
32. 30 April 1773, in Boswell, *Life*, I, 469–70. See also I, 467–69; II, 119, and the other references, and J. Boswell, *London Journal, 1762–63* (London, 1951), p. 285. Goldsmith himself honestly admits that "professed naturalists will, no doubt, find it [the *Animated Nature*] superficial" (Pitman, op. cit., p. 15). And in fact, again toward the middle of the nineteenth century, its illustrations of whales and narwhals were ridiculed by the experts, who found them more suggestive of a truncated sow and a hippogriff (H. Melville, *Moby Dick*, chap. 55; Modern Library ed., p. 265).

this bird alone."[33] But in the depths of the woods the profoundest silence reigns, broken if at all only by the echoing hiss of serpents.[34] Even the cuckoo, whose unchanging note evokes all the sweetness of summer, and which has also, the facetious naturalist reminds us, "a more ludicrous association . . . which, however, we that are bachelors need be in no pain about" — the cuckoo of Brazil succeeds only in making "a most horrible noise in the forests."[35]

Goldsmith shows no malice toward the Americans, save for the slightly negative feeling which is the corollary of the delight he finds in his own most perfect part of the world,[36] nor does he show any desire to solve scientific problems or propound startling paradoxes. His sole aim is to entertain the reader, and if he stresses whatever is surprising it is only to hold the reader's attention, not to turn all his ideas upside down. But in so doing he could not help showering the Americans with a few of the current slanders. He repeated Buffon's derogatory conclusions on American quadrupeds.[37] He was familiar with Juan and Ulloa, but he also possessed Raynal,[38] and although he gazes longingly on the simplicity of the rustic he was no less scornful than his friend and protector Dr. Johnson of the savages' crudity, their ridiculous superstitions, and their cowardly terror: "What a poor contemptible being is the naked savage!"[39]

IV. ROBERTSON AND THE AMERICAN NATIVE

Robertson's approach is considerably more subtle. When he reaches the American natives he is obviously reluctant to treat them with the same casual disdain as de Pauw. He studies them with great care, devoting one huge quarto page after another to the examination of their

---

33. Op. cit., pt. III, bk. VI, chap. 2 (ed. cit., II, 127). On the artificial contrast between the melodious mockingbird and all the other voiceless or strident birds, see J. Moore, op. cit., p. 325, and Frederika Bremer, *La vie de famille dans le Nouveau Monde* (1853; Paris ed., n.d.), I, 282, 313, 368, 380; II, 372, etc. This feathered songster had also been mentioned by the abbé Joseph de Laporte in his *Voyageur français* (1765–95), which earned him (1773) the ridicule of the *Allgemeine Deutsche Bibliothek* (Reed, op. cit., p. 62). It is referred to again as "America's nightingale" by Eugène A. Vail, *De la littérature et des hommes de lettres des Etats-Unis d'Amérique* (Paris, 1841), p. 381. And Thoreau (1840) laments its rarity in New England: John Aldrich Christie, *Thoreau as World Traveler* (New York, 1965), p. 89.
34. Op. cit., pt. III, bk, VI, chap. 1, and pt. III, bk, III, chap. 3 (ed. cit., II, 34, 121).
35. Ibid., pt. III, bk, V, chap. 6 (ed. cit., II, 103–04).
36. Singularly naïve comments in Pitman, op. cit., p. 122.
37. Op. cit., pt. II, bk. I, chap. 15 (ed. cit., I, 265).
38. On the former, see Pitman, op. cit., p. 50; on the latter, Sells, op. cit., p. 216. He also owned some *Recherches philosophiques*, 2 vols., 1773, which Sells identifies with Bonnet's work, *Recherches philosophiques sur les preuves du Christianisme* (op. cit., p. 212), but which could be de Pauw's. His friend and Robertson's, Edward Gibbon, owned all of de Pauw's works, including two editions of the one on the Egyptians and Chinese (*The Library of Edward Gibbon*, ed. G. Keynes [London, 1940], p. 215).
39. Cf. Pitman, op. cit., p. 133. On the inconsistency of his "philosophy," see Fairchild, op. cit., pp. 64–69, 329–30. On the savage, see the earlier *Letters from a Citizen of the World*, 1762, no. CXIV; and on the American, *Animated Nature*, pt. II, bk. I, chap. 11 (ed. cit., I, 235–36).

origins, their physical and moral qualities, their domestic customs, their arts of peace and war, their religions and customs; and when he has finished he heaves a sigh of relief at having completed this "laborious delineation" of their character.[40] He has been prosaic and prolix, he admits, but this is "one of the most important as well as instructive researches, which can occupy the philosopher or historian."[41]

The Greek and Roman philosophers and historians, our teachers in this as in every other field, never had a chance to meet any real savages: "In America, man appears under the rudest form in which we can conceive of him to subsist."[42] Likewise the early explorers were so ignorant and so prejudiced that they never thought to make any serious study of the natives. Almost two centuries were to pass before the "attention of the philosophers" became focused on them. But these philosophers were too impatient to reach their conclusions and thus confused or neglected the facts.

Struck with the appearance of degeneracy in the human species throughout the New World . . . some authors of great name [i.e., Buffon] have maintained, that this part of the globe had but lately emerged from the sea . . . and that its inhabitants, lately called into existence, and still at the beginning of their career, were unworthy to be compared with the people of a more ancient and improved continent. Others [de Pauw] have imagined, that, under the influence of an unkindly climate, which checks and enervates the principle of life, man never attained in America the perfection which belongs to his nature, but remained an animal of an inferior order, defective in the vigor of his bodily frame, and destitute of sensibility, as well of force, in the operations of his mind.

Yet others (Rousseau) have seen in the savages the most perfect models of the human race. And all these contradictory theories have been put forward with equal conviction and defended with unusual gifts of mind and tongue. The problem is therefore far from easy. One should proceed "with caution."[43]

And in fact Robertson proceeds with great caution, distinguishing between the savages of the tropics and those of the temperate zones, between primitive tribes and organized monarchies, between the general influence of climate and other factors not reducible to climate. He collects and evaluates a large body of testimony and rejects prodigies, monsters, and other peculiarities not sufficiently supported by certain and concordant proof.[44]

40. Op. cit., I, 414.
41. Ibid., p. 281.
42. Ibid., p. 282.
43. Ibid., pp. 286–87. Note that Robertson puts de Pauw on the same level as Rousseau and Buffon. He is however in marked disagreement with de Pauw when he maintains that America was thickly inhabited before the slaughter and cruelty of the Spaniards depopulated it (II, 345–51), but he rejects Las Casas as an "exaggerator" (II, 461; cf. below, n. 91).
44. Thus he denies the existence of the Patagonian giants, citing the careful collection of texts examined and rejected by de Pauw (ibid., I, 304, 465). Robertson also accepts the thesis of the American

He prepares questionnaires on the American native (Is he robust and vigorous? Is he naturally beardless? Is he deficient in amorous sentiment, etc.) and the same for the debated points relative to the animals (Have European animals improved or degenerated in America? Of those that are common to both continents, in which continent are they larger in size?), then he despatches these questionnaires to travelers and missionaries, to officials and inhabitants of the colonies, and collects up and stores away their replies.[45]

But all these excellent intentions and sound principles and diligent interrogations are, alas, not enough. Dr. Robertson is altogether lacking in sympathy for the subject of his researches, and although, as we have seen, he realizes the fundamental importance of the problem of the native, he never succeeds in approaching him with his heart, never feels his desires and fears; his interest is always cold, reserved, academic. So that all in all even Oviedo's savage ends up more alive than Robertson's; Oviedo was severe in his judgments, but understanding, a man quite capable of clapping the despised Indian good-naturedly on the shoulder. The same goes for de Pauw—a cruel observer, but amused and occasionally, albeit only in deference to fashion, compassionate; whereas Robertson's American is described dispassionately and humorlessly, without scorn, but with no hope either.

Was eighteenth-century historiography thus so limited as to be incapable of recognizing the worthiness of the primitive, trusting blindly instead in the proud myth of Progress? One would think not; for one thing there were other historiographers of the period, most notably Voltaire, Robertson's ideological mentor, who recognized and described in vivid terms certain essential characteristics of the naïve and naked savage, of the savage in all of us; and for another the very idea of Progress is almost totally absent from the *History of America*. Robertson's work shows civilization and barbarism face to face, in blatant opposition, each fixed within its own abstract formulas, with no point of contact, with no gradual transformation from one to the other. Nature makes men equal, and their possibilities of reaching perfection "seem" everywhere the same; but if we study the savage, we must agree "that the intellectual powers of man must be extremely limited in their operations."[46]

---

origin of syphilis, enough in itself to counterbalance all America's "benefits" (I, 307). De Pauw is also cited on I, 302, 328, 355, 458, 465.

45. Still unpublished, but examined by R. A. Humphreys, *William Robertson and His "History of America"* (London, 1954), pp. 6–7n., 20.

46. Op cit., I, 401–02. The Mexicans and the Peruvians are an exception, and the former are even conceded the quality of being "enterprising" (II, 18), but when compared with the peoples of the Old World "neither . . . will be entitled to rank with those nations which merit the name of civilized"; they too have remained in the "infancy of civil life" (II, 268–69). The vaunted works of art of the Mexicans are inferior to the roughest Egyptian sculptures: "the scrawls of children delineate objects almost as

The crude naïveté of this conviction of Europe's enormous superiority leads Robertson into a curious disregard for petty details, or what seem petty details to him, and one is reminded of a similar attitude in Buffon. For Robertson it would be "beneath the dignity of history" to give a minutely detailed description of the natives' dwellings, quite apart from being useless for his research![47] As for their ideas on religion, it should suffice to see whether they believe in the existence of God and the immortality of the soul; much work has in fact been wasted on this sort of inquiry: "The article of religion in P. Lafitau's *Moeurs des Sauvages,* extends to 347 tedious pages in quarto."[48] After all, religion "occupies no considerable place in the thoughts of a savage."[49]

His clearly expressed disdain for detail is not limited to particulars that in fact seem to be of considerable importance, such as questions of the homes and beliefs of the Indian; it is equally evident in many other areas of this "objective" study of the American. Thus it is indeed confirmed that he possesses all the attributes of humanity, but on two occasions he is summarily condemned as "a melancholy animal."[50] And though he is abundantly endowed with moral qualities, he lacks the one which ranks as the supreme virtue for an illuminist and a Scotsman: alacrity in his work, or the keen desire to achieve something useful and improve his own lot. The outstanding characteristic of the American is a constitutional apathy, due partly to the climate and partly to the ease with which he may exist without great effort; but it is a quality that is by now innate and indelible. The Americans are agile rather than robust and incapable under any circumstances of a sustained effort. Las Casas says so (and we know why: see above, p. 70), and what he says is confirmed by many other early chroniclers. Even as animals, then, "they resembled beasts of prey, rather than animals formed for labor."[51] True, they had no domestic animals to help them, but that was their fault; they never managed to domesticate the animals which would have been adaptable thereto, such as the bison. The savage in his natural state "is the enemy of other animals, not their superior. He wastes and destroys, but knows not how to multiply or to govern them."[52]

The American natives' real domestic animals were their women, whom

accurately" (II, 286–87); and those of the Peruvians, albeit superior, prove that they too "were not advanced beyond the infancy of arts" (II, 322; cf. II, 385–86).

47. Ibid., I, 373.

48. Ibid., pp. 380, 487.

49. Ibid., II, 302, 307.

50. Ibid., I, 398, 408.

51. Ibid., p. 290. In support of his thesis, so different from that offered "by very respectable authors," Robertson cites Bouguer, Juan and Ulloa, and La Condamine (I, 467).

52. Ibid., I, 332–33: confirming his nature of being a beast of prey. Buffon and Raynal are cited (the latter mentioned with high praise also on II, 300, 490–91). On America's lack of typically southern animals, such as camels, cows, horses, etc., see ibid., I, 272. For the llama ("its service . . . was not very extensive!") and the few animals domesticated by the Mexicans, see ibid., II, 268–69, 318.

they treated exactly like beasts of burden, and whom they still humiliate and despise, since these men are quite without any sentiment of love. Apathetic in this realm too, or rather torpid "to an amazing degree," blind to the charms of beauty, deaf to all domestic affection, their frigidity astonished even the austerest missionaries.[53] They are smooth skinned, indeed entirely without hair in every part of the body. And "truly [as a *femme du monde* was to say a century later], truly a man without a moustache is no longer a man."[54] This characteristic of meager virile ardor (although the Rev. Dr. Robertson does not linger over such a scabrous subject) reaffirms the judgment passed on the Americans for their meager will to work; they are "like children," and with childlike frivolity they leave the work they have begun, become distracted, and waste time in whimsical pursuits, or fall prey to complete idleness or give themselves up to sports, dancing, games, and drunkenness.[55] Even the most civilized of the American natives, those of Peru, have always been and still are weak, unwarlike, and unmanly: "Their feeble spirits, relaxed in lifeless inaction, seem hardly capable of any bold or manly exertion."[56] The Americans are children. For a rationalist, this was a verdict of guilty. Puerile was still a term of abuse in the mouths of those who worshiped a newly adult Reason and the steady glow of the lights by now all lit, dispelling all obscurity. But Diderot had already struck another note producing multiple reverberations: "the Tahitian brings us close to the origin of the world and the European to its old age,"[57] and already the first romantics, Hamann and Herder, had called attention to the primitive, basic, and unshaped powers in all peoples and were thus bringing about a revision or rather complete reversal of that eighteenth-century viewpoint which had seen the primitive as merely imperfect, immature, almost abortive (Buffon), or else, as with de Pauw's paradoxical contradiction, downright degenerate.

V. THE EXPLORERS OF POLYNESIA: JAMES COOK AND GEORGE FORSTER, HORACE WALPOLE AND LORD KAMES

England was not the most propitious terrain for these new ideas. The revolt of the colonies had led to a certain lingering resentment against the

---

53. Ibid., I, 292–93, 405–06, 482. The harsh necessities of his existence apparently prevent the savage, like the wretched laborer of the civilized nations, from cultivating the sentiments and passions of love. But this sociological explanation (I, 295 and II, 293) is contradicted by the observation (I, 326) that the easier it is for them to subsist the lazier and less enterprising the natives are. But in yet another place (I, 317) he states with despairing and contradictory insistence that the savage becomes more careless about providing for his needs, and more stolid and apathetic, in proportion to the increasing uncertainty and difficulty of the means he can find of satisfying those needs.

54. Guy de Maupassant, "La Moustache," 1883, in *Toine* (Paris, 1908), p. 60; cf. Robertson, *History of America*, I, 290.

55. Op. cit., passim, esp. I, 290, 315, 377–78: until the arrival of the Europeans, the women were even denied the satisfaction of getting drunk (I, 399–400).

56. Ibid., II, 324–25.

57. *Supplément au Voyage de Bougainville* (1772), ed. cit., p. 758.

Americans, while the industrial revolution convinced the proud citizenry of the "perfection" of their technical civilization. This very same period was also the era of the great voyages of discovery in the South Seas, whose reports were bringing to light savages even savager than the Americans and shifting the attention of the scholars and more learned public toward the tribes of Oceania.[58] It was Lord Monboddo who said that after three centuries of communication with the Americans, Europe could no longer hope to find there "people living in the natural state"; they should be sought instead in the barren wastes of the South Seas, still little frequented by European vessels.[59] And down there too the animals were smaller than those of the Old World, and the larger wild beasts were lacking completely: the only fierce animal is the native.[60] *"L'homme est, je vous l'avoue, un méchant animal!"*[61]

The accounts of Captain Cook's travels[62] reveal a considerable curiosity and even a certain sympathy with respect to the natives— Maori, Tahitian, Fijian, Vancouver Indian—but no idealization, in fact an emphatically realistic attitude that could only undermine the myth of the Noble Savage. There were of course repeated surreptitious revivals of this myth (the savage blessedly content with his natural state) and that of the romantic "primitive" (childishly restless, and destined to tread an eventful path on his progress toward civilization);[63] but the mental and figurative attitudes of neoclassicism, although they distort and overrefine the early image of the newfound Antipodes, are in the end themselves crushed beneath the weight of factual evidence, and dissolved in the prevailing current of scientific rigor. Hawkesworth, the first person to describe these journeys, was accused by some of having plagiarized and misunderstood Buffon and de Pauw, and by others of "immoral" crudity in his description of the manners and customs of the aborigines—which latter accusation apparently brought him to an untimely death![64] Poor Dr. Hawkesworth, so incautious in his pursuit

58. Just as in France the *Voyage autour du monde* (1771–72) of Bougainville (on whom see above, p. 128) attracted public attention to the Papuans and gave Diderot the stimulus for his famous *Supplément*, the extreme defense of the sanctity of all the instincts (without explicit reference but with frequent echoes from de Pauw: cf. for example what he says on "infibulation," ed. cit., p. 756, with de Pauw's *Recherches*, ed. cit., II, 139 ff.). But Bougainville, who spent his life fighting the English and took on board with him as chaplain our Americanophile friend Pernety (see above, p. 86) is much more sympathetically inclined toward the natives than the explorers serving under the orders of His Britannic Majesty.

59. B. Smith, op. cit., p. 91, n. 3.

60. *Sic,* John Barlow, *Encyclopedia Britannica,* 6th ed. (1823), s. v. "Australasia," quoted by B. Smith, op. cit., p. 203; cf. p. 253 (absence of animals useful to man).

61. Molière, *Tartuffe,* act V, sc. 6.

62. First voyage, 1768–71 (pub. 1773, edited by John Hawkesworth); second voyage, 1772–75 (pub. 1777); third voyage, 1776–80 (pub. 1784).

63. Ample documentation and acute comment in B. Smith, op. cit., esp. pp. 1–7, 251–52.

64. See *Encyclopedia Britannica,* 13th ed., s. v. "John Hawkesworth"; B. Smith, op. cit., pp. 86–87, 96, 126–27, and *The Voyages of Captain James Cook Round the World,* ed. Christopher Lloyd (London, 1949). See below, n. 73.

of Buffon and De Pauw that he fell an indirect victim of their thesis! George Forster, a German of Scots origin and Baltic upbringing, shows a much more complex attitude. He accompanied Cook on his second voyage, and in 1777[65] published a frank and highly colored account of it. In time this same Forster was to become the earliest and most influential teacher of the great Humboldt.[66]

Later, in the last tragic years of his brief existence, Forster took his place among the most convinced supporters of the French Revolution, but after sacrificing everything to it finished by denying it any moral justification. In very much the same way his first instinctive reaction to the savages of Polynesia was favorable,[67] but in his final judgment he reluctantly found he had to condemn them. The inhabitants of the Society Islands and Tahiti he finds at least classically handsome and happy in their innocence, but the American savages of Tierra del Fuego he considers brutalized.[68] He is openly contemptuous of Pernety, whom he describes as a writer with little regard for truth and totally inaccurate;[69] while Buffon is always spoken of enthusiastically (he also translated one volume of the *Histoire naturelle*), and for de Pauw, our "most learned canon," he has only the frankest admiration.[70] De Pauw's critical spirit (*Prüfungsgeist*) demolished a number of fantasies about America.

Thus Forster eloquently rejects Rousseau's thesis and reaffirms the superiority of life in civilized society over the "natural life" of the savage.[71] Not that this prevents him parading the customary humani-

65. George Forster, *A Voyage round the world, in His Britannic Majesty's Sloop "Resolution," commanded by Capt. James Cook during the years 1772, 3, 4 and 5*, 2 vols. (London, 1777); German translation, Berlin, 1778–80.

66. Forster was attracted to and influenced by Jacobi (ca. 1780), was a friend of William von Humboldt, but above all was friend and companion, on a journey through the Low Countries (1790), of Alexander von Humboldt, who always referred to him as his teacher and said that he had opened a new era of scientific travels, giving them the purpose of studying comparative ethnography and geography. "In George Forster we see in a certain sense the prefiguration of Alexander von Humboldt" (J. Löwenberg, in *Alexander von Humboldt, eine wissenschaftliche Biographie*, ed. by K. Bruhns [Leipzig, 1872], I, 95; cf. ibid., 94–108, 111–12, 382). Cf. Minguet, op. cit., 38n., 48, 71n., 333. On his sympathy for the American Revolution, see King, op. cit., pp. 54–56. On his activity during the French Revolution, see A. Chuquet, "Le révolutionnaire George Forster," in *Etudes d'histoire* (Paris, n.d.), I, 149–288; A. Stern, *Der Einfluss der Französischen Revolution auf das deutsche Geistesleben* (Stuttgart-Berlin, 1928), pp. 36–42; J. Droz, *L'Allemagne et la Révolution française* (Paris, 1949), pp. 187–216. For a general view, see the classic essay (1843) of Gottfried George Gervinus, *J. G. Forster*, in *Schriften zur Literatur*, ed. Gotthard Erler (Berlin, 1962), pp. 317–403, 515–17 (on his relations with Jacobi, pp. 238, 344n., etc.), Hermann Hettner, *Geschichte der deutschen Literatur im 18. Jahrhundert* (Leipzig, 1928), IV, 199–211; Doll, op. cit., pp. 471–72, and now Kurt Kersten, *Der Weltumsegler, Johann Georg Adam Forster, 1754–1794* (Berne, 1957), esp. pp. 38–42, and B. Smith, op. cit., esp. pp. 38–39, 62, 151.

67. On the Tahitians and the New Zealanders see *A Voyage round the World*, I, 321, 365–68; II, 109–12, 156–57, 480, etc.

68. Ibid., II, 606; cf. Gervinus, op. cit., p. 334.

69. Op. cit., II, 495, and esp. 515.

70. Ibid., I, 55, 435, 514; II, 412, 562; and in *Werke*, ed. cit., I, 67, 340, 382, 445–46, 850, 967; II, 122. This admiration for de Pauw on the part of the "great naturalist" Forster surprises and almost shocks Archbishop Moxo (see below, p. 300).

71. Op. cit., II, 503.

tarianism, quoting Las Casas and denouncing as worse than anything the savages ever did not only the cruelties of the early conquerors[72] but also the innumerable outrages of the highly civilized Europeans.

Admittedly, the New Zealanders are cannibals, and de Pauw's suggestion that they are driven to these excesses by *malesuada fames* is not very convincing.[73] There may be some exceptional cases,[74] but the most plausible explanation of this cannibalism seems to be rather an "excess of passion," which is of course the antithesis of all civilization, but not unnatural in itself. Do not the Europeans slit each others' throats by the thousand, "without a single motive, besides the ambition of a prince, or the caprice of his mistress!" Is it not sheer "prejudice" to have a horror of cannibalism when murder does not even arouse remorse? After all, these New Zealanders eat only their enemies killed in battle; they certainly do not devour their relatives, nor anyone who dies a natural death; nor do they take their prisoners to fatten them, "though these circumstances have been related, with more or less truth, of the American Indians."[75]

In short, human nature is what it is, in the Old World and the New, and even the newest of all. No continent can claim the right to instruct another or hold it responsible for its problems; nor was syphilis brought from America to Europe; it was born of itself all over.[76] Forster's impartiality foreshadows the sobriety and understanding of Alexander Humboldt's accounts; but it left him open, like Hawkesworth before him and all those who described the customs of the distant savages, to the cold lethal sarcasms of Dr. Johnson. So the explorers have found many new insects? What a splendid achievement! They could as well have stayed at home: there are more than twenty thousand species of insect in England alone.[77] They tell of extraordinary things? "I never knew before how much I was respected by these gentlemen; they told *me* none of these things."[78] Forster grips one's attention and carries one along?

72. Ibid., I, 518; II, 12.
73. Referring to the *Recherches sur les Américains*, I, 207, and recalling that this suggestion of his too was cribbed by Dr. Hawkesworth. Hawkesworth is frequently mentioned and severely condemned by Forster, because among other things he misunderstood and copied from de Pauw and Buffon without even naming them (ibid., I, 516–17; II, 562n., 602n.); cf. above, n. 64.
74. Ibid., II, 505–06.
75. Ibid., I, 516–18. A similar reflection on the vendettas of the savages and civilized peoples, ibid., II, 466; cf. II, 556; and Kersten, op. cit., pp. 232–33. On the fashions of Europe and those of the South Seas: *Werke*, I, 405, 484, 827. On the cruelty of the European soldier: *Werke*, I, 448. Elsewhere Forster tries in some way to justify the infanticides of certain Tahitians and prove the depravation of the civilized peoples with an announcement (1777) from some London midwives offering to procure abortions: ibid., II, 135n.
76. *A Voyage*, II, 160. Forster's breadth of understanding led him to be considered "among the founders of modern ethnological science" (*Enciclopedia Italiana*, XIV, 498c).
77. Against Hawkesworth: Boswell, *Life*, ed. cit., I, 478.
78. Against Hawkesworth: ibid., II, 9.

"No, Sir; he does not carry me along with him: he leaves me behind him: or rather indeed, he sets *me* before him; for he makes *me* turn over many leaves at a time."[79] And finally the classic reply to Boswell when the latter was enlarging on the abilities of the Tahitians and suggesting that they absolutely could not be considered savages: "Don't cant in defense of Savages."[80]

At the opposite end of the scale to Dr. Johnson is Horace Walpole, as liberal as Johnson was conservative, but equally skeptical about America's future.[81] It is true that as the Revolution dawns he looks across the Atlantic with warmly sympathetic gaze and produces one of the by now customary Berkeleyan or Galianian prophecies:

The next Augustan age will dawn on the other side of the Atlantic. There will, perhaps, be a Thucydides at Boston, a Xenophon at New York, and, in time, a Virgil in Mexico, and a Newton at Peru. At last, some curious traveller from Lima will visit England and give a description of the ruins of St. Paul's.[82]

With equally prophetic vision and similar prosopopoeic reference to the great names of antiquity, already in the mid-eighteenth century there had been talk of "Aristotles" and "Platos" in the New World. It was only reasonable to expect that from that immense and unknown land there might one day arrive on Europe's shores "some nation superior in intellect to all of ours, that will reveal to posterity as lunatics those great philosophers we admire today as oracles."[83] Walpole's image, resuscitated time and again in the poetic vogue for "ruins," the object of gloomy meditation on the caducity of empire (culminating in Volney's classic *Ruines*),[84] appeared once more in a poem by Thomas Lyttelton (who died in 1779), entitled *The State of England . . . In a Letter from an American Traveller, Dated from the Ruinous Portico of St. Paul's in the Year 2199, to A Friend settled in Boston,* published in London in 1780;[85] and

---

79. Against Forster, ibid., II, 132.

80. Ibid., p. 532; cf. also above, chap. 4, n. 5.

81. For Johnson's low opinion of Walpole, see Boswell, *Life,* ed. cit., II, 536; for Walpole's of Johnson, in the correspondence, especially from 1774 onward, there is an almost embarrassingly wide choice: just to give an example: "prejudice, and bigotry, and pride, and presumption, and arrogance, and pedantry are the hags that brew his ink" (letter of 7 February 1782, in *The Letters of H. Walpole,* ed. P. Cunningham [Edinburgh, 1906], VIII, 150; cf. ibid., VI, 109, 178–79, 302, 311; VII, 171, 484, 508; VIII, 26–27, 74, 361, 538, 557, 571).

82. Letter to Sir Horace Mann, 24 November 1774, ed. cit., VI, 153, quoted also by Brie, "Anfänge des Amerikanismus," pp. 362, n. 15a. For other, more specifically political prophecies, see Sumner, op. cit., pp. 46–51.

83. Sforza Pallavicino, *Del bene,* 1644, II, chap. 21, in *Trattatisti e narratori del Seicento,* ed. E. Raimondi (Milan-Naples, 1962), p. 231.

84. "Who knows if on the banks of the Seine, the Thames or the Zuyder Zee . . . a traveler like myself may not one day be seated on dumb ruins" (Volney, *Les ruines, ou Méditations sur les révolutions des empires,* 1791; ed. Paris, 1797, I, 16). Cf. Rose Macaulay, *Pleasure of Ruins* (London, 1954), and, for a related atmosphere, van Tieghem, *La poésie de la nuit et des tombeaux en Europe au XVIIIe siècle* (Brussels, 1920).

85. See Oliver Edwards, "The Wicked Lord," *The Times* (London), 26 July 1956.

it rapidly became a cliché, a *topos* in the comparisons between the two hemispheres. We find it paraphrased in a letter from Mme de Tessé to Jefferson: "When the Richness of its soil and the excellence of its government shall have brought North America to the highest degree of Splendor, and the south follows its example, and you have half the globe beneath your care, one will perhaps seek for traces of Paris as today one searches for those of ancient Babylon, and Mr. Jefferson's memoirs will guide travelers in their eager quest for Roman and French antiquities, which will by that time be confused."[86] And a few years later it was taken up both by De Giuliani, observing fearfully that "manufactures, sciences, the fine arts . . . are today seeking a different home . . . and, crossing the seas, they threaten to settle in America";[87] and, with more symbolic turn of phrase, by the botanist Labillardière (1799), referring to the South Sea Islands: "The period may arise when New Zealand may produce her Lockes, her Newtons, and her Montesquieus, and when great nations in the immense regions of New Holland may send their navigators, philosophers, and antiquaries to contemplate the ruins of *ancient* London and Paris, and to trace the languid remains of the arts and sciences in this quarter of the globe."[88] Dumont d'Urville managed (1826–27) to work it into a philosophy of history hinging on the succession and decline of civilization ("a few centuries hence . . . future members of the academy of New Zealand" etc.),[89] and last of all it appeared solemnly paraphrased by Macaulay (1840) in a celebrated passage in his essay on Ranke.[90]

But for Horace Walpole this awe-inspiring prophecy is little more than a *boutade*. He immediately goes on to joke about these "horoscopes of empires," and it takes little to make him change his mind. Thus even as in 1780 he is writing to his friend Sir Horace Mann that we live in "an age of abortions" and that England is exhausted, finished, extinct, he begins to suspect that perhaps the whole globe has now grown old. The world was young in Asia, mature in Europe, and even Africa, with Egypt and, momentarily, Carthage, produced a few gleams of light like the other continents. But now there is nothing more to be hoped for. America? . . . Yes, "America has begun to announce itself for a successor to old Europe, but I already doubt whether it will replace its predecessors; genius does not seem to make great shoots there." The reason he gives is very significant: "Buffon says, that European animals degenerate across the

86. Letter of 30 March 1787, in *Papers,* XI, 258.
87. "Saggio politico sopra le vicissitudini inevitabili delle società civili," 1791, in *Illuministi italiani* (Milan-Naples, 1958) III, 684. Cf. above, pp. 138–39.
88. Jacques Julien Houton de Labillardière, *Relation de voyage à la recherche de la Pérouse,* 1799; Eng. trans.: *An Account of a Voyage in Search of la Pérouse* (London, 1800), quoted in B. Smith, op. cit., pp. 111–12.
89. B. Smith, op. cit., p. 253.
90. *Essays,* p. 548.

Atlantic; perhaps its migrating inhabitants may be in the same predicament" — which is precisely what de Pauw had suggested. And with characteristic gloom Walpole concludes: "If my reveries are true, what pity that the world will not retire into itself and enjoy a calm age!"[91]

The same ideas, quite without any hint of deprecation, crop up again in Henry Hume, Lord Kames, one of eighteenth-century Britain's most interesting writers on aesthetics.[92] When Kames had published his famous *Elements of Criticism* in 1762, at the age of sixty-six, Dr. Johnson, his junior by thirteen years, had greeted it with superior and condescending disdain: "A pretty essay, and [one which] deserves to be held in some estimation, though it is chimerical."[93] But Johnson's lack of esteem was cordially reciprocated by the Scotsman, who in the worthy company of Adam Smith and other learned Caledonians found that there was nothing to Dr. Johnson, "nothing but Heaviness, weakness and affected Pedantry."[94] And one should also remember that the cantankerous lexicographer showed a marked antipathy for Scotsmen in general, an antipathy which makes the exception of his benign attachment to Boswell seem almost paradoxical. But this was a trait he shared with Walpole, his enemy in every other field, but like Johnson ever willing to pour scorn on the claims of the Scots to put the forgeries of an Ossian or "creatures" like our Lord Kames, Lord Monboddo, and Adam Smith, among others, on the same level as a Milton or an Addison, a Prior or a Gray.[95]

Here Kames finds himself in noble company indeed; and in fact he was not an insignificant "creature" at all, but a man whose brilliant if bizarre mind left its mark in other disciplines apart from that of aesthetics. Per-

91. Letter to Sir Horace Mann, 13 May 1780, ed. cit., VII, 364–65. Early in 1789 Walpole read de Pauw's work on the Greeks, and agreed completely with its slanders of the Greeks and its demolition of Lycurgus: "Mr. Pauw has proved it very doubtful whether any such personage existed; if there did, he only refined savages into greater barbarism" (letter to the Countess of Ossory, ibid., IX, 167, 171). Walpole admired Robertson, but found his *History of America* no more than an able compilation, lacking the acumen and fire of the *History of Scotland*, and he objected to the irony at the expense of the humanitarian Las Casas (letter to W. Mason, 10 June 1778; ed. cit., VII, 81; cf. also letter of 23 November 1791, ibid., IX, 361).

92. Cf. Croce's frequent references, particularly *Estetica* (Bari, 1922), pp. 288–90, 383, 487, 501, 518, 525–26; *Problemi di estetica* (Bari, 1923), p. 283; *Ultimi saggi* (Bari, 1935), pp. 139–40, 206; *Varietà di storia letteraria e civile*, I (Bari, 1935), p. 146. Cf. also G. E. Lessing, *Hamburgische Dramaturgie*, Allg. Bemerk., in *Werke*, ed. G. Witkowski, Bibl. Inst., V, 396–97; O. Elton, *A Survey of English Literature, 1730–1780* (London, 1928), II, 120–22; A. Ralli, *A History of Shakespearean Criticism* (London, 1932), I, 33–34.

93. Boswell, *London Journal*, p. 261: quoted also with minor variations by J. W. Krutch, *Samuel Johnson* (New York, 1945), p. 212. Cf. also *Boswell in Search of a Wife, 1766–69*, ed. Frank Brady and Frederick A. Pottle (New York, 1956), p. 153.

94. Related by Boswell, ca. 1762, quoted in Krutch, op. cit., p. 220. Adam Smith had a copy of Kames's *Sketches* in his library (*A Catalogue of the Library of Adam Smith*, ed. J. Bonar [London, 2d ed., 1932], p. 97); it was Kames who had induced him (1746) to teach literature at Edinburgh (A. Smith, *Lectures on Rhetoric and Belles Lettres*, ed. John M. Lothian [London, 1963], p. xiii); the *Sketches* is also referred to in the *Wealth of Nations*, ed. cit., p. 779.

95. Letter to Rev. William Mason, 5 February 1781, in *Correspondence*, VII, 111.

haps one should take with a pinch of salt the great admiration that the
petulant Boswell always expressed for Lord Kames; Boswell gained help
and protection from Kames, accompanied him on a tour of southern Scotland, aspired to write books "like Lord Kames," addressed a letter to
him which is an unlikely mixture of vanity and humility, and even hoped
to become his biographer; but at the same time he did not hesitate to fill
Kames's ears with praises of Dr. Johnson's intelligence, moral ardor,
learning, and manly virtues; nor did he offer any resistance to the approaches of Kames's only daughter Jean, who was no sooner married
than she invited the twenty-two-year-old James to the delights of love.
(He offered no resistance, but he did permit himself the luxury of some
remorse, and resisted quite successfully the temptation to reveal everything to her husband; one is thus left in some doubt as to whether this
need for confession may not have been motivated to a considerable extent by his customary exhibitionism.)[96]

Even without Boswell's adulation there remains much that speaks in
favor of Lord Kames, such as his weighty volumes on the law and his
idea of applying chemistry to agriculture. The latter notion provoked
the scorn of certain simple if sarcastic minds, who thought they were
making a laughingstock of Kames when they said that he had tasted personally all the manures with his fine philosopher's palate, so as to extract therefrom an essence which would save him the trouble of hauling
them down to the fields by the cartload;[97] they seem to have been unaware that in fact they were recognizing his achievement in having foreseen the possibility of chemical fertilizers. But apart from all this he is
deservedly remembered for his fearless opinions, his taste in the great
historical and philosophical arguments, and his animated relations, sometimes friendly, sometimes (as we have seen) more acrimonious, with the
great figures of his time. He was an assiduous correspondent and constant admirer of Mrs. Montague, the famous "Queen of the Blues";[98]
in 1748 he took the twenty-five-year-old Adam Smith under his wing, and
in 1771 entertained Benjamin Franklin at his home for five days.[99]
He earned a reply from Voltaire, and his lasting hostility, with cer-

96. See his *Tour to the Hebrides*, pp. 65n., 237, 362–63, and his diaries, esp. *London Journal*, pp.
10, 200, 323, n. 4; *Boswell in Holland* (New York, 1952), pp. 44, 87; *Boswell on the Grand Tour* (London, 1953), pp. 107–09, 164, 229.
97. See in *Boswell in Holland*, p. 87. The idea interested Jefferson (see Martin, op. cit., p. 10). But
Liebig's fundamental theses on chemical fertilizers date from 1840, the earliest "superphosphates"
from 1841. For the criticisms by Joseph Townsend (*A Dissertation on the Poor Laws*, 1786) of Lord
Kames's optimism on the inexhaustible fertility of the earth, see E. Halévy, *La formation du radicalisme
philosophique*, II, *L'Evolution de la doctrine utilitaire de 1789 à 1815* (Paris, 1901), p. 145.
98. *Mrs. Montague, Her Letters* . . . , ed. R. Blunt (London, n.d.), I, 154–55; II, 129–30 and passim
(see index).
99. D. Hume, *The Letters*, ed. Greig (Oxford, 1932), II, 251n.

tain charges in the *Elements of Criticism*.[100] He maintained friendly relations with Thomas Reid, who at his request wrote a long critique of Aristotelian logic to insert in one of Lord Kames's works.[101] But most notably he was one of the very first correspondents of David Hume, who as early as 1745 considered him "the best friend, in every respect, I ever possest";[102] the friendship, although it later became noticeably less warm, lasted right up until the death of the great skeptic.[103] In his youth Hume addressed some of his finest letters to Kames, and later on was always ready to praise and advise or defend him and recommend his work to publishers. It is actually from one such letter, to the publisher of the *Sketches of the History of Man*, that we learn that its author flattered himself that it would be resoundingly successful. Hume, doubting as ever, did not share "the prodigiously sanguine Expectations of the Author," but admitted that he might be mistaken, as he had been mistaken over the success of one of his friend's other books.[104] And in fact the *Sketches* ran into at least five editions[105] and are not completely forgotten even today.

What does Lord Kames have to say about America and the Americans? It is a long book, some eleven hundred pages, and the New World and its natives are mentioned frequently in it. One entire essay is devoted to the origin and progress of the American peoples, with particular reference to the Mexicans and Peruvians.[106]

For the most part Lord Kames makes use of the data and examples drawn from America to support his ideas on polygenesis. His prime aim is the demolition of the antihistorical and climatic thesis which claimed that the varieties of the human species, all springing from the single couple Adam and Eve, could be explained in terms of natural factors. In his efforts to combat this thesis, which fixed each race in an unvarying immobility, the shrewd magistrate does not hesitate to trespass into heresy, insisting instead on the original diversity of races and even on the successive creation of the different races coexisting on the earth.[107]

100. Ibid., I, 436; Boswell, *Grand Tour*, pp. 108, 264, 273, 294; E. C. Mossner, *The Life of David Hume* (Austin, Tex., 1954), pp. 412, 487–88.

101. *Sketches of the History of Man* (Dublin, 1779), II, 184–262.

102. Letter of 15 June 1745, in *New Letters*, ed. R. Klibansky and E. C. Mossner (Oxford, 1954), p. 17.

103. Mossner, op. cit., pp. 57–62, 118 (Hume submits his *Treatise* to Lord Kames), 410–12 and passim.

104. *Letters*, II, 289–90. For many other passages see the index of names, and, especially on the early years of the long friendship, see D. Hume, *New Letters*, pp. xiii–xiv, 1–10 and passim.

105. First edition: Edinburgh, 1774; the quotation is taken from the third "considerably improved" edition (Dublin, 1779); there exists a fourth, with additions, Edinburgh, 1788, and a fifth of 1807. German translation: Leipzig, 1778–83.

106. Op. cit., pp. 80–108.

107. For a prompt American reply (Philadelphia, 1787), see John C. Greene, "The American Debate on the Negro's Place in Nature, 1780–1815," *Journal of the History of Ideas*, 15, no. 3 (June 1954),

The Americans, in particular, must have been created in those "fertile and delicious plains [*sic*] of Peru and Mexico," which are found at the center of the continent and which were in fact densely populated when the Spanish arrived.[108]

He supports this thesis with a prolix accumulation of trivia, vague probability, and circumstantial evidence, which betray a lifetime on the bench and call to mind the cutting reply he received from Lord Monboddo when he asked him if he had read the recently published *Elements of Criticism* (1762): "No, my Lord!" replied the defender of the orang-utan's humanity, "you write much quicker than I can read."[109]

But whenever he is developing some theory of natural history Lord Kames adopts without question the theses of the great and unrivaled Buffon. Thus although he is familiar with Charlevoix and La Condamine, Gumilla and Bougainville, Garcilaso and Acosta and Ulloa, when he comes to the animals and men of America he still accepts the entire series of Buffon's disastrous propositions—that America was the last part of the world to emerge from the flood; that it has neither lions, nor tigers, nor panthers, nor other quadrupeds found in the warmer climate of Asia; that the natives, however brave under torture (passive courage), are lacking in active courage; that "there is not one single hair on the body of any American"; and that the savages are barren because they are frigid, both men and women, and because in particular "the males are feeble in their organs of generation," just as the animals, both indigenous and imported, "are of a diminutive size, compared with those of the Old World," while the Creoles surrender to the climate and degenerate irremediably, quickly lose and never regain their strength, their good looks and their agility, and are even soon reduced to speaking in undertones, with long and frequent pauses. South Carolina is the only exception to this rule: "Europeans there die so fast that they have not time to degenerate."[110]

For a man as capricious as Lord Kames, a man who prided himself on his originality—his friend Hume in 1751 called him "surely the strangest man in the world,"[111] and William Graham in 1764 described

---

pp. 384–85, n. 2, and William H. Hudnut III, "Samuel Stanhope Smith, Enlightened Conservative," *Journal of the History of Ideas*, 17, no. 4 (October 1956) esp. pp. 544–45. Kames had already ventured into heresy with his *Essays on Morality and Natural Religion* (1751), on which see J. M. Robertson, *A Short History of Free-Thought* (London, 1915), II, 186, the letters of Hume and those of Mrs. Montague, cited above, nn. 98 and 99, and Mossner, op. cit., pp. 336–53. His "heresy," anything but frivolous, was to suggest that free will does not exist, but that the Divinity wisely rooted in man the belief that he was free.

108. *Sketches*, II, 86.

109. Knight, op. cit., p. 28; for certain of Kames's scientific ideas, cf. ibid., pp. 97–98.

110. This apparently happens especially in the area around "Charlestown," because there is no "sea-breeze to cool the air" (op. cit., I, 12). But Charleston, the only city in South Carolina that Kames can be referring to (Charlestown is in West Virginia), is a well-known seaport. For the other expressions, see I, 26, 28; II, 80–81, 84–85, 88–89.

111. *Letters*, I, 162; also "the most arrogant Man in the World" and "an iron mind in an iron body" (Mossner, op. cit., pp. 410, 412).

him as "the most unequal-tempered man alive"[112] — this total acceptance of Buffon may seem quite inexplicable; but it can probably be explained by the simple fact that it was the very paradoxicality of these ideas which led them to be accepted so unquestioningly by the man who had put forward the so much more striking paradox that the Americans, like every other human species, are a race *sui generis*.

VI. TWO SUPPORTERS OF DE PAUW: DANIEL WEBB AND ANTONIO FONTICELLI

In England, then, de Pauw's ideas were to fall on fertile ground. There the myth of the Noble Savage had decayed rapidly, and with the outbreak of the Revolution in France even the radicalist Mother Nature was losing ground before the majesty of long-established institutions, the authority of the past, the slow constructive work of history. So de Pauw, in his slander of the savages, had hit on a formula that could not help but find favor among the English, with their traditional hostility for the Spaniards, their recurrent anti-Catholicism, and even their quite recent antagonism toward the Americans. True, that inverterate anglophobe, Thomas Jefferson, writing to an English friend in 1788, expressed his pleasure that the calumnies on American nature had not taken root in England: "I must do the justice to those of your country to say they have given less than any others into the lies of Paw, the dreams of Buffon and Raynal, and the well-rounded periods of their echo Robertson."[113] But it is none the less true that no British writer took it upon himself to attack de Pauw, that many Englishmen tacitly appropriated his theories for themselves, that the echoes of de Pauw are frequent in the romantic poets like Keats and Moore, and that de Pauw's frankest admirer was in fact an Englishman too, Daniel Webb.

Webb, like Lord Kames, is known chiefly for his ideas on aesthetics, and of course for his bizarre derivation of the Greek language from Chinese;[114] but he also compiled a sort of annotated anthology of de Pauw's *Recherches,* which he published first in 1789 in a limited edition of a mere fifty copies for his friends, and again in 1795 in a commercial edition.[115] His comments are almost always in the form of unrestrained

112. Boswell, *Grand Tour*, p. 264.

113. Letter to Benjamin Vaughan, 23 July 1788; *Papers*, XIII, 397.

114. See B. Croce, *Estetica*, p. 299; *Problemi di estetica*, p. 390; Elton, *English Literature, 1730–1780*, II, 135–36; Cordier, op. cit., I, 26.

115. The former is entitled *Selections from les Recherches philosophiques sur les Américains of M. Pauw*, by Mr. W. . . . (Bath, 1789); the latter *Selections from M. Pauw, with additions* by Daniel Webb, Esq. (Bath, 1795). The first has 211 pp., the other, with small additions (introduction, pp. 31–32, 56) has 235. To the latter is sometimes added, with fresh pagination, a *Sequel to the Selections from Pauw, in notes;* and later Webb also published *A general history of the Americans, of their customs, manners and colours. An history of the Patagonians, of the Blafards, and white Negroes. History of Peru. An history of the manners, customs, etc. of the Chinese and Egyptians, selected from M. Pauw by Daniel Webb, esq.* (Printed by and for T. Wood, Rochdale, 1806).

panegyrics. Even when he mentions having doubts or reservations,[116] he does so "with the greatest respect for the genius and learning of M. Pauw."[117] And in republishing the work this kind of praise is laid on more thickly; he had written before, for instance: "This statement of the subject is ingenious; it is happy."[118] Now this seems insufficient, and he adds: "Lively and profound; the genius of Pauw could reconcile the antithesis, and blend the vivacity of Montesquieu with the depth of Aristotle. When he seems to play on the surface, he is at the bottom of the subject."[119] As Webb reaches the end of the work he feels he cannot take leave of his author without expressing once more his profound respect for de Pauw's intelligence and learning, his critical acumen in matters which are subject to proof and the ingenuity of his conjectures in those which are not.[120]

One can hardly hope for any useful observations from such an enthusiast. Even if he repeats the usual parallel between the savages and European soldiers—of Marshal Turenne in the Palatinate: "could a Huron or an Iroquois have done more?"—he still looks on the primitive races as the rejects and victims of Nature. One can only smile at his pronouncements on the subject of cranial deformations, when he states that this is the savage's way of avenging himself for the cruel injustice which Nature has shown him "by defacing the fairest example of her art."[121] As if the savage's head were not an integral part of that body in which Nature had so misused him!

Antonio Fonticelli merits little more than passing mention, but one may refer to him here together with Webb, both because his small volume[122] appeared between the first and second editions of Webb's *Selections,* and also because he provides the exact Italian counterpart to the Englishman's uncritical compilation.

Americologia is an original title, but the promise it contains is not

116. For example, pp. 6, 65–66, 87, 89, 122, 131, 141, etc., of the 1st ed.; some, for example those on p. 6, are suppressed in the 2d ed.

117. 1st ed., p. 61.

118. Ibid., p. 108; cf. p. 12.

119. 2d ed., p. 112: a footnote admits the plagiarism of the expression from Voltaire!

120. 1st ed., p. 211, with reference to all de Pauw's works, including the most recent (1787) on the Greeks: cf. pp. 101, 153, 208.

121. 1st ed., p. 49. It is also curious to note the reason he gives for suppressing some pages on the cannibals: "The subject in general [*sic!*] is uninteresting [*!*], the details are often disgusting" (1st ed., p. 67).

122. *Americologia, ossia osservazioni storiche e fisiologiche sopra gli Americani con un breve ragguaglio delle ultime scoperte fatte dai Russi nel Mar Pacifico: Compendio di curiose notizie interessanti e scientifiche dato in luce da A. F. dedicato alla Società Patria* (Genoa, 1790). I have not been able to find any biographical details on the author, who was apparently afraid of the censors (pp. 5–6), possibly practiced medicine (pp. 6–7), and flattered himself that his work would run to a second edition (p. 19). No details on this mysterious personage are furnished by G. Rosso, "L'interesse americanista nell'Italia del settecento e l'americologia di Antonio Fonticelli," *Bollettino del Civico Istituto Colombiano* (Genoa), 1, no. 2 (April–June 1953), pp. 69–73.

fulfilled. From the epigraph (" '*studio disposta fideli,*' Lucret.") lifted directly from the *Recherches philosophiques,* right through to the penultimate article (the last one deals with the discoveries in the Pacific by the Russians), there is scarcely an article in the *Americologia* that is not a translation or rehash of the work of de Pauw. Fonticelli makes no secret of this: "My book has nothing whatsoever new about it," he says. But he refrains from spelling out the name of the author whose work he has ransacked. "Many things bear some relation to what may be read in three volumes printed in another language,"[123] he continues; here he seems only to be claiming a certain merit for himself as translator, but then one fails to understand why he should call upon the *Società Patria* (to whom he also dedicates the work) to provide their protection for his tract against "the slander and satire that are customarily hurled at national productions."

The *Americologia* cannot really be called a national production. Fonticelli's own contribution is limited to the insertion of a list of the principal discoverers and conquerors of America (freely sprinkled with errors), a comparative survey of the American colonies and states, a compendium of American imported products and some vegetables "which should be known in Europe," and finally two brief biographies, of Columbus and Vespucci (pp. 18–24). Following this there is a jumbled conglomeration of extracts from here and there in the *Recherches,* not excluding the most lurid passages, interlarded with occasional unedifying comments from Fonticelli; a section on sailors' tattoos (p. 35); two brief articles on coffee and cocoa (pp. 38–42); a variety of comments of sociopolitical nature on work and idleness (pp. 67–71); a brief list of the largest and heaviest diamonds known (pp. 106–07); and the work winds up — reiterating the view that the Americans are "stupid, ignorant and brutal" (p. 119), to the extent that they have even remained indifferent to the devoted attention and instruction of the Jesuits — with a typical little sensible savage's sermon, in which the "poor Caribee" gently reprimands the European for his thirst for gold, reminds him of the dangers of long voyages, and offers him Horace's old advice to be content to live out his days quietly at home![124] This incongruous accretion alone would be enough to show how impervious Fonticelli was to the problems and arguments of the American dispute; and, by the same token, it reveals his pamphlet for what it really is — a mere exercise in academic or rather journalistic composition.

---

123. *Americologia,* p. 5; cf. p. 10.
124. The motto repeated on the frontispiece and the last page is also taken from Horace (*Epistolae* I, 1, 45): *Impiger extremos currit mercator ad Indos* — "The eager merchant hastens toward the distant Indies."

VII. THE LONG-LASTING ANTAGONISM BETWEEN
SPANIARD AND CREOLE

If de Pauw had no enemies in England, in Spain he found himself without a single friend. This is explained partly by the same causes (his disparagement of the conquistadores, the missionaries, and the continent itself, so great a part of which was known as Spanish) having the opposite effect, and partly by the way in which other age-old arguments were merging into the dispute, giving it a new and bitterly impassioned tone, and also, by a curious paradox, providing de Pauw with some involuntary and reluctant allies, if no actual supporters.

In the very earliest decades of Spanish administration in the Indies there had arisen a serious internal conflict, the result of a spontaneous rift within the ranks of the conquerors: the conflict between Creoles and Spaniards (known also as *chapetones, gachupines,* and *godos*), or between white men born in the Indies of white parents, and white men who had arrived in the Indies from the mother country. It was this long-standing and constantly rekindled antagonism that finally razed to the ground the entire dilapidated superstructure of the Spanish American empire; the rift was renewed as each generation of Spaniards became Creole, even as a fresh generation of Spaniards was arriving. The virulence and bitterness of the dispute only increased as the Creole caste became more firmly established and more strongly unified, at first in stubborn defense of their rights, and later in fighting back against the continuous influx of their compatriots, all anxious to make their fortunes in America, greedy for their share of the rich profits reaped by the earlier colonists, and often disdainful of the character and capabilities of the Creoles.

The conflict therefore did not have the fixed and fatalistic quality of a racial clash. Spaniards and Creoles were both white, pure-blooded, of undefiled peninsular lineage. In fact in the matter of nobility the Creoles could often boast of more illustrious ancestors than the Spaniards recently arrived from Europe. As for money, it was quite normal for these gentlemen of the Indies to be considerably wealthier than the *hidalgos* and the royal officials; and for the latter on the other hand to arrive with a more voracious appetite, a conscious desire to get rich, very rich, and quickly; in short to display a harshness and energy considerably in excess of the Creoles, by this time satiated and exhausted, having often intermarried with the natives and become absorbed in the seven blessings of idleness.

The distinction then was not ethnic, economic, or social, but geographical. It was based on a negative *jus soli,* which took precedence over the *jus sanguinis.* A man born in the Indies, because of this single fact, found himself set apart from and subordinated to his countrymen, with whom he had everything else in common: the color of his skin, his religion, history, and language. If he was an official his chances of reaching the higher levels of the administration were only a fiftieth of those of a Spaniard. If an ecclesiastic, he might become a curate or rector, but the majority of the bishops and archbishops disembarked from Spain with their miters already on their heads. Solórzano states the case quite plainly: "Despite the many good qualities that they [the Creoles] possessed, they could never hope for more than the crumbs from the table."[125]

VIII. THE PRIDE OF THE CREOLES

It is not difficult to see how this rift between Spaniard and Creole contained the seeds of the polemic that was to reveal itself more clearly and to become more bitterly fought out in the second half of the eighteenth century. The natives of America were considered inferior to those of Europe. And not because they came of inferior stock. There was only one possible way of justifying this inferiority — by attributing it entirely to the Creole's surroundings, the climate, the milk of the Indian nurses, and other such local factors.[126] Many of the "calumnies" of the new continent derive originally from the jealously exclusive attitude of those born in the peninsula, and their consequent "disparagement" of the Creoles, almost as if the Creole's place of birth made him guilty of some crime and robbed him of every privilege he had acquired for himself by conquest or inheritance. "Climate" was stronger than "race," or as the nineteenth century put it, "geography" overcame "history."

The European despised the Creole. But the Creole replied resentfully by showing his passionate enthusiasm for his land. Thus his patriotism was born in the form of legitimate reaction; naturalistic in premise, it revealed itself as an attachment to the "country," to the land itself rather than to any traditions, as pride in the American soil. *Mancebos de la tierra,* "offspring of the land," the Creoles were once called.[127] And the first signs of their independence came with the societies of the *Amantes del Pais,* "the lovers of the country," societies whose avowed aim was a reverent understanding of their mineral resources, climatic peculiarities,

125. There were 18 Creoles out of 754 viceroys, governors, etc., of Spanish America; 105 Creole bishops (other authorities give 278 or 287) out of 706.

126. The honest Solórzano (*De Indiarum jure,* 1629–39; translated into Spanish under the title *Política indiana,* 1648) had already denied the validity of this type of argument, explaining the vices of a few Creoles in terms of a specific inferiority of the Americas (see Madariaga, op. cit., p. 477). See also the reprint of his defense *De los criollos y su Calidad y condiciones, y si deben ser tenidos por españoles,* in the *Revista de la Facultad de Derecho y Ciencias Sociales* (Buenos Aires), 5, 21–22 (1950), pp. 1309–1414 (summarized in *Revista de Historia de América,* 32 [1951], p. 357).

127. A. Rosenblat, *La población indígena de América desde 1492 hasta la actualidad* (Buenos Aires, 1945), p. 265.

and indigenous flora and fauna. On the eve of independence, they already had no hesitation in calling themselves quite simply "American."[128]

This specific expression of a feeling for the land was so spontaneous that it emerged not only in Spanish America but also in the English colonies. Pride in being American took shape as men began to boast of the physical blessings of their country, instead of glorying in some historic heritage or mythical antiquity. The Americans could not pride themselves on their past, the colonial past of recent times or the obscure theocracy of the more distant ages of tribal life and the native dynasties, an age anything but progressive or illuminated; a shapeless and lifeless past, in fact, totally out of tune with the new ideologies of humanity, tolerance, and civil liberty. What they could glory in was the richness and vitality of their natural surroundings; in their land Nature was fresh, luxuriant, plentiful in every kingdom, seeming to give abundant promise if not actual guarantee of a future that would know no bounds. The antihistorical elements in eighteenth-century political philosophy favored the acceptance of such a vision in areas relatively lacking in history or else ignorant of their history, as yet untouched and thus ready to be molded according to the new schemes of reason and enlightenment, though still possessed of a firm faith in their own wealth, natural perfection, and most blessed virginity.

The acclaim of the unquestionable richness of the New World in precious metals also frequently led on to the defense of the intellectual gifts of the Creoles, their religious virtues and scientific skill, their right to govern themselves and compete with the Europeans. This profusion of gold and silver seemed an irrefutable argument of the generous disposition of the land, a sure sign of its lavish fecundity in every type and quality of intellect, of heroic mind and faith, a promise of abundance in the glorious field of the spirit too. Garcilaso in 1617 found it logical, according to his own optimistic and baroque logic, that "a land so well endowed with rich minerals and precious metals . . . should breed veins of noble blood and mines of understanding."[129] Father Oliva (1631) and Father Calancha (1638) presented their biographies of virtuous Jesuits

---

128. Madariaga, op. cit., pp. 669–70. The Creoles too called themselves *españoles*, but in antithesis to *europeos* (the Spaniards of Spain!). Among the innumerable descriptions of the phenomenon suffice it to mention Juan and Ulloa, *Noticias secretas de América* (ca. 1750; London, 1826), I, 329; II, 93–95, and Robertson, *History of America* (1777), II, 366–67. On the societies of the *Amigos del País*, see Jean Sarrailh, *L'Espagne éclairée de la seconde moitié du XVIIIe siècle* (Paris, 1954), pp. 223–85; Richard Herr, *The Eighteenth Century Revolution in Spain* (Princeton, 1958), pp. 154–63, 355–57; Robert J. Shafer, "Ideas and Work of the Colonial Economic Societies, 1781–1820," *Revista de Historia de América*, 44 (1957), pp. 331–68. On the telluric pride of the Creoles, see Minguet, op. cit., p. 263.

129. Prologue to the *Historia general del Perú* (second part of the *Comentarios reales,* 1617; Buenos Aires ed., 1945), I, 10.

and Augustinians of Peru as spiritual treasures in no way inferior to the treasures of gold and silver.[130] Fra Juan de Melendez gave his collected histories of the canonized and beatified Dominican fathers of Peru the allusive title *Real Treasures of the Indies* (1681–82). And Francisco Antonio de Montalvo (1683) stated his positive expectation that Peru would give "more Saints to Heaven, than Silver to the Earth."[131] In time such pious hopes gave way to simple boasting, and the praises of America as a land "no less rich in noble intellects than in precious metals"[132] became ever more frequent.

One can detect the same sort of ideological-economic linking of metallic treasures and the values of the faith in the apologists of forced labor among the natives, whose arguments went something like this: without *mita,* no mines; without mines, no silver; without silver, no possibility for Spain of defending her overseas possessions or maintaining missionaries there![133] It was a rough choice for the *indios* — to commit their mortal bodies to the pits or their eternal souls to hell!

Any criticism of the soil, climate, or nature of America thus offended the innermost sensibilities of the Creoles, who had built their newfound faith and all their highest hopes precisely on the power of that same Nature. Every reference to any sort of weakness or insufficiency in the New World seemed to have as its main intent the undermining of their self-esteem, the tightening of the chains that bound them. In every theory that talked of degeneration, the Creole could see only an insult to himself, a pedantic and provocative sophism designed to convince him of his own inferiority in regard to the European.

130. Anello Oliva, *Historia del Perú y varones insignes en santitad de la Cia. de Jesús* (1631; Lima ed., 1894), xi, xvi, 137–46. The souls of the natives are the true silver treasures of the Indies, the sixteenth-century missionaries had already said (Hanke, *Aristotle and the Indians,* p. 20).

131. F. A. Montalvo, *El sol del Nuevo Mundo* (Rome, 1683), p. 16b; cf. ibid., p. 95a. In much the same way an English preacher had suggested (1610) that the Indians should be converted by barter and trade, by buying from them "the pearles of earth" and selling them "the pearles of heaven" (quoted in H. M. Jones, *Strange New World,* p. 191). In 1668 Joseph Glanville in his *Plus Ultra, or the Progress and Advancement of Science since the time of Aristotle* (in defense of the Royal Society) considered it likely that science, supported by artillery, would in time "inrich *Peru* with a more precious Treasure than *that* of its *golden* mines" (quoted by Roy S. Wolper, "The Rhetoric of Gunpowder and the Idea of Progress," *Journal of the History of Ideas,* 31, no. 4 [October–December 1970], p. 597). For other British antitheses (Lowley, 1656) between metallic (American) treasures and spiritual (British) treasures, see Blanke, op. cit., p. 178.

132. Examples from 1674, 1705, 1730, and 1737 are found just in J. J. Eguiara y Eguren, *Prólogos a la Biblioteca mexicana,* pp. 133–34, 140, 187, and cf. ibid., p. 113. See also my study on *Diego de León Pinelo contra Justo Lipsio,* nn. 13, 32, and 61. On the relationship in America between cultural development and material prosperity, see Bolton and De Gandia, in *Do the Americas Have a Common History?* ed. Lewis Hanke (New York, 1964), p. 132. The metaphorical equation: metals = treasures (of the spirit) enjoyed considerable success in baroque Europe too: see Mario Boschini, *Le Ricche Minere della Pittura Veneziana* (Venice, 1664 and 1674; reworked by A. M. Zancetti, Venice, 1733); Boschini was also author of *I Giojelli Pittorici, virtuoso ornamento della città di Vicenza* (1676).

133. See K. V. Fox, "Pedro Muñiz, Dean of Lima, and the Indian Labour Question," *Hispanic American Historical Review,* 42, no. 1 (February 1962), pp. 63–88, esp. 79–80.

IX. THE DEFENSE OF THE CREOLE: GARCILASO AND FEIJÓO

Now when even certain brilliant and learned Europeans had rejected and disproved the supposed inferiority, the Creole himself would hear no further mention of it. Garcilaso, the Peruvian son of a Spanish official and an Inca princess, had begun his *Royal Commentaries* with the statement that one spoke of an Old and a New World only because the latter was discovered by the former "and not because they are two, but *all one*"; and he dedicated the second part of the work to "the Indians, half breeds, and Creoles," in the hope that thus "the Old and Political World may understand that the New, although barbaric in the opinion of the Old, is not so, nor has it ever been so, except in its lack of culture."[134] In these same years Lope de Vega showed his high opinion of the "rare and subtle intellects" of the Americans.[135] And little more than a century later, Garcilaso's "lack of culture" had already been transformed into a highly developed culture, more splendid indeed in America than in Spain. Father Feijóo—known as the Spanish Voltaire or the Spanish Bayle, although he might be more accurately described as the Spanish Fontenelle (and not only because of his longevity)—took issue with the current opinion according to which the Creoles "become senile before they are actually old." He went on from there to an animated defense of "the excellency of American intellects," among which he then found "the intellects of Lima to be most excellent";[136] it was in fact this particular apology that brought down on his head the sarcasm and pity of de Pauw.[137] In his letters on the *Population of Spain*, Feijóo repeated with obsequious humility "that the development of every area of the field of letters among those who are not teachers by destiny is more rich in America than in Spain."[138] And again in the *Intellectual and Comparative Map of the Nations* he returned to this flattering comparison: "Many have observed that the Creoles, or sons of Spaniards born in that land,

134. *Prólogo* to the *Historia general del Perú*, 1617. Note the derogatory use of "political" in opposition to the young and barbarous world. Justus Lipsius had (in 1605) described America as barbarous, because it had no universities: his words were misunderstood and denied (1648) by the chancellor of the University of San Marcos in Lima, Diego de León Pinelo. After him the intellectual capacities of the Peruvian Creoles were defended (ca. 1760) by José Eusebio de Llano Zapata (for whom see my *Viejas polémicas*, pp. 239–52). Those of the Mexican Creoles had already found champions in the sixteenth century (Juan de Cárdenas), in the seventeenth century (Carlos de Sigüenza y Góngora), and the eighteenth (Velasquez de León). Toward the end of the century Concolorcorvo, having spent forty years studying "the particularities of the intellects of the Creoles," could assert: "I find no difference, in a general comparison, from those of the peninsular" (*El lazarillo de ciegos caminantes*, 1773, ed. Paris, 1938, p. 324).
135. See quotations in M. A. Morinigo, *América en el teatro de Lope de Vega* (Buenos Aires, 1946), p. 211.
136. *Obras escogidas* (Madrid, 1863), pp. 155a, 159b. For the Fontenelle-Feijóo parallel, see Marcelin Defourneaux, *L'Inquisition espagnole et les livres français au XVIIIᵉ siècle* (Paris, 1963), p. 131 and n. 4.
137. *Recherches*, II, 165–66; "Amérique," I, 351a.
138. *Obras escogidas*, pp. 594–95.

are of greater intellectual vitality and agility than those produced by Spain."[139] And in referring to the natives too, Father Feijóo maintained "that their capacity is not in any matter inferior to ours."[140]

In considering these solemn pronouncements of Feijóo one must of course make certain allowances for his constant involvement in the polemic against the ignorance, arrogance, and backwardness of his countrymen.[141] But we can still easily understand the vast reputation and long-lasting popularity of the Benedictine father throughout Spanish America, from Mexico and the Antilles to the River Plate. By 1730 he had received the praise and thanks of Mexico, and by 1732 the same of the city of Lima.[142] And although from 1759 onward his books were the object of frequent attention from the Mexican Inquisition[143] his ideas influenced the reform of the University of Havana (1761),[144] gained the enthusiastic appreciation of ecclesiastics in Guatemala,[145] and were studied with lasting pleasure by one of the foremost apologists of America — the Jesuit Clavigero (see below, pp. 196 ff).[146]

X. THE EXPULSION OF THE JESUITS

One item which received repeated mention was the suggestion that the American mind both matures and declines early in life, a theory which had already been the object of detailed discussion and which continued to be so even after Feijóo found it to be without foundation.[147] In 1746 Father Andrés de Arce y Miranda took up Feijóo's thesis and passed it in to

139. Ibid., p. 90b.
140. Ibid., p. 90a.
141. "Let us not exaggerate the decadence of Spain in order to increase the merit of Feijóo," protests Marcelino Menendez y Pelayo, *Historia de los heterodoxos españoles* (Buenos Aires, 1945), VI, 90. For a balanced judgment see Mario di Pinto, *Cultura spagnola nel Settecento* (Naples, 1964), pp. 123–73.
142. On his correspondence with Peralta y Barnuevo, see D. Valcarcel, "Fidelismo y Separatismo en el Perú," *Revista de Historia de América,* 37–38 (1954), p. 136. On his popularity in Peru, see Pablo Macera, "Bibliotecas Peruanas del Siglo XVIII," *Boletín Bibliográfico de la Biblioteca de la Universidad de San Marcos,* 35, nos. 3–4 (1962), pp. 124–37; in Venezuela, see A. Millares Carlo, review in *Revista de Historia de América,* 51 (June 1961), p. 210. In the North American colonies too his works were apparently quite widely read: cf. John Francis McDermott, *Private Libraries in Creole Saint Louis* (Baltimore, 1938), pp. 31–32, 44, etc.
143. M. L. Perez-Marchand, *Dos etapas ideológicas del siglo XVIII en México* (Mexico, 1945), pp. 59–60, 171. Against the slander of those who find him "suspect in the faith," see Menendez y Pelayo, op. cit., VI, 104–05.
144. Agustín Millares Carlo, "Feijóo en América," *Cuadernos Americanos,* 3, no. 3 (1944), pp. 157–59, citing J. M. Chacón y Calvo, *Literatura cubana, Ensayo crítico* (Madrid, 1922), p. 47.
145. H. Corbató, "Feijóo y los Españoles Americanos," *Revista Iberoamericana,* 5, no. 9 (May 1942), pp. 59–70, esp. 68–69.
146. See his biography written by his coreligionist and compatriot Juan Luis Maneiro, *De vitis aliquot mexicanorum* (Bologna, 1791–92), III, 33, 39; and the passages cited in the anthology *Humanistas del siglo XVIII* (Mexico, 1941), pp. 183, 184. Some details of his influence in upper Peru can be found in G. Francovich, *La filosofia en Bolivia* (Buenos Aires, 1945), pp. 49–54.
147. A. Millares Carlo, "Feijóo en América," pp. 151 ff.; and the *prólogo* to his selection of the *Teatro crítico universal,* 3 vols. (Madrid, 1923–25), I, 5–86 and III, 9–16; and the same to the popular edition of *Dos discursos de Feijóo sobre América* (Mexico, 1945), pp. xiii–xiv.

Eguiara, corroborating it with further Mexican examples and at the same time defending "the purity of blood of the literate Creoles," who should not really be given that name: "The name Creole . . . besides being ridiculous is denigratory and slanderous."[148] In his turn the fiery Aztec Eguiara y Eguren too produced an abundance of examples from Mexico to show that the minds of Americans not only do not decline prematurely but are even more startlingly precocious than Feijóo allows.[149] The shrewd Peruvian Concolorcorvo lent his support too, expanding (in opposition to Feijóo) the thesis of early maturity, and simultaneously rejecting (this time in agreement with Feijóo) the thesis of early onset of old age; on the grounds, he says, that the thick and humid vapors of Lima tend rather to "fortify the brain."[150] At most, the Mexican conceded, a certain dullness and laziness in learning "may perhaps be the custom in some part of *Peruvian* America."[151] The Peruvian, on the other hand, found that it was not altogether impossible to come across a certain decadence in *Mexican* brains, accounted for by the dry climate of their capital. And not only their climate, alas, "the Mexicans cannot help but weaken themselves greatly with their frequent hot-water baths"![152]

Feijóo's arguments against the theory of premature senility in the Creoles[153] were taken up in Argentina and in Spain itself, while in the very year that the United States won her independence a doctor of that country took it upon himself to affirm the precocious intellectual development of children born in South Carolina.[154] Even after the New World had begun to produce its own American-born defenders, among the first being the exiled Jesuits in Europe who were so directly opposed to de Pauw, Father Feijóo continued to have considerable influence by reason of his prestige as a European, a man of wide learning, and a man of the church.

Thus it was primarily as a result of Feijóo's work that there began to be a reappraisal of the opinions on the degeneration of the Creoles, which might perhaps have led to a more accurate statement of the problem. But this revision of ideas was overwhelmed at its outset by the explosive

148. Efrain Castro Morales, *Las primeras bibliografías regionales hispano-americanas — Eguiara y sus corresponsales* (Puebla, 1961), pp. 30–33.
149. Eguiara y Eguren, op. cit., pp. 128–29, 134–49.
150. *Lazarillo*, p. 334.
151. Eguiara y Eguren, op. cit., p. 136.
152. *Lazarillo*, pp. 353–54.
153. See Ricardo R. Caillet-Bois, *Las corrientes ideológicas Europeas en el siglo XVIII y el virreynato del Rio de la Plata*, in *Historia de la Nación Argentina*, vol. V (Buenos Aires, 1939), p. 11; and Juan and Ulloa, *Relación histórica*, I, 4 (ed. Madrid, 1748, I, 47–48). On the falseness of the reputation for obscurantism and ignorance given to Spanish America by the *philosophes* (and combated by Humboldt), see Minguet, op. cit., p. 270.
154. Cited in Kraus, *Atlantic Civilization*, p. 267. The precocious development of the North Americans was affirmed again in 1835 by a German immigrant, who attributed it partly to the climate, partly to the greater liberty they enjoyed (*A Mirror for Americans*, ed. W. S. Tryon [Chicago, 1952], p. 165).

force of the Buffon–de Pauw theories, reaffirming with apparent scientific precision the thesis of an inescapable decadence of men and animals in the New World.

On the other hand the very year of the publication of the *Recherches* witnessed an upheaval that was to have a profound effect on the subsequent course of the polemic: after a short stay in Corsica there were beginning to arrive in Italy, in the States of the Church (which had done everything in its power to avoid having to accept them), the Jesuits who the previous year had been expelled, or rather deported, from Spain and her American possessions; almost all of them were Creoles and among the outstanding representatives of the intellectual development of their native countries. They were men embittered by the harshness of their exile, resentful of the insults they had had to bear, and filled with a real and burning attachment to the lands from which they had been abruptly, even brutally, driven out; an attachment which one could not yet call patriotism, but which was certainly an essential element in patriotism, and in some cases even an embryonic form of it (inasmuch as it even included, alas, the seeds of the most narrow-minded nationalism).

On their arrival in Europe, the fathers were surprised and aggrieved to find how far the anti-American "calumnies" had spread. These calumnies offended not only their militant and strongly felt antirationalism but also the affection they felt for the lands where they had grown up and where many of them had taught for so many years. They had been reduced to a state of wretchedness and exile by an ideology armed with political power, and now they found themselves faced again with the same ideology, this time masquerading as scientific truth and pitilessly, jeeringly disparaging the soil where their young order had won its first claims to glory and the peoples who had been dear to them and to whom the exiles undoubtedly looked back with nostalgia.[155] After all, had it not been the Jesuit missionaries themselves who had created and spread abroad the legend of the Noble Savage of America? Had they not made themselves an obvious target for de Pauw's sarcasm for this very reason? It had been through their work, and particularly through their written relations, that the pastoral innocence of the classic idylls and the simple customs of the age of the patriarchs had come to life again in the forests of New France. It was through their work that the tradition of Ronsard

155. On the efforts and attempts of various Jesuits to return to America, see for example R. Vargas Ugarte, *Jesuitas peruanos desterrados a Italia* (Lima, 1934), passim, esp. pp. 160–62, and the pathetic appeal of four Chilean Jesuits exiled to Imola, failing in health and invoking the need to "breathe their native air" (quoted in Miguel Batllori, *El abate Viscardo: Historia y mito de la intervención de los jesuitas en la independencia de Hispanoamérica* [Rome, 1953], p. 123). But the ban was absolute; and they were even forbidden to communicate by letter with their countries (A. de Saint-Priest, *Histoire de la chute des Jésuites au XVIIIe siècle* [Paris, 1844], p. 62). On the recalcitrant patriotism of the Spanish fathers in exile too, see for example P. Hazard, op. cit., II, 246–47.

and Montaigne had lived on in the seventeenth century, that there had slowly been forged the "connecting link" between the wild cannibal of the sixteenth century and Rousseau's philanthropic man of nature. The Jesuits in particular had taken it upon themselves to explain the disconcerting innocence of the savages, and not by suggesting, as others had done, that they were exempt from Original Sin—for which incontrovertible "proof" had been found in the fact so much proclaimed as to become almost a cliché, that the female savages gave birth painlessly, in other words were exempt from the punishment inflicted on Eve (Genesis 3:16)[156]—but by pointing out that the ownership of private property was quite unknown to them, since they lived in tribal communities, like monks in a monastery.[157] And in Paraguay the fathers had even attempted, with some success, the synthesis of the monastery and the tribe, of Society and communism.

The Jesuits had also provided descriptions of the natural life confirming the opinion that America did have monstrous and ferocious wild beasts, particularly tigers, and melodious little songbirds too, and a profuse abundance of land that could be cultivated, and furthermore that European domestic animals multiplied prodigiously in America.[158] On other occasions however, pushed by the need to glorify their own missionary efforts, they had become de Pauwians *ante litteram,* exaggerating the horrors of American nature, the "marshy swamps" and "foul reptiles" that beset their apostolic path.[159]

Only by bearing in mind this complex of immediate and more distant causes can one fully understand the swiftness and forcefulness of the Jesuits' reaction to de Pauw, Raynal, and Robertson. In their attack on these minor lights of secular encyclopedism they brought to bear all the passion, all the technique of erudition that their order possessed, all the experience of lifetimes spent in America, bolstered by the firm conviction that they were fighting for a crucial point in the inseparable interests of truth, religion, and their motherland.

These defenses and counterattacks by the Jesuits who had taken refuge

---

156. See examples in G. Atkinson, *Les relations de voyages,* pp. 130–33, and cf. below, pp. 243–44, 621–22. The men in turn sometimes figure as exempt from the pain of labor inflicted on Adam (Genesis 3:17). Both male and female, then, are without shame for their nudity, while Adam and Eve blushed with shame after the Sin (Genesis 3:7). On the presumed exemption of America from Original Sin, see R. Remond, op. cit., pp. 491–92, and, for its literary reflections in the nineteenth century, the whole of R. W. B. Lewis, *The American Adam: Innocence, Tragedy and Tradition in the Nineteenth Century* (Chicago, 1955).

157. G. Chinard, *Les refugiés huguenots en Amérique,* "Le mirage américain" (Paris, 1925), pp. xiv–xv; *Le rêve exotique,* passim; introduction to Lahontan, *Dialogues curieux* (Paris, 1931), p. 46 (the Jesuits as Lahontan's source); Zavala, *América,* pp. 23, 172; and particularly the cited work of J. H. Kennedy, *Jesuit and Savage in New France.*

158. See L. Muratori, *Il cristianesimo felice,* passim.

159. See examples in Remond, op. cit., pp. 155–56.

in Italy had the incidental effect of providing their distant fellow countrymen with a whole battery of national traditions and glories; a paradoxical
result which Charles III could hardly have foreseen when he signed the
expulsion order, and thought that by so doing he could strengthen his
despotic and enlightened authority in both hemispheres. But it is a result
that agrees well with, or rather parallels (on the doctrinal level), the practical efforts made by a good number of the exiled Jesuits—who conspired
even with the Protestant English—to overthrow the Spanish rule in the
American colonies, and bring about their independence. When the great
revolt of Tupac Amaru broke out in Peru (1781–83) the Jesuits could be
seen burning with impatience and hate and making offers to the English
to rouse Mexico too into revolt against Spain.[160] In 1786 the Venezuelan
hero Francisco de Miranda, his mind ever fixed on the idea of emancipation, was busy in Venice and Rome compiling lists of names and addresses of the ex-Jesuits exiled almost twenty years earlier and still
living in Bologna and other cities, to show to William Pitt.[161]

XI. THE SPANISH JESUITS: FATHER NUIX MAKES USE OF DE PAUW

There was thus bound to be a divergence of opinion on the subject of
America between the Jesuits exiled from Spain and those removed from
the overseas territories: the former steadfast in their acclaim of the
metropolis, and so quite prepared to accept certain of de Pauw's arguments for the use that could be made of them in furthering their own
cause, but still attacking the author as an enemy of Spain; the latter de-

160. G. G. Gervinus, *Geschichte des XIX Jahrhunderts*, vol. III (Leipzig, 1858), p. 38. On the contacts established between the British government and the Jesuits already by 1767, see the document
published by Saint-Priest, op. cit., pp. 293–97, and Batllori, *Viscardo*, pp. 75, 77 n. 6, 93, 107–08, 137.
It is also known, of course, that protection was offered to them by other non-Catholic sovereigns, such
as Catherine II of Russia, and Frederick II, for whom it perhaps contributed to the reputation he earned
in Italy as a crypto-Catholic (Goethe, *Italienische Reise*, 25 October 1786: ed. Leipzig, 1913, I, 115).
161. W. S. Robertson, *La vida de Miranda* (Buenos Aires, 1938), pp. 73–74, 105, 110–11, 192; Madariaga, op. cit., pp. 774, 845, 869, 1004; and Batllori, *Viscardo*, p. 103. Menendez y Pelayo also
affirms that "the expulsion of the Jesuits helped to accelerate the loss of the American colonies," but
only because of the cultural and religious decay resulting in the colonies after their removal (*Los heterodoxos españoles*, VI, 192–94). On the Jesuits in general as precursors of the Latin American emancipation, see for example the Jesuit Vargas Ugarte, *Jesuitas peruanos*, pp. 124–25, 129–30, and his
polemic, centering on the figure of the Peruvian Jesuit Juan Pablo Vizcardo y Gusmán, with the Jesuit
Miguel Batllori; while the Peruvian Vargas Ugarte tends to exalt the role of the fathers in the struggle
for independence (see *La "Carta a los españoles americanos" de d. J. P. Vizcardo y Guzmán* [Lima,
1955], esp. pp. xiii, 42–53, 79–82, in which he sees the consequent application of the Company's
"democratic" and tendentially "monarchomachic" political theories), his coreligionist Batllori considers it a conventional myth, demolishes the figure of the exile Viscardo and denies that he knew,
let alone followed, the "populistic" doctrines of Suarez and Mariana (see *Viscardo*, pp. 82, 147)—one
more proof of the inextinguishable vitality of the diatribes whose story we are following. On the Jesuits
of New Spain, in whom Mexican patriotism, born with Cortes and Las Casas, supposedly reached mature and conscious form, see H. Corbató, "La emergencia de la idea de nacionalidad en el México colonial," *Revista Iberoamericana*, 6 (1943), pp. 377–92. On the converging of the cultural international-
ism of the Company with the "native" pride of the exiled fathers, see M. Picón Salas, *De la conquista a
la independencia* (Mexico, 1944), pp. 166–80, and Batllori, *Viscardo*, p. 83.

termined to reject the Prussian's slanders *in toto* and even suspecting the Spaniards of having prompted him to produce them. Such is the frequent fate of writers with the greatest aspirations to originality and paradox — to be taken over regardless by some political movement or other. They find themselves forcibly enrolled in the legions of propaganda, and this punishment of their impertinence is left as an example to posterity.

Father Juan Nuix is an outstanding example of the attitude of the first group, the Jesuits exiled from Spain. More than ten years had passed since the publication of the *Recherches* when, after questioning more than a hundred American Jesuits in Italy,[162] he wrote his lucid but none too impartial *Impartial Reflections on the Humanity of the Spaniards in the Indies, against the so-called Philosophers and Politicians, to serve as enlightenment to the histories of Messrs. Raynal and Robertson* (Venice, 1780). In the meantime the poison of de Pauw's thesis had passed into the much more widely known and respected writings of the abbé Raynal and the Rev. Dr. Robertson; but although the Jesuit father aims his attack primarily at these two — with some regard for the Scotsman and none at all for the Frenchman — he does not overlook Marmontel, too naïve a follower of Las Casas, nor de Pauw, who is indeed explicitly mentioned, among the authors who have recently attempted to besmirch the good name of Spain, by Nuix's brother José, in his preface to the Castilian translation of the *Reflections* (Cervera, 1783).[163]

In point of fact Father Nuix's thesis is concerned solely with history and not with physical or geographical problems. The purpose of the entire book, right from the title (so redolent of Jesuit urbanity and eighteenth-century philanthropy), is not only to exculpate the Spaniards from the accusations of cruelty toward the Indians but to show that they were much more humane than the humanitarians of the eighteenth century. They found the *indios* weak, certainly, but they managed to "give a much more just explanation for this weakness than did some of the recent philosophers":[164] they attributed it to their meager and unnourishing

---

162. Op. cit., pp. 6–7 (*Riflessioni imparziali sopra l'umanità degli Spagnoli nell'Indie contro i pretesi Filosofi e Politici, per servire di lume alle storie dei signori Raynal e Robertson* [Venice, 1780]. On Nuix, see Ezquerra, op. cit., pp. 232–35.

163. I have quoted some passages from this edition, which followed another (differently translated) edition from Madrid, 1782, with notes by P. Valera and Ulloa, also because it contains additions missing in the Italian edition, in which de Pauw, for example, is never mentioned. On these two translations and the success of the book, which was applauded in Italy and France (French ed., Brussels, 1788) but which in 1783 was still unknown in Spain, see the exchange of letters between Joseph Vega y Sentmonat and Juan Antonio Mayans, 5 and 12 August 1783, in *Revista Crítica de Historia y Literatura Españolas, Portuguesas y Hispanoamericanas*, 6 (1901), pp. 103, 105.

164. *Riflessioni*, p. 131 (Spanish ed., p. 219). For this die-hard Hispanism of his (which includes a good dose of anti-Semitism: *Riflessioni*, pp. 190–91), Nuix, already called an odious sophist by Humboldt (*Essai politique sur l'île de Cuba* [Paris, 1826], I, 153 n. 1), was admired by Menendez y Pelayo, who deplored the fact that his work had fallen into complete oblivion (*Obras completas*, IX, vol. IV of the *Estudios y discursos de crítica histórica y literaria* [Santander, 1942], pp. 29, 90–91; *Los heterodoxos españoles*, VI, 190); and redeemed and hailed by J. Juderías, *La leyenda negra* (Barcelona,

diet, not to any irremediable organic inferiority. And they were more humane in their general judgment too: "There has never been heard in Spain that which is calmly suggested in other areas, namely this Infamous comparison of the Savages with the Animals."[165] So the *indios* should consider themselves lucky to have been discovered and colonized actually by the Spaniards and not by the philosophers who criticize them so severely: "Oh wretched Americans, if the Spanish too had viewed you as Robertson and other philosophers did!"[166] They denied the Americans any intellectual capacity, any moral judgment, leaving them as idiot children, or animals, for whom enslavement was the only right and proper fate.

Thus Nuix defends the natives, but not because he has any sympathy for them. Nothing really interests Nuix except his own beloved Castilians.[167] The natives, "the most cowardly men that have ever been seen in the world,"[168] are no more than a mirror in which to reflect more gloriously the virtue and splendor of the kings and captains of Castile.[169]

It becomes clear then why Nuix is divided in his attitude toward de Pauw. On the one side he castigates him together with the other slanderers of the good name of Spain and wants to refute his "foolhardy" accusation that the dogs who hunted down the natives were in the pay of Spain or his imputations against Sepúlveda of having permitted their enslavement

---

1917), pp. 312–13. It is true that even an unshakable champion of Spain like Carbia (*La leyenda negra*, pp. 212–15) finds that Fr. Nuix's "impartiality" leaves much to be desired (on which see *ad abundantiam* Hanke, "The *Requerimiento* and Its Interpreters," *Revista de Historia de América*, 1 [1938], p. 31; Rosenblat, *La población indígena*, p. 15, n. 1; M. Batllori, "L'interesse americanista nell'Italia del Settecento. Il contributo spagnolo e portoghese," *Quaderni Iberoamericani* [Turin] 12 [1952], p. 167); but still in 1944, in the political climate of Francoist Spain, it seemed opportune to republish his book, with the abbreviated title *La humanidad de los españoles en las Indias* (2 vols., Madrid, 1944) and a prologue-apology by C. Perez Bustamante (reviewed in *Revista de Indias*, 17 [1944], pp. 539–44), and again in 1963 the venerable Ramón Menendez Pidal (*El padre Las Casas, su doble personalidad* [Madrid, 1963]), returned to his arguments to demolish the evidence of the Bishop of Chiapas (see L. Hanke, "More Heat and Some Light on the Spanish Struggle for Justice in the Conquest of America," *Hispanic American Historical Review*, 44, no. 3 [August 1964], p. 327). Further proof still of how far from being extinguished are the polemics whose first steps we are here tracing.

165. *Riflessioni*, p. 298 (Spanish ed., p. 471).

166. Ibid., p. 303. A footnote to the Spanish ed. (p. 479) cites "the author of the *Recherches*, etc.," in other words, discreetly, de Pauw.

167. But let him not be suspected of exaggerated patriotism! He is a Catalan, and "possibly among all those famous adventurers of the Conquests, there was not a single Catalan" (*Riflessioni*, p. 4). But Sommervogel (*Bibliothèque de la Compagnie de Jésus* [Brussels-Paris, 1894], V, 1836), says Nuix was born in Toca, in Old Castile!

168. *Riflessioni*, p. 82: an echo from Robertson.

169. His thesis was taken up, and quoted (pp. 42–44, 47, 68, 75–76), by another Jesuit deported to Italy, Mariano Llorente, in his *Saggio apologetico degli storici e conquistatori Spagnuoli dell'America* (Parma, 1804), in polemic with the Vespuccian researches of Francesco Bartolozzi (1789), and his disdainful comments on the Spanish historians, but incidentally also with Raynal (pp. 47–48, 61–63), Robertson, Marmontel, and especially Las Casas. Buffon, who was very popular and much respected in Spain (see Sarrailh, op. cit., pp. 459–61) is mentioned for his praise of the missionaries on pp. 81–82. On other Jesuits who undertook to defend Spain, even against their coreligionists (like Clavigero), see Miguel Batllori, "L'interesse americanista," p. 167.

and extermination.[170] This was also the attitude of the Spanish Inquisition, which first placed de Pauw's book on the Index (31 January 1777) and then pronounced it (28 August 1777) "full of insult to the Spanish nation, principally to the conquistadores, treating them and everyone as Barbarians and thieves, cruel and inhuman";[171] in other words the Inquisition too condemned its politico-historical ideas, which were not in the least original, and said nothing of its physicogeographical suggestions, whose novelty and extremism were nothing short of scandalous.[172]

But on other occasions Father Nuix finds it more convenient to make use of de Pauw; either, as we have seen, to show the benignly humane attitude of the Iberians in a better light, by contrasting it with the Prussian's cynicism, or else calling upon him to bear witness *ex campo adverso* to the good qualities of the Spaniards or the bad qualities of other colonists.[173] It was thus the incautious Nuix that initiated this use of de Pauw *ad majorem Hispaniae gloriam*, which in the end was to make him doubly suspect and repellent to the Creoles locked in battle with the mother country.

XII. DE PAUW'S FIRST AMERICAN OPPONENT

The reactions of the American Jesuits are of course much more significant. They were almost the avant-garde of Creole culture, and their vindications of America, though usually limited to the region from which each came—Mexico in the case of Father Clavigero, Chile for Father Molina, and the kingdom of Quito (now Ecuador) for Father Velasco—were taken over and repeated throughout the continent when echoes of de Pauw reached America too. But the very first American to react to the *Recherches* was not one of these at all. Preceding the Jesuits by almost a decade was a polemicist completely unknown as such, although

170. *Riflessioni*, Spanish ed., pp. 394, 474. The former charge, abundantly proved by an eyewitness like Oviedo (*Historia general y natural*, XVII, 23, and XXIX, 3; ed. cit., I, 547, III, 9–10), was repeated by Las Casas and Montaigne (*Essais*, II, 12; ed. cit., p. 445), taken up in the eighteenth century by Marmontel and Raynal, and admitted and deplored even by a defender of Spain like P. Moxó (for whom see below pp. 298 ff.), *Cartas mexicanas escritas . . . en 1805* (Genova, n.d., but 1837–38), pp. 140–41. At the end of the eighteenth century an admirer of the North American frontiersmen coldly reports that "these Americans have trained English dogs to hunt the savages" (J. P. Brissot de Warville, *Nouveau voyage dans les Etats-Unis* [Paris, 1791], II, 428n.). Such a hunt seems to have been recommended as early as 1703: Pearce, *The Savages*, p. 23.

171. *Archivo Histórico Nacional*, Madrid, Papeles de Inquisición, Legajo 4465, no. 4, quoted by Hanke, "The *requerimiento*," p. 30, n. 7. The Spanish Inquisition condemned it in 1787 (Defourneaux, op. cit., p. 174). In its turn the Mexican Inquisition too censored de Pauw's book (Perez-Marchand, op. cit., p. 170, n. 2); and that of Lima confiscated it (J. Torre Revello, "Libros procedentes de expurgos en poder de la Inquisición de Lima en 1813," *Boletín del Instituto de Investigaciones Históricas* [Buenos Aires], 15 [1932], p. 342). Again in our own day Carbia (*La leyenda negra*, pp. 134–39) treats de Pauw merely as a belated exponent of the accusations made against the Spanish conquerors and colonists. He hardly refers to his thesis of the degeneration of America (p. 134, n. 194).

172. There is an analogous attitude toward Raynal, condemned for anti-Hispanism and tolerantism (Defourneaux, op. cit., p. 113).

173. See for example op. cit., Spanish edition, pp. 345n., 420, 486–87.

very well known indeed on other counts. In 1771 Pernety wrote with satisfaction (and with his usual labored style):

M. le Comte Orcassidas, a Creole, son of a viceroy of Mexico, majordomo of the king of Spain, at present in Berlin, continuing a journey through all Europe, undertaken for his instruction, having lived some considerable time in the New World, which he has covered almost in its entirety, with the same intention, is a living proof against M. de P. He has read his *Recherches philosophiques* and the *Défense;* he has declared, and still declares to whoever wishes to hear it, that their author is mistaken in almost all items, particularly on those which he makes the basis of his hypothesis.

The count has seen at least a hundred thousand natives, of the north and south, and everywhere he found "the men extremely inclined for sex," and not one with milk at his breast; little hair, true, but this is because they remove their hair; and in short they are strong in body and mind. European fruits are better in America than in Europe. And the animals of like species reach such perfection there that the count's father had sent "several to the king of Spain, to try and breed such a fine race in Europe."[174]

And who was this "Count Orcassidas"? He was Juan Vicente— firstborn son of don Francisco de Guëmes y Horcasitas, Count of Revillagigedo, viceroy of Mexico from 1746 to 1755 — who pursued a military career in Spain and was later, from 1789 onward, viceroy of Mexico himself, indeed "a great viceroy, one of the greatest that New Spain ever had": the same who rebuilt Mexico City, had the Pacific coast explored as far as the Bering Strait, and devoted his unflagging energy to the improvement of the administration, education, finances, communications, defenses, and economy of his country.[175] Is it not almost symbolic that the great Revillagigedo himself, while still traveling and studying in Europe, should have been the first "American" to rise up against the accusations of Buffon and de Pauw? And is there not just a hint of irony in the fact that the cook he brought back with him from Europe, the Frenchman Jean Laussel, should have fallen foul of the Inquisition, which in 1794 confiscated several of his books, among which an "Interesting Memoir for the human race, with a dissertation on America and the Americans" — indubitably a copy of the notorious *Recherches?*[176]

XIII. THE AMERICAN JESUITS: FATHER CLAVIGERO

But Count Orcassidas contributed nothing to the debate in writing. It fell to the Jesuit refugees to produce the first published testimony in

174. *Dissertation,* II, 524–26.
175. Madariaga, op. cit., p. 748; cf. the praises of C. H. Haring, *The Spanish Empire in America* (New York, 1947), p. 129. The father had another son, Antonio Maria, who was made a count in 1781 by Charles III, and pursued a career in the diplomatic service.
176. Spell, op. cit., p. 219.

defense of America.[177] The most extensive and detailed of these is the voluminous *Storia antica del Messico* by Father Francesco Saverio Clavigero, published at Cesena in four large volumes in 1780–81, and quickly reprinted, translated into various languages, and widely read in both hemispheres, to the point that Prescott could later write that despite its longwindedness and the fact that it was bristling with Mexican terminology it created almost a "popular interest" in Aztec archeology.[178]

The work of the learned Jesuit, who left Mexico with his confrères in 1767 to take up residence in Italy and translated into Italian and in that language published his history—"persuaded . . . by certain Italian men of letters, who showed themselves extremely anxious to read it in their own language"[179]—remained the standard text on the ancient history of Mexico for over half a century. But even later it continued to be one of the most widely known and approved histories relating to the

177. A little later a statesman of no less standing than Revillagigedo, Thomas Jefferson, aligned himself with the Jesuits and published in Paris the first defense of North America (see below, pp. 252 ff.). And in Mexico, in Puebla de los Angeles, there also appeared the first American work on Rousseau, or rather *against* Rousseau, produced by a Dominican from Cuba, Christoval Mariano Coriche (Spell, op. cit., pp. 34–36).

178. W. H. Prescott, *History of the Conquest of Mexico,* bk. I, ch. 2, conclusion (Mod. Lib. ed., p. 35). Cf. also Jean-Jacques Ampère, *Promenade en Amérique* (Paris, 1856), II, 316, 364. F. de Miranda (Raynal's critic) bought Clavigero's *Storia* in Rome to have it translated in England, and in 1787 presented the copy to Prince Potemkine (W. S. Robertson, *La vida de Miranda,* p. 463). An English edition translated by Charles Cullen (who was helped by Clavigero) appeared in London in 1787, in two quarto volumes, and was reprinted several times also in America (Philadelphia, 1804; then Richmond, Va., 1806; London, 1807; Philadelphia, 1817): see A. La Piana, *La cultura americana e l'Italia* (Turin, 1938), p. 162; Bernstein, *Origins,* pp. 58, 62 n. 40. German trans. (from the English): Leipzig, 1789–90; Spanish trans.: London, 1826 and various reprints in Mexico (1844, 1853, 1861–62, 1868, 1883, 1917, 1944; on other unpublished Spanish translations, and for the original Spanish version, published in 1945 [2d ed. rev., Mexico, 1958, edited by R. P. Mariano Cuevas], see *Revista de Historia de América,* 26, p. 534, and C. G. I. (Cavazos Garza Israel), "Autores nuevoleonenses: Lic. José Alejandro de Treviño y Gutierrez," *Inter Folia* (1959), n. 61, pp. 1–3 (Treviño "left an unpublished translation of Clavigero's ancient history of Mexico"). In Madrid Clavigero's work could not get published, no doubt because of its "Creole" tendencies and its firm denunciation of the cruelty of the Spaniards—characteristics it shared with all the literature produced by the American Jesuits in exile (for its "caustic insults" to the Spaniards, cf. Vargas Ugarte, *La "carta,"* p. 34). But Clavigero also finds a just nemesis in the enslavement of the inhabitants of New Spain. See in particular the conclusion to the *Storia,* where he points to the wretchedness of the oppressed Mexicans as God's punishment for the sins of their pre-Colombian ancestors, "a fearful example of divine justice and the instability of the kingdoms of the earth" (III, 233–34), apocalyptic in tone and sounding more Augustinian and Jansenistic than Jesuitical. On the question of a French translation, see Maneiro, op. cit., III, 68. Even a Dane wanted to publish it (1787) in his own language! (Maneiro, ibid.). The anonymous author of the preface to the posthumous *Storia della California* (2 vols., Venice, 1789) says that the *Storia antica del Messico* was translated into French, German, and English (I, 3).

179. *Storia,* I, 2. Clavigero already knew Italian, and in 1762 had translated from the Italian a life of St. John of Nepomuk (see Maneiro, op. cit., III, 49, and Sommervogel), but he had his translation checked by an Italian scholar (Maneiro, op. cit., III, 67). On the long travail he endured (including a trip in summer in an open chaise from Bologna to Modena, to consult a book, from which he returned with a split head after being pitched out of the conveyance, but still content, *laetus admodum,* with his literary expedition) see ibid., III, 63–67. Further biographical data appear in C. V. Callegari "L'abate F. S. Clavigero," *Le vie d'Italia e dell'America latina* (July 1931); in José Miranda, "Clavigero en la Ilustración mexicana," *Cuadernos Americanos* (Mexico), 28 (1946), pp. 180–96; and in Batllori, *Viscardo,* pp. 105–06. On his modernistic scientific ideas and his philosophical eclecticism, ante 1767, see B. Navarro, *La introducción de la filosofía moderna en México* (Mexico, 1948).

ancient Aztec monarchy and the conquest of Cortes.[180] The learned Icazbalceta, writing sometime around 1852, described Father Clavigero as "the most popular of our writers and the most worthy of so being."[181]

A. *Fundamental aim of the work, the refutation of de Pauw.* It is all the more interesting then that his *Storia* should have come into being in direct polemic with de Pauw. Clavigero in his preface actually mentions three motives which induced him to write it. But the first—the desire to overcome the boredom and "shameful loafing" of his state of enforced idleness—is somewhat generic and would hold true for any occupation he chose. The second—his yearning to serve his country—is certainly more definite and sincere but coincides substantially with the third, which is precisely the aim of "restoring to its ancient splendor the truth which has been so obscured by an unimaginable swarm of modern writers on America."[182] Love of country is the positive side of that same animus whose negative form is the indulgence in polemics against whoever slanders the motherland. Or rather love of country, we could say, is the sentimental prerequisite which is transformed into acts and writing and becomes concrete and belligerent when enlisted in the fight against these impertinent scribblers in Paris, Berlin, and Edinburgh who dared to diminish the power of nature in Mexico, or the native civilization, or even the whole American race. Clavigero's first biographer relates how he had already gathered a lot of material but not yet begun to write,

when behold there began to spread throughout Italy, amidst great uproar, a muddled work entitled *Philosophical Investigations on the Americans,* by a certain German author from Prussia, whose style is fluent and not inelegant, but who misunderstands everything and errs at every step, even in the things that are clearer than daylight as soon as one sets foot in the New World. And this was what finally impelled Clavigero to ignore the difficulties and set to work, so that the truth might be established and defended and the history of the Mexicans properly portrayed.[183]

180. Cf. Prescott, op. cit., I, 1 (ed. cit., pp. 18–19), who gave currency to the term *Aztec* empire, actually introduced by Clavigero, to indicate the ancient Mexican state (L. H. Barlow, "Some Remarks on the term 'Aztec Empire'," *The Americas,* I [1945], pp. 345–46). The poet Postl drew on Clavigero for a novel he wrote in 1843 (see E. Castle, *Der grosse Unbekannte* [Vienna, 1952], p. 470). In Italy too his work earned a lasting reputation which continued into the second half of the nineteenth century: see G. Rosa, *Storia generale delle storie* (1864; 2d ed. Milan, 1873), p. 379. Again in 1880 Carducci turned to it for some Mexican terminology and a few touches of local color for the ode *Miramar* (Manara Valgimigli, *Carducci allegro* [Bologna, 1955], p. 50).

181. *Historiadores de México,* in *Opúsculos y biografías* (Mexico, 1942), p. 9.

182. Op. cit., I, iv, 1.

183. Maneiro, op. cit., III, 62–63. In a letter from Bologna to Mariano Fernandez de Echeverría y Veytia, of 25 March 1778, Clavigero informed him that his *Dissertazioni* were written to "rebut the errors of Mr. Buffon, Mr. Pauw, Mr. Raynal, and other celebrated authors" (quoted by O'Gorman, *Fundamentos,* pp. 118–19), and "to serve my country in as much as I am able" (quoted by J. Le Riverend Brusone, in the preface to the Mexican [1944] edition of the *Historia,* I, 8). Of the *Recherches* Clavigero knew the London edition of 1771, with Pernety's *Dissertation* and de Pauw's reply (IV, 8).

It takes no more than a brief glance at the *Storia antica del Messico* to see the accuracy of this. Of the four volumes that make up the work, the ten books of the history proper occupy the first three. The fourth (1781) and largest (almost 30 percent of the total) is dedicated to Count Gian Rinaldo Carli, another celebrated adversary of de Pauw (see below, pp. 233 ff.), and has nine dissertations on the earth, plants, animals, and inhabitants of Mexico, which constitute a formidable argument against de Pauw and, regarding the animals, Buffon, together with occasional shafts directed at Robertson[184] and Raynal[185] too. This last part in fact repeats in polemical and oratorical form what the first part had expounded in historical and didactic terms. Once he has established his truth in the "history," Clavigero descends to do battle with error in the "dissertations."[186]

De Pauw appears in the very first rank of the army of error. Already near the end of the preface de Pauw is cited together with Marmontel as the archetype of the foreigner who distorts the facts as an excuse "to be even more ferocious toward the Spaniards."[187] And in a long note on the supposed circumcision of the Mexicans, Clavigero attacks "the low-minded and sarcastic author" of the *Recherches,* not only for his blatant errors and his lack of reverence for the Bible but also for "his diligence in the minute description of any subject that has some affinity with the obscene pleasures."[188]

Another error to combat, and one that Clavigero finds himself running up against right from the first book of the history, is Buffon's thesis deny-

184. "Among modern writers on American matters the most famous and respected are Signor di Rainal and Dr. Robertson." But the former made "great blunders" about the present and is sceptical about all Mexico's past. The latter is also liable to error and contradiction, he "exaggerates the idiocy of the Conquistadors" and is mistaken in believing all sources to have been lost (I, 19–21). Against Robertson, who is however cited in other places as an authority, see for example I, 29n.; III, 3n., 9n., 17n., 19n., 25n., 38n., 42n., 85n., 128n., 200n.; IV, 185 ff., 223–26, 236–38, 269–76, 286–87. In the fifth edition of his *History* (1788) Robertson replied to the criticisms made by the abbé, whom he had immediately (1782) dismissed in a private letter as "a weak and credulous bigot" (Humphreys, op. cit., p. 28). Clavigero had read carefully (*potissimo studio*) Feijóo (see above, p. 186), and knew Bacon, Descartes, and the "Americanum Franklinium" (Maneiro, op. cit., III, 51; and *Humanistas del siglo XVIII,* ed. Gabriel Mendez Plancarte [Mexico, 1941], p. 191); but he pays scant attention to Feijóo's thesis on how the Americas were populated (IV, 25). Against the chronicler Herrera: IV, 66–67, 103, 201.

185. See for example II, 189–90n.; III, 128n.

186. There are in fact some indications (a greater frequency of references to the former in the latter) suggesting that the *Dissertations* was written at least in part before the *History.*

187. Op. cit., I, 18. Of de Pauw's other opponents Clavigero knows and quotes Pernety (IV, 8, 171); mentions with disdain the "rancid" preadamite theories of the "author of a miserable little work entitled Le Philosophe Douceur, printed in Berlin in the year 1775" (IV, 15); quotes Molina with homage (IV, 73n., 96n., 97n.); and admires G. R. Carli, to whom he dedicates the *Dissertazioni,* but whose *Lettere americane* (II, 267) is reproved for its anti-Spanish bias. Obviously the viewpoints of the exiled Jesuit and the enlightened encyclopedist, allies though they were in the fight against de Pauw, could hardly coincide.

188. *Storia,* II, 73n.; cf. IV, 315: "that great Researcher of America's filth." Other incidental attacks on the ignorant and insolent "Researcher": II, 132n., 151, 172. De Pauw's obscenity is indubitable, but nobody had remarked on it before the Mexican Jesuit father. Europe of the 1770s was not easily shocked.

ing the existence of lions, tigers, and rabbits in America. But his plan is already worked out, and he is not going to change it: this thesis, he says, is one "sufficiently contradicted by us in our dissertations," so that "it is not necessary to interrupt the course of our history to refute it."[189] The prologue of the *Dissertations* explains in fact that their intention is to dissipate the errors spread abroad by the "modern writers," and he goes on: "How many people, in reading, *for example,* the work of the *Researcher,* will not fill their heads with a thousand unseemly ideas and notions contrary to the truth of my history?" There follows a savage portrait of de Pauw:

He is a fashionable Philosopher, and erudite, and especially in certain matters in which he would do better to be ignorant, or at least to refrain from speaking of them [an allusion to his frequent digressions into scabrous topics]. He spices his discourse with buffoonery and gossip, ridiculing whatever should be respected in the Church of God, and sinking his teeth into whoever stands in the path of his inquiries, without regard for truth or innocence. He delivers his arbitrary decisions in magisterial tones, quotes the writers on America at every third word, and protests that his work is the fruit of ten years' labor.

His aim is to convince the world "that in America nature is completely degenerate in the elements, the plants, the animals, and the men," and thus to put together a monstrous portrait of the continent. Clavigero has chosen de Pauw's work as his target and victim "because like a cesspit or sewer it has gathered in one place all the refuse, that is to say the errors of all the others." Nor will he be moderate in the expression of his disapproval, since gentleness is out of place when dealing with "a man who slanders the whole New World and the most respected persons of the Old."[190] Among other authors he will have to impugn the worthy Buffon, a man of very great qualities, but who sometimes erred, or forgot what he he said earlier, or neglected details, and who bases himself on the supposed impossibility of the animals proper to the climates of the Old World passing over to the New.[191]

In the first dissertation—"on the population of America and particularly that of Mexico"—Clavigero does in fact take issue with Buffon, in sustaining the thesis of a formerly existing land link between the New

189. Op. cit., I, 69–70.
190. *Storia,* IV, 5–8. Note that de Pauw, introduced literarily only "as an example," is promoted within the space of two pages to become the summary symbol of all the anti-American literature. Other ponderous witticisms at the expense of de Pauw, "whose brain seems to have a particular organization for understanding things in a contrary fashion to all other men" (IV, 248), are dispatched by Clavigero with a certain schoolmasterly insistence. Cf. "if nothing of what we have said suffices to convince Sig. de P., I would charitably advise him to have himself removed to a hospital" (IV, 286); and another fleeting polemic allusion occurs when Clavigero shrewdly observes that "the Europeans never did less honor to their own reason than when they doubted the rationality of the Americans" (I, 120).
191. *Historia,* ed. M. Cuevas, I, 84–85. Cf. below, pp. 567–68.

World and the Old; and "the extravagant *Researcher*"[192] is mentioned only in passing. In the second dissertation—on the "main eras in the history of Mexico"—he attempts to fix the chronology of its various ethnic strata and ancient sovereigns. But already by the third—"on the land of Mexico"—the polemic can no longer be held in check, and Clavigero bursts out against the thesis of the sodden or ill-dried-out continent, of America as "a completely new country," as Buffon would have it, and, following in his footsteps, de Pauw too ("who largely copies the sentiments of M. de Buffon, and where he does not copy him, multiplies and enlarges the errors").[193] Against the thesis of the flooding of the continent, an earlier occurrence according to Buffon, and more recent and specific according to de Pauw, and against its dire physiological and psychological corollaries, even up to the "stupidity of the Americans and . . . a thousand other extraordinary phenomena, which he from his study in Berlin has observed better than we, who have spent so many years in America,"[194] Clavigero mobilizes arguments from the fields of geology, natural history, and political history.

   B. *The arguments reversed.*   One polemical gambit with which Clavigero is well acquainted is to take the arguments adduced by the Europeans and turn them back either on Europe itself or on the Old World in general.

   If America had its own little private flood, the Old World had nothing less than the universal flood. How come its animals did not degenerate? How come its soil was not left sterile, and its women too? "Was Europe conceded everything good, and everything evil sent to America?"[195] The Europeocentrism of the Buffon–de Pauw theses is laid bare in all its crudity. But Clavigero's polemic never gets to the root of the issue; he plays with corollaries; he falls into the same error as his adversary when he tries to demonstrate the inferiority of the Old World with respect to the New;[196] and he even gives way to almost humorous arguments, like that put forward to refute "the philosophical chimera" of the flood, that if there is one country which would have been able to save itself from Noah's flood, this country is Mexico, since it is situated very high up above sea level, and in fact marine fossils are very rare there.[197]

   To refute the supposedly harmful effects of the climate, which de Pauw

192. *Storia,* IV, 21.
193. Ibid., p. 65.
194. Ibid., p. 68. The irony at the expense of the philosopher judging things from afar is repeated several times.
195. Ibid., p. 73.
196. Although he writes that he has no wish to present America as superior to the Old World, these parallels are "too odious," and vaunting one's own country above all others "seems more proper to children fighting than men of letters disputing" (IV, 8).
197. Ibid., p. 77.

demonstrated with the diminutiveness of the quadrupeds, the abundance and magnitude of the insects, the feebleness of the men, and so on, Clavigero produces quotations from Buffon discrediting the witnesses brought forward by the "Prussian philosopher" or, more often, pointing out equal or worse phenomena in Europe. But although his reasons are good and his argument sound, one is left feeling bored as one always is after having been subjected to a deliberately and tenaciously pursued apology; nor can one help noticing the tone of legalistic courtroom eloquence, in which the winning of a point prevails over the honest desire to determine the effective reality of things. America, indicted before the tribunal of Reason, and accused by the public prosecutor de Pauw, finds in Clavigero a counsel deeply involved and well prepared, but not overscrupulous in his choice of oratorical weapons. It is difficult to justify, even in terms of reprisal, certain statements whose motivation falls somewhere between a malicious desire to overwhelm with insult and a puerile reaction of wounded vanity:

If America had no corn, nor did Europe have maize, which is no less useful or less healthy; if America did not have pomegranates, lemons, etc., at least it has them today; but Europe never had, nor has, nor can have Chirimoye, Ahuacati, Muse, Chicozapoti, etc.[198]

America is made to look like some little schoolgirl grasping in her fist the orange snatched from her playmate Europe, and spitefully waving in her face her own *chicozapote*, all hers and hers alone![199] Clavigero's rebuttal sinks all too easily into the grotesque and the ridiculous; in view of this, and its dialectical monotony, not to mention a certain very evident touchiness that has a whiff of provincialism, and his obtuse refusal to consider the historicizing point of view of the *Défense*,[200] we can abbreviate our account of the other parts of his reply.

The fourth dissertation—"on the animals of Mexico"—combats mainly the Buffonian theses according to which America displayed "a prodigious

198. Ibid., p. 103, where he pursues the line of reasoning: if America has barren parts, the Old World has even more barren and horrible ones (see below, p. 211). Here one notes a revival of the old debate as to whether the Old World's "contributions" to the New did or did not compensate for those the New World gave the Old, an ill-founded discussion possibly originated by Sepúlveda (L. Hanke, *Aristotle*, pp. 52–53, 87), and persisting loquaciously into our own times. It has obvious "structural" analogies on the one hand with the theories that saw America providing compensation for the losses suffered by the Faith in Europe (cf. above, pp. 134 and 136), and on the other with the question so much discussed in the eighteenth century, of whether the discovery of America was a good thing or a bad thing for the Old World: "or qual di voi sta peggio?" (G. Parini, in the sonnet "Ecco la reggia . . . ," in *Poesie e Prose*, ed. L. Caretti [Milan-Naples, 1951], p. 402).

199. Cf. also, for the *chicozapote*, op. cit., I, 51–52. With greater good sense and good humor another Jesuit, Fr. Acosta, had said long ago of the *chicozapote* that "some Creoles said . . . that it exceeded all the fruits of Spain. To me [he added] it does not seem so: as for taste they say that there can be no argument, and even if there were, it is not a worthy argument for writing about" (*Historia natural y moral*, IV, 25; ed. cit., p. 257). On Clavigero's polemic passion, see J. Le Riverend Brusone, *Prefacio*, I, 10–12.

200. See, for example, IV, 171.

scarcity of matter" in the animal species; Clavigero shows that they are neither as few nor as mean or as ugly as Buffon and de Pauw affirm,[201] and counters with the objection that such "statements, if the truth be told, are rather a censure of the conduct of the Creator, than of the climate of America."[202]

Among the birds there are nightingales and at least another twenty-two species of songbirds, including the "far-famed" *centzontli,* whose song is a miracle of softness and sweetness, harmony and variety of note, and which is known for the "ease with which it learns to express whatever it hears," and because it can imitate perfectly "not only the songs of other birds, but even the different sounds made by the quadrupeds." Even the sparrows, which are mute in Spain, sing quite well in America![203] In the New World, in short, the birds sing better too, and they sing more, and they all sing, even those which are not supposed to!

And so on. American ostriches have two toes too many? . . . The *unau* (the American sloth) boasts the beauty, the superfluous beauty, of forty-six ribs? . . . And all of this is supposed to be due to the American climate? Let these animals be brought to Europe, accompanied by their females, and let us see if in twenty generations the number of their toes or ribs is reduced. But if that does not happen, one will have to conclude "that the logic of these Gentlemen is more unhappy than the aforesaid quadruped" (the *unau*), and one will have to marvel "that in a country where matter was so scarce Nature should have sinned in excess of it in the ribs of the sloths and the toes of the ostriches."[204] As for ferocity, the American animals in no way take second place to the animals of Asia, whose aggressiveness and strength have probably been exaggerated: "I have seen with my own eyes the havoc wrought in my house by an almost-domesticated stag on a poor American girl."[205]

As for tails, the honor of America's quadrupeds is vindicated in the case of all except six, of which two are doubtful. And if some are ugly, because it is true that they do not all fit in with European ideas on the beauty of beasts, how much uglier are some of the animals of the Old

201. In IV, 118–19, he rejects the thesis of the animals being "one-sixth part smaller," and difficult to draw (see above, p. 55). Clavigero has seen a tiger "killed a few hours previously by nine harquebus shots," which was considerably bigger than the Comte de Buffon would have one believe (IV, 116–17). And that same very erudite Buffon, who counted the teeth and measured the tails of all the quadrupeds, quite simply forgot the very common Mexican coyote (I, 76–77; IV, 110).

202. *Storia,* IV, 119. True, of course, but the rationalist recognizes the climate and does not recognize the Creator. . . . On the Mexican bird called the *sensütl,* doubtless the same as our *centzontli,* and its warbling so lively and melodious that it gives singing lessons to the heroine of the vapid story, see already C. M. Wieland, "Koxkox und Kikequetzel," 1769–70, in *Sämtliche Werke,* XIV, ed. cit., p. 65.

203. Op. cit., I, 89; IV, 134–36. The latter boast is actually withdrawn in a footnote but left in the text!

204. Ibid., IV, 120–21, 123. Cf. Molina, below, p. 214.

205. Ibid., p. 131.

World, like the elephant for example![206] The camel, finally, recovers the normality of its genital functions, with only some slight qualification: "It is false to say that the camels transported to Peru left no posterity; since Father Acosta, who went there some years later, testifies to having seen them increased, *though little.*"[207]

C. *The defense of the Mexican Indian.* The fifth dissertation — on the "physical and moral constitution of the Mexicans" — enters into a full discussion on the thesis of the degeneration of the men. They are all degenerate, according to de Pauw, the *indios,* the Europeans settled in America, the Europeans born in America (*criollos*), and the mestizos of various extraction (*castas*). But Clavigero — after a quick thrust *ad personam* in the comment that if de Pauw had written his *Recherches* in America he himself might have been a good example of his own theories — limits his defense to that of the American natives, who are "both the most slandered and the most defenseless." It would have been much easier for him to defend the Creoles — and even more so since, as he writes with typical pride: "We were born of Spanish parents and have absolutely no affinity or consanguinity with the Indians."[208] But the defense of the *indios* is more pressing and proceeds along the lines by now well known. The men of America are neither weak, nor hairless, nor milk-bearing; nor do the women possess those peculiarities so indiscreetly pointed out by de Pauw. As for good looks, let de Pauw consider an African, "a stinking beast, whose skin is as black as ink, his head and face covered with black wool instead of hair, his eyes yellowish or bloodshot, his lips thick and blackish, his nose flattened"; let him look at a Lapp, a Tartar, or a Kalmuck; let him look — continues the intrepid Jesuit — at the Hottentots, who have "that monstrous irregularity of a callous appendage extending down from the pubic bone"; let him consider the

206. Ibid., pp. 128–29, with an animated description of the elephant, "a monster of matter." Even in this slander of the elephant one can detect a hint of reprisal. That particular pachyderm was, according to Buffon, the animal nearest to man in intelligence, "inasmuch at least as matter can approach the spirit" (*Morceaux choisis,* p. 139). Cf. above, p. 25. Buffon's follower, Oliver Goldsmith (for whom see above, p. 163), had gone further still: as a creature of noble mind and discerning nose, "the elephant gathers flowers with great pleasure and attention; it picks them up one by one, unites them into a nosegay, and seems charmed with the perfume": and its favorite, among all of them, is the orange blossom! (*History of the Earth and Animated Nature,* pt. II, bk. IX; ed. cit., I, 499; cf. Pitman, op. cit., p. 114). A veritable ancestor of Dumbo! Among the other animals that Clavigero finds ugly are the camel, the giraffe, and the macaco (ibid.). Molina too finds that "the camel is a monster, to tell the truth, compared with these quadrupeds" (auchenia) (*Storia naturale,* p. 312; *Historia natural,* p. 294; *Storia naturale,* 2d ed., p. 257), and Edmund Temple observes likewise that the llama, which "in the words of Buffon 'seems to be a fair diminutive' " of the camel, is in reality considerably more handsome and "without any of the deformity of the camel": *Travels in Various Parts of Peru, Including a Year's Residence in Potosi* (Philadelphia, 1833), I, 174 (cf. below, p. 297).

207. Op. cit., IV, 140 (my italics; cf. above, chap. 3, n. 18). A little farther on he ridicules the customary (see above, pp. 56, 147) affirmation that dogs cease to bark (I, 73, and IV, 138–39, 147–49).

208. Op. cit., IV, 160–61. Cf.: "The Mexican language was not that of my Parents, nor did I learn it as a child" (IV, 247).

tails of the Formosans and Mindorans; and then let him try and tell us, if he dare, that the Americans are ugly.[209] The Mexicans, in particular, are handsome, healthy, robust, and immune to many misfortunes and illnesses. And no Mexicans ever have bad breath.[210]

Suddenly the discussion echoes a note of truth learned by hard experience, as the old priest bursts out: "If M. de Pauw had seen, as I saw, the enormous weights that the Americans carry on their shoulders, he would not have been so bold in taunting them with weakness."[211] They till the soil, cut down woods, build roads and houses, dig the mines and "clean up the cities," and perform all the heaviest tasks and offices: "This is what the weak, cowardly and useless Americans do, while the energetic de Pauw and other indefatigable Europeans busy themselves hurling abuse at them."[212] And the same note is heard again when he is defending the intellectual gifts of the Indian:

I dealt intimately with the Americans: I lived some years in a seminary devoted to their instruction . . . later I had some Indians among my disciples . . . so that . . . I protest to M. de Pauw and to all Europe that the minds of the Americans are not at all inferior to those of the Europeans, that they are capable of all learning, even the most abstract.

If they were well taught, "one would find among the Americans Philosophers, Mathematicians, and Theologians to rival the most famous in Europe." The obstacle in their path is not natural but social. Not stupidity, but poverty: "It is very difficult, not to say impossible, to make great progress in learning in the midst of a wretched and servile life and continued discomforts." Let the haughty Europeans attend one of the meetings in which the *indios* discuss their affairs, and they will hear "how these satyrs of the New World harangue and declaim."[213] When

209. Ibid., p. 164–66.
210. Ibid., I, 118–23. That singular privilege had been attributed (1703) to the savages of North America ("the air which leaves their mouths is as pure as the air they breathe"; Lahontan, *Dialogues curieux*, p. 93). But it is curious that it should actually be another Mexican, Fr. Mier (who for that matter was familiar with Clavigero's work), that in polemicizing with de Pauw accuses the Europeans of having introduced into America plants like garlic and onions, that befoul the breath: anyone who has eaten them "cannot enter into a decent house" (José Guerra, pseudonym of S. Teresa de Mier, *Historia de la revolución de Nueva España* (London, 1813), II, 734–36; cf. my *Viejas polémicas*, pp. 266, 269 n. 4).
211. *Storia*, IV, 173. On the preceding page, with the usual *reductio ad absurdum:* "The Swiss are stronger than the Italians, and yet we shall not consider the Italians degenerate, nor shall we blame the climate of Italy" (IV, 172). Shortly after that there are mentioned the great constructions and demanding agricultural labor as proof of the robustness of the *indios* (in implicit polemic with Las Casas too: see above, p. 68). Defense of the giants: I, 125; IV, 10n., 42n.
212. *Storia*, IV, 175. Moxó will say the same thing (see below, p. 299), and Humboldt will write that the appearance of the robust Mexican miners would have made the Raynals and de Pauws, etc., change their minds (Minguet, op. cit., p. 373). And with an analogous polemical gambit Croce vaunts the muscles of a porter on the quay at Naples over those of any idealized "German" to reject Montefredini's accusations of a weakness in the "Italic race" (*Aneddoti di varia letteratura* [Naples, 1942], III, 374).
213. *Storia*, IV, 190–91. L. Hanke too ("Pope Paul III," 73, n. 18) mentions Clavigero's reply to de Pauw (I, 35–36) on the subject of the alleged Papal declaration that the *indios* are truly men. Of

he remembers his native country, his forlorn *peones* and his little disciples at the Jesuit college, the exiled father is overcome with emotion,
and the polemics and pedantry give way to a hymn of faith in all men.

The question of the Indians' aptitude for the study of letters and the
sciences already had a copious bibliography, and the capabilities of the
Mexicans had been especially defended and exalted (see above, n. 134).
What we really have here is in fact a restatement in secular and humanistic terms of the ancient question of the conversion of the heathen,
of their capacity to receive baptism, and their classification as men or
animals.[214] The motive force behind these debates was always a complete faith in the superiority of civilization (whether religious or scientific) over nature, a faith in Progress. They represent in fact the opposite
extreme to Rousseau's thesis of the advisability for the savage of not becoming civilized or constrained in society, and on the harmful consequences of the arts and sciences.

The Jesuits in particular always exaggerated the natives' capacities for
study and mastery of all the arts and sciences. It was on the basis of their
reports that Muratori wrote (in 1743) that the Americans might be stupid
and lazy, but were no more so than the miserable European peasantry,
and since they had excellent memories they could easily attain the highest
levels of learning, if—and here the limitation is not poverty, as it was for
Clavigero, but politics—"if there were not prudent considerations
militating against their further instruction."[215]

With the same acrid skepticism Muratori absolves America from the
charge of having no iron. It is true that "up until now no iron mine has
been discovered anywhere in America," but "I would almost be tempted
to suspect that European policy has not as yet wished to concern itself
with the discovery of such mines in America for various reasons which it
is not necessary to relate."[216] In other words even then European colonialism kept the natives in ignorance and neglected the natural resources of the countries administered!

The same ground is covered by Clavigero's comparison between the

---

the *indios* of Peru and their way of calculating with pebbles, Acosta had written conclusively: "If this
is not intelligence and if these men are animals, let any man who wishes be a judge, for what I deem to
be certain is that in the things to which they apply themselves they are much superior to us" (*Historia
natural y moral*, VI, 8, ed. cit., p. 412). And in preface to his comments on the Mexicans he had remarked that among other things these observations would "remove much of the common and stupid
scorn, with which the Europeans consider them, believing these peoples not to possess qualities of men
of reason and prudence" (ibid., VII, 1; ed. cit., p. 452).

214. On the difficulties that the discovery of the American peoples presented to the theologians already tormented by the ancient problem of the "salvation of the heathen," see Louis Capéran, *Le prob-
lème du salut des infidèles* (Toulouse, 1934), I, 219–25, 252–58, 288–90, 297–98.

215. *Il cristianesimo felice*, II, 94; cf. ibid., I, 142–45.

216. Op. cit., II, 247.

paganism of the *indios* and the no less deplorable paganism of the ancient Greeks and Romans: an old and abused apologetic device which Oviedo had already employed frequently. From the religious point of view the Americans were no worse than the august figures of the classical age.

The comparison with the Greeks and Romans, arising, as we have just seen, from the formulation of the problem of the salvation of the heathen, had also been common and indeed almost *de rigueur* in the literature of the missionaries and Jesuits. Father Acosta had prefaced his description of the native civilizations of the Incas and the Aztecs with the warning: "If anyone should marvel at certain of the rites and customs of the *indios* and scorn them as ignorant and foolish, or abhor them as inhuman and diabolical, he should note that in the Greeks and Romans who ruled the world one finds either the same customs, or others similar, and sometimes even worse ones."[217] Thus Clavigero takes up again and breathes new life into teachings and aspirations that date back to the sixteenth century.

D. Moral vices, religion, and cannibalism. The defense of the Indians' morals is something that comes far more easily to the missionaries' spiritual heir. De Pauw accuses the Indians of four vices—gluttony, drunkenness, ingratitude, and pederasty. Clavigero denies the first and third; he recognizes the second, but says that it only became widespread with the arrival of the Spaniards; and he is horrified at the vile slander of the fourth accusation, when that vice is so frequent in Asia and Europe.[218] However, he admits that in their family relationships "the love that the husbands bear their wives is less than that which the wives bear their husbands." Nevertheless, adds this curious Jesuit, "it is common, if not general, for men to be less interested in their own wives than in other people's."[219]

In the sixth dissertation—on the "culture of the Mexicans"—Clavigero easily refutes de Pauw's accusation that describes all Americans as "barbarous and savage."[220] The Mexicans had money (cocoa), iron and copper, bridges, ships, lime, writing (hieroglyphics), the calendar, civil and military architecture, goldsmithery, and more besides. They had a rich language and wise laws. And what they did *not* have proves nothing against their mental qualities, nor against the climate, given that

---

217. *Historia natural y moral,* 1590, prologue to books V–VII, ed. cit., 302; see also VI, 1; ed. cit., p. 396. On the repeated parallel between the Mexicans and the Graeco-Romans, see the observations of Le Riverend Brusone in the preface, ed. cit., pp. 20–21.

218. *Storia,* IV, 195–200.

219. *Storia,* I, 122: on marriage among the Mexicans, see however IV, 255–56.

220. Op. cit., IV, 203. The whole of bk. VII of the *Storia* (ed. cit., II, 100–228) is devoted to the culture and government of the Mexicans.

most inventions "are due more to fortune, necessity, and avarice than to intellect."[221] And if their education was in some way inferior to the Greeks' from the intellectual point of view, it was certainly far superior from the point of view of morals and virtue.[222]

The seventh dissertation too—"on the borders and the population of the kingdoms of Anahuac"—lingers a while to combat "the blunders of M. de Pauw,"[223] reaffirming that ancient Mexico was thickly inhabited. But when he comes to the eighth—on the "religion of the Mexicans"—he begins by saying that this time he will not attack de Pauw, since the Prussian recognized clearly the similarity between the ravings of the Americans and those of other nations of the Old World in matters of religion. However, the polemic proves stronger than the polemicist; and it takes him by the hand, setting the patriot against the Jesuit. Father Clavigero soon finds himself defending the paganism of the Mexicans as a religion that is "less superstitious, less unbecoming, less puerile, and less unreasonable than that of the most cultivated nations of ancient Europe,"[224] in other words preferable to the classical paganism of the Greeks and Romans. The good Clavigero even manages to defend their practice of human sacrifice, albeit with some uneasiness,[225] and only draws back, horrified at the audacity of his own argument, when he comes to the question of cannibalism; "I confess, that in that they were more inhuman than those other nations." But—but even in the Old World and among the most civilized peoples cannibalism was and is known. The argument continues with various examples of cruelty and the rhetorical question asking who was guiltier, the Mexicans who ate their fellowmen for reasons of religion, or the Greeks who (according to Pliny) ate them for medicinal reasons. "But no," he says, as common sense finally triumphs, "I cannot aspire to defend the Mexicans on this point." And he goes on to the ninth and last dissertation—on the "origin of the French disease"—where he finds the Americans not guilty of having transmitted syphilis to the Spaniards, contrary to the opinion of de Pauw and "almost all Europeans," who, terrorized by the disease, which they looked on almost as a divine and savage punishment for their "sins," had easily convinced themselves that it must be of American origin and had thus made the New World the source of a mysterious and treacherous corrup-

---

221. Ibid., IV, 239.
222. Ibid., p. 261.
223. Ibid., p. 265.
224. Ibid., p. 288; cf. II, 3. The rites of the Mexicans take up the whole of bk. VI (ed. cit., II, 3–99). This effort of Clavigero's to set the Mexican religion above all the other pagan religions, though below Christianity, of course, is warmly approved, for its Mexicanism and indigenism, by Gabriel Mendez Plancarte (pp. xiii–xiv of his preface to the anthology *Humanistas del siglo XVIII*).
225. See chap. 9, sec. 3, "The Mexicans' Human Sacrifices."

tion, even before it became the module of nature totally decadent and rotten.[226]

Clavigero's main significance in the history of the debate on the "weakness" of America lies in the forcefulness of his reaction, i.e., in the rich array of arguments he is moved to produce to counteract de Pauw's foolish accusations. In a half-baked paradox, spiced up with a few scandalous anecdotes, he found the polemic stimulus for the rehabilitation of one of the greatest of the continent's ancient civilizations.

E. *The precursors of his polemical technique.* Clavigero's favorite polemical tactic is the counterattack. His oratorical technique is the one which has been defined as the *tu quoque.* America is defended by listing in detail the weaknesses of Europe.

This process of parry and thrust is so instinctive, so easy, and so flattering in the impression it gives of the arguer setting himself above the contestants and without absolving the one denying the other any right to accuse, that it is still a common debating gambit even today.[227] But the origins of this approach go back at least as far as Pietro Martire, with his naked savages giving lessons to the Christians in morals and theology. The Protestant Jean de Léry, mindful of the wars of religion, observed: "These days one no longer feels the same abhorrence for the cruelties of the savage cannibals . . . for we see the same and even worse and more detestable things in our own midst."[228] Montaigne wields the same critical and biting weapon with robust relish. The cannibals consume their enemies for revenge, true; but you Europeans devour a man alive with your tortures, you roast him and feed him to the dogs and

226. See John Langdon-Davis, *Sex, Sin and Sanctity* (London, 1954), pp. 295–96, 326. Almost as a sort of appendix to the *Storia antica del Messico* Clavigero wrote, in Italian, the *Storia della California,* which was supposed to appear a few months after the former (*Storia antica,* I, 110n.), but was actually published only after Clavigero's death (2 vols., Venice, 1789; Spanish trans. by Garcia de San Vicente, Mexico, 1852). Just as in the former the author speaks as a Mexican, in the latter he speaks as a Jesuit, recounting the glories not of the Aztecs but of the missionary fathers of his order (and at the close, referring to the expulsion, he has a few harsh words for the other orders, Franciscan and Dominican, that succeeded them: II, 205). Nevertheless Clavigero is unable to restrain himself from ridiculing, in the preface, those authors who write about America without study and without knowledge, like de Pauw, Robertson, and other Europeans. The *Recherches* "in a single sheet, given over to the treatment of that peninsula, contains forty-eight falsehoods, which I have patiently enumerated, including simple errors, formal lies, and bold slanders." He lists only "some of them for demonstration," and refutes them (I, 16–21). He then proceeds to address a few well-chosen words to Robertson (I, 21–22) and Raynal (I, 23) too. Buffon is mentioned on I, 104. The existence of songbirds is reaffirmed, of "nightingales, though few, the famous Centzontli," etc., "who with their sweet and harmonious song bring some relief to those who travel through these arid and melancholy wastes" (I, 99).

227. A recent apologist of America is reproved by the reviewer of the *Times Literary Supplement* (11 March 1955, p. 143) because "against the sharper cuts at the United States that are habitually made by Europeans he has always the same childlike defence, a *tu quoque,* which is too often neither accurate nor an answer."

228. *Histoire d'un voyage faict en la terre du Brésil,* 1578, ed. P. Gaffarel (Paris, 1876), II, 52, quoted by J. C. Lapp, op. cit., p. 156.

swine, "and what is worse, under pretext of piety and religion."[229] Nor are examples of ritual and criminal anthropophagy lacking among we proudly civilized Europeans.[230]

A more refined literary form of this same attitude of penitent reflection and satire was to appear first of all in the seventeenth century, with certain Lucianesque *Dialogues of the Dead,* in which Fontenelle brings together Cortes and Montezuma, and contrasts the supposed barbarity of the Mexicans with the much-vaunted wisdom of the Athenians and Romans. "You could not reproach me," says the Aztec, "with any folly of our peoples of America, for which I could not find worse in your countries; and I even undertake to consider only the follies of the Greeks or Romans." A little later, at the beginning of the eighteenth century, and shifting our field of vision from ancient history to modern geography, the same attitude of critical mockery appears in yet another form in the *Lettres persanes,* where the prejudices and weaknesses of Europe are laid bare under the steady and ironic scrutiny of an extra-European. The imitations of the *Lettres persanes* were, as we know, innumerable, and not a few of them availed themselves of the Americans as frank and impartial though shocked observers of European customs. Typical, at least in its title, was the *Letters of an Exiled Savage (to his correspondent in America), containing a Criticism of the Customs of the Century, and some Reflections on Matters of Religion and Politics,* which appeared anonymously in 1738.[231] Similar criticisms of European society found expression in the utopias, many of which had American settings.

Voltaire was to handle the polemical antithesis with exceptional virtuosity, both in novel form (*Zadig,* for example) and in direct statement. Just one example: "We pour scorn on the credulity of the Indians, quite forgetting that more than three hundred thousand copies of almanacs are sold in Europe every year, which are full of observations that are no less false and ideas no less absurd."[232]

229. *Essais,* I, 31. At the end of the immediately preceding *essai* (I, 30) Montaigne had lamented, with European and American examples, the idea "of thinking to gratify Heaven and nature by our massacre and homicide, which was universally embraced in all religions."

230. Ibid., 30 and 36. The religious thesis of anthropophagy, which is not actually so far removed from the more recent theories on the magico-religious beliefs of the primitive peoples, goes back to Las Casas (see chap. 9, sec. 3, "The Mexicans' Human Sacrifices"). For its relationship to the liturgy of divine sacrifice, see J. Frazer, *The Golden Bough* (Mexican example on pp. 488–91 of the abridged ed., New York, 1940).

231. Long attributed to the Marquis d'Argens, author of the *Lettres juives* and *Lettres chinoises,* it is now thought to be by J. Joubert de la Rue. It is an imitation of the *Lettres persanes* and the stories and dialogues of Lahontan, who in his turn seems to have drawn his inspiration from Lucian (G. Chinard, in the introduction to his edition of the *Dialogues curieux,* pp. 45–46, 64). Similar polemic tendencies occur in an anonymous work of 1785: *An Historic Epistle from Omiah to the Queen of Otaheite: being his remarks on the English Nation,* on which see B. Smith, *European Vision,* pp. 59–60.

232. *Essai sur les moeurs,* chap. 157; ed. cit., V, 57.

Two items in particular in this antithesis deserve mention—the Europeans killing their enemies without eating them, and the poverty of European nature compared to the benign generosity of nature in America—because Clavigero too found them in his arsenal of possible retaliatory weapons; he declined to use the first, which was repugnant to his religious humanity, but he used and abused the second.

Montaigne, as we have seen, had managed to defend the American cannibals. And the philosopher La Douceur had commented ironically on the Europeans' noble trade of slaughtering men without eating them. Voltaire makes satirical use of the antithesis on more than one occasion. In *Candide* Cacambo approves of the anthropophagous Oreillons; "it certainly makes more sense to eat one's enemies than to leave the fruit of one's victory to the ravens and crows," as the Europeans do, since they have better things to eat.[233] The *Lettre de M. Clocpicre à Mr. Eratou,* after expressing "some horror" at the story of the hussar who had eaten a Cossack and found him very tough, observes that one should not argue from the particular to the general, that there are Cossacks and Cossacks, and one might perhaps find very tender Cossacks; but it closes with the hussar's words: "Really, gentlemen, . . . You are very sensitive; two or three hundred thousand men are killed, and everybody finds that good; one Cossack is eaten, and everybody cries out."[234] In the article *Anthropophages,* in the *Questions sur l'Encyclopédie,*[235] Voltaire refers to his interview with a female anthropophagite from Mississippi with whom he had spoken at Fontainebleau in 1725: "We kill our neighbors in pitched battle, or in unpitched battle . . . what does it matter when one has been killed whether one is eaten by a soldier or a crow or a dog?" And the same conversation with the dusky lady-cannibal is related in the *Essai sur les moeurs,* where Voltaire ends with this "moral": "The real barbarity is the killing, not the quarreling with the crows and worms over the dead man's body,"[236] and gives numerous examples of savage and religious cannibalism from Paris and Holland, from the Bible and the Tartars.

Kant condemns the fighting man of Europe in even more coldly ironic terms:

The difference between the European savages and those of America lies principally in this, that whereas many tribes of the latter have been completely consumed by their enemies, the former know how to make better use of their enemies

---

233. Chap. XVI, ed. Pléiade, p. 181; and see above, p. 44. Here one notes the link with the other theme of America's shortage of foodstuffs.
234. Op. cit., in *Oeuvres* (London, 1772), XXVIII, 111.
235. London ed., 1779, XLVII, 27–29.
236. Chap. 146; ed. cit. IV, 379.

than in eating them, and prefer to increase the number of their subjects and thus the quality of material available for yet more widespread wars.[237]

If the Europeans refrain from eating their enemies, it is because they are more utilitarian than the Americans. In more or less the same way Guerrazzi in the nineteenth century finds the barbarous lynch law preferable to the hypocritical civilization of the European governments, "under which murder is sanctified with a seal of legality."[238]

In modern times Shaw is following precisely in Voltaire's footsteps when in the preface to his *Saint Joan* he sympathizes sarcastically with the Marquesas Islanders' amazement at Joan being burned and then not eaten: "Why, they ask, should anyone take the trouble to roast a human being except with that object? They cannot conceive its being a pleasure. As we have no answer for them that is not shameful to us, let us blush for our more complicated and pretentious savagery."[239]

The literature of the Old World does not of course contain so many examples of denigration of European nature as compared to American. Any tendency in that direction is lost in the simple panegyrics of America's tropical exuberance, with no barren and insidious comparisons. But it was only very shortly after Clavigero that André Chénier's Inca, recounting the conquest of Mexico by the Spaniards, described the nature of Europe as "miserly." Europe has no fish in its rivers, nor birds in its forests. It has neither the "juicy acorns" of the cocoa tree, nor cocoanuts, nor bananas! "Leurs champs du beau maïs ignorent la moisson / La mangue leur refuse une douce boisson."[240]

But the historian is not entitled to poetic license. In Clavigero the quarrel between worlds is totally unbecoming. Yet viewed on a political rather than doctrinal level these moments of childish spite and pique, these reproaches of the Greeks for their pederasty and the Romans for their cruelty, and so on, are seen to contain the first whimperings of that moralistic exaltation of the New World, as polemically opposed to the Old, and corrupt, World, which was just then becoming the inspiration of the publicists of the newborn United States, and which would be taken up again and "propagandized" *ad nauseam* in the nineteenth century and a good part of the twentieth.

237. *Zum ewigen Frieden*, 1795, *Zweiter Definitivartikel*.
238. *Il secolo che muore*, IV, 343.
239. Op. cit., ed. Tauchnitz, pp. 53–54.
240. Fragment from the "Amérique," in *Oeuvres complètes*, Pléiade ed. (Paris, 1940), p. 418. In North American patriotic literature there are frequent eulogies of the abundance of crops and fruits in the New World (M. Curti, *American Loyalty*, passim, esp. pp. 30, 40–41, 69). Burke's impassioned words (1776) are well known: "for some time past the old world has been fed by the new," which has offered its aged parent its own swollen breast "with a true filial piety, with a Roman charity" (in *Works*, ed. World's Classics, II, 182). On the suggested scarcity of foodstuffs in America, see above, pp. 44 (Voltaire), 90 (de Pauw), etc.

XIV. FATHER MOLINA'S *NATURAL HISTORY OF CHILE*

Father Molina, who was a young man just turned twenty-seven when he left Chile for exile in Italy, is not to be compared with the learned and ponderous Clavigero. His main interest is not archeology but natural history. Not even the fierce Arawaks arouse any real passion in him. The patriotic fervor that inflames some of the Mexican's pages is here reduced to a nostalgic yearning for the beauty of the Chilean landscape and the mildness of its climate; Chile is "the Italy, which is to say the *Garden of South America.*"[241] Indeed in his anxiety to convince his reader of the benevolence of the land of Chile, Molina concludes by announcing that the lions, which are few in number and found only in the depths of the forest, "are timid and different from the maned lions of Africa," and have never dared to confront man but "rather flee from all the places that man frequents."[242] He also admits that there are only thirty-six indigenous species of quadrupeds in Chile. And although there are numerous in-

---

241. Giovanni Ignazio Molina, *Saggio sulla storia naturale del Chile* (Bologna, 1782), pp. 3, 29 and passim. Volney, *Oeuvres complètes*, p. 684n., actually took him for an Italian. Molina himself, for that matter, born in Concepción, after a long stay in Italy felt himself "more Bolognese than American" (*Memorie di storia naturale* [Bologna, 1821], I, 7, 56, 196; Clavigero too was taken for an Italian: *Catalogue of the Library of Jefferson*, IV, 269; Rosa, op. cit., p. 379).

Molina published first of all, anonymously, a *Compendio della storia geografica, naturale e civile del regno del Chile* (Bologna, 1776), which was translated into German by E. J. Jagemann (who attributed it erroneously to Felipe Gomez Vidaurre), and published in Hamburg, 1782; then this *Saggio sulla storia naturale* (which discreetly recalls the *Compendio*, p. 7), translated into German, 1786, and immediately quoted by Kant (Akad.-Ausg., XIV, 634); into Spanish by Domingo Joseph de Arquellada y Mendoza (Madrid, 1788), and into French by Gruvel (Paris, 1789); and finally a *Saggio sulla storia civile del Chile* (Bologna, 1787), translated into German in 1791 and into Spanish (by Nicolas de la Cruz y Bahamonde [Madrid, 1795]; on the possibility of another Spanish translation already in 1788, see Arnoldsson, *La conquista española*, p. 57). "All the cultivated nations of Europe demanded its translation [of the *Saggio*] into their own language," *Storia naturale*, 2d ed., p. iii, and Iturri asserts that it was admired by Spallanzani, translated into French, English, German, Russian, and Spanish: "The Letter of Francisco Iturri, S.J. (1789) — Its Importance for Hispanic American Historiography," ed. José de Onis, *The Americas* (Washington D.C., 1951), p. 87. The notes added to this last translation, together with the notes to the French translation, were utilized in the English translation (Middletown, Conn., 1808; London, 1809, 2 vols.) of the two *Saggi* from the Italian, by Richard Alsop and William Shaler, and entitled *The Geographical, Natural and Civil History of Chile*.

In 1792 Molina asked the king of Spain for an increase in the pension promised to him for his two works on the natural and civil history of Chile (Ricardo Donoso, *Fuentes documentales para la historia de la independencia de América*, I, *Misión de investigación en los archivos europeos* [Mexico, 1960], p. 93; cf. also 92) and later ardently embraced the cause of independence from the Spanish monarchy (see Vargas Ugarte, *La "Carta,"* p. 52). In 1810, finally, Molina, now seventy years old, published in Bologna a second edition of the *Saggio sulla storia naturale*: in large format, abundantly "increased" also by inclusion of information taken from Humboldt and the botanists Ruiz and Pavón, and embellished with a fine portrait of the author, thus bearing all the signs of a definitive edition, it turns out to be considerably less involved than the first edition in the polemic with de Pauw and his followers: "Their diatribes [in fact] have today fallen into the oblivion they deserved. The American Revolution has made all their [the Americans'] detractors fall silent" (op. cit., p. 272). De Pauw is still contradicted incidentally (for example on pp. 11, 24 and 29), but this is no more than a residuum. Other polemical remarks, such as that against Fr. Gilij (see below, p. 222), are omitted. But likewise abandoned, in compensation, are certain of the boasts of the edition of twenty-eight years earlier, relating to the succulent taste of the meat of the Andean cattle, the dimensions of the horns of the oxen (see below, p. 216), etc. There is also some attenuation in the homage paid to Linnaeus's classificatory system (for example, p. 254).

242. *Storia naturale*, pp. 51–52, 295–99; cf. *Memorie*, II, 185.

sects there, "nonetheless I am of the opinion, from what I can observe [one can almost see the good Molina scratching himself!] that land insects are more numerous in Italy."[243]

A. The rehabilitation of nature in Chile. Despite this ingenuous reexhumation of the "cowardly lion" and the paucity of the animal species, Molina too reacts with a vibrant enthusiasm for America when he comes up against de Pauw's slanders, and labors studiously to show that in none of the three kingdoms does the New World give way to the Old. Buffon can deny it as much as he likes. Even a great beast like the hippopotamus can reputedly be found in the rivers and lakes of Arauco—a hippopotamus with webbed feet "like the seals," and with its skin covered with a soft down "similar in color to the sea wolves'" (i.e., seals'). The cautious Molina never states positively that they exist; but it is "universally believed throughout the country" that they do.[244]

The preface speaks first of all in general terms of the great interest in America shown by Europe "at the present time"; he expands a little on the meager knowledge of Chile in Europe and presents the plan of the work. Then all of a sudden the anti–de Pauw polemic explodes: "Such of my readers, as are familiar with the Philosophical Researches on the Americans by M. Pauw, will be amazed to find a country of America described differently from what he would have us believe of all parts of that vast continent. But what can I do? Must I betray the truth, so as not to expose myself to the vulgar sarcasms which the author of the said Researches hurls at all those whom he finds opposed to his strange ideas?"[245] Pauw has seen nothing of the Americas and for reasons of his own, "which are not difficult to guess,"[246] has chosen to overlook anything said by any reputable author that might go against his theses, which

---

243. *Storia naturale*, p. 196. Cf. above, p. 105. But he cannot swallow that wretched little figure of thirty-six: "I am actually quite convinced that there are more" (ibid., p. 273). In the 2d ed. (1810) he still reaches "barely" thirty-eight species of mammals (ed. cit., pp. 172, 226). As for the insects, it could be mentioned that the illustrious Niebuhr too relates, on the word of an English traveler named Howse, that the Italians are much dirtier than the redskins, who may have lice, but no fleas, nor bedbugs (letter from Rome to M. Jacobi, 30 April 1817, in *Lebensnachrichten über Barthold Georg Niebuhr aus Briefen desselben und aus Erinnerungen einiger seiner nächsten Freunde* [Hamburg, 1838], II, 309).

244. *Storia naturale*, p. 274. In the 2d ed. (1810) the sea "wolves" become sea "calves" (*vitelli*).

245. *Storia naturale*, p. 12. Note that de Pauw is not even mentioned in the *Compendio*, Molina's first work, in which, however, it was affirmed that the European animals had been acclimatized in Chile "without degenerating in any way" (p. 91; for the plants, see p. 43). Of the nightingale of Chile, Molina admitted however that "it is smaller than the one over here, and its song is neither so continuous nor so harmonious" (p. 64). Of the lion, which is small and without mane, and attacks cattle but not men, see p. 8n.; cf. pp. 81–82. In the *Storia naturale* the nightingale disappears, but of the Thenca, a variety of the Centzontlatole (see above, p. 202), it is affirmed, among other wonders, that "its voice is higher, more varied and more melodious than the nightingale's" (p. 252).

246. This truly "Jesuitical" accusation of venality was to be taken up in the nineteenth century by the Peruvian Dávila Condemarín (see below, p. 306) and again in our own day by the American Echeverria, who supposes de Pauw agreed to work as an instrument of Frederick II's antiemigration policy (*Mirage*, pp. 11–12).

proceed from "incongruent premises" to "anti-American conclusions." His descriptions might be applicable to the moon or the selenites. But unfortunately for him America is not the moon; it has been visited by some learned men and studied by others who were moved solely by the love of truth, like Count Gianrinaldo Carli.[247]

As he develops his argument, which he does in fact somewhat aridly and scholastically, Father Molina's scorn falls impartially on everyone (which would include de Pauw) who thinks that the dogs of the New World could not bark;[248] but in particular he loses no chance of holding up to public ridicule that French "philosopher" who denies the Americas the capacity to produce peaches, apricots, cherries, and in general any kernel fruit,[249] or high-grade iron,[250] or long-lived men;[251] the same individual who confuses the homes of the various tribes of *indios*,[252] and believes that Atacama is in Chile[253] and knows nothing of the Chilean language,[254] nor of the climate, which is not at all as de Pauw describes it, because "Nature delights in transgressing laws which men make without consulting the location of the countries on which they try to impose them";[255] who, finally, considers the Chilean ostrich degenerate compared with the African ostrich "because the latter has two instead of three toes in front,"[256] whereas if anything, Molina retorts, the African ostrich would be the "bastard" with his one toe less.

247. *Storia naturale*, pp. 12–14; Carli is praised again in the closing lines of the *Storia civile*, p. 308, and in the *Memorie*, II, 190. Of the other authors that had their say in the polemic, Molina several times quotes Pernety (*Storia naturale*, pp. 148–49n., 161–62n., 165, 283), Robertson (*Storia naturale*, pp. 29–30, 322; *Storia civile*, pp. 73, 308), Raynal (*Storia naturale*, pp. 39–41, 48, 50, 62–63; *Storia civile*, pp. 77–78, 101–02, 273, 275–76; Raynal had praised the climate and nature of Chile: cf. above, p. 46) and Clavigero (*Storia naturale*, p. 270; *Memorie*, II, 185). He is also familiar with and makes extensive use of Fr. Acosta, Frezier, Feuillée, and Ulloa.

248. *Storia naturale*, p. 270; cf. above, pp. 56, 147, n. 207, etc.

249. Ibid., p. 194n.

250. Ibid., pp. 91–92; see also above, p. 57. In fact in his enthusiasm for the minerals of Chile Molina makes a very accurate prophecy on the great riches one day to be derived from the nitrates (ibid., pp. 70, 82, 85–86). But he also maintains as "a constant fact in America" that "when the mines are exhausted they are regenerated anew with the passing of time and are refilled as they were before" (*Memorie*, I, 181–82)—almost as if they were so many inexhaustible devil's purses. This is, of course, a derivation from the ancient idea, going back to Aristotle, that metals are products of the earth, like vegetables (see also Gerbi, *Viejas polémicas*, pp. 241–42).

251. *Storia naturale*, p. 333; *Storia civile*, p. 53. On this point Father Molina, who in fact lived to the age of eighty-nine (1740–1829), is particularly insistent. On the much-discussed longevity of the Americans, see L. Wright, *The Elizabethans' America*, pp. 69, 161; P. G. Adams, *Travelers*, p. 11, 183, 186. According to Molina the famous *Patagones* are none other than the tall and robust Indians of the Chilean Sierra, the Puelches, the "Antarctic Titans" (*Storia naturale*, pp. 9, 337; *Memorie*, I, 199–200; but cf. the *Compendio*, p. 226); and in the region they inhabit there grows the Chilean pine, "the most gigantic tree of the terrestrial globe" (*Memorie*, ibid.).

252. *Storia naturale*, p. 27.

253. De Pauw says that the army of Almagro suffered from hunger in Chile. No, replies Molina, "famine afflicted those troops in the desert of Atacama, which never had anything to do with Chile" (*Storia naturale*, p. 128n.). Is there a single Chilean today willing to renounce Atacama and its nitrates?

254. *Storia naturale*, p. 334; *Storia civile*, pp. 305–07.

255. *Storia naturale*, p. 41; on the extreme humidity of the Americas, cf. however the *Memorie*, II, 180.

256. *Storia naturale*, p. 261; cf. Clavigero, above, p. 202.

B. Respectful disagreement with Buffon. The tone of this last polemic thrust seems a throwback to Clavigero's technique of petty spitefulness, but its content—the comparing of the lives of animals perfect or degenerate, large and complete or small and defective—takes us right back into the Buffonian system. Molina is familiar with Buffon; but on his way past he respectfully rejects his authority: "This great man was badly informed on this point [the relationship between the *vicuña* and *paco*] as in many others concerning the natural history of America."[257] He even claims, does he not, that the South Seas "are incapable of producing Whales." In this ocean he admits only the existence of fish of modest dimensions: "This great man [he bows again], who sometimes gets carried away with his favorite systems, might at least have remembered the monstrous size of the false sea lions of the Juan Fernandez Islands, which he himself describes."[258]

In another passage Molina takes one of Buffon's own critical weapons —the formula "the names confused the things"—and turns it against one of the Frenchman's followers. All the evils came

from the abuse of the names of creatures of the Old Continent by the earliest Conquerors, who applied them whimsically and quite without discernment to the new objects they saw before them, which bore some slight resemblance to objects they had left behind in Europe. . . . The abuse of nomenclature, which still continues, has been most harmful to the natural history of America: it is the origin of the capricious systems on the degeneration of the quadrupeds in this immense continent, and likewise of the small deer, small boars, small bears, etc., which are cited in support of such systems. . . . A modern, respectable author, who claims that the degeneration of the animals in America is evident,[259]

fell into the same error. One could easily defend "all the American quadrupeds, struck down by this arbitrary sentence of degradation."[260]

Molina's defense is an effective one: American nature is not inferior

257. *Storia naturale*, p. 313; *Storia civile*, pp. 9–10.

258. *Storia naturale*, pp. 230–31. On the whales of the Antarctic, whose existence is denied by Buffon through "one of the most indefensible of his strange paradoxes," see also the *Compendio*, pp. 74–75, and the note on whales in the *Memorie*, II, 54, 61–63, quoting Pernety, Bougainville, etc. Buffon's false lions are "lamantins" (*Phoca elephantina*), who are delightfully described fighting furious battles for the females waiting on the sidelines "ready to applaud and follow the victor. Thus the most valorous [like so many broad-bellied pashas!] form themselves numerous seraglios, and accompanied by the sultanas taken from the weaker members travel triumphantly across the vast Ocean" (*Storia naturale*, p. 282).

259. Referring to Fr. Filippo Salvatore Gilij, for whom see below, p. 222. Against geologists who "through some mistaken analogy" were determined to extend to America's volcanoes the systems modeled on those of Europe, see *Memorie*, I, 26. Against the botanists: *Storia naturale*, 2d ed., p. 101.

260. *Storia naturale*, pp. 270–71. Cf. "I have never pretended to say that everything has improved in America. I am by nature opposed to odious comparisons" (*Storia civile*, p. 99). Thus, for example: "the fine arts in Chile are in a wretched state. The mechanical arts too are still very far from being perfected there" (*Storia civile*, p. 274; cf. already *Compendio*, p. 244). Or, to take another example, that of "comparison of animals," he is willing to "let the Alps have their lammergeyer and the Andes their condor, both champions worthy of entering the lists, and battling for the dominion of the skies" (*Storia naturale*, 2d ed., p. 225).

because it is different. And Molina is quick to note the differences. Even among the Americans of various nations he notices particular traits which make it impossible to classify them as "all the same." Nor can he restrain his scornful laughter at the expense of those who failed to observe them: "I laugh to myself when I read in certain modern writers with reputations as diligent observers, that all Americans look the same, and that when one has seen one of them one has seen all of them" (*Storia naturale*, p. 336). There is no mistaking the allusion to Antonio de Ulloa's celebrated statement: "Once one has seen an Indian of whatever region, one can say that one has seen all of them, as for color and build; but in the matter of size it is not so, as this varies according to the areas. . . . Almost the same as has been said for color can be applied to the manners and customs, character, spirit, inclination, and qualities, in some things such similarity being observable as if the most distant territories were one and the same."[261] Of the Creoles, on the other hand, Molina writes that they are all equal, from whatever European nation they descend: "The same ideas and the same moral qualities are noticeable in all. This uniformity, deserving of some attention, has never, I believe, been considered by any philosopher in its full extension" (*Storia naturale*, p. 272n.). The implications are clear: the superiority of *climate* over *race*, of *geography* over *history*. America produces natives that differ greatly one from another; but it reduces the offspring of the Europeans all to the same level.

His counterattack is less effective: nature in America is so good that the species of the Old World which have been brought there have at least maintained their "stature," and the individuals in many cases increased it and prospered "in their repeated propagation and long sojourn in this benign climate" (*Storia naturale*, p. 271). Nor did the oxen of Chile, domestic or wild, "ever have the misfortune to lose their horns, as the denigrators of America would have it believed." If they degenerate, "it is in excess rather than deficiency. Their horns become so large" that people make cups and flasks out of them, as large as eight inches in diameter![262] All the European plants transported to Chile "thrive there as if they were in their native country" (*Storia naturale*, p. 188). His apology echoes with the old ingenuous enthusiasm of the early chroniclers

---

261. *Noticias americanas*, 1772, entretenimiento XVII, ed. Madrid, 1792, p. 253. See analogous comments from La Condamine (above, chap. 4, n. 95), Gilij (below, p. 230), and Smith on the redskins: "The study of one of these nations suffices for forming an exact judgment on the others" (*Voyage*, I, 173). See also Humboldt (Minguet, op. cit., p. 374), and toward the middle of the nineteenth century Beltrami: "The peoples of the two Americas are all and everywhere of the same physical and moral type" (*Notizie e lettere*, pub. under the auspices of the Municipio di Bergamo and dedicated to the Historical Society of Minnesota [Bergamo, 1865], p. 122).

262. *Storia naturale*, pp. 330–31. The biggest horn of all was presented as a gift (and a very appropriate one) to Viceroy Manuel Amat, celebrated in literature as the lover of the voluble Perricholi. For Fr. Gilij's reply, see below, pp. 228–29.

and ancient historians of the Americas. But whether because of the new polemic tone, or because of the apology's limitation to the earth and skies of Chile, here too one notes a new feeling of attachment to country, some sort of embryonic and minuscule physical patriotism that finds more immediate and spontaneous expression in the exile.[263]

XV. FATHERS VELASCO, JOLIS, AND PERAMAS: QUITO, THE CHACO, AND THE RIVER PLATE

Two Jesuits had defended Mexico and Chile against de Pauw. Some years later an Argentinian Jesuit in Rome was to take up his pen to join the battle against the European slanderers (Father Iturri, see below, p. 295). Another father in exile, don Juan de Velasco, from the land which was to become Ecuador, completed in 1789, in Faenza, a *History of the Kingdom of Quito*, in which he unmasked the glittering and fraudulent works of de Pauw, Robertson, Raynal, Marmontel, and Buffon, whose influence had led to the formation of a veritable "modern sect of anti-American philosophers." De Pauw, the recognized leader of the sect, is politely described as a madman or degenerate himself, ill informed, given to reckless generalizations, and at every step contradicted by the facts. But for all this Velasco still cannot concur with Pernety's defense: "I know better than he does what those American nations [the *Indios*] are. I confess that they have many and great defects," he says, drawing thus a clear dividing line between himself and the primitivists and Rousseauians; however, he goes on, even the impious Raynal found he could distinguish between the real savages and the civilized Mexicans and Peruvians, and Dr. Robertson too avoided that mistake.[264]

263. Molina had by this time lost all hope of seeing his native land again: see *Storia naturale*, p. 7. Giovanni Fabbroni, in his *Scritti di pubblica economia* (1804), published under the pseudonym of Diego Lopez, already talks of Molina and Clavigero as excellent writers and "celebrated patriots" (Florence ed., 1847, I, 267). And Fr. Encina observes that Clavigero's and Molina's works should be considered not so much as elements of Creole patriotism, but rather as manifestations of the "blossoming, in the two ex-Jesuits, of an intense love for their countries," a love that in its turn acted on the spirit of the Creole and reinforced his "consciousness of his worth" and his desire for emancipation ("Gestación de la Independencia," in *Revista Chilena de Historia y Geografía*, 89 [1940], pp. 15–16). In the same way Arnoldsson (*La conquista española*, p. 36) sees in Molina and in Clavigero the first defenders of the ancient civilizations of the *indios*, the first "identification of Indian antiquity with modern Hispano-America."

264. Velasco's work (published in integral form only in 1841–44, in Quito; second part trans. in the Ternaux-Compans collection, vols. 18–19 [Paris, 1840]; rept. of vol. I [Quito, 1940], ed. R. Reyes) has always remained unobtainable to me. Ferd. Denis, librarian of Sainte-Geneviève, describes it (in G. Osculati, *Esplorazione delle regioni equatoriali lungo il Napo e il fiume delle Amazzoni* [1846–48, Milan, 1854], p. 330) as "precious" and "extremely rare in Europe." See however José Dávila Condemarín, *Bosquejo histórico de la fundación de la insigne Universidad Mayor de San Marcos de Lima* (Lima, 1854), p 67–69; M. L. Amunátegui, *Los precursores de la independencia de Chile*, III (Santiago, 1872), p. 113; M. de Mendiburu, *Diccionario histórico-biográfico del Perú* (Lima, 1931–34), VIII, 357; Carbia, *La leyenda negra*, p. 134. On Velasco's sources and the success of his work, ample details in N. Zuñiga, *Atahualpa o la tragedia de Amerindia* (Buenos Aires, 1945), pp. 42–76, and further information in Donoso, *Fuentes documentales*, pp. 29–30, 92.

It was Faenza, and the same year 1789, that saw the publication in octavo of the first volume (which regrettably remained the only one, although four were announced) of the *Essay on the Natural History of the Province of the Gran Chaco, and on the practices and customs of the Peoples dwelling there, together with three diaries of as many journeys made into the interior lands of those Barbarians,* the work of another exiled father, Father Giuseppe Jolis. More than twenty years had passed since the Jesuits' expulsion from America and since the publication of de Pauw's *Recherches.* But from the very first lines of his preface Jolis says how he was largely spurred into composing his essay by the "pitying and unflattering portrait of that whole continent presented by some authors, who describe its climate as so harmful that not just the men degenerate there, but the animals, the plants, and the trees brought over from Europe too: and the same holds true, they claim, for the wild beasts that originate there, and the heathen peoples living there, and finally the *criollos,* which is to say the sons of Europeans born in America."[265]

It is a precise résumé and there is no doubt that Jolis is well acquainted not only with Buffon's and de Pauw's writings, but also with those of their main adversaries, such as Pernety, Carli, Clavigero, and Molina.[266] Yet his major theme is antiencyclopedism, into which he introduces the defense of the regions he visited in America merely as a single episode. "Spanish America," he bursts out impatiently, "has been so badly treated by the Gentlemen of the *Encyclopedia* that it would have been better served if they had never mentioned it at all."[267] It is understandable then that the contempt he lavishes on the denigrators of America embraces both the greatest of the early naturalists of the New World, Oviedo, suspect perhaps for having furnished material to the newer writers,[268] and Buffon's "follower," the serene illuminist historiographer Robertson, "Dr. Robertson, a writer of great merit moreover, and careful," who is however rebuked for several blunders.[269] And one can under-

265. Op. cit., pp. 3–4 (cf. also 13–15, 19, etc.). The author apparently wanted to dedicate his work to a certain Pignatelli (the pugnacious Jesuit Giuseppe Pignatelli, 1737–1811, beatified in 1933?), who had encouraged him and perhaps helped him to publish it. On the subject of rays (the fish), Jolis invokes the testimony of other brother exiles from his order: "There are living, and at present to be found in this city of Faenza, those who have seen some in those rivers as big as a carriage wheel in circumference" (op. cit., p. 385).

266. Pernety is mentioned on pp. 5–6, 149, 152, 156; Carli on p. 6; Clavigero on pp. 98, 141, 143, 157, 180, 224, 231, 275, 285, 289, 313, 327; Molina on pp. 113, 140, 217–18, 231, 267, 285, 288, 290, 297, 306, 313. Jolis also refers to Muratori's *Il cristianesimo felice* ("his little History of the Missions of Paraguay," p. 156) and Fr. Gilij (pp. 100, 285).

267. Op. cit., p. 59; cf. p. 64.

268. "His History is woven with so many and such great exaggerations and fables that it seems to have been written by someone who never set foot in the New World, and in order to amuse the reader with Romances" (op. cit., p. 198; cf. also 194, 212, 285). On pp. 155 and 540n., Oviedo is suspected of having given rise to the current doubts about the existence of tigers and kernel fruit in America. He is also mentioned on pp. 268 and 275.

269. Op. cit., pp. 477–81; cf. pp. 7, 152, 162, 217, 297.

stand why although he is persistently attacking his enemies on the zoological and naturalistic fronts, so to speak, his interest is in fact wholly in the "nations," in the peoples among whom he has spent his missionary life. When he has completed his review of the plants, quadrupeds, avians, "and other unreasoning beings," his arguments embroidered with the usual polemical forays and decorated with picturesque descriptions à la Buffon, he seems to heave a great sigh: "Freed at last of this tiresome impediment, I will go on to speak of reasoning beings, which is to say the Nations" who inhabited the Chaco in the year 1767, "when by Superior disposition I was obliged to leave them."[270] And here the polemic ceases, the description becomes detailed and affectionate, Buffon disappears over the horizon, and de Pauw only reappears for a couple of hasty visits, in relation to circumcision,[271] fruits with stones,[272] or America's episcopal sees.[273]

A Spaniard, not an American; a missionary, not a professor—Jolis is more a man of action than a scholar. When Petrus Johannes Andreu wanted to send the Good News to the immense unwelcoming regions of the Chaco, he "chose . . . two men of intrepid spirit and staunch endurance, Roque Gorostiza and José Jolis, to penetrate to the depths of the Chaco. One can hardly believe and record the dangers and difficulties that beset these two men on the expedition they undertook. . . . Jolis took with him a great number of Tobas and some Mataguayos, with whom a settlement was established on the Golden River [the Río Dorado]."[274] At the time of the expulsion Father Jolis had been in America twelve years and was with Father Michele Navaz in the smallest (and one of the most recent and remote) "missions" of the Chaco, that of the Madonna della Colonna, in the vernacular Macapillo, in Tucumán, where were gathered some two hundred Pasaini natives, of whom forty-eight were Christians.[275] Yet this link, seemingly so tenuous, continued to bind the exiled Jesuit to the boundless expanse of the Chaco, spurred him into entering the debate and drafting an extensive treatise, and remained a factor in his life for almost twice as long as the time he spent in America, until his dying day, in fact, because Jolis died in Faenza "for the Chaco and his paper *indios*," as Diego Gonzales wrote, "since the uncompleted history of the Chaco took his life, and the first volume [*"grueso y flaco"*] ended up wrapping sardines, for want (by some

270. Ibid., p. 387; note that "leave them": Jolis thinks not about the land but about the people he was obliged to abandon.
271. Ibid., pp. 434–39.
272. Ibid., pp. 540–41n.
273. Ibid., pp. 564n., 567n.
274. Jos. Emmanuel Peramas, *De vita et moribus sex sacerdotum Paraguaycorum* (Faenza, 1791), p. 142.
275. See the table giving further precise details, between pp. 528 and 529 of his book.

way) of someone to take on the task of publishing the second, although the dead man left much residue." Indeed, it seems that the second volume was already prepared for the press, and Jolis was about to leave for or was on his way to Bologna when death overtook him.[276]

The character of the man, completely devoted to his "paper Indians," explains the curious limitations (and perhaps also the limited reputation) of his work. As a missionary he detests encyclopedism, but Buffon's and de Pauw's extreme anti-Americanist theories leave him intellectually unmoved. He does not begin his counterattack with exalted praises of America, not of the parts where he had lived, anyway. He never confronts his opponents directly. But on factual details he remains intransigent. He burns with a continual resentment at the flagrant errors and patent stupidity of these presumptuous observers, or rather these armchair scientists, these careless sedentary know-it-alls.

M. de Buffon, who is "certainly not fond of America," claims that the songbirds of the American forests can be reduced to some half dozen. There are, however, at least twenty-five, Jolis retorts, "and this may serve to show the reader what faith can be attached to this celebrated and renowned Naturalist, on the things of America."[277] His conclusion is respectful, but cutting: "I revere the much-praised Naturalist, yet I cannot but let the public know what an unsure guide he is in things relating to the savages who inhabit the New World, whom he usually either ignores, or misrepresents in such a way as to make them appear quite other than what they are."[278]

His manner toward de Pauw is usually less circumspect. The "Coryphaeus of the anti-Americans"[279] is a "modern German writer," or rather "Prussian," with a weakness for the miraculous and the excessive, and thus very fond, in many things, of exaggeration and hyperbole.[280] Many of his allegations are simply repudiated as false.[281] But on the denial of the existence of tigers — authentic tigers — in America, Jolis gives him a

---

276. Guillermo Furlong, "José Jolis, Misionero e Historiador (1728–1790)," *Estudios*, 46 (1932), pp. 82–91, 178–88, esp. 180, 185. The second volume was to be "considerably more curious [than the first], and more amusing for every sort of person" (*Saggio*, pp. 9–10). In the same review (*Estudios*, 18 [1920], pp. 294–302), Furlong published the third of the travel diaries, which were to complete Jolis's *Saggio*, and to which he often refers the reader for details, as for example on the tapirs, monkeys, and bats (*Saggio*, p. 221), on the crab lice and cochineals (ibid., p. 376) and on certain indigenous tribes (ibid., p. 471).

277. *Saggio*, pp. 222–27. The attacks on Buffon are so frequent as to become wearisome: see for example pp. 45, 138, 147–48, 151–61, 164–69, 173, 179–80, 183–84, 187, 196, 198–99, 207–08, 211, 213–15, 217, 219–21, 229–32, 236, 247, 249–50, 258, 262–70, 273–81, 287, 297, 299–301, 309, 314, 317, 321n., 335.

278. Op. cit., pp. 305–06; cf. p. 13.

279. Ibid., p. 126.

280. Ibid., pp. 320–21, where the same accusations are leveled at another "German," Fr. Martin Dobritzhoffer.

281. Cf. for example: pp. 36n., 100–01, 107–08, 124–25, 148, 150, 161, 167–69, 184, 215, 217, 235, 265, 297n., 322n., 330, 335, 375.

regular dressing down, just like some school principal with an impertinent little pupil: "It was thus very necessary, I say, my dear Canon Pavv, that even you should have deigned to study first American Zoography, so as to learn to know those animals, to be able to distinguish their genera and the species; and then to occupy yourself as a Philosopher in researches that were not useless, as so many of yours certainly are." The Jesuit admits to being no scientist: "I willingly and candidly confess that I am not a Naturalist." But he concludes delightfully: "I do not think I am taking too much upon myself if I assert that there are real tigers in America, where I have spent many years, and have had the convenience of seeing some of them, and eating not a few in the missions of the Chaco."[282] The table fork rings out its challenge to the goose quill. The outcome of the duel is a foregone conclusion. How dare de Pauw contradict this devourer of wild beasts? . . . Come now, what Buffon measured and observed could not have been the proud and fearsome tiger of America: it was "an American tabby cat."[283]

When Jolis left for America in 1755 he was accompanied by Father Giuseppe Emanuele Peramas, and when he returned from the broad lands of the River Plate to the sleepy provincial life of Faenza in the Papal Romagna, Father Peramas was still his companion. Peramas is more a man of letters than Jolis: he is a good Latinist, and quite at home in academic exercises, such as the one whose Castilian translation has recently revived his reputation along the River Plate—a comparison between the Guaranays and the Republic of Plato, no less.[284] But what interests us is that in this brief treatise de Pauw is attacked no less than seven or eight times, usually in relation to subjects completely extraneous to the attempted parallel, and with arguments of the most candid empiricism.

How can de Pauw claim that the dogs in America no longer have the strength to bark? "In fact I was once almost deafened by the barking of American dogs."[285] How can he talk about newborn children being killed because they are deformed, *more Lacaedemonio*, if in America no imperfect children are ever born? "I can bear witness to this myself, who have seen no small part of South America."[286] But he too is concerned

---

282. Op. cit., pp. 153–54. "Not a few," he says here, but possibly it is a matter of no more than a couple. Elsewhere, in fact, Jolis says: "In the absence of better food I fed at least twice, and with pleasure, on tiger's meat" (op. cit., 166).

283. Op. cit., pp. 158–59.

284. Published as an introduction to his *De vita et moribus tredecim virorum Paraguaycorum* (Faenza, 1793) and translated as *La República de Platón y los Guaranies*, with prologue by G. Furlong (Buenos Aires, 1946).

285. Op. cit., par. 149; ed. cit., p. 74; trans., p. 116. Cf. above, pp. 147–48.

286. Op. cit., par. 96; ed. cit., pp. 53–54; trans., pp. 88–89.

not so much with the scientific problem as with the defense of the clergy against the canon of Xanten's accusations. While he exalts the American tigers as bigger and fiercer than those of the Old World, he admits that "the lion on the other hand is so timid that any dog puts him to flight; he is small and does not have the majesty of the African lion."[287] In short Peramas abandons the lion to de Pauw's sarcasms. But when de Pauw finds fault with the tonsured clerics, as for instance when he writes in the *Recherches* that natives were burned alive by the Dominican Inquisitors,[288] Peramas explodes with protest: "O Pauw, O pious Pauw! Here I can only pause, not knowing whether I should have more pity for you or for those Indians whom you pity with such noble clemency. But it is you rather that arouse my pity and my anger, you who have lied so unashamedly and erred so crassly in your ignorance, or your anxiety for slander, as is your wont." The Dominicans were never inquisitors. Nor did the Inquisition ever have jurisdiction over the *indios*. Peramas concludes with a solemn anathema: "This I wished to say of de Pauw, so that it might be known what credence one can lend to these impious philosophers, when they rage against the religious, against the sacred authorities, the supreme head of the Church (for not even he is spared by de Pauw), with deliberate and cunning fables, and whether through hate or malice or ignorance of the matters treated, deceive the simple masses." How much wiser they would be to submit to the true faith with sincere humility![289] America fades away once more, and the polemic winds up as a sermon.

The most interesting case, however, is that of the exiled Jesuit who undertook to describe the Orenoco and the Terraferma, the territory of the present-day republics of Venezuela and Colombia. Father Gilij (a crude Latinization of Giglio or Gilli?) thus rounds off the regional apologetic geography of Spanish America (save for Peru, of which more later); but Father Gilij is something very different from all his fellow Jesuits. He is never mentioned, even in passing, by those who have concerned themselves with our debate,[290] and thus on more than one count deserves some

---

287. See G. Furlong, *J. M. Peramas y su Diario del destierro* (1768) (Buenos Aires, 1952), p. 119. The *Diario* was published in Spanish at Turin, translated into Latin by the author, and also into Italian, French, and German (Ricardo Orta Nadal, *Un aspecto de la historiografía y etnología jesuíticas del Litoral—La idea de cultura en José Manuel Peramas* [Santa Fe, 1953], p. 18).

288. Op. cit., I, 73.

289. Op. cit., par. 39; ed. cit., pp. 21–22; trans., pp. 45–46. Other attacks on de Pauw in pars. 121 (on the subject of *mate*), 170 (to refute his estimate of the Guaranay population), 187 and 245 (denying the ferocity of the Guaranays). Pars. 253–74 polemicize against "what the *philosophe* Raynal thought about Guaranay discipline." But the most curious thing is to see Fr. Peramas invoke in opposition to Buffon, as a witness of the benefits brought to the natives by the missionaries, the apocryphal La Douceur, "the martial philosopher Ladouceur, who turned his sword into stylus and pen, and takes a determined stand on behalf of the Guaranay inhabitants" (par. 251, p. 119; trans., pp. 169–70).

290. Forster does actually mention him in passing, in a review of a work on anthropology (*Werke*, III, 268), and his disciple, the great Humboldt, knew him well, and in his *Reise* cites him as an authority at least twenty times (thirty-seven, according to Minguet, op. cit., p. 345, n. 47, certainly not a mere nine,

belated recognition of his merits as an observer and of his unusual position in the polemic.

First of all Father Filippo Salvatore Gilij is an Italian, not a Creole; born near Spoleto in 1721, he lived for almost twenty-five years in America (1742–67), at first for six years in Santa Fé de Bogotá, which he reached in June 1743 after disembarking at Cartagena and going up the Rio Magdalena, and where he completed his theological studies and was later a teacher of belles lettres; and subsequently in the missions of the Orenoco, until the expulsion of the Jesuits. After his return to the Papal States he held rectorates in Montesanto and Orvieto, and died in Rome in 1789.[291] Thus for Gilij it was not a question of exile in the strict sense of the term; he was brought back to his own country, to die where he had been born; the expulsion brought to a close a long overseas interlude—"I was not there a short time, nor as a transient, but as one who expected to die there"[292]—maybe even fulfilling a secret hope, and certainly not meaning, as it did for an American Jesuit, a complete break with his own land, his friends, his disciples. With or without the decree of expulsion, Gilij would probably have returned to Italy. His pages, then, are not stamped with the same warmth of affection and sense of personal and spiritual tragedy as those of Clavigero and Molina. His outlook is always that of a European: if he sets out to describe only the provinces of Terraferma it is because they are the first that one comes to on arriving from Italy.[293] Gilij also refers sparingly and quite dispassionately to his quality as a Jesuit. At times he is even a shade ironical about his confreres: to show how rare and expensive wine is in Bogotá he tells us that

---

as the *Register* suggests); but he too confuses him, at least once (III, 56), with Fr. Gumilla, when he attributes to Gilij a *Storia dell' Orinoco*, printed in Rome, which can only be Gumilla's *El Orinoco ilustrado y defendido*, which when reprinted and translated into French became the *Histoire naturelle, civile et géographique de l'Orénoque*. . . . This book was however printed in Madrid in 1741 and again in 1745 and (at Barcelona) in 1791, while Gilij's *Saggio di storia americana* was produced in Rome. The error is repeated by Humboldt's biographer, Julius Löwenberg, who mentions in passing "Father Gili's fabulous 'Orenoco Ilustrado' " (*A. von Humboldt*, I, 390)—in other words attributes to Gilij the book by Father Gumilla, which is in fact a work endowed with a good number of fables (see below, n. 327), as was well known to Humboldt himself, who cites him a dozen times (in particular on his notorious tendency to exaggerate, see *Reise*, IV, 60). For recent rediscoveries, see below, Suggestions for Further Research, and on recent partial translations into Spanish of the "forgotten" Fr. Gilij, see *Hispanic American Historical Review*, 48, no. 2 (May 1968), pp. 288–90; *Aconcagua* (Madrid), 2, no. 4 (4th trim., 1966), p. 510.

291. I am completing and correcting the details given by Sommervogel with the autobiographical material furnished by Gilij himself in his *Saggio di storia americana, o sia Storia naturale, civile e sacra de' regni e delle provincie Spagnuole di Terra-ferma nell'America meridionale*, 4 vols. (Rome, 1780–84): for his journey to and sojourn at Bogotà, see esp. II, xi, 6; IV, iv, 24, 26, 29, 205, 327, 333, 351, 439; on his journey to and sojourn in the Orenoco, passim, but esp. I, xxii, xxvi, xxx–xxxiv, 122; II, xi; IV, 334; on the exile and return to Italy, I, vii, xxiii, 118. A few other details can be found in G. Kratz, S.I., "Gesuiti italiani nelle missioni spagnuole al tempo dell'espulsione (1767–68)," *Archivum Historicum Societatis Iesu*, 11 (Rome, 1942), p. 42. He should not be confused with the botanist and seismologist Filippo Luigi Gigli (1756–1821).

292. *Saggio*, IV, 131.

293. Ibid., I, xix–xx; cf. below, n. 338.

"even the Jesuits, whose life was not the hardest in the world" only drank a small cup of wine three or four times a year.[294]

In consequence, while not a few other Jesuits expelled from America were very bitter toward Spain and quite ready to help England or any other power who might open the doors of their country to them again (see above, p. 191), Gilij remains always a resolute hispanophile. Not only does he defend the reliability of the old Spanish chroniclers and historians—learned men whose nomenclature should not be taken lightly[295]—and declare that he will limit himself to the natural history, since the civil history can be read in the Spanish authors;[296] not only does he accuse the foreign writers of nationalistic fanaticism in their criticisms of the conduct of the Spaniards, both ancient and modern, in the territories conquered and controlled by them,[297] and, on the basis of Solórzano's words, extol the protection and privileges conceded to the natives by the Madrid government, in contrast with the treatment inflicted on them by other European powers;[298] but to top all this he accepts a pension from the same King Charles III who had expelled the Jesuits, as a reward for his history, which had freed the Spanish nation and government "from the calumnies with which the Foreign Writers endeavor to denigrate it."[299]

His highly original position is backed up by his vast reading among the describers of America, from Pietro Martire and Las Casas to his contemporaries (Buffon, Robertson, Raynal, Ulloa, La Condamine, Clavigero, and Molina); but more particularly by his own empirical good sense, which keeps him well away from all unilateral systems, whether the anti-Christian fanaticism of Rousseau or the Americanistic fanaticism of the Creole Jesuits, the rigid classifications of the modern naturalist or the arbitrariness of those who would preclude any possibility of comparison or generalization (see below, pp. 228–29). His favorite author is Oviedo, whom he quotes very frequently, and often with fulsome praise: the acute observer and unremitting experimenter, further removed than anybody from erudite constructions and slanderous or apologetic propositions;

---

294. Ibid., IV, 29.
295. Ibid., p. 89, with reference to Oviedo and the Jesuit Acosta.
296. Ibid., I, xix–xx.
297. Ibid., p. xvii.
298. Ibid., IV, 287, 292–94.
299. Ibid., IV, xi; the award is dated 27 March 1784. Thus he finds himself ideologically close to Fr. Nuix (for whom see above, pp. 191–94), who is not however among the very many authors whom he cites and knows. Sommervogel (*sub voce*), also, mentions the commencement of a translation into Spanish of the *Saggio di storia americana*, but of this a few fragments translated into German in 1785 and 1798 are all that are known (see Kratz, op. cit.). In Rome Gilij held friendly conversations and exchanged correspondence (in Latin) on the subject of the American languages with the historian August Ludwig Schlözer, of Göttingen (op. cit., III, 350–54), well known for his Americanistic interests and aversion for the American Revolution (see Doll, op. cit., pp. 441–43).

Oviedo, whose intellectual makeup was so quintessentially Italian and realistic. And just as Oviedo, anticipating Ranke's famous formula, had written that his sole intention was to write "what in fact happened," so Gilij announces that he will present America "in its true semblance."[300]

To do this, he finds that he has to fight on two fronts: against his European enemies and against the Creole defenders of the American continent, with which latter he casually groups the idealizers of the savage, who, with "enormous errors" and for the purpose of "using dreams and imaginations to establish the most detestable maxims of Atheism," put forward the Cannibals, Eskimos "and suchlike stolid nations" as our teachers.[301]

The first group he combats with simple candor bolstered by his firm conviction that they write to entertain the general public, either "in a spirit of novelty, or from some such other reason as I would prefer not to name":[302] they are frivolous or deceitful. This story that they have so often put about in their books "that America is an area freshly dredged up from beneath the waves, and in consequence generally wet, marshy, and almost all lakes and swamps," is an arbitrary and stupid suggestion. There are wet parts and dry parts of America; nor can one argue from the wet parts that it is a question of "new" lands. They are wet because of the rains, the great rivers, and the thick forests that cover the land And the earth there is usually very fertile. The reason for its not producing more is the indolence of the natives: "If only the cultivators of the earth were as industrious as the earth is rich! To become wealthy America would need no other mines than its fields."[303] To gain the maximum yield from the manpower (if we may borrow the economists' jargon) they should switch from an extractive to an agricultural economy. And in fact, insists Father Gilij a little later, even trade brought in more than the mining industry.[304]

But the basis of his argument is moralistic: even the "economic" conclusion can really be reduced to a condemnation of idleness, mother of all the vices. Idleness, whether in the native or the Creole, is his bête noire. "Industriousness," productive activity, is on the other hand, for him as for Robertson, the supreme virtue. This also explains his scientific utilitarianism: knowledge with no practical application is just so much trifling frivolity.

Thus with sublime nonchalance he excuses himself from any discussion

---

300. Op. cit., I, xix; cf. Oviedo, *Historia*, XLVII, 8 (ed. cit., IV, 292b); and also ibid., XXII, 1 (ed. cit., II, 156a) and XXXIII, 54 (ed. cit., III, 552b).
301. Op. cit., I, xvi; cf. II, 127.
302. Ibid., xii–xiv; IV, 19.
303. Ibid., IV, 19–22; cf. IV, 381.
304. Ibid., pp. 389–90.

of the problems raised by Linnaeus and Buffon: "I do not set up any canon of natural history, no classes, no orders, no kinds, no species, no variations, nor other such erudite subtleties of the north" [sic].[305] The comparison of American animals with those of the Old World has given rise to involved discussions. "Leaving aside this nonsense, which serves I know not what purpose," Gilij sets out to describe his system, "a system which is not Buffonian, not Linnaean, but true," true because it is based on twenty-five years of direct, attentive, and untiring experience.[306]

The essence of his system is simple: the *causa causarum* is climate. Everything depends on climate: "In a climate different from ours, our plants and our animals will of necessity suffer, weaken, become bastardized." Everything, of course, that belongs to the animal and vegetable kingdoms, because "the mineral kingdom is not subject to such variations." Man, however, the lord of the animals, is no exception to the rule; the races vary according to the temperature of their surroundings, and thus the Caldopolitans differ from the Lanigers.[307]

Not even Father Acosta is spared by the Jesuit of two centuries later: when Acosta extols the fruits and climate of America, Gilij objects that America lacks not only the most delicate of the European fruits, the pears and apples, peaches and apricots, but even the more rustic ones like the chestnuts, walnuts, and hazelnuts. And Acosta's well-known statement on the plants imported from Spain and improved in the Indies is greeted with wary reserve: "I leave aside this assertion, and we shall see in due course whether it is altogether true."[308]

So although, as we have seen, he rejects Buffon's conceptual construction, Gilij is quite prepared to accept his corollaries and experimental data. His concluding remarks on the fauna of the Orenoco are a precise echo of Buffon's sentences of condemnation. In those American animals that bear a similarity to European ones, their smallness is a noticeable feature. The deer are like Europe's roebuck, the wild boars appear in miniature edition, the bears in reduced format, "and what the naturalists say about this seems evident: namely, that in America nature is not as robust as in our countries." Perhaps it is because of their diet, perhaps because of the great heat they suffer, perhaps even the result of reasons "of which we are unaware." The fact remains that the animals of the Orenoco are pitiful in appearance. In fact so pitiful that they seem to be "al-

305. Ibid., p. 88.
306. Ibid., p. 90.
307. Ibid., pp. 92–94, 194. Gilij seems to be of the opinion that in minerals, in geology, America is no different from the Old World. A few years later Goethe was to stress the peculiarity of the New World precisely in its geological structure (see below, p. 359).
308. Ibid., pp. 14–15 (and cf. above, pp. xvii–xviii). Further on he discusses whether the meager variety of fruit and vegetables is to be ascribed to the earth or its cultivators (IV, 165 ff.).

most of a different type from ours." Except for the fox, "notably enlarged" (like Buffon's pig, the fox is the exception that proves the rule!), they seem "bastardized" in comparison with their European counterparts.

Also, we should note, this is no matter of some passing crisis, nor a recent fact: "This deterioration of Nature must have begun in them as soon as they arrived in America, and perhaps they had the misfortune to shrink, like the plants taken there from Europe." The animals brought from Europe within historical times, on the other hand, seem to resist this evil influence: horses and oxen stay "as fat and vigorous as before." But one cannot be too sure: already the pack mules "seem to have lost some of their original size." Father Gilij stares pensively at these poor little beasts of burden: "Who can say, whether with the passing of the years these animals too will not go into decline, as the first ones that came from the old continent did."[309] The sole consolation (but of doubtful value and more likely to invalidate the explanations suggested for it) is that in the snakes and reptiles, fish and even birds "nature is perhaps more vigorous and more luxuriant in America."[310]

On the question of singing birds, however, Gilij stays fairly close to the writers who insisted on the poor quality of their melody-making. His theory is curious: in the warm climates (Orenoco) the birds are either mute or strident, in the cold climates (the plateau) there are "most surprisingly" many that sing well, and which must therefore be classed as a group apart, "to the greater glory of America" and the truth. Then as for those in the torrid zone, they may *sing* less well than the birds of Europe; yet they *talk* better.[311] The parrot has his revenge on the nightingale. In the missionary's version it is not the splendor of their plumage that makes up for their lack of melody, but their instinctive verbal fluency. But why is it that they sing less well? It is because they are large and fat: "Nature, which seems in many things to have fallen off in the living beings of America, in the creatures of the air does not decline at all, but grows," which is precisely what makes their voices less pleasing, as M. Buffon has explained "very eruditely." However, it is not a fact that the small birds too are strident and inharmonious? Yes, of course, Father Gilij admits; and for the explanation refers again to M. Buffon.[312]

---

309. Ibid., I, 316–17. Gilij observes at this point that "man's industry does much to preserve them," but further on, beginning to argue with Molina, he changes his thesis: America's beasts of burden are indeed smaller than the European ones, "but it can be said of them that they are so not through alteration suffered there with the passing of the years, but by nature and race" (op. cit., IV, 138). On the European animals taken to America, see also ibid., III, 52–55.

310. Ibid., I, 317.

311. Ibid., pp. 292, 311–12 (citing the Centzontle); IV, 99–101, 184, 191–94, 196.

312. Ibid., I, 292–93. These voiceless great creatures remind one of Parini's "singing elephant" (the *castrato*) with his "reedy voice issuing from his great chasm of a mouth" (*La musica*, ca. 1769).

It is obvious then why on reading Father Gilij's first volume (1780) Molina became so upset with his brother Jesuit, who appeared to be lending his support to the declared enemies of American nature, and accused him of "stupidly" giving the names "deer" and "boar" to American animals which were in fact in classes by themselves.[313] And it is clear why, although he attacks him as "a modern, reputable author," he never mentions him by name (thus confusing us too, by the way, who in the first Spanish version of this work believed his attack to be aimed at Buffon).

When our good friend Gilij on the other hand produces a reply to his Chilean colleague, it turns out to be a maze of hairsplitting sophistry. No, he never said, as Molina accuses him of saying, that the naturalists' law on the smallness of animals "is" evident: he said it "seems" evident. He never said that the American anteater is a "degenerate species" of bear: he said that it is "a degenerate branch of the bear species." And why on earth does Molina relinquish the deer and the wild boar and insist on defending only the American bear, "this blessed bear, which I put in almost as a joke"? Does he think to frighten Gilij by parading this "formidable puppet"? But Gilij realizes that this bear is a dangerous beast, that his defense is weak; and reverts to his standard means of escape for such cases: "This question will be treated further when we have more time; that is to say when I shall publish my *American Anecdotes,* in a separate volume." For the moment, suffice it to say that that animal is *known* as a bear "and in some manner resembles one."[314] Yet again (see above, p. 98) we come back to the old question of arbitrary denominations, to the *te baptizo carpam,* and Adam's lexicological labors when God delegated him to assign names to all the beasts of the earth and air (Genesis 2:19–20).

So Gilij parries Molina's frontal assault as best he can, then proceeds to outflank his opponent by rejecting his thesis of "abuse of nomenclature" (see above, p. 215). The Chilean Father's long-winded criticisms lead Gilij to suspect "that he really believed I looked on the names imposed on American things by the Spaniards as if they were final and unchangeable definitions." With all the power of his arrogant empiricism, Gilij delivers what is tantamount to a challenge: this animal that the Spaniards called a *lion* "was classified by me, without my paying any particular attention to it,[315] because I do not play the philosopher too, with the

313. Op. cit., IV, 90.
314. Ibid., pp. 87–88 (cf. I, 250). It need hardly be said that Gilij never published the promised work (cf. also III, 416), nor does it figure among his unpublished works in Sommervogel's bibliography.
315. Gilij discusses the bear "as a joke" and amuses himself with tigers and lions. . . .

tigers; and if need be, I am ready to support my decision with my pen."[316]

The whole polemic on the names imposed on things by the early naturalists and chroniclers has one single aim of evident apologetic origin: to avoid talking about "small" deer, "small" wild boars and "small" bears in America, and thus to spare the susceptibilities of the Americans. But Gilij has no intention of sparing them and insists: "Let us add the little porcupines, the shrunken Spanish pumpkins, our bastardized vegetables, and a hundred other American variations which emerge from my history."[317] So much for Molina.

But he is not dismissed quite yet. Father Gilij seizes on him once more to ridicule his defense of American horns, "in which (and he will permit me to tell him the truth) the learned author of the history of Chile made no small error."[318] Molina, who finds everything improved in America, when he comes to the subject of oxen and cows, "adds (I know not to what purpose) this emphatic expression: 'But neither these nor the other domestic (cattle) ever had the misfortune to lose their horns, as the slanderers of America have suggested.'" And yet, in the vastness of America there are indeed cattle that are without horns. "I will say more," Gilij goes on ironically, "in some places there are even some [bovines] without hair. But he should not be afraid that by this America is left degraded."[319]

In loco doctoral tones Father Gilij also takes issue with the other great Jesuit apologist, Father Clavigero, whose superior authority he seems to accept implicitly. However, to stay for a moment with the horned cattle, when Clavigero asserts that bulls multiplied in Mexico, Paraguay, and other parts of America "more than in richly cattled Italy," Gilij counters with elaborate arguments about the more limited availability of pasture and the greater population of Italy and the fact, proved by the customs statistics of the city of Rome, that proportionately more meat is eaten in Italy than in America.[320] And when the Mexican Father enlarges on the physical bulk of the *danta,* one of the great beasts found in these climes,

316. Op. cit., IV, 89. Gilij had written that there were numerous ferocious tigers in the Orenoco (ibid., I, 242–43), in disagreement with the "distinguished" Dr. Robertson too, who charges them with being inert and timid (ibid., p. 314); Robertson is also mentioned in I, 7; II, 240–41, 379.

317. Ibid., IV, 89–90. Elsewhere, however, in the course of a lengthy discussion (IV, 113–143) on the animals imported from Europe, Gilij calmly discusses the opposing theories of those "who believe everything of ours to have deteriorated in America" and those who instead consider "its worth . . . to have increased enormously there" (IV, 127).

318. Molina is mentioned explicitly in a note.

319. Op. cit., IV, 139, following which he cites his authorities, transcribing entire letters (IV, 139–43); cf. above, p. 216. Elsewhere too Gilij observes that America should no longer be looked down on by the scholars for some of its defective products, since careful distinctions should always be made between different places and climates: op. cit., IV, 194.

320. Ibid., IV, 130–35; conclusions on the oxen, pigs, etc., ibid., IV, 137–38n.

Gilij observes obliquely that one should distrust what the American writers say about the size of their animals: this *danta,* for example, "what varied shapes it assumes in the histories of the New World! Some say it is the biggest quadruped in the kingdom of Mexico."[321] Others call it the *ourignac* and have it the size of a horse. "To me," Father Gilij concludes, "it seems more like a donkey, and I would not even go so far as to say a large donkey."[322]

In dealing with the plants and animals Gilij uses his common sense and manages to keep well away from either of the conflicting exaggerations; but he never transcends them, nor does he grasp their fundamental motivations. When he comes to the men, on the other hand, he has a number of very sensible things to say, and gives us a vivid and accurate picture of both the Indian and the Creole. It is one of his basic points, not of course discovered by him but frequently forgotten by the apologists and detractors of America, that there is not *one* America, but *two,* widely different from each other; the savage one, where there are only natives, and the civilized one, where the Indians live together with the Spaniards. Two separate worlds, and thus two quite separate subjects, "frequently confused in books and only skimpily treated up till now," that he will have to discuss: the savage Orenoco and the civilized Terraferma.[323]

Of the Indians he offers us a detailed, carefully considered, and very humane portrayal. One can feel how every page grows out of his long and close association with his subject and is imbued with a healthy distrust of all forcibly one-sided schemes. He is skeptical about the fantastic estimates of the original size of the native population, even though the figures were confirmed by such authorities as Oviedo and Gómara, and he puts forward good reasons for believing that all in all the Indian population has perhaps shrunk a little or else remained the same as it was, namely not very large, at the time of the Conquest.[324] In appearance and customs this native population is very homogeneous: Ulloa was right to say that when one has seen one Indian one has seen all of them, and Molina was wrong once again to reject and ridicule that statement.[325] The *indios* are more similar to each other than members of the same nation; they are as similar as members of the same family, and yet there is the inexplicable enigma of the fact that they speak very different lan-

321. And here the footnote refers to Clavigero, I, sec. 10, p. 75. Clavigero is also cited in II, v, 272, 331; III, 31; 281; IV, 130 ff., 195.
322. Op. cit., IV, 195. The "Dantas, o Gran Bestias" are also mentioned by Juan and Ulloa, in the *Relación histórica del viaje a la América meridional,* VI, 4 (Madrid ed., 1748, II, 491), a work known to Father Gilij. However the *danta* is not to be confused with the *ourignac.*
323. Op. cit., I, xxi–xxii; IV, vii.
324. Ibid., I, xiv; IV, 259–63, 322–23, 408–09.
325. Ibid., IV, 253–55; cf. above, p. 216.

guages, which do not even belong to the same type.[326] Tomás Ortiz
(see above, p. 65) was too hard on them, and Las Casas overidealized
them. Even Father Gumilla, his predecessor in describing the Orenoco,
was unnecessarily harsh in his judgment.[327] Nearer the mark was La
Condamine, for whom their basic characteristic was insensibility. "However," the careful missionary is quick to add, "I could never be quite sure
that the quality in the Indians, that people call *insensibility*, was not rather
either suffering or pride."[328] To tell the truth it is difficult to understand
them, because they have no spokesmen of their own; Garcilaso only
talks about the Incas, and "in his native arrogance" ignores the other
races. Their unofficial defenders with their misguided zeal often succeeded only in vilifying them. Marmontel slanders them[329] and Robertson
dehumanizes them, calling them even "very chaste . . . and I would
almost say, without incentive," while "the weak constitution of their
bodies, their imagined coldness and indifference toward the fair sex, are
things contradicted by the Spaniards and missionaries of the Orenoco,
who held the Indians to be very libidinous." It is true that they are neither
tender, nor gallant, nor courteous. But with this habit of theirs of going
about naked and bathing together, they have plenty of chances of "transgressing."[330]

So Gilij gives back the Indians their erotic vigor and definitively dis-

326. Ibid., IV, 257–58. Cieza de León had already observed of the *indios* that "although they are all
dark-skinned and glabrous and resemble one another in so many things, there is such a multitude of languages between them that at almost every league and every part there are new languages" (*Chrónica del
Perú*, I, ca. 1550, quoted by Leopardi, *Zibaldone*, ed. cit., II, 660; cf. II, 968. Cf. also Muratori, *Il
cristianesimo felice*, I, 37, 216, and Humboldt, *Reise*, II, 9, 29). Gilij collected abundant and detailed
information on the languages of the Americans, making use of some fairly unreliable authors too, like
Lahontan (op. cit., III, 265; Lahontan is cited also on I, 281, 310–11, 402–05; III, 280, 310–11, 403–
05), but drawing mainly on the knowledge of other exiled Jesuits, including Molina (cf. III, 234 ff.); and
he "left grammatical and lexical manuscripts of the Maipur and Tamanaca languages" (Kratz, loc. cit.).
A parallel contradiction to the one quoted from Gilij in the text can be found in his assertion that the
plants, wild animals, customs, errors, and ways "are more similar one to another (from one end to the
other of America) than in any other part of the world" (op. cit., III, vi) and the flowing prose in which he
describes the prodigious variety of the landscape, the fauna and flora of America (ibid., IV, 91), or informs his reader that in America, as in every other part of the world, there is good and bad, "healthy and
sick lands" (ibid., I, xviii–xix).
327. The ecclesiastical reviser says (I, xi) that Gilij corrects and completes Gumilla, who was also a
personal friend of his, and admired by Gilij even when he criticized him (op. cit., I, xxv–xxvi; II, ix,
302).
328. Op. cit., II, viii–x; cf. IV, 8. La Condamine, one of the authors most frequently quoted by Gilij,
had written in much the same way: "Insensibility is the basis of it [the character of the *indio*]. I leave
the decision open, as to whether one should honor it with the name of apathy, or degrade it with the
name of stupidity" (*Relation*, pp. 418–19).
329. *Saggio*, II, 240–41, referring to his *Incas;* see however the criticism of his eulogy of the state
of nature, ibid., II, 371–76.
330. Ibid., II, 240–41, 379–80 (also rejecting Robertson's theory—for which see above, n. 53—that
the comfortable and civilized life and liberty of conversation provoke and facilitate amorous relations).
The Indian women are also "warmer." Fr. Gilij relates several quite amusing anecdotes about his effort
to persuade them to dress (ibid., II, 47–49), and brings down on himself the irony of his admirer Humboldt for the way he boasts ingenuously of knowing "the secrets of the married women" (*Reise*, III,
156).

sociates himself from the Buffonian thesis. But this does not mean he considers them any more forceful or robust in their other day-to-day activities. Indeed he seems to be in complete agreement with the biblical Samsonian equation of hirsuteness and bodily strength. The Indians are either hairless or depilated. Now, "from beardless nations such as the Orenocoans what strength could possibly be expected? None, or very little. In fact, there is perhaps no other nation in the world which is gentler, weaker, or less robust than the Indians." These same Venezuelan savages, described by a terrified Vespucci, after his encounter with them on an offshore island, as brawny and gigantic cannibals, now to the good Jesuit "seem like flowers, that languish as soon as they are picked."[331]

In short Father Gilij considers the natives an uncultured but not ugly race, possessed of some strange habits, cruel, fickle, but "easily instructed" in the religion and customs of civilized life; a people who have not made great progress, "but who are capable of so doing, once they overcome their laziness."[332] What the missionary lacks of course is any sort of intellectual sympathy for the rites and customs of the savages. His skepticism is unshakable: "I have never watched the Indian dances without suspicion."[333] In more than one way they call to mind the rustic peoples of Europe: "I have frequently compared the Americans to our own peasants," especially as regards their dwelling places.[334] Their "cities" and "missions" could be called beautiful relatively speaking, but not in themselves: they are mere conglomerations of huts. But "their churches are really beautiful; they are rich, and are made no differently from those of the Spaniards."[335]

Then those of the Spaniards (and so we come to the Creoles)[336] are real works of art: the churches of Bogotá "would not be scorned in our own Italy."[337] Thus there is no decadence or precocious senility in the Spaniards of the New World. And they lack nothing to make life comfortable: everything is easily available there, "and in this respect America, provided one has money in one's pocket, is not perhaps inferior to Italy."[338] To close, Gilij pays glowing compliments to America's seats of

331. *Saggio*, II, 37–39, modified by a footnote that considerably attenuates the condemnation in the text, explaining that this weakness is due mainly to the lack of exercise (ibid., II, 365–66). But the thesis seems to be a belated echo of Las Casas's apologetic descriptions (see above, pp. 68–70).

332. Op. cit., II, xi.

333. Ibid., II, 289. He is also suspicious of the witch doctors who come in person early in the morning to bring their female patients the necessary potions for making them fruitful: "there must, as anyone can see, be something very evil beneath it all" (ibid., II, 99).

334. Ibid., IV, 278.

335. Ibid., p. 280.

336. Whom we shall discuss only briefly, because this subject is treated with greater knowledge and passion by the American Jesuits.

337. Op. cit., IV, 327; for the architecture, sculpture, and painting of the Creoles, ibid., pp. 362–65.

338. Ibid., p. 391. Note the continuous reference to the paradigm Italy.

learning, so despised by de Pauw: "Their universities are full of men of consummate wisdom."[339] Of his former disciples he speaks with unrestrained praise and pleasure. And even though neither of the universities in Bogotá teach medicine, this art and science of healing flourishes in Lima and Mexico.[340]

Thus the Jesuit exile from the forests of the Orenoco extends his eulogy to the illustrious capitals of the major viceroyalties, and in so doing compensates partly for the lack of defenders of Peru.

XVI. CARLI'S *AMERICAN LETTERS*

In fact one cannot but be surprised at the absence of Peruvian Jesuits in the polemics pursued with such ardor and persistence by fellow members of their order from almost every part of Spanish America.[341] This may well be one more sign of the cultural decadence of the Peruvian province of the order, which is frankly admitted by Father Vargas Ugarte and Father Miguel Batllori, and which resulted in an almost complete literary sterility, in every field, on the part of the Peruvian exiles.[342] It was actually left to an Italian to undertake the defense of Peru against

---

339. Ibid., p. 312.

340. Ibid., pp. 353–56, with anecdotes on the great fame of the French doctors in those parts.

341. Fr. José Sánchez Labrador wrote twenty volumes on the natural, civil, and religious history of Paraguay, but they are still unpublished, in Holland. Some extracts, referring to medicinal products, were published (in 1948) by a professor of the University of Tucumán, Aníbal Ruiz Moreno (see *Revista de Historia de América*, 30 [December 1950], pp. 533–35). Nor have I found anti-Buffonian references in the writings of the Jesuits expelled from Brazil (of which the most significant is Jose Rodrigues de Melo, *De Rusticis Brasiliae Rebus Carminum Libri IV* (Rome, 1781), possibly because they were removed several years before (1760) the explosion of the polemic (cf. M. Batllori, S.I., "L'opera dei gesuiti nel Brasile e il contributo italiano nella *Historia* del P. Serafim Leite," *La civiltà cattolica*, 102, no. 3 [July 1951], pp. 193–202). As a matter of fact the traces of anti-de Pauwian polemics are also very rare in Brazil, and for the most part confused with the general polemic against the "climatic" theory, according to which the inhabitants of the tropics are inferior men. Thus Azeredo Coutinho attacks (1794) Montesquieu "and the supporters of his climatic system," for whom the inhabitants of the torrid zone are weak, incapable of serving in the navy, etc. (E. Bradford Burns, "The Role of Azeredo Coutinho in the Enlightenment of Brazil," *Hispanic American Historical Review*, 44, no. 2 [May 1964], p. 151). But Buffon and Robertson (*History of America*) at least were found in Brazilian libraries at the end of the eighteenth century (E. Bradford Burns, "The Enlightenment in Two Colonial Brazilian Libraries," *Journal of the History of Ideas*, 25, no. 3 [July–September 1964], pp. 434–35). On other works (some unpublished) by Jesuits from Brazil, New Granada, Guatemala, the River Plate and Paraguay, all "implicitly, and even at times explicitly" in polemic with Buffon, de Pauw and Raynal, see references in M. Batllori, "L'interesse americanista," p. 169; *Viscardo*, pp. 168–69.

342. Ruben Vargas Ugarte, *Jesuitas peruanos*, passim, and esp. pp. 96–97; and the *"Carta,"* pp. 55–56; M. Batllori, *Viscardo*, pp. 26–27. The only exception would be that of the Trujillan Fr. Marcos Vega —author of a work on the origin of the Americans and of dialogues between a Spaniard and an American, works that are now lost—who however belonged to the province of Quito (*Jesuitas peruanos*, pp. 121– 22; *La "Carta,"* pp. 60–61). Nor strictly speaking can Fr. Juan (Giancelidonio) Arteta (1741–96) be called a Peruvian, since he was born at Guayaquil; Arteta was exiled to Italy and wrote there sometime before 1780 (date of the ecclesiastical approval) a *Difesa della Spagna e della sua America meridionale . . . contro i falsi pregiudizi, e filosofico-politici ragionamenti d'un moderno storico* (Raynal), as yet unpublished (cf. R. Altamira, "Los cedularios como fuente histórica de la legislación indiana," *Revista de Historia de América*, 19 [1945], pp. 91, 93). An incomplete *Noticia* of this work, drafted by the author himself, was published (from the manuscript in the Library of the Royal Palace in Madrid) by Jaime Delgado, "El padre Juan Arteta, impugnador de Raynal," *Boletin Americanista* (Universidad de Barcelona), 1 (1959), 3, 161–70.

de Pauw's slander, the illustrious Gian Rinaldo Carli, who did however use archeological and linguistic information given to him by an unidentified Peruvian ex-Jesuit. In the Italian economist and administrator's *American Letters* the debate rises to a veritable panegyric of the Inca government and its institutions, including its religion, such as could hardly have been produced by the Jesuit Fathers, even if they were more "patriotic" than Clavigero.[343] On the other hand Carli could not feel that same attachment to American nature that the exiled Jesuits felt, and his intellectual leanings are rather more historical and political than zoological and geophysical. This may account for the noticeable slant he gives to the polemic, and also, perhaps, to some extent, for the immense success enjoyed by the *American Letters,* so much more "human" and so much less anthropological.

Carli does not even bother to consider the problem of the inferiority or degeneration of the Americas. He simply does not believe in it, and for him it takes no more than the existence of the usual Patagonian giants to prove that nature in America, far from being degraded and "only producing weak, sickly, and delicate animals and men, in no way comparable to ourselves, is instead more generous than with us."[344] And if one wants to take a leaf out of Buffon's book and distinguish between old and new lands, "certainly America is an old country, as old as our own hemisphere, if not older." The height of the mountains of Peru would seem in fact to show "that America is the oldest country in the world."[345]

The animals are never mentioned, and of the plants Carli observes that America has furnished Europe with a large number of plants that have proved either medicinally or nutritionally very valuable. Is it not true that the "health-giving" cocoa makes a "delicious drink"? "Thus every morning we have the occasion to remember poor America."[346] What really concerns him is man: and at the very outset he announces that "little by little we shall see that the Americans were substantially men like other men," and that "the human race and the organized nature of America had the same seed and the same development in parallel progress with

343. Fr. Arteta (see preceding footnote) praises the gentleness and humanity of the Incas, but scorns the pre-Hispanic civilization of Perú, and defends Father Valverde (cf. F. Mateos, S.J., "Una versión inédita de la conquista del Peru," *Revista de Indias* [Madrid], 17 [1944], pp. 389–442), the same Valverde that Carli (see below, p. 237) sees reincarnated in de Pauw! He cannot have been Carli's informant, since his ex-Jesuit was born in Lima, descended on his mother's side from Orellana and had lived many years in Cuzco: *Lettere americane,* ed. cit., I, 60–61, 198. Fr. Vargas Ugarte guesses it was Miguel de Soto of Huaura (*La "Carta,"* pp. 60–62).

344. *Lettere americane,* ed. cit., I, 262–64. America's Amazons too enjoyed an advantage over those of classic times: they had "both breasts" (ibid., I, 271).

345. Ibid., I, 16; II, 78–79 (see *contra* above, pp. 112–13). The weakness of Carli's geographical knowledge becomes apparent when he describes America as "a vast continent, which is to say at least as large as Asia and Africa put together" (I, 33). Cf. above, n. 8.

346. *Lettere americane,* I, 209. Cf. G. Parini, *Il Mattino,* lines 134–36, 144–57.

us."[347] Their weapons were similar, their customs, their beliefs, and so on. If the Americans were less industrious and cultured than the more illustrious nations of the Old World, the other inhabitants of Africa, Asia, "and Europe itself have given us, both in ancient and in modern times, little enough reason to be proud of ourselves."[348]

With the substantial identity of earth, men, and their prehistory in the two hemispheres thus established, and having mentioned some of the earlier critics of de Pauw, such as Pernety and his friend Paolo Frisi,[349] Carli, with truly Vicoan confidence in the parallel paths of nations, proceeds to forget the savage and concentrate all his exuberance and wisdom on the defense of the ancient civilizations of America.

Enthusiasm for the savage could not really be expected from someone who had made it his life's work to combat the theses of Jean-Jacques, who while still young had authored the *Andropologia,* a brief poem on the happiness that can only be found in society; who almost simultaneously with the *American Letters* (1776) was writing *L'uomo libero,* "The Free Man," a refutation of the *Social Contract,* "that most fatal of all books"; and who with the revolution in full swing (1792) was to publish his pamphlet *On Physical, Moral and Civil Inequality among Men.* No, the savages, "the truly and positively savage peoples," Carli abandons to de Pauw's scathing condemnations.[350] When he receives Robertson's *History* he does find that their illustrious author, "currying favor with de Pauw," dwells unnecessarily on "the nature and weakness of the savage peoples," but he contents himself with objecting that similar savages abound throughout Africa, in a great part of Asia, and even in Europe.[351]

So Carli declines to defend the innocent primitives, but for the Mexicans and the Peruvians he will claim the highest level of civilization and administrative wisdom. He will make them giants in the art of government, the "Patagonians" of politics. What provokes Carli's response is only an incidental element in de Pauw's slanders. The denial of the greatness of ancient pre-Colombian civilizations spurs him into becoming their apologist. In the field of archeology he feels capable of meeting and

347. *Lettere americane,* I, 12, 20. His prime aim was to establish the prehistoric links between the Americans and the inhabitants of our hemisphere (letter of 27 November 1776, in Ziliotto, op. cit., p. 191), which he attempts in the second and third volumes with the help of the Atlantis hypothesis. The objection to such a hypothesis, based on America's lack of European animals, is rapidly discussed by Carli (op. cit., II, 210–11), but considerably more thoroughly by the French translator (*Lettres américaines* [Boston and Paris, 1788], II, 261–62), who mentions Pernety in a footnote.
348. Op. cit., I, 12.
349. On Pernety, I, 19 and II, 299 (allusion to Pernety's *Examen,* which the French translator confuses with the *Dissertation:* I, 423n.; cf. II, 262n.); on Frisi, ibid., I, 19, 105.
350. *Lettere americane,* I, 42, 233; on the *Andropologia,* cf. L. Bossi, *Elogio storico del Conte Comm. G. R. Carli* (Venice, 1797), pp. 86–88.
351. Op. cit., II, 279, 286–87. There is a warning, however, from "the Printers to the reader," paraphrasing Carli, that de Pauw's work overawed even "writers of the first rank, like abbé Raynal and M. Robertson" (I, 3).

overcoming his arrogant opponent. At first he is simply "terrified" of de Pauw. He treats him with almost reverent admiration:

The immense labor that this learned German has expended in scouring the accounts of travels, the clarity of his judgments, his skill in sustaining a system without appearing to be systematic, the eloquence with which he beautifies and strengthens each of his propositions — these are the particular gifts of a work which seduces and delights."[352]

His argument is limited in another way too. Although he speaks for both the Mexican and the Peruvian civilizations, in reality he concerns himself predominantly with the latter. The elective and feudal monarchy of Mexico in fact occupies hardly one full letter (the eleventh), and even that one closes by announcing that he will go on to speak of the adjacent republics, like Tlascala (to which he devotes the twelfth letter), "and then of the most regular and paternal of all the Empires of the world that have ever been or ever will be, namely that of Peru."[353] And referring to this point of the text there is a note in the accompanying letters, which he sent to Gravisi with each of the *American Letters,* telling his cousin: "Now we begin on a much more important subject . . . now we are beginning to get to the heart of the matter."[354] In fact all the rest of the book, which the author himself describes as badly and hurriedly put together (he dictated a letter a week to his secretary, in great haste, and sent it off to his cousin without even having it recopied, sometimes without even rereading it),[355] is given over to the study and panegyric of the empire of the Incas.

Carli is familiar with the recent historians of the Inca empire: Ulloa (in fact the *American Letters* was thought to be a "continuation" of Ulloa's *Cartas americanas!*),[356] Algarotti, de Pauw, Raynal, and "the incomparable painter of the human passions," Marmontel. But the first two "stay too much on the level of generalities"; de Pauw "writes with a pen poisoned by the black bile of a Cannibal" (a baroque expression which was to enjoy considerable success);[357] Raynal is "too succinct and too deferential to Pauw,"[358] and Marmontel too fanciful. The best

352. Op. cit., I, 2. Carli also knows the second *Recherches* and agrees with Voltaire's praises of de Pauw (ibid., II, 50–51).
353. *Lettere americane,* I, 113.
354. Ziliotto, op. cit., pp. 196n., 198.
355. Cf. Ziliotto, op. cit., pp. 194–95, 201–02 ("as fast as the pen would write," ibid., p. 225): Carli was in Milan, his cousin in Capodistria. The letters were however revised and corrected before publication: ibid., pp. 206–07.
356. Spell, *Rousseau,* p. 110, quoting a Spanish review of 1789. In fact in the French ed. (Boston and Paris, 1788) of Carli's *Lettres américaines* it is said that it can "serve as a sequel to d. Ullua's Mémoires."
357. "This expression is violent," notes the French translator, J. B. Le Febure de Villebrune (who also translated Ulloa), "but it is pure truth" (op. cit., I, 195n.). Cf. below, p. 314.
358. Carli had however the greatest admiration for Raynal's *Histoire:* see *Lettere americane,* I, 60; and Ziliotto, op. cit., p. 225.

thing is to go right back to the earliest sources, or rather to the one supreme and purest source: "I cannot deny my esteem and faith in Garcilaso de la Vega."[359]

Following in Garcilaso's footsteps, Carli describes in minute detail the system of government of the Incas, whose fundamental aim was "to oblige all their subjects to be happy. No empire ever attained an end so worthy and so useful to humanity."[360] De Pauw, who refuses to believe in anything we are told about the Incas, must "through some extravagant metempsychosis" have inherited the soul of Valverde. But Carli repeats that it was "certainly the best of all the political systems that have been imagined or followed in the whole of our hemisphere," because in it "men not only should have been happy, but it was such that they could not, even if they so wished, be anything but happy."[361] He goes on, letter after letter, lauding everything, until at the beginning of the nineteenth he comes tumbling out with this confession-cum-aspiration: "I am so full of the idea of the ancient government of Peru, that I feel like a Peruvian, or at least I seem to wish that in some other part of our globe a similar system could be designed, so that I might go there and enjoy full happiness in this part of my life which remains to me."[362]

De Pauw is by now almost forgotten, and the occasional generic barb launched in his direction is aimed more at the arrogance of the man who writes "from the depths of a German province" and "thinks everything outside of Breslau and Berlin barbaric and savage," and drinks beer, and perhaps, horror of horrors, is quaffing beer "at this very moment when I write"[363]—than at refuting his specific theses. In the end Carli himself seems to grow tired of sparring with this tailor's dummy, and on the famous subject of beards (the Americans') bursts out: "And do you think I have no other aim than to do battle with Pauw? I am certainly not so ambitious that I feel I need to seek out illustrious literary opponents to make my reputation";[364] but yet he cannot resist getting drawn into the debate and cites the smooth-skinned peoples of the Old World and hairy caciques in the New—the bearded cacique of Catarapa even had a hairy wife—and counts the hairs in the beard that adorned the chin of Montezuma.[365]

359. *Lettere americane*, I, 121; cf. ibid., I, 78, 81, 95.
360. Ibid., I, 125.
361. Ibid., I, 146.
362. Ibid., p. 182.
363. Ibid., I. 197, 207; II, 16.
364. Ibid., I, 251.
365. Were they six in number, or does Gómara mean that they were sparse? (op. cit., I, 253). Among the errors of de Pauw that Carli submits to particular criticism is this: the Prussian repeats Vespucci's statement that the American women "in order to remedy the organic defect" of the weakness of their men, "were accustomed to put an ointment on their virile member composed of spices and caustic insects, causing it to swell up enormously, and the men to become thus more capable of satisfying them,"

The reasons for this long eulogy of the Inca empire are clear enough. Carli himself recognized that his work deserved "no other name than the one which considering all aspects I gave it myself, which is to say that of a dream," the very same epithet that he applies several times to de Pauw's *Recherches*.[366] What Carli in fact saw in the government of the ancient Peruvians, as described in the most romantic of the chroniclers, was the perfect realization of his political ideas and aspirations.

The philanthropic and paternalistic despotism of the ancient Incas coincided only too well with the ideology of the erudite encyclopedist and zealous servant of Maria Theresa, the man protected and promoted by Joseph II, the fervent supporter of Peter Leopold of Tuscany's reforms, and author himself of important economic reforms in the Duchy of Milan, the student of censuses and statistics, and believer in a regulated economy and a state devoted to the economic welfare and increase of the population. One cannot quite say that Carli's Peru is a mere utopian projection of his own unsatisfied reforming zeal. But the enlightened minister, the firm believer in the beatific efficacy of well-organized institutions, often takes the archeologist by the hand, and pushes him into eulogizing that "menagerie of happy men," Inca Peru, and consequently into reviling equally the fanaticism of the ancient conquistadores and the modern *philosophes*. In suspecting de Pauw of having inherited the soul of Valverde, Carli sets up a continuum of hostility between the sixteenth-century enemy of Atahualpa and the eighteenth-century enemy of the ancient American civilizations, between the fanatical friar and the fanatical illuminist. And in so doing he also indirectly reaffirms the ideological link between the hispanophobe de Pauw and the most extreme hispanophiles; just as later the Americans were to accuse de Pauw's work of

---

and affirms that the latter prescription is lacking in Ramusio's Italian version (*Recherches*, I, 63–64). Carli replies, text in hand, that Ramusio too mentions the poisonous animals (*Lettere americane*, I, 14–16); but he does not bother to discuss either the truth of the fact nor the facile and extreme deductions that de Pauw extracts therefrom. Those peculiar "well-known drugs of the Americans" are also mentioned with horror by T. Porcacchi (*L'Isole più famose del Mondo* [Venice, 1572]), and with amusement by G. de Gamerra (*La Corneide* [Livorno, 1781]), II, 154 and 188, who quotes "*Les Améric. observ.*" (cited also in V. 363); but a little further on he quotes de Pauw too: II, 225, nn. 5 and 8; III, 346–47, nn. 5 and 6. They are also discussed, with mention of both Vespucci and de Pauw, by De Lignac (*De l'Homme et de la Femme considérés physiquement dans l'état du Mariage* [Lille, 1773–74], I, 401–02; II, 160), who several other times, and on topics no less scabrous, cites de Pauw as a respectable authority (op. cit., I, 395, 398, 456–57; II, 106, 110, 162, 248, 282, 347, 349, 352). See above, p. 146.

366. Letter of 25 March 1778. in Ziliotto, op. cit., p. 206 (cf. "a bundle of dreams," ibid., p. 194; "legend," ibid., p. 200; "trifles," ibid., p. 296); cf. *Lettere americane*, I, 38–39 and Isidoro Bianchi, in the Cremona edition, I, v. In fact the *Lettere americane* is not considered in any way authoritative as a work of history. It is significant that Prescott refers to it in his *Conquest of Mexico* (1843), and almost always as the work of an "enthusiastic" writer or a person of "lively imagination," but he does not mention it once in the following *Conquest of Peru* (1847), although it is a continuous apology of the Incas. Rota (*Enciclopedia Italiana*, IX, 30b) describes it as "a somewhat fanciful work." Baudin, who actually interprets the Inca Empire in very much the same way, writes that Carli "traces a cheerful outline of Peru, a gross deformation of reality" (*L'empire socialiste des Incas*, p. 252).

helping to serve the political ends of the supporters of Spain (for which, see below, p. 315).

Carli, on the other hand, is a convinced hispanophobe;[367] and although educated by a priest and himself a practicing Catholic, he never evinced any great love for ecclesiastical jurisdictions, and actively encouraged the suppression of the Tribunal of the Inquisition; but this did not mean he was anticlerical, nor even antireligious, in the fashion of the Paris or Berlin *philosophes*. On the contrary, with that intellectual background, his assiduous study of the ancient civilizations, and the Italianate historicism of his ideas, Carli naturally places great emphasis on religion as a measure of a people's civilization. The Americans were inferior to the Europeans in many techniques and arts, but they had the most elaborate religious systems and rites and cults. And this is what counts, morality and the fear of God, not mechanical tools or the perfection of luxury. De Pauw would have us believe that they were savages, because they had neither money, nor iron nor writing. But in that case the Spartans too were barbarous savages, and the Romans before the defeat of Pyrrhus, and the Muscovites until 1440; while Xerxes' effeminate Persians would be called civilized.[368]

The *American Letters*, written in 1777–78, and published in 1780, was sensationally successful. Clavigero's *Storia antica del Messico* came out in the same year, and the two authors exchanged profuse compliments. Already in the second edition of the *Letters* (Cremona, 1781–83), there are numerous references to the work of the learned Mexican; while the latter, having received the *American Letters* just as the last few pages of his second volume were coming off the press, praised the "very new and very erudite work" which gave "a true, although incomplete, idea of the culture of the Mexicans"[369] and went on to dedicate his anti–de Pauwian *Dissertations* (see above, p. 198) to Carli, with all due pomp and solemnity; he does so to thank him "in the name of the Americans," who are obliged to him for providing them with a champion of noble breed, renowned for the high offices he has filled "and above all famed for the brilliance of his writings," a man who "has had the courage to defend those maligned Nations against the many celebrated Europeans that revealed themselves to be their enemies and persecutors."[370]

367. Among his favorite authors is Correal, "the most diligent and patient of all travelers" (*Lettere americane*, I, 174, 180, 190), one of the classics of the *leyenda negra*.
368. Op. cit., I, 70–71, 107.
369. *Storia antica del Messico*, II, 267. Clavigero notes a few errors in Carli: "Sometimes a city is mistaken for a king" and "almost all the Mexican names appear in altered form, and some so disfigured, that not even I, so familiar with the language and history of Mexico, can recognize them" (ibid.); the same charge is extended to include all the European authors (ibid., IV, 146); but after discussing some details (II, 267–70), Clavigero refers back to the *Dissertations*.
370. *Storia antica del Messico*, IV, 4. Cf. ibid., p. 31 (Atlantis, defended by Carli "with an abundance of erudition"), 39n., 240.

XVII. FRANKLIN AND THE NORTH AMERICANS' STATURE

The Istrian polygraph's *Letters* was reprinted and translated, and soon became known throughout Europe.[371] It was used, as we have seen, by Molina, who like Clavigero dedicated his *Storia naturale* to Carli, and by other exiled Jesuits too. Among those who later appealed to its authority were men like de Maistre, Humboldt, Tommaseo, and Leopardi.[372] But its most particular significance lies in the fact that it was the first composition in the polemic to attract the attention of a North American; and not just any North American either, but Benjamin Franklin.[373]

The second (and first complete) edition of the *American Letters* was offered to Franklin by the publisher, Father Isidoro Bianchi of Cremona, as the work of "another illustrious author" (after de Pauw, La Condamine, Raynal, Robertson, Bailly, and Buffon) who was the first "in Italy ... to give us a more grandiose and adequate idea of that great continent, wherein you must be justifiably proud to have been born." The Romans are no more; no longer does one hear the solemn boast: *civis romanus sum.* "But every American will always and with more justification be able to say to the inhabitants of the other three parts of the universe: *I am a citizen of America.*"[374] Carli is an admirer of the learned American and has spared no pains to illustrate the history of Franklin's fatherland [*sic!*]. Franklin alone, then, "the glory of the Philosophers' Republic," can be "the competent judge of the merit of this Book."

Benjamin Franklin did in fact deliver his judgment in a letter to the Cremonese printer, in which he begged him to thank Carli "for his skilful defense against the attacks of that ill-informed and evil-minded Writer, who certainly never has a good word for anybody without regretting it immediately and retracting it soon after."[375] Already two years before

371. After the third Italian edition (Milan, 1785) it was included in the collections of Carli's complete works. German translation, Gera, 1785; French translation, Boston (actually Paris), 1788, and Paris, 1792; possible English translation, see Bossi, op. cit., p. 171, and Bartolome Gamba, *Serie dei testi di lingua italiana* (Venice, 1828), no. 1848; Spanish translation, Mexico, 1821–22 (on which see C. Radicati di Primeglio, *J. R. Carli, economista y americanista del siglo XVIII* [Lima, 1944], pp. 27–29). Still in our own time it is the subject of various monographs, such as that of Y. Abeniacar, *Sulle "Lettere americane" di G. R. Carli* (Milan, 1911), and of Radicati di Primeglio, cited above, and "J. R. Carli, el iniciador del estudio cientifico del problema de la Atlántida," *Documentos* (Lima), 1 (1948), pp. 44–72. Cf. also Franco Venturi in *Illuministi italiani*, III (Milan-Naples, 1958), pp. 419–57, and Ada Annoni, *L'Europa*, pp. 75–79, 505–09. Thus I would not really say that Carli the Americanist is "a forgotten man," as is suggested by E. Sestan, who devotes several good pages to him (*Europa settecentesca ed altri saggi* [Milan-Naples, 1951], pp. 138–43).

372. J. de Maistre, *Soirées de St. Pétersbourg*, ed. cit., II, 69, 118, 287 (criticizing the French trans. and its footnotes); A. Humboldt, *Vue des Cordillères* (Paris, 1810); Leopardi, *Dialogo della Terra e della Luna*. For Tommaseo, see F. De Stefano, *G. R. Carli* (Modena, 1942), pp. 212–13, 230.

373. Jefferson too owned a copy of them (*Catalogue*, IV, 165).

374. *Lettere americane* (Cremona, 1781–83), dedication. In 1940 Congress passed a law instituting the official observation of "I am an American citizen" Day, on the third Sunday in May.

375. From Passy, 19 November 1784. The letter is reproduced at the beginning of the second of the four vols. of the *Lettere americane* in the ed. of Milan, 1786, referred to by Bossi, op. cit., pp. 193–94, and republished by C. R. D. Miller in *Modern Philology*, 27, no. 3 (February 1930), pp. 359–60. On the

that, in 1782, he had listed among Raynal's errors the notion "that European Animals degenerate in America. That men are shorter liv'd,"[376] etc., in other words typically de Pauwian theses, and one of his Italian reviewers had already commented (1774) that Franklin by his very existence, with his sharpness of mind and universally recognized wisdom, "gave the lie" to de Pauw's theory.[377]

Franklin had represented the United States in Paris since 1776. But in 1782 the office passed to Jefferson, who in the same year in which Franklin addressed himself to Carli, 1784, produced in Paris his *Notes on Virginia*.

So once again the first response to the slanders of America came from Americans in Europe, in direct contact with the "denigrators," from men who had made their mark in various fields and were particularly sensitive to the accusation of inferiority. We have already seen how, while the Hispano-Americans resented above all de Pauw's suggestions of their ignorance and mental inertia, the Anglo-Saxon colonists reacted primarily against the insinuation of some organic inferiority in the natural environment of the New World. Thus they have no hesitation in going beyond de Pauw to assail the great Buffon. And they very often build on empirical arguments, on "practical examples," as indeed behoves a discussion based on measurements and dimensions and quantity, on questions of more and less — and not on the excellence of an ancient civilization, the attractions of an ideal political regime, or the refinement of some highly developed culture. It is a fact that, up until independence, the culture of the Hispano-American cities had maintained a superior level to that of the Anglo-American centers.[378] In the latter the libraries contained scarcely anything but works of theology and patristics, usually in the shape of Bible commentaries. In the Spanish colonies the Castilian classics were readily available, nor was there any lack of French books or European books in general, even on forbidden subjects.[379] But the in-

---

masonic brotherhood between Franklin, Fr. Bianchi, and the printer Manini (who published the *Lettere americane*), see Visconti, op. cit., p. 116, and Pace, op. cit., pp. 138–40. For his part Carli thought he had outlined a theory on lightning before becoming acquainted with Franklin's famous experiments (see De Stefano, op. cit., p. 14).

376. Max Hall, *B. Franklin and Polly Baker* (Williamsburg, 1960), p. 124.

377. Pace, op. cit., p. 124.

378. A. de Humboldt, *La Nouvelle-Espagne*, II, 10–11 (and his North American reviewer, 1811, quoted by Bernstein, *Origins*, pp. 64–65); M. de Oliveira Lima, *La evolución histórica de la América Latina* (Madrid, n.d., but ca. 1913), p. 67; P. Henríquez Ureña, *Literary Currents in Hispanic America* (Cambridge, 1941), p. 232, n. 41, quoting Humboldt.

379. See B. Fay, *L'esprit*, pp. 25–28, showing how French culture began to be known in the thirteen colonies only after 1750, and was even then treated with reserve and distrust. Cf. Bernstein, *Origins*, pp. 52–60, for the somewhat paltry and monotonous list of books on Latin America possessed by North American libraries, as compared to the inventories of those of Latin America at the same period, for example the collection of José Manuel Dávalos (see below, pp. 291–92), and the lists of books confiscated by the Inquisition. For the early period of Spanish colonization, see also the important re-

habitants of New England were a more impatient and energetic nation, prouder of their strength, confirmed once more by the success of their recent revolt. The anti-American slanders provoked replies from the two largest groups of Americans of European stock, each reacting with particular vehemence to the libels on its own most cared for, most visible and tangible qualities. When the Latin American protested that his land was "great," he meant great in the glories of the past, in the letters and sciences, great in faith and perhaps even in opulence. When the North American said the same thing, he meant that his land was boundless and the Anglo-Americans tall in stature. The "purchase" of Louisiana had barely been completed when the Americans began to "measure their future grandeur by the extent of their vast territory."[380]

As for the men, the ironic Franklin was one day entertaining the abbé Raynal to dinner, together with a number of other Frenchmen and Americans. The abbé set off on one of his usual oratorical tirades on the degeneration of men and animals in America. The host, good-humored as ever, suggested that the matter be tested empirically: "Let us try this question by the fact before us." He asked his guests to stand up, and it turned out that all the Americans were tall and well built, and all the Frenchmen singularly tiny: the abbé himself was "a mere shrimp." Raynal defended himself with flattering references to "exceptions," and, according to another not improbable version, by objecting that facts and examples count little in philosophy, where only concepts and ideas are valid: almost as if the Buffon-de Pauwian thesis had by then become a logical necessity serving to impose coherence on the world, and thus an article of faith, against which mere real facts were of little avail.[381]

---

searches of I. A. Leonard, gathered together in *Books of the Brave* (Cambridge, Mass., 1949). On the literary ignorance of New England, see M. F. Heiser, "Cervantes in the United States," *Hispanic Review*, 15 (1947), p. 409, quoting E. C. Cook, *Literary Influences in Colonial Newspapers, 1704–1750* (New York, 1912), p. 2; and T. G. Wright, *Literary Culture in Early New England, 1620–1730* (New Haven, 1920).

380. Félix de Beaujour, *Sketch of the United States of North America*, trans. William Walton (London, 1814), p. 284, quoted by Weinberg, op. cit., p. 48.

381. Raynal's thesis is very similar to those we have already seen in de Pauw (see above, pp. 89–90). The anecdote was apparently recounted to Jefferson by Franklin himself: cf. "Anecdotes of Benjamin Franklin" in *The Life and Selected Writings of Thomas Jefferson* (New York, 1944), p. 179, and in *Works*, ed. Paul Leicester Ford (New York–London, 1904), III, 458n. Another version of the incident occurs in a letter to Jefferson from William Carmichael: "I do not know whether Dr. Franklin ever mentioned to you what passed at a Dinner at Paris at which I was present, on that contested point. I think the Company consisted of 14 or 15 persons. At Table some one of the Company asked the Doctor what were his Sentiments on the remarks made by the Author of the Recherches sur l'Amerique. We were five Americans at Table. The Venerable Doctor regarded the Company and then desired the Gentleman who put the question to remark and to Judge whether the human race had degenerated by being transplanted to another section of the Globe. In fact there was not one American present who could not have tost out of the Windows any one or perhaps two of the rest of the Company, if this Effort depended merely on muscular force. We heard nothing more of Mr. P.'s work and after yours I think we shall hear nothing more of the opinions of Monsr. Buffon or the Abbé Raynal on this subject" (letter from Wm. Carmichael, Madrid, 15 October 1787; *Papers*, XII, 240–41). The episode was also used,

Franklin was tall, and his blow, passing over the head of the dwarf Raynal, caught the tall Buffon, who was so proud of his stature and noble bearing. For a moment the war of the worlds seems to shrink to the contest between the two venerable naturalists, as they stalk up to one another, arch their chests, draw back their shoulders, and exchange looks of bitter hatred. In the background lurk the sardonic shadows of the towering Patagonians. . . .

And not just their shadows. The north had its own Patagonians, the redskins. It is remarkable how frequently the Americans of the United States delight in recalling the Indians' tall stature and bold features, and how easily they go on to apply the redskins' physical attributes to themselves. In 1818 Lieutenant Francis Hall mentions again what "a considerable stumbling block" these brawny giants are to Raynal's thesis.[382] Men and women of European descent were generously made partakers in the gymnastic and genesic powers of the natives, both their real ones and those ascribed to the Noble Savage.[383] The Anglo-Saxon Creole does not merely, like the Spaniard, reject the accusations of degeneracy, but proceeds to claim for himself the physical and moral virtues of the Indians, who are immune from so many European diseases, whose beauty is the

---

and embellished with sarcasms at the expense of Europe, by John Bristed (*Resources of the United States of America, 1818*), who contrasts the "stout, well-proportioned, tall, handsome" Americans with the ridiculous Frenchmen, "all little, lank, yellow, shrivelled personages, resembling Java monkeys" (quoted in Martin, op. cit., pp. 210–11; cf. 190–91). On the importance of tallness also in the political life of the North America of those times and ours, see André Siegfried, *Tableau des Etats-Unis* (Paris, 1954), pp. 250–51, and Frank Thistlewaite, *The Great Experiment* (Cambridge, 1955), p. 110. On Franklin's anecdote, see also C. Van Doren, *Benjamin Franklin* (Garden City, 1941), p. 721; B. Fay, *Civilisation américaine* (Paris, 1939), pp. 54–55; G. Chinard, "America as a Human Habitat," pp. 40–41, who observes that there is nothing to prove that before Franklin went to Paris he was "particularly disturbed by the aspersions thrown by Buffon on the climate of America": another sign that the polemic, though intercontinental by definition, exploded in the tense climate of Europe. And it was here that it sprang to life again, in almost exactly the same terms, a couple of centuries later: "Here is Kennedy in Vienna, annoyed by Nikita Krushchev's description of the Soviet Union as a young nation and the U.S. as an old one, and replying, 'If you'll look across the table, you'll see that we're not so old' " (*Time*, 17 December 1965, p. 50).

382. M. Hall, *B. Franklin*, p. 134.

383. Kraus, op. cit., pp. 217–18, 254, 267; Martin, op. cit., p. 196; Chinard, "Le mirage américain," in *Les réfugiés huguenots*, pp. xix–xx; cf. B. Franklin, *Remarks Concerning the Savages of North America*, 1783–84 (which are not, however, according to Pearce, *The Savages*, pp. 138–39, to be taken seriously). Any denigration of the savage only served to undermine this patriotic pride. Thus all reformers and pedagogues defended the Indians, "whatever may have been advanced by European writers to the contrary," as healthier, happier, and more moral than the Europeans (R. Coram, *Political Enquiries*, 1791, quoted in C. and M. Beard, *The American Spirit* [New York, 1942], pp. 126–37). The "Indian constitutions" were taken as models by the rebelling colonists (see Blanke, op. cit., p. 263). "No such animal was ever seen in America, as the Indian M. de Buffon described in Paris" (Samuel Williams, 1794, quoted in Martin, op. cit., pp. 196–97; cf. Pearce, *The Savages*, p. 161). But when the great march westward began there was no lack of arguments to justify the extermination of the "savage" and "degenerate" Indians (see examples from 1810–11 and 1859 in Tryon, op. cit., pp. 492, 721–24). The history of the attitudes of the North Americans toward the redskins between 1609 and 1851 has been outlined with attention to every nuance and subtle, occasionally too subtle, consideration by the above-mentioned R. H. Pearce, *The Savages*.

"Greek" ideal, whose men have such a firm attachment to liberty and whose women such an enviable facility in giving birth.[384]

Thus the colonists of New England derive an indirect benefit from the Europeans' exaltation of the primitive and the savage. Already by 1803 Volney could observe that most North American writers seemed obsessed with the notion of refuting the Europeans, "as if by some bizarre fiction they set themselves up as the representatives and avengers of the natives, their predecessors."[385] And in fact the Englishman Hall, amazed at the extraordinary stature of the members of Congress from the western states, found that the only persons to whom he could compare these "Goliaths of the West" were six muscular and gigantic Indian chiefs, who reminded him of the mighty Greek heroes who had stood alone against the Trojan hordes and thrown them back.[386] The Americans of the west were already a match for the fierce Indians in physical prowess. In the novels of Fenimore Cooper, Chasles wonderingly noted, "the red savage and the 'squatter' meet, or rather merge," almost as if the North American climate had influenced the Puritans' descendants to the point where they were no different from the native population.[387]

The next easy step was taken a few decades later, when toward the middle of the nineteenth century the Atlantic coast community became unequivocally urban, industrial, and commercial and lost all further possibility of decking itself in the redskin's feathers. The attributes of the Noble Savage, dusted up for the occasion, were then transferred *en bloc* to the westerner. The "frontier" inherited the mythic prestige of the forest. Mark Twain's "innocents" trace their ancestry all the way back to that remote legend,[388] and the line of development continues unbroken

384. Cf., for example, among the earlier writers, Lahontan, op. cit., pp. 120, 131; and among the contemporaries Perrin du Lac, *Voyage dans les deux Louisianes* (Paris, 1805), p. 353. On the other hand the colonists inherited the "slanders" of the savages too. Talleyrand, raging against the ethical disposition of the inhabitants of Maine, writes that they are "lazy and greedy, poor but without needs, still too much like the natives they supplanted" (*Talleyrand in America as a Financial Promoter, 1794–96*, ed. H. Huth and W. J. Pugh [Washington, D.C., 1942], p. 82). See also Castiglioni (below, p. 276), Hilliard d'Auberteuil (below, p. 250), Kürnberger and Bremer, who suppose the strident shouting of the North Americans to be derived from the redskins' war cries (*Der Amerikamüde*, 1855, ed. Die Brücke, n.d., p. 384; *Vie de famille*, II, 290). And Mrs. Trollope, finally, was to explain the vanity of adornment and propensity for alcoholic drinks shown by the "yankees" in terms of the identical tendencies of the redskin and Negro (*Domestic Manners*, 1832; ed. cit., p. 423).

385. *Tableau du climat et du sol des Etats-Unis*, in *Oeuvres complètes*, ed. cit., p. 632b; cf. Chinard, *L'exotisme américain dans l'oeuvre de Chateaubriand* (Paris, 1918), p. 20; Pearce, *The Savages*, pp. 49, 54; Visconti, op. cit., pp. 43–45.

386. *Viaggio nel Canadà e negli Stati Uniti*, 1816–17, passage translated and reprinted in the *Raccoglitore* of Milan, 1818, and transcribed by Leopardi, *Opere*, ed. Gregoriana, p. 1153. The tallness of the New Englanders was eulogized (1812) by the chancellor of Yale, Timothy Dwight (Tryon, op. cit., p. 39). On the Jesuit precedents of this idealization of the redskins, see above, p. 64.

387. Philarète Chasles, *Etudes sur la littérature et les moeurs des Anglo-Américains* (Paris, 1851), p. 271.

388. H. N. Smith, "Origins of a Native American Literary Tradition," in *The American Writer and the European Tradition*, ed. M. Denny and W. H. Gilman (Minneapolis, 1950), pp. 67–70.

from the Good Huron and Leatherstocking to Buffalo Bill and Hopalong Cassidy.

XVIII. PAINE: THE PROMISE OF GREATNESS IN AMERICA'S NATURE

The eighteenth-century mind did not have far to go for the explanation of this dual and commingled excellence of native and immigrant, of redskin and Creole: it was the *climate*, this wonderfully healthy forest air, a third excellence corroborating and absorbing the others.[389]

Closely linked to the Americans' satisfaction over the (qualitative) generosity of Nature was the rejoicing in her (quantitative) abundance and vastness. The immense area of the continent was compared to that of the minuscule and shrunken Europe,[390] and a simple pseudological rule of three led to the conclusion that the animal species too must there be larger and heavier than in the Old World. An even more agile leap, from geodesy and zootechny to the philosophy of history, led to the corollary that a magnificent future must surely be in store for a land so spacious, fruitful, and imposing. The environment was a sure promise of glory.

This romanticizing type of landscape nationalism has been noted and commented on more than once, with reference both to literature[391] and the fine arts.[392] It followed and reacted against the lament of the early New England writers and poets—a lament still found in the young Hawthorne about the "prosaicness" or dumbness of the American landscape, lacking historical associations, shadows from the past, "romantic" apparitions.[393]

The later and polemical but no less "romantic" enthusiasm for America's virgin and potent nature emerges already in the propagandistic

389. See Samuel S. Smith's thesis concerning the influence of the American climate and way of life on the Europeans' descendants, who "had changed in complexion and hair texture . . . whites who lived like Indians began to look like them" (Kraus, op. cit., p. 181).

390. Examples are given in M. Curti, *American Loyalty*, pp. 4, 32 ff., 40 ff., etc. This theme is almost completely lacking in the early Latin American "nationalists." Later, and still in our own day, the position was reversed. The United States completed the occupation of its territory, and the Latin American republics "discovered" the vast regions of Amazonia, the Pampa, the *Llanos*, etc. Pride in spatial vastness is now no more than a secondary element in North American patriotism; in that of South America it is the primary and active element.

391. H. M. Jones, *Ideas in America*, p. 112; idem, *The Theory of American Literature* (Ithaca, 1948), pp. 72–73, 153, 191–92; and in general the whole of the above-mentioned large work by E. Vail, which aims to refute the widespread assertion "that poetry was a plant rejected by America's climate": see esp. op. cit., pp. 610, 612; C. and M. Beard, op. cit., pp. 165–66; C. L. Griffin, "Native Indian Culture," in *Concerning Latin American Culture* (New York, 1949), pp. 117–18; and with a greater wealth of precedents and development, Boorstin, *Genius*, pp. 23–27. See also the profound observations by Perry Miller, "Nature and the National Ego," now in his *Errand into the Wilderness*, pp. 204–16, and the criticisms by I. Löwenstern, *Les Etats Unis et la Havane—Souvenir d'un voyageur* (Paris-Leipzig, 1842), p. 20, of this vain boast of the North Americans.

392. S. Isham, *The History of American Painting* (New York, 1927), quoted in Jones, *Ideas in America*, p. 196; cf. also, for later examples, F. O. Matthiessen, *American Renaissance* (New York, 1941), p. 598.

393. Van Wyck Brooks, *The Flowering of New England* (New York, 1941), p. 47.

writings of the first Puritan colonists,[394] and in the early 1780s was being more and more vigorously asserted. In 1783 Webster demanded that America should make itself "as independent in *literature* as in *politics*," and in 1786 there were already critics (belated and unconscious initiates into the aesthetic of the *imitatio naturae*) upbraiding American writers for following European models instead of seeking their inspiration in the luxuriant, sublime, all-powerful nature of their own vast country (once more, nature against classical heritage, geography against history).[395] At the same time André Chénier too was extolling the educative power of America's unbridled nature: "et l'âme qui s'embrase à cet ardent modèle / Devient indépendante et sublime comme elle."[396]

On the political plane the argument is already exploited *ad nauseam* in Thomas Paine's *Common Sense* (1776). It is unnatural that a continent should be governed by an island. The satellite cannot rule a planet larger than itself. America is an eighth of the inhabitable earth, while England is closed within the "narrow limits of 360 miles." If America is young (and here we see the first signs of a reversal *in rebus politicis* of the thesis of the "new" and still sodden continent), if it is childlike, so much the better: "The *infant* state of the colonies as it is called . . . is an argument in favor of independence."[397]

In the *Rights of Man* (1792) the same prophecy is even more explicit, even more closely linked to telluric environment. America was predestined to be the cradle of the new liberty: "An assemblage of circumstances conspired not only to give birth but to add gigantic maturity to its principles. The scene which that country presents to the eye of the spectator has something in it which generates and enlarges great ideas. Nature appears to him in magnitude." The theater inspires the actors and lifts them to ever sublimer heights. The very "wilderness" stimulates the development of a totally human and brotherly society, without historical quarrels and political intrigues.

If the governments of Asia, Africa, and Europe had been developed on the same principles, the oft imagined visitor from another world, ignorant of history, "would take a great part of the old world to be new, just struggling with the difficulties and hardships of an infant settlement."[398]

---

394. Boorstin, *Genius*, pp. 23–27.

395. Henriquez Ureña, op. cit., p. 237 n. 8; Kraus, op. cit., p. 283; Jones, *American Literature*, passim, esp. pp. 48–71.

396. André Chénier, *Fragments de l'Amérique* (Pléiade ed.), p. 416.

397. T. Paine, *Representative Selections*, ed. H. H. Clark (New York, 1944), pp. 39–40. *Common Sense*, "an excellent work," made its author famous in America and all Europe (Marquis de Chastellux, *Voyage dans l'Amérique septentrionale* [Paris, 1788], I, 263–65). On Raynal's plagiarism of *Common Sense* and Paine's polemic against Raynal, see Feugère, op. cit., XXII, 416–19.

398. Thomas Paine, *The Rights of Man*, pt. II, Introd.; Conway edition (New York, London, 1906), II, 402–03 (*Representative Selections*, pp. 173–74). This second part is in particular polemic against

He would find widespread and incurable poverty, corrupt governments, and the inexorable grasping hand of the tax collector. The Old World is the "new" one, the imperfect, backward one. It is "childish," and in the worst sense, through having grown too old. It is decadent and incapable of meeting the needs of the new times. Only in America do nature and reason work in harmony to fix the rules and forms of a truer and more humane civilization, only there does virtue inimitable flourish, along with the promise of unlimited progress.

Unlimited for a thousand years, maybe. Then America will degenerate like Europe. But while the collapse of the ancient empires left us only the "mouldering ruins of pompous palaces, magnificent museums, lofty pyramids and walls and towers of the most costly workmanship," when "the empire of America shall fall," there will be seen a much sadder spectacle: the ruin of the most noble work of human wisdom, the most majestic scene of human glory, the sublime cause of liberty.[399]

The *Rights of Man* was drafted as a reply to Burke's famous *Reflections*, the most vigorous and impassioned defense of the values of tradition and history. The exaltation of nature unadorned formed part of the attack on the banner-decked ramparts of the past. Thus America as a political concept came into being as antihistory, as the power of nature — in spite of all the European Thersiteses — reaching out toward the future and already proud of its titanic primitivism. If Spanish America had boasted of its bands of saints, the jeweled and glittering trophies of religion, the abundant celestial gifts of grace, Anglo-Saxon America gloried in the mirage of the virgin purity, the boundless possibilities of its land. This delight the North Americans take in being so virtuous, and thus specially favored by God, and thus prosperous and happy, can of course be explained to some extent by Puritan impulses of universal validity. In *The Scarlet Letter* the tormented Reverend Dimmesdale, in his last sermon, rejoices in the conviction that his mission, unlike that of the prophets of Israel, is to "foretell a high and glorious destiny for the newly gathered people of the Lord."[400] But the specifically American form of that conceit was nourished on beliefs and arguments developed in Europe and now boldly turned back on their birthplace. The theme that proved its fecundity over three centuries, from Las Casas to the romantics — of

---

the *Appeal from the New to the Old Whigs*, published by Burke in 1791, and is thus under the immediate suggestion of the antithesis between old and new (cf., for example, "though it might be proved that the system of government now called the *new* is the most *ancient* in principle," ed. cit., p. 414; *Representative Selections*, p. 184).

399. *Representative Selections*, pp. 390–91. On Paine see also Brie, op. cit., pp. 364–66; and for his polemics against Raynal, Villard, op. cit., pp. 333–34, 391.

400. Nathaniel Hawthorne, *The Scarlet Letter* (New York: Books Inc., n.d.), p. 206.

America the rich in gold and guilt,[401] or of Europe's wronging of the innocent Americans and its ensuing punishment with mysterious and irremediable disasters, of Europe burdened with crime and misfortune – now
blossomed among the ingenuous patriots of the United States. One such
patriot drew his readers' attention (1794) to "this glad world remote
from every foe, / From Europe's mischiefs, and from Europe's woe";
another enumerated (1813) the abundant blessings of (North American) providence "while discord is tearing old Europe to pieces"; and yet
others suspected Europe's luxury goods of being bearers of moral corruption, as well as unwelcome competition for those produced by the austere
republicans across the Atlantic.[402] The best and worst in modern Western
thought – its scruples of conscience in the face of conquest and exploitation, its anxious insistence of its own pride of place in the world, and its
right to pass judgment on the rest – reappear, mixed together by the vicissitudes of the polemic, in the turbid and mystic nationalism of the doctrine
of the Manifest Destiny.[403]

The thesis of the New World's degeneration and impotence, on the
other hand, could hardly be made to fit in with any illusion of superiority,
indeed actively undermined such a notion. And almost all the Founding
Fathers of the United States loosed a few shafts in the direction of Buffon and de Pauw. Paine's and Franklin's comments have already been described. Thomas Jefferson actually attempted a formal refutation.[404]
John Adams, while still ambassador in London, mentioned in passing, in
the preface to his *Defence of the Constitutions of the United States*
(1786), how pleased he was that Paine had demolished "the mistakes of
Raynal, and Jefferson those of Buffon, so unphilosophically borrowed

401. V. Monti, *Il fanatismo*, 1797, in *Poesie liriche* (Florence, 1858), p. 363. The gold is American,
and the guilt European, of course. The theme reappears further complicated in Zacharias Werner's *Die
vierundzwanzigste Februar* (1810), where the gold, honestly earned in the New World, should serve to
wash away and redeem the crimes committed in the Old, but instead releases new and even more horrendous ones (Reclam ed., pp. 32, 39, 42).

402. See M. Curti, op. cit., pp. 30, 49, 100, and passim; and also the frank statements of two young
French officers, the Prince de Broglie and the Count de Ségur, who went (1782) to serve in the army of
Rochambeau (for whom see also Fay, op. cit., p. 122): *Deux Français aux Etats-Unis . . .* , in *Mélanges
de la Société des Bibliophiles Français* (Paris, 1903), n. 6, passim, and esp. pp. 169–71, 183, 185. For
other copious literary manifestations of faith in the sublime destiny of the United States and its universal
mission of redemption, see the above-mentioned early work by Sumner and the more recent cited work
by Friedrich Brie.

403. On the Darwinian-chauvinistic origins and racialist tendencies of this myth, see Weinberg's
classic *Manifest Destiny* and H. Wish, *Society and Thought in Modern America* (New York, 1952),
pp. 268, 390, 598; on its "Anglo-Saxon" and Puritan character, see L. B. Wright, *Culture on the Moving
Frontier* (Bloomington, 1955), pp. 92–95, 104; on the "messianism" of the young United States, Weinberg, op. cit., pp. 39–40, and R. Niebuhr, *The Irony of American History* (London, 1952), pp. 21–26,
40, 59–62: and in fact of the colonies even before the Revolution, A. Nevins and H. S. Commager,
America: The Story of a Free People (Oxford, 1943), p. 50.

404. In the same work, the *Notes on Virginia* (for which see below, pp. 252 ff.), he formulated his
political philosophy and outlined the destiny awaiting the United States (see G. Chinard, *Thomas
Jefferson: The Apostle of Americanism* [Boston, 1944], pp. 118–36).

from the despicable dreams of de Pauw."[405] And his wife, the pugnacious Abigail, while admitting Europe's superiority in the arts and sciences, claimed that America had a more widespread culture and more virtuous and more beautiful women (in London she finds only one girl of truly divine beauty and immediately points out that her father is an American and a very handsome man!), and went straight over to the counterattack, to the usual ritual slanderous counterattack on Europe's nature and society: "Do you know," she wrote in a letter to her sister in 1786, "That European birds have not half the melody of ours? Nor is their fruit half so sweet, nor their flowers half so fragrant, nor their manners half so pure, nor their people half so virtuous."[406] The same year saw the publication of the *Anarchiad*, a political satire composed by Barlow, the author of *The Vision of Columbus*, and Freneau, the future Jacobin, in which de Pauw is shown rejoicing over his invention of a telescope that makes things appear smaller the further away they are. With this miraculous instrument—a caricature embodying both the indictment of the "philosopher who judges from afar" and their own annoyance at being judged of minuscule stature—all the creatures of America are seen to be infinitely smaller than those in Europe.[407] It was the same Barlow who shortly thereafter read Jefferson's apologetic *Notes on Virginia* and hastened to congratulate him. "We are flattered with the idea of seeing ourselves vindicated from those despicable aspersions which have long been thrown upon us and echoed from one ignorant Scribbler to another in all the languages of Europe."[408] The exaggeration is clearly rhetorical—de Pauw's theses were not echoed in all the languages of Europe—but is obviously dictated by an irrepressible anger.

In its indiscriminate outbursts of indignation the *Anarchiad* inveighs

405. *A Defence of the Constitutions of Government of the United States of America, against the Attack of M. Turgot, in His Letter to Dr. Price, Dated the Twenty-second Day of March, 1778* (London ed., 1787; in *Works*, ed. C. F. Adams [Boston, 1851]), IV, 293. Adams reverses the order of the dreams: de Pauw derives from Buffon, and not vice versa. Jefferson, in his turn, read Adams's book "with infinite satisfaction and improvement" (letter to John Adams, 23 February 1787, in *Papers*, XI, 177; cf. ibid., XI, 189, 239–40). Cf. also a letter from Adams in 1755, in Brie, op. cit., p. 358.

406. "But keep to yourself," she added, "or I shall be thought more than half deficient in understanding and taste" (letter to Mrs. Shaw, London, 21 November 1786, in *Letters of Mrs. Adams . . .* [Boston, 1840], pp. 358–59; cf. also 305, 315–17, 387–88). The observation might have come to her from Jefferson, who on 21 June 1785 had written to her: "I heard . . . the Nightingale in all its perfection: and I do not hesitate to pronounce that in America it would be deemed a bird of the third rank only, our mocking-bird, and fox-coloured thrush being unquestionably superior to it" (*Papers*, VIII, 241). But Jefferson still tried to acclimatize the "delicious" European nightingale in America (E. Martin, op. cit., p. 60).

407. B. Fay, *Esprit*, pp. 145–46 (and on the prompt reception of de Pauw's and Raynal's books in the American colonies, ibid., p. 27). The same image of the reversed telescope is used in that same year 1786 by Mazzei to ridicule abbé Mably (*Recherches sur les Etats-Unis* [Colle, 1788], II, 23). On the precocious Americanism of Freneau (1771), and Barlow (1778), who had read Robertson's recent *History of America* (1777), but took the idealization of the pre-Columbian civilizations considerably further, see Brie, op. cit., pp. 359, 371–72, 375n., 378; and Pearce, *The Savages*, pp. 178–79.

408. Letter of 15 June 1787, in *Papers of Thomas Jefferson*, XI, 473.

against another writer, who was not only anything but a follower of de Pauw—indeed who admired the innocence and felicity of the savages, the fertility of the American soil, and the vast herds of cattle it supported[409]—but who had actually taken up the defense of the "Anglo-Americans" against the slanders of the English, who called the American troops cowardly and undisciplined. The trouble (for the Americans) was that this European publicist, however well intentioned—perhaps also because he was in the pay of the French government—appeared to be very familiar at least with Buffon's slanders; in fact his apology was too lenient toward America's enemies, and at the same time he let himself be led into attributing to the colonists not only the positive qualities commonly attributed to the savages, but the negative ones too:

While the Anglo-Americans [he wrote] are less robust than most European peoples, and the humid climate seems to weaken them, they do have more boldness, are less sensitive to wounds than the Europeans, and recover from them more easily. Although less ardent, less passionate, less spiritual than the Creoles of the Antilles, they are quick-witted in their youth . . . are fluent of speech, but are little capable of reflection, and cannot meditate a long while over something, and are in this quite the opposite of the English in Europe. They are fully formed at twenty and old men at fifty,[410]

and so on, with more ambiguous and qualified praise.

XIX. HAMILTON AND CRÈVECOEUR

But already in the year following the publication of the *Anarchiad* the polemic and its retortions had been taken up by a much more authoritative figure and in a manifestly political arena. In *The Federalist* Alexander Hamilton scoffed at Europe's arrogance:

Men admired as profound philosophers have, in direct terms, attributed to her inhabitants a physical superiority and have gravely asserted that all animals, and with them the human species, degenerate in America,—that even dogs cease to bark after having breathed awhile in our atmosphere.

409. Hilliard d'Auberteuil, *Essais historiques et politiques sur les Anglo-Américains* (Bruxelles, 1781–82; rpt. and expanded, Paris, 1783), I, 13, 31, 48; II, 394–96 (with polemic against Raynal, who limited the population of the United States to seven or eight million). See his letter to Jefferson (17 February 1786) in *Papers of Thomas Jefferson*, IX, 288–89, and his reply (20 February 1786), ibid., pp. 290–91.

410. Hilliard d'Auberteuil, *Essais*, I, 279–80. Cf. Fay, *Esprit*, pp. 102–04 (who suspects Hilliard of drawing on de Pauw; it is actually quite clear that his source is Peter Kalm: see the extracts from his *Voyage dans l'Amérique du Nord* [1753–61], in *This Was America*, ed. O. Handlin [Cambridge, Mass., 1949], p. 15; cf. below, n. 557), 128 (use of Chastellux), 146; *Bibliographie critique des ouvrages français relatifs aux Etats-Unis, 1770–1800* (Paris, 1925), p. 55; Villard, op. cit., pp. 327–28. The German translation was harshly criticized (1783) by the *Göttingische Gelehrte Anzeigen* as littered with errors (Doll, op. cit., pp. 446–47). And Jefferson too, who owned two copies of the *Essais*, one of which was presented to him by the author, considered it unreliable as a historical source (*Catalogue of the Library*, I, 203–04, 220). Further scornful comments appear in *Papers*, X, 10, 580 (cf. X, 4, 10, 582–83); XI, 80; XII, 62.

And in a footnote, just to make sure, "Recherches Philosophiques sur les Américains."[411]

In his famous *Letters from an American Farmer* (1782) Crèvecoeur does not explicitly combat de Pauw's slanders, but they are candidly and passionately refuted by the whole book. In the very first letter he vindicates the strength and energy of the seeds of American nature: "We are possessed with strong vegetative embryos" from which there grow luxuriant wild plants, "which an European scholar may probably think ill placed and useless."[412] Nor are the natives any less well endowed: "Let us say what we will of them, of their inferior organs, of their want of bread, etc. They are as stout and as well-made as the Europeans."[413]

In fact Bernardin de Saint-Pierre's providential benignness of nature is extended in full to the blessed American continent: the high tide facilitates navigation on the estuaries of the great rivers, the low tide makes it possible to go down to the beach and gather "that variety of shell fish which is the support of the poor."[414]

America is devoid of history, true, but history is one long series of crimes and acts of violence.[415] America is intact and uncontaminated: it has neither courts nor aristocracy, neither kings nor bishops, and no great industries—"no great manufacturers employing thousands"[416]—no hostile castles nor ancient monuments nor cathedrals nor gilded palaces nor soaring spires.[417] Thus the prophetic and auspicious corollary: America will be the home in exile of Europe's poor and oppressed, the salvation of her hungry and her unemployed, the workers' fatherland, the general refuge for the whole world.[418]

411. *The Federalist*, no. 11, 23 November 1787, ed. E. M. Earle (New York, 1941), p. 69. On the voiceless dog, see above, pp. 56, 147, n. 207, p. 214, etc., and Robin, *Nouveau voyage*, p. 42. The assertion can be traced back to Oviedo: see Enrique Alvarez Lopez, "El perro mudo americano," *Boletin de la Real Sociedad Española de Historia Natural*, XL (1942), pp. 411–17. Still in our own day D. W. Jeffreys has used the nonbarking dogs of the New World to support his thesis that the Arabs carried Negro slaves to America considerably before 1492 ("Pre-Columbian Negroes in America," *Scientia*, 88 [July–August 1953], pp. 202–18).

412. *Letters from an American Farmer* (Dolphin Books ed., Garden City, N.Y.), pp. 21–22. But Crèvecoeur's enthusiasm does not stretch to the tropics: below the equator everything is putrid, poisonous, and pestilential: ibid., letter IX, ed. cit., p. 174. On Crèvecoeur see D. H. Lawrence, *Studies in Classic American Literature* (Garden City, N.Y., 1953), pp. 31–43; *Catalogue of the Library of Thomas Jefferson*, IV, 199–201; V. L. Parrington, op. cit., I, 140–47; Claude-Anne Lopez, *Mon Cher Papa: Franklin and the Ladies of Paris* (New Haven–London, 1966), pp. 159–67.

413. Op. cit., letter XII, ed. cit., p. 220. Cf. letter VIII, p. 156, for the trees which would have been able to grow and thrive in Nantucket, if the inhabitants were not entirely devoted to fishing, *et alibi*.

414. Ibid., letter VIII, ed. cit., p. 159.

415. Ibid., letter IX, ed. cit., p. 171: of obvious derivation from Voltaire.

416. In that same year 1782 Mazzei prophesied a great industrial future for the United States (see below, p. 269), but Crèvecoeur was under the dual influence of his unwavering physiocrat agrarianism (much like Jefferson's, come to that) and his horror of the incipient industrial revolution in Europe.

417. Op. cit., letters III, IV, VIII, ed. cit., pp. 46, 70, 98, 161.

418. Ibid., letters III, IV, VIII, XI, ed. cit., pp. 63, 71, 93, 161, 194. A swift echo in Talleyrand (1794): "Is not every man who chooses a fatherland already an American in advance?" (in Michel Poniatowski, *Talleyrand aux Etats-Unis, 1794–1796* [Paris, 1967]), p. 207. See below, p. 550.

Free from ancestral ties, from age-old nationalistic disputes and the must of prejudice, the American is the new citizen of this earth, and as such carries on and at the same time rejects the whole heritage of the Old World. Once again the heliodromic theme blares out: "Americans are the Western pilgrims, who are carrying along with them that great mass of arts, sciences, vigour, and industry which began long since in the east: they will finish the great circle."[419]

XX. THOMAS JEFFERSON'S *NOTES ON VIRGINIA*

Of all these replies, however, by far the most important is Thomas Jefferson's, both on account of his thorough treatment of the problem, and because the *Notes on Virginia* was widely read in both Europe and America.[420]

The Secretary of the French Legation in Philadelphia, François Marbois (later the Marquis de Barbé-Marbois),[421] had presented Jefferson with a comprehensive questionnaire on the geography, the products, the social and political institutions, the religion, and the finances of Virginia. Finding himself with time on his hands after his resignation from the governorship of that state, and obliged to be idle after a fall from his horse, he took advantage of the circumstances to draft detailed answers to the

419. Op. cit., letter III, ed. cit., p. 49.

420. A private edition was produced in Paris in 1785 (falsely dated 1782); a French trans. was published in 1786, an English ed. in London, 1787, rpt. Philadelphia, 1788; a German trans., Leipzig, 1789 (see also Doll, art. cit., p. 464). There are innumerable other American editions. And already by 1791 the *Notes* was cited in support of a sermon on *The Blessings of America!* (*Catalogue of the Library*, II, 166). "The true history of that publication" is recounted by Jefferson in his *Autobiography* (in *Works*, ed. cit., I, 93–95; unless otherwise indicated all our citations will refer to this edition, which reproduces the *Notes on Virginia* in III, 349–517) and in a letter to John Page (4 May 1786; ibid., V, 98; cf. ibid., IV, 412–13; V, 301, 304). Further details and previously unpublished passages can be found in the recent edition by William Peden (Chapel Hill, 1955); cf. also *Catalogue of the Library*, IV, 301–30. On the history of the work and its editions, see also Ford in ed. cit., III, 313–45, and *Papers*, VII, 546, 563 (Jefferson could not get it printed in Philadelphia). On its distribution and diffusion in France, Holland, England, Spain, Italy, Switzerland, and the United States, see numerous passages in the *Papers*, vols. IX–XIII, and especially *Papers*, VIII, 147–48, 161, 169–70, 174–75, 184–86, 258, 260–61, 263–64, 324, 358, 462, 502–03, 562, 566, 631–32. On Morellet's French trans. (Jefferson, *Works*, III, 322 ff.; *Papers*, IX, 133; *Catalogue of the Library*, III, 357; F. Mazzei, *Lettere alla corte di Polonia*, ed. R. Ciampini [Bologna, 1937], p. 9). See also D. Barros Arana, *Notas para una bibliografía de obras anónimas y seudónimas, sobre la historia, la geografía y la literatura de América*, 1882, in *Obras completas*, VI (Santiago, 1909), p. 469, n. 375. Cf. finally *Alcuni libri piuttosto interessanti* (Florence, Sansoni, 1950), nn. 18–19, and below, chap. 9, sec. 5, "The Quakers, the Marquis, and the Girondist."

421. Barbé-Marbois, after a stormy career during the Revolution, became one of Napoleon's favorite ministers, and died a marquis and peer of France. By a singular coincidence it was actually to him, as Minister of the Treasury, that there fell the task of negotiating the famous sale of Louisiana to the United States, of which Jefferson was then president. The man who had furnished Jefferson with the occasion for the most powerful polemic in defense of the North American territory was an essential instrument of its greatest spatial and economic enlargement, realized by Jefferson himself. Jefferson wrote to him again thirty-seven years after receiving his questionnaire (14 June 1817, in *The Life and Writings*, ed. cit., pp. 681–82) reaffirming his faith in the future of the United States. The *Britannica* says that Barbé-Marbois served six governments "and all with servility"; the *Dictionnaire des Girouettes* (3rd ed., Paris, 1815) already assigned him no less than four weathercocks. See also R. Remond, op. cit., pp. 238, 318.

diplomat's queries (1781–82), based on notes that he had made some time earlier. Virginia, which the Elizabethans, in a frenzy of courtly admiration for the Virgin Queen, had already hailed as a new Eden,[422] was not for Jefferson just a state like any other: it was in his own warmly affectionate phrase, "my native country,"[423] and extended as far west as the Ohio and the Mississippi, taking in all of Kentucky.

"Virginia was by far the largest state in Confederation—claiming territory now comprising numerous states and embracing perhaps a third of the Continent," which leads him to identify it with all America.[424] In the heart of Virginia lay his house and his land: Monticello, truly, *praeter omnes ridet;* and as he boasts of its charms he finds himself instinctively repudiating the well-known calumnies of the European scholars, and in fact hurling them back against Europe: "Indeed, madam," he wrote to Angelica Schuyler Church, "I know nothing so charming as our own country. The learned say it is a new creation; and I believe them; not for their reasons, but because it is made on an improved plan. Europe is a first idea, a crude production, before the Maker knew his trade, or had made up his mind as to what he wanted."[425] America is creation's masterpiece. And Virginia, his Virginia, is an exhaustive compendium of all the United States, a representative section of the whole of North America. As the Virginian Colonel Byrd had biblically put it: "In the beginning, All America was Virginia."[426]

One of the very earliest readers of the *Notes* in fact wrote to Jefferson saying: "I consider it a most excellent Natural history not merely of Virginia but of No. America and possibly equal if not superior to that of any Country yet published."[427]

In describing Virginia, Jefferson thus found himself pushed into writing what was to be the only complete and formal book passed on to posterity by that prolific correspondent, orator, and publicist. And among the very few examples of American literature admitted by the disdainful Sydney Smith (1818) we find indeed "a small account of Virginia by Jefferson."[428] Directed at a French audience, and first published in Paris, the book was bound to examine the famous theories of Buffon, to whom

---

422. L. B. Wright, *The Elizabethans' America*, pp. 109, 161, 167, 205 and passim.
423. On the ambiguity of this expression, see Curti, *American Loyalty*, pp. 22–23; Boorstin, *Genius*, pp. 73–74; idem, *The Americans: The National Experience* (London, 1966), p. 402.
424. Peden, in ed. cit., xxi–xxii.
425. Letter of 17 February 1788; *Papers*, XII, 601.
426. William Byrd (1674–1744), quoted in Boorstin, *Colonial Experience*, p. 97.
427. Letter of Charles Thomson (secretary of the Continental Congress), 6 March 1785, in *Papers*, VIII, 16.
428. Article in the *Edinburgh Review* (December 1818), cited in Cunliffe, *Literature*, p. 44. It is not literature, but statistics, a recent biographer suggests, on the other hand; see Merrill D. Peterson, *The Jefferson Image in the American Mind* (New York, 1960), p. 406.

one of the very first copies was delivered at Jefferson's personal request.[429]

A. The mammoth and America's humidity.   Here again the point of departure is the size of America's animals. After brief reference to the minerals and plants of Virginia, Jefferson begins on the description of the quadrupeds,[430] introducing us proudly to the mammoth or great buffalo, without doubt the largest of all (p. 408), a great brute whose "cubic volume" was six or seven times that of the elephant, as Buffon himself has admitted (p. 412). Once having established its existence on the basis of fossil remains, and thus assured an overwhelming supremacy of the cold and temperate zones of the new continent over tropical Asia and Africa, which can barely support the minuscule elephant, Jefferson uses this hairy and puissant pachyderm as a lever, so to speak, to pry open and demolish the Buffonian thesis of America's zoological inferiority:[431]

It is certain such a one [such an animal] has existed in America, and that it has been *the largest of all terrestrial beings.* It should have sufficed to have rescued the earth it inhabited, and the atmosphere it breathed, from the imputation of impotence in the conception and nourishment of animal life on a large scale; to have stifled, in its birth, the opinion of a writer, the most learned, too, of all others in the science of animal history, that in the new world, "living nature is less active, much less strong." (p. 415)

The moment Buffon is quoted, before his ideas have even been properly outlined, Jefferson falls upon them and pronounces them downright ab-

---

429. Letter to Chastellux, 7 June 1785, in Jefferson, *Works,* III, 319. And Mazzei, Jefferson's friend, always talks of Virginia as the richest and most authoritative of the thirteen ex-colonies. But he is mistaken, or at least exaggerating, when he says that "the real reason" why Jefferson wrote the *Notes* was to fulfill his promise to furnish a reply to the written questions, "provided . . . they were restricted to the state of Virginia alone," which might be put to him by his friend the Duc de La Rochefoucauld (F. Mazzei, *Memorie della vita e delle peregrinazioni* [Lugano, 1845–46], I, 533–34). But Mazzei knows that the *Notes* had been drafted before Jefferson's arrival in France (see his *Recherches historiques et politiques sur les Etats-Unis . . .* [Colle, 1788], II, 115). Another Italian, Luigi Castiglioni, *Viaggio negli Stati Uniti dell'America settentrionale* (Milan, 1790), I, 355, recalls that Jefferson did not want to make his *Notes* public. Its true purpose — Vail says in fact — was to "refute the inconceivable supposition advanced by Buffon and abbé Raynal, that in America the animal species, including the human family, were, in comparison with Europe, reduced" (op. cit., p. 15).

430. Birds, fish, and insects are treated somewhat summarily, on pp. 462–69, since these creatures do not present any polemic interest like the quadrupeds.

431. Buffon (see above, pp. 15–16) was quick to catch the danger of Jefferson's argument. And his first reaction, on receiving the *Notes on Virginia,* was to reaffirm that the mammoth and the elephant were the same creature (letter from Jefferson to Hogendorp, 13 October 1785, in *Works,* III, 415n., and IV, 466–67, and in *Papers,* VIII, 631–32; and the exchange of letters with John Rutledge, Jr., 4 September and 9 September 1788, in *Papers,* XIII, 568, 592–93; but on the subject of the mammoth and against Buffon see already the correspondence from 1784 with Ezra Stiles in *Papers,* VII, 304–05, 312–17, 364–65; Martin, op. cit., pp. 62, 111–15, and passim, and below, p. 403); he was seeking in fact to remove the fulcrum of Jefferson's lever. On the American mammoth admitted also by Buffon, see already Clavigero, *Storia antica del Messico,* IV, 42n., 115 and the enormous monstrous dimensions he gives for it, and Pictet, op. cit., I, 150–52, who follows Jefferson. But Castiglioni was already dubious about this gigantic "unknown animal": op. cit., I, 387–88; II, 155. De Pauw, naturally, had made fun of the mammoth, "an individual more worthy of appearing in the mythology of the North than in the nomenclatures of natural history" ("Amérique," I, 348a).

surd: "as if both sides [of the earth] were not warmed by the same genial sun"; as if the earth of America had a different chemical composition; and as if this earth and sun gave birth to fruit or grain that was less nourishing or that brought about a premature surcease in the process of growth. No, the size of the animals is not dependent on their diet. The pygmy and the giant, the mouse and the mammoth soak up the same nutritive juices. The difference in growth depends on circumstances that remain impenetrable to creatures of our limited capacity:

Every race of animals seems to have received from their Maker certain laws of extension at the time of their formation. Their elaborate organs were formed to produce this, while proper obstacles were opposed to its further progress. Below these limits they cannot fall, nor rise above them.

The differences in climate, earth, food, and upbringing can influence the size of individuals, but always within the fixed limits of the species. Every species has its own dimensions, fixed *ab aeterno*. All the manna the heavens could provide would not suffice to make a mouse grow into a mammoth (p. 416).

Twenty-five years later Goethe repeated the same notion, ignoring any necessity of reconciling it with his transformism, and indeed took it a step further in setting Nature alongside the Maker, or God himself:

Zweck sein selbst ist jegliches Tier, vollkommen entspringt es
Aus dem Schoss der Natur und zeugt vollkommene Kinder . . .
Doch im Innern befindet die Kraft der edlern Geschöpfe
Sich im heiligen Kreise lebendiger Bildung beschlossen.
Diese Grenze erweitert kein Gott, es ehrt die Natur sie:
Denn nur also beschränkt war je das Vollkommene möglich.[432]

Thus Jefferson denies a priori any validity whatsoever to comparisons of stature, but having done so proceeds nevertheless to analyze the fragile basis of Buffon's "opinions." According to the latter, the inferiority of America is due (Jefferson simplifies somewhat) to a lack of warmth and an excess of humidity. But is America really wetter? Adequate statistics

---

432. "Every animal is an end to itself, springing forth perfect out of Nature's womb and begetting perfect progeny. . . . But the power of the nobler creatures is intimately limited within the holy circle of its living form. No God can extend these limits; Nature respects them: for only through such limitation is perfection possible." The harmony deriving from the proportion of parts to the whole, the perfection of balance, which Goethe here assigns to the animal species, is notoriously one of the fundamental concepts of his view of the world. Nature itself, Goethe writes elsewhere, cannot create monsters, like horned lions. He quite likely had in mind a celebrated passage where Kant admires the unity of the animal scheme in the innumerable variety of forms "through the shortening of one and the lengthening of another, through the wrapping up of this part and the unwrapping of that" (*Kritik der Urteilskraft*, pt. II, sec. 80; ed. Insel [Leipzig, 1921], VI, 316–17). Cf. also J. P. Eckermann's *Gespräche mit Goethe* (Zurich, 1948), 6 May 1827; E. Caro, *La philosophie de Goethe* (Paris, 1880), pp. 127–31, 388–90; W. Jablonski, *Goethe e le scienze naturali* (Bari, 1938), pp. 152–53, 160–61; and Lovejoy, *Chain of Being*, p. 369, n. 76. Haldane repeats and develops Goethe's thesis that "for every type of animal there is an optimum size" (op. cit., p. 25).

on this point are unavailable.[433] And is it really true that humidity is hostile to the growth of the animal species? There is no good reason to suppose so, and experience indicates the opposite. The more humid a land is, the more luxuriant its vegetation, and "vegetables are mediately or immediately the food of every animal; and in proportion to the quantity of food, we see animals not only multiplied in their numbers, but improved in their bulk, as far as the laws of their nature will admit."[434] Thus in the overall comparison of the two continents, America and Europe, America is certainly found to be warmer (a positive factor) and wetter (a negative factor) than Europe: they are thus "equally adapted . . . to animal productions" (p. 419). And in any case, Jefferson adds in a letter, perhaps one cannot even really say that America is *wetter:* did not Dr. Franklin find London and Paris wetter than Philadelphia? . . .[435] But in the *Notes*

433. In 1805 (8 February), writing to Volney, Jefferson compared the climates of Europe and America, and preferred the American, one of the reasons being that "though we have double the rain it falls in half the time" (Modern Library ed., p. 577; cf. Martin, op. cit., pp. 131–47). Virginia's climate, in particular, after having enjoyed for some time a legendary renown (cf. Spenser, *Fairie Queen*, I, "fruitfullest Virginia" [1589]; Michael Drayton, *To the Virginian Voyage:* "Virginia, Earth's only Paradise"; P. Chaunu, op. cit., p. 115; Blanke, op. cit., pp. 86, 101–03, 114, 117, 119–20, 141), had inexplicably (or through lack of the hoped-for gold?) acquired a terrible reputation. Some find it intolerably hot, others profess themselves bitterly disappointed in it, others still scorn and ridicule it (Blanke, op. cit., pp. 128, 157, 300). Thomas Burnet, after ascribing the longevity of the inhabitants of the Bermudas to the traditional mildness of its climate (see the famous poem by Andrew Marvell, "Bermudas," ca. 1653), continues: "And on the contrary in Virginia, as they call it, which is not far away, they are very short-lived and sickly, on account of the extremely intemperate climate" (*Telluris theoria sacra* [1681], II, 3; Amsterdam ed., 1699, p. 90). Jefferson owned a copy of this work, but despised its geological theories, and especially the inquiries into the antiquity and vicissitudes of the globe.

434. This thesis, that animal life thrives better in a thriving plant life, had already been put forward with precise reference to the Americas, by Pietro Martire (*Decades de Orbe Novo*, I, 10; III, 6, 7), but discussed and denied by Darwin, with the examples of the formidable fauna of arid South Africa and the mediocre animals of verdant tropical America (cf. below, pp. 448–49). Jefferson cites in support of his thesis an example given by Buffon, of a race of animals, the oxen, who prosper more the colder and more humid their surroundings are; and the thesis, likewise Buffonian, that "everything colossal and great in nature was formed in the northern lands" (p. 418n., citing *Epoques de la Nature*, pp. 255–63; and again in *Notes*, p. 458n.). In this phase of the polemic the separation between the two points of view comes out quite clearly. Buffon, when he spoke of American species, always had in mind those of South America and the Tropics (see above, chap. 1, n. 9). Jefferson was thinking first and foremost about the animals of North America, and took comfort in Buffon's thesis about arctic fauna in general. And his friend Madison reminded him that Buffon, in polemic with de Pauw, had already limited his denigration of the American fauna to that of South America (letter of 20 June 1786, in *Papers*, IX, 665).

435. Letter to Chastellux, 7 June 1785 (*Works*, III, 420n., and in *Papers*, VIII, 184–86), which concludes by bewailing the fact that the problem cannot yet be resolved, as the data is lacking: "in the meantime, doubt is wisdom." And a few years later: "I verily believe it will turn out in event that the atmosphere of our part of America is less humid than that of this part of Europe," which helps to refute Buffon, de Pauw, Raynal, and Robertson (letter to Benjamin Vaughan, 23 July 1788, *Papers*, XIII, 397; and cf. Vaughan's reply, 2 August 1788, ibid., XIII, 460). In the *Notes on Virginia* the climate (humidity, p. 472) is discussed in the course of a reply to the question: "A notice of all that can increase the progress of Human Knowledge?" (pp. 470–84). On Franklin's experiments, and their anti-Buffonian implications, see Chinard, "America as a Human Habitat," p. 41, and Martin, op. cit., pp. 176–77. On the defense of the climate of Pennsylvania undertaken by Dr. Rush, see already Brissot, *Nouveau voyage*, II, 118–29. The thrust of Jefferson's polemic is to deny any natural diversity between the two hemispheres (and, secondarily, to insist on the superiority of the American hemisphere in such differences as do exist), but later he seems to acknowledge it as an evident fact: "Nor is it in physics alone that we shall be found to differ from the other hemisphere. I strongly suspect that our geographical peculiarities may call for a different code of natural law" (letter to Dr. Mitchell, quoted in Weinberg, op. cit., p. 29).

on Virginia Jefferson points out somewhat more shrewdly that, in reality, the supposed wetness of South America is perhaps explained by the fact that it was visited and described almost exclusively by Spaniards and Portuguese, who came from countries that were among the driest in the world. An Irishman, a Swede, or a Finn would probably have found South America a dry and arid land.[436]

B. *The animals compared by volume.* We come next to the volumetric comparison of the European and American quadrupeds. Jefferson gives statistical tables of the animals common to the two continents, of those found only in one, and of those that have been raised domestically in both: all set out in order of volume, the biggest first, the tiniest at the very foot of each table, and beside each animal a note of its weight in pounds and ounces. Not all the weights are equally certain. Some refer to specimens of exceptional size. For Jefferson it is enough however to show that the law which Buffon maintained was valid "without exception" is unacceptable.

But then Jefferson gets carried away with enthusiasm at seeing so many of his champions, his reindeer and bears and wolves, defeating or at least equaling in weight the European champions; he is determined to rout his opponent completely, and onto the metaphorical scales he throws the vast American mammoth, bringing the balance crashing down on the side of the New World. And to objections that the mammoth is extinct he replies no, Nature never let a species become extinct,[437] and very probably the mammoth can still be found wandering somewhere in some remote part of the continent.

There are a number of other worthy animals of which we know too little. Buffon certainly never saw them or weighed them. He based himself on the tales of travelers, who described them as smaller than their European counterparts. But were these travelers qualified to judge? "Have they not been men of a very different description from those who

---

436. Op. cit., pp. 461–62n.; compare above, pp. 7–8. The argument was taken up and developed by Jefferson's friend Volney, in his *Tableau du climat* (1803), pp. 697–98. And it is found again, in its naïve form, so to speak, in the diary of a young American diplomat, journeying (1826) down to the Rio Magdalena: "In observing the rich luxuriance of the forests on this river and in different parts of America, we may well believe that the minds of the European discoverers were impressed with admiration. One who has seen only the sterility or at most stunted trees of many parts of Europe [where the author had never been] might well feel and express admiration at what is presented here" (E. T. Parks and A. Tischendorf, "Cartagena to Bogotà, 1825–26: The Diary of Richard Clough Anderson, Jr.," *Hispanic-American Historical Review*, 42, no. 2 [May 1962], pp. 217–31, esp. 227).

437. "Such is the economy of nature, that no instance can be produced, of her having permitted any one race of her animals to become extinct" (p. 427). Jefferson was unwilling to believe in the possible extinction of any species "since it would imply that the Creator had abandoned some of his creations" (*Times Literary Supplement*, 19 September 1968). It is the customary argument *ad absurdum* in defense of nature, that it cannot be so weak or impotent as to allow one of its creatures to be destroyed or canceled from the face of the earth. On Jefferson's interest, about this same period, in gigantic fossil carcasses and the mastodon, in polemic with Buffon's geological theories, see the Princeton edition of the *Papers*, VI; IX, 260–61, 476–78; XIII, 568, 593.

have laid open to us the other three quarters of the world?"[438] Did they measure or weigh the animals they wrote about? Did they in fact even see them? And did they really know the animals of their own countries? They were often such ignorant men that they even confused the species.[439] Their evidence must be rejected.

In the tables drawn up by Jefferson, based almost exclusively on Buffon[440] but completed by the Virginian with most deliberate and particular care,[441] the quadrupeds peculiar to America turn out to be four times more numerous and not a whit smaller than those of Europe (pp. 432, 436). Thus one more of Buffon's theses is shattered. The animals domesticated in both hemispheres are larger wherever they have been fed and raised better, and there is absolutely no call to conjure up some "imbecility or want of uniformity in the operations of nature" (p. 433); so that the third Buffonian thesis too "is as probably wrong as the first and second were certainly so" (p. 435).

C. The indios *and the redskins.* But worst of all, Jefferson continues, is the fact that Buffon extended his "hypothesis" to take in the men of America too. Fortunately his description (summarized above, pp. 6–7; Buffon, XV, 446–47) does not correspond to the facts. Of the South American Indian, Jefferson knows only what little he has read, which he finds as improbable as one of Aesop's fables. Of the North American native, he knows considerably more, through personal experience too, and he can vouch for his being quite the opposite of the way he is represented by the Europeans. "He is neither more defective in ardor, nor more impotent with his female, than the white reduced to the same diet and exercise."[442] The redskin is brave, shrewd, very much attached to

438. Op. cit., p. 428. Jefferson seems to want to imply that the traders' and adventurers' and missionaries' American tales cannot be accepted as being as valid as the exact geographical descriptions of the Old World (see below, n. 449). In a letter written some years later to the president of Harvard, Dr. Willard, Jefferson wrote: "The Botany of America is far from being exhausted, its Mineralogy is untouched, and its Natural History or Zoology, totally mistaken and misrepresented. As far as I have seen, there is not a single species of terrestrial birds common to Europe and America, and I question if there be a single species of quadrupeds (Domestic animals are to be excepted)" (Letter from Paris, 24 March 1789, in *Life and Writings,* pp. 467–68).

439. A note to the 1853 ed. comments: "Even Amerigo Vespucci says he saw lions and wild bears in America" (p. 428n.). As already with Molina (see above, p. 215), who was well known to Jefferson (*Catalogue of the Library,* IV, 293), the Buffonian (or rather Oviedian) argument of the "names" having confused the "things" (equally well known to Jefferson, ibid., p. 431n.) is turned against Buffon himself. The criticism of the travelers as inexperienced or naïve seems to be an echo of similar expressions in J. J. Rousseau, *Discours sur l'inégalité* (1754), note 8; ed. cit., pp. 128–31.

440. Clavigero too (praised by Jefferson for correcting the errors of Robertson: *Catalogue of the Library,* IV, 269; Martin, op. cit., p. 56; cf. above, n. 184) had drawn up tables of the American quadrupeds "recognized and admitted" by Buffon, confused by him with other species and ignored by him or "wrongly denied," to conclude that America, a third of the globe, had at least one hundred and fifty-two species against two hundred or three hundred at most counted by Buffon in the whole globe (*Storia antica del Messico,* IV, 151–59).

441. Letter of 25 September 1783 to Thomas Walker, *Catalogue of the Library,* IV, 304.

442. In the 1853 ed. (p. 438n.) the thesis of the eroticism of the savage is supported by the testimony (they are "immoderately lascivious") of that same Vespucci who a little earlier had been cited as the archetype of the unreliable traveler. Vespucci is cited several times in the following pages.

his children, loyal to his friends, alert and intelligent, and, like the white man, devoted to hunting and gambling. His shortcomings and those of his womenfolk, held to be less fruitful,[443] are due solely to his circumstances, not to nature. They are caused by his way of life, with its frequent hunger, constant danger, and backbreaking work. And as for their being smooth skinned, that is because they shave their skin. . . . The traders who married Indian women and succeeded in persuading them to abandon the habit "say [delightedly?!] that nature is the same with them as with the whites."[444] It is really not so surprising that a few years later (1797) one of Jefferson's critics ridiculed him for his zeal in "examining minutely every part of [the Indian's] frame," and thus ascertaining that even if his hand was smaller than the European's his genital organs were neither smaller nor less efficient.[445]

Nor are the redskins mentally inferior. Oratory is their strong point. Neither Demosthenes nor Cicero, nor any other of Europe's most famous orators, whoever he might have been, ever made a better speech than the Mingo Chief Logan's address to the governor of Virginia, Lord Dunmore, in 1774 (pp. 444–46).[446] Jefferson never doubts its authenticity and

443. At one time Jefferson had seemed to accept the thesis of the meager fecundity of the redskin women, but later corrected the manuscript, referring only in general terms to "obstacles" to proliferation (see Peden ed., pp. 96, 281 n. 3).

444. *Notes*, p. 445. But not even if they were naturally glabrous, Jefferson concludes paraphrastically, "is the consequence necessary which has been drawn from it" (ibid.). Montaigne already knew that the Mexican women "remove their hair from their whole body" except their foreheads (*Essais*, II, 12; Pléiade ed., p. 461), certainly on the word of Lopez de Gómara ("They all remove their hair and anoint themselves, so as not to have any hair except on the head and brows": *La conquista de México*, chap. 223; Mexico ed., 1943, II, 245). Brereton gives a delightful story (1602) of Indians making false beards with animal hair, "and one of them offered a beard of their making to one of our sailors for this that grew on his face" (L. B. Wright, *The Elizabethans' America*, p. 143). "No beards" is also the comment of another English traveler of 1612 (A. L. Rowse, *The Elizabethans and America* [London, 1959], p. 167; Wright, *The Elizabethans' America*, p. 216). The Mexicans have almost no beard (C. M. Wieland, "Koxkox und Kikequetzel," p. 70). "The Indians are generally glabrous" (Lévi-Strauss, *Tristes tropiques*, p. 244; they painstakingly remove their hair, ibid., p. 296). And "the Indians [redskins] are supposed to have been beardless" (Edmund Wilson, op. cit., p. 66). And Humboldt (*Reise*, II, 22) and innumerable others. See also above, p. 124, and below, n. 500. On the lack of Indian monuments and also of such public works as irrigation ditches, Jefferson expresses himself quite frankly on p. 500; on his reluctant acceptance of civilization, in the *Second Inaugural Address* (1805), in X, 131–33; on his attitude in general, see Pearce, *The Savages*, pp. 91–96, and the bibliography in Martin, op. cit., pp. 279–80.

445. Quoted in Martin, op. cit., p. 224. B. Rush, in his *Autobiography*, ed. G. W. Corner (Princeton, 1948), manages to trace a curious parallel between the redskins and the French, "the most civilized of any nation in the world."

446. This famous speech, published in America in 1775, was already brought to the Europeans' notice by Raynal, in the 3rd ed. of his *Histoire* (1780); by Pictet, op. cit., I, 191; by abbé Robin, *Nouveau voyage*, pp. 147–48; and by Ferdinand M. Bayard, *Voyage dans l'intérieur des Etats-Unis . . . pendant l'été de 1791* (1797; 2d ed., Paris, 1798), pp. 217–18. See also E. D. Seeber, "Diderot and Chief Logan's Speech," *Modern Language Notes*, 60, no. 5 (March 1945), pp. 176–78; idem, "Chief Logan's Speech in France," *Modern Language Notes*, 61 (June 1946), pp. 412–16; F. Mazzei, *Recherches historiques*, IV, 153–55; and the long notes and appendices in Jefferson, *Works*, III, 444–55, in the Peden ed. of the *Notes*, pp. xxiv n., 226–58, in the *Catalogue of the Library*, IV, 214, 224–27; V, 209, 210, and in H. Melville, *Moby Dick*, ed. L. S. Mansfield and Howard P. Vincent (New York, 1952), pp. 680–81. The redskins' eloquence was proverbial, on the reliable evidence of those masters of eloquence, the Jesuits (see Kennedy, op. cit., pp. 138–39; E. A. Vail, "Orateurs Indiens," in op. cit., pp. 467–76; Wright, *The Elizabethans' America*, p. 185) and Diderot too had recognized "the eloquence of those people" (*Voyage de Bougainville*, p. 759). But this characteristic too seems to be of classical derivation: the fiery elo-

chooses it, deliberately, to combat "the contumacious theory of certain writers . . . that our country from the combined effects of soil and climate, degenerated animal nature, in the general, and particularly the moral faculties of man," because he knew that it had been suggested by some that he had made it up himself "to support an argument against Buffon."[447] No, the speech is genuine, and Logan the savage is a master of eloquence.

The oratorical invention ascribed to Jefferson recalls the case of Polly Baker, whose speech was almost certainly the work of Benjamin Franklin. Polly's fictitious defense, when she went on trial for having brought five bastards into the world, had been an attempt to convince her judges of her "merit" in having increased the colony's population; thus it represented a counterattack in the name of natural law (supported by economic law) against society and its false and hypocritical laws, and had been utilized as such by publicists and *philosophes,* including even Raynal, Diderot, and Brissot.[448] The redskin chief and the little Connecticut strumpet spoke out with one voice in favor of a simpler, more human, more acceptable justice than the one codified in Europe's laws. This *indignatio* created new myths and new characters, which were immediately accepted as authentic and reliable.

Thus there is a solid core of truth to back up Jefferson's more sophistic arguments, as he advances fearlessly to the reduction of Europe's arrogance.

The barbarians of northern Europe, so much more numerous than the scattered Indians, did not produce a single genius; and then it took sixteen centuries to form an Isaac Newton. Certainly there are differences among men: some races are stronger and more intelligent than others. But what has which side of the Atlantic one is born on got to do with it?

---

quence of the Scythians and other barbarous peoples was a commonplace among the ancients: see Lovejoy and Boas, op. cit., pp. 336–40; and, sarcastically, Voltaire, "Discours préliminaire," *Essai sur les moeurs* (the section "Des Scythes, et des Gomérites"), I, 64. On the humanitarian facundity of the Brahmins, Calanus and Dindymus, see Bernheimer, op. cit., pp. 107–10. From the time of Las Casas, for that matter, the natives had been put on a level with the Greeks and Romans, or if anything a little higher (cf. Hanke, *Aristotle and the Indians,* p. 54; Romeo, op. cit., p. 52). For Lafitau, cf. P. G. Adams, op. cit., pp. 187, 199. Classicistic representations of the redskins are frequent in Beltrami (1823): *Alle sorgenti del Mississippi,* pp. 32, 52, 76, 79, 81 (oratory), 89, 104, 141, 203. Tocqueville too comments on the "Spartan" natural eloquence of the Redskins (*Voyages en Sicile et aux Etats-Unis* [Paris, 1957], p. 73), and Ampère (op. cit., I, 188) goes into ecstasies over their "veritable eloquence." On the Spartan eloquence of the pioneers of the West ("which will remind you of the orators of antiquity") see Thoreau, in Lawrence Willson, "The Transcendentalist View of the West," *Western Humanities Review,* 14 (1960), p. 190. For the natives of the South Seas and Australia, who were likewise compared to the ancient Greeks and Romans, see B. Smith, op. cit., pp. 24, 26, 127, 251, 255.

447. On this curious controversy, ample details in *Catalogue of the Library,* III, 308–15, 357. Cf. also Pearce, *The Savages,* pp. 78–80, 94.

448. The history of this humorous invention has been wittily told by Max Hall, op. cit. (cf. also G. Spini, in *Rivista storica italiana,* 73, no. 2 [1961], pp. 331–32), and Wolpe, op. cit., pp. 93, 164).

Is it seriously suggested that nature "has enlisted herself as a Cis or Trans Atlantic partisan?" Come now, let us admit it; Buffon may be an eminent and inspired zoologist, but here he let reason give in to a ready tongue, a lively imagination, and his magic style (p. 455).

Coming back to the subject in a letter of 1785, Jefferson observes that the only respectable author ever to affirm the inferiority of the *indios* was "Don Ulloa." Robertson is a mere copyist, a translator of Buffon. And "Pauw, the beginner of this charge, was a compiler from the works of others, and of the most unlucky description."[449] And Ulloa may have had direct experience with the Indians, but only those of South America, and after ten generations of humiliating slavery. The pre-Colombian *indios*, and the redskins, are quite another matter. "I believe the Indian then to be in body and mind equal to the white man."[450]

449. In fact "he seems to have read the writings of travellers only to collect and republish their lies. It is really remarkable that in three volumes in 12mo of small print it is scarcely possible to find one truth, and yet that the author should be able to produce authority for every fact he states, as he says he can" (letter to Chastellux, 7 June 1785, in *Works*, III, 418n., and in *Papers*, VIII, 184–86; Raynal too, Jefferson recounts, was quick to put forward an "unquestionable authority" for each of his American fairy tales: see *Catalogue of the Library*, I, 215; and cf., against Raynal, *Papers*, X, 299, 302). Jefferson was very familiar with the *Recherches*. In 1783–84, at Annapolis, he talked of it to a Dutch merchant, G. K. van Hogendorp, who, on returning home, obtained a copy for himself, but never managed to get through more than a third, as it seemed to him so absurd, and contradictory to everything he had seen in America (and anyway, he protested: "Why is nature smaller, or rather less great, in the forming of one animal than of another?" [letter to Jefferson of 8 September 1785, in *Papers*, VIII, 502]). On 10 May 1784 Jefferson sold his copy of the *Recherches*, in 3 volumes, to James Monroe, for sixteen shillings (ibid., VII, 240). He bought another copy in 1788 (*Catalogue of the Library*, IV, 164–65). Later he became familiar with Clavigero's reply. But it seems that he too is unwilling to cite de Pauw in a work destined for the public; and even when writing to his friend Rutledge he resorts to a periphrasis: one must do as de Saussure (who was to be praised by Cuvier precisely for his resistance to the temptation to formulate a "system"), or first of all ascertain the facts, and then construct the theories: "the contrary disposition in those who call themselves philosophers in this country classes them in fact with the writers of romance" (letter of 9 September 1788; *Papers*, XIII, 594; cf. *contra*, above, p. 89).

450. *Notes*, III, 420n.; cf. p. 439n., and 443 (and now *Papers*, VIII, 174–75, and in the Peden ed., p. 273). The Negro *is* inferior, but if he were educated he *would* perhaps, after several generations, be the equal of the white man. And although the Negroes are by nature less hairy than the whites, "yet they are more ardent" (p. 443; see also Greene, op. cit., pp. 386–87, and Donald J. D'Elia, "Dr. Benjamin Rush and the Negro," *Journal of the History of Ideas*, 30, no. 3 [1969], pp. 413–22). David Ramsay, when he read the *Notes*, although he congratulated Jefferson on his antislavery, wrote to him that he had "depressed the negroes too low. I believe all mankind to be originally the same and only diversified by accidental circumstances. I flatter myself that in a few centuries the negroes will lose their black color" (letter of 3 May 1786, which continues however: "You have given M. Buffon a decent but a merited correction. Europeans affect to under value Americans," while their inferiority is due to "the state of society": *Papers*, IX, 441). With their expressions of antislavery sentiment Jefferson feared that the *Notes* would be badly received in Virginia; and he limited its distribution to one or two trusted friends, men like James Madison or James Monroe (whose opinion he solicited: see letter to Madison, 11 May 1785, *Papers*, VIII, 147; to Chastellux, 7 June 1785, ibid., p. 184; and to James Monroe, 17 June 1785, ibid., p. 229; for other signs of his timidity on the slavery question, see Fay, *Esprit*, p. 159, and Peterson, op. cit., pp. 177 ff.). Madison reassured him, and Jefferson then distributed in America all the copies he had left (letter of 8 February 1786, *Works*, V, 79; letter of 13 August 1786, V, 151); see also copious details in Coolie Verner, *Mr. Jefferson Distributes His Notes* (New York, 1952). He also expressed a desire (letter to William Carmichael, 15 December 1787, *Papers*, XII, 426), that the book should be read by Ulloa, if still alive: "a person so well acquainted with the Southern part of our world, and who has given such excellent information on it, would perhaps be willing to know something of the Northern part." (Note that Jefferson once again implicitly denies that Ulloa's criticisms could refer to the North American Indian.)

D. The white man in America. With the thesis of the American native's degeneracy thus successfully rejected, Jefferson drops Buffon and turns abruptly on Raynal, whom he considers responsible for the thesis of the degeneration of the white man in America.[451] Buffon never stated outright that the European degenerates in America: "He goes indeed within one step of it, but he stops there. The abbé Raynal alone has taken that step."[452]

The accusation is unfounded. Despite its extreme youth, America has already given the world a Washington, a Franklin, and a Rittenhouse.[453] To the geniuses of the time "America contributes its full share." And America has only three million inhabitants. France, which has twenty million, Jefferson goes on, as precise as a bookkeeper balancing his books, should therefore have eighteen. A quick mental calculation — Voltaire, the Encyclopedists, Buffon, Raynal himself — and France is approved: "We . . . have reason to believe she can produce her full quota of genius." England — ten million inhabitants and nine geniuses short — England, no. Her "philosophy" has emigrated to France, her liberty to America. "The sun of her glory is fast descending to the horizon" (p. 461). She is on the brink of a fearful ruin. . . .

After offering us so many shrewd observations on the animals and the redskins, Jefferson concludes by indulging in just these contagious comparisons and parallels that he had shortly before condemned. And we would be tempted to smile ironically and call *tu quoque,* if we did not know that when he did this he was merely picking up and continuing the American colonists' lofty and almost messianic expectations of becoming heirs designate of Britain's fast-fading genius — the prophets in prose and verse had already looked forward to the birth of a Newton or a Shake-

---

451. Cf. in fact his *Histoire philosophique et politique,* bk. XVIII (Geneva ed., 1775), III, 410. But Raynal does not always support the thesis (see above, p. 46, and cf. for another retraction on Raynal's part, M. Hall, op. cit., p. 77), and even the passage quoted by Jefferson (and transcribed by Brie, op. cit., p. 357, in Chinard, "America as a Human Habitat," pp. 37–38, etc.) notes mainly the lack of geniuses, and is followed by optimistic hopes, reinforced in the successive editions and translations. However a note of Jefferson's recognizes that Raynal withdrew his censure of the "Federo-Americans," while sticking to it for the South Americans (cf. *Catalogue of the Library,* III, 203). But the latter groan beneath their burden of slavery, superstition, and ignorance. Whenever they succeed in gaining their freedom "they will probably show they are like the rest of the world." Still in 1798 Washington recalled and repudiated Raynal's thesis on the lack of geniuses in America (see M. Hall, op. cit., pp. 77–78). A recent renewed proof of the passionate feeling in such methods: the same computation of "geniuses" in relation to population, as index of civilization, attempted with anti-German intent by Rom Landau, *We Have Seen Evil* (London, 1941), pp. 78–79.

452. Letter to Chastellux, 7 June 1785, in *Works,* III, 418n., and in *Papers,* VIII, 185. Jefferson also owned some of the works of Delisle de Sales (*Catalogue of the Library,* II, 15, 49), Boulanger (ibid., II, 18–19, 88), Horn (ibid., III, 35), etc.

453. The famous self-taught astronomer who thanked Jefferson (28 September 1785) enthusiastically for the gift of the *Notes:* "an inestimable Treasure" (*Papers,* VIII, 566). On Rittenhouse, see Boorstin, *Colonial Experience,* pp. 246–51, 407. John Adams wrote to Jefferson with amiable flattery: "Your Argument in favour of American Genius, would have been much Strengthened, if a Jefferson had been Added to a Washington, a Franklin and a Rittenhouse" (letter of 16 July 1786, in *Papers,* X, 140).

speare "on the shores of Ontario," and the landing of the nine muses in Connecticut[454] – if his political hatred of Britain was not all too apparent,[455] and finally if we failed to remember that the *Notes on Virginia* was addressed to a French diplomat.

  E. Buffon, the panther, and the elk. On his arrival in Paris, Jefferson immediately sent a copy of the *Notes*, through Chastellux, to Buffon,[456] and as soon as the latter returned to the capital formed "a particular acquaintance" with his erstwhile adversary in polemic.[457] Their first meeting seems actually to have been somewhat cool. The American was introduced to Buffon as "Mr. Jefferson, who, in some notes on Virginia, had combated some of his opinions." Buffon's only reply was to present his transatlantic critic with a copy of his own latest work, with the observation that "when Mr. Jefferson shall have read this, he will be perfectly satisfied that I am right." Jefferson, to convince him that he had confused the panther with the jaguar, showed him "an uncommonly large panther skin" which he had purchased for sixteen dollars shortly before leaving America, and assures us that with this fine piece of work he managed to make Buffon reconsider his opinion.[458] But when he tried to exploit his

454. See examples in Jones, *American Literature*, pp. 34–38. Chastellux, writing to Jefferson (2 June 1785, *Papers*, VIII, 175), confessed himself totally convinced that America had produced and would produce "in every field more great men, in proportion, than the other parts of the world."
455. An Englishman in fact protested, and Jefferson produced a dignified apology: "The passage relative to the English, which has excited disagreeable sensations in your mind, is accounted for by observing that it was written during the war, while they were committing depredations in my own country and on my own property never practised by a civilized nation" (letter to Francis Kinloch, 26 November 1790, *Works*, VI, 152). See also his letters on returning from London, in 1786 ("that nation hates us, their ministers hate us, and their king more than all other men. . . . We are young, and can survive them; but their rotten machine must crush under the trial," *Papers*, IX, 446, 462–63, 474; and again *Papers*, X, 201, 370, 447; XI, 90, 143; XII, 193).
456. Letter from Chastellux, 2 June 1785 (*Papers*, VIII, 174–75; cf. ibid., p. 184), who optimistically adds that Buffon "will certainly not be surprised that your opinion is different from his and he will equally approve both the reasons that you use for support and the honest and philosophical manner in which you advance them." Hogendorp too confessed himself convinced (8 September 1785) that Buffon would retract: "Did you, Sir, ever talk on that subject with Count Buffon, or any one of his Disciples? I should be very happy if You would inform me of the success of Your reasonings, and whether You expect a palinodia in a future edition of the great natural Historian's immortal works" (ibid., VIII, 502–03). Jefferson replied that he had not yet seen Buffon, but that he had heard it said that on at least one point, the identity of the mammoth with the elephant, he persisted in his opinion (see above, pp. 254–55, and below, p. 266).
457. Letter to Archibald Stuart, 25 January 1786, in *Works*, V, 75.
458. Buffon, instead, had written to him, thanking him certainly, but adding: "This Pennsylvania Cougar does not differ from the one described by M. Colinson except for the fact of its shorter body, more or less in the proportion of 13 to 16. It also has a longer tail, and in the matter of size seems to be intermediate between Colinson's Cougar and the South American one" (letter of 31 October 1785, in *Papers*, IX, 130–31); in other words he persisted in his opinion. Jefferson tried to get him other American animals (ibid., IX, 148–49) and Madison, while doubting that "the fallow and Roe-deer" could be numbered "among the native quadrupeds of America," as Jefferson had done in his *Notes*, wrote to him sophistically: "As Buffon has admitted the fact, it was, whether true or erroneous, a good argument no doubt against him" (letter of 12 May 1786, in *Papers*, IX, 520), promised to send him other animals, and from the detailed comparison between the European marmot and the American monax, between the American weasel and Europe's *belette* and *hermine*, and the moles of both hemispheres, extracted other arguments against Buffon (ibid., p. 521–22; letter of 19 June 1786; ibid., IX, 661), and in particular against his "assertion that of the animals common to the two continents, those of the new are in every instance smaller than those of the old" (ibid., pp. 664–65).

initial advantage, to broaden the scope of the argument and convince Buffon of the respectable dimensions of the American deer (or elk or mouse deer) too, telling him that a European reindeer could walk underneath an elk's belly, and its head was adorned with antlers two feet long, the Frenchman "replied with warmth, that if I could produce a single specimen, with horns one foot long, he would give up the question."[459]

Even before he left America (1783–84) Jefferson had been interested in finding out the measurements, habits, etc., of the moose, and the ways in which it differed from the elk and the *orignal*, and had been told that it could reach a height of six feet and more and that its antlers were so big they were used as cradles for children;[460] convinced he was on to a sure thing, Jefferson immediately sent off for the antlers, skeleton, and pelt of the finest elk that could be found in America: "I have a great desire," he wrote to his friend Stuart, "to give him [Buffon] the best idea I can of our elk."[461]

It was a rash agreement. Half a century earlier William Byrd had praised the goodness of the meat of the elk, but had had to admit: "They are however not quite as large as the European ones."[462] But Jefferson stubbornly refuses to give up hope. He had already written to Archibald Cary, and after explaining to him that Buffon was quite ignorant about the elk and the American deer had asked him: "Will you take the trouble to procure for me the largest pair of bucks horns you can," or better still, a whole stuffed buck? "With respect to the Elk, I despair of your being able to get for me anything but the horns of it. David Ross I know has a pair; perhaps he would give them to us"; and if one could get the skin and skeleton too, "they would be most desirable."[463] And again the very same day he addressed the same urgent request to John Sullivan and William Whipple: skins, skeletons, and horns of the moose, caribou, and elk "would be an acquisition here, more precious than you can imagine."[464]

But all these requests produced no immediate effect, and Jefferson complained of the fact in a letter to Hopkinson, who had written to ask if

459. "Anecdotes from Mr. Jefferson's conversation," in *Private Correspondence of Daniel Webster*, I, 364, rpt. in *Works*, XII, 391n. Pernety too had vaunted the "Mouse-deer," a gigantic American stag (*Dissertation*, II, 526–27).

460. See *Papers*, VII, 21–24, 28–30, 317–20.

461. Letter to Archibald Stuart, 25 January 1786, *Papers*, IX, 218; and letter to Buffon, 1 October 1787, *Works*, V, 352–49, accompanying the gift; cf. Jameson, op. cit., pp. 50–51. H. F. Osborn, *Cope: Master Naturalist* (Princeton, 1931), pp. 11–12 (cited in Smallwood, op. cit., p. 125) tells how Jefferson "sent to Vermont for the skeleton of a moose. This was hunted down by Jefferson's friends [and] shipped to him at a cost of Lg. 50" (the yankee's arguments are always rounded off to the nearest [higher] figure: the exact cost was £ 46.7.10½).

462. Quoted in Boorstin, *Colonial Experience*, p. 104.

463. Letter of 7 January 1786, *Papers*, IX, 158.

464. Ibid., pp. 160, 161–62.

he should send Jefferson a foot and a feather from a strange bird that might however be known to a great naturalist like Buffon: "You must not presume too strongly that your comb-footed bird is known to M. de Buffon. He did not know our panther. I gave him the stuffed skin of one I bought in Philadelphia and it presents him a new species, which will appear in his next volumes. I have convinced him that our deer is not a chevreuil: and would you believe that many letters to different acquaintances in Virginia, where this animal is so common, have never enabled me to present him with a large pair of their horns, a blue and a red skin stuffed, to show him their colours at different seasons. He has never seen the horns of what we call the elk. This would decide whether it be an elk or a deer."[465]

Sullivan on the other hand was writing back reassuringly; he paints an almost surrealistic picture of the "whole Skeleton" of a moose waiting on the Connecticut River to be loaded onto a sled and transported over the snow to Portsmouth as soon as the roads become passable;[466] except that when it finally arrives, with a huge bill for carriage and without the bones of the head, it is half rotten. Sullivan thought it could be patched up with other horns *ad libitum:* "The Horns of the Deer, the Elk and the Caribou I also send. They are not the Horns of this Moose but may be fixed on at pleasure," even if they have not reached their full size and if one of the horns of the elk has been cut away.[467]

It is understandable then that when Jefferson at last found himself in possession of the zoological remains he felt some doubt about the impression they would make. And in particular the antlers of the elk sent from Virginia, the antlers on which the whole argument hinged, seem to have left him a little disappointed. They hardly appeared big enough to impress Buffon, and when sending him the specimen with assurances of his deep esteem and respect, he wrote almost apologetically: "The horns of the elk are remarkably small. I have certainly seen of them which would have weighed five or six times as much."[468] Worse still, the deer

465. Letter to Francis Hopkinson, 23 December 1786, in *Papers*, X, 625. On the bird, see *Papers*, X, 78. It finally arrived, "but the comb which you mentioned as annexed to the foot has totally disappeared," perhaps as "the effect of it's drying": letter of 1 August 1787, *Papers*, XI, 656.

466. Letter of 26 January 1787, *Papers*, XI, 68.

467. Letter of 16 April 1787, *Papers*, XI, 295–96; and of 26 April 1787, ibid., IX, 320–21; cf. also ibid., XI, 326, 328, 359, 384; XIII, 41, 194–95, 197, 287–88, 333.

468. Letter to Buffon, 1 October 1787, *Papers*, XII, 194–95 (and Martin, op. cit., pp. 183–86). According to Webster's version, Jefferson was on the other hand quite satisfied with the stag, "a very good specimen," with horns 4 feet long. Buffon was supposedly persuaded, and promised a correction, "but he died directly afterwards" (XII, 393–94; Buffon actually died on 15 April 1788). In point of fact Jefferson complained to Sullivan too: "Unluckily, the horns of them [the elk and deer] now received are remarkably small," and asked him whether he could not perchance procure him some bigger ones, especially of the Moose, "for I understand they are sometimes enormously large indeed" (letter of 5 October 1787; *Papers*, XII, 208–09). On returning to America Jefferson repeated to Benjamin Rush (17 March 1790) that he had convinced Buffon "that most of the animals in Europe were of different

antlers too turned out to be unsatisfactory in size: "I must observe also that the horns of the Deer, which accompany these spoils, are not of the fifth or sixth part of the weight of some that I have seen," and Jefferson almost begins to sound like a racehorse trainer trying to scratch his colts before the race begins. He mentions that he has asked for further samples "and therefore beg of you [Buffon] not to consider those now sent as furnishing a specimen of their ordinary size."[469]

This was not however the end of the Moose's adventures in Europe. Young John Rutledge noticed its huge skin in Jefferson's house in Paris, and the following year, finding himself at Geneva, mentioned it to the famous naturalist and traveler Horace-Bénédict de Saussure, the climber of Vesuvius, Etna, Mont Blanc, and the Monte Rosa, whereupon the latter, his curiosity aroused, sent off to Jefferson for more details.[470] And Jefferson replied immediately that the skin was indeed that of the Moose shown to M. de Buffon; adding that it was seven feet tall, although at times they reached ten feet; and complaining once again about the huge amount of money it had cost him.[471]

But Jefferson continued to interest himself in the problem. His *Notes,* he wrote in 1788, "are very light sketches on a subject, which fully detailed would have filled volumes."[472] Alongside the weapons and Indian relics in the entrance hall of his home hung the antlers and head of an elk and the skull of a mammoth.[473] In 1789 he wrote to President Willard of Harvard exhorting him to encourage the study of the natural history of America, "to do justice to our country, its productions and its genius."[474] On the basis of some fossil remains found in Virginia, probably belonging to a prehistoric anteater, he invented (1796–97) an American super-lion or super-tiger, three times bigger than the African lion, and thus as superior to these Old World felines as the mammoth to the elephant. He baptized and presented it to the scientific world as the *Megalonyx,* "the Great Claw," which must have existed, indeed must still exist, in some part of the United States, if for no other reason than to intimidate and reduce to silence those who denied the existence of great carnivores in

species from the same [*sic*] animals in this country . . . particularly the Buck and doe. The American Buck has horns three feet long, and the French or European Buck only one foot" (B. Rush, *Autobiography,* p. 181).

469. Letter of 1 October 1787, *Papers,* XII, 194–95.

470. Letter to Jefferson from John Rutledge, Jr., 4 September 1788; *Papers,* XIII, 567–68.

471. "The experiment was expensive to me, having cost me hunting, curing and transporting, 60 guineas": letter of 9 September 1788; *Papers,* XIII, 593. Cf. however above, n. 461.

472. Letter to La Blancherie, 28 April 1788, *Papers,* XIII, 112.

473. Ticknor, op. cit., I, 28; Howard C. Rice, Jr., "Jefferson's Gift of Fossils to the Museum of Natural History in Paris," *Proceedings of the American Philosophical Society,* 95, no. 6 (1951), p. 610. On Jefferson's interest in America's large fossil skeletons, see also *Papers,* IX, 260–61, 476–78.

474. C. A. Browne, "Thomas Jefferson and the Scientific Trends of His Time," *Chronica Botanica,* 8 (November 1943), p. 23, quoted by Kraus, *Atlantic Civilization,* p. 278.

the New World.[475] He continued to work ceaselessly to amass material supporting his points of view, sent mastodon fossils to the naturalists of Paris (1808), and still in 1809 was planning a new edition of the *Notes*, though he doubted that the rest of his life would suffice to complete it.[476] And in fact, though he lived another seventeen years, he never managed to publish it.

Among the favorable reactions to the *Notes on Virginia* one should mention that of the Englishman (though of partly American descent) Benjamin Vaughan, the first publisher of Franklin's works, and editor of the English version of the *Rural Socrates* (for which see above, chap. 4, n. 33);[477] his comments appeared only in a private letter but are noteworthy since they cover several general points. Vaughan in fact wrote to Jefferson that "many mistakes respecting the animal and vegetable productions of America have arisen from the precipitancy of European philosophers in deciding upon slight evidence; as well as from the propensity of mankind to extend partial into general conclusions," and concluded: "Your notes on Virginia furnish ample proofs of this."

Europe itself received animals from other climates. The English do not have a single edible plant that is indigenous to their islands. If the eastern part of North America had been populated and civilized a few centuries before Christ and had thus had time to acclimatize the animals and plants of the rest of the continent, and maybe even those of China and Japan, and had *then* discovered Western Europe, its philosophers would probably have made the same critical comments "on the rude and ill provided condition of the New World (as our part of it would then have been called)." And a contemporary Chinese philosopher might well say the same of the western part of North America. Certainly – and thus Vaughan sums up and reasserts his comparativist and historicizing

---

475. Martin, op. cit., pp. 107–11, 113; and in this connection he resumed the polemic with Buffon, who had denied the existence of large animals in America, and reduced the mammoth to an elephant: ibid., pp. 188–89 (cf. also *Papers*, XIII, 568, 593). But in reality he was following in the footsteps of Buffon, who had preferred large animals to small ones; and just as Buffon had been unaware (see above, pp. 16–19) of the ancient and more recent assertion that divine power shone forth in the most minuscule creatures, Benjamin Rush extolled (1811) in a letter to Jefferson the "wondrous skill and power" of the Creator in forming creatures of the size of the mammoth and "megalonyx": "This animal is an astonishing effect of God's power. He seems to have produced him merely to show what he could do . . ." (quoted in Martin, op. cit., p. 236). But in precise retribution his theories on the megalonyx have recently been judged "just as fantastic as any which Buffon had offered" (N. Schachner, *Jefferson*, I, 227, quoted by Peden, p. 270, n. 56). Humboldt had already spoken doubtingly of the "Megalonyx" (*Reise*, I, 324, 367), but Darwin believed in it (A. Moorehead, *Darwin and the Beagle* [London, 1969], p. 83). See G. Forster, *Werke*, II, 712; Ampère, op. cit., I, 98–99, 256, and the picture by Charles W. Peale of the megatherium found near Buenos Aires in 1789.

476. Letter to John W. Campbell, 3 September 1809, *Works*, XI, 115; cf. Martin, op. cit., pp. 114–15 and passim, and Peden, op. cit., pp. xx–xxi; *Catalogue of the Library*, IV, 324–29. On the gift of fossils see abundant details in Rice, op. cit., pp. 597–627. On Jefferson as "father of American paleontology," see Peterson, op. cit., pp. 403 (with references to Buffon), 515–16.

477. *Catalogue of the Library*, I, 331.

view of the varying civilizations—certainly "Europeans in general do not at present think worse of America than some of the Greeks and Romans formerly thought of those parts of Europe, which now make the most brilliant figure of any countries upon the globe."

Climates can vary, and considerably, but the so-called humidity of America is almost certainly a mistake, and in fact "there is nothing peculiar and ill-fated in your own climate and soil, compared with that of the globe *at large*." Thus Jefferson did well to combat "the opinions of certain European philosophers on some of these subjects regarding Eastern America." "Certain" European philosophers? . . . In the rest of the sentence he drops the generalizations and comes out bluntly with the names of the leader and his disciples: "I think the *Recherches sur Les Américains* contain nearly three volumes of error, believed in Europe because boldly asserted, and till lately never controversed [which is certainly not true]. Monsr. de Buffon and the abbé Raynal in particular among the French, and Dr. Robertson and others with us, have largely imbibed these errors [which is even less true, for Buffon]; but the time has arrived when science, industry and art on your side of the water, will soon furnish materials to overthrow the whole of them, and even to efface their memory [which is instead a fairly accurate forecast of things to come]."[478]

XXI. FILIPPO MAZZEI: EXPERIENCE AGAINST IDEALIZATION AND CALUMNY

Filippo Mazzei's four volumes defending the United States against the European slanders are an obvious derivative, an appendix almost, of the *Notes on Virginia*, but still fail to provide what Jefferson had so much wished for, the resumption of the war against Buffon. Mazzei—devoted friend of Jefferson; citizen and diplomatic agent of the state of Virginia; the adventurous Florentine who lived at one time or another in Constantinople, Smyrna, London (where he apparently gave Italian lessons to Edward Gibbon, who was trying to read Machiavelli),[479] in the depths of Virginia, in France, Amsterdam, and Warsaw; who in 1793 was looking for a house in Pisa for Vittorio Alfieri; and who at the ripe age of seventy-two traveled from Pisa to St. Petersburg[480]—in 1785 found him-

---

478. Letter of 26 January 1787, *Papers,* XI, 69–72; cf. above p. 179. Yet another correspondent, Wm. Carmichael, wrote to him from Madrid: "I think you have victoriously combatted Buffon, Monsr. de P. and the Abbé Raynal" (letter of 15 October 1787, *Papers,* XII, 240).

479. S. Rotta, "Il viaggio in Italia di Gibbon," *Rivista storica italiana,* 74, no. 2 (June 1962), p. 330.

480. The principle source for his life is his autobiography: *Memorie della vita e delle peregrinazioni del fiorentino Filippo Mazzei, con documenti storici sulle sue missioni politiche come agente degli Stati Uniti d'America, e del re Stanislao di Polonia,* 2 vols. (Lugano, 1845–46; on which see B. Croce, *Aneddoti,* II, 323–31), supplemented by the unpublished letters and reports contained in F. Massai, who came into possession of a part of the Mazzei archives and prepared a new edition of the *Memorie:* "Un

self in Paris without employment and without a penny to his name. Luckily for him Jefferson had arrived shortly before, as representative of the United States, succeeding Franklin; Mazzei had known Franklin too and had at one time been on very good terms with him, but the two had later fallen out and some ill feeling remained between them.[481] So it was to Jefferson that Mazzei turned immediately for help, and it was Jefferson who suggested he write a reply to Mably's criticisms of the American constitution. A man of proven and unshakable attachment to the cause of the United States, already author of several propagandistic and polemical pamphlets, and a man who at that particular time could ill afford to lose what friends he had, Mazzei set to work with aggressive enthusiasm.

He had been attracted to the New World ever since he was young, and before moving to Turkey had seriously considered seeking his fortune in South America. Of North America he had known the very best it could offer in both men and nature. He had been friendly with Franklin, Thomas and John Adams, Madison, and Monroe, had been close to George Washington, and had had Jefferson's help and advice in his attempts to establish vines, olives, and silkworms in Virginia (which as a matter of fact had already been done a century and a half earlier).[482] The success of his vineyards and other agrarian enterprises had convinced him of the goodness of the soil and climate of the state. "America produces everything," he wrote prophetically in 1782, "and could manufacture everything with ease," should its farmers decide to devote themselves to industry.[483] So the champion that descended into the lists to do battle with the pedantic old abbé Mably was well accoutered, clad in the invincible armor of experience and firm convictions.

---

dimenticato: Giuseppe Timpanari," *Rassegna Nazionale,* yr. 42, 2d ser., vol. 29 (1920), p. 284–97; "Due autografi inediti di Vittorio Alfieri," *Nuova Antologia,* 6th ser., vol. 210 (1921), pp. 371–74; in R. C. Garlick, *Philip Mazzei, Friend of Jefferson: His Life and Letters* (Baltimore, Md., 1933); in Howard R. Marraro, ed., *Philip Mazzei, Virginia's Agent in Europe. The Story of His Mission as Related in His Own Dispatches and Other Documents* (New York, 1935); Marraro has also translated the *Memoirs* (New York, 1942, furnishing it with a preface and copious bibliography); in R. Ciampini, ed., *Lettere di F. Mazzei alla corte di Polonia, 1788–92* (Bologna, 1937; first and only volume published, covering the period up to March 1790, and incorporating almost all the letters formerly included in idem, *Un osservatore italiano della rivoluzione francese* [Florence, 1934]; and in the cited vols. of the *Papers*). See also E. Bonora, in *Letterati, memorialisti e viaggiatori del '700* (Milan-Naples, 1951), pp. 761–68; Sara Tognetti Burigana, *Tra riformismo illuminato e dispotismo napoleonico: Esperienze del "cittadino americano" Filippo Mazzei* (Rome, 1965); Carlo Bernari, "Filippo Mazzei, un toscano fra due rivoluzioni," *Letteratura,* 29, nos. 76–77 (July–September 1965), pp. 3–15; the notes in Visconti, op. cit., pp. 68–75, 133–34, 142, and in the cited unpublished thesis of A. Violo, esp. pp. 114–29.

481. On the causes of the quarrel see below, n. 502; M. Hall, op. cit., p. 130; and especially Pace, op. cit., pp. 3–4, 104–09, 358–88, who reveals Franklin's faults; Tognetti Burigana, op. cit., p. 30, n. 59.

482. *King James Told How to Ensure Prosperity in America* (1622), in Wright, *Elizabethans' America,* pp. 254–58.

483. *Memorie,* II, 260; the prophecy was repeated half a century later by Miss Martineau (see below, pp. 492–93).

The first essays in his rebuttal, somewhat lighthearted in tone, earned the approval of Marmontel, who begged Mazzei to go into the matter properly. Others insisted — Pitobie, a translator of Homer; Short, Jefferson's secretary; and Morellet, though the latter disapproved of the notes on general matters that Mazzei added in an attempt to make his work "less arid."[484] But up to this point the argument was restricted to constitutional questions; the discussion revolved around the mechanisms established by a political document, with no reference to the reality of America and the Americans.

A first amplification of perspective was due to the abbé Raynal. While still in Virginia, Mazzei had heard of the "great uproar" the *Histoire philosophique* was causing in Europe "especially on account of its pompous title," and having chanced to meet the author in Paris, Mazzei addressed himself to Raynal in person to obtain a copy of the new edition. When he received it he confined his reading to the parts about North America, and horrorstruck at finding so many mistakes and lies decided to "unmask him" and print a simultaneous "refutation of both abbés," together with some additional notes agreed on with Jefferson.[485]

So the polemic expands its horizons but remains linked to the authors under attack; it is still an attempted rectification or retort, a work inspired by the occasion. The final step was taken on the advice of the illustrious Condorcet, who — as Mazzei writes to Madison — "said that I did too much honor to the two abbés in making them the *Heroes of my Poem*" and recommended that the book be enlarged so as to become a complete description of the United States and a defense of its revolution. "So the rebuttal is no longer principal but accessory," and the work is doubled, but all his friends, Condorcet, La Rochefoucald, Lafayette, are enthusiastic about the idea;[486] Jefferson puts at his disposal the notes and materials collected for the *Notes on Virginia* and writes repeatedly to his American and European friends with anticipated praise and recommendations of the book that Mazzei is writing; from New York and Philadelphia come some "very wise and prudent reflections" and observations on the part of Madison;[487] the republicanistic Mme de Tessé, Lafayette's aunt, reads him a letter just received from Jefferson (then at Nîmes) "as no

484. *Memorie*, I, 528–29; Garlick, op. cit., pp. 97–100; cf. the comment in G. Procacci, "L'abate Mably nell'illuminismo," *Rivista storica italiana*, 63, no. 2 (1951), p. 220.

485. Op. cit., pp. 532–33; and the introduction to the *Recherches*. His friend John Adams wrote to him already in 1785 (15 December) to defend abbé Mably, "as honest a Man and as Independent a Spirit as you will find among them [the French writers]": Jefferson, *Papers*, VIII, 679n. Later on some of his pungent criticisms of the "dotard" Raynal earned him a gentle correction from the abbé Scipione Piattoli (included in A. D'Ancona, *Scipione Piattoli e la Polonia* [Florence, 1915], pp. 258–60). But for Mazzei, Mably remained an ignorant bungler and Raynal "a willful lyer" (*Papers*, ibid.).

486. Op. cit., I, 535; letter of 14 August 1786 in Garlick, op. cit., pp. 104–06.

487. Letter of 21 December 1787, in Garlick, op. cit., pp. 113–14; cf. Ciampini, *Lettere*, p. 252. On Jefferson's contributions, see Garlick, op. cit., pp. 100, 102, 104–05, and *Papers*, IX, 67–72.

doubt the apostles' letters were once read to the assembled early Christians";[488] and already there is talk of three editions, in Italian, French, and English. Meanwhile the French translation is checked by Morellet, Dupont de Nemours, and others too: the beautiful Marquise de Condorcet is not happy with it and would like her husband to redo it, but he does not have the time, and finally she does the translation of one chapter and her husband the next ("You will see in one the style of a truly sensitive soul," writes Mazzei delightedly, "and in the other the living voice of geometry").[489] Jefferson solemnly announces to his friend Hogendorp: "There will be another good work, a very good one, published here soon by a Mr. Mazzei who has been many years a resident of Virginia; is well informed, and possesses a masculine understanding."[490] In short the whole Americanophile coterie joins in the work, as if collaborating on the construction of some massive weapon of war.

When the book is still at the press Jefferson announces it to a correspondent in Milan, adding that it will also be translated into Italian and published in Florence.[491] Printing begins in April 1787,[492] and January 1788 finally sees the appearance of the four volumes of the *Recherches historiques et politiques sur les Etats-Unis de l'Amérique septentrionale*.[493] The first is given over to a historical-constitutional study of the United States, the second to refuting Mably, the third to the rebuttal of Raynal, and the fourth to the treatment of a number of individual subjects such as the redskins, slavery, emigration, and especially the economic situation in North America: in all over thirteen hundred pages, a "large work" in truth, even an "enormous work," as it was called by a recent bibliographer, who however seems to have been overawed by its bulk and adjudges it a boring, solemn, overprecise, and quite unreadable compendium of assorted information on the United States.[494]

488. Letter of 30 March 1787, in *Papers*, XI, 258; G. Chinard, *Trois amitiés françaises de Jefferson* (Paris, 1927), pp. 100–01.

489. Op. cit., I, 538; the two chapters are VIII and IX of the fourth part (ed. cit., IV, 102–26). Mazzei first thought of Marmontel as translator (see Jefferson's *Papers*, VIII, 475n.)

490. Letter of 25 August 1786, in *Papers*, X, 209, which goes on: "I should rather have said it will be published in Holland, for I believe it cannot be printed here."

491. *Papers*, XII, 39.

492. "M. will be satisfied if he is finished in August" (*Papers*, XI, 298).

493. A title which calls to mind Hilliard d'Auberteuil's above-mentioned *Essais historiques et politiques sur les Anglo-Américains*, against which Mazzei too breaks a few lances (*Recherches*, I, vii–viii) and for which see above, pp. 249–50. As place of publication the *Recherches* bears the legend "at Colle," a press location unknown to all the bibliographers, who have therefore never asked themselves the relevant question: *Colle* was the name of Mazzei's property in Virginia, near Jefferson's famous Monticello (see also Ciampini, *Lettere*, p. 256).

494. B. Fay, *Bibliographie critique des ouvrages français relatifs aux Etats-Unis* (Paris, 1925), pp. 24–25, 64–65; cf. the same author's *Esprit*, p. 136 ("an almost unreadable work," though the fourth volume is "very interesting"), pp. 161–62. "Superficial and disconnected," written too hastily, "of no great importance or usefulness," in Ciampini's opinion, *Lettere*, p. xviii; "superficial, badly planned and poorly constructed," according to Marraro, in the preface to the *Memoirs*, p. xiii. Cf. also Tognetti Burigana, op. cit., pp. 34–35.

It did not in fact all come from Mazzei's pen; apart from other people's notes and the many passages transcribed *in extenso* from the authors refuted and from historical documents, the *Recherches* includes Franklin's observations on the redskins and his advice to emigrants,[495] and an essay by Turgot[496] and two by Condorcet[497] — inserted to boost the explosive charge for his "broadside" — which add up to a total of two hundred and forty-three pages. What remains is however still sufficient to reveal the anonymous author, "a citizen of Virginia," as a man full of good sense, careful, assured, and as alien to the idealization of America as he is critical of the continent's slanderers.

His source is not of course the Jesuit missionaries, nor the armchair naturalists, but the years spent in working the earth of Virginia, arranging exchanges of products and supporting the cause of the insurgents, finding money to lend to and men to work for the United States. So that whether he is lavishing sound advice on immigrants and removing their naïve illusions,[498] or showing up the exaggerations in the descriptions of Pennsylvania or Virginia as "promised lands,"[499] or portraying the natives sympathetically but without indulgence, admitting their "insurmountable aversion for work," their shrewdness and irascibility, and that they are undeniably on occasion cannibals too;[500] or following in Jefferson's footsteps and discussing the sad and shameful problem of slavery,[501] or removing the aura of sanctity from Penn and his Quakers;[502] or defending

495. *Recherches*, IV, 76–92, 171–83. Jefferson wanted Mazzei to run him off three hundred copies of the chapter on the emigrants, to help him to get rid of people pestering him (Ciampini, *Lettere*, p. 279).

496. *Reflections . . . sur la manière dont la France et l'Espagne doivent envisager les suites de la querelle entre la Grande-Bretagne et ses colonies* (*Recherches*, III, 109n., 217–82), an important memoir (1776) that Fay (*Esprit*, pp. 32, 44, 49–50, 70, 106, 108) knows only at second hand.

497. The first is composed of the four *Lettres d'un bourgeois de New-Heaven* [*sic*] (Condorcet was an honorary citizen of New Haven in Connecticut: Fay, *Esprit*, p. 139) sur l'unité de la législation (*Recherches*, I, 267–71; Fay, *Esprit*, pp. 161–62) in favor of the one-chamber principle; the second, considerably more interesting, is the essay *Influence de la révolution de l'Amérique sur l'Europe* (*Recherches*, IV, 237–83) sent (under the pseudonym P. B. Godard) to the famous competition of the Lyon Academy, and which, already rare in Mazzei's time ("it is impossible to find it," *Recherches*, IV, 213), is considerably more so today: "quite rare," Fay calls it (*Bibliographie critique*, p. 66), and Zavala, *América*, p. 20, failed to find and read it. It is however known to Morandi, *L'unità politica*, p. 41, n. 3, and Echeverria, *Mirage*, pp. 153–54. Cf. also F. Acomb, *Anglophobia in France, 1763–89* (Durham, N.C., 1950), pp. 102–04.

498. *Recherches*, IV, 76–102 (esp. 98); cf. Echeverria, *Mirage*, p. 146.

499. *Recherches*, III, 40, 85–89.

500. Ibid., II, 183–84; III, 19–21; IV, esp. 150, 153, 170–71; but they are not glabrous, as was thought by "some careless writers and travelers": they simply remove their hair (ibid., pp. 162–63). This facile defense is used, before and after Mazzei, on innumerable occasions (see above, p. 259), at least up until the times of the explorer of the Mississippi, the ingenuous Giacomo Costantino Beltrami: *La découverte des sources du Mississippi* (New Orleans, 1824); Italian trans.: *Alle sorgenti del Mississippi*, ed. Luciano Gallina (Novara 1965), p. 30.

501. *Recherches*, IV, 127–40.

502. Ibid., I, 72–84, 223–45; III, 49–71 ("the principal merit of the Quakers consists in economy and their devotion to business," but as for hypocrisy "they are unrivalled, and in the matter of commerce, delicacy and equity are not their favorite virtues": III, 63). These opinions, which certainly also reveal his irreligious fervor, caused Mazzei to be sharply attacked by Brissot de Warville (*Memorie*, I, 538–39; II, 277–78; Garlick, op. cit., p. 115; and chap. 9, sec. 5, "The Quakers, the Marquis, and the Girondist"). Reciprocal distrust led to very strained relations between Mazzei and Franklin, who appeared to the Europeans as the prototype of the Quakers (Fay, *Esprit*, p. 94; Visconti, op. cit., pp. 133–34, 142).

almost, in the face of Raynal's hyperbole and eulogies, the architectural mediocrity of Virginia's buildings[503] — Mazzei shows himself so averse to any Americanistic fanaticism that his own position becomes correspondingly stronger, both in arguing with the critics of the newborn United States and (what concerns us more) with those of the physical nature of the American continent.

For Buffon Mazzei has all the respect and admiration he deserves,[504] and when he comes up against his theories on the inferiority of the animals in America he refers back to Jefferson's *Notes*, which unmasked the error fallen into by "certain writers, *including M. de Buffon himself* . . . this celebrated naturalist."[505] But on the basic point he refuses to budge. The explanations of America's peculiarities in terms of "climate" and "soil" leave him totally unconvinced: "The difference is moral, not physical."[506] America's climate is not much better or much worse than any other. Nature, by and large, has showed no favoritism. And to demolish the numerous romantic (*romanesque*) theories on degeneration in plants and animals, it will be enough "to tell things as they are."

The European animals degenerated wherever they were not carefully raised; and "the contrary occurred where they were tended properly": the Rhode Island cattle and Virginia horses have won great renown, the pigs have thrived on the abundance of acorns, and the sheep on the rich variety of available pasture.

As for edible plants, Mazzei has come across almost all of them in America and has found some to have done better than in Europe, and none worse. Should one then conclude that America is a favored land? Not a bit of it: "This does not show any superiority of soil and climate; the same thing happened to several [of the plants] that I sent from America to Europe." It is a known fact that a change of environment is generally beneficial to plants and animals. It would help farmers everywhere if instead of using the seed from their own crops they exchanged it for seed from some distant area.[507] So what the Poggio a Caiano agriculturalist derives from the comparison of two worlds is no corollary of telluric superiority but a lesson in the benefits of crossbreeding.

Here however, even though he has just got through writing that a

---

503. *Recherches*, III, 34; these modest disclaimers probably derive at least in part from the scruples of "republican simplicity."

504. *Memorie*, II, 46–47; on a curious dialogue with Buffon, see *Papers*, VII, 123.

505. *Recherches*, III, 92 (my italics); IV, 209n. Buffon, he writes to John Adams (23 January 1786), "has been unwillingly induced into error," but Jefferson showed him his error "most masterly and completely" (Jefferson, *Papers*, VIII, 679n.).

506. *Recherches*, II, 32; cf. I, 118; see also Chinard, "America as a Human Habitat," p. 44.

507. *Recherches*, III, 84–95; the plants of any country degenerate in any other country if one neglects to study the terrain and climate most suited to them: "If laziness or ignorance take the place of intelligence and attention, a very considerable deterioration will certainly result therefrom" (III, 95). Roubaud, to justify the degeneration of European plants in America, in the face of de Pauw's accusations, asserts: "It is the customary result of transplanting" (*Histoire*, XIII, 131). On the "ancient practice" of the "change of seed," see *Enciclopedia Italiana*, XXXI, 344b.

simple outline of the true facts will be enough to refute all these ill-informed writers, and despite his intention, stated at the outset, of ignoring the criticisms of writers less known than the two abbés,[508] Mazzei passes rapidly over Buffon and Raynal and commences an explicit attack on Monsieur de Pauw—de Pauw, who outdoes even Raynal with his blunders and who has managed to beget three volumes with hardly a word of truth between them, "although almost everything in them is based on some authority." It must certainly have cost him a considerable effort, and in a way it constitutes something of an achievement on his part to have put together such an indictment of every creature and object of America—even if most of his information was drawn from the most ignorant scribblers and travelers.

Mazzei follows this shrewd summing up of de Pauw's work[509] with a surprising piece of information: "I have learned that M. Pauw finally became aware of his error, and as I have this from someone whose word I cannot doubt, and who assured me that the words were addressed to none other than himself, one may hope that the author will use the same frankness toward the public."[510] Alas, that selfsame year, 1788, saw the publication of his latest *Recherches philosophiques sur les Grecs,* whose very first page reiterated his remarks of twenty years earlier on those brutalized savages, the Americans. Mazzei's hopes were disappointed.

Similarly disappointed were the general expectations of a great success for his book, although Jefferson recommended it to his French friends and almost one might say thrust it down their throats ("a good work . . . one can rely on his facts with absolute confidence").[511] In France it got just one review; in America, where Jefferson thought it would sell at least one hundred and seventy-five copies, it seems that ten years later it had not even sold one;[512] a single copy sent to one of Jefferson's friends in England apparently went astray,[513] and fifteen hundred copies, which

508. *Recherches,* I, xiv.
509. Deriving from Jefferson, however: cf. above, n. 449.
510. Ibid., III, 93–94. For a similar illusion of Pernety's, see above, p. 99.
511. *Papers,* XIII, 631: letter of 27 February 1787 to Lormerie.
512. See letters in Garlick, op. cit., pp. 116–17, 121, 125 (a few copies sold in Virginia?) n. 70 on pp. 125–26 and p. 146. Jefferson, who owned various of his friend's works, bought his copy in Paris for 12 livres (*Catalogue of the Library,* III, 221; cf. ibid., 54–55, 86, 137, 170, 326–27). One copy is found in one of the *Private Libraries in Creole Saint Louis,* for which see McDermott, op. cit., p. 123. A valid reason and almost an excuse for the meager success of the work can be found in the remark of Brissot de Warville, Mazzei's bitter adversary, about the goods importable into the United States: "*French books:* The best will not be a success here. There are very few people familiar with the French language" (*Nouveau voyage,* II, 376; see also *Mémoires,* III, 53, and H. M. Jones, *America and French Culture, 1750–1848* [Chapel Hill, 1927], pp. 186–200, 572). And in fact James Madison wrote immediately to Jefferson: "Tell him [Mazzei] I have received his books and shall attempt to get them disposed of. I fear his calculations will not be fulfilled by the demand for them here in the French language" [*sic*] (letter of 10 August 1788: *Papers,* XIII, 499).
513. *Papers,* XII, 602–21. By 1837 Mazzei was almost forgotten: see Ticknor, op. cit., II, 93.

the author left in Paris in 1791, were eventually lost.[514] Mazzei remained as poor as ever. The only indirect benefit he derived from the book was that it served to bring him to the attention of King Stanislas of Poland,[515] who a few months after its publication (July 1788) named him his correspondent in Paris, and later called him to his court in Warsaw.

XXII. THE BOTANIST CASTIGLIONI AND THE LASCIVIOUS
NORTH AMERICAN COLONISTS

Mazzei had devoted his efforts to introducing olives, vines, and silkworms in his adopted country, and in 1785–87 another Italian, Luigi Castiglioni, traveled across the whole of North America in search of nutritive, decorative, and officinal plants to acclimatize in Lombardy. Though at first sight they appear contradictory, the intentions of the Florentine and the Milanese in fact coincided: fundamental to their complementary efforts was a firm belief in the substantial identity of nature and climate in the two hemispheres.

They were equally critical of the writers who assumed a radical difference between one world and the other, and even more so when from this difference they went on to deduce an absolute superiority of the Old World over the New. Castiglioni waits almost until the closing pages of his work[516] before discussing briefly the current opinions on the Amer

---

514. Garlick, op. cit., p. 141, and Tognetti Burigana, op. cit., p. 39, n. 81: which may explain the book's rarity; though four years after its publication the author still had so many copies left. It was however analyzed in the *Correspondance* of Grimm, Diderot, etc. (Tourneux ed., XV, 251–53), and consulted by Botta for his *Storia della guerra della indipendenza degli Stati Uniti d'America* (1809). See G. Mira, "Un italiano del Settecento collaboratore dell'indipendenza americana," *Nuova Antologia*, 6th ser., vol. 192 (1917), p. 235.

515. Stanislas had not read it however; at least four times, after being named correspondent, Mazzei offered it to him in homage (*Lettere*, Ciampini ed., pp. 9, 42, 64, 121), and then suggested to him (ibid., p. 252) that he should "make public" in Poland a discussion by Madison on freedom of worship, which was included in the work (II, 239–52), and read what was said there (IV, 141, 165–66) on the goodness of the savages, even though they did not believe in an afterlife (*Lettere*, pp. 252–53), or Franklin's advice to immigrants (ibid., p. 279). Stanislas instead had pp. 372–73 of the first volume translated into Polish (dealing with a permanent committee of six people which would prepare the agenda for legislative assemblies), and replied to Mazzei that his comments on the savages would provide material for a "theological discussion" between the two of them, whenever Mazzei came to Warsaw (*Memorie*, II, 50, 83, 323). On his relations with Stanislas, see copious details in J. Fabre, *Stanislas Auguste Poniatowski et l'Europe des Lumières* (Strasbourg, 1952), pp. 507–22 and relevant notes. Jefferson tells Madison what really happened: King Stanislas sent a trusted secretary (Grimm perhaps? see Tognetti Burigana, op. cit., p. 41) to Paris to find him a correspondent: "A happy hazard threw Mazzei in his way. He recommended him, and he is appointed. He has no diplomatic character whatever, but is to receive Eight thousand livres a year as an intelligencer. I hope this employment may have some permanence. The danger is that he will over-act his part" (letter of 31 July 1788; *Papers*, XIII, 441).

516. *Viaggio negli Stati Uniti dell'America settentrionale fatto negli anni 1785, 1786 e 1787*, 2 vols. (Milan, 1790); German trans., Memmingen, 1793. See Doll, op. cit., pp. 471, 500. The actual journey terminates on p. 168 of the 2d vol.; pp. 169–402 contain an alphabetical listing of "Observations on the most useful Plants of the United States." The author (1765–1832) describes himself as Patrician of Milan, knight of the Order of St. Stephen Protomartyr, member of the Philosophical Society of Philadelphia and the Patriotic Society of Milan (of which he was also President); he was later director of the Royal Printing House (1807), President of the Academy of Fine Arts, and holder of the Order of the Iron Crown. It was he that introduced the American locust tree into Lombardy. His book was still being

icas: he admits that the climate in the United States is more severe than in the corresponding latitudes in Europe, but he accepts Carli's explanation of the fact,[517] and the "hypothesis of the degeneration of the animals in America, adopted by the Count de Buffon and exaggerated by M. Pauw and other writers," is dismissed with the simple assertion that "it has been sufficiently disproved in the fine work of Mr. Jefferson."[518]

In passing, Castiglioni pauses to explain certain other peculiarities of American nature which had been pointed out as marks of degeneration, as for example the lack of deep roots to the trees — which as a result are easily knocked down or even fall over by themselves[519] — and the well-known lack of songbirds; he himself has seen plenty of black and yellow sparrows flittering about, who sing "very melodiously" in captivity, and he describes the appearance and the habits of the mockingbirds, and the excessive prices they command for their excellence of song;[520] but he recognizes that in general the American birds "while they are not commonly endowed with sweetness of song, are on the other hand dressed in feathers of the most beautiful colors"[521] (the usual dumb technicolor!).

More original is his attitude toward the inhabitants of the United States. Castiglioni (like so many others) praises the courage and intelligence of the redskins and considers them very superior morally to the so-called civilized men,[522] but he does not limit himself to this cliché: he draws the due corollaries therefrom, and just as the North American had arrogated the inimitable virtues and prowess of the redskin (see above, pp. 243–44), so Castiglioni transfers to the colonists, these progressive New England colonists, the insinuations and accusations once applied to the natives. The latter, as we have seen, were found to be both frigid and lustful at the same time. And this is exactly the way Castiglioni represents the North Americans in some of his pages on their sexual behavior that could almost qualify as an early version of the Kinsey report.

---

sought out in 1844 by Alessandro Manzoni, *Lettere,* ed. Cesare Arieti (Milan, 1970), II, 326. On his relationship with Franklin, to whom he was recommended by Paolo Frisi, see Pace, op. cit., pp. 35, 88, 143, 371, according to whom "the whole of Castiglioni's journey, even its scientific aspect, can be interpreted politically in a way in which Franklin himself probably envisioned — namely, as a rebuttal of Pauw's perverted views on America," ibid., pp. 134–35. See also Visconti, op. cit., pp. 59–60, 75, 117, and the previously cited unpublished thesis by Violo, esp. pp. 91–93.

517. Op. cit., II, 154–55. Carli and Clavigero are also cited on the subject of the Mexican pyramids, ibid., I, 391n.

518. Op. cit., II, 155: Robertson and Carli "proved the same with great clarity." On the writers who not only wanted to find the human race and the animals degenerate in America, "but strove to discredit even the fruitfulness of its earth" (which like any other after a few years needs fertilizing or fallow periods), see *Viaggio,* II, 167n. Buffon is also cited in I, 150n., 154n., 171, 285n., 334n.; II, 156, etc. Castiglioni admits (op. cit., I, vii–viii) to not having studied either zoology or mineralogy.

519. Op. cit., I, 116–17; cf. already Oviedo, above, p. 40, and abbé Robin, *Nouveau voyage,* p. 44.
520. Op. cit., I, 44, 357.
521. Ibid., II, 156.
522. On the valor of the savages and the wrongs they suffered: ibid., I, 87–88; II, 48, etc.

After so many agonized Quaker and Puritan sermons on the corrupt ways and senile debauchery of an enfeebled Europe, it is nice to learn from an eyewitness, and a friendly one at that, that

love in United-America . . . is neither so vivacious nor so refined as in most of Europe. Abominable vices weaken the power of amorous passion in the maidens, and the young men purchase elsewhere the daily satisfaction of their appetites. From which there results either a total indifference, or else a brutal eagerness in seeking the most delicate proofs of love. The women, rendered almost insensitive, present themselves like statues at the court of Cupid, and make modesty and virtue to consist in receiving with indifference the most lively proofs of affection.[523]

What Buffon, de Pauw, and Raynal had said of the savage, of his stupid inertia and cold insensibility, is now repeated with vengeful precision of the exterminators of the redskins, the compatriots of Washington and Franklin. Castiglioni dwells in particular on the widespread practise of "bundling" — the custom among young people of opposite sex of "passing the night together and even sleeping in the same bed," with her undressing "down to her petticoat," and him keeping only his undershirt and breeches, and "everything being permitted, which cannot have consequences" (*tout, mais pas ça*). As for the origins of this "strange custom," which to him seemed hardly to be believed, especially "in a people otherwise so rigid," until he had "the occasion to see incontrovertible proof thereof," Castiglioni is quite at a loss, "unless we were to attribute it to the imitation of the savages" (thus revealing that he notices at least a certain mental link between what he actually saw among the citizens of Connecticut and the squalid physiology attributed to the natives) "or to the necessity in which the earliest colonists found themselves of inviting their young people to marry early and augment the population of the colony."

The trouble with this latter explanation is precisely in its demographic ends: they lead Castiglioni on to further explanations that leave us in some doubt as to the rigorous observation of the rule of *tout, mais pas ça*. It happens in fact that "when the promises of marriage are broken off on account of some accident, the girls are often obliged to retire into the countryside to leave the anticipated fruit of their loves."[524]

It is far from easy to trace the origins and history of this prurient custom. The clues that emerge from the shadowy alcoves are few and uncertain. On the one hand a certain form of bundling is already found

523. Ibid., II, 92–93. The ladies of Virginia, with their mincing and wheedling ways and their naked breasts, are described (1791) with republican outrage by Brissot, who visited the United States in 1788 (see chap. 9, sec. 5, "The Quakers, the Marquis, and the Girondist"), and Moreau de Saint-Méry (in E. S. Turner, *A History of Courting* [London, 1954], p. 186; see below, pp. 280–81).
524. *Viaggio*, II, 92–94.

among Lahontan's Hurons, who practiced it with the girl savages wrapped in chemises from the neck to the "calf of the leg";[525] and this indigenous derivation is reconfirmed by Barbé-Marbois (for whom see above, pp. 252–53) in certain letters of his (1779–85) where bundling is described "as borrowed from the Indians," widespread in Connecticut, and after its abolition in that state, persisting in Boston and New York.[526] On the other hand there is no lack of indiscreet testimony on the diffusion of the custom in old England, in warm-blooded Wales, and in most Puritan Scotland itself. Our own Lord Kames discourses on the chaste promiscuity common (about 1770) "among the temperate Highlanders of Scotland; and it is not quite worn out in New England."[527] And the *Shorter Oxford English Dictionary* mentions under the date 1781 that *bundling* "once was customary with persons of opposite sexes, in Wales and New England."[528]

In any case it is certain that New England in the period we are discussing witnessed the golden age of bundling, that ambiguous confirmation-cum-denial of the notion of the North Americans' scarce virility. The examples multiply and reinforce each other. Bundling is mentioned as a current practice in 1747 among the people of the lower classes in Massachusetts and Connecticut.[529] A generation later Berthier, Rochambeau's historiographer, records with amazement (ca. 1780) that it was customary for two lovers to lie together for hours in bed taking of their happiness, without anything at all incorrect happening:[530] a record for continence that outdoes even the abbé Robert d'Arbrisselle, a second (but voluntary) Tantalus, who spent his nights caressing two provocative little nuns, "and all without sinning."[531]

The abbé Robin relates with candid admiration that "the Americans are very hospitable; they have only one bed; the chaste wife, should she be alone, shares it with her guest without fear and without remorse";[532]

525. *Dialogues curieux*, pp. 35–36, 230.

526. Reynolds, op. cit., p. 201, who is however inclined toward a Dutch origin: cf. below, n. 536.

527. *Sketches*, I, 328. The reviewer in the *Times Literary Supplement* (15 June 1967), discussing Gerald Carson's book, *The Polite American* (London, 1967), repeats that " 'bundling' was practised enthusiastically in Old England before it was transported to New England."

528. *Sub voce*. The Oxford English Dictionary defines it as "formerly" common in Wales and New England, and produces examples from 1781 (Connecticut), 1807 (New England), 1809 (Washington Irving) and still in 1842 (Wales) and 1878 (Celtic peoples). On the extreme lasciviousness of the Welsh and their "trial nights," see comments in Eugen Dühren (pseudonym of Iwan Bloch) *Das Geschlechtsleben in England mit besonderer Beziehung auf London* (Charlottenburg-Berlin, 1901–03), III, 230–32.

529. M. Hall, op. cit., pp. 35, 37.

530. "Journal de la Campagne d'Amérique," in *Bulletin de l'Institut Français de Washington*, new ser., n. 1 (1951) quoted by Echeverria, *Mirage*, p. 105.

531. Voltaire, *La Pucelle d'Orléans*, IV, who took the edifying anecdote from Bayle, *Dictionnaire historique et critique*, s.v. "Fontevraud" (6th ed. [Basle, 1741], II, 479–85, with detailed "casuistics"), who had already mentioned it in the *Nouvelles de la République des Lettres*, April 1686 (in *Oeuvres diverses* [the Hague, 1737], I, 529–33). Cf. also Reynolds, op. cit., pp. 170, 184.

532. *Nouveau voyage*, p. 42.

thus letting himself be wrongly numbered among the contented witnesses of that interrupted embrace.[533]

But not always interrupted. Castiglioni's scepticism seems to be confirmed by a ballad of 1785 describing a pair of bundlers who took all the ritual and required precautions, but "so provoked was the wretch / That she of him a bastard catch'd."[534] Thus it surprises one somewhat to learn that even the rigorist John Adams was willing to allow bundling as the lesser of two evils, in the matter of excessive amorous passion: ". . . yet, on considering the whole of the Argument on each side, I cannot wholly disapprove of bundling."[535] And even Washington Irving (1809) finds a place for this "superstitious rite" among the healthy customs of Connecticut and holds it partially responsible for the extraordinary increase of the Yankee race.[536] A further "semibundling" among Canada's youth is recorded by Head (ca. 1820),[537] and yet another, in Ohio (1821), gives rise to shocked comment on the part of Zerah Hawley,[538] while a few years later (ca. 1832) the Perfectionists adopted a religious form of bundling "permitting unmarried couples to do their courting in the wallbed with the lower parts of their bodies secured in sacks."[539]

And so it continues, at least up to the "California caress" — "coition without consummation" — of the end of the nineteenth century[540] and the petting of our own day. The reference to the Kinsey report (p. 276) was not accidental. In his inquiry into *The Sexual Behavior of the Human Female* (1953) the biologist Kinsey in person informs us that petting, apparently indulged in by the whole of the American youth of today, is nothing but a variant of the ancient practice of bundling.[541] Castiglioni is proved right, and what started as scandalized gossip is confirmed by the voice of Science.

It is curious however that it should be precisely and solely the sexual

533. Fay, *Esprit*, p. 121; cf., *contra*, Fanny Varnum, *Un philosophe cosmopolite du XVIIIe siècle: Le Chevalier de Chastellux* (Paris, 1936), pp. 187–88.

534. H. L. Mencken, *The American Language, Supplement One*, ed. cit., pp. 211–14, with further bibliography. More little rhymes are carried by L. L. Matthias, *Die Entdeckung Amerikas anno 1953 oder das geordnete Chaos*, trans. into French with the title *Autopsie des Etats-Unis* (Paris, 1955), pp. 237–38n. On the other hand J. F. Smith recounts (1784) a "tender and respectful" love growing out of a promiscuous environment, op. cit., I, 125–27, 131, 135–37.

535. Quoted in the *Times Literary Supplement*, 6 July 1962, under *The Adams Family*.

536. In *A History of New York*, in *An American Reader*, ed. B. Rascoe (New York, 1938), pp. 279–80. But the custom becomes "hideous" a few pages further on (p. 283), and Irving accuses the yankees of having spread it among the good Dutch boys of Connecticut.

537. George Head, *Forest Scenes and Incidents in the Wilds of North America* (1829; London ed., 1838), pp. 240–41.

538. Tryon, op. cit., p. 504.

539. Taylor, op. cit., p. 278.

540. Langdon-Davis, op. cit., p. 183.

541. *Time* (Atlantic ed.), 24 August 1953, p. 36. Other details in M. Hall, op. cit., pp. 43–46 (with bibliography); Turner, op. cit., pp. 122–27; Reynolds, op. cit., pp. 185–210; E. J. Dingwall, *The American Woman: A Historical Study* (London, 1956), p. 40; Wish, op. cit., pp. 132, 234.

life of the colonists that persuades Castiglioni to join hands with the slanderers of the New World, who were always such careful and sceptical measurers of the Americans' virile capacities; curious both because Castiglioni in his conclusion emphatically rejects the thesis of the New Englanders' precocious senility and intellectual sterility,[542] and also because when all is said and done his basic interest is not in the human race but in the plants, trees, bushes, herbs, and other "useful vegetables."

Another writer to discuss the sexual mores of the American men, and even more the women, was Moreau de Saint-Méry, who found himself in complete agreement with the Milanese botanist. Moreau lived in the United States some ten years later (1794–98), and his bookshop and printing house in Philadelphia became a meetingplace for a number of émigrés and refugees, most notably Talleyrand.[543]

In summing up his transatlantic experiences, Moreau tells us that the young ladies of America, and in particular those of Quaker Pennsylvania, are anything but chaste and well behaved, and it is not out of any burning love — "for the American women are not tender" — but so as to have a few more trinkets and baubles that they allow themselves liberties, or rather "digressions," on which their parents close both eyes. Frigid and without passion, they submit for hours on end, in total impassivity, as if they were doing sums, to intemperances which could be forgiven only in moments of unbridled frenzy. Worse yet, they masturbate at a very early age and are not unfamiliar with the base pleasures of Lesbos. As soon as they marry they immediately become model wives, although they still remain rather dirty and unkempt. And in any case after the age of eighteen they lose their charms and shrivel up: "Their newborn bosom has already disappeared."[544]

542. Op. cit., II, 160–64, esp. against Raynal, with Jefferson's arguments: but of the inhabitants of Massachussetts, both men and women, he had said that they age more quickly than the Europeans (ibid., I, 92).

543. Moreau de Saint-Méry, a native of Martinique and related to Josephine Beauharnais, a man renowned in France as jurist and lawyer (later Napoleon entrusted him with the administration of the Duchy of Parma, 1802–06) took an active part in the early phases of the Revolution; but to flee the enmity of Robespierre he found himself obliged, toward the end of 1793, to embark for the United States, where he remained until August 1798: see his *Voyage aux Etats-Unis de l'Amérique, 1793–1798*, ed. St. L. Mims (New Haven, 1913); Fay, *Esprit*, pp. 269–70; Remond, op. cit., p. 82; Poniatowski, op. cit., pp. 79, 164, 316, 333; and Turner, op. cit., pp. 186–87. On his time in Parma, see abundant details (and bibliographical references) in A. Levi, "Spigolature romagnosiane: Moreau de Saint-Méry e Romagnosi," *Aurea Parma*, 19, nos. 4–5 (1935).

544. *Voyage*, pp. 304–10, 334, and Poniatowski, op. cit., p. 164; and the Pulszkys, who (1853) reject the "prejudice that the bloom of American ladies is but short," in Handlin, ed., *This was America*, p. 236. Moreau also comments occasionally on bundling, op. cit., pp. 335–39, more frequently on prostitution (on which see also his friend Talleyrand, in Huth and Pugh, *Talleyrand in America*, p. 82) and the free customs of the Quakers and Quakeresses. Still in our own time his references to the dirtiness of American women are mentioned and used (together with Simone de Beauvoir's criticisms, *L'Amérique au jour le jour* [Paris, 1948]) by Matthias, op. cit., p. 248n.

The males are certainly no better off. The climate enervates the domestic animals: "The horse has less vigor, the bull less of the impetuosity that he commonly exhibits in his lovemaking and fighting." The dog is without generosity and chivalry, bites and beats [*sic*] his mate, and is subject to syphilis. The cat is extraordinarily meek. And finally "man also receives from this climate an impression which robs him of part of his energy, and which disposes him to indolence."[545] Spineless men and shameless women—the picture is complete. The French jurist from Leeward America fails to reject the current climatic-degenerative theories; and the *de facto* morality prevailing in the *de jure* prudish Philadelphia appears in even darker hues than in the portrayal of the learned Milanese naturalist.

XXIII. THE VINDICATION OF AMERICA'S YOUTH

The emergence of the United States, of an America unquestionably new—new politically speaking, though with an ideology rooted in the untamed vastness of the continent, and thus confirming America's titanic adolescence—was accompanied in Europe by a revolution in attitudes toward primitivity and young races. The *Sturm und Drang* raged against rules, traditions, and hierarchies, inherited laws and conventional idolatries. Its antihistorical and abstractly revolutionary spirit prevented it from absorbing the heliodromic theories, although they concurred in the prophetic exaltation of "young" lands and peoples. America, the Western Hemisphere, is never particularly stressed in the *Sturm und Drang* (or in the early Goethe) as Europe's heir apparent. But the *Sturm* did however take up Rousseau's glorification of nature and the savage, his disdain of the Enlightenment, and his faith in immediate sentiment. Thus the naturalists' and historiographers' maledictions lost their meaning or even provided the impatient new generation with the basis for their panegyrics. Childish, immature, incomplete, still sodden? . . . The slanders, repeated word for word, were converted into hymns of praise. Buffon and de Pauw found themselves on Balaam's ass.

The American continent, with all its animals and nations, was merely a "particular instance" of the vindication of nature over history, of the "virgin" and "pure" over the formed and traditional, a process characteristic of early romanticism, and preparatory to that synthesis of history and nature, of man and world, which was proper to mature romanticism.

Montaigne's rapt and spontaneous enthusiasm rose again, enriched by two centuries of polemics:

---

545. The same picture of spineless and lethargic Americans appears in Claude C. Robin, *Voyage dans l'intérieur de la Louisiane* (Paris, 1807) (quoted by Echeverria, *Mirage*, p. 250).

Our world has just found another . . . so new and so young that it is still being taught its alphabet: less than fifty years ago it knew neither letters nor weights, nor measures, nor clothes, nor wheat, nor vines. It was still naked in its mother's lap and lived only on its mother's nourishment. If we conclude rightly of our own end, and that poet [Lucretius] of the youth of his own age, this other world will only enter into light when our world leaves it. The universe will fall into a paralysis: one member will be crippled, the other in full vigor.

There was heard again, though more bitterly now, his sorrow at the corruption or rather contagion brought to this world by the cultured Europeans: "It was an infant world."[546] And there rose again, more fervent, more ardently religious, his yearning for young and unspoiled lands; for "these new lands," Montaigne had written, "discovered in our time, still pure and virgin in comparison with ours."[547]

In 1754 Rousseau had bewailed the sad lot of the human race, that once having lifted itself from absolute primitivism to the civilization of the savages had not halted at that point. That was "the true youth of the world," and all further progress had carried the individual nearer to an apparent perfection, but the species to a veritable decrepitude. For Jean-Jacques that was our species' Golden Age; not (as it often thought) the merely natural state in which the centuries ran by uselessly and "the species was already old, and man still remained a child."[548] The good savage is clearly distinguished from the primitive brute, and as serenely superior to his crude ancestor as he is to his corrupt descendants.

In this new climate of opinion a simple follower of Rousseau like Bernardin de Saint-Pierre, an ecstatic naturalist, could infuse Buffon's pessimistic theory with new and more hopeful possibilities. Bernardin saw the four parts of the world as "harmonically" representing the four ages of man: Asia his old age, Europe his manhood, Africa his effervescent youth, and America, of course, his infancy: "Nature appears to have assigned the character of infancy to America. She has given it in general a mild and humid temperature, like that of children."

Here Montaigne's imposing "child-world" becomes a "children's world," or a "childish world." Nature has provided the inhabitants of

546. *Essais*, III, chap. vi (Pléiade ed., pp. 874–75). Montaigne speaks of the infancy of the American *civilizations*, not the lands, nor the ethnic stocks. Further on he speaks of "souls so new, so hungry to learn" and of their "ignorance and inexperience" (ibid., p. 876). But later he seems quite simply to renounce even this limited infantility, when having described the wise and courageous reply of the natives he adds: "Here is an example of the babbling of this infancy" (ibid., p. 877).

547. Ibid., I, chap. XXX, ed. cit., p. 209. But there had already been so much talk of these "new lands" that one of Montaigne's contemporaries could jokingly observe that "the New World is not new now, but old, considering how much has been said and written about it" (Acosta, op. cit., *Proemio*, p. 11). On some precursors of Montaigne's attitude (André Thevet, Jean de Léry, Jodelle, Ronsard) see Lapp., op. cit., and P. Henriquez Ureña, op. cit., pp. 22–23. Still in the nineteenth century Cesare Correnti discussed the various meanings of the New World, which from *new* by nature becomes the new world of humanity (Pace, op. cit., p. 169).

548. *Discours sur l'inégalité*, pp. 61, 75; cf. Lovejoy, *Essays*, pp. 14–37.

America with a food that is easily gathered and well protected against bad weather and birds, the *manioc* tubers, and potatoes; she has given them clothing, with the cotton plant; and furniture and dishes with the calabash gourds, "from which one can make any sort of vessel"; and shelter too, "under the porticoes of the prickly pear." Dangerous animals are rare; on the other hand there are plenty of monkeys, "which give themselves up to a thousand innocent games," and multicolored birds of sweetest song. . . .

In Bernardin's extreme anthropocentrism the "imperfection" that Buffon wrote of is diluted into a maternal tenderness of Nature toward her creatures. The continent's "weakness" is not now objective, so to speak, but subjective, the "weakness" of a mother for her children: "These vast and peaceful countries seem reserved for the infancy of the world."[549] America is still characterized by a physiological incompleteness, but this is then allegorized, and no longer has any deprecatory implications. De Pauw had thought to ridicule the vaunted happiness of the savage by describing it as being like that "enjoyed among us by children, who are savages in the midst of society, until such time as their reason develops and instruction enlightens them."[550] Now this ignorant happiness of the child is precisely what is yearned after as preferable by far to the maturity of instructed and enlightened reason.

The reversal of opinions about the continent was facilitated by a parallel revolution in attitudes toward the savage. The question of whether he shared in Original Sin—which cropped up in various guises, for example whether he was pure like Virgin Nature or, like Nature lacking Grace, decadent and degenerate, or whether he was "inferior" because unredeemed or "superior" because without guilt, whether he was pagan like the Infidel or innocent like the newborn child—was eliminated with the progressive dissolution of the dogma of Sin.

The early romantics had opposed the current dogma of Original Sin with the popular myth of the sin of Adam and Eve[551] and had looked on the biblical "Fall" as the source of history and progress. The savage, consequently, could also be "fallen,"[552] without being decadent or degenerate or corrupt. Far removed from our level of civilization, he could figure

549. Bernardin de Saint-Pierre, *Harmonies de la nature*, 1796, bk. VI, *Science des enfants*, in *Oeuvres posthumes* (Paris, 1833), pp. 294–95. On the extremely varied usefulness of the plants of America, cf. ibid., pp. 69–70, and the *Fragments de l'Amazone*, ibid., p. 517.

550. *Recherches*, I, 128; on the radical change of opinion about infancy, see first my *Politica del Settecento* (Bari, 1928), p. 46, and E. Mâle, *L'art religieux après le Concile de Trente* (Paris, 1932), p. 327; then my *Romanticismo*, pp. 160–61.

551. See my *Romanticismo*, and *Il Peccato di Adamo ed Eva* (Milan, 1933).

552. This dissolving of the dogma of sin anticipated the undermining of the thesis of the savage as degenerate, as nature abandoned to itself after sin, that would later be developed by de Maistre (see below, pp. 389–90).

equally well as Adam, in his youthful innocence before the coming of sin, or as Adam immediately after sin, naked and lost on the earth stretching out endlessly before his gaze, outside the Garden of Eden. Sin no longer counted. Before or after "sin" the human condition remained the same, and the spiritual value of the savage-Adam the same too. Sin, in fact, no longer existed, no longer weighed on the conscience of Europe. And in a sudden burst of affection and sympathy the weakness or childishness of the Americans finished by becoming desirable in itself, without reference to a previous state of divine grace, and no longer compared either favorably or unfavorably with the cultivated and learned society of Europe.

XXIV. HERDER AND THE AMERICAN PROBLEM

The preromantic theories found their most eloquent defender in Herder. In many ways he is the antithesis of de Pauw. He believes in the unity of the human race, in the providential course of history, in the virgin genius of the primitive. He detests the fatuous complacency of the Age of Enlightenment, its blatant frivolity, and its unquenchable optimism. In a passage that seems to contain an echo of the ill-famed *Recherches,* Herder even denies illuminism's boast of having promoted liberty, pointing out that European trade—that worldwide trade so enthusiastically approved by Voltaire and Raynal—in fact *enslaves* the other three continents and "civilizes" them by corrupting and poisoning their inhabitants, to get in exchange their "silver and precious stones, spices, sugar—and hidden maladies." These days, the young Herder goes on, the "peoples' pastors" are known as "monopolists."[553]

These are variations on themes by Rousseau, to be sure. And Herder's tone too, always so fiery and agitated and sermonizing, takes us back to the spiritual climate of Jean-Jacques. Yet Herder, unlike Jean-Jacques, believes in Society, and even more in Progress: the progress of all mankind, excluding and favoring no one, and with but few occasions of local and accidental decadence. What counts for him is not, as it was for the impassioned Genevan, the earthly happiness of the individual, but the lasting improvement of the human race.[554] The individual may suffer and perish, but the species' upward progress is inflexible, unswerving, and infinite.

If despite these sentiments Herder never made any direct assault on de Pauw, it is possibly because he did not consider him a worthy adver-

---

553. *Auch eine Philosophie der Geschichte,* in Gerbi, *Romanticismo,* p. 123. In this fundamental work of his, Herder, who had already broken with Nicolai, reacts against the *Aufklärung* (which was suspicious of primitivism) represented by Isaak Iselin's *Geschichte der Menschheit* (1764; see Reed, op. cit., p. 65).

554. On the new sense of "Glückseligkeit" in Herder, as "realization of the ideals and aspirations of man," see the acute observations of Meinecke, *Historismus,* pp. 438-39.

sary; or more probably because Herder in turn, in the grip of his unitary vision of universal history, represents it as a single strand, from the patriarchs of Israel to the philosophers of Paris, ignoring, or worse, both the Islamic and Far Eastern civilizations, and those of America. To justify his exclusion of China Herder makes it a simple reflection of Egypt, the latter on the other hand being included in his providential plan;[555] and America serves him merely as a paradigm of primitivism, curious in itself, but contributing nothing to the incomparable European civilizations. The Patagonian savages and the New Zealand savages are dry and barren branches of the tree of life.[556] America is raw nature, not organized society.

In Herder's major work the striking ideas sketched out in his youth are forced into a system and diluted with moralism. The famous *Ideas of a Philosophy of the History of Mankind* (1784–91) do, of course, include a whole chapter, the sixth of the sixth book, on the Americans.[557] But Herder contents himself with describing the present condition of the natives. He tells us that according to many reports the most advanced American nations are those of the northern part of the Continent. The ancient Mexican empire is mentioned only to inform us that it had ten times more inhabitants than the corresponding Spanish viceroyalty, and that the oppressed peoples are seething with hatred under that "iniquitous tyranny." The Peruvians, "these sweet children of Nature, once so happy under their Incas," are likewise afflicted and boiling with resentment. And Herder's heartfelt eulogy goes to those Americans and other natives of the interior who managed to keep themselves barbarous and free.[558]

Despite these differences between the various peoples of America, and although he recognizes that the continent includes widely divergent

555. According to Schulin, op. cit., p. 69, n. 104, Herder derived his negative opinion on China from P. Sonnerat, *Reise nach Ostindien und China* (German trans., Zurich, 1783).

556. *Ideen*, IV, 4, trans. cit., I, 186.

557. Ed. cit., I, 291–301. A little further on (VII, 5) Herder discusses the influence of climate and accepts the observations of Pehr Kalm (*En resa til Norra Amerika* [Stockholm, 1753–61], II, 233–35; cf. also III, 240–41) on the premature maturity and senility of the Europeans in America and the Creoles in comparison with the vigorous and long-lived natives: "It is incorrect to attribute that to the unhealthy climate of America; it is only to foreigners that it has shown itself unkind" (I, 342). Which gives rise to a suggestive quandary: could the weakness of the present inhabitants of Mexico, Peru, etc., derive in part "from the fact that one has changed their country and way of life, without being able or wanting to give them that of Europeans?" (I, 343). On the breadth of the concept of climate in Herder, see H. A. Korff, *Voltaire im literarischen Deutschland des XVIII Jahrhunderts* (Heidelberg, 1917), pp. 368–69; Rouché, op. cit., pp. 23–24, 268.

558. The Spanish found themselves obliged to "honor" them with the title of *bravos!* (*Ideen*, I, 6; ed. cit., I, 53). A further passionate apology of the "barbarian" peoples' rights of self-defense (with invocation to Las Casas and other numerous references to America) in *Briefe zur Beförderung der Humanität*, Zehnte Sammlung, no. 115 (Frankfurt-Leipzig ed., 1798), pp. 29–34 (on which see Robert T. Clark Jr., "The Noble Savage and the Idea of Tolerance in Herder's *Briefe sur Beförderung der Humanität*," *The Journal of English and Germanic Philology*, 33, no. 1 [January 1934], pp. 46–56). "In a young people, fighting for freedom, he [Herder] also condoned resorting to power politics" (Meinecke, op. cit., p. 456).

climatic zones, nations of giants and nations of pygmies, warlike tribes and peace-loving tribes, and so on, Herder reaffirms the substantial affinity of all Americans, an affinity even greater than that observable among the Negroes; an affinity which he proves with quotations from Ulloa and other travelers and from which he manages to deduce the unalloyed purity and single remote Asiatic origin of all the tribes of the hemisphere.

Which is all very well, but what exactly is this "general character" of the American? It is an "almost childish goodness and innocence." *Childish* — the very adjective used by Montaigne and shortly to be taken up again by Bernardin de Saint-Pierre; but which with Herder contains a promise of development, of adulthood and maturity to come, while Montaigne had yearned after this innocence *qua talis,* as the antithesis of civilization's decadence, and Bernardin's tenderhearted picture of America would be more like some scene of cherubs romping in cloud-cuckoo-land. Herder instead, his acute mind aimed ever in the same direction, points out that these peoples' greatest claim to our attention is in the spectacle they offer us of a civilization which took its first steps alone, without any help from the rest of the world, and whose fragile debut can thus show us a rich and instructive aspect of human nature.

Naïve and ill informed as it may be, this sympathy is certainly superior to Robertson's cold analysis and de Pauw's erudite disdain. In the essay of 1774 Herder had ridiculed Robertson along with the other historiographers of the Enlightenment, but in later works he came to recognize the Scotsman, together with Voltaire and even Gibbon, as his companions-in-arms in the defense and vindication of Humanity, and was warm and lavish in his praise of them.[559] The venomous and mediocre de Pauw, on the other hand, is never explicitly mentioned by Herder. But to our now practiced ear there is no mistaking the target of a number of barbed comments delivered in passing, even though no names are given:

And these are the men that are supposed to be a race of weaklings, of veritable abortions? . . . I believe the reader will decide to reject that prejudice according to which the *indios* are weak and good for nothing . . . neither they [the Tupinambas] nor their valiant neighbors can be considered bastardized creatures,

and so on.[560]

---

559. Meinecke, op. cit., pp. 448, 476–77.

560. De Pauw is cited by name only for his theories and "bold hypotheses" on China and Egypt (see *Ideen,* XI, 5; Suphan ed., XIV, 33; French trans., ed. cit., II, 225) concerning which Hamann wrote to him already in 1774, expressing his hearty agreement (letter of 2 April 1774, in *Briefwechsel,* ed. cit., III, 79). But there is no shortage of probable references to the *Recherches sur les Américains.* Apart from the current cliché of syphilis as the recompense of the conquest (cf. de Pauw's "Discours préliminaire"), see Herder's discussion of the insensibility of the Americans (*Ideen,* VIII, 1; trans. cit., II, 9–10), in implicit polemic with the *Recherches,* I, 72–74 (only mentioning Robertson and Ulloa, true; but de Pauw too cites Ulloa in the passage mentioned). And cf. de Pauw: "Until now we have only had false notions on the northernmost peoples of America" ("Discours préliminaire") with Her-

Yet when Herder has to make up his mind which part of the earth may claim the supreme honor of having been the cradle of man, America is immediately set aside, and precisely because of a series of "Buffon-de Pauwian" deficiencies: because its mountains are precipitous and inhospitable, its volcanoes active, its plains humid, its fauna inferior to that of the Old World, and its indigenous societies "formless outlines" of governments. The comparison of one hemisphere with the other "poses a serious problem for the philosopher." But the philosopher Herder evades the problem by repeating ambiguously that the human race cannot have been born "in the rich valley of Quito" (Western Hemisphere) nor yet "in the Mountains of the Moon, in Africa" (Eastern Hemisphere).[561] And unwilling to abandon the biblical thesis of Adam's single progeny he resigns himself to treating all the other races as degenerate varieties of the white race.

Taken all in all, the significance of these "critical exertions" is mainly symptomatic. They reveal the rapid maturing of a problem that was already implicit in the polemic between the budding historicism and the rationalism of the age, but which was becoming ever more alive and immediate in the image of the Americas: the problem of the relationship between history and nature, between civilization and innateness, tradition and spontaneity. To prevail decisively over the philosophy of the Enlightenment it was necessary to revive a feeling for the past, the whole past, even the remotest past back to the age of primitivism, and at the same time to eliminate the idea of humanity as invariable and identical in all places at all times. Herder energetically supported each of the two tendencies, without bothering to reconcile them, indeed almost without noticing any antithesis between the idolization of the primitive and an enthusiasm for progress.[562]

His discoveries, and still more his weaknesses, make Herder the most typical exponent of this radical conflict. On one side he is the most

---

der: "We only know these peoples [of the North] . . . through imaginary accounts." See also the condemnation of the authors that feed Europe's pride by slandering the savages: *Briefe*, loc. cit., p. 34. A methodical survey would, I think, reveal other textual traces.

561. *Ideen*, X, 2; trans. cit., II, 141. Cf. the Buffonian-sounding eulogy of the majestic elephant and the noble lion, in contrast with the inert and shapeless *unau* (*Bradypus* or American Poltroon) of America (III, 3; ibid., I, 119–24); the deploring of the American fauna, poor in large animals, and rich in bats, mice, insects, toads, etc., with sad consequences for the history of man (II, 3; ibid., I, 87–88); the ingenious explanation of America's weakness and inferiority, at the moment of discovery, by the fact that it possessed almost no domestic animals (VIII, 3; ibid., II, 37–39; X, 3; ibid., II, 147, an idea which would also seem to come from Buffon and Reimarus: Rouché, op. cit., p. 290). A series of no less than eighteen derivations of Herderian theses from Buffon (including those referring to the American fauna) can be found in E. Sauter, *Herder und Buffon* (Rixheim, 1910), summarized in Rouché, op. cit., pp. 207–08n., 219 n., 2, 669. On Herder's relationship with the geographical and naturalistic theories of the century, in general, see Meinecke, op. cit., p. 462 and Rouché, op. cit., pp. 276–77, quoting Grundmann, *Die geographische und völkerkundliche Quellen und Anschauungen in Herders Ideen* (Berlin, 1900).

562. R. G. Collingwood, *History*, pp. 86–87; A. O. Lovejoy, "Herder and the Philosophy of History," in *Essays*, pp. 167, 181.

ardent defender of primitivism, on the other the most effective promoter of the idea of development in history. He stresses even more than Montesquieu the importance of physical and climatic factors, the link between man and nature, but assigns a religious value and a transcendental end to the evolution of the human race. America was the reagent that revealed these strident contradictions.

Although Herder's gaze is always turned toward the East, toward biblical antiquity and the peoples of Asia, he finds himself unable to shake off these nagging doubts and unanswerable questions presented by the extreme West. The epithet "childish," used by Herder to describe the Americans, had served him once already and would do so again, to designate the most ancient East, "the infancy of the human race." The New World deluges him with claims and queries which leave him troubled and unhappy. Thus one moment he is repeating Berkeley's famous prophecy and seeing Europe's moribund learning born again in the Anglo-American colonies (1780),[563] and a moment later going on to reject it and reply to the "good bishop" that Europe is not yet at the fourth act, but barely at the third, and may yet recover her youth, revive and not abdicate.[564] Poor Herder! If he silences the American "barbarians" he is denying his optimistic exaltation of young and ingenuous nations. If he admits them *plenis titulis* into the course of human history, he sees the ruin of all his hopes of having shown a uniform meaning, a universal value, in the passing of the centuries.

De Pauw's charges aggravate the problem by offering a paradoxical solution that is doubly unacceptable for Herder. A "degenerate" American has no place either among the child-races or among the educated nations. His instinctive reaction is thus to rehabilitate the native, to bring out the qualities in the Americans which had already appealed to his Rousseauian admiration of the pure and natural — a feeling reinforced in this case (and here he agrees with de Pauw) by the contrast with the hypocritical violence wrought on these peoples by the Europeans — which was in constant danger of being swallowed up and submerged in the Europeocentric maelstrom of his system or carried off and likewise drowned in the impetuous and uniform current of his mystical Progress. Herder cannot bear to give in to the cynic de Pauw, and lingers a moment to put in a good word for the Americans. He agrees, albeit unwillingly and unproductively, to discuss their theoretical case. And thus, in passing, with absentminded benevolence, he bestows on them too the blessing of humanity's muddled theologian.

---

563. *Vom Einfluss der Regierungen auf die Wissenschaften und der Wissenschaften auf die Regierungen* (1780).
564. Texts (1780, 1792) in King, op. cit., pp. 68–70.

The Reaction to de Pauw
in Spanish America

I. CHARACTERISTICS OF THE LATIN AMERICAN REACTION TO THE EUROPEAN SLANDERS

THERE are several good reasons why we can speak of reaction to de Pauw in Latin America, rather than a "polemic" on his theses. Polemic implies a dialogue: maybe even with someone already dead, but still a dialogue, the opposition of two theories, a dispute—which may suggest violent controversy, but does mean a colloquy too. It was a dispute that involved the exiled Jesuits and the American founding fathers. The Latin American authors, writing on the eve of and immediately after the liberation of their countries, react belligerently, angrily, and resentfully to Buffon's and de Pauw's notions, but without producing any organic corpus of argument and factual data to oppose them. They reply to the all-embracing condemnations with disjointed dithyrambs. To the serious problems raised by Buffon they make no reference at all, and de Pauw is only mentioned for his more scandalous aspects and wilder exaggerations. The "Prussian" was classed quite simply as an enemy of America and the Americans, an enemy to be showered with abuse whenever the occasion offered. If Voltaire accuses the Americans of being unindustrious, the fiery Vidaurre protests that "this is a greater insult than those thought up by the imbecile de Pauw."[1]

De Pauw had once been the focal point of so many of the discussions, but now these same conspicuous exaggerations of his relegate him to the rank of convenient and unmistakable target. The essence of his theories was not even examined, but the glories of America shone out more resplendent in contrast to his black insinuations. The fundamental question, so richly suggestive as originally formulated, faded and dwindled on reaching the cultural environment of the overseas colonies, so much

---

1. Manuel de Vidaurre, *Suplemento a las Cartas americanas* (Lima, 1827), p. 13 (ibid., p. 117, a dubious allusion to the second *Recherches*).

poorer in scientific tradition and interest; but at the same time it became more bitter too, as the political aspect rose to preeminence.

Sometimes its opponents are content to refer back to the defenses of America published in Europe, as more authoritative and "impartial." And usually, as we have seen, their susceptibilities seem more sensitive to the slanders on their intellectual capacities than the denigration of the Americans' physical prowess. But their logical pattern is still that of later rationalism and shows almost no trace of the new concepts elaborated by historical thought and romanticism. All one notes — and this confirms rather than invalidates these writers' immaturity — is an unsparing and disorganized use of the boasts of youth, newness, and vigor on the part of their lands and nations. In other words their replies are belated, often incidental, and for the most part no longer relevant, incapable of producing any useful result, and spoiled among other things by a characteristic limitation of outlook.

And yet they are not by any means without interest, either in themselves, or in the history of the polemic: not in themselves, because they are almost always the work of men of wit, learning, and eloquence, men who were among the finest minds in their respective countries; and not in the history of the dispute because these replies brought about the acceptance throughout Latin America of the anti-Buffon anti-de Pauw thesis that is still valid and triumphant today — the thesis or rather article of faith establishing the excellence of the American continent and its mission in the vanguard of humanity. Each viceroyalty and captaincy general of the Spanish Empire, each of the future republics raises at least one voice to rebuff the "Prussian's" vituperation and to announce present and future glories, virtues of unimagined splendor and destinies of unmeasurable greatness. In the Old World, the Revolution's roar and shriek drowned out the erudite squabbles of abbés and adventurers, and two decades of war were refocusing the world's attention on the struggles and aspirations of fever-ridden Europe; Napoleon was selling Louisiana, and the whole continent, from California and Florida to the Straits of Magellan, was slipping from Spain's grip. But in America the accusations of inferiority were becoming ever more widely known, and matched by a growing patriotic anger that went hand in hand with the political revolt and merged with the resentment of the Creoles against the Godos.

Up until the close of the century the protests come from Americans who have been or still are in Europe, and thus continue the Jesuits' polemic. But from 1800 onward the voices of the Americans of America are more and more frequently heard.

II. DÁVALOS AND THE CLIMATE OF PERU

José Manuel Dávalos was a doctor from Lima, a rich mulatto with a restless turn of mind who had been unsatisfied with what he had learned in his homeland, had betaken himself to France, and in Paris and at the illustrious university of Montpellier had spent several years (1784–88) in the untiring study of botany, chemistry, and anatomy, graduating from the "Augustissimo Ludoviceo Monspeliensi" on March 5, 1787, with a dissertation (or *specimen academicum*) *De morbis nonnullis Limae grassantibus ipsorumque therapeia* (Monspelii, 1787).[2]

The work is devoted to the city of Lima, *in Peruvia*, and from its very first lines Dávalos protests against the writers who were pleased to "defile thee [Lima] with poisonous slanders." A note follows immediately explaining that these ill-intentioned writers can be reduced to de Pauw, who slandered the University of San Marcos, and dared to write that the mathematician Godin found not a single student there who could understand him.[3] Thus Dávalos's first polemical objective is the vindication of the scientific glories of Lima: Herrera, Peralta, Olavide, Bravo del Castillo, Joseph Baquíjano, and many others.

But a more far-reaching anti-de Pauwian criticism is implicit in the principal thesis of his little work ("a creditable little work," Unánue called it, somewhat condescendingly).[4] He maintains in fact that the climate of

2. On Dávalos, see Mondibuiu, op. cit., VIII, 357; cf. ibid., IV, 351; Medina, *Biblioteca Hispano-Americana* (Santiago, 1898–1907), V, 239–40 (see also *La imprenta en Lima* [Santiago, 1904–07], III, 184; IV, 177); H. Valdizán, *Apuntes para la bibliografía médica peruana* (Lima, 1928), pp. vi–vii, 213–21, 223, 235–36; Juan B. Lastres, "El doctor José Manuel Dávalos (1758–1821)," *Documentos* (Lima), 3, no. 1 (1951–55), pp. 155–82. Of some interest is the catalogue of his well-stocked library (which includes neither de Pauw nor any of his contradictors), published by Fr. R. Vargas Ugarte in the *Cuadernos de Estudios* of the Instituto de Investigaciones Históricas de la Universidad Católica del Perú, 2, no. 5 (Lima, 1943), pp. 324–42. The difficulties put in front of the mulattoes who wanted to study medicine in Lima (on which see Rosenblat, op. cit., pp. 274–76) "had the curious effect of driving some of the most independent mulattoes abroad, especially to Montpellier, to study medicine," and of thus bringing it about that on their return to their native country they contributed to the progress of Peruvian medicine ("The Case of José Ponseano de Ayarza: A Document on the Negro in Higher Education," *The Hispanic American Historical Review*, 24, no. 3 (August 1944), p. 433; cf. ibid., p. 557). The fact was mentioned already in a speech printed in Lima in 1812, and was quoted the following year by Fray Servando Teresa de Mier (fictitious name: José Guerra) in his *Historia de la revolución*, II, 599, 665, actually mentioning a mulatto from Lima earning his doctorate in Montpellier, almost certainly our Dávalos.

3. *De morbis*, pp. iv–v. This savage insinuation by de Pauw which, as we shall see, was to offend Unánue too (below, p. 304) and José Maria de Salazar (below, n. 58), angered another doctor from Lima, José Pastor Larriñaga, who in the *Prólogo* to his *Apología de los cirujanos del Perú* (Granada, 1793), rejected the assertion of "Mr. Pauw in his *Averiguaciones filosóficas sobre los Americanos del Perú*" (*sic*, quoted in Valdizán, *Apuntes*, p. 301).

4. The relations between Unánue and Dávalos do not always seem to have been wholly cordial. Medina, op. cit., V, 239–40, mentions a curious begging letter from Dávalos, in which he modestly writes that in Lima "if I am not the first doctor, I am one of the first," and complains about having applied for a chair in medicine, which "the viceroy, exerting his authority and disregarding the laws and constitutions, gave to D. D. Hipólito Unánue." Unánue was also "honorary doctor" to the royal household, the precise position sought by Dávalos in his letter. And, an apparently even more serious indication of academic or professional rivalry, Unánue does not even mention his colleague's dissertation in

Lima, and of Peru in general, is extremely healthy, and cannot in any way be blamed for the sicknesses of the inhabitants of the city. These infirmities are due, he says, to their diet of oily, sticky, heavy foods, and to the fact that they eat too much and badly, and stuff themselves with pork, potatoes (which Dávalos suspects of containing some harmful element), yucca (which is poisonous in its raw state), and pungent spices and seasonings.[5] But about the air and climate in general, on the other hand, Dávalos is enthusiastic. The soothing breezes of Miraflores are enough in themselves to cure both tertian fever and pulmonary disorders. Tetanus is completely unknown there.[6] A simple note goes on to furnish the extraordinary information that "there is in Peru a place by the name of *Piura*, where syphilis is remedied solely by the healthy influence of the climate" (p. 105, n. 1).

A few years later the satirical Esteban de Terralla y Landa, writing under his pseudonym of Simón Ayanque, published his savage poem *Lima por dentro y fuera* (1792), and he too wrote of Piura: "City that looks like a village, / Good only for curing venereal disease."[7] But it is surprising to find that Piura's antiluetic reputation has lasted almost into our own times:[8] maybe an ideological reprisal for those ancient charges accusing America of having given Europe venereal disease?

III. SALAS AND THE HAPPY EARTH OF CHILE

The Chilean economist and patriot Manuel de Salas likewise defended his country on the climatic plane.

As early as 1796 Salas had been implicitly quarreling if not with

---

his own major work, despite the close relevance of its subject. Later, however, Unánue had Dávalos named professor of medicine, which should suffice to relieve him of the accusation made against him "of having been a bitter enemy of D. J. M. Dávalos (L. Avendaño, *Discurso por el centenario de la Escuela de Medicina;* H. Valdizán, *La Escuela de Medicina,* in *Obras científicas y literarias de Unánue* [Barcelona, 1914], II, 450, 482; cf. Lastres, op. cit., pp. 160–61). Further indication of Dávalos's difficult character: when another Lima mulatto, José Manuel Valdés, presented himself for the degree of bachelor (1807), José Manuel Dávalos, who was on the jury, told him that without the Sovereign's grace, "for the half-breed José Manuel Valdés . . . the doors of this school would always have been of bronze," to which Valdés replied with an allusion to Dávalos's being a mulatto too (J. A. de Lavalle, "El doctor, don José Manuel Valdés," 1858–86, in *Estudios Históricos* [Lima, 1935], 443–81, see pp. 450–51).

5. *De morbis*, pp. 11–12. Other factors responsible for the disease rate are *guarapo* and brandy, and the cemeteries and hospitals in the middle of the city. The toxicity of the yucca is mentioned already by the earliest chroniclers of America, such as Pietro Martire; and the potato, whose genus, *Solanum*, includes various highly toxic plants, was still suspected of being poisonous in the second half of the seventeenth century.

6. Op. cit., p. 118; cf. p. 9.

7. Paris ed. (1924), p. 12; and in a footnote, p. 196, which seems to have been added to the 1834 edition: "[Piura] is such an excellent place for those who fall ill from this malady, that there are very few who die from it, despite the multitude of people who go there for the cure from many parts of the republic."

8. The climate of Piura provides a "radical cure" for rheumatics and syphilitics, we are assured by C. B. Cisneros and R. E. Garcia, *El Perú en Europa* (Lima, 1900), p. 19, a little book which also informs the reader that the ostrich (*"avestruz,"* p. 14) lives on the *puna* together with the *llama* and the *vicuña!*

Buffon, whom he always mentions with great respect,[9] at least with his version of American nature. Chile is a privileged land, the American country "most adequate for human happiness . . . capable of all the products and animals of Europe, of which none have degenerated and some improved, where wild beasts are not known, nor insects, nor poisonous reptiles." And going on to the men he echoed Father Feijóo's defense: "The weakness and effeminacy attributed to these peoples is a mistake."[10]

Again a few years later (1801) he protested vehemently against the thesis that the Americans were inferior and incapable of raising themselves to the level of the exact sciences. Against the slanders of Sepúlveda and de Pauw he mentioned men like Peralta, Franklin, and Molina, and their achievements in the fields of astronomy, electricity, and history. To combat the thesis of decadence he returned to Garcilaso's favorite motif and flaunted the youthfulness of the New World, whose continental civilization could now exist independently of that of tired old Europe.[11] Again in 1815, when confined by the Spaniards on the Isle of Juan Fernandez, Salas described how the captain of the frigate taking him there had praised the richness of that island, which bred (among other things) "oxen of such a size that they cannot be included in the proofs of the degradation of all America's species, so boldly asserted by the frivolous and caustic Mr. Pauw, in his *Investigations*."[12]

IV. ITURRI AND MUÑOZ'S *HISTORY*

We find a more complicated reaction in the *Carta* written in Rome in 1797 by the former Santa Fé Jesuit, Francisco Iturri, exiled to Italy along with his confrères: an opuscule that gained a certain political notoriety when, with independence won, the American nations were intent on vaunting their homegrown glories, but which for the most part consists of a sustained attack on Robertson and de Pauw, as plagiarized, according to Iturri, in the *Historia del Nuevo Mundo* (1793) of Juan Bautista Muñoz, the apparent target of the diatribe.

9. M. de Salas, *Escritos . . . y documentos relativos a él y a su familia*, 3 vols. (Santiago, 1910–14), I, 249; II, 162; III, 41; and in M. L. Amunátegui, *Don Manuel de Salas* (Santiago, 1895), I, 258; II, 213; III, 194. This work fills out the pages devoted to Salas in *Los precursores de la independencia de Chile*, III, 343–457.

10. *Representación sobre el estado de la agricultura, industria y comercio del reino de Chile*, 1796, cited in Salas, *Escritos*, I, 152–53, and Amunátegui, op. cit., I, 118–21. Similar expressions: Salas, op. cit., I, 190–91; II, 320, 366–67; Amunátegui, op. cit., I, 126, 240; II, 107 (1796) and passim.

11. H. Bernstein, "Some Inter-American Aspects of the Enlightenment," in *Latin America and the Enlightenment*, ed. A. P. Whitaker (New York, 1942), pp. 55–56; and *Origins*, pp. 56n., 65.

12. Salas, *Escritos*, II, 207; Amunátegui, II, 206–07. De Pauw's geological theories are also cited in a work mentioned by Salas, op. cit., II, 162, and in Amunátegui, op. cit., II, 213. The Chilean scholar was a great admirer of the wisdom and simplicity of Galiani's *Dialogues sur le commerce des bleds* (see ibid., II, 196).

Robertson's *History of America* had had a singular reception in Spain. First of all the Academia de la Historia named the Scotsman a corresponding member (8 August 1777), and at the suggestion of its president, the renowned Campomanes, entrusted one of its members, Ramón de Guevara, with translating the work into Castilian. But as soon as they became aware of its anti-Spanish tendencies their attitude changed rapidly from favor into persecution. The Inquisition put it on the Index (although we are assured by Menendez y Pelayo that this was "merely a formality");[13] subsequent royal edicts banned it in Spain and in the Indies, in the original version (23 December 1778) and in the French translation (20 December 1782),[14] and the king himself, ignoring the opposition in the Academia de la Historia,[15] on 17 June 1779 charged Juan Bautista Muñoz with the task of using original documents to write the *Historia del Nuevo Mundo,* whose first and only volume in fact appeared fourteen years later. The Academia in its turn, recognizing "the necessity for a General History of the Indies to be drafted by some authorized person from Spain, using sure and incontestable documents," took steps leading to the establishment of the invaluable Archivo General de Indias[16] — another beneficial and lasting scientific result, like the reappraisal of Mexican history in the wake of Clavigero's work, of the often frivolous and incoherent discussions we are here narrating.

The purpose of Muñoz's work, in the intentions of his sponsors, was to correct the anti-Spanish rather than the anti-American errors of Robertson. Thus his *Historia,* as an official undertaking, could not satisfy the Americans, like Iturri, for whom the defense of Spain mattered little (even though he proclaimed himself a faithful subject and boasted of being Spanish), while the defense of their native countries mattered very considerably. And Muñoz did in fact go on undaunted to repeat that "the great quadrupeds of the old continent were not found in the new; but in return [*sic!*] they have an infinity of insects and vermin."[17]

13. *De los historiadores de Colón,* 1892, in *Estudios y discursos de crítica histórica y literaria,* VII (XII of the *Obras completas,* Santander, 1940-), pp. 100–02. In Guatemala however it was confiscated by the Inquisition: Ernesto Chinchilla Aguilar, *La Inquisición en Guatemala,* (Guatemala, 1953: *Revista de Historia de América,* nos. 35–36, 1953), p. 246.
14. I. A. Leonard, *Hispanic American Historical Review,* 23 (1943), p. 30, n. 18; Defourneaux, op. cit., p. 188; cf. ibid., pp. 113n., 148.
15. "Not without strong opposition from the Academy of History, determined to uphold its prime claim to be chronicler of the Indies": on the ensuing polemic, see Rómulo D. Carbia, *La Crónica oficial de las Indias occidentales* (La Plata, 1934), pp. 240–65, and *Historia de la leyenda negra,* p. 211.
16. J. Torre Revello, *El libro, la imprenta y el periodismo en América durante la dominación española* (Buenos Aires, 1940), pp. 85, clxxxiii–clxxxvi; and the ample study by A. Ballesteros Beretta, "J. B. Muñoz: La creación del Archivo de Indias," *Revista de Indias,* 2, no. 4 (1941), pp. 55–95, followed by others, in the same review, on Muñoz and his researches. Cf. also Carbia, *La Crónica oficial,* p. 109 and n., 113–15, and Humphreys, op. cit., pp. 26–27 and nn.
17. J. B. Muñoz, *Historia del Nuevo Mundo,* I (only volume published; Madrid, 1793), p. 10, etc. See also Richard Konetzke, "A. von Humboldt als Geschichtsschreiber Amerikas," in *Historische Zeitschrift,* 188, no. 3 (December 1959), pp. 551–52.

But this is still no reason to suppose, as some have done, that Iturri wrote his *Carta critica sobre la Historia de América* [*sic*] *del Sr. Juan Bautista Muñoz* — completed in Rome on 20 August 1797, and printed in Madrid in 1798 — at the instigation of Campomanes (a jealous and bitter enemy of Muñoz),[18] or that he was prompted by spite and vexation that the eminent official cosmographer and historian had dealt with a topic which he had been thinking of discussing himself.[19] One need only remember that embryonic patriotism characteristic of the exiled Jesuits. In fact the same polemical position (arguing against Robertson, Raynal, de Pauw, Marmontel, Buffon, and La Condamine) and the same enthusiasm for Father Molina appear already in his letter to Alcedo of 1789;[20] and Iturri's *Carta* (like other apologetic writings of exiled Jesuits) — a work which was probably never intended for publication, and which certainly did *not* bring about the interruption of Muñoz's *Historia*[21] — was republished in Buenos Aires in 1818, and in Mexico, at Puebla de los Angeles, in 1821, as a manifesto of Americanism, a posthumous chastisement of the *godo* Muñoz. And the Mexican Mier, although a friend and admirer of Muñoz, mentioned delightedly that Iturri, another friend of his, and "an American of Paraguay . . . gave Muñoz a real hiding, for including various of de Pauw's, Raynal's, and Robertson's idiocies in his historical outline."[22]

18. See Carbia, *La Crónica oficial*, p. 251n. So it would seem from two manuscript notes of Dr. Soloaga, one transcribed by Carbia, op. cit., p. 262; the other almost identical, by Jorge M. Furt, "De arte historica," in *Contribuciones para el estudio de la historia de América: homenaje al dr. Ravignani* (Buenos Aires, 1941), p. 274n. Campomanes is cited with hyperbolic praise in the *Carta*, pp. 83 and 90–92. The notorious anti-Jesuitism of the encyclopedist Campomanes raises some doubt; but does not Iturri himself mention the *Encyclopédie* as a work of unquestionable value (p. 31)?

19. There is considerable doubt about the existence of the *Historia natural, eclesiástica y civil del virreynato del Plata* which Iturri (according to the *Enciclopedia Espasa*; see also Sommervogel, *sub voce*) wrote in 1798 in collaboration with Gaspar Juarez, in three folio volumes supposedly kept in the Archives at Pisa. Carbia, op. cit., pp. 256–57n., believes it lost. It is certain that Iturri was writing a defense of America's glory in the arts and sciences. "My work," he writes in the *Carta*, p. 116, "will pass in review all the objects of the Human Sciences." He alludes to the same work on p. 56. And on p. 5 he gives the title of the same [?] work: "The damage that must come to Spain through the liberty with which her colonies are slandered." But note that hispanophilia is conspicuously absent from all the rest of the letter.

20. "The Letter of Francisco Iturri, S.J.," pp. 87–88.

21. This is affirmed by Iturri himself, and repeated in the manuscript notes quoted above, n. 18. But see Carbia, op. cit., p. 264. When Muñoz's *Historia* was presented to the Academia de la Historia for the required examination before printing permission was granted "there were varying opinions" (Ricardo Donoso, *Fuentes documentales*, p. 30). Several chapters at least of the second volume of the *Historia del Nuevo Mundo* were completed when Muñoz was struck down by apoplexy, in 1799. There is a copy in the New York Public Library (J. de Onis, "Alcedo's Bibliotheca Americana," *Hispanic American Historical Review*, 31, no. 3 [August 1951], p. 356, n. 24). And in the *Boletín del Archivo General de la Nación*, Ciudad de Trujillo (Santo Domingo), 3, n. 11 (31 May 1940), pp. 169–220, there appeared the unpublished part relating to Santo Domingo (J. Torre Revello, *La expedición de Don Pedro de Mendoza y las fuentes informativas de . . . Herrera*, in Furt, *Contribuciones*, p. 606, n. 1). Muñoz did actually reply to Iturri with a *Satisfacción a la Carta crítica sobre la Historia del Nuevo Mundo* (Valencia, 1798), which Iturri in his turn countered with the *Vicios de la Satisfacción a la Carta crítica* (unpublished, Academia de la Historia, Madrid): Carbia, op. cit., p. 262, and n. 1.

22. *Memorias* (1818; Madrid, n.d., Biblioteca Ayacucho), p. 318, with evident allusion to Iturri's *Carta*. This "plagiarism" by Muñoz "stirred up the bile of my very dear friend the American ex-Jesuit

In point of fact the defense of the American peoples, and in particular of the Mexicans and Peruvians, takes up only a few pages toward the end of the *Carta* (pp. 110–16), following one of the usual "retaliations" enumerating the vices and barbarities of numerous races of the Old World (pp. 96–110). The major part of the pamphlet is a polemic against Muñoz, accusing him of having defamed the old historiographers of America, Fernando Colón, Las Casas, and particularly Herrera, and finally of having been an undiscerning plagiarist of Robertson and the "liar" de Pauw, for everything regarding the soil of America and its inhabitants. Even Muñoz's criticism of earlier Spanish historiographers is found to be a plagiarism of de Pauw (p. 33). Muñoz's history, Iturri repeats twenty times, consists of slavish translation from an Englishman's history and a Prussian's investigations. His insistence is significant, if for no other reason because it shows how easy it was to assimilate Robertson's theses to the so much more radical and outrageous suggestions of de Pauw. It may be only a polemical convenience, but Iturri, who was familiar with the works of almost all the principal critics and defenders of America, beginning with the "great" Buffon (p. 52), the first to reduce the slanderous notions to a system,[23] sums up all the opinions on the inferiority of America in terms of the de Pauw-Robertson binomial, the former more rabid and mendacious, the latter more popular and widely known.[24] He barely considers the substance of the accusations. And he never deigns to discuss the details: "Let it suffice us to know that his [Munōz's] picture of the Americans is a servile copy of de Pauw and Robertson. That is enough to discredit it and set it among the fables" (p. 80).

Iturri's only attempt to refute these accusations consists in the quotation of extracts from historians and naturalists that speak enthusiastically of the New World. Don Bernardo Ibáñez (*Reyno jesuítico del Paraguay,* quoted on pp. 55 and 69–70) tells us that "all animal and vegetable nature manifests itself there with greater strength and size." Is not this testimony enough "to discredit a million de Pauws, Robertsons, their trans-

---

Iturri; who loosed off a fiery letter against it," but Muñoz was quite capable of defending himself: S. T. de Mier, *Escritos inéditos,* ed. J. M. Miguel Vergés and Hugo Diaz-Thomé (Mexico, 1944), p. 148. On this question see also G. Furlong, S.J., *Francisco Javier Iturri y su "Carta crítica,"* 1797 (Buenos Aires, 1955).

23. P. 45. For Pernety, p. 69; La Douceur, p. 35; La Condamine, p. 45; Jefferson, p. 44; Carli, p. 39; Raynal, pp. 102, 110. Ulloa too is quoted several times.

24. Carli had already attacked de Pauw and Robertson together. Iturri insinuates that Muñoz could not even be original: "but he knew that Pauw had done it in French, and that *since that language was little known in Spain,* his translation could seem new" (p. 118). Elsewhere he reduces Muñoz's plagiarism to his physical description of the New World (bk. I); the rest would then be compilation and plagiarism from the Spanish historiographers, often in open contradiction with the slanderous assertions of that first book.

lators and imitators"?[25] The ex-Jesuit's sole argument is the by now familiar gambit of the counterattack. America is new? Europe and parts of Africa and Asia are a lot newer. It is marshy and swampy? There are bigger lakes in Prussia alone. It is a sandy desert? The Old World has the Arabian desert, and (rather more curious examples) the "vast sands" of Bordeaux and the shifting dunes of Mont Saint-Michel (p. 60). America has no great quadrupeds? But fortunately nor has Europe, nor in many other parts of the Old World do we find "those hideous great mountains of flesh," such as elephants, camels, and dromedaries (pp. 65–66: echoes of Clavigero, see above, p. 202). As for plants and their degeneration, finally, is it not remarkable that all American fruits, except the prickly pear, degenerate "while all European fruits flourish over there" (p. 72: echoes of Acosta, see above, pp. xvii–xviii)? Whose soil is more decadent and corrupt? . . .

So Iturri too puts himself on his opponent's ground: and the supremacy of America, of her fertility, beauty, and vastness, her physical elevation and temporal antiquity, is for him an article of faith. Thus his position ends up as a double anachronism: for its unwaveringly eulogistic apotheosis of the continent, quite out of place alongside the already developing scientific approach to the problem of America, and for the antiquated character of most of its arguments. Iturri was still defending and boasting of the venerable age of the Americas when others were already exalting the youthfulness of the continent as its supreme virtue.

One curious feature remains—the direction of his attack. Iturri is a typical example of the Creole who sees in de Pauw the ideological instrument of the Bourbon monarchy, and he reveals an equal aversion for the writer who had slandered his country and the government that held it in subjection. When de Pauw states that the Creoles are degenerate, he is providing ammunition for the mother country. In fact, the Americans go on, de Pauw did not even invent his "insults"; they were suggested to him by the Spaniards, and he contented himself with summarizing them. And this same de Pauw—who a few years earlier had been held up by Nuix as a sworn enemy of Spain, and whom the same Father Nuix had still sought to utilize, *malgré lui*, to defend Spain against the illuminists, the leaders of the current to which de Pauw indubitably belonged—was now "accused" of helping Spain to maintain her transatlantic dominion, and of being one of the favorite authors of the *godos*.

25. On p. 64 Ibañez is said to be superior "to millions of de Pauws." Don Gregorio Mayans "is worth more than a hundred million de Pauws, Robertsons, and their Translators" (p. 116).

The pugnacious Mexican polemicist, Fray Servando Teresa de Mier, could write in 1813:

Ever since the Prussian Pauw worked for nine or ten years, like a beetle concocting his pellet of dirt, collecting together everything bad their rulers had said about America and its inhabitants, the Spaniards have persisted in making merry with this putrefaction, and throwing it in our faces as if we were the *indios* of old.[26]

First, it seems, de Pauw plagiarized the Spanish slanderers of America. And then the Spaniards exploited de Pauw's theories to make political capital.

V. MOXÓ: MEXICO DEFENDED BY A SPANIARD

Father Móxo is a special case; he was not American by birth, but a willing defender of Mexico and the Mexicans against de Pauw and his followers.

The *Cartas mexicanas* of the Catalan[27] Benito María de Moxó, future Archbishop of Chuquisaca, was written in Mexico City shortly before the author's departure for Peru (p. 253) and attempt the rehabilitation of the climate and the physical and spiritual qualities of the Mexicans, but most particularly the civilizing virtues of the Spaniards, in the face of the slanderous attacks on everything American. Father Moxó is decidedly more hispanophile than Americanophile; and his apology, though following on in a direct line from Father Nuix and Clavigero (the two of them are mentioned conjointly on p. 38), leans particularly on the arguments of the former, which are often quoted verbatim. Moxó's sole criticism of Father Nuix is that he did not make use of Garcilaso de la Vega

---

26. Fr. S. T. de Mier, *Historia*, "Prólogo," 1, xv. On his ideas, a distortion and residuum of these polemics, see the study in appendix to Gerbi, *Viejas polémicas*, and below, pp. 312–15.

27. With evident pride Moxó, born at Cervera, calls Father Nuix "my famous compatriot" (*Cartas mexicanas*, p. 38), and writes: "my country Catalonia" (ibid., p. 311). On his life see R. Vargas Ugarte, *D. Benito María de Moxó y de Francolí arzobispo de Charcas* (Buenos Aires, 1931; Facultad de Filosofía y Letras, Publicaciones del Instituto de Investigaciones Históricas, LVI); see also Ezquerra, op. cit., pp. 265–66. The *Cartas mexicanas* is dated from Mexico, between August and October of 1805, where Moxó, already elected (1 January 1805) to the archbishopric of Charcas, was impatiently awaiting a chance to get there. Having finally left on 23 December 1805 (though on 16 February 1806 he dated a letter from Mexico, *Cartas*, p. 348) he landed at Tumbez (*Cartas*, 2d ed., p. 398) and, arriving in Lima on 8 May 1806 a few days later (20 June 1806), despatched the manuscript from that city to Madrid to have it printed there (Vargas Ugarte, *Moxó* pp. 53–54). But the work remained unpublished (and the original has possibly been lost) until another copy of the manuscript was taken from Bolivia to Europe in 1836 by the Spaniard Father F. Andrés Herrero, where it was printed in Genoa, at the expense of the Genoese Don Juan Bautista Jordán, between 1837 and 1838 (the license is dated 16 September 1837). But of this edition "almost all the copies" were "sent to America" (translator's preface to the Italian edition, Genoa, n.d., p. ii). A second Spanish edition was printed in Genoa at the end of 1839 (license dated 4 December 1839) and the Italian translation "by S. B." also appeared about that same time. One last event was to befall the adventurous little book. A nephew of Moxó, Don Luis Maria de Moxó y de Lopez, published a counterfeit edition of it in Barcelona in 1838, with the picturesque title of *Entretenimientos de un prisionero en las provincias del Rio de la Plata: por el Barón de Juras Reales siendo Fiscal de S. M. en el Reino de Chile* (Vargas Ugarte, *Moxó*, pp. 69–70).

in his defense;[28] Clavigero on the other hand is rebuked for various errors, resulting mainly from his immoderate Creole patriotism.[29] The criticisms of Robertson come from Father Nuix; but it is of course Clavigero who provides Moxó with the bulk of his arguments against de Pauw.

Out of the twenty almost two entire letters—the fourth and fifth—are aimed at the Prussian philosopher. As always, when the Spaniard girds himself up to deal with the philosophers that defame his country, he sees them in an enormous Babelic throng: "An almost infinite number of French, Dutch, German, and English writers appear before my mind at this moment. . . ." But de Pauw is once again their most representative exponent. "Be so good . . . as to open the celebrated book of the philosophical investigations on the Americans written by Mr. Pauw" (p. 25): at whatever page it is opened, one finds some abuse of the Americans.

Moxó does not however waste his time repudiating those insults one by one. Nor, one need hardly say, does he go into the really essential problem of the degeneration of the continent and its natural species. To de Pauw's assertions of the physical weakness of the natives he is content to reply, à la Clavigero (see above, p. 204), that he has seen them, these *indios*, "bearing enormous weights over very great distances." He has seen them, and can still see them: "As I write these lines an Indian is passing below my window, his shoulders bent under a great load of firewood he is going to sell" (p. 26).

From this same panoramic balcony Father Moxó sees another living disproof of de Pauw's words. The Prussian had written that corn grows only in a few corners of North America;[30] but "from one of the windows of the study where I am now writing this letter, I can detect a considerable piece of ground covered entirely" with corn (p. 32, and see above, chap. 5, n. 240). The fragility of this line of reasoning, empirical almost to the point of puerility, reveals how little effort Moxó made to understand the deeper motivations of the de Pauwian polemic.

Equally unconvincing is his reply to de Pauw's substantially accurate assertion that what little progress agriculture in general has made in America has been due to Europeans and Africans,[31] not to the Americans themselves: "Anyone," Moxó replies with sincere but misplaced fervor,

28. *Cartas*, p. 128; see also pp. 151, 162, etc.

29. Ibid., pp. 2, 33, etc.; on Moxó's criticisms of Clavigero, see J. Le Riverend Brusone, preface, pp. 23–24.

30. Moxó talks of "corners." But de Pauw: "Our rye and our wheat have not taken hold, except in some areas in the north" (op. cit., I, 14). And in the *Défense* he is in fact even more moderate, recognizing that "wheat and rye . . . in the northern provinces . . . have produced quite good crops" (op. cit., p. 108).

31. De Pauw does actually say something like this in the *Défense*, p. 53.

"who like me has watched the dedication of these poor Indians; anyone who has seen them, as I have, laboring almost all day to tickle the palates of the Europeans and Creoles," while "for themselves they are content with the crude juice extracted from the agave or pita, and a few tortillas" cannot restrain his scorn when he reads the slanders of a philosopher against "a nation whose industry, patience, and carefulness have been and still are so useful to Europe" (pp. 30–31). As if the not always spontaneous sobriety of the Mexican Indian and the usefulness of his labors were arguments against the technical superiority of Europe's agriculture!

Some of de Pauw's other characteristic and by now almost proverbial "calumnies" are more swiftly despatched; the suggestion that the *indios* are much subject to baldness, that the American men have milk at their breasts, that there are no fossil shells in America; that the meat of the iguana causes syphilis, or that there are frogs which "roar like heifers" (pp. 33–34).[32] He justifies his delaying so long over these fairy tales by the fact that "Forster, although such a great naturalist, often refers to the philosophical investigations as a very sound and exact book";[33] and the letter concludes by agreeing with Buffon's severe but respectful judgment on de Pauw.

The following letter, the fifth, revives the polemic that seemed already dead. Moxó summarily denounces the "specious and ridiculous system of the degeneration of the Americans," which he attributes to de Pauw's antireligions fanaticism, refutes his interpretation of Pope Paul III's

32. De Pauw, following Oviedo and Gómara, says (op. cit., I, 17) that the meat of the iguana is harmful to anyone who already had syphilis, in overt or latent form. He affirms the existence of fossils (I, 23–24). He says that the Americans are hairless, not bald (I, 37–38). For the milk in their breasts, see I, 43–44. One would actually think Father Moxó had not read more than thirty or forty pages of de Pauw's book. The inventory of his library (in Vargas Ugarte, op. cit., xxix–li) includes the works of Nuix, Clavigero, and Molina, and others referring to America, but *not* de Pauw's book. And lastly as for the "frogs . . . whose cry imitates the lowing of bullocks," see de Pauw, op. cit., I, 8, quoting Dumont, *Mémoires sur la Louisiane,* 1753 (a sentence, I, 103, transcribed by Church too, op. cit., p. 185). De Pauw (and Pernety, who agrees with him on this point of fact: *Dissertation,* p. 42) had already been contradicted by Clavigero, *Storia antica,* IV, 83. But even in 1697–1698 a Bostonian had written about a fat local frog crying "exactly like a Bull" (Kraus, *Atlantic Civilization,* p. 175). In 1773 the German translation of *Le voyageur français* (*Reisen eines Franzosen,* the collection of the Abbé de la Porte, for whom see J. M. Quérard, *La France littéraire, sub voce,* IV, 2, 551), comes back to the frogs as big as young goats (see Reed, art. cit., p. 62). Smith assures us that the bullfrog "emits the most terrible bellows, stronger than the roaring of the bull" (J. F. Smith, *Voyage,* I, 19, 32). And an attentive observer like Castiglioni repeats that near Lake George (now Horicon Lake, New York) he heard croaking among the thousands of frogs "that one peculiar to America called the *Rana Bovina* (Linnaeus: *Rana boans; Bullfrog* in English), which . . . with its cry imitates very closely the roaring of an ox" (*Viaggio negli Stati Uniti,* I, 159). See also Kant, *Reflexionen zur physische Geographie,* Akad.-Ausg., XIV, 634–35; Chateaubriand, *Les Natchez,* in *Oeuvres complètes* (Paris, 1826), XX, 149; *Voyage en Amérique,* and "A. Mackenzie," in *Mélanges littéraires* (ed. Paris, 1859), pp. 78, 412; E. Quinet, *La Création,* in *Oeuvres complètes,* XXII–XXIII (Paris, n.d.), I, 142. On the bullfrogs imported into the Bassa Mantovana from Brazil in 1930, and thought by the terrified peasants of the Ferrarese to be some fearful monsters, see *Corriere della Sera,* 21–22 May 1957, and 30–31 July 1964.

33. *Cartas,* p. 34; cf. above, p. 171.

bull (pp. 36–37), and passes on to other matters, without however forgetting the vexatious Prussian philosopher.[34]

The remainder of the book discloses the real aim of his apology and the incidental character of his quarrel with de Pauw. Moxó maintains that the ancient Mexicans, and the Americans in general, attained a high level of civilization and social organization; that they are neither inferior to the Europeans, nor degenerate, nor forced to live on a dry and barren soil — and this is where he takes issue with the slanderers of America. But despite all these natural advantages, or at least equivalencies, they were addicted to bloody human sacrifices, cannibalism, and anthropophagy. (In his twelfth letter Moxó gives a curious analysis of "four classes into which anthropophagy can conveniently be divided," in the third of which, religious anthropophagy, he includes the Mexicans). What did they lack then? The answer is obvious: Christian religiosity, and Spanish arms to enforce it.[35]

The uncertainty of Moxó's position, defending Spain one minute and the *indios* the next,[36] in a frank attempt to reconcile his patriotic feelings for his country with his pastoral feelings for his flock, comes out clearly in an item of biographical detail. In 1806, when he sent the *Cartas mexicanas* to the still all-powerful minister Godoy, Moxó wrote: "My love for our country . . . made me take up my pen . . . but I was inspired above all by my anxious desire to assure our Sovereign, in the only way I have yet been able to, of my undying gratitude."[37] The *Cartas* was a homage to Spain and the king.

Nine years later, in May 1815, the Argentinian general Rondeau successfully invaded Upper Peru, and ordered the arrest and deportation of the loyalist Archbishop Moxó. On his enforced journey to Salta, Moxó drafted (18 September 1815) an impassioned "letter to the Americans, written on the road to exile," reminding them of his many services and his constant affection for America, "my second and sweet fatherland."[38]

34. In fact he still quotes him frequently, on the subject of Robertson, p. 52; the Mexicans' writing, p. 57; and on pp. 60–63, 69, 75, 173, 181, 216, etc. Moxó also mentions Humboldt's arrival in Mexico in 1803; but he expresses some doubt about what this other Prussian will manage to write (p. 6). The contrast between the good Prussian Humboldt and the bad Prussian de Pauw can be seen in Caldas, Valle, and other Americans.

35. Elsewhere (p. 298), Moxó inconsistently defends the human sacrifices of the Americans by recalling those practiced by the illustrious nations of the Old World, which should make us excuse "some poor savages dwelling in the furthest corners of the world," if they did the same. Cf. below, chap. 9, sec. 3, "The Mexicans' Human Sacrifices."

36. But after being in Peru he characterized the indios — with further and even more flagrant inconsistency — as being weak in body (those once robust porters passing below his balcony!), melancholy, timid, sluggish, in fact downright lazy, apathetic, and puerile (*Cartas*, 2d ed., pp. 384, 398–99, 400).

37. Vargas Ugarte, *Moxó*, pp. 53–54.

38. *Cartas*, p. xxii. A little further on, in fact, his second fatherland actually becomes his first: "My country Catalonia can surely not be offended if I give to this soil and to you a preference dictated by reason, ordained by Religion and demanded by gratitude and honor" (ibid., p. xxvi). Moxó is praised as a "victim of Spanish loyalty" by Menéndez y Pelayo, *Los heterodoxos españoles*, VI, 447n.

Foremost among the services rendered, the Archbishop mentions his *Cartas mexicanas*. No sooner had he arrived in America than he saw that it suffered "great and cruel hardships. Then I took up my pen in its defense, and spent many days and nights composing the two thick volumes of the *Cartas mexicanas*." Not a word about his defense of Spain and the king. Instead, with pardonable opportunism, the patriots' prisoner-archbishop writes: "Love and zeal for the interests of America overcame all considerations of flesh and blood, in an age when because of the intrigues and colossal power of the favorite Godoy, the whole monarchy shook constantly with the destructive tremors of arbitrariness." In further equally orotund phrases Moxó goes on to assert that it was his writing which lifted the veil that for many years had kept hidden a long and oppressive series of disorders, political errors, repeated insults and misdeeds; it was he who restored the true and sacred rights of man, described the wretched state of the agriculture, industry, and trade, and invoked liberty and equality for the Americans; and who from Lima, having signed the work "with my own hand," sent it "to the Court of Madrid with a fat letter of credit" and firm instructions to his procurator to get it printed as soon as possible.

The manuscript, still unpublished, which in 1805 had been offered to Godoy as a reply to the foreigners who had dared to criticize Spain's work "both in the matter of the *conquest* of those vast *colonies,* and in the matter of her new policy and government" (pp. 53–54), now becomes a denunciation of the evils of the Spanish administration, and an invitation to recognize the fact "that America was *not* a *colony,* but an integral part of the kingdom."[39]

The archbishop died barely six months later. Thus the letter to the Americans should be read as an apology *in extremis.* Its inconsistencies are to be ascribed more to the loose thinking and occasional straightforward shallowness of the writer than to any improbity on the part of the man, who in many other accounts is seen as a pious, charitable, and honorable person.

VI. UNÁNUE: LIMA'S CLIMATE AND HER COLLEGIANS' ERUDITION

At the same time that Moxó was composing his *Cartas,* a distinguished doctor and patriot of Lima, Hipólito Unánue, a colleague and rival of Jose Dávalos, was putting the finishing touches to his classic *Observations on the Climate of Lima and Its Influence on Organic Beings,*

---

39. Op. cit., pp. xxii–xxiii; my italics. On Moxó's pusillanimous ambiguity, see G. René-Moreno, *Bolivia y Perú—Más notas históricas y bibliográficas* (Santiago, 1905), pp. 173–88. His first editor, Andrés Herrero, in his turn rejects the *leyenda negra,* recalling the "horrific crimes" committed by the rebellious Creoles, not against "savage Indians," but against the Spanish, "very worthy persons, and related by flesh and blood" (prologue to the Genoa edition, 1837, s.p.).

Especially Men, which was published in that same city in the following year, 1806.[40]

Unánue in general does not believe in the decisive influence of climate: even if in warm climates there are physical factors tending to induce laziness and inertia, there are moral factors in man which are enough not just to counterbalance them, but to nullify them completely. And with an ingenious transposition of Montesquieu's thesis (see above, chap. 2, n. 27), he goes on to tell us that it is not climate that enslaves men, but slavery that makes them cowardly and idle.[41]

In the case in point, however, Peru's climate is not tropical, but temperate and benign. Buffon's and de Pauw's theories have no possible application to Peru. Unánue, who has read the Italian Gian Rinaldo Carli's *American Letters* (pp. 19, 73, 78) and the North American Jefferson's *Notes on Virginia* (pp. 54, 65, 77), is firmly opposed to the French naturalist, and has nothing but scorn and contempt for the German abbé. The cold which according to de Pauw[42] destroys American vegetation "is one of those deductions born of prejudice and ignorance" (p. 49). And to the "farfetched imagination of certain overseas Philosophers" who dipped their brushes in "black and acrid shades" to portray these areas as an accursed land, a "dismal refuge of snakes, crocodiles, and other poisonous monsters," the wise physician does not even deign to reply: his irony is satisfied when he annotates the thesis with a quotation from Horace: "Quale portentum neque militaris / Daunias latis alit aesculetis / Nec Jubae tellus generat, leonum / Arida nutrix" (p. 54).[43]

Buffon's theories are summarized and discarded in the same page. But a little further on Unánue accepts Humboldt's word for it that in America the domestic animals too, the dogs for example, are "of more tractable disposition, or even possibly more cowardly than those of Europe" (p. 40). Which is commented on and justified with one of his wry poetic reminiscences, the well-known couplet from the *Gerusalemme liberata* (I, 62): "The soft and happy and delightful earth, / Produces inhabitants

40. I am quoting from the edition of Barcelona, 1914 (vol. I of the *Obras científicas y literarias*). A further edition, prepared by C. E. Paz Soldán, and based on the 2d ed. (Madrid, 1815), appeared in Lima in 1940. Moxó read it as soon as it was published and mentions it with glowing praise in one of the appendices of the *Cartas*, 2d ed., pp. 387–88.

41. *Observaciones,* I, 68; *Discurso sobre si el clima influye o no en las costumbres de los habitantes,* ibid., II, 53–55.

42. See in fact the *Recherches,* I, 9.

43. *Observaciones,* p. 54; Horace, *Carmina,* I, 22, lines 13–16: "Such a beast as neither warlike Apulia / Nourishes in forests of oak trees spreading / Nor the land of Juba has ever borne, that / Dry nurse of lions" (trans. H. R. Henze). But the quotation is hardly appropriate: Buffon specifically denies that America is "dry," and even more that it is the "nurse of lions." Buffon is quoted also in various other writings: see *Obras,* II, 159, 173, 283, 285. Unánue mentions Raynal in passing (I, 78; II, 230–31) and knows A. de Ulloa's *Entretenimientos* well (I, 18, 92, 115, 137; II, 8–9, 12, 16, 109–10, 156, 186, 282–83, 287, 291).

like unto itself," applied to the dogs!—the usual melodious resolution of his scientific arguments.

Metastasio's heroes had the same habit of winding up their recitatives, mixtures of septenaries and hendecasyllables, with a musical ditty in octosyllables. These aphoristic little verses rob the dramatic tirade of all forcefulness, and dissolve the rhetoric in a proverb. Unánue's lines are one more proof of the traditional familiarity of Aesculapius with the Muses, and reveal the good man of letters beneath the doctor's cloak, the humanist's elegance waiting to seep through between the cracks in the physicoclinical dissertation.

In a work written a few years before the *Observations*, Unánue had described the great Inca highways and noted sarcastically how "Mister [*sic*] Pauw and certain others denied the existence of these roads";[44] to refute them, he reverted to the usual tactic of rhyme:

> Pero quien podrá convencer
> Las testas en que el tino
> Perdieron, de tal modo,
> Que acaso restaurarle no podría
> El eléboro todo
> Que en tres islas Antícirias se creia?[45]

Yet Unánue recognizes a singular virtue in de Pauw: that of having so provoked the susceptibilities of the Peruvians with his attacks that he brought about a remarkable improvement in the study of the exact sciences in Lima: "De Pauw took it into his mind, among his many errors, that Godin did not find a single person in Lima who could understand a lesson in Mathematics" (p. 123; see above, p. 291). This is indeed what de Pauw says (*Recherches*, II, 166). But the accusation cannot have been altogether undeserved. Already in 1689 the viceroy Duke de la Palata was bewailing the fact that the chair of mathematics in the University of San Marcos did not have a single student, so that "the incumbent cannot comply with his obligation to read [mathematics] because he has no one to read it to."[46] Scarcely two months before the publication of de Pauw's *Recherches* a prominent Liman, José Eusebio de Llano Zapata, was lamenting that mathematics,

44. De Pauw denies all Garcilaso's assertions *en bloc* (op. cit., II, 176–77), but I do not believe he *ever* speaks of the undeniable Inca roads.

45. *Discurso histórico sobre el nuevo camino del Callao, año de 1801*, in *Obras*, II, 186n. 2. The lines are attributed to "Iriarte A. P." (Tomás de Iriarte, author [1777] of a famous paraphrase of Horace's *Poetic Art;* cf. *Ars Poetica*, line 300). For further defense of the Inca roads against the denigrations of encyclopedists and lying cosmopolitan philosophers, see the *Idea general de los monumentos del antiguo Perú*, in *Obras*, II, 197, n. 2. And on the false descriptions of Peru produced in Paris or London, see *Una idea general del Perú*, ibid., II, 291–92. But Unánue is an admirer of that "philosopher worthy of this title," Bernardin de Saint-Pierre, and quotes a typical passage from his *Etudes de la Nature*, referring to the evils brought to Asia and America by the Europeans (II, 324–25).

46. F. Barreda Laos, "Vida intelectual del virreinato del Perú," *Historia de la nación argentina*, ed. R. Levene, vol. 3 (Buenos Aires, 1937), pp. 142–43.

that science so useful to the military, has there [in Peru] been not only ignored, but actually unknown. Our people have contented themselves with a slight smattering of astrology, which has been enough for them to obtain the chair of mathematics. There has never been any competition for it, the first person to present himself with letters of recommendation gaining it on his own word.[47]

And again in 1794 and 1795 the Rector of the College of San Carlos, Dr. Toribio Rodríguez Mendoza, addressed himself repeatedly to the king of Spain and the viceroy Taboada y Lemos to deplore the fact that the study of mathematics was once again completely neglected; that "there have never been rival candidates presenting themselves to compete" for the chair in question; that the students had looked on mathematics with "boredom and disdain," so that its teaching had been abandoned "for lack of listeners"; and to request finally, as a remedy to such a "shameful experience" and a stimulus to useful discoveries ("the American soil is very fertile, and contains an immense unknown treasure"), that a new chair might be endowed in the Caroline College.[48]

But Unánue claims that on becoming aware of these charges of ignorance, "the honor of Peru was roused, and to give proof of the contrary it embraced this study with much diligence. It is amazing to see the children of the Caroline College present themselves for the examinations in Mathematics and Physics, proficient in an incredible number of propositions, even the most difficult ones."[49]

And so the debate continues, from Buffon's tragic deductions trampling underfoot the whole animal kingdom, and de Pauw's terrifying sentences of degeneration oppressing and dragging down all America, all the way to these infant prodigies, these little pupils so well prepared that no exam worries them, from cowardly lions to prize classroom grinds — and another subtly humorous contrast emerges from the successive stages of the polemic's progress.

VII. DÁVILA CONDEMARÍN: A BELATED APOLOGY OF THE UNIVERSITY OF SAN MARCOS

Here we must digress and momentarily disregard chronology to consider a sort of postscript to Unánue, as expressed in the writing of another

47. Letter of 16 December 1766 to Don José Perfecto de Salas in *Revista Chilena de Historia y Geografía*, 92 (1942), pp. 214–15.
48. See the curious documents published in *Anales de la Universidad Mayor de San Marcos*, n. 2 (1950), pp. 12–25. In 1802 Humboldt is still found complaining that very few natives take an interest in the sciences (Minguet, op. cit., p. 175).
49. Op. cit., p. 123. This paragraph too closes poetically with the white swans rescuing from oblivion "the worthy names, which lasting praise should gain" (*Orlando furioso*, XXV, 14). In a letter to Jeremy Robinson (1818?) Unánue again defends the scientific worthiness of the American territories "once held to be barbarous"·(letter in R. Vargas Ugarte, *Manuscritos peruanos en las bibliotecas de América* [Buenos Aires, 1945], p. 321). On the brilliance of the young Carolingians, which apparently astounded Malaspina and various European professors, see also the other *Informe* of the above-mentioned Rodríguez de Mendoza, quoted by R. Porras Barrenechea in *Revista Histórica* (Lima), 17, p. 217 (cited in the *Anales*, loc. cit., p. 13).

learned Peruvian who resumed and continued the defense of Liman culture in the middle of the nineteenth century.

There is in fact a clear if belated echo of these academic reactions, these polemics revolving round the prestige of an institution rather than the truth of an assertion, in the historical eulogy of the University of San Marcos composed by its rector, José Dávila Condemarín, immediately after his election, for the purpose of interesting public opinion in the reform of the atheneum, which by then was in a state of decay and impoverishment.[50]

No sooner has Dávila Condemarín completed his listing of its scientific glories than he reminds his readers that in spite of everything there were "foreign writers" who sought to obscure them. And as usual these many or few "foreign writers" are quickly reduced to "one of them, the Prussian Mr. Pauw," on whom the Peruvian unleashes his full fury. Dávila Condemarín is aware that Pauw bases his theories "on the physical constitution of the earth of America," and its climate which favors only poisonous snakes and animals (p. 16). But he concentrates his attack on two of the Prussian's charges: that San Marcos never produced anyone capable of writing even a bad book, and that Godin found no students there capable of following him. To these charges he replies with facts, examples, and quotations from numerous other adversaries of de Pauw, and also with the surprising insinuation, attributed admittedly to "an erudite Mexican," that de Pauw's hatred for the Americans was only equaled by his love for America's *pesos* and doubloons (p. 17).

Dávila Condemarín's work is singularly well documented. He knows the details of de Pauw's life and recognizes his talent. But de Pauw misused this talent with his calculations and conjectures on the physical and moral characteristics of the Americans, in which he disregarded historians and eyewitnesses and insisted "on using only his own bad judgment" (p. 66). But his ideas certainly did not go unopposed or uncriticized! Dávila has read the replies of abbé "Crocier" (*sic,* for Croizier, p. 18), of Unánue (pp. 18–19), Carli (p. 20), Pernety (p. 66), and José Manuel Dávalos (p. 66). But de Pauw's notions still rankle with him. When he has completed his polemic note, a friend brings to his attention "the curious *History of the Kingdom of Quito,*" by Juan de Velasco, and he happily proceeds to copy out from it a number of vigorously anti-de Pauwian passages (pp. 67–69).

He finally decides that that must terminate his digression, particularly since "this is not the main object of this work"; but immediately afterward he returns to the attack with the observation that if de Pauw had

50. J. Dávila Condemarín, *Bosquejo histórico de la fundación (y progresos) de la insigne Universidad Mayor de San Marcos de Lima . . .* (Lima, 1854).

lived longer he would have changed his mind, inasmuch as "in these last years" the Europeans have come to realize "that divine providence lavished every sort of benefit on the soil of America."[51] Then as for spiritual goods, or the literary productions of the learned men of Lima, Dávila Condemarín unloads on the unfortunate de Pauw nothing less than the entire works of Peralta y Barnuevo, nineteen of them already printed and some twenty more, mostly treatises on mathematics and law, as yet unpublished. The Prussian disappears from sight beneath this avalanche of folios: "What answers will de Pauw be able to find," Dávila Conde-marín concludes with a sneer, "when he sees the large preceding list, which includes the works written *only* by the Peruvian Peralta?" (p. 71). If perchance he should have anything else to add, the Chancellor is ready with a long list of other authors, some of them no less prolific than Peralta,[52] one final thrust in the form of a couple of anti-de Pauw quota-tions, and as the *coup de grâce* Juan and Ulloa's eulogy of the Creoles' in-telligence.

This time the note really is finished. But the insuppressible polemic crops up again in the following note, which speaks of a sort of solemn ritual of exorcism of de Pauw's slanders, celebrated in Lima in 1793:[53] and further on again, with the explicitly anti-de Pauwian references in the praises heaped on the culture of Lima by the Frenchman Vanieri,[54] and an English journalist in 1826.

Enough? Not yet. "Lastly, to corroborate what has been said to im-pugn de Pauw's falsehoods," the Chancellor of San Marcos invokes other authorities: León Pinelo's bibliographical *Epitome*, the "Diccionario de América de Salcedo" (more properly Alcedo, or rather Antonio de Al-cedo Herrera), a sort of antique *Reader's Digest:* "The Essence of the Best Papers,"[55] and last of all d'Orbigny's *L'Homme américain* (pp. 84–85).

So eighty-six years after its publication de Pauw's *Recherches* still

51. Ibid., p. 70: an allusion to Peruvian guano, or Californian gold? In 1854 de Pauw could have been even more savage than in 1768! Dávila forgets that he himself had bewailed the University's decline in prestige and wealth with the coming of Independence (op. cit., pp. 26–28).

52. Ibid., pp. 72–75. The list seems to be derived from Montalvo: it includes only authors of the six-teenth and seventeenth centuries, among whom are Juan de Castellanos, Garcilaso, Calancha, Antonio de León Pinelo, etc., to which he adds Olavide, but no contemporary authors (ibid., p. 75).

53. "The Seminary of San Carlos dedicated to the University in the year 1793 a public act of *philoso-phy and mathematics* under the presidency of the *immortal Señor Moreno* (José Ignacio Moreno). . . . In the dedication, after praising the vast erudition in the sciences of which the academy could boast in all times, he limits himself to the refutation of Pauw and particularly his proposition concerning Mr. Goudin, giving also an idea of the state of advancement in which the sciences are found in the country. See the *Mercurio Peruano*, VIII, 280 ff., in which notice is given of this literary ceremony" (op. cit., p. 76).

54. In other words the Jesuit Jacques Vanière, author of the *Praedium rusticum* (1730), already cited for this eulogy of the culture of Lima by Eguiara y Eguren too. *Prólogos*, pp. 140–41.

55. On this review, which lasted until 1791, and its diffusion in America, see S. de Madariaga, *Cuadro histórico*, pp. 198, 804, 813; R. Herr, op. cit., pp. 190–98.

had its venom, and could still provoke replies aimed personally and directly at its author, though no longer with the same air of anger and outrage. But we must get back to the beginning of the nineteenth century.

VIII. CALDAS AND THE COLD IN NEW GRANADA

Two years after Unánue had brought out his shrewd *Observations on the Climate of Lima* the eminent naturalist José Francisco de Caldas, astronomer and botanist, disciple and continuator of the great Mutis, and in Quito companion of Humboldt[56] (whom he tried desperately but vainly to follow on his travels to Peru and Mexico), began publication in Bogotá of his *Semanario del Nuevo Reino de Granada* (1808), in whose first number he included an apologetic description of its physical and economic geography.

In contrast to the other American naturalists Caldas fully accepts Buffon's zoological theories. Interested primarily in the New World's physical nature and flora, he makes no attempt to defend its fauna. His memorandum *On the importance of naturalizing the vicuña of Peru and Chile in the kingdom* (1810) begins: "When we compare the animals of the old Continent with those of the New, we have to agree with Buffon that ours are dwarves, mutilated, weak. . . . The llama, the alpaca, and the vicuña show us the dromedary and the camel in miniature." However, the practical-minded naturalist goes on, this is no reason why we should neglect these auchenia, which are so useful for transportation, food, and in the case of the vicuña, for very fine wool, "the silk of the new Continent." "Yes, the vicuña is a treasure," Caldas repeats, and goes on to examine ways of acclimatizing it in the New Granadan *sierras* of Santa Marta and Sante Fe.[57]

But when he comes to the description of his country the patriot Caldas—who died before a Spanish firing squad in 1816—finds there is plenty to content him. In more than one place the report becomes a plain panegyric. In particular the geographical position of New Granada (present-day Colombia) arouses the publicist's enthusiasm. It "occupies the center of the new continent," so that it seems destined to have "all the world's trade." The mineral riches of Peru and Mexico are equaled by those of the Granadan Andes. And how can Peru "tucked away on a barren part of the Pacific coast," and Mexico, which is a little better placed between the tropic and the temperate zone, hope to compete with

---

56. On Humboldt and Mutis, see *Revista de Historia de América*, 48 (December 1959), pp. 488–505; on Mutis, J. Sarrailh, op. cit., p. 443, etc. On Humboldt and his *brouille* with Caldas, see Minguet, op. cit., pp. 169, 268–69.

57. *Obras de Caldas*, ed. Eduardo Posada (Bogotà, 1912), pp. 481–93. But see below, p. 311. On the recent attempts to acclimatize the auchenia in Colombia, see W. Hellmich, "Die Bedeutung des Andenraumes im biogeographischen Bilde Südamerikas," in *Tier und Umwelt in Südamerika*, esp. p. 89.

the situation and the hydrographic system of the most blessed vice-royalty of Sante Fe? "We have to agree: there is nowhere in the old or the new World better situated than New Granada."[58]

As for climate, Caldas insists especially on the diversity of zones and their products: from the fertile torrid zone, where man "acquires gigantic stature," but is slow-moving and weak, to the Andean areas with their robust inhabitants and beautiful, fine-complexioned women," to the barren and frozen plateaus. And this variety shows him yet another singular privilege of his country: "There are few points on the surface of the globe more advantageous for observing, and one might say touching, the influence of climate and diet on the physical constitution of man, his character, his virtues, and his vices" (p. 7).

This decisive influence attributed to climate aroused the displeasure of one of Caldas's compatriots, don Diego Martín Tanco, who hastened to write him a clever and lively letter (10 February 1808), showing that climate has no influence on either the moral or the physical growth of man: everything depends on man's beliefs and upbringing. Instead of laboring to demonstrate that America's climate is not harmful to man, as was suggested by de Pauw and the slanderers of the continent, or even that it is favorable and beneficial, as maintained by her defenders, Tanco cuts short the argument at the outset by insisting, in open contradiction of Montesquiou, but leaning to some extent on Bernardin de Saint-Pierre, that the climate, whether of America or the Old World, has absolutely nothing whatsoever to do with character. Extreme heat and extreme cold are equally capable of stimulating great passion. But the effect of heat, which is real enough on the generation and development of animals and plants, is nonexistent for man. In any part of the world, whatever the reading on the thermometer, women take nine months to produce their young.

In rebus politicis, there is no foundation for the thesis that ferocity dwells in the north, or liberty in the high mountains. There are "monarchical mountains" (Savoy, parts of the Alps, etc.) and republics in the

---

58. *Semanario de la Nueva Granada* (Paris, 1849), pp. 7–8. And again toward the end of the essay: "We can unite in one point the attractions and riches of all the dwelling places of this vast continent" (p. 29). With similar patriotic devotion Mutis defended the superiority of the New Granada's *quina* over Peru's, and argued fiercely with the findings of the Spanish botanists Ruiz and Pavón (review of Arthur Robert Steele, *Flowers for the King: The Expedition of Ruiz and Pavón and the Flora of Peru* [Durham, N.C., 1964], in *Hispanic American Historical Review*, 45, no. 3 [August 1965], p. 486). Another contributor to the *Semanario,* José Maria de Salazar, who published therein his *Memoria descriptiva del pais de Santa Fé de Bogotá,* complained instead that the position of New Granada was not propitious for civil progress, "since we are separated by an immense sea from Europe and have to exist in obscurity." But he added immediately, as if to reject a damaging suspicion: "This does not mean that we accept the paradox of the Prussian Pauw, who makes us incapable of reason and finds not a single person among us able to compose a book" (cf. in fact the *Recherches,* II, 166–67). Indeed the genius of America will one day offer the world "works of the spirit as admirable as those of nature" (*Semanario,* p. 407). Cf. above, pp. 184–85.

lowlands of Holland, Poland, the Venetian lagoons, and (New?) England. And all these territories, moreover, whether lofty or low-lying, have known a succession of liberal and despotic governments. "Neither cold nor heat give men the strong desire for liberty, and even less the unjust ambition to rob others of theirs." The same can be said for amorous passion, which the "climatist philosophers" distribute among the various peoples — but always reserving for their own nation the qualities of war-like valor and erotic vigor.[59] The truth is that "in all countries love is a torrid zone for the heart of man"!

And not only that: in the same climate there are actors and anchorites, who are certainly more different from each other than a Swede and a Chinese. Also, Tanco continues astutely, with an even more surprising antithesis: "What an enormous difference we find between the Greeks of our day, full of wind, flattery, and trickery, and such lovers of life, and their masters the Turks, so silent, proud, sincere, and ever ready to face death!"[60] Yet for centuries they have been living in the same climate and eating the same food.

To those who would suggest that the explanation lies in race, Tanco replies by resolutely denying that blood has any more significance than climate. Those formidable Turks are usually Janissaries of pure Hellenic stock. The *bayadères* and the ascetics of India belong to the same race. And every criminal or tyrant is the brother or son of a philanthropist or philosopher. Man is always free to lean toward vice or virtue. Both reason and moral sense demand as much.[61]

In reply to Tanco's extreme objections, Caldas composed what is per-haps his best-known work, *On the Influence of Climate on Organic Beings,* in which he looks for a middle way between those who "concede

---

59. Robertson too had held that "cold and temperate countries appear to be the favourite seat of free-dom and independence" (*History of America,* I, 343) and de Maistre had repeated that "it is in the midst of the forests and the ice of the North that our governments were born" (*Etude sur la souveraineté,* in *Oeuvres inédites* [Paris, 1870], p. 319). And Melville too was to return to the same theme (1849) with his assertion that "freedom was born among the wild eyries in the mountains," while the plains favored slavery: *Mardi,* CLXI, in *Romances* (New York, 1931), p. 667. But Tanco comes back to Hume's criti-cism (see above, pp. 41–42), in fact in a way completes it by pointing out the occult *political* motive of so many pseudoclimatic theories. Aristotle had already deduced from Greece's climatic position, in a temperate zone, its capacity to live in liberty and also "dominate all others, as soon as it was joined to-gether in a single state" (*Politics,* 1327b). The Spaniards easily persuaded themselves that the climate of the West Indies predisposed its inhabitants to be enslaved to the Iberians (see above, pp. 74–75), and later they held firmly to the belief that even the descendants of Spaniards, the Creoles, enfeebled by the climate, were less capable of governing than the peninsulars (see above, pp. 182–83).

60. Cf.: "The Greeks, their enemies tell us, are lying, perfidious, miserly, cowardly, and skulking; and in contrast with this picture we are shown . . . that of the good faith of the Turks, and their singular virtues" (Chateaubriand, *Itinéraire de Paris à Jérusalem,* Avant-Propos [ed. Paris, 1854], I, 22). The idealization of the Muslims, that had come into vogue at the beginning of the eighteenth century, is quite evident in these passages (Henri Baudet, *Paradise on Earth: Some Thoughts on European Images of Non-European Man* [New Haven, 1965], pp. 47–48, 50).

61. *Semanario,* pp. 49–55. Cf. Dante, *Paradiso,* VIII, 130–33.

nothing to climate" and those who give it "an unlimited power."[62] Climate *influences* man's physical development, quite obviously, and thereby *contributes* to his moral character. The human will is still free to choose between good and evil. Race exists too, without a doubt: common physical and moral features characterize many families; but on this point, which he did not cover in his original work, Caldas feels he is under no obligation to reply.[63] He dwells instead on the matter of heat and cold, which "are what separated out all the animals on the earth," and modified their qualities. "What is the American leopard or lion compared with the animals that bear these same names in the old continent?" The plants are likewise subject "to the imperious laws of heat and cold" (pp. 121–22). Only man lives and rules in all corners of the earth.

The Buffonian original of this rigorous exclusion of man is unmistakable: the French naturalist is frequently and lavishly praised, there are verbal coincidences,[64] and finally, in the passage immediately following, de Pauw—the writer who first extended Buffon's climatic degeneration to man—is assailed with a ferocity quite out of proportion to the point under discussion, a quite incidental and unimportant one. Caldas points out that the annual temperature range in the higher regions of New Granada is considerably smaller than in the Old World. But after these precise thermometric observations he bursts out with this sudden tirade:

We do not wish to infer from this, as does de Pauw, that obstinate enemy of all things good in America, that the cold of this vast continent is extraordinary, that it has caused the extinction of the larger animal species, that it has so weakened man that he has lost his beard and all interest in the propagation of his kind, that lactation lasts ten years, and finally, that the native of these regions, ever stupid, in every way insensitive, never sheds a tear, never heaves a sigh even amidst the most cruel torments. We shall never subscribe to these ravings of the Prussian philosopher.

New Granada may not be equatorial Africa; but it is still a lot warmer than Europe. Let de Pauw measure the difference, "and tell us whether New Granada is colder than Prussia, Germany, and all those countries in

62. *Semanario*, p. 111; cf. A. P. Whitaker, "The Americas in the Atlantic Triangle," in Hanke, ed., *Common History*, pp. 148–49, and Andrés Soriano Lleras, "F. J. de Caldas y la medicina," *Boletín Cultural y Bibliográfico* (Bogotà, Banco de la República), 9, no. 10 (1966), pp. 1953–55.

63. *Semanario*, p. 115n. Thus one is amazed to see attributed to Caldas the paternity of "the theory of the formation of the human races under the influence of the earth, the climate and atmospheric pressure, which has become one of the commonplaces of contemporary ethnology and philosophy" (J. Mancini, *Bolivar et l'émancipation des colonies espagnoles des origines à 1815* [Paris, 1912], p. 21n., which quotes M. Vergara y Vergara, *Historia de la literatura en Nueva Granada*, 1867, pt. I, p. 393).

64. Cf. Buffon, in passage quoted above, chap. 1, n. 55, and Caldas: "Black below the line, olive-colored in Mauretania and Egypt, dark in Italy . . . the color of his face has a constant relationship to the latitude" (ibid., pp. 123–24). And cf. Buffon on the decadence of the domestic animals, and the resulting variability of their coloring (cf. also above, p. 26), with Caldas: "The domestic animals . . . have become corrupted in their natural qualities. . . . Their skin colors have varied remarkably, and they have lost the simple and uniform clothing that nature gave them" (ibid., pp. 153–54). In Caldas there is however no deploring of this variability.

which man has reached perfection; whether here the cold can produce the dreams and fancies he invented, without warrant or knowledge, about the most beautiful and fruitful country in the world" (pp. 126–27).

Now as a matter of fact de Pauw does indeed write that "it is readily noticeable that the air in the New World is less warm than in the old continent," but from this observation, which appears at the very beginning of the *Recherches*,[65] he does not actually derive the series of consequences mentioned by Caldas, which come instead, as we know, from a whole theory of humidity, putrefaction, and fermentation, in which "the heat of the sun"[66] is implicitly an essential factor. So we have one more confirmation of the fact that de Pauw was considerably more famed as a typical slanderer of America than he was ever actually read and studied. At the mere mention of his name the learned Creole was overcome with rage, and drawn, regardless of relevance, into unburdening himself of his patriotic ire at the expense of the chosen sacrificial victim. Buffon's distinguished profile had seemed hardly a fitting target, so it was on the Prussian's head that the rain of missiles fell.[67] The transformation of the polemic is complete: it is no longer a scientific debate but a symbolic execution in effigy.

IX. THE MEXICAN S. T. DE MIER AND DE PAUW IN THE *CORTES* OF CADIZ

Another resounding symbolic execution was the one performed by Mier, the Mexican patriot and sworn enemy of the Spaniards, who main-

65. Op. cit., I, 11. For the reference to large animals, see ibid., I, 4, 12; for beards, etc., I, 37; for decennial lactation, I, 54. The passage on the insensibility of the savages seems to derive from the *Recherches*, I, 71–72. On this latter subject note that Caldas himself avoids describing the habits and customs, virtues and vices of the inhabitants of New Granada: "This object . . . would bring down on us the odium and indignation of our compatriots" (*Semanario*, p. 128); and that in a work of 1803 he wondered what "sad causes and what influences contrary to our happiness" accounted for the demographic decline of the *indios* (*Viaje de Quito a las costas del Oceano Pacífico*, in D. Mendoza, *Expedición botánica de J. C. Mutis al Nuevo Reino de Granada y Memorias inéditas de F. J. de Caldas* [Madrid, 1909], II, 62).

66. *Recherches*, I, 5; cf. ibid., I, 184–85, 190, etc. Caldas also mentions Carli ("what sort of upset would [the archeological exploration of America] bring about in Carli's ideas?" *Semanario*, p. 547); Saint-Pierre, whom he considers very inferior to the "French Pliny," or Buffon (although, as an American, Caldas should have sympathized, like Unánue, rather with the former than the latter); Muñoz (ibid., p. 547) and Unánue (p. 482, 501–02); and even Raynal (ibid., p. 115n.; quoted also by Salazar, ibid., p. 396n.) for the passage quoted above, chap. 2, n. 51. As early as 1782 an official of Victoria (in present-day Venezuela) was asking a French officer to get him the abbé Raynal's famous work (*Journal de voyage du Prince de Broglie* . . . , in *Mélanges publiés par la Société des Bibliophiles Français* [Paris, 1903], p. 140, n. 6).

67. Cf. Moxó, pp. 327–30n. Buffon had been well known in America for decades. And if he was in general much respected there were not infrequent reservations, from the point of view of orthodoxy. In a curious letter (anonymous; the letter is signed: "The doctor who is the same forward as backward," followed by a flourish), addressed to Don Mariano Ioseph de Alcozer, and dated Lima 24 March 1772, there are cited "the works of Monsieur Buffon, which are very common, and which contain fourteen propositions, for which he was justly condemned by the theological faculty at Paris, for having overreached himself in matters outside of his own domain, as usually happens with these fashionable charlatans" (p. 7 of the autograph in a miscellany of manuscripts and prints of the eighteenth century, in the Archives of the University of San Marcos).

tained that Christianity was already known to the Americans before Columbus,[68] and thus they owed nothing to Spain and the Old World.

With Mier we are of course a long way from the discussions of zoological species and the races of the continent (and even further from any enthusiasm for the young world, to be shaped *ex novo*). But de Pauw was so much read and his thesis so subtly corrosive that more than once Mier reveals at least an indirect knowledge of his work, acquired most probably through the replies of Carli and numerous other critics, whom Mier mentions and often quotes directly.[69]

Count Carli, we may remember, finding de Pauw so scornful of all the achievements of the ancient Incas, had suspected him of being the reincarnation of Fray Vicente de Valverde. Fray Servando, quoting Carli, says several times that de Pauw relied on a Spanish correspondent, or wrote at the suggestion of a Spaniard,[70] or quite simply at the dictation of the Spaniards. In his major work, after mentioning how grateful the Spaniards are to de Pauw for collecting together all their calumnies on America,[71] Mier sums up:

68. Chapman (1613) had already supposed that the American natives were acquainted with the Gospel (A. L. Rowse, *The Elizabethans and America*, pp. 201–02) and today again Prof. Corrado Gini, following in Heyerdahl's footsteps, writes of the mythical Quetzalcoatl: "Everything leads one to believe that he was an Irish monk" (art. cit., p. 1407). On the question of the Cross being known in Mexico before "Christopher" Columbus, see Frances Calderón de la Barca, *Life in Mexico* (Garden City, N.Y., n.d.), pp. 364–65. Mier's thesis (for which see Gerbi, *Viejas polémicas*, pp. 275–78) came back, after a century's interval, to those of the seventeenth-century apologists who had affirmed that the religion of the Chinese (Confucianism) coincided with Christianity. Thus already Matteo Ricci and "Père Louis Lecomte, in his Mémoires sur la Chine, one of the most bitterly attacked works of Jesuit sinophile propaganda, declared in 1686 that for five thousand years the Chinese had had a knowledge of the true God" (Arnold H. Rowbotham, "The Jesuit Figurists and Eighteenth-Century Religious Thought," *Journal of the History of Ideas*, 17, no. 4 [October 1956], p. 473). Lafitau had already tried "to do for America what the Figurists had tried to do for China, that is to say, to bring the country, historically, within the circle of Judaico-Christian tradition" (ibid., pp. 482–83). The originality of Mier consists in having tried to utilize the obviously apologetic and historiographical thesis for patriotic and nationalistic ends.

69. Mier was acquainted with and calls himself a friend of Iturri (*Memorias*, p. 318; *Historia de la revolución de Nueva España* . . . , II, 726), of Hervás y Panduro (*Memorias*, p. 318; *Historia*, II, 732, 773; App., xxix; *Escritos inéditos*, p. 252) and Muñoz (*Memorias*, pp. 14, 148, 182, 196–98, 220, 222, 224–25: "my protector"; p. 376; *Historia*, I, 146, 150, 578n.; App., xix). Besides the authors already cited he knows Feijóo (*Escritos inéditos*, p. 265), Buffon (*Historia*, I, 149; *Escritos inéditos*, pp. 273, 346) whose "dreams" on the poverty of American fauna were refuted by Azara (*Historia*, II, 733; cf. in fact E. Cardozo, *Historiografía paraguaya* [Mexico, 1959], pp. 424–25; and on Azara in general, ibid., pp. 401–35), Montesquieu (*Historia*, II, 746: America more important than Spain) and Rousseau (*Historia*, II, 566, or the Social Contract; cf. *Escritos inéditos*, p. 214), and, among the other characters in our polemic, Marmontel (*Historia*, I, 342n.), Father Molina (*Historia*, II, 619, 726, 730, 734); Jefferson (*Historia*, II, 726, 730), abbé Raynal (*Historia*, II, 742–44; *Escritos inéditos*, pp. 100, 199, 312), Robertson (*Historia*, I, 151 ff.; II, App., p. vii), Thomas Paine (*Historia*, II, 743n.; *Escritos inéditos*, p. 359), Unánue (*Historia*, II, 622, for an article in the *Mercurio peruano*, and *Escritos inéditos*, pp. 330, 337, for the *Observaciones*); and various minor figures. For the bibliography, see Gerbi, *Viejas polémicas*, p. 266n.; and also A. Reyes, "Fray Servando Teresa de Mier," in *Obras completas*, III (Mexico, 1956), pp. 433–42.

70. *Memorias*, p. 99.

71. *Historia*, I, xv; the passage quoted below, p. 314. The *Historia* is Mier's greatest literary and theoretical effort, and he was particularly pleased with its fourteenth book (see ibid., II, 563; *Escritos inéditos*, pp. 63, 132, 234n., 249, and 272). But one cannot disagree with Gervinus, who called it a "prolix and clumsy polemic" (*Geschichte des neunzehnten Jahrhunderts*, III, 69), nor with the Mexican Lorenzo de Zavala, who described it as "an indigestible work" (quoted by O'Gorman, "Prólogo" to his anthology of S. T. de Mier [Mexico, 1945], p. xiv).

It is impossible to imitate the picture they paint of them [the Americans] with their pens dipped in cannibals' blood, piling up against America and its natives all the idiocies and insults dictated to de Pauw by these same Spaniards.[72]

It is therefore "necessary to take a broom to this obnoxious beetle, to crush them in their own filth, and provide my compatriots with a little manual of exorcisms against such *antuerpias* [*sic*]."[73]

So what did he actually say, this accursed de Pauw? Ever picturesque rather than precise, Mier tells us: "He said that America is a continent but lately emerged from the waters, and therefore full of foul-smelling and deadly swamps and lagoons" and that "from its putrid marshes have sprung a breed of frogs called *indios*." But these, he concludes impatiently, are "ravings worthy of the padded cell."[74]

Thus whoever attacks de Pauw, the archenemy of the Americans, is greeted enthusiastically by Mier; and whoever defends him or carries on his thesis is Mier's personal archenemy. Fray Servando never tires of expressing his admiration for the most learned philosopher Carli.[75] Although he professes himself ever the devoted friend and admirer of Muñoz, he takes pleasure in referring to Iturri's polemic *Carta*. And when Pedro de Estala compiled his *Universal Traveler* and "copied down all the absurdities and inaccuracies against America and particularly Mexico produced by de Pauw and his successors Raynal, Robertson, and Laharpe," Mier could, of course, no longer contain himself, and assailed him with the sarcasms that were to reopen his long history of trouble with the law.[76]

But the culminating episode in this mortal struggle came in 1811 when the Mexican *Consulado* suggested to the Cortes of Cadiz that the parliamentary representation of New Spain should be cut down, since out of its six million inhabitants, three were *indios,* two were mestizos, and half of the million whites were unworthy of political privileges; and because Mexico was "pervaded by a mood or spirit of indolence and sensuality" and the natives were generally "base and stupid." Enraged at this sudden stab in the back, Mier stepped forward as echo or rather

72. *Historia,* I, 285; *Escritos inéditos,* p. 341.

73. *Historia,* p. xvi. Pauw is "the Prussian beetle" also in *Escritos inéditos,* p. 297. "The *Antuerpia* is a marine boar of which one specimen was seen in '37" (1537: A. de Torquemada, *Jardín de flores curiosas* [Salamanca, 1570], quoted by A. Reyes, "De un autor censurado en el 'Quijote' (Torquemada)," *Cuadernos Americanos,* 6, no. 6 [1947], p. 219).

74. *Memorias,* pp. 99–100. I am omitting some expressions that are repeated identically in the passage quoted below.

75. *Memorias,* pp. 100, 258; *Historia,* II, 726, 730 ("such a great philosopher as Carli"), 737; App., p. xxi, and half a dozen times in the *Escritos inéditos.* Other Italians of his age are mentioned approvingly: Muratori (*Escritos inéditos,* p. 146), Filangeri (*Historia,* II, 629; *Escritos inéditos,* p. 113) and the Italian who wrote on the *quipus* (*Historia,* II, App., p. xviii), i.e., the Conte di San Severo, the anonymous author of the *Lettera apologetica* (Naples, 1750)—while he practically ignores Humboldt (Minguet, op. cit., p. 215n.).

76. *Memorias,* ix, 375–76.

amplifier of the American delegates' indignation, and with his usual vehemence and pertinacity accused the spokesman of the *Consulado,* Francisco Javier Lambarri, of having taken over de Pauw's worst slanders to justify the subjugation of the Americans.

What happened at Cadiz, "that dark and dismal scene," writes Mier, who watched it from up in the tumultuous galleries of the assembly, "deserves a detailed and thorough description." And the description follows, with a new paragraph of its own, and an almost classical fairy-tale opening: "There was once an incredulous man called Pauw, who hailed from Prussia. . . ." But he must have written his book somewhere "beyond the polar circles," such is the "abysmal and absolute" ignorance he demonstrates on the subject of America and things American. In the Prussian's fertile mind

America was in effect a new continent, recently emerged from the waters of the ocean; and being consequently still only half dried out and impregnated with its salts, it was incapable of producing wood or of bringing any fruit to ripeness. All that could be found in it were rushes, fungi, thorn trees, and reptiles. And from its miry ponds and swamps which filled the land crawled forth a species of frogs called *indios,* who managed to speak some rude gibberish, and were thus to be placed in some intermediate position between men and the orangutan apes.

Here again the final conclusion is that Pauw should be put away in an asylum. Yet such was the ungodly frivolity of the age that Voltaire praised the sceptical spirit of that "philosopher"; and furthermore Robertson and Raynal, "two such elegant writers," wrote "at de Pauw's direction." True, there were others that came forward to combat him, men like Carli, Clavigero "in the dissertations attached to his *Historia de Mégico Antiguo,*" Molina, "Madisson in *The* [History] *of Virginia,*"[77] Iturri, Valverde,[78] "and many others." And it is likewise true that a Berlin academic, "M. Pelletier,"[79] twice entered the lists against de Pauw, and the second time forced him to defend himself with the plea "that his Spanish correspondent had misled him." Spanish? Fray Servando smirks contentedly, like a judge who has finally extorted the desired confession: "I had already been thinking that only under such influence could a foreigner write against the Americans, with a pen, as Carli put it, soaked in cannibals' blood."[80]

---

77. *Sic,* but there is no work by James Madison corresponding to this reference. It seems probable that Mier, who was always confusing things, wrote Madison (who for that matter did collaborate on the *Federalist,* for which see above, p. 250) for Jefferson, the author of the *Notes on Virginia.*

78. On Antonio Sánchez Valverde (*Idea del valor de la Isla Española . . . ,* 1785; *Disertación sobre el origen del morbo gálico,* polemicizing with de Pauw: see *Escritos inéditos,* p. 316) see also *Historia,* II, 734, 744.

79. This again seems to be a slip on Mier's part: Pelletier for Pernety.

80. The same metaphor is used by Mier in the *Historia* too, I, 285 (passage quoted above, p. 314) and in the *Memorias,* p. 99. The *topos* of the pen dipped in blood (which Mier gets from Carli; see above,

X. OTHER REACTIONS IN LATIN AMERICA: THE YOUTHFULNESS OF
THE NEW WORLD

Among the patriots of the River Plate, men less rich in cultural traditions, less involved in theological controversies, less sensitive to slanders
of their climate, the reactions to the Europeans' calumnies came mainly in
the form of eulogies of the American nations' dynamic youthfulness. In
1810 Mariano Moreno, a fervent disciple of Rousseau,[81] republished in
the *Gaceta de Buenos Aires* Jefferson's defense of all Americans as a
lusty and energetic race.[82] The Creoles were not the Spaniards' inferiors. The Creoles are not the "yankees'" inferiors.

In the *Lira Argentina,* the 1824 collection of poetic and patriotic compositions dating from 1810 onward, published in Buenos Aires, the New
World–Old World antithesis is repeated with tedious insistence, with all
the facile unquestioning monotony of the timeworn cliché. The New
World figures as humanity's refuge and hope, its supreme citadel. The
same concept appears in Venezuela and Peru, tinged with equivocal
Rousseauian sophisms. Bolivar's teacher, for example, managed to convert Rousseau's axiom on the ethical superiority of the state of nature
over corrupt society into a seal of approval of the continental destiny of
the Americas, as innocent and pure and deserving of independence as
Europe was civilized and therefore decadent.[83]

Once independence had been won the publicists of the new republics
were more than ever convinced of their state of virginal purity. For
these men, nurtured on Rousseau's schemes, the severing of the political
link with Spain represented a sort of resolution of the "social contract,"
a sort of *restitutio in pristinum,* "a return to primal innocence." In 1826
the Peruvian Vidaurre, exaggerating as usual, wrote: "The inhabitants
of those Americas which used to be Spanish . . . restored to the state of
nature, free and independent . . . are more perfect than in the days near

---

p. 236) was current, and usually referred to Draco. In the prologue to the *Jew of Malta,* Marlowe has
Machiavelli say: "Laws were then most sure, when like the Draco's, they were writ in blood." A Spanish
paper of 1765, in mentioning the projected constitution for Corsica prepared by Rousseau, said it was
sure that "Señor Rousseau will not have dipped his pen in blood as Draco did" (Spell, op. cit., pp. 43–44).
Note the deformation of the image on the part of the furious Mier, at first an enemy and then a follower
of Rousseau (ibid., pp. 218, 244–45).

81. Spell, op. cit., pp. 235–38.
82. H. Bernstein, "Some Inter American Aspects of the Enlightenment," in *Latin America and the
Enlightenment,* p. 64. Cf. above, pp. 187–88.
83. Mariano Picón Salas, *Rousseau en Venezuela,* communication to the First Interamerican Conference of Philosophy (1943), reviewed by M. Bunge in *Minerva,* 2 (1944), pp. 163–64. Following the
same ideological line in Europe the Hegelian Michelet saw "the final future of the human race, the extreme development of democratic self-government" precisely in the islands between America and
Oceania, which Hegel had already branded as "immature" (see Croce, *Saggio sullo Hegel,* p. 140).

the creation."[84] They are like Adam, with experience added. They are like Emile, grown-up, victorious, his own lawmaker.

This rhetorical transfiguration of course did little to justify the claims of the Americans, whether of North or South, whether Protestant colonists or Catholic Creoles, that they had a right to be left alone to govern themselves, to try and make their own civilization. But it did give their demands that same absurd half-physiological half-goliardic justification, by which the "young" have greater rights than the "aged," and the assault of the "new" is more legitimate than the resistance of the "old."

This same ardent frenzy had already been satirized by Goethe, in general terms, in the scene of the Baccalaureus (1826–30). And the philosophers teach us that "history . . . knows not old age and youth of peoples nor of individuals in the physiological sense."[85] But the episode is interesting and significant precisely because of its illogicality. So vain and meaningless is the epithet of an age of life applied to a nation or a continent, that in the case of America the same factual data were used to deduce without difficulty both its "youth" and its "decrepitude"; and contradictory corollaries—a glorious future before it or an incurable immaturity and total incapacity for progress—were extracted with equal ease from its supposed "infancy." It was the same ambiguity in this latter term, with its possibility of interpretation as a synonym either of divine innocence or of precocious senility, or dotage, that lent itself to the alternatives in the polemic and the variations of myth, and which continued for some time to stand in the way of a more exact understanding of America and the Americans.

XI. THE HONDURAN J. C. DEL VALLE AND THE MISSION OF AMERICA

These polemics were followed, chronologically though not ideologically, by the criticisms of de Pauw which blossomed in Central America

84. M. de Vidaurre, "Discurso a la Asamblea de Panamá" (22 June 1826), in *Suplemento a las Cartas Americanas,* p. 144.

85. B. Croce, "False lezioni attribuite alla storia," *Il carattere della filosofia moderna,* p. 231; Frédéric Le Play, *Economie sociale,* ed. F. Auburtin (Paris, 1891), pp. 24–27; R. G. Collingwood, *The New Leviathan* (Oxford, 1942), pp. 158–59. "There are no such things as old countries and young countries," repeats Luigi Einaudi in 1948 (*Lo scrittoio del presidente* [Turin, 1956], p. 39). On the anguished doubt of the Italians, on reaching the status of nationhood, as to whether they were old or young, see F. Chabod, *Politica estera,* pp. 25 n. 6, 528, 637 n. 2, 642. In particular "the notions of *old Europe* and *young America* are a permanent source of error" (J. B. Terán, *La salud de la América Española* [Paris, 1926], p. 170). And L. Romier (*Qui sera la maître, l'Europe ou l'Amérique?* 1927) sets out from the principle that "a people is neither young nor old" (quoted by W. T. Spoerri, *The Old World and the New* [Zürich-Leipzig, 1937], p. 131); a thesis taken up again, in polemic with the Europeans, by the American Malcolm Cowley (*New York Times Book Review,* 24 February 1946). But another North American seer had already written: "Those who say, Dominora [i.e., England] is old and worn out, may very possibly err. For if, as a nation, Dominora be old—her present generation is full as young as the youths in any land under the sun" (H. Melville, *Mardi,* 1849, CLIX; ed. cit., p. 663).

as the movement toward independence gathered force. Even if they have read Humboldt, these writers still live in the intellectual atmosphere of the eighteenth century; with them it is a sense of patriotism, not the new scientific spirit, which reacts to the Prussian slanders. Their arguments are thus still those which had served de Pauw's very first opponents, occasionally enlivened by the heated oratory and that greater fervor of the apologist *pro domo sua*. They are tropical and politically impassioned echoes of the diatribes of a previous generation; and they completely ignore the developments and revisions of the original thesis.

When the Creole empire of Agustín Itúrbide was established in New Spain, the rector of the University of Mexico, Agustín Pomposo Fernandez, brought out a translation of Carli's *American Letters*. The Italian's defense, by then almost half a century old, still served for the "rehabilitation" of America.

The secretary of state for foreign affairs in this same Mexican Empire (1823), the Honduran José Cecilio del Valle — famous for having drafted Central America's Declaration of Independence (15 September 1821), and after his opposition to the incorporation of Central America into Mexico elected president of the new Central American Republic, and thus one of the most distinguished of the "founding fathers" of the New World — is still more typical in his refutation of de Pauw and other Old World writers.

A widely read man, politically a conservative up until independence, and thereafter almost a utopian, a publicist of lively wit, ever eloquent and persuasive with his air of moderation and sweet reason learned from the study of French models, Valle is a perfect disciple of the illuminists. There is no reference in him either to the romantic "youthfulness" of America;[86] no enthusiasm, ever, for revolutions. Everything could be brought about by gradual reform and the wise actions of the authorities.[87] No less typical than his preromantic ideology is his glorification of the mathematical sciences, for their usefulness and (let the *âmes sensibles* rejoice) for their humane and philanthropic tendencies. So much blood has been spilled in America because the masses "have not been guided by the spirit of mathematics," which (who would have guessed it?) "are eminently sensitive to all the [ills] suffered by our species. Wherever there are tears, there stands mathematics, meditating and calculating to

---

86. "Youthfulness" is still for him (as for the *philosophes*) a negative quality. See for example the wish (1831) that "this age of youthfulness, volubility, exaltation and commotion may be succeeded by one of maturity, experience, fixity and tranquillity" (*Obras* of José Cecilio del Valle [Guatemala, 1929–30], I, 220).

87. Prudence, circumspection, and caution are repeatedly recommended to Governments as highly necessary qualities: see the example that is given in *Obras*, I, 37 (1824); I, 47 (1824–25); I, 102 (1825).

reduce their number," masterminding the strategy and tactics, deciding the battles scientifically, etc.[88]

His study of political economy, of Adam Smith, of Ricardo and Jean-Baptiste Say, widened his intellectual horizons and gave him a certain realism in his view of the "poverty" of the American nations in the midst of the "richness" of their natural surroundings. But the doctrines of his revered master and friend, and regular correspondent, Jeremy Bentham, the philosopher of utilitarianism, reinforced his fundamental belief in the sovereign power of Reason as illuminator of the world, dissipating evil and promoting the progress of all peoples along an undeviating path toward infinity.[89] Wise institutions, well-conceived laws, and the paternal administration of government—these are the things that assure the happiness and greatness of peoples. To religion Valle pays the lukewarm respects of the deist; and clerical obscurantism he abhors above all things.

America's nature is paradisiacal. But Spain's political system was wicked. And human laws act like the laws of nature. The errors in human laws destroy the benefits of nature's laws.[90] This is why America is so

88. *Obras*, I, 220. Cf. Gerbi, *Il Settecento*, pp. 97–98. The idea that scientific warfare is more human and less bloody is already suggested by Donne (*Sermon* XXXVI, ed. cit., p. 710), greeted with irony by Thomas Bastard (1598) and La Bruyère (*Des jugements*, sec. 119, in Pléiade ed., p. 403), taken up again by Montesquieu (*Lettres persanes*, CVI) and Helvétius (*Epître sur les arts*, ed. of the *Poésies*, 1781, p. 93), contested by Bonneville (*Les Lyonnaises* pp. 6, 208–09, 249) and again in Valle's time upheld by Louis Napoleon, who wrote (1835): "The more the art of war has been perfected the less bloody the battles have become" (P. E. Schazmann, "Napoléon III précurseur de la Société des Nations," *Revue historique*, 179 [1937], pp. 368–71). A related idea, that was current toward the middle of the seventeenth century, was the defense of firearms on the grounds that they represented an "advance" since they lessened the savagery of war and saved human lives! (Wolper, art. cit., pp. 593–98, with contemporary references to chemical and biological warfare, and the claims that they too would "save" human lives!).

89. On Bentham's singular popularity in Spanish America, see E. Halévy, *La formation du radicalisme philosophique*, II, *L'évolution de la doctrine utilitaire de 1789 à 1815*, pp. 277–78, 364–65; R. H. Valle, "J. Bentham en el pensamiento americano," *La Prensa* (Buenos Aires), 25 May 1947; A. Rojas, "La Batalla de Bentham en Colombia," *Revista de Historia de América* (Mexico), 29 (June 1950), pp. 37–66. On his interest in the United States, see Chilton Williamson, "Bentham Looks at America," *Political Science Quarterly*, 70, no. 4 (December 1955), pp. 543–51; and Boorstin, *National Experience*, p. 36. Ballanche had already noted that for the Americas Montesquieu was an ancient author: "He is their Aristotle: Delolme and Bentham are their Justinian" (*Palingénésie sociale, Prolégomènes*, etc., pt. II, sec. 5: Paris ed., 1830, III, 27, 224). In Guatemala his works, like other books in Valle's possession, were prohibited and confiscated by the Inquisition (E. Chinchilla Aguilar, *La Inquisición en Guatemala*, p. 247). Bolivar had them in Peru (ca. 1825): M. Perez Vila, *La biblioteca del Libertador* (Caracas, 1960), pp. 19–20. On his influence in Mexico, particularly on J. M. L. Mora, see Charles A. Hale, "J. M. L. Mora and the Structure of Mexican Liberalism," *Hispanic American Historical Review*, 45, no. 2 (May 1965), p. 206.

90. "The consequences of such a sad system were as necessary as the effects produced by the laws of nature" (article of 1822 in *Obras*, II, 166). There is no complete collection of Valle's numerous articles, studies, discourses, and letters. Thompson, who visited him in 1826, reports: "He had all the mania of authorship about him: proofs and revises and lumps of manuscript, folios and quartos and octavos, opened or interlarded with scraps of memoranda, were scattered, in profusion, over the table: it was as though he were inordinate in his requisitions at the feast of intellect" (G. A. Thompson, *Narrative of an Official Visit to Guatemala from Mexico* [London, 1829], pp. 209–10). In 1881 the government of Honduras promoted an edition of his works that was to be in three volumes, but only the first ever appeared, published in Tegucigalpa in 1913, though printing had begun in 1906 (the date that figures on the frontispiece). Valle's descendants began another collection, which was to be in *four* volumes, two of

backward, despite its physical advantages. It is poor and undeveloped, though very beautiful. The alternative in Filicaia's famous line in the sonnet to Italy (1690), *"Deh fossi tu men bella, o almen più forte"* — "Oh that thou wert less fair, or at least more strong" — would hardly have pleased the Honduran. For his America, Valle wants strength and beauty together: *"What we desire is that this half of the globe should be as noble politically as it is physically."*[91]

This gives rise to a double polemic: against America's real political deficiencies, and against her supposed physical deficiencies. The first can be remedied, as we know, with wise laws: the intellectual and paternalist Valle dreams again the ancient Platonic dream of the philosopher-king, though with some doubts as to whether this ideal is compatible with those other ideals, of liberty and democracy, on which the recent independence of America was based.[92]

But the others, the physical deficiencies, simply do not exist. Central America is a land blessed of the Lord. Considered from any point of view, Guatemala (the former *Audiencia,* which comprised the territory of the five present-day republics situated between Mexico and Panama) is the pearl of the continent: "It is its fair center; it is its most distinguished portion."[93]

Thus when Valle runs into de Pauw he has no difficulty in recognizing the Enemy. Right from the first issue of his paper *El Amigo de la Patria,* he personifies the scientist, "el sabio," in the figure of Humboldt, who visited the two Americas, to his great pain and peril, "to give the lie to those who composed horrifying pictures of that fair half of the earth, to defend us from the insults of de Pauw and those who said that we Americans are condemned to ignorance by the influence of the climate."[94]

---

which were published in Guatemala, 1929–30. See also Rafael Heliodoro Valle, *Bibliografía de d. José Cecilio del Valle* (Mexico, 1934); and an article by the same author in *Revista Mexicana de Sociología,* 6 (1944), pp. 7–18; the old biography by Ramón Rosa (1882) which prefaces both the modern editions (and was reprinted in Tegucigalpa in 1943 and 1948); the study by Virgilio Rodriguez Beteta, *El Amigo de la América,* 1917, reprinted in *Obras,* II, v–xxxi; and F. D. Parker "J. C. del Valle: Scholar [?] and Patriot" [deals only with his political activity], *Hispanic American Historical Review,* 32, no. 4 (November 1952), pp. 516–39.

91. *Obras,* II, 189 (article of 1820). Among the means proposed one might mention the opening of the Nicaragua Canal, from which Valle expected portentous results ("the population of the world would double or triple"), but which he considered premature in 1826, on account of Nicaragua's political weakness (op. cit., I, 134, 138).

92. "I dare to forecast it. If Europe's civilization continues in the present direction the wise men or kings that are wise will in the end hold the scepters, and the nations will be less unhappy. . . . America is in a different position from Europe. What will be its destiny, in view of the step that it has taken?" (ibid., II, 329n.; a study of 1830). In the delirium of the illness that was to bring him to his deathbed Valle repeated his plans for the Presidency: "I shall surround myself with wise men from Europe, my friends, whom I shall bring here to ensure the well-being of our country" (Rosa's biography, I, xcv–xcvi). And see the explicit quotation of the famous passage from Plato's *Republic:* I, 187 (1829).

93. *Obras,* II, 88 (1821). Cf. Thompson, op. cit., p. 295, on Guatemala's boast of "centrality."

94. Ibid., p. 9 (1820).

Among all the Europeans who wrote of the New World, de Pauw is chosen as the typical exponent of that senseless phobia: "Casas wept, and de Pauw raved."[95] José del Valle, then, plants himself squarely in de Pauw's path, prepared to defend (as Caldas for New Granada) the geographical situation of Guatemala, which he claims to be preferable to that of France and Spain, and in value "superior to that of Europe's mightiest kingdoms." Men who were unfamiliar with the torrid zone disparaged it out of vain pride and wicked ignorance. Muñoz called its soil "barren, debased and poor," Buffon found it had few regions that could be tilled, and de Pauw saw in it "a degraded nature . . . rich only in harmful animals, in insects and mosquitoes, in snakes and vermin. It is the land of putrefaction, writes another,[96] of sweat and ulcers, of diarrhea and putrid fevers."

Valle replies that the European "lives blithely content in the land of horror and death . . . he raises cattle in the land of serpents"; and that Humboldt, the most distinguished and modern of the great naturalists, never tires of admiring the majesty and noble vigor of American nature.[97] The soil of the continent is prodigiously fertile. All (or almost all) the plants of the Old World have prospered splendidly in America. "There were writers who scandalized the world saying that these lands, the most fertile that God's power ever created, are unproductive. Pauw, the slanderer of America, a man of systems and never of reason, dared to assert that our soil is sterile."[98] But these insults are proved false in a lengthy enumeration of the rich and varied products of the most prolific and blessed of continents. "Let us remember it with pure joy: America is the country that has most expanded the boundaries of Botany."

All the greatest naturalists of Europe came to collect plants and press

95. Ibid., p. 58. Also: "There are shameful errors in them [the works written about America]."

96. In a footnote Valle cites "Wilson, Observaciones relativas al influjo del clima," by which he probably means the work of Alexander Wilson, referred to with the title *Influencia del clima en los cuerpos animados* in a thesis defended by the Bachelor Micael Benegas, a disciple of Unánue, concerning the influence of the moon on diseases (Lima, 1798). On his return from Mexico Valle brought with him, among other books, "Williamson, Hugh, Observaciones sobre el clima en diferentes partes de América, comparado con el clima de las partes correspondientes del otro continente" (op. cit., I, 85), in other words the memorandum "An Attempt to account for the change of climate which has been observed in the Middle Colonies of North America," presented to the Philosophical Society in 1770, which was highly optimistic about the benign influence of the North American climate, whose improvement it attributed to the more intense cultivation of the land (Chinard, art. cit., 1947, p. 45; cf. Martin, op. cit., p. 207). Herder (*Ideen*, VII, 5, Fr. trans. cit., I, 344) cites both "Williamson, *Essai sur les causes du changement de climat*, Recueil de Berlin, vol. VII," and (ibid., VIII, I; ed. cit., II, 14) "Wilson, *Observations sur l'influence des climats.*"

97. Op. cit., II, 80 (article of 1821). Besides the authors cited in the text Valle is familiar with the works of other defenders or denigrators of America: among the ancients, Fr. Acosta, Garcilaso, Fr. Cobo; among the moderns, Raynal, Ulloa, Bernardin de Saint-Pierre, Fr. Clavigero (I, 112), Fr. Molina and Fr. Iturri (II, 94).

98. *Obras*, II, 112 (1821). Elsewhere too Valle opposes "system" or "prejudice" to "reason"; on the subject of de Pauw he writes: "The systematic spirit of Europe can still be found in the books of the philosophers" (II, 58).

flowers in this "inexhaustible" continent. Valle, "the plants' constant friend,"[99] names these visitors one by one "with pure joy," and parades them before us with their herbariums, their boxes of seeds, and their specimen cases over their shoulders. Today America possesses plants from all parts of the world; and among them those most useful to an afflicted humanity. "The human race suffers less as a result of America's products and her children's labors."[100]

When the English diplomat G. A. Thompson was about to leave Guatemala, Valle, who had become friendly with him, suggested that he take with him "specimens of the different woods of the country," and gathered together no less than thirty-seven of them; the Englishman ordered a case to put them in; but the carpenter regretted he did not have the time: he was busy building a new pulpit . . . and Thompson left without the precious samples.[101]

Valle's defense of the mineral riches of America is somewhat more succinct, either because the abundance of precious metals was undisputed and almost proverbial ("let it be said with sweet satisfaction: *Gold, silver, America,* are words that mean one and the same thing");[102] or else because some of the insinuations about the useful metals were quite simply ridiculous, as for example the notion that America's iron was less hard than Europe's: "metal is one in all of nature."[103] Only the animals and wild beasts of America are left undefended; and these Valle seems never to have bothered about.

The reason for this omission may have been the difficulty of presenting a richness in the animal kingdom comparable to the abundance of minerals and the opulent generosity of the soil, in other words in terms of an enormous potential wealth at the disposition of the Central American peoples (once they establish sound laws), and described delightedly by Valle in an unceasing display of colorful and prophetic detail.

99. Op. cit., I, 167 (1826).

100. Ibid., II, 105; cf. the preceding pages. The economist and patriot does not miss the chance of advising his fellow citizens to treat themselves with homegrown simples, instead of enriching the European pharmacists by buying their specifics (or patent medicines) which are already old and lacking in any therapeutic value by the time they reach America!

101. Thompson, op. cit., p. 352. Thompson translated into English and considerably enriched the *Diccionario geográfico-histórico de las Indias Occidentales ó América* of Antonio de Alcedo (Span. ed.: Madrid, 1786–89; English ed.: London, 1812–15). On Valle, see also op. cit., pp. 184–86 ("Valle is . . . passionately addicted to literature, and is a great patron of science"), pp. 208–11 (the visit to the study of Valle, this "Cicero of the Andes," which is "so completely filled with books, in large masses, not only around the walls but on the floor, that it was with difficulty we could pick a way through the apartment," and how Valle deluged him with documents and memoranda), pp. 215, 222, 319, 321 (Valle outlines the boundaries of the five Central American states on a map brought to him by Thompson: the map is reproduced in Thompson's book), pp. 324–25, (he declines a diplomatic mission to England), p. 450.

102. *Obras,* II, 95 (1821); cf. ibid., pp. 72–74 (1821).

103. Ibid., p. 100 (1821); cf. above, pp. 57–58.

Unlike so many other figures in the polemic, driven by their annoyance with de Pauw to denigrate Europe, Valle, faithful to his intellectual upbringing, has nothing but enthusiasm for old Europe's civilization, her inexhaustible spiritual wealth and unrelenting progress. How long will it take, he wonders, for America to be as "enlightened" *as Europe?*[104] But the political situation in Europe, under the yoke of the Holy Alliance, terrifies the free American. The intervention of absolutist powers to put down insurrections and abolish constitutions prompts Valle to the dire prophecy: "If some states want to meddle in the administration of others, America will be *like Europe,* a chaos of blood, death, and horror."[105]

Valle, as a republican and illuminist, has no sympathy whatsoever for the great empires, nor for political enterprises. He quotes Machiavelli with apparent disapproval, and with the customary reservation that perhaps "he intended to render tyranny hateful by revealing its horrors."[106] Of Russia he says that "it will be ill administered as long as it continues to be huge";[107] of the British Empire, that Guatemala will one day dominate the oceans and seize "from the Britons the scepter with which they ruled the seas,"[108] not so differently from Gabriel Pepe who in the *Nuova Antologia* (1830) predicted "that Montezuma's ancient empire will in the future be the Tyre and Great Britain of the new continent."[109]

Valle is also a biting critic of the Roman Empire. the city was "the fatherland of the tyrants who in the darkness of the night, in the midst of the storms, calmly shared out among themselves the whole expanse of the earth."[110] But he is also capable of acute observations on the relationships between the geography of a country, its politico-economic organization and its history, for which he might well be included among the precursors of "geopolitics,"[111] and he is convinced that economics is the basis of politics, and that the best way for the American republics to make themselves really independent, free, and sovereign, will be for them to get rich.[112] Indeed, if America will but answer her vocation, and make herself more and more united and independent — Valle invoked an American federation at the same time as Bolivar, and the principle of the exclusion of the European powers from American affairs before Mon-

104. Ibid., p. 120 (1821); cf. ibid., p. 51 (1821). And again: "Europe is the most beautiful ornament of the civilized world" (I, 171 [1829]; cf. I, 174 and 212–13 [1831]).
105. Ibid., II, 360 (1823); on the principle of nonintervention, cf. also I, 126–30 (1826).
106. Ibid., I, 245–46; II, 293n. (1824).
107. Ibid., II, 85 (1821).
108. Ibid., p. 81 (1821).
109. See N. Tommaseo, *Di Giampietro Vieusseux e dell'andamento della civiltà italiana in un quarto di secolo,* in *Ricordi storici intorno a Giampietro Vieusseux e il tempo nostro* (Florence, 1869), p. 106.
110. Op. cit., II, 160 (1822).
111. See for example ibid., pp. 81, 291, etc.
112. See I, 214 (1831). Cf. above, pp. 92–93.

roe[113]—if she can bring her civilization up to the sublime level of her nature, her example will be a challenge to all tyrants and an aid to all oppressed peoples, "and America's liberty will in the end make the whole world free."[114]

113. On the Pan-American federation, see II, 206–09 (1822) and on Valle as a "Pan-Americanist," see for example P. Leonard Green, *Pan American Progress* (New York, 1942), pp. 10–11, and Parker, art. cit., pp. 528–29. The Congreso Interamericano was to take as its first problem "the most useful plan to ensure that no province of America is beset by external invaders, nor becomes victim of internal disorders." Monroe formulated his famous doctrine on 2 December 1823.

114. *Obras*, II, 199 (1821).

Hegel and His Contemporaries

I. THE AMERICAS POLITICALLY DISMISSED AND THEIR ZOOLOGICAL PROBLEMS DISSOLVED

AFTER Herder the dispute seems to lose emphasis and dramatic interest. The American revolution recedes into the past, the French revolution commands the attention and emotions of all Europe, the Latin American revolutions are still to come, and when they do in fact come they arouse neither the passionate hopes nor the violent reactions of the first two. America retreats to the very edge of Europe's visible horizon. Interest in the overseas dominions fades almost to the point of extinction. "Perish the colonies rather than a principle!" the reiterated cry of Dupont de Nemours and Robespierre (1791), means this too: that the economic interests of the slave owners and the very existence of the West Indian plantations did not and could not count for anything compared with the revolution's maxims as ordained in Paris. A few years later (1803), in an almost symbolic act, the first consul Napoleon sold the Louisiana territory to the United States for some fifteen million dollars, a stretch of land four or five times bigger than France, and large enough to provide the North American union with a dozen new states. And even his implacable adversaries, the Idéologues, were unanimous in their approval of this peaceful alienation.[1]

A few years more, and Spain saw almost all her American empire crumble, and Portugal lost Brazil. One after another the European powers were expelled from the continent and reduced to lurking on the islands near the coast, or in semiinsular areas like Guiana or Canada, where the climate was extreme and the resources, at the time, practically nonexistent. Monroe's threat of 1823 gave final sanction to a state of affairs that was by then irreversible. The United States, in the person of its first president, George Washington, had already declared that it had no desire to meddle in the affairs of Europe; now it drew the first corollary from that maxim, and in the person of the fifth president warned Europe

---

1. Cf. Echeverria, *Mirage*, p. 276.

not to meddle in America's affairs. The two hemispheres were to ignore each other, to turn their backs on each other. England, mistress of the seas between the two continents, immediately indicated its willingness to adhere to Monroe's isolationist and tutelary "doctrine." And the Americans were left to seek their destiny alone. Europe, almost relieved of political responsibility, no longer felt America's problems so acutely, or dissolved them in those of a more general nature, the problems of primitive peoples, colonization, and civil progress.[2]

Talleyrand's case is typical, if somewhat complicated by personal resentments. He comes to the United States not as a pilgrim, but as a fugitive in search of temporary asylum, and disembarks unwillingly, already out of sorts. And in the course of his two years' sojourn (1794–96) he grows ever more vexed at Washington's failure to receive him, more disappointed at his failure to make a lot of money quickly, and more irritated at the distance placed between himself and the courts and drawing rooms which constituted the natural arena for his talents. His inborn liveliness and intelligence, sharpened by necessity, are all for nothing. True, his English is not good. In conversation, writes one of his friends and admirers, he "makes little parsonish witticisms, that are quite lost on everybody," and which in fact would be hardly more appreciated in Paris.[3] As for business, at first he criticizes and almost ridicules the currently fashionable speculations on virgin territory, and instead enthuses about the great possibilities of rapid arbitrage in stocks, and forward-dealing operations on merchandise and commodities; later, however, he turns all his dialectical and rhetorical skill to recommending speculation on the land still to be colonized, as the best way of getting rich in the United States, and finally suggests short-term credit-financing of the lucrative export trade in English manufactures to the ex-colonies; all of which would seem to be an indication not so much of any particular ability as salesman, as someone put it, but rather of real and repeated disappointments, and the restless activity they resulted in.[4]

2. On the decadence of the *Amerikakunde* in Germany (but not in the English-oriented Göttingen) toward the end of the century, and its resurgence after 1830, cf., with caution, Doll, op. cit., pp. 436, 454, 464, 470, 507, 511. On the dissolution of the "American mirage" too in France after 1793, and the diminished interest in the United States, see Echeverria, *Mirage*, pp. 175–224 (esp. 215–16), 235.

3. Duc de Liancourt, *Journal de voyage en Amérique et d'un séjour à Philadelphie . . . ,* ed. J. Marchand (Paris-Baltimore, 1940), p. 68. Liancourt himself (the author of that remarkable story on Louis XV's last illness found in C. A. Saint-Beuve, *Portraits littéraires* [Paris, 1862–64], III, 512–39) notes several times that Talleyrand and his friends did nothing but speak ill of the Americans: "It is impossible to have a lower opinion of them in all respects, to speak worse of them, and yet they adulate them whenever they meet them" (ibid., p. 73; cf. pp. 62, 66, 71, 76); against which he objects that when all's said and done they have the defects of all other men, and are certainly no worse than the Europeans (pp. 97–98, 112), in fact those of the country areas and the interior are better (p. 147).

4. *Talleyrand in America as Financial Promoter, 1794–96,* trans. and ed. by H. Huth and W. J. Pugh (Washington, D.C., 1942), passim, but esp. pp. 21–23, 33–57 (against land speculation), 137–75 (in favor of the same); Poniatowski, op. cit., p. 267; G. Pallain, *La mission de Talleyrand à Londres, en 1792* (Paris, 1889), pp. 421–44 (letter to Lord Lansdowne, 1 February 1795, on Anglo-American trade).

Constitutionally indifferent to nature (in his *Memoirs* he even forgets to mention that he went to see Niagara Falls!) and bored by this vain and oversensitive society, so completely involved in its concern with business, *dépassionnée*, "devoid of passion" ("the American people are perhaps the people least acquainted with passion in the whole world"), and incapable, in short, of forming a true nation, with the race composed as it is of clumsy *parvenus* who use Sèvres porcelain as hat racks for those awful hats of theirs that a European peasant would not be seen dead in, of vagrant woodcutters and fishermen that go wandering the seas with no more homeland than the cod-fishing ground, disgusted with a country that has "thirty-two religions and only one dish," and even that one inedible, desperate to return to France — "If I stay here another year I shall die," he wrote in 1795 to his friend Mme de Staël; and to M. Olive in 1796: "Here I am off course" — no sooner does he return to France than he expresses his certainty that Europe will lose all her transatlantic possessions. To compensate for this he suggests an immediate search for others in the warm countries (hence his encouragement of the Egyptian expedition), and then for the rest of his life, with a consistency quite remarkable for him, he continues to urge that France should direct her expansion toward the Mediterranean and Africa, and renounce her American dreams.

The discovery of America has already proved to be nothing but a nuisance. Of its various climates, that of the state of Maine is frigid and stimulating, and in accordance with the rule of Nordic climes will no doubt give birth to a race of conquerors; but New York in summer is downright noxious for Europeans.[5] The soil is better in the Old World, and whenever slavery is abolished agricultural products will cost more in America than in Europe or Africa. Furthermore the products that originated in the Old World — sugar, coffee, cotton — are superior to the same products in the Americas (a far-off echo of certain Prussian "slanders"?).[6] In any case there can be no doubt of the danger that as the United States continues its implacable expansion it may seize all the European colonies. Then if the Europeans emigrate to the New World there is the risk

---

5. Poniatowski, op. cit., pp. 122, 303.

6. It is by no means certain that he had read it (in fact he admits that before going to America he had rather vague ideas about the United States: Huth and Pugh, op. cit., p. 139) but it is worth noting that his library, auctioned in London in 1793 with dismal financial results, contained almost the entire *corpus* of our polemic. In addition to Buffon, of course (two copies: and on May 21, 1795 Talleyrand was acquiring another copy: G. Lacour-Gayet, *Talleyrand* [Paris, 1928–34], IV, 41) and de Pauw, and besides La Condamine and Raynal, Talleyrand owned Pernety's and Cook's travels, Jefferson's *Notes*, Robertson's *History* (original and translation), Carli's *Lettere americane*, Mazzei's *Recherches*, Chastellux's journey with Brissot's criticism, and numerous other works dealing with America (*A Catalogue of the Entire, Elegant, and Valuable Library, Late the Property of Mons. De Talleyrand Périgord . . .* [n.p., but London, 1793]: nos. 25, 260, 352, 571, 742–43, 860, 931, 936, 1008, 1213, 1260, 1276, 1293, 1354, etc.). For this library, which certainly does *not* prove that Talleyrand was really informed about our polemic, see Poniatowski, op. cit., pp. 17, 41, 63–64.

of depopulating the Old. From every point of view, in fact, "forget America," the diarist-diplomat repeats: the Old World offers us sufficient land and resources and problems, and (but this is taken for granted) a much pleasanter way of life.[7]

At this same time, around the turn of the century, the sciences of living nature too, in fact, were beginning to move away from the questions set forth or sketched out by Buffon and his contemporaries, and concerning themselves far more with the genesis and variations of the species in time than with their distribution over the face of the earth: biology, and in particular embryology, took the place of "natural philosophy" and ecology. Cuvier was revolutionizing comparative anatomy (1799–1805), rejecting the sublime speculations on the essence of life, and the closed and rigidly coordinated systems. And his study of fossils led him to some surprising conclusions, which among other things necessitated a revision of the very terms of Buffon's original problem: the Indian elephant is a very different species from the African elephant, and the fossil remains of the American elephant actually dictate its classification in a genus of its own, the mastodons.[8]

Fourcroy, who in 1794 had denied the objective validity of natural classes, but defended the compact continuity of the scale of creatures, is by 1804 converted to Cuvier's school, which denied any possibility of forming such a scale or chain, and in its place saw in nature an infinite diversity, "thousands of independent chains, continuous in each of their series, but conflicting with or broken off from each other, and incapable of coordination."[9]

The result of these new attitudes was the slow but irreversible dissolution of the basic antithesis between the fauna of the Old and New Worlds. When the Spaniards were exploring South America, Cuvier

7. See *Mémoires* (Paris, 1891–92), I, 70–79, 229–47; letters to Lord Lansdowne, in Pallain, op. cit., pp. 419–54, esp. 425, 432 ("money is the only universal cult"), p. 443; and cf. Sainte-Beuve, *Nouveaux lundis* (Paris, 1863–70), XII, 12–133; A. Leroy, *Talleyrand économiste et financier* (Paris, 1907), pp. 125–41; B. de Lacombe, *La vie privée de Talleyrand* (Paris, 1910), pp. 63–107; A. Schalk de la Faverie, *Napoléon et l'Amérique* (Paris, 1917), pp. 99–102; Fay, *L'esprit*, pp. 270–72; idem, *Bibliographie critique*, p. 85; F. Baldensperger, "Le séjour de Talleyrand aux Etats-Unis," *Revue de Paris*, 31, no. 6 (November–December 1924), pp. 364–87, which should now be studied in conjunction with the notebook, which is published, regrettably only in translation, in Huth and Pugh, op. cit.; Lacour-Gayet, op. cit., I, 181–206, 302–12; IV, 40–48; D. Cooper, *Talleyrand* (Turin, 1938), pp. 59–67; J. Gaulmier, *Volney* (Paris, 1959), p. 203, and Poniatowski, op. cit., esp. p. 182 (loss of colonies).

8. Nordenskjöld, op. cit., pp. 334, 337; G. Cuvier, *Discours sur les Révolutions du Globe* (1825; Paris, 1867), pp. 210–11. He remains close however to many eighteenth-century theories with his explanation of the disappearance of so many species as a result of "cataclysms," volcanic eruptions and subsequent floods (ibid., pp. 338–39).

9. Texts quoted by L. Febvre, "Un chapître de l'histoire de l'esprit humain: Les sciences naturelles de Linné à Lamarck et à Georges Cuvier," *Revue de Synthèse Historique*, 43 (1927), pp. 42–43; and in *Civilisation: Le mot et l'idée*, Première Semaine Internationale de Synthèse (Paris, 1930), pp. 28–29.

admits, they found not a single European, Asiatic, or African quadruped; but that continent, like all the others, like the newly discovered New Holland, had its own animal species, which were a source of endless wonder to the naturalists who did not know them. If there were other continents to discover, other species would be found in them perhaps more similar to those whose fossilized remains have been discovered. But by now the whole earth is known, and the greatest problem remaining is to learn "in which strata one finds each species," to assign to each animal its geological age, not its present whereabouts.[10]

II. KANT: A NEW OPINION OF THE AMERICAN

With the reforms of Kant philosophical thought too turned away from the antinomies between empirical concepts, like those of Europe and America, and from the disquisitions on the virtues and vices of the savage. Already perhaps by the end of the century nothing in de Pauw's *Recherches* can have seemed quite as inappropriate as its claim to be *philosophique*. Yet the thing that Kant himself had admired in de Pauw's writing, a few decades earlier, had been precisely the "philosophical" spirit, the attempt to examine the facts and reduce the confused mass of data to a system.

I am certainly not going to turn my head to parchment [the philosopher had written with vigorous disdain] searching the archives for old semiillegible details to scribble down about this. There are people who make the record office their business, but sooner or later someone must make some sensible use of it. In Pauw, even if nine-tenths of his material is unsupported or incorrect, the very effort of intelligence deserves praise and emulation, as making one think and not simply read thoughts. After all [Kant's lecture notes insist] we do not want to turn our brains into mere picture galleries or registries for the storage of the names and faces of natural phenomena.[11]

And in fact if we review what Kant wrote about the Americans, de Pauw's influence seems undeniable.

In 1764 Kant still had a very high opinion of the savages, of those of North America anyway; and without inquiring into whether this was due to climate or chance or political regime, he described them as endowed with a strong sense of honor, frank and honest, proud and freedom-

---

10. Cuvier, *Discours*, pp. 42–43, 59–60. For Cuvier, Buffon's sole claim to distinction would be in the field of literature! (see A. Comte, *Cours de philosophie positive* [Paris, 1864], VI, 381).

11. *Reflexionen zur Anthropologie*, sec. 890, Akad.-Ausgabe, XV, 388–89 (cf. sec. 1482; ibid., XV, 671). The lines which follow extend the eulogy to Buffon, whose considerable influence on Kant's knowledge in the natural sciences is well known. The editor E. Adickes refers, for Kant's knowledge of de Pauw, to his *Untersuchungen zu Kants physischer Geographie* (1911), pp. 120, 189, 206; and suspects other derivations from de Pauw in secs. 987 (ibid., p. 431) and 1371 (ibid., p. 597). Kant was also familiar with Ulloa and with Cook's travels (Akad.-Ausgabe, IX, 316; XV, 536–38, 785, 795). And finally one should remember his notorious preference for authors of originality, even when their originality bordered on paradox (Akad.-Ausgabe, II, 516).

loving, like the ancient Spartans. All they lack is a Lycurgus to create a model republic. And chief Attakakullakulla is inferior to Jason only because he does not have a Greek name. Then again the women in Canada enjoy a rank and influence unequaled even in most civilized Europe. In the rest of America, on the other hand, the natives have no well-defined character and are distinguished only by an "extraordinary insensibility."[12] All in all, Kant's debt to the Jesuit missionaries' tales and classical comparisons seems obvious—just as there is no mistaking the Rousseauian coloring of his considerations on the pure and noble humanity of savages in general.

But in 1775 Kant gives us an altogether different picture of the Americans; and in the new portrait we see emerging the very notions of decadence, imperfection, and coldness that de Pauw had theorized and put forth seven years earlier. The Americans are *"eine noch nicht völlig eingeartete (oder halb ausgeartete) hunnische Race"* "a not yet properly formed (or half-degenerated) subrace," from the stock of the Huns or the Kalmucks. Both their physical appearance and their "frigidity and insensibility of temperament" give proof of their ancestors' long residence in the glacial regions of the North: their vital force is almost extinct ("eine halb erloschene Lebenskraft . . ."), and they are too feeble for any sort of agricultural labor.[13]

Again in the notes for his lectures on *Menschenkunde, oder philosophische Anthropologie,* which in their early versions belong to the pre-Critical period (they began in 1772–73), Kant describes the torpid Americans in absolutely de Pauwian terms:

The American people are incapable of civilization. They have no motive force; for they are without affection and passion. They are not drawn to one another by love, and are thus unfruitful too. They hardly speak at all, never caress one another, care about nothing, and are lazy.[14]

Nor does his opinion change in the essay of 1788, *On the Use of Teleological Principles in Philosophy,* where the climate is said to make

---

12. *Beobachtungen über das Gefühl des Schönen und Erhabenen* (1764). IV Abschnitt. in Akad.-Ausgabe, II, 243n., 253–55. In the notes for his course in physical geography of ca. 1758, Kant, relying on collections of travels and on Bouguer and La Condamine, had described Chile and the Chileans in the most favorable light: the people are of a happy and lively character, Spanish horses become swifter and more beautiful there. The Peruvians on the other hand are found to be incredibly lazy and indifferent to everything (Akad.-Ausgabe, XIV, 632–33).

13. *Von den verschiedenen Racen der Menschen* (1775), Akad.-Ausgabe, II, 433, 437; the words in parenthesis were removed in the 1777 version; see E. Adickes, *Kant als Naturforscher* (Berlin, 1924–25), II, 412–14. On his sympathy for the cause of the American rebels, see King, op. cit., pp. 86–89.

14. *Menschenkunde oder philosophische Anthropologie,* ed. F. C. Starke (Leipzig, 1831), p. 353 (in the pages that follow there are various concordant opinions on the "savage"). In the notes the substance of his verdict was the same: "The Americans insensitive. Without affection and passion, unless for revenge. Love of liberty is here mere idle independence. They do not speak, do not love, care about nothing. Mexico and Peru accept absolutely no culture" (Akad.-Ausgabe, XV, 877). The Americans incapable of governing themselves and destined for extermination: ibid., p. 878.

the American race "too weak for hard work, too indifferent to pursue anything carefully, incapable of all culture, in fact lower even than the Negro."[15] An even more synthetic form of the same notion appears when Kant sets himself the question of whether the human race is young or old, and concludes that it is young, observing, among other proofs, that "one whole continent [is] half brutish and scarcely populated."[16]

But in the definitive version of the *Menschenkunde* (1798) he omits the whole section referring to the various races, the Americans included.[17] Not through any change of heart, however. In the *Metaphysik der Sitten* (1797), the American natives are again said to be inclined to indolence, but even if this were not so they would still be few and scattered "in the deserts of America" through lack of a state, and thus of any juridical organization, and thus of any adequate supply of food—with which the ancient thesis of a shortage of food in America is no longer deduced from the sterility of the soil, but from the absence of organized societies.[18] And finally the late work on *Physical Geography* contains scattered references to America, still considered to be very little known, especially in its southern part.[19] Kant repeats that the Patagonians are not true giants (p. 428),[20] mentions the flattened or spherical skulls of the redskins (pp. 433–34), and reaffirms that *some* American tribes represent the lowest level of humanity (p. 316). He notes that all domestic animals and European fruits have been quite successfully acclimatized in America,[21] but that there are no lions (p. 336) and the birds, though beautiful and richly colored, do not sing well (pp. 354, 430). Man, lastly, develops precociously in the tropics, though he never reaches the perfection of

15. Quoted by Adickes, *Kant als Naturforscher*, II, 415n., recalling the concurring opinions of Buffon and de Pauw, and the disagreement of Clavigero, cited by J. Unold, *Die ethnologischen und anthropogeographischen Anschauungen bei Kant und Forster* (Leipzig Inaugural Dissertation, 1886), p. 32.

16. *Reflexionen zur Anthropologie*, sec. 1453, Akad.-Ausgabe, XV, 634–35. On the animal character of the savages, cf. ibid., sec. 1260 (XV, 555). The passage from savage to civilized life, from the minority to the majority of the human race, is the most arduous of all history, from which one can deduce: "The world is still young. One half of it is barely discovered" (ibid., secs. 1423, 1498, 1500–01; XV, 621, 779, 789). Cf. "The Americans: rough, wild, barbarous," ibid, sec. 1497; XV, 771.

17. Akad.-Ausgabe, VII, 320; *Werke*, ed. Cassirer (Berlin, 1912–22), VIII, 214; Kant simply refers back to the work of H. R. Girtanner, *Ueber das Kantische Prinzip für die Naturgeschichte* (Göttingen, 1796; see also Adickes, *Kant als Naturforscher*, pp. 104–08). On the various versions of the part referring to the races, see also Akad.-Ausgabe, XV, 875–76n. References to the inertia of the Carib: Cassirer ed., VIII, 122 (and Akad.-Ausgabe, XV, 339, 817), and to the meager eroticism of the American men (?) in a marginal note, Cassirer ed., VIII, 578 Cf. in Akad.-Ausgabe, XV, 554: "The savages are not at all disturbed by sexual inclination."

18. *Metaphysik der Sitten*, secs. 55, 62.

19. *Physische Geographie*, ed. and reworked by F. T. Kint, p. 802, Akad.-Ausgabe, IX, 229, 233–34. Several times, for example ibid. p. 430, Kant says that great discoveries can be expected from Humboldt's travels.

20. He had already written in a note of 1758 that Patagonia "is reportedly inhabited by giants, but this is not known for sure" (Akad.-Ausgabe, XIV, 631–32).

21. Op. cit., p. 431. In Africa, on the other hand, the animal species are found to have degenerated: ibid., pp. 314, 317.

the temperate zone[22] — all clichés by now mechanically repeated without any particular emphasis,[23] but with a power of suggestion so strong that not even the mighty intellect of a Kant could resist them.

It should be said that he was effectively helped in this by the most renowned naturalists of his time and his circle, those whom he would naturally draw on for factual data and critical judgments. Far from scornfully rejecting de Pauw's libels, they discussed his opinions with all due solemnity and happily accepted his pronouncements and conclusions.

The famous Blumenbach, the *magister Germaniae* of academic memory (but who is still recognized in today's textbooks as the founder of physical or comparative anthropology), mentions de Pauw a dozen times[24] already in the doctoral dissertation which won him immediate fame, the *De generis humani varietate nativa* (Göttingen, 1775), and accepts his criticisms of Linnaeus on the subject of the orangutan, although he does find them to be "severe censures" toward a man so deserving of the highest esteem for his many other merits.[25] And Kant read and studied Blumenbach, wrote to him that "your works have taught me much"[26] and referred to him in glowing terms in a celebrated passage of the *Critique of Pure Reason*,[27] while Blumenbach, for his part, openly admitted his great debt to Kant's minor writings, and in particular to the one which dealt with the races of humanity.[28]

Even more significant than these ideological relations between the anthropologist and the philosopher are perhaps those between Kant and Zimmermann, author of some of the earliest treatises on zoological

22. Ibid., p. 316. Negative verdicts on the mulattoes and the Creoles in the *Anthropologie:* Akad.-Ausgabe, XV, 598, 601, 760, 878.

23. Being largely unaware of the precedents, Adickes concludes that Kant's verdicts on the Americans in the period 1775–88 show clearly "how perfectly hypothetical are both the point of departure and the deductions" and that Kant delights in building "castles of fantasy" (*Kant als Naturforscher*, II, 416; but cf. II, 459, 491–92: Kant's theories on race among his claims to fame) in support of his general thesis "that Kant was no more than a brilliant amateur when it came to matters of scientific detail" (P. P. Wiener," Jeans's *Physics and Philosophy," Journal of the History of Ideas*, 4 [1943], p. 487, and Adickes, op. cit., II, pp. 483–85, 492–93). For Haldane, on the other hand, Kant "understood the nature of scientific thought in a manner which is entirely impossible to the mere student of science and its history" ("Kant and Scientific Thought," in *Possible Worlds*, p. 129). Cf. also B. M. Laing, "Kant and Natural Science," *Philosophy*, 19, no. 74 (November–December 1944), pp. 216–32.

24. Op. cit., p. 34n. (correcting an error of his relating to the *membrana nictitans*); 47 (on the Patagonians); 55 (on the Portuguese in Africa becoming like Negroes); 56 (on the mestizos and the quadroons); 27 (on the "Ochavones" and the *Puchuela*); 67 (on the Americans' mania for deforming, disguising, or in some way modifying their bodies); 75 (on the hairlessness of the men of America). On Blumenbach, see the article in the *Enciclopedia Italiana*, and ibid., III, 583, and Nordenskjöld, op. cit., pp. 306–09. The elder Forster, J. R., father of Georg, was familiar with his works: B. Smith, op. cit., p. 63. On his contacts with the younger Forster, see Kersten, op. cit., pp. 173–74 and passim.

25. Op. cit., pp. 81–82.

26. Letter of 5 August 1790, in *Briefwechsel*, ed. H. E. Fischer (Munich, 1912), II, 155.

27. *Kritik der Urteilskraft*, 1790, sec. 81, ed. Insel (Leipzig, 1921), p. 324. The passage immediately caught the attention of Salomon Maimon, and inspired him to lofty and audacious speculative rhapsodies (cf. his letter to Kant, 15 May 1790, in *Briefwechsel*, II, 150–53).

28. Letter of J. H. I. Lehmann to Kant, 1 January 1799, in *Briefwechsel*, III, 264.

geography, who had borrowed a number of theses, arguments, and observations from the acrid and outspoken *Recherches*. It was actually Zimmermann's opinion of his essay about the races of humanity that inspired Kant to reflect further on the subject.[29] While Kant finished up by appropriating de Pauw's pronouncements on American humanity, Zimmermann, in his major work, either respectfully discussed or openly supported de Pauw's assertions on the quadrupeds, the inhabitants of the various continents, and in particular on that midpoint between man and beast, the *homo sylvestris*, the orangutan of the forests of Borneo and the Congo.

Based on extensive documentation from travelers, naturalists, and scientists of every period and academy, the *Specimen zoologiae geographicae, quadrupedum domicilia et migrationes sistens* (Leyden, 1777) is a real monument of learning and "natural philosophy": a fine quarto volume of more than seven hundred pages, rounded off by the first geographical map of the distribution of the mammals over the globe.[30] In this meticulous and pioneering work it is hardly surprising that Buffon is quoted on very nearly every page; what is surprising is that de Pauw's scandalous work is mentioned already in the preface, and then at least fifteen times more, usually with the author's agreement and always with his deepest respect. Zimmermann agrees with de Pauw concerning the greater frigidity of the American environment (p. xiii), the characteristics of the Nordic peoples (p. 63), the factors of degeneration inherent in the climate, food, or customs (p. 58), the beautiful Acansas, the Danes of America (p. 66), the Negroes' woolly hair (p. 78), the monstrous albinoes (p. 231), the men that change color (p. 79n.), and the spreading of rodents from Lima throughout all America (p. 223)—a just reward, the professor says, for the many maledictions that the New World heaped upon the Old (one can just picture Mickey Mouse scuttling around taking revenge for venereal disease and punishing America for the revolution in prices).

De Pauw is numbered among the authors "fide dignissimi" (p. 74), and it is repeatedly said that no one observed such and such a phenomenon better than he did, or resolved such and such a problem more acutely than him. When Zimmermann finds himself obliged to contradict de Pauw, or even just to question one of his statements, he prefaces his

29. Letter of 4 July 1779 to Johann Jacob Engel, in *Briefwechsel*, I, 215.
30. Cf. Oscar Peschel, *Geschichte der Erdkunde* (Munich, 1865), pp. 673–74 (cf. also 650, n. 1). Part of the map is reproduced in the *Enciclopedia Italiana*, XXXV, 1009. Jefferson possessed a copy of the French translation of the first part of the work (*Catalogue of the Library*, I, 469–70), and cites Zimmermann in the *Notes on the State of Virginia* (ed. Peden [Chapel Hill, N.C., 1955], p. 26) and in a letter of 14 May 1809.

objection with a series of profound obeisances: "I certainly would not wish to contradict a man possessing the erudition and intellect revealed by de Pauw, who so acutely explained natural matters in accordance with the purest rules of philosophy" (p. 39). On the other hand he is ready to side with de Pauw, even when he is attacking celebrities like Boerhaave (ibid.), or, simultaneously, such a venerable and imposing pair as Buffon and Linnaeus — although, come now, he might have shown a little more respect for the latter at least! De Pauw is right, without a doubt, on the matter of the orangutan, but why does he rail against the illustrious Swede as if he was intent on abusing and ridiculing him?[31] And it is all very well to refuse to believe in the Patagonian giants, and point out the very valid arguments against the legends of their existence, but why the bared fangs, why such acrimony (mordace dente), "when the truth could have been defended without insult and vituperation"?[32] The peace-loving Brunswick zoogeographer (as previously the Göttingen anthropologist) is scandalized by de Pauw's notorious insolence and aggressive zest, but still sees no reason to make common cause with his detractors. Pernety and his "prolix" Examen are dismissed in a footnote.[33]

All in all, de Pauw's iconoclastic outburst did some good. It subjected ancient fables, myths, and mirages to the coldly ironic eye of Reason. And the most learned Eberhard August Wilhelm Zimmermann deigns to offer the support of an argument of his own — the cowardice of the Peruvians in the face of the Spaniards, compared to the valor of the Cafras against the Portuguese — to the many proofs with which de Pauw "showed the natives of America to be feebler than all the other inhabitants of the earth."[34] Thus the science of the day, in its most "official" form, was not content merely to adopt the shameless and savage slanders of a man like de Pauw, but proceeded eagerly to produce new evidence to support his thesis.

But his mischievous delight in raising Cain and winning a cheap laugh at the expense of learned and painstaking researchers was still repellent to serious writers, indeed to all serious people. All right, so Linnaeus made mistakes. Nobody is arguing about that. But in the attitude toward the error, what a difference between the publicist and the professors!

31. Specimen, p. 400; cf. in fact the Recherches, II, 57, 71-72.
32. Specimen, p. 68.
33. Ibid., p. 72n. The Histoire (1770) is mentioned on p. 669, because it confirms, on the subject of the seal, "what I had already previously suspected in my first chapter [see, in fact, Specimen, p. 253], before examining Pernety's travels." In a note on the German translation of William Bartram's Travels, Zimmermann affirms with de Pauwian peremptoriness that "the Tiger is actually found nowhere in America," on which see N. Bryllion Fagin, William Bartram: Interpreter of the American Landscape (Baltimore, 1953), pp. 90–91.
34. Specimen, p. 592. Elsewhere too Zimmermann, meditating on the fact that the Americans had not yet domesticated the wolf into a dog, deduces therefrom a Buffon–de Pauwian thesis: "Perhaps this can produce a new argument to show that neither America itself nor its inhabitants, who have not yet tamed such a useful animal, can be as ancient as some have believed?" (p. 91).

They know very well that there is no call to turn the place upside down over a single error, however serious. Making mistakes is mysteriously coessential with the very search for truth. Whoever seeks is liable to err. Whoever thinks will wander and stray.

For someone like de Pauw, convinced of the infallibility of Reason, error deserves only scorn and disgust. Blumenbach and Zimmermann, on the other hand, even while they are defending the authors of laws and rigid systems, like Linnaeus and company, seem to remain more open to the libertarian entreaties of the *Sturm und Drang,* with their demands for respect and reverence for the fallible and fallacious geniuses of scientific inquiry, great even in their aberrations, almost as if they were so many storm-tossed heroes or blinded supermen.

In any case, this is really not the first time that the unconventional boastful blusterer turns out to be more timid and enslaved to the conventions of his time, more the captive of torpid fashion, and less revolutionary in deed, than the careful and unambitious drafter of plodding treatises, and maybe even the compiler of college notes. "Les esprits forts savent-ils qu'on les appelle ainsi par ironie?"

III. THOMAS MOORE: A WRETCHED PEOPLE IN A SPLENDID LAND

In this new political and intellectual climate, then, one might reasonably have expected to see the dispute wither and die, disappearing without trace. Instead it is precisely at this period that the "slander" of America achieves its fullest (and least significant) triumph, with its adoption by Hegel; it is precisely now that Humboldt opposes it with renewed energy; and even if in fact it seems to be somewhat forgotten by pamphleteers and scientists, its work goes on, both as a persistent source of irritation to the Americans, as we already saw, and in evoking frequent echoes, sometimes querulous, sometimes prophetic, in two specific groups of writers, one of poets and one of mystics. Neither could of course bring anything new to the debate; even their main sources often remain uncertain, so that we shall not be overscrupulous about the occasional breach of chronological order. But with them the polemic flares up again, in one more belated irridescent glow, so that Hegel's harsh and unrelenting condemnations, rather than blazing alone in the desert, are accompanied and heightened by the occasional expression of pity or horror, a few wholehearted vituperations, and the odd ingenuous and innocuous apocalypse.

Blake was both poet and mystic. But his rhapsody *America* (1793) contains only an impassioned and inflated exaltation of the revolt of the colonies. Washington, Franklin, Paine,[35] and Hancock appear amidst

---

35. Blake was a friend of Paine, and protected him (Howard Fast, *Citizen Tom Paine* [New York, 1953], pp. 215 ff., 239).

the smoke and glare of crimson meteors, like gigantic figures planted on the American shore of the Atlantic, rampant with anger and prophetic fury, while a number of divinities constructed *de toutes pièces* flit across the stormy scene punctuating the angels' tears and the stirring blasts of apocalyptic trumpets with ambiguous prophecies. Yet even Blake's poem is a sign of a newly acquired poetic dignity for America—the following year he wrote another "prophecy," *Europe*—now admitted into the company of the great lyric themes, not only as object of discovery and conquest, but as concrete symbol and theater of a new destiny.

At this same time André Chénier was drafting his *Amérique,* which was to be a work of twelve thousand lines; and Viscount Chateaubriand was heading toward Niagara and the Mississippi, and clouding their exoticism with tones of morbid sentimentality, but presenting French literature and the redskin tribes with a pathetic Cornelian heroine and a kindly old patriarch dripping with Christian wisdom;[36] while Goethe was introducing America into the reworked *Meister* as the antithesis of Europe, and the land of the Future.[37]

Clearly the concept of America grew steadily richer and more complex through these widely varying expressions and interpretations, so that almost without the need of any polemics as such it could escape the crude alternatives of the dispute and resist all attempts at summary definition. The vigorous political affirmation of the United States in particular brought a new and disconcerting element into the discussion. It was the first time that a European "colony" had won its freedom and indeed boasted of being the equal in everything of the continent from which it had sprung, and capable, with its untapped and unlimited resources, of surpassing and defeating it. Europe, like any elderly parent confronted with an offspring's youthful feats and precocious insolence, was split between a benign and approving pride and an impatient all-holy desire to let go with a few hearty clouts round the ears — or at least a few grave words of wisdom on the conduct expected from the scion of a decent family.

On the other side of the Atlantic, as we have already seen, the theories of Buffon and de Pauw were no longer discussed, but derisively and angrily cast in the faces of the Europeans: they were held up as the proof of the incapacity of the inhabitants of the Old World to understand the

---

36. "I took with me [on returning to France] . . . two savages of an unknown race: Chactas and Atala" (*Mémories d'outre-tombe,* I, bk. VIII, chap. 12; ed. Levaillant [Paris, 1950], I, 359). On the nonreality of Atala, see already Volney, "Eclaircissement sur les sauvages," in *Oeuvres,* p. 727n. (and now Gaulmier, op. cit., p. 274). On Chateaubriand see below, pp. 352–58.

37. See E. Beutler, "Von der Ilm zum Susquehanna: Goethe und Amerika in ihren Wechselbeziehungen," in *Essays um Goethe* (Leipzig, 1941), pp. 401–02. On Goethe, see below, pp. 358–72.

men and things of America, and thus, by one of those logical somersaults in which the acrobatic genius of politics so cheerfully excels, as one more argument to exalt the greatness and glory of the new state.

All those in Europe, on the other hand, and particularly in England, who still nurtured some feelings of bitterness or distrust toward the too recent and already provocative sovereign independence of the United States, were quite prepared to make use of geophysical arguments to rebuff their boasts and aspirations. Typical, in this regard, is the case of Thomas Moore, the Irish bard, who, in 1803–04, crossed the whole of America from Bermuda to Canada. On the one hand Moore is filled with enthusiasm for the imposing grandeur of the American landscape, for the richness and magnificence of a placid but powerful nature—and thus far from accepting the concepts of the slanderers of the continent. But both his writings and his letters, on the other hand, express a complete disdain for the new society, which he finds to be miserly, quarrelsome, and uncouth, and shamed by the comparison with the surroundings in which it grows and of which it is unworthy—so that his conclusion, and almost his *coup de grâce,* is an explicit reference to Buffon's and de Pauw's picture of the American Indian, a "very humiliating" picture, but much more exact than the "flattering representations" of Mister Jefferson in his *Notes on Virginia.*[38]

The actual result of this compromise between romanticizing exoticism and patriotic anger is the disintegration of the whole Buffon–de Pauw system. The formula "an ugly race in a sublime country" is the necessary transformation of the classic anti-American thesis "an ugly race in a horrendous country" resulting from a double ideological influence: on the one hand the corrosive romantic rehabilitation of nature wild and unbounded, on the other the criticism leveled at the arrogance and political moralism of the North Americans. This reversal is however so symptomatic that Moore goes on to repeat the facile antithesis ten times over, until it begins to sound like a banal mechanical inverted echo of the climatic theories—the excellent earth produces the worst of men—and there come flooding into one's mind other similar clichés, like the "paradise inhabited by devils," for example, the label applied for many centuries to Naples and its kingdom.[39] America too is depicted as a land thrice happy, a haven of peace "far from the shocks of Europe"—safe even from

---

38. "To Thomas Hume Esq. M. D.," in the *Poems Relating to America* in *Poetical Works* (ed. London, 1865), p. 101 and n., published for the first time in *Epistles, Odes and Other Poems,* 1806. Moore too had admired, near Niagara, the statuesque build and the athletic activities of the Tuscarora redskins ("Preface to the Second Volume," ibid., p. xxi).

39. See B. Croce, *Uomini e cose della vecchia Italia* (Bari, 1927), I, 68–86. The contrast "between the advantages of the climate and the savagery of the inhabitants" was noted and wondered at by the first describers of Brazil (Romeo, op. cit., p. 121) and later by the earliest explorers of the Austral regions (B. Smith, op. cit., p. 247).

those fiery and death-dealing comets that have so often "into chaos hurled / The systems of the ancient world"![40] America is a new Eden of unconfined vastness, a miracle "which man / Cag'd in the bounds of Europe's pigmy span, / Can scarcely dream of."[41] And yet this world, where only demigods should walk, is destined to produce nought but a "half-organised, half-minded race / Of weak barbarians," and worse, to take to its bosom "the motley dregs / Of every distant clime / Each blast of anarchy and taint of crime / Which Europe shakes from her perturbed sphere."[42] All this immense and bewitching America, with its mountains and gardens, with its great shining lakes and rivers rushing onward like conquerors, behold, as soon as it is filled with inhabitants " 'tis one dull chaos, one unfertile strife / Betwixt half-polished and half-barbarous life."[43]

It is useless then to nurture hopes for the "future energy and greatness of America." Its early degeneration, "this youthful decay," announces its approaching ruin: "Even now, in dawn of life her sickly breath / Burns with the taint of empires near their death; / And, like the nymphs of her own with'ring clime / She's old in youth, she's blasted in her prime."[44]

Again in the last composition of the collection Moore recalls the long pleasant evenings spent in conversation and song, when he would tell his American friends of the poets and heroes and glory of Europe, and they would listen in silence and resign themselves with a sigh: "They have listen'd and sigh'd that the powerful stream / Of America's empire should pass, like a dream / Without leaving a relic of genius. . . ."[45]

One can imagine the angry response that Moore's lines drew from the North Americans — and he himself, with obliging compunction, mentions it several times.[46]

---

40. "To Miss Moore," loc. cit., p. 88.

41. "To the Lady Charlotte Rawdon," ibid., p. 105. Note the characteristic contrast with tiny agitated Europe, which soon became a cliché.

42. "Oh . . . say, was world so bright, but born to grace / Its own half-organised, half-minded race [here the references to Buffon and de Pauw] / Of weak barbarians swarming o'er its breast, / Like vermin gendered on the lion's crest? . . . to nurse / The motley dregs / Of every distant clime / Each blast of anarchy and taint of crime / Which Europe shakes from her perturbed sphere?" ("To Thomas Hume," loc. cit., p. 101). America, Europe's Elysian refuge *sub specie naturae*, becomes its jail and cesspit *sub specie societatis!* Hence Moore's mockery of Brissot's "revolutionary" enthusiasm (loc. cit., pp. 86, 89 n. 1; cf. below, chap. 9, sec. 5, "The Quakers, the Marquis, and the Girondist"). An immediate precedent for his attitude can be found in Dietrich von Bülow, *Freistaat von Nordmerika in seinem neuesten Zustand* (Berlin, 1797), who describes the North American citizens as the dregs of Europe and the climate of the United States as extremely healthy, but rejects the generalizations of "Raynel" on the barrenness of the soil (Doll, op. cit., p. 497).

43. "To the Hon. W. R. Spencer," loc. cit., p. 103.

44. Preface; "To the Lord Viscount Forbes," ibid., pp. 86, 99. A slender and forlorn possibility of America yet becoming great is discussed in the lines "To the Hon. W. R. Spencer," ibid., p. 104.

45. "To the Boston Frigate," loc. cit., p. 108.

46. See *Poetical Works*, pp. xxii, 86, and *An attempt to vindicate the American character, being principally a reply to the animadversions of Thomas Moore* (Philadelphia, 1806), cited by G. Vallat, *Etude sur la vie et les oeuvres de Thomas Moore* (Paris, 1886), p. 50n. Moore is again accused of sus-

IV. VOLNEY AND PERRIN DU LAC: CRITICISMS OF THE
NORTH AMERICANS

On the very eve of Moore's American journey the same ideas were expressed with less passion and less poetry by Volney in his *Tableau du climat et du sol des Etats Unis* (1803). Volney, a belated *philosophe*, had spent several turbulent years (1795–98) in North America, and had been a friend of Jefferson. His thoughts had turned to America even before he set out (1782) on his famous expedition to Syria and Egypt: "I was tempted by the newborn America and the Savages."[47] He was also very familiar with the *Notes on Virginia*, had been advised by Jefferson in the preparation of his own book, and like him (see above, p. 256) at a certain point mentions Franklin's meteorological observations as blatant contradiction of the assertions of "Dr. Pauw."[48] At this point the reader is referred to a footnote, where the author adds the curious comment: "It is a strange book, M. Pauw's Researches on the Americans." He himself read it only on his return from America, "to profit from the great enlightenment ascribed to him" (as a matter of fact de Pauw's reputation was in full decline by the end of the century), but he dropped the book in horror when he discovered its author's frivolity, presumption, love of paradox, and polemic acrimony.[49]

But although he rejects the geophysical pessimism of the *Recherches*, quotes Molina and Humboldt,[50] and carries out an objective analysis of the soil and climate, winds, and rainfall of North America, which in fact earned him recognition as the real founder of American scientific geography,[51] Volney still sees no reason to share the optimistic visions of the

pecting "sordid motives" beneath America's enthusiasm for liberty by Prof. Ephraim Douglas Adams, *The Power of Ideals in American History* (New Haven, 1913), p. x; and another American observes obliquely that Moore made only "a brief tour of the Eastern cities" [*sic*] and spent most of his time "with British naval officers whose ships were in port and with wealthy Federalists, who bitterly resented Jefferson's control of the government" (D. Smalley, in a note to his edition of F. Trollope, *Domestic Manners*, p. 244n.). Which does not however explain Moore's particular attitude, nor his explicit reference to the thesis of the degeneration of man in America. Cf. also Jones, *Strange New World*, pp. 304–05.

47. Quoted in Gaulmier, op. cit., p. 31.

48. On his relations with Franklin, see Gaulmier, op. cit., pp. 28, 49, 65, 205.

49. *Tableau*, X, sec. 2, in *Oeuvres complètes*, p. 680b; on his relations with Jefferson, cf. the *Catalogue*, IV, 211–14, and J. Gaulmier, op. cit., pp. 204, 210, 218, 247, 255, 258–59, 260, 264, 268, 293, 298. In the *Observations générales sur les Indiens et sauvages de l'Amérique-Nord* too, Volney mentions the fact, well known to all travelers, that the savages remove their hair, "but of course the paradoxical Dr. Pauw seized on this anomaly to support the edifice of his dreams" (ibid., p. 713b; cf. Jefferson already, above, p. 259, and Mazzei, p. 272). Volney also rejects de Pauw's thesis attributing the savages' resistance under torture to a supposed physical insensibility: "Truly, they would need to be more insensible than oysters and trees!" The real cause is their exaltation, substantially the same as the fanaticism of the religious martyrs (ibid., p. 723). Cf. also Gaulmier, op. cit., p. 274 (against the "good savage").

50. *Oeuvres complètes*, p. 648a. "He has read everything one could have read in his time on the geography of America" (Gaulmier, op. cit., p. 269).

51. Remond, op. cit., p. 255; and Humboldt? and Oviedo, then? . . . . On his climatic theories, cf. Gaulmier, op. cit., p. 57. On his rejection of the American illusion that the climate of the United States is the best in the world, ibid., p. 273.

free citizens of the new republic. Brissot's and Crèvecoeur's idyllic portraits provoke only his irony.[52] Like Moore, in fact, he actually begins his work with a denunciation of "the romantic error of the writers who refer to a collection of the inhabitants of Old Europe — Germans, Dutchmen, and especially Englishmen of all three kingdoms — as a *new* and *virgin people.*" This fundamental objection was to be diligently taken up both by Gobineau — "But who are these new arrivals? They represent the most varied specimens of those races of old Europe from whom least is to be expected. They are the products of the refuse of all times; Irishmen, Germans, so frequently half-breeds, a few Frenchmen who are no less so, Italians who surpass them all"[53] — and by Proudhon: "The people of the United States, . . . is not a young people at all . . . it is an agglomeration coming from all corners of Christendom, principally England and Germany," and is indeed the dregs of those countries.[54]

To the Americans' boast of their national virtue par excellence — their youth — he replies with typical eighteenth-century harshness, and in accord with his constant mockery of Rousseau and his model savages, that with this vaunt America "conceals her present weakness behind her plans for future greatness," and that her people do indeed deserve the epithet *young,* but only "for their inexperience and the enthusiasm with which they surrender to the pleasures of fortune and the seductions of flattery."[55]

Their progress cannot be explained by the excellence of their political institutions — Volney brought down on himself the wrath of John Adams for his severe criticism of Adams's defense of the constitution of the United States — and in any case they have been moving steadily further away from the principles of the revolution. The North Americans' prosperity is due to geopolitical circumstances, to their insular location, to their lack of powerful neighbors, and their remoteness from every theater of war. In fact — Volney goes on, with considerable insight — every European war brings the United States more advantages, and reinforces "the natural and progressive direction of her ambitions toward the archipelago of the Antilles and the surrounding continent."[56]

The target of criticism shifts decisively from the continent to the new

52. Gaulmier, op. cit., pp. 199, 209, 216.
53. *Essai sur l'inégalité des races humaines* (1854; 4th ed., Paris, n.d.). II, 536.
54. *La guerre et la paix* (1861; Brussels, n.d.), I, 71.
55. *Tableau, préface,* ed. cit., p. 631, and Gaulmier, op. cit., pp. 271, 273. Cf. above, chap. 6, n. 86. See also Sainte-Beuve, *Causeries du lundi,* VIII, 424–27; F. Baldensperger, *Le mouvement des idées,* I, 195–06, and G. Chinard, *L'homme contre la nature,* pp. 76–77, 115. And, for later echoes, Miss Martineau, for whom see below, pp. 491–95.
56. *Tableau, préface,* ed. cit., pp. 631–32. Volney also mentions, and rejects, the boasts of the Americans based on the vastness of their territories: ibid., p. 633. On his fame and influence, see Remond, op. cit., pp. 254–55.

state that had arisen therein, from the physical to the sociopolitical sphere, even though Volney never managed to complete the political and social part of his study, perhaps also for personal reasons.[57]

The same period saw the appearance (1805) of a book by another Frenchman, a minor official very little known and certainly less read then and today than the illustrious Volney, but a man not lacking in good sense and almost always diametrically opposed in his viewpoint to the author of the *Tableau*. As explained in the far from brief, indeed antiquatedly long-winded title of his account—*Journey to the two Louisianas and to the savage Nations of the Missouri, through the United States, the Ohio and the Provinces bordering it, in 1801, 1802 and 1803, together with an outline of the manners, usages, character and religious and civil customs of the Peoples of these diverse countries*—Perrin du Lac is more interested in the savages than the colonists and citizens of the United States. But his account of the North Americans' political institutions presents a picture of liberty, order, and supreme happiness. The young republic is in every way different from and superior to Europe. In their manners and customs too, her citizens "seem to have as their fundamental rule to do nothing like us."[58]

However, in one way at least they are like the Europeans: in their fierce national pride and the embryonic but already vehement imperialism. Forgetting the help they received from France, "they think themselves the finest warriors in the world, because they obliged a few savage nations to sue for peace, or because they have a fleet (so they call their wretched little flotilla) in the Mediterranean, laying down the law to the beys of Tunis and Algiers."[59] One can be sure that they will soon claim their "natural boundaries," will then eject the Spanish and French from the new continent, and finally, after a violent revolution, will aspire to occupy the place that has so far been denied them "in the political balance of the world."[60]

57. For which see Gaulmier, op. cit., p. 265.
58. *Voyage* (Paris, 1805), pp. ii–iv, 103.
59. Op. cit., pp. 99–100; further irony at the expense of the "formidable American army," ibid., p. 151.
60. Op. cit., pp. 438–42: the revolution will shake their fine but fragile constitution, and "the most advantageous result of this struggle will be the separation of the states of the North from those of the South" (ibid., p. 101). For other prophecies of a schism between North and South in the United States, see Remond, op. cit., pp. 539 (1814, 1817, 1818), 672 n. 27 (1842), 711 n. 53 (1831, 1844), 712 (1833), 735 (1829). The city of Washington will be the theater "of troubles which will surely divide or rend the most beautiful lands of the new continent" (ibid., p. 91). For other contemporary fears about the expansionism of the United States, whose final triumph will bring about the end of civilization, see Echeverria, *Mirage.*, pp. 243–44, who also mentions the criticisms of Perrin du Lac in the organ of the *Idéologues*, the Americanophile *Décade philosophique*, ibid., p. 259.

In wholehearted contrast to this radiant prophecy is Perrin's description of the physical, psychological, and social conditions of the North American citizens. Addicted to the most vulgar pleasures, they are unworthy of the freshness and grace of their young womenfolk: to whom the Frenchman pays the compliment of likening them to his own compatriots, finding them less seductive perhaps, but more serious and sensible. Unfortunately they age quickly, lose their bloom before twenty, and usually their front teeth before they are even eighteen! And what causes this premature decay? "Most travelers attribute it to their habit of drinking very hot tea." But Perrin has an even more singular theory: "I am inclined to believe that this sort of malady is the result of the infrequency with which they wipe their noses." It's all a question of mucus. And in fact the upper incisors are the first to decay and fall out.[61] A little more use of the handkerchief—this is the real remedy for pyorrhea! And —if we may paraphrase a once-famous toothpaste commercial—a smile will be enough to reveal the virtues of blowing one's nose.

Among the men there is not the smallest sign of genius. Franklin and Washington alone, perhaps, can really be called great men. Of Jefferson, who had been at such pains to combat this very accusation of America's want of genius (see above, pp. 262–63), of Thomas Jefferson, so much admired by Volney, and incumbent President, the *sous-préfet* Perrin du Lac has nothing good to say at all: he is a factionalist, a jealous and suspicious demagogue, with a mania for agriculture, a mean and pusillanimous man. Certainly he wrote the *Notes on Virginia,* but "he has hardly more merit as a writer than as President of the United States."[62]

The *Notes,* "a work on the statistics of Virginia," is almost the only text quoted by Perrin du Lac.[63] But it seems to me that there can be little doubt of a familiarity with de Pauw, and/or some of his echoes or opponents, in an author who could say of the savages' beards that *"some writers* have claimed that nature withheld from them the mark of virility,

---

61. *Voyage,* pp. 30, 35, 104–08. The charge against warm tea, made by Volney too (*Tableau,* pp. 688–89; Gaulmier, op. cit., p. 202), can probably be traced back to Peter Kalm, quoted in O. Handlin, *This Was America,* pp. 15–16, and is faithfully repeated by abbé Robin, op. cit., p. 39: "The loss of their teeth . . . is attributed to the tea." The good abbé was also persuaded that tea weakened the fiber (ibid., pp. 167, 185) and is disappointed to note the early onset of old age among American women (ibid., pp. 15, 39–40). Other writers blamed warm bread and cakes (Dingwall, op. cit., p. 40). On premature old age in the redskins, see Beltrami, op. cit., p. 31.

62. "Caring little about rendering his country respectable in the eyes of the foreign nations, he would like to condemn it to being merely agricultural, without trade or political solidity," op. cit., pp. 87–89, 438–39; in short a sort of precursor of the Morgenthau plan for Germany! Cf. also, below, chap. 9, sec. 5, "The Quakers, the Marquis, and the Girondist."

63. There are fleeting references to Liancourt (*Voyage,* p. 95) and the naturalist Michaud (more properly Michaux, François André: ibid., p. 243), whose *Voyage à l'ouest des Monts Alléghanys . . .* (Paris, 1804), was recommended to Jefferson by John Vaughan (8 July 1806) with the vindictive comment: "Abbé Raynal would have (if alive) to reverse his stigma of Degeneracy . . ." (in *Catalogue of the Library of Jefferson,* IV, 210).

which is the external characteristic of man in all countries; but this is a gross error";[64] who denied the existence of fierce quadrupeds in America — the black bear, and the jaguar, or panther, are not at all dangerous — and who vaunted rather the goodness of the meat of those inoffensive beasts; and who on the other hand extolled the presence in the New World of all the game species found in the Old, while admitting that they showed differences that embarrassed the naturalists: "The most remarkable thing is their smallness."[65]

V. KEATS: THE FLIGHT OF THE DRYADS

Moore and Volney became the target of violent attacks from the North Americans, but there was no transatlantic reaction whatever to the dismal portrayal of North America by a slightly later and much loftier poet than Moore, John Keats. Not that the Americans looked with benign indulgence on an occasional outpouring from the mournful, sublime cantor of autumn and the Grecian Urn. Not that they were grateful to him for that famous image of his — the earliest lyrical effulgence prompted by the New World — in which the sudden revelation of Homer's poetry is sublimated into the wonderment of Balboa and his companions when they first gazed down from a Darien mountaintop on the vast gleaming expanse of the Pacific.

No, the reason is more banal: until a few years ago nobody had realized that those particular lines of Keats (the "Lines to Fanny," 1819, first published in 1848) actually described America. All the most authoritative critics, including even Colvin and Middleton Murry, two Keats specialists, believed them to be a poetic delineation of some imaginary wilderness, a somber cheerless fantasy, quite unrelated to any geographical reality. The very extravagance of the description precluded any possibility of recognizing the territory of the North American union in that savage satire. While from one point of view this shows that the Buffon–de Pauwian theories and descriptions fell into total oblivion in the second half of the nineteenth century, from another it is a clear indication that they were so much "in the air" at the beginning of the century that they could furnish a whole arsenal of disparaging motifs to

---

64. Op. cit., pp. 345–46. The other defenses, of the savages' pure breath, strong teeth, agility, etc., are a mere paraphrase of Lahontan, op. cit., p. 93: curiously secondhand, for a traveler who had observed the savages in person. For that matter various other of Perrin du Lac's "observations" (p. 184, for example, on the savages' marriage customs: cf. Lahontan, op. cit., p. 230) are more redolent of the oil lamp than of pure springwater. And in fact quite recently Perrin du Lac has been accused of copying word for word from the manuscript of a certain J. B. Trudeau, who had traveled in Missouri: F. Grenier, "Un plagiaire illustre, F. Perrin du Lac," *Revue d'histoire de l'Amérique Française,* 7 (1953–54), pp. 207–23. A copy of Perrin du Lac's book is to be found in one of the *Private Libraries in Creole Saint-Louis:* see McDermott, op. cit., p. 154.

65. *Voyage,* pp. 249–52.

anyone who for one reason or another felt ill disposed toward the New World.

Keats was never in America. And though it occasionally crossed his mind to visit it he was always repelled by the idea of taking up permanent residence in America, even when his beloved brother and sister-in-law settled there: "It is quite out of my interest to come to America. What could I do there? How could I employ myself?"[66] But the absence of his loved ones leaves him desolate, and anxious about their fate in such a distant land (Kentucky!); Keats reread Robertson's *History of America*,[67] and in his feverish and agonized imagination conjured up a whole vision of squalor and hidden threats to his dear ones "dungeoned" in "that most hateful land."

Nature, the great infallible Nature, for once seems to have erred. America is malformed and bereft of poetry. The dismal currents of this "monstrous" land harbor no divinities with weed-strewn locks; the winds are frozen scourges, and the thick and sunless forests would fright a dryad.

If we turn from mythology to natural history, and from wood nymphs to domestic animals, Keats's plaintive verses carry an echo of more familiar charges: the prairies of dry weeds starve the famished oxen searching for sustenance, the flowers are bad[68] and perfumeless, the birds without the sweetness of song.[69]

This want of melodious birds was, as we well know, one of the commonest and most typical charges laid at America's door. But for the poet whose masterpiece was the "Ode to a Nightingale" this muteness was a sinister compendium of everything silent and repulsive. "Thou wast not born for death, immortal Bird!" Where that magic voice is lacking, death and despair reign supreme. And how does Keats invoke the nightingale, from his very first stanza? "Thou, light-winged *Dryad* of the trees." So:

66. Letter to George and Georgiana Keats, 17–27 September 1819, in *The Letters of John Keats,* ed. M. Buxton Forman (London, 1948), p. 423. For his dreams of travel, ibid., pp. 194, 448.

67. Copious documentation in Harold E. Briggs, "Keats, Robertson and 'That most hateful land'," *PMLA*, 59, no. 1 (March 1944), pp. 184–99, which was the first work to identify Keats's source. In 1949 Prof. Häusermann, of Geneva, furnished the unapprized Middleton Murry with the same interpretation (see the *Times Literary Supplement*, 18 November 1949, p. 751), whereupon it was included in the fourth and last edition of the latter's *Keats* (New York, 1955), p. 50.

68. Keats's editors, such as Buxton Forman (*The Poetical Works of John Keats* [Oxford, 1934], pp. 438–39), are surprised at the epithet "bad" applied to flowers, and develop the curious notion that the poet may have written "buds" and then forgotten to remove it! Other, perhaps rather too ingenious, explanations of the "*bad* flowers" in Briggs, op. cit., p. 192, n. 43. One might also consider Keats's declared insensibility to the beauty of exotic flowers (letter of 14 February 1820, in *Letters*, p. 465).

69. "And no birds sing" is also the refrain of the celebrated "Belle Dame sans Merci," written by Keats about this same time and possibly containing other echoes from Robertson (see Briggs, art. cit., pp. 195–97, and *contra*, "Ten Days in the Life of Keats," *Times Literary Supplement*, 14 March 1952). In a letter to the *Times Literary Supplement* (25 November 1949), A. D. Atkinson confirms that Keats was probably familiar with the works of Buffon, and Cook's travels (see also *Letters*, p. 456), and that traces of them can be found in his poetry. But there is no need to look further: Robertson mentions those negative characteristics of the American fauna too.

and the dark forests of the "Lines to Fanny" "would fright a *Dryad.*" It is not an accidental echo: it is a thematic refrain.

In fact the motif reappears once again, right at the beginning of "Lamia" (1820).[70] The poet evokes the mythical age when the Fates had not yet driven the nymphs and satyrs from the woods, nor the glittering Oberon *"frighted away the Dryads* and the Fauns." Thus for Keats the flight of the dryads represents the twilight of classical nature, the corruption of everything beautiful, the death of the eternal Pan. There is no place for the dryads in the grim forests of America.

And there's more yet. The setting of some extemporaneous and half-humorous lines included in a letter from Keats to his brother and sister-in-law in America[71] is at the same time "both fairyland and America,"[72] just as the "hateful land" was simultaneously America and some bewitched country. There too the woods are sad and mute: "so lone and wild, / Where even the Robin feels himself exil'd." There too, rivers and streams scurry by dark and frighted like the dryads: "the very brooks as if affraid / Hurry along to some less magic shade." And there is even a talking mule from Tahiti, a strange quadruped that seems instead to have escaped from the pages of the *History of America,*[73] and even some real savages, evil "Monkeymen," that live in the trees.

Of the men, on the other hand, the "Lines to Fanny" say nothing: they suffer rather than share the "errors" of nature. Evidently Keats was thinking then of his brother and sister-in-law, rather than the redskins or the citizens of the young republic. But there are other places where he gives his opinion of each of these groups. Some of his incidental comments on the savages have seemed closer to Robertson's realism than Rousseau's idealization.[74] And he refers to the North Americans quite bluntly and without admiration in a letter to his brother, which in fact makes fun of his friend Dilke, a naïve believer in Godwinian perfectability, who imagined—and was not the first to do so; there had been a Berkeley to give voice to the same prophecy—"that America will be the country to take up the human intellect where England leaves off." No, one should not delude oneself. America has had great men certainly, a Franklin, a Washington, but when all's said and done, these gentlemen were vulgar people: the first a philosophizing Quaker given to banal and miserly maxims, the second so mean he even sold the horse that had car-

---

70. In the same poem one notes other curious derivations from Robertson (R. Gittings, *John Keats: The Living Year* [London, 1954], pp. 171–72).
71. "When they were come into the Faery's Court" in *Poetical Works,* pp. 349–52, and *Letters,* pp. 321–24.
72. Gittings, op. cit., p. 108.
73. Ibid., p. 109.
74. Cf. Briggs, op. cit., pp. 197–98.

ried him through all his campaigns. How could they have the mark of true greatness? "The humanity of the United States can never reach the sublime."[75] Let the young couple, George and Georgiana, infuse a little "Spirit" into the "Settlement," and Keats will pray—prays, in fact, in gay and nimble lines that are at the same time both chant and spell—that their expected child may be the first American poet: "Little child / O' the Western wild / A Poet now or never!"[76] The couple duly produced the awaited child—and then another, and another, and another—eight in all, counting both sexes. But never a single poet.

VI. BYRON AND SHELLEY: THE *RECHERCHES SUR LES GRECS* AND THE RADIANT DESTINY OF THE UNITED STATES

Just how personal and unusual these outpourings of Keats are becomes clear when we compare them with the convinced and fervent approval of America shown equally by his bosom friend Shelley and his critic Byron. In both one and other, so much at variance in their judgment of Keats's poetry, but united in their sorrow at his squalid end,[77] the enthusiasm for the liberty secured and successfully defended by the North Americans overrides all other considerations: a political and occasional motif, but one framed and gloriously reflected in the ancient vision of the world's destiny marching inexorably westward (see above, pp. 129 ff.).

Lord Byron hailed Washington as "the Cincinnatus of the West,"[78] and in the United States' rise to power saw the last hope for liberty, so trampled down in Europe.[79] His hopes are supported on the one hand by memories of great deeds of classic times, summoned up to embellish the latest triumph of America and her first president;[80] and on the other by a muffled echo of the naturalistic theories, with the twice-repeated reference to the United States as a region—"one great clime"—whose "vigorous progeny" hold high the banner of liberty across the far Atlantic ("Ode on Venice").

75. Letter of 14–31 October 1818, in *Letters*, p. 235.
76. Ibid., p. 237; cf. Gittings, op. cit., pp. 19–21.
77. See Byron's letter to Shelley, Ravenna, 26 April 1821, in *Works*, ed. T. Moore (London, 1832–36), V, 144–45.
78. "Ode to Napoleon Buonaparte" (1814); ed. cit., X, 15.
79. "Childe Harold's Pilgrimage" (1817), IV, 96; ed. cit., VIII, 233; "Ode on Venice" (1818), ed. cit., XI, 181–86. Cf., on the other hand, the diffidence of the aging Wordsworth, a conservative and moralist: even if he set no store (1833) by the vulgarity of the Americans' manners—"that comes from the pioneer state of things"—he regretted their attachment to money and base politics. Worse still, there were no "gentlemen" among them, and their morals were poor. So said the venerable poet to the young enthusiastic Emerson (see his *English Traits*, XI, in *Selected Essays*, ed. Nelson, pp. 224–25); and some years later he composed two sonnets against the Americans as degenerate descendants of the Pilgrim fathers and the Pennsylvanians who had become forgetful of the morality of the Quakers (*Poetical Works*, ed. T. Hutchinson [London, 1895], p. 515).
80. "Don Juan," 1819–24, VIII, 5 (ed. cit., XVI, 214) and the closing lines of the above-mentioned "Ode on Venice." On his idealization of the Polynesian natives, see "The Island, or Christian and his Comrades" (1823), in *Works*, ed. cit., XIV, 299–356, and B. Smith, op. cit., pp. 249–50.

An even more explicitly optimistic prophecy appears in Byron's diary of a few years later, in a passage transcribed by Thomas Moore, the selfsame slanderer of the Americans, in his life of the poet. After mentioning his pleasure in accepting the homage of a young American, Byron adds that he is always glad to receive the visits of citizens of the United States, in particular because he respects the people that managed to win their independence with firmness and without excess, but also because it gives him a feeling of talking with his own posterity: "In a century or two the new English and Spanish Atlantides will be masters of the old countries, in all probability, as Greece and Europe overcame their mother Asia in the older or earlier ages, as they are called."[81] History has not lost its bearings; it marches ever onward to the West.

Byron was no less flattered when an American squadron dropped anchor in the port of Leghorn, and he received the invitations and compliments of the officers, as well as the flirtatious attentions of some of the ladies, although he was not slow to realize that all this obsequious adulation was due more to his reputation as an anglophobe than his fame as a poet. He concludes, nevertheless, "I would rather . . . have a nod from an American, than a snuff-box from an emperor."[82] The American captain—the celebrated Chauncey who carried the United States flag "to the shores of Tripoli"—also offered Byron a passage to the New World, and the artist Edward West, who painted Byron's portrait on the commission of the American officers, actually gained the impression that the poet was on the point of accepting the offer.[83] It is certainly true that Byron wrote to a friend just at this time to ask for precise information on the situation in South America, "I mean Bolivar's country," where he was thinking of buying some land and settling down. Although he insists that his friend be absolutely objective, it is quite clear that he hopes to be told something that will encourage him in his project. He concludes, in fact: "I have read some publications on the subject, but they seemed violent and vulgar party productions."[84] Could it possibly be that he was referring to the violent and "party" *Recherches* of our own de Pauw? . . .

---

81. Extract from 1821: ed. cit., V, 200–01.
82. Letters to Murray and Moore of May and June, 1822; ed. cit., V, 335–37, 341–42.
83. Ibid., V, 346; on the commission, V, 336, 341. Other details in *His Very Self and Voice: Collected Conversations of Lord Byron*, ed. J. E. Lovell (New York, 1954), pp. 290, 296–301, 321. Already in 1815 Byron told Ticknor that he intended to visit the United States, but his American interlocutor remained sceptical, with justification, about the seriousness of this proposal (*Life, Letters and Journals of G. Ticknor*, I, 59, 68).
84. Letter to Mr. Edward Ellice, 12 June 1822, ed. cit., V, 342–43. Later, in fact on the eve of his death at Missolonghi (1824), while continuing to admire North American institutions, he told Parry that the Americans, conceited and egocentric because they lacked a glorious national past, had brought with them from the Old World "some of the worst vices of European society," which had then become aggravated in the soft climate of the slave-owning South, and concluded: "I have no love for America. It is not a country I should like to visit" (*His Very Self and Voice*, pp. 570–71).

One thing is sure: that Byron knew and as a good philhellene despised de Pauw's third *Recherches,* on the Greeks, published in 1787: a considerably more cautious and less scandalous work than the previous ones, in which de Pauw exalted the Athenians as the sole creators of Hellenic civilization, and treated the Spartans, Aetolians, Thessalians, and Arcadians on the other hand as plain barbarians, delightedly vilifying the bloody institutions of the illiterate Lycurgus, a lawmaker without genius or originality, and showing that the Spartan women were base and dissolute, and their men belligerent, maybe, but not brave.[85]

The *Correspondance* of Grimm, Diderot, etc., in describing these *Recherches,* deplores de Pauw's weakness for paradox and absolute lack of respect, but goes on to admit that he is learned and clever—"in the matter of erudition, he is perhaps the finest mind of the age"—and concludes with the opinion that the third *Recherches* is "a real libel" on the Lacedaemonians. But it was studied by the young Wilhelm von Humboldt;[86] and mentioned again, disdainfully, by Antonio Padovani, professor of statistics at the University of Pavia, who rejected its estimate of the population of Attica—"such calculations are as false as the rest of his researches"[87]—and then by Macaulay in 1838.[88]

Dr. Johann Bernard Merian, on the other hand, better known as a participant in the debates on the "Homeric question," immediately recommended it to his friend Cesarotti: "Some *Researches on the Greeks* by Abbé Pauw have just come off our press, a work very worthy of your interest. In it you will see ancient Greece in a new light, and you will have no difficulty in recognizing the author of the Researches on the Americans, the Chinese and the Egyptians"; and on yet another occasion he spoke to him of "The *Researches* on the *Greeks* by Abbé Pauw, a most singular book, filled with paradoxical novelties, where among other things the great legislator Lycurgus and the whole republic of Lacedaemon are very much mistreated."

Cesarotti replied somewhat cautiously: "He [Pauw] is a bold thinker, he has new ideas, and subtle thoughts, but he abounds, and superabounds, in defending his own opinions, and might one not sometimes apply to him what Horace said: *Mihi res non me rebus submittere conor*—'I try to submit the things to myself, not myself to the things'? However that may be, I am grateful to him for having first dared to defy the general

85. *Recherches sur les Grecs,* II, 307–24, 326–27 (English translation: *Philosophical Dissertations on the Greeks* [London, 1793]). The third *Recherches* also figures, in the original edition, in the library of Adam Smith, who possessed only the third volume, the *Défense,* of the first *Recherches,* on the Americans (*A Catalogue of the Library of Adam Smith,* p. 139).

86. R. Leroux, *G. de Humboldt—La formation de sa pensée jusqu'en 1794* (Paris, 1932), p. 379.

87. *Delle finanze di Atene e di vari mezzi di accrescerle—Discorso di Senofonte tradotto ed illustrato da A. P.* (Pavia, 1821), p. 89.

88. "Sir William Temple," in *Essays and Lays of Ancient Rome,* p. 466.

prejudice of other writers, who follow one another like sheep on the subject of the Spartans, whom I love and respect no more than he does, despite their fierce patriotism, their savage virtues and political capuchinism." Merian in turn wrote back: "You might depict M. l'abbé de Pauw equally well in the simple phrase, *mihi res, non me rebus.* I have known him personally, it was I that previously published his *Americans,* and more recently his *Greeks,* not without suppressing a considerable amount of material in the one and the other. I must do him the justice of saying that he did not take offence at all. He is a very good man, basically. And his pungent and somewhat ruthless tone is only the result of his retired and solitary way of life. Here is an anecdote that will make you know him rather better, and to his advantage. He had spent a year at Potsdam, during which our King Frederick sent for him every evening, because he was very fond of his conversation. At the end of the year the King, of his own accord, awarded him a pension of a thousand crowns. From that moment abbé Pauw found it impossible to stay there: he renounced the pension, left Potsdam, and went back to Xanten. Despite the paradoxes strewn throughout his book on the Greeks, it still seems to me to contain wider and more philosophical views than M. Barthélemy's" (i.e., the famous *Voyage du jeune Anacharsis*).[89]

Our abbé's warlike and sarcastic spirit had thus lost none of its vigor. Not only do we find him picking quarrels with all his old enemies: with Rousseau, "the most inconsequential reasoner that ever appeared,"[90] with the sects of mystics and illuminists that were to be found everywhere at the close of the eighteenth century,[91] with the congenital stupidity of the Spanish and Portuguese aristocrats,[92] and the very latest theories on the cooling of the terraqueous globe and the existence of Atlantis.[93] Not only does he persist with his polemic naïvetés, as for instance where he opposes the exaggerated descriptions of the Athenians' luxury with the supremely obvious fact that in Athens "the individuals' dwellings, compared to the principal houses of London and Paris, were no more than hovels."[94] But he expands his field of criticism to include Winckelmann and Mably,[95] recent fashions (see above, pp. 87–88), and the ancient coats of arms of Europe, "these Gothic and barbarian hiero-

89. 3 February 1790, in Melchiorre Cesarotti, *Epistolario,* III, (vol. 37 of the *Opere* [Florence, 1811]), pp. 57, 95, 119, 126–27. On Merian see the *Enciclopedia Italiana, sub voce;* B. Croce, *Bibliografia vichiana* (Milan-Naples, 1947), pp. 386, 388–90; F. Nicolini, *Divagazioni omeriche* (Florence, 1919), pp. 77–92, 95–112.
90. *Recherches sur les Grecs,* II, 167; cf. above, p. 53.
91. Ibid., p. 151.
92. Ibid., I, 144.
93. Ibid., p. 87; allusions to Buffon and Carli?
94. Ibid., p. 281; cf. the descriptions of Cuzco, above, p. 57.
95. Ibid., p. 89, 113, 365n.; II, 163–64.

glyphics, which the princes of Europe call their arms";[96] and even manages to treat the noble English thoroughbreds as he had treated the quadrupeds of South America: "the English have very much degraded the strain of their horses with the races at New-Market"—a statement that was to scandalize Lord Byron[97]—and to defame the University of Oxford as he had defamed that of Lima: "In these sumptuous palaces, known in Oxford as the schools, one can only with difficulty and at enormous expense form a mediocre man in a hundred years."[98]

De Pauw does not of course forget the Americas, nor the American savages, nor does he modify his basic opinion of these "savage and brutalized peoples"; but he does eventually point out certain features that they share with all primitive peoples, and in particular their keen feeling for music, however crude. He recalls Forster's account of the bagpiper whose playing drove the South Sea Islanders into incredible ecstasies; and the well-known fact that a missionary in South America gained much better results with his guitar than with theology.[99] They also have war songs, which have the opposite effect, spurring the savages on not to acts of bravery but to bloodthirsty vendettas, just as the songs of Tyrateus and other warrior-bards fed the passion and ferocity of the Lacedaemonians.[100]

But in effect, as he struggles to bring the Spartans down to the level of the savages, de Pauw finds it impossible to avoid bringing the American natives up a little toward the level of the crudest of the ancient Greeks. Thus to prove that the Spartans could have been cunning without being intelligent, he refers back to Robertson's observation that even the most

---

96. Ibid., I, 363; cf. *contra*, Phorkyas's reply to the question of the Coretides: "What are arms?" (*Faust*, II, 3). Viscount Chateaubriand, on the other hand, mocks the heraldic mania of the North American *parvenus*: "They display the chivalric blasons of the Old World, decorated with the serpents, lizards, and parakeets of the New" (*Mémoires d'outre-tombe*, ed. cit., I, 353).

97. *Recherches*, I, 155; cf. Byron, note to "Childe Harold's Pilgrimage" (1811) in *Works*, ed. cit., VIII, 123.

98. *Recherches*, I, xv; cf. above, pp. 304–05.

99. Ibid., II, 121; on Forster, see above, pp. 171–73.

100. Ibid., p. 332. Already in the article "Amérique" in the *Supplément à l'Encyclopédie* de Pauw had likened the savages' custom of killing their deformed children to the analogous and "barbarous" custom of the Spartans (loc. cit., p. 350b). The comparison between the crudest of the ancient Greeks (and also of the Scythians: see above, chap. 5, n. 446, and Horn, op. cit., pp. 459–60) and the American natives was almost instinctive, for that matter. Volney, having seen the savages of America, found that everything Thucydides had written of the Spartans could be applied to them—to the point where "I would happily call the Spartans the *Iroquois* of the ancient world" (*Leçons d'histoire*, VI, in *Oeuvres*, p. 593, n. 1; cf. also H. N. Smith, op. cit., p. 294, n. 57). Melville compares the Lacaedemonians to his idolized Polynesian natives (*Typee*, XXIX, in *Romances*, ed. cit., p. 150). Other examples from 1705, 1766, 1810, 1820–57 in Pearce, *The Savages*, pp. 43, 100, 170, 190–91. Curious parallels between the Scythians and the savage Irish, on the one hand, and between the latter and the ferocious Indians of the New World on the other, are found in Jones, *Strange New World*, pp. 170–71. But the comparison was also utilized in a negative sense, to pronounce the Spartans and the Indians equally despicable (Elizabeth Rawson, *The Spartan Tradition in European Thought* [Oxford, 1967], pp. 177–79, 259–60, mentioning Voltaire's scepticism on the subject of ancient Sparta, and accepting as valid de Pauw's thesis, even though he had been rebuked by Heyne for being far from meticulous in his work: ibid., p. 312).

degraded savages sometimes reveal "an astonishing sagacity," when their lives are at stake—as in fact do certain animals, instinctively.[101] Examples and arguments of this sort, not to mention the very tone of the work, could only exasperate Byron, the glorifier of eternal Greece and a little later soldier and martyr in the cause of the Hellenes' revolt against the Turks.

With Shelley all trace of polemic disappears; but the vision of the New World's future greatness is even more precise and iridescent. It occurs not in the "Ode to the West Wind"—despite the suggestive title—nor in the "Ode to the Lark," that joyfully warbling spirit so different from Keats's magic nightingale, just as the skies where it hovers and soars differ from the shadowy groves where the nightingale pours out his plaintive melody; nor in the elegy on the death of Keats, the "Adonais"; but tucked away in that tedious poem, the "Revolt of Islam" (1817).

This work too takes its point of departure from the Hellenic restlessness under the Turkish yoke. The liberty sought by the Greeks found a sure omen, for Shelley as for Byron, in the liberty already won in America. Over there, beyond the Western seas, there dwells "a people mighty in its youth," worshiping, albeit with the crudest rites, the ideals of liberty and truth. England, glorious but strife-torn parent, "turns to her chainless child for succour now . . . That land is like an Eagle . . . whose golden plume . . . in the blaze of sunrise gleams / When earth is wrapped in gloom." The radiant destiny of this people will be "an epitaph of glory for the tomb of murdered Europe." They will be numberless like the grains of sand, will grow as rapidly as day succeeds the night, and all the world, with all its races, will sleep in their shadow.[102]

The most fanatical supporter of the Manifest Destiny could hardly ask for more. But the rapt vision includes one realistic feature: the new state will be a refuge and asylum: a meeting place for myriads of men, driven from their homes by the cruelty of proud and frightened tyrants. The decades which followed did in fact see the beginning of the great European migration to North America, and the blossoming in the United

---

101. *Recherches*, II, 356. Is this perhaps why the anti-de Pauwian Caldas approvingly cites the *Recherches sur les Grecs* (*Semanario*, pp. 152–53n.)? See also Tanco's unusual verdict on the Greeks and Turks, above, p. 310. No less surprising is the citing of the *Recherches sur les Grecs* (I, 131 ff.) by the learned W. Rehm (*Griechentum und Goethezeit* [Bern, 1952], pp. 104, 402) as anticipating Herder's discovery of a mournful quality in Greek poetry. Herder talks of the sweet, most human melancholy in face of the fleetingness of life and youth. The "melancholic afflictions" referred to by de Pauw are misanthropy and misogyny! On de Pauw's denigration of the modern Greeks, see Byron, *Works*, VIII, 120. See also T. Spencer, *Fair Greece Sad Relic: Literary Philhellenism from Shakespeare to Byron* (London, 1954), pp. 109–10, 224–25, 241, 288.

102. "The Revolt of Islam," canto XI, stanzas 22–24; cf. Jones, *Ideas in America*, p. 271. Of Shelley's American dreams H. N. Brailsford wrote in 1913: "How ironical the vision seems to us" (*Shelley, Godwin and Their Circle* [London, n. d.], p. 247). But after the Marshall plan and all the rest, one no longer knows to whom the irony is most applicable!

States of socialistic communities and religious, anarchical, and economic experiments, resulting in a radical revision of the image of America in the hearts and minds of the tormented sons of ancient Europe.

VII. CHATEAUBRIAND: AMERICA'S PERNICIOUS SPLENDOR

Chateaubriand is a more complex case. It is established that he was in America, from 10 July to 10 December 1791, but still a matter of argument whether in those five months he could have traveled, as he would have us believe, from Baltimore to the Niagara, and from there to the Mississippi and the Natchez.[103] Whatever the truth of the matter, he continued to exploit the American theme throughout his life, from the *Essai historique sur les révolutions* (1797) to *Atala* (1801) and *Les Natchez* (1801-26), and then again in the *Voyage en Amérique* (1827) and the *Mémoires d'outre-tombe* (pt. I, bks. VI-VIII), and in fact, as a source of comparison and reminiscence, in all his writings. "Throughout his life he will proudly call himself the Savage, but he will use the prestige of savagery to conquer the most civilized of the old societies."[104] It is not without reason, then, that he is looked on as the popularizer, if not the actual inventor (being preceded at least by Marmontel and Bernardin de Saint-Pierre), of American pathetico-religious exoticism.

This is both his greatest glory and his limitation. America for him is never more than a marvelous decor, a brilliantly colored backcloth for heroes and heroines of a confused and restless sentimentalism; but the basic issues of our dispute remain completely foreign to him. His redskins are features of the landscape, and his landscapes, often nocturnal and always of exquisite literary craftsmanship, are mere melodious "states of mind." True, he was familiar with the Jesuits' letters and many of the travelers' descriptions, had read Buffon and waxed enthusiastic about Raynal, quotes Carli's *American Letters* and recommends Robert-

---

103. See J. Bédier, *Chateaubriand en Amérique: Vérité et fiction* (Paris, 1900); and in the Levaillant edition of the *Mémoires d'outre-tombe* (Paris, 1949), I, 593–610, an overall survey of the various problems relating to this journey. See also: A. Reyes, "Chateaubriand en América," in *Obras completas*, III, 426–32; and, particularly destructive, P. Martino, "Le voyage de Chateaubriand en Amérique: Essai de mise au point—1952," *Revue d'histoire littéraire de la France*, 52, no. 2 (April–June 1952), pp. 149–64; Henri Guillemin, *A vrai dire* (Paris, 1956), pp. 49–56; P. G. Adams, op. cit., pp. 85–86; Richard Switzer, in the introduction (pp. vii–lxxiii) of his critical edition of *Voyage en Amérique*; Raymond Lebègue, "Structure et but du *Voyage en Amérique* de Chateaubriand," in *Connaissance de l'étranger: Mélanges offerts à la memoire de J. M. Carré* (Paris, 1964), pp. 273–78, which analyzes the mechanism of Chateaubriand's "whimsical inventions." The accent of exoticism, especially in *Atala*, is traced in R. Lebègue, "Chateaubriand révélateur de l'Amérique," *Cahiers du Sud*, 47 (1960), n. 357, pp. 173–82; see also idem, "Poésie et vérité: Le voyage de Chateaubriand en Amérique," *Bulletin de la Société Chateaubriand*, 21 (1964), pp. 12–21, and the summarizing article (with bibliography) "Réalités et résultats du voyage de Chateaubriand en Amérique," *Revue d'histoire littéraire de la France*, 68, no. 6 (1968), pp. 905–34; and also Manfred Gsteiger, "Chateaubriand in Amerika," *Neue Zürcher Zeitung*, 5 September 1968. Last of all, doing everything possible (and impossible) to bridge Chateaubriand's "credibility gap," Christian Bazin, *Chateaubriand en Amérique* (Paris, 1969).

104. A. Maurois, *Chateaubriand* (Paris, 1938), p. 69.

son's "excellent" *History of America*.[105] But both his youthful belief in Rousseau[106] and the attachment of his middle and later years to sumptuous and formal Catholicism keep him remote and immune from any argument that might cast doubt on the goodness of Nature or the Supreme Deity. De Pauw is mentioned just once, in a contemptuous footnote contradicting an opinion expressed in the *Recherches sur les Grecs* about the Mainotes or Maniottes.[107] In Chateaubriand even the most typical themes of the dispute lose their edge. Their deprecatory overtones are subdued in a sigh, obscured in some flash of wit, or lost altogether in some factual observation.

Of the theories on the degeneration of the American fauna—never accepted, *et pour cause*, by an anthropocentric finalist like the viscount, who moreover contrived to extract ethicoreligious arguments from the law that "man diminishes where the animal grows"[108]—one catches a deformed and almost grotesque echo when he talks of America's carnivorous insects. These insects,

seen under the microscope, are formidable creatures: they were perhaps these winged dragons whose skeletons one finds: reduced in size as matter was reduced in energy [whatever that may mean!], these hydras, gryphons and others, are today found, it seems, in the shape of insects. The antediluvian giants are the little men of today.[109]

Our miserable little present-day species are sextodecimo reductions of some massive prototypes, organic leftovers of the primitive world of monsters and titans.

And as for singing birds, while it may be true that the first travelers found few in America, and those displeasing to the ear, today there are several species that sing as sweetly as Europe's thrush.[110] In any case Chateaubriand's forests (even if he once speaks of the "dumb solitude" of the Canadian forests,[111] and on another occasion of the "absolute silence" which reigns at noon in America's woods[112]) are anything but

105. See particularly the *Essai historique sur les révolutions,* in the *Oeuvres complètes,* I, 29n. (Buffon: and II, 229, 340 and passim in the *Génie* and elsewhere), 30n. (Carli), 31n. (Robertson), 143n. (Raynal: and 211n.; II, 281, 332, 367). On the influence of Raynal, see also A. Dollinger, *Les études historiques de Chateaubriand* (Paris, 1932), pp. 272–75; Villard, op. cit., pp. 318–19. On the literary influence of Fabre d'Olivet and Delisle de Sales on Chateaubriand: L. Cellier, "Chateaubriand et Fabre d'Olivet—Une source des 'Martyrs,'" *Revue d'Histoire Littéraire de la France,* 52, no. 2 (April–June 1952), pp. 194–206.
106. "I was then, like Rousseau, a great partisan of the savage state" (*Essai,* I, 299n.; II, 97, 416 ff.).
107. *Itinéraire de Paris à Jérusalem* (1811; ed. Paris, 1854), I, 75n.; cf. in fact *Recherches,* II, 414 ff. (see also T. Spencer, op. cit., pp. 224–25). Possible traces of de Pauw's anti-Spartanism in the *Itinéraire,* II, 255–56?
108. *Génie,* ed. cit., I, 149. See below, p. 356.
109. *Mémoires d'outre-tombe,* pt. I, bk. VII, chap. 3 (ed. cit., I, 293).
110. *Voyage en Amérique* (1827), ed. cit., pp. 51–61, 108 (ed. Switzer, p. 213). God reserved the nightingales to Europe "to charm civilized ears" (passage quoted by Olschki, op. cit., p. 19, n. 17).
111. *Essai,* quoted by Switzer, in the critical edition of the *Voyage,* p. xiv.
112. Quoted by R. Lebègue, "Réalités et résultats," pp. 928, 932.

quiet: they are filled with murmurs and trills, whisperings and rustlings, and transfused with mysterious harmonies echoing the distant thunder of mighty cataracts. "The forest is all harmony." The dryads, far from fleeing in terror, fill these woods with their eternal chorus.[113]

As for these unexpected dryads, we are obviously dealing with a particular instance of the famous romantic polemic on the poetic value of ancient deities and mythological beings, whether pagan or Christian (Schiller, Monti, Wordsworth, Keats, Platen, Aleardi, etc.).[114] Moore bewailed the fact that there were no classic dreams to endow the landscape of America with an aura of immortality.[115] America's "poeticity" was left anemic by its lack of nymphs and allegorical personifications of the aspects of nature. Writers did all they could to furnish the rivers of the United States, for example, with tutelary deities. Fantoni sang of the Delaware's "proud horns."[116] For Chateaubriand the Mississippi too has a forehead adorned "with twin crescents," and an "old and muddy" beard.[117]

These scholastic mythologies and lyrical fantasies affect everyone. The European finds them gripping, stirring, intoxicating, and the unwitting native is plunged into them as into his natural element. For Chateaubriand the savages and the redskins are most convenient heroes, and, whenever the occasion demands, dewy-eyed preachers. Chactas is a final incarnation of the sententious Antillean cacique; and he strikes us as strangely anachronistic at a time when the robust, athletic, and anything but Lascasian characters of Fenimore Cooper are about to emerge from

113. *Voyage en Amérique* and *Mélanges littéraires*, ibid., pp. 78, 412. The objective Tocqueville was to note that Chateaubriand portrayed the forests "with false colors. In America he seems to have traversed without seeing it that eternal forest, damp, cold, mournful, somber and soundless," etc. (letter of 14 February 1851, in *Oeuvres et correspondances inédites* [Paris, 1861], II, 174; cf. *De la démocratie en Amérique* [Paris, 1951], I, 21; in the *Voyages en Sicile et aux Etats-Unis*, pp. 167, 169, 336–37, the dominant note is admiration mixed with dismay and uneasiness; see below, p. 378). But Volney had already stressed the silence and monotony of those forests, the fallen rotting tree trunks, the swarms of gadflies, which certainly do not produce "the charming effect dreamed about by the romantic writers in the bosom of our European cities" (quoted by Gaulmier, op. cit., p. 268). For the silence of the South American forest, see Darwin, in Moorehead, op. cit., p. 51.

114. Cf. for example B. Zumbini, *Studi sul Leopardi* (Florence, 1909), I, 264–80; and, on the attempt to furnish nature with a new mythology, O. Walzel, "Nikolas Lenau," in *Vom Geistesleben des 18. und 19. Jahrhunderts* (Leipzig, 1911), pp. 333–42.

115. *Works*, p. 103b. On the possible transmigration of the Muses to the New World, cf. the even earlier prophecies and hopes of seventeenth-century English poets in Blanke, op. cit., pp. 311–13.

116. G. Fantoni, *Poesie* (Bari, 1913), p. 22 (in point of fact the horns belonged first to all to the Thames: on the curious transplantation, see Visconti, op. cit., pp. 98–99; and Pace, op. cit., p. 252).

117. Chateaubriand, *Atala*, prologue, etc. See also the lament of Keats, above, p. 344, and, on classicism in the spiritual and political formation of the United States, the whole chapter "Roman Virtue," in Jones, *Strange New World*, pp. 227–72. On the sixteenth-century travelers' tendency to find in the New World everything recounted by the ancient Greek and Latin writers, see already the pertinent observations of Humboldt, *Reise*, III, 397. On two later phases of the dissatisfaction over America's lack of easy poetic symbols (this time no longer classicist, but medieval) and for the destruction of myths and legends brought about by Columbus's discovery, cf. below, pp. 363–65 and 381 respectively. See also pp. 547–48.

the American woods.[118] But the viscount is no longer satisfied with the old parallels with the Scythians and rude Helvetians and other such Rousseauian prosopopeias,[119] and, to find a place for these savages in the plans of Divine Providence, strains orthodoxy to its limits in imagining a total palingenesis in America: "The Eternal revealed to his well-beloved son his plans for America: he was preparing for the human race, in this part of the world, a renewal of existence," the gradual and effective recovery of that primitive "sublimity" lost with Original Sin, and only potentially accessible to man by virtue of the redemption.[120]

The reality, unfortunately, as opposed to this truly sublime theological delirium, is totally discouraging. No, the United States is *not* the Kingdom of God on earth. Already in the *Essai* of 1797, the very same work that talks so freely of "American empire" and endows the battlefield of Lexington with the title of "philosophical land," Chateaubriand includes a ferocious satire against the Quakers—"and even a little against all Americans," as he was to write in self-excuse thirty years later.[121] The cities of the United States are new, cold, monotonous; the customs—if indeed one can talk of customs, since "what they have there are habits rather than customs"—are frivolous, corrupt, very different from the expected Republican austerity. "With each passing day I thus saw my dreams dissolve, one by one, and that hurt me deeply." In the New World there are no monuments or traditions, although this at least is compensated for—Chateaubriand is a real virtuoso in logical and stylistic equilibria and *balancements*—by the forests, which are ancient, and by liberty, which is eternal: the former the daughters of the earth, the latter the mother of society.[122] As he sums up, taking the Americans into his confidence, or at least the few to whom he feels he can bare his soul, the young Chateaubriand makes things quite clear: "I love your country and

118. These too, one need hardly say, no little "romanticized." One should reread those other beautiful, frighteningly beautiful pages of Tocqueville describing his first encounter with the redskins, which begin: "I do not think I ever experienced a more complete disappointment than on seeing these Indians. I was full of memories of M. de Chateaubriand and Cooper" (*Quinze jours au désert*, 1831, in *Oeuvres et correspondances inédites*, I, 175–77; and now in *Voyage en Sicile et aux Etats-Unis*, pp. 223, 343; but cf. G. W. Pierson, *Tocqueville and Beaumont in America* [Oxford, 1938], pp. 287–89, and Fabian, op. cit., p. 22). Cooper himself rejected the accusation "that he was a Chateaubriand dreaming of noble savages" (Pearce, *The Savages*, p. 211). And a more recent scholar: "ethnologically Chateaubriand's American works can not be taken seriously" (H. F. C. Ten Kate, *The Indian in Literature*, in *Annual Report of the Board of Regents of the Smithsonian Institution . . . for 1921* [Washington, D.C., 1922], pp. 513, 527).

119. For example, in the *Essai historique sur les révolutions*, ed. cit., I, 285–86; in the same work, however, Chateaubriand points out that the Americans have not progressed at all since the time of the discovery, and that already by then they were fairly far from the pure state of nature (ibid., I, 26; cf. A. Maurois, *Chateaubriand*, p. 64).

120. *Les Natchez*, in *Oeuvres complètes*, ed. cit., XIX, 117. For other variations on this mystical theme, see below, pp. 357 and 394.

121. *Essai*, I, 210–13; *Voyage en Amérique*, p. 54.

122. *Voyage*, p. 53; cf. pp. 59, 210.

your government, but you I do not love at all."[123] Volney and Moore were
to say the same thing, in prose and in verse, without all the mystery.

Coming back forty years later to his study of the difficulties threatening
the United States, Chateaubriand, now an aging diplomat made wiser by
life and de Tocqueville, characterizes the North Americans as sordid,
harsh, and humorless, and in looking for the causes of this settles on one
that is crudely naturalistic and transparently de Pauwian in flavor:
"Could it be that the Americans, without knowing it, suffer the law of a
climate where vegetable nature seems to have profited at the expense of
living nature, a law resisted by some distinguished minds, but not beyond
the bounds of possibility despite that refutation?"[124]

One feels like retorting with a few questions for the viscount: does he
really not think a vegetable is alive too? and why ever should a vegetable
be more mean and miserly than an animal? But it seems more appropriate
to reflect on the vitality and vegetude of certain ancient and conspicuous
errors.

Chateaubriand, in fact, had already welcomed them and subjected
them to further revision in the passage of the *Génie du christianisme*
where he refutes various objections to the thesis that morality is not conceivable without a life after death. The penultimate objection is that which
stresses the influence of climate on the mind, and in so doing "mate-
rializes" the spirit. Chateaubriand feels so sure of himself on this point
that he turns to his audience like a conjurer or juggler and invites them to
watch closely while he performs his amazing tour de force: "Instead of
resolving an objection, we are about to extract a proof of the immortality
of the soul from the very thing with which they oppose us."

As an awed silence falls upon the public the apologist begins by observing that nature is "stronger" in the extreme latitudes, in the tropics
and the arctic regions: animals, plants, rivers, and mountains assume
gigantic forms there. Only man is exempted: his physical and moral
faculties do not "expand" like the elephant's near the equator or the
whale's at the pole. Man stands thus in an inverse relation to nature:
"Man . . . grows feeble by reason of the increase of animal creation [the
other two kingdoms are forgotten about] all around him." Look at the
Indian, the Peruvian, and the Negro in the south, the Eskimo and the
Lapplander in the north. What mean and flaccid creatures compared to
the elephants and the whales! (Truth to tell, one's thoughts turn irrev-

---

123. *Essai*, I, 212n.; cf. G. Chinard, *L'exotisme américain dans l'oeuvre de Chateaubriand*, pp. 95–
96; and A. Bellessort, "L'Enchanteur en Amérique," in *Reflets de la vieille Amérique* (Paris, 1923),
pp. 113–49, esp. 120–23.
124. *Mémoires d'outre-tombe*, pt. I, bk. viii, chap. 11; ed. cit., I, 354; cf. M. Stathers, *Chateaubriand
et l'Amérique* (Grenoble, 1905), esp. pp. 127–29. On this bizarre law, see above, p. 256.

erently to Ragazzoni's "pacific Lapps," with their "bellies bloated, gorged on whale fat, nodding gently off to sleep.")[125]

This is not enough? The *coup de grâce* follows:

There is something else: America, where the mixture of silts and waters gives the vegetation the vigor of a primitive land [the magician waves his wand, the animals vanish, and the earth and plants reappear], *America is pernicious to the races of men,* although it becomes less so each day, by reason of the weakening of the material element.

In short, man possesses something antithetical to "passive nature": "now, this thing is our immortal soul," the soul that languishes in affliction when nature is all-powerful, and causes the weakness of the body. "The body, which, if it had been alone, would have thrived in the heat of the sun, is thwarted by the prostration of the spirit." The immortal soul does not like sunbathing. The mental and physical weakness of the peoples of the extreme south and the extreme north is nothing but "a veritable intellectual sadness, produced by the position of the soul and its struggles against the forces of matter." The soul works best where matter acts least: this is the Good Lord's way of demonstrating "almost mathematically" the immortality of our being.[126]

The reasoning is childishly sophistical. But what interests us is not so much that as the discovery, indeed the remarkable revelation beyond the antithesis of body and soul, strength and weakness of matter, contrasted, coupled and counterbalanced, of a large undigested residuum of our polemic. De Pauw is chased away from the front door, and comes in at the back. Defeated by the luxuriant and multicolored vision of American nature, he lends himself to the support of a laborious metaphysical corollary. The American's decadence however is no longer justified by physical causes, but rather by the oppressive exuberance of the natural surroundings. All in all, then, Chateaubriand's law reechoes on the one hand the Buffonian exception of man as compared to the other animals (see above, pp. 154–56), perhaps also the more distant Renaissance exaltation of man's antiphysical actions, while on the other hand it falls in with Moore's and Volney's formula, and Chateaubriand's own in the *Essai:* "a pitiable people in a splendid land." But while that formula had been intended to point out a stupefying contrast, Chateaubriand uses the two terms as the necessary and connected aspects of one and the same reality. In America the men are flabby and mean *because* the earth is

---

125. E. Ragazzoni, *Poesie* (Turin, 1927), p. 56: "ciascun preso già dal sonno / Perché ha l'epa troppo piena / Già di grasso di balena."

126. *Génie du christianisme* (1802), pt. I, bk. VI, chap. 3 (ed. cit., I, 148–49). On the subject of these proofs Lanson talks of "incomparable ingenuousness" (*Histoire de la littérature française,* p. 884).

vigorous and prodigal. Only as it becomes very gradually less so does man begin to raise his head. And again Chateaubriand finds himself agreeing with de Pauw, who had imagined (above, pp. 91–92) the decadence of the Americans being arrested and converted into slow progress with the leveling of the forest and the reclaiming of the swamps; while his radical pessimism on the fate of America makes one more appearance in a letter he wrote in his later years to the Bergamasque explorer Costantino Beltrami: "I fear, Sir, that the transatlantic world that you have seen and so well painted *is itself approaching some catastrophe like the old world.*"[127]

Chateaubriand finds the same contrast between a luxuriant nature and a worthless humanity in South America. But here the decadence has a supernatural rather than physical cause. While he waits for the Jesuits to bring him the Good News, the savage of Paraguay is totally lacking in Grace, crushed beneath the weight of Original Sin. The landscape varies between sublime desolation and magical beauty, but "the Indians that one met in these retreats resembled it only in their horrific aspects. An indolent, stupid and savage race, showing primitive man degraded by his fall, in all his ugliness. There is no greater proof of the degeneration of human nature than the smallness of the savage in the greatness of the desert."[128] Not therefore "small" because nature is too "big," but because one day Adam ate an apple. The first principles of Paraguayan geography and ethnography should be sought beneath a tree in the Earthly Paradise.

VIII. GOETHE: AN AMERICA WITHOUT BASALT OR MANOR HOUSES

In the very same year (1827) that saw the publication of the most complete if not actually the definitive version of Chateaubriand's *Voyage en Amérique,* Goethe was condensing his ideas on the New World into the twelve brief lines *Den Vereinigten Staaten,* "To the United States," one of the most pregnant and extensively annotated texts in our whole rigmarole.

127. Letter of 3 March 1833 (my italics), which goes on ambiguously: "We live in an age of social transformation: we sow painfully; the future will harvest" (in Costantino Beltrami, *Notizie e lettere,* p. 96). Cf. also Eugenia Costanzi-Masi, "Notizie di Giacomo Costantino Beltrami sugli Indigeni Americani," in *Atti del XXII Congresso internazionale degli Americanisti* (Rome, 1928), II, 685–96. Chateaubriand utilized Beltrami's works to describe the regions of the Mississippi that he had never seen: cf. Lebègue, "Structure et but," pp. 277, 282.

128. *Génie,* pt. IV, bk. IV, chap. IV; ed. cit., II, 200, with the intention of magnifying the work of the missionaries. One might note the Robertsonian characteristics of the native, and remember that a little further on Chateaubriand transcribes, with fulsome praise (as Manzoni was also to do, *Osservazioni sulla morale cattolica,* chap. VIII; ed. *Opere varie* [Milan, 1943], p. 85), the page in which Robertson defends the missionaries' work: *History of America,* II, 350–51; *Génie,* ed. cit., II, 248–49; cf. also Stathers, op. cit., pp. 125, 137. De Maistre's very similar portrait of the savages has an analogous origin: cf. below, pp. 389–91.

Strictly speaking, Goethe has no place in the dispute: he certainly does not slander America, nor does he indulge in polemics against her slanderers. But how can he possibly be left out? How can one possibly leave out Goethe in narrating the story of any intellectual current or trend that made itself felt or even just hovered about in Europe at the end of the eighteenth and beginning of the nineteenth century? One would be lacking an essential point of reference, a necessary gloss, or the radiant reflection of a mind that had no need to set itself above the strife to achieve a lucid but still sympathetic serenity. After all the petty squabbles and conventional panegyrics one is suddenly in a different world when one's ears first echo with Goethe's allocution and ardent wish, the first addressed to the continent, in the singular, the second to the United States, in the plural:[129]

> Amerika, du hast es besser
> Als unser Kontinent, das alte,
> Hast keine verfallene Schlösser
> Und keine Basalte.
> Dich stört nicht im Innern,
> Zu lebendiger Zeit,
> Unnützes Erinnern
> Und vergeblicher Streit.
> Benutzt die Gegenwart mit Glück!
> Und wenn nun eure Kinder dichten,
> Bewahre sie ein gut Geschick
> Von Ritter-, Räuber- und Gespenstergeschichten.[130]

What is the image of the New World that emerges from this epigram? America is a blessed land. Its contrast with old afflicted Europe is total. On the geological level, it has no basalts. From the point of view of history, it has neither feudal remnants nor age-old grudges. Its poetry will thus be able to remain immune to literary romanticizing. "It is no cemetery of romanticism," as Heine was to write of Europe in 1851, "no ancient pile of rubbish."[131] The United States lives in the present and is truly united — a doubly valid guarantee of its future health and prosperity.

Each aspect of this rapid vision, spanning the ages from the most dis-

---

129. The sudden change in number takes the listener from the *physical* and *historical* vision of the New World to the *ethical-literary* vision of its peoples, from the past to the present and the future. The tone too changes perceptibly from the solemn beginning to the playful smile of the close.

130. Some sort of translation may seem opportune, since these verses have often been partly misunderstood (see for example Thomas A. Riley, "Goethe and Parker Cleaveland," *PMLA*, 57, no. 4 [June 1952], p. 350; C. A. and M. R. Beard, *The American Spirit*, pp. 147–48; F. Amoroso, *Lirica e gnomica dell'ultimo Goethe* [Bari, 1946], p. 210): "America, thou hast a better lot than this old continent of ours. Thou hast neither ruins of castles nor basalts. Thou art not disturbed within thy inner self, when the moment comes to live, by useless memories and futile strife. Use ye the present with all good fortune! And if some day your sons compose poetry, may a benign fate preserve them from the stories of knights, brigands, and ghosts."

131. Heine, *Vitzliputzli*, in *Werke*, ed. O. Walzel, III, 58.

tant prehistory to the remotest future, demands and deserves a few words of comment.

The basalts are dark-colored volcanic rocks. For an ordinary mineralogist they are just rocks, to be studied and classified like any others. But Goethe was no ordinary mineralogist. For him basalts were witnesses of the earth's long-distant revolutionary past, the geological age when the surface of the planet was shaken by eruptions and catastrophes. Basalts were thus associated in Goethe's mind with everything that most horrified him, confusion, violence, the blind fury of uncontrolled forces. The man who would rather commit an injustice than tolerate disorder[132] felt an instinctive aversion to admitting that Nature, the divine lawmaker, could commit or tolerate disorder: "Nature, then," Geogony was to repeat in a poem of 1828, "is throughout its wide kingdom ever true to itself, logical and steady." And Goethe, calm and steady on his immovable granite base, will continue until 1823 to look on volcanoes as late and superficial manifestations of Nature ("oberflächliche Spätlingswirkung der Natur").[133]

Wherever he found basalts and volcanoes, black rocks and eruptive cones, Goethe immediately imagined that the people were bound to be quarrelsome and violent, and their history strife-filled and tormented. This mineralogical determinism allowed him to establish a harmonic link between nature and history; but it also linked him indissolubly both to those ancient naturalists who used the globe's millennial vicissitudes to explain the events of the last few centuries (see, for example, above, pp. 49, 58–59), and to a somewhat more recent naturalist, Benjamin Franklin, who in 1781 justified the Cévennes Protestants' rebellion in terms of the telluric revolutions in the South of France;[134] in fact it caused him to subordinate the inexhaustible development of mankind to fixed and inscrutable geological factors.

Granite was for him the legitimate sovereign. But as a *Xenie* of 1827 shrewdly whispers, "As kings are toppled, so is granite now deposed." The Plutonists are real revolutionaries of the chasms. "Pluto's pitchfork now doth threaten Revolution in the depths." And who emerges from the tumult? "Basalt, the black Devil-Moor, breaks out from the depths of Hell," exfoliating rocks, stone, and clay, and reversing the

132. *Belagerung von Mainz,* 25 July 1793, in *Werke* (Berlin, 1873), XXV, 161.

133. P. Niggli, "Goethes Schriften zur Mineralogie von 1812–1832," *Neue Zürcher Zeitung,* 7 (and 10) (October 1950). Humboldt's book on volcanoes obliged him to reconsider his convictions; but in 1828 he was again raging against Humboldt's Plutonism, and preferred to side with the minority against similar "absurdities" (*Gespräche* [Zürich, 1949], II, 532). Cf. already the Neptunist Forster, *Werke,* II, 396–97 (on basalt and volcanoes); C. G. Carus, *Goethe, zu dessen näherem Verständniss* (1843; Zürich, 1948), p. 127; substantially repeated by P. Witkop, *Goethe* (Stuttgart-Berlin, 1931), pp. 225, 323–24; E. Cassirer, *Goethe und die geschichtliche Welt,* pp. 33–34, and one and all, but particularly Wilhelm Emrich, *Die Symbolik von Faust II* (Bonn, 1957), pp. 286–89, 375–78.

134. Alfred Owen Aldridge, *Franklin and His French Contemporaries* (New York, 1957), p. 68.

natural order of things: "and so then the whole dear world would be turned upside down, geognostically too."

Goethe had already been probing these recondite relations on his journey to Italy. And when in 1816 he came across Cleaveland's treatise and began to study the mineralogy of America—in reality that of North America to the East of the Mississippi—and learned that the region had no basalts nor volcanoes, he was much impressed by this sign of telluric stability, and thus of calm and regular development.[135] "That continent is fortunate [almost the same words as the epigram], since it is without volcanic phenomena, so that the geology of the New World shows a much more stable character than that of the Old, where it seems there is no longer anything that remains stable."[136] And again in a note of 1819, with even closer approximation to the text we are considering, one reads: "Lucky the North Americans to have no basalt, no ancestors, and no classic soil."[137] The American continent is no longer characterized, as for Buffon, by its fauna, nor, as for others, by its vegetation, but by its geological structure. As early as 1795, in fact, Pictet had noted how "very regrettable" it was "for the European Naturalists, that the North American continent has not yet been studied from the geological point of view."[138]

America's present and future rested on firm foundations. Her progress had proceeded without interruption since the beginning of the world. *Keine Basalte.* But this is not all. The absence of these rocks also saved America from a ferocious and inconclusive scientific dispute. It was indeed one of the most significant advantages of not having basalts, that a country so deprived was automatically excluded from discussion of their origin. And the formation of the basalts had been precisely the point at issue in the famous quarrel that burst out in the closing decades of the eighteenth century, between the Neptunists and the Plutonists, the former steadfast in attributing the primary role in the forming of volcanic

---

135. See Riley, art. cit., pp. 350–74, esp. 359–64 (for Italy), 365–70 (for the United States). In 1818 Goethe was given P. Cleaveland's book, *An Elementary Treatise of Mineralogy and Geology* (Boston, 1816), which became his principal source of information on the minerals of the United States. Cf. also Niggli, op. cit.; and, for observations in Italy, the academic essay of G. Rovereto, *W. Goethe geologo in Italia* (Rome, 1942).

136. Quoted by Beutler, op. cit., p. 419. The Lisbon earthquake (1755) had given the boy Goethe the first violent emotion of his life (*Dichtung und Wahrheit*, I, 1; ed. Insel, Leipzig, 1922, pp. 35–36).

137. Weimar ed., Abt. *Naturwissenschaftliche Schriften*, XIII, 314, quoted by F. Strich, *Goethe und die Weltliteratur*, (Bern, 1946), p. 186, and Riley, op. cit., p. 367. Goethe held that America's crystallizations too were "different, larger, on a greater scale" than those of the other continents (conversation with J. G. Cogswell, 27 May 1817, in *Gespräche*, I, 870). Cf. *contra*, Fr. Gilij (above, p. 226); and cf. Kürnberger, who instead *bewailed* the fact that the North American landscape was so little varied and picturesque: "Nowhere have they [the Alleghanies] been lifted and torn apart by volcanic action" (op. cit., pp. 305–06). The late romantic sees monotony where Goethe admired a classic, firm simplicity of structure.

138. Pictet in a note in the *Tableau*, II, 170.

rocks to the waters, while the latter resolutely insisted on assigning it to the planet's internal fire, and more specifically to volcanoes. The great geologist Werner, Goethe's teacher, had been one of the strongest supporters of Neptunism, and his pupil, ever averse to explosions and cataclysms, had in general followed the same theories.[139]

His interest in these problems had been revived just a few months before he wrote the lines to the United States by an essay and some samples sent to him by the geology professor Karl Cäsar von Leonhard, to whom he immediately replied telling him that his "delight and pleasure in noble Mineralogy" had been rekindled, and asking him for more samples of certain sandstones and "the basalt accompanying them."[140] In *Faust,* the doctor inclines to Neptunism, while Mephistopheles, of course, is a fiery Plutonist. Goethe is on the side of God's servant, and has his adversaries speak through the mouth of the devil.

But even in that same scene Faust shows signs of losing interest in the argument: "I ask not whence? nor why?"—preferring to observe nature simply as it is.[141] Goethe was growing weary of the whole thing. Already by 1824 the bigotry shown by both sides reminded him of the wars of religion,[142] and in 1828 finally, tired of decades of "futile controversy,"[143] he lost patience with both parties. In the second part of *Faust* the polemic between Neptunists and Plutonists has a curious retrospective echo in the argument between Thales and Anaxagoras, which the former concludes with the words: "How much further does this get us? . . . Such quarrels only waste our time and leisure."[144] And just about the time he was writing those lines (ca. 1829), Goethe was asked precisely what Plutonist and Neptunist meant, and replied:

Thank the Lord that you know nothing about them; I cannot say either; one could lose one's wits trying to unravel them. But in any case these party labels

139. "I cannot give up my Neptunism" (conversation with Boisserée, 2 August 1815, in *Gespräche,* I, 794–95); and again: "much declaiming against the geologists who think they can explain everything by the action of fire," to Soret, 26 January 1828, loc. cit., II, 527. And see also the *Xenien* of the same time "The worthy Werner scarcely turns his back" and "No flames, no seas." Besides, the Neptunists were closer to the biblical account, and naturally admitted the Flood, while the Plutonists based themselves on the principles of the rationalist and "vulcanist" Buffon (*Epoques de la nature*)—so that the scientific dispute was aggravated by an *odium theologicum* (Glass, *Forerunners of Darwin,* pp. 243–44).

140. Letter of 13 February 1827, in F. Soret, *Zehn Jahre bei Goethe,* ed. H. H. Houben (Leipzig, 1929), pp. 194–95. Cf. the letter to same, 18 September 1819, quoted by Riley, op. cit., p. 369.

141. *Faust II,* act IV, opening: cf. E. Kühnemann, *Goethe* (Leipzig, 1930), II, 505–06.

142. Conversation with Eckermann, 18 May 1824, in J. P. Eckermann, *Gespräche mit Goethe,* p. 555. His rejection of the two extreme theses is already indicated by Bielschowsky (*Goethe* [Munich, 1918], II, 442, 535) and underlined by R. Magnus, *Goethe als Naturforscher* (Leipzig, 1906), pp. 275–82, who partially utilized (see pp. 260–61) G. Linck, *Goethes Verhältniss zur Mineralogie und Geognosie* (Jena, 1906), and by K. Viëtor, *Goethe* (Bern, 1949), pp. 410–12.

143. These words, that translate so precisely Goethe's "vergeblicher Streit," are those used by A. Geikie to describe the debate in his article "Geology" in the *Encyclopedia Britannica,* 11th ed., XI, 644b.

144. *Faust II,* act II, scene "Am obern Peneios"; see also the final scene, with Thales's hymn to water and the later astute remarks of Kühnemann, op. cit., II, 438–41.

are certainly meaningless by now, just so much smoke; people don't even know any more what they mean when they use them.[145]

Verily "useless memories and futile strife." In conclusion, then, America is a country without trace of prehistoric convulsions, with no fatuous pedantic squabbles. O lucky country!

But no less lucky in its want of feudal ruins and age-old grudges. Here two of Goethe's profoundest spiritual tendencies coalesce: on the one hand, his lack of sense of history, which makes him condemn as vain and frivolous all ancient quarrels, racial conflicts, and worship of tradition;[146] on the other, his aversion for sickly romanticism (romantic means "sick," classic, "healthy"), the picturesque vogue for ghost stories and anything medieval. The absence of castles in America is an eloquent symbol of the special newness of the country. Born of Renaissance Europe, it never knew a medieval period. The institutions of the Dark Ages (apart from a few transplants in Spanish America, such as the *encomienda*) and the architectural expressions of that time would ring false in America's landscape, just as in fact the neo-Gothic cathedrals, Florentine palaces, and French cloisters copied or rebuilt stone for stone on the banks of the Hudson clash with their surroundings.

Of all the emblems of old Europe, nothing caught the American imagination like the "castle" and all it implied—the serf's submission to his feudal lord, the parasitism and heraldry and the warlike defiance of that closed and fortified compound, the "conspicuous waste" and hidden domestic splendor. Zwangs-Uri, the Bastille, and the Tower of London were already symbols for the Europeans, and the Rocca Paolina too would soon become another symbol, in the poetry of Carducci. A history of the "castle" in the New World, and the approval or disapproval of its existence or nonexistence, with or without ghosts, would reflect every little nuance in the ever-changing life-ideals and worldly tastes of North American society. If we follow the path back from the manor house to the reality it symbolized, we shall find that its moats and turrets were the poetic crystallization of the fortified citadel of European history and culture.[147] It was a synthetic image, a picturesque abbreviation. And did not Dante, for that matter, gather the great minds of antiquity and the Arab world within a "noble castle"?

145. Conversation with the art critic and historian Johann Heinrich Meyer, 6 March 1828, in *Gespräche*, II, 532. In act III of *Faust II* Seismos boasts of having created the varied beauty of the earth by means of shocks. I called the debate "inconclusive"; but perhaps I should have said "inconcluded." It has had a recent revival with the classification of rocks exactly into plutonic, neptunic, and volcanic, proposed (1939) and defended by the English geologist H. H. Read. Now we can expect the new *Xenien* . . .

146. See B. Croce, *Goethe* (Bari, 1946), II, 205–07, polemicizing with Meinecke.

147. On the "castle" as symbol of the "tyranny of expired traditions": see Helmut Kuhn "Amerika—Vision und Wirklichkeit," *Anglia*, 73 (1955), p. 478.

Thus it is easy to understand why the very earliest American writers felt a hiatus between the literary conventions to which they were bound, inherited entirely from Europe,[148] and the "American" subject and setting of their creations: between the tradition in which they had been raised and which shaped both their own and their public's tastes, and the world they were to represent. Almost all the more reflective authors show an awareness of this typical contrast between form and content, and suggest ways of resolving it, either by adapting the style to the subject or claiming a classical dignity for the material.[149] Longfellow could not bear the tales of frontier adventures (the first Westerns!), and groaned: "Ah, the discomforts!" Hawthorne mentioned in 1860 "the difficulty of writing a romance about a country where there is no shadow, no antiquity, no mystery, no picturesque and gloomy wrong" (almost paraphrasing Goethe's *Xenie*).[150] And in 1862 Thoreau compared the panorama of the Rhine with that of the Mississippi: the former rich in ancient fortresses, ruins harking back to the Crusades, and the spirit of heroism and chivalry, but the latter full of a fervor of life that turned men's thoughts more to the future than the past or present. "I saw," the poet concludes, in tones that even Goethe would have approved, "that this was a Rhine stream of a different kind: that the foundations of castles were yet to be laid . . . and I felt that *this was the heroic age itself.*"[151] True, there was also a Henry James, with his inveterate nostalgia toward the Old World, who referring in fact to Hawthorne and his artistic problems repeated (in 1879) his lament that there were no feudal castles nor ivy-covered walls, nor numerous other "items of high civilization";[152] and one is hardly surprised to find Matthew Arnold echoing him, in 1888, from the Old World, with his judgment of America as "uninteresting," since among other things it lacks cathedrals, parish churches, and medieval castles.[153] But today's

148. Nor did the North Americans have ballads, popular songs, nor a folklore of their own, not to mention a primitive epic: everything had to be drawn from Europe (Stanley T. Williams, "Cosmopolitanism in American Literature before 1880," in M. Denny, *The American Writer and the European Tradition* [Minneapolis, 1950], p. 49; Cunliffe, *Literature*, p. 47 [the fact deplored in England, 1819], p. 306; and cf. above, pp. 354–55). Hence Goethe's fears of a "contagion" of romantic nonsense.

149. The first formulation of the deprecated absence of castles, fortresses, and cathedrals is found in Richard Flower (1819), according to Jones, *Strange New World*, pp. 349–50, but can in fact already be seen in Crèvecoeur (1782): see above, p. 251. Cf. also Strout, op. cit., pp. 78, 80–81, 83, 90.

150. H. James, *Hawthorne* (London, 1879), p. 42; cf. Williams, art. cit., p. 46, and H. N. Smith, "Origins of a Native American Literary Tradition," in Denny, op. cit., pp. 65–66. But Hawthorne deplores its absence: Goethe had rejoiced at it as a fortunate predisposition for the development of a healthy classical poetry!

151. H. D. Thoreau, *Walking* (1862) in *Walden and Other Writings*, ed. Brooks Atkinson (New York, 1937), pp. 612–13; author's italics. There is also a vision of the Rhine and its castles in "Civil Disobedience," ibid., p. 652.

152. H. James, *Hawthorne*, p. 43, also quoted by Jones, *American Literature*, pp. 64, 121, 150; and by Williams, op. cit., pp. 46–47. Cf. below, pp. 547–48.

153. M. Arnold, *Civilization in the United States*, 1888, in *Five Uncollected Essays*, ed. K. Allott (Liverpool, 1953), pp. 54–55, 102–03. On American reactions, and more on his influence in the "uninteresting" United States, see John Henry Raleigh, *Matthew Arnold and American Culture* (Berkeley

Americans are more in the tradition of Goethe and Thoreau, and usually ready to extol the natural beauties of their vast country as superior to the monuments and ruins of the Middle Ages.[154] "It is better to turn directly to Nature than to busy oneself laboriously with the dross of past ages," sounds like a very "American" statement, but it was actually Goethe who said it.[155] (Australia too, for that matter, a country whose cultural development came even later than that of the United States, relied on the worn-out motifs of European romanticism as its models until the end of the nineteenth century. Crawford recalls that even after 1880 the Australians "turned away from Australia for artistic or literary inspiration," and wrote Tennysonian lyrics about fields and skylarks since "colonial life was regarded as too crude to serve for artistic inspiration," and adds in a footnote: "I remember seeing a sketch-book filled with drawings made in the early 1880's by my mother as a pupil in a little up-country school. The drawings, beautifully done, were of tottering ruins of *Old World castles* and abbeys, covered with ivy.")[156]

Goethe's final shaft against the tales of knights, brigands, and specters can obviously be linked to his approval of the fact that America lacks the required scenario for these romantic fancies, but it belongs no less evidently to the current literary polemic: it is the sting in the tail of the *Xenie*, added as a postscript to the lyric. For the "basalts" too, in fact, we saw that the term refers both to a (prehistoric) fact and the (current) arguments about the fact. And likewise we saw that the danger of ghosts appearing on America's soil existed precisely because of the absence of other neutralizing literary interests. American poetry might have been born spectral and romantic by default. The same disturbing possibility had occurred to people in the United States too; and it was actually in 1828[157]

---

and Los Angeles, 1961), esp. 43, 78, 151, 180; and Henry F. May, *The End of American Innocence: A Study of the First Years of Our Own Time, 1912–17* (London, 1960), pp. 32–33. But already half a century earlier Mrs. Trollope from Britain, while admiring the banks of the Ohio and the Monongahela, had regretted that they were not adorned with feudal castles and Gothic abbeys (*Domestic Manners of the Americans*, 1832, IV and XVIII, and cf. below, chap. 8, n. 220), while another European traveler, who was in America from 1849 to 1857, after having discovered that the Hudson had neither castles nor ruins, added: "I do not regret the ruins and the legends of the Rhine," and indeed admired the Mississippi's imposing natural "castles": "The ruins of the Rhine are wretched compared to these gigantic remains" (Frederika Bremer, *La vie de famille*, I, 38; II, 263; cf. also I, 144, and, on the absence of popular songs and legends, ibid., pp. 66–67, 361; III, 256, 368). On the commonplace of the parallel between Hudson and Rhine (in Melville, Parkman, James, etc.), useful references in Christof Wegelin, *The Image of Europe in Henry James* (Dallas, Tex., 1958), pp. 170–71.

154. Example: "Our mountain passes are as picturesque as feudal castles" (Nevins and Commager, *America*, p. vi). Other examples in "Castles and Culture—America and the Gothic Tradition," *Times Literary Supplement*, 17 September 1954 ("American writing Today," p. xliv). The title of the article is taken from chap. 40, "Castle and Culture," of Mark Twain's *Life on the Mississippi*.

155. *Tag- und Jahreshefte*, 1812, in *Autobiographische Schriften* (Leipzig, 1910), III, 521 (concerning G. Bruno). Cf. Meinecke, op. cit., p. 551.

156. My italics: R. M. Crawford, "The Australian National Character—Myth and Reality," *Cahiers d'histoire mondiale*, II, no. 3 (1955), pp. 715–16.

157. Goethe's epigram was translated into English already in 1831 (Riley, op. cit., p. 350), but German authors were beginning to be read in the original.

that the young F. H. Hedge, later to become famous as a theologian and Germanist, included the following lines in an address he was giving to an academic gathering:

> Let foreign climes their varied stories unfold:
> And German horrors rise in dark array,
> And German names more horrible than they.
> Amazed we hear of Werke and Gedichte,
> Of Schlegel, Schleiermacher, Richter, Fichte,
> And thou, great Goethe, whose illustrious name,
> So oft mis-spelt and mis-pronounced by fame,
> Still puzzles English jaws and English teeth,
> With Goty, Gurrte, Gewter, and Go-ethe.[158]

Goethe would doubtless have read these verses too with amusement and pleasure. How irritated he used to get, in fact, whenever he recalled the puns that Herder had allowed himself on his name, so many decades earlier: "der von Göttern Du stammst, von Goten oder von Kote, Goethe?"![159]

By some vengeful and ironic twist of fate, however, it came about that all the most successful works of the new poets of the United States bore the clear imprint of those very features so passionately deprecated by Goethe (and by Hedge): and so we find specters and horrors galore in Irving and Poe (and even James), nobles and prostrated sinners in Hawthorne, legendary figures of sea dogs and brigands in Melville and the tales of the Far West[160] — the "romantic material" in its entirety, in fact, reworked with relish and liveliness, and often with a seriousness of approach and a poetic inspiration that would have frozen the smile on the lips of the seventy-eight-year-old Goethe.

But there is one more element we must not neglect in those lines he wrote in 1827. America is politically united: it has no internal discords nor old scores to settle, and is thus assured of a happier destiny.

This theme, the lauding of its freedom from strife as America's supreme gift, is one that can be traced back at least to the times when America offered itself as a refuge to the persecuted Europeans. An almost pre-Goethian tone can be detected already in Andrew Marvell's previously cited poem on the wondrous "Bermudas" (ca. 1653: see above, chap. 5, n. 433): "a grassy stage, / Safe from the storms' and prelates' rage";[161]

---

158. Williams, op. cit., p. 55.

159. Dichtung und Wahrheit, pt. II, bk. X; ed. cit., p. 432.

160. Even the rites and customs of the Ku Klux Klan have been held to be traceable back to the tribunals of the Holy Vehme represented by Goethe in his Goetz von Berlichingen: cf. J. Urzidil, Das Glück der Gegenwart: Goethes Amerikabild (Zürich, 1957), pp. 23–24.

161. In the Oxford Book of English Verse, 1250–1918 (Oxford, 1939), pp. 404–05. The expression seems to echo the words of John Milton, who had seen so many good Christians obliged to flee England, "whom nothing but the wide Ocean, and the savage deserts of America could hide and shelter from the fury of the Bishops" (Of Reformation Touching Church Discipline in England, 1641, in Works, ed. F. A. Patterson [New York], III, 138).

and even, I would say, in Ronsard: "If religion and the Christian faith bring such fruits, I prefer to leave it. And to go off and live in exile in the Indies, under the Antarctic pole, where the savages dwell and happily follow the law of nature";[162] or, a few years later, in Lescarbot (*Histoire de la Nouvelle France,* 1609), who mentions among the motives for emigrating to the New World the desire "to flee a corrupted world" and leave behind "the strife, quarrels, and trials."[163]

But the elderly Goethe's faith in the future of the United States, of this nation so little burdened down with history, can be linked to his historical pessimism, or rather nihilism.[164] Yet it is also part of his religious addiction to harmonious development, uninterrupted by sudden jolts or setbacks. While Hegel, as we shall see (cited below, p. 437), points to this lack of internal tension and class conflicts as a *weakness* of the United States, Goethe instead looks on it as a sure *promise* of ascending progress. The very thing which to Hegel seems a deficiency of *dialectic* is admired by Goethe as fullness and *harmony.*

What else? In the same year in which he wrote the lines to the United States Goethe was explaining to Eckermann that the United States was bound to expand beyond the Rocky Mountains, and thence to the Pacific, and thus to develop an immense trade with the Orient, and thus to secure the isthmus of Panama, and open a canal through it which would take warships and merchant ships of any tonnage, with incalculable consequences for all the civilized and uncivilized world.[165] The vision is so well argued that Goethe seems to have the gift of prophecy.

The prophecy in its turn caught fire in the poet's eager mind, gathered round it other hopes and other dreams, smouldered in secret and then exploded again in a new vision. The image of Europe strewn with black rocks, ruins, and specters lurked in the depths of Goethe's saddened spirit.[166] And just about that same time another creature emerges and takes shape in the poet's imagination, the restless, insolent, surprising little figure of the *Homunculus.* The *Homunculus,* the completely artificial man, born in a test tube from a crystallized mixture, a creature without history and without parents, not to mention ancestors, speaks to his cousin Mephistopheles as the American of the epigram might speak

162. *Oeuvres,* ed. P. Laumonier (Paris, 1914–40), VIII, 14–15, quoted by Lapp, op. cit., p. 155.

163. Quoted in G. Atkinson, *Les nouveaux horizons de la renaissance française* (Paris, 1935), pp. 105–06.

164. It is significant that Alexander Herzen quoted (1 January 1868) the first eight lines of Goethe's *Xenie* to greet America as the land of the future, devoid of historic relics or petty squabbles or feudal influences, and thus equal to Russia in revolutionary possibilities (Max M. Laserson, *The American Impact on Russia – Diplomatic and Ideological – 1784–1917* [New York, 1950], pp. 231–32).

165. Eckermann, *Gespräche,* 21 February 1827, pp. 599–600. 1827 is also the date of a proposal for reworking L. Gall's *Auswanderung nach den Vereinigten Staaten* (in *Schriften zur Literatur* [Leipzig, 1914], II, 321–22), a violently anti-American work, "the product of a disappointed immigrant" (Doll, op. cit., p. 508).

166. On Goethe's melancholy at the time of composition (June 1827), see Riley, op. cit., pp. 356–57.

to our old continent: "Thou, from the North, / And in the age of mist brought forth, / In knighthood's and in priesthood's murky den, / How should thy sight be clearer, then?" All around is blackened crumbling stone, ogival and repellent, grotesquely florid. Away, right away, to the Thessalian Walpurgisnacht! Mephistopheles, who a little earlier, when he had said that he saw nothing of Faust's dream, had earned the reply "How should thy sight be clearer, then!" now objects that he has never heard of such goings-on, and is then mocked for being not only blind but deaf: "How should it reach your ears?" The ears of the *vieux jeu* devil are only attuned to the skeletons and ghosts of the romantic ballads. "Romantic ghosts are all you know." Chivalry, ruins, specters, the low literature of current fashion: nothing is missing. . . . Even the science of the schools, even the good Wagner is dismissed. Farewell, and away, quickly, to the banks of the Peneus, to the Pharsalian plains! America and the Hellad serve equally well as vigorous antitheses of senile and medievalizing Europe.

Nor does this exhaust the hidden ferment of his imagination. The *Homunculus* is or at least claims to be superior to Mephistopheles, whose creature he is, however. He is the spirit that sees the present (*die Gegenwart*) in all its clarity and transparency, and thus represents the life of intense activity as opposed to intellectualism: he is an impatient Faust, without inner discords.[167] On one side, then, he can be the mouthpiece of the new, unhistoried, and strife-free continent, the continent which in fact symbolizes "*die Gegenwart*."[168] In another way he foreshadows Faust's last yearning, which is only satisfied when a new land is torn from the water, half paradise and half artifice, a land where millions of men may be able to pursue free and active lives.

It has often been suggested that there are elements in Faust's dreamland that seem to draw their inspiration from the deeds of the American pioneers,[169] and it is also known that messages and suggestions from the

167. Eckermann, *Gespräche*, 16 December 1829, ed. cit., pp. 374–76; F. Gundolf, *Goethe* (Berlin, 1917), pp. 770–71.

168. See Urzidil, op. cit.

169. One can perhaps glimpse an anticipation of Goethe's land torn from the waves and covered with gardens, meadows, and villages in Barlow's lines on "the glad coast . . . Won from the wave" that "presents a new-formed land, yields richer fruits and spreads a kinder soil" and the "free-born souls" that inhabit it, etc. (*Vision of Columbus* [1787], canto IV, quoted in Brie, op. cit., p. 376, n. 36). See also M. Kerbaker, *L'episodio di Bauci e Filemone nel Fausto del Goethe* (Naples, 1903), p. 31 ("a certain tint of Americanism"); F. Strich, *Goethe und die Weltliteratur* (Bern, 1946), p. 188; Beutler, op. cit., pp. 405, 449; T. Mann, *Goethe und die Demokratie* (Oxford, 1949), p. 21; Viëtor, op. cit., pp. 368–69; H. A. Korff, *Geist der Goethezeit* (Leipzig, 1953), IV, 647–48 (for the analogy suggested by the conclusion of the *Wanderjahre*, the liberating "Auswanderung nach Amerika"). W. Mommsen (*Die politischen Anschauungen Goethes* [Stuttgart, 1948], p. 214n.) notes then that in the *Paralipomena* (act IV, Insel-Ausgabe, p. 551) Faust refers to the "advantages of society in its beginnings" and wants to associate himself with the natives. In act V of *Faust*, on the other hand, the natives are massacred and primitive society destroyed. The conqueror replaces the farmer. But even before that Kerbaker had seen

New World besieged Goethe's mind in these last years, contributing to that prodigious creation of myth and plastic symbol. Faust concludes his supreme vision of a free people on a free soil with the words: "*If I could but see* such a swarm," saddened by the certainty that he will *not* see it. The eighty-seven-year-old Goethe prophesies that the United States will stretch out from ocean to ocean, and sighs: "*If only I might live to see that;* but I shall not."[170]

It remains to be seen how Goethe arrived at this vision of America, so conceptually prolific and reechoing with deep poetic chords. It was not the polemic with Buffon or de Pauw that led him there. The degenerative laws formulated by Buffon were the very antithesis of Goethe's whole zoological philosophy (see above, p. 255) and more generally of his resolute reluctance to historicize nature. Of de Pauw he knows and quotes the later works, the study of the Egyptians and Chinese,[171] and that of the Greeks;[172] never the most famous one of all, of the Americans. But in any case he would never have approved of its explanations in terms of cataclysms and earthquakes and terrifying convulsions of the globe, and the anti-Neptunism of his theory of rocks.[173] The poet who, like Thales, saw humidity as the fount of life and shaper of the world — "All things sprang from Water! All things are sustained by Water!"[174] — could only remain impervious to the classic and fatal image of America as a wet, indeed sodden world.

But his overall opinion of de Pauw is singularly benevolent. Visiting Pempelfort, on his way back from the excursion into France, Goethe's thoughts linger on that "marvelous" time, hardly more than a generation ago, but already almost impossible to conjure up vividly. Voltaire had freed humanity from the fetters of ancient superstition and opened men's minds to doubt; and while he fought to bring down the authority of the clergy, "and cast his eye particularly on Europe, so de Pauw stretched his conquering spirit over further continents." Our muchmaligned de Pauw is held up by Goethe as the Voltaire of the extra-European world! "He would allow neither Chinese nor Egyptians the

in the episode of Baucis and Philemon the parabola of the innocence of whoever lives in conformity with Nature and is swept away by the inexorable violence of Progress.

170. Eckermann, *Gespräche*, 21 February 1827, ed. cit., p. 600.

171. *Kampagne in Frankreich* (Pempelfort, November 1792) in *Werke*, ed. Berlin, XXV, 99.

172. *Italienische Reise* (28 May 1787; ed. cit., II, 60), confirming that one can apply to the *lazzaroni* what de Pauw said of the cynics, namely that given the climate of Greece they did not, when all is said and done, have such a miserable life. "There are today in Naples," De Pauw goes on (*Recherches sur les Grecs*, ed. cit., II, 148–49), "beggars who would refuse the viceroyalty of Norway, if it was offered to them." Goethe translated almost the whole passage: de Pauw's book, remember, came out exactly in 1787.

173. *Recherches sur les Américains*, II, 326–51 (*Sur les vicissitudes de notre globe*), esp. p. 343; cf. above, p. 58.

174. *Faust II*, act II, scene "The rocky coves on the Aegean Sea," toward the end.

honor which age-old prejudice had heaped upon them." As canon of
Xanten, near Düsseldorf, he was on friendly terms with Jacobi (see
above, chap. 4, n. 285). And how many others should be mentioned along
with these three, Goethe goes on, though in fact he mentions precisely
three more; only three, but neither obscure nor mediocre men: Hemster-
huis, Diderot, and Rousseau.[175] De Pauw—like Dante, "a sixth among
this band"—is indeed in good company. . . .

Thus if Goethe never speaks of the *Recherches sur les Américains,* it
is probably for another basic reason: at the time of its appearance and
in the immediately subsequent years of fiercest polemics, America was
completely beyond his mental horizons. The young Goethe ignores the
New World. Klopstock, then already advanced in age, hails the American revolution with hymns of praise. Klinger, still a very young man,
uses America as the setting of his *Sturm und Drang.* Goethe remains
cold and indifferent.[176] His beloved Lili tells him she is ready to flee to
America with him. Goethe will not leave his native land.[177] America is
"accursedly far away." He sighs only for Italy; and even when he sails
from Naples to Palermo on a beautiful yacht built in America, his gaze
never looks beyond the shores of the Mediterranean: "Sicily points me
toward Asia and Africa."[178]

In Brunswick in 1784 he attends a pantomime with "Soldiers returned
from America disguised as savages," tattooed and painted after the
fashion (apparently) of the redskins; and though they strike the persons
of the *beau monde* as terrible or repulsive, Goethe remains quite unmoved. Resolutely anti-Rousseauian and not in the least "primitivist,"
Goethe sees in the spectacle merely "the efforts of the human race to
rejoin the class of animals." The tattoos are no more than imitations of
the fleeces of quadrupeds and the multicolored feathers of the birds;
when the redskins compare themselves to these creatures they are
ashamed of going about naked, with this smooth uninteresting skin that
nature gave man. Then as for their dances and mimicry, "that is very
like the behavior of monkeys."[179]

America does not interest him, the native bores and disgusts him. It
almost seems as though the savage, poised thus between man and beast,
tending in fact to degenerate, though not yet fallen from human dignity,

---

175. *Kampagne in Frankreich,* loc. cit. Goethe read or reread the second *Recherches* in 1813–15
(see R. Michéa, *Le "Voyage en Italie" de Goethe* [Paris, 1945], p. 366, n. 34; cf. ibid., pp. 19, 66, 372).

176. "However I only took an interest in all these happenings insomuch as they touched upon the
greater society. I myself and my narrow circle did not busy ourselves with newspapers and news"
(*Dichtung und Wahrheit,* IV, bk. 17—the book of Lili!—Insel ed., p. 750).

177. Conversation with Soret, 5 May 1830, in *Gespräche,* II, 671n. (in Houben ed., p. 389n.).

178. *Italienische Reise,* 26 March 1787; ed. cit., I, 229.

179. Letter of 21 August 1784, in *Goethes Briefe an Charlotte von Stein,* ed. J. Fraenkel (Jena, 1908),
II, 224–25. There is a certain de Pauwian flavor about Goethe's words: the *Recherches* describes the
character of the redskin "by reducing the American savage to his animal instinct" (ed. cit., I, 123), but
on the question of tattooing de Pauw is much more realistic (ibid., I, 202–06).

fills Goethe with a muffled horror, a secret dread of instability. When he writes to his friend Charlotte von Stein he tries to make fun of the savage, but his irritable tone betrays his uneasiness.

The crisis, or rather the beginning of a slow but complete transposition, came in '89. Disturbed and ever more anxious at the terrible developments of the Revolution, the unleashing of the rage of the populace and the glowering threat of the organized masses, Goethe looks anxiously around for a new land where man may freely develop all his faculties. The various parts of *Wilhelm Meister* reflect the phases of this search, the progressive concentration of his yearning, from generic *Wandern* to necessary emigration (*Auswandern*), which still however smells of flight, and finally to the ideal of a community in America, which is both flight and conquest, escape and palingenesis. Already in the *Lehrjahre* (1795) America shines forth as the embryonic fatherland of a new humanity: and immediately acquires all the characteristics of a promised land, a world of the future, a sure refuge from the ills weighing down on the men and values of this too agitated Europe.[180]

In the years that follow this faith is nutured on extensive, substantial reading, on the words and writings of the recently returned Humboldt (1804),[181] and conversations with the long series of Americans who come to visit him at Weimar from 1793 onward, among whom are many extremely distinguished men: Trumbull (1797), Ticknor (1816), Bancroft (1819), Calvert (1825), and a select group of other scholars and politicians.[182] In 1818 he writes to Voigt that he is absorbed in a number of works on the United States: "Such a growing world is well worth the trouble of looking into."[183] And the following year, 1819, the year when the idea of the epigram is beginning to take shape, Goethe is already sighing: "If I were twenty years younger, I would set sail for North America."[184] In the same year he sends his works as a gift to Harvard University, to feel himself closer (as he says in the dedication) to

---

180. Copious and precise documentation in Beutler, op. cit., pp. 396–408; cf. also Bielschowsky, op. cit., II, 542–44, and, on the development of Goethe's interest in the United States after 1815, Mommsen, op. cit., pp. 175–79, and Castle, op. cit., pp. 184–85, 253–54, 406; on the character of America in the *Meister*, Mommsen, op. cit., p. 275, and Viëtor, op. cit., pp. 289–90, who brings out well how Goethe's enthusiasm for America did not for a moment imply any *Europamüdigkeit*, was indeed bound up with his devotion to the Old World. Riley, op. cit., p. 364, asserts too summarily that the United States "came to mean to the older Goethe something of what Italy had meant to the younger man."

181. Kuhn (art. cit., p. 477) quoting Wadepuhl (Walter, *Goethe's Interest in the New World* [Jena, 1934], p. 18) is however too peremptory when he asserts: "Goethe's discovery of America occurred, so it seems, very late, around the year 1807, and the impulse was given to him by an offprint of Alexander von Humboldt's 'Ideen zu einer Physiognomik der Gewächse,' sent to him by the author."

182. Beutler, op. cit., pp. 408–19. These visits flattered Goethe the way those of other North Americans did Byron (see above, p. 347).

183. Quoted in Riley, op. cit., pp. 352–53.

184. Conversation with F. von Müller, 10 May 1819, in *Gespräche*, II, 54; cf. conversation with Boisserée, 2 August 1815, ibid., I, 798 (and, jokingly, conversation with Müller, 13 July 1818: ibid., II, 36). Further sighs are heard by Eckermann on 15 February 1824: see Eckermann's *Gespräche*, p. 84.

"that wonderful country that attracts the attention of the whole world with its sober system of laws promoting a development that will know no bounds."[185]

In 1826, finally, Prince Bernard of Weimar, the brave and brilliant second son of the Grand Duke, came home from extended travels in the United States, full of enthusiasm and admiration for the young American republic. In the lines that Goethe wrote to welcome him back, infused with a borrowed distillation of all the young prince's optimism, more than one expression anticipates or echoes the lines in the last part of *Faust* that relate the feverish activity of the aged but indomitable doctor: "There's a buzzing like a beehive, / With the building and carrying in." And Baucis says: "By day in vain the workers raged, / Pick and shovel, blow on blow." And Philemon: "Wise lords set their serfs in motion, / Dikes upraised and ditches led."

Goethe to Bernard: "The river's current now is ruled, / Through the scarcely peopled land." And the bewildered old woman: "Where the fires at night were swarming, / Stood the following day a dike . . . Burning torches leading seaward, / On the morrow a canal."

The *Wanderer*, when one day the tempest throws him up on the "dunes," finds that now there is a "garden" there. And "a garden blooms in the sand," in the America from whence the prince returns.

One final echo of his yearning for ideological incorporation with the United States – "He feels the joy of the noble land, he gives himself up to it" – is revealed in Faust's impatience to see the people flooding into the new and splendid land he has torn from the waves, and living there in perfect liberty: which liberty is not a gift of heaven, but something to be earned, like one's living, with each day's work. The masonic song for the returning Prince Bernard closes with two solemn chords, each echoing the same theme: "The earth becomes free through love, and great through deeds."[186]

IX. LENAU: THE PROMISED LAND BECOMES THE ACCURSED LAND

Nikolas Lenau's first notion of America, of the United States, formed at about the same time, differed little from Goethe's. But he can more

185. Beutler, op. cit., pp. 418–19.
186. One could find other parallels, particularly with the words of Faust in his exhortations to work (as in Urzidil, op. cit., pp. 10–11), but perhaps they would be just a little too subtle. Suffice it to recall that Faust's last undertaking is a canal, a ditch (*Graben*): and Bernard was particularly interested in the vast network of canals in the United States (Beutler, op. cit., p. 427). His book was published in Weimar in 1828, and in the same year, in English, at Philadelphia (Doll, op. cit., p. 515, and Castle, op. cit., pp. 207–08, 253). Again in 1830 Goethe reminded an American of Duke Bernard's "enthusiastic attachment to America" (conversation with J. B. Harrison, 25 March 1830, *Gespräche*, II, 681), despite certain unpleasant experiences he suffered, which are joyfully recounted by the spiteful Mrs. Trollope (*Domestic Manners*, XXVIII).

easily be linked with the travelers and naturalists of the previous century than with the poets and philosophers of his time, inasmuch as he insisted on going to see America for himself, and returned filled with loathing and anguish.

Lenau was always a restless and tormented spirit, but intensely sincere in each of his successive enthusiasms; he can pass for one of America's most ardent apologists or most stubborn slanderers, the only difference being in whether he is writing before or after his arrival in the United States. A man of essentially uncritical temperament, he combines the most extreme poles of the polemic in one person. He contributes no new opinions or elements to the debate, indeed relies exclusively on the motifs already present in the eighteenth century. But by reliving the polemic sentimentally within the space of a few months he shows once more how the apologists and slanderers actually operate on the same scientific level, or rather on no scientific level, but on that other level, be it higher or lower, more fiery or more celestial, where love and hate, dislike and ardent longing, meet face to face and take each other's places.

Disappointed and saddened at the repression of the liberal movements of 1830, and in particular at the harsh repression of the Polish revolt (September 1831), Lenau mentally turns his back on the Europe of Metternich and Czar Nicholas. He is suddenly seized with the idea of emigrating to another world, and all his dreams "crystallize" around that notion.[187] America is a divine flame, Liberty, the prosperous strand where tyrants cannot reach, the fatherland, the true fatherland of the poet: "New World, free world, on whose richly flourishing shore the wave of tyranny shatters, I greet thee, my fatherland!"[188]

The journey will be safe and easy. And in America, land of plenty, there are neither thieves nor beggars and the wild animals are less to be feared than Europe's mad dogs. Over there all his desires will be fulfilled. He will hear no more talk of this "damned politics," this "truly revolting politics that we have here." He will learn more in the school of the virgin forests than the learned naturalist Schubert can teach him. Five years will scarcely suffice to exhaust this "enormous storehouse" of natural beauty. His song lives and throbs with nature, "and in America nature is more beautiful, more powerful than in Europe": his poetry will be renewed and raised to fresh heights. "I need America for my education." The latent and half-conscious forces of his spirit will be aroused and

187. A letter of 17 February 1832 talks about literary projects for the summer (ed. Eduard Castle [Leipzig, 1911], III, 139); the following one, of 11 [?] March 1832 shows him determined and enthusiastic about emigrating, impatient to get to know "the American monkeys" and the treelined banks of the Missouri (ibid., III, 141). According to V. Errante, (*Lenau* [Messina-Milan, 1935], p. 52) on the other hand, the idea was first conceived while he was still in Vienna (1824–30).

188. *Abschied, Lied eines Auswandernden*, ed. cit., I, 121–22.

shaken by the great thundering voice of Niagara: "How beautiful the mere name Niagara is! Niagara! Niagara!"[189]

America will benefit not only his lyrical resources but his economic resources too: he will buy a thousand acres of land, and install his good manservant Philip as tenant; the steward will be a certain Ludwig Häberle, another very honest and capable emigrant who was a carpenter at home: the contract will of course be ratified by the courts — everything is in order: "in three or four years the value of my property will have multiplied at least six times" — and there's no call for laughter, the accounts have been worked out down to the last detail — and he will then be able to live off his income in Austria without lifting one finger.[190] . . . Even La Fontaine's Perrette, with her milk pail on her head, was never more ironically optimistic: "Everyone has daydreams; there is nothing sweeter."

In vain his friends and relatives and even his beloved sister seek to dissuade him. In vain the government makes a public announcement of its lack of faith in the organizer of the expedition the poet is joining; in vain the faithful Kerner warns him against the seductions of the same man, a hairy devil with a great beard "like a prehensile tail" and a belly like a wrinkled purse: we must save Lenau, he wrote to Mayer, "from the prehensile tail of this American specter!"[191] Even the Stuttgart wit that trills away to him: *"Missouri, Missouri, ubi vos estis pecuniam perdituri"* — "Missouri, Missouri, where your wealth will turn to penury"[192] — is wast-

189. Letters of 13 and 16 March 1832, ed. cit., III, 142, 145–46. Lenau had just finished reading Gottfried Duden, *Bericht ueber eine Reise nach den westlichen Staaten Nordamerikas* (Elberfeld, 1829; ibid., VI, 226). Duden had "romantically described" Missouri "as a wilderness paradise," thus making it a center of attraction for the German emigrants (H. Wish, *Early America*, pp. 326–27). Even the great Niebuhr immediately gave it a warm recommendation, but particularly for what it had said "about the Germans there, and about the evil consequences of the persistence of the English structure in a barbarian isolation" (letter of 14 June 1829, *Lebensnachrichten*, III, 235). Later Kürnberger too (op. cit., p. 319) mentions "Duden's Missouri and similar fantastic works about America," although by 1837 Duden himself had published a repentant "self-criticism," a *Selbstanklage wegen seines amerikanischen Reiseberichtes zur Warnung vor fernerem leichtsinnigen Auswandern* (Castle, op. cit., pp. 209–10, 408); cf. also Eckhart G. Franz, *Das Amerikabild der deutschen Revolution von 1848–49: Zum Problem der Uebertragung gewachsener Verfassungsformen* (Heidelberg, 1958), p. 32.

190. Letter of 27 July 1832 (from Amsterdam, in other words when he was already on his way), ed. cit., III, 184–85. The contract can be read there, III, 204–07; on Lenau's subsequent sad adventures with American real estate, see Errante, op. cit., p. 118; *Werke*, ed. cit., IV, 271; V, 73, 329, 389–90, 395, 425–26. On the joys of return, which he then thought to be imminent, cf. also the letters in the Castle ed., III, 146, 151–52, 169–70, 191–92, etc.

191. *Werke*, III, 143–44.

192. C. Schaeffer, in the Leipzig edition, Bibliographisches Institut, I, xxxvi, xlii; cf. Castle ed., III, 148, 153, and Errante, op. cit., pp. 53–55. A few years later (1848) an American was to refer to "Missouri, or 'Misery', as disappointed emigrants call The State" (J. L. Peyton, *Over the Alleghanies* [London, 1870], in Tryon, ed., *A Mirror for Americans*, p. 596). One can gain some idea of the hyperboles used to laud the virgin lands of America already in the seventeenth century from the passages collected by Blanke, op. cit., pp. 299–300, and in Lenau's time from the novel of F. Kürnberger, said to have been inspired by the poet's American adventure; in particular "the luxuriousness of the lower Missouri defies all belief" (*Der Amerikamüde*, p. 70). That Lenau did provide the inspiration for the work is denied on the other hand by Karl J. Arndt, in an essay seeking to demonstrate that in America, and

ing his breath. His company is on the road to ruin. Its passport has expired. No matter. His first collection of poetry is handed over to the printers, a sort of farewell salutation to Europe and the past, and Lenau sets out for the future, toward the New World. He sails from Holland, and no sooner does he get a glimpse of the ocean from the mouths of the Zuyder Zee than he is convinced he will fall madly in love with it; in fact, he already feels a new lyrical afflatus upon him.[193]

Baltimore, 8 October 1832 (a little more than a year since another rebel, Edgar Allen Poe, had sought refuge there; the fateful earthly trajectories of the two poets skimmed past each other, but never touched): seen from the ship, the coastline is pleasant, but the first encounters with the people are enough to shock and repel the young German. They offer him cider, but he does not like it. "Cider," he jokes, "rhymes with '*Leider*'" ("alas"). They have no wine, and no nightingales. Developing this latter theme, of purely eighteenth-century flavor (see above, pp. 161 ff.), Lenau immediately weaves a lament on the unhappiness of American nature. The nightingale is right to shun these wretches whose only thought is making money. The silence has a deep significance. It is a sort of "poetic curse" (*ein poetischer Fluch,* three times repeated) weighing down upon America. It would take the voice of Niagara to rouse these boors, to remind them that there are other gods than those coined in the mint. One glimpse of them in a restaurant is enough to make one detest them for ever. Quickly, away up to Niagara, and then home again at the first opportunity.[194] The mirage of America fades at the first sight of these merchant-ridden shores, but reappears again further off, in the glittering spray that climbs from the thundering cataracts. Will it prove any more real up there?

No: the winter passes, and Lenau—already suffering from gout and scurvy, and nursing a head wound caused by a fall from a sled—is attacked by rheumatism; his aversion for the people and the place gets stronger by the day: a rough climate and a rough people; and not boldly and powerfully rough, like the primitives, but feeble, meek and thus doubly repugnant. *"Buffon is right* when he says that in America men and animals decline from generation to generation. Here I have not yet seen

particularly through the influence of the Harmonists of Economy, Lenau recovered his faith in a personal God, and abandoning his liberal radicalism became a moderate and conservative: this would thus be "The Effect of America on Lenau's Life and Work," (*Germanic Review,* 33, no. 1 [February 1958], pp. 125–43).

193. Letter of 1 August 1832, ed. cit., III, 187; and on arrival: "The sea has gone to my heart" (letter of 16 October 1832, ed. cit., III, 190).

194. Letter of 16 October 1832, ed. cit., III, 192–94. And a few months later, ratifying the first verdict: "The formation of the Americans is a mercantile and technical one. Here the practical man develops in his most frightful emptiness" (letters of 6 and 8 March 1833; ed. cit., III, 201; VI, 7).

a courageous dog, a fiery horse, or a man full of passion. Nature is terribly languid (*matt*). There are no nightingales, indeed there are no real songbirds at all." And there are none because nature in America is never so happy or so sad that it must sing. It has no feelings, no imagination, and thus cannot give them to its creatures. The lines of the mountains, the folds of the valleys, everything there is monotonous and unimaginative. The American women are totally unattractive. The men pay them every sort of reverence and compliment, but then there are hill dwellers in Germany who venerate cretins. And, oh dear, when these women sing in society, they are worse than the birds: the sounds they emit remind one of what one gets by wetting one's finger and rubbing it along the edge of a glass — a truly horrifying thing, because every note reechoes the frightening emptiness of their minds.[195]

Even the American men of European descent have become enfeebled and spineless. The Germans that have lived there some years have lost all their energy, and even their burning fever of nostalgia. The emigration to America is the bitterest fruit of the sad situation in Germany. Lenau, in a delightfully spontaneous emotional reaction, fears that he too might lose his memory of home, his desire to go back. Return he must, at the earliest possible moment. "In this vast fogbath [*Nebelbade*] of America, love's veins are quietly opened and its lifeblood drained slowly away, and it notices nothing. I really do not know why I longed so much to see America."[196]

The wheel comes full circle: America plunges from "promised land" to "accursed land. . . . Here are noxious airs, creeping death."[197] Everything is inconvenient and displeasing, the streets, the beds, the desks, the pens, the ink: everything.[198] By the time he returns, the radiant United States of his departure has become the "Swinish States of America" — "ver-

195. Letters of 6 and 8 March 1833; ed. cit., III, 200–01; VI, 6–7 ("It had already occurred *to many naturalists* that here men and animals further deteriorate from generation to generation. It is literally true!") (my italics). But, let us remember once more, Buffon does *not* extend the degeneration to man. In the above-mentioned novel of Kürnberger, however, the degeneration of the Europeans in America is considered proverbial ("and so let anyone deny the transatlantic degeneration of the races!" op. cit., p. 385), even if it is sometimes treated ironically (ibid., p. 200) or extended from the United States to the whole tropical world (ibid., pp. 260, 394, 414).

196. Letters of 5 and 8 March 1833, ed. cit., III, 196–97; IV, 7–8; cf. also the letter of 6 March 1833, ibid., III, 203; and Chateaubriand: "An abrupt reversal occurred within my mind . . . I suddenly interrupted my journey, and said to myself: 'Return to France'" (*Memoires d'outre-tombe*, ed. cit., I, 340); and the moving story of Kurt (in Zacharias Werner's *Vierundzwanzigste Februar* [see above, chap. 5, n. 401]), who in savage America hears the call of the Swiss lakes, the waterfalls, glaciers, alpine bells, like a chorus of voices inviting him to return home: "Come! Come!" (ed. Reclam, pp. 31–32). The *locus classicus* of this anxious fear is obviously the *Odyssey*, bk. IX, where Ulysses chains his two weeping companions and flees from the lotus-eaters to prevent others tasting the sweet lotus and "the fatherland falling from their hearts."

197. Letter of 5 March 1833, ed. cit., III, 197; cf. "sad soil" in the letter of 8 March 1833, ed. cit., VI, 8; and the de Pauwian visions of Moorfeld-Lenau in Kürnberger: "From every gorge, from every lowland, swamp, and fen the fever wriggles loose" (op. cit., pp. 398, 405, 408).

198. Letter of 6 March 1833, ed. cit., III, 203.

schweinte, *nicht* vereinte *amerikanische Staaten.*"[199] The fatherland of liberty is no longer even a fatherland: the American is only interested in money. "What we call a fatherland is here simply an instrument for guaranteeing one's capital."[200] America is one big disappointment, "a land full of chimerical deception."[201] It is the real land of the sunset (*Untergang*) of all things, mankind's Occident (the culmination and reversal of the heliodromic theory). The Atlantic insulates it against the spirit and every superior form of life.[202] Lenau's condemnation is total: nature and society, the surroundings and the men, are all just as violently repellent to love's disappointed pilgrim.

In the lyrics inspired by America the echoes of Buffonian themes return again — less explicit, true, but no less certain to listeners like ourselves, to whom they have become not merely familiar but downright tedious. In the primeval forest an aura of death envelops and oppresses life; after a struggle of thousands of years death has been victorious, and the rotting tree trunks are like bony fingers choking every living shoot; there is no more rustling of foliage, no glitter of greenery, no happy warbling of birds to enliven the forest, that tomblike symbol swallowing up everything in its mysterious silence and gloom.[203]

The musical Lenau is particularly grieved at the lack of trills and warbles; or rather, he takes it as a supremely simple metaphor of all his grief and melancholy. The birds are his own songs: "and even the birds, my songs, have fled away."[204] Lenau, who in fact used to amuse himself capturing live birds,[205] in poetry adores, extols, allegorizes, and transfigures them, like his great fellow-spirit Leopardi: "The Nightingale is a profound creature, a singing mystery."[206] It is the living emblem of divine liberty. The earth is dying of cold, its extremities, the poles, are already frozen and the nightingale has now left the rose gardens of Ireland. Its

199. Said to Kerner: see Bibliographisches Institut ed., I, xlii.
200. And not even a sound guarantee: that "idiot" President Jackson, with his struggle against the *Spezialbanken*, will ruin credit and bring about a terrible crisis (letters of 6 and 8 March 1833, ed. cit., III, 202; VI, 7) — which seems a strange misrepresentation of the battle Jackson was then waging against the (second) United States Bank and in support of the banks of the separate states. The crisis did however materialize, and prove duly severe, in 1837. On the causes of Lenau's dislike of Jackson see Arndt, op. cit., pp. 132–33. On other anti-American reactions provoked by business misfortunes, see Remond, op. cit., p. 647, n. 70.
201. "Der Urwald," I, 268.
202. Letters of 5 and 8 March 1833; ed. cit., III, 199; VI, 6. To Errante, unaware of the historical precedents of Lenau's extreme anti-Americanism, this seems "acute neurasthenia," Freudian anguish and a symptom of his future madness (op. cit., pp. 112–16).
203. "Der Urwald," ed. cit., I, 268–70; VI, 329–30.
204. Ibid.: cf. also the verses of some of his friends Uhland, Kerner, etc., "like sweet birds" in the virgin forest (letter of 13 March 1832; ed. cit., III, 143). And the plea that if his American poems have something insipid (*abgeschmackt*) about them, it should be attributed to the American climate (ibid., III, 199).
205. Bibliographisches Institut ed., I, 241, note on "Das Lied vom armen Finken," written in 1834 or 1836; see also the letter of 2 April 1844, ed. Castle, V, 167.
206. Letter of 6 June 1838; ed. cit., IV, 288. Cf. for example Leopardi's *Elogio degli uccelli,* toward the end (their perfection greater than that of all other living things).

song is the lament for a lost homeland, and a prophetic warning of approaching death. "Oh destiny of Liberty, so like the fate of the Nightingale!"[207] *Kein Vogelsang* — "no song of birds" — is Lenau's first brushstroke when he sets out to portray a deserted valley.[208] And in the American forest, literally *"kein Vogel sang"* — "no bird sang."[209]

On the eve of his departure the poet wove an idyllic vision round the song of the lark and the nightingale;[210] and when he heard the song of a caged nightingale it awoke his yearning to explore ever more distant climes.[211] On his return, after the long journey, what strikes him about his homeland? At first, the trees, "like the dreams of youth grown green again"; but immediately afterward, "dear to me and softly familiar as never before, the song of the birds sounded in my ear."[212] The dumbness of the American forest is much more the reflection than the cause of his disappointment and repugnance and the spiritual silence that envelops him in the New World, in this world where he had dreamed of a new blossoming of his song and a feast of hymns of liberty.

The echoes of this bitterness are heard not so much in the poems on the traditional theme of the redskin driven from his lands and filled with proud resentment toward the white man,[213] but in the impulsive reversal of the Goethian aspiration. Oh happy America, Goethe had just finished saying, you have no ruined castles and useless memories; and may a benign destiny save you from the stories of knights, brigands, and specters. Lenau, on the banks of the Ohio, seems to retort with his lines on "The Ruins of Heidelberg."[214] So much for the *new* poetic material that

207. Letter of 16 January 1832; ed. cit., III, 134.

208. "Die Marionetten" (1831–32); ed. cit., I, 204; "Asyl," ibid., I, 43, and passim.

209. "Der Urwald," ed. cit., ibid., I, 268. See also Kürnberger, op. cit., pp. 218 ("*vogelsangloses Land*"), 317, 343, 346 (but Cuba does apparently have feebly amorous nightingales: ibid., p. 258). Cf. our Beltrami, who traveled extensively (before 1824) "these preadamite forests, these immense solitudes where a silence of death is only interrupted by the roaring of wild animals or the croaking of the crows" (*Notizie e lettere*, p. 122), and more radically still, Tocqueville: "Here . . . the very voices of the animals are never heard . . . everything is silence" (*Quinze jours dans le désert*, 1831, in *Voyages*, p. 370; cf. above, n. 113). Echoes of this silence, if such things are possible, are heard in de Vigny: "The wind alone murmurs . . . the birds are hidden in the hollows of the black pines" (*La sauvage*, ed. Nelson, pp. 228–29), and, for the forests of Brazil, in Darwin: "Within the recesses of the forest a universal silence appears to reign" (quoted in Christie, op. cit., p. 123), and again today in Lévi-Strauss: "The voice does not carry . . . an extraordinary silence reigns" (*Tristes tropiques*, p. 310).

210. "Reise-Empfindung" (1832), ed. cit., I, 5–6; cf. also "Frühlings Tod" (1832), ibid., I, 48; "Warnung und Wunsch" (1832–33), ibid., I, 137, etc.

211. Letter of 16 May 1832, ed. cit., III, 145; on the Rhine he is already disturbed by the total lack of water birds (letter of 2 July 1832; ed. cit., III, 173–74).

212. "Wandel der Sehnsucht" (1833), ed. cit., I, 22. It is symptomatic that in the poems and letters of the years after his return the references to America are extremely rare and insignificant (see examples in ed. cit., IV, 136; V, 73, 178, 349). The New World is "repressed."

213. See for example "*Der Indianerzug: Die drei Indianer*," ed. cit., I, 108–13; equally negative verdict in Walzel, op. cit., p. 358 and in Errante. op. cit., p. 144.

214. Ed. cit., I, 98–101 (cf. III. 62; V, 188). See also the famous poem "Der Postillon" (ibid., I, 105–07), also written in America, in which the nostalgia for his Swabian countryside, cemetery and all, breathes life into his verse (Errante, op. cit., p. 146, and "Gravitation nach dem Unglück — Zu Lenaus Gedicht *Der Postillon*," *Neue Zürcher Zeitung*, 14 July 1963). It is typical of Lenau, for that matter, to compose his lyrics far from the places they represent (ibid., pp. 71–72, 335; ed. Castle, VI, 232).

he had gone to America to find! Flowers springing up again on crumbling walls, moonlight on the multicolored houses, and watching over the affairs of human beings, from high above, the fortress of another age, "the ruin there, in its stony silence, like the scornful laughter of the past." Then suddenly the mocking laughter is pierced and overcome by a dulcet sweet lament, recalling the great company of departed souls: it is the nightingale, prodigious Philomel, at whose notes the shades return to the scene of their all-too-brief happiness, and having no voices of their own pour out all their inexpressible love for this land through the notes of the little bird's song. Isn't it clear? Isn't Lenau himself entrusting the burden of his nostalgia to the voice of poetry? Is the gulf between Lisbon on the Ohio and Heidelberg on the Neckar any less than that which separates the dead from the living?[215]

In the purity of this yearning toward the Old World, Lenau's American lyrics reach their loftiest vein. He explains it to us himself. In the wilderness of America, without friends, without nature(!), without pleasure, he is forced to turn inward upon himself and think how best to plan his future: "As a school of privation, America is really very much to be recommended."[216] There is more remorse than regret in his tone when he admits that "faithless I deserted my dear land, where joy bloomed for me as nowhere else"[217] — and at times something closer to stubbornness or defiance. The picture of Nikolas Lenau, tramping the virgin forest with his feet shod in "spotless patent leather shoes" and the hand that brandishes a hatchet in white kid gloves,[218] is not a grotesque vignette, but a bitter symbol of an unyielding rejection. The lyrical images that assail him are no less incompatible with the reality of America. Left alone to spend the night in a *Blockhaus* in the depths of the forest, the poet downs another bottle of Rhine wine and begins to read aloud his friend Uhland's romantic ballad, *Held Harald*. As the fable unfolds it conjures up the light irresistible scampering of elves and the hero's comrades' fatal attraction to the fairies. Outside a furious storm bursts, and in the woods, "the tall woods of the republic," that seem to be an extension of Harald's "wild woods," the trees blasted by the tempest groan angrily with the voices of the vanquished defenders of German liberty.[219] The deeper Lenau penetrates into America and nature, the tighter he clings to his links with historic Europe.

---

215. Errante, on the other hand, considers the whole part of the nightingale and its "disturbing song" false, an extraneous accretion: op. cit., p. 145. But the nightingale here is the poetry itself, that which understands the past and brings it back to life; in complete antithesis to Goethe's longing, Lenau invokes its song over the feudal pile: "Well dost thou understand ruins."
216. Letters of 5 and 8 March 1833, ed. cit., III, 197; VI, 6.
217. "Die Rose der Erinnerung," ed. cit., I, 107–08.
218. See Errante, op. cit., p. 111.
219. "Das Blockhaus," ed. cit., I, 273–75. Even before his departure, Lenau intended to declaim the poems of his friends in the American forests (ed. cit., III, 143, 146–47).

But even these links could not bring him lasting peace. The poem was composed a few years after his return. Another change of heart brought him closer to the feelings of the time before his departure. And he penciled in a comment above the *Blockhaus* that echoes the Goethian epigram: "Europe's rattling of chains may be more poetic, but America's clinking of coins is more consoling." He added it, and then, wavering, scratched it out.[220] The incurable poet could never resign himself to abandoning his dreams, nor could he stop himself destroying them with his own hand.

X. LEOPARDI: AMERICA'S DECADENCE BECOMES UNIVERSAL

While with Lenau the reminiscences and highlights borrowed from the dispute of America serve to accentuate his own personal tragedy, leaving the polemic more intense but so much reduced in scope as to almost disappear, with Leopardi it dissolves in a problem that is more far-reaching and tormented in a different way—the question of the ideological relationship between civilized and savage life, which involves a judgment on the progress and whole history of the human race.

Leopardi was certainly familiar with the arguments of the slanderers of the New World: he read Robertson's *History of America*, Carli's "so well-known" *American Letters*, and various writings of Buffon, Raynal, and Ulloa. He was not without curiosity about the ancient American civilizations (relying mainly on Pedro Cieza de León, Garcilaso, and Algarotti in regard to the Peruvian, and Solís for the Mexican), nor about the psychic and somatic characteristics of the inhabitants of the New World, whose indolence and slothfulness he comments on, as also on their heads being deformed and uniformized from infancy, their beardlessness and great height, the latter with particular reference to the redskin chiefs and the Americans of the western states as compared to the easterners (see above, p. 244).[221] Nor could Leopardi, the poet who so

---

220. Ed. cit., VI, 334. Another great liberal disappointed by America, without even having been there, was Heinrich Heine, who adjudged its life monotonous and its democracy oppressive (cf. Castle, op. cit., pp. 408–09) and represented it as a gigantic prison, a land cursed by God, tyrannized by the dregs of humanity, inhuman with the Negroes, hypocritical and plutolatrous (letter from Helgoland, 1 July 1830, in *Ludwig Börne: Eine Denkschrift*, 1840, ed. Walzel, VIII, 386–88).

221. For Robertson, see G. Leopardi, *Opere* (ed. Gregoriana, Milan, 1935), p. 312; *Zibaldone*, ed. cit., II, 945, 951. For Carli, *Opere*, ed. cit., p. 312; *Saggio sopra gli errori popolari degli antichi* (Florence, 1859), pp. 190, 306. For Ulloa, *Opere*, p. 312. For Buffon and Raynal, *Zibaldone*, analytical index, and, for the former, *Saggio*, pp. 288, 306, and *Pensieri*, LIV (ed. cit., p. 351; though he apparently only read the extracts carried in an anthology: see N. Serban, *Leopardi et la France* [Paris, 1913], p. 139). For Cieza de León, *Opere*, p. 312, and *Zibaldone*, analytical index. For Garcilaso, Serban, op. cit., pp. 91–94, 470, and possibly (*Historia de la Florida*) *Saggio*, p. 311. For Algarotti, *Zibaldone*, II, 792. For Solís, *Zibaldone*, analytical index. For Cieza, Algarotti, Robertson—and Franklin too—see Manfredi Porena, "Un settennio di letture di Giacomo Leopardi," in *Scritti leopardiani* (Bologna, 1959), pp. 419–38, nn. 90, 92, 232, 413. On the habitual idleness of the "*uomo silvestre*" (an echo of Robertson?), see *Elogio degli uccelli*, in *Opere*, ed. cit., p. 252. On heads, *Dialogo della Moda e della Morte*, loc. cit., p. 132; beards, *Zibaldone*, II, 739; gigantic Americans, *Opere*, pp. 1152–53. Leopardi also knows

rapturously extols the song of the birds, have been unaware of or indifferent to that unhappy particularity of American nature whereby its birds were less melodious than Europe's.[222] Nor, finally, was he unfamiliar with the theories that explained a rapid improvement in climate in terms of the cultivation of the fields, the reclaiming of the land and the establishment of centers of population, "which effect has been and still is particularly evident in America, where, so to speak, within living memory, a mature civilization has succeeded what was partly a state of barbarism, partly mere emptiness."[223] But America in itself, as a new world, as Europe's future or Europe's caricature, as the world's hope or the fatal omen of its ruin, did not interest him at all. For him, in fact, the continent held little intrinsic significance.

Of the discovery of that "huge unknown land" — an event that Gómara and others had hailed as the most significant in world history after the Incarnation — Leopardi's only comment is that it has shrunken the world and destroyed a whole "other world" of "pleasant dreams" and "beautiful imaginings" and "supremely poetic" geographical illusions, in other words America's presence is a lethal threat to poetry![224]

And of Columbus's undertaking, hailed by Campanella, for example, as the vast conquest of the Ocean and the throwing of a bridge "for Caesar and for Christ, from one world to the other," Leopardi has the navigator himself say that the enterprise may or may not succeed, but it will at least serve to keep himself and his companions "from getting bored" for a while — as if it were just some sort of game or frivolous

---

"very well that in America there are not and there never were lions" (*Zibaldone*, II, 1098); and he has read Charlevoix (*Saggio*, p. 289; Serban, op. cit., p. 463). De Pauw does not figure in the library of Monaldo Leopardi, which until 1827 fed Giacomo's curiosity and thirst for knowledge: possibly because that extensive collection of books was formed almost entirely after 1795 (Serban, op. cit., pp. 16, 30n., 452), or in the period of the almost total eclipse of de Pauw's reputation.

222. "Some say . . . that the voices of the birds are gentler and sweeter, and their songs more modulated, in our part of the world, than in the regions where the men are savage and rough" (*Elogio degli uccelli*, loc. cit., p. 249). Among the "some," G. Reichenbach identifies "the highly regarded Buffon" (idem, *Studi sulle Operette morali di Giacomo Leopardi* [Florence, 1934], p. 121).

223. *Pensieri*, XXXIX (after 1832; ed. Gregoriana, p. 342); cf. above, pp. 91–92.

224. *Ad Angelo Mai* (1820) and the relevant notes: cf. F. Montefredini, *La vita e le opere di Giacomo Leopardi* (Milan, 1881), pp. 417–19. This position coincides substantially with the notion of the Americas' intrinsic lack of poeticity (see above, n. 115). Sainte-Beuve already indicated its affinity with what Chateaubriand had written in his youth in the *Essai sur les révolutions* (*Chateaubriand et son groupe littéraire sous l'empire*, ed. M. Allem [Paris, 1948], I, 103n.). But even more surprising is the coincidence of Leopardi's lament over the disappearance of myths ("Where have they gone, our pleasant dreams, of the unknown refuge of unknown inhabitants . . . ?" "Ad Angelo Mai" [1820], and in the hymn "Alla primavera o delle favole antiche" [1822]: "Once the streams and liquid springs were a haven, a placid haven and mirror for snow-white nymphs," with Diana going down to wash therein, and rustic Pans, etc.) with Poe's charge against science in a sonnet of 1829–30: "Hast thou not dragged Diana from her car? / And driven the Hamadryad from the wood? . . . Hast thou not torn the Naiad from her flood, / The Elfin from the green grass . . . ?" (*Works*, ed. cit., V, 62), and with Melville's similar lament: "Columbus ended earth's romance: no New World to mankind remains!" "Clarel," 1876, in *The Oxford Book of American Verse*, ed. F. O. Matthiessen (New York, 1950), p. 405: cf. also Kuhn, op. cit., p. 481, and below, chap. 8, n. 362.

diversion.[225] The words put into the admiral's mouth are actually so out of keeping with what is known of his religious and almost hallucinatory character that they provoked De Sanctis to the sarcastic rejoinder: "This is not Columbus talking, but Leopardi, and Leopardi would not have discovered America."[226]

And in fact, far from dwelling on America, Leopardi's glance passes swiftly over the peculiarities of that continent to come to rest instead on the unhappy destiny of all mankind, within which destiny the deficiencies and weaknesses peculiar to America become absorbed, as it were, and thus lose all individual significance. Leopardi also substantially accepts de Pauw's basic thesis on the corruption or degeneration of the savages, but he extends it to cover all the peoples of the globe, so that in point of fact, America is absolved from its own particular malediction. And while the North American republic is not spared the poet's sarcasm — "the other shore of the Atlantic Sea, new font of purest civilization" — there is really no reason to see this as anything more than a particular instance of that generic mockery of the "glorious and progressive destinies" of the whole world, which Leopardi poured out from his perch on the stony slopes of the havoc-wreaking volcano, whose thunder and lightning merely served to give further proof of the miserable fragility and stupid hopes of the human race.[227]

Already in the *Dialogue Between Two Beasts* (1820) he had imagined the extinction of the whole human race, which had moved so far away from the state of nature that it had lost its native felicity, and decayed physically too: "the men too had changed considerably . . . because at first they were much stronger and bigger and bulkier, and lived longer than they did later, when by dint of vice they became weaker and smaller," just as the animal species they domesticated became weaker and bastardized.[228] This theory calls to mind the seventeenth-century theologians who among the consequences of Original Sin had stressed man's physical decadence and reduced longevity (above, pp. 59–60), and it takes

225. *Dialogo di C. Colombo e di P. Gutierrez*, ed. cit., pp. 245–46. On the general enthusiasm, besides that of Campanella, Bembo, Guicciardini, Ramusio, Tasso, Botero, etc., see Romeo, op. cit., pp. 125–26.

226. Cf. F. de Sanctis, *Giacomo Leopardi*, ed. W. Binni (Bari, 1953), pp. 301–02, and *contra*, Reichenbach, op. cit., pp. 112–15, and L. Giusso, *Leopardi e le sue due ideologie* (Florence, 1935), pp. 17, 19, 222, who in Leopardi's Columbus, sailing boldly on simply to escape from boredom, discovers no less than a romantic and Faustian hero.

227. *Palinodia*, ca. 1834; and "La ginestra," 1836. To the founder of the American republic, George Washington, Leopardi elsewhere pays the singular compliment of setting him alongside Timoleon of Corinth and a little higher than Andrea Doria, as a hero not greedy for power (*Paralipomeni*, III, in *Opere*, pp. 539–40): cf. S. Cassarà, *La politica di Giacomo Leopardi nei Paralipomeni della Batracomiomachia* (Palermo, 1886), pp. 415–18.

228. *Opere*, 1145–50: cf. *Zibaldone*, I, 1302 (1821), where Leopardi recalls that the church fathers, and St. Paul, and even the pagan philosophers, had noted "a degeneration and corruption of man, known and preached even in the most ancient mythologies."

or rather keeps Leopardi very close to them, rigorous pessimists, with their denial of all progress and scholarly despair at the irreparable loss of Grace. But this theological theme becomes curiously interwoven with the other quite rationalistic and naturalistic theme of the degeneration of the domesticated animal species (see also above, p. 26); and more generally with the Rousseauian notion of the evil influence of civilization. "Forty or fifty years ago," says Timandro, "the philosophers used to grumble about the human race; but in this century they do quite the opposite." Eleandro, however, the poet's mouthpiece, agrees with the philosophers of 1774–84.[229]

In his anxiety to systematize the world's unhappiness, to show the wretchedness of man's condition as necessary and at the same time absurd, Leopardi seized hungrily on any arguments that come to hand: and only the violence of his despair can mold such logically heteroclite material into any sort of unity. In the *Wager of Prometheus* (1824), the demigod alights first of all in the region of Popayán, near the river Cauca, an area now sodden and deserted although clearly inhabited earlier, and concludes by condemning the cannibalistic savages of the "new world" and the Indian widows who in the "older" continent sacrifice themselves on their husband's funeral pyres as equally barbarous; while Momo underlines the slowness and haphazardness of the "civilized" Europeans' progress, recalling that the other classes of creatures, the animals, have no need of progress because "from the very beginning they were perfect each one in itself," and that even such an imperfect civilization as man has achieved is extremely precarious: it may easily fall, in fact has already fallen several times.

Here Leopardi does not yet state that the savages or the Europeans are "decayed"; but in every relative "perfection" he sees included every sort of imperfection: and as the dialogue ends the London dog lover, whose boredom drives him to infanticide and suicide, reinforces his sarcastic doubt on the value of our civilization.[230] But there were other factors already inclining him toward a decadentistic interpretation of universal history—the projection onto the life of the human race of his own life, which passed so abruptly from the dreams and fables of childhood to a premature old age,[231] and even more his resolute and so frequently reinforced conviction of the superiority of the ancients over the moderns,

229. *Dialogo di Timandro e di Eleandro* (1824), loc. cit., p. 265. Typically Rousseauian—ibid., p. 266; in *Parini, ovvero della gloria* (1824), loc. cit., pp. 194–95 and in the *Zibaldone* (ed. cit., I, 203; II, 24; *contra*, ibid., II, 1298, 1301)—is the aversion for the corrupting metropolises.

230. *Opere*, pp. 156–64, 312–13.

231. M. Losacco, *Indagini leopardiane* (Lanciano, 1937), pp. 18–19, quoting G. Barzellotti, "A. Schopenhauer e Giacomo Leopardi" in *Santi, solitari e filosofi* (Bologna, 1886); cf. *Pensieri*, CII (loc. cit., p. 376).

of the classical world over the present-day world, proved also by the ascertainment of man's "noticeable shrinking," and often justified with the "greater strength of Nature, being also not corrupt or less corrupt" at the time of the Greeks and Romans;[232] or with the splendid explanation that the ancients, although not more long-lived than the moderns, were however "more full of vitality . . . better adapted to the functions of the body, more powerful physically."[233]

The poet becomes even more resolute and coherent in his denial of all progress in certain sections of the *Zibaldone,* which coalesce and issue forth in a pungent digression in the *Paralipomeni della Batracomiomachia.* The starting point is still, as it was with the *Dialogue Between Two Beasts,* the comparison between the happy or at least ignorant state of the animals (the state of nature) and the corrupt and unhappy state of modern man (see also below, n. 242). But it is better to look at the simpler and more dogmatic arguments in the *Zibaldone* since the *Paralipomeni's* Aesopic conventions, whereby frogs and mice are people too, together with the coating of veiled irony and not always successful sarcasm, can somewhat cloud one's vision.

In the *Zibaldone* Leopardi openly acknowledges the religious derivation of his attitude: "One of the principal dogmas of Christianity is the degeneration of man from a happier and more perfect primitive state: and linked to this dogma is that of the Redemption and, one may say, the entire *Christian* religion. The principal teaching of my system is precisely the said degeneration."[234]

This degeneration is greatest whenever man moves away from nature: the most primitive societies, which is to say those of the savages, are also the most barbaric and unnatural; to approach civilization, "a state, which is not at all contrary to nature," man has a long and painful path to reascend.[235] Here again, then, the pattern is the biblical one: a sudden fall followed by a long and difficult recovery. The state of innocence is the purely savage state. "Barbarity supposes a beginning of civilization, an inchoate, imperfect civilization; in fact it includes it." The savage tribes of America are so cruel and ferocious because they have a beginning of civilization, "because they have started to become civilized, in short because they are barbarous. . . . Their ills come from a beginning

---

232. *Zibaldone,* I, 299 (1820), 300–01 (1820); cf. ibid., I, 399 (1821).

233. Ibid., I, 896–97 (1821). On the thesis that history is decadence, cf. Giusso, op. cit., pp. 123–26.

234. *Zibaldone,* I, 674–75 (1821). The passage goes on to say that the demonstration of man's original happiness and his increasing unhappiness as he moves further away from nature are so many "direct proofs" of the truth of Christianity: cf. ibid., I, 337 (1820). Kerbaker (*Scritti inediti* [Rome, 1932]) and Losacco (op. cit., p. 305) admit that the biblical account of Original Sin is the "theological basis" of Leopardi's system. But cf. below, p. 386.

235. *Zibaldone,* II, 662–63 (1823).

of civilization. There is nothing worse, certainly, than a civilization either inchoate or past maturity, degenerate, corrupted."[236]

But does there exist anywhere on the face of the earth a completely savage people, altogether untouched by civilization? It would have to be totally without society, even if this favors civilization which is also "an approach to Nature." Without society, because society, even the most rudimentary, is corruption — corruption which is indeed already apparent in the first expressions of organized society, the cities. Here Leopardi's thought reveals an extraordinary *contaminatio* of biblical and Rousseauian motifs. For Jean-Jacques the cities, and particularly the big cities, were the abhorred quintessence of political civilization, of bourgeois luxury, of the fatal progress of the arts and sciences: they were the antithesis of Nature, the antithesis of the country, the antithesis of Virtue.[237] They were the result and culmination of man's decadence in society.

But they were not Original Sin. For Leopardi, however, they were: "the vile urban consortia" ("To Spring") were invented by the fratricidal Cain ("Hymn to the Patriarchs," 1822, quoting Genesis 4:17), and it was he, not the mild-mannered Adam, "the human family's ancient leader and father," that introduced evil into the world. For our moral consciences, let the Bible say what it will, the theft of an apple is much less serious than the murder of a brother. For Leopardi, then, the first cause of mankind's damnation is not the fruit that Eve stole but the blood that Cain spilled. That and that only is the true "ancient error that offered up the seed of man to the tyrant power of disease and disaster," and it was committed after Adam's departure from the seat of paradise, which when he left it was therefore "unacquainted with sin and sad events." ("Unacquainted with sin" — the home of the first sin! And "with sad events" — the garden where physical and spiritual death first entered the world!) And when finally Jesus Christ came down to redeem mankind, he came not to erase the guilt of out first forefathers, but that of the "first malefactor," the "first founder of societies," the killer of Abel. The city is Cain's invention, and "in a way the effect and daughter and solace of sin," and thus by its very nature "corrupter" and "source of the greater part of our vices and crimes."

---

236. Ibid., II, 1013–14 (1826). This whole historical scheme can be traced back to the words written in a book that Leopardi knew well, the *Génie du christianisme:* "man, . . . by a law of Providence, the more civilized he becomes, the closer he approaches to his first state . . . the perfect arts are nature . . . between the centuries of nature and those of civilization there are others that we have named centuries of *barbarism*" (op. cit., pt. III, bk. V, chap. 2; ed. cit., II, 90). What we have here is in essence one of the usual attempts to reconcile the theology of the Bible with the positivity of human history, the pessimism of the Fall with the optimism of Progress. Cf. also above, p. 358 (a particular instance of this thesis) and below, p. 390 (the de Maistrian version of the same); and J. Moras, *Ursprung und Entwicklung des Begriffs der Zivilisation in Frankreich (1756–1830)* (Hamburg, 1930), p. 65, and n. 96.

237. Cf. Gerbi, *La politica del Settecento,* pp. 286–89.

With this twist of Christian myth and theology Leopardi made our corruption a historical consequence of the crime of fratricide, and no longer a mystic heritage of Adam's fault.[238] As he put it, while St. Paul and the Fathers saw "an immense imperfection in the primitive system and order of man," and thus judged the Creator's work "substantially imperfect, that is to say composed of contradictory elements," he himself finds the imperfection in man's "acquired qualities . . . repugnant to the natural ones," or in "corrupted natural qualities, repugnant to each other, only because they have been corrupted." While they "in effect put man almost outside of nature," where everything is perfect, "I replace him there, and say that he is outside of it only because he has abandoned his primitive being."[239]

In transferring Adam's sin to Cain, Leopardi thought in fact to elude the strident contradiction of a benign God immediately permitting the Fall of his creatures, and to find a more satisfactory explanation than the biblical one for the vexed problem of the origin of evil in the world. He humanized the fearful mystery of Original Sin, and could thus delude himself that his implacably rationalistic doctrine was founded on the deepest spiritual truths of Christianity. In fact the rationalization and secularization of Original Sin were in tune with the most marked tendencies of modern thought, and its interpretation as a sociopolitical wrong, in particular, harmonized with the dominant preoccupations of the eighteenth century, that age assailed by recurrent doubts on the value of civilization and state-ordered systems. Leopardi is so imbued and tormented with these notions that he remains quite unaware of his heresy.

One inevitable corollary of his line of reasoning was the freeing of America from the curse of Original Sin, or at least those peoples of America who had no cities, societies, or civilizations. But do they exist? . . . Yes, they exist. Among all the tribes of the world, perhaps the Californians alone still live in conformity with nature, because they have almost no society between themselves, no language, and so "they are savages and not barbarous."[240] They resist civilization, are ignorant of clothing

---

238. G. A. Levi, *Storia del pensiero di Giacomo Leopardi* (Turin, 1911), p. 58, appropriately citing the *Zibaldone* (ed. cit., I, 203–04): "the first author of the city, which is to say society, according to the Scripture, was the first criminal, that is to say Cain . . . and as the first criminal was the first founder of society, so the first to combat it decisively and curse it was the redeemer of guilt, which is to say Jesus Christ" (cf. ibid., I, 454–55). For the identification of Original Sin with civilization, and the substitution of Cain for Adam — a thesis which has deep roots in a crucial passage in Saint Augustine, *De Civitate Dei*, from bk. XIV, chap. 28, to bk. XV, chaps. 1 and 2 — see also A. Aleardi, *Le prime storie* (Verona, 1858), p. 14; Giusso, op. cit., pp. 132, 138, 174–75; A. Sorrentino, *Cultura e poesia di Giacomo Leopardi* (Città di Castello, 1928), p. 135. As for Rousseau and his half-hearted efforts to dilute Original Sin along the course of history and thus have it coincide with "civilization," see for example Guillemin, op. cit., pp. 39–40.

239. *Zibaldone*, I, 1302–03 (1821).

240. *Zibaldone*, II, 665 (1823); cf. ibid., II, 306, 376, 577, and the *Storia del genere umano, Opere*, ed. cit., p. 118; the footnotes to the *Inno ai patriarchi*, ibid., p. 111: "It is held [by whom?] that the

and unacquainted with fire, and eat everything raw. The pious Californians—last heirs of the venerable title of "Noble Savage" after the caciques of the Antilles and the guileless Hurons. The Californians—their fantastic image looms up gigantic in the furthest West. . . . And lo, the quibbling arguments are drowned in the swelling notes of the "Hymn to the Patriarchs" (1822): "Amid the vast Californian woods, are born such a blessed race. . . ."

But not even they are safe from our "wicked boldness": "The shores and caves and quiet woods are stripped before our fury; the violated peoples taught new toil, unknown desires; and naked, fleeing Happiness, chased to the setting sun." Leopardi wakes swiftly from the brief dream of the natural life and flays "our" so-called civilized world with renewed bitterness. The hymn to the patriarchs finishes with a burst of Parinian invective against the tyrant Europe devastating innocent America and in her fury poisoning herself with her own prey.[241]

But not even this slow reconquest, this convergence of civilization and nature at infinity, satisfies Leopardi. In another place he affirms that civilization is so little in conformity with nature that there exist "hundreds of savage and barbarous nations of America, Africa, Asia, and Oceania" that have not only not yet reached civilization, but "have taken no step toward reaching it" and will never reach it unless they are violently forced to do so by the civilized peoples. More than half the human race is without civilization. Thus one cannot believe that civilization comes about naturally. Or would someone like to suggest—implies Leopardi, with the usual argument *ex absurdo*—that nature was "so stupid and so improvident that more than half the time it missed its mark"?[242]

With the passing of the years Nature changes from benevolence to enmity or indifference,[243] and the poet's whole philosophical system

---

Californians are, among the known races, the furthest from civilization, and the most recalcitrant to the same" (the same verdict is given by Mrs. Frances Calderón de la Barca: "The savages [of California] were the most degraded specimens of humanity existing . . . more degraded than the beasts of the field," op. cit., p. 225); ibid., pp. 968–69; the bibliographical announcement (the hymn "contains in substance a panegyric of the customs of California": pp. 970–71), and the lengthy description of the Californians (based on information from "travelers") in the prose outline of the hymn (*Puerili e abbozzi vari* [Bari, 1924], pp. 246–47), where the danger threatening them is personified in the missionaries, and thus in Christian religiosity itself (see also Zumbini, op. cit., II, 21–22). On the forests of America, with other reminiscences of Chateaubriand too, see *Puerili*, F. Neri, *Il Leopardi e un "mauvais maître"* (Rome, 1915: offprint from *Rivista d'Italia*) and A. Omodeo, in *Critica*, 38 (1940), p. 164.

241. See also Guerrazzi, below, p. 544.

242. *Zibaldone*, II, 1099 (1827). See chap. 9, sec. 4, "The Impotence of Nature," below. For (human) nature spoiled and weakened by civilization, and other contrasts between civilization and nature, see *Zibaldone*, I, 99, 627. One need hardly mention the oft-asserted greater happiness (or lesser unhappiness) of the animals compared to man (see above, p. 384). The "*blessed* offspring" of the Californians, over whom "impends all unsuspected the black day of death" are blood brothers of the "*blessed*" flock envied by the wandering shepherd of Asia for their ignorance of death and boredom.

243. On this reversal, see the whole of the cited work by Giusso, esp. pp. 57 ff.

comes apart: or rather crumbles and dissolves a little more with each succeeding effort he makes to use it to interpret life and the universe.

His fundamental inconsistencies reappear confused and blunted by a vein of humor and satire in the fourth canto of the *Batracomiomachia,* where the poet describes the degeneration of the savages. Savages only in a manner of speaking, because as the scholars have recently discovered, "those that the populace call savages . . . lead no natural and primitive life, as was hitherto believed, but through corruption a defective life, having fallen from their former perfect state, in which their father's fathers ever lived, as in their proper native ambience."

The other alternative is too absurd even to think of. The ever-benevolent Nature cannot have imposed upon her chosen creatures a life so hard and a path so long as that leading from the forests to civilization. "We are left to conclude that the wild and uncouth life must be not nature but corruption," and that man is born civilized and falls from there into the savage state.

But all this, Leopardi continues and objects, is no more than an aprioristic argument. The real truth is that Nature is evil, "our greatest enemy and tormentor," concerned with other matters than our good or ill, and treating men just like the animals; and all zoological species are today equally decadent and wretched. The men are like the mice and the mice are like the men. Even the mouse's fear and anxiety-ridden existence "must be not nature but corruption," Leopardi repeats word for word, and goes on to compare it to Israel's historical Diaspora, and the ill-tolerated exile: "and she remembers the temple of Jerusalem and the countryside of Palestine, and weeps." Every barrier falls before Leopardi's impetuous and all-pervasive pessimism. Nineteenth-century Europe is as primitive as the ancient kingdom of the mice. Poverty, weakness, and terror pervade the human race, just as they do "every animal that lives in the earth or sky."

That "weakness of America," born as a Europeocentric explanation for the infinite variety of the world, as an attempt at mental systematization of these remote and singular countries, strange animals and natives so curiously human, ends up, bloated with its various turbid additions, by being turned against the same deluded and embittered Europe, to weaken what little pride she has left, to sweep away her centuries of painful progress, to sully her triumphs and her conquests, rob her of her august signs of civilization, and reduce her men to the level of savages and both to the level of the croaking frogs, the ridiculous mice.

Parturient montes. . . . And Rodipane is crowned king and grasps the golden scepter with its globe on top "because then the mousely species thought it ruled the whole world."[244]

XI. DE MAISTRE: THE DEGENERATION OF THE AMERICAN SAVAGE

When Leopardi describes the American and non-American savage as a living example of degenerate and corrupt humanity he adds that the reader will no doubt wonder at this thesis as a great scientific novelty, a "strange and unusual" deduction. But even leaving aside the more disastrous interpretations of the biblical dogma of the Fall, and even if we ignore de Pauw's malevolent generalizations, we still do not have far to go to find at least one recent and exact precedent for Leopardi's gloomy picture: a notion born precisely from the coalescence of Christian and naturalistic pessimism, and formulated once again almost in scorn and defiance of current opinion.

Joseph de Maistre, a deliberately paradoxical thinker, draws the elements of his theory on the depravation of the savages from de Pauw, either directly or through Robertson.[245] For him, as for Leopardi, man's primitive condition is a state of happy perfection. His state of nature is civilization and science. At the beginning of all history is the Golden Age. The state of the savages, on the other hand, is not even comparable to the Iron Age. It is the barbarity of "some tribes that degenerated and then

---

244. *Paralipomeni della Batracomiomachia*, 1830–37, chap. IV (ed. Gregoriana, pp. 544–49). The comment of Cassarà, op. cit., p. 435, is insufficient. On that of Zumbini, see below, n. 245.

245. Leopardi's derivation from de Maistre has been indicated by Zumbini, op. cit., II, 249–53, but he holds that Leopardi uses the thesis of the degeneration of the savages ironically, to attack de Maistre and to defend the ideas of the eighteenth century, and particularly those of d'Holbach, against de Maistre: a thesis which, although it may seem plausible in some details (for example the satire on the balance of power, admired by de Maistre: *Soirées*, II, 29–30; *Paralipomeni*, II, 32–35), seems to me impossible to reconcile with the many passages from the *Zibaldone* (not yet published when Zumbini wrote his study) and other writings of Leopardi, all in agreement in upholding the degeneration of the human race and mocking the idea of Progress (see for that matter Zumbini too, op. cit., II, 278–79, and P. Hazard, *Leopardi* [Paris, 1913], p. 195). It remains true however that in the *Paralipomeni* the intermingling of ridicule and sarcasm ends up by revealing all the uncertainties and internal contradictions in the system of the scoffer himself. Another possibility is that Leopardi became aware of the thesis of de Maistre—whose works were actually very well known in Italy, and particularly in the Papal States, around 1830—through Gioberti, a great friend of the poet and constant admirer of the politician (cf. V. Gioberti, *Meditazioni filosofiche inedite* [Florence, 1909], pp. 184–92, esp. 191: "It was possible for men to become savage," 231–32, 245, 388–92; G. A. Levi, *Giacomo Leopardi* [Messina, n.d.], pp. 309–10; E. Gianturco, *Joseph de Maistre and Giambattista Vico* [New York, 1937], pp. 221–24). Even for the well-known octave on "learning," which is no more than "the child reacquiring, at great pains, the knowledge which age has withdrawn from ourselves" (*Paralipomeni*, IV, ed. cit., p. 547), it is no problem to find precedents in de Maistre or even Saint-Martin: "All our discoveries are only in some way reminiscenses," one learns from the *Tableau naturel des rapports qui existent entre Dieu, l'Homme et l'Univers*, 1782, in *Gnostiques de la Révolution*, ed. A. Tanner (Paris, 1946), I, 51–54. There is nothing on the de Maistrean origin of Leopardi's expressions in N. Serban, op. cit. (where the only references, pp. 22–23 and 478, are to the possibility that Leopardi read the *Soirées* and the *Lettres d'un gentilhomme russe sur l'Inquisition espagnole*), nor in F. Flora, *Leopardi e la letteratura francese* (Milan, 1947), nor in the general studies on Leopardian thought by G. A. Levi, Paul Hazard, Karl Vossler, and Giovanni Amelotti. Vague references in Giusso, op. cit., pp. 180, 228–29. De Sanctis, op. cit., p. 28, points out that in 1815 Leopardi was unacquainted with de Maistre.

painfully made their way back *to the state of nature,* which is civilization."[246]

But how did they slip down to such depths? Some chieftain must have committed a dreadful crime, one of those crimes which we can no longer even conceive of today (just like Leopardi's patriarchal Cain). "This chieftain . . . handed down the anathema to his posterity." And since every constant force, de Maistre muses fancifully, has a coefficient of acceleration ($g = 9.8$?!), this degradation "weighing down continuously on his descendants, in the end made them what we call *savages.*" From this miscellany of theology and algebra, ethical genetics and rational mechanics, there emerges a great ethnographic truth: "What Rousseau and the like call *the state of nature* is the last degree of brutalization."

That the opposite was generally believed was partially the result of the charity of the missionaries, who idealized the savage with the intention of protecting him (but they were right, those Europeans, when they refused to recognize the natives found in America as men), and partially of the bad faith of the *philosophes,* who made use of the savage to rail against the social order. But just look at him, this savage. The anathema is written not only in his mind but in his body: "He is a misshapen child, robust and ferocious, in whom the flame of intelligence glows with no more than a pale and intermittent flicker." He is neither provident nor perfectible. Even our vices have degenerated in the savage, just as "the most abject and revolting substances" are still susceptible of a further degeneration. He is thieving, cruel, and dissolute, but in a different way from us, because he does not have to overcome his nature: "He has an appetite for crime, but no remorse for it whatever."

But who are these savages, anyway, that de Maistre describes so harshly? A footnote provides the answer: "Robertson (*History of America,* vol. II, bk. 4) has perfectly described the brutalization of the savage. It is a portrait as true as it is shocking."[247]

---

246. *Soirées* (written 1809, pub. 1821), I, 77–78; II, 179; cf. Leopardi, above, pp. 384–85; Chateaubriand, p. 358 (and also, for savages degenerated "naturally" rather than mystically, Humboldt, below, n. 346). On the difficulties in this thesis, and its relations with the "ferine wandering" of Vico and other authors, see F. Nicolini, *La religiosità di G. B. Vico* (Bari, 1949), pp. 90–92; on its relations with remoter theosophical doctrines, A. Omodeo, "Cattolicismo e civiltà moderna nel secolo XIX," *Critica,* 34 (1936), pp. 115–16 (and in *Un reazionario: Il conte G. de Maistre* [Bari, 1939]). The point is barely touched on in Emile Dermenghem, *Joseph de Maistre mystique* (Paris, 1946), pp. 181–82, 194.

247. *Soirées,* I, 80–82. Carli's *American Letters* is also cited, ibid., I, 71n.; II, 69, 118, and 287, and in *Du pape* (Paris, 1918), pp. 278 n. 1, 281 nn. 1 and 2. Further eulogies of Carli in the *Oeuvres inédites* (Paris, 1870), p. 339 n. 2. In the course of the demonstration that war is the natural condition of the human race and that "human blood must flow uninterruptedly over the globe, somewhere or other," de Maistre produces in passing these Lascasian words: "The Discovery of the New World: the sentence of death for three million Indians" (*Considérations sur la France* [1796; ed. Lyon, 1873], pp. 33, 39). A little further on (p. 41) Buffon's thesis "that a great part of the animals are destined to die a violent death" (cf. also above, p. 10) is extended by him, with flamboyant savagery, to include man, and verified by man's history. Raynal and his declamatory philanthropy, on the other hand, were greeted only with disdain (Saint-Beuve, *Portraits,* II, 399).

He does not stop with this. In another passage, for example, he writes:

The savages of America are not quite *men*, precisely because they are *savages* [and at this point de Maistre tears to pieces Pope Paul III's famous bull recognizing their full humanity] and they are moreover beings visibly degraded both physically and mentally; and on this point at least, I do not see that there has been any reply to the ingenious author of the *Recherches philosophiques sur les Américains*.[248]

It is all very well for Rousseau to set them up as exemplary models. His defense relies on various successive and superimposed states of nature, and fails through its own internal contradictions. In fact the savage is a long way from the first and genuine "state of nature," still moist with innocence and virtue. "Every moral and sensitive man is revolted by the brutalization and cruelty of these American savages whose happy existence Rousseau dares to boast to us about: hordes of brutalized men wandering in the wilderness . . . having all the vices, except those for which they lack the materials," and so on for line after line. "What frightful pictures!"[249]

The truth of the matter is that the savage is just the opposite of the primitive. But the profound mystery of his existence has still to be explained: "Perhaps if one knew what a savage is, and why there are savages, one would know everything." One sure fact is that the savage is "necessarily subsequent to civilized man." The proofs? One glance at the New World is enough: "Look at America, for example. This country shows all the signs of a new land"—a clearly Buffonian feature. "Now, since civilization is of great antiquity in the Old World, it follows [*sic!*] that the savages living in America at the time of its discovery descended from civilized men!"

De Maistre, however, seems to have slight doubts about the solidity of his thesis, and hastens to bolster it up with one of the usual arguments *ex absurdo:* if one did not accept it one would be saying "that they have been savages father and son since the time of the creation, which would be absurd." And why absurd? Because, apparently, the Almighty cannot have created savages. The book of Genesis talks about a primitive life, but it says nothing about savages. The *Odyssey,* following some time after the Bible, describes barbarous and ferocious beings, but no brutalized savages. "This state has only ever been observed in America." The American native is the sole prototype, the fundamental paradigm of the savage. America, degeneration, brutal violence, and base and loathsome corruption form a single complex of ideas, the complex of the sole au-

---

248. *Etude sur la souveraineté,* ca. 1794–96, rev. 1815, in *Oeuvres inédites,* p. 333.
249. *Examen d'un écrit de J. J. Rousseau sur l'inégalité des conditions parmi les hommes,* in *Oeuvres inédites,* pp. 454–55.

thentic savage. "At least there is no proof that he ever existed elsewhere." And thus, after an unsuccessful excursion in search of a primitive state of animality anywhere in the rest of the world — everywhere the kingdom of the gods and heroes preceded and lit the way for those of men some millennia earlier — America's private curse is reaffirmed. The savage state is a real "anomaly" — it is subsequent to the social state and "has existed incontestably only in America."[250]

In this mystical transformation of the specific de Pauwian condemnation, America even seems to escape the bonds of the first sin, and be afflicted only by those "second-order original sins," which in the *Soirées* in fact serve to justify the existence of the savages.[251] Which means in fact, to reduce the essence of the tortured de Maistrean dissertations to plain terms, that America is devoid of those ancient traditions which give historic coherence to the peoples of our civilization, poor in national myths and literary monuments, and outside the orbit of the great geogonies and religions of the Old World. It is America, and neither Europe nor Asia.

De Maistre had a well-developed sense of the dignity of the past, and although he scorns man-made history he is always ready to bend a reverent mental knee before the ancient institutions, the truths revealed in the depths of the distant past, the sublime veiled knowledge of the sanctuaries: "The true system of the world was perfectly known in remotest antiquity."[252] Where there is no "antiquity" the conservative mystic passes by without a second glance. The America of the savage fills him with a sort of horror and physical repulsion. And as for his pontifications

---

250. *Examen*, pp. 482–86. Saint-Martin, from whom de Maistre drew many of the general principles of his system, had already indicated the American savages as the extreme point of debasement and torpification of the human race (A. Franck, *La philosophie mystique en France à la fin du XVIIIe siècle* [Paris, 1866], p. 105).

251. *Soirées*, I, 58–59 (these secondary and repeated falls too, in fundamental contradiction with the dogma of Original Sin, seem to be Saint-Martinian in derivation, and thus, in the last analysis, cabalistic and Gnostic: see Franck, op. cit., pp. 160–61, 172; Viatte, op. cit., II, 38). The idea of degeneration, with or without Original Sin, preys on the Count's mind. As main cause of the French Revolution he points (*Considérations sur la France*, p. 175) to the moral degradation of the French aristocracy, and fishes out from Bernardin de Saint-Pierre (*Etudes de la Nature*, X [ed. Paris, Firmin-Didot, n.d.], pp. 199–200) an argument demonstrating the degeneration of the French nobility with respect to their forbears. These forbears were the "great lords of the court of Louis XIV." In little more than a century "one can see from the evidence how these races have degenerated!" The same argument, evidently drawn from the same source (although it is not cited) is used by Chateaubriand to demonstrate the drying up of France's genius under the influence of the philosophy of the eighteenth century: "Impiety, which makes everything sterile, is also demonstrated in the impoverishment of physical nature. Cast your eyes on the generations which followed the century of Louis XIV. Where are these men with the calm and majestic faces? . . ." (*Génie de christianisme*, pt. III, bk. IV, chap. 5; ed. cit., II, 87). A slightly later echo (but referring to an earlier epoch) of this supposed shrinking of current generations in respect to their forbears can be heard in the words of don Ruy Gomez before his ancestor: "His giant armor would be ill-suited to our build" (V. Hugo, *Hernani*, act III, in the famous "portraits" scene). Cf. also Whitman, below, p. 534.

252. *Soirées*, I, 73–76.

on the subject of the North American colonists, the more apocalyptic and inflexible they get, the more they make one laugh.

He discusses, for example, the possibility of universal suffrage; and at the mere mention of America his tone becomes magisterially disdainful: "People quote America; I know nothing more exasperating than the praises heaped on this babe in arms; wait for it to grow up."[253] A babe in arms cannot even be considered an example. It is true that the Americans have made use of the democratic traditions of Old England and those of the refugees that fled from the wars of religion, and that "the Americans built on the plan of the three powers that they took from their ancestors, and did not by any means start out anew, like the French," but what is new in their Constitution, what comes from popular deliberation, "is the most fragile thing in the world; it would be difficult to gather together more symptoms of feebleness and caducity."[254]

Something similar had been said by other critics of the young republic, though without the same acute insight into the traditional elements incorporated into the American constitution. But de Maistre goes further, goes as usual just that bit too far, and lays himself open to ridicule. In view of their disagreement over the choice of a capital, the Americans have decided to build one *ex novo*, to erect it on the banks of a great river, and to call it Washington; and already all Europe has been informed of the "master plan" of the new capital. But a capital constructed *de toutes pièces* is something unthinkable to the stubbornly traditionalist count. Lord, no, it is not strictly speaking a task beyond the powers of mortal men:

One can easily build a town: however, there is too much deliberation, too much *humanity* in this business: one could lay a thousand to one that the town will not be built, or that it will not be called Washington, or that it will not become the seat of Congress.[255]

253. *Considérations sur la France*, p. 56; cf. ibid., p. 102. And see below, p. 395. The thesis of America as infant can obviously be traced back to Montaigne (see above, p. 282). But Montaigne's emphasis is different *toto coelo:* "child," reinstated at the end of the eighteenth century, and by the romantics, for his freshness and innocence, is again vilified (like "youthfulness": see above, pp. 282–83, 286, 318) by the reactionaries and the worshippers of antiquity and whatever is "old." Forty years later (1834) Guizot caused a sensation in the Chamber by declaring à la de Maistre that the United States was "a society being born . . . an infant society" (Remond, op. cit., pp. 663–64 n. 20, also noting the echoes of de Maistre, p. 685, n. 7), and again in 1848 a legitimist reverted to the metaphor to reinforce his polemic (ibid., p. 142).

254. Ibid., p. 103; sneers at Paine, ibid., p. 82n. The same thesis—that the American Revolution "has come down, so to speak, to a transference of executive power from England to America," with the further advantage, as compared to the French Revolution, that "the Americans are a new people, good, religious, and calm," which will not however prevent grave upsets in their political organism—is expounded in the third of the *Fragments sur la France* (in *Oeuvres inédites*, pp. 39–40). In his youth de Maistre had in fact taken a sympathetic interest in the progress of the American Revolution (Sainte-Beuve, *Portraits*, II, 396; Paolo Treves, *Profeti del passato* [Florence, 1952], p. 49).

255. *Considérations*, pp. 103–04.

The count lost his bet. But beneath his disdain is there not something like an echo of de Pauw's scornful remarks on the capitals of other Americans, the proud city of Cuzco, which (according to him) could not have been more than a heap of smoky little huts, or the Babylonian city of Mexico, which he reduced to a wretched little hamlet, whose vaunted palace was simply a barn where the Aztec emperors huddled?[256] The land of America is not fitted for the splendors of a metropolis.

Grotesque as these exaggerations seem, they are basically less serious, less doctrinally inhuman than the debasement of the savage to the rank of wild ignoble animal. Nor can one deny that with this summary condemnation de Maistre was really putting himself on a higher level than that of the naturalists and travelers. The question of whether the savages are innocent or degenerate was removed from the diatribes between the devotees of Nature and the fanatics of Progress, and raised to the level of theology. The concept of Original Sin (see above, pp. 283 and 358) became once more the ruling factor in weighing the value and the destiny of man.

But by this time there were already many North Americans, and men of authority, who sought to anchor the historicocosmic dignity of their fellow countrymen — not now the rejected and broken native, but the citizen of the United States — to a presumed or at least vigorously asserted exemption from Original Sin: a theme that was taken up again, with more or less conscious awareness, by almost all the major writers of the American Renaissance. The New World figured as the Garden of Eden, the Old as the land of vice, crime, and degeneration through want of Grace. Innocent of history and unburdened with tradition, the American appeared to Noah Webster, for example (1825), as God's immediate offspring, the new Adam.[257] A candid primitivistic heresy, that in the atmosphere of dauntless faith soon evolved into a notion of linear Progress, without tragedies or falls.

De Maistre, on the other hand, loyal to Catholic dogma, saw all the world's history as a picture of futile struggles, fatal massacres, and unavoidable decadence from a state of original perfection. He did not believe in Civilization, like de Pauw; nor in Nature, like Leopardi. And he

256. *Recherches*, II, 178, 202. The absence of capital cities or at least of real metropolises in the United States alarmed Chastellux (1786), who found the five largest cities (Boston, New York, Philadelphia, Baltimore, Charleston) too maritime and mercantile; and the same defect, noted in Boston and Philadelphia, worried Brissot too (1791), who however, as a perfect Rousseauian in detesting the big cities in general, concluded with a prophecy agreeing with de Maistre's bet: the fortunate America would never have enormous cities like London and Paris (Stark, op. cit., pp. 79, 90, 93, 96, 100; and below, chap. 9, sec. 5, "The Quakers, the Marquis, and the Girondist"). But it is also worth noting that American cities, even state capitals, are in fact extremely unstable, and that many urban centers do have a certain ephemeral and vagabond character about them (Boorstin, *National Experience*, pp. 93–97, 454).
257. For quotations and copious details, see Lewis, op. cit., esp. p. 72.

could thus, with paradoxical logic, see the savage as the most "evolved" and thus the most "decadent" of man. In the historian's texts, and the events of his own day, he sought and found the experimental confirmation of his rigorously antihistorical thesis and its consistent denial of any sort of Progress.

XII. FABRE D'OLIVET: AMERICA REJECTED BY THE THEOSOPHISTS

America reappears in very similar though usually rather less emphatic guise in the writings of the other reactionaries and mystics; it reappears foreshortened, and merely glimpsed in passing, so that it is impossible to say with certainty whether the basic inspiration of the condemnation should be traced back to de Maistre, to his teacher, Saint-Martin, to that teacher's teachers, Martinez de Pasqualy and Jakob Boehme, to remoter and vaguer rabbis or theosophists, or whether it derives in fact from doctrines predating the discovery of the continent by several centuries. What is clear is that the Buffon–de Pauw formulas proved their extraordinary malleability yet again, lending themselves to the support of apocalypses, escatologies, and palingenetic visions that would only have amused the author of *Recherches* and bored the writer of the *Histoire naturelle*. But all these hallucinated "prophets of the past" consider that they write at God's direct dictation, and would thus feel they were betraying their vocation if they were to quote their profane sources with any exactitude: particularly when the sources in question are very common and very recent, and accessible to everyone without need of any special initiation ceremonies.

Historical exactitude is in any case the least of their concerns. "Buffonians" in this too, the immensity of the prospects they outline so fascinates them that they recoil in horror from defining them, from fixing chronologically ascertainable points of reference. Dates are shackles on the winged feet of the fates. The measuring of geographical distances is an insufferable bore, a mean and useless task for those who devour space while standing still and halt immobile in their flight, like the arrows of Zeno of Elea.

America, the continent with an unarguable birthdate, separated from Europe by just so many thousand miles of ocean, is the first victim of this Sybilline and charismatic impulse. With a gesture of indifference even the meek and whimpering Ballanche excludes "the young Americans" from his evolutionary laws, which he formulates according to the scheme of the biblical Fall, and thus rejects them from the apex of history, residing, for him, in a socially redeemed humanity, because they have no past to point the way to the future. These little three-hundred-year-old orphans will have to wait for their salvation, or at least some prophet of their salvation, until they are a bit older; until, shall we say, they can count three thousand years behind them, like Europe. . . .[258]

They never went through the initiations that the east imposed on our civilized world. They have no fabled times, no cosmogonic cycles, and *thus* (a bold leap that was to enjoy spectacular success, from the contemporary Goethe right up to Henry James) they have no poetry of their own, either in literature or the arts. One day they will have, certainly, when they have assimilated the heritage of their imported tongues and the traditions of the Bible (in other words when they are thoroughly Europeanized, and no longer the virgin Americas).[259] And then, although unfamiliar with Roman law and the civil code, and born under the (unhappy) sign of the "social contract," then they will perhaps find a civil mission too, that of bringing back the unfortunate Negroes to the one common humanity: "Do we not see that there are already more ideas of civilization in the blacks who have reached social emancipation than in the colonists brutalized by the unlimited power of the master over the slave?"[260]

But the most complete and explicit repetition of the thesis of the Americas' physical immaturity occurs in that esoteric rhapsody — whose glimmerings of a sense of history can hardly compensate for its incredible critical liberties — the *Histoire philosophique du genre humain*[261] of Fabre d'Olivet, untiring unveiler of mysteries, intrepid linguist, dialectal poet and author of historical dramas and tragedies, novelist and musicologist,

---

258. P. S. Ballanche, *L'homme sans nom*, 1820, in *Oeuvres*, ed. Paris-Geneva, 1830, III, 26–28, 221–25; ed. Paris, 1833, III, 164 (cf. de Maistre, above, p. 393); *Palingénésie sociale: Prolégomènes*, 1827, ibid., IV, 26–26, 249–52; cf. also ibid., III, 28, 221, cited by R. Mauduit in his introduction to *Le Vieillard et le Jeune Homme* (Paris, 1929), p. 36–37, who reminds the reader that Comte too wanted to reason solely on the basis of the "Western world" (without the Americas: cf. also below, p. 461). The influences of the mystics and reactionaries on the Saint-Simonians and Comte are in any case well enough known. But one should not generalize; a fervent admirer of Ballanche, Michel Chevalier (see his *Lettres*, II, 401–06) sees America assured of a lofty destiny, since it will be the meeting place of the two great currents of civilization, that of our civilization going from east to west and that of the civilization of the Far East going from west to east, each with its path frequently diverted by the effect of two other impulses, Semitic to the south and Japhetic to the north (op. cit., I, pp. iii–viii): a real double parallelepiped of forces, which on colliding in America however apparently join forces rather than canceling each other out! The most curious thing is that Chevalier was actually an engineer, who went to the United States (1833–35) to study public works and the early railways (he composes a delightful hymn to the locomotive, that huffs and puffs and snorts and charges off just like a racehorse, no less! [*Lettres*, I, 223]) and who had a very acute insight into the immense technical and industrial possibilities of the country. On his work and its diffusion in France, cf. Remond, op. cit., pp. 375–77; in Germany, see Franz, op. cit., pp. 36–37, n. 31.

259. P. S. Ballanche, *Oeuvres* (Paris-Geneva, 1830), III, 26–28.

260. Op. cit., III, 223. On the Negroes, cf. below (Hegel), p. 433, and (Schopenhauer) pp. 458–59.

261. In its first edition (1822) the work was entitled *De l'etat social de l'homme, ou vues philosophiques sur l'histoire du genre humain*, and in the second (identical) edition of 1824 *Histoire philosophique du genre humain, ou L'homme considéré sous ses rapports religieux et politiques dans l'etat social, à toutes les époques et chez les différents peuples de la terre . . . [sic]*. The insistence on the terms *man* and *social* betrays the theosophical (man is God) origins of the work and the political humanitarian tendencies of the age. Its basic concepts, as antithetical to historical materialism [!], are praised by Tanner, in his introduction to the *Gnostiques*, I, 39–40, though he recognizes that for Fabre the "facts" sometimes serve as proofs "for the support of the preconceived idea."

liberal interpreter of oriental wisdom, and in short the greatest polygraph of scientific occultism.

And not only polygraph – Fabre d'Olivet was no armchair theosophist; he insisted on putting his esoteric learning into practice, with results that were unfortunately not always the happiest for him. His curing of two deaf-mutes "according to the method of the ancient Egyptian priests" got him into considerable trouble, with the police among others. When he arranged a performance of an oratorio he had written according to the musical system of the ancient Greeks, as rediscovered by himself, it was pointed out to him that it was neither more nor less than the old plagal mode still preserved in Gregorian chant. And when (apparently) he sought to use his beloved wife's powers as a medium for the purpose of extending his knowledge of Pythagorism, it seems he succeeded only in ruining her health and scandalizing her religious faith, whereupon she left him and obtained a decree of separation. But even heretics and sorcerers have a benign Providence watching over them. And Fabre found some consolation in a zealous (female) disciple, who also restored his posthumous reputation, and even more in assuming a contented attitude of persecuted martyrdom, in daring experiments in necromancy, and in the foundation of the Universal Theodoxic Cult.[262]

In drafting the *Histoire philosophique* the extempore historiographer's Providence took the form, in general, of the major compilations of the eighteenth century, taken over *in toto,* right down to their schemes and ideologies,[263] and in particular, for his information on the Americas, the literature of the dispute, used quite indiscriminately; for the continent's natural and geological history, Fabre d'Olivet draws on Buffon and perhaps Carli; for its people, on de Pauw; for the history of the European conquest, on Raynal and the noisier repeaters of Las Casas and the *leyenda negra* – showering the lot with abundant references to the Flood in the secular versions of Bacon and Boulanger.

His references, however, are precious few, and although Buffon[264] is named, de Pauw[265] never is. But can one doubt the provenance of a passage like this?

262. The previous biographies, brief and dated, are completely superseded by the fundamental work of L. Cellier, op. cit.: see, in particular, on the deaf-mutes, pp. 163–82, 244–48; on Greek music, 98–102; on conjugal relations, 256–62. It contains nothing, however, about Fabre's ideas on America, not even in the long analysis, pp. 263–93, of the *Histoire philosophique.*

263. Fabre d'Olivet believed in linear Progress, in a Europe enlightened after the Dark Ages, in the continual "evolution toward perfection" of sciences, arts, and languages (see *La langue hébraïque restituée* [Paris, 1815–16], I, 194; II, 7).

264. *Histoire,* 3rd ed. (Paris, 1910), I, 289–90n.; and cf. *Les Vers Dorés de Pythagore expliqués* (Paris, 1813), pp. 397–98, and Cellier, op. cit., pp. 76–77. Boulanger is also mentioned several times in the *Langue hébraïque* (for example, I, xxvii, xxix, xxxiv).

265. Fabre d'Olivet had however certainly read at least the *Recherches sur les Grecs,* which he mentions with undisguised disdain (while revealing that he knows other works by the same author) on the

The new hemisphere . . . was a rather new World, compared to the old; younger, more recently emerged from the bosom of the seas, producing, in each of the three kingdoms, substances or creatures on which nature visibly impressed all the signs of youth.

And up to here everything is beautifully new, fresh, and solid. But immediately afterward, without a word of explanation, this youthfulness splits up, to become a positive attribute in inanimate nature, and a negative one in living nature.

The general and geological forms displayed a remarkable magnificence there, but the principle of life, undeveloped, languished still. There were higher mountains than in the other hemisphere,[266] greater rivers, more numerous and vaster lakes: and yet the vegetable kingdom lacked sap and vigor there.[267] One met no species of animal there, that one could compare to that [sic] of the old World. Even the lions and the tigers, or rather the pumas and the jaguars that were given these names, had neither the courage nor the voracity of those of Africa. The very climate itself was quite different from that of the other hemisphere. It was respectively [?] more humid and colder. Only the pliant and "latescent"[268] plants, the poisonous reptiles, the noisome insects reproduced abundantly, and with astonishing rapidity.[269]

But how and when did this "recent" emersion occur? Fabre d'Olivet cannot resist the illustrious myth of Atlantis, and before allowing America to rise from the waters he dunks it in the ocean, plunges it in up to its neck, then fishes it out wet and dripping. . . .

It is a quite certain fact (*bien certain*) that the continent today known as America is none other than the island of Atlantis; peopled by the red race, it was on the point of making itself master of the world when a "horrible catastrophe" or flood occurred, the result, on the metaphysical plane, of the absolute perversion of these peoples and their consequent abandonment on the part of Providence. But even when one admits this primordial and biblical-type cause, "there still remain great difficulties in the matter of the secondary and physical causes."

---

subject of impertinent critics of antiquity: "Further off I see, as the height of singularity, a maker of Researches who finds . . . that the first editor of Homer's poems, the manly lawgiver of Sparta, Lycurgus in short, was an ignorant and unlettered man, who could neither read nor write" (*Vers Dorés*, p. 281, quoting "Pauw, *Recherches sur les Grecs*, vol. II, p. 355"; in fact, *Recherches sur les Grecs*, ed. cit., II, 379–81, and above, pp. 348–53).

266. An echo of Delisle de Sales (see above, pp. 111–17), another author well known to Fabre d'Olivet (see for example *Vers Dorés*, pp. 36n., 117n., etc.), and one who figures among the subscribers to the *Langue hébraïque;* cf. Viatte, op. cit., II, 169–70, 181, 187; and especially Cellier, op. cit., pp. 60–63, 78–81, 109–11, 119–20, 205, etc., according to whom the friendship with Delisle played "a large role, larger than has been suspected until now" in Fabre's tormented life (pp. 54–55).

267. Fabre d'Olivet forgets the forests of the North and Amazonia, perhaps influenced by the usual laments over the meager fertility of the earth and the scarcity of edible fruits.

268. *Sic:* the word is not found in any dictionary. If it derives from the Latin *latesco* it may mean that these plants hid themselves, shrunk up (*lătescere*), or that they broadened out in exuberant growth (*lātescere*). Or could it just be a slip of the pen, *latescent* for *lactescent?* . . . The *lapsūs* of the initiates create insoluble hermeneutical problems.

269. Op. cit., II, 181–82.

To resolve them Fabre d'Olivet does not hesitate to imagine a sudden movement of the terraqueous globe, which raised the North Pole, perhaps with several successive shocks, until the earth, forcibly straightening itself out, turned back the waters toward the South Pole, submerging Atlantis and leaving stagnant swamps in the lower areas thus rinsed. All the red men were drowned, except those few who at the time of the flood were on the highest mountains, the Appalachians, the Cordilleras, or the Tapayas,[270] and who were thus beyond the reach of that vast tidal wave.

But this whole story seems so unconvincing to Fabre d'Olivet himself that he deems it wise to call on the support of other authorities: "Bacon thought as I do that America had been part of the old Atlantis"; Boulanger, "who carried out considerable research in this matter," sees savagery as having originated with terror of the Flood; and "many scholars have since amplified and commented on these ideas."[271] Beneath all this, however, one catches a glimpse of another picturesque and unscientific element, namely the esoteric tradition of the four races (black, white, yellow, and red) competing throughout the millennia of prehistory for the mastery of the world[272] — a tradition which repeats in its formal scheme and translates into naturalistic terms the biblical parabola of the four monarchies (see above, pp. 131–32). The white race, according to Fabre d'Olivet, makes its appearance when the black, "an older race, reigned over the earth and held the scepter of knowledge and power," ruling Africa and the greater part of Asia, where it had brought the yellow race under its sway:

Some remnants of the red Race languished in obscurity on the summits of the highest mountains of America, and survived the horrible catastrophe which had just struck them; these feeble remnants were unknown: the red Race, to which they had belonged, had only a short while ago possessed the Western Hemisphere of the globe.[273]

270. If it were worth the trouble of arguing, one might point out that the Appalachians reach a mere 6700 ft., and the Tapajoz, in Brazil, is a river, a tributary of the Amazon.

271. Op. cit., II, 190–96. For Bacon, see above, pp. 60–62; for Boulanger (disliked for his rationalism by other occultists, like Saint-Martin, who is frequently quoted with reverence by Fabre d'Olivet), see above, p. 59.

272. See Papus (G. Encausse), *L'occultisme et le spiritualisme* (Paris, 1902), pp. 114–19, who sums up the tradition "following Fabre d'Olivet," who is for him "the angel of this current of erudition and philosophy . . . one of the most learned men produced by occultism" (ibid., p. 125).

273. *Histoire philosophique*, I, 167. The immediate source of this succession of races seems to be a group of articles ("Animal," "Nature," "Quadrupède") in the *Nouveau Dictionnaire d'Histoire Naturelle* (1816), quoted by Fabre d'Olivet with glowing praises, and wherein one reads, among other things: "Possibly the Negro race . . . was once the queen of the earth, before the white race was created. . . . The Negro, once king of the animals, fell under the yoke of the European; will the latter in his turn bow his head before a more powerful and intelligent race?" (*Vers Dorés*, pp. 398–402). But the question is answered in the negative by Fabre d'Olivet (see below, p. 401). See also the extract quoted in Tanner, op. cit., II, 247, and cf. below, pp. 458–59. Schopenhauer's attribution of racial primacy to the Negroes. Gioberti, on the other hand, maintains (1851) that "the red man of America is superior to the Ethiopic," and is in his turn surpassed by the "bronze-colored" [?], the yellow, and the supreme Caucasian races (*Rinnovamento civile*, I, 128).

After the catastrophe the continent was left sterile and incapable of feeding a numerous population. In fact, when the Europeans arrived they found only two "entirely formed nations," the Mexicans and the Peruvians: two childlike nations of whom Fabre d'Olivet tells us in one place that their development, which perhaps promised something, was stifled before it bloomed by the European Will, and in another, instead, that they had had, at least the Peruvians, "a precocious intellectual development," perhaps the result of the teachings of Chinese sailors that had landed near Panama, but a "slow and stunted physical development." For Fabre d'Olivet, these stunted sages first serve as a confirmation of the cyclical thesis that the decrepit nations are just like the childish ones,[274] and are then compared to hothouse fruits, "beautiful to the eye, but flaccid and tasteless to the tongue." The result is easily foreseeable (very easily, three centuries after the fact): since the Peruvians, with all their literary culture, were unwarlike, it could present no problem for a handful of rapacious, shrewd, and cruel brigands to annihilate "this race too involved in ideas beyond their reach."[275]

Alongside these dreamy Incas, physically Lascasian but mentally heirs of a mysterious oriental wisdom, the simple natives cut a poor figure: they too are of scarce bodily strength, and furthermore (or less) have no intellectual endowments. They remained in the infancy of the social state, and "none of their faculties were fully developed: they were feeble both physically and mentally."[276] Even their color is of low quality. They belonged to the red race, certainly, but they were not of pure stock: polluted by mixtures and crossings of blood, their traditions preserved the memory of the disaster of Atlantis and the migration of Europeans, via Iceland–Greenland–Labrador–Canada–Louisiana–Mexico:[277] today then, three hundred years after the discovery, they are still more bastardized and crossbred, just as the animal and vegetable species show signs of changes resulting from the importation of European specimens and zootechny. Yet the type described is indelibly familiar to us: beardless, "their constitution was moist and without manly strength. There

274. Old age and infancy come together again, but this time in antithesis, in the reference to the Negro slave trade to America: "A decaying race came to share the misfortunes of an infant race" (op. cit., II, 199; and Tanner, op. cit., II, 257–58).

275. Op. cit., I, 152–53; II, 182, 197, 200. Other savagely antihispanic statements and sacramental references to the "expiation" owed by the Spanish nation for its crimes: op. cit., I, 341n.; II, 129–30, 179–80, 184, 187–89, 201n., 204. On the Mexicans, cf. also II, 200–02; on the Peruvians, II, 203–04. The monarchy of the former was imperial-feudal, of European type, that of the latter, theocratic, of Oriental type (op. cit., II, 383).

276. *Histoire philosophique*, II, 186. Other derisive comments about Rousseau's idealized American natives (Caribs, Algonquins, peoples on the banks of the Mississippi) are mentioned by Cellier, op. cit., p. 275.

277. Op. cit., II, 186–88, 200. The idea of human sacrifice is also said to have come to the Mexicans from the Europeans, via Iceland! (ibid., I, 201).

were men who had milk at their breasts."[278] Their women were unfruitful and enslaved to the men,[279] who were however feeble, without ambition and strong passion, childlike, uncaring. In the whole hemisphere there was not one shepherd: "Not a single animal was known that had been submitted to the yoke of domesticity."[280]

As for the nations of European stock that are now established throughout the hemisphere, Fabre d'Olivet looks on them with ill-disguised antipathy: North America is Protestant, South America is Jesuit: sooner or later they are bound to come to blows, "and then we shall see the real trial of strength between Luther and Loyola."[281] No glorious destiny for the West then, and no question of a transfer of political power from the Old to the New World: instead Fabre d'Olivet sees Europe, ancient Europe, bound together in a holy alliance and led by a Supreme Pontiff, marching "to the conquest of the World, by the sole strength of things."[282]

An optimist in all things, from Europe's destiny to the success of his book, Fabre d'Olivet was convinced that it would have been difficult "to set forth more clearly, rapidly and perhaps agreeably the history of the human race over the last twelve thousand years, according to an entirely new system combining physics and metaphysics." Even superficial readers, he relates, have found his book interesting. If his "contemporaries" refuse to accept the truth he offers them, and which alone can save them from the terrifying disasters threatening them, so much the worse for them: "Posterity will avenge me."[283]

The ritual appeal for posterity's vengeance has not yet been answered. But what are one hundred and fifty years for the historian of one hundred and twenty centuries? Of his contemporaries, it is known that he was occasionally visited by Ballanche, who had read his works and who (according to another critic and contemporary) felt himself strangely drawn to his ideas, although he found them "permanently dug in behind a barrier of scarcely verifiable science and guarded by a haughtiness which never delivers its final judgement."

278. Ibid., II, 186n. We might have expected to hear this detail reported in shocked tones by anybody rather than the orphic and Pythagoric Fabre d'Olivet, who should have remembered the mammae of his distant predecessor Tiresias! Note however that in Fabre d'Olivet, as in de Maistre and the other frowning "prophets," de Pauw's scandalous and erotic details are decorously left in the background.
279. Ibid., II, 187n.; cf. de Pauw, *Recherches*, I, 54: "They procreated little."
280. Op. cit., II, 187n.; cf. de Pauw, *Recherches*, I, 111 ("The natives of North America did not have the spirit to subdue these animals, nor to reduce them to pasture . . . the Bisons, which the Tartars domesticated, likewise remained wild with the Americans").
281. *Histoire philosophique*, II, 256; cf. Hegel, below, pp. 436–37.
282. Ibid., p. 468 (and Cellier, op. cit., p. 305–06). It was this augury or prophecy, of course, formulated in the political terms topical at the time, that was generally misunderstood, and earned Fabre d'Olivet a reputation as theocratic reactionary that he did not really deserve. In the united world one single language will be spoken, which Fabre d'Olivet hopes will be French (*Langue hébraïque*, I, 197).
283. Letter of 15 May 1822 (in Tanner, *Gnostiques*, II, 9–10).

This at least is plain speaking. In defining "this philosopher who could have dispensed with being a charlatan," Sainte-Beuve had not yet learned to tempor his venom.[284]

XIII. THE REACTION OF THE SCIENTISTS: BARTON AND HUMBOLDT

A. Benjamin Smith Barton and the learned North Americans. Now the fact of the matter is that it needed a lot more than the instinctive scepticism of a Sainte-Beuve, the ingenuous enthusiasm of a Bernardin de Saint-Pierre or, going back a few decades, the caviling concern of the odd Jesuit father, to destroy the thesis of America's inferiority propounded by naturalists and historians of considerable fame. What was needed was the word of Science. And the amazing thing is that this word had already been pronounced back at the very beginning of the century, and yet neither poets, nor mystics, nor (as we shall shortly see) the great Hegel, seem to have paid it a blind bit of notice.

We have already observed the development of a lively reaction to the specious accusations of Buffon among the proud rebellious citizens of North America. The development of the West and the increase in traffic with the Far East were seen as further reasons to reject the French naturalist's thesis. In 1818–19 a disciple of Jefferson, the well-known politician and publicist, T. H. Benton, one of the prophets of the Manifest Destiny, dusted off Columbus's grandiose illusion and pointed to the United States as the bridge thrown across to the riches of the Indies, indeed to all Asia. When they reach the Pacific and stand within sight (so to speak) of the continent where Adam and Eve were created, the Americans will have completed the "circumambulation of the globe." And thus having gained control of the traffic with Asia, despite the English, they will make themselves independent of Europe and will no longer be servile copyists and imitators, branded *by Buffon* with a stigma of biological inferiority.[285]

More serious in their aims were the geologists, ornithologists, and ethnographers who were patiently gathering data and making observations which without being overtly polemic, indeed largely because they were not formulated as explicit contradictions of the thesis of America's telluric inferiority, succeeded in discrediting its basis of fact. The naturalists of the New World found fossil strata of undeniable antiquity, birds of

284. Sainte-Beuve, *Portraits contemporains* (1834; ed. Paris, 1855), I, 324; cf. E. Faguet, *Politiques et moralistes du dix-neuvième siècle* (Paris, n.d.), II, 137. Fabre d'Olivet had already been adjudged a charlatan or a ruffian by Volney, by the circle of Benjamin Constant, and later by Renan (Cellier, op. cit., p. 242 n. 1).

285. H. N. Smith, *Virgin Land*, pp. 22–26. Several times, in the early years of the century, politicians, professors, and journalists raised paeans to Jefferson for his decisive victory over the errors and calumnies of Buffon (see examples in Martin, op. cit., p. 26).

tolerably melodious song,[286] and Indians capable of being infected by civilization—such civilization, at least, as was presented to them in the form of intoxicating beverages and thunderous firearms.

When in 1801 two fossilized mammoth skeletons were found near New York, a son of the discoverer took one of them to London, and put it on display for the astonished Europeans, describing it in the publicity hand-outs as the *"great* American incognitum . . . a non-descript carnivorous Animal of *immense size,* found in America"; he also sent a copy of the leaflet to the President of the United States, who was an old friend of his, Thomas Jefferson.[287]

These naturalists and scientists, like Jefferson, were inspired by a sense of love and affectionate curiosity toward their land and all its prod-ucts. The Creoles have already been mentioned (above, pp. 184–85). In the former British colonies political independence preceded the methodi-cal study of local peculiarities and resources, which could thus develop unaffected by the defensive and eulogizing attitude too frequently ob-servable in the scientific literature of Spanish America at the turn of the century. But even if they are more coldly objective the naturalists of the United States set out from the conviction that their "material," the min-erals, plants, animals, and peoples of North America, are just as worthy of study, just as important in themselves and for themselves, as those of any other part of the world.

The idea of America as a continent only recently emerged from the waters and still not dried out, "a marshy wilderness inhabited by croco-diles and snakes," was scornfully rejected by the eminent Philadelphia botanist, Benjamin Smith Barton, who had studied in Europe, at Edin-burgh and Göttingen, and who in 1802 became president of the American

286. See, for example, after Jefferson (*Papers,* VIII, 241, for whom the nightingale is a third-rate songster in comparison with the mockingbird and the American thrush: see above, chap. 5, n. 406), Gilbert Imlay, 1792, who praises the sweetness of song of the birds of Kentucky (H. N. Smith, *Virgin Land,* p. 130), and the disciple and friend of the famous W. Bartram (*Travels* . . . [Philadelphia, 1791]; on whom see N. B. Fagin, *William Bartram; Interpreter of the American Landscape* [Baltimore, 1933], esp. p. 96), Alexander Wilson, *American Ornithology,* 1808–13, polemicizing with Buffon (J. R. Moore, op. cit., p. 326; Martin, op. cit., p. 195; Vail, op. cit., pp. 374–88).

287. Cf. *Catalogue of the Library of Jefferson,* I, 475–76; Martin, op. cit., 115, 125, and above, pp. 241–42. The find was also depicted by the discoverer, Charles W. Peale, in a vast canvas of banal grandiosity (1806), whose apparent inspiration was the simultaneous effort to show the picturesqueness of the power excavators and the drama of the discovery—a painting that is a classic of its genre. The enormous skeleton was put on display in the Philadelphia Museum, where it was attentively examined by Perrin du Lac (*Voyage dans les deux Louisianes,* pp. 253–56), scientifically discussed (1815–16) by Montlezun (Remond, op. cit., p. 331), and where a quarter of a century later (1829) it was seen, though leaving the viewer "greatly disappointed in its appearance," by the lady-traveler Anne Royall (Tryon, *A Mirror for Americans,* pp. 62–63, and Martin, op. cit., pp. 119–20). Löwenstern too, op. cit., p. 198, saw and admired mastodon skeletons in Philadelphia, "the largest and most complete ones known." In 1833–34 a museum in Cincinnati put on show some "enormous organic remains" (Tryon, *A Mirror for Americans,* p. 553); while in Columbia, South Carolina, Frederika Bremer saw (1850) "some skeleton fragments of gigantic animals, the megatherium and mastodon, found here" (op. cit., I, 383; cf. II, 263).

Philosophical Society. Dr. Barton accepted the challenge of Buffon, de Pauw, and Robertson, retraced the path to the very first sources of Indo-American civilization,[288] and in the opening pages (I, 4) of his *Fragments of the Natural History of Pennsylvania* wrote:

I cannot but deem it a puerile supposition, unsupported by the evidence of nature, that a great part of America has probably later emerged from the bosom of the ocean than the other continents.

In the *Notes on Virginia* (which was well known to Barton) Jefferson had already demolished the hypothesis of an American flood, indeed had even doubted that the atmosphere contained enough humidity for the Bible's universal flood; and managed to remain true to his faith in the Old Testament and America at the same time by suggesting that there may well have been some little flood over there "in the country lying around the Mediterranean sea."[289] In much the same way the Rev. Timothy Dwight (1752–1817) found it best to defend the climate of the United States, and protect its past from the slander of a post-Noachic flood and its animals from the charge of degeneration, by heaping gross sarcasms on Buffon and his credulous follower, de Pauw.[290]

With equal zeal and determination Dewitt Clinton denied (in 1814) that the air of America had a harmful influence on the body or spirit of man, and went on to exalt the American "race" as a happy mixture of the best European stock.[291]

The geographer Jedidiah Morse (1761–1826), in describing the United States, set himself the task in his turn of correcting the many errors committed by the Europeans, the only ones who until then had concerned themselves with American geography, and drew largely on Jefferson's *Notes*. It was from the *Notes* that he took the polemic against Buffon and Raynal, who is said to have "extended . . . to the inhabitants transplanted in America" the thesis worked out by Buffon "to ennoble the species and individuals of Europe, at the expense of the corresponding species and individuals in the New World"—a task actually carried out by de Pauw—and in several places he defends the healthiness of the climate of the United States, the longevity of its inhabitants, its richness in natural

288. H Bernstein, "Inter-American Aspects," p. 58, and *Origins*, pp. 61–62. The translation (1808) of Molina's Chilean history was dedicated to Barton (ibid., p. 64), and Jefferson, who owned various of his works (*Catalogue of the Library*, I, 318–19, 468–69; III, 357; IV, 185–87, 219), sent him some of his notes on Indian vocabularies (see Ford ed., IV, 120; IX, 177; *Life and Writings*, ed. Modern Library, pp. 598–99, and Peden, in a note to his edition, p. 282, n. 13). On Barton, cf. Smallwood, op. cit., pp. 289–93; Pearce, *The Savages*, pp. 77–78; Martin, op. cit., 194–95, 247. (He should not be confused with William Barton, who [1791] defended the climate, salubriousness, and virtuous disposition of America against Buffon and the other European denigrators, and on whom see Chinard, "America as a Human Habitat," pp. 47, 49; *L'homme contre la Nature*, pp. 63–66 ff.; and Martin, op. cit., pp. 200–02).
289. Martin, op. cit., p. 128.
290. Ibid., pp. 153, 158, 170, 194–96, 204.
291. Curti, *American Loyalty*, pp. 66, 71; C. and M. Beard, op. cit., pp. 214 ff.

products, and even the virtue of the redskins, whom he absolves from the accusation of sexual frigidity (a characteristic of all nomads and hunters); but he does not hesitate to class as lazy, idle, and despotic, the rich planters of the South, who have been softened by the climate and more especially by their great number of slaves.[292] Thus although his references to Latin America reiterate the superficial judgments of Buffon and de Pauw, he describes the natives of North America quite sympathetically, in an accurate and detailed picture that concludes with an attack on Buffon and de Pauw; and toward the end of his life (ca. 1824) he founded the American Society for Promoting the Civilization and General Improvement of the Indian Tribes in the United States.[293]

B. Humboldt's enthusiasm for tropical America. But Jefferson, Barton, Clinton, and Morse wrote in America. And in Europe (as Sydney Smith was asking at that very time) "who reads an American book"?[294] In Europe too, however, America just then found a defender, and someone of much superior standing to these worthy North Americans. Alexander von Humboldt did, in fact, quote and praise Barton as an "acute naturalist," before going on (1806–07) to take up on his own account, from a more elevated standpoint, the criticism of the well-known, indeed too well known, assertions:

Too often writers generally praised, and rightly praised, have repeated that America is in every sense a new continent. That luxuriant vegetation, the enor-

---

292. See the elaboration in Pictet, *Tableau,* I, 180–81, 186; II, 134; against his severe judgment on the inhabitants of Maryland, ibid., II, 140, see Bayard, *Voyage,* pp. 190–91.

293. See M. A. Kraus, *A History of American History* (New York, 1937), pp. 151–55; H. Bernstein, *Origins,* p. 63; Pearce, *The Savages,* pp. 60–79, 96, 97, 187. And, for other examples, Martin, op. cit., pp. 192–96; in defense of the Americans' longevity, see ibid., pp. 202–03.

294. "In the four quarters of the globe, who reads an American book or goes to an American play, or looks at an American picture or statue?" (Sydney Smith, in the *Edinburgh Review,* January 1820; much the same expressions occur in an article by Smith in the same periodical, December 1818: see Cunliffe, *Literature,* p. 44). The saying, frequently quoted and becoming almost proverbial (see Basil Hall: in England "the great mass of the people never read an American volume, and never even see or hear of one," *Travels in North America in the years 1827 and 1828* [Graz, 1965], II, 49), is taken up again with increased savagery with the revival of anti-Americanism in England after the insolvencies of the American states in 1839–42 (Thistlewaite, op. cit., p. 78). In point of fact the general ignorance in Europe about North American things and writings was really quite extreme at that time (Curti, *Probing Our Past* [New York, 1954], pp. 193–94), and the same was even more true of Latin America (A. P. Whitaker, *The Western Hemisphere Idea* [Ithaca, N.Y., 1954], p. 9). A quarter of a century after Smith's barbed remark an American publisher could answer him that a very large number of American books, 382 within ten years, had been reprinted in England (G. P. Putnam, "Literature in America," 1845, in *An American Reader,* pp. 291–92). When *Uncle Tom's Cabin* appeared, and gained its well-known resounding success, another American countered facetiously: "Who reads an American book, did you inquire, Mr. Smith? Why . . . who does not?" (C. F. Briggs, *Uncle Tomitudes,* 1853, ibid., p. 383). And in 1859 the *Boston Post* published a study with statistics on "Who Reads an American Book" (Carl Bode, *The Anatomy of American Popular Culture, 1840–61* [Berkeley–Los Angeles, 1959], p. 115). Finally Melville, in his essay on Hawthorne, announced that the day was near when it would be asked: "Who reads a book by an Englishman that is a modern?" (Matthiessen, op. cit., p. 372, still smarting from the insolent remark, points out that those very years 1820–21, with the appearance of Irving, Bryant, and Cooper, saw the birth of the literature of the new American nation—which in fact amounts to admitting the Englishman to be right).

mous sweep of its rivers, the restlessness of its powerful volcanoes are a proof (they say) that there the earth, still shaking and not yet dried out, is nearer to the primordial chaotic state than the Old Continent. Already long before I went there I found such ideas as antiphilosophical as they were contradictory to generally recognized physical laws. Fanciful images of youth and restlessness, of growing aridity and inertia [*Trägheit*] of the aging earth can arise only in those who find it amusing to go in search of contrasts between the two hemispheres and make no effort to gain an overall view of the structure of the terrestrial globe.

It would be as much as to say that southern Italy was "newer" than northern Italy, because it had so many more earthquakes and volcanic eruptions:

The idea that a certain peace must reign in Nature in an older land is based on a mere trick of our imagination. There is no reason to suppose that one entire part of our planet is older or newer than another.[295]

Goethe, with his faith in the countries without eruptions or earthquakes being more stable socially too, had let himself be seduced by this same trick of imagination. Humboldt does not. Even his primitive Neptunistic convictions undergo a change in the glow of America's volcanoes. Instead of hailing the New World as Goethe did for its lack of basalt and seismic disturbances, Humboldt is happy to admire its complexity, the alternating fury and contorted couplings of natural phenomena. Tension is more productive than harmony, the dialectic of the challenge is the mainspring of progress.[296] It is not the calm peace of the geological strata that attracts him, but life, the unforeseeable variety of life, including the life of the earth, the violent play of elemental forces. His heart stirs not to the ethereal serenity of the universe but to the impetus and impulses that keep it in motion and agitation, and compose themselves into a superior harmony of discords.

In the convulsive darkness of prehistory, the world was infinitely more tempestuous and violent than this "tranquil world of ours, in which we live." The animals were gigantic, the plants differently distributed, the rivers broader and deeper.[297] And America offers us still the spectacle of those times (*Urzeit*) and those noisy conflicts, with erupting subterranean fires, raging torrents, and thundering hurricanes. "The struggle

295. A. von Humboldt, *Ansichten der Natur, mit wissenschaftlichen Erläuterungen,* 1807, 3rd ed., (Stuttgart-Tübingen, 1849), I, 16 (the statement on crocodiles and snakes), and n. 19; ibid., pp. 167–71, which cite, apart from Barton, the article "Über die Urvölker von Amerika" by the same Humboldt, in the *Neue Berlinische Monatsschrift,* 15 (1806), p. 190; cf. Minguet, op. cit., pp. 371, 633–34. The French edition (*Tableaux de la Nature* [Paris, 1808]), was presented with the author's compliments to Jefferson, who already had a very high opinion of Humboldt and replied with heartfelt thanks (*Catalogue of the Library,* I, 305; cf. also ibid., IV, 290–92, and below, n. 323).
296. Minguet, op. cit., pp. 60–61, 615.
297. *Reise,* III, 122.

of the elements with each other is the real characteristic of the natural scene in the New World."[298]

Thus it is not only America's slanderers that discover and denounce unique and contradictory deficiencies in the continent. The admirers too, like Goethe and Humboldt, find and admire in it what they themselves most intimately worship, the former the sovereign calm of nature, the latter its eternal creativity, which eludes the dichotomies and dilemmas of the professors.

The volcano Tunguragua belches forth more mud and water than lava: "So here we have a volcano," jeers Humboldt delightedly, "with which Nature wishes to reconcile and unite the Neptunists and Vulcanists!"[299] He says it jokingly, but this volcano and its liquid charge go a lot further toward resolving the scientific conflict than the so-much-later bored indifference of the aging Goethe.[300]

In the polemic between Neptunists and Plutonists, as in the quarrel over America's geological age and humidity, the empirical objectivity of the new natural science, imbued with the critical spirit and a sense of history, could not but reject all such temporal schemes, value judgments, balances and symmetrical contrasts that showed even a hint of aprioristic systematizing. But any futile condemnation found an even stronger enemy in Humboldt's alert and sympathetic spirit, his yearning for an organic vision of the world and his romantic longing for totality: "In America," Chateaubriand was to write, "the great Humboldt has described and said everything."[301]

It was in fact for the purpose of conscientious study — quite unmixed

---

298. Ibid., p. 191; III, 321.

299. Letter to von Zach, from Cumanà, 1 September 1799, in K. Bruhns *Alexander von Humboldt, eine wissenschaftliche Biographie* (Leipzig, 1872: hereafter cited as Bruhns), I, 323. On another volcano, Cuchivano, which possibly within its belly separates the water into its elements and belches forth burning hydrogen, see *Reise,* I, 331–33. On the Neptunism of Humboldt's younger days and his successive oscillations, see Bruhns, op. cit., I, 238–39; III, 102, 108, 182–83. His first work, *Mineralogische Betrachtungen über einige Basalte am Rhein* (1790), was to show "that this rock is of Neptunian origin" (H. Klencke, *Alexander von Humboldt* [Leipzig, 1851], p. 29). Still, on his return from America, Humboldt believed that his travels provided further confirmation of Werner's system: letter to Freiesleben, from Bordeaux, 1 August 1804, in Bruhns, I, 397. On his balanced position, see Minguet, op. cit., pp. 43–44, 73, 551.

300. See above, p. 362. On the resulting conflict of ideas between Goethe and Humboldt see also above, n. 133, and exhaustive details in Bruhns, op. cit., I, 192–97; but see also Friedrich Muthmann, *Alexander von Humboldt und sein Naturbild im Spiegel der Goethezeit* (Zürich-Stuttgart, 1955), esp. pp. 16–17, 63–64 and Minguet, op. cit., pp. 28n., 50, 72–74, 78–80. Jefferson too, substantially a Neptunist, professed an absolute disinterest in the rival boasts of Vulcan and Neptune (Martin, op. cit., pp. 45, 127–28). Considerably later, but still in the spirit of Humboldt, is the irony of an American journalist who in the upper valley of the Mississippi found clear signs that it had once been subject to powerful volcanic and diluvial action, "and neither the Neptunian or Vulcanian theory can advance a superior claim" (E. Flagg, *The Far-West* [New York, 1838], in Tryon, ed., *A Mirror for Americans,* pp. 571–72).

301. *Voyage en Amérique,* p. 27.

with morbid exoticism—that Humboldt had set sail (in 1799) for the equatorial regions of the New World—the part of America said to be most unhealthy, the fearsome tropics around the Caribbean Sea. And from the moment of his arrival he had found himself completely enchanted. He had no difficulty at all in getting acclimatized. Quite the reverse, he experienced an immediate and powerful sensation of being in some vast theater, extraordinarily rich and bright, and with his mind tense and reaching out he was ready to examine and enjoy its every aspect. In his descriptions the enthusiasm of the first discoverers seems to come alive again, so much more surprising after three centuries of travel and exploration, and rendered more serious and solemn by nineteenth-century Europe's scientific maturity. It is no injustice to his innumerable precursors, both ancient and recent, from Oviedo to La Condamine, to say that with Humboldt Western thought at last achieves the peaceful conquest and intellectual annexation to its own world, the only Cosmos, of the regions which until then had been hardly more than an object of curiosity, amazement, or derision. And as Humboldt moves toward this conquest his mind is open and excited, touched with that slight euphoria that still today comes over any one of us leaving behind the problems and the unnumbered ancestral voices of our civilization, and seeing for the the first time the mute and dazzling horizons of tropical America, the parched coastal deserts and the untouched flamboyant margins of the great continental forest. One feels reborn. And if remote little Europe is then torn in war, Napoleonic or Hitlerian, it is only too easy for the delighted exile to discover a crude rationality, a naïve perfection, a possible imitation of ancient Eden in this landscape of low thick woods furrowed with vast rivers, and soaring white peaks dropping into the sea.

Humboldt's first impressions, and his second ones too, are in fact never without this quality of exaltation: "I cannot repeat to you enough," he writes to his brother, "how very happy I feel in this part of the world where I am already so accustomed to the climate that I feel as if I had never lived in Europe."[302] By night the whole sky sparkles: "I think that right here the starry sky presents the most beautiful and magnificent spectacle."[303] By day, plants and animals glow with a thousand colors: the birds, the fish, even the crabs, blue and yellow, contribute to the overall impression, spattering the emphatic green of the vegetation with chromatic harmonies: "Only here, here in Guayana, in the tropical part of South America, is the world really properly green."[304] Mexico's moun-

302. Letter to his brother, from Cumanà, 17 October 1800, cited in Bruhns, op. cit., I, 332. Cf. Minguet, op. cit., pp. 58, 192, 195.
303. Letter from Cumanà, 1 September 1799; Bruhns, op. cit., I, 322.

tains are the most beautiful in the world. Chimborazo (Ecuador) is the most majestic peak on earth.[305] The dream of Humboldt's life has come true. "The tropics are my element." He remains always in excellent health. He even enjoys the company of the Creoles more every day,[306] and in a witty and beautiful Mexican lady he actually finds "a sort of Western Mme de Staël."[307]

When he has to return to Europe his heart grows heavy; he cannot tear himself away from this "stupendous world of the Indies."[308] And still in later life he will yearn for the tropics, the climate of the palm trees and the bananas; and as an old man he will demand that his rooms be kept at a "tropical" temperature, about twenty degrees Réaumur.[309]

C. His criticisms of Buffon and de Pauw. Now the curious thing is that Humboldt's exact intention in visiting America had been to investigate the Buffonian problem, the problem of the relationship between living creatures and the natural environment. He proposed to collect plants and fossils, of course, and make astronomical observations, and chemical analysis of the air, yes—all of this was part of the traveling naturalist's regular routine, "but all this is not the main purpose of my journey. My attention will always be focused on the convergence of forces, on the influence of inanimate creation on the living animal and plant world, on this harmony."[310]

But here already it becomes clear that the problem was Buffonian only in name, because with this stress on harmony and convergence of forces it is immediately tinged with romantic and philosophical hues. Rather than dwelling on quantitative and qualitative comparisons between the two hemispheres, Humboldt tries to understand each organism and each environment in itself and in its relation to the universe. And more than once he finds himself in the position of having to take issue with some of the French naturalist's most famous statements.

Buffon, for example, was completely wrong to treat the jaguar as a sort of lesser tiger. The jaguar is a much more formidable animal than people think. Humboldt himself met one as he was making his way up the Apure river, and it was bigger than any of the Bengal tigers ever seen in Europe's menageries: "The natives themselves were amazed at its prodigious

304. Letter to his brother, from Cumanà, 16 July 1799, and to Willdenow, from Havana, 21 February 1801, in ibid., I, 319–43.
305. Ibid., II, 441.
306. Letter to Baron von Forell, from Caracas, 3 February 1800, ibid., I, 329; cf. ibid., I, 333, 341, 342. On the question of his health, see ibid., I, 341, 396–97, 398; II, 440.
307. Ibid., I, 391.
308. Letter to Freiesleben, from Bordeaux, 1 August 1804, ibid., I, 397.
309. Ibid., I, 426; II, 476.
310. Letter to von Moll, from La Coruña, 5 June 1799, in ibid., I, 274.

length."[311] And as for the reptiles, there are not just alligators but real crocodiles: Humboldt measured one which was twenty-two feet and three inches long.[312]

So much for the wild animals. Humboldt is just as explicit on the subject of the domestic animals. In fact he deals Buffonian theory an even more stunning blow simply by laying bare its literary origins (see above, p. 21) and certain reasons for its success in Europe:

> It would be superfluous for me to refute here M. de Buffon's hazardous assertions on the alleged degeneration of the domestic animals introduced into the new continent. These ideas have spread easily, because while flattering the vanity of the Europeans they could also be linked to glittering hypotheses on the ancient state of our planet. As soon as one examines the facts with care [this care that so tried Buffon's patience] the physicists recognize harmony where this eloquent writer announced nothing but contrasts.[313]

This does not mean, of course, that Humboldt failed to observe the alterations suffered by an animal type under the influence of environment. Monkeys of the same species are domesticated and trained more easily in some places than in others. Here the crocodiles are ferocious, there they are cowardly. But the domestic animals that were brought over from Europe and became wild in America have multiplied in number although surrounded by all sorts of threats and dangers;[314] and in the tropics (but not the American tropics alone) Europe's minuscule and nimble lizard swells into the colossal, weighty, armored body of the crocodile, and the domestic cat figures in the vastly aggrandized forms of the tiger, lion, and jaguar.[315] In other words nature in the tropics is exuberant and the wild species are more robust and prolific than the domestic ones—two theses that are not new, but are at least revitalized by a personal experience; two theses not without truth, but never fully developed, whether because Humboldt refrained from formulating general laws of zoological

311. A. de Humboldt and H. Bompland, *Viaje a las regiones equinocciales del nuevo continente . . .* (Paris, 1826), II, 490; and *Reise,* III, 28–29; cf. also III, 43; IV, 129–30 and passim. The enormous creature is also mentioned by an English traveler of the same period, Edmond Temple: see *Travels,* I, 140. The Prince de Broglie too saw a vast young tigress in a cage in Caracas in 1782 (*Journal de Voyage,* p. 144; cf. ibid., 136, etc.). On a certain confusion on Humboldt's part among the South American felines, see Bruhns, op. cit., III, 290–91.

312. Bruhns, op. cit., III, 294. On crocodiles and tigers as big as Africa's, ibid., I, 323, aggressive and powerful, ibid., I, 328, 334, 340; and cf. Minguet, op. cit., p. 136, and below, p. 417, and also Humboldt's *Cuba,* I, 345–53 (with reference to "Buffon's law relative to the distribution of the species among the tropical regions of the two continents"). Cf. Minguet, op. cit., pp. 104, 108.

313. A. de Humboldt, *La Nouvelle-Espagne,* III, 224–25; the accent still falls on the harmony that absorbs the contrasts (see above, pp. 406–07).

314. A Buffonian thesis, inasmuch as it establishes a superiority of the wild species over the domestic ones (see also above, p. 26), anti-Buffonian inasmuch as it affirms the prolificity of the American animals (cf. below, p. 412). The return to the savage state, in America too, of the cultivated plants, which he compared to the domestic animals, was something which occupied Humboldt's mind years before his departure for the New World (letter to Schiller, 6 August 1794, in Bruhns, op. cit., I, 204).

315. Bruhns, op. cit., III, 273–76.

geography, and moreover lacked the knowledge of the new systematic zoology (Cuvier and Lamarck made their first discoveries while he was in America),[316] or because of his absolute and unshakable distrust of evolutionary theories:

Everything which relates to the origin of the species, to the hypothesis of one variety becoming constant, or of a type perpetuating itself, belongs to problems of zoonomy, on which it is wise to make no categorical pronouncement.[317]

His position in the history of the dispute is thus anomalous. In many ways his enthusiasm for the Americas is more scientific than the slanders current in his time. On the other hand, he simply abandons a number of promising leads and possibilities, and by and large remains outside the mainstream of zoological thought, exercising only a belated and lateral influence on the discussions on America; his journey lasted from 1799 to 1804, but the publication of the writings revealing his results extended over several decades, from 1808 to 1834 for the *magnum opus*, and for the *Kosmos*, until 1858. The final version of the *Reise in die Aequinoctial-Gegenden des neuen Continents* has a preface dated 26 March 1859, forty days before his death.

Yet there can be no doubt that Humboldt was perfectly familiar with all the literature of the polemic, beginning with Buffon and de Pauw. And although in his enthusiasm for the opulence and generosity of tropical nature, he accepts and repeats certain typical de Pauwian extravagancies, such as the abundantly lactiferous Indian males;[318] although at times he rejects the ingenuous idealizations of the primitive and the savage, whether Carib or Tahitian, whether from the Orenoco or Mississippi, and notes paradoxically that the cannibals are not the worst nor the wildest of the savages;[319] although he frequently repeats that most of the savage tribes have declined from higher levels of civilization,[320] he reserves his

316. See above, pp. 328–29, and Bruhns, op. cit., III, 271, 273.

317. *La Nouvelle-Espagne*, III, 246.

318. Assuring the reader, for example, that "in this province of New Andalusia there is a man living who has so much milk that as his wife cannot herself suckle her child he has fed him himself all alone for the last five months. And his milk is not in the least bit different from women's milk." And adding as if to reinforce the credibility of the fact: "The billy goats of old also gave milk" (letter to von Zach, 1 September 1799, from Cumaná, in Bruhns, op. cit., I, 323); and cf. also Minguet, op. cit., p. 112; *Reise*, I, 310–12, where Humboldt adds: "Among the remarkable elements in the so-called weakness of the Americans, the travelers also cited the fact that the men have milk at their breasts," which he counters with the example of virile and sturdy milk-bearing Russians, and other abundant examples. And Lincoln for that matter once told a general, who had expressed doubt about the usefulness of certain precautions, that he had ordered them for the same reason for which God had given man mammae: so that if he should have a child he might be able to suckle it (J. Langdon-Davies, op. cit., p. 163n.). Even as late as 1889–90, on the subject of the *couvade*, there were quoted in *Notes and Queries* "numerous instances of men suckling children" (R. Reynolds, op. cit., p. 41).

319. *Reise*, I, 159; III, 89; IV, 18.

320. "Most of the savages . . . are only races that have become savage, the relics that escaped some great general shipwreck" (op. cit., IV, 324): "Most of the tribes, that we call savage, came very probably from peoples who once had a considerably higher cultural level" (ibid., II, 2 [the passage goes back to the French edition: see below, n. 346]).

admiration for the advocates of the Americas' and the Americans' physiological normality. He respects the missionaries' reports in particular and almost seems to be answering de Pauw, who had described them as "never truthful" (see above, chap. 3, n. 2), when he comments ironically: "The *philosophe* seemed to feel in duty bound to deny everything the missionaries had observed";[321] he defends the civilization of the ancient Mexicans against de Pauw, Raynal, "and even Robertson,"[322] and sets great store by the writings of Jefferson and Clavigero, who defended North America and Mexico;[323] he mentions and frequently quotes Father Gilij (above, pp. 223 ff.); he knows Carli's *American Letters;*[324] and he avails himself on a number of occasions of Volney's more recent and "excellent work" on the United States.[325] It has already been mentioned that he always revered his teacher George Forster, an attentive reader of de Pauw, and that he was acquainted with Dr. Barton's works,[326] but it should be added that he also read those of the South American apologists like Father Molina, whom he sought out personally in his house in Bologna,[327] Hipólito Unánue, and Francisco José de Caldas.[328] At Madrid he was able to examine the immense collection of documents assembled by J. B. Muñoz.[329] Ulloa and other historians are used and discussed frequently.[330] In fact, Raynal becomes the target of a number of polemic sallies which would more properly have been directed at de Pauw, possibly because Raynal's *History* was better known, or else because Humboldt like all the more serious writers was reluctant to get involved in a fight with someone like de Pauw. Thus Humboldt declares Raynal's assertions on the sterility of the domestic animals of Portobello to be "devoid of all truth."[331] But in another passage, where he criticizes

321. Quoted in Minguet, op. cit., p. 326.

322. Minguet, op. cit., p. 438 and see n. 330.

323. In the *Nouvelle-Espagne,* ed. cit., III, 224–25n., Humboldt mentions Jefferson's "excellent work" on Virginia and Fr. Clavigero's *Storia.* For Jefferson, who sent him a formal invitation to Washington (1804), and with whom he spent three weeks (Bruhns, op. cit., I, 393–94, 396, 398), see also *Nouvelle-Espagne,* I, 82 ("classic work on Virginia"), 222 ("excellent *Essay on Virginia*"); II, 435–36n., 448; III, 219, etc.; Doll, op. cit., 507 (Humboldt contrasts the United States with the "melancholy" and "immoral" spectacle offered by Europe); and above, chap. 5, n. 295. For Clavigero: *Nouvelle-Espagne,* I, 217, 318 ("judicious observations . . . directed against Robertson and Pauw"), 321, 379; II, 113, 115, 165–66, 172, 177, 292, 350, 450; III, 55, 144, 191, 198, 213, 216, 221, 253, 300; IV, 305, 481, etc.; Bruhns, op. cit., I, 378; III, 220; Minguet, op. cit., pp. 330, 669.

324. Bruhns, op. cit., III, 220.

325. *Nouvelle-Espagne,* I, 292, 383 (a "faithful picture . . . of the Indians of Canada"), 388, 390, 399; II, 448; IV, 490, 544; *Reise,* III, 89.

326. *Nouvelle-Espagne,* I, 293, 375; II, 448; and cf. above, pp. 170–71.

327. Without however finding him, to Molina's regret, since he was out in the country: *Storia naturale,* 2d ed., p. 225.

328. See for Molina, *Nouvelle-Espagne,* III, 54, 114; for Unánue, highly praised, I, 350; II, 48 (and Minguet, op. cit., pp. 174, 226, 227, 628); for Caldas, Bruhns, op. cit., I, 390; II, 529. The Spanish Jesuit Hervás y Panduro is also mentioned: *Nouvelle-Espagne,* II, 448; III, 195.

329. Minguet, op. cit., pp. 59, 585.

330. On his knowledge of Robertson, cf. Konetzke, op. cit., p. 543; Minguet, op. cit., pp. 327, 381.

331. *Nouvelle-Espagne,* I, 251. Raynal is also cited in that work, II, 400; III, 43, 201, 213, 219–20; IV, 182, 185, 227, 230–34, 265, 404, 466.

Ulloa's and Raynal's estimates of the production of the precious metals of America, Humboldt condemns the exaggerations of Ulloa and the "famous author of the *philosophical Researches.*"[332]

As a matter of fact there is no shortage of places where de Pauw becomes the main target and is assailed with the arguments put forth by Father Clavigero, which were as familiar to Humboldt as they are to us. Though he is not named it was de Pauw surely enough who had affirmed the extreme scarcity of edible plants in America,[333] and it is certainly de Pauw that Humboldt has in mind when he says:

America was not, by any means, so poor in edible plants as has been suggested by some scholars, with their false spirit of system — scholars who were acquainted with the new continent only in the works of Herrera and Solis.[334]

One detects an even more Clavigerian tone in the defense of the muscular Mexican miners:

The sight of these strong hardworking men would soon have changed the opinion of the Raynals, the de Pauws and all those authors, worthy men besides, who have been pleased to declaim on the degeneration of our species in the torrid zone.[335]

Humboldt, in short, thinks there is no further need for a detailed rebuttal of the lurid system of his notorious "compatriot." His admirable *Political Essay on the Kingdom of New Spain* already in itself completely refutes it. On the culture of the Americans, for instance, the learned naturalist expresses himself in terms that are quite incompatible with even the least scornful of de Pauw's comments.[336] But when the occasion arises he loses no chance of indicating his marked disagreement with both Buffon and de Pauw, and often permits himself a little urbane mockery at their expense.

The point on which he *seems* to come closest to the degenerative thesis is his profound and troubling conviction that the savage fell to his condition from a higher and more civilized one, that he is thus not a primitive, and even less a prototype, but a brutalized and barbaric creature: "The barbarity which dominates in these regions is perhaps not so much the expression of a complete and native lack of civilization but rather the effect of a long decadence. Almost all the tribes which we call savage probably descend from peoples that once possessed a considerably higher

332. Ibid., IV, 188–89. One might have thought it a slip of the pen for "author of the *Histoire philosophique*," if it were not that the criticism applies exactly to a passage in de Pauw, *Recherches*, I, 85.
333. See, for example, *Recherches*, I, 108–10.
334. *Nouvelle-Espagne*, III, 140–41. Both Herrera and Solis are cited in de Pauw's *Recherches*.
335. *Nouvelle-Espagne*, I, 362, and IV, 37; cf. above, p. 204. And already in 1801: "The Caribs are the largest and the most strong-muscled nation that I have ever seen; they alone are enough to contradict Raynal's and de Pauw's fantasies about the weakness and degeneration of the human race in the new world" (letter of 21 September 1801 to his brother, in *Briefe Alex. von Humboldts an seinem Bruder Wilhelm* [Stuttgart, 1880], p. 30, quoted by Konetzke, op. cit., p. 532, n. 2).
336. See for example *Essai*, II, 10–11, 18, and the passages quoted above, n. 306.

level of civilization. And perhaps there is some truth in those oriental doctrines that see the savages as races driven into the woods by civilized society."[337] It is easy to persuade oneself that the natives with their greased and painted bodies are the fragments of some great shipwreck,[338] "a degenerate race, the weak remnants of peoples who lived for a long time scattered in the forests, and in the end sank back into barbarity."[339]

The thesis may sound de Pauwian, or even biblical (even Adam fell!), but the emphasis is quite different. For Humboldt it serves mainly to reaffirm his belief in the substantial natural identity of all men, at both ends of the scale of civilization. And at the same time it awakens in civilized man, the target of his discourse, a subtle doubt on the value of the process of civilization and its arrogant boasts; he flashes before his eyes the lability of its conquests and the precariousness of its vaunted triumphs. But most of all he historicizes, without pseudoreligious apriorisms, the slow and troubled path of humanity, and thereby cuts short all possibility of primitivism. The man of the nineteenth century peers at the savage as if he were the disinherited descendant of more illustrious and glorious ancestors, indeed as if he were the possible fearful image of his own remote and guilty progeny. The ancient "barbarity" is enriched with new allusive meanings, and "civilization" caught in an angry threatening glare. It is not so surprising that the theory of the degeneration of the savage proved so attractive to mournful and meditative souls like de Maistre, Chateaubriand, Schlegel, Leopardi, and Schopenhauer.[340]

Nor is it surprising that Humboldt, though accepting the thesis, refused any adherence to the theories of de Pauw. In another well-known

337. *Reise*, II, 1–2; cf. above, n. 320.
338. Ibid., IV, 324.
339. Ibid., III, 89 (quoted also by Febvre, op. cit., 55, n. 119, and Konetzke, op. cit., p. 559); IV, 399; cf. Minguet, op. cit., pp. 143, 336. Against the distinction between "savages" and "civilized" peoples, ibid., pp. 354, 439.
340. Above, pp. 358, 387–88, 389–90, 448, 457. Supposed references to the thesis of the degeneration of the savages (or rather the tendency of a "natural" society without "civilization" to degenerate), have been found in La Condamine and Wieland: see von Hofe, "Jacobi, Wieland and the New World," p. 188. For the former see above, chap. 4, n. 96; for the latter, it is true that in a series of anti-Russeauian works of 1769–77, gathered under the title *Beyträge zur geheimen Geschichte des Menschheit* (in *Sämmtliche Werke*, vol. XIV, pp. 1–241), there are hints of a polemic against the excellence of the pure state of nature, talk of "men degenerated into savagery" (p. 207) and "children become savage" (p. 191), and the statement that the descendents of Koxkox and Tlaquatrin (two characters in "Koxkox and Kikequetzel, eine mexicanische Geschichte") "sank to mere animality" (p. 86); but these are never more than generic expressions, describing a degeneration that is merely and completely ethical. Wieland, though he knows, then, among others, La Condamine (p. 175) and Buffon (pp. 71, 73, 147), dutifully repeats that Mexico's nature is benign (pp. 63–64). And the savages Rousseau speaks of are *not* primitives: through the enormous sufferings inflicted on them by the Castilians they "have been terrified into a certain wildness, which was not natural to them" (p. 100); the lapse into savagery is always casual (ibid.). The last essay, then, eloquently entitled "Ueber die vergebliche Abnahme des menschlichen Geschlechts" (of the human race, therefore, not of the savage Americans), after pointing to the fakirs as the last grade of degeneration (p. 220) and after moralistically lamenting that we are all inferior to our great ancestors and the heroes of the past (p. 223) concludes by decisively rejecting the thesis "of an ever-increasing *debilitation of Nature* and weakening of *humanity*" (p. 233).

work, he condemns these pseudotheories *en bloc* with overt irony and undisguised polemic:

Certain celebrated writers, more struck by the contrasts than the harmonies in nature,[341] have been pleased to depict all America as a land of swamps, hostile to the multiplication of animals, and newly inhabited by tribes as little civilized as the inhabitants of the South Seas. In the *historical researches on the Americans* an absolute skepticism had taken the place of a healthy criticism.[342]

The italicized words are almost a literal transcription of the title of de Pauw's book, with an alteration which is certainly involuntary but actually characteristic of the change from the age of the *philosophical lights* to the age of *history*.[343] To remove any possible doubt in our minds Humboldt quotes him a little further on, together with Raynal and Robertson, deploring the fact that not one of these three managed to appreciate the civilization achieved by the Aztecs: "These authors regard as barbaric any state of man that differs from the notion of culture that they have formulated for themselves with their systematized ideas. We cannot accept these sharp distinctions into barbaric and civilized nations"[344] — which is perfectly in line with the romantic attitude to primitive peoples, and a valid criticism not only of the three authors quoted, but of all rationalist historiography.

The same expressions reappear in his major work, the *Kosmos*, of which this part dates back mainly to the lectures of 1827–28. There Humboldt emphatically denies the "unpleasant hypothesis of higher and lower races of men. There are more docile, more civilized races, races improved through intellectual culture, but no nobler races," and admits[345] only that in the tropics there exist "causes which in many parts of this happy region work against the local formation of higher civilization."[346] It is true that in the later *Examen critique* (1836–39) Humboldt seems to

341. One seems to catch here and in the passages quoted on pp. 406 and 407, an echo of the influence of Bernardin de Saint-Pierre. His *Harmonies de la Nature*, with their universal sympathy, could well have absorbed and superseded, in Humboldt's mind, the severe verdicts of Buffon and de Pauw. Humboldt in fact preferred Bernardin de Saint-Pierre's sensitive descriptions to those of Buffon, which lacked any perception of the emotive affinities between the naturalist and nature (*Kosmos* [American ed., 1868], III, 8, quoted by Jones, *Ideas in America*, p. 290, and Muthmann, op. cit., pp. 28–29).

342. A. von Humboldt, *Vues des Cordillères et monuments des peuples indigènes de l'Amérique* (Paris, n.d., but 1816), I, 10–11. On one occasion de Pauw calls his book "Recherches sur l'Histoire Naturelle des Américains" (*Recherches*, II, 99).

343. Already in 1789 Jolis (op. cit., p. 375) had cited de Pauw as the "Author of the Historical Researches."

344. *Vues des Cordillères*, II, 98. One can also recognize a Herderian note in this insistence on a common humanity (Humboldt quotes Herder in the *Nouvelle-Espagne*, II, 161, etc.; and Muthmann, op. cit., p. 47, underlines the identity of their points of view on the races).

345. *Kosmos* (Stuttgart, 1845), I, 14; cf. Bruhns, op. cit., III, 221.

346. Ibid., I, 385. The *Kosmos* was assiduously studied (1850) by Miss Martineau (Vera Wheatley, *The Life and Work of Harriet Martineau* [London, 1957], p. 295, and H. Martineau, *Biographical Sketches* [London, 1869], pp. 278–89), who seems to have found her inspiration therein for the thesis described below, p. 493.

accept the "great law of nature, recognized by Buffon in the disparity of the animal Creation proper to these regions (South America and in general the whole tropical part of the New World) and to Africa," and considers it applicable "within certain limits" to the vegetable kingdom. But this same extension to the plants shows how he only half understood or half remembered Buffon's zoological thesis. Buffon stresses the *difference* between South American and African fauna. Humboldt brings out the analogies and *similarities* between the flora of the two continents, South America and Africa, and their absolute diversity from the European, Asiatic, and North American flora.[347]

Here too then the nineteenth-century naturalist fails to get to the root of the problem that had concerned the eighteenth-century naturalist. The differences that puzzled Buffon were between two hemispheres, separated by so many degrees of longitude; those that occupy Humboldt are between climates, or parallels. The former made America a special case, in complete antithesis to the Old World. The latter formed part of a general climatic law, valid for all continents, and acting uniformly from the poles to the equator. In the tropics, in fact, nature is more exuberant, varied, extravagant, and fruitful.[348]

But while in one way (as we have said once and as we see here again) Humboldt remains marginal to the polemic; even though from the chronological point of view too it seems he should perhaps come *before* almost all the authors in this chapter—in another way, from a higher point of view, he belongs even *after* Hegel. Humboldt was in fact perfectly aware of the antiquated arbitrariness of that philosophy of nature that reached its full flowering in the Hegelian condemnation of America, and did not hesitate to ridicule it. His position in respect to Hegel follows precisely, and significantly, that of his teacher Forster toward Kant, respectfully rebuked by the naturalist-explorer because in his works on anthropology and physical geography he had formulated general principles on the basis of an absolutely insufficient knowledge of the facts.[349] One of his lectures of the period 1827–28 begins with a "protest" or "warning" (*Verwahrung*) against Hegel, whose philosophy of nature "without knowledge and without experience" is a "schematism more rigid than that imposed upon humanity by the Middle Ages." It gives the "intoxicating illusion of having a firm grip on the truth, but dissolves in the "short sweet saturnalia of a merely mental science of nature," in a ludicrous "masked ball of mad philosophers."[350] Again in 1841, having

347. *Examen critique*, II, 76–78.
348. See B. Smith, op. cit., pp. 152, 192–93, etc.
349. *Noch etwas uber die Menschenrassen* (1786), in *Werke*, II, 74; G. G. Gervinus, op. cit., p. 363; Kersten, op. cit., pp. 167–78; cf. above, pp. 172–73, 330–31.
350. Bruhns, op. cit., II, 139–40, 147–49; R. Buchwald, *Goethezeit und Gegenwart* (Stuttgart, 1949), pp. 177–78.

made up his mind to include these sarcasms in the *Kosmos*—"one must have the courage to print what one has said and written for thirty years" —Humboldt listed some amusing little samples of these romantic definitory and hermeneutic lunacies, as for example: "America is a female form, long, thin, watery, and at the forty-eighth parallel ice-cold. The degrees of latitude are years—woman becomes old at forty-eight."[351] Canada is the continent's menopause!

Then Hegel himself becomes the personal target when Humboldt reads his *Philosophy of History* and finds so many "abstract statements and completely false judgments" on the Americas (and the Indies); reading these lies—he writes to Varnhagen von Ense—he feels depressed and disturbed. And to shake himself out of this mood he adds an ironic postscript at the bottom of the letter: "I have organized my life very badly, and soon I shall have completely lost my senses. I would willingly renounce the European beef that Hegel tells us is so superior to American beef, and I would love to dwell beside these weak and inoffensive crocodiles of his which are however, unfortunately, twenty-five feet long."[352] Certainly, the whole Hegelian philosophy of nature must have seemed grotesque to Humboldt; but no part of it more so than the part referring to the New World, which Humboldt knew so well and which he was busy describing in minute detail in his imposing series of scientific works. All that remains to us, then, is to see what America chose to wear for the masked ball; or rather how it was turned away, because its costume was not pretty enough.

XIV. HEGEL: AMERICA IMMATURE AND IMPOTENT

A. Overall judgment, severe and impassive. The dispute of the New World reaches its peak in the antithesis between Humboldt and Hegel, and at the same time the point of widest divergence between the two extremes. In the decades that follow all America's enthusiasts rely on the vigorous assertions of the Prussian naturalist, and all its slanderers take comfort in the pronouncements of the Swabian philosopher. There are almost no new developments. Humboldt, the veteran of the tropics and the dying viceroyalties, establishes the idea that will stand for generations, of an America rich in physical strength and glutted with stupendous vis-

---

351. Letter to Varnhagen von Ense, 28 April 1841, in *Lettres de Humboldt à Varnhagen von Ense, 1827–1858*, trans. C. F. Girard (Geneva, 1860), pp. 63–64; and in *Correspondance de Alexandre de Humboldt avec Varnhagen von Ense*, trans. M. Sulzberger (Brussels, 1860), p. 125. Humboldt does not give, nor do I know, the source of this gem. From another letter to Varnhagen von Ense (4 May 1841) it seems to belong to a follower of the Schellingian Henrik Steffens. Cf. Minguet, "L'Amérique et les *Leçons sur la Philosophie de l'Histoire*," *Les langues néo-latines*, 54, no. 4 (December 1960), pp. 42–43.

352. Letter to Varnhagen von Ense, 1 July 1837; Geneva ed., pp. 32–33; Brussels ed., pp. 73–74. "To a man like myself, as fascinated as an insect by the earth and its natural diversity, an abstract assertion of completely false facts and opinions concerning America and the Indian world is both oppressive and disturbing" (letter of 1 July 1837 to Varnhagen von Ense [Leipzig, 1860], pp. 43 ff., quoted in Konetzke, art. cit., p. 540). The passage from Hegel is transcribed below, p. 428.

tas. Hegel, who is struck by the vision of the North American republic's rapid rise to manhood and the repeated and successful outbursts of revolution in Spanish America, but uncertain how to include the continent in his dialectical triads with their Europeocentric tendencies, confirms the American peoples' claims to the glorious title of youth, and thus also the possession of the Future; but physical America is once more damned as immature.

The vast apparatus of his system could not ignore such an abundantly evident "phenomenon"; but in his efforts to rationalize it and resolve its antithesis the whole mechanism creaks. Hegel recognizes no accidentality: neither in individual continents, nor in the different areas of the American continent, nor in the phases of its history. Reason must blaze forth in every part of reality, and reduce it, willy-nilly, to crystalline exactitude, to the polished and glittering symmetry of what is necessary, has always been necessary, and can suffer no change. Thus he dialectalizes and polarizes everything, parts of the world, differences in climate and fauna, the gorgeous feathers and false notes of America's birds, the varied destiny of her peoples, the pre-Columbian civilizations, and the contemporary religious affiliations. In this mechanical but still immensely powerful yearning for a single explanation for the infinite diversity of the world, one law to explain the nature of the two hemispheres, Hegel takes up and continues the efforts of Buffon, indeed carries his theses to their extreme consequences, extending them from the animal kingdom to all American reality.

Thus without even realizing it Hegel goes much further than de Pauw himself. But his judgment is expressed quite without acrimony, and he does nothing to stimulate further inquiry and scientific debate. From one point of view, then, he is at the apex of the "polemic," from another completely outside it. Although he knows a considerable amount about America and demonstrates a familiarity with the current and contrasting theses, one cannot really say that he ever tackles the overall question of the "dignity" or "value" of the New World, or that he makes any specific use of the arguments that we have met so far. His path is different, even if the conclusions to which it leads end up by reconfirming and aggravating the harshest pronouncements of America's denigrators. We must now see if we can follow that path, without getting bogged down in the subtleties of the pseudological passages or lost in the interpretation of the minor differences between one work and the next. All in all, the Hegelian concept of the Americas is consistent and shows no signs of having undergone any modification from earlier to later versions. But to understand it we have to see how it fits into the system.

  B. *The restoration of the philosophy of nature.* America is first and foremost a natural fact. It belongs thus in the first instance to the philosophy of Nature. Now Hegel has an extremely lively and dynamic concept of nature, but one that is at the same time so rigidly antihistorical that it forces him to admit shortcomings in nature whenever the individual phenomenon does not fit in with the scheme established *ab aeterno*.

In his youth the accent falls, as is only right, on the indomitable vitality of nature. Hegel defends Schelling against Reinhold, and to demonstrate the legitimacy of the philosophy of nature and its perfect compatibility with religion and ethics emphasizes the new attitude of the modern science of nature, that sense of the spirituality of nature which the ancients lacked, "that instinct deeply inculcated in the feelings of the later world, to bring back into nature the life that had fled from it." Nature is all alive, indeed nature coincides basically with life itself and there is therefore good reason and justification for the enthusiasm "with which all living manifestations of universal nature, which were almost unknown or little observed by the ancients, are accepted by the moderns as so many signs of the life enclosed in nature."[353]

But in his maturer years, having moved away from Schelling and tired of the romantics' mystic rhapsodies, Hegel dispassionately confirms the disrepute into which the so-called philosophical science of nature has lately sunk.

What has recently been known as the philosophy of nature, consists for the most part of a futile game of empty and irrelevant analogies, which are, however, meant to be taken as profound discoveries. The philosophical consideration of nature has thereby fallen into deserved discredit.[354]

The task he sets himself is thus a real *restauratio* of the philosophy of nature on new foundations, on the unshakable basis of pure logic. The philosophy of nature will be an applied logic (*eine angewandte Logik*). The essence of the syllogism consists in the statement that the particular is the median, which comprises within itself the extremes of the general and the individual. All things are "particular" which bracket a universal with an individual.[355] The whole world, the universe with all its phenomena and all its creatures are realized syllogisms, logic in action. Thought palpitates in things, and in all phenomena, from the greatest to the smallest, the same spark glitters, that synthesis of universal and individual which is the very rhythm of the Spirit.

Such a vast and lively conception, all throbbing and resounding with

353. *Über das Verhältniss der Naturphilosophie zur Philosophie ueberhaupt* (1802), in *Werke* (Berlin, 1845), I, 309.

354. *Enzyklopädie der philosophischen Wissenschaften*, sec. 190 Zus. (*Werke* [Berlin, 1842–43], VI, 358; the *Enzyklopädie* is hereafter cited as *Enz.*, followed by section number, and location in cited edition of the *Werke*).

355. *Enz.* 24 Zus. 2 (VI, 49–50).

echoes of Plotinus and Leibniz, led on necessarily to a complete absorption of nature in the Logos, to a generous philosophical consecration of all facts and all creatures—and thus to be strictly rational ruled out any possible condemnation, classification or comparative judgment of merit between this and that aspect of the globe, indeed of the whole universe.

But the infinite variety and incoercible diversity of natural phenomena prevent Hegel sticking to his safe and omnivalent formula, and induce him on the one hand to deny nature any development, to freeze it in a staticity of invariable species and laws, almost as if to make it easier for him to grasp, and on the other hand, to admit that Nature can sometimes fail or make mistakes (the logical corollary of its abstract personification, but absurd if it is by definition thought in act and living syllogism), and thus "produce" beings that are aberrant from the type, either abnormal or subnormal. With the first expedient Hegel denies the possibility of alterations in time, with the second he finds the remedy for the inequality evident even in the simultaneous manifestations of this single Nature. The former leads him to a rigid antievolutionism, the latter expresses itself in the crude accusations of "impotence" leveled at the Mother of all Beings.

C. Radical antievolutionism. Hegel's antievolutionism is radical: the species are what they are, and what they have always been, and every form, every law, every phenomenon of nature repeats itself in time without any change, in perfect and static uniformity. Nature has no history.[356] Nature is antihistory. Thus the system that insisted so energetically on unity is surreptitiously reinfiltrated by an irremediable dualism; the system that did away with Kant's a priori forms of sensibility, by a violent antithesis between space and time; the system that hinged on the category of the Future, by a perpetual immobility. All the aporiae of the Hegelian dialectic come reeking to the surface in his treatment of nature.

Nature in fact knows no true evolution, only the development of the concept, a development clearly visible in the organic world: thus the plant develops from the seed, thus the winged insect from the caterpillar; but the chrysalis and the butterfly are the same individual: "With individuals there can easily be temporal development, but with the race it is otherwise."[357] The individual has a development, belongs to history; the species, no, the species never moves:

It is completely senseless to suggest that the races evolve little by little in time: the time difference has absolutely no interest for the thought. . . . The land ani-

356. On the Hegelian antithesis between nature and history, see Collingwood, *Idea of History*, pp. 114–15; on his antievolutionism, ibid., pp. 128, 211. On his indifference to merely temporal developments, see also Jerome Rosenthal, "Attitudes of Some Modern Rationalists to History," *Journal of the History of Ideas*, 4 (1943), p. 454.
357. *Enz.* 249 Zus. (VII, I, 35); cf. ibid. 161 Zus. (VI, 317) and 166 Zus. (VI, 328).

mal did not evolve . . . from the water animal, . . . nor did the land animal take to the sky nor the bird come down to earth again.

The attempts to explain the chain of being by means of the creatures' transformations are fashionable, indeed "all the rage," under the stimulus of current natural philosophy, but in reality they explain nothing:[358] "Man did not evolve from the animal, nor the animal from the plant; each is what it is, once and for all."[359] Each animal is irreparably enclosed within its own rigid pattern: "Every single animal belongs to a particular and thereby fixed and limited kind, beyond whose boundaries it may not trespass."[360]

This same approach, rather more than the polemic against the theories of spontaneous generation, accounts for his derisive comments (already mentioned in relation to Buffon, see above, p. 13) on those "nebulous and basically sense-derived descriptions, such as the *birth* of the animals and plants from water"[361] — an attitude which among other things prevents Hegel drawing any pernicious deductions from the "humidity" of the New World, but does not stop him writing some beautiful pages describing the pullulating life of the sea, despite the falseness of the "ancient representation" of life emerging from the sea.[362]

The same reluctance toward generic explanations reappears finally in his rejection of the rival theories of Neptunism and Vulcanism, which attempted to reconstruct the remotest annals of the globe and understand the play of forces which had shaped its structure over the millennia. Hegel admits that the earth suffered violent revolutions, but he ridicules those who interest themselves in the succession of the geological strata, or produce specious theories to show that the deepest are the oldest, thus translating contiguity (*Nebeneinander*) into a hypothetical succession (*Nacheinander*).[363] Basalt may well, as the Vulcanists claim, be of igneous origin, yet that only means "that it belongs to the principle of fire — but it is no more born from fire than from water."[364] The very principles of the

---

358. "This quantitative difference," writes Hegel, ". . . however . . . explains nothing" (*Enz.* 249 Zus.; VII, I, 34). But in fact those differences are not "quantitative" at all. Hegel himself in any case, had asserted that quantity is more important in nature than in the Spirit, although, however, "so to say," that same quantity is more important in inorganic nature than in organic (*Enz.* 99 Zus.; VI, 199–200).

359. *Enz.* 339 Zus. (VII, I, 440). Strictly speaking there are no intermediate species either: the aquatic mammals, the amphibians, etc., are "only mixtures, and not higher inclusive intermediate species" (*Vorlesungen über die Aesthetik* [hereafter cited as *Die Aesthetik*], ed. H. G. Hotho, in *Werke*, ed. cit., X, I, 87).

360. *Die Aesthetik*, ed. cit., X, I, 189–90. Cf. Goethe, above, p. 255.

361. *Enz.* 249 (VII, I, 33); on this passage cf. the comments of B. Croce in *Critica*, 37 (1939), p. 144 n. 3.

362. *Enz.* 341 Zus. (VII, I, 459–62), in polemic against spontaneous generation and with references to putrescence linked to life; on the sea as the spur to adventure, etc., see *Vorlesungen über die Philosophie der Weltgeschichte*, ed. Lasson (Leipzig, 1920), I, 187–89.

363. See for example *Enz.* 339 Zus. (VII, I, 438–39).

364. *Enz.* 340 Zus. (VII, I, 448).

famous polemic are uncertain and can no longer be told apart. Both Vulcanists and Neptunists are right and wrong at the same time, because the two explanations are equally essential and made mutually interdependent. Volcanoes are subterranean storms, accompanied with earthquakes. Hurricanes are volcanoes exploding in the clouds.[365]

D. *The impotence of nature.*   It would seem that a nature so devoid of development and internal dialectic should be a mirror of motionless perfection. Time can in no way add to it or improve it. No part, no moment of it is preferable to any other. Faced with this logical consequence, which would oblige him to worship the unvarying perfection of creation, Hegel flees to the opposite pole and, precisely because he is incapable of seeing nature as history, ascribes to it a spasmodic and enigmatic "impotence." Where reality seems to offer no reflection of the divine image of the rational, rather than seeking a deeper or still latent rationality in it he makes do by hypothesizing a defective power of realization — just as the theologists had explained the failure of the God-created man by a loss of Grace.

The "impotence of nature" is the translation into physiological terms of the ancient Original Sin. And just as the latter had served to explain besides man's expulsion from Paradise the decay of the whole physical world,[366] the corruption of the heavens, the disappearance of the giants, and nature's universal loss of vigor, so the Hegelian "impotence," with no attempt at justification in terms of punishment for a crime of any sort, helps to account for whatever in the Cosmos is not as it ought to be or as we think it ought to be. Quite simply "the impotence of nature brings about the impure presentation of logical forms."[367] "Impure": the impurity of presentation consists in this, that in the sphere of nature the determination of the concept comes from outside, in abstract and therefore accidental form. This accounts for its apparent richness and variety, which on closer inspection turn out to be no more than arbitrariness and disorder, and for the impossibility of "deducing" philosophically (as he challenged Krug to do) the casual particularities and oddities of nature. The impotence of nature marks a "limit" to philosophy[368] — which means, in fact, that the impotence is not in nature but in philosophy, in its incapacity to surpass that limit.[369]

---

365. *Enz.* 288 Zus. (VII, I, 182): cf. ibid., 339 Zus. (VII, I, 433). Cf. Humboldt, above, p. 406.

366. See above, pp. 59–60, 382–83, and the learned article of Joseph E. Duncan, "Paradise as the Whole Earth," *Journal of the History of Ideas,* 30, n. 2 (1969), pp. 171–86 ("the whole earth fell under the curse after the Fall," p. 177).

367. *Enz.* 24 Zus. 2 (VI, 50). And in the *Philosophie der Geschichte,* ed. cit., I, 151: "The impotence of Nature is such that it is not able to hold firm its overall classes and species against other elemental impulses and forces." His disciple C. L. Michelet also said that in natural reality the rational turned out "variously distorted and stunted through the form of its external appearance."

368. *Enz.* 250 (VII, I, 36–37).

369. Croce, *Saggio sullo Hegel,* p. 117. An ingenious defense of the "impotence of nature," which would integrate the "power (and astuteness) of Reason" and in a way actually anticipate the statistical theory of natural laws, is attempted by N. Hartmann, *Die Philosophie des deutschen Idealismus,* II, *Hegel* (Berlin-Leipzig, 1920), pp. 286–88, 294.

Just as the mind can wander off in vain and incoherent daydreams, so Nature pursues its whims in the multiplication of the genera and species.[370] It has no firmness and precision in its workings, and this is why it is often impossible to discover certain lines of demarcation between its creatures. Every classification has much that is arbitrary in it. And so the desired reduction of nature to an absolute system is absolutely impossible. The animal species are mere accidentalities, and particularly for the inferior ones one must leave to nature "the right of hazard and accident," that is, of external and unforeseeable determination.[371] There are abortions in the human race too. There are hybrid and monstrous creatures among the animals, and yet all these are as "natural" as the indefinable type from which they deviate. Nature, incapable of realizing logical forms, falls prey to incoherence and dislocation. Everything material is so recalcitrant (*so widerspenstig*) to the unity of the concept![372] And the animal still has a certain organic unity, because its organs and its limbs cannot exist separately from each other; but for the plant one cannot even say that much. Its parts are independent. The plant is thus even more impotent than the animal: "This independence of the parts is the impotence of the plant!"[373] Impotent, then, for Hegel, means inorganic, incapable of being deduced, fundamentally accidental, devoid of internal necessity. When he comes to deducing the continents and their natural species and inhabitants, Hegel will be able to get round any difficulty and incongruence by denouncing anything that offers any serious resistance to his deductive arrogance as "impotent."

E. *Deduction of the hemispheres and the continents.* Nothing can shake Hegel's confidence in his triads, not even the sight of a world divided into five or six different parts; Europe, Asia, and Africa are all he needs to construct a system of cosmic, mythological, and geophysical relationships so compact and coherent, indeed so perfectly rational that its center turns out, as is only right, to be Germany! Which enables him to confirm delightedly that "the divisions of the world then are not accidental, and separated according to convenience; there are in fact substantial differences."[374]

But above or beyond this organic structure there remains a vaster antithesis, that between the Old and New World: which is in part deduced, in part denied as empty and fictitious. To deduce it Hegel comes back to the theories of Treviranus, for whom every living form is the result of physical forces still operating, a thesis which Treviranus however had

370. Hegel, *Lu scienza della logica*, trans. A. Moni (Bari, 1925), III, 52.
371. *Enz.* 370 Zus. (VII, I, 653, 670).
372. *Enz.* 376 Zus. (VII, I, 696); cf. 250 (VII, I, 38) and 270 Zus. (VII, I, 653, 663, 665–66).
373. *Enz.* 345 Zus. (VII, I, 489).
374. *Enz.* 339 Zus. (VII, I, 442), satirized by Croce, *Saggio sullo Hegel*, pp. 125–26; cf. *Enz.* 393 Zus. (VII, II, 65–66): "the differences between continents . . . not accidental, but necessary."

applied only to the plants and the animals.[375] Thus a plausible naturalistic explanation of the flora and fauna is extended to the geographical parts of the world, and immediately afterward to the races inhabiting and characterizing them. The Northern Hemisphere has a more compact landmass, the Southern Hemisphere on the other hand is more broken up, and mostly ocean: and so the structure of the globe takes on a new polarity, of unlimited consequences.

Where did this polarity come from? And how is the antithesis between north and south related to the division of the world into two hemispheres, Western and Eastern? Hegel moves effortlessly back into prehistory and outlines for us the forces that determine this process of formation, a "past process" by which the terrestrial body built its limbs. Nature left these forces "beyond the earth" as independent factors; they are in fact the position of the earth in the solar system, its solar, lunar, and cometary life (which is somewhat obscure, particularly if one remembers that only Africa is "lunar" and Asia "cometary," and that moreover the earth is the lunar element and the sea the cometary element),[376] its inclination to the ecliptic and its magnetic axis. There is a close relationship between these axes, and their polarization—not to be confused with the polarity of north and south!—and "the division of the sea and the land, and the latter's compact expansion in the north, the fragmentation and sharpening and contraction of the parts to the south [so this is the difference between Northern and Southern Hemispheres—and finally, but completely unexpectedly] *the further division into an old and new world."*

Once this is admitted, the final deduction is easy too: "The further division of that [Old World] into regions, distinguished one from another and from the new world by their physical, organic, and anthropological characteristics, to which a younger and less mature part has now been joined":[377] from which casual allusion to Oceania we get our first hint of the New World being younger and less mature than the Old!

F. Old World and New World. But once he has proposed this theme of the antithesis and dialectical relationship between the two worlds — a precariously balanced dyad superimposed on the triad of the Old World — Hegel seems reluctant to let it go; in fact he orchestrates it and weaves around it a whole series of variations, in many of which we shall recognize the tritest themes of the polemic.

The main division of the earth is actually this: into New World and Old

---

375. *Enz.* 393 (VII, II, 64). On Treviranus, see *Encyclopedia Britannica,* 11th ed., *sub voce.* Hegel cites him fairly frequently (for example VII, I, 476, 478–80, 484–87, 515, 563, 571–72, 592–95, 612–13, 623–25, 627–28, 634, 638, 657–58, 663).

376. *Enz.* 340 Zus. (VII, I, 462).

377. *Enz.* 339 (VII, I, 431).

World.[378] They differ in everything: the latter curved around the Mediterranean like a horseshoe, the former elongated in a north-south direction. The Old World is perfectly separated into three properly articulated, connected, and integrated parts; the New, improperly and incompletely split up, showing only, like a magnet, the generic difference between north and south, with a miserable little hinge joining the two parts. In the Old World the mountain chains generally follow an east-west direction, or sometimes southwest-northeast; in America, on the other hand, in this Old World's understudy (*diese Widerlage*), the Cordilleras run north and south (remember Raynal and Herder? see above, p. 47); and the rivers, finally, through some inordinate oddity and arbitrariness, and particularly the South American ones, flow toward the east!

Even the distinction between "new" and "old" represents a marked opposition. The date of discovery is an accidental fact (although America is new from this point of view too, since its existence is "real" only from that time) and thus of no interest. What matters is its essential character, and in this sense one has to admit that America has "a more youthful look" (*ein jüngeres Ansehen*) than the Old World — which has also a more complete historical formation. Everything there is new, and by new here Hegel means immature and feeble: its fauna is weaker (*"die Thierwelt ist schwächer"*), but to make up for that it has a monstrous vegetation. Its civilization lacked the two great instruments of progress, iron and the horse.[379] While no continent of the Old World was ever brought under the sway of another, the whole of America fell prey to Europe. Its indigenous peoples are disappearing: there the Old World is renewing itself, recovering its youth (*"die alte Welt gestaltet sich in demselben neu"*). From this lamentable geophysical "newness" Hegel goes straight on in one bound to the continent's promising sociopolitical "youthfulness." The ambiguity in the word "new" had never been used with greater shrewdness and abandon.

But Hegel has still not quite squeezed it dry. In the *Philosophy of History* the search for the real meaning of the New World's "newness" takes another step forward. The newness that in the *Encyclopedia* was not just accidental but substantial is enriched by another qualification, when he calls it "not just relative, but absolute." The New World, in which Hegel includes America and Oceania, is so called, true, because it was dis-

---

378. *Enz.* 339 Zus. (VII, I, 441–42) and 393 Zus. (VII, I, 64–72), to which the following passages also belong. Cf. also A. Vera, *Philosophie de la Nature de Hegel* (Paris, 1864), II, 376. Note that in some passages (for example *Philosophie der Geschichte*, I, 116) the antithesis between "the Old and the New World" obviously refers to the ancient world and the modern (Christian) world.

379. Iron and the horse are the basic elements on which supremacy is founded; their absence characterizes the weakness of the American societies (*Philosophie der Geschichte*, I, 193–94). Montaigne had already (*Essais*, III, 6; ed. cit., 875–76) indicated iron and the horse as the essential factors in the European conquest of the Americas.

covered later,[380] but it is new not only in respect to the Old but in a full and absolute sense, in everything relating to its physical and political and spiritual qualities. Hegel continues—and by this time we can appreciate the full ironic and polemic substance of his words—"It is not its geological oldness which interests us. Nor would I want to deny it the honor of having emerged from the waters at the precise moment of the creation of the world.[381] But it is a fact that the archipelago between South America and Asia betrays a physical immaturity [*eine physische Unreife*]." Almost all these little islands are physically immature then, these slender strips of land lined with coral rock, emerging from the deepest abyss. And no less mature is New Holland (or Australia), with its enormous (?) rivers that have still not succeeded in digging themselves beds.[382]

The qualification of *immature* is thus applied by Hegel more to Oceania than to America. Buffon did not know Oceania and called America *immature*. Immature, in each case, meant the not yet systematized, the imperfectly known, or the continent of which man's knowledge was *immature*. But America's privilege of impotence remains intact: "America has always shown itself and still shows itself physically and spiritually impotent."[383]

G. The impotence of America in its fauna. Where is this impotence revealed? Hegel does not even consider a telluric weakness, and in the plants he recognizes a vigorous exuberance. Which leaves the animals—and man. As for the animal species, we know already that their mere existence is a whim, a weakness of nature (see also above, p. 423). To want to organize them into an organic system is mere folly. Instinct alone, not right or idea, ranged the animal classes in series: "But the whole conception of series is unphilosophical and against all logic. For nature does not set up her forms in such ladders, one after another, but in a mass." The twenty-four classes outlined by Linnaeus are Linnaeus's system, not nature's (one remembers Buffon's antisystematism and his particular aversion for Linnaeus). Jussieu did better, but Aristotle had already done something similar with the animals![384]

---

380. This too is imprecise: *later* than what? The Old World was never discovered. It would have been enough to say quite simply that America is the New World because it was discovered: a statement of the obvious, in any sense. The Old World became so when it found another world, a "new" one. Not because it had grown old, but in fact when it showed itself capable of new and formidable enterprises and conquests.

381. Cf. Humboldt: "It would be impossible to admit that the New Continent issued from the waters later than the Old" (*Vues des Cordillères*, I, 18); and Barton, above, p. 404; and later Emerson, below, p. 511.

382. Chateaubriand too was to call Australia immature, Lucretianly *ébauchée*, because it had black swans, rivers that ran from the coast toward the interior, kangaroos that jumped like grasshoppers, and other zoological oddities (*Voyage en Amérique*, ed. cit., pp. 26–27; ed. R. Switzer, I, 42).

383. *Philosophie der Geschichte*, ed. cit., I, 189–91.

384. *Enz.* 281 Zus. (VII, I, 156–57).

And Hegel, in fact, comes back to underlining the specific importance of the dimensions of an animal or plant—a corollary of the thesis that quantity is more important in nature than in the Spirit (see above, p. 422), which he tries to work in with Kant's and Goethe's theory of organic harmony and the internal limitations of each animal: "The different species of plants and animals have a definite bulk both in the totality and in their single parts."[385] But immediately afterward he observes that the lower creatures, those nearer to inorganic nature, are distinguished from the higher animals by their greater indifference toward dimension: the ferns and the ammonites vary in size within much ampler limits than the mammals and the more complex beings.[386] So size, apparently, loses indicative significance while gaining in quantity, the nearer organic nature gets to inorganic.

This tangle of contradictions shows how acutely aware Hegel was of the problem of the size of animals; but it was a problem he never solved, not even in the cursory fashion of Buffon; and it was left unsolved because Hegel was much less interested in the zoological species' dimensions than in their diversity and stability and the law governing them.

What is this law? It is formulated in very general terms, so that it applies to America too, and particularly South America, from which Buffon had drawn his examples, but not only America. For Hegel there exists only one perfect type of animal that completely realizes the concept "animal," and all the varieties of creatures are modifications thereof.[387] In the higher animals these modifications correspond to the environment wherein their lives evolve; the lower animals, on the other hand, are less related to the elements and remain indifferent to their great diversity. Hegel, then, unlike Buffon and Haldane (see above, pp. 25–26), seems to look on the lower animals as precisely the ones that are least subject to the influence and caprice of the elements.

There is, however, a geographical discrimination interfering with this general rule. The further south one goes, toward where the continents taper off and break up into archipelagoes, the more the animal species too become modified, differentiated, peculiar to and typical of that part of the world.[388] The southernmost points of the continents have very different species, much more different from each other than those of the northern parts of the same continent. The zoological species are thus a reflection,

---

385. *Enz.* 107 Zus. (VI, 216–17); cf. Goethe, *Metamorphose der Thiere* (1806), cited above, p. 255.
386. *Enz.* 107 Zus. (VI, 216–17); but in inorganic nature quantity is *more* important than in organic: see *Enz.* 99 Zus. (VI, 199–200). How then does it become *less* important and almost indifferent in the creatures closer to inorganic Nature?
387. *Enz.* 352 Zus. (VII, I, 558) and 370 Zus. (VII, I, 653). One need hardly be reminded of Goethe's speculations on the *Urthier* and *Urpflanze*.
388. *Enz.* 339 Zus. (VII, I, 441).

or rather a parallel, of the diversification of the parts of the world, which in its turn is the result of mysterious cosmic forces (see above, p. 424):

Since in the north the continents are more connected, animal and vegetable nature too is more linked there; whereas the further south one goes in Africa and America, where the continents divide, the more the animal species too [and not the vegetable ones?] move away from each other in type.[389]

In its northern part the earth has an ample bosom, as the Greeks used to put it, and can properly be the theater of universal history; in its southern part it subdivides and scatters into innumerable capes and peninsulas, "like America, Asia, and Africa"; now, in these slender prolongations the natural creations too diversify and "specialize," while the northern zone, where most of the animal and vegetable species are found, remains the most important part from the zoological and botanical point of view.[390]
This phenomenon is due to the climate — which in the south, apparently, is more effective than in the north,

since in the south the animal world [but not the vegetable world?] is more specialized than in the north, on account of differences in climate and terrain: thus the Asian and African elephants are significantly differentiated one from another, while America has none [a curious form of Particularization or Individualization, this total lack!]; and likewise the Lions and Tigers, etc., are different,[391]

as is only appropriate for higher animals subject to the influence of the elements, without it being suggested, however, even implicitly, that one variant or creature is superior to another. But the *Philosophy of History* is more radical and consequential. In America the inferiority observable among men is reflected in the animals:

Its fauna shows us lions, tigers, crocodiles; but these have only a certain similarity to the creatures of the Old World, while they are in every way smaller, weaker, more cowardly. We are assured that the meat of the animals there is less nourishing than in the Old World; enormous quantities of cattle do in fact exist there, but a piece of European beef is a delicacy.[392]

The echoes of Buffon and de Pauw are unmistakable, even though the immediate source is not identifiable.[393] The men are as badly off as ever, although it seems curious and almost paradoxical that it should be man himself, the highest of the higher animals, that is released from the domination of climate, more divorced from the natural environment than any other creature, and permitted to live happily in any latitude, although the

389. *Enz.* 370 Zus. (VII, I, 654, 670).
390. *Philosophie der Geschichte*, ed. cit., I, 182.
391. *Enz.* 370 Zus. (VII, I, 654, 670).
392. *Philosophie der Geschichte*, ed. cit., I, 191; cf. Humboldt's criticism, above, p. 417, and Ortega y Gasset, "Hegel y América," *El Espectador*, VII, in *Obras*, 3rd ed. (Madrid, 1943), I, 597.
393. "Hegel was undoubtedly not insensible to de Pauw's arguments," Minguet states bluntly ("L'Amérique" [cit. above, n. 351], p. 41).

Eskimo and the tropical native are very different from the inhabitants of the temperate zone![394]

H. The American birds and their song. Thus in Hegel the inferiority of the American animal species is not so much deduced as postulated: and postulated quite incidentally, more as an accepted fact than a notable oddity of nature. There is only one particular instance of inferiority that attracts the attention of Hegel, the avid music lover and *bel canto* enthusiast: the raucous voices ascribed to the American birds. He never doubts the fact[395] and provides an amusing explanation for it.

Heat brings out the colors in plants: their individuality (*Selbst*), attracted by the light, pours itself into existence as light. Animals have darker colors, but among the birds the most multihued and wonderful are those of the tropics, which are almost plants, and whose proper essence is expressed, thanks to the light and heat of their climate, in their vegetative covering, their plumage. In this the birds of the north cannot compete, "but they sing better, the nightingale and the lark for example, which do not exist in the tropics." Heat destroys the voice and replaces it with the metallic splendor of color. Sound perishes in the heat. And the voice too, even if it is something higher than sound, suffers from this opposition in the torrid zone.[396]

Thus the aphonia of the tropical birds would seem to be constitutional and incurable. But in a footnote Hegel makes a curious conjecture, which if it turned out to be true would destroy his thesis. He says, in effect, that the meager musicality of American birds is acquired, and thus remediable: "When the day comes that the forests of Brazil no longer resound with

394. *Enz.* 370 Zus. (VII, I, 654) and 392 (VII, II, 58); *Philosophie der Geschichte*, ed. cit., I, 231. The exception goes back to Buffon (and had been sustained by Caldas; see also above, p. 311). But elsewhere (*Philosophie der Geschichte*, ed. cit., I, 180–83) Hegel confirms the importance of the influence of climate and denies that in the frigid or torrid zone, among the Lapps or the Africans, liberty could ever flourish or man raise himself above the struggle with natural exigencies to the point where he might make these lands a "theater of world history"; and even more pessimistically he reaffirms (*Die Aesthetik*, ed. cit., X, I, 187) the animal's absolute dependence on the soil and climate and hints at the possibility that the poverty of its surroundings robs it of the flower of its beauty, makes it shrivel and shrink and reflect the indigence and meanness of surrounding nature in its appearance. But he does not refer to the species of America.

395. Although the zoologist J. B. von Spix and the botanist C. F. von Martius, in the account of their journey (1817–20) to Brazil (*Reise nach Brasilien*, 3 vols. [1823–31], I, 191; rpt. Wiesbaden, 1969) attested to the existence there of singing birds (*Enz.* 303 Zus.; VII, I, 225–26). The journey of Spix and Martius is cited also ibid., 254, 451–52, 513–14. It was Martius himself, in his dissertation *Como se deve escrever a historia do Brasil* (1843, pub. 1845 and carried *in toto* in *Revista de Historia de América*, 42 [December 1950], pp. 433–58) who recommended (p. 446) that there should be excluded "a multitude of extravagant allegations, of facts that are entirely false (like those put about in the scandalous work of Mr. de Pauw, for example)"—a parenthesis which if not unique is certainly one of the very small number of "Brazilian" protests against de Pauw.

396. On the relationship between *Klang* and *Wärme* see also the sections following 303; on that between *Klang* and *Stimme*, and on the song of the birds, which is not the manifestation of any need, but expression without desire, the immediate enjoyment of themselves, see also *Enz.* 351 Zus. (VII, I, 554–55), 365 Zus. (VII, I, 639), and 370 Zus. (ibid., 667–68). On the relationship between the multicolored feathers and light, cf. 361 Zus. (VII, I, 610–11).

the almost inarticulate tones of degenerate men, then many of the plumed songsters too will bring forth more polished melodies."[397] From which one deduces that these American birds must have ruined their voices listening to the shrieks of the degenerate savages, and being so stupid as to imitate them instead of singing in their own way. Once the natives are exterminated or reduced to silence, the birds will begin to pour forth sweeter melodies (like the nightingale? or the lark?).

In this example too we find that an arguable and indeed openly doubted factual item serves to illustrate an arbitrary conceptual relationship, that of heat, sound, and color. And although the example is American, classically American, Hegel draws no anti-American corollary from it: he does not interpret this dumbness as the poets did, as a sign of nature's sadness or insensibility in the New World. Only in the reference to the natives, from whom the birds supposedly first learned their discordant shrieks, can one detect any anti-American prejudice.

I. The savage as man of nature.   So how did Hegel arrive at this implicitly negative opinion? The savage, the spoiler of nature's innocent voice, is actually at first defined by Hegel as man of nature, the Rousseauian primitive living out his days in intimate contact with nature, and seeing it as the expression of God's spirit.[398] Just as the simpler organisms live in closer symbiosis with their environment, so the more primitive peoples, less evolved in spiritual liberty, remain in closer communion with the nature that surrounds and looms over them. The animals sleep by instinct; the savages rest at night; only the Spirit turns night into day.[399]

The application of these ideas to the "historical" peoples proceeds along strictly Rousseauian lines. The ancient Greeks and Romans were closer and more devoted to nature than the modern nations. And of these modern nations the Italians and the Spaniards live much more a life of nature than the Germans and the races of the north.[400]

But here already one can see the primitivistic premise losing ground; there is no doubt whatever that for Hegel the German is a superior human

397. *Enz.* 303 Zus. (VII, I, 225–26). A stubborn defender of the virtues of the American natives, L. A. Muratori, had instead admired the euphonic speech of the savages of Paraguay, offering also a curious dietetic explanation for the phenomenon: "They have excellent voices, and contributing to make them so, and even more harmonious than in other countries, are the waters of the rivers Paraná and Uruguay, inasmuch as even we can see how the voices of some of the inhabitants of the mountains are more melodious, because they drink only water, provided it is pure and healthy water" (*Il cristianesimo felice,* I, 97). Cf. above, chap. 5, n. 13.
398. *Philosophische Propedeutik,* sec. 151 (ed. Karl Rosenkranz, *Werke* [XVIII, 184]); *Vorrede zu Hinrichs' Religionsphilosophie, Werke,* XVII, 295.
399. *Enz.* 361 Zus. (VII, I, 608) and 392 (VII, II, 58). The animal's intimacy with nature can also be seen in its anticipatory sensitivity to earthquakes (*Philosophische Propedeutik,* 151, loc. cit.); *Enz.* 392 Zus. (VII, II, 62, 63–64); the savage, in his turn, has an almost animalish instinct and at times "has a knowledge of things that happen a thousand hours away" (*Vorlesungen über die Philosophie der Religion,* ed. Marheineke [Berlin, 1840], *Werke,* XI, 274).
400. *Enz.* 392 Zus. (VII, II, 62–63) and 406 Zus. (VII, II, 179).

type to the Italian or the Spaniard; thus as he moves away from the condition of nature, man gets progressively nobler and more perfect. The man of nature is a creature that is all sentiment, but if he is all and *only* sentiment, man is no longer distinguishable from the animal. If his whole religion were to be reduced to sentiment, or more precisely to the feeling of his dependence on a superior being, the best Christian would be the dog.[401] So this savage so perceptive to the voice of God is in fact only listening to "his master's voice."

Thus the modern prototype of the savage, the American native, can hardly hope to be looked on with indulgent sympathy. Yet the sentence pronounced upon him is particularly severe precisely because he inhabits the American continent, the continent that lacks any real *raison d'être*. The various races are closely correlated to and dependent on the parts of the world: their characteristics are tellurically conditioned and necessary like those of the continents themselves (see above, pp. 423–24). It is therefore right that Europe, Africa, and Asia should contain the Caucasian, Ethiopian, and Mongolian races, but to these three recognized, authorized, and legitimate races, Hegel reluctantly adds two more, the Malaysian and the American, "which constitute however more a collection of infinitely different peculiarities than a sharply defined race." They are much less well defined (*weniger . . . scharf ausgezeichnet*) than the three races of the Old World. Even their coloring is vague: with white, black, and yellow, one knows where one stands: but the epidermis of the Americans is "copper colored."

J. The American aborigines. What can one expect from such poorly tinged people, in the land of weakness and imprecision? Certainly nothing good: the American aborigenes are "a weak and vanishing race." Their rudimentary civilizations were necessarily bound to disappear on the arrival of the incomparable European civilization. And just as their civilization was of lower quality, so those among them who are still savages, are so to an extreme degree, the very archetypes of barbarism. Only in America are there still savages as dull and idiotic as the Pescheräh (or Fuegians)[402] and the Eskimos. It has recently come to light that the Iroquois, Eskimos, and other savage peoples have songs, but they contribute

---

401. "So wäre der Hund der beste Christ," *Vorrede* (XVII, 295). On the stupid religion of the savage, his "innocence" and accidental meekness because of his dependency on the climate, see *Die Philosophie der Religion,* ed. cit., XI, 273. On his inattentiveness, see also *Enz.* 448 Zus. (VII, II, 213).

402. Probable origin of this abysmal reputation of the Fuegians (see also Chastellux and Schlegel): the descriptions of the de Pauwish Hawkesworth (1775) "these people appeared to be the most destitute and forlorn, as well as the most stupid of all human beings" (*An Account of the Voyages Undertaken by the Order of His Present Majesty, for Making Discoveries in the Southern Hemisphere* [Dublin, 1775], p. 23, quoted by S. Samuel Trifilo, "British Travel Accounts on Argentina before 1810," *Journal of Inter-American Studies,* 2, no. 3 [July 1960], p. 246), and of G. Forster, *Reise um die Welt,* 1777, xxiii, ed. Gerhard Steiner, in *Werke,* ed. cit., I, 918–24, 1033.

nothing whatsoever to the charmed circle of poetry. And as for heroism, the subject is best not even mentioned; the Caribbeans themselves, these valiant Caribbeans, were extinguished by the combined effect of spirits and firearms.

The Americans of the south are even more unwarlike. The natives could never have thrown off the Spanish yoke (it was the Creoles that rebelled). In Paraguay they were like ignorant children (*unkündige Kinder*) and were treated as such by the Jesuits. All in all, the Americans are clearly no match for the Europeans (*"die Amerikaner sind daher offenbar nicht im Stande, sich gegen die Europäer zu behaupten"*). It will be up to the Europeans to develop a new civilization in the conquered lands.[403]

Hegel paints the same picture in the *Philosophy of History*. As soon as he has affirmed America's physical and spiritual, congenital and incurable, impotence, he goes on to illustrate it simply with examples of the impotence of the American:

In fact [he writes] after the Europeans landed in America, the natives gradually faded away before the onslaught of European activity. In the free states of North America all the citizens are men of European descent; the former inhabitants could not mix with the Europeans and were driven out by them. Truth to tell, the natives learned certain arts from the Europeans, among others the drinking of spirits, which had a disastrous effect on them [on the redskins this time, while it was on the Caribbeans before]. In the south the natives were treated much more violently and put to heavy labor, for which their strength did not suffice.

Here there is an echo of Las Casas, perhaps reinforced by the more recent memory of de Pauw or one of his followers.

Meekness and inertia, humility and groveling submission to the Creole, and even more so to the European, are the essential characteristic of the Americans of these parts, and it will be quite some time before the Europeans succeed in awakening a little dignity [*Selbstgefühl*] in them. We have seen them, in Europe, devoid of all spiritual life [*geistlos*] and barely susceptible to instruction. The inferiority of these creatures, from every point of view, even in their build, can be recognized in everything

—always excepting the rough, wild, and powerful Patagonians (the same old *Patacones!*), but not the Jesuits' disciples, who "even had to have a bell rung in the middle of the night to remind them of their conjugal duties. . . ."[404]

These summary condemnations echo the tones of crude and even cynical realism, the overbearing arrogance too, one might well add, that Hegel lavishes on other peoples that have suffered defeat, and, as van-

---

403. *Enz.* 393 Zus. (VII, II, 64–72); and for the aborigenes' songs (already appreciated by Oviedo), see *Die Aesthetik*, X, III, 438. On the rudimentary religion of the Eskimos, see *Die Philosophie der Religion*, XI, 286–87.
404. *Philosophie der Geschichte*, ed. Brunstäd, p. 128; ed. Lasson, I, 192.

quished, have been judged and sentenced by the "tribunal of the world": in fact there seems to be no good reason why the massacre of the Antilleans by arquebus fire should be ascribed to some presumed organic and spiritual inferiority on their part. The Spanish jurists of the sixteenth century had been more humane, inasmuch as they had at least considered the question of the legitimacy of the war of extermination, and sought to justify it, either by vaunting the incomparable spiritual gifts brought by the conquistadores, or by debasing the native to the level of subhuman or quite simply animal being. Hegel instead begins with the historical fact of the conquest by violence, and turns it into an argument proving that the aborigenes were worthless and therefore bound to disappear in any case.

Among the consequences of the weakness of the American natives, Hegel includes the Negro slave trade. And it is strange to note the relative sympathy he shows toward these other "primitives," who come however from the Old World. Their dark color is a result of climate, heat, and light—the very same factors which in the birds, on the other hand, produced the brilliantly glittering polychrome plumage![405] And the Negroes transported to America are credited with discovering the therapeutic value of Peruvian bark, and with the merit of having successfully established in Haiti "a state built on Christian principles."[406] So despite a touch of "childishness" in their spirit, the historical dignity of the Ethiopian race is safe.

K. Contemporary America: America and the "spirits of peoples." Hegel's attitude to America's contemporary political institutions revolves around two concepts: firstly that of the *Volksgeister,* the "spirits of peoples," each dominating in turn and then disappearing for ever, and secondly that of a radical antithesis between North and South America. The first concept sanctions the definitive eclipse of the pre-Columbian civilizations, the second comes back to the contrast between northern and southern regions which, as we have already seen, is of greater significance in the deduction of the continents than the contrast between east and west.[407] The civilizations of Mexico and Peru were merely natural;

---

405. "The black hair (*Haar* maybe for *Haut*, "skin") of the Negro also depends on the climate, the warmth, and the light" (*Enz.* 345 Zus.; VII, I, 489).

406. *Enz.* 393 Zus. (VII, II, 68); *Philosophie der Geschichte,* ed. Lasson, I. 193. The characterization of the Negroes is much less favorable when Hegel is discussing Africa (ibid., I, 215–18).

407. Hegel too, see above, p. 141, follows the heliodromic theory and has history marching from East to West. On the limited sense of this thesis of his see however B. Croce, *Discorsi di varia filosofia* (Bari, 1945), I, 141–43; Löwith, *Von Hegel zu Nietzsche* (Zurich, 1941), p. 45; A. Lasson, *Hegel als Geschichtsphilosoph* (Leipzig, 1920), p. 130; Schulin, op. cit., pp. 52–53. But there remains a reflection of it in his accepting for America the qualification of land of the future, and in his embarrassment as he recognizes that Asia is to America's West but toils to reassert the thesis that Europe is the absolute West, the center and culmination of the Old World, and Asia, therefore, the absolute East! (See also Hegel's denunciation of Görres's mystical philosophy of history, judged to be vacuous and formalistic, in his review of *Ueber die Grundlage, Gliederung und Zeitenfolge der Weltgeschichte, Drei Vorträge . . . von J. Görres* (Breslau, 1830): "so one can run endlessly on and on without saying anything" (*Werke,* XVII, 268).

on the approach of the spirit, they could only perish.[408] This is a particular instance of the law that assigns each nation a moment in history and then thrusts it back outside reality, into the void: a law so rigidly mechanical that one can only wonder at its acceptance and stubborn application by a mind as open as Hegel's to the organic and dynamic, though its "fiercely distrustful"[409] rejection by Humboldt comes as no surprise at all; a law that precludes all possibility of nations living together, of civilizations being reborn or assimilated or grafted onto one another, and thus substantially denies historical development, which it would apparently like to replace with a parade of the sort of symbolic figures that one sees on old clock towers following each other out of little doors when their hour comes, swaggering a few seconds in the sun and then returning to the darkness by another little door; a law, in fact, that is the counterpart in the field of history of the resolute antievolutionism of the philosophy of nature.

Already in one of his earlier works Hegel asserts the absolute necessity of the position that falls to each people, and the uniqueness of its "moment," conditioned by history on one side and geography on the other;[410] and in the *Propedeutik* the fatal law is formulated in its full inflexibility. "Not all peoples count in world history. Each has, according to its principle, its own point or moment. Then, it seems, it passes away forever. Its turn does not come accidentally."[411] When it does come the spirit of the world is mirrored completely in that people, subjected to that climate, and bound to that period, but mirrored in a completely naturalistic way, just as the totality of life is found complete in the polyp, the nightingale, and the lion: each of which is enclosed within itself, does not develop from anything else or into anything else, and is absolutely itself, an individual quite without relation to the others, a single step above which there floats (*schwebt*) the idea of totality.[412] The peoples are thus like the natural species, multiple incarnations of the Logos, with the single difference, one would hardly say advantage, that while the animal species more or less coexist, and are not condemned to extinction, the

---

408. *Philosophie der Geschichte*, ed. cit., I, 184 ("Chile and Peru are narrow coastal strips, they have no culture," and see below, p. 436), 190–91; *Enz.* 393 Zus. (VII, II, 64–72), and above, p. 432. Antonio Martinez Bello avails himself of Hegel's thesis on the immaturity of the Americas to deny the derivation from Hegel of the Cuban patriot and orator Rafael Montoro (*Origen y meta del autonomismo — Exegesis de Montoro — Ensayo de filosofia de la historia de Cuba* [Havana, 1952], pp. 61, 89).

409. Letter to Varnhagen von Ense, 30 May 1837 (Geneva ed., p. 31; Brussels ed., p. 72).

410. "Thus to speak in the most general terms the particular climate of a people and its moment in the development of the universal race are a matter of necessity, and from the far-extended chain of climate and history one single link determines its present: which is to be understood on the one hand by geography and the other by history" (*Ueber die wissenschaftlichen Behandlungsarten des Naturrechts*, 1802–03, *Werke*, I, 403).

411. *Philosophische Propedeutik*, sec. 202 (*Werke*, XVIII, 201).

412. *Naturrecht*, op. cit., I, 404.

nations must ceaselessly give way one to another in the guidance of the human race. The geographical and anthropological bondage of each nation, understood in the Montesquieuian sense, leads on irrevocably with its naturalistic unbending plurality to the conclusion that only once in history may a people be bearers of the Spirit, the "overlords."[413]

From this one could equally well argue that America has still to enjoy its moment of world supremacy, that the future is hers, or that it will never be invested and invaded by the Spirit, since its civilization is merely natural. For the natives, whom he considers extinct or on the point of extinction, Hegel opts for the second alternative. But for America in general, he seems to incline toward the first. When he arrives at the subject of epic poetry he remarks that the wars it celebrates must not be just any wars, but must have some universal historical significance (*universalhistorische Berechtigung*). Such were the wars that Homer sang of the Greeks and Trojans, and those of El Cid against the Moors, the Christians against the Saracens (Tasso and Ariosto), and the Portuguese against the Indians (Camoens). In all these wars and all these poems Europe, the golden mean, and individual beauty triumph over the gaudy and amorphous greatness of Asia. What will tomorrow's epics be, then? Not those of wars between the European nations, which are all now limited, and none of them thus strictly speaking capable of starting a war "of itself" (!). The epics of the future, when they come, will only be able to represent "the victory of a future living American rationality over [European] imprisonment in measurement and detailing, produced to infinity. . . . If today one wants to get beyond Europe, one can only go to America."[414]

Thus Goethe's dream of a virgin poetry being born across the sea appears again, with the added qualification that this poetry shall contain the epic exaltation of the triumph of life over limitation, reason over history, America over Europe, just as the epic poetry of the past sang the struggles of Europe to impose its will on Asia.

L. The United States and South America. But which nation of the New World will receive this mission and this laurel crown? With the natives excluded, there remain the societies and tribes of European origin. But in regard to them Hegel finds himself embarrassed by his repudiation of the American continent. He experiences some difficulty in

413. *Grundlinien der Philosophie des Rechts,* secs. 246–47. On the concept of the organic totality of peoples and states and on the necessariness of their characteristics, with ample recognition of the "immortal work" of Montesquieu, see *Naturrecht,* I, 406–07. In the *Enz.* too the characters of peoples are said to be fixed like those of the races, and among the corollaries it is repeated that in the warm countries the sense of liberty is weak (*Enz.* 393 Zus.; VII, II, 72–73; cf. above, pp. 415–16 and 512; *contra,* p. 310).

414. *Die Aesthetik,* ed. cit., X, III, 351, 354–55. On the prosaic contemporary world's incurable lack of epic character, see *ibid.,* p. 417.

combining the contrast between physical immaturity and physical maturity (New and Old World) with the distinction between a merely natural (physical) civilization and a spiritual one. Is the natural civilization to the spiritual as the immature continent is to the mature? Hegel never quite says so in so many words, but his verdict on the United States suggests something very similar: that they have not yet reached political maturity, that they do not form a solid state, because they still have enormous spaces to fill with waves of farmers, colonists, and immigrants. This continual draining off and the absence of powerful neighbors prevent the formation of those internal tensions, those class conflicts and urban and industrial agglomerations which are the necessary basis of an organic state. North America, in fact, is still too natural, and therefore too "unpolitical" and unspiritual; it has too much space, and therefore too few problems; too much "geography," and therefore too little "history." If Europe had still the great Teutonic forest, there would have been no French Revolution.[415]

Its real history is still to begin. When this continent came into contact with Europe it was in part already deceased, and in part, still not complete and "ready" (*fertig*). Its natives have practically disappeared. And Hegel is quick to appreciate the quite "European" character of the new North American civilization ("what happens in America derives from Europe"; "America is a dependency that has taken Europe's overflow")[416] – and the possibilities it offers for the energies that find no outlet in Europe.

But North and South America are "very decisively separated." To the south of Panama the strip of land between the mountains and the sea, where Peru and Chile are situated, is "narrower and offers less advantages than that of North America" (between the Appalachians and the Atlantic: see above, pp. 433–34). Republics have appeared in the whole of South America except Brazil, but if we compare them with North America we find "a surprising antithesis." In the north, order and

---

415. *Philosophie der Geschichte,* ed. Lasson, I, 198–99. In commenting on the passage quoted in the text Ortega y Gasset believes one can quite simply formulate this *Hegelian* law: "The History or spiritualization of the Universe is a function of the density of population." The Europeans too, when they are scattered across the continent of America, recede in their spiritual evolution and become like a primitive people: *Hegel y América,* I, 602. On the relations between history and geography, see *Obras,* I, 419 ff.; *El espectador,* IV, 1922 (denying geographical determinism), and "En el centenario de Hegel," 1931, in *Ideas y creencias, Obras,* II, 1695 (admitting instead that "history . . . is born from geography," and citing his essay *Hegel y América*). See also the aphorism about the earth influencing "the development of history" (*El espectador,* VIII, ed. cit., I, 747). There is a clear affinity between this thesis and that of the tropicalization of the white man, and also Turner's theories on the decisive influence of the "frontier" in North American history (cf. also below, chap. 8, n. 346).

416. *Philosophie der Geschichte,* ed. Lasson, I, 194–200. On America as incompleteness and its incapacity for completion (*Nichtfertigsein und Nichtfertigwerden*), ibid., I, 202. But Europe is even too complete: it is a "cage" (quoted by Gollwitzer, op. cit., p. 440, n. 63a).

liberty; in the south, anarchy and militarism. In the north, the Reformation; in the south, Catholicism. The north was "colonized," the south, "conquered."

Here Hegel outlines a new polarization, no longer between mature and immature, natural and spiritual; but between the two Americas, between the mutual confidence (*Zutrauen*) that reigns among the industrious, faithful, and liberal Protestants,[417] and the violence and suspicion prevalent among the quarrelsome, arrogant Catholics.[418] He introduces thus a dynamic, indeed explosive, element into the inert and impotent continent and goes on to say that perhaps the struggle between the two Americas will prove to be the focal point of future history:

America is the land of the future in which there will be revealed, in the times that stand before us, and maybe even in the conflict between North and South America, the center of gravity of universal history [*die weltgeschichtliche Wichtigkeit*];[419] it is the land of yearning for all those who have wearied of Old Europe's historic armory.

But after such a hopeful beginning, with its promise of a critical revision of the thesis of America's "youthfulness" and a more determined and deeper examination of the Goethian epigram (see above, p. 435), Hegel suddenly leaves us standing. As land of the future, America interests neither the historian, who is solely concerned with the past and the present, nor the philosopher, who bothers himself neither with what merely has been, nor with what merely will be, but exclusively with what is eternal, which gives him "quite enough to do."[420] And thus, rather

417. But of the merchants of the United States Hegel writes (*Philosophie der Geschichte*, ed. Lasson, I, 197), that they are notorious for cheating their neighbors under the lofty protection of the Law. . . .

418. Op. cit., ed. Lasson, I, 195–96. On the political contrast, in Hegel's time, between the well-defined South American republics and the uncertain conformation and vague boundaries of the United States, see useful observations in Boorstin, *National Experience*, p. 269. But as usual Humboldt had already softened and rectified the (Hegelian) thesis: "One is always hearing it asserted that the Hispano-Americans are not far enough advanced in culture for free institutions" (*Reise*, IV, 400).

419. Raynal had already effectively outlined the natural, social, and political antithesis between North and South America (*Histoire philosophique*, XIII [Geneva ed., 1775], II, 530–31); and on the outbreak of war between England and the colonies had already noted the "latent germs of discord between North and South America" as a grave danger for the political balance of the whole world (*Histoire*, 10 vols. [Geneva ed., 1780], IX, 364 ff., cited by Morandi, *L'unità politica*, p. 25). See also Chateaubriand, *Voyage en Amérique* (1827), p. 211, and Bazin, op. cit., pp. 225, 231. Gioberti (after Fabre d'Olivet, see also above, p. 401) came back (1851) to the theme of the "contrast" observable in America "between the poor and agitated republics of the South and the flourishing state of the North" (*Del rinnovamento civile d'Italia*, II, 251): the latter, "America *borealis* . . . an example of civil virility, both in political experience and the genius proper to its inhabitants" (ibid., I, 103; cf. II, 313); the former on the other hand condemned to "a dreary alternation between military rule and an idle and turbid license" (ibid., II, 362). A similar antithesis, but between the North and South of the United States, appears already in Jedidiah Morse (Pictet, *Tableau*, II, 180–81), anticipating a polemic motif that will be current during the Civil War.

420. *Philosophie der Geschichte*, I, 200 (cf. above, p. 21). The future is not an object of knowledge (*Enz.* 406 Zus.; VII, II, 180), and for this very reason Hegel washed his hands of the future of the Slav peoples too. Gollwitzer, op. cit., pp. 263–64, has some apt and precise observations which only lack the historical perspective here outlined.

abruptly, Hegel bids farewell to the "New World and the dreams that are attendant upon it," and returns to the more familiar waters of the Mediterranean.[421]

M. The character of Hegel's error.   Hegel's disdainful and arbitrary dismissal of the American continent is thus not an inevitable outgrowth of his system. The system stamped the errors with its own typical form. The Hegelian dialectic, applied to empirical data, made look like logically necessary corollaries of the structure of the universe. But the root of these errors is more remote. It consists in the substantial falsity, also and especially on the empirical level, of much of the factual data that Hegel struggles to deduce dialectically.[422] Hegel's error is thus an error to the second degree, an error squared. The facts on which he bases his argument are wrong, and the logical form in which these facts are presented and argued is improper. He could just as well, or just as badly, have dialectalized the thesis of America's insuperable perfection and the Old World's miserable decrepitude.

Why then did he choose to condemn the New World? The choice was certainly not a conscious and deliberate one. But in the eyes of the philosopher who thought of the development of the Spirit, or the Absolute, in the historically conditioned terms of the East, Greece, Rome, and Christianity, the Old World certainly had more reality, more consistency, more life than the vast strange lands whose appearance at the end of the fifteenth century upset that perfect and organic line of evolution. To admit America into his system, Hegel would have had to dismantle his whole historical-dialectical apparatus, and thus reveal just

---

421. Nor does Hegel reopen the question when he is characterizing the discovery of America (*Philosophie der Geschichte*, ed. cit., II, 856, 871) nor where he talks of the ancient Welsh songs that refer to "Wanderungen nach Amerika" (*Die Aesthetik*, X, III, 406); nor does he come back to it in discussing various other details of American geography with which he shows himself familiar. He mentioned for example Chile's afternoon storms (*Enz.* 288 Zus.; VII, I, 183); the iron deposits in Brazil and Baffin Bay (ibid., p. 185); the woods, shells, and fossil snails found in America and in the Andes (*Enz.* 339 Zus.; VII, I, 435–36); the mammoth bones Humboldt found in Peru, Quito, and Mexico, and the skeleton of a gigantic animal found by him in the region of the Plate (Humboldt was never there) (ibid., 436); the theories on the origin of syphilis and the endemic character of yellow fever in America (*Enz.* 371 Zus.: VII, I, 676); the "descensus lapidum in Europa et America" (*Dissertatio Philosophica De Orbitis Planetarum*, 1801), etc. Hegel also makes perceptive observations on the unifying function of the waters, both fluvial and oceanic, by which "Cadiz is more tightly linked to America than it is to Madrid," and "the communication between America and Europe is much easier than in the interior of Asia or America" (*Philosophie der Geschichte*, ed. Lasson, I, 186–87; the same notion occurs in a letter from Humboldt to Varnhagen von Ense, 17 May 1837).

422. Dilthey has observed that in Hegel's time Lavoisier, Galvani, Volta, and Brown had already revolutionized the natural sciences, but Hegel was quite happy to subordinate all that to the structure of his system (Spanish translation, *Hegel y el idealismo* [Mexico, 1944], p. 257); and his teaching thus remained without issue in this part: "Where an Alexander von Humboldt reigned . . . there was no longer any room for such an outdated treatment of nature. This was the Achilles' heel of his system" (ibid., p. 270). A more indulgent discussion of Hegel's attitude toward the natural sciences appears in Hartmann, op. cit., II, 24–25. Essential among contemporary works is M. J. Petri's very erudite commentary on *Hegel's Philosophy of Nature*, 3 vols. (Oxford, 1970), which does not however alter my conclusions.

how fragile and artificial it was, how rigidly incapable of adapting itself to new realities and finding a place for them within itself. America, with its enormous and undeniable presence, *naïve et péremptoire*, would have uncovered and betrayed one of the weaknesses in the system. To gain entry into the triadic pattern the five parts of the world, whether they liked it or not, had to be reduced to three, just as with Hegel the five senses had become three, and the five traditional arts.[423]

So Hegel must have been intellectually delighted to come across the thesis of America's weakness. And he no doubt derived a vengeful pleasure from taking over a thesis that made it easy for him to rid himself of the vexatious obstacle, which in fact moved it right outside the realm of reality and history, reducing it to the miserable condition of some gigantic abortion.

N. The thesis less vigorous in Hegel than in Buffon. But precisely because with Hegel the theory serves a practical purpose, the masking of a deficiency in his system, and not for the solution of a problem, it has with him that much less freshness, less force than in Buffon. In the French naturalist the biological inferiority of America was an imperfect but provocative explanation for the diversity of the species in the various continents. It was an attempt at synthesis, an effort to relate the living nature of the two worlds to a single principle. It was a sincere and concrete effort, and it showed its fecundity first of all in arousing the polemics and reactions already discussed, and again in providing Humboldt and Darwin with the point of departure for some of the most important theories of the modern science of nature. The Swabian philosopher's rejection of America, on the other hand, was so sterile that it remained as a blot on his system, as a typical and flagrant example of error, and was never again seriously considered or discussed. True, some of the empirical elements that had served to underpin it were occasionally used to support this or that biological or sociological thesis. But the basic theory of "America's weakness," the immaturity of the hemisphere, died in the very moment of its consecration as a necessary aspect of the Logos.

Buffon's theses, so boldly suggestive if interpreted evolutionistically, in accord with the historicist tendencies of his thought, lost all vitality once they were implanted in Hegel's rigid antievolutionistic system. They shriveled up, fossilized. And their ambiguous but fruitful alterna-

---

423. According to Ortega y Gasset, on the other hand, Hegel's systematic embarrassment and his consequent condemnation of America derive from his conception of reality as history and history as the past. America, "which if it is anything is something future," having no history would thus have no reality either (*Hegel y América*, op. cit., *Obras*, I, 594, 600). Nor does Ortega y Gasset allow Hegel to be charged with ignorance of the empirical facts: indeed, he writes, he was excellently informed; he saw "acutely" the "weakness and immaturity" of the typical South American species; and his limitations are those "suffered by all empirical knowledge" (ibid., pp. 598–99; but they were not suffered just then by Clavigero, nor Jefferson, nor Humboldt, nor many other naturalists).

tive of immaturity and decadence gave way once more to the dry antitheses and static comparisons of the first denigrators of the continent.

O. The historicization and dissolution of the thesis.   As the nineteenth century advanced and historicism pervaded the natural sciences and transformed them from sciences of immobility and uniform laws into sciences of the eternally changing and creative,[424] a corresponding revision of viewpoint was required for that massive object of natural science, the American continent. Its age could no longer be translated into qualitative terms: young equals immature, old age, decadence. Nor could it be compared to the Old World any more as if they were two static entities, two measurable quantities, and thus comparabie with one serving as the yardstick for the other.

In the flow of becoming, every phenomenon reacquired its autonomy, its personal dignity. If America was adjudged degenerate, it could only be so described in respect of its *own* past. If it appeared immature, this only meant that it had not yet achieved its *own* destiny. As Zanella was to say of the whole world: *"se schiavi, se lagrime | Ancora rinserra | È giovin la terra"* — "if it still has slaves, if it still has tears, then the earth is young" (*La conchiglia fossile*).

In short the fictitious antithesis that opposed the New World to the Old, America's geography to Europe's, was fated to disappear as soon as geography, like every other natural science, became reabsorbed in history, as soon as spatial determinations, extrinsic one to another by definition, and thus prone to pose as polar dyads, faded away before an organic concept of the sole and unnumbered reality, in Humboldt's vivid picture of the *Kosmos*.

P. The chain of being and the old metaphysics.   But in yet another way, Hegel's repudiation of America shows just how much antiquated and fragile and scientifically dead matter remained in his thought. A considerable residue of medievalism is abundantly evident among the materials he uses to construct his massive system.

In the kingdoms of nature every species exists solely inasmuch as it embodies a moment of the Logos. But the American natural species turn out to be deficient embodiments, the rejects or crude first attempts of the Logos. It is not difficult to recognize in these half-ingenuous, half-pedantic explanations the *caput mortuum* of the old metaphysics. The forms of existence that Hegel labors to deduce and develop one from another in a necessary chain are the transparent reincarnations of those species and ideas which Western thought, from Plato onward, had stubbornly per-

---

424. On the penetration of historical thought into the natural sciences (the influence of biology and the beginnings of evolutionism), see above, p. 408, and Collingwood, *The Idea of Nature*, pp. 12–13, 133–36.

sisted in ordering in an uninterrupted and necessarily complete chain from the Supreme Deity right down to the humblest creature. Hegel's Logos makes the journey in reverse; but great and significant as this inversion of movement is, it does not alter the typical age-old scheme.

The "temporalized" (Lovejoy) form of the chain of being, developed in the eighteenth century to reconcile the static and rigid character of the eternal chain with a new faith in Progress, served as a bridge between the Platonic and Neoplatonic systems and the new historicizing dialectic.

Hegel seeks to give life and movement to just this same inert natural chain, to saturate it with active spirituality. But the dead weight of the scheme adopted crushes, suffocates, paralyzes the new principles. The continents refuse to be ordered as categories and antinomies. The animals cannot bring themselves to be mere variants of the Animal, modified and enfeebled exemplaries of an imaginary *totem* postulated by a professor of philosophy. The resounding failure of the attempt, with its strident disharmonies of an "impotent nature," its limping triads, its Spiritless facts and beings, reveals clearly the unsuitability of a mythicomystical structure, such as that of the infinite scale of prototypes, as a vehicle for the concepts of historical thought, which sees the one in the individual, not in the species or the idea; and the infinite in the same concrete one, and not in its multiplication to infinity, along a graduated, continuous, interminable scale.

The whole Philosophy of Nature, in any case, rests on the concept of "being other than oneself," an invention or formula of clearly Scholastic flavor, and develops along almost naïvely anthropocentric lines.[425] The earth is the supreme theater of the Spirit. In this pre-Copernican or rather essentially biblical[426] vision of the universe it is not surprising that all the stress is on the Old World, and that America, Oceania, the whole remainder of the globe pales and almost loses its *raison d'être*. The ideological link between the discovery of America and Copernicus's discoveries, a link so acutely realized by Bruno, for instance, and shortly to be taken up by Gioberti,[427] asserts itself again in Hegel's double disregard of the New World and the infinite worlds.

425. Cf. Dilthey, op. cit., pp. 235–36. Strong traces of Wolfianism were already noted by Schelling, and are recognized by Dilthey, ibid., pp. 246, 296. On the mechanistic character remaining in "Hegel's nature," see Collingwood, *The Idea of Nature*, p. 128. But the best criticism of the concept of nature as "other than itself" can be read in Hegel himself, where he is blithely illustrating the metaphysics of excrementa and defines them as "the abstract dropping of it from itself" (*Enz.* 365; VII, I, 632–34).

426. Dilthey, op. cit., p. 263.

427. "Christopher Columbus did for the ordering of the earth what Copernicus did for that of the heavens" (*Del Rinnovamento Civile*, III, 80). Parallel and analogous is the recognition of the link between "plurality of worlds" (Epicurus–Bruno–Fontenelle) and "discovery of the new [earthly] world" — noted already by Montaigne (*Essais*, II, xii, quoted in M. Bataillon, *Montaigne et les conquérants de l'or*, offprint from *Studi francesi*, 9 [1959], p. 356).

The Dispute's Trivialization and Obstinate Vitality

I. DISLOCATION OF THE TERMS OF THE POLEMIC AFTER HEGEL

THE internal contradictions and fundamental hesitation in Hegel's ideas on America show how by this time the traditional terms of the dispute were no longer sufficient to contain the problems presented by the New World. On the one hand the natural sciences had broken free from the volumetric schemes and the rigid limitations of the climatic theories, and on the other the political and social development of the United States and the turbulent vitality of the Latin American countries quickly obliterated the memory of their colonial past, recent as it was, and contradicted the usual characterizations of the Creole as sleepy and spineless and the North American as physically decadent and barbarously uncouth.

So Hegel finds himself on the horns of a dilemma. He struggles conscientiously to provide a coherent picture of the two worlds and their ideal relationship, but the harder he tries, the more he exasperates and confuses their intrinsic and reciprocal antinomies. America is physically and morally impotent, but it is also the Future, or "potency" by definition. Europe is the perfection of the Absolute, it is the west that cannot be overcome by another west more western still (nor is Asia, which is the essential east, allowed to be America's west!), but it is also an ancient armory, a "cage," a prison where boredom reigns and where the lofty strains of the epic will never again be heard.[1] Universal history reached its peak in the Germanic and reformed world; but its center of gravity, attracted by a new polarity, between North and South America, shifts toward the point where a new fatal conflict may flare up.

After Hegel, then, the dispute could not have and did not have any further developments of interest; and this chapter is more in the way of

1. Cf. above, p. 435; Hegel, *Philosophie der Geschichte,* Lasson ed., I, 225, 232–33, and Gollwitzer, op. cit., pp. 262–65 and notes.

an appendix. The knowledge of the new continent, and particularly of the United States and the pre-Columbian civilizations, went steadily forward, and the names of Michel Chevalier, Tocqueville, Prescott, and hundreds of travelers and archeologists became deservedly famous on both sides of the Atlantic; but the specific themes of the polemic provoked by Buffon disappear, and the name de Pauw falls into the most complete oblivion. America, however, both as land and people, continued to occupy the European mind, and from time to time became the embodiment of political, technical, economic, religious, and generally human ideas deriving from the heart of the Western tradition; and also occasionally served as target for Europe's intolerance toward certain ways of life and customs, toward the boastful ignorance and commercial sharp practices, that were certainly common enough in the whole world and at all times, but which toward the middle of the nineteenth century were particularly conspicuous in the transatlantic states.

The nations of America in their turn, and the United States in particular, sought to legitimize their existence, their recent admission into the community of nations, with claims of special missions and manifest destinies, with talk of their function as place of refuge or field of experiment, of their physical or spiritual supremacy and portentous privileges of ethical purity or literary virginity

Thus the European criticism shifts rapidly from the physical nature of the continent to the society formed therein. A change of target, but not always of method and arguments. In fact the verdict pronounced on the new American nations and their "civilization" often takes on the tone and coloring of the diatribes on the animals and natives. The new scientific concepts show their strength in the way they sweep aside dozens of misstated problems, and reveal their fecundity in their acute and impartial explanations of the phenomena and creatures of the five continents and other places. But they were inapplicable, or at least not yet applied, to historical concepts such as nations, popular mentalities, political institutions, and the ideologies and ideals that had emerged so rapidly and were now fermenting and bubbling in the Americas. It came about in this way that at a time when the soil and skies of the New World had already been redeemed by Science, its people and states were still measured with the yardstick of simplistic comparisons, contests of merit, polarizing parallels.

Typical in the admiration of America is the little-known case of A. Thierry, who, tormented by the problem of the races and the age-old question of the relationships between dominators and dominated, transfigures the United States into a supremely happy nation without conflicts of race, language, or religion—a land dedicated to the cult of liberty, a common refuge for all humanity, because there "the men know only how to look on each other with fraternity and love."[2] America has thus realized Europe's noblest dreams. The United States belongs to Europe's spiritual world: it is the close and providentially happy terminus of all her long disastrous history.

This foreshortening of the focal distance between the two hemispheres was complicated and at the same time aggravated by an accompanying critical reappraisal of European civilization, indeed of the whole concept of civilization. Coming into being almost simultaneously with Europe's awakening consciousness of itself, the idea and the very word "civilization" entered the thought and lexicon of the West in the second half of the eighteenth century at the very time when the antithesis between "society" and "nature," between Europe (civilized by definition) and America (savage par excellence), between the optimistic dogma of Progress and the recurrent terror of the Fall, was becoming most crude and striking. And we have already seen in how many ways the polemics of the New World were interwoven with the efforts to define and better understand the nature, history, and destiny of the Old World, and how often and how fatally the opposition between the two hemispheres finished up by coinciding with those alternatives of future and past, space and time, which held and hold within themselves the most tormented enigmas of human destiny.

The reexamination of those ideas came about through the revolutionary crisis, felt as a break with the past, as a threat of civilization's total ruin, as expiation and palingenesis, as the liberation of forces as yet scarcely understood and menacingly impetuous;[3] and it was carried out, with no less revolutionary results, in both the sphere of the natural sciences (see pp. 442 ff.) and in the realm of speculation, causing the dissolution of the old "philosophy of history," through the analysis of those very same concepts of civilization, culture, progress, evolution, and primitivism, into sociology on the one hand and integral historicism on the other.

But this whole process, although of considerable interest for the intellectual history of the two worlds, and despite its frequent echoes of some of the diatribes or apologies that we have examined, lies outside our subject. Here it will suffice to mention, and very summarily, such texts and theses as show the clear imprint, right up to and beyond the middle of the nineteenth century, of the condemnations and calumnies born in the middle of the previous century.

2. Augustin Thierry, "Sur l'antipathie de race qui divise la nation française, à propos de l'ouvrage de M. Warden, intitulé Description statistique, historique et politique des Etats-Unis de l'Amérique Septentrionale," 1820, in *Dix ans d'etudes historiques* (Brussels, 1835), pp. 299–307.
3. L. Febvre, op. cit., pp. 30–32, and, in general, the whole essay.

II. FRIEDRICH SCHLEGEL: THE ZOOLOGICAL AND ANTHROPOLOGICAL POVERTY OF AMERICA

Friedrich Schlegel was a contemporary of Hegel, but a convert to re-action and even less sensitive than Hegel to the prestige, albeit only verbal, of the New World and the young nations. In 1810 he had defined North America as a "nursery" (*Pflanzschule*) of humanity and European liberty, but by 1828 he was defining it as the veritable "nursery" of all destructive principles, a school of revolutionism for France and the rest of Europe.[4] The reversal is an obvious corollary of Schlegel's growing sympathy with reactionaries and right-wingers. And in fact his judgment on the future destinies of the two hemispheres is reversed in perfect and synchronic parallel.

In his lectures on universal history Schlegel still sees the Americas in "Kantian" terms. The Americans are not yet sufficiently well known.[5] But of America we do know that it is completely and radically detached from the physical nature of the Old World, in its vegetable and animal products, "not to mention its organic products, since many animals are lacking there which exist in the Old World." The latter, despite its in-finite variety, when compared with America forms a physical unity, even if Africa in particular is to be distinguished from the other two continents of the Old World on account of its "lack of rivers" [*sic!*], in other words of the particular item in which America is so stupefyingly exuberant.[6] As for the men, it is possible that in America there are Asiatic races: cer-tainly the present-day Americans are not the original inhabitants of America, and "from the organic point of view they seem to be the weakest of men." The savages, the cannibals, these are the only autochthonous Americans.[7]

But these comments remain unconnected, also because Schlegel does not believe in the fundamental equality of peoples and constantly rejects the climatic theories, which have so much influenced his predecessors, including Herder.[8] For him the Germans are the bearers of the purest and highest traditions, and will be able to carry forward their educative task in all climates, beginning naturally with Europe, which gradually becomes his sole concern as he proceeds with his lectures on universal

4. Gollwitzer, op. cit., p. 254; F. von Schlegel, *The Philosophy of History*, trans. J. B. Robertson (London, 1873), p. 453; on the lethal germs and the infectious turmoil of dissidence and civil war fer-menting in the United States, see *Vorlesungen über Universalgeschichte*, 1805–06, ed. J.-J. Anstett (Zu-rich, 1960: vol. XIV, pt. 2 of the *Kritische Ausgabe*), pp. xlvii, 244.

5. "The Americans, who are however not yet sufficiently well known to us" (*Vorlesungen*, p. 13; cf. above, p. 331). Kant is cited a few lines above.

6. Ibid.: an echo of the customary "humidity" of the New World. A little earlier (p. 7) and a little further on Schlegel dwells on the plurality of Floods, all, except the last, having happened before man's appearance on Earth.

7. Ibid., pp. 15, 17, 68.

8. Ibid., pp. xxxvii, xlv.

history.[9] Italian civilization flourished mainly in those regions, Tuscany and Lombardy, where German domination lasted longest and German influence was strongest![10]

The discovery of America is effectively characterized by its insertion into the European movement of scientific progress and commercial expansion, and the demonstration of its influence on the human spirit in general and the restlessness of the peoples, even though these peoples were distracted by the tumults and crises of the Reformation. Unfortunately, and once again as a result of the Reformation, Christianity was not able to permeate America, so that "the existence of the Europeans is not assured in any part of the New World," nor has European civilization been able to acclimatize itself over there. North America has been more or less colonized, but this colonization, which led to the separation from the mother country and had an evil influence in Europe, is to be considered a harmful secondary effect of that great event.[11] If only there had still been the Jesuits the spark from the American Revolution would not have been able to lead to the conflagration of the French Revolution, but the order had been suppressed and thus the path opened to anarchy![12]

The problem of the relationship between European civilization and the overseas nations continued however to ferment in Schlegel's mind, and indeed logically presented itself to him again, more vividly, when the Napoleonic empire crumbled and everyone was asking himself on what basis and in what form Europe could be rebuilt and the Western heritage saved. And in fact in 1816, according to a recently discovered fragment, Schlegel was again considering Berkeley's and Herder's auspicious doubts: with Europe devastated and destroyed, could not a new era arise in America?

Why not? And the Germans too could take part in this palingenesis, not with one of the usual colonies, but with a migration of a chosen band of scholars and scientists. This academic dream (which is not a little grotesque, when one conjures up the image of all these *Herren Universitätsprofessoren* disembarking for their apostolic mission) immediately becomes precise and insistent; what incalculable changes could one not produce in America with thirty or forty German philosophers of nature, but good ones (*von der guten Art!*)! And thus perhaps one will be able to catch two fat birds with one stone: the reconstruction of Europe after the catastrophe, and the maturing of a humanistic civilization in America.[13]

9. Ibid., pp. xlvii, 87 (with explicit denigration of Africa and America), 147, etc.
10. Ibid., p. 164.
11. Ibid., pp. 221–25, 228, 230.
12. Ibid., pp. 238, 241.
13. "Friedrich Schlegel, Fragmente aus dem Nachlass," ed. Alois Dempf, *Merkur, Deutsche Zeitschrift für Europäisches Denken* (Stuttgart), 10, no. 106 (December 1956), p. 1180.

At this time, anyway, Schlegel still saw America as the refuge of an elite at least of European culture, which would be able to produce a singular development there. A few years later the prescription was radically altered: Europe had no further need of being reborn in America, when it could become young again by impersonating the Slavic supremacy of Russia.[14] And in his later lectures on the *Philosophy of History* (1828), in Vienna, Schlegel repeated that Polynesia "counts for nothing in history," that America's history dates only from its discovery and is merely "passive" history, as "dependance," or "adjunct," of Europe until the last fifty years.

Physically the earth can be divided horizontally, so to speak, into a Northern Hemisphere and a Southern Hemisphere, or vertically, into a Western and an Eastern. With the former division, the Southern Hemisphere is found to be clearly inferior to the Northern: it is watery and desolate, and lit by less stars and those few less bright (its "inferiority" stretches out into ethereal space). The northern half on the other hand, rich in land and peoples, the legendary seat of the happy and virtuous Hyperboreans, is the globe's positive pole.[15]

If now we stand the dividing line on end, vertical instead of horizontal, we find in a perfect and revolving symmetry of values that the Western Hemisphere is clearly inferior to the Eastern: the latter is predominantly land (excepting its southern extremity, true, but here a chain of islands stretches out to the fifth continent, Oceania, making it a "dependency" of Asia—a sort of bonus of land thrown in for good measure), while in the former water predominates, and not only in the south but in the center too, so that the area of America, big as it is, cannot be compared with that of the other continents [*sic!*], and its population is meager—equal at most to that of a single European state, such as France or Germany.[16] One hesitates to think how "imperfect" the southern part of the Western Hemisphere must be. Schlegel never says so, but it seems it must really be the veritable pit of the universe.

America, in any case, is all one imperfect continent, simpler and more

14. Thus in his review *Konkordia* (1820–23), cited by Gollwitzer, op. cit., p. 252; see also *Vorlesungen*, pp. 200–01. There is practically nothing added in Harold von Hofe, "Friedrich Schlegel and the New World," *PMLA*, 76, no. 1 (March 1961), pp. 63–67.

15. On the superiority of the Northern Hemisphere, cf. already the *Vorlesungen*, ed. cit., pp. 7–8, 16–17, which however limited the opposition between east and west, which "are only relative notions" (p. 8)—and north and south are not, then? . . .

16. Schlegel, *Philosophy of History*, pp. 80–81, 109–10. In point of fact the American continent, around 1825, did have only thirty-four and a half million inhabitants (Rosenblat, op. cit., pp. 36, 129–53). The immediate sources of Schlegel's ideas on America can more easily be guessed at than documented. Von Hofe (op. cit., p. 66) and Anstett (in the introduction to his edition of the *Vorlesungen*, op. cit., p. xxx) mention the influence of Georg Forster. Rather more certain would seem to be the influence of Buffon, and Kant's *Physische Geographie* and the essay on the races. The repeated references to Atlantis (*Philosophy of History*, p. 81; *The Philosophy of Life*, trans. A. J. W. Morrison [New York, 1848], pp. 83–84) seem to come from Bailly, *Lettres sur l'Atlantide de Platon* (Paris, 1779; see also *Vorlesungen*, p. 261).

rudimentary in shape than the Old World. Possibly the Old World resembled it a little when Europe was separated from Asia by a "ditch"
extending from the White Sea to the Caspian and was joined to Africa on
the other hand by an isthmus at Gibraltar (Schlegel has no hesitation in
cutting up and pasting together continents and hemispheres). America,
anyway, was inhabited by men and animals of inferior quality. It lacked
the noblest and finest zoological species, and others it had only in degenerate and unpleasant-looking forms. The few indigenous animals of
the New World are "a poor recompense" for such grave deficiencies.

As for the men, they suffer from a double malediction: physically they
are less robust and less agile than the Africans, less long-lived and less
fertile than the Asiatics; morally they are as degenerate as any other
savage, and even more so. After the loss of Grace, there is no limit to the
Fall of man. He can descend to mere animality. Of all men, the American
native has come closest to the animals. And at this point, although he
mentions Humboldt's objective findings, Schlegel advances boldly far
beyond even de Maistre and Leopardi to assign the last step in the scale
of humanity to the "monstrous" Patagonians, the semiimbecile Pescheräh, and the horrendous cannibals of New Zealand.

Once again Rousseau finds himself in the line of fire. Jean-Jacques was
quite wrong to identify the savage with the man of nature. The truth is
quite the reverse: the civilized state is natural, while the savages are the
exemplary victims of a second fall, perhaps not as sudden and total as the
first, but slow and progressive: "The tribes which we call savage have the
same origin as the nobler and more civilized nations, and it is only gradually that they have sunk to their present condition of brutalization and
degeneration."[17] The perfection of the American, and the completion of
America's historical life, which Hegel projected into the far-distant future,
are thrust back by Schlegel into an inscrutable past: once again the real
antithesis concerns not America's reality, but the two opposing dogmas,
of Progress and Original Sin.

But present-day America is still supreme in one thing, its luxuriant
vegetation. And Schlegel does not hesitate to proclaim it as a general law,
which is as certain as it is precise, that in the Old World the animal force
prevails, and in the New the vegetable force.[18] But this, which he announces as his own discovery, and almost as a paradox of nature, was

17. *Philosophy of History,* pp. 92–93, 111; on the Pescheräh, see also above, p. 431. Cf. the similar
expressions of Leopardi (above, p. 388) and de Maistre (above, pp. 390, 392). To support his thesis of a
gradual fall of all humanity, Schlegel falls back on stale theological arguments, recalling the longevity of
the patriarchs and the existence in ancient times of gigantic men and animals (ibid., pp. 101 ff.). But of
the Patagonians, both giants and Americans, he says that they may be tall, but they are very ugly, and
seem taller when they are on horseback because they have short legs (like the lies of the Italian proverb?!)

18. *Philosophy of History,* p. 110; cf. Hegel, above, p. 425.

actually a commonplace, indeed an echo of the earliest chroniclers of the Indies. The exuberance of the American flora had aroused amazement, admiration, and terror almost, even in earliest times. Oviedo had described the virgin forest in preromantic accents. Father Acosta had specified that in the humid surroundings of the Indies not only are the wild trees much more numerous and varied than in the Old World, but even roots and tubers have a much richer growth than in Europe, where on the other hand fruit trees and garden vegetables are much more in evidence;[19] and each succeeding generation experienced the same surprise. A few years later a contemporary of Schlegel, the naturalist William John Burchell, wrote to Darwin that nothing had so struck him in Brazil (where he had spent the years from 1826 to 1829) as the magnificence of the vegetation, in contrast with that of South Africa (which he had visited between 1810 and 1815), and the simultaneous absence of large quadrupeds[20] — which moved Darwin to describe the idea that "large animals require a luxuriant vegetation"[21] as an outdated prejudice. Thus the naïve antithesis between a more robust fauna in the Old World and a richer flora in the New contained the germ of one of the most profound and fruitful truths of zoological geography.

III. ZOOLOGISTS AND ANTHROPOLOGISTS: GUANO AND THE SAVAGES

In Schlegel there were still some pretensions to system, justifying a few moments' attention. But it is certainly not worthwhile gathering up all the accidental or mechanical repetitions of more or less openly Buffon–de Pauwian theses that appear in writers and travelers and publicists of all sorts, and are thus totally devoid of any meaning or conceptual content. So we shall not waste time either with the restless Flora Tristán, who found the chickens of Arequipa (Peru) to be tough and saw the cause of this leathery meat in the influence of the volcano Misti;[22] nor with the careful Cattaneo, who mentions America's lack of the "big and strong [animals] of Asia and Africa. . . . The lion, the tiger, the crocodile, are represented in America by less powerful species: by the puma, the jaguar, the alligator. In place of the camel, the horse, and sheep, America had the llama, the alpaca, and the vicuña."[23] Nor with Cesare Correnti,

19. *Historia natural y moral,* IV, 18–19, 30; ed. cit., pp. 242–46, 267–70.
20. These were his specialty, and zoologists have given the name Burchell to one variety of rhinoceros and two sorts of zebra.
21. Darwin, *Voyage of a Naturalist round the World,* V; ed. cit., I, 111. Cf. above, chap. 5, n. 434. Still in our day Lévi-Strauss thrills at the sight of the Brazilian forest, thick with "plants more copious than those of Europe" (*Tristes tropiques,* pp. 74–75, 83).
22. *Pérégrinations d'une Paria* (1833–34), 1838, L, 8; Santiago ed., 1941, p. 116, Lima ed., 1946, p. 200.
23. *Corso di filosofia* (1852 ff.), in *Opere,* ed. Lemonnier, vol. VII (Florence, 1892), p. 314. In the lines which follow Cattaneo describes the animal offspring of Australia as even weaker and more strange, and in the subsequent pages (315–27) he gives a realistic Vico-like description of the American savages,

although there is even less chance of mistaking the provenance of his ideas when he writes of America that "the inferior forms of the organism seem to grow there with too bold a vigor, and with their inexhaustible profusion to prevent the development of superior forms," so that the insects, the reptiles, and the monkeys (inferior forms too?) had there "preoccupied the field of life," and the Europeans found nothing there but "bald and bastardized lions, puny tiger cats, pigmy camels."[24]

Nor, on the other hand, shall we attach too much importance to an amusing defender of America against Hegel, even though his poem seems to indicate that the philosopher's anti-American attitude had become proverbial and was talked about in much the same way as the "calumnies" of Buffon and de Pauw half a century earlier.

It was soon after 1840 that boats began to arrive from the Pacific with cargoes of Peruvian guano, that miraculous nitrogenous fertilizer whose natural virtues brought new life to the worn-out fields of old Europe. The imperfect and immature continent finally produced a product that was undeniably more effective and more potent than anything Europe could produce to compete with it. So Hegel was contradicted to his face by the birds of the Pacific. The facetious poet Scheffel, a Swabian like Hegel, was quick to catch the humor of the situation, and closed his quatrains "Guano" (ca. 1845) with the unlikely but pungent words of the rustic cabbage grower of Böbling (near Stuttgart, where the philosopher was born):

> God bless you, you excellent birds,
> Remote on your far Guano shore,
> For despite neighbor Hegel's harsh words,
> You produce the most perfect manure![25]

Is Scheffel really referring to the Hegelian thesis of America's impotence? The learned commentators of his lyrics leave us in doubt.[26]

---

basing himself on a number of authors both ancient (Oviedo, Pietro Martire, etc.) and modern (Robertson) and affirming in his turn, against Rousseau, that man's natural state is civilization, and that "the savage life is really the childhood of the human race."

24. Cesare Correnti, "Il Nuovo Mondo," in *Il Nipote del Vesta-Verde*, vol. VII (1854), pp. 53–57, and in *Scritti scelti*, ed. T. Massarani (Rome, 1892), II, 357–62; a probable derivation from Herder (cf. above, p. 286), who is cited, together with Humboldt, on p. 359.

25. "Gott segn' euch, ihr trefflichen Vögel, / An der fernen Guanoküst, – / Trotz meinem Landsmann, dem Hegel, / Schafft ihr den gediegensten Mist!" (J. V. von Scheffel, *Werke*, ed. K. Siegen and M. Mendheim [Stuttgart, 1917], II, 180–81). A Castilian translation of the entire poem was published in the *Boletín de la Compañia Administradora del Guano* (Lima), 20 (1944), pp. 113–14. The guano had served as polemic argument against de Pauw too (see above, chap. 6, n. 51).

26. See the editors cited in the Bong edition; Adolf Hausrath, "J. V. von Scheffel und Anselm Feuerbach," *Deutsche Rundschau*, 52 (July–September 1887), pp. 97–122, esp. 111; and E. Stemplinger, who includes "Guano" in his anthology of *Kulturhistorische Dichtung: Scheffel, Julius Braun, Lingg* (Leipzig, 1939), pp. 177–78, 262.

But the context and a number of circumstantial indications make our interpretation quite permissible.

The birds' burlesque and malodorous reply to the philosopher—"birds are all philosophers," says an earlier line of the same poem—repeats the answer that the touchy "Comet," mistreated by all the stars, makes to Humboldt, the "old man of searching powers," in the immediately preceding poem, because Humboldt too was somewhat unkind, and wrote in the *Kosmos* that the comet was slighter than froth and that it filled the greatest space with the smallest mass. Just let them wait a little, these evil old astronomers; they don't know what a comet can do; if it ever catches them, it will unload a whole hailstorm of meteorites on the lenses of their telescopes! The birds of the Pacific in their turn, in contented solitude and perfect digestion ("blessed is their digestion, and as fluent as a poem") will finish by damming the ocean with towering mountains of guano.

With the same goliardic irreverence Scheffel pokes fun at the disputes between the Vulcanists and Neptunists (see pp. 361–62); "Granite" says he is tired of being eaten away by the waters, and becomes eruptive, and "Basalt," enamored like some "geological Romeo" of the maiden Molassa, turns the terrestrial strata upside down, erupts in fury and destroys everything—including his sweet Molassa.[27]

But did Scheffel know of Hegel's peculiar attitude toward America? It seems more than likely that he did, if in the summer of 1845 (exactly when "Guano" is generally supposed to have been written)[28] he was following one of Professor Eduard Röth's courses in the "exposition and criticism of Hegel's system" at Heidelberg, and in the following summer took a course on Shakespeare given by the Hegelian Karl Werder;[29] and if after his youthful loss of religious faith he sought a successor to it in the Hegelian philosophy,[30] although being more temperamentally inclined to levity and jest than any sort of speculation he never succeeded in plumbing its profounder depths.[31] If we remember too that his teacher Röth did not belong to the Hegelian school,[32] and that his liberalizing

---

27. *Werke*, II, 171–72, 175–77. On basalt, see also "Pumpus von Perusia," ibid., II, 189, ll. 9–12.

28. See the life which prefaces the *Werke*, ed. cit., I, lxxxiv, lxxxvii, and the preface to the collection *Gaudeamus*, ibid., II, 165; and also Hausrath, loc. cit.

29. See the life cited above, I, xiv, xix. In the *Säkkinger Episteln* (1850) there is also a derisive mention, as cousin of an *Erdmännlein*, or dwarfling, of the "great" Johann Eduard Erdmann, the Hegelian professor of philosophy (*Werke*, ed. cit., V, 47; VI, 255). Röth, an Orientalist, convinced that the origin of our knowledge should be sought not in India or China but in Egypt and Zoroaster's Persia, published a *Geschichte der Philosophie* (1846–58), described by Scheffel as "having great influence at the time on the young students" (Stemplinger, op. cit., p. 93). But the *Allgemeine Deutsche Biographie*, the source of these details, gives no precise indication of his philosophical position.

30. *Werke*, I, xcvii.

31. Ibid., I, xiv.

32. Hausrath, loc. cit.; and see n. 29, above.

anti-Prussian and pro-Austrian leanings were the very antithesis of Hegel's political ideas, we shall be near to understanding how Scheffel could simultaneously possess a certain acquaintance with the philosopher's theories and little sympathy with the man.

Of the various little rivulets which are all that remain of the broad stream of the dispute after Hegel one at least must be mentioned, since in its turn it goes on to merge with one of the major currents of nineteenth-century scientific thought. Zoologists and anthropologists reconsidered the problem of the natives and the animal species of North America in the light of the new concepts of evolution and natural selection; and under the influence of the dominating and partly misunderstood historicism often confused the "primitive" in the chronological sense with the logically "primitive": they assigned the characteristics of an extreme antiquity to the most rudimentary species and uncultured tribes, and vice versa attributed to the remotest past customs thought to be anterior to those of our civilization, and zoological forms differing from the surviving ones.[33]

By this confusion they could see the South American mammals of the Tertiary period as the last belated examples of a vastly protracted evolution, at the end of which they had found themselves furnished with formidable and ancient armor-plating, which had not however saved them from extinction, and perhaps had even rendered their demise more swift and total;[34] and, even more curiously, allowed a subtle "biographer," quoted but not named by Ortega y Gasset, to maintain that the weakness and immaturity of the species characteristic of South America are due precisely to the fact that they are "the primigenial" and the most archaic: "The oldest species is, as a species, and while it survives, young in relation to the newer and more complex ones"[35] — an ingenious reversal offering the vanity of the South American a consolation for the biological inferiority of his fauna by exalting the antiquity of its lineage: a typically *hidalgo viejo* justification.

As for the natives, the discussion broadened and merged into the general discussion on the character of primitive peoples, with particular stress on the point of whether they were degenerate, as so many theo-

---

33. See E. De Martino, *Naturalismo e storicismo nell'etnologia* (Bari, 1941), pp. 77–82, 205–06, and passim.

34. "Some Tertiary mammals, especially in South America, were immense and bizarre creatures; and one wonders how long a period of evolutionary history was needed for them thus to arm themselves" (E. W. Barnes, *Scientific Theory and Religion* [Cambridge, 1933], pp. 474–75, quoted by Toynbee, op. cit., IV, 423).

35. Ortega y Gasset, 1928, op. cit., I, 600–01 (3rd ed., I, 599), who alludes perhaps to J. von Uexküll, *Ideas para una concepción biológica del mundo* (1913), which was translated into Castilian, in 1922, at the instigation of Ortega himself.

logizing and nontheologizing writers maintained,[36] or whether they shared in the progressive ascent of all humanity. The anthropologists of the Victorian era, Lubbock, Tyler, Pitt-Rivers, devoted no small part of their tracts to repudiating the accusation of degeneration,[37] and even the thoughtful Droysen, confronted by the material accumulated by Klemm (1843) on primitive peoples, reconsidered the question of whether the savage should be looked on as immature or degenerate.[38] In America the evolutionist Morgan came out in open opposition to the theory of the savage as degenerate,[39] but the thesis of "decadence" once again played an important role in the system of Elliott Smith, for whom civilization was born in Egypt and became more "diluted," lost, or degenerate the further it spread from its land of origin.[40]

These theories too, obviously, sought to reconcile the only too evident deviations or interruptions of that supposedly uniform movement with the dominant dogma of universal progress; and thus reflected the uneasiness of advanced rationalism when faced with the too many and too flagrant and conspicuous examples of incurable backwardness or shameful decadence. True, these theories refer in general to all primitive peoples, and have nothing specifically American (or should we say anti-American) about them. But one cannot forget that these very same American natives were actually the first that Europe had known and studied as such, and that thus throughout the eighteenth century *primitive, American* and *savage* had been almost synonymous terms.

So the theories of the nineteenth century represent the orchestration, on an anthropological and universal plane, of "American" themes and problems proposed mainly on the sociological and political plane in the preceding century. But this enrichment of sonority, to stay with the metaphor, is accompanied by a corresponding weakening and fading of the melodic line. Progress toward civilization, the leitmotiv of the En-

36. Still in 1862 Robert Knox was asserting (*The Races of Men,* London) that even the Americans of European stock showed signs of physical and mental degeneration (Curti, *American Loyalty,* p. 66). Cf. above, chap. 3, n. 52; chap. 7, n. 245; and passim.

37. Lowie, op. cit., p. 20, with quotation. At the beginning of this century Frederick Pollock added in a footnote to Maine's *Ancient Law* (London ed., 1906, p. 181): "It is perhaps needless at this day to refute the formerly current opinion that the customs of savages are the result of degradation from a more ancient state of innocence or civilization."

38. J. G. Droysen, *Historik* (Munich-Berlin, 1937), pp. 212–13. Klemm, one of the founders of ethnology, was decidedly pessimistic about the natives in the interior of South America (Lowie, op. cit., pp. 11–16).

39. It is curious however that Morgan, in his anxiety to demolish the idealizations of the Spanish chroniclers, sometimes seems to echo de Pauw, as when he reduces Montezuma's palace to a "joint tenement house of the aboriginal American model, owned by a large number of related families, and occupied by them as joint proprietors" (quoted by R. A. Humphreys, "W. H. Prescott: The Man and the Historian," *Hispanic American Historical Review,* 39, no. 1 [February 1959], p. 12; cf. above, pp. 57 and 394).

40. Lowie, op. cit., pp. 160–69.

lightenment, disappears, transformed into the new theme of biological evolution. The problem of the savage, a historical and philosophical problem, becomes the problem of man, taken in the naturalistic sense, as species or race.

IV. DARWIN: THE SOUTH AMERICAN FAUNA AND THE EVOLUTION OF THE SPECIES

However, when the physical and metaphysical condemnations of America fell on the fertile soil of a critical, original, and constructive mind they showed that they could still bear scientific fruit of surprising freshness.

Take the Buffonian discovery of the inferiority of the American species. When fossil remains of gigantic quadrupeds were found in South America—and of species considerably more numerous than those surviving— yet belonging to creatures clearly related to the small and scattered animals existing in that continent, Charles Darwin, possibly still under the influence of his enthusiastic reading of Humboldt[41] and with his Humboldtian enthusiasm for the exuberant nature of the tropics,[42] suggested an acute revision of Buffon's thesis (1833-34): "He might have said," he noted in the diary of his journey, "with a greater resemblance of truth, that the creative force in America had lost its power, rather than it had never possessed great vigour."[43] Innumerable mastodons, megatheres, and elephants populated the vast spaces of antediluvian America; their bones "tell their story of former times with almost a living tongue."[44] Darwin's curiosity, as is evident also from the letters and diaries of his voyage, was constantly attracted to the remains of large animal fossils in South America.[45]

But how did whole species and indeed whole genera come to disappear? The obvious answer is a catastrophe of some sort. But what a terrifying catastrophe it would have had to be! . . . It would have turned the whole world upside down. And geology does not permit such a theory. Nor can it have been a change in climate: it is definitely known that the great quadrupeds lived in America *after* the Ice Age. Nor can one reasonably

41. See B. Smith, op. cit., pp. 152, 155, 183n., 235. ("Darwin was a great enthusiast for Humboldt and took copies of his works with him to read on the *Beagle*. It was Humboldt who opened Darwin's eyes to the beauties of tropical scenery.") Cf. below, nn. 48, 59.
42. *Charles Darwin and the Voyage of the Beagle*, ed. Nora Barlow (New York, 1946), p. 76.
43. *Journal of Researches into the Natural History and Geology of the Countries visited during the Voyage of H. M. S. Beagle round the world*, more commonly known as the *Voyage of a Naturalist Round the World*, 23 December 1833, vol. I, chap. 8; ed. cit., I, 222–26. The first hints of this train of thought occur in chap. 7, and are dated 5 October 1833: see ibid., I, 166–69. The "loss of vigor" of American nature and the early conjecture about a catastrophe recall de Pauw's pessimism.
44. Barlow, op. cit., p. 96.
45. Ibid., pp. 76, 91, 95–96, 105, 194n., 206–08, 216.

postulate the destructive action of man, nor a severe drought. In any case, the *small* animals would have been exterminated before the larger ones.

Darwin's provisional conclusion is a question mark, with a pregnant confession of ignorance: we know nothing of the conditions of each animal's existence. Nature maintains mysterious checks which prevent the unlimited propagation of the species. The same species can be abundant in one zone, and very thin in another, even though the two zones are exactly similar in their physical conditions. The most stable animal species of Europe have gone wild and multiplied in America.[46] Causes that are in general unfathomable determine the profuseness or.paucity of a given species. So we should not be surprised that species die, just as individuals die. A constant and cumulative action, as yet unknown, but whose results are evident, can produce the same effect as a cataclysm or any other violent factor excogitated without logical necessity.[47]

There are further reminders of the climate of our polemic in the numerous references to the geological newness or recent emersion from the waters of the South American continent,[48] a fleeting mention of voiceless lions ("the lions never roar"),[49] the coldly scientific attention bestowed on the Fuegians and Patagonians,[50] and, perhaps more significantly, the repeated quotations from one of the cassocked gladiators of the dispute, the Jesuit Father Molina.[51]

So Darwin must have been aware of the "slanders" to which America had been subjected. But the notional link with Buffon, who is always mentioned with reverence,[52] is particularly clear in the way he so insistently returns to the problem from which he set out, that of the geographical distribution of the species, and in particular the even more ancient and typical one (see below, pp. 567–68), of the presence of animals similar to those of the mainland in remote archipelagoes, both the Falkland Islands and the Galapagos:[53] "The zoology of Archipelagoes would be worth examining," Darwin noted in 1835, "for such facts would undermine the stability of species"[54] — a sudden flash of lightning on the path

---

46. See Peter Vorzimmer, "Darwin, Malthus and the Theory of Natural Selection," *Journal of the History of Ideas*, 30, no. 4 (October–December 1969), p. 540 (a passage from 1845). Cf., *contra*, above p. 26.

47. *Journal*, ed. cit., I, 222–26.

48. Barlow, op. cit., pp. 96, 110, 117, 228, 233, 238, 245. On his Humboldtian enthusiasm for tropical nature, see Moorehead, op. cit., pp. 51, 55, 57.

49. Ibid., p. 202.

50. Ibid., pp. 80–81 (in the savage in the state of nature "with difficulty we see a fellow creature"), 97, 172 ("innocent, *naked*, most miserable").

51. Ibid., pp. 192, 242. Darwin probably read Molina in Richard Alsop's translation (cf. Barlow, op. cit., p. 269, and above, chap. 5, n. 241).

52. Cf. above, pp. 32–33, and Barlow, op. cit., p. 258.

53. Barlow, op. cit., pp. 177–78, 217, 245, 259. The problem of island animals had already worried Forster, *Werke*, I, 61, 81, 808.

54. Ibid., p. 247. Cf. also Moorehead, op. cit., pp. 187, 202.

that would in time lead to the revolutionary and fundamental theses of twenty-four years later.

Buffon's problem, the problem of the South American fauna, thus directed Darwin toward the most basic exploration of his scientific life. As soon as he returned home, in his first book of notes on the "Mutability of the Species" (1837), Darwin described his observations on the American fossils and the animals of the Galapagos as "the origin of all my views."[55] And the examples and reflections of the *Journal* were taken over almost in their entirety in his major work (1859), only modified so as to exclude that "degeneration" of the animals from *large* to *small* that the earlier works seemed to admit.[56]

This reversal too is present in embryo in the notes of the voyage, which tend to exclude the extinction of a species "by change of circumstances" and boldly suggest "not *gradual* change or degeneration from circumstances; if one species does change into another it must be per saltum — or species may perish."[57] And to think that his friend, the captain of the *Beagle,* and fundamentalist, Robert Fitzroy, continued instead to believe that if the mastodons disappeared from the face of the earth it was because they were too large to enter Noah's ark![58]

In the climate of optimism and evolutionary progress proper to the new times the theory that had once been pursued to the point where it condemned a whole continent to a fatal decadence and corruption was now reversed, and acted as mainstay for a grandiose systematic construction in which all the species, from all the regions of the world, were developing toward ever more perfect forms.

In very much the same way the young Darwin rejected the gloomy pessimism of the Rev. Robert Malthus: in the theory of natural selection the mortal struggle, and unequal contest, between sustenance and proliferation, rather than leading to decadence and the extinction of the species provokes a gradual, permanent, and modificatory adaptation of the same species, and brings about a step forward in Evolution.[59]

V. SCHOPENHAUER: AMERICA'S ANIMALS AND SAVAGES AS DECADENT OR IMPERFECT FORMS

But in the same year that saw the publication of the *Origin of Species,* 1859, Arthur Schopenhauer, with only a short time still to live, added a

55. See *The Origin of Species* (1859), introd. to Modern Library ed. (New York, n.d. but 1936), p. 11; and the article on Darwin in the *Encyclopedia Britannica,* 11th ed.; also Glass, op. cit., p. 260; B. Smith, op. cit., pp. 240–41.

56. *The Origin of Species,* chap. XI, ed. cit., pp. 273–74; and chap. XII, ed. cit., pp. 278 ff.

57. Barlow, op. cit., p. 263.

58. *Times Literary Supplement,* 19 September 1968.

59. See Vorzimmer, op. cit., pp. 527–42, esp. 536–40. On Lyell's influence, ibid.; on Humboldt's, Minguet, op. cit., p. 348.

few more pages to his major work, whose first edition he had published more than forty years earlier. In the chapter added on "Matter" (*Von der Materie*) the old philosopher proved himself convincingly and disastrously behind the times. He refused to accept the evidence of Pasteur's decisive experiments, and favored Pouchet and spontaneous generation. On the subject of Darwin's fundamental problem he had already lent his support to theories that even his own enthusiastic disciples defined as "somewhat puerile" and "mythological."[60] Now he suddenly comes up with Buffon's "discovery," found heaven knows where, and uses it just as his archenemy Hegel had done, to fill in and plaster over one of the most evident flaws in his system.

For Schopenhauer nature is of course the objectivization of the will to live. The will to live is one and eternal. How then can we explain the variety of the species? Even for our own little planet he finds himself forced to admit that "the will to live has run the gamut of its objectivization three times, in three series independent one of another." In fact, he goes on, everyone knows that the Old World, America, and Australia each have their own particular series of animal species, detached and completely different from those of the other two zones. Only the genera are the same, usually, because we are all on the same planet.

This relationship is particularly evident in the comparison between America and the Old World:

America always shows us the inferior analogue [*das schlechtere Analogon*] in regard to the mammals, and in compensation the superior analogue in regard to the birds and reptiles. Thus it doubtless has the advantage of possessing the condor, the macaws, the hummingbirds and the great batrachians and Ophidia; but instead of the elephant, for example, it has only the tapir, instead of the lion the cougar, instead of the tiger the jaguar, instead of the camel the llama, and instead of the monkeys proper it has only the Barbary apes.

From this Schopenhauer concludes that it is inadmissible that nature could have created man in America. Only three races are *primitive:* the Caucasian, the Ethiopian, and the Mongolian—all three belonging to the Old World. The Americans are climatically modified Mongolians.[61] In

---

60. Hans Herrig, *Schopenhauer und Darwin* (1872), in *Gesammelte Aufsaetze ueber Schopenhauer,* ed. Grisebach, Leipzig (Reclam 3187), pp. 42–72; see esp. p. 52. No less curious are his etymological lucubrations on "Coluber" and "Kolibri," on the name Atlantis found in the Mexican ending "atlan," and that of Mount Soraktes, of Horatian memory ("Italian Sorate," Schopenhauer goes on), which *is* the same as Sorata in Peru! (*Parerga und Paralipomena,* chap. 25; Insel ed., V, 629–30). Leaving aside the fact that the Sorata massif belongs to Bolivia, a considerably more entertaining practitioner of this sort of attempt to link America's physical reality to the memories of classical geography was the fanatical Mexican Mier (see above, pp. 312–15), who on finding himself before Vesuvius noted delightedly that the Neapolitans called it *Montezuma* (*Monte Somma*)! (*Memorias,* p. 282).

61. A. Schopenhauer, *Die Welt,* supplements, chap. 24; Insel ed., II, 1061–63; French trans., A. Burdeau (Paris, 1896), III, 124–26. Like Hegel before him Schopenhauer promptly sets aside Australia as a country too poor in fauna to pursue in the analogy. Cf. A. O. Lovejoy, "Schopenhauer as an Evolutionist" (1911), reprinted in Glass, op. cit., pp. 415–37, esp. 428.

short the will to live, on its objectivization in the Western Hemisphere, felt itself very serpentine and very avian, not very mammiferous and not at all human.

Schopenhauer produces similar mythologies, in the *Parerga und Paralipomena*, to explain the varieties of the animal and the vegetable species in the different climatic regions of the globe. Of America he laments only its lack of tailless monkeys and anthropoids, which he sees as further confirmation of his theory on the origin of man. Man appeared on the earth in the tropical zone of the Old World. The only true and primigenial race is thus the black or dark brown race. The yellow and white races, the Mongolians and the Caucasians, are in reality only faded and washed out Blacks or Ethiopians. The Americans are Chinese who migrated to the Western Hemisphere and are thus not as dark as they should be.

The savages of the Brazilian forest are dark brown, true. Schopenhauer almost seems inclined to consider them therefore as primitive and autochthonous men, or at least to let his reader so conclude from his chromatic racial premises. But in a footnote of strongly de Pauwian or de Maistrean flavor he deprives even the obscure Brazilian savages of this privilege:

The savages are not primitive men [*Urmenschen*], just as the wild dogs of South America are not protodogs [*Urhunde*]; but the dogs are dogs that have gone wild, and the men are men that have gone savage, descendants of men of some civilized race, strayed or shunted down there, and who were not capable of maintaining their civilization.[62]

So alas, the white and the yellow are degenerations of the black: a white complexion is an unnatural degeneration ("die weisse Gesichtsfarbe eine Ausartung . . . unnatürlich"). The black savage is a degeneration of the yellow. The white is driven to civilization by his organic decadence. The savage is rejected by civilization when he returns to the maternal bosom of tropical nature. This endless circle of malediction reflects the antihistorical premises of Schopenhauer's philosophy. His rigorous exclusion of any sort of progress induces him to define each race as a degenerative form of another. Reality is decadence. So the old eighteenth-century theses, surviving the romantic revolution intact, serve to endow his cosmic pessimism with some sort of scientific appearance.

Schopenhauer's brutal description of the United States is not directly

---

62. *Parerga und Paralipomena*, II, *Vereinzelte, jedoch systematisch geordnete Gedanken über vielerlei Gegenstände*, chap. VI ("Zur Philosophie und Wissenschaft der Natur"), sec. 92, Insel ed., V, 180–85; and *Die Welt*, pt. II, chap. 44 (Insel ed., II, 1344; Fr. trans., III, 358–59). On the savages, who lead a life scarcely a step higher than the monkeys', see also *Parerga*, chap. 26, sec. 333; ed. cit., V, 648. Schopenhauer's lasting sympathy for the black slaves in the United States (see also Insel ed., III, 253n., 625; V, 228), and his profound admiration for Indian philosophy (the Hindus are for him "dark brown," almost black) are obviously linked to his racial theory. Cf. Hegel, above, p. 433.

connected to these Buffonian corollaries and variations, but is perfectly in tune with their fundamental premises. The republic's political constitution is based on pure and abstract juridicality: it would be fine for any other creatures than men, who are for the most part egotistical, bullying, untruthful, wicked, and largely witless. Look at what in fact happened: the country is materially prosperous, but its predominant tone is a base utilitarianism, with its ever-present companion, ignorance, leaving the way open for stupid Anglican bigotry, foolish conceit, and brutal vulgarity, together with an idiotic veneration of women.

Nor is Schopenhauer content with these broad sweeps of the brush: he recalls the horrors of slavery, the discrimination against Negroes, the lynch law, the hired murderers who often go unpunished, the unbelievably savage duels, the bold-faced disregard of law and order, the repudiation of public debts, the scandalous political trickery (*politische Eskrokerie*) of a neighboring province and the subsequent thieving raids into the neighbor's rich territory, which are later justified by the supreme authority with lies that everybody knows and ridicules as such (an allusion to the Mexican War, 1846–48), the ever-growing ochlocracy and the deleterious influence on private morality of the public disregard of the law. . . . Then as for the "imitations" of the North American republic in Mexico, Guatemala, Colombia, and Peru—they do not even bear talking about![63] All America is rotten with hypocritical legalism.

All exaggerations, true: but how often repeated in later years, in the most widely differing accents, and linked in how many subtle ways to the summary condemnations of the putrid and harmful nature of the continent! And, we might add, how hopelessly outdated by this time in relation to the objective knowledge of the New World and its twenty republics!

VI. THE SAINT-SIMONIANS AND AUGUSTE COMTE

In the theocrats and early Saint-Simonians, in Michel Chevalier for example, there are in fact already signs of a new attitude toward America, and particularly toward the United States, whose ever-expanding image tended to obliterate the other lands and nations of the continent. America is characterized by the application of the most modern techniques to limitless spaces; Europe's accumulated heritage can be applied even more productively in a land so vast and empty. The question of merit or superiority no longer arises: it is agreed that the untapped resources of the New World, exploited with the experience and machines of the Old World,

---

63. *Parerga*, chap. IX, sec. 127: Insel ed., V, 274; cf. ibid., chap. VIII, sec. 117: ed. cit., V, 248 (the Americans are descendants of an English penal colony), and chap. XXI, sec. 252, ed. cit., V, 528 (egoism in the Mexican republic).

guarantee these countries a continuing and formidable progress. Attention is no longer focused exclusively on the political institutions, which had so much interested men like Volney and Tocqueville, but on the relationship between prices and costs, the statistics of iron consumption, navigation on the Mississippi, the canals and locomotives, mines and plantations.

This rapid assimilation of the industrial revolution made the process of absorption of European culture and customs seem correspondingly slower: the crudeness of American manners was described and caricatured by such writers as Mrs. Trollope and Charles Dickens, and in fact by almost all the travelers *emunctae naris*. But their disdain for the social life of the United States no longer leans on inflexible laws of nature, nor is it enriched by fatuous references to degeneration. Indeed, the rough manners and vigorous economic development combine to form a picture of promising barbarity, a good omen underlined with innumerable curses. In a certain way these criticisms too thus contributed to the immunization of America against fatal condemnations and lethal slanders.

It is surprising then to find that an author belonging to this intellectual current, the direct disciple of Saint-Simon, Auguste Comte, rebels against it and pronounces verdicts of de Maistrean harshness on America and the United States. Comte was in fact a great admirer of the illustrious de Maistre and his theologizing rigor; and somehow managed to integrate de Maistre's theories on the philosophy of history with those of no less a person than Bossuet. His system, secular in intention, is totally biblico-Catholic in structure and intellectual reference. Thus, despite a brief youthful flirtation,[64] America for Auguste Comte, from its savages to the federal republic, from the atheists to the Protestants, could only be a source of annoyance or indifference.

The reliance on a Catholic philosophy of history, frequent enough in the *Cours,* becomes even more so in the *Système de politique positive,* and the other works of his old age. Of particular interest is Comte's letter to his American apostle John Metcalf, of New York, urging him to solidify the "spontaneous" alliance of Catholics and positivists against the Protestants, and for this purpose to maintain "special contacts" with the American Jesuits—whom Comte rebaptizes "Ignatians," to free them "from a name as harmful in itself as it is generally discredited."[65]

As is well known, Comte states openly from the *Cours* onward that his study will not cover the whole human race. His interest is confined to the more evolved populations, "to the elite or avant-garde of humanity," excluding "with scrupulous perseverance" each and every "digression" on the centers of civilization which for one reason or an-

---

64. See Remond, op. cit., pp. 641, 682 n. 23.
65. *Système de politique positive,* in *A. Comte conservateur* (Paris, 1898), pp. 255–56, 277–78.

other have remained at an imperfect stage. In practice, as he admits, that means restricting himself to the white race in Western Europe, and ignoring the intellectuals' frivolous curiosity about India, China, etc., and coming back to the fundamental scheme established by that "great genius, Bossuet."[66]

But he does not even manage to include the whole historical reality of the Christian West. Out-bossueting Bossuet, Comte begins by reducing and compressing it into five great nations, France, England, Germany, Spain, and Italy;[67] and then, anxious for sociological uniformities, he throws out as insignificant all their "exceptional events or all the too minor details, so childishly pursued by the irrational curiosity of the blind compilers of sterile anecdotes," and aspires to the ideal of "a history without names of men or even names of peoples,"[68] a pure mechanism of conceptual abstractions.

On his own account, finally, Comte proceeds to other reductions, and in the very middle of his philosophy of history boasts "I have never read, in any language, either Vico, Kant, Hegel, or Herder, etc." He is convinced in fact that "this voluntary negligence has contributed much to the purity and harmony of my social philosophy." Now however that this philosophy is irrevocably formed, and he need no longer worry about contaminating influences, Comte sets himself a new task: "to learn, shortly, in my own way, the German language," so as to see how far the German systematizers agree with him.[69]

To a mind so proudly egocentric, and only by condescension limitedly Europeocentric,[70] the problems of the Americans were bound to remain

66. *Cours de philosophie positive,* 2d ed. (Paris, 1864), V, 7–8. The *cours* was given for the first time in 1826, with Humboldt among its listeners (I, 3). Vol. I was written in 1830, II in 1834–35, III in 1835–37, IV in 1838, V in 1840–41, and VI in 1842. Bossuet is also mentioned and praised in V, 31, 187–88, 306, 418 ("the most powerful mind of modern times, after Descartes and Leibnitz"), 458–59; VI, 257–58, 260, etc. The "illustrious" de Maistre is mentioned by Comte fairly frequently, for example on IV, 34, 64, 135n., 138n. (with ample acknowledgment), 352; V, 95, 149, 250, 256, 284–85, 306; VI, 129n., 348n., 401. See Hans Barth, "Die Theologie Joseph de Maistres als Urbild der Soziologie von Auguste Comte," *Neue Zürcher Zeitung,* 4 August 1956.

67. But sometimes the United States is thrown in with England (see below, p. 463).

68. *Cours,* V, 12, 14; VI, 534. Cf., *contra,* Humboldt's impartial interest (above, pp. 415–16). The sophistical absurdity of these limits is well caught by Faguet, *Politiques et moralistes,* II, 356–57.

69. *Cours,* VI, 34–35n. On his ignorance of German philosophy, see R. Flint, *Historical Philosophy in France . . .* (Edinburgh, 1893), pp. 582–83. It is known that even before completing his *Cours* Comte, confident of having sufficient material by then at his disposition, decided to read no more newspapers or reviews or scientific acts, but only two or three poets (including Dante) and the *Imitation of Christ* (see Morley's very fine article in the *Encyclopedia Britannica,* 11th ed.). Rigidly consistent in this too, he even abstained from rereading his own works (which he wrote out at great speed, making almost no corrections). It is curious to note his reaction on rereading after an interval of fifteen years (1842–57) "the best part of the *Philosophie positive,*" in other words the chapters on the philosophy of history: "Apart from their moral dryness, which immediately sent me to read a canto of Ariosto to revive myself, I was profoundly struck by their mental inferiority, in comparison with the true point of my philosophy where my heart has fully established me" (*A. Comte conservateur,* ed. cit., p. 293).

70. The destiny of the world should be entrusted to a Comité Positif Occidental of 30 members (8 Frenchmen, 7 Englishmen, 6 Italians, 5 Germans, 4 Spaniards): "Moreover this committee would naturally have its seat in Paris" (ibid., VI, 544n.). On these anachronistic claims to "French hegemony in the coming utopia," see R. Niebuhr, op. cit., p. 59.

closed with seven seals. On the climate and animal variations Comte obstinately refuses to accept Montesquieu and Buffon (just as in historiography, for that matter, he rejects the achievements of Voltaire): the former because he exaggerated the environment's social influence, the latter its biological influence.[71] The species, both animal and vegetable, are substantially fixed and invariable, all of them, even those domesticated in Europe and taken thence to America. Buffon was a great man, but he would have done better to follow the teachings and rigid classifications of Linnaeus.[72] As for the savages, whom he considers as useful comparative material for studying the phases of the history of society,[73] Comte repeats Robertson's summary verdicts: they are greedy, feebly erotic, improvident, indomitably opposed to all regular labor, devoid of religion, and gloomily sad.[74] Of the winning of independence on the part of the provinces of Spanish America, he confines himself to the sybilline comment that these wars of liberation (which were of course encouraged by the shrewd politicians in London) were a manifestation of "the natural antipathy of the Catholic peoples toward a Protestant or rather British policy."[75] And his comments on the North American Union echo the sad forecasts of de Maistre. The American Revolution brought the world no new principle: in essence it was only a "simple extension" of the other two Protestant revolutions: of the Dutch in its beginnings, of the English in its final results. And where did it lead?

To the complete political supremacy of the metaphysicians and legists being more firmly established than anywhere else, among a population where innumerable incoherent cults consistently exact a tribute (that has no real social destination) much superior to the present budget of any Catholic clergy.[76]

The future of the United States is thus obscure. Although it enjoys considerable temporal advantages, this "universal colony" is in fact

71. *Cours*, VI, 237–38: Montesquieu's instinct, to make the course of political events subject to natural laws, was sound, but his attempt failed because it was premature (i.e., because there was as yet no *philosophie positive*): IV, 178–85, 320–21; VI, 264.

72. Ibid., III, 395–96; on Lamarck's theories, ibid., III, 430–32; IV, 276–77; on the modifications to the domestic animals, see also III, 581–82. Note how Comte, working as an apologist in reverse, defends Linnaeus against Buffon, and Buffon against Cuvier (ibid., VI, 381, 579).

73. Comte thus makes clear the element of sound historicism contained in the eighteenth century's preoccupation with the savage: a need was felt to remove the too exiguous limit of five or six thousand years of recorded history, and at the same time to demolish the biblical chronology; the peoples without history were scrutinized for the first glimmerings of a complete and organic history of the human race, that could not be gleaned from the accessible texts and monuments.

74. Ibid., IV, 318, 444–46, 505–06; V, 27. Robertson is cited and warmly praised on V, 158; VI, 64.

75. *Système de politique positive*, III (1853), in *Auguste Comte conservateur*, p. 186.

76. *Cours*, V, 470–71. On the proliferation and intolerance of the Protestant sects in the United States, ibid., IV, 51, 94; V, 486; VI, 344. Comte's philo-Catholicism leads him to illustrate – as Humboldt had already done, for that matter (Bruhns, op. cit., II, 294) – the more humanitarian treatment of the slaves in Hispano-Catholic America than in Anglo-Protestant America (V, 242, 287), although he severely condemns the Spanish colonial system, with its slaughter and oppression (ibid., VI, 129–32).

much farther away from a real social reorganization than the peoples from which it emanates,[77] and through which it will, in due time, have to receive this final regeneration, whose philosophical initiative could not possibly come from within the colony.

One's mind goes inevitably back to the reactionaries who advised America to wait until she was a little more grown up, and meanwhile denied her any spiritual meaning or message. But Comte advances boldly to denounce

the childishly illusory claims of political superiority for a society where the various essential elements proper to modern civilization are still so imperfectly developed, saving only industrial activity.[78]

At most the United States can be considered, together with Scotland and Ireland, as a natural appendage of England; in fact its civilization,

basically devoid of originality, is no more than a simple direct expansion of the English civilization, modified by local and social circumstances, especially before the present century.[79]

The same notion figures in the previously mentioned instructions imparted (1857) by Comte to his American disciple John Metcalf, for accelerating the conversion of the American proletariat to positivism. It is first of all vital to separate them "carefully . . . from all European Intruders, not excepting even the best of them." Leaving just the redskins and their descendants, right? No, the apostle will have to discern "within the bosom of the Yankee population, the true descendants of the worthy collaborators of the great Cromwell, who preferred to emigrate to America in their thousands rather than submit to the British monarchy." But the fact is that the bulk of the Puritans emigrated to America between 1629 and 1640, or before Cromwell's protectorate. Thus for Comte the elite of the North American population is composed not of the Daughters of the Revolution or the descendants of the Pilgrim Fathers, but of that handful of Presbyterians who left England after the Restoration?!

In any case, they are the exclusive material that Metcalf is to work on. They are inert and passive? No matter: "It is morally impossible that this noble race can ever have abandoned their social aspirations, the sort that one does not renounce until they are satisfied." They are re-

---

77. An echo of Volney? See above, p. 340. The United States would be substantially "older" than the single nations from which it drew its population.

78. Ibid., V, 471, with a promise of development "in the following chapter," which remains unfulfilled. On the slight or nonexistent influence of the American Revolution on the French, see also VI, 283–84. One might remember that in his youth Comte was dissuaded from going to the United States by a friend who warned him against the mercantile spirit of that nation: "If Lagrange came to this country, he would not be able to earn his living as a land surveyor" (J. Morley, in *Encyclopedia Britannica*, 11th ed., s.v. "Comte"). This was in fact to be Thoreau's professional destiny.

79. *Cours*, VI, 60n.

sponsible for the successful outcome of the war of independence, but after that they took no further part in American politics: "Having then returned to their purely industrial activity, they await a systematic doctrine capable of realizing the spontaneous program of the Cromwellians." It will suffice to present them with positivism as the doctrine they are waiting for, as the fulfillment of their political and religious aspirations — and the die will be cast.[80] Under Cromwell's shadow Comte's ideas will infiltrate the ranks of the American proletariat.

A single doubt remains — what of the alliance with the Catholics? Relations between Puritans and Jesuits have never been very cordial. How are the positivists going to use both of them? Is it not actually more likely, just to take an extreme hypothesis, that Cromwellians and Ignatians are going to make a combined assault on the verbose and systematic apostles of Universal Religion? The social regeneration of the New World faces new and serious risks.

VII. EDGAR QUINET: THE INSULARITY OF AMERICA AND THE TRIUMPH OF THE HUMBLEST CREATURES

As a young man Edgar Quinet had translated Herder's *Ideas,* and absorbed the more "American" parts of Chateaubriand.[81] And following in Chateaubriand's footsteps, and in singular anticipation of Comte, had had a vision of the possible palingenesis of Christianity (or at least religiosity) in the Americas; "only recently emerged from the waters of the flood," the new continent will shake itself free from the decrepit arms of a ruined society, and will carry mankind to loftier destinies and the ecstatic vision of God.[82] Later in life, during the long years of exile, Quinet read Schopenhauer and Emerson, and nourished himself on Darwin. His last great work, the *Creation* (1870), is an introduction to the philosophy of universal history written in the poeticoprophetic style of Herder, but in the spirit of evolutionism, while its resolute faith in the revelations of the most positive science set its author in the logical sphere of the followers of Auguste Comte.

Quinet reaches the conclusion that history and nature are woven into a single harmonized tissue. And only the laws of nature can give us the key to the secrets of history. Geology illustrates the events of recent centuries. Our destiny is written in the Jurassic.

80. *Auguste Comte conservateur,* pp. 304–05. Note that despite his merciless criticism Auguste Comte earned an extraordinary reputation and lasting popularity throughout the American continent (Whitaker, *The Western Hemisphere Idea,* p. 64); and the coat of arms of Brazil is adorned with his device "Order and Progress," but actually in the United States his influence was almost nil (Whitaker, in Hanke, ed., *Common History,* p. 162).

81. Cf. *Une lecture des Mémoires de M. de Chateaubriand* (1834), in *Allemagne et Italie* (Brussels, 1839), II, 28–69, esp. 29–31, 54–59.

82. *De l'avenir de la religion* (1831), in *Allemagne et Italie,* II, 25–27.

Such yearnings after unity and universality are always dangerous for a simple understanding of the differences that meet our gaze. And even more dangerous when they make their appearance in a poetic and mystic temperament, providing it with a pseudotheoretical, fictitiously logical foundation for its inflamed and passionate flights of fancy. Attention shifts away from the individual characteristics of the single creatures, which are "explained" and "leveled out" in grandiose *laws* just too beautifully uniform.

In Quinet—limiting ourselves of course to his ideas on America[83] —this ardent desire for synthesis leads him to nothing less than the re-discovery of the discoveries of Buffon.

America's fauna belongs to the type that he has called "insular."[84] The large land mammals cannot develop on islands. No large mammal is autochthonous to an island. And this explains the relative inferiority of America's animals. When the islands fused into one, the small toothless marsupials originating in Guiana and Brazil grew to the stature of the megathere and spread throughout the continent.[85] In the Tertiary period the two hemispheres came together. And the mammoth and mastodon wandered over both. Once they were separated, those great beasts "which were not indigenous to America, being separated from the mother stock, disappeared." They disappeared, Quinet explains, like "a tree separated from its roots, or a river from its source."

In just the same way (*de la même manière*) we can explain "this extraordinary fact of the smallness of the American mammals." South America in fact was once "an oblong island." When the Andes lifted, a second great island emerged. It was then that "the South American fauna took on the insular type," the indigenous type, the type that survived the invasion of the great European quadrupeds and their extinction after the rupture of the two continents.

And there is more yet. The insular type left its mark also on the habits of the American mammals, which is why they are so domestic and sedentary. "With them we do not find the cosmopolitan instinct, the migratory habits" of other animals like the Bengal tigers, that push up as

83. On Quinet in general, see the brilliant study by Faguet, *Politiques et moralistes,* II, 175–227 (on the *Création* in particular, pp. 206 ff.).

84. *La Création* (in *Oeuvres complètes,* XXII–XXIII), Paris, n.d., I, 187. "Insular" corresponds to Jurassic (ibid., I, 142–48); but "the Tertiary flora and fauna have left their principal traits in the fauna and flora of contemporary America" (ibid., I, 170). In short Quinet would seem to assign to America a Jurassic fauna and a Tertiary flora, which when the geological terminology is translated into everyday terms is equivalent to restating the old antithesis between a meager fauna and an exuberant flora. This concern of his over the "insular fauna" already had a long history too (see below, chap. 9, sec. 1, "The Originality of Buffon").

85. Ibid., I, 188–89, 277. These zoogeological metaphors and parallels, including the example of the gigantic edentates of the pampas, had a curious and belated revival in the *Meditations* of Keyserling (on which see below, p. 560: *Südamerikanische Meditationen,* p. 20, etc.).

far as Siberia. The larger animals of America are quite content to ramble over the pampas "without leaving the basins where they were born." They still observe the invisible terrestrial limits of the "islands" of their birth.

In any case, Quinet goes on, the Americas are still a system of islands today. Situated in the middle of the oceans, almost separated in the middle by the isthmus of Panama, partitioned by the spinal column of the Cordilleras and gigantic rivers, they form in fact an archipelago, and the "insular type" has been perpetuated in the fauna, with its reduced dimensions and degenerate or archaic types. Elephants, camels, apes, and giraffes disappear "in favor of the reptiles, who alone have maintained their size, and strength, such as the snakes, boas, caymans, and alligators." The snakes are in fact the fauna proper to the islands, just as the larger mammals belong to the large continents and the small mammals to the continents "of lesser extent." In America the quadrupeds shrink and lose their strength, their milk, and their wool, but the reptiles and the insects retain such dimensions that they bring to mind the secondary (or Jurassic) age "where reptiles were the kings of the insular world."

Man is an exception (as he was for Buffon) because he moves from one island to another, and if an isthmus disappears he can still use his ships to repair "the ruins of the World, for his own advantage."

But after so many Buffonian derivations one is amazed to find Quinet imagining that he was the first to discover the corollary "that the quadruped mammals taken to America today must become smaller there." He reached the point, he writes, by pure deduction, "without knowing if it ["this strange fact"] was really confirmed by experience." And when he learns that it is in fact so, he tells us about it in a voice so bursting with jubilation and candor that we are tempted to an irreverent smile:

The simple confirmation of this phenomenon caused me a heartfelt joy . . . this phenomenon . . . reveals itself to my eyes like the star whose necessary existence the astronomer had first arrived at with his calculations, and which finally appeared in reality at the end [sic!] of his telescope. That day I really tasted the joy of truth anticipated and confirmed. It must count as a great day for me: it is October 11, 1867.

Albo signanda lapillo! — a real red-letter day.

Encouraged thus by his first speculative success, Quinet pushes on and prophesies that the European animals introduced into Australia, the sheep for instance, will also diminish in stature and strength;[86] and in a

---

86. The example was a most unhappy choice. The sheep had already been acclimatized in Australia, and this country was one of the major wool producers of the world. In 1851 there were 17.3 million sheep, and by 1860 20 million, which despite Quinet's theories grew to more than 100 million by 1891 and to about 165 million today. The production of wool per head, which was initially 3½ to 4 lbs., increased to more than 11 lbs., and fleeces of 30 or 40 lbs. are not uncommon. Quinet might have remembered that Chateaubriand had already admired the sheep in Australia: "The pure merinos in particular have become of a rare beauty there" (Voyage en Amérique, p. 29; Switzer ed., I, 45–46).

footnote he adds the recent confirmations (1868) of Darwin, Dr. Roulin, and Andrew Murray. But in the text, on the very next page after the announcement of his discovery, he admits that "Buffon had noted the shrinking of the great quadrupeds in America"; yes, but he had not been able to explain it! He had spoken of nature being neglected by men, while these great beasts existed in America long before man![87]

Man, the highest of all creatures, originated in the Old World: he must have been born where the great continental masses are found. Only lower animals thrive on islands. It is a logical corollary of Quinet's ideas, on the other hand (and some small solace to his republican feelings), that migration from the "continent" to the "island," the influx of peoples of all races into America, confers on the continent "a power of increase and a social fecundity which astonishes the world." A hundred million men are there molded into a new order merely by Nature's immensity.[88]

From all these comparisons of insular and continental, unimpressive and imposing faunas, it becomes clear that Quinet too, like Buffon, considers the large animals to be preferable to the small. In point of fact his reasons seem somewhat utilitarian (more wool, more meat, more milk), in keeping with the mercantile spirit of his times, rather than aesthetic, philosophical, and hierarchical, like Buffon's. Indeed, we cannot suppose for one moment that the republican Quinet wanted to establish such a radical inequality between the creatures. His sympathies are instinctively with the mean and lowly. The systems which "believe only in the power of the giants" are false. "Nature's first lesson to Man is that the infinitely small is equal in power to the infinitely large." Nature does not depend on the colossi, the leviathans, the behemoths, but on the imperceptible microorganisms. The weakest and most defenseless creatures have outlived all their enemies and all ages. Series of cosmic cataclyms could not annihilate them, "so that it is true that the small is the equal of the large, that he is at least his ancestor and almost always outlives him."[89]

Buffon too, we remember (see above, pp. 10–11), noted the indestructibility of the inferior species, but with a certain aristocratic shudder of horror at the pervasive swarms of these baser creatures. Edgar Quinet, democrat and evolutionist, sees in the myriads of protozoa instead the basis of all nature and the key to its mysteries. Buffon, ever mindful of the thinly scattered natives, had described a barren and poverty-stricken

---

87. *La Création*, I, 268–80 (cf. the beatific pride of the "Préface"). Quinet believes America to be older than the Old World (I, 270).

88. Op. cit., II, 303–04. Quinet's heartfelt sympathy for all the free republics of America, of both North and South, kindles the fiery eloquence of his anti-Napoleonic pamphlet, *L'expédition du Mexique* (1862).

89. *La Création*, I, 105–07. Nature attaches no importance to dimensions: ibid., I, 120. One whole chapter (I, 7–12) is devoted to the thesis: "the large explained by the small": the imperceptible Foraminifera possess the secret of the proud mountains, etc.

America. Quinet sees it raised to undreamed-of heights by the waves of immigrants arriving in their millions. The *Creation* offers us thus one more example of the persistent vitality and extraordinary adaptability not of some ordinary protozoon, but of the ancient thesis of America's weakness.

VIII. BRITISH CRITICISMS OF AMERICAN SOCIETY: FRANCES WRIGHT AND MRS. TROLLOPE

The echoes of the aging debate lasted until well after the middle of the century, becoming less clear, maybe, but even more vociferous and persistent, and equally evident in the opinions pronounced by the English on American society and the offended or enraged reactions of the Anglo-Americans. The naturalistic and biological themes recede ever further into the background, to be replaced by increasingly substantial and insistent social and political notions, criticisms of the young nation's way of life, its prejudices, its own special arrogance, and constitutional defects. As Talleyrand had already observed prophetically (1794): "It will take a whole generation and a new reign for the Englishman to look on the American as his equal."[90] The more thoughtful Europeans—an American liberal, Charles J. Ingersoll, noted bitterly in 1810—admit that the Revolution was a glorious happening and the rebels showed splendid gifts of energy and heroism, but they presume that they must have since become flabby in thirty years of peace and prosperity: "An expansion of population, of resources, of territory, of power, of information, of freedom, is supposed to have degenerated the Americans. Is this the course of Nature?"[91] And with this interpretation *ex absurdo* of what nature does and does not do, Ingersoll arrives at a proud and vigorous North American nationalism.

There is somewhat less passion and less irony in the comment of another American, Washington Irving, who betook himself to Europe among other reasons for the purpose of meeting some really great men, greater than those he had met by the cartload in America, "for I had read in the works of various philosophers, that all animals degenerated

---

90. Poniatowski, op. cit., p. 206.

91. Charles J. Ingersoll, *Inchiquin, the Jesuit's Letters . . . Containing a Favourable View of the Manners, Literature, and State of Society, of the United States* (New York, 1810), in Tryon, op. cit., pp. 22–23, 785. In the curious fiction invented by Ingersoll, who attributes his work to an unknown Jesuit, one seems to catch a distant echo of those energetic defenses of the American Jesuits against the Europeans' accusations of "degeneration." Ingersoll was quite familiar with Buffon's and Raynal's insulting theories and the abrasive criticisms of the early English travelers, and marveled that they had survived so many repudiations (see Martin, op. cit., p. 202, Curti, *Probing Our Past*, p. 194, and Fabian, op. cit., p. 8n.). For too long, he writes, "the soil of this enviable country has been represented in Europe as parsimonious and abortive; the climate as froward and pernicious; the creatures as stunted, stupid, and debased below their species; the manners, principles, and government, as suited to this universal depravity. These absurdities appeared engraved with the stamp of knowledge and authority; their circulation was general and accredited" (Tryon, op. cit., p. 28).

in America, and man among the number." The geniuses of Europe must tower over those of America like the Alpine peaks over the Hudson plains. Away then, he thought, and let us visit "this land of wonders . . . and see the gigantic race from which I am degenerated."[92]

On the opposite shore of the Atlantic, on the other hand, the preconception of an essential inferiority of the New World never completely disappears, not even when the European limits his vision to the United States alone, ignoring Latin America, and excluding even Canada from all reproof. Thus new elements come into play, superimposed on the age-old themes, and combine with them, however incongruous the assortment, to form corrosive and virulent amalgams: humanitarian zeal, national pride, moral rectitude, and the cult of good manners, the hallmarks of the Victorian era, find easy and enjoyable outlet in the criticism of a country that legitimizes slavery, tolerates spitting on the ground or on the carpet, derides old England, rejoices in any sort of violence, and seems to take perverse pleasure in parading its lack of breeding.

The democratic and egalitarian republic had yet another grievous fault in the eyes of English writers: it did not recognize British copyright, and never paid a penny for the piratical reprints of any book that was successful.[93]

Not that there was a total lack of English writers benevolently disposed toward America. But the diminishing current was so strong that it dragged democrats and conservatives along with it, and turned even an impassioned admirer of the United States like Frances Wright into the unconscious instrument or ironic occasion of the American adventure of Frances Trollope, the most notorious vivisectionist of transatlantic society.

In Frances Wright (born 1795) the enthusiasm for the United States,

---

92. Washington Irving, "The Author's Account of Himself," in *The Sketch-Book*, 1819, ed. Paris, 1846, pp. 2–3, where there is also a gibe at the English travelers, who are insignificant people in their own country and yet look down on the inhabitants of the United States: cf. below, n. 133. Other contemporary comments on the English writers' anti-Americanism in Löwenstern, op. cit., pp. vi, 60, 121–22.

93. On the question of copyright, which caused Dickens so much anguish, cf. already B. Hall, *Travels*, II, 355 ff.; idem, *Voyage dans les Etats-Unis de l'Amérique du Nord . . .* (1829; Brussels, 1835), II, 5–8; Thomas Hamilton, *Men and Manners in America* (Edinburgh, 1833), I, 371; H. Martineau, *De la société américaine*, trans. B. Laroche (Bruxelles, 1838), III, 198; idem, *Retrospect of Western Travel* (London, 1838), II, 10, 236; Frederick Marryat, *A Diary in America* (Paris, 1839), II, 77–85; Florence Marryat, *Life and letters of Capt. Marryat* (Leipzig, 1872), pp. 165 ff.; H. Allen, *Israfel: The Life and Times of Edgar Allan Poe* (New York, 1926), II, 497–503, 521–22; U. Pope-Hennessy, *Charles Dickens* (London, 1945), pp. 73–74, 159–61, 164–65, 167–68, 171, 174, 179–81. Even the *Notes* of the American Jefferson, as his London publisher bitterly complained, were immediately reprinted in a pirated edition in Philadelphia (*Papers*, XI, 677; XII, 35, 73, 116). Add to that the fact that precisely around 1840 thanks to technical advances "prices for novels fell from two or three dollars to as little as fifty cents or even a quarter" (Wish, *Early America*, p. 453). The American law was reformed only in 1891, but even today the protection it provides is held to be insufficient (*New York Times*, "Topics," 19 January 1954; *The Times* [London], 23 October 1954; letters of David Daiches and T. Besterman to the *Times Literary Supplement*, 25 September 1970, p. 1094, and 2 October 1970, p. 1134).

its political institutions, and its way of life, was the result of a conventional but by no means sterile adoration of classical antiquity, as it appeared in its traditional image, austerely republican. Miss Wright was rich, a proud, solemn, very good-looking woman, Graeco-Roman in both appearance and upbringing, and a liberal by family tradition (her father, a friend of Adam Smith and Jeremy Bentham, had distributed Thomas Paine's *Rights of Man* and "French" or "subversive" political writings in Dundee, and a second "adoptive" father was to be sought fanatically by the young lady in Lafayette) — who at the age of eighteen wrote a defense of Epicurean philosophy and at twenty read (in Italian) Botta's *History of the War of Independence of the United States* (1809).

The effect was remarkable. To us Botta's writings may seem deathly cold. But, one might say, *nullus est liber tam frigidus, ut non animulam inflammatur.* And in our own review too we have seen cases of perfect pedants fulfilling a revolutionary function. Botta's icy work, which in its English version of 1820 was immediately greeted enthusiastically by John Adams and Thomas Jefferson, and accepted by Americans of all parties as the best guide on the history of the Revolution,[94] seems to have preserved and handed down, deep-frozen as it were, an experience that the fervent Miss Wright took to her bosom, thawed out within her ardent soul, to the point where she felt this experience to be completely and terribly her own, to the point of martyrdom, and, alas, apostolate. And it was possibly the very thing that seemed to Jefferson (as it seems to us) the major defect in Botta's work, the rhetorical device of giving his characters reconstructed or invented speeches, that fascinated the talkative Miss Frances who, her biographers tell us,[95] to assure herself that her political neoclassical ideal was really and recently incarnate on this earth, looked in her atlas to see whether this mythical country of the United States really existed.

To see for herself with her own eyes she crossed the ocean in 1818, and having spent a couple of years in the new republic published (in 1821) her *Views of Society and Manners in America,* her only extant work, although she was such an indefatigable propagandist and lecturer. In fact she did not really need to write any more, since she remained dedicated to the American ideal throughout her life, which she devoted to humanitarian causes, such as abolitionism, the redemption of the Negroes, votes for women, the reform of the institution of matrimony and of the relations between the sexes, and the diffusion of the socialist ideas of Robert Owen.

In America she sought to attract the venerable Lafayette, and to Amer-

---

94. Boorstin, *National Experience,* p. 368.
95. Richard Garnett, in *Dictionary of National Biography, sub voce:* M. Sadleir, *Trollope: A Commentary* (London, 1947), esp. pp. 70–77; U. Pope-Hennessy, *Three English Women in America* (London, 1929), pp. 28–32, 44–47, and passim to 101.

ica she directed, or rather dragged, her friend Frances Trollope. In New York and in Philadelphia she had a play of hers given, apparently a Schillerian-tyrannicidal tragedy (*Altorf*), which all the London theaters had refused to present, and went from one city to another reeling off cycles of oracular and radical sermons, declaiming them "with gesture small and staid / so pretty in her vehemence" (as a satire of the times admits),[96] and sometimes surrounded by "a bodyguard of Quaker women in the full uniform of their sect." In America, finally, at Cincinnati, she died at the end of 1852. Carlo Botta's literary exercise had aroused the most warlike panegyrist of the young North American state.

Her book is thus a frankly partisan apology, which is sometimes amusing, sometimes touching. When she was still on the ship bringing her to America Miss Wright had already been pleased at the excellent English of the American sailors,[97] and at the end of the journey confesses to us that because of her repulsion for slavery she has not visited any of the states of the South.[98] She wants to see or hear nothing that could disturb the image that she has made for herself of that new and happy world. She herself later confessed that she wore rose-colored spectacles.[99] And in fact she indulges in continuous polemics against the malicious travelers, mainly English, who had criticized or mocked the United States,[100] and furthermore often succeeds in unmasking their Tory prejudices or narrow nationalism.

Of the more ancient slanderers who had denigrated the physical nature of the continent she never speaks, and seems to have no direct knowledge of them. But she does mention that certain scientists suppose that America was less ancient than the Old World, and does not hesitate to ascribe this hypothesis to an American naturalist, "but I soon saw that its antiquity could no more be called into question than its goodness," and since there can be no doubt of this she closes the subject.[101] She admits that the lark has no rivals in America, but lists various other birds of delightfully melodic song.[102] She repeats the anecdote of the disdainful English traveler who scorned everything American — "the beef, the mutton, the fish, the game, everything was superior in his own country" — until a storm breaks out and at the formidable thunderclap an American

96. Pope-Hennessy, *Three English Women*, p. 98. The play was however apparently read and admired (1826) by Stendhal! (*Correspondance* [Paris, 1962–68], II, 829, 1104).
97. *Voyage aux Etats-Unis d'Amérique*, trans. J. T. Parisot (Paris, 1822), I, 14.
98. Ibid., II, 334.
99. Pope-Hennessy, *Three English Women*, p. 31. *The Westminster Review*, the Tory organ, defined the work quite straightforwardly as a "prostitute rhapsody" (cited by Fabian, op. cit., p. 9, n. 12).
100. Against Fearon: I, 60–62, 104–05n., 169, 339–40; II, 218n., 266–69. Against Ashe: I, 169. Capt. Basil Hall is excepted, partly: I, 105–07, 242–43n.; II, 6n., 218–19n. Against the English travelers, in general, I, 29, 168–69, 287; II, 169–70n., 284–86, 309–10.
101. Op. cit., I, 215. She is familiar with Volney: II, 246–47.
102. Ibid., II, 243–44.

companion of the Englishman asks him seriously: "And do you have better thunder in England too?"[103] She often talks about marshes and malarial regions,[104] but the miasmas recede as cultivation advances, and in any case, the Americans are a fine race: the men, tall, robust, and long-lived,[105] and the girls, very beautiful, at least until the age of twenty-four or twenty-five, when they begin to decline[106] (actually the florid Miss Frances was just about twenty-three or twenty-four herself at that time), and in fact—the highly cultured Miss Frances adds—they are still just a little bit ignorant.[107] As for Washington, she admits that the capital does not yet exist, is scarcely an embryo of a city and it will take who can tell how many centuries [sic!] before it takes on the aspect of an imperial metropolis. But is it not better that it should be thus? God guard America and its capital from losing the adorable imprint of youthfulness too quickly![108]

But our interest in Miss Wright is not so much in these thin polemical residues as in the precocious spontaneity with which she believes in the superior culture of the United States, and its inevitable development. To the European who says to America: "Yes, you are rich and prosperous, but where are your ruins, your poetry?" the American did right to reply by pointing to a veteran of the Revolution, Cincinnatus-like with his hoe: "Here are our ruins," and to a landscape of healthy pastures, herds, farms, and villas: "Here is our poetry."[109] The fine arts will follow. In the preface to her tragedy Miss Wright, almost foreseeing the coming of O'Neill, announces that America "will one day revive the sinking honor of the drama." Painters and architects there are already, and of excellent quality;[110] writers too will blossom if peace lasts.

Her unfortunate friend, follower, and victim, Frances Trollope, was not such an optimist. This energetic lady (mother of the novelist Anthony), after losing her last penny in an attempt (1828–30) to promote a sort of bazaar-atheneum in Cincinnati, a mixture of philological club, art gallery, restaurant, theater and fashion house,[111] was confirmed in her

103. Ibid., pp. 309–10.
104. In the South: I, 84–85; the North: I, 227–28; the West: I, 240, 294–95, 299; in Canada: II, 8–9.
105. Ibid., I, 242.
106. Ibid., p. 42.
107. Ibid., p. 44.
108. Ibid., II, 311–12, 323. Clear echoes of a Rousseau- and Jefferson-type antiurbanism.
109. Ibid., I, 239–40.
110. Ibid., p. 112. Her neoclassical taste is revealed in her aversion for the "Gothic" and her admiration of Canova (I, 176–77; II, 270, 323). As soon as her book appeared it was used by the polygraph Alexander Lips, in his Statistik von Amerika (Frankfurt, 1828); see Eckhart Franz, op. cit., p. 10.
111. One would be grateful for further details of this strange, indeed extraordinary undertaking, this attempted violent grafting of "civilization" onto the "frontier," (see however Pope-Hennessy, Three English Women, pp. 82–87; M. Sadleir, Trollope [London, 1947], pp. 78–80; Eileen Bigland, The In-

conviction that the men and women of America were ignorant boors, and wrote her report on the *Domestic Manners of the Americans* (1832). The vaguely zoological title[112] is matched by the irony of the contents. All in all the country is beautiful, the air fresh, and the climate good, the stars brilliant and the animal and vegetable life exuberantly rich; but the people, save for "a small patrician band," the people in general, rich and poor, in north and south, are really unbearable: "I do not like them. I do not like their principles. I do not like their manners. I do not like their opinions."[113] Ten years later the discerning Löwenstern expresses admiration for the Americans, foresees that the United States will exercize

---

domitable Mrs. Trollope [London, 1953], p. 96; particularly the bibliography in L. P. and R. P. Stebbins. *The Trollopes* [New York, 1945], p. 362; and Donald Smalley, in the important introduction to his edition of Mrs. Trollope's work [New York, 1949], pp. xl–li). The building was described by Miss Martineau as "the great deformity of the city" and built, according to her, in a Gothic-Greco-Turco-Egyptian style (*Retrospect*, II, 249, and Wheatley, op. cit., p. 190); but Hamilton, op. cit., II, 169, defines it as Greco-Moorish-Gothic-Chinese," Mrs. Trollope's friend Timothy Flint as "a queer, unique, crescented Turkish Babel," that one could not look at without laughing (Smalley, loc. cit., p. xlv), and Marryat as being "composed of many varieties of architecture; but I think the order under which it must be classed is the *preposterous*" (*Diary*, I, 168). And finally a modern art historian classifies it as "a composite of Gothic, Classic, Moorish, and Venetian": O. W. Larkin, *Art and Life in America* (New York, 1949), p. 148, while Brooks (*Dream of Arcadia*, p. 46n.) says that it had "an Egyptian portico, Grecian pillars, Gothic windows, a Turkish dome and the tower of a Norman castle." See also Stebbins, op. cit., p. 39. It was immediately baptized (Smalley, loc. cit., pp. lii, 69n.) and subsequently remained known as "Trollope's folly" (but even Fulton's steamship was derided as "Fulton's folly": Bremer, op. cit., I, 53), and passed through diverse hands, though nobody ever succeeded in making it pay. Marryat, loc. cit., I, 169, who also criticizes the commercial prospects of this chimerical enterprise, says of the building that it is "now [ca. 1838] used as a dancing academy, and occasionally as an assembly room." Over the years it was subsequently used as hotel, Presbyterian church, and military hospital. Frances's son, Anthony Trollope, found it (1861) occupied by a "Physico-medical Institute" run by a quack and a council of suffragette lady doctors (*North America* [Leipzig, 1862], II, 239; *An Autobiography* [Oxford, 1924], p. 7). Later still it was the seat of the Ohio Mechanics Society and a "popular bawdyhouse," until it was demolished in 1881 (*Time*, 20 August 1945, p. 54).

112. But possibly inspired by the above-mentioned (p. 470) work (in favor of America) by her friend Frances Wright; and echoing Bayard's intention of forty years earlier: "I propose to depict the manners of the Americans and their domestic habits" (*Voyage*, p. xiii). But it was only a little earlier that Hall warned: "A traveller should speak with great caution—I may say with reluctance—of the private manners and customs of foreign countries" (*Travels*, III, 149).

113. *Domestic Manners*, XXXIV ("Conclusion"), ed. cit., p. 404. On the author's bourgeois, moralistic, snobbish, and nationalistic prejudices, see the biography, sympathetic as it is, of Bigland: op. cit., pp. 57, 83, 196. Nor is she altogether innocent of anti-Semitism (*Domestic Manners*, XII, ed. cit., p. 123), an outlook abundantly developed and theorized in *Vienna and the Austrians* (London, 1837), I, 373–74; II, 5–7, 220–27. It is also curious that this "moralist" should quite unnecessarily include a line from Parny's obscene *Guerre des Dieux* (*Domestic Manners*, XXVI, ed. cit., p. 274; cf. E. Parny, *Oeuvres complètes* [Brussels, 1824], I, 34). But the book that resulted from her economic misadventures was the beginning of her long-lasting literary fortune. Among her three dozen novels, all three-deckers, there are several that contain at least some scenes inspired by her American experience: (a) *The Refugee in America* (1832), "an artificial and stilted account of an English family in America, with much exaggerated sensibility and a priggish heroine" (Sadleir, op. cit., p. 89; this same heroine is described by the American Smalley [loc. cit., p. lxiv] as "an American, an unspoiled, adaptable maiden," etc.); (b) *The Life and Adventures of Jonathan Jefferson Whitlaw: or Scenes on the Mississippi* (1836; rpt. in 1857 with the title *Lynch Law*), which opens with a fearsome description of the vast and mournful river, and depicts New Orleans as the horrific metropolis of Slavery and Fever: Paris ed., 1836, pp. 1–2, 180–81; cf. Smalley, loc. cit., pp. lxvii–lxviii; (c) *The Barnabys in America* (1843; cf. Smalley, loc. cit., p. lxxi); and (d) *The Old World and the New* (1849; cf. Smalley, loc. cit., pp. lxxii–lxxiii), etc.: see Sadleir, op. cit., pp. 96, 102–03, 403–05.

"a happy influence on the happiness of the world," but concludes that he "would not want to live there."[114] And yet Cincinnati, which was later to become an important printing and publishing center, was already then one of the most cultured and progressive cities of the west, and one that paid particular attention to the advanced education of young ladies.[115]

Mrs. Trollope's impressions had been negative from the moment of her disembarkation at New Orleans (1827), and as she went up the muddy Mississippi (1828) the marshes, the wretched little shacks lining the river banks, the fevers, the crocodiles (about which she tells hair-raising stories), and the river's "indescribably dreary" appearance combined with the shocking promiscuity of shipboard life to form a picture of absolute moral and physical repulsiveness. And her horror knows no bounds when an attack of fever lays her low, and she thinks that she and the three young children that she has with her might be condemned to finish their lives "in this hateful land that breathed fever and death."[116]

Thus it took only the slightest and most casual stimulus to persuade her into giving public expression to her feelings, and this was provided by the *Travels in North America in the years 1827 and 1828* of Capt. Basil Hall, an account filled with such biting satire, although the author had traveled with reasonable comfort and been received in the best society, that it stirred up violent and lasting reaction in the American press and public opinion.

In his conclusion Hall declares that despite the best will in the world and the help he received spontaneously from his American friends, he found no trace in the United States of that superior intelligence so loudly boasted of by its writers, and he repeats that it is an old country, although it thinks itself young, offspring of a Europe which it denies; and worse, it is a country laid waste in some remote epoch by a glacial flood, coming down like a torrent from the north and ruining and destroying everything in its path, tearing up forests and peeling the rocks, scattering shapeless boulders and puddles of lakes in the furrows opened with its blind force, and finally, on reaching the sea, forming with the detritus and rubble that natural breakwater, Long Island!

Although Hall declares himself absolutely sure about this "de Pauwian" cataclysm he is honest enough to confess his disappointment at failing to find any trace of it in the Alleghenies, which are regrettably

114. See L. B. Wright, *Culture*, pp. 92–95, 104.
115. *Les Etats-Unis*, p. 225.
116. See Bigland, op. cit., pp. 48, 56, 110–11. A few years later Marryat used the same horror-struck tone to describe the Mississippi, a putrid stream of mud and driftwood, a fetid sewer for the continent (*Diary*, I, 166; II, 91–92). But the story of the crocodiles, according to Mark Twain, is no more than a humorous invention of some joker intent on having a little fun at Mrs. Trollope's expense (Smalley, loc. cit., pp. 21–22n.).

covered with dense woods. No traces of this scourge have been found, but they must be there somewhere; the good Englishman trusts that some member of one of the swarms of philosophical societies in America will take on the task of further careful research in this matter. Apparently no American scholar has yet accepted the ambiguous invitation of such an unfriendly critic.

Hall, a Tory like Trollope, is frequently and eulogistically quoted in the *Domestic Manners,* and was even thought to be its author.[117] Hall, however, poses more as reactionary and jingoist than Tory: he goes to great lengths[118] to defend corporal punishment, approves the tight discipline of the Church of England;[119] and when he visits the famous factories at Lowell is pleased to note that they cannot compete with those of Manchester or Preston.[120]

The indignation against the indiscreet retired captain was still rampant when Mrs. Trollope left the United States (July 1831). Mrs. Trollope based her book on the diary she had kept during a long tour through the states of the Atlantic coast, and hastened to submit the manuscript to Hall, who was delighted to find this unexpected support for his thesis, which had been attacked even in England by liberal critics, and he arranged its prompt publication.[121]

For the purpose of our present chronicle Mrs. Trollope's main interest is in her adherence to certain characteristic biological theses, and in general to the concept of America as "quantity not quality," or rather, quantities of bad and very bad qualities. The natural phenomena are magnificent (as already mentioned), but the abundance of foodstuffs, for example, is not matched by the goodness of that most delicate of edibles, the fruit. In the whole of the Cincinnati market there is not one peach, not one apricot or plum, the strawberries are miserable, the raspberries even worse, the redcurrants uneatable, the grapes too tart, the apples unworthy to appear on an English table, the pears, the cherries, and the plums detestable. The same goes for the flowers. And whose fault is all this, the soil's or the farmer's? Well, a gentleman who seemed to know about these things assured her that in the whole of the state of Ohio there was not a single indigenous flower or fruit.[122]

117. Sadleir, op. cit., p. 86; Smalley, loc. cit., pp. 359–60n.
118. Op. cit., II, 87–102.
119. Ibid., I, 211–12.
120. Ibid., p. 219. On his influence in France, see Remond, op. cit., p. 278.
121. Bigland, op. cit., pp. 118–19, 133–34; slightly different versions in Pope-Hennessy, *Three English Women,* pp. 96–97, 102; Sadleir, op. cit., pp. 86, 88–89, and Smalley, loc. cit., pp. lvii–lxi; cf. also Fabian, op. cit., p. 9, n. 14.
122. *Domestic Manners,* VII, ed. cit., p. 61. Thompson too, though no "de Pauwian," had noted (1826: op. cit., pp. 293–94) that the peaches in Guatemala were "by no means equal to the peaches cultivated in the common gardens of England. . . . The delicious quality of what may be termed European fruits, found in these countries, has been greatly over-rated."

What about the men? The natives are perhaps of Egyptian origin[123]—but she came across few of them. The colonists of Kentucky are a fine race, tall and strong, but of atrocious habits, given to thieving, gambling, drunkenness, and swearing.[124] And if the American men all have such tight thin lips, this is not a congenital feature of their physiognomy, but a result of the nauseating custom of chewing tabacco and then violently spitting out the stinking juice.[125] The women are often very beautiful, but totally without charm; they may be the most splendid women in the world, but they are certainly the least attractive, and grow old at a ruinously early age.[126] After two years in Cincinnati—which, we should remember, was still rather more chaotic and turbulent a society than the cities of the Atlantic coast[127]—Mrs. Trollope is enchanted with Washington and New York: she disagrees with criticisms of the incompleteness of the capital and boldly predicts that New York will keep expanding until one day it covers the whole of Manhattan Island![128]

But her antipathy for American institutions gets the upper hand and finds an easy outlet in the repeatedly exploited antithesis between the maxims of liberty and the existence of slavery—these Americans, with one hand waving the Phrygian cap and the other whipping the poor Negroes![129]—until that antithesis is simultaneously extinguished and aggravated in the Trollopian verdict that the slavery of the Negro is less

123. Ibid., XXXV, ed. cit., p. 272.

124. Ibid., III, ed. cit., pp. 17–18.

125. Ibid., XX, ed. cit., p. 234. At least twenty times, if not more, Mrs. Trollope denounces the American vice of spitting everywhere, even in the theater and Congress chambers (see ed. cit., index, to which should be added at least three other references: pp. lvi, 260n., and 330n.!); in this she followed Hall too, *Travels*, II, 406.

126. *Domestic Manners*, XII and XXV, ed. cit., pp. 117–18, 267; cf. Bremer, op. cit., I, 39; II, 331–32; III, 253, etc.: Löwenstern, op. cit., p. 174; E. S. Turner, op. cit., pp. 188–89. On the premature senility attributed to the American women, see examples in Martin, op. cit., p. 201.

127. "It is there," noted a very sharp contemporary observer, "that one must go to have an idea of this social state so different from ours; in Boston, New York, and Philadelphia, in all the big cities of the Coast, there is already a class which . . . wants to enjoy fortune, not to toil to make one. In Ohio, . . . they do not even know yet what the upper classes are, the chaos is complete. Society in its entirety is a kind of workshop!" (Tocqueville, *Voyage*, 1831, ed. cit., pp. 281–82; cf. pp. 284–85, 324; and Löwenstern, op. cit., p. 238). It was precisely this that disconcerted and scandalized Mrs. Frances Trollope.

128. *Domestic Manners*, XIX and XXX, ed. cit., pp. 207, 267. Did she perhaps recall the words of her friend Frances Wright? Cf. above, p. 472.

129. Ibid., XX, ed. cit., p. 222; cf. ibid., II and XXII, ed. cit., pp. 8–9, 14–15, 247, and the preface to the 5th ed., ibid., pp. 442–43. The same contrast, a flagrant proof of democratic hypocrisy, in T. Hamilton, op. cit., II, 142–43; in Fanny Kemble (on a white minister who was himself a slave owner: Pope-Hennessy, *Three English Women*, p. 191, and cf. ibid., p. 296); in Kürnberger, op. cit., p. 392, and in many other places (cf. G. D. Lillibridge, *Beacon of Freedom: The Impact of American Democracy upon Great Britain, 1830–1870* [Philadelphia, 1955], pp. 111–13). But cf. already Humboldt's scorn for the (Venezuelan) colonists who "with their copy of Raynal in their hands maltreat the slaves," and while they "talk enthusiastically of the cause of liberty," sell "the Negroes' children when they are scarcely a few months old" (letter from Cumanà, 17 October 1800, in *Lettres américaines* [*1798–1807*], Paris, n.d., but 1904, p. 87; and in Bruhns, op. cit., I, 333). In fact this facile *topos* goes back at least as far as Diderot (ed. cit., p. 760), where he refers to the missionary disembarking at Tahiti with a wooden crucifix in one hand and an iron sword in the other; and it subsequently became proverbial.

harmful to the customs than the egalitarianism of the whites. To come to a particular but conspicuous example, there is an equally strident contrast between the democratic Jefferson's "sophism" according to which "men are born free and equal" (a sophism which, as we know, is at the basis of the Declaration of Independence) and the dissolute, irreligious, tyrannical life of this same Jefferson. Mrs. Trollope declines to "criticise his written works," but loses no chance of criticizing his principles and character.[130] In the United States liberty is hypocrisy, democracy a lie, and by logical extension Thomas Jefferson, the defender of America's soil and one of the Founding Fathers, is the basest of scoundrels.

It is hardly surprising then that at this point the good lady enthusiastically quotes Thomas Moore, indeed transcribes a good thirty lines of the letter to Viscount Forbes that gathered together all his vituperations of the American republic and, in a note, of its then president, Thomas Jefferson.[131] Mrs. Trollope actually insists that she wishes to make no rash judgments on the country's political stituation; that she is only a woman wanting to give her impressions of the social life; and that America will be outstanding in the arts too when it seeks inspiration within itself and stops imitating Europe;[132] but all in vain — her acrimony, and the very persistence of her acrimony, the limitations of her mental horizons and the consequent spontaneous sharpness and acidity of her intolerance result in that sort of jovial savagery, that imperturbable complacency and British self-assurance which could not fail to appeal to her compatriots.

Her book was in fact an immediate and massive success. Some ten reprintings sold out within the year, and translations were published in French (1833), Dutch (1833), Spanish (1834), and German (1835). And

---

130. *Domestic Manners*, VII, XXII, XXIV, XXIX, ed. cit., pp. 71–73, 244, 263–64, 316–17 (where it is precisely his written work she criticizes!); *Life and Adventures of J. J. Whitlaw*, p. 208; Bigland, op. cit., p. 89. Cf. Perrin du Lac, above, p. 342, T. Hamilton, below, p. 490, and Marryat, *Diary*, I, 251–52; II, 311. On the probable British origin (ca. 1800–02) of the viler accusations against Jefferson, repeated with gusto by enemies of the Democratic party and President Jackson, see Smalley, loc. cit., p. 72n. (the text of the insulting article by the Englishman James Thomson Callender is reprinted in *The Jefferson Reader*, ed. F. C. Rosenberg [New York, 1953], pp. 109–11). See also M. D. Peterson, op. cit., pp. 181–87. Still in 1853 — "slander away, slander away, something will always stick" — these accusations reechoed in the theoretician of the pure races, Gobineau (*Essai*, II, 532), obviously as averse to the natives, a turbid mixture of strains (ibid., II, 494, 505), as he was to the North American citizens, a conglomerate jumble of heterogeneous immigrants (ibid., II, 535–56, 538); and, a few years later (1857) they revealed their sinister influence at work on such a severe critic of the American constitution as Macaulay ("What did Macaulay Say About America? Text of Four Letters to Henry S. Randall," ed. H. M. Lydenberg [New York, 1935], 15, 25, 27). On the violent attacks of the bigots, who were suspicious of Jefferson's scientific and antiscriptural ideas, see Bremer, op. cit., I, 331–33; III, 312; Martin, op. cit., pp. 236–40.

131. *Domestic Manners*, XXII, ed. cit., pp. 244–45; cf. also above, p. 338. (It is in the following epistle that Moore describes Buffon and de Pauw as being considerably more truthful than Jefferson.)

132. Ibid., V and XX, ed. cit., pp. 43, 219–20 (and the bold prophecy on pp. 430–31); but the reading of Cooper's indigenous "American" novels gives her terrible nightmares and horrible visions, to free herself from which she follows this cure: (a) an ounce of calomel, (b) novels of civil and sentimental criminals (Bulwer Lytton), and (c) chivalric novels (Walter Scott).

even if in America it provoked legitimate outbursts of protest,[133] in Europe it earned the fifty-five-year-old literary novice a welcome in the most intellectual salons of Paris and Vienna and the goodwill and interest of conservatives everywhere, including men of the stature of Metternich and Chateaubriand;[134] it was read by the Emperor (Nicholas I) and Empress of all the Russias,[135] irritated a liberal spirit like Giovanni Berchet,[136] and even influenced writers like Tocqueville, Proudhon,[137] and Stendhal.

The authoress herself, on the other hand, seemed almost to forget, or to want to have forgotten, the scandalous tract which had earned her such notoriety. In her book on *Vienna and the Austrians* (1837) America is practically ignored: a waterfall near Salzburg is said to be superior to all the waterfalls in America, with the exception of Niagara;[138] a period of exceptional cold reminds her of the frost on the Potomac,[139] and the

133. On the reaction in America, and the custom of shouting "Trollope" in the theater to bring unruly spectators to order, see examples in Smalley, loc. cit., p. 134n., and G. P. Putnam, "Culture in America," 1845, in B. Rascoe, ed., *An American Reader*, pp. 293–94. Already in 1835 Richard Cobden used the verb "trollopise" in the sense of "speaking ill of the Americans" (and was immediately followed, 1836, by the publisher Harper: see Wheatley, op. cit., p. 174), and to sit "legs à la Trollope" meant to put one's feet rudely up on the table and slouch back (Tryon, ed., op. cit., p. 306: New Orleans). Vail (op. cit., p. 317) describes (1841) the satire that Paulding wrote of the English travelers in America (*John Bull in America* (London, 1825) as written "in the trollopist style." While on the other hand a New York reporter visited Cincinnati immediately after the publication of the book, and after praising the culture and refinement of the Cincinnatians added that "the picture of life and manners here by an exceedingly clever English caricaturist has about as much vrai-semblance as if the beaux and belles of Kamschatka had sat for the portraits" (C. F. Hoffman, *A Winter in the West* [New York, 1835], rpt. in Tryon, op. cit., p. 553; see also Marryat, I, 169–70). Cf. also Frances Trollope, *Vienna*, II, 407 ("If I show myself in the Western world, I shall be promptly executed by Lynch law"); Bremer, who was rejected by an American sailing ship because it was suspected that as a writer she would write Trollope- or Dickens-type slanders (op. cit., pp. 266–67); A. Trollope, *Autobiography*, pp. 21–27; Sadleir, op. cit., pp. 101–03, 225; Pope-Hennessy, *Three English Women*, p. 163; Bigland, op. cit., p. 142; Smalley, loc. cit., pp. viii–x; and Frederick W. Shelton, *The Trollopiad, or, Travelling Gentlemen in America: A Satire by Nil Admirari* (New York, 1837). Still in 1883 Mark Twain excised from his *Life on the Mississippi* all the passages defending the honesty, candor, and exactness of "Dame Trollope" (Smalley, loc. cit., p. v; cf. ibid., p. xii). This "very-respectable lady" saw almost no one in America, but nonetheless wrote "an outrageous book, which in Europe has charmed the aristocratic vanities into whose service she found herself somewhat singularly pressed" (Ampère, op. cit., I, 207–08, 216).

134. Who cites her as "Mrs. Troloppe," in the *Mémoires d'outre-tombe*, ed. cit., I, 345. On the other hand there were of course those – apart from Berchet, mentioned below – who ridiculed her, such as the Whigs and liberals (for the *Edinburgh Review*, see Remond, op. cit., p. 273: for replies from Jouffroy and other Frenchmen, ibid., pp. 276–77, 716, 720). Replies from Italian travelers to Trollope, Dickens, Marryat, and others, in Andrew J. Torrielli, *Italian Opinion on America, as Revealed by Italian Travelers, 1850–1900* (Cambridge, Mass., 1941), pp. 14, 23, 224, 256. And Michel Chevalier perspicaciously pointed to her British aristocratism as the poison lying at the root of her ill humor (*Letters*, I, 313, 315; II, 17).

135. Bremer, op. cit., I, 261–62.

136. He met her at Baden, and was obliged to act as interpreter between her and certain noble gentlemen (presumably reactionaries) who found her "quite delightful"; he dismisses her with the laconic comment: "She appears to me to be a woman corresponding to the book she has written (rather vulgar)" (*Lettere alla marchesa Costanza Arconati*, ed. Robert van Nuffel, vol. II [Rome, 1962], p. 10 [letter of 8 August 1833]).

137. *La guerre et la paix*, I, 74.

138. *Vienna*, I, 171.

139. Op. cit., II, 254.

Americans are rebuked for devoting themselves to political struggles rather than to healthy and carefree pastimes.[140] The society of Vienna is compared only to that of other great European cities like London and Paris. Mrs. Trollope almost seems to be ashamed of having belonged to the society of a place like Cincinnati. At the same time her reactionary tendencies become more noticeable, leading her to make a curious apology for the amenities of Spielberg, which is a prison, true, but whose prisoners are well cared for and well fed, enjoy fresh air and healthy physical exercise, etc.[141]

IX. ECHOES OF MRS. TROLLOPE: PRO-AMERICANISM AND ANTI-AMERICANISM IN STENDHAL AND JACQUEMONT

Stendhal is not a participant in our polemic. He is not so much un-aware of as completely indifferent to the problems of American nature. But the vivacity of his reactions to Mrs. Trollope's book obliges us to make a brief illustrative digression. The *Domestic Manners,* in the French translation (Paris, 1833), was read and annotated by Stendhal between 6 and 9 September 1834.[142] And it made such an impression upon him, a person ill inclined to tolerate American materialism, but even less to put up with British cant—of which he found a conspicuous example in the lady with the equivocal name, and perhaps for that reason so much the more puritan (Mrs. Trollope: "Mme le Traînée")—that he covered it with marginal comments and already the next day, 10 September, asked his friend Colomb to buy him (at a discount) Mrs. Trollope's other book on "Belgium Manners."[143]

Four years earlier Stendhal had reviewed Captain Hall's *Travels in North America,* judging the author a witty reactionary and America a country of mortal boredom.[144] The same attitude can be found in his notes on Mrs. Trollope's works, where three times he repeats the phony proportion: "Americans : English = English : French,"[145] meaning that to an elderly English lady, a die-hard moralist, the Americans were bound to seem as devoid of grace and spontaneity as the English themselves appeared to the French.

Stendhal's pseudomathematical formula, which as a matter of fact Mrs. Trollope would have accepted[146] and which descends directly from

---

140. Ibid., pp. 29–31, 140.
141. Ibid., p. 202; Pellico's *Le mie prigioni* had come out in 1832.
142. René-Louis Doyon, "Stendhal: Notes sur l'Angleterre et l'Amérique," *Table-Ronde,* 72 (December 1953), pp. 9–28.
143. *Correspondance,* ed. Divan, VIII, 348; Pléiade ed., II, 693.
144. *Mélanges de littérature,* ed. Divan, III, 315–28; *Correspondance* (Pléiade ed.), II, 177–78, 991.
145. Doyon, op. cit., pp. 18, 19, 24.
146. *Domestic Manners,* XXVIII, ed. cit., p. 305.

his review of Hall's book: "The gravity of the Americans . . . shocks the English, as the gravity of the English shocks us,"[147] was to be taken up again shortly afterward by Tocqueville, who, similarly inspired by Mrs. Trollope's book, was to write (1840) in his *Democracy in America:* "The English have made merry at the expense of the Americans' manners: and what is really strange is that most of those who painted this amusing picture for us belonged to the middle classes in England, to whom this same picture is highly applicable. So that these merciless slanderers usually present the example of what they blame in the United States: they don't realize that they are railing against themselves."[148]

In reality Stendhal's ideas on the United States modified with time, which helps us to understand certain of his ambiguities, inconsistencies, and contradictions. Back in 1820 Stendhal is an enthusiast: "North America seems to me a perfect model,"[149] Jefferson's commentary on Montesquieu "contains exactly my political credo,"[150] and he even signs a letter to his friend Adolphe de Mareste[151] with the pseudonym "Thomas Jefferson." His recurrent longing is to emigrate to the United States: "Oh! How happy I would be if I had eight thousand francs. I would go to America for six months."[152] With only two thousand francs he would still be able to spend three months in Philadelphia:[153] "I boil for Philadelphia."[154]

His faith in America persists: several times Stendhal prophesies that the United States, about the year 1900, will be the first power in the world; and he actually insinuates, through the mouth of one of his characters, that the republics of South America will give Europe back its liberty.[155] But if he still thinks of America as a place of escape, he says so in joking tones which reveal a weakening of his childhood enthusiasm: "If it weren't for seasickness I would willingly set sail for Amer-

147. *Mélanges,* III, 322. Cf. Victor Jacquemont, *Lettres à Jean de Charpentier* (Paris, 1933), p. 107 (1825): "An Englishman . . . is not just a serious animal. He is a sad animal" (and p. 164).

148. *Démocratie en Amérique,* II, 226. Mrs. Trollope might have subscribed to this last observation too: see her note (1839) in *Domestic Manners,* p. 257n. Tocqueville's opinion was already implicit in a comment he made in 1832: "America presents the most perfect image, for both good and bad, of the special character of the English race. The American is the Englishman left to his own devices" (*Voyage en Sicile et aux Etats-Unis,* p. 203).

149. *Correspondance,* Pléiade ed., I, 882.

150. Ibid., I, 943; cf. pp. 894, 898 (1818). On the commentary on Montesquieu, written by Destutt de Tracy, translated and distributed by Jefferson (1806–11), see F. Picavet, *Les idéologues* (Paris, 1891), pp. 377–83, Henry Dumolard, "Stendhal et la politique," in *Annales de l'Université de Grenoble* (Grenoble, 1929), Section Lettres-Droit, vol. VI, no. 2, pp. 136, 139, and Victor Jacquemont, *Lettres à Jean de Charpentier,* p. 21. Stendhal had a copy of the *Histoire de la peinture en Italie* sent to Jefferson (1817: *Correspondance,* I, 861), but the book does not figure in the catalogue of the President's library.

151. Op. cit., I, 923.

152. Ibid., p. 1022 (1820).

153. Ibid., p. 1023.

154. Ibid., p. 1009; cf. the similar intention (in 1805) of his friend Cheminade, ibid., p. 1128, when Stendhal was thinking of going to New Orleans in Louisiana (ibid., pp. 1121, 1169).

155. *Le rouge et le noir* (1830, ed. Divan), II, 112–13.

ica."[156] Republican government is horrible everywhere, except in America (1831).[157] Which doesn't mean to say that it's beautiful there.

Meanwhile the unpleasant impression America makes on his great friend Victor Jacquemont (1827), his reading of critics and scoffers at American society (and perhaps also the behavior of certain uncouth Americans whom he meets in Rome) nourish and increase his aversion for that mercantile Boeotia,[158] reactivating and generalizing the old hatred for the North Americans' exclusive interest in money and their blasphemous judgments on the arts,[159] the sad puritan America's incapacity for laughter,[160] and the tyrannical stupidity of public opinion in the United States.[161] "What in fact has reasonable America produced in the way of art?"[162]

Thus one can understand Stendhal's pungent pleasure in reading the *Domestic Manners*, and his willingness to overlook the reactionism of its author. Stendhal freely admits that she is an acute observer, and when he attempts to "dispatch her" with a single bon mot—she is *"un sot ultra avec de l'esprit"*[163]—his epigram turns out to be ambiguous: for Stendhal *esprit* had always redeemed even the greatest crime. So when Mrs. Trollope repeats[164] Talleyrand's judgment: *"Les Américains sont de fiers cochons et des cochons fiers,"* Stendhal, as a long-standing admirer of the Bishop of Autun, adds quite simply *"Bien."* Further traces of this fundamental agreement are found in almost all his successive works, which missed no opportunity of expressing his irritation at the demagogy and vulgarity of the North Americans, their mania for the dollar, their lack of *esprit*, etc.[165] The Republic itself loses its proud classicist fascination, because it obliges people to pay court to mediocrity, as in fact hap-

156. *Souvenirs d'egotisme* (1832, ed. Divan), V, 48; other references in the novels.

157. *Correspondance* (Pléiade ed.), II, 217.

158. Remond, op. cit., pp. 879–82, with reservations, corrections and slight alterations of emphasis. Cf. James F. Marshall, "Stendhal and America," *French American Review* (Institut Français de Washington), 10–12 (1949), pp. 240–67.

159. *Marginalia* (1814, ed. Divan), I, 332; *Journal* (1817, ed. Divan), V, 303; *Du romanticisme dans les beaux-arts* (1819), in *Racine et Shakespeare* (ed. Divan), pp. 269–70; *De l'amour* (1822), chap. 50 (Lyon, 1922), II, 50; *Promenades dans Rome* (1828, ed. Divan), III, 278–81.

160. All of chap. 50 in *De l'amour* (1822), and *Vie de Rossini* (1824, ed. cit.), I, 286; II, 20–21.

161. *Le rouge et le noir* (1820), from the first chapter (Divan ed., I, 9) to the note on the very last page (II, 499).

162. *Vie de Rossini*, II, 287; an echo perhaps of the famous comment by Sydney Smith (above, p. 405), a writer admired by Stendhal, and whose words had been printed (1820) in the *Edinburgh Review*, of which Stendhal was an assiduous reader.

163. In Doyon, op. cit., p. 11; cf. above the similar verdict on Hall.

164. *Domestic Manners*, XXVIII, p. 310.

165. An American scholar has counted no less than three hundred and fifty allusions to the United States in Stendhal's work (Remond, op. cit., p. 680). Suffice it to mention: Doyon, art. cit., pp. 10, 21–28; *Lucien Leuwen* (1833–36, ed. Divan), I, 3, 22, 58, 101–02, 113–19, 175; II, 255; III, 369 (citing Talleyrand and Tocqueville, and mentioning Cincinnati and the "boring" President Washington); *Mémoires d'un touriste* (1838), ed. Y. Gandon (Paris, 1927), I, 3–4, 34–35; II, 49; *Mélanges* (1836, ed. Divan), III, 441–42; *La chartreuse de Parme* (1839, ed. cit.), I, 212; II, 355, and the *Chroniques italiennes* (1833–39, ed. cit.), I, 3.

pens in America, and "brings people to their knees before money, as in the United States."[166]

Quite different from this attitude, where he is half Coriolanus and half Tocqueville, and in some measure closer to our debates, is Stendhal's judgment on the American native, the redskin. In general he follows Volney, whom he quotes fairly frequently and mentions, among other places, at the precise point where he simultaneously rejects the idealizations of Rousseau and the degradations of de Pauw.[167] The true Greeks are not to be found in the dusty manuscripts of a library, but in America, with rifle in hand, "hunting with the Wabash savages": the climate is "less happy" than in Hellas, but only there can one today find the Achilles and the Hercules.[168] Read Thucydides and his description of ancient Greece: "Change the names and this fragment could be the history of the savages of America toward the time when the Europeans came and disturbed their nascent society. The Pelagians were no more than the inhabitants of the Wabash."[169] Volney's description of the savage, he says, has definitely cured him of any exalted admiration for military virtues, because the bravery of the savages is "the same as that of Homer's Greeks."[170] And if in the middle of the lecture our professors were suddenly to see Pelid Achilles appear before them, they would get a good fright.[171]

No less curious, and even more remote from the "slanders" of Buffon, is the attitude of that pleasant spindleshanks Victor Jacquemont, the protégé of Lafayette. He was on terms of amicable bantering with Stendhal[172] — they never missed a chance of a dig or a wisecrack at one another's expense — but he was also a close friend of Mérimée,[173] the de Tracys, and Delacroix.[174]

166. *Lucien Leuwen,* quoted by Dumolard, op. cit., pp. 133–34, 138–40.

167. *Journal* (1813), II, 168; cf. above, chap. VII, n. 49.

168. *Histoire de la peinture en Italie* (1817; ed. Divan, n.d.), II, 11 ("Where can we find the ancient Greeks?"). On the idea of America as New, or quite simply Greater Greece, a yet more "Magna Grecia," obviously linked to the idea of America as refuge or palingenesis of European civilization (Berkeley, etc.), see Echeverria, *Mirage,* pp. 76–77, 112–13, who quotes Chastellux, the abbé Brizard, Louis Mercier, and abbé Raynal. Following the same lines, but making America the heir of Rome rather than a "Greek colony," are the comments of Melville in his lecture on "Roman statuary": the ancient busts of Julius Caesar and Seneca foreshadow the physiognomies of North American businessmen and managers.

169. *La peinture en Italie,* II, 133–34.

170. *Molière, Shakespeare, la comédie et le rire* (1803–23; ed. Divan), p. 276.

171. *La peinture en Italie,* loc. cit.

172. François Michel and Yves Laissus, "Jacquemont et Stendhal," in *Jacquemont* (Paris, 1959), pp. 31, 74, etc.; Jean Dutourd, *L'âme sensible* (Paris, 1959), pp. 15–19, 47–50.

173. A quarter of a century after Jacquemont's death Mérimée wrote: "He was one of those people who gain on being intimately known" (*Correspondance générale* [Paris, 1941–64], in which Jacquemont is named more than forty times: VIII, 148; XI, 242), and still in 1863 he calls him "my best friend" (ibid., XI, 574) and in 1867 "the noblest and most amiable character that I have ever known" (ibid., XIII, 671; cf. ibid., p. 698). See also P. Mérimée, *Portraits historiques et littéraires,* ed. Pierre Jourda (Paris, 1928), 93–110; Pierre Trahard, *La jeunesse de Prosper Mérimée* (Paris, 1925), esp. I, 97–103 and II, 258–70.

174. See Eugène Delacroix, *Diario,* ed. Lamberto Vitali (Turin, 1954), III, 403 and n.; and the monu-

A naturalist by vocation, an untiring traveler, a lover of flowers and music, a lively spirit filled with lay and illuministic fervor, firm in his faith in the philosophy of the eighteenth century and its *idéologues,* and a great admirer of the young Werther and the Schillerian Marquis von Posa,[175] Jacquemont passed several months (interrupted by a journey to Santo Domingo) in the United States, visited New York and Philadelphia, took a brief trip as far as Niagara Falls and almost drowned there,[176] and after three and a half years of scientific travel in India and Tibet died with serene clearheadedness and "stoic" firmness[177] at Bombay, at the tender age of thirty-one.

Jacquemont left for America toward the end of the autumn of 1826, after an unhappy love affair,[178] at the insistence of his father and brother,[179] interrupting his studies in medicine when he was already near to taking his degree, and surprising his friends,[180] but without nourishing any great illusions. On the ship he observes already that the Americans are sad, glacial, and arrogant: "Such a permanent pressure of authority! I am expecting to find everything like this in America: I mean the people mixing there less than anywhere else, and society the absolute reverse of democratic government."[181] And his arrival is no more encouraging: "Only with reluctance did I set foot on the soil of America. The appearance of everything displeased me . . . I would have liked to leave again for Europe on the instant."[182]

---

mental, exhaustive biography by Pierre Maes, *Un ami de Stendhal: Victor Jacquemont* (Paris, 1934), pp. 137, 600–01.

175. *Lettres à Charpentier,* pp. 145, 152. *Correspondance inédite avec sa famille et ses amis, 1824–1832* (Paris, 1867), I, 27; and Maes, op. cit., p. 190. His father was persecuted by Napoleon (ibid., I, 312–13), he himself is a liberal and "revolutionary" (ibid., II, 222; cf. *Lettres à Charpentier,* pp. 130, 188–89), waxes enthusiastic over the *trois glorieuses* (July 27–29, 1830 – the revolt against Charles X: ibid., II, 40, 71), and ridicules Napoleon, hates and despises him (in Stendhal, *Correspondance* [Pléiade ed., II, 796–800, 823]), earning a rebuke from his friend Stendhal (Victor Jacquemont, *Lettres à Stendhal,* ed. Pierre Maes [Paris, 1933], pp. 36–37). Waterloo was "the greatest battle, in its results, of modern history" ("Lettres inédites de V. Jacquemont à Sutton Sharpe," ed. Adolphe Paupe, *Revue d'histoire littéraire de la France,* 14 [1907], pp. 696–711, esp. 696). See also *Lettres à Charpentier,* pp. 173, 186–87, 194; Maes, op. cit., pp. 101–10, 456; Michel and Laissus, op. cit., p. 45.

176. Prosper Mérimée, introduction to V. Jacquemont, *Correspondance inédite,* I, 5; Maes, op. cit., p. 294; Chinard, Pierre Huard, Jean Theodoridès, in *Jacquemont,* ed. cit., pp. 172–73, 259. Larousse would have us believe that he "traveled throughout North America."

177. "He who best represented the Greek Stoic," Mérimée wrote of him (*Correspondance générale,* XIII, 698), followed by all the others.

178. Copious details in Maes, op. cit., pp. 181–247, 253; Michel and Laissus, op. cit., p. 47.

179. *Lettres à Charpentier,* p. 171.

180. On the circumstances, see *Lettres à Stendhal,* pp. 66–69.

181. *Correspondance,* I, 53, 63, 66. Thus I would not say he came back "disappointed" (Remond, op. cit., pp. 634, 677–79). In fact he recognized that the visit to the United States had had a favorable effect on him, and that his ego was the better for it: *Correspondance avec sa famille et plusieurs de ses amis pendant son voyage dans l'Inde, 1828–1832* (Paris, 1833; in 1869 there appeared a sixth edition, not counting three counterfeit editions that appeared in Belgium, three in English and one in Italian; see the eulogy of Sainte-Beuve, *Causeries du lundi,* XIII, 422), II, 124, 246–47; cf. *Lettres à Stendhal,* p. 72; *Lettres à Charpentier,* p. 182; Maes, op. cit., p. 276 ("I congratulated myself on having left Europe"); Gilbert Chinard, Henry de Villenoisy, and Alexander W. Brown, in *Jacquemont,* pp. 137, 159, 173, 195, 416.

182. Maes, op. cit., p. 255; Chinard, in *Jacquemont,* p. 145–46.

On his return journey, in fact, he wrote to his friend Victor de Tracy a long severe letter (a good forty-three pages), in which he summed up his impressions and here and there anticipated Tocqueville. For the political institutions of the United States he has a reasoned admiration: the citizens are hardworking, industrious, and lovers of order, and have made an "admirable usage" of liberty.[183] The public manners — "that is the best side of America, although it is far from being perfect."[184] George Washington was worth little as a general or an orator, but he was really a fine man and a good citizen.[185] And Franklin's simplicity is worthy of admiration.[186]

All in all, America is a country "more made for exciting the curiosity of somebody who doesn't know it than satisfying that of the man who has seen it. By and large American manners do not please me." The vices of government can be imputed to society, in which two things particularly irritate him: religious intolerance and the widespread ignorance and lack of taste.

As for the former, Jacquemont comes back "cured" of all sympathy for Protestantism: "Our Jesuits are philosophers compared with these Puritans!"[187] If he were a journalist of the *Compagnie,* what a fine time he could have at the expense of the religious tolerance of the Americans! Rather European religion than to be bored for fifty-two Sundays in a row.[188] The sectarian fanaticism pervades every place: "The Bible seems to me to be the bane of America."[189]

Jacquemont is no less acrid when he speaks of American culture. "The pleasure of study is almost unknown in America." The newspapers are silly: the Americans would do better to read the *Commentary on Montesquieu* (see above, n. 150). And as for learned and literary society, it is worthless.[190] In the salons, the Americans "are slaves. They look as if they are bored to death, which must be true, considering what is said there."[191] From the intellectual point of view, New York "is more wretched than Pontoise or Melun." These American are really repellent creatures: "Disgusting! Disgusting! It is shameful to speak of them: these animals are below criticism . . . good heavens, sir! What wit we

183. *Correspondance avec sa famille,* I, 29, 36–38, 49–51. Referring to this letter Mérimée wrote to an American friend (in 1866) saying ambiguously that it would "amuse" him (*Correspondance générale,* XIII, 35). Cf. Michel and Laissus, and Pierre Josserand, in *Jacquemont,* pp. 40, 114.

184. *Correspondance inédite,* I, 307.

185. Ibid., p. 313.

186. Stendhal, *Correspondance,* II, 817; *Lettres à Stendhal,* pp. 40, 170; Picavet, op. cit., p. 487; Maes, op. cit., p. 89n.; Michel and Laissus, *Jacquemont,* p. 72.

187. *Correspondance inédite,* I, 156–60.

188. Ibid., pp. 137–38, 310; *Lettres à Charpentier,* p. 166; Villenoisy and Brown in *Jacquemont,* pp. 134, 371, 392–96.

189. *Correspondance inédite,* I, 158. "It's the Bible that makes them so hypocritical and serious, those English" (*Lettres à Charpentier,* pp. 108, 164, 188–89).

190. *Correspondance avec sa famille,* I, 221–23; *Correspondance inédite,* I, 166–70.

191. *Lettres à Charpentier,* pp. 189–90; cf. p. 214.

have in Paris!"[192] The populace is amorphous, devoid of any national character: "No population is as antipicturesque." The United States is a "free and boring country."[193]

And yet, just a few months before his death, he was seized by a curiosity to analyze that attractive and monstrous community: it would please him, he writes, to be an ambassador in Washington: "I would love to stay four or five years in the United States in order to know perfectly the mechanism of this singular society and its national customs, and to make a faithful picture of it for the governments and the governed of Europe. This work would be extremely useful." He certainly did not expect to lead a pleasant life in Washington, but in truth nobody finds pleasure in the stench of the carcass that he sometimes has to dissect, "and yet the dissection of this carcass interests me very much."[194]

Rarely have there been such biting and severe judgments on the United States: often one is reminded of the verdicts of de Pauw on the degenerate, enfeebled Americans. It is so much more surprising then that Jacquemont, unlike (for example) Lenau, and all those who had used the soft nature of America as a justification for the vices and weaknesses of the Americans, is eternally exalting the beauty, strength, and exuberance of American nature, in the north, the south, and particularly the center. Certainly, it is without charm,[195] or that "picturesque" and human character that he had so much liked in Switzerland and Lake Maggiore, but it is powerful and sublime: admirable, for instance, are Lake George, Santo Domingo, and the woods of Haiti,[196] the American forest during the period of the magic Indian summer,[197] and of course the proud bay of Rio de Janeiro,[198] which prompts Jacquemont to an explicit contrast between the splendor of tropical nature and the terrible anarchy of the government and society of Brazil: "Is that a nation?"[199] No: it is "a country for which nature had done everything, and which men have spoiled, irreparably

192. *Correspondance inédite*, I, 141–42; Chinard, in *Jacquemont*, pp. 142, 184. On the intellectual attractions of Paris, see also V. Jacquemont, *Lettres à Charpentier*, pp. 28, 34, 53, 103, 107, 166. The Americans are incapable of appreciating the genius of Canova (Chinard, in *Jacquemont*, II, 273). Cf. Stendhal, *Correspondance*, II, 825.

193. *Correspondance inédite*, I, 175, 343. More frequently he condemns the Americans' greed for money.

194. Ibid., II, 229–30 (letter of 18 June 1832). Further defense of the "dissection" in Maes, op. cit., p. 148. On the projected work, see also the *Lettres à Charpentier* (1827), pp. 171, 181; Chinard, in *Jacquemont*, pp. 195–96.

195. *Lettres à Sutton Sharpe*, p. 704; Maes, op. cit., p. 289. Of the Antilles: "This beautiful nature seemed unpoetic" (Chinard, in *Jacquemont*, p. 156; on Rio: ibid., p. 176).

196. *Correspondance avec sa famille*, II, 15, 75. "I stayed barely more than three months in Haiti, but this country will always be dear to me" (Chinard, in *Jacquemont*, p. 154).

197. *Correspondance avec sa famille*, II, 245.

198. Ibid., I, 27; II, 245. "He gives us a fine portrait of Rio Janeiro" (Stendhal, *Correspondance*, II, 165).

199. *Correspondance avec sa famille*, I, 30; II, 95; *Correspondance inédite*, II, 213–20. All the other South American states are in the same condition and will become depopulated and sink into poverty (*Correspondance avec sa famille*, I, 28–29; *Correspondance inédite*, II, 24, 114, 132).

ruined."[200] And a little later he mentions with accents of pleased surprise: "Tropical vegetation was quite new for me,"[201] as it had been for Humboldt. And in fact the America described by Humboldt is the most beautiful thing in the world.[202]

The really curious thing is that this admiration, rather than fading as Jacquemont tramps up and down the fabled India, actually burns more brightly and strongly. The men and nature of America glow in the memory and comparison. Even before leaving for Asia his brief journey to America seems to him "a useful preparation for this voyage to India."[203] To exalt the governor-general, Lord Bentinck, his friend Jacquemont finds no better comparison than that with Franklin and the Quakers.[204] Then as for nature, "the jungles are no more than a flat caricature of the virgin forests of Santo Domingo and Brazil."[205] The countryside of Kashmir is worth nothing.[206] The island of Salsette (above Bombay) certainly cannot be compared with Cuba.[207]

At each step Jacquemont uses the marvels of America to degrade the nature of the Old World. As he comes in sight of the Himalayas — a chain of mountains of tedious monotony — he exclaims: "Oh, how I envy M. de Humboldt his Cordilleras, his virgin lands unequaled in the world."[208] Vast and various as the world is, "the majestic solitudes of Santo Domingo . . . will always be for me the ideal type of equinoctial nature. I have seen Brazil since: it is no less admirable, but it did not give me the same feelings of surprise and tenderness." The forests of North America too are monotonous, of course, yet sublime and poetic.[209] But compared with Haiti, "I find in India neither grandeur, nor grace, nor originality."[210]

200. Chinard, in *Jacquemont*, p. 175.
201. *Correspondance inédite*, I, 99. On the "tedious lushness of the vegetation" in the tropics, *Lettres à Charpentier*, p. 209.
202. *Correspondance avec sa famille*, I, 225. Like Humboldt, in fact (see above, pp. 408–09), Jacquemont feels extraordinarily well in the tropics (*Correspondance inédite*, I, 105, 109–10, 114; Maes, op. cit., pp. 283, 285–87). For Humboldt, with whom he is in correspondence (ibid., I, 239–44, 257–58; Maes, op. cit., p. 354), Jacquemont has at the same time a great scientific admiration and an unlimited moral and literary scorn: his book on Central Asia is unreadable, and the author undoubtedly a great man, but "the most arrant charlatan I know" (ibid., II, 240–41; *Lettres à Charpentier*, pp. 31, 40–44, 73, 148, 169). Cf. Theodoridès in *Jacquemont*, pp. 218–19.
203. *Lettres à Charpentier*, p. 179. From Haiti he writes: "Here I am most happily experiencing the climate under which I must go and live for several years" (ibid., p. 199).
204. Chinard, in *Jacquemont*, pp. 193–94; Brown, ibid., p. 389.
205. *Correspondance inédite*, I, 347, 371; II, 332; Maes, op. cit., pp. 415, 421; Chinard, in *Jacquemont*, pp. 154, 157–58; Jean F. Leroy, ibid., pp. 323–24.
206. *Correspondance inédite*, II, 99. A lake in Kashmir "would cut a poor figure in the Alps" (in Stendhal, *Correspondance*, II, 878); cf. Maes, op. cit., p. 499; *Jacquemont*, p. 413.
207. *Correspondance inédite*, II, 271.
208. Ibid., I, 372; cf. II, 28; Trahard, op. cit., II, 265–66; Augustin Lombard in *Jacquemont*, p. 300; Alexander Brown, ibid., pp. 413–14.
209. *Correspondance inédite*, I, 348; cf. Maes, op. cit., p. 291. But the "Jersey shore," at first sight, seems to him "flat, sandy, and sterile . . . this desolate scene was made even uglier by the hand of man" (Maes, op. cit., pp. 253–54).
210. Chinard, in *Jacquemont*, p. 158; Brown, ibid., p. 413.

As for the natives, the redskins, he has no illusions however. He sighs at their extermination—"the discovery of Columbus was quite fatal for a large part of the human race!"[211]—but one has to admit that they were refractory to Western civilization.[212] In short, his overall judgment on the Americas is very close to the thesis of the "paradise inhabited by devils" (see above, pp. 337–38), so dear to Volney and Thomas Moore (who were two of his favorite authors),[213] and essentially accepted also by Mrs. Trollope (see above, p. 473).

And in fact, when at Poona, in Maharashtra, his host, "a very continentalized Englishman of French origin, a Huguenot of the Cévennes" gets him to read, one evening after dinner, a very recent novelty, "a small and very witty book by Mrs. Trollope on the Americans: *Domestic Manners of the Americans*," Jacquemont is very amused to recognize in it the Americans that he had met five years before: "These are often caricatures, but good likenesses. The book seems to me deliciously written. All the antirepublican deductions of this aged lady are not equally logical: but certainly all the facts that she recounts speak with the voice of reality for those of us who have seen this country. I seem to recognize all of my friends from the other side of the Atlantic. Read these two small volumes if you have the chance,"[214] repeating thus, at a distance of four months, the swift advice that he had already given, as soon as he read the book, to a cousin of his, in reinforcement of the thesis that the American women, enclosed in a sort of caste, remained isolated from the men from every point of view: "Read an English book in two volumes: *Domestic Manners of the Americans*, by mistress Trollope."[215]

X. OTHER CRITICS OF THE RIGHT: ANTHONY TROLLOPE AND THOMAS HAMILTON

There are further echoes of Mrs. Trollope's book, as was almost inevitable, in the three volumes that her son Anthony wrote about the United States after visiting the country at the beginning of the Civil War. His aim, pondered over for many years, was to correct and at the same

211. *Correspondance inédite*, I, 193.

212. Ibid., I, 119. Jacquemont is always firmly convinced of the exemplary value of European civilization. He has seen the "marvels" of Delhi, Agra, etc., and comments obliquely: "Ah! What a great people we are, we Europeans"; ibid., I, 361; cf. *Jacquemont*, pp. 12, 87, 406, 408, and above, p. 484.

213. But the "Oriental perfume" of Moore's *Lalla Rookh* was not his "hobbyhorse" (*Lettres à Sutton Sharpe*, p. 704). For Volney, cf. Maes, op. cit., p. 280. On Jacquemont's relationship with the Idéologues, see the excellent work by Picavet, op. cit., pp. 479, 484–89.

214. *Correspondance inédite*, II, 272–73, letter of 13 October 1832 to Joseph de Hezeta, in Calcutta. On the Englishman, no details even in Maes, op. cit., p. 534. Is he possibly to be identified with the Mr. Shortreed described on his departure from Poona, "a man of superior intelligence . . . but a fanatical Puritan, his soul desiccated by his horrible Bible" (quoted in Maes, op. cit., p. 541)?

215. *Correspondance avec sa famille*, II, 325; letter of 7 June 1832 to Mlle Zoé Noizet de Saint-Paul.

time complete the picture left by his mother.[216] Almost everything she said was true and was worth saying. But she was a woman, interested only in social and domestic life, and thus (he confirms) she did not concern herself with political institutions and their consequences: he, on the other hand, Anthony Trollope, is a man, and will try to do so, though he recognizes his limitations: it would take a Tocqueville to do the job properly.[217]

In point of fact there had already been a Tocqueville, and there was no need of another. At least Trollope, whose aim is to write something light to entertain the general public, says nothing that could take the place of *Democracy in America*. But with the additional complication of his prejudices on the subject of slavery and secession, and the anti-English *animus* of the northern states, the only ones he visited, the outcome of his inquiries is paradoxically the confirmation, in its general outlines, of his mother's diagnosis. He almost seems to be mimicking her words (see above, p. 473) when he writes: "I do not like the Americans of the lower orders," even if he adds: "but I respect them";[218] or else: "I do not like the West . . . I do not love the Westerners. They are dry, dirty and unamusing."[219] Thus even if he extols the scenic beauty of the Green River or the upper Mississippi, finding them far superior to the Rhine,[220] he shudders with horror at the unwholesome regions of the middle Mississippi,[221] and takes a savage pleasure in demolishing the Englishman's conventional image of the great virgin forest as some sort of magic Forest of Arden:

But these forests are not after that fashion; they offer no allurements to the lover, no solace to the melancholy man of thought. The ground is deep with mud,

216. She was still alive, in Florence, but almost completely feebleminded. When she was told that her son Anthony had gone to America: "Anthony!" she exclaimed, "who is Anthony and where, pray, is America?" (Bigland, op. cit., p. 212). The outbreak of the Civil War made his researches more difficult, but provided "an occasion on which a book might be popular" (*Autobiography*, p. 147) — an occasion which Trollope, always so concerned about the proceeds from his books, certainly did not want to let slip! On his sources, see the introduction by D. Smalley and B. A. Booth to their edition of *North America* (New York, 1951), p. x. On the history of the book, see Stebbins, op. cit., pp. 189–90, and the whole of the chapter significantly entitled "American Manners — Revised Version, 1861–62," ibid., pp. 191–209.

217. *North America*, I, 2–3; *Autobiography*, pp. 22, 30, 147.

218. *North America*, II, 89.

219. Letter to Kate Field, from Cairo, "the dirtiest place in the world," in Sadleir, op. cit., p. 233. Nature wanted to make of him, Trollope, an American, and he would have been a good American, "yet I hold it higher to be a bad Englishman, as I am, than a good American, as I am not" (ibid., p. 236).

220. *North America*, I, 214–15; II, 307; his mother had found the Hudson superior to the Rhine and the Danube (*Domestic Manners*, pp. 402–03). The same comparison (to the advantage of the Hudson over the Rhine) occurs in Löwenstern, op. cit., pp. 41–42 (cf. 52–53), and, in some aspects, in Ampère, op. cit., I, 315.

221. "Fever and ague universally prevail. Man and women grow up with their lantern faces like spectres. The children are prematurely old; and the earth which is so fruitful is hideous in its fertility" (*North America*, II, 286). The young Rothschild too, using a metaphor from plant life, found (1860) the United States to be like a fruit that spoiled before it was even ripe (*A Casual View of America — The Home Letters of Salomon de Rotschild, 1859–61* [London, 1962], p. 46).

or overflown with water. The soil and the river have no defined margins. Each tree, though full of the forms of life, has all the appearance of death. Even to the outward eye they seem to be laden with ague, fever, sudden chills, and pestilential malarias.[222]

And he concludes with a pitiless onslaught on the bad manners of the men and women of America.[223] The men spit, boast continually of "our glorious institootions, sir," but have absurd laws on authors' rights and brutally maltreat the workers.[224] Then when someone unconsciously reechoes Clavigero's polemic gambit and criticizes England not for submitting to the yoke of a "bloody tyranny" but for having no edible vegetables, Trollope is scandalized: "No vegetables in England!" The accusation, based on the absence of squashes, fills him with the most comic indignation: and it is amusing to watch him bury the unfortunate critic under a whole cartload of greengrocery, twenty or more different varieties of "vegetables" — not to mention the cabbages that grow all the year round, and the potatoes![225] The lists of one or the other hemisphere's products or "contributions" are among the most naïve and yet most persistent spectacles in the history of the polemic: they would seem to be an outdated curiosity in 1862, if they were not still so frequent in our own day.

But although Trollope criticizes the men for their arrogance and crudity, while recognizing their energy and military valor, the women are complimented on their respectability, learning, intelligence, and alertness, even if he never ceases to complain about their rudeness and haughtiness: "Their manners . . . are to me more odious than those of any other human beings that I ever met elsewhere."[226] And on the faces of all of them, finally, men and women, he sees the signs of premature

222. Op. cit., II, 295; cf. Tocqueville, against Chateaubriand (above, chap. 7, n. 113).

223. Note however that in his novels the American characters are usually treated sympathetically (cf. Willard Thorp, "Trollope's America," in *Two Addresses Delivered to Members of the Grolier Club, New York* [New York, 1950]); that in Boston he found a galaxy of great men (op. cit., III, 68) and that every now and then he has curious moments of "repentance" (e.g., III, 256). He himself, for that matter, calls his book "tedious and confused" and without informative value (*Autobiography*, pp. 149, 151), an "attempt . . . not . . . altogether successful" (in Sadleir, op. cit., p. 235).

224. Op. cit., I, 190–91, 316–17. The law on copyright, or rather the situation resulting from the lack of any protective law, is unjust to the English and harmful to the Americans: ibid., III, 242–47. Despite his wariness Trollope found himself cheated of his author's rights on *North America* too! (Smalley and Booth, op. cit., introd., pp. xxiv–xxv; Stebbins, op. cit., pp. 213–14), as he had already been of those on his book on *The West Indies* (Stebbins, op. cit., pp. 168, 200).

225. *North America*, I, 232–33; cf. above, p. 201, and Stebbins, op. cit., p. 193. But he might have remembered that his mother had extolled the abundance of vegetables in Cincinnati, praised the large juicy blackberries of America (*Domestic Manners*, p. 426), and bewailed the fact that in England the exquisite lima bean was unknown! (ibid., p. 61).

226. Op. cit., I, 301–02; cf. ibid., pp. 37–38. Trollope exempts from his criticisms a small group belonging "to the aristocracy of the land" (his mother had made an exception for a "small patrician band": *Domestic Manners*, p. 404). Some praise in I, 251–52. In the West even the girls are "hard, dry, and melancholy." Though energetic and often beautiful, they are really the most pretentious of tyrants, with whom it would be impossible to fall in love (ibid., I, 213–14; II, 282–83).

senility: a problem caused, he says, not by the climate, but by the radiators! "Hot air is the great destroyer of American beauty."[227] Which taken literally is very true even today—and not only of the women of America. . . .

Another composition very similar to Mrs. Trollope's, both in its title and its conservative and frankly insular approach, is the immense work published by the retired Captain Thomas Hamilton, *Men and Manners in America,* whose two volumes, amounting to almost eight hundred pages, appeared in New York in 1833. Hamilton has met Mrs. Trollope personally (in New York and at Niagara Falls), and admires both the lady and her writings: he has read Captain Hall's book and the poems of Thomas Moore,[228] and composed the account of his rapid but extensive tour, which took him from New Orleans and Charleston to Quebec, to refute the arguments of the members of the British parliament who flaunted American institutions as examples for the English.[229]

One can imagine what to expect from this anti-Tocqueville *ante litteram.* Nor, in particular, are we surprised at his savage portrait of Jefferson—a superficial writer, a man of dogmatic and prosaic temperament, a morally repulsive character, and, what is worse, an unremitting hater of the English.[230]

But Hamilton too wants to trace the effects back to the causes, and find some infallible physical reasons to confirm his condemnation of democratic American society. If the Yankees, for all their intelligence, are so unpleasant;[231] if the American girls, often very beautiful, fade so rapidly that at twenty-two they are "matrons" and at thirty in full decline;[232] if even the partridges and the grouse are tough and insipid,[233] this cannot be blamed, or not entirely, on republican principles. The

227. Op. cit., I, 298; cf. ibid., p. 322. The heating is excessive everywhere: "To this cause, I am convinced, is to be attributed their thin faces, their pale skins, their unenergetic temperament,—unenergetic as regards physical motion,—and their early old age" (ibid., p. 210). Bremer had had the same criticism to make some years earlier (op. cit., II, 361).

228. Thomas Hamilton, *Men and Manners in America* (Edinburgh, n.d., but 1833), I, 23 (Moore), 167 (Hall); II, 169 ff., 189 (Trollope). Some years later (1839) Mrs. Trollope almost drowned in Lake Windermere through her insistence on going out sailing with the "intrepid" Capt. Hamilton (Bigland, op. cit., p. 196). The book was translated into French (Brussels, 1834), into Italian (n.d.) and twice into German (Quedlinburg and Mannheim, 1834). On its influence in France, see Remond, op. cit., pp. 278–79.

229. *Men and Manners,* I, iv, 238.

230. Ibid., I, 46, 315–18, 357–58; cf. above, p. 477.

231. Ibid., I, 225, using expressions similar to Mrs. Trollope's, above, p. 473. But Hamilton has a clear prophetic sense of the great industrial future awaiting the United States: ibid., pp. 298–300.

232. Ibid., pp. 32, 270; II, 15: "an aggregate of straight lines and corners altogether ungraceful and inharmonious." Cf. above, p. 476, and Dingwall, op. cit., pp. 41, 76n. This ungallant verdict (on which see already above, p. 342) was widespread in France during the first half of the century: Remond, op. cit., pp. 476–77, 722.

233. Ibid., I, 21n.

generally sad state of New England society can be attributed largely to the spiritual heritage of the obnoxious Pilgrim Fathers and only minimally to the climate.[234]

But having reached these conclusions, it is precisely the climate that Hamilton blames for the evident physical wretchedness of the North Americans. The extreme change in temperature, together with the exhalations from the swamps, and alcohol and tobacco, are the true culprits of the skinny and sickly appearance of the *whole* population of the United States. Only in the Tuscan Maremma or the Roman Campagna could you find such unfortunate wretches as these. Everywhere fever rules unchecked. The inhabitants are weak and emaciated (once again, three centuries after Las Casas, this ambivalent qualification!): Hamilton never met a single farmhand with those well-toned muscles that are seen everywhere in England! And yet, although it is obviously ridiculous to want to compare such a climate with Britain's, this is exactly what the Americans do, all the Americans, feeling themselves offended and insulted if a foreigner does not go into raptures over every aspect of the nature of their country, if he does not praise the hurricanes as zephyrs, and the boiling sun as dispenser of a sweet tepidity.[235]

This telluric nationalism surprises the Englishman, who finds no way to account for it, and ascribes it to a generic and insatiable vanity particular to the American character.

XI. CRITICS OF THE LEFT: MISS MARTINEAU AND CAPTAIN MARRYAT

There was actually yet another contemporary of Mrs. Trollope who found the American climate enervating, a young actress later to become famous, Fanny Kemble, who described her experiences in her *Journal of a Residence in America* (1835); and she too, having set out for the United States (1832) in a spirit of extreme reluctance and almost despair, with a basic abhorrence for a country lacking ancient cathedrals and august ruins, immediately protested against the primitive and uncivilized customs and excessive drinking.[236] She had not read Mrs. Trollope's book,

234. Ibid., pp. 257–58.
235. Ibid., II, 371–77. On Hamilton, and in general on the criticisms of the United States on the part of the British conservatives, see Lillibridge, op. cit., pp. 10, 29, 38, and the cited work of Fabian, passim.
236. On Miss Kemble, who however immediately recognized the agricultural riches of the United States, an offering from Divine Providence to the poor, "wearied of the Old World" (Heine's expression, coined by him in 1828 [*Englische Fragmente,* X, "Wellington," in *Werke,* ed. O. Walzel, op. cit., V, 155], taken up again by Immermann, etc. [cf. ibid., III, 475] and Heine himself [1851: ibid., III, 62], was current in Germany, and in 1838 Ernest Willkomm published *Die Europamüden:* see Gollwitzer, op. cit., 446, n. 150; G. G. Gervinus, *Einleitung in die Geschichte des 19, Jahrhunderts* [1853: Leipzig ed., 1864], p. 175. "Europamüde? Weltmüde?" [*Neue Zürcher Zeitung,* 16 February 1969]), see A. Craven, *La jeunesse de Fanny Kemble* (Paris, 1882), pp. 207–10, 234–37, 268–69; and Pope-Hennessy, *Three English Women,* pp. 113–208. Her (Miss Kemble's) "whimsical and poetic volume . . . although a little harsh on American manners" (so that she later mentioned having repented of her "impertinences") was what stimulated J. J. Ampère to undertake his *Promenade en Amérique* (ed. cit., I, 4–5).

but as soon as she heard the vituperation that the Americans heaped upon her, she was convinced that she must be right. Certainly if that lady, Captain Hall, or Major Hamilton were to set foot in America again, they would be stoned, and "I myself," she adds with a certain bold coquettishness, "live in daily expectation of martyrdom."[237] Yet before publication her book had been subjected to the censorship of a fervent Americanophile, Harriet Martineau, already famous for her works on economics and labor questions, who made her suppress some thirty printed pages.[238]

But even the poor Miss Martineau, who had neither hearing, taste, nor smell, and was thus impervious to many of the more unpleasant aspects of North American life, after spending two years (from September 1834 to August 1836) in the United States, broke out in scandalized protest against slavery (*Society in America*, 1837; *Retrospect of Western Travel*, 1838) and against the unbearable vulgarity, in a republic, of an "aristocracy of mere wealth."[239]

Unbound by filial tenderness, and even less by any feminine indulgence toward the Europe of her day, the severe Miss Harriet was not tempted to hold it up to the Americans as a model. She drew no comparisons between the two worlds, and limited herself to measuring the divergence between the reality and the sublime ideals of the United States, finding it considerable: "The civilization and the morals of the Americans fall far below their own principles."[240] The American institutions deserve the highest praise, but their literature is worth absolutely nothing.[241] No less evident is the dichotomy between the economic possibilities and the actual conditions of the people. The zealous lady reformer is filled with admiration for the immense natural resources of the United States and filled with scandal at what North American society has succeeded in deriving from them. The landscape could not be more pleasant, or the country more fertile,[242] but the prosperity that could have resulted from these splendid gifts is jeopardized by the speculative spirit and crudeness

---

237. Pope-Hennessy, *Three English Women*, pp. 144–45, 162–63.

238. Ibid., p. 178; Wheatley, op. cit., p. 184.

239. *De la société américaine*, III, 26. For the exact itinerary and the list of persons Miss Martineau visited, see Wheatley, op. cit., p. 161 and passim, and William R. Seat, Jr., "Harriet Martineau in America," *Notes and Queries*, n. s. 6, no. 6 (June 1959), pp. 207–08. Her book was translated into German (*Die Gesellschaft und das sociale Leben in Amerika*) and published twice, in Kassel in 1838 and in Quedlinburg in 1846 (Franz, op. cit., p. 35); and also into French (1838), though this version had little influence (Remond, op. cit., p. 279). On Miss Martineau's lasting interest in the USA, manifested in articles, lectures, extensive correspondence and exchanges of books, see Wheatley, op. cit., pp. 202, 279, 324, 373–74, 382, 386.

240. Op. cit., III, 275 (cf. also ibid., I, 9, 11; III, 272).

241. Wheatley, op. cit., p. 182; but note for example her cordial relations with Emerson: ibid., pp. 157, 192, 277.

242. Op. cit., I, 240, 303. Cf. Wheatley, op. cit., p. 339.

of the pioneers. How come? The country is new and the republic is new, yes, but the races that people it are old, and still imbued with the rancid notions of the countries that the immigrants left.[243] This is a criticism we have encountered before, in Moore, Volney, and Captain Hall (see above, pp. 338–40 and 474), but which with Miss Harriet is tempered by her constant and pugnacious faith in progress. Even the savages — who should be called "young" if the European refugees are "old" — are susceptible of civilization.[244] And the Union has a radiant future before it: the Democrats say that it will be an agricultural country, the Federalists (Republicans) that it will be industrial; but the truth of the matter is that the United States is "predestined to be everything": the great central valleys will supply the whole world with agricultural products, the states of New England (and a few others) will develop their already prosperous industry and commerce.[245]

But this potential is as yet unrealized: while the land is well-tilled and the tillers are often admirable examples of the new society, the cities, on the other hand, are totally devoid of interest. Miss Martineau excuses herself from even discussing them: "If I have said nothing of the cities, it is because the life of the cities in America, considered from a *general* point of view, offers nothing *special*" [sic].[246] In Washington, more than six hundred people leave their visiting cards in a single day, and invitations rain down upon her.[247] But the only city where she unreservedly praises the natural beauty, the cultivated and pleasant society, the good manners and even the museum, is Cincinnati — in obvious implicit polemic with Mrs. Trollope.[248]

On a different but parallel level the young lady from England admires the almost universal (natural) beauty of the American women;[249] but is sorry to see that although they are offered the most maudlin compliments, they are for the most part treated in a way quite inconsistent with demo-

---

243. Op. cit., III, 8.

244. Ibid., I, 374–75. Miss Martineau knew by heart almost all of Moore, on whom see above, p. 337.

245. Op. cit., II, 3–4, 181–82; cf. Mazzei already, above, p. 269; Miss Wright (1821), *Voyage*, II, 161–62; Richard Cobden (1835): "here will one day be the headquarters of agricultural and manufacturing industry," quoted in Lillibridge, op. cit., p. 96, and the prophecies of Sismondi and other Frenchmen, quoted by Remond, op. cit., p. 763, n. 2. With her radical's faith in North American institutions, Miss Martineau is clearly set off from Mrs. Trollope, to whom she was "frankly hostile" (Sadleir, op. cit., pp. 86–87, 90, 105; Pope-Hennessy, *Three English Women*, pp. 77–78, 80; Stebbins, op. cit., p. 49; Wheatley, op. cit., p. 146), and whom she makes fun of concerning her difficulties over domestic help (Smalley, op. cit., pp. 53–54n.; but on many other particular points the two found themselves in agreement: Pope-Hennessy, *Three English Women*, pp. 299, 303), and from Comte, of whom she later (1857) translated a summary of the *Cours* (cf. Wheatley, op. cit., pp. 315–16, 319–22).

246. Op. cit., I, 384; my italics.

247. Wheatley, op. cit., p. 150.

248. *Retrospect*, II, 220, 222, 234–35, 254.

249. In that same year Chevalier is delighted to see (1835) that America has no extremely ugly women, "these repulsive creatures who are feminine only to the physiologist, that are so frequent in our cities" (*Lettres*, II, 227).

cratic principles, and even worse than in certain European countries;[250] and that their terrible hygienic habits give them poor health and unpleasant voices, either whining or strident. These magnificent creatures with their grating accents cannot but remind one of the gorgeously arrayed birds which lacked the gifts of melody! But the women of America too will get over their troubles in time: "the day will surely come" when their voices will have a soft, sonorous silver timbre.[251] And then, hopefully, they will also take better care of their persons, and will be less given to drunkenness;[252] and the American men, with reciprocal chivalry, will refrain from this nauseating habit of spitting with assiduous pertinacity on the wooden floors of hotels, the decks of ships, and the carpets of the Capitol.[253] But it is regrettably obvious that neither the men nor the women are going to grow up healthy and upright, if they do not start taking a little physical exercise. In America, it seems, everybody is hunchbacked, and the women more so than the men: the doctors say that among the boys and girls "it is difficult to find a perfectly straight spinal column."[254]

Although Miss Martineau contrasts and extols the good gymnastic and ambulatory habits of the English, the wary pedagogue misses no other chance of rebuking her compatriots too,[255] and particularly those whose antirepublican prejudices provided an excuse for the outrageous boasting

250. Op. cit., III, 95 ff. In vain she had been advised "not to embark on the thorny topic of American women" (Wheatley, op. cit., p. 176). On the reactions in America, see also ibid., pp. 183–84, 193, 196. In her book on Egypt (*Eastern Life, Past and Present,* 1848) she showed more caution in her judgments (Wheatley, op. cit., p. 266).

251. Op. cit., III, 65–66. Mrs. Trollope too complains that all Americans, both men and women, are tone-deaf and sing without the basic elements of the art (*Domestic Manners,* XXVIII, ed. cit., p. 299). And the criticism appears again in her son's book, as well as in Frederika Bremer's (op. cit., I, 345; II, 246). But how could Miss Martineau, who was notoriously deaf, notice this defect? And how could she be so terribly upset by the tinkling of the sleigh bells (*Société,* III, 140; *Retrospect,* III, 171), that very same silvery music ("Hear the sledges with the bells – Silver bells!") that was to inspire (1848–49) the first joyful stanza of one of Edgar Allan Poe's finest poems?

252. On the inevitable filth on board the steamers, on which the women, for four or five days running, washed only their faces and hands, see op. cit., III, 138; on their intemperance in drink: III, 145–46 (denied by Marryat, *Diary,* II, 120–21). Perrin du Lac too had noted: "The American women are usually criticized for their lack of cleanliness" (op. cit., p. 108), recalling perhaps the Americanophile but indelicate Bayard: "Their [the American women's] cleanliness is all exterior. A false modesty forbids them those salutary ablutions which preserve the health: the men, without having the same excuse, imitate the women in that" [*sic!*] (*Voyage,* p. 66); cf. also Huth and Pugh, *Talleyrand in America,* p. 91; Wheatley, op. cit., p. 181, and above, p. 476).

253. *Société,* I, 360; III, 65–66; *Retrospect,* I, 38, 64; III, 213; Pope-Hennessy, *Three English Women,* p. 299. Some pungent comments from an American, Melville, on spitting in the Senate: *Mardi* (1849), CLVIII, ed. cit., p. 660; and from another American, J. M. Mackie, on the monumental spittoons of the White House (1856): Tryon, ed., op. cit., p. 399n. Cf. also Fabian, op. cit., p. 126, and above, n. 125, p. 476, etc.

254. *Société,* III, 141–42: they are all pale and thin, etc.; cf. *Retrospect,* I, 93, 166 (consumptive and toothless; infant mortality, etc.). The cause of these ills, according to the Americans themselves, is "the languor due to the climate" (*Société,* III, 141–42; *Retrospect,* I, 166–68, 195–96). But there is hope that the climate will improve with the cultivation of the earth (ibid., III, 196; cf. above, pp. 91, 381). Hall had already found almost all the cadets at West Point hunchbacked! (*Travels,* I, 91).

255. On the class consciousness of the English, op. cit., III, 25; on the age-old abuses, their useless or harmful institutions (including the monarchy), etc., III, 46–47. Cf. Wheatley, op. cit., p. 186.

of the Americans: "They entered the United States with an idea that a republic is a vulgar thing: and some take no pains to conceal their thought. To an American nothing is more venerable than a republic."[256]

The same thought was expressed at more or less the same time by the venerable Coleridge, though he did recognize that the Americans cordially disliked the English: "How deeply to be lamented is the spirit of hostility and sneering which some of the popular books of travel have shown in treating of the Americans!"[257] And his complaint could have been repeated over and over again in the years that followed, referring both to the writings of the aforementioned ladies and to the work of the valiant Captain Marryat, who spent two years in the United States studying "the effects produced upon the English character and temperament by a different climate, different circumstances, and a different form of government,"[258] and then published a voluminous *Diary in America, with Remarks on its Institutions* (1839),[259] which, with the help of arguments taken from Tocqueville's recent work (1835) among others, arrived at the conclusion that England, although a monarchy, was considerably more "republican" than the United States: that the latter, strictly speaking, did not even form a nation but the most curious chaos; and that the disappearance of such little aristocracy as existed at the time of Independence had led to the moral corruption of both government and society, and reduced the Republic (capital *R*) to a democracy.[260] By now, Marryat

256. *Société*, I, 155; III, 21–22; *Retrospect*, I, 54, 157. The radical Miss Martineau finds her compatriots insolent toward the Americans, just as the radical Brissot had found the Frenchmen of his time to be (cf. Echeverria, *Mirage*, p. 137). On "self-contentment" as the national characteristic of the North Americans, *Société*, I, 150; III, 59, 274; *Retrospect*, III, 293; cf. also Löwenstern, op. cit., p. 51.

257. *Table Talk* (1832). On Miss Martineau's widespread unpopularity in America, see Pope-Hennessy, *Three English Women*, p. 303; Fabian, op. cit., pp. 15–16; F. Calderón de la Barca, *Life in Mexico*, p. 199 (ridiculing her idea of a police force of old ladies!); Van Wyck Brooks, *The Life of Emerson* (New York, 1932), p. 66, and Dickens himself in Pope-Hennessy, *Dickens*, p. 161 (and ibid., p. 165). In England, where her book was eagerly pushed by the radicals (Lillibridge, op. cit., p. 34), even such a great liberal lady as Lady Holland judged her "a highly vain person, restless when not before the public" (The Earl of Ilchester, *Chronicles of Holland House, 1820–1900* [London, 1937], p. 341); Charles Darwin gently made fun of her (Barlow, op. cit., pp. 148, 264; Wheatley, op. cit., pp. 135, 202); and even a kindred spirit like John Stuart Mill found her unbearable; her very ally and friend Charles Dickens, in fact, finally quarreled and broke off all relations with her (see *Letters from Charles Dickens to Angela Burdett-Coutts*, ed. E. Johnson [London, 1953], p. 292n.); while Matthew Arnold, for all his admiration for her, eventually (1877) concluded that she was totally uncongenial: "What an unpleasant life and unpleasant nature!" (*The Portable Matthew Arnold*, ed. L. Trilling [New York, 1949], p. 632). On the more reserved opinions of Sydney Smith and Carlyle, see Wheatley, op. cit., p. 179, etc.

258. *Life and Letters*, pp. 189–91; cf. ibid., p. 153.

259. I have before me the Paris edition, Baudry, 1839, in 2 vols. in octavo, totaling 700 pp. The original edition is in five or six volumes. It was twice translated into German, and published in Brunswick in 1839 and Stuttgart in 1845 (Franz, op. cit., p. 35).

260. Op. cit., I, 9, 11; II, 166. Tocqueville is frequently quoted, esp. in the 2d vol., and always with full agreement. Marryat is basically a Whig, but his aversion for demagoguery, added to a certain "racism," often incline him toward the opinions of a Hamilton or a Mrs. Trollope (cf. Ampère, op. cit., I, 208; Lillibridge, op. cit., pp. xiv, 21–22, 38–39). The thesis of the moral decadence of the United States after 1776 has a whole long history: see Remond, op. cit., p. 678 and esp. 704, where it is linked to the more general de Pauwian thesis of a degeneration of the whole continent (of which in fact it echoes only an occasional pessimistic touch): cf. also Confalonieri (1837), in *Carteggio*, ed. G. Gallavresi (Milan, 1913), pp. 727–30, and Jones, *Strange New World*, pp. 274, 309.

concludes, "the standard of morality is lower in America than in any other portion of the civilized globe."[261]

Such a profound political and social pessimism brings him very close to Miss Martineau, with whom he also agrees on certain particular details, such as the beauty of American girls, "the prettiest in the world," and that precocious decadence at the age of thirty;[262] though he refers to her usually with the most bitingly critical and hardly chivalric comments — "that old woman was *blind* as well as deaf"[263] — treating her in fact with almost the same acidity he displays for the society of North America.

This society is actually endowed with many valuable qualities and prodigious natural resources, but is inclined to decadence, as already seen in its institutions, by a constant and ominous factor: the climate, that same old fatal climate of the North American continent that makes Illinois, Indiana, and the western parts of Ohio, Kentucky, and Tennessee exceedingly unhealthy, but which is particularly lethal along the Atlantic coast, from Maine to Baltimore, "the most unhealthy of all parts of America."[264]

The race is of excellent quality, the best in the world: suffice it to say that it is substantially English, with a few German, French, Irish, and other Nordic additions. But has it improved or degenerated since the landing of those first precious progenitors? Captain Marryat examines the problem with the utmost care and concludes severely "that the American people are not equal in strength or in form to the English." There are men among them who are tall and robust, but they too are "not well made," just like de Pauw's animals that were *mal tournés*, "ill shapen." While Miss Martineau had found them hunchbacked, Marryat shakes his head sadly at "one particular defect in the American figure common to both sexes, which is, *narrowness of the shoulders*, and it is a very great defect." Exactly how this results from the climate, the captain is unable to explain. "I leave to others" the provision of the relevant clarification. Nevertheless, he repeats, it is certain, absolutely certain, that the whole

261. *Diary*, II, 163.
262. Cf. above, pp. 476, 489–90, etc.; *Diary*, I, 47, 76, 102, 177, 325; II, 112–13 (the climate of the Eastern states is such that "when a female arrives at the age of thirty, its reign is, generally speaking, over").
263. *Life and Letters*, p. 171; in the *Diary* Miss Martineau is attacked more than thirty times, often for several pages at a time, among other things for her intransigent abolitionism (Marryat's father, Joseph, wrote in defense of the Negro slave trade and the son brought back a young Negro as a gift for the Duke of Sussex [*Life and Letters*, p. 96], and in his *Diary* he reasserts the inferiority of the Negro race, I, 105–14). See particularly his sarcastic reply (ibid., II, 306–16) to the *Edinburgh Review*'s notice on the first part of the *Diary*, which Marryat thought was the work of Miss Martineau. "This Solon in skirts" is there depicted surrounded by a circle of American damsels, to whom she recounts at great length the frenzies and desperations of her many admirers, and how she managed to resist them, and remain still "Miss Martineau": continuing until the sun goes down, the fireflies begin to flit about, and the frogs set up their full-throated chorus.
264. *Diary*, I, 187, 325.

thing *is* the fault of the climate: the climate that is harmful to both body and spirit, "enervating the one and tending to demoralize the other."[265]

It was not, however, this picture of fatal decadence that earned Captain Marryat the obloquy of the Americans of his time[266] and a place even in today's American textbooks, but his gaily sarcastic comments on the "Puritan"[267] hypocrisy and prevailing prudery of the young republic. It was Marryat that gave Europe the news that the word "legs" was considered indecent in the United States and was replaced by "limbs," as also the story of a convent school where the "limbs" of a piano were concealed beneath decorous drawers with fringed edges.[268] They were just funny stories, maybe, but with their implicit suggestions of sexual inhibitions and effeminate bashfulness they were more offensive to North American public opinion than any sort of political or climatic slander.

XII. DICKENS: NATURE AND SOCIETY EQUALLY PUTRESCENT

When Charles Dickens left for America he had already read the works of Mrs. Trollope and Miss Martineau, had been treated to further details on the disgusting habits of the Americans by the former, and was already friendly with Captain Hall and Captain Marryat. Yet the violence of his

265. *Diary*, I, 330; II, 142 (the American climate causes beauty to wither and destroys the nervous system). We need hardly seek the "sources" for this widely held theory. Suffice it to recall that similar corollaries had been deduced by Hamilton, an author to whose authority Marryat frequently appeals (op. cit., I, 106n., 305–06, 337n.; II, 65–68, 136, 147, 311). As for the narrow shoulders stressed by Marryat, we know that he himself was "broad shouldered for his height" (*Life and Letters*, p. 223).

266. Already while he was traveling in the United States Marryat's frankness of speech, and the distrust nurtured by the Americans toward yet another European writer coming to "inspect" them and refusing to deliver his opinion before seeing the whole country and returning to England, caused him considerable difficulty, culminating in a hanging in effigy and his novels being ceremonially burnt. "I am not in very great favour with the Yankees here on the borders," Marryat wrote to his mother from Detroit, "they are terribly afraid of me, and wish me away" (*Life and Letters*, pp. 157–58, 170–71, 176; cf. *Diary*, I, 5; *Letters from C. Dickens to A. Burdett-Coutts*, pp. 49, 139n., and see above, p. 478, n. 133).

267. *Diary*, I, 92–94; malicious doubts on the supposed chastity of the Shakers: ibid., I, 42–44.

268. Ibid., I, 203–04; cf. Wish, *Early America*, pp. 286, 572–73; Henri Herz (1866) in Handlin, ed., *This Was America*, p. 190; Bayard had already noted (1791) that "the words chemise, foot, thigh and stomach are equally (like the word breeches) removed from the ladies' dictionary" (*Voyage*, pp. 33–34). Mrs. Trollope mentions that the word *corset* could not be pronounced in the presence of ladies (*Domestic Manners*, XIII, ed. cit., p. 136; cf. ibid., XIV, ed. cit., p. 159, and XXIX, p. 326; and Marryat, *Diary*, loc. cit.). In the *Clockmaker* (1836) by T. C. Haliburton, a Canadian, an art lover has a pair of short trousers and some lace-up boots painted on the indecently naked legs of a Christ child (H. Widenmann, *Neuengland in der erzählenden Literatur Amerikas* [Halle, 1936], p. 112). The sculptor Greenough was criticized for the excessive nudity of his cherubim (copied from the singing angels in Raphael's *Madonna of the Baldachin*), and for the comparatively unclothed state of a statue he executed of George Washington wearing a toga; and Hawthorne maintained that nakedness was not suited for the sculptural representation of modern figures, since everyone now wore clothes (Baker, op. cit., pp. 132–33, 139, 150–51). Kürnberger (op. cit., p. 105, etc.) has some entertaining comments on the "dressing" of pictorial and statuary nudes and the scandal provoked by the waltz. But our own age, more versed in psychoanalysis, has discovered in those prudish wrappings the sign of a sexual obsession: "To conceal the piano-leg is, of course, to sexualise it" (G. R. Taylor, *Sex in History*, p. 215), and "Victorian prudery was only a different form of sex-appeal" (E. S. Turner, op. cit., p. 150). And in fact Capodistria, in Lawrence Durrell's novel, sees a feminine form in every object: "Under his eyes chairs become painfully conscious of their legs" (*Justine* [London, 1961], p. 39).

diatribe—both in the account of his journey, the *American Notes for General Circulation* (1842), which Marryat helped him to compile, and in the notorious "American chapters" of *Martin Chuzzlewit* (1844)—is so sustained and supercilious, and goes so much beyond almost everything else that had been written against the New World, from de Pauw onward, that his biographers have insistently sought for some personal motive behind such acrimony. Now, whether it was because Dickens had been cheated by the American speculators who had launched the Cairo City and Canal Company;[269] or, as is generally believed, because the North American publishers never paid him a penny in author's rights and got rich at his expense;[270] or whether it was because of his theatrical red

---

269. See Pope-Hennessy, *Dickens*, pp. 152, 173. On his American tour (from January to June, 1842), Dickens, on reaching the confluence of the Ohio and the Mississippi, where Smith had already (1784) observed that "the land is so low that it is always flooded and covered with reeds" (*Voyage*, I, 183), and where there should have risen the city of Cairo, he found a horrendous marsh, "a breeding-place of fever, ague, and death; vaunted in England as a mine of Golden Hope, and speculated in, on the faith of monstrous representations, to many people's ruin" (*American Notes* [London, 1907], p. 169); and he observed that "such gross deceits" could only destroy the confidence of people overseas and discourage the investment of foreign capital (ibid., p. 243).

One catches an echo of the hopes that were reposed in the great future of Cairo when Drouin de Bercy, op. cit., I, 83, copied by Compagnoni (*Storia dell' America* [Milan, 1820], I, 19), tells us that the point of confluence of the Ohio and the Mississippi "is equidistant from Pittsburgh and New Orleans, two great commercial centers," a fact which later (1846) gave rise to the project of founding a great business metropolis there (the Rothschilds too were interested in the project: Remond, op. cit., p. 212, n. 122; Boorstin, *National Experience*, p. 298). But it had been realistically described ("the dullest, dreariest, most uninviting region imaginable . . . banks low and swampy, totally unfit for culture or habitation") five years before Dickens saw it by the American E. Flagg (*The Far-West* [New York, 1838], in Tryon, op. cit., 570–71); see already Hall (1828; *Travels*, III, 369 ff.). Later on Bremer described it (1850) as a heap of ruins: "It was supposed to become a great commercial city," but malaria drove away the inhabitants: op. cit., II, 346, and Melville found it the seat of the "old-established firm of Fever & Ague," as well as Typhus, Yellow Fever, etc. (*The Confidence-Man*, 1857, XXIII [ed. London, 1948], pp. 160–61). Its sad reputation comes back in the caricature (1856) of the "Western cockney" (a type that seems to have come right out of *Martin Chuzzlewit*), who has a little nest egg in virgin lands, "and owns a few corner lots in Cairo, and other cities laid down in his maps. These he will sell cheap for cash" (J. M. Mackie, *From Cape Cod to Dixie and the Tropics* [New York, 1864], in Tryon, op. cit., p. 614). The sarcastic references to these cities that exist only on the map and in the fraudulent fantasy of the speculators are far from infrequent (examples in Hall ["Embryo City," *Travels*, III, 280–87], in Löwenstern [1842, op. cit., pp. 65–66, 83], and in L. Oliphant [1855, quoted in Cunliffe, op. cit., p. 157]), and at times seem to be a grotesque echo of those equally frequent jibes directed at the projected and phantomlike metropolis of the Union, Washington (see above, pp. 393, 476).

Cairo is clearly the original for what becomes in the novel the colony and city of Eden. Everyone knew it in the United States, and even in England there were those who had already made the easy identification when Anthony Trollope visited the place (1862), which he found, in the middle of winter and occupied by Northern troops, even more desolate and horrendous than in Dickens's description (*North America*, II, 284, 286; other allusions to *Martin Chuzzlewit*, ibid., III, 258; a somewhat acid reference to Dickens, ibid., III, 238; on Cairo, cf. Stebbins, op. cit., pp. 207, 276, and above, n. 219. And see finally Mark Twain, *Huckleberry Finn*, 1884, chap. XVI [ed. London, 1950], pp. 86, 88, 93). The area to the north of Cairo was for decades the theater of frightful massacres and bloody vendettas (see P. M. Angle, *Resort to Violence: A Chapter in American Lawlessness* [London, 1954]). Still today the city, though an important railroad junction and the river port for a rich region, has little more than 6,000 inhabitants: "once a vast arena for swaggering river men, [Cairo] is to-day a tidy little city that is usually fast asleep behind its giant levees by midnight" (M. Schumach, "New Life on the Mississippi," *New York Times Book Review*, 18 April 1954, p. 15).

270. George Orwell, the author of *Nineteen Eighty-four*, remarks justly that the American chapters of Chuzzlewit are "the only grossly unfair piece of satire in Dickens's works, and the only occasion when he attacked a race or community as a whole," and adds: "No doubt the unpaid royalties were at the

and green waistcoats and the freedom with which he combed his gorgeous locks and artificial curls at table and expressed his frank opinion on certain ladies, features that rapidly succeeded in alienating the Americans, who had been waiting to lionize the wildly popular author of *The Old Curiosity Shop* (whose heroine, little Nell, a "connecting link" between Goethe's Mignon and Mary Pickford, had touched the hearts of the whole populace, from the most illustrious men of letters to the Colorado miners) — whatever the reason, the fact remains that these two books of his contained a barely revised but powerfully enriched compendium of almost all the slanders ever hurled at the American continent. The fact that Dickens concentrates them all on the United States is hardly an extenuating factor.

He did, however, have a precedent in Lenau (see above, p. 372). The young Martin Chuzzlewit's American adventure follows the parabola of the German poet's experience much more closely than that of the English novelist who created him and gave him his own experiences. Dickens left for the United States wrapped in a new and glowing halo of celebrity; he left for a triumphal tour, amply paid, accompanied by his wife in a specially purchased fur coat and their faithful servant, himself furnished with an abundant wardrobe enriched for the occasion with new pins, rings, and chains, and convinced that a writer like himself, deeply concerned with social problems, "involved" one would say nowadays, would feel more at ease among the New World republicans than among the aristocratic Europeans.[271] Martin, on the other hand, like Lenau, decides to betake himself to America in a moment of exasperation and despair. When the good Tom asks him in puzzlement: "Oh, where will you go?" he replies: "I don't know . . . yes, I do. I'll go to America."[272] And immediately America is transformed before his very eyes (as previously before Lenau's) into the land predestined for the fulfillment of his fortune, where he will finally be able to realize his talent as an architect, achieve great things, and for which he must therefore leave at the earliest possible moment, before someone else goes there and forestalls him.[273]

---

bottom of the trouble" (*New York Times Book Review*, 15 May 1949). O. Elton (*A Survey of English Literature, 1830–1880* [London, 1948], II, 210) calls them a "ghastly but specious caricature." Sadleir writes that one might think them derived from Mrs. Trollope's travel notes! (op. cit., pp. 73–74; cf. also E. Johnson, *Charles Dickens: His Tragedy and Triumph* [London, 1953], pp. 442–43; 471–76 and 479).

271. Pope-Hennessy, *Dickens*, pp. 152, 155–56; E. Johnson, op. cit., pp. 357 ff., 404; Bode, op. cit., pp. 156–62.

272. *Martin Chuzzlewit* (Oxford ed.), p. 264: the idea of going abroad is suggested to Martin by his friend John Westlock, who thought that he might find some possibility there, which he did not at home, of earning his livelihood (ibid., p. 251). But it seems that his spiritual father, Dickens, decided to send him there because the sales of the novel, which came out in monthly sections, were running very much below what had been hoped, and also perhaps to give vent to the resentment he harbored as a result of the poor reception accorded to his *American Notes* in the United States (E. Johnson, op. cit., pp. 453–55).

273. *Martin Chuzzlewit*, pp. 280–85; cf. above, p. 374.

But no sooner does he arrive than he is overcome with "a strong misgiving that his enterprise was doomed," and in the diamond ring that his Mary gave him he sees not a glitter of hope but a sparkle of tears.[274] Like Lenau, he experiments with colonization in the hinterland, fails disastrously, a simultaneous victim of the smooth-tongued and shameless swindlers and the pestilential climate, falls ill, and before he is even fully cured, as soon as he can speak, admits that he embarked on a mad undertaking, and that the only thing to do is "to quit this settlement forever, and get back to England. By any means! Only to get back there, Mark."[275]

He does in fact succeed in getting back, but not in freeing himself from the horror of America. In the rest of the novel, every mention of America reintroduces the theme of fever and barbarity. Even the jovial Mrs. Lupin, the prosperous hostess of the Blue Dragon, bewails the fact that Martin went to a country where one goes to prison for helping a poor Negro to escape: "How could he ever go to America! Why didn't he go to some of those countries where the savages eat each other fairly, and give an equal chance to everyone!" So the Yankees are worse than the cannibals. And the unfailing optimist Mark Tapley too has to admit that it takes some effort to remain in a good mood in the United States.[276]

The scene described is the one by now familiar to us, but nobody since Buffon had presented it with such literary virtuosity and richness of color. Humidity dominates the picture: "no end to the water!"[277] The closer Martin and his faithful Mark come to the colony of Eden—a sarcastic designation that becomes even more symbolic when Dickens has one of his characters describe it as "a reg'lar little United States in itself"[278]—the more desolate and monotonous the landscape grows. The two travelers begin to feel that they have stumbled into the horrendous realm of the Great Slough of Despond:

A flat morass, bestrewn with fallen timber; a marsh on which the good growth of the earth seemed to have been wrecked and cast away, that from its decomposing ashes vile and ugly things might rise; where the very trees took the aspect of huge weeds, begotten of the slime from which they sprung, by the hot sun that burnt them up; where fatal maladies, seeking whom they might infect, came forth at night in misty shapes, and creeping out upon the waters, hunted them down like spectres until day; where even the blessed sun, shining down on festering ele-

274. Ibid., p. 358.
275. Ibid., p. 618; cf. Lenau, above, p. 376. Dickens himself, in America, played "Home, Sweet Home" on his accordion every night, "with great expression and a pleasant feeling of sadness" (E. Johnson, op. cit., p. 405), and on the ship bringing him back to England noted quite a few returning emigrants, disappointed, hungry-looking and half naked (*American Notes*, pp. 220–21).
276. *Martin Chuzzlewit*, pp. 762, 848, 851.
277. Ibid., p. 345.
278. Ibid., p. 609. And a little further on (p. 626): "Is the Eden Land Corporation . . . an Institution of America?" And again toward the end: "Neighbours in America! Neighbours in Eden!" (p. 953).

ments of corruption and disease, became a horror; this was the realm of Hope through which they moved.

At last they stopped. At Eden too. The waters of the Deluge might have left it but a week before: so choked with slime and matted growth was the hideous swamp which bore that name.[279]

It seems to be Keats's "hateful land," but with Dickens the emphasis falls on the decomposition of organic matter, the miasmas, the mire and slime, the deadly vapors and endemic fevers, with all-too-evident allusion to the parallel state of society.[280]

And here the question has to be asked: where did Dickens find those characteristic features of the picture of a degenerate and decomposed America? The first and obvious answer is that he took them from life. Already on his first train journey, from Boston to Lowell, Dickens had gazed out on mile after mile of deforested land, and sheared off tree stumps, some neatly severed and others with the trunks half collapsed and leaning on their neighbors, but

many more logs half hidden in the swamp, others mouldered away to spongy chips. The very soil of the earth is made up of minute fragments such as these; each pool of stagnant water has its crust of vegetable rottenness; on every side there are the boughs, and trunks, and stumps of trees, in every possible stage of decay, decomposition, and neglect.[281]

And as he gradually goes farther south and moves inland toward the Ohio and the Mississippi, Dickens grows more and more horrified at each successive panorama of gloom and decay, ghostly solitude and dismal silence.[282]

At the confluence of the two rivers, the supposed site of the metropolis Cairo (Cairo, if we remember our equation, = Eden = USA), his horror reaches its peak: "The forlornest places we had passed, were, in

---

279. *Martin Chuzzlewit*, p. 447. All around are rotting tree trunks, scrawny dogs and pigs, half-naked children, and a fetid putrescence (ibid., p. 451).

280. See for example pp. 611, 621, 622; on malaria ("Eden . . . the settlement a grave") ibid., pp. 608, 953.

281. *American Notes*, p. 62. An occasional pleasant view is found, however, from time to time: p. 141 (the Susquehanna valley), 151 (canal near Pittsburgh), 170 (twilight on the Mississippi). But as Harry Stone has noted ("Dickens' Use of His American Experiences in *Martin Chuzzlewit*," *PMLA*, 72, no. 3 [June 1957], pp. 467, 469–70 and passim: it is his central theme), not a single item that is mentioned with approval in the account of his travels becomes part of the American chapters in *Martin Chuzzlewit*, where instead the negative aspects of the country and people are insisted upon to the point where they come to typify them.

282. For example, *American Notes*, pp. 152, 158, 192 (fantastic shapes of the tree stumps), 248 (unhealthiness of the climate), etc. The passage on p. 158 is the source of the quoted description in *Martin Chuzzlewit*, p. 451. Other parallels would be easy enough to find; but I imagine the boundless Dickensian bibliography already includes a "chart of concordances" or of "parallel passages" for a precise demonstration of this "source" of the novel. (So I thought in 1955, but I see that Harry Stone, in presenting the article cited above, observes that "strangely enough, despite the immensity of the Dickens bibliography, one hunts vainly for such a study" [p. 464]. But Stone is in fact wholly unaware of our polemic, and his sound observations are thus robbed of much of their impact.)

comparison with it, full of interest." All the previous themes return with full orchestra, and a new one emerges to dominate and drown them: the traditional theme of absolute silence — "no songs of birds were in the air" — reinforced this time with references to a monotonous, insipid immobility: "no pleasant scents, no moving lights and shadows from the swift passing clouds."[283]

Once this diapason is reached the horror continues in a prolonged echoing rumble throughout his journey down the Mississippi, which flows through Dickens's pages like some fetid acheron, quite unrecognizable to anyone who remembered it from Chateaubriand's melodious description. Disgusting, monstrous, intolerable, lurid, are some of the labels that Dickens attaches to this vast nightmare river, to this "father of the waters," which, thanks be to heaven, has no offspring like it![284]

Dickens' inspiration then, seems to have been his personal contact with the new continent rather than the reading of one or other of the classic texts of anti-Americanism, and his contribution is thus original, adding a new little "rivulet" to the "Mississippi" of our polemic. But although Dickens is obviously quite uninterested in problems of geography and biology, and even less concerned with theories about the savage or the origin of the continent or the path of civilization, he did in fact absorb something of the vast literature of the debate.

Even the very earliest describers of the Americas had perceived it through the screen of literature and the memories of legendary journeys! It is not impossible that Dickens knew Goldsmith's very popular treatise on natural history;[285] and at the end of the chapter, when Martin finally comes across an "American gentleman," Dickens adds the not too mysterious allusion:

> It was perhaps to men like this . . . that a traveller of honoured name, who trod those shores now nearly forty years ago, and woke upon that soil, as many have done since, to blots and stains upon its high pretensions, which in the brightness of his distant dreams were lost to view, appealed in these words:

283. *American Notes,* ed. cit., p. 169. The most striking sound, at the foot of the Alleghanies and near St. Louis, is the "almost incredible noise" of the frogs (op. cit., pp. 145, 175, 181); cf. above, chap. 6, n. 32.

284. Ibid., pp. 170, 184–85.

285. On which see above, pp. 163–65. Dickens was of course familiar with *The Vicar of Wakefield* (cited also in the *American Notes,* p. 97); and in a speech in New York (1842) even claimed that he read Goldsmith, or his "blood brother," the American Washington Irving, at least five evenings of the week! (Pope-Hennessy, *Dickens,* p. 167). The typical expression "animated nature" occurs twice in *Martin Chuzzlewit* (pp. 265, 478), used precisely in the Goldsmithian sense of "living nature." Dickens also mentions (ibid., p. 341) a line of Jarvis, in the *Good-Natured Man* (act IV: "I won't bear to hear anybody talk ill of him but myself"). His library included a copy of the *Animated Nature,* all Buffon's works, and McKenney and Hall's monumental work on the redskins, as well as the writings of almost all the more recent critics of American society, Marryat, Martineau, Trollope, etc. (*Catalogue of the Library of Charles Dickens . . . ,* ed. H. J. Stonehouse [London, 1935]).

> *Oh but for such, Columbia's days were done;*
> *Rank without ripeness, quickened without sun,*
> *Crude at the surface, rotten at the core,*
> *Her fruits would fall before her spring were o'er!*[286]

And who was this honored traveler? None other than Thomas Moore, whom we have already had occasion to mention twice in relation to the very poem from which Dickens quotes (see above, chap. 7, n. 38, and p. 477); the aged Thomas Moore, who as a good friend of the young Dickens met him after his return from the United States and lent an attentive ear to his outpourings of heartfelt anti-Americanism.[287] Moore's verses had of course exalted the vigor of American nature, but vigor in everything, in both its solemn magnificence and lethal sadness. So that alongside the hymns to Niagara and the glittering lakes, we find the ballad of "The Lake of Dismal Swamp" and the song of "The Evil Spirit of the Woods," all saturated with humidity, fever, and foul exhalations.[288]

Dickens could well have caught something from such contagious material. But he comes closest to Moore in his verdict on the society of the United States—a verdict, or rather sarcastic invective, in which all the traveler's pent-up disdain is released in the *vis comica* of the novelist.

Dickens was very much aware of his reputation as a writer specializing in the study of the underprivileged and lower classes, and of what the Americans expected from the author of *Oliver Twist* and what might interest Miss Angela Burdett-Coutts, and thus in the early chapters of the *American Notes* he talks about his visits to reformatories and prisons, schools and universities, lunatic asylums and homes for the blind, factories and hospitals.[289] But as he moves slowly south and west his disillusionment increases,[290] he gradually weakens in his zeal as inspector of institutions of charity, learning, and repression, and the satirist takes over. One has only to compare the sympathetic description of Boston with the grotesque portrait of Washington, this stupid city where "very

286. *Martin Chuzzlewit*, p. 338.

287. Pope-Hennessy, *Dickens*, pp. 82, 178–79, 190. Dickens owned all his poetical works (*Catalogue*, p. 82).

288. *Works*, pp. 89, 102; cf. "o'er lake and marsh, through fevers and through fogs," ibid., pp. 101–02. It is quite clear however that in these compositions, as in the lines written "On Passing Deadman's Island" (ibid., p. 107, 2d st.), Moore is indulging in the current romantic-funerary fashion.

289. Like almost all the other travelers he notes the general prosperity of the working classes, the lack of pauperism and begging, the fine looks and the relative culture of the workers of both sexes (op. cit., pp. 65, 67); and also the extreme courtesy of manners, particularly toward women (*American Notes*, pp. 55, 145). In fact in a letter to Lady Holland (Baltimore, 22 March 1842) he openly recognizes the good manners of the Americans in general: "I am bound to say that travellers have grossly exaggerated American rudeness and obtrusion" (Ilchester, op. cit., pp. 242–43). With equal chivalry Dickens repeatedly praises the beauty of the women of New York ("the ladies are singularly beautiful," op. cit., p. 95), and a little more ambiguously those of Boston: "The ladies are unquestionably very beautiful—in face: but there I am compelled to stop" (ibid., p. 55).

290. Cf. Pope-Hennessy, *Dickens*, pp. 165, 168, 179, 191. On his initial enthusiasm, which soon waned, see E. Johnson, op. cit., pp. 371, 382–83, 392–93, 404.

little fuss was made"[291] at the presence of the distinguished author. Dickens sees the federal capital as one vast squalid suburb, dreary, half empty, unhealthy. It could be named "the headquarters of tobacco-tinctured saliva."[292] They call it "the City of Magnificent Distances," but it would be more correct to name it "the City of Magnificent Intentions," intentions left unrealized, half completed, abortive. Washington is an abandoned project. And Dickens too, like de Maistre, Thomas Moore, and Perrin de Lac, hazards the prophecy that it will never develop further: "Such as it is, it is likely to remain."[293]

Then in *Martin Chuzzlewit* not a trace remains of the visits to social institutions. The United States is characterized with the usual formula: "geography and not history," in other words a brief past preceded by no dark ages and blood-filled centuries, and vast empty lands.[294] In England it even enjoys the reputation of being an egalitarian democracy.[295] But such a claim could be disproved by the mere existence of slavery, the theme that the writer constantly comes back to, in each of his many

291. Pope-Hennessy, *Dickens*, p. 170.
292. "The head-quarters of tobacco-tinctured saliva" (*American Notes*, p. 111, and E. Johnson, op. cit., pp. 396, 400, 407, 414–15, 443). In the travelers' descriptions the Americans' spitting almost achieves the dignity of a disgusting national rite: see already the diary (1704–05) of Sarah Kemble Knight ("spitting a large deal of aromatic tincture": quoted in Cunliffe, *Literature*, p. 33), above, p. 476, and *American Notes*, pp. 95–96, 111–12, 121–22, 147, 187; *Martin Chuzzlewit*, p. 629, etc.; B. Hall, *Travels*, III, 1; T. Hamilton, op. cit., I, 35, 133; II, 164–65, 190; F. Kürnberger, *Der Amerikamüde* (Frankfurt, 1855, but the novel takes place in 1832), 70, 101, 108, 168, 233, 390, 460; Wish, *Early America*, p. 376; Michel Chevalier, *Lettres*, I, 117; Remond, op. cit., pp. 475, 723, 726. On board a steamer going from New York to Philadelphia a young Irishman found a dense and evil-smelling crowd, "all huddled together in glorious equality . . . and in the most independent manner spitting and smoking almost in each other's face" (Thomas Cather, *Journal of a Voyage to America in 1836* [London, 1955], p. 23). Cf. for 1842, Löwenstern, op. cit., p. 60, for 1851, Ampère, op. cit., I, 185; II, 42–43 ff.; for 1859–71, S. de Rothschild, op. cit., pp. 32, 90; for 1863, G. Capellini, *Ricordi di un viaggio scientifico nell'America Settentrionale nel 1863* (Bologna, 1867), p. 207. The general dirtiness of the Americans while traveling is denounced as the cause of a number of diseases (for Miss Martineau, see above, p. 494; and *American Notes*, p. 156; Johnson, op. cit., p. 408).
293. *American Notes*, p. 116. Cf. the disdain of Volney (Gaulmier, op. cit., p. 206), Talleyrand's cold refusal to be shocked (Poniatowski, op. cit., pp. 328–29); Thomas Moore's "premature ruin" (*Poems*, ed. cit., p. 100, n. 5); the disgust of his young friend Fanny Kemble (Pope-Hennessy, *Three English Women*, pp. 161–62); the scepticism of Löwenstern, op. cit., p. 201; Perrin du Lac (*Voyage dans les deux Louisianes*, 1805, p. 82): "The plan of this town would be superb, if it could be executed; but everything leads one to believe that centuries will pass before this end has been achieved"; and the irony of Capt. Marryat: "Everybody knows that Washington has a Capitol, but the misfortune is that the Capitol wants a city" (*Diary*, I, 115). The same pessimism pervades the above-mentioned Irishman Cather: "Washington is the mere skeleton of a city. The original place . . . will never . . . be filled up" (op. cit., p. 33); Michel Chevalier: "Washington, with its plan designed for a million inhabitants, will probably not have forty thousand fifty years from now" (*Lettres*, II, 197; in fact by 1885 Washington had more than two hundred thousand inhabitants); Miss Martineau: "The city is a grand mistake. Its only attraction is its being the seat of government; and it is thought that it will not long continue to be so" (*Retrospect*, I, 266–67; cf. I, 236–37; the future capital could be Cincinnati; cf. I, 267, II, 240); the bored diplomats mentioned by Remond, op. cit., p. 328; the young Rothschild (1860): as dusty as the Sahara, a lot of new streets, "but not one has been completed; the houses seem to have an unfinished look" (op. cit., p. 33); and the Italian Francesco Carega di Muricce (1875), quoted by Torrielli (op. cit., p. 221), for whom Washington is a stretch of countryside "waiting for houses and people to become a city." Cf. however above, p. 476.
294. *Martin Chuzzlewit*, pp. 340–41.
295. Ibid., p. 270.

guises—Dickens the humanitarian, Dickens the Englishman, Dickens the political economist,[296] and particularly Dickens the sardonic orator: "They're so fond of Liberty in this part of the globe, that they buy her and sell her and carry her to market with 'em. They've such a passion for Liberty, that they can't help taking liberties with her."[297] Nor should we be unduly surprised that on the outbreak of the Civil War, Dickens provoked the wrath of Fanny Kemble (an extreme abolitionist, her views reinforced by her personal acquaintance with slavery on her husband's Georgia plantation) by telling her that he sympathized with the South: he did so "to the extent of not believing in the northern love of the black man nor that the northern horror of slavery had much to do with the war."[298] The northerners were opposed to slavery, yes, but they were still Americans. And the Americans are basically an intolerant people, conceited, indeed arrogant and boastful, ludicrously infatuated with the excellence of their "institutions," conformist, presumptuous and quick to pronounce their proud Catonian condemnations of the corruption of the Europeans, the haughtiness of the enfeebled Britons and anyone in general who nourished the smallest doubt on the excellence of any single aspect of the Union.[299]

Martin Chuzzlewit's summary opinion is related to and almost, I would say, allegorizes the image of the putrid and stinking land: the Americans shirk their minor social duties, and then boast about this as if it were "a beautiful national feature," and thus go on to violate more serious and fundamental obligations. Where it will all end, heaven only knows, but it will certainly be the natural development of an organism rotten at the root.[300]

Rotten at the root: once again one is reminded of Lenau's nausea and terrified reaction. Just as the German poet had sullied the very name of the American nation ("the Swinish States") Dickens organizes a facetious and clownish club of *United Vagabonds* on board the sailing ship that is

296. *American Notes*, pp. 24, 113, 118–19, 126, 132–33, 136, 225–41; *Martin Chuzzlewit*, pp. 350–51, 431–32, 762; Johnson, op. cit., pp. 402–03.

297. *Martin Chuzzlewit*, p. 346. Cf. also ibid., p. 612 ("he always introduced himself to strangers as a worshipper of Freedom; was the consistent advocate of Lynch law, and slavery") and cf. already Moore: "Oh Freedom, Freedom, how I hate thy cant!" (like that of the Americans who "Strut forth, as patriots, from their negro-marts, / And shout for rights, with rapine in their hearts" ("To the Lord Viscount Forbes," in *Works*, p. 100, 1st st.).

298. Pope-Hennessy, *Dickens*, p. 413.

299. On conformism and intolerance: *Martin Chuzzlewit*, pp. 337–38, 612; on the unfailing and fatuous optimism: ibid., pp. 603, 609, 611, 615, 624; on the "institutions," ibid., pp. 613, 626, 629 (Miss Martineau had analyzed the very singular "national contentment" of the Americans [see above, p. 495] and Tocqueville had already produced his definitive pronouncement on it: *Démocratie en Amérique*, ed. cit., II, 233); on anti-European moralism: ibid., pp. 353–55, 611, 613, 615, 626–27. In the *American Notes* Dickens mentions various anti-British boasts (op. cit., p. 196), but also judges the English residents in America with extreme severity (the earth ruining the men?): op. cit., p. 111.

300. *Martin Chuzzlewit*, p. 629.

taking him back to England and mocks the Americans' flag and crest. The stars and stripes had "the remarkable quality of flouting the breeze whenever it was hoisted where the wind blew";[301] and the great American eagle "is always airing itself sky-high in purest aether, and never, no never, never tumbles down with draggled wings into the mud."[302]

The most sacred emblems are ridiculed. The land, the men, the institutions, the symbols and the ideals are dismissed in a single cruel and violent summary condemnation. It is hardly surprising that in these chapters Dickens quotes or refers several times to the cynical Swift. And it is certainly not necessary to examine all the minor criticisms one by one.[303] Nor can we be surprised at the violent reaction that the two books provoked, nor attach too much importance to the recantations which Dickens added later on, in the form of prefaces and postscripts, apparently hoping the indigestible material might prove more palatable when sandwiched between two such slices of good white bread.

Their tone and almost deliberate display of condescending mockery aroused displeasure even in England. Macaulay professed himself shocked at their "vulgar and flippant" style and refused to review the *American Notes,* a work that managed to be "at once frivolous and dull,"[304] The good-natured Longfellow, incapable of a bad word for anybody, who was in London as Dickens's guest, read the volume presented to him by his friend and host at one sitting; he was already pondering over his *Poems on Slavery* (1842), which were to take a number of ideas from the indignant perorations of the Englishman, and paid him the ambiguous compliment of saying that his *Notes* was "jovial and good-natured," although "at times very severe."[305] Of the novelists's other friends, Sydney Smith was enthusiastic about *Martin Chuzzlewit,* but

301. Ibid., p. 634; cf. also p. 335.

302. Ibid., p. 603, and cf. below, p. 515. Mark Tapley, if he had to paint the American eagle, would make it "like a Bat, for its short-sightedness; like a Bantam for its bragging; like a Magpie, for its honesty; like a Peacock, for its vanity, like an Ostrich, for its putting its head in the mud." "And like a Phoenix," Martin replies, happy to be leaving America, "for its power of springing from the ashes of its faults and vices, and soaring up anew into the sky!" (ibid., p. 639). For Dickens's antipathy toward the rapacious American eagle, see H. Allen, op. cit., II, 527.

303. See, however, on the worship of the dollar, *Martin Chuzzlewit*, pp. 334–35; on the bank failures, *American Notes*, p. 96, *Martin Chuzzlewit*, p. 270; on the aggressive and scandal-loving press, *American Notes*, pp. 22, 86, 345, *Martin Chuzzlewit*, pp. 314–15; on the abuse of titles and the boring ceremoniousness of the levees, *American Notes*, pp. 124–26 (and Pope-Hennessy, *Dickens*, pp. 169, 189), *Martin Chuzzlewit*, pp. 333–34; on the Quakers, *Americans Notes*, p. 96 ("the Quakers would have none of him," Pope-Hennessy, *Dickens*, p. 173); on the transcendentalists, whom in fact he should have respected, as followers of his admired Carlyle, *American Notes*, p. 56, *Martin Chuzzlewit*, pp. 634–35. Even the American language is wittily parodied.

304. Pope-Hennessy, *Dickens*, p. 182, who agrees with Macaulay's opinion. Cf. also E. Johnson, op. cit., p. 442, who mentions in addition the foreseeable compliments Dickens received from Mrs. Trollope and Capt. Marryat.

305. E. Johnson, op. cit., p. 441, Parrington, op. cit., II, 441. The *Poems of Slavery* were in Dickens's library (*Catalogue*, p. 94), together with various pamphlets on slavery and copyright, and the early works of other American writers such as Emerson, Melville, Thoreau (*Catalogue*, p. 87).

warned: "You must settle it with the Americans as you can"; and in fact, as Carlyle put it, "The novel provoked all Yankee-doodledum to fizz like one universal soda-water bottle."[306] Carlyle's own wife, the lively and good-hearted Jane, read the copy of the *American Notes* that the author had sent to her husband; at first she found its humor forced and its narrative sections dull, but on reaching the second of the two volumes she became reconciled to the book and found it amusing and instructive.[307] But when she was introduced to a comic American general the terrible Jane could no longer restrain herself: "He seemed then as a living confirmation of Dickens's satires on the American *great men* and several times I burst out laughing in his face."[308]

As for the Americans, Dickens was already well aware that the *American Notes* would not be received with open arms, nor indeed looked on kindly at all.[309] So it surprises us that he was surprised at *Martin Chuzzlewit*, which outdid even the *Notes*, being symbolically de-

---

306. Pope-Hennessy, *Dickens*, p. 190 (in 1867 Carlyle defined current literature as "a poor bottle of soda-water with the cork sprung": *Shooting Niagara: and After?* in *Critical and Miscellaneous Essays* [London, 1907], VII, 221). "At one time, he had inquired and read a good deal about America," and one of his favorite books, in his youth, had been Robertson's *History of America;* now he knew that the workers ate meat there, but he feared that its (political) "principle" was "mere rebellion" (1833: *English Traits*, XI, in *Selected Essays*, p. 222). When Carlyle died Whitman wrote (1881) that he "didn't at all admire our United States," adding to himself, with unusual self-criticism, that perhaps Carlyle did not think or say "half as bad words about us as we deserve" (*Specimen Days*, in *Poetry and Prose*, ed. L. Untermeyer [New York, 1949], p. 679).

307. Jane Welsh Carlyle, *Letters to Her Family, 1839–1863*, ed. L. Huxley (London, 1924), p. 35.

308. Ibid., p. 177.

309. *American Notes*, p. 249; E. Johnson, op. cit., pp. 433–34; Fabian, op. cit., p. 16, n. 51, mentioning that Dickens suppressed a particularly anti-American introduction. A deliberately acid and viperish letter of his referring to the United States (1 April 1842) was published only recently (*The Times*, 31 March 1970; *Herald Tribune*, 31 March 1970). The *Notes* was translated into German three times (1843; 1845): Franz. op. cit., p. 35. And in France, although it was not translated, exercised widespread influence: see Remond, op. cit., pp. 279–80, 739. An immediate reply (1843), published under the title *Change for the American Notes, by an American Lady*, is one long criticism of the English nation and its society, on which see Philarète Chasles, *Etudes sur la littérature*, pp. 329–30. Another pamphlet in reply was attributed to Poe (H. Allen, op. cit., I, xiii). On the relationship between Poe and Dickens, see idem, op. cit., II, 522, 527–29, 615; Pope-Hennessy, *Dickens*, pp. 169–70. Further sarcastic comments (1845) in Tryon, op. cit., p. 191, and E. Johnson, op. cit., I, 442; cf. Bremer, op. cit., I, 19, 40, 189, 266; Chasles, op. cit., pp. 331–32. The verdict of Emerson and his contemporaries is shrewdly paraphrased by Brooks: "All praise to Dickens for showing so many mischiefs at home that Parliament had not been able to remove. But what was the *American Notes?* A lively rattle: too short, too narrow, too ignorant, too slight and too fabulous" (*The Life of Emerson*, 177; cf. pp. 202, 206). Emerson's essay *Social Aims* (in *Selected Essays*, pp. 439 ff) begins: "Much ill-natured criticism has been directed on American manners," but continues: "I do not think it is to be resented," and goes on with due contrition. As for Whitman, after visiting the West himself he had to admit that "Dickens had not been so far wrong after all!" (H. S. Canby, *Walt Whitman: An American* [New York 1943], p. 75; cf. above, n. 306). But still Mark Twain "felt outraged when he read that Dickens denied that the steamboats were magnificent floating palaces" (Wish, *Early America*, p. 379; for some examples, 1827–29, of the hyperbolic American enthusiasm for those "sublime, majestic, phantasmagorical" steamboats, see H. N. Smith, op. cit., pp. 157–58; but Thackeray too had made fun of them, describing them as made of papier-mâché, or consisting of a motor and ten thousand dollars' worth of wooden baubles: Cunliffe, *Literature*, p. 155; but in another work [*The Nation Takes Shape* (Chicago, 1959)], Cunliffe brings out the efficiency and practicality of these vessels, "a distinctively American creation"; cf. also the criticisms of Chevalier, *Lettres*, II, 13–18). Henry James, on the other hand, mentions, and approves, Dickens's passionate protest against the Philadelphia penitentiary (*The American Scene* [London, 1907], pp. 299–300).

stroyed on a New York stage by being thrown into the witches' cauldron in a parody of *Macbeth!*[310] Still twenty-five years later, on the eve of his second and still more triumphal tour through the United States, Dickens had some misgivings about the reception that awaited him.[311] But times had changed, the old polemics were almost forgotten, and the new ones fought out on a higher plane. Property speculation, the cheating of pioneers, the failure to pay authors' rights, the spitting and slavery were no longer in the forefront of the problems of the day. Largely through the good work of a number of native American writers who took up the question of the dignity and mission of their country, the discussion was eventually brought back to first principles and to more rational prejudices.

XIII. REACTIONS IN THE UNITED STATES

A. Emerson and the freshness of American culture. Already back in 1837 Ralph Waldo Emerson, steeped in Germanic idealism filtered

310. Pope-Hennessy, *Dickens,* p. 190; E. Johnson, *Letters to Burdett-Coutts,* pp. 48–49n.; other scornful anti-American expressions in the cited *Letters,* pp. 59 (1843) and 177 (1850).

311. Pope-Hennessy, *Dickens,* p. 421. Even the gentle Hawthorne had recalled (1863), in the preface to his book on England, affectionately entitled *Our Old Home:* "Not an Englishman of them all ever spared America for courtesy's sake or kindness" (quoted by James, *Hawthorne,* p. 151; Pope-Hennessy, *Dickens,* p. 161; and Cunliffe, *Literature,* p. 216). But it is also to be noted that no English critic had been spared by the Americans. See the Americanophile Englishwoman Frances Wright (op. cit., I, viii; see above, p. 470), as well as the already cited writings: against Capt. Basil Hall: [Richard Biddle], *Captain Hall in America, by an American* (Philadelphia, 1830; and London, 1830); Anne Royall, *Mrs. Royall's Southern Tour* (Washington, 1838). Against Major Marryat: William T. Thompson, *Major Jones's Sketches of Travel* (Philadelphia, 1848). Against all the ill-willed travelers: Washington Irving, "English Writers on America," in *The Sketch-book,* pp. 44–52; Robert Walsh, *An Appeal from the Judgements of Great Britain respecting the United States of America,* 1819 (see E. Castle, *Der grosse Unbekannte,* pp. 184, 232, and Curti, *Probing Our Past,* pp. 200–01); James K. Paulding, *The New Mirror for Travellers* (New York, 1828), who, according to Reynolds (*Beds,* p. 203), is decidedly anti-American in his *John Bull in America,* in which he attacks even Chastellux as an infatuated Americanophile. On Paulding, who also wrote *The United States and England* (New York, 1815) and *A Sketch of Old England, by a New England Man* (New York, 1822), see Curti, *Probing our Past,* p. 200. See also Asa Greene, *Travels in America by George Fibbleton, Ex-Barber to the King of Great Britain* (New York, ca. 1830–32); Calvin Colton, *The Americans by an American* (London, 1833); Caroline Gilman, *The Poetry of Travelling in the United States* (New York, 1838; see Tryon, op. cit., xi, 167, 613, 783–91); the Frenchmen Michel Chevalier, *Lettres,* I, 156–57, and Gustave de Beaumont (Fabian, op. cit., pp. 126–28); the American Catherine Sedgwick (Pope-Hennessy, *Three English Women,* p. 230); and the Canadian Thomas Chandler Haliburton, *The Clockmaker,* 1838–40; and cf. Vail, op. cit., pp. 311–18, and the almost contemporaneous essay by P. Chasles, "Les Américains en Europe et les Européens aux Etats-Unis," in his *Etudes* (see n. 309), pp. 237–81, besides pp. 405–06. The most interesting reaction however is seen not in these displays of pique and petty susceptibility but in the replies that came from Emerson and the other spokesmen of a new American consciousness, operating on a considerably higher level. One of these men, moreover, Melville, wrote the most laconic satire (a work that I have not seen mentioned elsewhere) of the works of the British travelers, imagining that the library of Oh-Oh contained a manuscript entitled *Three Hours in Vivenza* [i.e., the United States], *containing a Full and Impartial Account of that whole Country by a Subject of King Bello* [i.e., the King of England]: *Mardi* (1849), cxxiii, in *Romances,* p. 587. Nevertheless, after the painstaking studies carried out by Fabian, one cannot ignore the fact that these malevolent English travelers contributed a number of polemical observations and themes to the philosophical and systematic mind of no less a person then Tocqueville: see Fabian, op. cit., esp. pp. 6–27, 31–32, 46, 121–28.

through Coleridge and Carlyle and rebaptized "transcendentalism" (the Transcendental Club had just been founded in the previous year), had apostrophized his compatriots with his Fichtian discourse on the mission of the intellectual in the United States, *The American Scholar,* which was hailed, in the terms of Oliver Wendell Holmes, as "our intellectual Declaration of Independence," although it strikes today's reader as a curious emulsion of messianic oratory, academic pedagogism, and faith in naturalistic predestination.

The destiny of the "American scholar" is watched over by the propitious stars of the New World.[312] The end of his apprenticeship is in sight. He no longer has anything to learn from the traditions of the European world. Nature and his solitary soul will offer him a higher wisdom, a more universal image. Books themselves, the symbol and incarnation of inherited learning, are dangerous instruments: "I had better never see a book than to be warped by its attraction clean out of my own orbit, and made a satellite instead of a system." The function of the scholar, then, is not to study and teach, no: the scholar must be prophet and patriarch; he must encourage, relieve, and guide men, showing them the "facts" among the "appearances." He will not ignore the past, but will use it as a sort of extended echo chamber for his prophecies. "Whatsoever oracles the human heart, in all emergencies, in all solemn hours, has uttered as its commentary on the world of actions—these he shall receive and impart. And whatsoever new verdict Reason from her inviolable seat pronounces on the passing men and events of today—these he shall hear and promulgate."[313]

Emerson's mysticism, strongly colored by the myths and maxims of the ancient orient, rivets him in a radically antihistorical viewpoint. His divinities are the Soul (or the "Oversoul"), Harmony, Nature, the abstract "representative" or typical individuality—everything least his-

312. *The American Scholar* (1837), in *Complete Works,* Centenary ed., I, 114, 414–16. On some of its precedents (C. J. Ingersoll, 1823, on whom see above, p. 468; W. E. Channing, 1830, on whom see Fabian, op. cit., pp. 19, 58–79)—to which one might add Chastellux, *Voyages,* II, 286; Longfellow's *Defense of Poesy* (1832); and Timothy Dwight's thoughts on *Nationalism in Literature and the Arts* (1834), included in Tryon, ed., op. cit., pp. 120–29—see Jones, *Ideas in America,* p. 276, n. 13; Cunliffe, *Literature,* pp. 44–45; idem, *The Nation Takes Shape,* pp. 182–83; Lewis, op. cit., p. 78. Miss Martineau immediately spoke of it with prolix enthusiasm (*Retrospect,* III, 52–53, 229–40). On its agreement with Longfellow's convictions ("importance of native themes") and influence on Lowell, Melville, Thoreau, see Brooks, *New England,* pp. 208–09, and Matthiessen, op. cit., pp. 13n., 37, 191, 648, who still (1941) dedicates his *magnum opus* to the ideals deriving from *The American Scholar* (ibid., p. xvi). Boorstin, *Genius,* p. 194, finds that *The American Scholar* "still speaks to us," and Cornell University Press reprints it (1955) because it is "remarkably pertinent to the scholar's position in today's world." Its fundamental theme, that of the existence, or promise, of an original American culture, independent and historically valid, is in fact frequently and loudly repeated in our own time: see among others, the numerous writings of the Mexican Leopoldo Zea, and especially *América en la historia* (Mexico, 1957).

313. Cf. Brooks, *Emerson,* pp. 74–80; A. Schalk de la Faverie, *Les premiers interprètes de la pensée américaine* (Paris, 1909), esp. pp. 314–20, 330–35.

torical and concrete. History, he once said, is basically biography;[314] the biography of representative men, mannequins of ideas, schemes of functions, allegories of the spiritual faculties. Europe, burdened down with tradition, pales into insignificance before America, the potential pattern of the future. The mystical—or, if you like, transcendental—union of America with the soul of the Universe has no need of priests or secular liturgies. The Protestant Emerson is quite happy to do without clergy, links with the past, or assistance from Europe.

What was the most pressing problem, then, for the Transcendental Club? It was still the same old problem of the discrepancy between the virgin immensity of the continent (geography) and the modest products of American genius (history). Where Goethe saw a happy uncontaminated purity these Americans bewailed their impotence, their lack of violent passion and futile (but energetic) strife: "not one drop of the strong black blood of the English race! No teeth and claws, nerve and dagger" (almost a paraphrase, though unconscious of course, of the *Ritter- und Räubergeschichten*,[315] "the tales of knights and brigands"). America is a mediocre and uneasy country, "a country without an aristocracy"; and its great men? "Staid and timid mostly—no fiery grain." They are inconclusive, superficial, presumptuous.[316]

But the English too had once been uncouth and savage, and they had produced a Shakespeare, a Milton, a Carlyle. Perhaps the brute insensibility of the Americans harbors the seeds of their future Genius. The more he suffers at the squalid situation of the present, the more the "transcendentalist" Emerson burns with faith for what America will be. "We have yet had no genius in America . . . yet America is a poem in our eyes; its ample geography dazzles the imagination, and it will not wait long for metres."[317] Obviously this ideal transcends not only the crude

314. Cf. Thoreau, "We do not learn much from learned books, but from true, sincere, human books, from frank and honest biographies" (*A Week on the Concord and Merrimack Rivers*, 1849, in *Walden and Other Writings*, p. 351).

315. And, in fact, on the "Gothic" inspiration of Emerson's reverence for the fierce Saxon, see Samuel Kliger, "Emerson and the Usable Anglo-Saxon Past," *Journal of the History of Ideas*, 16, no. 4 (October 1955), pp. 476–93.

316. Brooks, *Emerson*, pp. 108, 194–99 (and cf. idem, *New England*, pp. 269–70; while the nationalist Ingersoll had fiercely denied [1810] that there was "more ferocity in the English than in the American character": Tryon, op. cit.). Even the Americans' bodies are physically incomplete! (*Emerson*, pp. 196, 208). And see also the *English Traits*, "Race" (*Selected Essays*, Nelson ed., pp. 229, 241–45) recalling, apparently, the polemics on the stature of the Americans (see above, pp. 242–44). Still toward the end of his life (1873) Emerson contrasted Egypt, "the land of eternal composure," to nervous America (*Emerson*, p. 305; cf. below, n. 384), but his scorn for Egypt ("Egypt is uninteresting") scandalized Henry Adams (letter to Oliver Wendell Holmes, 4 January 1885, in *Henry Adams and His Friends*, ed. Harold Dean Cater [Boston, 1947], p. 135).

317. *The Poet*, in *Selected Essays*, pp. 148–49. And again: "Massachusetts, Connecticut River and Boston Bay you think paltry places, and the ear loves names of foreign and classic topography. But here we are; and, if we will tarry a little, we may come to learn that here is best" (*Heroism*, ibid., p. 108). Curtius sees the passages quoted from *The Poet* as the announcement, typical of the new American genius, of a union of nature with the spirit, of an eternal Revelation with the daily toil, industry, and traffic ("Emerson," in *Kritische Essays zur europäischen Literatur* [Berne, 1950], pp. 130, 133–35).

America of his time but the highly cultivated Europe too. Emerson, despite his boundless admiration for England—he goes so far as to say that the English are taller and stronger than the Americans, almost as if he himself were one of those innumerable English travelers in the United States!—accuses that same country of the very fault that the Europeans say and will continue to say is the besetting sin of the Yankees, an excessive commercialism, a too-exclusive interest in mechanical arts and moneymaking techniques. Later, in the essay *Culture,* he will bemoan the fact that "all educated Americans, first or last, go to Europe. . . . Can we never extract this tapeworm of Europe from the brain of our countrymen?"[318]

As the years pass Emerson grows ever more convinced of the promise of a glorious destiny in the very bareness and barren grandeur of America. Already in 1844 he casually transmutes America's telluric characteristics into messianic omens. It is to be believed "that here shall laws and institutions exist on some scale of proportion to the majesty of nature. To men legislating for the area betwixt the two oceans, somewhat of the gravity of nature will infuse itself into the code."

But this whole discourse is typical, with its contrast between the "young" American and the ancient Europeans, between democratic railroads and the medieval culture of the Old World, the virgin soil of America as remedy for the "errors of a scholastic and traditional education," and Commerce (capital *C*) destroying the forces of Despotism, Feudalism, and Autocracy. Emerson's peroration, like Paine's before him, triumphantly opposes England's burden of feudal traditions to the freshness of American civilization:

Our houses and towns are like mosses and lichens, so slight and new; but youth is a fault of which we shall daily mend. This land too is as old as the Flood [a subconscious polemic against the thesis of the immaturity of the Continent?], and wants no ornament or privilege which nature could bestow. Here stars, here woods, here hills, here animals, here men abound, and the vast tendencies concur of a new order . . . a new and more excellent social state than history had recorded.[319]

Once again the very "stars" are invoked to guarantee the continent's destiny. Astrology swims up from the depths of the past to surface in the dreams and homilies of the utopian.

But the more immediate natural factors offer a somewhat less certain

318. *Selected Essays,* p. 382, echoing, apparently, Jefferson's proud repudiation (letter to J. Bannister, Jr., 15 October 1785, Modern Library ed., pp. 385–88); on the futility of travel, cf. *Selected Essays,* pp. 31–33. Similar expressions (e.g. "Forget Europe wholly,") in J. R. Lowell, *A Fable for Critics,* 1848, in Rascoe, op. cit., p. 363.

319. *The Young American,* 1844, in *Complete Works,* I, 370, 395; cf. C. and M. Beard, op. cit., p. 197, and above, chap. 5, n. 391. Walt Whitman too, in his discourse on Lincoln (1879), was to speak of the "western star," the planet Venus, shining "as if it told something, as if it held rapport indulgent with humanity, with us Americans" (quoted in Matthiessen, op. cit., p. 619).

guarantee. As he grows older Emerson is more and more tepid in his repetition of the German metaphysics, and instead begins to absorb and brood over the teachings of the all-triumphant natural science, and, unfortunately, its Buckleyan applications to history.[320] Although he continues to admire and praise Humboldt, who resolved the old causal and deterministic relationship between creature and environment in "harmony" (see above, p. 409), Emerson almost goes so far as to allow that climate "controls" man, unless the latter is some ethical genius:

The highest civility has never loved the hot zones. Wherever snow falls there is usually civil freedom. Where the banana grows, the animal's system is indolent and pampered at the cost of higher qualities, the man is sensual and cruel. But this scale is not invariable. High degrees of moral sentiment control the unfavorable influences of climate; and some of our grandest examples of men and races come from the equatorial regions.

And he concludes, with a typical logical compromise, that for civil progress "temperate climate is an *important* influence, though not quite indispensable";[321] or that "the expression of character . . . is, *in a great degree,* a matter of climate. In the temperate climate there is a temperate speech, in torrid climates an ardent one."[322]

On the subject of his own America in particular, the patriot Emerson found that it possessed "a happy blending of advantages" including the warm equatorial summers, favorable to the growth of genius and cucumbers;[323] but, ever wavering, he later regretted, albeit jokingly, that in America men had not learned to repair "the exhaustions of our climate," while the "mental power" of the *literati* was restored by wine in England, whiskey in Scotland, beer in Germany, etc.[324]

And finally, during the Civil War, his old aversion to slavery (said by some to be apt and suitable to the soft climate of the south)[325] reappears

320. In his *History of Civilization in England* (1857; trans. A Baillot, Paris, n.d., I, 111–38), the Comtean Buckle attempted to show with physicoclimatic reasons why such a great part of America had remained without a shadow of civilization and only in Mexico and Peru were there formed social and political organisms that were relatively evolved. In America, as in the other parts of the world (with the exception of Europe, the center of his historical universe), Nature weighs down on man, keeps him in a state of savagery and misery, exalts his "imagination" and depresses his "reason," and is thus more an obstacle than a stimulus to civilization.

321. *Civilization,* in *Society and Solitude,* 1870: *Complete Works,* ed. cit., VII, 25–26; but the essay cited is from 1861–62; see ibid., pp. 351–52; cf. C. and M. Beard, op. cit., p. 191, and Weinberg, op. cit., p. 94 (the economic and thus political incapacity of the inhabitants of the Tropics). Raynal had already exempted man from tropical degeneration thanks to his "morale" (cf. above, p. 46).

322. *The Superlative,* in *Works,* X, 176.

323. *Journal,* 28 June 1847, ed. cit., VII, 294. Berkeley (*Alciphron; or the Minute Philosopher*) had compared "the southern wits to cucumbers, which are commonly all good in their kind, but, at best, are insipid fruit; while the northern geniuses are like melon, of which not one in fifty is good, but when it is so, it has an exquisite relish"; and Hume had accepted Berkeley's observation (*Essays,* p. 215).

324. *Journal,* August 1861, ed. cit., IX, 333. Cf. the earlier statement of Crèvecoeur on the Americans: "As northern men they will love the cheerful cup" (*Letters,* III, ed. cit., p. 51).

325. Referring to slavery an imprudent Detroit politician made the curious statement (1848): "[I] think it the best thing for the nigger, the master, and the unhealthy climate of the South" (J. L. Peyton, *Over the Alleghanies, and Across the Prairies* [London, 1870], in Tryon, op. cit., p. 596; when the Civil War broke out Peyton loyally served the Confederacy and subsequently remained in England until 1876).

in tones that are strangely reminiscent of the old theories, used by Montesquieu and Voltaire but already criticized by Hume: "Freedom . . . long . . . loved the northern well; / Now . . . she will not refuse to dwell / With the offspring of the Sun."[326]

Liberty, faithful lover of the snowy north, will not easily adjust to life in the tropics. She does not like bananas or cucumbers. At least in the north when she felt her strength failing she could get back on her feet with a quick pull at the bottle.

B. Lowell and Melville: messianism and desperation. This mystic faith in the privileged destiny of the new continent, in an arcane and messianic predestination, reappears in all the major North American writers of the period (apart from Poe, of course), though not as carefully argued as in Emerson. Some, like Thoreau and Whitman, can be considered direct disciples of the sage of Concord. Others, like Lowell and Melville—the former as rich in waggish humor as Emerson was lacking therein, the latter calvinistically impervious to the transcendentalist's fluent optimism—draw on other remoter sources too, or on more personal experience, but merge into the same current. All of them show at least some signs of the polemic against Europe, and a sometimes worshipful, sometimes fearful deification of nature. Even when they exalt the new society of the United States, new because recent or quite simply because it is still only on the threshold of realization, they take pains to "deduce" it from the physical environment, and make an article of faith of its pre-established harmony with the immensity of the continent, the virgin power of the forests and the mighty surge of the great rivers. They anchor their often hesitant or despised ideals to the tall unshakable stanchions of a prodigiously lavish nature.

"Forget Europe wholly," advised James Russell Lowell in 1848, "let her sneer." Thank your God that there is a whole ocean between you and Europe; and forgetting all tradition, freed from all chains, stand up like the pine trees in your woods, build your plans on the scale of a whole hemisphere, remain faithful to yourselves, to this nineteenth century, and to your own American sentiments—"to your New-World instincts contrive to be true"—and what you do will be something unheard-of, brand new, provided you keep your ears cocked for the first peals of the Future.[327]

---

326. *Voluntaries,* October 1863, ed. cit., IX, 206. On a lecture given in 1861, in which he scarcely mentioned abolitionism and exhorted his audience to revere the American Eagle but not the American Peacock, see the account of a skeptical member of his audience, Anthony Trollope, *North America,* II, 7–8.

327. *A Fable for Critics,* loc. cit., pp. 363–64. Lowell "as an undergraduate had listened eagerly to *The American Scholar*" (Matthiessen, op. cit., p. 37). Later (1869), he published his famous satire against those Europeans, and especially the English, who had mocked American culture: *On a Certain Condescension among Foreigners* (which gave Matthew Arnold the cue for saying his *Word about America,* 1882, in *Five Uncollected Essays,* I, 22). Already the eighteenth-century Pennsylvanian poet

The early Melville (1846–47) takes us back along Bougainville's well-marked trail to a slightly more western west, to the archipelagoes of Polynesia, to witness the rebirth of the myth of the Noble Savage, serene and affable, gentle and discreet, unacquainted with strife and crime and internal spiritual torments: the savage who remains anthropophagous and happy until the arrival of the French or English missionaries, followed in due course by rapacious merchants,[328] the savage who will eventually attain the living form of art in the shape of the noble cannibal Queequeg, in *Moby Dick*.

But in Melville the yearning for primitivism as the symbol of innocence and spontaneous goodness was held in check by his conviction of man's original wickedness, and innate depravation.[329] The tension of the dilemma was released in the indictment of the "white man" who came and disturbed the innocent purity of the "native." Melville, filled with prophetic anger and solomonic despair, but still the spiritual son of Jean-Jacques,[330] is shocked at this presumption of "civilized" people, as the vainest of hypocrisies.

Nathaniel Evans had warned: "we are in a climate cast / Where few the muse can relish" and that "a shining heap of gold / Alone can man embellish" (quoted in Cunliffe, *The Nation Takes Shape*, p. 188); and one might mention the analogous indeed slavishly imitative justifications of the *Revue encyclopédique* (1820: Remond, op. cit., p. 301); and then of Charles J. Ingersoll (1823: ibid.; cf. also pp. 671, 763–64), of Basil Hall, 1828, *Travels*, II, 305, and Francis Lieber, who explained (1834) the lack of an American literature by saying that a nation or individual "could not at the same time attend to arts and letters and to a thousand things more directly connected with the well-being of life" (Curti, *Probing Our Past*, p. 144), and, almost in our own times (1908!), the incredible opinion of the Hungarian Vay de Vaya und Luskod: "their (the United States') most distinguished thinkers have produced hardly any influential book" (quoted in Handlin, *This Was America*, p. 417). Thus Lowell replies to the famous question of Sydney Smith (see above, chap. 7, n. 294), which still smarts, that America had *first* to grow rich, and could then cultivate letters: "The arts have no chance in poor countries. The *Edinburgh Review* never would have thought of asking: 'Who reads a Russian book?' " (quoted in Tryon, op. cit., I, xiii): a fine example of special pleading, taken up, without however any apologetic intent, by Henry James (cf. below, p. 547). Still in our own day an editorial in the *Times Literary Supplement* ("Wholly American," 6 November 1959) quite candidly absolves the Americans for their artistic sterility: "For the past century the Americans have been so busy building their own society to meet their own needs that they might excusably have neglected the arts for the practical sciences."

328. Matthiessen, op. cit., p. 376: Melville quickly realized that "all the pretences of civilization might be no better grounded" than those of the missionaries, and was thus also suspicious, convinced antislavist though he was, of the propaganda of the abolitionists (ibid., p. 383). Other justifications of the savage *qua talis* in Pearce, *The Savages*, p. 244.

329. "That Calvinistic sense of Innate Depravity and Original Sin, from whose visitations, in some shape or other, no deeply thinking mind is always and wholly free," wrote Melville himself, on the subject of Hawthorne (quoted in Matthiessen, op. cit., p. 190; cf. ibid., p. 243). And Pearce: "Something like Original Sin becomes the prime fact of our political and social history. Adam's Fall and the Idea of Progress become not two myths but one" (R. H. Pearce, "Hawthorne and the Sense of the Past, or, The Immortality of Major Molineux," *English Language History* [December 1954], p. 330; cf. p. 339). Bergson had already begun his last great work with the same assertion: "The memory of the forbidden fruit is the oldest thing in the memory of each one of us, as in that of humanity" (*Les deux sources de la morale et de la religion* [Paris, 1932], p. 1).

330. Parrington, op. cit., II, 264; Matthiessen, op. cit., pp. 377, 463. The "savages," says Melville, do not exist. There are pagans and barbarians that the bloody European aggressors have made fierce to the point that they became savage (*Typee*, IV, loc. cit., p. 27; cf. ibid., XVII, 91–92; XXVI–XXVII, 137–44; *Omoo*, XLVII–XLIX, loc. cit., pp. 291–98). The sympathetic Larry has nothing but enthusiasm for the "free and easy" life of the people in their natural state; and his "sentimental distaste

After the success of their revolt, the Americans have raised "a vaunt-ful crest."[331] They are free, yes, but only because in their youth they challenged the powers and conventions of the past, and now with the passing years they are already losing their liberty and threatening other people's: "He, who hated oppressors, has become an oppressor him-self,"[332] maltreating the poor Negro slaves in his own country and threatening neighboring countries, and those farther off too, with an ag-gressive expansionism worthy of any czar.[333]

Melville has his countrymen cry out with words that bear a remark-able resemblance to those Dickens put into the mouths of the ridiculed Americans of *Martin Chuzzlewit:* "Saw ye ever such a land as this? Is it not a great and extensive republic? Pray, observe how tall we are [the old boast of stature!]; just feel of our thighs; are we not a glorious peo-ple? Here, feel of our beards [no beardless wonders, these Americans!]." England's mountains are barely perceptible bumps in the ground com-pared to ours: her rivers, mere trickles, her empires villages, her palm trees mere bushes.[334] And like Dickens before him Melville spares nei-ther badge nor banner of the United States: red like the stripes on the flag are the stripes left by the whip on the Negro's back,[335] and that vaunted bald eagle is barely distinguishable from a blood-soaked vul-ture.[336]

---

for civilized society" moves him to "some illiberal insinuations against civilization," which conclude with the refrain: "Blast Ameriky, I say!" (*Redburn*, 1849, XXI, loc. cit., 1529; cf. the "unhandsome notions" of the cripple in *The Confidence-Man* "about free Ameriky, as he sarcastically called his country": XIX, ed. cit., p. 124). And Melville concludes: "We may have civilized bodies and yet bar-barous souls" (*Redburn*, LVIII, loc. cit., 1648; cf. below, n. 342).

331. *Mardi*, 1849, CXLVI, loc. cit., p. 635.

332. Ibid., CLXI, loc. cit., p. 666.

333. Ibid., CLXI, loc. cit., p. 669; CLXIV, 674, 676. On slavery and the secessionism of the South, ibid., CLVII (p. 659) and CLXII (pp. 669–72). On the iniquitous oppression of the redskins, ibid., CXLV, loc. cit., pp. 633–34; and *The Confidence-Man*, XXV–XXVII, ed. cit., pp. 173–89.

334. *Mardi*, CLXVIII, loc. cit., p. 659; cf. the comments of Van Wyck Brooks in *The Times of Mel-ville and Whitman* (London, 1948), p. 120n., and Matthiessen, op. cit., pp. 382–83. See also the whole of the proud and frenzied speech by the representative from Ohio, in *Mardi*, ibid., pp. 661–62. Parring-ton (op. cit., II, 266) makes it absolutely clear that Melville's criticisms of American civilization were so radical ("he outran Thoreau in contempt for current material ideals") that the America of his time could not even understand him: "It turned away and ignored him." And more generically Wish, *Early America*, p. 464: "His novels seemed too pessimistic for the optimistic 1850's." Even the characters in *The Confidence-Man* (1856–57) have been said, by John Freeman (*Herman Melville* [London, 1926]) to "support Dickens' worst charges in *Martin Chuzzlewit*" (see also L. Mumford, *Herman Mel-ville* [New York, 1929], p. 253, and cf. p. 281, which however rejects the assertion). In point of fact, despite the similarity of some scenes, such as that of the lot-salesman in the yet-to-be-built city of New Jerusalem (*The Confidence-Man*, IX, ed. cit., pp. 71–72; cf. *Martin Chuzzlewit*, pp. 423–24), Dickens satirizes the Americans, while Melville sprinkles his sarcasm over all humanity. *Martin Chuzzlewit* and Mrs. Trollope are also named, though with some confusion, by Roy Fuller, in his introduction to the cited ed. of *The Confidence-Man*, p. xii.

335. *Mardi*, CLVIII, loc. cit., p. 659. Already at least one American, James Fenimore Cooper, had found the flag with its stars and stripes ugly, just as he found the beauties of the American landscape in-significant in comparison with those of Switzerland or Italy (Castle, op. cit., pp. 417–18).

336. Ibid., CLXI, loc. cit., p. 667. Volney had already pronounced a quite precise verdict on the

These are always random and unargued outbursts, of course. But they fit perfectly into his radically pessimistic view of the civilized society, a vision fed on the sight of a world where slavery, tyranny, and arrogance prevailed: and which in turn reinforced his tragic sense of the fearful power of evil — that obstinate obsession that was to become incarnate in the hunt for the white whale, and which was to be the very life and ultimate ruin of the fearless and accursed Captain Ahab, that dismal hero so irrevocably damned.

Melville could thus hardly go into ecstasies over Emerson's gushing sermons, despite his sincere and reverent admiration for the man.[337] But the ideal that Emerson projected into "transcendental" time, in other words outside of time, never ceased to be Melville's mirage, his impossible and necessary dream.

America, the free *Vivenza*, the prodigious isle of *Mardi*, is a land blessed of the Lord, the chosen home of the free spirits, the country of youth, spring, and love, "the best and happiest land under the sun."[338] And in his "first really mature work,"[339] *White Jacket* (1850), Melville joins in the chorus of the predestination of the American people: an elect and priestly people, "the Israel of our times," who having shaken off the yoke of bondage a bare seventy years earlier, in obedience to God's command, already figure as the pioneer of humanity, the ark of refuge for the "political pagans," the oppressed and the exiled, a race strong in its youth, wise in its inexperience, the vanguard opening a new path in the

---

Americans' heraldic boasts: "Their bald eagle looks like a vulture" (Gaulmier, *Volney*, p. 281). Not even Hawthorne, for that matter, approved of that heraldic predator: "This unhappy fowl, she appears, by the fierceness of her beak and eye, and the general truculency of her attitude, to threaten mischief to the inoffensive community" (*The Scarlet Letter* [New York, 1850], pp. 2–3). And Franklin himself had suggested half jokingly that the turkey would have been a better choice, being "a much more respectable bird, and withal a true original native of America" (Cunliffe, *Nation Takes Shape*, p. 126).

337. See Mumford, *Melville*, pp. 140–41; Matthiessen, op. cit., pp. 181–82, 184–86, 472 n. 1. His expressions of exultation over the birth of a genuine American literature, owing nothing to Europe — "let us away with this leaven of literary flunkeyism toward England" — have been likened by Matthiessen again (op. cit., p. 191) to the tone of *The American Scholar*. But in the bitter *Confidence-Man* there is the satire of a mysticizing and sententious philosopher in whom it seems possible to recognize Emerson (op. cit., pp. xxxvi–vii, 224–35).

338. *Mardi*, CLIV, CLXI, pp. 652–53, 667. In his masterpiece too people have seen an expression of his enthusiasm for the vastness of the United States: "Melville reflected the physical size of his country in the vast conception of *Moby Dick*, giving the chapter on the ocean the title of 'The Prairies'" (*Times Literary Supplement*, 18 April 1952; but chap. LXXIX, "The Prairie," in the singular, describes the flat, uniform forehead of the whale; the Pacific Ocean is compared to the prairies in chap. CXI, "The Pacific"). On the lyrical alliteration between Ocean and Prairie, see B. Hall, *Travels*, III, 385; Lewis, op. cit., pp. 92, 99; and Viola Sach, "Le mythe de l'Amérique et *Moby Dick* de Melville," *Annales*, 25, no. 66 (November–December 1970), esp. pp. 1548–49.

339. G. Baldini, *Melville, o le ambiguità* (Milan-Naples, 1952), p. 6; on its success with the public, ibid., pp. 215–16. One of the greatest admirers of the book (and of all Melville, for that matter) was T. E. Lawrence, who wanted to write one like it on the Royal Air Force in 1920, "a much finer show than the States' of 1820" (*Letters*, ed. Garnett [London, 1938], pp. 402, 458).

new world which is hers, hers alone by right of birth: "The rest of the nations must soon be in our rear."[340]

What we have is thus not a variation of the old theme of "a terrible race in an excellent country," because Meville has absolute faith in the future resolution of the harsh contrast of the present. His anger at the political reality of his time is not unleashed in sarcasm and grotesque caricatures, but just melts away, because the poet immediately turns his gaze to the glowing visions and prospects of the future: to the new world that the bards have promised to the "new" race of the Americans, and to the ties of blood which will unite the United States and England, the present bursting with future and the past laden with glory, so that the whole earth will bow down before them![341]

This is the dream he loves to dream, and always without indulgence toward the America he knew and without worry for what America will be. When he girds himself up to describe the famous, almost legendary naval encounter in which John Paul Jones in his little *Bonhomme Richard* forced the surrender of the English ship *Serapis* (1779), he lingers for a moment to see what prophetic signs he can find therein:

Sharing the same blood with England, and yet her proved foe in two wars—not wholly inclined at bottom to forget an old grudge—intrepid, unprincipled, reckless, predatory, with boundless ambition, civilized in externals but a savage at heart, America is, or may yet be, the Paul Jones of nations.[342]

In the fury of the battle the Englishman sees the American ship sinking and calls on Jones to surrender, and the American replies with the famous classic phrase: "I have not yet begun to fight." But Melville is not

---

340. *White Jacket* (1850), XXXVI, loc. cit., p. 1199, at the end of the digression against the whip as a means of punishment on American warships, and a little later an elaborate antithesis between the Past, the enemy of humanity, and the Future, its hope. The forcefulness of this tirade is due to Melville's polemical motivation of wanting to bring out the incongruity of corporal punishment in the navy of a country so blessedly predestined. But the lyricism of the prophecies in *Mardi* is actually incidental too, and can be taken as a counterweight to the savage criticisms of North American political society, which are dependent in their turn on the satire applied to all the other states in the world. Brooks quotes the passage in *White Jacket* and other similar ones in *Redburn*, and compares them to the ideas of Emerson and Whitman (op. cit., pp. 121–23). But Matthiessen limits the applicability of the prophecy in *Redburn* and contrasts it with the bitter prophecy in *Israel Potter* (see below, p. 518) on the predatory and unscrupulous America of the future (ibid., p. 444): cf. also *Moby Dick*, Modern Library ed., pp. 63, 396.

341. *Mardi*, CXLVI (p. 636) and CLIX (pp. 662–63). On English as the language of the new Eden to be created in America: *Redburn*, XXXIII, loc. cit., p. 1572. On the august majesty of a simple President of the United States, *White Jacket*, XL, loc. cit., p. 1207. On America as Future (= Good) and Europe as Past (= Bad) cf. also Pearce, "Hawthorne," p. 345.

342. *Israel Potter* (1855), XIX, loc. cit., p. 1430 (see the end of n. 330, above). In the same book there is (VII–VIII, loc. cit., pp. 1376–90) a malevolent portrait of Franklin. On America colonized by various peoples, and therefore the heir of all periods and cosmopolitan, "we are not a nation, so much as a world," see *Redburn*, XXXIII, loc. cit., pp. 1571–72. America must therefore remain open to all immigrants, "for the whole world is the patrimony of the whole world": ibid., LVIII, loc. cit., p. 1647.

carried away by any heroic enthusiasm and concludes with the comment: "In view of this battle — one may ask — what separates the enlightened man from the savage? Is civilization a thing distinct, or is it an advanced stage of barbarism?"[343]

The theme of civilization's poison and hypocrisy reappears, rises again *ex medio leporum*, erupts from the very middle of the exultation. And when in later life Melville speaks (in *Clarel*, 1876) of the "impieties of Progress," and of the hundred thousand degenerate demagogues who will found an inert "Anglo-Saxon China" on the vast plains of America, a society born dead, and moved solely by a blasphemous haste and anxiety for mechanical novelties,[344] he actually seems to renounce his belief in the America of the Future too, to deny Columbus's enchanted enterprise (see also above, pp. 381–82), and to join forces with the continent's harshest judges and persecutors.

But it is perhaps more accurate to interpret the triumphant predictions of his youth as an instinctive reaction to the gloomy European prophecies: a resentful polemic boast, the exact parallel, on the fashionable level of the philosophy of history, of the retorts of the naturalists who contrasted the delectable fruits of the tropics to those insipid imported items that the unfortunate inhabitants of the Old World had to make do with; and to see his later disillusionment and bitterness instead as the price resentfully paid for a too willing, obstinate, and wholehearted infatuation with (and, at the same time, a senile nostalgia for) the Rousseauian dream of a blessed natural simplicity that he had dreamed long ago among the Polynesian cannibals. "Keep true to the dreams of thy youth" — was this not his motto?

Thus in Melville, as previously in Emerson, the two opposite extremes of the polemic — America a blaze of light and America the negation of all light — appeared commingled and exasperated, exasperated because commingled. The contest is no longer transatlantic but internal; and thus that much more tortured and uncertain. The arguments adduced *ex utraque parte* are by now so familiar that they alternate, come to grips and wrestle in the conscience of any American who faces the question of the

---

343. *Israel Potter*, ibid., p. 1438. Other expressions of hate for war, and distrust of standing armies and fleets, in *White Jacket*, XLIX, loc. cit., pp. 1233–34.

344. Cf. Parrington, op. cit., II, 266–67; Mumford, op. cit., pp. 313–20; Matthiessen, op. cit., pp. 495–96; Baldini, op. cit., pp. 174–75; H. N. Smith, op. cit., pp. 208–10 (and for other older [1853–55] expressions of horror at mechanization, Matthiessen, op. cit., pp. 400–01, and Brooks, *Melville and Whitman*, pp. 189–90). Sarcastic comments on the locomotive, "that old Dragon . . . that gigantic gadfly of a Moloch, . . . the chartered murderer! the death monopolizer!" in "Cock-a-doodle-doo!" (1853), in *The Complete Stories of Herman Melville*, ed. J. Leida (New York, 1949), p. 121, *et alibi*. It is not difficult to see why T. E. Lawrence, as an assiduous reader of Melville, considered the completely forgotten *Clarel* "one of his finest works" (*Letters*, p. 458).

real nature and meaning of his country in the world, his nation in history.[345]

It should not be forgotten, finally, that Melville had long cherished the myth of the superiority of the geographical west, the Far West[346] and even the Pacific islands; nor that it is the monstrous size of *Moby Dick,* even more than his startling whiteness, that fascinates him as it would have fascinated Buffon and Father Molina (see above, chap. 5, n. 258); nor that some aspects at least of our polemic must have been known to him, since he was acquainted not only with Cook's[347] and Ulloa's travels, but with Buffon,[348] and Goldsmith's *Animated Nature.*[349]

C. Thoreau: primitivism rediscovered. Thoreau and Whitman are a different breed. It is possible that deep down they are just as tormented as Melville, but in appearance at least they are positive to the point of dogmatism, so confident in themselves and their "message" that they appoint themselves supreme judges of who is good and who is bad, what is light and what is darkness; and thus seem to feel it their bounden duty to proselytize, to issue warnings and pronounce anathemas.

Men of considerably humbler origin than Emerson and Melville, they are much more "democratic" than the latter two, both in the sense that they set the criterion of all spiritual value in common man, and also that the economic aspects of modern society interest them and concern them to the point where (in Whitman's case) they would like to crush them in a passionate and prolonged embrace, or (in Thoreau's) escape them by doing away with machines and even with division of labor.[350]

345. With facile dialectical irony one could show that on the logical plane the thesis of America's sublime superiority coincides with that of its irremediable weakness, since both theories isolate it and assign it to a position outside of history and progress, in the inertia of a primitive limbo, or the unsurpassability of what is complete and perfect.

346. See the hymn to the mystic and cosmic West, *Mardi,* CLXVIII, loc. cit., p. 680. In *Israel Potter* too, one reads of Ethan Allen that "his spirit was essentially Western; and herein is his peculiar Americanism; for the Western spirit is, or will yet be (for no other is, or can be), the true American one" (XXII, loc. cit., p. 1450; forty years before Turner, but a good seventy years after Crèvecoeur: "He who would wish to see America in its proper light . . . must visit our extended line of frontiers where the last settlers dwell"; *Letters,* III, 52–53, 57). Note, both here and on p. 517, the expression "or may yet be," which throws open the refuge of the Future. In *Redburn* too, Melville says poetically that Columbus's sounding line, on touching the bottom, brought up from the sea the soil of the Earthly Paradise, "not a Paradise then, or now; but to be made so, at God's good pleasure, and in the fullness and mellowness of time" (XXXIII, loc. cit., p. 1572).

347. *Typee,* XXIV–XXV, loc. cit., pp. 126, 130–31; *Omoo,* XVIII, loc. cit., p. 227; XLIX, 297; LXI, 321; LXXX, 358.

348. "Whence, in the name of Count Buffon and Baron Cuvier, came those dogs I saw in Typee?" (*Typee,* XXIX, loc. cit., p. 146); cf. *Mardi,* XII, loc. cit., p. 399.

349. See *Moby Dick,* Modern Library ed., pp. xvii, 264–65; and *Typee,* XI, ed. cit., p. 64; cf. Pitman, op. cit., p. 95n. He seems to have known it in reduced or abridged editions (see the edition of *Moby Dick* with commentary by Luther S. Mansfield and Howard P. Vincent [New York, 1952], pp. 584, 748). Goldsmith, as a novelist and playwright, is mentioned in *White Jacket* (1850), XII, loc. cit., p. 1137.

350. See Matthiessen, op. cit., pp. 77–78, 374.

Whitman is more fervent and high-sounding, but Henry Thoreau, the solitary sentimental Franciscan Thoreau, is much more acrid and incisive. America the land of liberty? Come now, replies Thoreau, thinking not only about the slavery of the blacks, but also and particularly about that of the whites: "Even if we grant that the American has freed himself of a political tyrant, he is still the slave of an economical and moral tyrant." The American is the slave of King Prejudice and has no idea how to utilize his political liberty to achieve true liberty, moral liberty: "Is it a freedom to be slaves, or a freedom to be free, of which we boast?"[351]

The government of the United States is worthless, and so for that matter is every other government. And there is no call for so much fuss about the glory and God's blessing in being American: "I would remind my countrymen that they are to be men first and American only at a late and convenient hour."[352]

Serious matters must be attended to first, and then if there's any time left it can also be used for toying with national whims. This dissolving of a specific Americanism in common humanity seems to preclude any possibility of paroxysms on the more or less manifest destiny of the Union and the Continent. The Manifest Destiny is a repellent and meaningless slogan.[353] And there is yet another quality in Thoreau, indeed the very core of his spiritual being, which would seem to be even more refractory of the coveted harmonies between awesome distances and memorable deeds — this capacity for losing himself and finding himself all within the smallest and most limited of worlds, to see Walden pond as an undreamed-of and unbounded universe, to be expanded at will into the broad current of the Ganges, the Sargasso Sea, or the Pacific Ocean,[354] and maybe to see in the individual Henry David Thoreau the compendium and prototype of the only genuinely human race.

His scorn of travel, and even of means of locomotion, is typical. An avid reader of the tales of exploration and adventure, he in fact preferred to travel through his books, sunk in his armchair. His oceanic circumnavigation was regularly reduced to a journey around his room.[355] There is nothing in him of the curiosity of Ulysses, but instead a stubborn adherence to Horace's maxim: *Coelum, non animum mutant qui trans mare currunt.* What matters the West, what matters Africa? The only journeys which count are those made within ourselves, opening new ways not to commerce but to thought. The sources of the Nile, the Niger, or

351. *Life without Principle* (posthumous, 1863), in H. D. Thoreau, *Walden and Other Writings,* ed. Brooks Atkinson (New York, 1937), pp. 727–28.
352. *Slavery in Massachusetts* (1854), ibid., p. 673.
353. Christie, op. cit., pp. 108–09.
354. Ibid., pp. 202, 240, 270.
355. See Christie, op. cit., illustrating every little turn in the paradox expressed in the title.

the Mississippi, the Northwest Passage—these are futile goals: "Are these the problems which most concern mankind?" It is not worth the trouble of going around the world to count the cats in Zanzibar.

The Emersonian vanity of the trip to Europe is extended to include the whole world—and America too. The man who loves his land more than his spirit, the land which will receive his bones more than the spirit that animates his clay, may be a patriot, if you like, but he has a worm in his brain: "Patriotism is a maggot in their heads."[356] Any single village contains all history and all geography: "The characteristics and pursuits of various ages and races of men are always existing in epitome in every neighborhood."[357]

The locomotive, the conqueror of distances, the unbridled hero of the new times right up to Carducci,[358] and Honegger, thus becomes in Thoreau's eyes the very symbol of the evils of technical progress, a veritable monster, but a monster out of Hell, massacring and laying waste: with grotesquely effective hyperbole Thoreau foresees and announces the time when its smoke will dissipate and its steam condense, and then men will realize that "a few are riding, but the rest are run over."[359] Alfred de Vigny, for that matter, had had much the same vision in 1844, describing the bestial railroad which "with its fangs of fire, devouring its boilers, pierces the cities and leaps the rivers." This savage monster of progress even consumes the hapless passengers, cast as hostages into the blazing belly of this Carthaginian bull, "which hurls them out again as ash at the feet of the god of gold."[360]

One last indication of Thoreau's scarce interest in far-off places: in 1845 he retired into the woods to lead a life as simple and primitive as possible. At that time the United States had no shortage of virgin forest where a would-be Tarzan or sylvan Robinson or practicing Rousseauian

356. *Walden* (1854), loc. cit., pp. 286–87; cf. "the tapeworm of Europe" in the brains of Americans, according to Emerson (above, p. 511).

357. *A Week on the Concord and Merrimack Rivers* (1849), loc. cit., p. 315. Thoreau could thus write with pride and compunction: "I have travelled much in Concord" (the small county where he lived for almost his entire life), and with sarcasm reinforced by his disdain for money describe the authentic pioneers of the extreme West, the old seekers emigrating to California, as in fact taking themselves three thousand miles nearer to Hell (*Journal*, 1 February 1852, Boston ed., 1949, III, 266).

358. On the difference in the exaltation of the locomotive between Carducci and Whitman (but not Thoreau), see Chabod, *La politica estera*, pp. 378–79.

359. Quoted by Joseph Wood Krutch (*New York Times Book Review*, 20 May 1951), from the 1951 ed. of the *Journal*, but I have not been able to find the passage even with the help of the excellent analytical index in the fourteen volumes of the edition of 1906–49; see however *Journal* (Boston, 1949), V, 266–67 (1853); see also *Walden*, loc. cit., pp. 105–11, and the passages quoted by Lawrence Willson, art. cit., p. 185 (C. A. Tillinghast goes over the same ground again in "The West of Thoreau's Imagination: The Development of a Symbol," *Thoth*, 6 [1965], pp. 42–50). At the end of *An Excursion in Canada* (1853) Thoreau sums up: "In short, the Canada which I saw was not merely a place for railroads to terminate in, and for criminals to run to" (*American Reader*, p. 483). Cf. Melville, quoted above, n. 344; and Christie, op. cit., p. 287, n. 35.

360. *La maison du berger*, I.

might "return to the woods" and pursue his whims away from any human contact. Thoreau builds his hut on Walden Pond, a couple of miles from Concord, on a piece of land lent to him by the owner (Emerson), with an axe borrowed from another neighbor; and there he hosts periodic gatherings of his friends, and almost every day goes into town, following the railroad tracks, to see to his affairs and pick up the latest gossip.

He flees into the woods, a stone's throw from home. But his undertaking is no childish escapade, no brief experiment in camping without the benefit of motor transport and canned food, nor an early attempt at the commuter life, as practiced today by such a large proportion of the inhabitants of the major metropolises (although it has something of all of these in it). At Walden Thoreau really turns his back on civilization and with extraordinary freshness feels the thrill and delight of proximity to the earth, to water, to the animals. It is not a poet, or a naturalist, or a poet-naturalist who speaks to us in the pages of the famous book, but a delicate moralist abandoning himself to a vividly sensual attraction for the virginity of nature, and deriving therefrom, and matching thereto, albeit with somewhat consciously skillful insistence, supposedly practical lessons and cheerful, contented, and egocentric daydreams.

Thus it is not easy to define his personality. His cargo of ideas is modest and almost all secondhand. The more he tries to crystallize it into epigrams, aphorisms, biblical verses, the more his originality fades. His gestures are greater in intent than in realization; they are symbolic acts, exorcisms, ritual formulas. A spiteful English critic compared the recluse of Walden to a hermit in Hyde Park. When he wants to protest against slavery and the Mexican war and refuses to pay a minimal tax, and gets thrown into prison, he only stays there one night, his friends bail him out, and his account of the adventure closes with words intended to be humorous but which are actually harshly grating in their allusion to Pellico's decade-long incarceration: "This is the whole history of *My Prisons.*"[361]

---

361. *Civil Disobedience* (1849), loc. cit., p. 654. That night in prison, and the work that resulted from it, did however have an influence truly worthy of a master magician. In the *Encyclopedia Britannica*, 11th ed., the article on Thoreau (by William Sharp) begins thus: "Henry David Thoreau, American recluse. . . ." Gandhi draws on Thoreau for themes and techniques in his revolt. Tolstoy and some of the founders of the Labour Party become his disciples. *Walden* was given (1886) by Frau Helbig's mother to Tolstoy, "to provide a first point of contact" before going to make his acquaintance in person; the count kept it in his pocket and had marked a number of passages and whole pages, when mother and daughter went (July 1887) to visit him (Lili Morani-Helbig, *Jugend am Abendrot, Römische Erinnerungen* [Stuttgart, 1953], pp. 248–50). But he had, apparently, completely forgotten it when Andrew W. White (*Autobiography*, 1905) went to see him in March 1894 and discussed a number of American writers with him: see *Discovery of Europe: The Story of American Experience in the Old World*, ed. P. Rahv (Boston, 1947), pp. 359–83. The Walden experience later fascinated writers as different one from another as Sinclair Lewis and Marcel Proust. See Agostino Lombardo, "L'arte di H. D. Thoreau," *Belfagor*, 14, no. 6 (November 1959), pp. 674–85, and Walter Harding in *The Boston Public Library Quarterly*, Boston, April 1959.

His attitude is romantic, but his mental framework, despite links with the transcendentalists, goes back to an earlier epoch, is substantially of the eighteenth century, rationalistic, consequentialist, and anarchic. Thoreau's anarchism probably derives from his fundamental egocentrism (which moved Lowell to say that Thoreau accepted even his defects and weaknesses as peculiar virtues and powers), but it comes complete with all the required trappings. Typically anarchic are his deification of nature; his abstract humanitarianism, his flight from the city, and anathema of corrupt metropolises; his cult of friendship and reverence for heroes and in general for the "examplary" literature of the Graeco-Roman world.[362] Some of his negative attributes too, like the complete obliteration in all his work of women, love, and family affection, the extremist social interpretation of the Christian message, his disdain for past history and the naïve radicalism of the remedies he offers for society's present ills, are part of the framework of the eighteenth-century systems and utopias. His whole political philosophy, it has been said, is implicit in Godwin's *Political Justice*.[363]

Considered from any aspect, then, Thoreau seems impervious to nationalism, to the charms of territorial vastness, to antitheses between continents, to certain climatic theories[364] and the dimensional comparison of animals. Which makes it all the more significant and surprising to find Thoreau himself restating with unusual clarity the themes of the organic and historical supremacy of the New World, and refuting its denigrators in the person of their archetype Buffon.

Already in an early pamphlet on the *Advantages and Disadvantages of Foreign Influence on American Literature* (ca. 1836–37), Thoreau expresses his deeply personal regret that his fellow American poets prefer to celebrate the hedgerows full of larks and nightingales rather than the native redbreasts on the fences of their own country.[365] This generic "indigenism" becomes more precise and developed as the years pass, as

362. On friendship, see the long digression in *A Week*, loc. cit., pp. 371–96; on Thoreau's familiarity with the classics (he took with him to Walden Pond even an *Iliad*, which was in fact the only object stolen from the cabin which was always left open), see for example *Walden*, loc. cit., pp. 91–93; Parrington, op. cit., II, 402, and the whole of E. Seybold's book, *Thoreau: The Quest and the Classics* (Yale, 1951: for the political ideas especially, pp. 16–17, 66, 85). On his affinities with, and derivations from Rousseau, see François Jost, "Rousseau en Amérique du Nord," in *Essais de littérature comparée*, I, *Helvetica* (Fribourg, 1964), pp. 271–72, 284–87, 293–97, 302–06. Typical also is his Leopardian regret for the lack of a mythology to animate and express nature (*Walking*, 1862, loc. cit., p. 620); cf. *A Week*, loc. cit., pp. 338, 344 (fusion of poetry in a dead language and living nature) and the affirmation that Pan is not dead (ibid., cit. in Parrington, op. cit., II, 404). On some precedents, see above, chap. 7, n. 224.

363. See Parrington, op. cit., II, 409–11.

364. He rejects in fact the thesis that nature produces the best human species between the tropics, where the vegetation is richer and there is more warmth: "The temperate zone is found to be most favourable to the growth and ripening of man" (quoted by Christie, op. cit., pp. 210, 215).

365. Matthiessen, op. cit., p. 82.

his familiarity with American nature gradually increases, and finally, in a posthumous and barely studied essay (*Walking*, 1862, but written in 1851), appears as a major restatement of the old thesis of a fated and glorious destiny for the west and an irreversible march of history along the (apparent) trajectory of the diurnal star.

The west was bound to emerge as myth and promise in the society of New England, whose whole way of life was turned toward the west. To the east the Americans had nothing but the Atlantic, and beyond the sea nothing but ancient Europe from which they had pushed themselves away like the swimmer kicks away from the shore. To the east then they saw, in the distance, only the past, and nearby the physical limitation of all development. To the west, on the other hand, a whole boundless continent stretched out: chains of friendly hills, broad valleys, plains, gigantic rivers and lakes, prairies roamed by herds of bison, stony deserts and more mountains, taller and more forbidding, in keeping with perspective, and beyond more valleys, away in the furthest distance, but glittering with gold dust—and then down to the immense whale-filled ocean.

This rapidly expanding society thus found itself forced by geographical necessity to look to the west; and the west, with good reason, climbed through the successive levels of virgin literary republic,[366] biblical Promised Land, earthly prefiguration of the heavenly Jerusalem, new *civitas mundi* for all free and united men, intact wilderness,[367] and dazzling and confused symbol of all the powers of history and life. In Thoreau this whole process is seen in abbreviated and concentrated form.

When he leaves the house to take a walk he instinctively heads west, or even southwest, with a very occasional deviation to south-southwest! "Eastward I go only by force; but westward I go free." To the east lies the city, to the west the Wilderness. "I must walk toward Oregon, and not toward Europe."

The horizons have already expanded, the cardinal points are projected over the two hemispheres. And immediately his own personal experience or caprice too is projected onto universal history: "And that way the nation is moving, and I may say that mankind progresses from east to

366. One single typical prophecy: "The American mind will be brought to maturity" along the Great Lakes and in the Mississippi basin. "There, on the rolling plains, will be formed a republic of letters, which, not governed, like that on our seaboard, by the great literary powers of Europe, shall be free indeed," suited to the vastness of the country and independent of any European influence. The Lord of the prairies (not of course the bison, in this case) will receive the homage of all the arts. "He will be the American man, and beside him there will be none else" (Mackie, *From Cape Cod to Dixie*, quoted in Tryon, op. cit., p. 613). See also the cited work of H. N. Smith, *Virgin Land:* for Thoreau, esp. pp. 77–78; for the West as "garden of the world" (= Eden), pp. 123 ff. The West had already been mythicized by Frederika Bremer: "The West is the biblical Paradise crossed by four great rivers, and containing the tree of life and death" (op. cit., II, 158, referring to Genesis 2:10–14; but cf. her disappointment on returning, ibid., II, 381).

367. See Christie, op. cit., pp. 116–17, and below, pp. 525–26.

west." Just as the Muslim bows to Mecca, Thoreau prays, perambulates, and prophesies with his eyes turned to the last rays of the setting sun. But at this point a curious doubt besets him, over the fact that just recently there has been a southeastern movement of history in the colonization of Australia. But Thoreau soon gets round it: it is obviously "a retrograde movement." Australia is peopled by convicts and paupers, and their descendants (as de Pauw had said of the Americans) are already degenerate: "judging from the moral and physical character of the first generation of Australians," one cannot say that the experiment was successful.

To the west then! "We go eastward to realize history and study the works of art and literature, retracing the steps of the race: we go westward into the future, with a spirit of enterprise and adventure."[368] The Atlantic is a river Lethe: one has only to cross it (going east to west, of course) "to forget the old World and its institutions."[369]

The migratory animals too obey some mysterious instinct like the one which directs Thoreau in his casual strolls. The sun too migrates daily to the West: "He is the Great Western Pioneer that the nations follow." And Columbus did the same, with the result that we see all around us: "Where on the globe can there be found an area of equal extent with that occupied by the bulk of our States, so fertile and so rich and varied in its productions, and at the same time so habitable by the Europeans, as this is?" There follow the prescribed quotations from European geographers and explorers, Michaux, Humboldt,[370] Guyot, Francis Head, and last of all, bringing us fairly and squarely into the atmosphere of the polemic, the closing stab at Buffon: "This statement will do at least to set against Buffon's account of this part of the world and its productions."[371]

Then come the expected corollaries and variations. The absence of wild animals is not a sign of inferiority, but one of America's privileges: one can fall asleep without fear almost anywhere in the forests.[372]

---

368. *Walking*, loc. cit., pp. 607–08. Cf.: "Literature speaks how much still to the past, how little to the future; how much to the East, how little to the West" (*Thomas Carlyle and His Works* quoted by Parrington, op. cit., II, 413), as well as the cited article of Willson, esp. pp. 186–87 and 191. A few years before, "the Swiss-American scholar, Arnold Guyot, in his enormously popular Lowell lectures of 1849, demonstrated that civilized man was born in Asia, reached his youth in Europe, and his manhood in America" (Pearce, *The Savages*, p. 158); cf. also H. N. Smith, op. cit., pp. 41–43, and the exhortation of Hester Prynne, the heroine of the *Scarlet Letter*, to penetrate into the Wilderness: "There thou art free!" (Hawthorne, op. cit., XVII, 161) and Christie, op. cit., pp. 104–17, 222, 234.

369. Cf. Lowell, above, p. 513.

370. For the influence of Humboldt, see esp. Christie, op. cit., pp. 44, 121–24; for that of Darwin, ibid., pp. 74–81.

371. Op. cit., p. 611. The reference to the perfect habitability of the United States should be taken in conjunction with Thoreau's thesis that in the southern latitudes man degenerates, in the long run, and falls easy prey to the more northern races (*A Week*, loc. cit., p. 333; cf. *Walking*, loc. cit., p. 613).

372. Which does not prevent Thoreau, in accordance with his naturism, finding the wild animals superior by far to the domestic ones (ibid., pp. 617, 621); and elsewhere too (*The Natural History of*

America's fortunate lack of wild beasts is an old theme of the continent's apologists (see above, for example, pp. 343, 373, 608). As early as 1666, George Alsop had written of Maryland: "As for the Wolves, Bears, Panthers in this country, they . . . do little hurt or injury worth noting, and that which they do is of so degenerate and low a nature (as in reference to the fierceness and heroick vigour that dwell in the same kind of Beasts in other Countries)."[373]

Just as the defense of the native had resulted in his humiliation, and his being passed back and forth between apologists and slanderers, both confirming his stigmas of inferiority, so a century later the animals of America, made meek and innocuous to soften the image of the New World, became living examples and irrefutable proofs of its corruption. But this was only a particular instance of the "heritage" of myth and superstition being passed on *in toto* from the redskins to the Yankees (see above, p. 243): their virtues became an apanage of all Americans,[374] their defects already since de Pauw's time had been extended to the colonists, and even the parallel with the ancient Greeks and Romans was now transferred to the European settlers.[375]

For Thoreau, even infectious marshes have their *raison d'être:* even the Dismal Swamp (of Thomas Moore's ballad) is preferable to a man-made garden — nature ruined by the human hand[376] — because the swamp with its fetid slime is Nature's very womb: "I enter a swamp as a sacred place — a *sanctum sanctorum,*" he says, even when he sinks up to his neck in it.[377] But he forgets that the Dismal Swamp had always been taken

---

Massachusetts, 1842, in *Works,* ed. H. S. Canby [Boston, 1946], p. 649) writing with satisfaction that the state contains forty different quadrupeds, "and among these one is glad to hear of a few bears, wolves, lynxes, and wildcats."

373. *Character of Maryland,* ed. N. D. Mereness (Cleveland, 1902), p. 37.

374. Remond., op. cit., pp. 488, 492.

375. Ibid., pp. 504–06; cf. above, chap. 5, n. 446.

376. "Almost all man's improvements, so called, as the building of houses, and the cutting down of the forest and of all large trees, simply deform the landscape, and make it more and more tame and cheap" (ibid., p. 602). Man's work, rather than improving the environment (as even de Pauw had admitted, in fact, and as had been repeated *ad nauseam* by the apologists of that decisive improvement in the climate that could be obtained by cutting down the forests: see Ampère, op. cit., I, 132; Chinard, *L'homme contre la nature,* the whole second part, "La Forêt Américaine," and Remond, op. cit., pp. 264, 516 n. 26), ruins it by removing its genuineness and original strength.

377. *Walking,* pp. 616–18; and cf. Seybold, op. cit., pp. 77, 108; "Dismal Swamp" had become a proverbial expression: see *Walden,* loc. cit., p. 107; Melville, *Redburn* (1849), XI, loc. cit., pp. 1501–02; *Israel Potter* (1855), XXIII, loc. cit., p. 1453; H. Beecher Stowe, *The Dread: A Tale of the Great Dismal Swamp,* 1856. Already in 1763 *Dismal,* as noun, was "a local name of tracts of swampy land on the eastern sea-board of the U.S." (*Shorter Oxford English Dictionary, sub voce*). In 1784 Hugh Williamson wrote to Jefferson that very little had been done "in the Plans for improving the great Dismal" (*Papers,* VII, 569), and Smith, also referring to the land-reclamation works, paints a horrible picture of it (*Voyage,* II, 52, 117–20). Curious details on its history and on recent attempts, Thoreau-style, to maintain it intact, appear in *Time,* 30 November 1962, p. 17. "Swamp" is a typical Americanism (*Shorter Oxford English Dictionary, sub voce,* and Mencken, *American Language, Supplement One,* 496–97; *Supplement Two,* 574). Cf. also B. Hall, *Travels,* I, 111 ff.; Frances Trollope, *Domestic Manners,* XX, ed. cit., p. 228; and Brooks Atkinson in the *New York Times,* 29 October 1963.

as a poetic symbol of stagnant waters and lethal vapors, as Tasso had painted it even before it had been known in reality; "ne l'ozio l'acqua è pigra e torpe; / E là dov'ella s'impaluda e stagna, / Da neghittoso grembo esala intorno / Vapor grave e nocente, e fieri spirti / D'aure maligne, onde perturba il cielo, / E quasi l' aria infetta," so that "lo sfortunato abitatore ammorba."[378]

There even seems to be an apologetic allusion to the Americans' derided hairlessness when Thoreau recalls and translates the words of Linnaeus, *"Nescio quae facies* laeta, glabra *plantis Americanis,"* and applies them to the faces of his compatriots: "Perchance there will appear to the traveler something, he knows not what, of *laeta* and *glabra,* of joyous and serene, in our very faces."

And when will this be? One need hardly ask. It will come about when American civilization matches the luminous depths of America's skies, the splendor of her stars. If the Englishman Francis Head found that the moon seemed bigger in Canada than in Europe, "probably the sun looks larger also. If the heavens of America appear infinitely higher, and the stars brighter, I trust that these facts are symbolical of the height to which the philosophy and poetry and religion of her inhabitants may one day soar."[379] And here Thoreau quotes (incorrectly) Berkeley's prophecy (see above, p. 137), and turning into "a true patriot" extols his country as preferable to the Earthly Paradise.

But immediately afterward the politico-nationalist theme is abandoned, and the west that embodied the future of the United States is sublimated and simultaneously anaemicized, to become a synonym of that generic and primeval Wildness in which "the preservation of the world" resides. And with an agile bound, which by now should no longer surprise us, the Wildness, which used to be the west and the future, now reappears as extreme antiquity: "our ancestors were savages," and such were the founders of Rome and every other state, and this is man's "natural" condition, his only way to physical and spiritual salvation. By the same token the savages, the redskins, are very ancient; burnished by time,

378. *Il mondo creato,* III, 117–25, ed. cit., p. 65: "in idleness the water is lazy and dull; and where she stagnates in swamps, from her inert womb [a far cry from Thoreau's "fertile wombs"!] a heavy and malefic vapor breathes she forth, and fiery spirits and evil airs that foul the sky . . . infecting the unfortunate inhabitant"; cf. *Gerusalemme conquistata,* VI, 116–18.

379. Loc. cit., pp. 611–12, and already in the *Journal,* III, 268 (1852); "our intellects generally on a grander scale, like our thunder and lightning, our rivers, and mountains and forests"; for other "astrological" prophecies, see above, n. 319. But it is to be noted that Goethe's and Hegel's forecast, of an American poetry shortly to come into being, is put off by Thoreau to the end of time: the valleys of the Ganges, the Nile, and the Rhine have given their harvest of poetic myths (always the obsession with largeness: why not refer to the valleys of the Arno, the Avon, or the Main?!). Let us see what the Amazon, the Plate, the Orenoco, the St. Lawrence, and the Mississippi will give: "Perchance, when, in the course of ages, American liberty has become a fiction of the past . . . the poets of the world will be inspired by American mythology" (loc. cit., p. 620, and see below, n. 432).

learned in all of nature's secrets, they can look pityingly on the ignorant and arrogant white man.[380] Civilization is decadence and finally death. Wildness is life itself, the urge to go further and higher, and thus no longer past but once again future: "Hope and the future for me are not in lawns and cultivated fields, not in towns and cities, but in the impervious and quaking swamps."[381] Life is in those stagnant waters. America has not just emerged therefrom as de Pauw and company insisted. It has still to emerge.

In these confused rhapsodies the fundamental concepts overlap and merge into one another. The America whose soil Thoreau treads is not the America discovered by Columbus and Vespucci: "You may name it America, but it is not America." It is a land of myth, the divine Nature of the old poets and prophets.[382] But this nature, thus animated, is Life itself, elemental life, in vain oppressed and coerced by the arts and techniques of so-called civilization. But then again—it sounds almost like the monologue of Faust, that uncompromising translator of the Word—Life can be hard, painful, miserable; how can one see it as the very essence of creation? Thoreau replies that life is action and should never be cursed: "However mean your life is, meet it and live it; do not shun it and call it hard names."[383]

The gospel of activity without illusion, of simple and serene toil, is perhaps his most lasting message, and has in fact become part of the everyday religion of the North American. Thoreau found the Old World's fervor tepid, its culture tired and bookish, its society frivolous and over-refined. Although Emerson admired the "composure" of the ancient Egyptians (see above, n. 316), Thoreau shuddered at their embalmed and mummified immobility, "the death of that which never lived."[384] And while Emerson envied the sanguine energy of the English, to Thoreau they seemed flabby, tame, overcivilized—all of them, even Shakespeare—and out of touch with nature.[385] Even the age-old *querelle des anciens et des modernes* finds a place in this elastic *Weltanschauung*, so pessimistic about history and optimistic about man:

380. Brooks, *New England*, pp. 370–71; cf. *Walden*, p. 31 and passim. On the ideological significance of this "antiquity" attributed to the redskins, see Pearce, *The Savages*, pp. 147–50, 160. But Thoreau, consistent with his candid anarchism, is never "primitivist," nor indigenist (Christie, op. cit., p. 217).
381. *Walking*, loc. cit., pp. 614–15, 617.
382. Ibid., p. 604.
383. *Walden*, loc. cit., p. 292; *Walden* "is a book in praise of life rather than of Nature" (Parrington, op. cit., II, 406). On Horace's *carpe diem*, taken by Thoerau as an invitation to action, see Seybold, op. cit., p. 36.
384. *A Week*, loc. cit., p. 348. On the futility of the Pyramids, tombs for a few ambitious imbeciles who would have been better drowned in the Nile and fed to the dogs see *Walden*, loc. cit., p. 52. Melville too ridicules Emerson's enthusiasm for ancient Egypt and its mummies (*The Confidence-Man*, XXXVI, ed. cit., pp. 229–30).
385. *Walking*, loc. cit., p. 619. On the "Old Europe" impression he gained from French Canada, see *An Excursion to Canada*, loc. cit., p. 482.

Some are dinning in our ears that we Americans, and moderns generally, are intellectual dwarfs compared with the ancients, or even the Elizabethan men. But what is that to the purpose? A living dog is better than a dead lion. Shall a man go and hang himself because he belongs to the race of pygmies, and not be the biggest pygmy that he can? Let everyone mind his own business, and endeavor to be what he was made.[386]

With this show of modesty, with this heroic antiheroism, Thoreau manages to reconcile his veneration for the classics with his required faith as a modern and particularly as an American in the world in which it befalls him to live: to live a dog's life maybe, but better a live dog than a dead lion.

D. Walt Whitman: the athletic Democracy's emphatic oracles. At first sight Whitman's Americanism seems much more robust and resonant. The bard never tires of proclaiming the greatness of the United States, its nature and society and landscape, but also and particularly the teeming metropolises; and in a series of panting orations he magnifies its democracy, its arts and crafts, the courage of its soldiers in the Civil War, its laws on patents, the length of its goods trains and its wide assortment of agricultural, zootechnical, and mineral products.[387]

But on closer examination, or rather as soon as one manages to escape from the whirlwind of images and the martial tramp of the enumerations, this glorious assurance becomes shapeless and blurred; the verbal immensity of the themes can no longer mask the paucity of lyrical afflatus (in fact reveals it in all its nakedness) and only with some effort can one recognize and fish out from this murky torrent of tumid and complacent oratory the ancient apologetic motifs of the continent's supremacy, its ideological opposition to the Old World, the harmony prescribed, if not preestablished, between its nature and society, and its wholesale projection into a future of unlimited prospects, bathed in the diffused light of technical progress and sterilized by universal love: a neon-lit future, all properly chromed and nickel-plated.

One can understand why Thoreau was never quite convinced by Whitman, although he admired him. This verbal "sensuality" of his, that provoked such scandal when *Leaves of Grass* appeared (1855), had no effect on a real and refined sensualist like Thoreau: "It may turn out," he wrote, "to be less sensual than it appears." Nor was Thoreau impressed when he heard Whitman proclaiming to a group of friends, with his usual arrogance, that he represented America; Thoreau tells the story himself, and one can almost see his smile: "I chanced to say . . . that I

---

386. *Walden,* loc. cit., p. 290; cf., in disparagement of Progress, ibid., p. 295.
387. "Song of the Exposition," 8, in *Poetry and Prose,* ed. L. Untermeyer, pp. 227–29.

did not think much of America or of politics, and so on, which may have been somewhat of a damper to him."[388]

Thoreau was certainly no thinker, and we have already seen what a mess he got into whenever he attempted to develop an intuition, to give systematic structure to the whims and impulses of his mind. But Whitman was even less capable than Thoreau of organizing his thoughts and facing their contradictions. Like Victor Hugo, he delights in the play of cosmic antitheses and polarities, never hesitates to set side by side on the same altar, in mystical interpenetration, body and soul, male and female, youth and old age, richness and poverty, victory and defeat, expression and silence, life and death (all capitalized, of course);[389] by democratic profession averse to all hierarchy, caste, or distinction (an attitude reflected catastrophically in his literary form too, that so often degenerates into mere lists and rigmaroles)—Whitman surrenders with gay abandon to the most incompatible ideas—just so long as each one gleams and jingles to order on its own account.

On the spatial plane Whitman is by and large a cosmopolitan. Albeit in the name of America, whose authorized spokesman he feels himself to be, he launches his "Salut au Monde!" where even the French title has a purpose; all must give ear and understand him when he passes them in rapid review: "and I salute all the inhabitants of the earth."[390] The real and particular greatness of the same United States is not in its union, its richness, its military or naval power, or its genius in every field, but in its promotion of fraternity over the whole globe, the filling all nations and all humanity with a spirit of Comradeship.[391] And the more time passes the more the United States of the early *Leaves of Grass* is transformed into an ideal fatherland of the free and the good, into the most immense and tepid and vaporous of literary utopias.

On the temporal plane, Whitman accepts and respects the past, the whole past. Far from playing the primitivist and condemning the slow centuries of civilization, Whitman, although his eyes are completely fixed on the future and he considers "modern" a synonym for "sacrosanct," repeats over and over again (like Marx eulogizing the bourgeoisie) his thanks to his forebears for the treasures they have handed down, and

---

388. Letter to Harrison Blake, 7 December 1856, in Untermeyer, *Poetry and Prose*, pp. 965–66. For another colorful description of the same encounter between the two, with "each . . . planted fast in reserves, surveying the other curiously," ibid., p. 968. Whitman in his turn could not abide the individualist Thoreau's haughty indifference for the common man, his "disdain for men (for Tom, Dick and Harry): inability to appreciate the average" (quoted in Matthiessen, op. cit., p. 650; ibid., pp. 651–52, a lucid comparison between the two; another parallel in Canby, op. cit., pp. 148–55).
389. See for example "Great Are the Myths" (loc. cit., pp. 483–85).
390. "Salut au Monde!" loc. cit., p. 182.
391. *Independent American Literature* (1847), loc. cit., p. 557.

sings hymn after hymn to "the infinite greatness of the past."[392] Even if it is the task of American democracy to express "the peerless grandeur of the modern," it must not forget that it contains and carries with it the whole past, the whole earth's heritage.[393] Thus in Whitman there is neither any sentimental cherishing of the redskin, nor the violent resentment against him as an obstacle to the march of progress. In fact he always delights in calling New York and Long Island with their corresponding Indian toponyms, as if there were no break of continuity between the aborigines and the citizens of the new metropolises. Those who had seen America as future without a past were bound to judge its intractable natives as mere past without future: antithesis and integration all at the same time.[394] But someone like Whitman who squeezes and welds past, present, and future into one single process has to be just as ready to embrace the savage native as the pioneer that hunts him down and destroys him, as welcoming to the new poetic world about to bloom in America as to the unnumbered worlds already accumulated and piled up, like pyramids of granite cannonballs in the courtyards of the Old World's castles. The treasures of English literature are more precious to Americans than all the royal treasures.[395] And nobody was in a better position to know that than Whitman, who although he rejects the traditional poetic themes and studiously avoids even any reference to or quotation from other writers had actually absorbed not a little from English authors, like Blake, Walter Scott, and Carlyle, and from non-English authors, too, particularly nineteenth-century Frenchmen, not to mention the Bible and Homer.[396]

392. *Passage to India*, loc. cit., p. 379 (did Whitman give the title to E. M. Forster?); see also *With Antecedents*, loc. cit., pp. 256–57, and the quotations and observations by F. Stovall (1932), loc. cit., pp. 1132–35.

393. "Thou Mother with thy equal brood," loc. cit., pp. 411–12; "To-Day and Thee," ibid., p. 451; the opening of the first preface to *Leaves of Grass*, loc. cit., p. 487; and *Democratic Vistas* (1871), loc. cit., pp. 845–46. Later Whitman traced the true origin of the United States back to the ferment of the Elizabethan era, *A Backward Glance O'er Travel'd Roads* (1888), loc. cit., p. 510n. In general as Whitman got older he became more and more generous in his recognition of the importance of tradition and history: loc. cit., pp. 514, 546.

394. See Pearce, *The Savages*, p. 135.

395. *Independent American Literature*, loc. cit., p. 547. His debt to English literature is later widened (*Poetry To-day in America*, 1881) to include all the literatures of Europe and the East (loc. cit., p. 560). Whitman says he agrees with Longfellow in recognizing that the New World will only be "worthily original" after it is "well saturated with the originality of others" (*Death of Longfellow*, 1882, loc. cit., p. 797; cf. also *A Backward Glance*, p. 513).

396. The affinities with Blake were noted by Swinburne already in 1868 (loc. cit., pp. 996–98). For Scott, see his own admissions: *Specimen Days* (1882), loc. cit., p. 749, and *A Backward Glance*, loc. cit., pp. 514–15 (although Scott exhales a spirit of caste; ibid., p 550). For Carlyle, see the pages written on his death (*Specimen Days*, loc. cit., pp. 768–79; cf. also ibid., pp. 40, 551). The French influences are less certain; those of Rousseau (loc. cit., pp. 57–58) and George Sand (ibid., pp. 58, 755, 833n., 1204; Matthiessen, op. cit., p. 557; Brooks, *Melville and Whitman*, pp. 105–06; R. D. Faner, *Walt Whitman and Opera* [Philadelphia, 1951], pp. 45–48), seem secondary. With Hugo, another poet so much an extrovert that he seems to have nothing inside, there are obvious affinities of temperament and ideology (humanitarianism, democracy, etc.), and as early as 1867 W. M. Rossetti compared *Leaves of Grass* to

On the philosophical plane Whitman knows only Love. Love is "the basis of all the metaphysics," love of comrade, friend, consort, child or parent, love of cities and countries for each other.[397] But what moves him is not just love, whether of immediate or less immediate neighbor, but a sort of love of love, a covetous yearning for love, whose universality is postulated through the very experiencing of its absence: "When I hear of the brotherhood of lovers, how it was with them . . . Then I am pensive—I hastily walk away fill'd with the bitterest envy."[398]

His exaltation of sex too has something frigid and abstract about it— and if we are not mistaken represents a belated (and of course only half conscious) protest against the charge of impotence leveled at the Americans. In Whitman's work there is not the least suggestion of the figure of a lover, of either sex—because even if it is not certain that he was homosexual he was certainly childishly androgynous and disguised the object of his desire beneath dense veils. It is all very well for Walt Whitman to present himself as Adam redivivus in the new Paradise of the West, "lusty, phallic, with the potent original loins . . . bathing my songs in Sex," and to call these his songs "the offspring of my loins";[399] all very well for him to protest, in his youth, against the disgustingly philistine law that bans from literature whatever concerns sex, desire, libidinous themes, organs and acts,[400] and to boast, in later life, that *Leaves of Grass* "is avowedly the song of Sex, Amativeness, and even Animality";[401] and in a hundred different places, in every stage of his career, to exalt the body, the naked body, and all attributes of the human or to be

the *Légende des siècles* (loc. cit., pp. 981–82). But Whitman also reveals a familiarity (1881) with some of the critical writings of Sainte-Beuve and Baudelaire (loc. cit., p. 555), in whom he rediscovered, or so he thought, his ideas of 1855: Matthiessen, op. cit., p. 543. On his debt to Volney, see D. Goodale, "Some of Whitman's Borrowings," *American Literature*, 10 (May 1938), pp. 202–13; and Canby, op. cit., p. 368. "From the old world . . . that he barely knew," Chinard concludes ("L'esprit national dans la poésie américaine," *Revue de synthèse historique*, 29 [1919], p. 176), "he borrowed almost nothing."

397. *The Base of All Metaphysics*, loc. cit., pp. 165–66.

398. "When I Peruse the Conquer'd Fame," loc. cit., p. 171. It is also worth noting that Whitman is at his most sensual and ardent whenever he expresses the typically feminine emotion of abandoning himself to the music of opera, in particular to the full-throated notes of a soprano or contralto (affinities with Stendhal?): see Faner, op. cit., passim, and esp. p. 231.

399. "Ages and Ages Returning at Intervals," loc. cit., p. 157; cf. "As Adam Early in the Morning," ibid., p. 159; and that cry to the impenetrable future: "I merely thee ejaculate!" ("Thou Mother," loc. cit., p. 413).

400. "To Emerson, August, 1856," loc. cit., p. 528, and even more energetically, the anonymous review of 1855, loc. cit., pp. 534–35. But after 1860 Whitman set aside sexual themes and removed from his poems some particularly crude lines and passages (K. Campbell, 1934, in *Poetry and Prose*, pp. 1113–14). On his basic Quakerism, which became more acute after 1860, see Matthiessen, op. cit., pp. 534–40; Canby, op. cit., pp. 31–36, 356–57; Brooks, *Melville and Whitman*, pp. 94–95, 143.

401. *A Backward Glance*, loc. cit., pp. 518–19. "Amativeness," like "Adhesiveness," is a term with a suggestion of phrenology: Gall's phrenology had of course been popularized in the United States by Spurzheim (1832), enjoyed a tremendous vogue (see also Frances Trollope, *Domestic Manners*, VII, ed. cit., pp. 67–68; Martineau, *Retrospect*, II, 66, 91; III, 201–02, 281), and was one of Whitman's fixations.

more precise male body. His nudism is hygienic, physical, from the world of the sunbather, not the afternoons of the faun.[402] This sort of "new Priapic cult," which, according to one of his admirers was what Whitman was trying to establish,[403] is a rational and intellectual cult, frigid as frigid can be. And when he repeats Diderot's arguments on the purity and innocence of nature in all its manifestations, he reduces the vehemence and vigor of the philosophe to a scholastic lecture. With Whitman's bodies, the more he undresses them the less flesh they show. He could skin them and they would not produce a drop of blood. They are athletic patterns, and in fact on closer examination turn out to be modeled not on the citizens of Manhattan or Paumanok, but on the legendary Patagonians and the tall robust Americans of Franklin and Jefferson.

In the same way when Whitman surrenders to a moment of bad temper and ridicules the worthless Americans of his own day (1870) his abuse reminds one of the sort of sarcasms expended by Pernety, for example, on the civilized and artificial Europeans.[404] But when he goes into raptures over America, as he usually does, he finds that its inhabitants are all "superb persons," a "splendid race" with "perfect physique" and "majestic faces"; they are all "musical . . . athletic . . . gymnastic." All America is an "athletic Democracy."[405] And in that healthy environment the ordinary people become handsomer too,[406] while France's political convulsions reduced the stature of the French!

Exactly that: to those who believe that all the French are tiny, five or five and a half feet, Whitman replies first of all it is not true and then immediately admits it as a fact: "The bulk of the personnel of France,

402. Typical: "A Sun-Bath—Nakedness," loc. cit., pp. 694–96. Brooks too notes that "there was something austere . . . in Whitman's sexuality" (op. cit., p. 140), but L. L. Hazard is perhaps going a little far when she says that Whitman's most "daring" poems "are decorum itself" compared to the *Song of Songs* or Shakespeare's plays (*The Frontier in American Literature* [New York, 1941], p. 171).

403. John Burroughs, in *Poetry and Prose*, p. 1027.

404. "Unhealthy forms, male female, painted, padded, dyed, chignon'd, muddy complexions, bad blood, the capacity for good motherhood deceasing or deceas'd, shallow notions of beauty," etc., says Whitman (*Democratic Vistas*, loc. cit., p. 815). And Pernety: "As for . . . the ideas relative to what we call charm and beauty, each Nation attaches them to different things according to caprice and the prejudices of their upbringing" (*Dissertation*, ed. cit., p. 123). For specific criticisms of fashions and facial makeup, see above, pp. 87, 96, and 97.

405. "To Foreign Lands," loc. cit., p. 76; for the other expressions, see for example "For You, O Democracy" (loc. cit., p. 163), "Myself and Mine" (loc. cit., p. 254), "Thoughts" (loc. cit., p. 438), "So Long!" (loc. cit., pp. 445–46), etc. Several times Whitman boasts of being tall and vigorous, of having "perfect health" and of having never taken a purgative! (loc. cit., pp. 538, 540, 952, 967). But his real nature was feminine, and even his physical appearance had something womanly about it (see Mark van Doren, "Walt Whitman, Stranger," basing himself on the testimony of John Burroughs, loc. cit., p. 1151; Brooks, *Melville and Whitman*, p. 141; Hugh L'Anson Fausset, *Walt Whitman, Poet of Democracy* [New Haven, 1942], and Canby, op. cit., pp. 14, 355, the latter however producing a subtle defense of Whitman's quasi normality, describing him as mainly "autosexual," egolatrous; op. cit., pp. 182–206). The vast beard he wore—we might suggest, remembering one of the most typical accusations leveled at the natives of the New World—must have served to conceal his milk-bearing breasts.

406. "The people are getting handsomer," in *The Boston of To-Day* (1881, loc. cit., pp. 781–82).

before the Revolution, was large-sized. . . . The Revolution and Napoleon's Wars dwarfed the standard of human size, but it will come up again."[407] To a text as clear as this one can only add one comment: that more than a century after de Pauw these Europeans that shrink and stretch like bubble gum are just a trifle anachronistic; and furthermore that at the very time when Whitman was writing, his America with its arms open to all the peoples of the world was receiving the first elements of what was to become a flood of Russian, Polish, Italian, and Hebrew immigrants, all on average shorter than the Anglo-Saxons, Germans, and Scandinavians that made up the greater part of the North American population of the time.

But when Whitman looks around him he sees no puny, ugly, or inadequate man. The American citizens are fine and robust and pleasant-looking men. The women, possibly, leave a little to be desired. You want to know the weak point of the United States? *Cherchez la femme.* . . . After his repeated announcement of Man's advent in America, Whitman realizes that what the country really lacks is Woman: "With all thy gifts America . . . what if one gift thou lackest? . . . The gift of perfect women fit for thee . . . what if that gift of gifts thou lackest?"[408] And it is literature, the new health-giving literature that he calls on to provide his United States with "a strong and sweet Female Race, a race of perfect Mothers."[409] And what should they be like? The ideal American male is easily described: "But the other sex in our land requires at least a basis of suggestion." And Whitman makes himself clear with a few examples from life: a capable housemaid, chaste and independent (she has good health, moreover); the manageress of a workshop, who knows how to win the respect of workers and clients alike (nor has she lost "the charm of womanly nature"); a worker's wife with two children, who is a good cook and laundrywoman, with a bent for music and entertaining (Whitman certifies her "physiologically sweet and sound"); and finally an eighty-year-old grandmother who specializes in settling quarrels, an educated woman, but full of "native dignity," and a "peculiar personal magnetism":[410] these are just a few prototypes for America's womanhood of tomorrow.

But when the good Walt heads west (1879) his disappointment grows: there too the males are not too bad, but "I am not so well satisfied with what I see of the woman of the prairie cities." Neither in Kansas City nor in Denver do the women have "any high native originality of spirit or

407. *Millet's Pictures—Last Items* (1881), loc. cit., p. 784. For another too rapid degeneration of the French, before the Revolution, see de Maistre, above, chap. 7, n. 251.
408. "With All Thy Gifts" (1876), loc. cit., p. 372.
409. *Democratic Vistas,* loc. cit., pp. 816, 829–30.
410. Ibid., pp. 839–41.

body," while the men are full of it. The women are elegant, intellectual, but they have a dyspeptic and doll-like complexion. Not at all what is needed "to tally and complete the superb masculinity of the West"![411] Not till he gets to Boston does this new Diogenes in search of perfect specimens of feminity finally come across a number of *fine looking gray-haired women* (his italics), the attentive audience of a lecture he is giving, during which he pauses several times to gaze at them, "healthy and wifely and motherly, and wonderfully charming and beautiful."[412]

Whitman's ideal is thus confirmed as the vaguely Hellenistic notion of a young republic of well-built youths and venerable pensioners, an ideal nourished on the one hand by nationalistic pride and on the other by the poet's "misplaced leanings." In the perfect republic men are passionate friends. There "adhesive" love will prevail over traditional "affective" love. The true democracy "infers such loving comradeship . . . without which it will be incomplete, in vain and incapable of perpetuating itself."[413] Whitman's passionate attachment to the men of America, to his muscular compatriots, is thus for him the lyrical expression of a perfectly healthy political aspiration. The meeting of a (polemic) ideal with a (deviant) instinct? Even one of Whitman's admirers has admitted that he was quite wrong "when he tried to translate his homosexuality into national character."[414] And there is no doubt that that is what he was naïvely trying to do: "I will plant companionship thick as trees along the rivers of America . . . I will make inseparable cities . . . By the love of comrades, / By the manly love of comrades . . . O Democracy, to serve you ma femme!"[415] And again in the last canto: "I announce adhesiveness, I say it shall be limitless, unloosen'd, / I say you shall yet find the friend you were looking for."[416]

Whitman's democracy is thus a democracy *sui generis:* and although he identifies it with America, it could not be further from the *Democracy in America* that Tocqueville studied.[417] On the institutional level too it is

411. *The Women of the West,* loc. cit., pp. 751–52.
412. *The Boston of To-Day* (1881), loc. cit., pp. 781–82.
413. *Democratic Vistas,* loc. cit., p. 853n. The individuals will then be "unprecedently emotional, musical, heroic, and refined"!
414. L. Untermeyer, in the introd. to *Prose and Poetry,* p. 55, following M. van Doren, ibid., pp. 1157–58. There is some significance in both the immediate agreement with Whitman and the later repudiation of his ideas and poetry on the part of another disordered humanitarian, Algernon Charles Swinburne ("To Walt Whitman in America," in *Songs before Sunrise,* 1871; cf. L. L. Hazard, op. cit., pp. 176–77; G. Lafourcade, *La jeunesse de Swinburne* [Paris, 1928], I, 202–03; II, 553–54).
415. "For You, O Democracy," loc. cit., p. 163. Democracy is the only woman among all those loving comrades!
416. "So Long!," loc. cit., p. 445.
417. Tocqueville had in fact foreseen (*Démocratie en Amérique,* ed. cit., II, 71–72, 82–83) some of the vacuous and bombastic aspects of the democratic poetry of someone like Whitman (Matthiessen, op. cit., pp. 533–34, 651) and of its projecting of itself toward the future (*Démocratie en Amérique,* II, 77–79; Matthiessen, op. cit., pp. 543–44).

a democracy without organs, of no particular type, and thus vaguely related to Thoreau's anarchic humanity. Whitman gives its ideological justification in a purely negative characteristic: precisely in that lack of great men, of geniuses, for which America had so often been criticized and which had provoked among other reactions the *indignatio* and retort of a democrat like Jefferson. "America has yet morally and artistically originated nothing."[418] Whitman is quite happy to let the other countries have their great men: "Our leading men are not of much account and never have been, but the average of the people is immense, beyond all history." The leaves of grass are what count — not the mighty oaks or pines. In literature and art too American superiority is one of mass: "We will not have great individuals or great leaders, but a great average bulk, unprecedently great."[419]

This statistical enthusiasm — which is also contradictory in terms because an "average" can never be immense or sublime — is matched by the wholly quantitative concept of greatness as area and multitude. A hundred million men, splendidly handsome men, is Walt Whitman's perfect Utopia, waiting to be realized in his United States. Whitman tempers the inevitable exaltation of the West with his graphic perception of the swarming cities and the feverish movement of the ports, and thus effortlessly overcomes the Rousseauian-Thoreauian conflict between Forest and State, and once again dissolves the antithesis between desert and urban agglomeration, pioneer and merchant, in a single indiscriminate panegyric. In the West he sees "strong native persons," and a growing density, although the inhabitants, strangely "friendly," are "threatening, ironical, scorning invaders";[420] and to the pioneers he dedicates one of his most melodious and auspicious poems.[421] But the East too has its timeless wonders, its unfailing promise. And not only the distant East of Asia,[422] but the immediate East of the Union, and particularly the city where its heart beats, New York, the mighty, menacing, many-souled Manhattan, with

418. *Democratic Vistas*, loc. cit., p. 853; cf., in the same work, pp. 813–14.

419. "An Interviewer's Item," 17 October 1879, in *Specimen Days*, loc. cit., p. 751 (cf. in defense of the "average" against Thoreau, above, n. 388). And, stressing the physical and "solar" aspect of this "democracy," ibid., pp. 803–04. Whitman thus adheres *in toto* to the Herderian theory of poetry as expression of the soul of a people, "the result of a national spirit, and not the privilege of a polish'd and select few" (*A Backward Glance*, p. 521); and he thinks himself democratic, American, modern, and philosophical all at the same time when he combats and eliminates "that old claim of the exclusively curative power of first-class individual men, as leaders and rulers, by the claims, and general movement and result, of ideas" (*Carlyle from American Points of View*, 1881–82, loc. cit., p. 773n.). On the other hand on the necessity, if a perfect democracy is to be brought about, of the "extreme business energy" and the "almost maniacal appetite for wealth prevalent in the United States," see *Democratic Vistas*, loc. cit., p. 825n.; and cf. Brooks, *Melville and Whitman*, pp. 197–98.

420. *Our Old Feuillage*, loc. cit., p. 203; cf. *A Promise to California*, ibid., p. 172.

421. "Pioneers! O Pioneers!," loc. cit., pp. 248–51. The lack of emphasis on the West and the pioneers in Whitman (see also above, p. 534) has been noted by L. L. Hazard, op. cit., pp. 171–72 (*contra*, insisting on Whitman's faith in the West, Smith, *Virgin Land*, pp. 44–48). On the compensatory attraction exerted on him (almost alone among Northern writers), by the romantic South, see Canby, op. cit., pp. 167–68, 207–08.

422. *Hours for the Soul* (1878), loc. cit., p. 713.

its cascades of men more powerful than Niagara,[423] the most convincing demonstration of the triumph of democracy.[424] Its vast navigable rivers, its docks, its busy markets convince him "that not Nature alone is great in her fields of freedom and the open air . . . but in the artificial, the work of man too is equally great."[425]

It may be because of the relative novelty of the literary motif, but it is a fact that Whitman manages to be considerably more effective in describing cities, the citizens and their manifold trades, the confused murmur of the streets, the web and tangle of unnumbered, unknown destinies, than in depicting the physical aspects of the continent. But among the latter he is careful to include the noisome marsh, which had emerged in the eighteenth century as the abbreviated symbol of the whole hemisphere. In the late afternoon the voice of the mockingbird carries over the Great Dismal Swamp,[426] and the poet tries to express "the strange fascination of these half-known half-impassable swamps, infested by reptiles, resounding with the bellow of the alligator, the sad noises of the night-owl and the wild-cat, and the whirr of the rattlesnake."[427] A few insects, and Buffon's swamp would be complete.

But by and large American nature is vast and wholesome, heroic and inviting; and it demands, and in time will have, a society and a literature not a whit inferior to it, indeed sublime and perfect, as being the pure reflection of the country. In the lands of the Far West Whitman hails the promise of a new millennium, "the new society at last proportionate to Nature."[428] And all America is a poem ("these states are the amplest poem")[429] waiting to be expressed, an incandescent lyrical material, ready to be molded into epics of cosmic dimensions, songs of unlimited and unprecedented loftiness and intensity: "Think, in comparison, of the petty environage and limited area of the poets of past or present Europe, no matter how great their genius."[430] The individual poet's talent is not what

---

423. "Rise O Days from your Fathomless Deeps," 2d st., loc. cit., p. 294; cf. "Mannahatta," loc. cit., pp. 425–26.

424. "Manhattan from the Bay" and "Human and Heroic New York" (1878), in *Specimen Days*, loc. cit., pp. 709–11; cf. also pp. 728–29.

425. *Democratic Vistas*, loc. cit., pp. 814–15; cf. the 1855 preface to *Leaves of Grass*, ibid., p. 488 ("here at last is something in the doings of man that corresponds with the broadcast doing of the day and night").

426. *Our Old Feuillage*, loc. cit., p. 204.

427. "O Magnet-South," loc. cit., p. 425; cf. Thoreau, above, pp. 526–27.

428. "Song of the Redwood Tree," loc. cit., p. 233.

429. "By Blue Ontario's Shore," 5th st., loc. cit., p. 330. On his "geopoetics" ("he tried to produce poems in the physical image of America") and his reputation, which was greater in Europe and in Japan than in the United States, some amusing observations in Malcolm Cowley, *New York Times Book Review*, 24 February 1946.

430. *A Backward Glance* (1888), loc. cit., p. 511; but the argument (already outlined in 1849 by Longfellow, and in fact familiar to the transcendentalists: see Lewis, op. cit., pp. 79–80; Jones, *Strange New World*, pp. 346–47, 351) is repeated in a hundred places. A few examples should suffice: "Thou Mother with Thy Equal Brood," 5–6, loc. cit., pp. 413–14; *The United States to Old World Critics*, loc. cit., p. 461; 1855 preface, p. 489. The Civil War in particular is put forward as a fruitful poetic theme (pp. 557, 669, 848), which in fact gave Whitman the inspiration for some of his very best works, such as that on the death of Lincoln.

counts: what makes poetry great is its object, its content, its adaptability "for the use of the democratic masses."[431] In comparison to this imminently expected American literature, all the rest seems mean and ridiculous; it may do for the diminutive kingdoms and empires of Europe where it was born, but "the genius of all foreign literature is clipped and cut small, compared to our genius, and is essentially insulting to our usages, and to the organic compacts of These States."[432]

So Whitman wrote to Emerson in 1856, and not unintentionally, because in substance he was only reemphasizing the fundamental theme of *The American Scholar,* which became and remained the canon and first principle of his poetics.[433] He consistently rejects the old poetry, as romantic, sentimental, maudlin.[434] Even the sublime Shakespeare "belongs essentially to the buried past."[435] His works give off a whiff of death: "What play of Shakespeare, represented in America, is not an insult to America, to the marrow in its bones?"[436] His tragedies come from a feudal world and taint the pure air of the republic: "The great (foreign) poems, Shakespeare included, are poisonous to the idea of the pride and dignity of the common people, the lifeblood of democracy."[437] One could be listening to the pedagogic banning of the poets from Plato's republic.

What is Europe for Whitman, then? It is the past, of course, first of all; but we have already seen (above, pp. 530–31) that Whitman shows a certain filial respect for the past. More precisely Europe for Whitman is antidemocracy: caste, court, feudalism, a den of quarrelsome monarchs,

431. Loc. cit.; cf. above, p. 536.

432. "To Emerson," 1856, loc. cit. p. 525; cf. the 1855 preface ("of all nations the United States with veins full of poetical stuff most needs poets and will doubtless have the greatest and use them the greatest," p. 491). Thus Carlyle was not far wide of the mark when he sarcastically summed up the message of *Leaves of Grass* as: "I'm a big man because I live in such a big country!" (M. D. Conway, in *Poetry and Prose,* p. 975; cf. Matthiessen, op. cit., p. 373), nor Sidney Lanier, with his ironic suggestion that it could be expressed: "Because the Mississippi is long, therefore every American is God" (quoted in Cunliffe, *Literature,* p. 121). Lowell follows in the same path (1867): if the Avon gave birth to a Shakespeare, "what giant might we not look for from the mighty womb of Mississippi" (ibid., p. 142). And Sinclair Lewis is still found longing for an American literature "worthy of her vastness"! (quoted by Strout, op. cit., p. 192).

433. See L. Untermeyer (who utilizes the research of E. Holloway), preface to ed. cit., p. 56; Wish, *Modern America,* pp. 337–38; Curtius, op. cit., p. 134; Canby, op. cit., pp. 105, 108. On Emerson as a supreme poet (and listed in one breath with Job, Homer, Aeschylus, Dante, Shakespeare, and Tennyson!), see pp. 457, 782; doubts and reservations, described by Untermeyer as "ungrateful" and "dishonest" (p. 873), on pp. 886–88. On his person and death, ibid., pp. 792–94, 800. Whitman denies (1887) having read Emerson before writing *Leaves of Grass,* loc. cit., pp. 957–58. But his derivation from the transcendentalist is unquestionable: cf. Brooks, *Emerson,* pp. 287–88; Canby, op. cit., p. 120.

434. "Song of the Exposition," 2 and 7, loc. cit., pp. 222, 226; "By Blue Ontario's Shore," 5, loc. cit., pp. 329–30, 333; "Thou Mother with Thy Equal Brood," 3, loc. cit., p. 412; *A Backward Glance,* loc. cit., p. 521; *Art Features,* loc. cit., p. 742; *The Prairies and Great Plains in Poetry,* loc. cit., p. 747; *Democratic Vistas,* loc. cit., pp. 847–48, etc., and cf. Matthiessen, op. cit., pp. 534, 543.

435. *A Backward Glance,* loc. cit., p. 513.

436. *An English and an American Poet* (1856), loc. cit., p. 542.

437. *Democratic Vistas,* p. 829; cf. also *Poetry To-Day in America,* p. 550, and, for the significant total rejection of Matthew Arnold, Raleigh, op. cit., pp. 58–61.

and a nest of loves and affections that are anything but "adhesive." So that even if in the vision of the unfulfilled future America and Europe both pale and retreat into the shadows behind the poet's back,[438] and if in a senile *embrassement* the poet sees east and west "inseparably fused,"[439] much more often the New World and the Old World are contrasted as present and past, life and death, progress and decadence: "See revolving the globe, / The ancestor-continents away group'd together, / The present and future continents north and south, with the isthmus between."[440] Europe is an old dynastic slaughterhouse, a theater of conspiracy and regicide, with the stench of battlefield and scaffold still in the air:[441] it is a heap of feudal ruins, of royal skeletons, of weary clowns, priestly tombs, ruined palaces, and crumbling cathedrals.[442] Whitman scorns it, pities it, but also, logically, admires its indomitable revolutionary spirit whenever it flickers into life again;[443] and all in all he does not condemn it: "We do not blame thee elder World, nor really separate ourselves from thee." America is the Old World's daughter and will build something better:

> Mightier than Egypt's tombs,
> Fairer than Grecia's, Roma's temples
> Prouder than Milan's statued, spired cathedral,
> More picturesque than Rhenish castle-keeps,
> We plan even now to raise, beyond them all,
> Thy great cathedral sacred industry, no tomb,
> A keep for practical invention.[444]

If the terms of comparison are conventional picture-postcard stuff, the architectural project which is to surpass them is of naïve cumbersome insipidity: a vast palace, the biggest ever seen, all glass and iron, and painted pretty colors, topped with a row of flags and surrounded by a

438. *Years of the Modern*, loc. cit., pp. 435–36.

439. "I see that this world of the West, as part of all, fuses inseparably with the East, and with all, as time does" (*Poetry To-Day in America*, 1881, loc. cit., 552).

440. "Starting from Paumanok," loc. cit., p. 85. But the ship of democracy is on one occasion entrusted by Whitman with a most ancient and glorious cargo too, "Venerable priestly Asia . . . And royal feudal Europe" ("Thou Mother," loc. cit., pp. 412–13). It is a cargo, not ballast; consistent with what has been said above, pp. 530–31, about Whitman's respect for the past.

441. "Song of the Redwood Tree," I, loc. cit., p. 231.

442. See the review of 1855, p. 532; *A Backward Glance*, p. 517; *A New Army Organization Fit for America*, loc. cit., p. 637 (Whitman considers the European armies feudal in type and origin, and in general makes no distinction at all between "feudal" and "monarchical" or "royal"!).

443. See the youthful poem "Resurgemus!" (1848) celebrating the 1848 revolutions (in Canby, op. cit., p. 80); "O Star of France" (1870–71), loc. cit., pp. 368–69; "To a Foil'd European Revolutionaire," ibid., pp. 351–52 (which at first—see Matthiessen, op. cit., p. 554—had the title so typical of Whitman's nomenclatory insatiability: "Liberty Poem for Asia, Africa, Europe, America, Australia, Cuba, and the Archipelagoes of the Sea": one is irresistibly reminded of the *Hôtel de l'Univers et des Pays-Bas!*); *Spain*, 1873–74, ibid., p. 430; and the "consolatory" poem for Ireland reborn in America: "Old Ireland," ibid., p. 348.

444. "Song of the Exposition," 5, loc. cit., p. 224.

group of other buildings equally bright and splendid, but not so tall: in short some sort of exposition hall, or rather, as becomes clear when we get to the description of the inside, a cross between international trade fair and science museum complete with working models.

Whitman is especially fascinated by machines: not so much the locomotives of a generation earlier, but agricultural machines. Invented in America, rapidly proliferating and revealing their superiority over European rivals (1850–69), these new "crawling monsters" cut the hay, shell the cotton, thresh the grain, husk the rice, and with this saving of man's labor make possible the conquest of the vast prairies.[445]

His poetry seems to be modeled on these machines, setting out like them to conquer the world. Many of his poems are less "leaves of grass" than "crawling monsters," advancing from invocation to invocation, from image to image, loose-jointed, mechanical, intricate; sometimes they seem like a row of lithographed vignettes, other times a rapid film sequence or an auctioneer's catalogue,[446] a program for the opera season[447] or the colored tables in a popular encyclopedia—"costumes of the world," or "wild and domestic animals," "flags" or "ships, ancient and modern"; and sometimes, as when he holds a march past of all the arts and crafts, like some sort of spurious trade-union litanies. And then, when this prophet, this Brooklyn Homer, finally finds himself running short of breath at the end of some excessively prolix tirade, he excuses himself like a society columnist fearful of having omitted the name of some prickly dowager: ". . . and you each and everywhere whom I specify not, but include just the same!"[448]

In Whitman there is always this reaching for totality, and he does not

445. "The Return of the Heroes," 8, loc. cit., p. 345; Wish, *Early America*, p. 371; Curti, *Probing Our Past*, pp. 253–54; and Stewart Holbrook, *Machines of Plenty: Pioneering in American Agriculture* (New York, 1955); Ampère, op. cit., I, 200, 416. But there had to be a song "To a Locomotive in Winter" too (loc. cit., pp. 423–24), to that little old "fierce-throated beauty" (a symbolic representation, according to some critics—see Canby, op. cit., p. 6—of Mrs. Gilchrist, the ardent Briton who crossed the ocean and did everything within her power to marry the poet!); and the recognition of the civilizing function of the railroads ("Upon Our Own Land" [1879], loc. cit., p. 754). More curious still is the almost Madison Avenue eulogy of the comfort offered to the traveler "in the luxurious palace-car," i.e., the *wagon-lit* ("In the Sleeper" [1879], loc. cit., pp. 735–36). Cf., *contra*, the unpleasant experiences of Anthony Trollope (1861–62) in that "thoroughly American institution of sleeping-cars," *North America*, I, 177–79, 249.

446. Emerson, recommending the book to Carlyle, and calling it precisely "a nondescript monster which yet had terrible eyes and buffalo strength," admitted that to the Englishman it might seem "only an auctioneer's inventory of a warehouse" (letter of 6 May 1856; loc. cit., p. 964). True, replies an enthusiastic defender of Whitman, but the auctioneer is the Almighty Father! (R. M. Bucke, in *Poetry and Prose*, p. 1024). Similar expressions: ibid., pp. 59, 69.

447. "Proud Music of the Storm," loc. cit., p. 376 (for the source of inspiration, see pp. 372, 600, 932–33, 967; Matthiessen, op. cit., pp. 558 ff.; L. Pound, "Walt Whitman and Italian Music," *American Mercury*, 6 [September 1925], pp. 58–63). A demonstration of how much Whitman took from the opera, especially the Italian opera, both in inspiration and in the formal structure of his poetry, has been attempted, with a wealth of detail and an impressive array of statistical tables and musical examples, by Faner, op. cit.

448. "Salut au Monde!," loc. cit., p. 183.

realize that it is not to be grasped simply by piling element on element. If his immense vanity saves him from having to recognize his true measure as a poet of scarce and intermittent, impressionistic and elegiac vein (and thus far from possessing the dominant accents proper to the self-appointed bard of America and the universe), his basic good sense is enough to show him the enormous distance between his ideal democracy and the United States, and when the Civil War ends, and is followed by a wave of cynical opportunism, and the contrast becomes even more crude and strident, Whitman does not hesitate to express his disappointment in the grimly bitter *Democratic Vistas* (1871).

Throughout the decade 1870–80, that "dreadful decade" that witnessed violent economic crises, ever more widespread and more festering public corruption, the rise of the "dinosaurs" and the appearance in America's "egalitarian" society of an arrogant and bullying caste of multimillionaires, Whitman frets and sighs. The final proof of his bewilderment and his need of the support and reassurance of some valid philosophy when America, thirty years after his message, seems further than ever from realizing it, appears in his interpretation of Hegel. True, he seems only to have known Hegel through Gostick's summary.[449] But it is typical of both his speculative levity and his messianic candor that it should be none other than Hegel, the thinker who had pronounced the most total condemnation on America, that Whitman sees as the most typically American philosopher of the Old World; that he should hail the conservative and Prussian Hegel as the man whose formulas furnished "an essential and crowning justification of New World democracy in the creative realms of time and space." In his enthusiasm Whitman does not hesitate to make Hegel a sort of honorary citizen of the New World. Carlyle, of course, is the sort of philosopher one would expect from Europe. But Hegel — Hegel should have been born in America! His theories contain that something "which only the vastness, the multiplicity and the vitality of America would seem able to comprehend . . . or even originate. It is strange to me that they were born in Germany, or in the old world at all."[450]

What did Whitman find so genuinely American in Hegel? His explanations are obscure. He begins by wondering why on earth Carlyle, who had always been hostile or indifferent toward America, managed by the

---

449. *Sic*, but more properly Joseph Gostwick; on Gostwick as one of Whitman's sources, see also Floyd Stovall, "Notes on Whitman's Reading," *American Literature,* 26, no. 3 (November 1954), pp. 348, 351, 353–54, 361. In "Roaming in Thought (After Reading Hegel)," op. cit., p. 282, there are no more than four lines on Good and Evil in the Universe ("a singularly flatulent poetic reflection," according to Lewis, op. cit., p. 51).

450. *Carlyle from American Points of View,* 1881–82, loc. cit., p. 778n. Hegel is mentioned various times, almost always in general terms as one of the great philosophers: see *Democratic Vistas,* loc. cit., pp. 845, 856 n., etc.

time of his death to be more alive and influential in the United States than in England: and he thinks he can find the answer to the enigma in "a much more profound horoscope, that of Hegel."[451] The basic question, of all times and all places, he says, is the relationship or link between the (radical, democratic) "I" with its intellective, emotive, spiritual capacities, and the (conservative) "non-I", the complex of the objective and material universe and its laws. Kant left the question unresolved. Schelling tried to make man and the external universe, mind and nature, mutually convertible, resolvable the one in the other. But only Hegel turned this crudely formed answer into a coherent metaphysical system, a system that could be improved, but which "at any rate beams forth to-day, in its entirety, illuminating the thought of the universe, and satisfying the mystery thereof to the human mind, with a more consoling scientific assurance than any yet."

Hegel showed that the whole earth and its infinite phenomena and contradictions are nought but necessary manifestations and aspects, steps or links in the endless process of creative thought, which is essentially one and carries along with it every accident, fault, defect, or infirmity. In politics, this means that in the long run evil, oppression, cruelty, and sly injustice *non praevalebunt*. In theology, that the man who welcomes all faiths and accepts the world as it is, is more religious and more of a philosopher than the one who sees only darkness and despair in the work of Providence, and is thus, pious and devout as he may be, the most radical of sinners and unbelievers.

At this point Whitman feels some need to justify himself: "in recounting Hegel a little freely here," he did so to neutralize the letter and spirit of Carlyle and the maxims of Darwin and the evolutionists. It is a real shame that German metaphysics lacks the poetic afflatus, the prophetic ardor, those flashes of exaltation that one finds in the Bible and the great poets of every country.[452]

---

451. Ibid., pp. 771–72. A footnote insists on the paradox that although neither Hegel nor Carlyle ever concerned themselves *ex professo* with the United States, the chief works of both could be collected and bound together under the title (actually rather more Carlylean than Hegelian): *Speculations for the use of North America, and Democracy there, with the relations of the same to Metaphysics, including Lessons and Warnings (encouragements, too, and of the vastest) from the Old World to the New.*

452. Ibid., pp. 776–78. Little different, and if anything even more superficial, is the interpretation of Hegel in another passage (from the 1870s?) quoted by Matthiessen, op. cit., p. 525: "He [Whitman] declared that 'only Hegel is fit for America,' since in his system 'the human soul stands in the centre, and all the universes minister to it'" (cf. also p. 624). Somewhat vaguer are Parrington, according to whom (op. cit., III, 78–79) "Whitman . . . dwelt much with Hegel and the German idealists, and with their help he penetrated curiously to the core of things, discovering there an inner spiritual reality that is the abiding substance behind the external manifestation," and Myers, for whom Whitman illuminates "Hegel's notion of the escape from the State of isolation and 'unhappy consciousness' by identification of self with reality" (1934); *Poetry and Prose*, pp. 1141–42. One can form an idea of how the Americans of the 1850s understood Hegel when one reads in J. M. Mackie (*From Cape Cod to Dixie*, in Tryon,

One is thus left with the impression that only a poet like himself, Walt Whitman, could instil the necessary vitality into the technicalities of modern philosophy. And doubtless this is just the impression that Whitman wanted to leave us with; was it not Whitman who a few years earlier had appealed for "a class of bards" for America and the world, that would be as epic and impassioned as Isaiah, Homer, and Shakespeare, "but consistent with Hegelian formulas, and consistent with modern science"?[453]

Yet again, as when he was distributing his respectful greetings to the universal world, the bearded cantor is caught in the none too priestly act of embracing everything and holding nothing. The apostolic message addressed to the great mass of mediocre people goes unheard, and men continue to worry about their own affairs.[454] The implicit and explicit reply to the European insults, broadening into oracle, becomes generic and ambiguous; the polemic, confused to the point where the enemy is mistaken for an ally; the prophecy, vacuous and vapid.

XIV. THE POLEMIC'S LAST METAMORPHOSIS:
IMMIGRANTS AND EXPATRIATES

With this last rhapsodic broadside from the American shore, the history of the polemic properly speaking can be considered closed. The exaltation of the New World will continue from decade to decade, right up into our own day, with its constant even if involuntary accompaniment of criticism or compassion toward Europe and the rest of the world. And many Europeans, travelers, novelists, and sociologists, will in turn delight in pronouncing the most malicious or disdainful judgments on America and its past and present civilizations. But there are no new developments; this is already the afterlife of the polemic, beyond its final agony.

op. cit., p. 609): "The society of a Western hotel is in a constant flux. The universe, in the Hegelian philosophy, is not more fluid," and remembers that already an Elisha Mulford, "an Episcopalian clergyman," had "applied Hegel's political philosophy to the development of American civilization" (Curti, *Probing Our Past*, p. 122n., quoting [Francis] Lieber to [Charles] Sumner, 11 September 1870; 14 April 1871 [New York] in Huntington Collection). There is no mention of Whitman, but a good survey of the play of forces, the interweaving and overlapping of heterogeneous influences in the America of the late nineteenth century, in the essay by David F. Bowers, "Hegel, Darwin and the American Tradition," in *Foreign Influences in American Life*, ed. D. F. Bowers (Princeton, 1944), pp. 146–71, with bibliography, pp. 235–54.

453. *Democratic Vistas*, loc. cit., p. 859. On the frequently expressed hopes for the coming of a bard in America, see Brooks, *Melville and Whitman*, p. 135, and, with explicit reference to Whitman, Enrico Nencioni, *Saggi critici di letteratura italiana* (Florence, 1898), p. 235 (article from the *Fanfulla della Domenica*, ca. 1884).

454. Cf. M. van Doren, loc. cit., pp. 1155–57. A French bibliographer actually included him among the mad writers (Junior Philomneste [pseudonym of Jacques-Charles Brunet], *Les fous littéraires, Essai bibliographique* . . . [Brussels, 1880], pp. 195–96). On his (better) fortune in Italy, see G. Getto, "Pascoli e l'America" in *Carducci e Pascoli* (Bologna, 1957), pp. 161–64, and Glauco Cambon, "Walt Whitman in Italia," *Aut-Aut*, 39 (May 1957), pp. 244–63.

While the logical fault remains basically the same, the animating spirit is quite different. The United States, freed from the blemish of slavery, was climbing to a level of power and wealth never before seen in the history of mankind, and toward the end of the century was occupied on the one hand with a vigorous expansion in the Caribbean and the Pacific, on the other with the arrival of wave after wave of Italian, Jewish, and Slavic immigrants, coming to populate the hungry metropolises, the glowing factories, the relentless horizons of the West. The myth of America as refuge of the oppressed was revived in economic terms: the Statue of Liberty, dominating the port of New York, hailed and welcomed Europe's helpless masses, offering "A shelter for the hunted head / For the starved laborer toil and bread."[455]

Along the coastlines of South America other Europeans, mostly immigrants from the peninsular nations of the Mediterranean, were consolidating the bridgeheads already established there, which were, of course, rudimentary nuclei of civilization, market centers for cereals, coffee, meats and skins, fibers and minerals, but of a rarefied and timid culture, and an uncertain and turbulent political structure, and thus incapable of attacking the central mass of the continent, whose massive, solid, elemental nature seemed to defy penetration except the occasional foray in search of rubber or rare essences.

Europe, in turn, far from feeling itself weakened by the emigration, still unconscious of the ripening imbalance of power, intent on completing the conquest of Africa and colonizing the ancient lands of Asia and the virgin lands of Oceania, prided herself, with reason, on the unaccustomed rhythm of her progress; and in the arts, philosophy, and science confirmed and refurbished her time-honored supremacy. With renewed boldness she could thus refuse to recognize any privileged destiny for the Western Hemisphere, however manifest and breathtaking its ascent, and forgot, or revoked, the abdication implicit in the theory of History's westward progress.

Each hemisphere's knowledge of the other increased as communications of all sorts became more frequent and more rapid: but overall opinions, actually complicated by this greater mass of factual data to be absorbed, tended more and more toward the distortions of sentimental outpourings or allegorical self-criticism. Europe, in particular, began to criticize America's mechanism, standardization, obsession with quantity and the greed and arrogance of capitalism, which were the direct and immediate results of her own civilization, industrial revolution, and political

455. *Sic,* already before 1850, William Cullen Bryant, quoted in Weinberg, op. cit., p. 123. Cf. below, pp. 550–51.

ideologies.[456] Europe saw America as an extreme and shocking case of the ills afflicting herself, and thus found it easier to denounce them, and immediately afterward, with a facile sophism, to ascribe them to America herself and put Europe on her guard against the danger of contagion. (Just as people had spent centuries discussing whether syphilis was Europe's gift to America or vice versa; and Guerrazzi, polemicizing with the priests, wrote that the New World had given the poison of the *mal français* in exchange for "the infamies of the Catholic religion," with which it had been poisoned by the Europeans.)[457]

It was easy for all the worst aspects of European civilization to take solid shape in the image of an America where these evils were or at least seemed to be so conspicuous; as once the New World had summed up all the dreams and hopes of the Old in a single plastic symbol, so now it became the incarnation of all her legitimate fears, her torments and repulsions. The "dialogue" once again became merely the literary version of a substantially self-accusing "monologue."

On the American or at least North American side, the attitude is similar. We have seen how as the polemic shrank from the antithesis between two hemispheres to that between England and the United States,

456. Thus it will suffice to mention, teetering here on the edge of a footnote, the memorable sarcasms of a Niebuhr (an American-style republic is "the most trivial and disgusting that one could imagine": letter to Dora Hensler, from Rome, 14 October 1820, in *Lebensnachrichten über Barthold Georg Niebuhr*, II, 449; cf. also the letters of 1 July 1827, and 14 June 1829, ibid., III, 191–92, 235); of a Baudelaire, on the Americans' preoccupation with business and their faith in the omnipotence of industry (they believe, these ingenuous folk, "that it will finally eat the Devil": preface to his translation of Poe, *Histoires extraordinaires*, 1856); of an eighty-five-year-old Humboldt, comparing the United States to a Cartesian vortex reducing everything to the same level of boredom, and where liberty is no more than a useful implement, devoid of educative value (letter to Varnhagen von Ense, 31 July 1854 and 28 May 1857: Geneva ed., pp. 212–13, 264; Brussels ed., pp. 366, 452); of a Hebbel likewise disgusted with the pseudoliberty of the United States and the real "yoke" burdening men and things, the lack of poetry and ardor (letter of 29 December 1855, in *Tagebücher*, ed. R. M. Werner [Berlin, n.d.], IV, 61, n. 5410; cf. ibid., IV, 234, n. 6017 [1862]); of a Proudhon, on that "so-called young nation," a degenerate parasite of Europe, that never bestowed upon humanity a single great man, or work, or idea, having assumed as life's object a stercorary "wealth" (*La guerre et la paix*, I, 68–72); and of a Burckhardt on the North American barbarians, who are devoid of historical sense, but to whom there remain appended as relics the leftovers of European history; on their new physical type, of doubtful kind and longevity (*Weltgeschichtliche Betrachtungen*, 1868–70, pp. 9–10, 68–69); and on their total dedication to business (ibid., 1873, ed. cit., p. 203; cf. also Gollwitzer, op. cit., p. 403). With some justification Remond sees in these European criticisms of the pallid, mechanical United States an echo and a particularization of the general criticism leveled by romanticism against rationalism (op. cit., II, 725). But a North American theologian, who actually investigated the strident ironies resulting from the discordance between the ideal principles infusing the society of the United States and its actual practical acts and deeds and directives, complained: "Europe accuses us of errors of which the whole of modern bourgeois society is guilty and which we merely developed more consistently than European nations" (R. Niebuhr, op. cit., p. 50). And the same thesis is developed in Lewis Mumford's article "The America in Europe," *Comprendre*, 10–11 (May 1954), pp. 161–64, with such impetuous eloquence that he almost succeeds in destroying and annulling the specific originality of North American culture.

457. Thus one cannot be surprised at the fact that "the comparison between Europe and America," as Gollwitzer puts it, op. cit., p. 443, n. 99, "is found to be among the favorite themes of nineteenth-century publicistics." Cf. also Strout, op. cit.

the physical and biological themes receded into the background, or else completely disappeared, while political and social themes emerged into the limelight; and these too, given the substantial ethnic affinity of the two nations, were based on differences of government and economic structure — aggravated, of course, by the memory of two recent armed conflicts and the awareness of a present and increasing commercial competition, and therefore easily made to play the part of symbolic support for any other real or imagined polarity.

Thus the ideological collision occurred between Republic and Monarchy, Rebellion and Legitimacy, Liberty and Order, between savage roughness of manners and the polite conventions of civilized existence, the rush to open or rather cave in the doors of the future, and the reverent guardianship of the past, the watchful vigilance over its tombs and parchments. The conflict was no longer "geographical," but, as we have said several times, of "geography" against "history," and thus, by a swift and inevitable jump, of two antinomial and coessential spiritual attitudes; now, in short, a conflict of "history" against "history," the clash which is the soul of all history. The heritage (Europe's) and the mission (America's) cannot be separated, and in fact — this too we have seen (in Melville and Whitman) — are not separated. Criticism of the present and faith in the future heat and kindle one another, fan each other's flames in mutual function. And in the consciousness of the more thinking Americans the polemic becomes internal, intimate, and the more it burns the more fruitful it becomes. The sediment left by the ancient argument lives on.

The most exalted and significant example of the spiritualization of the ancient conflict can be seen in the greatest of the expatriates, Henry James: both in his literary work, so often inspired by the trials and temptations of the American in Europe, which more than once he endows with an aura of lucid and tormented poetry; and, even more transparently, in his critical works, so rich in autobiographical matter. Henry James, who spent almost all his life in Europe (leaving America after completing his studies, in that bitter decade 1860–69), is the most European of the American writers; and the unmistakable stamp of later French realism, the *fin de siècle* aestheticism and the refined richness of his style in the novels and short stories can easily make us forget that they were written by a native of New York. But when he speaks *ex professo* on some American topic, such as the novelist Hawthorne (1879) or the spectacle of *The American Scene,* (1907), or even Rupert Brooke's few letters from America (1916), James becomes or reverts to being the most American of the "European" critics. In him the contrasted positions symbolized in these continental toponyms form a natural dialogue, speaking to him, without polemic violence, in alternating tones of nostalgia, disappointment, bored irony, or anxious optimism.

He himself confirms this: when he was young Europe seemed to offer more rich and varied promise than his native country. In middle age, when Europe was no longer any novelty, America seemed to beckon him as a new source of surprise and wonderment: "Nothing could be of a simpler and straighter logic: Europe had been romantic years before, because she was different from America; wherefore America would now be romantic because she was different from Europe."[458] Thus it was not a question of an alternative between two hemispheres; but between reality and yearning, between the two souls constantly being renewed in the breast of Henry James.

In his study on Hawthorne, the last and most conspicuous example of American literary primitivism,[459] the fundamental theme is the by now familiar question of whether the United States will ever give birth to great art. The prospects are poor. The flower of art blooms only where the soil is deep. It takes a lot of history to produce a little literature, and America has had other things to do than busy herself with gardening: "Before producing writers, she wisely busied herself with providing them with something to write about."[460]

America's nature too is singularly lacking in history: it has a bold imprint of youth that obliterates any trace of an all too brief past. The very air there is new and young, and the vegetation seems not to have reached its majority.[461] The American landscape is consequently uninteresting, unpicturesque, anything but romantic. Hawthorne himself had lamented the fact (already in the period 1835–40, or before he ever went to Europe, and again in 1860), and James pursues and strengthens his case with an enumeration, tinged with sarcasm, of the many "items of high civilization" that America lacked:

No State, in the European sense of the word, and indeed barely a specific national name.[462] No sovereign, no court, no personal loyalty, no aristocracy, no church, no clergy, no army, no diplomatic service, no country gentlemen, no palaces, no castles, nor manors, nor old countryhouses, nor parsonages, nor thatched cottages nor ivied ruins; no cathedrals, nor abbeys, nor little Norman churches, no great Universities nor public schools—no Oxford, nor Eton, nor Harrow; no

458. Henry James, *The American Scene*, pp. 365–66. Cf. Strout, op. cit., pp. 119–33.
459. Henry James, *Hawthorne*, pp. 162–63.
460. Ibid., pp. 2–3; cf. above, n. 327.
461. Ibid., pp. 12–13.
462. Here one catches an echo of an ancient complaint, already voiced by Francis Lieber, who when he found the legitimate name of Columbia already "taken," suggested for the United States the "Norman" term Windland! (Curti, *Probing Our Past*, pp. 143–44).

literature, no novels, no museums, no pictures, no political society, no sporting class—no Epsom nor Ascot!"[463]

On the other hand this same picturesque Europe weighed down on Hawthorne—"he was oppressed with the burden of antiquity in Europe"[464]—and reinforced his radicalism and candid faith in the destiny of America, in that very special providence which would surely guarantee its prosperity and free institutions and unlimited progress *per omnia saecula saeculorum.*[465]

It was only shortly afterward that the Civil War delivered a rude shock to this puerile optimism—a strange companion, in any case, to his doubts on the artistic and literary possibilities of the North Americans. And at the end of the conflict—which seems to James to mark "an era in the history of [the] American mind"[466]—he did not hesitate to define the attitude of his compatriots as extremely touchy, nationalistic, and distrustful toward Europe. They think that all the other nations of the world are involved in some plot to despise them: and they are painfully conscious of being the youngest of the great nations, of not belonging to the European family, of being not at the center but on the edge of civilization, and of having something experimental about their political structure. And this feeling, this sense of relativity and precariousness, accounts for their inferiority complex toward the English and French; as also for their nervousness and provincialism.[467]

Another sign of this provincialism is the exaggerated reverence for the arts and letters, activities cultivated in America by beings of superior breed, by strange and almost monstrous geniuses, while in Europe they thrive naturally:[468] with which the circle is complete, and he comes back to the question of what poetry, if any, will come into being in the New World.

463. *Hawthorne,* p. 43: note that the comparison, postulated with Europe, is actually effected with England. On the absence of the picturesque and the lack of architectural beauty in Salem, see the beginning of the *Scarlet Letter* (ed. cit., p. 5). The protagonist, the Reverend Dimmesdale, had brought from the English universities "all the learning of the age into our wild forest-land" (op. cit., III, ed. cit., p. 53). On Hawthorne's attitude toward "historic" Europe, halfway between Irving's reverence and Mark Twain's scorn, see G. Möhle, *Das Europabild Mark Twains* (Berlin, 1940), pp. 93–96; on James's, see Christof Wegelin, op. cit. On the relationship between the two, see R. P. Blackmur, *The American Literary Expatriate,* in Bowers, *Foreign Influences,* pp. 129–32. Cf. *Hawthorne,* p. 85, and above, p. 364, and, for a better understanding of the implications of James's expressions, Wegelin, op. cit., pp. 46–47; also May, op. cit., pp. 34–35. Almost the same items were noted as lacking by Crèvecoeur (1782), who arrived however at the opposite conclusion, that American society was the most perfect and rational (see above, p. 251; and quoted in Cunliffe, op. cit., p. 48); while William Cullen Bryant found (1825) favorable auspices for the birth of American poetry precisely in the absence of myths and literary conventions: see Lewis, op. cit., pp. 87–88; and cf. above, chap. 7, nn. 114–17.

464. *Hawthorne,* p. 71.

465. Ibid., p. 142. In 1860, however, Hawthorne lamented that the United States, excellent in so many ways, was "not fit to live in" (quoted by Strout, op. cit., p. 104).

466. *Hawthorne,* pp. 142–44.

467. Ibid., pp. 153–54.

468. Ibid., pp. 29–31.

In the account of his visit to the United States, after an absence of twenty-five years, the accent shifts from literature to society. The problem of American art, if not actually forgotten, is viewed only from afar, and merges into the question of the environment. With trepidation and foreboding, pathetically reflected in the turgid complexities of his syntax, James looks bewilderedly around at the trends, distortions, and dangers of the *American Scene.* "Quantity" prevails decisively over "quality."[469] Everywhere, in the landscape, the cities and the lexicon, he is struck by the lack of historical and poetic "associations." Even the universities are itinerant; nothing is allowed to "accumulate" a little history, indeed nothing is allowed to accumulate anything, except the bank-accounts interest.[470] Almost the only faces he sees about him are those of pure and simple businessmen.[471]

James still indulges in the dream of the immense poetic possibilities implicit in the unbounded spaces and absolute liberty of America:

The ground is so clear of preoccupation, the air so clear of prejudgment and doubt, that you wonder why the chance shouldn't be as great for the aesthetic revel as for the political and economic, why some great undaunted adventure of the arts, meeting in its path none of the aged lions of prescription, of proscription, of merely jealous tradition, should not take place in conditions unexampled.

But the dream does not last. Immediately James begins to talk of mysterious factors frustrating that happy combination of elements, adds, with belated compunction, that plain size is no cause for complacency, and sadly refers to the vanity of mere "hugeness."[472]

Thus we come back to that "quantity" which cannot replace, let alone generate, "quality." But now there is also a metaphysical basis to the frequent attacks on the manifestations of quantitative mechanical genius, ranging from the repudiation of the arrogant skyscrapers, conglomerations of floors and windows,[473] to the exasperated outbursts against the Pullman train, which goes rampaging across the uninhabited stretches of virgin nature, ruining them irreparably, and converting all things healthy and pure "one after another to crudities, to invalidities, hideous and unashamed": it claims to bring a new civilization, but in fact it only destroys the beauty and the charm of the unspoiled, primitive, and solitary land.[474]

469. *American Scene,* pp. 18–19.
470. Ibid., pp. 31, 143. By way of exception, "I saw the lucky legacy of the past, at Philadelphia, operate" (p. 291).
471. Ibid., p. 64; cf. pp. 236–37.
472. Ibid., pp. 445–47, 462–63.
473. Ibid., pp. 76–78, 95–96; cf. Larkin, op. cit., p. 324. The skyscrapers with their illuminated advertisements are called "the vertical business blocks and the lurid sky-clamour for more dollars" in the introduction to Rupert Brooke's *Letters from America* (New York, 1916), p. xxxii, perhaps because Brooke liked them (ibid., pp. 7–8).
474. *American Scene,* pp. 463–64.

The theme goes back at least as far as Thoreau (see above, p. 521), for whom James confesses a revealing admiration,[475] but in James it is linked to a much richer experience, and a more thoroughgoing pessimism. And that historical barrenness of the American countryside, which in the essay on Hawthorne had still been decorated with the attribute of youth, now acquires a more serious and sacred character (that much more sacred, as the sacrilege of its violator is more flagrant), and with a leap that cannot possibly surprise us at this point in our story, turns into extreme antiquity, absolute primitivism. Florida reminds him of the Nile, but a prehistoric Nile, not just pre-Cleopatra, but pre-Pyramid: California is a sort of pre-Italy, an unconscious and inexperienced Italy, its "primitive *plate* in perfect condition, but with the impression of History all yet to be made."[476]

Then again—and let this be a warning to us, whenever we may be tempted to too facile classifications of such an agile and contradictory spirit—James is anything but a "primitivist." The chaste and naked nature could *vera patere dea* to Thoreau's eyes, but not to his, to the eyes of the man who wrote to the last of the real "primitivists," his friend Stevenson: "Primitive man doesn't interest me, I confess, as much as civilized."[477] At the opposite pole of the "American scene" we have indeed the great cities of the Atlantic coast, invaded and submerged by the inexhaustible and apparently necessary flood of immigrants, particularly Italians and Jews.[478] The phenomenon was then at its height, and James, although never especially interested or involved in it, did not fail to grasp the basic contribution it made to the dialectic of European-American relations.[479] The messianism of the "melting-pot," God's crucible, in which all the

475. *Hawthorne,* pp. 96–97; *American Scene,* p. 264.

476. *American Scene,* p. 462.

477. Letter of summer 1893, in *Henry James and R. L. Stevenson,* ed. J. Adam Smith (London, 1948), p. 231. The concept and form are very reminiscent of Dr. Johnson (see above, p. 173), another author for whom James had the highest admiration (see ibid., p. 277). A more detailed examination of James's attitude occurs in Wegelin, op. cit., substantially in agreement with this paragraph, and only at fault (though mentioning "our" polemic) in not sufficiently stressing that one cannot understand James's image of Europe without simultaneously analyzing his "image of America." Cf. also R. H. Heindel, *The American Impact on Great Britain* (Philadelphia 1940), pp. 303–04.

478. Ibid., pp. 123–30; Cunliffe, *Literature,* pp. 193–94.

479. Thus America resumed, among other things, its providential role of safety valve for Europe's excess population, the role it had played once before in the seventeenth century ("the poor man's best country in the world," wrote John F. Smith in 1624: Blanke, op. cit., p. 293, and Milton in *Animadversion*), again in the years of Malthus and Goethe, and again after the Restoration, and which had in fact already found in Crèvecoeur (*Lettres,* pp. 93, 161, 194) a clear and prophetic formulation (see above, p. 251). The emigrant, who at that very time had found his status changed from that of deportee, adventurer, and fugitive (see what Mrs. Montagu wrote about the Americans in 1777) to that of pioneer and bringer of arts and technology, finally assumed, and not without some difficulty, the image of the Worker (exploited possibly, but idealized) and brother and companion in forging the highest destiny of the country with a richer human amalgam. See also the inscription on the pedestal of the Statue of Liberty, and the lines quoted above, p. 544.

races of Europe were dissolved and refined,[480] and which was to produce a new and perfect humanity, was one of the national myths of the United States, at least up until the time of the laws restricting immigration (1921–24):[481] a myth that translated into positive and indeed original terms the ancient opposition between "space" and "tradition," by making environment prevail over heredity, social climate over race, geography over history.[482] But it was a cruel myth, because it tended to make men forget just how painful and costly this process of fusion was to the peoples forcibly amalgamated by being tossed into the melting pot. The first contacts between different peoples, of equal or unequal levels of civilization, are usually lethal for at least one of the elements involved. The American natives learned this when the Europeans first arrived on the scene. But in every period and in every corner of the world, this process, disguised by the anthropologists under the euphemism of "transculturation," has always been accompanied by infinite physical and spiritual sufferings. The assimilation of European immigrants into the United States passed through a first phase of intensification of national and racial tensions (aggravated by the presence of the Negro, and the associated inferiority complexes and defensive reactions that he aroused in the American white man, who almost seems to be still atavistically afflicted and humiliated by the de Pauwian condemnations), then on to a second, more lasting phase, of animosity on the part of the "naturalized citizen," or more often his sons, toward his country of origin and its traditional values.[483]

Instead of forming a link between the ancient European nations and their adopted country the immigrants sought to merge into their new environment, shouting its slogans with the zeal of neophytes, becoming "more American than the Americans"; they rejected and abjured the Old World, of which they had nothing but bad memories anyway. The antithesis between two worlds thus reappeared in the simplified guise of the perpetual and salutary opposition of son to father and grandfather: the ordinary rancor of one generation toward its predecessors was transferred into and reflected in one continent's judgment of the other. And just as the Puritan refugees had become the tormentors of the Quakers and ferocious witch hunters, so Europe's persecuted exiles lost no time in taking over

480. See I. Zangwill, *The Melting Pot* (1910), quoted in Wish, *Modern America,* p. 217. On the crisis this myth underwent in face of the growing flood of Slavic, Jewish, Italian, etc., immigrants, see Strout, op. cit., pp. 136–37.

481. In 1924 immigration from the Old World was virtually cut off, and American citizenship conceded to the last redskins. The United States withdrew into itself and became reconciled with its autochthonous past.

482. Siegfried, op. cit., pp. 33, 39.

483. Cf., for example, Spoerri, op. cit., pp. 16, 34, 47 and passim. "Their children are another matter" (Henry James, *The American Scene,* p. 120).

the role of persecutors and unyielding guardians of a rigid "Americanism."[484] In the contemporary isolationism of a MacCormick or the anti-Communism of a McCarthy it is not difficult to detect the traces of a violent prejudice directed more against Europe in general than Britain or Russia in particular.

XV. THE YOUNG WORLD QUITE OLD

The arrival of historicism on American soil and the resulting "transmutation of values" of the Old and New led to an even more radical disgregation of the very terms of the dispute. The inhabitants of the Western Hemisphere had always looked on this title of New World as a cause for pride and hope (even after the Buffon-de Pauwian criticism had translated this "new" into "recently emerged from the waters").[485] But when the cult of the past and its traditions rose to preeminence in Europe, and antiquity began to seem a more glorious attribute than youth, the Americans were quick to discover and proclaim themselves actually very old, much older, stabler, and surer of themselves than the troubled and turbulent Europe.

This took various forms, from the (mainly North American) quest for an autonomous and unitary principle for all American history,[486] to the

484. Which was already deplored by Melville in 1849; cf. above, p. 514, and Boorstin, *Genius,* p. 14. For the particular case of the Irish Catholics, see Wish, *Early America,* pp. 315–17, and A. C. Jemolo, "Nemesi storiche?" *Il Ponte,* 9, no. 10 (October 1953), pp. 1358–63.

485. See above, pp. 281–84, 316–17.

486. This tendency toward an "Americocentric" (and no longer Europeocentric) historiography drew additional impetus and integrating force from "historical Pan-Americanism," i.e., the thesis affirming the historical unity of all the Americas, transcending the limitations of nationality and of European derivation (English, Spanish, Portuguese, French America, etc.) and the restrictions imposed on North American historiography by the theory of the "frontier" (F. J. Turner, 1893), applied with provincial and painstaking pedantry (a theory which, in its turn, had arisen in reaction to the European historiography taught and fostered until that time in the North American universities: see H. H. Bellot, *American History and American Historians* [London, 1952], pp. 17–24; and, with greater acumen, H. N. Smith, *Virgin Land,* pp. 250–60). The tendency had a precise antecedent in "anthropological Pan-Americanism," or the theories proposing the original unity of the various races of natives (a nineteenth-century resumption and transformation of the old long-winded debates on the provenance of American man: see below, pp. 568–69) and thus affirming the necessity of a comparative and coordinated study of the autochthonous civilizations (see H. Bernstein, "Anthropology and Early Inter-American Relations," *Transactions of the New York Academy of Sciences,* 2d ser., 10, no. 1 [November 1947], pp. 2–17). But the first person to insist that the history of the United States could not be adequately studied if one failed to take into account the history of Latin America was Herbert E. Bolton ("The Epic of Greater America," paper read at Toronto, 28 December 1932, in the 47th annual session of the American Historical Association, summarizing the syllabus [1928] of his course in American history; published in the *American Historical Review,* 38 [1933], pp. 448–74; Castilian translation [Instituto Panamericano de Geografia e Historia, Mexico, 1937]; cf. also his *Wider Horizons of American History,* 1939). For the diffusion of his ideas, enthusiastically received in Latin America, see E. O'Gorman's article in *Universidad de la Habana,* 22 (January–February 1939); E. de Gandia, "El panamericanismo en la historia," *Boletín de la Academia Nacional de la Historia* (Buenos Aires), 15 (1941), pp. 383–93; preceedings of the 56th session of the American Historical Association (Chicago, 29–31 December 1941); *The Canadian Historical Review,* 23 (1942), pp. 125–56; E. O'Gorman in *Filosofia y Letras,* no. 6 (1942), pp. 215–35; A. P. Whitaker, "La América Latina en la mentalidad del pueblo norteamericano (1815–23)," *Revista de la Universidad Católica del Perú,* 9 (1941), p. 299, tracing back the continental solidarity of Americans to their European detractors in the eighteenth century, etc. For a recent

(mainly Spanish American) boasts of a more venerable origin and more quarterings of nobility than any European nation.[487] That singular character Gioberti had already noted that "some scholars hold the new world to be the old one," on the basis of the Toltec antiquities, "a concept paradoxical as history, but . . . plausible as prophecy."[488] And one of the first describers of Maya antiquities concluded his reflections on those and other vanished civilizations with the exclamation: "We call this country the New World. It is old!"[489] In the same way Beltrami, the explorer of the upper reaches of the Mississippi, claimed to have been the first to show that *"what one improperly calls the New World* is perhaps older than ours," and it was also spared the universal flood![490]

That same denomination of "New World," once taken as blessing on the birth and ascendance of the young republics, underwent such a transformation that it finally appeared to the later defenders of the native American element as an insult, a sign of Europeocentric presumption. The New World—if you just look closely enough—is the Oldest World:

A long time after Europe vibrated under the goad of its medieval antiquity with the romanticists, we vibrated under the spur of our ancientness, which conferred upon us the title of Oldest World instead of New World, since such newness existed only for the Europeans—an external evaluation—and not for us nor for reality *per se* (for history *per se*) into whose dominions we had made our actual entry thousands of years before the Spanish, French, English, and Dutch established their respective communities. The appearance of that sentiment of autochthonous pride coincided with various corroborating facts: the frustrated attempt of Florentino Ameghino to validate the theory of the *homunculus patagonicus* or *homo pampeanus*,[491]

the victory of the United States (the New World) over Spain in 1898, the fall of Porfirio Diaz "with its foreign influences" and the Mexican social revolution, the commemoration of the centennials of independence, and Europe's loss of prestige after the First World War. At that precise

restatement, see Philip C. Brooks, "Do the Americas Share a Common History?," *Revista de Historia de América* (Mexico), 33 (June 1952), pp. 75–83, and the articles in the same journal, no. 34 (December 1952), pp. 469–89; also Clifton B. Kroeber, "La tradición de la historia latino-americana en Estados Unidos: apreciación preliminar," *Revista de Historia de América*, 35–36 (1953), pp. 21–58, esp. 34–35; Silvio Zavala, "Colaboración internacional en torno de la historia de América," ibid., pp. 209–26.

487. Analogous thesis for the animals: cf. above, p. 452. The "dossier" of the polemic on the Bolton theory, which among other things obviously tends to remove the age-old antithesis between Anglo-Saxon America and Iberian America, has been excellently put together by Lewis Hanke, ed., *Common History*.

488. *Del rinnovamento civile*, II, 248–49.

489. Benjamin Moore Norman, *Rambles in Yucatan . . .* (New York, 1843), p. 173.

490. Letter to Signor de Monglave, in Beltrami, *Notizie e lettere*, p. 120; cf. p. 36.

491. In his book *La antigüedad del hombre en el Plata* (1880), Ameghino attempted to show that Argentina, or somewhere very near there, had been the cradle of the human race. But the anthropologists did not and do not agree: "A critical scrutiny of American data led to the conclusion that man was not nearly so ancient in the New World as in the Old" (Lowie, op. cit., pp. 86–87). Nor can we manage to see how a "frustrated attempt" can be a "corroborating fact."

moment "our ancient lineage brought about the reinforcement—perhaps it would be appropriate to say, the creation—of our historic consciousness."[492] And again, with a formula that manages to be simultaneously more concise and more all-embracing: "As old or older than Asians or Europeans, according to the most recent archaeological discoveries, we constitute, nevertheless, a New World, in regard to our debut in world influence, in regard to our discovery of our destiny."[493]

In fact, that "historic consciousness," that discovery of their own destiny, had come into being as antithesis and challenge to "old" Europe. It is hardly surprising that poor Europe began to feel quite bewildered. One has only to observe the agile acrobatics Ortega y Gasset indulges in to stay with the current and reverse his position.

In his essay of 1928, *Hegel and America*, he had written that America, *"if it is anything is the future,"* thus justifying its incomprehensibility to a philosopher as completely submerged in the past as Hegel. He had concluded then by suggesting that if Hegel were to return to earth today he would appreciate in the American soul "a type of *primitive* spirituality, a *beginning* of something original and non-European," with marked traits of "new and wholesome barbarism,"[494] which amounted to a confirmation of America as the land of the future.

But the ambiguity of this term "primitive," the translation into anthropological terms of the no less ambiguous "infancy" of the time of the emancipation, makes it an antithesis of both the tired European civilization, as in the passage quoted, and the progress which is the development and maturing of civilization, and thus allows Ortega, ten years later, to completely reverse his position almost without noticing what he is doing. In 1937, in fact, he could boast that around 1928, when "the old cliché that America is the future" was generally accepted, he himself had withstood the tide of fashion:

I had the courage then to oppose such an inaccuracy, maintaining that America, *far from being the future,* was, in reality, a remote past, because it was *primitivism.* And also, contrary to current belief, North America was and is much more so than South (Spanish) America.[495]

---

492. Luis Alberto Sanchez, "A New Interpretation of the History of America," *Hispanic American Historical Review,* 23 (August 1943), pp. 442–43. Emerson (above, p. 511) had been more cautious, claiming for America an antiquity as remote as the Flood.

493. L. A. Sanchez, *Existe América Latina?* (Mexico, 1945), p. 277. But he too had admitted more prudently (ibid., p. 45) that the distinction between New World and Old World was one "that we non-Europeans have difficulty in understanding and accepting."

494. *Obras,* I, 591–603.

495. *Prólogo para Franceses* (1937) to *La rebelión de las masas,* loc. cit., II, 1180, citing exactly *Hegel y América* and the articles on the United States published shortly afterward. The same essay, *Hegel y América,* is cited, in the same regard, a little further on when Ortega writes: "America is strong

A primitivism which is *not* future is in fact a more terrible condemnation than anything Buffon and de Pauw ever suggested. It is an organic, incurable infantilism. We point this out not to ascribe such a notion to Ortega y Gasset, who certainly holds no such catastrophic view of America,[496] but to show the dangers inherent in the reckless use of such fluid and ill-defined concepts; and because the final assertion that "contrary to current belief" North America is of a greater primitivism and a remoter past than South America, finds a curious confirmation-cum-denial in the words of an Argentinian historian—a historian, that is to say, of one of the nations of the New World that insisted most clamorously on its boasts of "youth." De Gandia, jealous of historical values, accuses the great North American republic of being young, and implicitly immature ("primitive," yes, but without "past") compared to the "old" Latin American republics! "If we compare the history of the North and the South we reach the unarguable conclusion that the old countries are the Spanish ones."[497]

But these paradoxes are really no more original either. The claims of a greater age with respect to Anglo-Saxon America were and are very common among the Ibero-Americans, both through their latinity and descent from Rome, in its time the conqueror and civilizer of rude Britannia, and through their Catholicism, for which Protestantism was a mere recent heresy. Already at the beginning of the previous century Fray Servando Teresa de Mier, as firm a believer as any man in historical prerogative and with nothing but respect for the claims of the ancient past, of however dubious authenticity, had contrasted the *young* United States with the *old* Latin America: "They were a new people . . . we are an old people."[498] And the Mexican and the Argentinian have been followed by a Colombian, Carlos Lozano y Lozano, who repeated: "We are older than the North Americans, much older."[499] Need it be said that the North Americans, in their turn, were goaded by these challenges into providing themselves with forebears? Today they are at pains to show

---

through its *youth* . . . America is younger in years than Russia. I have always, fearing to exaggerate, maintained that they were a primitive people *camouflaged* by the latest discoveries. Now Waldo Frank, in his *Redescubrimento de América*, declares it openly. America has not yet suffered; it is illusory to think that it can possess the virtues of the world" (*La rebelión*, p. 1264). Other variations on the American, this time "devoid of past" and gravitating "toward the future," in *Las Atlántidas* (1924), loc. cit., II, 926.

496. There is in fact an aphorism in the *Espectador* where Ortega, attacking the above-mentioned book by Waldo Frank, says to the hasty Americans: "Young men, not yet! . . . Strictly speaking . . . you have done nothing yet. America has not yet commenced its universal history." And once again he cites the essay *Hegel y América* (*El espectador*, VIII, loc. cit., I, 736).

497. E. de Gandia, *Panamericanismo*, p. 387.

498. *Profecía sobre la Revolución Mexicana* (1823), in *Antología*, ed. O'Gorman, p. 127.

499. Quoted in *Time*, 29 December 1947.

that they too have a glorious past, magnificent traditions, and so, so much history![500]

In fact the New World could not and cannot be "without history." Nothing can be without history, spirit, or rationality. What these charges really mean is that the New World cares too little for its own history, is motivated mainly by practical ambitions and instincts; it aims at setting its mark on the nature around it rather than at concentrating on itself, the better to understand both itself and nature. "Without history" thus defines not an unthinkable want of fact, but a spiritual attitude, a detached and resigned immersion in nature, an unconsidered battle against reason. When it wanted to have a history, America naturally found one, an ancient, indeed very ancient one. And when it reflected on its history, it produced some excellent historiography. The slogan "geography not history" is thus simply a formula of *Völkerpsychologie*. And the rival claims of every region to a past of its own, more past than any other part of the continent's, are the mark of a newly reached, or at least longed for and now glimpsed, spiritual majority.

XVI. DE PAUW'S OBLIVION AND SECRET IMMORTALITY

In this rivalry for roots in the past and the discovery of separate historical personalities, it is curious that no American went to look for arguments — be it even for their shock value — among the eighteenth-century authors who had assigned the New World an antiquity at least sufficient for it to have degenerated to the lowest level of humanity. Already by the second half of the nineteenth century de Pauw's reputation had gone into the complete eclipse that has lasted right up until our own time — and which is proved not so much by the absence of references to his *Recherches* as by the gross inaccuracy of even the most fleeting mention of his work or ideas. In Europe already in 1867 Dauban, though aware of de Pauw's merits, could assert that "de Pauw's books are no longer read."[501] In America the learned Amunátegui still mentions and summarily rejects his ideas on the harmful influence of America's climate and soil.[502] But when Garcia quotes these pages he refers to them vaguely as an attack on the "philosopher Pawo [*sic!*],"[503] and the

500. See for example the fine and by now in its turn "historic" account by Erich Marcks, in the "Historische und akademische Eindrücke aus Nordamerika" (1913), in *Männer und Zeiten* (Leipzig, 1916), I, 415; and the more recent articles by Max Lerner, "Are We a People Without History?" *The Virginia Quarterly Review*, 22 (1946), pp. 5–19, and Clare Booth Luce, *Europe and America* (USIS, Rome, n.d.), p. 26. But nor has there been any lack of critics of the United States, of people like Duhamel, for example, who *accused* the North Americans of being senile, not young, prematurely aged, without ever having been mature, as a result of material progress (Spoerri, op. cit., p. 87; cf. Strout, op. cit., pp. 176–77).
501. Dauban, *Lettres de Mme Roland*, I, 423.
502. *Los precursores de la independencia de Chile*, III, 109–15.
503. Agustín Garcia, *La ciudad indiana*, 5th ed., n.d., p. 74.

Chilean bibliographer Barros Arana, after mentioning de Pauw's main repudiators, adds (1882) that his book is now completely forgotten or "only consulted out of mere curiosity."[504] Claude Bernard quotes de Pauw on the subject of curare, at second or third hand, from a German encyclopedia.[505] One of Jefferson's most recent biographers, Saul K. Padover, makes no mention at all of his polemic against Buffon.[506] And a recent reprint of Clavigero's *Historia antigua de México* (Mexico, 1944) completely suppresses the Jesuit's long polemical *Disertaciones* against de Pauw and Buffon, which even Juan Bautista Muñoz had admired more than the *Historia* itself.[507] Then when a recent editor of *The Federalist*, Professor Max Beloff, comes across Hamilton's noted jibe directed at the author of the *Recherches philosophiques sur les Américains* (see above, pp. 250–51), he believes the work mentioned to be identical with Raynal's *Histoire philosophique et politique!*[508] Moras only mentions de Pauw to tell us that although he has "thoroughly examined" the *Recherches,* he has not been able to find therein the word "civilization,"[509] but he does not even point out that the whole book is basically an attempt to investigate that very same concept!

Fay[510] has certainly read de Pauw, and gives an adequate summary of him, but believes that Buffon plagiarized him. The great historian Herbert Eugene Bolton, on the other hand, asks himself the rhetorical question: "Who has written the history of the introduction of European plants and animals into the Western Hemisphere as a whole?"[511] and seems to forget Buffon's mighty effort. In 1933 Mme Edith Bernardin makes passing reference to "the books of C. de Pauw, today completely forgotten."[512] Spell fails to recognize the subtitle of the once famous *Recherches.*[513] Pearce takes him for a Frenchman,[514] while Stark seems to think he is a German, and says that he has "the point of view of the explorer who is out to solve the riddles of an exotic sphere of life":[515] when in fact a publication of 1768 should not even have been mentioned in a study deal-

504. *Notas para una bibliografía,* p. 503, n. 399.
505. Claude Bernard, *Leçons sur les effets des substances toxiques et médicamenteuses* (Paris, 1883), p. 245.
506. Which also surprises a reviewer in the *Times Literary Supplement,* 30 January 1943.
507. Fray Servando Teresa de Mier, "Manifiesto Apologético" in *Escritos inéditos,* p. 148.
508. Oxford ed. (Basil Blackwell, 1948), pp. 53n., and 478 n. 4.
509. J. Moras, op. cit., pp. 35 n. 58, 52 n. 83. Like others before him, de Pauw however makes current use of *civiliser* and *se civiliser,* "to civilize" and "become civilized": examples in *Recherches,* I, 108, 110.
510. Fay, *Civilisation,* p. 55; *Esprit,* pp. 13–14, 331–32 and passim.
511. In Hanke, *Common History,* p. 99.
512. *Les idées religieuses de Mme Roland,* p. 79n.
513. See above, chap. 5, n. 176.
514. Pearce, *The Savages,* p. 78, who cites B. S. Barton's attacks on de Pauw, "with his picture of beardless Indian males with milk in their breasts."
515. *America: Ideal and Reality,* p. 15.

ing, according to its subtitle, with *The United States of 1776 in Contemporary European Philosophy.* In another volume of over four hundred pages illustrating the "exchanges and encounters" between France and the United States de Pauw is mentioned only once (and does not even figure in the bibliography): between 1763 and 1776, "Buffon, Raynal, and the grotesque [*sic*] de Paw are almost alone [?] in pronouncing occasionally [!] unfavorable judgments on America."[516] Even the recent and most erudite researcher of the relations between Europe and America in the eighteenth century simply ignores de Pauw, and confines himself to remarking in a line and a half of footnote that "there was much talk in Europe (and even in America) about people and animals degenerating in the colonies" [*sic*].[517] Nor is there a single word on the American polemic and its variations in the work of the latest diligent chronicler of the Americans' notions of the Old World.[518] And the Italian journalist Indro Montanelli candidly confesses: "I do not know who, with scornful voice, described Argentina as 'the country where the camel becomes a llama, the lion a puma, the eagle a condor, and the Spaniard an Argentinian'."[519]

Rarely, I think, has the harshness of posterity rendered such meager justice to an author admired by the loftiest spirits of his generation, opposed by historians and publicists of talent and immense repute, read and assimilated by philosophers, scientists, and poets of sure and sublime inspiration, and who even in our own day, after decades of having been the summary symbol of the European "calumnies," the eponymous hero and scapegoat of an embittered ideological conflict, still acts as an acid, invisible ferment in the opinions, ideologies, and clichés of such a large proportion of the human race.

There is perhaps nothing so striking to the European who crosses the ocean and seeks to familiarize himself with the intellectual atmosphere of America as the widespread, if not universal, conviction of a special destiny, be it good or bad, allotted to the Western Hemisphere. America is not a continent like any other. The laws of history common to the rest of the human race are invalid there. America is either afflicted by some special curse, or marked out for the seal of some divine investiture.

Even the old accusations of recent emersion from the waters and weak-

---

516. Villard, op. cit., p. 225. Berveiller's comment is less imprecise, in op. cit., pp. 301–02.

517. Kraus, *Atlantic Civilization,* p. 218 n. 7. Just as imprecise are Visconti, op. cit., p. 44, and Eric W. Cochrane, "Il Gazzettiero Americano di Livorno e l'America nella letteratura del Settecento," *Quaderni di cultura e storia sociale,* 3, no. 1 (January 1954), p. 52. Precise, on the other hand, but later than the works by Church (1936) and myself (1st ed., 1943), are the cited studies by Chinard (1947) and Martin (1952), the rapid outline by E. Sestan, "Il mito del 'buon selvaggio' americano e l'Italia del Settecento," 1947, in *Europa settecentesca ed altri saggi,* pp. 137–38, and Claude-Anne Lopez's *Mon Cher Papa,* p. 14.

518. Strout, op. cit.

519. "Il lama, il puma, il condor," in *Corriere della Sera,* 26 July 1955. A writer in the *Economist* does however know: 22 April 1961, p. 319.

nesses in the fauna are converted into claims to excellence: Gonzales Prada exalts America Anadyomene, rising beauteous from the waves, "displaying her flora without thorns and her fauna without tigers."[520] And the lament on the hemisphere's late emergence from the sea, at a time when the others were already dry, reechoes in more general terms, in the bitter sighing over the South American republics arriving "too late in a world too old,"[521] and again in the sarcasms aimed at the same republics with their "great future behind them."

Oscar Wilde's cruel irony had already (1893) laid bare the paradox implicit in that boast of stalwart youthfulness, so tiresomely dredged up again with each successive decade: "The youth of America is their oldest tradition. It has been going on now for three hundred years. To hear them talk one would imagine they were in their first childhood. As far as civilization goes they are in the second."[522]

Yet still today, in our so-called arid and prosaic age, the dream of Berkeley, Galiani, and Melville reappears in a thousand different forms to comfort the hearts of the North and South Americans. The ambiguous fascination of the "novelty" of the New World has Roosevelt saying in 1942 that it is necessary to assure "the survival of a hemisphere—the newest hemisphere of them all";[523] and at the Chapultepec Conference a diplomat calls on a quite specific but no better identified "God of America"[524] to watch over the labors of the delegates.

520. "Discurso en el teatro Olimpo," 1888, in *Pájinas Libres* (Lima, 1946), p. 46. On the (metaphorical) tiger as a savage creature fortunately unknown "in the fauna of Peru," see ibid., p. 73, in an article "Perú y Chile," also dating from 1888.

521. The words are de Musset's (Rolla: *"je suis venu trop tard dans un monde trop vieux"*), but the sentiment it expresses is considerably older: "to feel oneself born in 'an age too late' was the great emotional aftermath of the Renaissance" (G. Williamson, op. cit., p. 135; cf. p. 148). The first to apply it to America—although the notion had already been expressed by Lowell: "O strange New World, that yet was never young"—seems to have been R. Poincaré (preface to F. Garcia Calderón, *Les démocraties latines de l'Amérique* [1911; Paris, 1914], p. 3). Frequently used proverbially (for example in Somerset Maugham, *Of Human Bondage* [Modern Library ed., 1915], p. 253), taken up again by other poets, like Francis Jammes ("Je suis venu trop tard dans un monde trop vieux," *De l'Angélus de l'ombre a l'Angélus du soir*, 1838) and Guido Gozzano (*"sento / D'essere nato troppo tardi"*—"I feel I was born too late," *Torino*), it was adopted and repeated by numerous Latin American authors, among whom suffice it to note two such authoritative figures as Alfonso Reyes ("Notas sobre la inteligencia americana," 1936, in *Última Tule*, p. 143; cf. also pp. 201, 219) and Jorge Basadre ("¿Han existido historicamente influencias de origen americano en la cultura occidental?" *Proceedings of the 8th American Scientific Congress*, 9 [Washington, D.C., 1943], p. 250; and *La promesa de la vida peruana* [Lima, 1943], p. 23). In the thesis that America passed abruptly from childhood to old age, without passing through maturity (for example: "culturally America had become rotten before it was ripe," Thistlewaite, op. cit., p. x, and Clémenceau, quoted by Art Buchwald: "They have gone from barbarians to decadence without the intervening period of civilization") Chinard detects the last echoes of the theories of Buffon and Hegel (*L'homme contre la nature*, p. 143).

522. Oscar Wilde, *A Woman of No Importance*, act I, in *Works* (London, n.d.), p. 599. Further sarcasms at the expense of George Washington and America, in *Intentions* (1891), ibid., p. 1085.

523. Sic, quoted by C. and M. Beard, op. cit., p. 569.

524. For this tribal divinity, see *El Comercio* (Lima), 22 February 1945. Curious "prayers of a man of the New World," with the old heresy of an America created by God for the Redemption of the human race, can be read in the *Erial* of the Argentinian Constancio C. Vigil (trans. into English from the 14th Spanish ed.; *Times Literary Supplement*, 14 September 1946). But—and yet again we see how every

Following in de Pauw's now fading tracks Freud, Rathenau, Spengler, and then Papini pronounce American culture an "abortion."[525] And the extreme theses of Buffon, under the guise of psychoanalysis and decadentism, begin to circulate again in the work of the turbid Keyserling. The first of his *Südamerikanische Meditationen* is simply a web of variations on Buffon's basic theme. South America becomes the continent of the third day of the Creation, the day when God made the sea and the land, the plants, the trees and the fruits. But it is at the same time the continent of "cold blood," of the reptiles, toads, snakes—all creatures which in fact appeared only on the *fifth* day of the Creation. It is the continent of poisonous grasses and edible plants, but also of crocodiles, ferocious ants, putrefaction, and unrestrained sexuality. Buffon's flexible naturalistic schemes are overlaid with images from second-rate romanticism, tinged with the dark macabre hues of the literary genre deriving from de Sade. The thesis of comparative zoology winds up as a prurient discussion of the South American's frigid and frenetic sensuality.[526]

XVII. THE SCIENTIFIC REVISION OF THE BUFFONIAN CALUMNY

On the scientific level there are of course no further defenders of the notion of America's earth or sky bringing about the degeneration of men and animals. But in the review of the specific arguments that had served to construct this edifice of error, there is raised the question of whether

---

theme in this polemic habitually reemerges turned upside down and inside out, and its "contrapuntalistic" possibilities are still not exhausted—another Argentinian sees America not as redeemer but as afflicted by a second Original Sin all of its own (H. A. Murena, *El pecado original de América* [Buenos Aires, 1954], esp. p. 164); with which on the one hand he upsets Chateaubriand's mystical geographies (see above, p. 355), and on the other comes back without knowing it to the thesis assigning America the sad privilege of a private Flood or some other custom-made curse.

525. G. Papini, "Lo que la América no ha dado," *Revista de América*, June 1947. Papini takes issue mainly with Latin America, with curious de Pauw-style arguments: St. Rose of Lima is not worth a St. Theresa of Avila or a St. Catherine of Siena! The Inca Garcilaso is not of the same level as the Spaniard Garcilaso de la Vega! America has squandered the cultural riches it received from Europe, etc. But no less curiously anachronistic were the replies of the South Americans, quick to recall that they were still young, and yet had already had some great men, like, for example, a Caldas praised by a Humboldt, and dangerous heretics too, and even quicker to vaunt the raw materials of their continent, the rubber, the cereals, the cattle, products to feed "the decadent, corrupt, and troubled Europe." Their scorn verges on the grotesque when, to prove America's spontaneous disinterested generosity, they write: "Américo Vespucio himself . . . *if our continent had not existed*, would have been no more than a dreamer lost at the crossroads of the unknown" (*La Prensa* [Lima], 17 and 30 July 1947; my italics). . . . Well, true enough, if America hadn't been there, Columbus too *"che ce scopriva? Li mortacci sui!"* (Cesare Pascarella, *La scoperta dell'America*, son. 50). See also Papini's article dated 12 July 1947, in *Corriere della Sera*, 30 August 1959. On Rathenau and Spengler, see Fraenkel, op. cit., pp. 258, 299–300.

526. H. Keyserling, *Südamerikanische Meditationen*, 2d ed., esp. pp. 19, 21, 22 (entitled: "unbridled sensuality is cold," and particularly filthy; but the link is essential), 24, 26, 31–32. Cf. also ibid., the typical pages 41–43 and the inevitable Original Sadness: over all South America "there now reigns the completely unadulterated *Ur-Traurigkeit*" (p. 280). On p. 285 we meet the devil too, to complete the trinomial that Mario Praz gathered in the title of his famous work.

they did not in themselves contain some glimmer of truth. The ingenious Vidal de la Blache struggles to explain how on earth the southern extremities of the continent should be relatively unpopulated, while there are Eskimos and Lapps in the same latitude in the north: he cites Tierra del Fuego and Graham's Land facing it in the Antarctic, and concludes: "The effort languished for lack of space; and the relative inferiority found in the mammals of the austral hemisphere seems to have been extended to the men."[527] And within this same period, or a half century after Edgar Quinet, another Frenchman, a sailor and explorer, rediscovers yet again the "discovery" of Buffon, and announces it with all due and deliberate solemnity: "The study of the fauna of the New World leads one to a very curious revelation: it is, in almost every example, a reduction of that of the Old Continent: the puma and the jaguar, here baptized the "lion" and "tiger," are diminutive versions of the lion and tiger, as the llama and tapir are of the camel and the elephant . . . [a few more examples follow] . . . *I do not know that this anomaly in the American fauna has ever been mentioned*"![528]

In somewhat more subtle but basically no less peremptory form the shrewd historian of the Americas, Pierre Chaunu, gravely repeats: "The feebleness of the American man in America, the irreversible degradation of the Indian, is one of the most important rules of this early human past in the New World."[529]

The ancient theories on the influence of climate were taken up again by geographers reaching out restless tentacles in their eager effort to transform themselves into naturalists and biologists, and by racist-inclined philosophers of history—like the American Ellsworth Huntington —with works which outlined ever so subtle, sophistically subtle, necessary relations between climate and civilization. And there were historians of real merit too, as we know, like Terán, who studied the stages and the social and political consequences of the "tropicalization of the white man" in South America. Even a subtle and open-minded spirit like Bernard Berenson finds himself wondering if the climate in the United States is not pernicious for the white race, as it probably was for the redskin. The uneasy critic discovers in his compatriots the traces of a rapid and irreversible decadence: "Some of our oldest settlers are now represented by offspring too frequently consumptive, queer, or otherwise in decline—

527. P. Vidal de la Blache, *Principes de géographie humaine* (Paris, 1922; pub. posthumously, written between 1905 and 1917), p. 24.

528. M. Rondet-Saint, *Randonnées transatlantiques* (Paris, 1921, though the passage quoted is from 1914), pp. 257–58; my italics.

529. *L'Amérique et les Amériques*, p. 15.

if not quite degenerate."[530] But why should the climate of North America be so lethal? The answer is curious, or rather might seem curious to anyone forgetting that it exactly reproduces an explanation provided by Raynal and Hegel: America's mountains run from north to south, and in the absence of the sort of transverse mountains found in Central Europe, the way is left open to the icy winds from the Arctic, and the torrid vapors of the Caribbean.[531] Modern technology may be able to delay the catastrophe, but not prevent it. It may take centuries, but the end result is inevitable: *the depopulation of America.*

Less well known in Europe is the scientific revision of the idea that the climate of America brings about the rapid degeneration of men and animals coming from Europe: an elaboration initiated by the Peruvian physiologist Carlos Monge, who showed[532] that the effort to acclimatize themselves to a mountain environment resulted in the Europeans, and at least some of the higher animals, suffering at least a temporary reduction in vitality and generative capacity. And when the mountain dweller descends to the plain he suffers the same difficulties in acclimatization, and analogous pathological phenomena. De Pauw had actually been aware of this process. In his reply to Pernety he recalls that in 1732, of sixteen thousand Salzburgers that moved to Prussia, four thousand died in the first year, "as happens to mountain dwellers who are suddenly settled in the plains."[533]

But although for preference Monge quotes the ancient chroniclers of Peru,[534] who furnish him with vivid historical examples of sterility and organic decadence, his theory is clearly applicable, and applied by the author himself, to all upper mountain regions, at whatever latitude (the

530. *Sketch for a Self-Portrait* (New York, 1949), pp. 66–67; my italics. The idea that the Americans have degenerated from the time of Independence onward (on which see above, pp. 495, 515) also goes back to the first half of the nineteenth century (see Remond, op. cit., pp. 678, 705; and Jacquemont, *Correspondance inédite,* I, 142–43, 168), and is prolonged into the second half of the century: see examples from Nievo (1850) and Colajanni (1884), in Torrielli, op. cit., pp. 6, 108. The now wary reader may feel he can detect a slightly vengeful echo of the famous thesis of the decadence and degeneration of the native (see de Pauw, de Maistre, above, pp. 389–91; Chateaubriand in Bazin, op. cit., p. 216; etc.).

531. *Sketch;* cf. above, pp. 46–47, 425; and Ampère, op. cit., II, 35.

532. We quote from the summary exposition of his long inquiries dictated by Monge under the title *Influencia biológica del Altiplano en el individuo, la raza, las sociedades y la historia de América* (Lima, n.d., but 1940). A greater abundance of citations and examples can be found in the other writings of Monge, "Política sanitaria indiana y colonial en el Tahuantinsuyo," extract from the *Anales de la Facultad de Ciencias Médicas* (Lima), 17 (1935), pp. 231–76, and "Aclimatación en los Andes: Confirmaciones históricas sobre la agresión climática en el desenvolvimiento de las sociedades de América," *Anales,* 28 (1945), pp. 307–83; English trans.: Baltimore, 1948. For similar researches on North Americans, inhabitants with "an intermediate degree of adaptation," in Leadville, Colo. (10,200 ft.), see R. F. Grover, "The High Altitude Resident of North America," in *Scientia,* 62 (1968), nos. 1–2, pp. 9–25.

533. *Défense,* ed. cit., p. 238.

534. Cieza de León, Garcilaso, Fr. Calancha, Fr. Cobo, Acta de la Fundación de Lima, etc.: op. cit., pp. 25–28, 48–49. And in the "Política sanitaria": Miguel de Estete, Fernando Santillán, M. Cabello Balboa, Fernando Pizarro, Pero Sancho, P. Falcón, the Prince of Esquilache, Gómara, etc.

Alps, Tibet, etc.). Thus the antithesis is no longer between Old World and New World, but between the climate of the plain and the climate of the plateau.

The Europeans discovered the first striking examples of this illness of incipient acclimatization (a sickness that could sometimes be lethal, to either individual or species), as soon as they came into contact with the civilizations of the Mexican and Andean plateaus. Later, generalizing naïvely and theorizing quite arbitrarily, they transposed the sufferings and defects of some of its human or animal inhabitants to the whole of the new continent. But the warning implicit in their observations, and formulated explicitly in various Spanish laws for the protection of the *indios*,[535] began to fade away with the end of the viceroyalty, although it was recognized again by San Martín and other generals of the wars of independence;[536] and then, as Monge wonderingly observes,[537] it fell into complete oblivion in the republican period. It seems probable that the violence of the young republic's reaction to the calumny of America's telluric inferiority even swept away such undeniable elements of fact as had served to support it.

It would not be the first time that the fight against a mistaken idea had worked to the detriment of the most evident facts. The pursuit and achievement of any certainty calls for more countermarching and circuitous maneuvering than many a vicious and tortuous machination. It was actually on the subject of America that Humboldt declared that "not infrequently do error or hazardous theories lead to the truth."[538] But here a gnawing uncertainty halts our train of thought—uncertainty at this minute but exasperating enigma of history, even if we see it as no more than a particular instance of the dialectic that only through negation achieves a greater positiveness. But can the dream have the same substance as reality? Does reality have no other means of growing and gaining recognition than to immerse itself repeatedly in myth and legend, in the violent alternatives and arbitrary excogitations of diatribe?

The mind hangs in suspense, and a sense of frustration pervades anyone who still tries to seek some light in the past. And yet, unless we have been blinded by a turban of proud vanity and complacency that has

---

535. *Influencia,* pp. 59–60; "Política Sanitaria," pp. 262–68.

536. Monge, "Aclimatación en los Andes: Influencia biológica del Altiplano en las guerras de América," *Revista de Historia de América* (Mexico), 25 (June 1948), pp. 1–25.

537. "It is reasonable to ask how it is possible that they were ignored in the republican life of South America, to the point where whole armies were led off to be massacred by the climate" ("Política Sanitaria," p. 262; cf. ibid., pp. 236, 244, 271, etc.; and "Aclimatación en los Andes: Influencia," p. 350; offprint, p. 45).

538. *Reise,* IV, 282.

slipped down over our eyes, it seems to us that not even this long review will have been totally in vain, if—showing us the far distant roots of a typical "calumny" in the Bible and Aristotle, and the modifications and modulations it suffered under the influence of theological prejudice, historiographical theses, legal argumentation, scientific and pseudoscientific investigation, dubious natural laws, biological hypotheses, libertine curiosities, social criticisms and countercriticisms, political passions and poetic transformations—if by relating this story it has taught us how complex is the life of an idea—and how simple, how unilateral, in comparison, the brief span of those who supported or assailed it; if, from so much bitter dispute we are thus left with more than one good reason for impartial indulgence toward all the contestants, and for inexorable severity toward ourselves who dare to judge them; and if this bitter sort of lesson carries with it at least this last consolation: that just as the chicken emerges chirping from the broken shell, so might some poor, diminutive, timid truth creep forth whimpering its message even from the tormented history of an insignificant error.

9

Supplements and Digressions

I. THE ORIGINALITY OF BUFFON

REFERRING to his "discovery" Buffon says that "the greatest fact, the most general, the least known to all naturalists before me . . . is that the animals of the southern parts of the old continent are not found in the new, and that reciprocally those of South America are not found at all in the old continent."[1] In another context Buffon repeats that "this general fact, which it seems was not even suspected" is so important that it must be corroborated with all possible proof.[2] And later, satisfied, he will say: "I have demonstrated this truth by such a great number of examples that it can no longer be called into question."[3]

Such insistence on the glorification of his thesis can be explained both by the extraordinary vanity of the man — to which Hérault de Séchelles's *Visite à Montbard* is a more than ample literary monument — and by his conscious awareness that what he says completely contradicts traditional opinions on the wonders and portents of America. Reason, good sense, and the criterion of relativity all recoiled from the legends of giants and prodigies. The cold pervasive light of analysis eliminated the shadows cast by the first amazed reactions. Mellin de Saint-Gelais knew already in 1556 that everything in America was different: "Different cattle, different fruits and vegetables, and a different people inhabiting the land"; but it was all more beautiful.

At the end of the century Juan de Cárdenas wrote in his *Problemas y secretos maravillosos de las Indias:* "In the Indies everything is portentous, everything is surprising, everything is distinct and on a larger scale than that of the Old World."[4] And another half century later the same

1. Ed. in quarto (de l'Imprimerie Royale), VII, 129, suppléments, quoted by Flourens, op. cit., p. 143.
2. "Animaux de l'ancien continent," in *Oeuvres complètes,* XV, 407–08.
3. "Epoques de la Nature," 1779, in *Oeuvres complètes,* V, 221.
4. Quoted by R. Iglesia, *La mexicanidad de don Carlos de Sigüenza y Gongora,* in *El hombre Colón y otros ensayos* (Mexico, 1944), p. 123. The physician Juan de Cárdenas, born in Spain but a resident of Mexico from an early age, was one of the first to maintain that the Creoles had superior minds to the Spaniards: *Primera parte de los Problemas y secretos maravillosos de las Indias* (Mexico, 1951), quoted in García Icazbalceta, *Bibliografía mexicana del siglo XVI,* ed. A. Millares Carlo, pp. 399–405. In this work he discusses themes by now very familiar to us, such as the humidity of the Indies, the lack of trees with deep roots, the natives' beardlessness, the spread of syphilis (originating in America through arcane telluric-astrological circumstances), the meager fierceness of the animals ("the animals in the Indies never rage") and the scarce toxicity of the reptiles and other poisonous creatures (see also below, n. 180).

awestruck rapture was expressed at some length in the refrains of an ornate Castilian prose. Antonio de León Pinelo devoted the whole of the fourth book of his *Paraíso en el Nuevo Mundo* (1656) to the "strange" animals, strange "trees" and "spices," the strange "minerals," including gold "and its strange abundance in the Indies," and to the richness in gold, silver, and pearls, a "strange and portentous" product of the Indies.

In our own day, for that matter, Claude Lévi-Strauss, on first approaching South America, expects to find a world totally different from his own, the antipodes in fact and substance: "I would have been very astonished if I had been told that an animal or vegetable species could look the same on both sides of the globe."[5]

But, for Buffon, American nature is "different," yes; but not "wondrous." It is diverse, but on a lesser scale. It is certainly "strange," but not in the least portentous.

To what extent Buffon's thesis is really something new to the history of science I leave to the judgment of the competent authorities. Brunetière states quite peremptorily that between 1757 and 1764, in studying the animals of the Americas, Buffon "chemin faisant" founded zoological geography.[6] And Remond adds that the theory of American degeneration has an illustrious guarantor in Buffon, "who . . . gives its first systematic exposition (1761)."[7]

But my immediate impression is that Brunetière exaggerates. Zoological geography was born with Marco Polo, or perhaps even with Julius Solinus. Confining ourselves to the Americas, the zoological geography of the New World comes into being with the observations of Columbus, and, in conscious and organic form, with Oviedo's *Summary*. In 1648 Jean de Laet published (in his *Historia rerum naturalium Brasiliensium*) the zoological observations made in Brazil by G. Pison and G. Marcgrav: "They established that the Quadrupeds, the Birds, the Snakes, the Fish, the Insects of America, while being obviously related to those of the Old World, are however distinct from them."[8] But already hardly a century after the discovery Father Acosta, one of the authors most widely known throughout Europe, was well aware that the fauna of the Indies was very different from that of the Old World, and was anxiously wondering whether one should think that God had continued the Creation after the six days of Genesis, and how those animals could have found their

5. *Tristes tropiques*, p. 33. On this radical antitheticity of the inhabitants and the fauna in the two worlds, see the sound observations of Charles G. Griffin, *Unity and Variety in America History*, in Hanke, ed., *Common History*, pp. 252–53.

6. *Manuel de l'histoire de la littérature française* (Paris, 1898), p. 375. Cf. already Perrier, op. cit., p. 63: "Buffon has deserved to be considered the founder of zoological geography"; and then Mornet (op. cit., p. 45): "the problem which made it possible for Buffon to create zoological geography. . . ."

7. Remond, op. cit., p. 261.

8. "Which posed an embarrassing question on the subject of their origins," Guyénot continues, op. cit., p. 58.

way into Noah's ark, since if they did not go into the ark "there is no reason to resort to Noah's ark," and if they did go into the ark how on earth did it happen that when they came forth with the other animals not a single specimen remained in the Old World?

Father Acosta is besieged by doubts and queries, which have kept him "long perplexed." But he has no doubt of the fact that these animals of America are absolutely different: "What I say of the *guanacos* and *patos* [rectius: *pacos*] I will say of a thousand varieties of birds and fowl, and mountain animals that have never been known either by name or appearance, nor is there any memory of them in the Latins or the Greeks, or in any nations of our world over here." And anyone who attempts "to explain the dissemination of the animals of the Indies and fit them into European patterns will be taking on a task that he will find difficult to accomplish. For if we are to judge the species of animals by their properties, they are so different that to wish to reduce them to species known in Europe will mean calling a chestnut an egg."[9]

This doubt about the origin of the American species which so tormented Father Acosta, and which was mentioned and paraphrased by Burton too,[10] is substantially analogous to Saint Augustine's concern over the problem of islands and their animals. Noah's three sons could easily have populated the whole earth and the islands, "for who doubts that when the human race multiplied, men could cross over by boat and settle the islands?"[11] But the animals? . . . Augustine leaves aside the domestic animals, which man could take with him in his boats, and the animals like the frogs that "are born from the earth." Which leaves the wild animals, the wolves "and others of that sort" who reproduce "only by the conjunction of male and female." Those who were not in the ark, even if they were on islands, were drowned. The others must be descended from the animals of the ark. And how did they reach the islands? By swimming, of course, if the islands were near land. Otherwise one can only presume that they were taken there by men to form "game reserves" (*venandi studio*). But although that is not entirely incredible, one cannot absolutely rule out either that "they may have been transferred . . . by God's order or permission, or by the work of the angels."[12]

9. *Historia natural y moral*, IV, 36; ed. cit., pp. 325–26. Fueter (op. cit., p. 292) credits Acosta with the first "hesitant attempts at comparisons" between Europe and America. On Acosta see also the short notice by Menéndez Pelayo in *Estudios y discursos*, VII, 137–39; and a good article by E. Alvarez Lopez, "La filosofia natural en el Padre J. de Acosta," *Revista de Indias* (Madrid), 12 (1943), pp. 305–22.

10. *Anatomy of Melancholy* (1621), ed. Dell and Jordan-Smith (New York, 1938), p. 415.

11. *De Civitate Dei*, XVI, 6.

12. Ibid., XVI, 7, ed. E. Hoffmann (Vienna, 1900), II, 137–38. In the last part of the chapter Augustine, noting the fact that some animals were taken into the ark which would not have been able to return to the islands in which they were created, according to Genesis 1:24, finds further proof that the ark was not ordained by God to save and preserve the races of animals, but is to be interpreted allegorically as an image of the Church welcoming all peoples; cf. *De Civitate Dei*, XV, 26, where he also cites his works against Faustus Manichaeus.

With the discovery of America and the emergence of the problem of its fauna Father Acosta sought to provide an answer by quoting and discussing this same Augustinian thesis, arriving at the conclusion that there must be a land link or at least some *narrow* strait between the Old and the New World.[13]

In the eighteenth century, Father Sánchez Labrador comes back to the problem of Augustine and Father Acosta, with explicit reference to America: "In that part of the world there are found species not seen in other parts of the world; who took them there, and by what paths of land or water?"[14] The enigma which opened the way to indiscreet conjectures on the plurality of creation and dangerous imaginings about preadamite species, and thus to doubts about biblical chronology, and which for this same erosive virtue is mentioned by Diderot too,[15] became the object of various apologetic writings. One might mention Giannone's *Triregno*, which follows Horn's *De originibus americanis* in inclining to the notion of the Phoenicians having populated the New World;[16] Feijóo's *Solución del gran problema histórico sobre la población de la América . . .* (secs. 12 ff.) which denies the idea of Atlantis and the intervention of the Angels, and preadamite creation, and suggests a land link that once existed between Asia and America (the Bering Strait) which later collapsed through some cataclysm or through the erosion of the waves; and the work of the Jesuit Father Francisco Xavier Alexo de Orrio, published in Mexico in 1763 and entitled similarly; *Solution to the great problem of the population of the Americas, in which on the basis of the Holy Books there is discovered an easy path for the transmigration of Men from one Continent to the other; and how there could pass to the New World, not only the Beasts of Service, but also the wild and harmful Animals; and by this occasion one completely settles the ravings of the Pre-Adamites, which relied on this difficult objection until now not properly solved;*[17] and the

13. See 1590 ed., pp. 69–71 and 81, quoted by Alvarez Lopez, op. cit., pp. 316–18. On the problem in the seventeenth century, see Glass, *Forerunners of Darwin*, pp. 32–33, and my *Diego de León Pinelo*, p. 12, n. 18 (referring to the year 1604).

14. Julio Rey Pastor, *La ciencia y la técnica en el descubrimiento de América* (Buenos Aires, 1942), p. 143. Similar doubt in Pernety, *Examen*, II, 219.

15. *Supplément au Voyage de Bougainville* (1772; Pléiade ed.), p. 755. Curious information on some precedents from the sixteenth and seventeenth centuries in D. C. Allen, *The Legend of Noah*, pp. 130–32. The Buffonian theory of the degeneration of the animals allowed a reduction in the number of prototypes and thus made it once more credible that Noah's ark could have contained them all (see Mornet, op. cit., p. 40).

16. *Il Triregno* (ca. 1731–32; ed. A. Parente [Bari, 1940]), I, 69, 87–95. Cf. A. Ricuperati, "Alle origini del *Triregno*: La *Philosophia Adamito-Noetica* di A. Costantino," *Rivista storica italiana*, 77, no. 3 (1965), pp. 628–29.

17. Pamphlet reproduced by Nicolas León, in *Bibliografía mexicana del siglo XVIII*, sección primera (Mexico, 1902), pp. 379–409. Frontispiece reproduced in Diaz Alejo and Joaquín Gil, *América y el Viejo Mundo* (Buenos Aires, 1942), fig. 175. The origin of the *indios* of America, and their possible provenance from other parts of the world, has an enormous bibliography, from the sixteenth century down to our own day: see the notes in Zavala, *América*, pp. 155–57; Rowse, op. cit., pp. 201–02;

work of the other Jesuit, Father Saverio Clavigero, which reaffirms the thesis of a land crossing.[18]

Humboldt too, finally, paraphrases the famous Augustinian passage somewhat liberally in the *Kosmos,* where he says: "If the animals were not taken to the distant islands by angels or by these enthusiastic huntsmen, the inhabitants of the continent, then they must have sprung directly from the earth; whereupon the question arises, to what end were all the animals gathered in the ark?"[19]

But to come back to Father Acosta, we should note here that he does not consider the animals of America in any way inferior, indeed many of them he finds to be "perfect animals and of no less excellence than those others known."[20]

On the other hand Acosta, who figures in these passages as a precursor of Buffon and even as an anticipated critic of his theory on the inferiority of the American fauna, has rather vague notions about this same fauna; and relying on Oviedo and other chroniclers he confidently asserts the existence in the Indies of a number of savage carnivores: "There are in America and Peru many wild animals, such as lions, although these do not equal the famous lions of Africa in size and courage and the same tawny color; there are many tigers and very cruel ones, although they are more commonly so with the Indians than the Spaniards. There are bears, though not so many; there are wild boars; there are innumerable foxes. . . . The mainland of the Indies abounds in all these sorts of animals, and in many others that will be described in their place."[21]

However—admits the honest Acosta—those American lions that he personally *saw* were not exactly like the lions described in the texts: they did not "correspond," either physically or temperamentally. . . . "There are lions, tigers, bears, boars, foxes, and other wild animals and savage beasts. . . . The lions that I saw over there are not red, nor do they have the manes with which they are customarily depicted: they are

---

Blanke, op. cit., p. 205. On their presumed affinity with the Hebrews (examples from the end of the seventeenth century and from 1876!) see Marion, op. cit., pp. 259–60, and Marianne Mahn-Lot, *La découverte de l'Amérique* (Paris, 1970), pp. 86–87.

18. *Storia antica del Messico,* IV, 31–36, and idem, Cuevas ed., I, 84; IV, 30–53.

19. Cotta ed., 1845, I, 489. On more recent scientific theories relative to the presence of animal species in islands or in lands separated by stretches of sea, see Darwin, *Origin of Species,* chap. XIII, ed. cit., pp. 304 ff., and the article "Zoological Distribution" in the *Encyclopedia Britannica,* 11th ed. More recently the problem of the existence of similar species in continents separated by immense oceans not spanned by any terrestrial bridges (isthmuses) has served as solid support for Alfred Wegener's rash theories on continental drift (see his *The Origin of Continents and Oceans* [London, 1970], pp. 6, 15, 98–99, 110). On the oddity of the marsupials being found only in Oceania and America ("how these animals got from one continent to the other"), see W. M. McGovern, *Jungle Paths and Inca Ruins* (New York–London, 1927), p. 79.

20. *Historia natural y moral,* IV, 36.

21. Ibid., I, 21; ed. cit., pp. 80–81.

brown, and they are not as brave as they are painted."[22] But Justus Lipsius, as we saw (above, pp. 28–29) was already specifying that every region had its own individual fauna, and demanding that every variety should be identified by a name of its own, and not by crude analogies.

Another great name among the ancient chroniclers of American nature, Father Bernabé Cobo,[23] is also perfectly aware of the basic differences between the fauna and flora of the Old and New World.

In general he too admits that the Indies was as poor in plants and animals as it was rich in minerals and precious metals, in which he sees a mysterious design of providence, using gold and silver to draw the greedy Europeans to the Indies and induce them to bring domestic animals and edible plants with them.[24] Two centuries later Humboldt as well was to point to the oft-deplored scarcity of the native population of America as a providential factor permitting its large-scale European colonization.[25] Naïve as they are, these efforts to discover the rational, or God's handi-work, in reality, and in even a partially artificial reality such as the de-population of America, one must recognize therein an urge for logic, the need for explanation, a stubborn cosmic optimism.

Cobo's main stress however falls on the qualitative differences, and not on the quantitative inferiority. The first chapter of book 4 teaches "how the natural plants of this New World are to be distinguished from those that have been taken there, either from Spain or from other regions";[26] and of the trees in particular Father Cobo notes that "there were very few trees which the Spaniards on their arrival in this country found to be similar in type to those of Spain."[27]

Chapter 45 of book 9, entitled "Of the kinds of perfect animals that were found in this New World similar to those of Spain," begins: "There

22. Ibid., IV, 34; ed. cit., p. 321. Oviedo, even before Acosta, had already emphasized the meager courage of the American lion: "In Tierra-Firme there are real lions, no more or less than those of Africa, but they are somewhat smaller and not so brave, in fact they are cowardly and run away; but this [Oviedo adds curiously] is common to lions, who do no harm if they are not chased or attacked" (*Sumario*, I, 488). On the tigers, on the other hand, "which are very fierce in the Indies" and "braver and crueler" than the lions, see Acosta, *Historia*, III, 15 (ed. cit., p. 180) and IV, 34 (ed. cit., p. 322).

23. Fr. Cobo need be mentioned only in passing, since his *Historia del Nuevo Mundo* remained un-published until the end of the nineteenth century. The first part was edited and annotated by Marcos Jimenez de la Espada, for the Sociedad de Bibliófilos Sevillanos. The 1st vol. bears the date 1890; the 2d, 1891; the 3rd, 1892; and the 4th, 1893. The other two parts of the work (on Peru and Mexico in particular) seem to have been lost (R. Porras Barrenechea, "El Padre Bernabé Cobo," *Historia*, 2 [1943], pp. 98–104).

24. Bk. X, chap. 43; ed. cit., II, 441. Fr. Cobo's contrast between the third realm of nature and the first two foreshadows the antitheses between animal and vegetable kingdom that were later to become quite common.

25. *Examen critique*, III, 155–56, 226; *Cosmos* (Madrid ed., 1874), II, 293. Cobo talks about ar-cane [?] design, Humboldt about "mysterious," though beneficial, causes.

26. Ed. cit., I, 329–35.

27. VI, 2; ed. cit., II, 11. Similar considerations for the fish (VII, 1; ed. cit., II, 128–29); for the birds (VIII, 1; ed. cit., II, 193 ff.), etc. Of the men Fr. Cobo tells us "that America was little populated" and seeks "for what reasons" (XI, 1; ed. cit., III, 5). The first cause, he finds, is the "lack of waters" in some places. The second, "the excess of waters that other places have" (ibid., III, 7).

was *not* found in the whole New World a single species of the tame and domestic animals of Europe," excepting certain small dogs or *gozques*.[28]

The lion is as always the object of very special attention and careful comparison. Father Cobo observes elegantly: "The animal which throughout the world is accorded the princedom among creatures is the Lion, but if it owes this title to its ferocity and the spirit with which it dominates most animals, then the ordinary Lions of these lands do not merit it, since they do not have the nobility, valor, and boldness of those of Africa."[29]

But even if in the matter of the wild beasts Father Cobo to some extent anticipates Buffon, for the domestic species he remains far away from him. The whole of the first chapter of the tenth book is devoted to a complacent discussion "of the causes through which the animals and plants which the Spaniards brought to this land have increased and multiplied so well there."[30]

The point where Father Cobo shows himself most removed from Buffon, however, seeming to precede him in time not by a mere century (1650–1750) but by several, is that where he discusses the problem which as we have seen troubled Father Acosta, of how the animals of America could have entered Noah's ark, and after the flood left it and gone home. After a quick foray against the other explanations, Father Cobo adopts as certain the extreme and desperate hypothesis of Saint Augustine, and informs us that the Angels of the Lord came down to the animals, guided them to the patriarch's floating menagerie and later accompanied them back to their native lands.[31] The couriers of Thomas Cook could hardly offer a more complete service!

II. THE TROPICALIZATION OF THE WHITE MAN

The "tropicalization of the white man" is the name given by Terán to that degenerative process by which the Spanish conquerors, first of all, under the "telluric and social influence of America,"[32] suffered "a moral reversal" and became cruel, savage, inhuman toward the natives and each other. Terán's account lays much greater emphasis on the "social" than on the "telluric" influence. The savagery of the Spanish conqueror appears there as conditioned by his encounter with an environment devoid of civilization (at least of any civilization accessible to him), with a society defenseless against exploitation, and cut off by immense distances from any other part of the world, thus leaving no possibility of the

28. Ed. cit., II, 302.
29. IX, 70; ed. cit., III, 337.
30. Ed. cit., II, 341 ff.
31. XI, 13–14; ed. cit., III, 67–77.
32. Giovanni B. Terán, *La nascita dell'America spagnola* (Bari, 1931), p. 68; cf. 27, 55, etc.

echo of his many misdeeds being heard, nor of any word of censure or effective protest reaching there, nor of any circulation of ideas or reciprocal influence being established there.[33]

Thus strictly speaking it is not a matter of deterioration due to the harmful influence of America, of a degeneration similar to that supposedly recognizable in animal species or indigenous tribes. But since the natural environment is mentioned by Terán too, and his thesis appears at first sight to contain a good proportion of pessimistic truth, we cannot but mention it in going back over the polymorphic "weaknesses" of America and consider it summarily in its more ample and complex formulation.

One must, in fact, beware of simplification. At the end of the sixteenth century Carletti actually noted a moral improvement among the Spaniards who had emigrated to America. They are not given to the infamy of robbery, writes the Florentine merchant, "and it seems somehow that that sky does not wish it, seeing that even those who were known in Spain as men of evil life, once they arrived in the Indies totally changed condition, and became virtuous, and sought to live civilly, so that one can say of these men that in changing skies they change nature."[34]

This rare and optimistic theory was repudiated, very shortly afterward, by the hispanophobe pen of Traiano Boccalini. It had already been said, in his time, as we have just seen, that the savagest and fiercest animals of the Old World lost their spirit and vigor in the Indies, and wild animals there became meek and the dogs no longer had the breath to bark. But Boccalini imagines that "the dogs which the Spaniards (or their soldiers and officials) had ferried to the Indies to protect their flocks against wolves, had become such rapacious wolves that in devouring sheep they outdid the voracity and cruelty of the very tigers." But there is no tropically climatic motivation in Boccalini: a little further on the men of Flanders announce that "in their countries too the dogs that the Spanish shepherds had sent to watch over the Flemish flocks had become such rapacious wolves that they devoured the sheep with appalling bestiality."[35]

Despite these contradictory and self-annulling judgments we certainly would not want to cast doubt on the reality of the "tropicalization," nor even simply to set it aside as a "naturalistic theory."[36] But it would be as

33. Spain called its viceroys and functionaries to account for their administration. And occasionally a voice was heard in the wilderness, like the desperate and irrepressible cry from Las Casas. But still in the middle of the eighteenth century Juan and Ulloa could not report openly on the things they had seen that were less flattering to the Spanish government.

34. F. Carletti, *Ragionamenti* (ca. 1606 [Carletti was in the Indies in 1594–95]; Milan, 1926), p. 30, with evident allusion to Horace, *Epistolae*, I, 11, line 27.

35. *Pietra del paragone politico* (1617; ed. E. Camerini [Milan, 1862]), pp. 88, 90. And Sister Mary of the Incarnation, an Ursuline nun in Quebec, observes sadly in the middle of the seventeenth century that "a Frenchman becomes savage rather than a savage becoming a Frenchman" (Marion, op. cit., p. 122).

36. G. Doria, *Storia dell'America Latina* (Milan, 1937), p. 23.

well to relieve the general phenomenon of that negative moral qualification, not in order to give it a positive one, as Carletti would like to do, but to reserve the condemnation of ethical judgments instead for the particular cases that turn out to be really blameworthy.

As a general rule one can often recognize in the tropicalization of the white man a positive element overlooked by the moralists: the adjustment of the white man to this equatorial nature, so limitlessly superior and almost intoxicating in comparison to the environment he knew before and in which he had grown up. The white man does not let himself be intimidated by it, nor does he "adapt" to it passively like the native, does not allow it to dominate and "control" him. But in a sort of contest of romantic folly he vies with it and challenges it; and with enormous crimes, with a practical *Sturm und Drang* of passion, with unbelievable excesses and bold endeavors (*hazañas*) pulls himself up to its level of unbridled exuberance. A formidable moral mimetism, in truth, in which the "Sed de oro," the *codicia,* the Christian mission and the glory of the king of Spain are no more than episodic forms, secondary pretexts, the phenomenic and phenomenal superstructure of a typical affirmation of the West.

The theory of "tropicalization" had appeared in outline as early as the time of Sepúlveda and Solórzano, but as a justification, an extenuating factor for the Creole.[37] And some time later the romantic Prescott went even further, discovering "a Quixotic enthusiasm," in other words not sub- but superhuman qualities, in the deeds of the conquistador of remote and marvelous lands.[38]

But despite these legalistic distortions and subsequent literary idealizations the theory had already attained a certain degree of scientific impassivity in Montesquieu. After first adducing the "strength of the climate" as an *excuse* for whoever had allowed the monks and priests of the Spanish Indies "a sort of concubinage," in his major work, as we know, he makes climate one of the typical elements of his system of geographical explanation of laws and customs.[39]

Raynal, a few decades later, comes back to this theory and develops it with explicit reference to Mexico and Peru, and with almost "Teranian" phraseology:

Beyond the equator, man is neither English, nor Dutch, nor French, nor Spanish, nor Portuguese. Of his own country he keeps only the principles and prejudices

---

37. Rufino Blanco Fombona, *Il conquistatore spagnolo del secolo XVI* (Turin, 1926), p. 260.

38. "The life of the adventurer in the New World was romance put in action. What wonder, then, if the Spaniard of that day, feeding his imaginations with dreams of enchantment at home, and with its realities abroad, should have displayed a Quixotic enthusiasm – a romantic exaltation of character not to be comprehended by the colder spirits of other lands" (Prescott, *Conquest of Mexico,* p. 292).

39. *Pensées inédites* (Bordeaux, 1899), I, 188, quoting Frezier, *Geographica,* p. 376. Cf. *Esprit des lois,* bk. XIV.

which authorize or excuse his conduct. Cringing when he is feeble; violent when he is strong; feverish for gain, impatient for pleasure; capable of any crime that will bring him rapidly to his ends. Thirst for blood seizes him. He is a tamed tiger returning to the forest.[40]

And his words are swiftly echoed by the physiocrat Roubaud, at first with the same accents of horror and disapproval, but later with a confused enthusiasm that already reminds one of Schiller's contemporary *Brigands* (1781). The first mention, referring to the buccaneers, is a literal "variation" of Raynal's tirade: "These pirates, so savage that they even drank their prisoners' blood, were born among almost civilized peoples, gentle enough in their countries. . . . These transplanted Europeans, becoming brigands by necessity, more barbarous than the barbarians themselves, because of their familiarity with peril and crime . . . by what signs would one have recognized them for Englishmen, Frenchmen, or Dutchmen, etc? . . . by their habits? They were like wild beasts."[41]

But when toward the end of his work Roubaud begins to speak *ex professo* of buccaneers and pirates, he changes his tune. Their customs, he says, mixing in a "violent ferment, rendered them monstrous or prodigious." They were just and pitiless, cruel and generous: "As soon as they met, they joined forces despite their differences, and even their national antipathies. In these distant countries they were compatriots."[42]

Compatriots in an ideal republic of supermen: "The fire of the climate, which had enervated the old usurpers of America,[43] only inflamed the blood of these robust men, kindled their courage. When these ruffians assembled, their, imaginations spurred each other on, took flight, and soared beyond the confines of humanity."[44]

I say again: who presides over this assembly, the pirate Henry Morgan or *der Räuber* Karl Moor? Certainly one can hardly conceive, without a little private smile, that the fiery orator is the abbé Roubaud: "Whoever, having energy, pays no heed to the present, and fears nought for the future, may be an extraordinary man, if he wishes to. They [the corsairs]

---

40. *Histoire philosophique,* ed. cit., V, 2–3; cf. ibid., pp. 172–74. On the other hand Raynal denies the degeneration of man in America. Cf. above, p. 46, and Chinard, *Le rêve exotique,* p. 392. An assiduous reader of Raynal, Senancour resorts to the influence of the tropics to explain the conversion of the restless European into "these agitated and turbulent men whose madness is watched by the rest of the world with a never-failing astonishment" (*Rêveries sur la nature primitive de l'homme,* ed. J. Merlant [Paris, 1939–40], I, 236 n. 11). Encina too refers to the tropicalization as a natural phenomenon, with a single ethico-social qualification, the emphasis on the rivalry and dissension between Creole and Spaniard: "The direct influence of the climate and soil of America, especially in the tropical regions, has been the modification, in the long run, of the Spanish temperament and character, even if there had not been the *mestizaje"* (Encina, op. cit., p. 7).

41. *Histoire,* XIII, 5–6.

42. Op. cit., XV, 218. The obliteration of national characteristics, in Roubaud as in Raynal, stands for the loss of every tradition and inherited custom, the escape from history into presocial nature.

43. An attempted reconciliation with the thesis of the debilitation of the Creoles. And a little further on: "Europe recruited the filibusters, as Spain had recruited the first conquerors of America" (op. cit., IV, 223).

44. Ibid., p. 219.

were the most extraordinary of men, because their sentiments in this regard reached the point of folly."[45] Madman, beast, demigod, outlaw — behold man freed and stripped of all inhibitions and all the dross of past ages in the incandescent crucible of the tropics.

Later, with varying modalities, but all attuned to the resurgence of the tiger in the citizen, the thesis was repeated by Humboldt, with almost Raynalian expressions;[46] by Robert Louis Stevenson and Joseph Conrad[47] in their tropical novels; by Turner, referring to the frontiersmen of the Middle West; by Bowman, talking of the inhabitants of the eastern valleys of Peru;[48] and by the apocalyptic *aprista* Orrego, who extended it to all Europeans in all America;[49] while the positive and civilizing aspects of the struggle against climate are stressed by Huntington, who is quoted approvingly by Toynbee,[50] and by Toynbee himself, who emphasizes the "possibilities" offered by the corrosive effects of overseas emigration.[51]

All in all then the tropicalization of the white man is a political rather

45. Ibid., pp. 222–23.

46. "On the other side of the ocean, everywhere, where the thirst for gold leads to the misuse of power, the European peoples have developed the same character in every phase of history" (*Reise*, I, 285–86).

47. Of the former it is customary to mention (G. Cocchiara *l'eterno selvaggio. Premesse e influssa del mondo primitivo nella cultura moderna* [Milan, 1961], p. 240) *The Ebb-Tide* (1894), with its Polynesian background (but the "tropicalization" is scarcely mentioned in it); of the latter, one could name the stories set in the heart of Africa (*Heart of Darkness*, 1902) and in Malaya (*An Outcast of the Islands*, 1896; *Lord Jim*, 1900), in the Caribbean and South America.

48. "The wilderness masters the colonist . . . it strips off the garments of civilization" (F. J. Turner, *The Frontier in American History* [New York, 1935], p. 4); I. Bowman, *The Andes of Southern Peru* (New York, 1916), pp. 28, 106–08. And on the "renegade" white man who goes wild and identifies himself with the redskins, see Pearce, *The Savages*, pp. 224–25. The study by Hans von Hentig, *Der Desperado: Ein Beitrag zur Psychologie des regressiven Menschen* (Berlin-Göttingen-Heidelberg, 1956), though rich in picturesque detail, refers only to the North American West, in the decades following the California gold rush (ca. 1850–1900). Although he also mentions climatic and telluric factors, Hentig insists mainly on the social, or asocial, economic and merely criminal ones. He does not of course talk of "tropicalization," but many of the excesses he records, such as the unlimited slaughter of the natives (redskins), and the cases of cannibalism (examples on pp. 15, 38, 221–22) find an easy counterpart in the history of the conquest of other parts of America, nearer the Equator.

49. "The telluric environment of America acts on the European like a corrosive solvent, both physically and psychically or mentally. The Latin American Creole, the product of the collision of the two races and two cultures, is the degradation of both, to an incredible degree. He is the human gangue, returning to chaos" (A. Orrego, *El pueblo continente. Ensayos para una interpretación de América Latina* [Santiago, 1939], pp. 33–34).

50. "In the process of adjusting themselves to a hard environment they (primitive men) advanced by enormous strides, leaving the tropical part of mankind far in the rear" (Ellsworth Huntington, *Civilisation and Climate*, 3rd ed. [New Haven, 1924], pp. 405–06, quoted by Toynbee, *A Study of History*, I, 292). So the adaptation of the tropical savage to the cold and fog of the North is a step forward just as much as the adaptation of the European to the tropical forest.

51. "The very process of transmarine migration has a disintegrating effect upon the migrants' social heritage which offers an opportunity for new social creation . . . transmarine migration is merely a possible stimulus" (Toynbee, op. cit., III, 135; the thesis of a stimulus generally deriving from transoceanic migration is developed with examples, ibid., II, 84–100). But elsewhere (ibid., V, 179), revealing an uncertainty by no means infrequent in his monumental work, Toynbee quotes Turner on the subject of the "barbarizing effect of the American frontier." And finally in the article by Hilgard O'Reilly Sternberg, "Land and Man in the Tropics," *Proceedings of the Academy of Political Science*, 27, no. 4 (May 1964: "Economic and Political Trends in Latin America"), pp. 11–22, the "tropicalization of the white man" is found to be a "myth," a cliché destined to disappear.

than ethical phenomenon; an affirmation of life, not of good or bad. If in the Indies it seemed to Terán a terrifying thing, this is to some extent because a crude affirmation of life, a bite, a rape, a war, almost always has repugnant aspects; and also partly because too often the mind of the tropicalized conquistador was bursting not only with Life but with a bullying arrogance, an instinctive urge to crush. When he had conquered both men and nature, in the twice-defeated tropics, the Spaniard was bound to be inclined to consider himself the model of all perfection — which is the surest road to decadence — and to impose on the country his own perfection, all his own unarguable perfection, with a rigid cultural and commercial exclusivism.

III. THE MEXICANS' HUMAN SACRIFICES

In the sacrifices, writes Clavigero, "I confess that the Religion of the Mexicans was too sanguinary, that their sacrifices were very cruel and their severities exceedingly barbarous, but every time I begin to consider what the other Nations of the World have done, I am confounded by the imbecility of the human mind, and the deplorable errors into which it is plunged when it is not guided by the light of true Religion, and I give infinite thanks to the Almighty for having preserved me from such evils." And elsewhere: "This is a subject that we would willingly pass over. . . ."[52]

Another Mexican Jesuit exiled in Italy, Father Pedro Marquez, an equally fervent admirer of the ancient Aztec civilization, and as anxious as Clavigero to put an end to the "ugly depictions both of the ancient and present Americans, put forth without due examination by some writers," defended the ancient Mexicans against the imputation of sacrificing men, saying that the offerings were few: "the custom these gentiles have of sacrificing men to their Gods . . . was neither so continuous, nor of such an exorbitant number as some writers have exaggerated"; and those few were "usually prisoners of war, and others deserving death"; and that "furthermore, they offered not only human victims, but also rabbits, quails, turtledoves, and other animals," and *copalli* incense — as if the simultaneous sacrifice of a rabbit or a turtledove lessened the cruelty of the human sacrifice.

Conscious perhaps of the weakness of such arguments, Father Marquez hastily turns to the counterattack: the Romans too used to sacrifice prisoners of war to Jove.[53]

The embarrassment is obvious in Marquez too. On this point Las

52. *Storia antica del Messico*, IV, 295; II, 45.
53. *Due antichi monumenti di architettura messicana* (Rome, 1804), pp. 19–20 (and in Plancarte, op. cit., pp. 137–38). The same themes and retortions occur already in Clavigero, of course, op. cit., IV, 295–99, who concludes that "the Mexicans did no more than follow in the tracks of the most celebrated Nations of the Old Continent."

Casas had been much bolder than the two Mexicans. Human sacrifices, he said, show a most lofty concept of the Deity, to whom the people who practice them sacrifice whatever they hold most dear: in many cases their own children. The Aztecs were wrong in thinking that their gods were God or true gods, but by offering them "the most excellent and most precious and most costly and naturally most loved by all, and most fruitful of creatures, especially if those that they sacrificed were their sons . . . they had a better and more noble concept and estimation of their Gods," and by the lights of their natural religion, provided better for the public welfare and common prosperity "than the [republics] that did not do so and forbade the sacrifice of men."[54]

Las Casas excuses anthropophagy too as a natural monstrosity,[55] not innately wicked, like a disease, or an excess of hunger, or as a means of disposing of the bodies of those sacrificed: "In New Spain they did not eat it [human flesh] so deliberately, from what I understand, except that of those that had been sacrificed, as something sacred, more for religion than anything else. . . ." (ibid.) The gap between the humanitarian Las Casas, who offers a laborious legitimization of cannibalism, and the Jesuit Father Clavigero, who simply looks away in horror, measures the progress of Europe's conscience over two long centuries.

Vico, pursuing a different ideological tack, unites within himself both the horror and the need to understand and explain. Human sacrifices are due to "a fanaticism of superstition" (*Scienza nuova,* p. 395) and are a "monstrous custom" (p. 392), but they cannot be looked on as a sign of mere evil or savagery. They are a universal phenomenon, and thus proper to a certain phase in the development of all civilizations.[56] The Phoenicians practiced them, sacrificing "their own children"; so did the Carthaginians, "soliti suos sacrificare puellos"; the Greeks, with Agamemnon sacrificing his daughter Iphigenia; the Romans, the Welsh, the English, and Tacitus's ancient Germans; and finally the Americans, unknown "until two centuries ago to all the rest of the world"; who, as Oviedo relates, not only used to sacrifice men, but "fed on human flesh" (pp. 391–93). These nations, barbarians, and "superstitious and ferocious gentiles" possessed "instinctive virtues mixed with religion and monstrosity" (p. 389). They had "bloody religions" (p. 134), but this was part of the "design of Providence; for that is what was needed to educate the

54. *Apologética historia,* chap. CLXXXIII, quoted in Las Casas, *Doctrina,* pp. 19–20. Precisely the same argument is used in a more recent and authoritative study of Aztec civilization (George C. Vaillant, *Aztecs of Mexico* [Garden City, 1941], pp. 204–05), citing other religious systems, our concept of martyrdom, and the example of Jesus Christ. But Sepúlveda already pronounced this audacious doctrine "impious and heretical" (Zavala, *La filosofía política,* p. 83).

55. *Apologética historia,* chap. CCL, in *Doctrina,* pp. 21–23.

56. Though not of the biblical one, which Vico tries to show, with apologetic incoherence, as exempt from human sacrifice, despite Abraham and Jephthah (see n. 4 to the *Scienza nuova,* pp. 390–91).

sons of the Polyphemes and reduce them to the humanity of men like Aristides or Socrates, Lelius or Scipio of Africa" (p. 135).

Human sacrifices, as Las Casas had dimly realized, are a sign of religiosity and thus an element of progress. The indissoluble link between their horror and their providentiality is so strongly felt by Vico that in discussing them he repeatedly resorts to verbal antitheses; the custom of making sacrifices was "impious piety" (p. 390), it was "the most inhuman humanity" (p. 394). Thus Plutarch errs in posing himself the (prematurely rationalistic and almost Voltairian) problem of "whether it were a lesser evil to worship gods so impiously, or not to believe in gods at all." He errs because with that "savage superstition . . . there arose some glorious nations, but with atheism there was not a single one founded in all the world" (p. 395).[57]

It is clear that Vico's theory is more humane, and also more philosophical, than the sighs and scandalized groans and legalistic expedients of the Mexican Fathers. And likewise its unabashed pessimism soars above the apologetic lucubrations that de Maistre wove around the notion of human sacrifice almost a century later.

In his *Eclaircissement sur les sacrifices* or *Traité sur les sacrifices,* published in 1821, de Maistre illustrates the universality of belief in the efficacy of human sacrifice, in the virtue of spilled blood and the expiatory capacity of the victim: a belief that is linked to the equally mysterious and bitter notion of the original corruption of flesh and blood. De Maistre recoils with horror from the appalling sacrifices of the Mexicans, but bends a reverent knee before the same idea sublimated in the dogma of the Eucharist;[58] which parallel, given the added stimulus of his love of savage paradox (theory of war, of the executioner, etc.), provides him with an argument of Catholic apologetics: "Wherever the true God is not known and served, by virtue of an express revelation, man will always immolate man and often devour him."[59]

The defense of the Mexicans' sacrifices by means of the example of other and greater sacrifices has continued right up into our day, and has often served for political polemics. Cattaneo compared the Aztec sacrifices with Radetzky's gallows and the death penalty in general.[60] A recent ethnologist, arguing with Montandon, who saw the dreadful human sacri-

---

57. Cf. Croce, *La filosofia di G. B. Vico* (Bari, 1922), pp. 91 ff.
58. Op. cit., printed with *Soirées*, ed. cit., II, 286–87, 323. The expression seems to echo de Pauw's, quoted above, p. 101. The Mexican patriot Fr. Servando Teresa de Mier contrasts the Aztec sacrifices to the propitiatory sacrifices of the Spaniards themselves, and the savage "roast offerings" of the Spanish Inquisition (*Historia de la revolución*, II, 723–24, 731). And in our modern national religions too we find a mystique of blood sacrifice, in the exaltation of the "fallen" and the belief in the redeeming virtues of their slaughter (see for example in Curti, *American Loyalty*, p. 171).
59. Op. cit., II, 296.
60. "Gli antichi Messicani," in *Opere*, III, 430.

fices of the Amerindians as a proof of "spiritual aberration," retorts in almost Voltairian tones: "The ritual killings of the Aztec seem paltry indeed beside the wholesale massacres of European warfare."[61] Keyserling finds the Mexicans' human sacrifices considerably superior, spiritually speaking, to the massacres of the Soviet Ceka, since the Aztecs' bloody cult "expressed the ecstasy of the flesh."[62] But in a recent American left-wing review they are preferred to the massacres of the reactionaries: "Though having no such religious motivations . . . Hitler and Franco sacrificed . . . an infinitely greater number of victims."[63]

IV. THE IMPOTENCE OF NATURE

The argument of the impotence of nature, implicit in one of de Pauw's incidental replies, and accepted systematically, in its profoundest sense, by Hegel, has so frequently played a part in the polemics on America that it is perhaps not out of place to recall that it too, like certain theses implied by Buffon, has a remote Aristotelian origin.

All terrestrial bodies, teaches the Stagyrite, are accidental and unstable combinations of the four elements. Unlike the celestial bodies, which move in a perfect circle, earthly things and creatures are subject to the law of rectilinear motion, to the law of gravity which draws them downward and to the center. The earth is the center of the cosmos, but at the same time its lowest point. Weighed down by matter, the earth is "almost condemned to a physical unworthiness."[64] It is the universe's lowest pit (Dante, *Paradiso*, XXXIII, 22–23). "Here we are in the feces of the world."[65]

The eternal forms cannot fully realize themselves in such a deaf and stubborn magma. The final causes endeavoring to set their stamp on matter are obstinately resisted by the mechanical causes which rule the matter itself. And it is this struggle, like the artist's struggle to mold matter according to his idea, that gives birth to all the chaotic aspects of a nature without law or plan, "where all things are constantly and rapidly inter-

---

61. Lowie, op. cit., p. 186.
62. Op. cit., p. 289.
63. Rafael Sanchez Ventura, "Flores y Jardines del México Antiguo y del Moderno," *Cuadernos Americanos*, 2 (1943), no. 1, p. 137. Lévi-Strauss too, in explaining, if not justifying, anthropophagy, resorts to the examples of the concentration camps and dissection rooms (*Tristes tropiques*, p. 348), while in polemic with the same Lévi-Strauss, Soustelle reaffirms the universal human tendency to cruelty (J. Soustelle, *Les quatre soleils: Souvenirs et réflexions d'un ethnologue au Mexique* [Paris, 1967], pp. 236–38).
64. G. De Ruggiero, *La filosofia greca* (Bari, 1921), II, 38, underlining the Platonic derivation of this negative concept of matter (ibid., p. 68). Already David G. Ritchie, after noting that the infinite and free variety of nature is considered by Hegel "not the glory, but the defect and impotency of Nature," recalled (1891) that this concept of the contingency and weakness of nature "is a survival in Hegel of the Platonic and Aristotelian conception of matter" (*Darwin and Hegel* [London, 1893], p. 57).
65. Fernán Perez de Oliva (1494–1533), *Dialogo de la dignidad del hombre* (Buenos Aires, 1943), p. 36.

changing."[66] In the order of natural things one meets *accident* at every turn; and there is no science of accident.[67] Nature is powerless to realize completely the lofty designs of the Spirit.

Despite its deep-seated contradiction with the most vital principles of his philosophy, for which there is no matter without form, no power without act, this duality and consequently this often imperfect fusion of form and matter remained in Aristotle as an obscure mythological presence, a symbol of the drama that is in things, a sign of the incomprehensibility of the contingent and the defective in a world that is absolute spirit, of the incurable antinomy between the Eternal Principle and the wretchedness of all that passes and dies. Like the God Mahadöh in Goethe's ballad, Aristotle's God "accustoms himself to living down here, lets everything happen to him" ("Der Gott und die Bajadere").

In Christian philosophy, with its lofty new concept of a God who is Creator, this dualism is transferred into nature, the allegorical fiction interposed between the Omnipotent and his creatures. Nature is perfect inasmuch as it is the work of God. Nature is incapable of repeating the miracle of Creation in giving perfect form to the variety of real things. With endless wavering, according to the alternating stress laid on one or another aspect of this ambiguous nature, and along the whole chain of being, each creature receiving its apportioned share of perfection and imperfection, omnipotence and impotence — the medieval concept of nature is characterized precisely by its capacity to absorb and tolerate these contradictory demands within itself, to be simultaneously the projection of the Almighty and the shadowy matrix of the species and things of this base planet.

In the *Divine Comedy* it is Saint Thomas Aquinas in person who explains and illustrates to Dante (*Paradiso*, XIII, 52–87) this power and powerlessness of nature. The eternal and contingent things are both reflections ("splendor") of the divine Idea, which "descends to the last power, / Down from act to act," creating all the objects of the material world, in a chain of being ever more removed from God. But the matter of these objects and the virtue of the heavens molding this matter are not always equal. Thus the Divine Idea shines in it sometimes more and sometimes less. The same plant gives "better and worse fruit; and you are born with diverse intellect." Or, as the Poet says elsewhere, "circular nature, which sets the seal on our mortal wax, plies well her art, but does not distinguish one receptacle from another." And from the same seed

66. Perez de Oliva, loc. cit.,
67. *Metaphysics*, bk. E (VI), 2, 1026–27; cf. W. Windelband, *A History of Philosophy*, trans. J. H. Tufts (New York, 1896), pp. 144–47. On the resistance or "recalcitrance of matter" (or nature) in Aristotle and the Neoplatonists, see Collingwood, *The Idea of Nature*, pp. 72, 92, 125.

she produces an Esau and a Jacob, and brings forth a Romulus, a founder of the City, from the loins of the most humble parent (*Paradiso*, VIII, 127–33; cf. *Purgatorio*, XXVIII, 112–14).

If matter were always perfect, and the formative virtue of the skies ever supreme, every created thing would be a precisely exact reflection of the divine idea. But "many times form does not match the intention of the art, because matter is dull in response" (*Paradiso*, I, 127–29). Nature operates like an artisan, or an artist who is master of his craft, but whose wrist is not quite firm. The execution does not always correspond to the concept. Nature can thus show herself impotent, powerless to impress upon the wax all the "light of the seal." She operates, as was said, like the artist "well-practiced in his art, but whose hand trembles" (*Paradiso*, XIII, 77–78).

Only what issues directly from the hand of God, from the hand that does not *tremble,* from the Word to which nothing remains *without response,* is invariably perfect: "Thus was the earth already made worthy of all animal perfection." But the animals are products of nature, and like the plants, not always equally successful.

This whole explanation dictated by Saint Thomas, and of clear Aristotelian derivation right down to the metaphors of the wax and the artist, represents the Christian version of man's long-standing endeavor to reconcile divine infallibility with the varied imperfection of the existing world. Nature is the executrix of the Creator's command, but "her hand may tremble": she may sometimes fail where before she has succeeded and will yet succeed again.

When the Renaissance dawned and nature rose to the supreme rank, to paradigm of rationality and perfection, honored and studied for herself, and finally even hypostatized as God, the *impotence* or *negligence* of nature should have disappeared. But the dualism, however much refuted and suppressed, continually reemerges from the bosom of that physical unity postulated and proclaimed as absolute. Except that instead of generically investing all creation it insisted on its critical principle in specific reference to this or that section of the universe. Instead of being evenly diluted, so to speak, over the infinite scale of beings, from God all the way down to the last grain of sand, it concentrated on the recent impressive acquisitions of geography and physics, and expressed itself in characteristic form in the duality of Old and New World, the one mature and the other immature, or the one perfect and the other imperfect, one the creation of the fully realized power of nature, the other an unhappy abortion of its impotence, or later, with the positions reversed, the one afire with youth and pregnant with future, the other sterile and heading for the ultimate impotence of death.

In point of fact this conception of the earth as a unit composed of two parts, one mature and perfect and the other deficient and degenerate, meant its transformation into a creature consisting, like all the others, of mixed divine and corporeal parts, spirit and matter. On the dissolution of the old hierarchical conception of the Cosmos, each of its elements, including that large element our own planet, became a Cosmos itself, and was thus bound to contain the opposing principles of the universe.[68]

It is this polarity — emerging contemporaneously with the very beginnings of the critical knowledge of the new regions, and undoubtedly representing a necessary step for this knowledge, which in its turn contributed to the better understanding of the regions already known — it is this polarity, so laden with passion and hope, that becomes the new vehicle of that same aporia that had beset the medieval mind faced with the whole series of creatures, all children of God, and yet so imperfect, at least when compared one to another. The differences, before being understood as necessary aspects of the totality, and even when they were postulated in principle as such, figured sometimes as degrees of greater or lesser perfection, sometimes quite simply as antinomial oppositions of perfection and imperfection, reality and impotence.

But it was a somewhat slow and uneven process. Only in the eighteenth century did it reach a distinct self-awareness, the clarity of formula or "law" of nature. The early describers of the Americas are still under the sway of their enthusiasm, which prevents them seeing the American differences as inferiorities in comparison to the Old World, and which indeed obscures their vision of these differences and makes them assimilate America's nature to that of the other hemisphere.

Thus with them the stress falls always on the fertility and vigor of the Americas, and consequently on the universal power of nature. Las Casas refuses to recognize that there could be signs of negligence in creation (whereas Raynal will find exactly that): to those who saw the Americans as so many barbarians, unsociable and irrational, he replies triumphantly that it is absurd to imagine that Divine Providence "could have been *neglectful* in the creation of such an immense number of rational souls, letting human nature go wrong."[69] Oviedo, for all his acute insight into the natural peculiarities of America, does not give in to generic anti-

---

68. For a more general formulation of this thesis, see A. Koyré, "Galileo and Plato," *Journal of the History of Ideas*, 4 (1943), p. 404. The conception of the Earth as a living organism, and subject to disease and wounds, already familiar to Kepler, Bruno, and Shakespeare, was amply developed in the seventeenth century.

69. *Apologética historia* in *Colección de documentos inéditos para la historia de España*, LXVI, 237–38, quoted in Zavala, *Servidumbre natural*, p. 54 n. 1. See also idem, *La filosofía política*, pp. 81, 91, 98, with reference to the difficulties of Christian philosophy when it has to reconcile the omnipotence of God the Creator with the imperfections and deficiencies of creation and the creatures.

theses, and pours forth his admiration in a perpetual hymn to Nature and the inexhaustible variety of its phenomena. It would never have occurred to him that there could be limits to its power, or that it could err. Oviedo, almost pantheistic if we compare him to the Scholastic philosophers, worships nature as the most complete and imposing manifestation of God, adores God in nature. And Father Acosta found everything so perfect in the Lord's physical work that he inveighed against the sacrilegious idea that it could be improved, and threatened the judgment of heaven on whoever might sever the Isthmus of Panama.

It is only when the polemics on America begin to appear in systematic form, with the blossoming of the criticisms of such a conspicuous part of creation, that the concept and argument of the impotence of nature swiftly reemerge. It is true that it is often repeated almost without memory of its metaphysical origins, and used ingenuously by Raynal and de Pauw for example, as a fashionable figure of speech.[70] But the metaphysician Hegel himself, however, Hegel who in his moments of most robust realism will repeat that the ideal is not so "impotent" then as to *have to be* only, and then not *be* in effect, resorts to the facile metaphor in his moments of systematic embarrassment. He resorts to that "delightful contrivance" (Croce), but not contrived by him, of the impotence of nature, "of its weakness, its fainting and swooning, in the harsh task of realizing the rationality of the Concept!"[71] He does even more, and worse, in respect to the animal and vegetable species, and to America, saying of the former that "the multiple natural genera or species cannot be considered in any way superior to the *whimsical* caprices of the spirit in its representations";[72] and of the latter, America, describing its nature as imperfect through incapacity of the Spirit and extending the same epithet of impotent, in its proper sense of "lacking strength," to its primitive civilizations, which could not resist the Europeans.

By way of curiosity we might mention finally that de Pauw's same

70. See also Leopardi, above, p. 387. Likewise current and in fact proverbial was the opposite thesis, of the omnipotence of nature. Let one example suffice: polemicizing with Robinet's biological theories Delisle de Sales wrote: "Nature produces no half-finished works; why ascribe to her our feeble efforts, our own patterns and impotence?" (*Philosophie de la Nature*, IV, 161; but cf. ibid., V, 44–45, on the subject of "half-finished" creatures near the Poles and in the torrid zone). This is also valid against Galiani's thesis of a "half-finished" America.

71. *Saggio sullo Hegel*, p. 117. For Hegel "the forms of nature . . . are, so to speak, Utopian forms, at once demanding realization and yet having in them something which makes realization impossible" (Collingwood, *Idea of Nature*, p. 125). Thus one can understand Hegel's adherence to the Aristotelian classification of the animals (above, p. 426).

72. *La scienza della logica*, trans. A. Moni (Bari, 1925), III, 52, where the "impotence of Nature" is defined as "the incapacity to hold firm and present the rigor of the concept and . . . the getting lost in this inconceptual and blind multiplicity": cf. above, pp. 420–21 and cf. Aristotle's *accidental*, of which there can be no science (or knowledge). Whitehead too, so "Aristotelian" in his metaphysics, is led to admit that the natural laws are not always observed and the physical universe presents "instances of failure" and disorder (Collingwood, *Idea of Nature*, pp. 168, 170).

formal argument reappears in an American polemicist of the middle of the nineteenth century, who, to show the maturity and originality of the American, a really new human type and not a mere European immigrant, wrote: "Why should Europe go three thousand miles off to be Europe still. . . . It would seem like a *poverty* in Nature, were she unable to vary."[73] For de Pauw, Nature would have been impotent if she had not finished making American man, who is so different from the European, and thus must have degenerated from the perfection to which Nature brought him. For Lowell Nature would be impotent if she had not succeeded in making the American a different individual from the European, and thus equal to him in dignity. For the European, Nature was impotent if she could not make Europeans. For the American, Nature was impotent if she could not make Americans. . . .

V. THE QUAKERS, THE MARQUIS, AND THE GIRONDIST

The Quaker, like the Huron before him, had been called upon to personify the myth of a pure, simple, tolerant, and benevolent humanity, a humanity moreover burning with exemplary religious spirit and untiring industry. The "Friend" combined the native virtues of the savage with the more easily assimilated ones of the good Christian and the industrious citizen: and with this special faith of his, mystical, maybe, but philanthropic too, that needed neither theology nor clergy nor sacrament, he was also an appealing figure to the less Rousseauian philosophers and deists. Even in the charming literature of the epoch (which is never solely and simply charming) the Quaker is idealized and conventionally presented as the enemy of ceremony and convention, of the "ye" to which he prefers his "thee," of all the hat-raising and solemn oath-taking. One might note for example Chamfort's *La jeune Indienne* (1764),[74] or Calzabigi's *Amiti e Ontario, o i Selvaggi* (ca. 1770),[75] both works considerably more antislavery than prosavage, dripping with noble sentiment, with enthusiasm for the naïve innocence of nature and a derisive scorn for gold,[76] and both deriving, probably, from the legend of Inkle and Yariko, which attracted the attention of the young Goethe too.[77]

To certain easygoing and realist Italians, on the other hand, (like Mazzei and those mentioned above, chap. 4, n. 185)—who were ready to approve a more undemanding Catholic-type religiosity or a sharper and more reasoned incredulity—the Quaker remained a singularly dif-

---

73. James Russell Lowell and others, article in *Atlantic Monthly*, 1858, quoted by C. and M. Beard, op. cit., p. 215.
74. In *Oeuvres complètes*, 2d ed. (Paris, 1808), II, 379–412.
75. In *Poesie* (Livorno, 1774), pp. 125–70.
76. Cf. Chamfort, op. cit., p. 392, with Calzabigi, op. cit., p. 160.
77. Cf. Beutler, op. cit., pp. 380–88.

ficult and suspect figure. His ostentatious display of virture smelled of hypocrisy and was often denounced as Jesuitical. This Protestant, this strict pietist, this preacher of morals turned out to be just too much like a homegrown "priest."

Thus the polemic on the Quaker would merit a more extensive study, apart from the fact that the Philadelphia "Friend" was the first exemplar of the modern American civilization to be idealized or ridiculed in Europe.[78] Voltaire too, who had mocked the English Quakers (*Lettres anglaises*), is full of respect for those of America (*Questions sur l'Encyclopédie*). But for now it will suffice to mention that it was actually the differing verdicts on the Quakers that separated and caused such strife between two of the most convinced apologists of the United States, Mazzei and Brissot de Warville: the former as temperate and irreligious as the latter was blunt and fervid and sanctimonious.

Jean-Pierre Brissot, the future Girondist, the friend of the Rolands and the Clavière,[79] had even as a youth shown that superficial and generous temperament, that undaunted incoherence and stubborn polemical punctiliousness that were to lead him into so much trouble and bring about the ultimate ruin of both himself and his Girondist followers. Even Mme Roland, although she was very fond of him and was herself no little inconsistent, found in him "a sort of lightness of spirit and of character" that pained her.[80] The son of a rich provincial innkeeper, a restless autodidact and an adventurous publicist in the capital, or rather in two capitals, Paris and London, passing from one infatuation to another, from the reform of penal law to the emancipation of the Negroes, from the abolition of private property to projects for interoceanic canals, from the development of Franco-American trade and his hopes (1790) of independence for all South American Creoles to revolutionary war as the regenerator of the nation and as crusade for liberty; who after being imprisoned in the Bastille was offered the fortress keys in homage when it had been destroyed by the fury of the populace, and who after being a good friend of Doctor Guillotin left his head on the machine invented by

---

78. Remond (op. cit., pp. 169–71) effectively illustrates the contrast between the Quaker of legend, the instrument of polemic, and the Quaker of reality, very little known.

79. Clavière signed his name as fellow author of the pamphlet *De la France et des Etats-Unis, ou De l'importance de la révolution de l'Amérique pour le bonheur de la France* (1787), paid the costs of Brissot's trip to America, collaborated in drafting the account of the trip (*Nouveau voyage dans les Etats-Unis de l'Amérique septentrionale fait en 1788* [Paris, 1791; German trans. 1792, utilized by Karl von Rotteck]), where he was copiously praised, and was presented by Brissot with the portfolio of the Treasury in the first Girondist ministry (March 1792). In the same ministry Roland (referred to with deep reverence in the *Nouveau voyage*, III, 77n., 167–71, 184, etc.), had Home Affairs, again on Brissot's designation. On Mme Roland's pro-Americanism, actually expressed to Brissot, see above, chap. 4, n. 281, and Gidney, op. cit. On the same sentiment in Brissot (and on his practical and economic motives), Gidney, op. cit., passim, esp. pp. 23–33, and below, p. 596.

80. *Mémoires*, I, 97.

that same philanthropist—his life is a series of whimsical coincidences and catastrophic encounters with men and things greater than himself.

Marat had Brissot as companion in study and scientific research, treated him with almost feminine tenderness of affection—"you are aware, my very dear friend, of the place you occupy in my heart"—but did not follow up his proposal for their collaboration on a translation of *Paradise Lost,* and later attacked him with his customary virulence, although with almost Loyolan "regret" at having to denounce a man whose early writing "had not placed him among the ranks of distinguished writers, but had caused him to be looked on as a patriot."[81]

When the revolution came he was one of its most fervent and convinced supporters. At the beginning of 1791 his cry of alarm is almost prophetic: "The bourgeois aristocracy, they are the ones that will be most difficult to uproot."[82] But he was soon overwhelmed and trampled underfoot by the political energy and oratorical ardor of the enemies he had so assiduously collected. André Chénier abused him publicly and repeatedly.[83] Camille Desmoulins, for whom he had stood witness at his wedding to the tender and proud Lucille (1790), settled on him (1792) as his favorite target[84] and fashioned the word *brissoter,* which the *Grand Larousse* still explains as a synonym of *voler, filouter,* "to steal or scrounge."[85] Danton himself admonished him humorously: "Brissot, you are a *brissotin,*" while friends and enemies agreed that he was the least *brissotin* of all possible *brissotins.*[86]

Brissot himself tells us how and why he undertook the defense of the Quakers, and how this defense later procured him a hearty welcome in America, a welcome that led him to adopt the United States as a new fatherland, where he would certainly have gone to settle if the revolution that exploded in France had not kept him in his old fatherland. All things are concatenated, and there is no danger of Brissot trying to underemphasize the importance of anything he ever said or did. His review, for example, the *Courrier de l'Europe,* "has contributed more than one thinks to the success of the war in America and thus to the French revolution." And its value is not only as *res gesta,* but as *historia rerum gestarum.*

81. J. P. Marat, *Pamphlets* (Paris, 1911), p. 187 n. 1. The expansive and affectionate comments occur in a letter from 1782, included in Brissot's *Mémoires,* I, 352–54, and in Marat's *Correspondance* (Paris, 1908), pp. 8–10.

82. *Nouveau voyage,* I, xv. A (hostile) summary of his (youthful, 1780) ideas on theft and property (which he renounces in the *Mémoires,* ed. cit., I, 114–15, as an academic paradox, a scholastic exercise, and which Proudhon denied having known) in A. Sudre, *Histoire du communisme* (Brussels, 1849), pp. 222–39; see also Stark, op. cit., pp. 82–90.

83. *Oeuvres,* ed. Pléiade, pp. 280–81, 350–51, 685, 689–90.

84. *Jean-Pierre Brissot démasqué,* 1792; *Histoire des Brissotins,* 1793.

85. Cf. C. Desmoulins, *Le vieux cordelier,* ed. A. Mathiez and H. Calvet (Paris, 1936), p. 191 n. 2, and passim.

86. A. Aulard, *Histoire politique de la Révolution Française* (Paris, 1901), p. 405.

Its author insinuates modestly that one day it will perhaps be "the only monument to consult to know the history of the revolution of America."[87]

With this lively awareness of his historical mission Brissot was thus filled with scorn and irritation when he read the frivolous *Voyages dans l'Amérique Septentrionale dans les années 1780, 1781 et 1782* of the academician Marquis de Chastellux;[88] and no less than scandalized at the success obtained by their flippant, derisive, and coolly "philosophical" tone.

Chastellux was a nobleman and a man of letters under Voltaire's protection, he was a friend of Gibbon,[89] but he was before all else a soldier, a senior officer under Rochambeau's orders. The account of his journey is in the form of a dairy and in that tone of superior badinage that a man of the world retains even on the very edge of the world—even when he lands up in an inn so poor and ill equipped that a single miserable tin pot is used to serve food to the innkeeper's family, his guests, and his servants: "I dare not say for what other purpose it was suggested we might use it, when we went to bed."[90]

But a little further on, in a Richmond hotel, Chastellux finds excellent lodgings, food in profusion magnificently served, and very honest prices.

---

87. *Mémoires*, ed. cit., III, 276, 280–81.

88. I am quoting from the Paris ed., 1788. A partial first luxury edition of twenty-four copies was printed in 1781, on the presses of the printing house of the French fleet, in Newport (and was partly reproduced in the Gotha *Journal de Lecture* edited by Grimm); another, apocryphal and incomplete, came out in Cassel in 1785; a third, complete and acknowledged by the author, in Paris in 1786 (and, translated into English, in London, in 1787 and 1792; on 17 March 1786 David Humphreys wrote to Jefferson: "I have begun to translate the Travels of the Marquis de Chattelus in America," in *Papers*, IX, 330; on the various reprintings and translations, see the edition by Howard C. Rice mentioned below, pp. 25–26). Already on 3 October 1782 the Comte de Ségur wrote to his wife, in France, that he had been received by Washington: "If you want to know him, reread the portrait painted of him by the Chevalier de Chastellux in his journal, and it will be as if you had seen him" (*Mélanges*, p. 168; cf. *Voyages*, ed. cit., I, 11n. and 121–25). The frivolity of the details recounted in the book (1786 ed.) was already criticized by Grimm, Diderot, etc., *Correspondance*, XIV, 380; and deplored by Jefferson, who while exhorting Chastellux to offer the public the account printed in only a few copies had amicably suggested (24 December 1784) that he should cut out the offensive comments about various ladies (*Papers*, VI, 550–51; VII, 580–83, 584–86; cf. also VIII, 467–70, 471–72, and *Catalogue of the Library*, IV, 201–03). He was again rebuked for their lightness and complacency (1797) by the revolutionary Bayard, op. cit., xv, 37–38, who instead enthusiastically admired Brissot (ibid., pp. xvii–xviii, 199) and repeated his antiurbanism, moralism, etc. On the excessive gallantry of Rochambeau's officers, see abbé Robin, op. cit., p. 31. Although Franklin, who should have known how things stood, praised the "handsome likeness" Chastellux had given of the United States (Echeverria, *Mirage*, p. 120), it is still true that in America "General" Chastellux's book was not enthusiastically received: it was criticized for the inaccuracy of its military accounts (Jefferson, *Papers*, XI, 230), and the Rev. James Madison drily reported to Jefferson that he had received a complimentary copy: "I find it is but little relished by most here" (letter of 28 March 1787, in *Papers*, XI, 253). But Ezra Stiles read the book and found it very satisfying, and wrote to Jefferson: "I am ashamed that any of our countrymen should take Umbrage at some of his free and humorous Remarks upon our American customs, especially when the most of them are very judicious, and the greater Part of his Travels are most excellent" (letter of 30 April 1788, in *Papers*, XIII, 188). After having one more edition in 1828 the book has again been reprinted in our own day: *Travels in North America in the Years 1780, 1781 and 1782*, with an introduction and copious notes by Howard C. Rice, Jr. (Chapel Hill, N.C., 1963).

89. Edward Gibbon, *The Letters*, ed. J. E. Norton (London, 1956), II, 264.

90. *Voyages*, II, 60.

And we rejoice to learn that the examplary hotelier was a Neapolitan, Formicalo by name, who had worked first in Russia and then as Lord Dunmore's butler, following him to Virginia. He owned a fine house, furniture, slaves, and everything led one to believe that he would soon become an important personage in his new fatherland; "however, he still remembers his former one with pleasure" and is grateful to Chastellux for speaking to him only in Italian.[91]

The diary is rich in pleasant little anecdotes and swiftly drawn character sketches, like margin illustrations, of soldiers and tavern keepers, woodmen, and lawmen, but it never lingers over general reflections. Even the bold vignette of Chastellux and Jefferson drinking with friends until late at night, quaffing great cups of punch and taking excited turns to quote passages from Ossian, and having the volume brought and laid reverently alongside the steaming bowl[92] — remains a "vignette."

The philosophical deductions are conveniently gathered at the end, in a long letter "to M. Madisson, Professor of philosophy at the University of Williamsburg," with whom Chastellux had held long conversations on the presumable progress of science and the arts in America.[93] In point of fact two thoughts alone occupy the mind of the canny major general as he wanders across America: the making of war and the making of love. Time and again, when he is on the road, he informs us about the state of the fortifications, the tactical and strategic advantages of a position, the possibilities of transit for cavalry or the best sites for the emplacement of batteries — and he completes a careful reconnaissance of each of the recent battlefields.[94] But with nightfall he halts his journey and then, when he has told us how he dined, he describes what is known in the vernacular as "the woman situation."

His admiring gaze comes to rest on the guests' wives and the hosts' daughters, and lingers with particularly pleasure on the freshness and innocence of the young girls, the little lady republicans whom he is delighted to find endowed with the same ambiguous attraction as the maidens of Greuze. ("Ma passion predominante è la giovin principiante," as Leporello was shortly to say of his master, Don Giovanni). A little girl

91. Op. cit., II, 121–22. On Chastellux's attachment to Naples, which he visited in 1773, see Croce, *Bibliografia vichiana*, p. 353; and also Chastellux's *Félicité publique* (Bouillon, 1776), II, 180–81n.
92. *Voyages*, II, 36–37.
93. Op. cit., II, 261–301. The Rev. James Madison should not be confused with his cousin, the famous James Madison, one of the Founding Fathers of the republic and fourth president of the United States: Howard C. Rice, Jr., in his edition of the *Travels in North America*, n. 1. Jefferson advised (1784) Chastellux to arrange for the translation of this letter "on the probable influence of the revolution on our manners and laws, a work which I have read with great pleasure and wish it could be given to my countrymen" (loc. cit., VII, 581). The work on *Félicité publique* (for which see below, n. 101) also concludes with "a chapter of pure theory" (I, xvi; II, 266–322).
94. He had not brought any books on natural history with him, but only those necessary "for the political and military knowledge of the continent where I was going to wage war" (op. cit., II, 324). On Rhode Island he had a fort built, Fort Chastellux (Varnum, op. cit., p. 156 n. 34).

of twelve is no longer a child, nor yet a young lady: "She is rather an angel in the habit of a girl."[95] Heaven knows for what reasons — certainly not climatic — physical maturity in England and America is so swift and premature, "with the result that in the young people, even in the girls of twelve or thirteen, a roundness of form is found together with freshness of complexion. . . ."[96]

His descriptions go no further: and he does not really seem to be much changed from the way Mme d'Epinay had described him ten years earlier: "such a good boy," incapable of offending anyone, "possessed of wit, grace, and considerable good looks," but at the same time "some simplicity and guilelessness."[97] In fact, being the gentleman that he was, he never tells us about his "successes," nor, for all his familiarity with some very dubious and shady taverns, does he ever mention bundling.[98] But when we remember the care he takes to point out "the extreme liberty which reigns between persons of different sexes in this country, as long as they are not married,"[99] we shall find at least a hint of coquettishness in his insistence that nobody should think badly of his observations, glances, and comments, since his advanced age puts him above suspicion. Was he really so very old? In 1781 the Chevalier de Chastellux was precisely forty-seven — and a bachelor.

Nine years earlier he had published his major work, which earned its author, already known and befriended by Voltaire, the Patriarch's warm admiration and unreserved benevolence, and, with the electoral assistance of Mlle de Lespinasse, the coveted *fauteuil* in the Academy (the

95. *Voyages*, II, 222. Later he was to compose a gallant verse fable with the expressive title: *Les trois grâces du Nouveau-Monde* (in *Correspondance* of Grimm, Diderot, etc., XIII, 247–49; and in Varnum, op. cit., pp. 141–42).

96. Op. cit., II, 97–98. Pleasantly deceived by his sensuality Chastellux extends the current thesis of the precocious maturity of the Creoles to the North American females, and accepts also its complementary and compensatory thesis, that of their precocious senility and mortality: "Longevity is not common" in America (II, 86; cf. also Liancourt, *Journal*, p. 42). On this point he was answered by Mazzei, *Recherches*, IV, 199–200.

97. Letter to Galiani, 7 November 1770, in *D'Epinay e Galiani*, ed. Nicolini, pp. 115–16. Mme d' Epinay several times mocks Chastellux's mania for puns and plays on words (ibid., pp. 21, 138; cf. also Julie de Lespinasse, *Lettres*, ed. G. Isambert [Paris, 1876], I, 214; Marmontel, *Mémoires*, II, 91; Marquis de Ségur, *Julie de Lespinasse*, ed. Nelson, p. 199; Varnum, op. cit., pp. 23, 27, 133). Sainte-Beuve (*Causeries du lundi*, XI, 484–85) relates an amusing anecdote of Chastellux's inconsistency and malleability (but he was dealing with Mme de Staël, poor man!). Mrs. Montagu, on the other hand, "The Queen of the Blues," proclaimed him (1776) "ye most Pleasing of all ye beaux esprits" (*Mrs. Montagu . . . from 1762 to 1800*, ed. R. Blunt [London, 1923], I, 322, 330). On his relations with Mme Brillon and the Countess Golowkine, see C.-A. Lopez, op. cit., pp. 109, 195–97.

98. In fact he contradicts abbé Robin, who described it as very common: Varnum, op. cit., pp. 187–88; cf. above, chap. 5, n. 532. Jefferson too, for that matter, considered abbé Robin an absolutely unreliable author (*Papers*, XII, 62). Cf. Reynolds, *Beds*, p. 203: "Chastellux never even mentioned the subject," though his English translator refers to it in a note (1787, ed. Rice, I, 283).

99. Op. cit., I, 136–37. On his numerous lovers, in France, and his marriage, at 53, to a young Irish girl, see for example Grimm's *Correspondance*, XV, 219. In 1795 the Duc de Liancourt met two sisters in America called Dickinson, who had known Chastellux, but who "like several of our ladies in Paris . . . could not forgive him at all for having married a young lady that he loved, because previously he had loved an elderly lady who still loved him a little" (*Journal*, pp. 90–91).

fauteuil which had belonged to none other than Montesquieu!); the work for which he is still most often remembered today—the two volumes with the frankly eudaemonistic (and unwittingly Muratorian[100]) title *De la félicité publique*,[101] which see the object of the art of politics as being the assurance of "the greatest happiness of the greatest number of individuals" and thus anticipate Jefferson's inclusion of the "pursuit of happiness" among the innate and inalienable rights of man and citizen.[102]

The title lent itself too easily to irony, and there were many readers so discouraged by the almost eight hundred pages of text that they got no further than the title. From Paris, where according to Laharpe the book was not much read, there came the swift rejoinder:

> To Chastellux, a seat in the Academy!
> And what did he produce? A well-wrought book;
> Its name? *On Public Happiness!*
> The public's happy: it never heard of it.

In Grimm's and Diderot's *Correspondance,* the *Félicité publique* is judged an "estimable work, whose only fault is the very real one of being quite unreadable."[103] Two years later Thomas wrote of it to the Duke of Alba: "The book is not as well known in Paris as it could be."[104] The elderly Garat observed in 1820 that "this book on *Public Happiness . . .* has so far produced only the happiness of Voltaire," who was fulsome in its praise, in fact, and effective in the protection of his adoring and rev-

---

100. The coincidence does not go much further than the title. The work *Della pubblica felicità* (1759) is a sort of Christianizing utopia, even though already concerned with the practical aspects of society, the *Félicité publique* a universal history with a markedly materialistic-utilitarian outlook.

101. *De la félicité publique, ou Considérations sur le sort des hommes dans les différentes époques de l'histoire.* The first edition is from Amsterdam, 1772 (rpt. 1774?); I am quoting from the "new edition," corrected and augmented, Bouillon, 1776 (rpt. with short unpublished notes of Voltaire in Paris, 1822). Translations were made from the first edition into English (1774) and German (1780); and some chapters were also published in Italian (Naples, 1782). On Chastellux's relations with Vico and his theory of progress, see V. Cuoco, *Scritti vari* (Bari, 1924), I, 67, 304, 312; B. Croce, *Conversazioni critiche,* V (Bari, 1939), pp. 321–29; *Bibliografia vichiana,* pp. 352–53 (with other references); Lavergne, op. cit., pp. 279–330; J. Delvaille, *Essai sur l'histoire de l'idée de progrès jusqu'à la fin du XVIIIe siècle* (Paris, 1910), pp. 419–23 (quoting Voltaire's fulsome praise); J. B. Bury, *The Idea of Progress* (London, 1924), pp. 186–91. A brief summary of his works, including the *Voyages,* is given in Stark, op. cit., pp. 58–79. Although Lavergne describes his book as "too much forgotten these days" (1870; op. cit., p. 285) and Varnum assures us that Chastellux "does not deserve the oblivion into which he has fallen" (op. cit., p. 6) and Croce (*Conversazioni critiche,* p. 326) repeats that he is "now forgotten," the bibliography on him is not really so meager (see Varnum, op. cit., pp. 237–57).

102. Op. cit., II, 82, 93. On the Jeffersonian concept see however Wish, *Early America,* p. 197; Villard, op. cit., pp. 240–41; H. M. Jones, *The Pursuit of Happiness* (Cambridge, Mass., 1952), pp. 13–17, 61–98, citing Josiah Quincy, Jr., who defined (1774) the goal of society as "the greatest happiness of the greatest number" (op. cit., pp. 4, 6–7). On the vanity of this pursuit, also and especially when successful, see R. Niebuhr, op. cit., pp. 37–55.

103. *Correspondance,* XV, 102. The work on poetry and music (see below, n. 126) was also said to have failed to make a "sensation" because of its coldness (ibid., VII, 44; and Diderot, *Oeuvres complètes,* ed. Roger Lewinter, IX [Paris, 1971], p. 941).

104. Quoted in Sarrailh, op. cit., pp. 158–59.

erent disciple.[105] Our friend the abbé Galiani found the "idea" of the book (i.e., its subject, its title) very fine and very original, but he confessed to Madame d'Epinay that he had not yet read it.[106]

But the content, however prolix and singularly lacking in the wit that made Chastellux so sought after in the salons of Paris, is anything but insipid. Vague as his notion of "public felicity" is, and despite the hopelessness of the author's efforts to measure it and thus be able to make comparisons between one country and another and one epoch and those preceding or following it — his criteria come down in the end to the question of population increase and progress in agriculture, in keeping with the canons of the physiocrats — there is no denying that the book is more than just a glowing profession of faith in the beneficial power of Reason and the effective grace of Progress and represents in fact an effort to widen the horizons of historiography and include therein, following of course in the footsteps of Voltaire's masterpieces, the study of the economic and social conditions and the opinions and sentiments of the lowest and least vocal classes.

It was not such a different design from that which moved Adam Smith, at very much the same period, to begin the inquiry, which was to lead to so much more striking scientific results, into "the nature and causes of the wealth of nations" (1776); and the problems touched on by Chastellux were soon to occupy the labors of men like the revered Malthus (1798), Jeremy Bentham, and, in times closer to our own, the theorists of the welfare state.[107]

The ideological accouterment of the *Félicité publique* includes nothing that was not already present in the *Essai sur les moeurs:* "It is in that immortal work that one must seek out the germ of all the truths which we do no more than develop."[108] Of his own, Chastellux contributes a crudity of contrast on which he bases a more firm and universal hope. In every epoch, in every climate, men were more unhappy than in eighteenth-

105. Cf. in fact Voltaire's opinion on the author of the *Félicité publique* ("he makes mine") in Varnum, op. cit., p. 124. See examples of eulogies of Voltaire in *Félicité publique*, ed. cit., II, 56, 73, 85, 183–84. For Voltaire's constant praises, and his daring to put Chastellux above Montaigne and Montesquieu, see Varnum, op. cit., pp. 30–31, 43–44, 74, 94–95, 116, 120–25, 127–28.

106. Letter of 15 May 1773, in *Correspondance*, ed. cit., II, 204–05. In Galiani's and d'Epinay's letters there are numerous other references to Chastellux: see for examples Mme d'Epinay's criticism of the *Félicité publique* in Nicolini, *Gli ultimi anni*, pp. 10–12; and the desire expressed by Galiani to have Chastellux's opinion of his *Dialogues* (*Correspondance*, ed. cit., I, 70–71).

107. Bentham, who thoroughly enjoyed (at least one other person did!) the treatise on *Félicité publique*, and got in touch with the author (Halévy, op. cit., I, 25, 289), found Chastellux's glorious certainty to be poetic fancy however, and considered perfect happiness to be as chimerical as the philosopher's stone and the universal elixir (Bury, op. cit., p. 230). Nevertheless Chastellux's economic ideas, in particular those on the public debt and the influence of state expenditure on employment (op. cit., II, 323–55), if original, would merit the charitable attention of some "Keynesians."

108. *Félicité publique*, ed. cit., II, 184n.

century Europe. History offers us a picture of terrible sufferings even in the centuries of Pericles and Augustus, even after the advent of Christianity,[109] right up until the Renaissance. We are thus at the dawn of a palingenesis. There is little to admire in our ancestors. But our lovable contemporaries offer us some consolation. And great things can be expected from our grandchildren.[110] So, *tout va très bien, Monsieur le Marquis?* Not exactly, but *ça ira.* Already a contemporary could write: "If Jean-Jacques was the *philosophe Tant-Pis,* M. de Chastellux persists in his desire to be the *philosophe Tant-Mieux.*"[111] And indeed, after a glance round at the various nations of Europe, Chastellux concludes: "I would not say, all's well, but all is better. There is some progress: the world gives cause for hope."[112] Do we smile a bitter smile? . . . or should we delude ourselves still, as Zanella's great refrain runs through our heads: "If the earth still enfolds slaves and tears, it is because it is young"?

Among the most certain signs of the imminent *instauratio* of a better order are the insurrection and new institutions of the thirteen colonies. Here again the present is all dazzling light, dispelling the thick shadows of antiquity, ignorance, and despotism. The American continent too has had a most unfortunate history. In the geological past it was submerged by the oceans that split it in two and tore off the Antilles. Its flora developed, but—and with this facile antithesis Chastellux approaches Buffon's most perilous theories—the fauna there suffered "a slow degradation in the species."[113] The savages, and particularly their women, lived a wretched life, migrating en masse to search for food. Many of them are still "almost animals," and it seems unlikely that the Fuegians and the Patagonians will ever emerge from that humiliating state. But the impatient philosopher turns his back on them: *"There is nothing obliging us to fix our gaze on such sad objects,* and only the progress of the per-

---

109. Chastellux's irreligion is not aggressive, but radical. When invited to contribute an article to the *Supplément de l'Encyclopédie* on his speciality, "public happiness," he found his work suppressed by the censor "because the name of God did not appear in it even once" (Quérard, *sub voce;* Varnum, op. cit., p. 116).

110. Chastellux admires Frederick II, for example (op. cit., I, 137), considerably more than Alexander the Great (I, 176–78, 238–39; II, 134). And he is as savage as de Pauw was to be against the supposed virtues of the Spartans (I, 53–61). On the Chinese he finds himself in some embarrassment, caught between his inclination to dismiss them as the people least susceptible to progress (they remained in a "reasonable infancy") and Voltaire's unshakable sinophilia (cf. above, pp. 150–54): and he gets out of it by excusing himself from "entering into more detail on the subject of a people on whom several modern publications, such as the travels of Anson and the observations of M. Pavgh [a curious spelling of our friend de Pauw!] have cast so much obscurity that it is still very difficult at the present moment to judge them in a solid and impartial manner" (op. cit., I, xxii n.). If he read the first *Recherches* the bitter pessimism and de Pauw's insistence on the degenerative processes must have struck him as blasphemy.

111. *Correspondance* of Grimm, Diderot, etc., XV, 103.

112. *Félicité publique,* II, 82, 131.

113. Ibid., I, 174.

fected species can concern us."[114] The savage is not a man. If he were, he would be at least a little civilized. But then he would not be "the abominable savage.". . .

When the Europeans arrived they destroyed the wretched natives. The accursed thirst for gold, which is ever opposed to the "true economy," drove them to those bloody conquests. Did they not bring Christianity, at least? In South America the converts are actually still idolaters.[115] But this is time past. Today America too shares in the progress of liberty and reason. Solon and Lycurgus can retreat into the shadows when a John Locke and William Penn appear on the scene.[116] And every true philosopher must long for an end to the war between England and the colonies so that "America might continue to people and perfect itself; for reason and legislation and the happiness resulting therefrom can never spread too far on this globe where everything is linked together."[117]

With this favorable disposition barely tempered by his maturer age Chastellux crossed the Atlantic in 1780 and made three long tours through the United States. His general opinion is unchanged. A faithful follower of the great Buffon, "the most illustrious figure of our age," and moreover one of the naturalist's oldest friends[118] — Chastellux accepts his geological theories and follows him in repeating that America is a part of the world only recently emerged from the waters.[119] Its earth is in general unproductive and is particularly sterile in Virginia.[120] The climate of the warmer areas brings an inclination to laziness; and the natives, or at least those that Chastellux came across, are "hideous," not infrequently stupid, and react to the oppression of the white man by becoming crueler than ever. One of the consequences of peace — prophesies Chastellux accurately — will be their total destruction or their complete banish-

---

114. Ibid., I, 232; II, 270, 286–87; my italics. "The progress of the perfected species"? No need to wait for Leopardi and his sneers at our "golden age" (*Palinodia*) and its "magnificent and progressive destiny" (*La Ginestra*). A contemporary of Chastellux, the caustic Chamfort, an idealizer of the savages out of hate for society, a sympathizer with the Quakers as a result of his polemics against the rabble of priests, bursting with vitriol and epigrammatic rancor, prefaced his collection of maxims, vignettes, and anecdotes with the sarcastic title: *The Products of Perfected Civilization.*

115. Op. cit., I, 47, 232; II, 101.

116. Ibid., II, 137; cf. Lavergne, op. cit., p. 292.

117. Op. cit., II, 236.

118. Ibid., p. 330; cf. Varnum, op. cit., pp. 17–18, 32, 180, 201; Bertin, ed., *Buffon*, p. 40 ("He is Demosthenes writing the observations of Aristotle"). Buffon had welcomed Chastellux into the Academy, showering him with the ritual eulogies (*Correspondance* of Grimm, Diderot, etc., XI, 66–70; Lavergne, op. cit., p. 302; Varnum, op. cit., p. 132); and it was Chastellux that would introduce (1787) Jefferson to Buffon (Villard, op. cit., p. 334; but cf. above, p. 263, and, more significantly, Buffon's letter of 31 October 1785, inviting Chastellux and Jefferson to dinner: *Papers,* IX, 130). The science of nature, says Chastellux, emerged whole from Buffon's head like Minerva from Jove's (*Félicité publique,* ed. cit., II, 124n.; cf. Lavergne, op. cit., pp. 319–20).

119. *Voyages,* I, 41–42; II, 309; Buffon praised the *Voyages* highly: Varnum, op. cit., pp. 180, 182.

120. Op. cit., II, 144; on this point Mazzei replied to Chastellux (*Recherches,* IV, 193–94) explaining that the Virginians called any land not fit for tobacco "poor land."

ment from the region between the sea and the Great Lakes.[121] As for the American animals, and the relative ease with which they can be domesticated, the subject is discussed at length when the marquis visits Jefferson, who at that very time was busy drafting his *Notes on Virginia*.[122] And on Jefferson's estate he is particularly interested to see some specimens of the elk, the only wild animal of the region, that he finds to be quite unlike any European species. Its antlers are short, one and a half feet at most; however, he adds in a footnote, he has been assured (doubtless by Jefferson himself; see above, pp. 264–65) that when the elk is old his horns are as long as a deer's.[123] And lastly, when he finds an extraordinarily large and savage-looking caterpillar, he presents this "splendid insect" to abbé Robin, who offers us an admiring and minute description of it.[124]

But his scarce interest in these problems comes out more clearly when he touches on America's much-discussed lack of songbirds. Chastellux does not bother to explain this singularity, nor does he show any distress over this muteness of the vast forests, in fact jokes about the fact that "the nightingale does not sing in America." The great musicians, as we know, frequent the courts of despots, not the fora of republics. ("Beside Kings will he sit and sing, / Adorned with gold and jewels," had already been said of one melodious castrato.)[125] In free America there is thus no reason why one should find either "the gracious *Millico,* or the pathetic *Tenducci.*" But America does have, and rightly, "le bouffon *Caribaldi,*"[126]

---

121. Op. cit., I, 338–39; II, 154; and cf. Varnum, op. cit., p. 189. Very shortly afterward, in 1789, Henry Knox, Secretary for War and thus the person responsible for relations with the Indians, confirmed that they had disappeared completely in the more civilized parts of the republic: and announced that "in a short period, the idea of an Indian on this side of the Mississippi will only be found in the page of the historian" (quoted by Pearce, *The Savages,* p. 56; cf. p. 59). Toward the white men (cf. also above, pp. 588–89) Chastellux displays an attitude of indulgent superiority: of the astronomer "Rittenhausen" (*sic,* for Rittenhouse, of course, who had been lauded by Jefferson: cf. above, p. 262) he speaks as of someone with a natural talent for mechanics and clockmaking: he knows a little astronomy too, but "he is not a mathematician of the order of the Eulers and the d'Alemberts": op. cit., I, 193–94. In any case, he adds, in a somewhat de Pauwian spirit, the almanac is almost the only book of astronomy studied at Philadelphia. . . .

122. Chastellux mentions that in 1781 Jefferson composed "an excellent memorandum . . . of which he had a few copies printed last year [1785?], under the modest title *Notes on Virginia,* or rather without any title, for this work has not been made public." But a well-known scholar was able to use it, and is about to publish some *Observations sur la Virginie,* which Chastellux warmly recommends (op. cit., II, 304n.; cf. Varnum, op. cit., p. 175). The *Observations* are none other than the French version of the *Notes* by the very well-known Morellet (who also wrote against Brissot, in defense of Chastellux, a reply that remained unpublished: Varnum, op. cit., pp. 20, 183).

123. *Voyages,* II, 39–41; on the American rabbit, and its difference from the European one, ibid., II, 78–79.

124. Charles Robin, op. cit., p. 114.

125. G. Parini, *La musica,* written ca. 1769, but published only in 1791.

126. These names mean nothing to us today, but they were once household words. *Millico* is the Apulian composer and soprano Giuseppe Millico (1739–1802), who was very much admired by Gluck, Fanny Burney (see Charles Burney, *An Eighteenth Century Musical Tour,* ed. Scholes [London, 1959], II, 90), and Mlle de Lespinasse (a good friend of Chastellux): "Never, no never, has perfection of voice been joined with so much sensitivity and expressiveness. What tears it brings to the eyes! What agitation he brings to the soul! I was overwhelmed: nothing has ever made a deeper, more touching, more heartrending impression on me; but I would have liked to listen to it until I died from listening.

though heaven knows why the baritone belongs in a republic, and the sopranos not; perhaps because he has not suffered the eviration which, Parini would say, debases human dignity?—and the bird in question would be the famous mockingbird, which however, if the truth be told, does not sing: "He has no song and consequently no sentiment properly his own," but of an evening imitates to perfection what he has heard during the day;[127] which really parrotlike quality one would think more fitted to the gossiping antechambers of an absolute monarchy than the debating halls of a free senate.

One can readily understand that a man of such lighthearted and playful spirit cared little for the Quakers: on one occasion he mentions in passing their greed for profit;[128] and after describing a cordial and almost affectionate conversation with one of them, Bénezet, a mild-mannered little old man but aglow with love for the human race—"he is, without doubt, a respectable creature"—he devotes a couple of pages to the sad "sect," which he considers hypocritical, mean, and shamelessly fraudulent, and attends a meeting where—to his utter amazement and disbelief—a woman addresses the gathering,[129] then one of the men holds forth on mystical enlightenment, and finally an old man utters a most pedestrian prayer.[130]

Oh, how preferable this death would have been to life!" (letter to the Comte de Guibert, 29 August 1774, in *Lettres de Mlle de Lespinasse*, ed. cit., I, 123, 217–18).

Of the "celebrated sopranist" from Siena, G. F. *Tenducci* (1736–1800, according to the *Enciclopedia Italiana*) Giacomo Casanova tells us how one evening he took his five pretty Hanoverians to hear him at Covent Garden, and was very much surprised, but not by his voice so much as by the fact that although he was a *castrato* he had a wife and two children—which was apparently possible thanks to a generous anatomical peculiarity described in the *Mémoires*, Garnier ed., VII, 43 (on these two, see also Sir George Grove's *Dictionary of Music and Musicians*).

On *Caribaldi* (Gioacchino, 1743–?), who sang in the house of another of Chastellux's lady friends, Mme d'Epinay, the latter wrote to Galiani: "Ah, what a singer, this Caribaldi! I have heard him twice in my house: truly, he makes my head spin" (Nicolini, ed., *Gli ultimi anni*, pp. 221, 291). On a certain Garibaldi, who was however a tenor, with "a pleasing voice, and much taste and expression," see Burney, op. cit., I, 69, 76.

Chastellux's passion for music and singing is known and documented (see his *Essai sur l'union de la poésie et de la musique*, 1765; and, on the "union of a Pergolesi with a Metastasio," also the *Félicité publique*, ed. cit., II, 126; Varnum, op. cit., pp. 35–48, 66–67, 152). Jefferson, who owned a copy of the *Félicité publique*, dedicated his *Thoughts on English Prosody* to Chastellux (*Catalogue of the Library*, III, 33; see frequent mentions in the *Papers*, vol. IX–XIII, esp. X, 498–99).

127. *Voyages*, I, 132–33; Chastellux did not hear it then, but later he delighted in its song. On other melodious birds, cf. ibid., II, 18, and esp. II, 79, on the thrush, "America's nightingale."

128. Op. cit., I, 155. Anti-Quaker expressions occur already in the first *Voyage* of 1781. Even the "very American" Lafayette, much admired by Chastellux, derided that "ugly race of people, the stupid Quakers" (André Maurois, *Adrienne, ou La vie de Madame de la Fayette* [Paris, 1960], pp. 85, 123).

129. Twenty years earlier, when Boswell told him that in a Quaker meeting he had heard a woman preach, Dr. Johnson retorted with the famous remark: "Sir, a woman's preaching is like a dog's walking on his hind legs. It is not done well; but you are surprised to find it done at all" (31 July 1763; Boswell, *Life of Dr. Johnson*, ed. cit., I, 286–87). Dr. Johnson too, like Chastellux, said "that he liked individuals among the Quakers but not the sect" (22 March 1776: ibid., I, 624; cf. also 28 April 1784, ibid., II, 463). One of the plates illustrating the greatest curiosities in the New World, in Compagnoni's *Storia dell'-America* (Milan, 1821–23, 29 vols.), represents a "Quakeress preaching" between two spellbound (or sleeping?) coreligionists (vol. XXV, pp. 102–03).

130. *Voyages*, I, 240, 244–46. Another noble writer, the Catholic Vicomte de Chateaubriand, was to satirize the American Quakers and their supposed unselfishness (*Essai sur les révolutions*, 1797; cf. above, p. 355).

And that's all. Apart from one or two other passing jibes[131] Chastellux pays no further attention to the Quakers, of either sex. The Moravian Brothers and the Negroes, for example, are discussed at much greater length.[132] But these few phrases were enough for Brissot. They offered him the occasion or rather the excuse to attack this fortunate narrative (and simultaneously its noble author, the Academy to which he belonged, and the moderate ideas it expressed) with his *Examen critique* (or, as he was to call it later, his *Réfutation*) of Chastellux's journey: a small work which right up until the eve of his execution he considered to be among the best that had issued from his indefatigable pen.[133]

From that moment the Quakers are his benjamins, the perfection of all gentlemanly virtues, the victims of a libertine's insolence. After five years and the short visit to America (and after Mazzei's new attack), the portrait is enriched with fresh and glowing colors. The Quakers are virtuous and therefore happy, philanthropic and industrious, egalitarian, well brought up, clean, and rationalist.[134] In homage to their austerity, Brissot stops powdering his hair.[135] It is through their work, and particularly the apostle Bénezet's, that Negro slavery will soon be abolished throughout the continent.[136] Nor is it true that the Quakers are melancholy. This is what the French say, for whom anyone is sad who is not bursting with joviality. The Quakers have the serenity of the wise, for whom silliness is no cause for laughter. They don't play the fool.

Whoever slanders them can only be either evil-minded or stupid. Mazzei is the spokesman of the slave-owning plantation men, Chastellux is a

131. Cf. ibid., I, 278, 280; II, 140–41.
132. On the former, see op. cit., II, 250–59; on the latter, II, 145–51, with some sensible comments: already in the *Félicité publique* Chastellux had ridiculed Aristotle's thesis on natural slavery (cf. above, pp. 67 ff.).
133. Brissot's *Mémoires*, ed. cit., I, 46; III, 211–12. The full title of the pamphlet is in fact: *Examen critique des Voyages dans l'Amérique septentrionale de M. le Marquis de Châtellux ou Lettre à M. le Marquis de Châtellux dans laquelle on réfute principalement ses opinions sur les Quakers, sur les Négres, sur le Peuple et sur l'homme. . . .* On this opuscule, which I have not seen, cf. Varnum, op. cit., pp. 180–83; Stark, op. cit., pp. 80–81; Villard, op. cit., pp. 330–31; *Catalogue of the Library of Jefferson*, IV, 219. In 1786 Chastellux, together with a select group of friends of America, like the Duc de La Rochefoucald, Lafayette, Condorcet, Mazzei, and Crèvecoeur, had heard a lecture or "discussion on American politics and commerce by a Mr. Warville: the tendency of whose performance is good," wrote David Humphreys to Jefferson (letter of 17 March 1786; *Papers*, IX, 330), "some of the observations new, many of them just and ingenious: but perhaps there is too much declamation blended with them." And Jefferson wrote back, some months later: "A violent criticism of Chastellux's voiages is just appearing. It is not yet to be bought" (letter of 14 August 1786; *Papers*, X, 251). He must certainly have been referring to the work by Brissot, to whom Jefferson wrote two days later to congratulate him on his volume *De la France et des Etats-Unis, Papers*, X, 261–63; cf. X, 385; and on Jefferson's dealings with Brissot, again in X, 514–15, 623, 630, 637, 638–39.
134. *Nouveau voyage*, I, xxv, 103, 117–18, 239–40, 272–76, 295; III, 443–44; and especially II, 167–249 in direct polemic against Mazzei and Chastellux on pp. 190–211. Garat was to say that Brissot's supreme ambition was to be "Europe's Penn . . . to convert the human race into a community of Quakers, and to turn Paris into a new Philadelphia" (*Larousse*).
135. Gidney, op. cit., p. 45.
136. *Nouveau voyage*, I, 443.

conceited ignoramus. Brissot devotes a whole chapter to considering which of the two was more unjust and malevolent toward that worthy sect.[137] And of Chastellux he states with error of fact but accuracy of insight into his weak points that he "never heard and never saw" a single Quaker in America, and that it is only to keep in fashion "and to please the pretty girls that he jokes about interior grace. What faith can one have in such a traveler?"[138]

But the Quakers are not the only subject on which the commoner impugns the Marquis. He makes it almost a point of honor to contradict him, if not precisely in everything, at least on every fundamental question. Brissot had spent only four months in America; but the very title *Nouveau voyage* seems designed to supersede and suppress the academician's *Voyage*. Rousseau's disciple stands up boldly to the follower of Voltaire. Thus the skirmishing is no novelty to us, but does contain some interest, as further proof of the universality of that radical antithesis and the facility with which America became involved, or rather used, in an essentially European dispute.

If Chastellux showed himself satisfied, at least relatively, with the "magnificent and improving fortunes" (to borrow Leopardi's phrase) of the Europe of his day, Brissot sees nothing but decadence: "Almost everywhere, in Europe, the villages and towns are falling into ruin, rather than growing."[139] While the Voltairian is full of enthusiasm for the life and luxury of the big cities, and sceptical about the rustic virtues of the plough, Brissot, mindful of Jean-Jacques (and herein more than ever a Girondist *avant-lettre*), rejoices that in America there are absolutely none of "these capitals, these monstrous excrescences, which, being no more than a product of degradation, defile everything they contain."[140] There are not "and there will never be, in America, big cities." The population there will multiply, but it will remain spread out "and yet communicating from New Hampshire to Quito,"[141] forming a sort of immense gar-

---

137. Ibid., II, 190–211, 215n., 237n. Mazzei praises Chastellux's *Voyages*, though with reservations (*Recherches*, IV, 185–204), and recognizes in particular: "His observations on the way of life of the inhabitants are very true; *the same can fairly be said for everything he states about the Quakers*" (ibid., pp. 185–86, my italics).

138. Ibid., II, 193. Brissot, on the other hand, admits that he never attended a meeting (*Nouveau voyage*, II, 227).

139. Ibid., I, 238; cf. Galiani, above, p. 178.

140. *Nouveau voyage*, III, 435; cf. also I, 214 (less poverty and less bad faith in the country than in the city); *Mémoires*, I, 248, and passim. Along the same lines are his admiration for Bernardin de Saint-Pierre (see *Nouveau voyage*, I, 308–09; *Mémoires*, III, 132) and his antipathy for Beaumarchais and his "scandalous farce" of *Figaro* (ibid., III, 17n.).

141. Ibid., II, 437–38; cf. de Maistre's no less audacious prophecy, above, p. 393. Even Philadelphia seems to Brissot (as it had to abbé Robin: see *Nouveau voyage*, p. 94; and cf. Varnum, op. cit., p. 186; and as it was to seem a few years later to Bayard, who insisted more however on commercial dishonesty: *Voyage*, pp. 243–47) to be tainted with some hints of libertinage; but the foreign sailors are responsible, of course! (*Nouveau voyage*, I, 294–95).

den city, in which the age-old virtues of the farmer will be kept intact. Even if there were two hundred million men in America they could all be landowners, they could all be free and independent.[142]

This "agrarian idealism" was perfectly in line with the political maxims of the founding fathers, who had nothing but admiration for the intact gifts of the tillers of the soil, and likewise for those physiocratic theories so easily translated into allegories of the richness of the earth and panegyrics of the peasant, and who thus hoped to see the new republic based on agriculture, and who could therefore object with equal energy to the Indian on the one side, despised as a nomad and hunter,[143] and the Englishman on the other, for his dependence on trade and navigation. They felt themselves to be heirs of Abel, not of Cain; of Jacob, not of Esau; not of Nimrod, but of Cincinnatus, in whose name they founded an order of chivalry; and as the contrite and grateful recipients, at this peak of so much ethical purity, of a God-given mission to exterminate the redskins and drop British merchandise into the sea. Thus one can understand Jefferson's enthusiasm over the Brissotian demonstration that the United States would be "more virtuous, more free, and more happy, employed in agriculture, than as carriers or manufacturers," and the copious compliments he heaped on its author.[144]

There was another polemical suggestion in Brissot that must have pleased the author of the *Notes on Virginia*. If Chastellux had referred (see above, n. 96) to the Americans' precocious senility and short lifespan, here was Brissot standing forth and demonstrating with an impressive display of statistical and actuarial tables that they were if anything more longeval than the Europeans. This notion then, of the very high

142. *Nouveau voyage*, I, xv.

143. Cf. Pearce, *The Savages*, pp. 66–67, 220, 235, indicating in the book of *Genesis* and in Vattel (ibid., pp. 70–71) the authorities legitimizing a natural supremacy of agricultural societies over hunting societies. For Franklin too, agriculture was the only honest means of earning money (see Jones, *Pursuit of Happiness*, pp. 91n., 151). This line of reasoning follows the Aristotelian argument of the natural supremacy of the free man to the brute slave (on which see above, p. 67). Thus in order to justify their subjugation of the American natives of North and South the invaders enrolled in their ranks the highest spiritual authorities of the European West, of biblical and classical antiquity, when in point of fact they needed no more than their firearms, a little technology, and alcoholic beverages. But their concern with providing a rational justification of the conquests, even if it led to an abuse of truly sacred texts, was fundamentally to the credit of those conscientious and tormented bearers of civilization. The "white man's burden" is, in comparison, a crude, barbarous, and hypocritical thesis.

144. Letter of 16 August 1786. Jefferson owned copies of almost all Brissot's works: see *Catalogue of the Library*, I, 128; II, 56, 59–60; III, 26–27, 57–58, 72, 81–82, 85, 97, 213–14, 454 and esp. 463. On the relations between them see also *Papers*, vols. IX–XIII, with a hint of distrust on Jefferson's part: "I don't know Warville's business in America. I suspect him to be agent of a company on some speculation of lands," etc., written in cypher to Madison (letter of 3 May 1788, *Papers*, XIII, 131–32). "Those who labour in the earth," Jefferson pontificated, "are the chosen people of God if ever He had a chosen people" (*Writings*, II, 229, quoted by R. Niebuhr, op. cit., p. 27; cf. above, chap. 7, n. 155, and on the precedents for Jefferson's agrarianism, H. N. Smith, *Virgin Land*, pp. 125–28, 203. On its physiocratic origins, *The Correspondance of Jefferson and Du Pont de Nemours*, with an introduction on Jefferson and the Physiocrats by Gilbert Chinard (Baltimore, 1931), pp. xliv–lx. On Jefferson's Rousseauian aversion for that refined form of urban civilization, the theater, see *Papers*, XII, 498–99.

mortality rate among American men and the visible old age of American women over twenty-five, is one more prejudice that must be destroyed, even if it was put about by the abbé Robin.[145] As a matter of fact, "I believe M. Paw had spun these yarns before he did."[146]

Brissot, like the Marquis, pays careful attention to the figure, complexion, and feminine charm of the American woman: but here too he is definitely more austere than the nobleman, disregarding the young girls, and his admiration stretches to include even the seventy-year-olds: "I have carefully observed the women between thirty and fifty; most of them are buxom, in good health, charming even. . . . I have seen this same good health shine in the women of sixty or seventy."[147] He is quick to criticize the elegance of those of less venerable age however, and even more their mincing ways, their affectations and flirtatiousness. When invited to dine with the Virginian Griffin, President of Congress, he is quite upset when he finds

seven or eight women, all decked out in large hats, feathers, etc. I noted, with regret, much pretension in some of these women. . . . Two of them had their bosoms quite revealed. I was scandalized by such indecency among republican women.[148]

A delightful scene—and not unfamiliar, surely: "Cover that breast, for I have no wish to look upon it. Such objects wound the soul, and lead to guilty thoughts."[149]

If at times the good Brissot blushes and averts his gaze, there are other moments where he quite gives himself away. In his polemic and apologetic zeal he was bound to go too far sooner or later: and this is exactly what happens for instance when he comes to the defense of a certain lady that Chastellux had portrayed in these malicious terms:

I was introduced to a rather ridiculous personage, one who however plays a particular role in the town; a certain Miss V——, famous for her coquetry, her wit and spitefulness; she is thirty, and does not seem to be about to marry. Meanwhile she covers herself with rouge, and white and blue and every color imagi-

145. A self-confessed mason, at that, and admirer of the Quakers, and author of a *Nouveau voyage dans l'Amérique septentrionale en l'année 1781 et Campagne de l'armée de M. de Rochambeau* (Philadelphia–Paris, 1782), on whom see Fay, *L'esprit*, pp. 120–21 ("he takes up the old tales of abbé de Pauw and Raynal"), p. 165; idem, *Bibliographie critique*, p. 53; Varnum, op. cit., pp. 185–88.
146. *Nouveau voyage*, II, 140: de Pauw is not cited any further. Because Brissot too prefers to ignore him?! The climate of the United States strikes him as being fairly similar to that of Paris: op. cit., I, 30, 374; III, 122.
147. Ibid., loc. cit., see also *Mémoires*, II, 237.
148. *Nouveau voyage*, I, 247–48; see also II, 81–82.
149. Molière, *Tartuffe*, III, 2. Bayard is similarly horrified: "I have learned, since the publication of my *Voyage*, that the women wore diamonds." A bad sign: soon those innocent little Republicans will be trading their charms "to have the stupid pleasure of decorating their arms with a few rocks, whose glitter doesn't even equal the glow of a candle" (*Voyage*, p. 266).

nable, dresses herself and her hair in the most extraordinary fashion, and as a good Whig in everything, sets no bounds to her liberty.[150]

This last touch in particular sends Brissot into a fury: he forgets the discretion so carefully observed by the marquis, and screams to the whole wide world that it is all slander, that the agreeable Miss *Vining* in Wilmington, although she may perhaps have been a little flirtatious, was never anything but unreproachable in her conduct. Even the Quakers admit it! And a Frenchman should be the last person to slander her, since Miss Vining, "pretty, amiable, affable, witty, . . . always showed much partiality for the French nation," and opened her house to all the officers of Lauzun's legion. Chastellux himself "received only politeness from Miss Vining. If she painted herself red or white, what did it matter to him?" The paladin Brissot, in short, is ready to thrust his hand into the fire to prove that the girl is a model of modesty and reserve. Chastellux's jibes — one can only hope it was not Brissot himself that passed them on — wounded her deeply.[151]

With the same sanguine self-assurance Brissot maintains that it is quite possible to educate and civilize the savages,[152] and that the commercial servitude imposed by the English justifies certain somewhat "primitive" customs of the inhabitants of Virginia, such as blowing their noses with their fingers — "I observed this habit among very well-brought-up Americans" — or using for that purpose a silk handkerchief which later serves as cravat, table napkin, etc.[153]

Anyone remembering Chastellux's comment (p. 587) and inclined to include too much else in this all-embracing textual "etcetera," and holding his nose at such a crude spectacle of the colonists' civilization, finds

150. *Voyages,* I, 269–70. In the 1st ed., destined for a few friends, the name of the lady was printed in full. Accepting or rather forestalling a suggestion from Jefferson, Chastellux softened several other "strictures on some . . . ladies" in the edition for release to the public (see *Papers,* VII, 580–83, 584–86; cf. above, n. 88, and Varnum, op. cit., pp. 146–49). But still forty years later there was somebody who felt impelled to come to the defense of the young ladies of America against the impertinent Marquis: the beautiful and fiery Miss Wright, though she admired "the respected author of the *Félicité publique,*" fails to recognize him in the mocking aristocrat who "permits himself to speak ill of the women who indulge their innocent gaiety in his presence, and to pour scorn on those who had impressed him with their reserve." She does not however go so far as to agree with Brissot's verdict on Chastellux's book (*Voyage,* II, 219–20n.).

151. *Nouveau voyage,* I, 253–54. Brissot does not however mention Chastellux's most serious crime: describing a lady as thirty when in fact she was seven or eight years younger: "Miss Vining . . . who *at 25* was the belle of Philadelphia *in 1783,* spoke French fluently and with elegance, a fact which 'made her a general favorite with the French officers' who wrote to Paris about her, and excited the curiosity of Marie Antoinette" (Jones, *French Culture,* p. 194, citing in footnote: "Griswold, R. W., *The Republican Court, or American Society in the Days of Washington.* New York, 1855, p. 85 [?]. She corresponded with many distinguished men, and Lafayette was attached to her"). An occasional malicious little reference to Miss Vining occurs also in Liancourt, op. cit., p. 64, and possibly 98.

152. *Nouveau voyage,* I, 107–08. Ingenuous as he was and totally impervious to irony, Brissot took Polly Baker's notorious speech (see above, p. 260) quite seriously, and, with his usual impetuosity, had Polly asking, in his translation, not for "*a* statue" — as the original text jokingly said — but "*some* statues," no less! (M. Hall. op. cit., pp. 73–75).

153. *Nouveau voyage,* II, 275.

himself obliged to think again when he comes to Brissot's comparison of American and European latrines, to the full advantage of the former. "Have you observed," he begins in doctoral tones, "the places in our countryside where men and women go to satisfy their needs?" And he describes them to us, and to counteract any possible objection that after all one cannot really be too demanding in the country, he pursues his refrain — "Have you observed these same places in the houses of our dainty Parisians, in the homes of the great lords themselves, who think they can make up for cleanliness with luxury?" (Anything and everything becomes ammunition in his polemic against the big cities and the great lords — even toilet sewage!) In America, on the other hand, wherever one goes, even in the depths of the forest, one can find in the garden of every house, but thirty or forty paces removed from the building, "a little hut that is very clean, often decorated even, destined for this operation": and always containing, through a delightful "fatherly attentiveness . . . a lower seat for the children."[154] In the bathroom contest America leaves Europe a long way behind. And its victory represents the consecration and exaltation of its prime ideals (worshiped today more than ever), Technology and Hygiene, gadgets and conveniences.

In the matter of the fine arts and useful crops, on the other hand, Brissot reverts to the most austere severity, to a worse than Spartan rigorism. Chastellux, as we saw (above, n. 126), was a lover of music and song. Brissot even finds it suspicious that music is so carefully fostered in Europe, that its taste is spreading, that it is becoming part of the school curriculum. "Is the same true for America?" No, fortunately. "I believe that this gift is no use for anything, except possibly to the other frivolous studies with which it is associated." The study of music actually hinders any other study: "Music leads to ceaseless study, to seeing always beyond what one knows [Brissot did not know how right he was!]; and what good can come to men from something so foreign to the useful sciences, and which occupies the time most properly given to study?" At this point the arguments reflect the Platonic condemnation of poetry; but the conclusion echoes Rousseau's anathema for the theater: "Does America need spectacles too?"[155]

Unfortunately a fatal attraction for music has already seized hold of

154. Ibid., I, 162–63; the ship that took him from Newport to New York also had at the stern "two very comfortable recesses, to serve as privy places" (ibid., I, 221). Another malodorous tale: I, 277.

155. Ibid., I, 31. Brissot is delighted to note that Philadelphia, through the work of the Quakers, has been spared the danger of theaters (ibid., II, 227; cf. III, 176, etc.). On some reactions aroused by Brissot's Catonism among the young North Americans, see Villard, op. cit., p. 256. In Europe one of the first reviewers, Forster, although lavish in his praise of the work, commented shrewdly on the author's "Spartan rigor," his aversion for rugs and high-class ladies' lingerie, and the "democratic disdain" of his criticisms of that "fine wit" Chastellux, the "mocking" Mazzei, etc. (*Werke*, III, 375–403, esp. 382–83, 390).

Boston. "In some rich homes [it's always the "rich" that introduce these vices!] the pianoforte can be heard." The girls play pretty badly, true – but so much the better! "May Heaven see to it that the ladies of Boston are not like our own Frenchwomen, struck down with the malady of perfection in music! It is only ever acquired at the expense of the domestic virtues."[156] Wrong notes become the Vestals.

Following much the same lines is the polemic against the cultivation of the vine: the vine that Mazzei had acclimatized in Virginia and in which Jefferson too placed so much hope; but which was grown by man to make wine, which is in the first place a dangerous beverage, and which in the second place is already and will continue to be exportable from France to the United States at unbeatably competitive prices. So let the Americans heed the advice of the best qualified commentators, learn from others' experience, and not plant vines: "They will scrupulously avoid the culture of the vine. Wherever it is practiced it has led to the wealth of a few and the wretchedness of a great many." The vine is antiegalitarian, not in the least democratic or republican. "In the wine-growing countries the fatal influence of the vine extends even to those who do not grow it": low-priced wine, in fact, leads to drunkenness, and poisons and brutalizes all social classes, but particularly those who seek to drown their misery therein. The only way to moderate its use is to make it expensive: "rationing by the purse," we should say today. A free republic cannot of course want its citizens to get drunk too easily. "From all these observations, it becomes clear that the free Americans must proscribe the culture of the vine."[157]

And what should they grow, then? Potatoes, of course! "The potato – that's the food of the man who wants and knows how to be free." This "plant of liberty" grows anywhere and requires little attention: so the laborer is left with more time to attend public meetings.[158]

With politico-agronomic notions of this sort, it is obvious that Brissot

156. *Nouveau voyage*, I, 112–13; cf. Jones, *French Culture*, p. 335. His follower Bayard admitted on the other hand that among the American ladies there were some with good voices, but all lacked expression and sounded as if they were singing psalms even when intoning most impassioned love songs (*Voyage*, pp. 90–91). True, Bayard also admired the warbling of the American birds (ibid., pp. 13, 16, 29, 163), while he accepted the thesis that European fruits degenerated in America, and went so far as to add that if one might generalize such an observation "one would be led to conclude therefrom that Buffon's assertions, against which M. Jefferson argued so heatedly in his notes on Virginia, have more reality than the American philosopher thinks" (ibid., pp. 121–22).

157. *Nouveau voyage*, III, 129–34. Brissot recognizes however that the country people sometimes make excessive use of wine and brandy to augment the calories in their wretched diet (which in 1790 was called "remedying the lack of substantial foods"): "give them meat and potatoes, and they will easily do without wine" (ibid., III, 136). On the introduction of the vine into North America, through the work of the French peasants, see Villard, op. cit., pp. 47–66. On the excellent prospects for the culture of the vine in Virginia, see Mazzei, *Recherches*, III, 95–96, 101–02. Jefferson in his turn wrote to Brissot that drunkenness was not so widespread in America as he thought (16 August 1786, in *Catalogue of the Library*, III, 464).

158. *Nouveau voyage*, I, xv n.; III, 135n. Another verbal example of his frank utilitarianism is the eulogy of Franklin (whom he met "chez Marat": *Mémoires*, I, 249–54) for "his such philosophical dissertations on the way of preventing chimneys smoking" (*Nouveau voyage*, I, 323).

has neither understanding nor sympathy for the so much more rustic and simple Mazzei. He met him in Paris and recounts a conversation, which seems authentic, during which the Tuscan advised him good-naturedly to soften the tone of his criticism so as not to make too many enemies.[159] The reaction of the proud Brissot was to call Mazzei a hypocrite, coward, and slanderer of his "friends" — that is, the Quakers.[160] But as always his fury blinds him. If Mazzei observes in passing that the lunatic asylum in Philadelphia was probably not the first to be founded in America, and in any case "such curiosities are not of sufficient concern for one to want to take the trouble to verify them,"[161] in other words he has no interest in the question of priority, Brissot misunderstands or misrepresents his words, and talks sarcastically of his visit to that hospital "which the humane M. Mazzei regards as a mere curiosity, not worth the trouble of seeing.". . .[162]

And so the polemic proceeds — I'm sorry, so the polemic proceeded at the end of the eighteenth century.

VI. A LATECOMER AND HIS DISCIPLE: DROUIN DE BERCY AND GIUSEPPE COMPAGNONI

A "Latecomers" is a title that could be applied to a good number of the authors already reviewed, whether in regard to philosophy, historical thought, or the natural sciences. The polemic itself, in its fundamental form, debating whether the Old or New World is "better," is an intrusive logical fossil in late eighteenth-century Europe. Thus to call any disputant a "latecomer" we must have a good specific motive. The motive is this: Drouin de Bercy discusses and attacks de Pauw's thesis in 1818 as if its author had not been dead twenty years, indeed as if the *Recherches sur les Américains,* published half a century earlier, was hot from the press and demanding an immediate reply.

Not that Drouin de Bercy is unacquainted with de Pauw's numerous critics: he is familiar with them all, even the most minor and least-known ones, like the abbé Frisi, "the learned and judicious abbé Frisi, who remained unmoved by M. Paw's fantasies" and "noted several of his errors,"[163] and he makes use of them all, indiscriminately, either scholastically opposing authority to authority, or judicially crushing one witness with two, and two witnesses with four. But in the almost nine hundred pages of his work there is no trace of the least effort to see whether there were not some element of truth in the anti-American slanders, nor to

---

159. Op. cit., II, 190–92n.
160. Ibid., II, 239.
161. *Recherches,* IV, 101.
162. *Nouveau voyage,* I, 306, and using almost the same words, *Mémoires,* II, 62; cf. also *Nouveau voyage,* I, 324n. (a probable allusion).
163. *L'Europe et l'Amérique comparées* (Paris, 1818), II, 91.

understand, if they were really a total error, how this could come about and what significance it might have: thus there is no attempt at critical confutation, and the target of the polemic, de Pauw, is shown as so steeped in falsehood that the reader is left wondering what point there can be in quarreling so violently and at such length with an adversary so evidently inept and innocuous.

Drouin de Bercy's persistence thus seems inexplicable, and even disregarding the chronological question militates against his theories, leaving his arguments mechanical, insignificant, and boring. For all the wealth of documentation, reference, and quotation, Drouin de Bercy, the last of the "Creoles," reminds one of those Hispano-American polemicists discussed in chapter 6: one sees in him the same intransigence, the same obstinate refusal to see anything from his opponent's point of view, the same delight over the possibility of utilizing the debate to launch into panegyrics of the Americas or satire of poor little tormented and accursed Europe. Just as Mexico is defended against de Pauw and exalted against everyone by Clavigero, and Chile by Molina, and Central America by Valle, so Drouin de Bercy, "Settler and Landowner at Santo Domingo,"[164] can be looked on as the champion firstly of the Great Antilles, and then of the whole American continent.

Ensconced on his island home, the same where for decades Oviedo had patiently waited to collect accounts and depositions from whatever adventurers passed between one continent and the other, Drouin de Bercy feels himself in a position to "compare"—as the title of his book says—nearby America and distant Europe, and to pronounce his verdict in the case for slander brought by the former against the latter: guilty on all counts.

After spending, as he says, thirteen years in various parts of America, and reading the chroniclers, travelers, scientists, historians, and apologists of the continent—I have found more than seventy authors quoted in his pages—Drouin, convinced that America, rather than inferior, is in

164. So he proclaims himself on the frontispiece, and adds "Acting Lieutenant Colonel of the General Staff in the French Army, at the time of the expedition under General Leclerc" (the expedition of 1802, sent out by Napoleon to quell the revolt of the Negroes led by Toussaint Louverture). Neither qualification adds much luster to his obscure name (which remains so to Church too, op. cit., pp. 204–05, and to the diligent Remond, op. cit., pp. 259, 263, 334). Referring to "the French property owners who have homes and slaves" in Santo Domingo a Milanese businessman, Carlo Mantegazza, had written at just this time (in his *Viaggio a S. Domingo nell'anno 1802* [Milan, 1803], p. 84) that "while they do not lose in the Colony any of the defects of the mother country, they do not acquire either any of the virtues of the colonies, and in a short time their pride is pushed to such an extreme that they become ridiculous and barbarian." Of his officers on the General Staff the valiant Leclerc had such a low opinion that when he knew his end was near he called on the first consul to send someone to succeed him because "there is no-one here capable of taking my place" (T. L. Stoddard, *The French Revolution in Santo Domingo* [Boston–New York, 1914], p. 340). Drouin's other works: *De Saint-Domingue, de ses guerres, de ses révolutions, de ses ressources et des moyens à prendre pour rétablir la paix et l'industrie* (Paris, 1814); *Histoire civile et commerciale de la Jamaïque* (Paris, 1818).

everything and for everything superior to Europe, steps out at the head of this great band of authorities, against the solitary, lost, abandoned de Pauw. Once again the apology of the New World sets out from an individual polemic against the author of the *Recherches;* indeed for hundreds of pages it survives and nourishes itself solely on the unceasing hand-to-hand combat with this insolent writer.[165] The repeated rejection of de Pauw's malicious comments serves as the connecting thread binding together the Antillean landowner's panegyric. Already in the preface Drouin reminds his readers that some authors spoke badly of this or that part of the Americas, but that de Pauw thought to distinguish himself by slandering it *in toto* and *in omnibus partibus.* In him the sins of all the denigrators come together and take solid shape: he is the ready-made scapegoat, complete and willing.

The comparison-cum-bill-of-indictment proceeds methodically. Drouin compares the two hemispheres first of all from the point of view of climate and nature, then as regards the soil and its useful and harmful products. There follows the inevitable parallel of the animals, and lastly the defense of the natives, both physical and spiritual. The recapitulation of "America's advantages over Europe" culminates in hymns of praise to the former and a correlative depiction of the unhappiness and barbarity of the latter, afflicted by innumerable evils, among which Drouin lists at random the taxes,[166] the idiocies of the scholars, the infanticides, the trials for a husband's impotence, spies, the social inequalities, and the crimes resulting from poverty.

The time comparison is to America's advantage: although Drouin finds himself short of ancient traditions and leaves us in doubt as to which hemisphere might have a greater "historical" antiquity, he has no hesitation in asserting that "America is the oldest terrain on the globe"[167] and that its products facilitate the civilizing of its peoples, of those innocent natives, so sweet and goodnatured that they should be the ones called "civilized" in comparison with the "savage" Spaniards.[168] With this deliberate reversal of the current antithesis there emerges the idea of an American "civilization," wholly indigenous, tightly bound to the environ-

165. Drouin says yes, de Pauw did uncritically copy Buffon (II, 30), but none of his thunderbolts fall on the latter, though he is mentioned several times—once in fact to contradict the assertion made by de Pauw and others that America's land is cold and humid (ibid., I, 374). Of Robertson, on the other hand, who gave the weight of his authority to many of de Pauw's verdicts, he suggests that he denied a good number of unarguable facts "to pay court to M. Paw" (II, 390, 393).

166. The European pays the treasury for "the windows of his home, the rays of sunlight that cross his room" (according to the notorious French tax on "doors and windows," introduced precisely in year XII), "the electuaries destined for the maintenance of his teeth," and even his burial! (II, 440).

167. *L'Europe et l'Amérique,* I, 29; a little earlier, I, 18, he had cited Barton and Humboldt and their rejection of the thesis that America had emerged from the waters later than the Old World (see above, pp. 404, 406); cf. also II, 56.

168. Ibid., I, 15–16; II, 296, 446.

ment and disturbed or interrupted in its course by the appearance of swarms of bearded thundering savages.

The space comparison is to America's advantage: "The New World is a little [*sic*] larger than Europe." It has a better climate, higher mountains,[169] and its volcanoes too are in every way preferable to the European ones. Not that they are mightier and more violent, no, "M. Paw will not be able to say that America is more tormented than Europe by volcanoes" — but they are more beautiful, Cotopaxi, for example, and they contribute to the ventilation of the air. The "playful earthquake" of the little poem finds its precursor in those serviceable breezes. In America, in fact, "by an unparalleled bizarreness, nature has allowed the volcanoes to spew forth air instead of fire," so that they spread a delightful coolness in the heat of the tropics.[170] With the breath of these eruptive craters, what need of air conditioning?

Drouin expresses the same ingenuous admiration for the natural phenomena and curiosities, the prodigies and the marvels of America: it has bigger caves, more surprising echoes, infinitely richer mines, lakes and rivers that make it the "best-irrigated" region in the world (the final transformation of the old accusation of extreme humidity: from "sodden" and rotting, America becomes "well irrigated" and flourishing), cataracts, saltpans, natural bridges, and better winds than Europe, more numerous, wider, and deeper bays. As Rossetti put it: "Everything of thine is great, / Great are thy trees, thy mountains, rivers, seas!"[171] The passages from one sea to another are *nine* in America as against *three* in Europe (9–3, what a trouncing!). And where there is no channel, what a jewel of an isthmus! "Europe cannot flatter itself that it offers, as America does at Panama, an isthmus unparalleled in the whole world."[172] Nor certainly does Europe, nor the whole world, contain another spring like that found to the South of Coquimbo (in Chile), which gushes only once a month "through an opening similar to that part of the woman whose periodic flow it imitates."[173] Even America's fireflies are miraculously bright. God sent them so that the Americans might not remain in the dark. Just so: "It was the Creator's preference for the New World that made him want everything, right down to the insects, to be useful to the inhabitants of this fortunate climate."[174]

169. Ibid., I, 31–37; see above, pp. 112–13; Drouin does not seem to be acquainted with Delisle de Sales.

170. Ibid., I, 47–48.

171. Gabriele Rossetti, *Il veggente in solitudine* (Italy, 1846), p. 272. All the verses from p. 261 to p. 277 of the "polymetric poem" are dedicated to America.

172. *L'Europe et l'Amérique*, I, 141; see ibid., pp. 55–64 (caves), 64–65 (echoes), 65–69 (mines), 69 (natural bridges), 71 and 104 (lakes and rivers), 106 (waterfalls), 131 (gulfs), 142 (straits), 145 (winds).

173. Ibid., I, 51, citing *Voyageur français:* the detail could well have been used by the German who judged America essentially feminine (above, p. 392).

174. Ibid., I, 186, with evident reminiscence of Bernardin de Saint-Pierre's benign and providential Nature (quoted in I, 137, 183–84; II, 285).

By dint of this same benevolent protection America is, in the matter of natural calamities, one of the world's least troubled dwelling places. We have already heard of the refreshing influence of its volcanoes. Earthquakes and landslides are much less frequent there than in Europe, where Etna for example, after engulfing Nicolosi, threatens "the little town of Catania" with the same fate. And what will "M. Paw" be able to say when Drouin presents him with the list of the earthquakes suffered by the English, more than forty between A.D. 951 and the present time? The same goes for the frosts, avalanches, floods and droughts, pestilences and famines, grasshopper plagues, epidemics, wars and invasions: from every point of view, "Europe is worth even less than the New World."[175] Europe is crumbling and drying up: and there is also a danger of its being destroyed by a downpour of bolides and aerolites.[176]

Let us hope that does not happen, but its very atmosphere is pestilential. Everybody talks about America's swamps, and there are of course some, like the Dismal Swamp and others, but they are not at all unhealthy. In Europe, on the other hand, does de Pauw really think the air of Rome or Mantua is healthy? And what about the atmosphere of the murderous coal-mining areas? And what are the barren stretches of the New World compared to the sandy deserts of Asia, the steppes of Eastern Europe, the uncultivated and uncultivatable parts of France itself? The yield on European land is often nil and at the most touches 3 percent; in America, it goes from 5 to 6½ percent. American products, in fact, are of excellent quality, whether those transplanted, like the vine and the fruits, or those proper to the tropics, like coffee, rubber, tobacco, and sugar. Europe, strictly speaking, does not even have products of its own: its fruits and its flowers come from Asia. "What can Europe boast of?" Nothing, of course. In his anxiety to lower Europe in comparison with America, Drouin humiliates it with regard to Asia too, and thus breaks the traditional dichotomy of two worlds and two hemispheres, but opens the way to a new rivalry, between America and Asia, both bursting with autochthonous berries and corollas.[177]

When he comes to discussing the fauna Drouin again shifts his position of defense and counterattack. He denies, of course, that the American animals are smaller or decadent—indeed, the oysters are "four times bigger than the European ones"[178]—but he gets carried away by his an-

175. Ibid., I, 156.

176. Ibid., pp. 188–89.

177. Elsewhere, however, he reaffirms America's climatic superiority over Asia: the European, in fact, barren in India, is very fruitful in the New World (op. cit., I, 165–66).

178. Ibid., II, 58. But oysters are mollusks. And the slanderers of America had always admitted, indeed stressed the fact that the lower animals, the reptiles, insects, etc., were very numerous there and often of enormous dimensions. Drouin ridicules the story of the frogs bellowing like oxen (see above, chap. 6, n. 32); but he goes on to say that when he was in Pennsylvania he heard a "flying toad . . . whose cry was something like the baying of a bullock" (ibid., I, 381–82): ox or bullock, for a batrachian

thropocentric utilitarianism and is soon admitting that America has no wild beasts and monstrous animals. Thus he recognizes the fact, but only to discover therein one more of America's "excellences": de Pauw, instead of criticizing the Creator, should have thanked him for supplying the New World with animals that could be domesticated, and not with creatures like those of the Old World, untamably savage, and thanked him for destroying its elephants, rhinoceroses, and hippopotamuses, and "substituting" them with tapirs, peccaries, and anteaters.[179] All this refers to the land, of course, since in the waters of America, as is well known, there are no whirlpools nor marine creatures, and the sharks never harm swimmers: "They even touch them, without ever attacking them."[180]

The men are thus the Lord's beloved, and the three kingdoms of nature in America are disposed to increase their well-being and happiness. The continent was densely populated at the time of its discovery, and its inhabitants prolific and very healthy. Syphilis is a European disease, the fruit of inveterate lasciviousness and uncleanliness: twenty-two authors, from Moses and David to modern times, are quoted to free America from the suspicion of contagion.[181] The so-called hairlessness of the savage is a question of capillary topography: just let de Pauw take a look how much hair they have on their heads! As much as Europe's women.[182] The asserted cowardliness of the Americans is belied both by the natives' heroic resistance and by the colonists' recent rebellions, in the north and in the south. As for the former, then, how can de Pauw accuse them of being fainthearted and indolent? Look at the famous peoples of old, the Persians, the Greeks, the Romans, the Egyptians: what are they today? "Today they are the softest people, the most frivolous, the most cowardly."[183] With similar *tu quoque*'s Drouin exalts the American's mental gifts: if they are barbarians because they do not have iron the Spartans were barbarians too; if they are savages because they do not know how to

---

it's still quite some voice! With similar inconsistency Drouin vaunts the marvelous multiplication of the domestic animals, but of the famous camels, that de Pauw had described as having become barren in America (see above, pp. 57–58), all he can tell us is that two of them were brought to Santo Domingo, but ended up being eaten by the French soldiers in 1803.

179. Ibid., II, 68. Cf., for that matter, above, pp. 343 (Perrin du Lac), 373 (Lenau), 525 (Thoreau). A few pages previously, however, Drouin had accused de Pauw of "slandering" the valiant and fierce American felines (II, 58). . . .

180. Ibid., I, 126. Gómara had already admitted that there were very many and very large snakes in the Indies, but these *culebras* "were not so brave nor so poisonous as ours and the African ones" (*Historia general de las Indias,* quoted by M. Bataillon, "Un Chroniqueur Péruvien retrouvé: Rodrigo Lozano," *Cahiers de l'Institut des Hautes Etudes de l'Amérique Latine,* 2 [1961], p. 20). Cf. above, n. 4.

181. *L'Europe et l'Amérique,* II, 85–123; on the twenty-two authors, ibid., II, 96–97. Drouin also touches on the scabrous question of the artifices used by the native women to remedy a certain deficiency in their consorts (on which see above, chap. 5, n. 365): II, 107–09.

182. A two-edged argument, obviously; but Drouin uses it quite openly: II, 138–40. Cf. below, p. 624.

183. Another argument of dubious implications, because it seems to admit the previously denied present-day cowardliness of the American natives.

draw, the Chinese and Japanese are too, since "they still do not know how to draw correctly."[184]

In his fervor of enthusiasm Drouin occasionally chances to strike a new note, to discover some previously unmentioned excellence in America, as when he insists on the *intrinsic* literary value of the continent, listing the romances and tragedies and operas that it has inspired, from *Alzire* to *Atala:* or when he reverses and demolishes the traditional question of the benefits and the ills accruing to Europe from the discovery by maintaining that America assuredly lost a large amount by being discovered by the Europeans:[185] even the huge numbers of immigrants that come flocking to America are a real scourge — they are "restless and troublesome" elements, and when Europe got rid of them she gave a poor exchange for the tangible and tinkling treasures of the American mines.[186]

But these flashes of paradox are lost in the gray wasteland of the two volumes, which can lay claim to one single true originality — that of conjoining a minutely detailed knowledge of all the particulars of the polemic to an absolute insensibility for its general themes and basic problems. Progress and decadence, primitivism and degeneration, the westward march of history, the function of civilization, the relationships between animal life and physical environment, are concepts and motives that make no impact whatsoever on Drouin's mind. So impoverished does the dispute become with him, that despite his almost continuous polemic with de Pauw we would not even have allowed him this supplementary mention if he were not an important source, in fact I would say the most important source, as regards overall value judgments, of Giuseppe Compagnoni's *History of America.*

B. As "inventor of the tricolor" or actual "author of the Italian Flag"[187] Giuseppe Compagnoni is assured his pigeonhole — niche might be just too strong a word — in the hagiography of the Risorgimento. In celebratory pamphlets and urban toponymy his name is identified with and almost enveloped in the nation's banner.

But even apart from the fact that the "tricolor" was already in existence when Compagnoni proposed to the Congress of Reggio, on 7 January 1797, that it be adopted as insignia of the Cispadane republic, whence

---

184. *L'Europe et l'Amérique,* II, 370, 376. De Pauw (*Recherches sur les Égyptiens,* I, 217) mentions "the ridiculous drawing and frightful daubing of the Chinese." To our own taste, refined precisely through our study of Chinese and Japanese painting, there is an almost paradoxical ring about his other statement: "There are no painters in Asia who know how to render the foliage of trees properly" (ibid., I, 220). Cf. above, chap. 4, n. 40.

185. *L'Europe et l'Amérique,* II, 136, 141–42.

186. Ibid., pp. 427–29: the idea of this exchange, men for metals, was a commonplace in the Spanish authors of the time of the viceroyalties.

187. See M. Rossi, *Giuseppe Compagnoni, autore della bandiera italiana* (Lugo, 1941). "Inventor" is the term used by Luigi Rava, C. Casadio, etc.

it passed to the Cisalpine,[188] and even ignoring the wider question of whether the proposition of an emblem is a just title to immortality (albeit the limited immortality of school texts and street names) — Compagnoni has other merits and other claims to defy the obscurity and oblivion that befell Drouin de Bercy.

He is certainly not a great man: either in what he did or what he wrote. Self-educated, in fits and starts, according to the varying needs of the moment, he exercized the honorable profession of polygraph, as it was once called, or journalist, to use today's term, and his literary output is more remarkable for the diversity of subject treated than for any novelty of ideas or nobility of form. With a style that is smooth and fluent to the point of slovenliness, and excusably facetious, one would say he had kept the urbane facility of his Jesuit teachers,[189] even after abandoning the order and the cowl and indeed making the prescribed move to the ranks of the more advanced freethinkers and sansculottes.

Before the Revolution Compagnoni was editor and director of various periodicals in Bologna and Venice, a secretary in Ferrara and Turin, annotator and translator of Cato's *De re rustica,* author of a short poem on the "Fiera di Sinigaglia," of verse apologies, almanacs for women, topical pamphlets, and collections of fictional correspondence. As late as 1791 he called himself abbé on the frontispiece of the *Lettere piacevoli, se piaceranno,* written together with Francesco Albergati Capacelli, which was fiercely attacked by another Jesuit, the elderly Saverio Bettinelli,[190] and which contained among other things that comparison between the Greeks and the Jews, to the full advantage of the latter, a work defined by himself as a "paradox," but which in fact oscillates between journalistic "gimmick" and academic exercise, and yet remains a long way from that real paradox, but sustained by acid erudition, with which de Pauw had three years earlier assailed the conventional image of the ancient Hellenes.[191]

188. C. Spellanzon, *Storia del risorgimento e dell'unità d'Italia,* vol. I (Milan, 1933), p. 148; G. Piccinini, *Giuseppe Compagnoni e il Tricolore* (Reggio Emilia, 1943), pp. 8–10. On the precedents of the tricolor, in polemic with V. Fiorini ("Le origini del tricolore italiano," *Nuova Antologia,* 16 January and 16 February 1897), but with full recognition of Compagnoni's faith in the triumph of the tricolor, see also Nicola Ferorelli, "La vera origine del tricolore italiano," *Rassegna storica del Risorgimento,* 12 (1925), pp. 654–80 (on Compagnoni in particular, p. 679 n. 1). Note however that not even in his *Memorie autobiografiche* (ed. A. Ottolini [Milan, 1927]), which brings out every possible merit and distinction to which he could lay claim, does Compagnoni make the slightest reference to the adoption of the tricolor.

189. He is actually called an "ex-Jesuit" by E. Masi, *La vita, i tempi, gli amici di Fr. Albergati* (Bologna, 1878), p. 407. But the order was of course suppressed in 1773. The earliest biographers say that Compagnoni, ordained priest in 1778, was not accepted by the canons of Lugo and was prevented from entering the cloister as a minor conventual. Thus he remained a secular priest, adorning himself with the title of abbé.

190. Masi, op. cit., pp. 431–33.

191. Compagnoni and Albergati, *Lettere piacevoli* . . . (Modena, 1791), pp. 167–94 (and reprinted in a more authentic text the following year, at Venice, in a pamphlet of 36 pages). On the fortune of this letter, see the *Vita letteraria del cavaliere Giuseppe Compagnoni scritta da lui medesimo* (Milan,

Between 1795 and 1797 he was still busy publishing a poem on the *Grotta di Vilenizza*, an Algarotti-type *Chimica per le donne*—a casual compendium with a mixed stuffing of physics, geology, mineralogy, theology, medicine, and meteorology—and that *Mercurio d'Italia* where Foscolo cut his teeth. But once he became immersed in political life the various posts he was called upon to fill in rapid succession—as government secretary, deputy, teacher of "constitutional democratic law" at Ferrara, and finally, after the Directorate had had the eighty most radical elements (including Compagnoni) barred from the legislative assembly, judge of the Court of Cassation in Milan—diverted him from literature, although not from publicistics (he was founder and joint editor of the *Monitore Cisalpino*, 1798),[192] nor from advancing other "paradoxes," such as that of the injustice, harmfulness, and immorality of the very principle of progressive taxation,[193] and that other so exquisitely illuministic proposal, that polygamy should be instituted so as to increase the population, and also because in any case monogamy, wherever established, "was everywhere belied by fact" (1798)—until the Austro-Russians made him flee to Paris.

And here he immediately took up his pen again, joined Dandolo in drafting the greater part of *Les hommes nouveaux*,[194] and produced the *Veglie del Tasso*, another pastiche along the lines of the already published letters of Sappho and Cagliostro, which were to enjoy such long and unlikely success.[195] Returning to Italy after Marengo, throughout the Napo-

1834), p. 24; and the cited *Memorie autobiografiche*, pp. 127–28. Although Compagnoni exalts the poetry of the ancient Hebrews, I can find no trace in him of Herder's famous work *Vom Geiste der ebräischen Poesie*, 1782–83.

192. A selection of articles from this review has been published by L. Rava, "Giuseppe Compagnoni e il suo *Monitore Cisalpino* (1798) col *Vocabolario del nuovo linguaggio democratico*," *Rassegna storica del Risorgimento*, 14, no. 3 (1927), and, in offprint, Aquila, 1927. On his "Jacobinism" see Delio Cantimori, ed., *Giacobini italiani* (Bari, 1956), I, 416–23 (on pp. 3–96, writings by Compagnoni).

193. *La tassa progressiva, Riflessioni del cittadino Giuseppe Compagnoni* (Ferrara, 1797), containing such prophetic gems as this: "Industry is coming to a halt; the public wealth is becoming constipated; speculative genius itself is becoming paralyzed" (p. 16). The essay is included in L. Rava, *Il primo Parlamento elettivo in Italia, il Parlamento della Repubblica Cispadana a Bologna, aprile-maggio 1797* (Bologna, 1915), pp. 32–37; cf. also L. Rava, *La costituzione della Repubblica Cispadana del 1797* (Bologna, 1917). Compagnoni is called "one of the most industrious and loquacious members of that assembly" by T. Casini, "I Deputati al Congresso Cispadano, 1796–97," *Rivista storica del Risorgimento Italiano*, 2, nos. 1–2 (1897), pp. 138–210, esp. 138 n. and 164–65.

194. *Memorie autobiografiche*, pp. 255–56; F. Luzzatto, "Vincenzo Dandolo, Giuseppe Compagnoni e *Les Hommes Nouveaux*," *Nuova rivista storica*, 21 (1937), pp. 39–50. See also for certain (dubious) suggestions of the concept of punishment as social defense and of the desirability of considering the criminal rather than the crime, the article by F. Luzzatto again, "Precursori della scuola criminale positiva: Giuseppe Compagnoni," in *Scuola Positiva: Rivista di diritto e processo penale*, n. s. 15, nos. 1–2 (Milan, 1925).

195. One enthusiast set it in verse, and another to music! It went through various genuine and counterfeit Italian editions, and was translated numerous times, into French already from the first edition, and also into German, Polish, Russian, and possibly even English, says Compagnoni (*Memorie autobiografiche*, pp. 261–62), who, ever insatiable, adds that it could profitably have been translated into Spanish too. Before he died Cabanyès did in fact publish (1832) a free Spanish version. And soon after his death the Englishman William Keegan translated it into Latin (Naples, 1835).

leonic period he held important governmental and academic positions, culminating in 1810 with the post of Counsellor of State, but the Restoration obliged him to withdraw a second time from public affairs and, on the rebound, to devote himself once again completely to literary work. He needed to earn his living, which was not so easy for an aging former civil servant, with ideas that were suspect to his new masters; and he was soon reduced to writing articles, translating and abridging historical texts, composing school primers, college grammars and manuals, or pamphlets on domestic and professional morality.[196] It was a lowly existence, but dignified enough, and it earned him the admiration, sympathy, and friendship of men of liberal views: suffice it to mention two of the most outstanding, Stendhal, who in praising Compagnoni's excellent translation of Destutt de Tracy calls him "a man of letters worthy not of translating but of composing original works,"[197] and Giacomo Leopardi, who lists him among the "men of worth," writes to his uncle Antici that he has "become great friends" with Compagnoni and, in his letters to the Stellas, father and son, frequently sends him the warmest greetings.[198]

Compagnoni had in fact already been working for the publisher Stella for some years. The latter had begun to bring out the Italian version of Ségur's *Universal History* in monthly fascicules: but at a certain point

196. See *Degli Offici della Famiglia. Dialoghi VIII* (Milan, 1826); and *Lettere a tre giovani sulla morale pubblica* (Milan, 1829), in which he lists the duties of the citizen, the state employee, the taxpayer, the scholars, the young toward the old, the living toward the Dead and Posterity, the lawyers and litigants, the doctors and patients, etc., disavowing also (p. 117) his defense of gallantry contained in the youthful *Lettere piacevoli* (see in fact ed. cit., p. 78). An anonymous publication, but according to Compagnoni notable "for its singularity," was the work with the vaguely Leopardian title: *Vita ed imprese di Bibì uomo del suo tempo (Biografie autografe ed inedite di illustri italiani di questo secolo,* ed. D. Diamilla Müller [Turin, 1853], p. 112), which E. de Tipaldo (*Biografia degli Italiani illustri . . .* [Venice, 1835], II, 181–89) describes as unfinished.

197. H. Stendhal, *Des périls de la langue italienne,* 1818, in appx. to *Racine et Shakespeare,* Divan ed., p. 257n. An autograph letter of Destutt de Tracy, offered in a catalogue of autograph papers, says however: "I don't know if he [Compagnoni] really understood everything I was trying to say about it, nor if he dared to transcribe it; I am afraid he wasn't able to do either." Destutt de Tracy's *De l'amour* has been translated back into French (from Compagnoni's Italian) by G. Chinard (Paris, 1926). See also Stendhal's *Correspondance* (Pléiade ed.), II, 775–76, 1086; III, 662, 780.

198. G. Leopardi, *Le lettere,* ed. F. Flora (Milan, 1949), pp. 555, 569, 571, 578, 583, 592, 619, 629, 678, 911. Unaware that certain criticisms of Giordani published in the *Nuovo Ricoglitore* were by Compagnoni, Leopardi wrote however that "they reveal a profound ignorance of language and style." Just as hostile are the verdicts of Tommaseo (see below, n. 268; "a frightful bungler" he is called in the *Memorie poetiche,* 1838, ed. G. Salvadori [Florence, 1916], p. 221; for that matter Compagnoni referred to himself as a "furious scribbler" in his *Vita letteraria,* p. 18); and of Monti — even though in 1797–98 he professed himself his friend and held him in high esteem (*Epistolario,* ed. A. Bertoldi [Florence, 1928], II, 3, 16) — against whose *Sermone sulla mitologia* he had composed, under the pseudonym Giuseppe Belloni, an *Antimitologia* (see *Discussioni e polemiche sul romanticismo,* ed. E. Bellorini [Bari, 1943], II, 364–68). A little later Monti wrote to Gian Giacomo Trivulzio lamenting the poverty of his inspiration (30 August 1826), and complaining that now his lyre produced sounds "so rude and wretched / That poorer verses would not be made / By Tommaseo, Mangiagalli, and Compagnoni" (*Epistolario,* VI, 209, 215, and *Opere,* ed. Ricciardiana, p. 1270). Equally hostile is C. Cantù, *Monti e l'età che fu sua* (Milan, 1879), pp. 114n., 298n. Carlo Porta and Tommaso Grossi on the other hand seem to have been friends of his (see *Le lettere di Carlo Porta e degli amici della Cameretta,* ed. Isella [Milan-Naples, 1967], pp. 333, 382–83, 390, 393).

Ségur, whose health was poor and who was heavily involved with his political responsibilities, had slowed down the pace of preparation of his work, and the Milanese publisher who had precise obligations to his "associates" (subscribers, we would call them today), having reached volume XXV which completed the *History of the Late Empire,* saw himself obliged to find a substitute for the *History of France,* which should have come next, but which Ségur did not yet have ready.

In the meanwhile, to stop the gap, and—he says—in agreement with Ségur, Stella decided to offer the public a *History of America,* and entrusted the task to an unnamed Italian writer "who for meticulousness, clarity of style, and soundness of philosophy" gave hope of a work which would be not at all inferior to the celebrated product of the Count and Peer of France.[199] The writer in question was our friend Compagnoni, who must have been delighted to set out on a task which would keep him busy for many many months: nor does he in fact seem to have had a moment's hesitation when faced with the task of providing a volume of some two hundred pages every thirty days, on a subject which up until then— and he was sixty-six—had not interested him the least little bit.[200] In these circumstances it is hardly surprising that Compagnoni availed

199. "L'editore a chi legge," unnumbered pages at the beginning of vol. I (XXVI of the *Storia universale*) of the anonymous *Storia dell'America, in continuazione del Compendio della storia universale del sig. Conte de Ségur* (Milan, 1820; from vol. VI onward the date is 1821, and from XVII to XXVIII it is 1822). I have seen only this edition, which had almost 1700 subscribers, according to the list published in vol. XXIX (two thousand according to the last volume of the *Storia universale,* the 180th in the series [Milan, 1830], p. 30); but the publisher Stella complained already in 1823 about "a reprint violating the copyright produced in another city in Italy" (op. cit., XXIX, 10) and C. Morandi ("Giuseppe Compagnoni e la Storia dell'America," *Annali della R. Scuola Normale Superiore di Pisa— Lettere, Storia e Filosofia,* ser. II, vol. 8, no. 3 [1939], pp. 252–61) relates that "there were subsequent Milanese editions and also one in Naples in 19 volumes: Naples, Iride, 1842–45" (p. 254 n. 3). On the other hand it seems that the bulkiness of the work came in for some criticism ("some found it too extended": Compagnoni, *Vita letteraria,* p. 42) and somewhat worried the subscribers and the publisher, who excuses and justifies himself in vol. XXIX, pp. 5–9, promising that he will not do the same again ("I shall not produce any more . . . histories . . . of such length"), and, to make it sell better, divides it "into fourteen particular histories, each of which stands by itself, and is sold separately" (G. Belloni [G. Compagnoni], *Storia dei Tartari* [Milan, 1825], I, 12n.).

200. Although Compagnoni claims that in his youth and in the few moments free from the demands of public life he read works pertaining to America (*Storia dell'America,* XXVIII, 254), the subject is almost entirely absent from his vast literary output. Apparently in 1777 he wanted to dedicate a small volume of verse on Washington to Benjamin Franklin (see Visconti, op. cit., pp. 109–10, 113, 120; Pace, op. cit., pp. 237–38, 349, 405–06; on his admiration for Franklin, see ibid., pp. 172–74). But the manuscript of his *Washington,* "a poem new in form and subject" (and certainly to be identified with that "sort of poem new in form and subject, entitled the *Wosleyron,*" referred to in the *Memorie autobiografiche,* p. 192) got lost (E. de Tipaldo, op. cit., II, 187). Fleeting references to the American Revolution occur in his *Prospetto politico dell'anno 1790* (Venice, 1791), pp. 11, 30. At the Congress of Modena he mentioned, on the subject of jurors, the constitutions of America and other countries (17 February 1797: in C. Zaghi, *Gli atti del terzo Congresso Cispadano di Modena* [Modena, 1935], p. 200). In the little poem on the "grotta di Vilenizza" he describes the huts of Corgnale, which remind him of "the houses the busy beavers raise, by the banks of the freezing rivers where America lifts her brow toward the pole" (in L. Rava, *Giuseppe Compagnoni da Lugo, inventore del Tricolore italiano, e il suo poemetto "La Grotta di Vilenizza"* [*1795*] [Rome, 1926], p. 24). And in the *Chimica per le donne* there are a few references to natural phenomena of the Americas (Venice, 1797, I, 183; II, 27, 29, 192, 201).

himself almost exclusively of secondary and tertiary sources, and that in composing the first volume particularly, to get under way, he brazenly ransacked and plagiarized a recently appeared and thus very little known book, which hailed from Paris and possessed every appearance of great seriousness and authority: *L'Europe et l'Amérique comparées*, by M. Drouin de Bercy.

He actually mentions his name, or half his name, only once, and on a very specific question.[201] But in a couple of other places there are veiled references to the "writer that we have particularly followed in this picture of America"[202] and to the "modern writer that we have very often followed in this Introduction."[203] It takes no more than a rapid comparison, however, to discover a mass of parallelisms and nonfortuitous coincidences,[204] and to become convinced that where Compagnoni "followed" Drouin was not really so much in the factual details as in his indiscriminate enthusiasm for everything American, and in his naïve acceptance of astonishing virtues and prodigious phenomena, which take us right back to the pre-Buffonian era.[205]

But being the skillful man of letters that he was, and as a conscientious compiler of a work intended to be pleasantly instructive and popular in tone, Compagnoni succeeds in transforming Drouin's continental fanaticism into an acceptable enthusiasm for the beauty of the theme he has undertaken to develop: he completely abandons the polemic against Europe (except for the usual moralistic tirade against European avarice and savagery, an essential part of the humanitarian ideology) and of course eliminates almost entirely the tiresome and anachronistic attacks on de Pauw.

Of him, Compagnoni knows only what he has read in Drouin, and despatches him with a single blow: "We shall not waste our time repudiating the deliberate slanders published against the Americans by M. Paw, fifty years ago, which have been justly refuted by many better-qualified

201. "It has been justly observed by M. Bercy, an even more recent writer [than Humboldt], that the American languages are at least as different one from another as the Greek language is from German, and French from Polish" (*Storia dell'America*, II, 173; cf. also I, 109). The passage Compagnoni quotes is repeated in XIII, 153, and occurs in fact in Drouin, op. cit., II, 320–21. On the languages of the American savages, and quoting himself, see also G. Compagnoni, *Dell'arte della parola* (Milan, 1827), pp. 21–22; on the Mexican hieroglyphics and the Peruvian *quipus*, quoting Garcilaso, ibid., pp. 54–55.

202. *Storia dell'America*, II, 210–12, before interpolating a long passage translated from *L'Europe et l'Amérique*, II, 425.

203. *Storia dell'America*, II, 111–13, before interpolating a long passage translated from *L'Europe et l'Amérique*, I, 267–68.

204. Cf. for example *Storia dell'America*, I, 83–85 and 87–88 with *L'Europe et l'Amérique*, I, 159–61 and 166 respectively; the list of authors on the "lues" (*Storia dell'America*, I, 127–37; *L'Europe et l'Amérique*, II, 96–97), etc. And could Drouin also be that "ingenious author" who described "a morning in the Antilles in the time of the heavy dews" (XX, 17–19)?

205. If I am not mistaken the *Storia dell'America* never mentions Buffon, for that matter.

and most worthy writers."[206] Compagnoni knows a good number of these refuters, however, be it only through having found them drawn up for battle in Drouin's two volumes, but he does not use or even mention those who wrote mere rebuttals, like Pernety (whom Drouin calls Prenetty) or Frisi, nor even Jefferson, while he makes extensive use of those who, even if they take their polemical cue from the *Recherches,* made some positive contribution to the knowledge of the Americas, such as Clavigero,[207] Molina[208] and Gigli,[209] and particularly the great Humboldt.[210] About Carli there is still some doubt: his *American Letters* must certainly have been known to Compagnoni, since he had referred to its theory on Atlantis in the *Chimica per le donne,*[211] and then again they were mentioned several times in the work of his American mentor, Drouin, even in relation to subjects that he himself skimmed over;[212] but Carli is never actually named at all in the *History of America,* possibly for the usual reason that Carli indulges in polemics and propaganda rather than describing or relating, or else because Compagnoni found him politically antipathetical.[213] Compagnoni's main source for Peruvian history remains Garcilaso, as much a nostalgic idealizer of the Inca empire as Carli, who for that matter was always ready to swear by the word of the most noble mestizo.[214]

The shift in Compagnoni's interest is already clear from this choice of authorities. He is much less concerned with revenging the outrages in-

206. *Storia dell'America,* I, 94; de Pauw is named only once more, a little further on I, 98, as witness of the sobriety of the natives.

207. The first few times (ibid., I, 87, for example) Clavigero is quoted secondhand (cf. Drouin, op. cit., I, 164); but later, when he begins to discuss Mexico, Compagnoni refers directly to this author "whom we have followed in the exposition of all these matters, as the most experienced in the things of Mexico, where he was born and passed most of his life" (op. cit., VI, 92; cf. ibid., II, 30, 87, 197; VI, 93, 115, 147, 153, 158; VII, 70, 73, 75, 115, 119).

208. Cf. ibid., II, 74, 80, 136; XII, 36, 44 (identification of the Chileans with the Patagonians).

209. Cf. ibid., XVII, 150; XVIII, 121, 199.

210. Cf. ibid., I, 9, 15, 48, 80, 86, 95–96, 99–100, 102; II, 54, 129–30, 132, 141, 173; XVII, 126; XXIII, 157. Simplifying somewhat, Morandi ("Compagnoni," p. 257) says that the use he made of Humboldt is "Compagnoni's real strength as compared with the writers of the eighteenth century, what made it possible for him to render less rigid, if not actually to break, the schemes previously followed." But Humboldt is already cited very often in Drouin's first volume; and, on the other hand, as we shall shortly see, Compagnoni did not derive that much "strength" from him.

211. *Chimica per le donne,* II, 18–19 ("if you read Buffon, Baïly, Carli, you will hear of the marvelous revolutions suffered by the sea in the past ages").

212. *L'Europe et l'Amérique,* II, 107–08 (on the delicate practice referred to here, see above, n. 181), 154 (in defense of the Amazons), 173 (on the Peruvians), 189, 191.

213. Morandi does in fact cite a passage from the *Storia dell'America* (XXVIII, 262), which he compares with one of the *Lettere americane* (ed. cit., I, 5), but he draws no conclusions therefrom, and rightly.

214. See above, p. 237. Garcilaso, and his source Blas Valera, are cited in the *Storia dell'America,* VIII, 24, 62, 70–74, 148; IX, 10–12, 20, 24–25, 28, 32, 34–35, 38, 44, 77, 120, 217, 232; X, 115–16, 128, 155, 160–61, 165, 178, 180; XII, 29. Drouin cites him a half-dozen times. For the United States Compagnoni follows mainly Botta, another author completely foreign to the polemic, mentioned as "an illustrious Italian" who "outlined with much diligence" the details of the war of American independence (op. cit., XXVI, 219; cf. also XXVII, 20, 22).

flicted on America than with describing it region by region, with exhaustive detail and willing sympathy. The further he gets from generalities, the more he becomes a narrator, though hardly a historian; as the polemicist recedes, so the compiler reemerges.

One detects a certain vacillation in the principles followed in the writing of the *History of America;* Compagnoni actually boasted of having set about its composition "not as compiler, but as original historian,"[215] and informs us in the letter that acts as preface to his *History of the Russian Empire* (Milan, 1824): "History is properly narration." But, "dry narration never pleased me, and I feel sorry for those Historians who have been so easily satisfied." The historian cannot withhold "the feeling" that the events "make on his mind." On the other hand "he must temper this feeling, and not forever be running ahead of the mind of the reader," because that would seem like arrogance and would be irritating. True, the progress of philosophy has now made it possible to treat history "I would almost say scientifically," to make of it "a noble amalgam with morals and politics," thus creating "a sort of philosophical, or if you like political, history, completely unknown to previous centuries." But this is a task reserved for the powers of a few men and is not what is required either to continue Ségur's history or to satisfy the publisher Stella and his subscribers.[216]

His boasts, in short, are the standard ones of the popularizer and especially the compiler: that he makes no claim to be saying anything new, that his intention is not *ad litteram* "to discover America," but to provide an exhaustive treatment of the subject, to gather facts and information, wherever they can be found, moral "examples," and scientific curiosities, and set them out in neat order, so as to fill in even the remotest corners of the picture he has undertaken (or been required) to paint. Compagnoni goes into moving detail over the "troubles" he went through in obtaining his sources, particularly the foreign ones, and his travails in concluding the investigations on each particular topic: "The difficulties mentioned crowded about me, and not infrequently I saw them swarm and multiply, and drag me on toward an ever sharper and more grievous regret, and I perceived only too clearly how I was in great danger of finding myself considerably behind the point that I must perforce reach."[217] But he is just as ardent when he comes to expressing either his satisfaction over the

215. *Storia dei Tartari,* I, 13; cf. below, p. 617.
216. *Storia dell'Impero Russo,* I, 8–11. The latter, obviously, wanted to be entertained; and Compagnoni to furnish them with pleasant reading and basing himself on the example of Diodorus Siculus (whose *Historical Library* he had translated), inserted into his American *opus* "certain cases and certain peculiarities which writers of just repute do not seem to have thought suited to the solemnity of history" (op. cit., XXVIII, 268–69).
217. Letter to Petronilla Reina née Gorini, in *Storia dell'America,* XXVIII, 258–60.

completed work — which only shortly before his death he was to describe as his "most important," and "original" — while the histories of the Russians and Tartars, Turks and Austrians would be qualified by the author himself as "compilations";[218] or his pride and delight at being the first person to give the public the whole history of all America, without betraying "such a lofty subject."[219] And publishers, reviewers, and biographers have, in dutiful admiration, echoed his boast and recognized his primacy.

Now here too, as with the tricolor, one might cavil: it remains to be seen whether a historiographer can claim any merit in having tackled a theme so vast that it obliges him to treat it in the most superficial way (one seems to hear the whispered word of the proverb, about grabbing for everything and catching nothing); and it would also be quite legitimate to question the objective validity of this boast of primacy, since Oviedo, in the middle of the sixteenth century, had outlined the history and geography of all the American lands then known. Compagnoni limits himself to rejecting Robertson's claim, who, he says, in the so-called *History of America* concerned himself solely or almost solely with the deeds of Columbus and the civilizations and conquests of Mexico and Peru, the best-known and easiest parts of the history of the continent.[220]

But if we pry a little more carefully, disregarding the questions of area or volume or difficulties overcome, we find ourselves forced to admit that Compagnoni's prolix compilation has a particular and intrinsic merit: it gives the history of America from the point of view of the Americans themselves, not from the European's. The vaunted geographical completeness is a corollary of this commitment to the history of the continent. Once America, in itself and for itself (Ségur and his collaborators took care of the other parts of the world) is accepted as a subject "full worthy of poem and of history," as Tasso said of Columbus' exploit, all its different regions become equally interesting, equally necessary for the completion of the picture.

In this sense Compagnoni is thus really the precursor of that "historiographical Pan-Americanism" that has been so much discussed in recent years,[221] and in particular since more than once he reveals a conscious awareness of his originality and "Americocentrism." Commenting on the deeds of the American pirates, incredible but true, he remarks that "as the sky, the waters, and the earth of that vast part of the globe" present us with new wonders, so the "men that have shared in the many vicissi-

---

218. See his brief autobiography (1830) in *Biografie autografe*, ed. cit., pp. 109–14; cf. above, p. 616.
219. And he goes on: "Whatever most noble, most important, and indeed most curious can be found scattered in a thousand books about America, here has been more or less conveniently either exposed or indicated" (*Storia dell'America*, XXVIII, 258–60).
220. Ibid., pp. 256–57.
221. See above, pp. 552–53.

tudes of which America has been the theater" offer us examples that have no equal in the history of the Old World. Compagnoni does not distinguish here between natives and invaders, and attributes this prodigious virtue to the soil—in other words confirms the "telluric messianism" of so many American writers. But then he goes straight on, expanding on this attitude: "We would not wish to dissimulate the fact that the things occurring in America have both taken some impulse from Europe, and reverberated on Europe, no less than on the other two parts of the old continent. *But in America they had their center;* and it seems that the air of that New World has given a particular spirit to everything from the Old with which it came into contact," including the savage passions and massive crimes of the Conquistadors and pirates:[222] with which Compagnoni also gives us an outline of the thesis of the "tropicalization of the white man" and presents the history of America not just as a series of popular colored posters, filled with exotic marvels, but as the extreme manifestation of Europe's exuberance and energy. But it is always the native that most attracts his interest, and several times he warns us that their facts and customs "must with every right take first place in this History, in which the facts of the Europeans, if we see them in their true light, are of no more than secondary and accessory significance."[223]

This sympathy for the natives is reinforced by his hostility toward the Spaniards, nourished in its turn by humanitarian and irreligious ideals. It is well known that always and everywhere men have cruelly slaughtered each other with all the rage of African lions, "but what had the Mexicans done to the Spaniards?"[224] And let not anybody say—Compagnoni goes on elsewhere, contradicting the thesis of tropicalization—that the climate can explain or excuse the savagery that history justly rebukes in the Iberians. "In the plains of Lapland the Portuguese and the Spaniards, if they had found mines there and managed to overcome the natives, "would have imposed the same rule over the Lapps as they did over the Americans. If the influence of climate came into it at all, it would be the climate they were born in. Everything resulted from a moral perversity contracted through their ancient customs."[225]

Race, not climate, history, and not geography, are thus the real culprits of these excesses. Among which, however, Compagnoni seems to establish certain degrees of guilt; and while he is relatively sympathetic

222. *Storia dell'America,* XX, 161–64 (my italics). The passage was quoted in a review by the *Ricoglitore* (no. LXIV, 15 June 1822), which was in turn reprinted in its entirety in the *Storia dell'-America,* XXI, 273–76.

223. *Storia dell'America,* XXV, 227; for the occasional reference already in Drouin, cf. above, p. 605.

224. Ibid., V, 198–99. And elsewhere, concerning the massacres of the natives: "What verdict can reason pronounce on the Europeans?" What would the noble Columbus say? (ibid., XXVI, 120).

225. Ibid., XIV, 198. The vices belonged more to the age than to the men, Compagnoni says elsewhere to excuse them (XI, 47).

toward the heroic adventures of the early invaders, he has nothing but burning disdain for the later exploiters. The adventurous Gonzalo Pizarro is looked on with understanding, but his conqueror, the cunning Pedro de la Gasca, is called a swindler.[226] Francisco de Toledo is vilified considerably more than Francisco Pizarro; the despot is hated more than the conquistador.[227]

The old Jacobin's hostility for the Spaniards and coolness toward the Catholic religion (to which he did however return, dying reconciled with the Church) thus predispose Compagnoni to a fondness for the natives, pagan or idolatrous as they might be, which can be linked to Rousseau's primitivism. His prejudice against the Jesuits and missionaries is as strong as de Pauw's. Of Guaranay women, brought up by the good Fathers, he relates that they give themselves to any man, of any age: there is no single example of an Indian woman "over the age of eight having ever refused a man's proposal."[228] Pombal is lavishly praised for having banished the Jesuits,[229] who are charged with slandering California so as to be able to enjoy it for themselves and make a virtue out of living there, as they would have it, out of mere missionary zeal,[230] and so on.

But for the religions of the natives he has a benevolent curiosity that degenerates into polemical indulgence. The human sacrifices are defended with the customary argument that they were celebrated by all peoples, who thought to placate their Gods by the sacrifice of the thing most precious, life itself (someone else's!).[231] Cranial distortions, once said to be "a most eccentric custom," are justified and defended as a rite or ceremony of war, and better still by their almost universal practice among the most distant tribes.[232] And even the use of poisoned arrows is justified and defended.[233] Thus, between Father Gumilla, who abuses the savages,

226. Still ten years later Compagnoni said of a certain French captain that he came into the Cisalpine Republic "with all the wariness Gasca once showed in entering Peru; but without the fraud and the cold cruelty of that Spanish commissar" (*Memorie sulla vita e sui fatti di Giuseppe Luosi mirandolano* . . . [Milan, 1831], p. 23).

227. A reflection of Compagnoni's undying admiration for Napoleon? In the will drafted on St. Helena, 21 April 1821, Napoleon fondly imagined that his heirs might be able to ask for an accounting of the liquidation of his properties in Italy from Prince Eugène and "the Crown Administrator, Compagnoni" (Las Cases, *Mémorial de Sainte-Hélène*, ed. J. Prévost [Paris, 1935], II, 838) – the latter having never been crown administrator and being busy at that time writing about Chileans and Patagonians. It seems that Napoleon meant Costabili, keeper of the crown properties (T. Dandolo, in the preface to Fozio's *Biblioteca*, translated by Compagnoni [Milan, 1836], I, vii).

228. *Storia dell'America*, XII, 182. The "proposals" cannot however have been so frequent, if the Guaranay men had to be awakened from their sleep at midnight to be invited to fulfill their marital duties: ibid., XIII, 147. Cf. Hegel, above, p. 432.

229. Ibid., XVII, 78–85.

230. Ibid., XXII, 97–98, 100, 113. On the missionaries as allies of the adventurers in New Granada, ibid., XIX, 190–93. Compagnoni is very sympathetic on the other hand toward some Protestants, such as the Quakers (XXV, 103–05, 138–48, 202–03) and Moravian Brothers (XXII, 40–58; cf. *Lettere a tre giovani*, p. 129).

231. *Storia dell'America*, VII, 95–105.

232. Ibid., I, 199; IX, 179, 214; XVI, 55; XXIII, 80, 91, 190.

233. Ibid., XVIII, 172–74.

the scientist La Condamine who judges them insensitive and incapable of civilization, and the kindhearted Father Gigli, who recognizes their fundamental humanity, Compagnoni says that he sides with the latter, and in fact goes even a bit beyond him with his conclusion: "The savage then is closer than anyone else to what we call happiness."[234]

This is the starting point for his only polemic, directed not against naturalists or "philosophers," but against that historian of America who had slandered the savages, that familiar figure William Robertson (see also above, p. 617). Although Compagnoni is a very great admirer of the political institutions of the recent American republics—and although in general his history seems to proceed with mechanical smoothness from barbarity and cruelty to the luminous wisdom of civil systems—precisely for the study of the natives America's history is "more beautiful and more important and more instructive than all the ancient and modern histories of our continent."[235] Robertson, "availing himself, as he asserts, of the studies of a learned friend of his,[236] embellished the *History of America* with a fine picture representing the savage nations," which is the most famous part of his work. But Robertson is a simplifier and a "systematizer," while he, Giuseppe Compagnoni, presents "the facts as they are," in all their immense variety. In this way, by clarifying the primitives' way of life, and in other respects too (which in their turn one would like clarified), America's history "serves as key for the understanding of the History of the early nations of the old continent, and sheds light on the obscure traces remaining of our own barbarian ancestors."[237] The comparativistic theme was not new but one hardly expected to see it served up again by Compagnoni, who had so insisted on the autochthonous dignity of America's history. Does this history have any interest of its own, then, or is its value solely in its assistance for the understanding of Europe's?

As a matter of fact this is not the only point where Compagnoni vacillates somewhat in his pronouncements: driven by the need to push for-

234. Ibid., p. 122, evidently mindful of the passage in Fr. Gilij, quoted above, pp. 230–31. The only natives treated really badly by Compagnoni are the wretched inhabitants of the extreme North: the Greenlanders, reported to have some foul and stinking habits (op. cit., XXII, 84, 195); the Chippewa, among whom a girl, to be considered attractive, must have "more than anything else pendulous breasts" (XXII, 219); and the filthy savages of Alaska, whose houses are "absolute sewers" (XXIII, 45). Compagnoni finally apologizes for having dwelt so long on such squalid and desolate peoples, but they are men, after all! (XXII, 6–9).

235. *Storia dell'America*, XXVIII, 261.

236. In his preface Robertson says he obtained extremely valuable information on the natives from the Chevalier de Pinto, the Portuguese Minister at the court of London, who had lived for several years in the Matto Grosso ("I have often followed him as one of my best instructed guides"), from Bougainville, Godin, and various other missionaries and travelers (op. cit., I, xiii–xiv), and also cites, in the notes to the text, a large number of authors, more or less learned. Drouin had seen Robertson as a follower of de Pauw (see above, n. 165).

237. *Storia dell'America*, XXVIII, 264–65.

ward with his narrative, to spin off one volume after another, he has little time to worry about the internal coherence of his ideas; and even if he often seeks to give a rational explanation for surprising facts and discusses incredible stories and descriptions in terms of ordinary common sense,[238] much more often he is not even aware of the uncertainty he creates in his readers' minds. Particularly when he approaches the themes of "our" polemic, so totally unprepared to deal with the weighty problems of geophysics, logic, and historiography that it contained, Compagnoni quite casually throws together the most contradictory opinions. Raynal, for example, is scoffed at for believing the Jesuits and pursuing "the alluring fantasies of his imagination";[239] but he is covered with praise for his sentimental philanthropy,[240] and then again contradicted on the matter of a volcanic cataclysm in Guiana.[241] As for the animals, Compagnoni only just stops short of accusing the great Buffon of bad faith: "Those who thought that the soil of America was not capable of animals of the size of those that are found on the old continent have certainly dissembled such proofs as exist to the contrary . . . and then if one is talking of large animals still existing, America in that regard is certainly very well off in relation to the old continent."[242] But he goes on to admit, with Clavigero, that "in Mexico there were not originally a large number of animal species."[243] On the classic question of whether the discovery of America helped or harmed the Old World, Compagnoni refrains from giving us his opinion.[244]

But most confused of all are his ideas on the physiological qualities of the natives. His instinctive propensity for finding them to be good, happy, and interesting leads him to magnify the climate too[245] where they

238. He believes, among other things, in the existence of the Amazons (op. cit., I, 118–26; some years later de Pauw was rebuked by another Italian precisely for having denied the Amazons: F. Predari, *Le Amazzoni rivendicate alla verità della storia* [Milan, 1839], p. xxii), and of giants, both Patagonian (I, 95, 117–18, 139; II, 7, 36; XII, 45–47, 59–66) and non-Patagonian (II, 53–55; IX, 217; XXIII, 75). On his uncertain historiographical principles, see also above, p. 616.

239. *Storia dell'America*, XXIII, 114.

240. See for example XXI, 197; XXVI, 118–19.

241. Ibid., XVIII, 6–9.

242. Ibid., II, 53, 55; on the nondegeneration of the domestic animals imported from Europe, ibid., II, 104, 106–07.

243. Ibid., II, 87.

244. Ibid., II, 203 (cf. Drouin, above, p. 603). Of his naïveté, which was the negative aspect of the frankness he often boasted about and the good-heartedness and cordiality of manner that his contemporaries found so praiseworthy, one can detect signs even in his more meditated political works: see C. Morandi, "La politica estera della Repubblica Italiana e il Compagnoni," in *Problemi storici italiani ed europei del XVIII e XIX secolo* (Milan, 1937), pp. 93–99, summarizing the *Considerazioni sulle relazioni politico-diplomatiche della Repubblica Italiana* which Compagnoni presented (1802) to Vice-President Francesco Melzi d'Eril. Naïve expressions of delirious nationalistic enthusiasm for the eternal primacy of the genius of the Italians occur in the *Orazione sulla Pace di Lunéville* (Milan, 1800), pp. 8–9.

245. At the same parallel North America is colder than Europe or Asia (*Storia dell'America*, I, 72), but with the extension of cultivation "the climates of the United States . . . will come to the condition of our countries of milder temperature" (an old observation, see pp. 91–92, which Compagnoni takes

live and vegetate until a ripe old age. "If there is any country where there are many men and women that live happily to an age of a hundred and more, this country is America."[246] On the other hand his care to relate each picturesque little detail induces him to present a portrait of the Americans that is very similar to that of their slanderers: the men hairless and poorly endowed with every manly attribute; the females lascivious, insatiable, easy of childbirth, but of poor fecundity. Nature was generous with these women regarding "the construction of the organs of their sex, which in those [*sic:* the chaste Giuseppe Compagnoni stumbles over his syntax] of the men are said to be of a quite disproportionate mediocrity."[247] One is left in some doubt as to whether the native women's supreme facility in delivery depends on this factor,[248] but it is at least probable that it was this generous particularity that induced them to seek an artificial remedy to the inadequacy of their men and to react enthusiastically instead to the conspicuous vigor of the Spaniards. As a matter of fact Compagnoni, contradicting himself within a few pages, denies the first consequence with equivocal and elaborate circumlocutions, namely that the American women "were in the habit of having recourse to irritant philters, or to the corrosive action of insects as a miserable supplement for something in which, doubtless solely through strange and incompetent comparisons, nature has been slandered as having been ungenerous with the men of America."[249] But to discuss the second he descends to even more scabrous considerations: the Guaranay women have "abundent bosoms, small hands and feet, wide buttocks . . . just as with the other Americans in the parts which distinguish them, nature was very moderate in the dimensions of the males, exuberant in that of the females: whence the argument has been drawn to suppose that this was why the Americans were driven by internal frenzy to become so affectionate toward the Spaniards ["The white man was quite a success down there!"],[250] that through the women it was thus easier for those Spaniards to conquer the country; without taking into account another generally recognized

---

from Drouin, op. cit., I, 179–80, who quotes "Bonnet, Tableau," i.e., J. E. Bonnet, *Tableau des Etats-Unis de l'Amérique au commencement du XIXe siècle* [Paris, 1816]; on other works by Bonnet, cf. Quérard, op. cit., *sub voce; Fay, Bibliographie critique*, pp. 41, 88; idem, *Esprit*, p. 299).

246. *Storia dell'America*, I, 88; cf. VI, 61–62 (Mexico); XIII, 156 (Paraguay); XXVIII, 180 (United States). Cf. also below, n. 262.

247. Ibid., I, 116.

248. Ibid., I, 116; II, 20; X, 126; XIII, 104, 157; XVIII, 143; XIX, 68. In Chile the delivery of twins is an everyday event: XII, 36. The Canadian women are an exception, apparently not giving birth easily: XXIV, 167–68. Agostino Codazzi also refers to the native women's ease of delivery (*Memorie inedite di Agostino Codazzi sui suoi viaggi per l'Europa e nelle Americhe, 1816–22*, ed. Mario Longhena [Milan, 1930], p. 326).

249. *Storia dell'America*, I, 126–27, adding that from the very beginning the two sexes were seen to be "generally proportioned in their own respects" and that men who allowed themselves to be polygamous cannot be accused of "feebleness." Cf. also I, 146, and above, n. 181.

250. C. Pascarella, *La scoperta de l'America*, sonnet XXXVI.

particularity, which is that of the scarcity of their monthly purgations: a fact which considerably diminishes the force of the alleged supposition [?]; so that it is really not at all certain that the disproportion spoken of is necessarily connected with an irritation likely to produce such a great effervescence." And he opposes to it likewise the "infecundity of the American women in comparison particularly to the Spanish women," together with other lubricious considerations and impure speculations.[251]

One fact that remains certain, however, is the erotic aggressiveness of the native women. Compagnoni, usually so scholastic and reserved, actually tries to be a little facetious in telling about the two gay and easy-going Tupi girls (who are even shown in an engraving so that we may know them better!) who never wanted to sleep alone, and became quite vexed "if anyone wanted to oppose them . . . in the complex of which things one can see clearly how these young ladies have certain quite strange customs, and all the ignorance of the savages, but a most happy nature and a great disposition to kindness."[252]

And how do the American men come out, compared to these bold and friendly maidens? Rather badly. For almost all of them the emphasis is on an inauspicious total hairlessness.[253] But the hunt for the savages' hair does meet with occasional success, and Compagnoni never fails to indicate the few sprouts that are thus distinguished, to point triumphantly to every little tuft caught by the sun's rays; the Guaranay have little hair, true, but they do have some, certain Mexicans and the inhabitants of distant Alaska (so some travelers say) wear moustaches, and the Chileans, smooth-faced as they may be, are however robust and very hairy at the pubis.[254]

All in all, however, our good historian admits at least that "the Americans of the torrid zone have very little beard, and many of them can be

---

251. *Storia dell'America*, XII, 171–72. On the impossibility of attributing the meager fecundity of the native women to the climate, since the Spanish women are very prolific, cf. ibid., XIII, 156. Compagnoni is more inclined to believe that they are less prolific because of the hard life they lead: ibid., I, 115. But immediately afterward he gives us another explanation based on the scarce eroticism of the Americans: to satisfy the "physical need" two individuals have to come together "equally stimulated by the same." But, "if such is the natural constitution of the Americans, that this physical need is rather moderate in them, one can only presume that in their domestic unions many couplings take place without the woman being suitably disposed, which is the only way she becomes likely to conceive [!]. Which sufficiently explains the meager fecundity of those women" (*Storia dell'America*, I, 117). Or is it rather to be explained by Compagnoni's confusion-wreaking hastiness?

252. Ibid., XIII, 47–48. The Mbaya women, then, "among all the Indians are most obliging" (ibid., p. 86). The most attractive of the native women, on the other hand, are those of Virginia, which have "the peculiarity . . . of small, round breasts, so firm that even in old age they are never seen with pendent breasts" (ibid., XXV, 58).

253. For the Haitians see ibid., III, 121; for the Mexicans, VI, 60; for the Peruvians, IX, 105; for the Patagonians, XII, 65; for the Guanà, XIII, 65, 161; for the Bogotans, XIX, 68; for the Caribs, XX, 24; for the Iroquois, XXIII, 191, etc. This feature of hairlessness is one of the most persistent traits of the image of the native: Codazzi too says that the redskins have "bodies completely smooth, without hair" (op. cit., p. 229).

254. *Storia dell'America*, I, 104; XII, 37, 171.

seen completely hairless, perhaps because they are in the habit, having so little and such scattered hair, of quickly removing it";[255] he admits it and then straight away sets about justifying this lack, as if it were a certain mark of radical inferiority. He recalls, with Humboldt, that when they shave "their beards grow," and goes on unperturbed: "But nobody among those who have taken so much delight in exaggerating either this lack or tenuity of beard of the Americans took into consideration something which they should have remembered,[256] which is, that the Americans have an abundance of hair on their heads: so that having such a mane, if they had thick beards too, they would with respect to the European peoples, for this part, differ by excess; compared to it [?] as they are, they cannot reasonably be held to differ in defect." They are not underendowed in the "honor of the chin," because they are physically overendowed in the scalp. And Compagnoni in fact concludes and solidifies his demonstration with this "singular piece of information": that even "our women do not have the abundance of hair on the chin, that we have, and only because they have more hair on their heads than we do";[257] with which the clumsy Compagnoni destroys the whole of his own defense, and strengthens the thesis of the slanderers who saw the natives' hairlessness as a mark of femininity.

Nor is the picture of them that follows soon after very different, where he tries to convince us that the American is not weaker but more "temperate" than the inhabitant of the Old World, and that since nature gave him few needs and a not overly-warm temperament and "few desires, and those placid and such as are easily assuaged," he is "further along the path toward happiness than any other being."[258] But when he wants to exalt the Creoles, whose blessed constitution is partly the result of America's favorable climate, they are described as handsome and well built—the men robust and the women fascinating, in the north "tall and slender, with high firm bosoms," in Peru (so says an abbé) slim and light, so that they seem "to throw themselves into the arms of love with every movement,"[259] and in short certainly not such as to find happiness in the limitation of the appetites.

The picture he paints of the great cities founded by the Europeans is stupefying, hyperbolic: at Lima, "the queen of South America," he discovers even "a fine river" that is "sensible to the ebb and flow of the sea";[260] in Washington, which so many travelers had derided and still

255. Ibid., I, 104.
256. No one? . . . Drouin de Bercy, op. cit., II, 138–40; cf. above, p. 609.
257. *Storia dell'America*, I, 104–05. Cf. already Drouin de Bercy, above, p. 609.
258. *Storia dell'America*, I, 145–46.
259. Ibid., pp. 102–03. On the Creoles, mestizos, mulattoes, etc., cf. also XII, 185–87.
260. Ibid., VIII, 210–11; XI, 187. The Rimac is little more than a trickle of water (and no more than a stream even in the rainy season); not even a canoe could sail down it.

derided, he finds all the splendors of a metropolis.[261] But even these Americans of European descent, these perfect examples of humanity perfected by the climate and by the wisest of political institutions, cannot altogether escape the sprinkling of the poison that their critics had distilled and spread abroad, so that the glowing prophecies on the future of the United States are followed by the reminder that the country is devastated by yellow fever and scurvy, and that over there "the prettiest and freshest girls from fifteen to twenty, if they have not lost all their teeth, have at least spoiled them."[262]

Will these United States really become the most powerful nation of the continent and the world? Compagnoni seems to think so when he tells us grandiosely that they will, constitute "without exception the vastest empire ever created on the earth, not by chance and force, but by industry,"[263] and when he calculates its demographic progress by extrapolation, with only a small error of excess: "By the end of the century the United States will have no less than one hundred and twelve million inhabitants . . . in 1925 the entire population could be two hundred and twenty-four million men."[264] But with his usual incoherent overlapping of promises and qualifications, Compagnoni elsewhere reserves this future primacy for Brazil: Brazil, which to become the most powerful state in the world, to balance the United States "with considerably greater ad-

261. Ibid., XXVIII, 58–60; cf. above, p. 393, etc.

262. Ibid., p. 181; cf. above, p. 342 (Perrin du Lac). Compagnoni, who had taken from Clavigero the belief that the Mexicans never suffered from any sort of catarrh ("the pituitary excretions of their heads are meager, and they spit rarely": VI, 61), and from the chroniclers the happy conviction that the public women of Peru, the *pamparunas*, bore "no disease" (X, 130; on the non-American origin of syphilis, cf. I, 127–37), borrows or rather translates from Drouin (op. cit., I, 159–61, 166) a fine-sounding harangue to the effect that nobody in America is squint-eyed or hunchbacked, and there are no blind or dumb people (*Storia dell'America*, I, 83–85, 87–88), a fact which he then repeats severally for the Mexicans (VI, 61), for the Paraguayans (XIII, 156–57), for the Orenocans (XVIII, 125), for the Virginians (XXV, 58), etc. In Europe, on the other hand, what a lazar house! There are more than four hundred different and horrible diseases! And, he could have added, quoting himself (*Orazione sulla Pace di Lunéville*, p. 7), how many filthy beggars! European cities are infested with a "swarm of wretches, who have been allowed till now, to the shame of public decency, to trade on their own disgusting filth."

263. *Storia dell'America*, XXV, 7.

264. Ibid., XXVIII, 160–61, 188: they will be as populous as China! (Another calculation, bringing the number "irreparably" to 136 million in 1915 and 272 million in 1940, was made in 1846 by Cesare Balbo, *Lettere di politica e letteratura* [Florence, 1855], p. 346). But in Compagnoni there is almost no inkling of the formidable development industry would have in the United States. Of the Isthmus of Panama, so much admired by Drouin (above, p. 606, and cf. *Storia dell'America*, II, 125), he says that it is now and will always be impossible to sever it (op. cit., I, 57–58). Of Pennsylvania, whose rich coal deposits were already generally known, he reports that "in minerals it has only an oil spring; whose oil is excellent for rheumatism"! (ibid., II, 151). He sees very well, on the other hand, some of the economic effects that the independence of Latin America will have on Europe: at first the slowing down or stopping of the flow of precious metals, and then, with the progressive economic autonomy of the new republics: "The mass of things that they can seek from Europe will gradually decrease and the mass of things that America can provide for Europe will, on the other hand, increase" (XXIII, 158). As things continue in that way, Europe might "one day suffer the humiliation of becoming a colony of America after having held America as her colony" (ibid., II, 210–12, following Drouin, op. cit., II, 425). In fact the idea of the impoverishment that would befall Europe as a result of the independence of the Ibero-American colonies, the producers of precious metals, was current in those years: see C. F. von Schmidt-Phiseldeck (1821), in Gollwitzer, op. cit., p. 244.

vantages," lacks nothing but a good administration, and it seems already on the point of obtaining it, since the great revolutions occurring in Latin America (and which he does not discuss)[265] are tending certainly "to give the more classical parts of the New World a moral configuration of much more lively character" than that of the thirteen colonies.[266]

Thus it was not so much the long-windedness of certain parts, nor the fact of its forming part of the unwieldy compilation of Ségur and company,[267] nor the typographical modesty of the edition, but these directional uncertainties and inconsistencies that robbed Compagnoni's work, which as we have seen was otherwise not without its moments of inspiration, of that vital sap that assures success. Although reprinted, the *History* to which Compagnoni had entrusted his reputation remained quite without influence, without echo, without even being remembered by anyone, except its author and a few close friends. Compagnoni retorted to certain of his critics with futile pride: "I await a fairer judgment from time, and I know I shall not be disappointed." The young Cushing referred to it flatteringly (in 1829) in Vieusseux's *Anthology*,[268] and as early

---

265. His history is otherwise very much up to date, and discusses geographical discoveries and cataclysms that occurred in 1820 (XXIII, 29–30, 37). Cushing already noted, with approval, that Compagnoni had stopped his history of the Spanish American countries on the eve of their revolutions, through a lack of accessible materials (see Vieusseux's *Antologia*, Florence, vol. XXXIV [1829], n. 101 [May], pp. 83–84; cf. already *Storia dell'America*, XXVIII, 267–68).

266. Op. cit., XVII, 111–12, 135.

267. For the same *Compendio della storia universale* of Ségur and his continuers Compagnoni subsequently wrote and published under his own name a *Storia di casa d'Austria*, 6 vols. (Milan 1823: a compendium taken from the work by Will. Coxe), a *Storia dell'Impero Ottomano*, 6 vols. (Milan, 1823), and a *Storia dell'Impero Russo*, 6 vols. (Milan, 1824), i.e., "of the three Empires whence Europe is honored" (*Storia dell'Impero Russo*, I, 5), and under the pseudonym of "Giuseppe Belloni, an old soldier of Italy," a *Storia dei Tartari* (7 vols., Milan, 1825).

268. In answer to an explicit request from the director of the review, who preferred to address himself to an American scholar, like Cushing, "who in the *North American Review* had shown singular love and unusual understanding for Italian letters" (in 1824 he had published therein an essay on the *Decameron*). Such a review had already been published however, precisely in the *North American Review*, 27, of July 1828 (see mention in Miguel Gonzales-Gerth, "The Image of Spain in American Literature, 1815–1865," *Journal of Inter-American Studies*, 4, no. 2 [April 1962], who cites it curiously as a "review of *Storia d'America*, by Giuseppe Compagnoni, Conte di Segur [Milano]"!). Cushing (1800–79), a democratic politician whose public life was characterized by a "marked inconsistency" (*Encyclopedia Britannica, sub voce*), says that a "careful reading of the whole work" allows him to assign it "a high grade of excellence"; he recognizes its merit of being "the only truly complete and regular work . . . that exists in any language"; he justifies its inclusion of curious details and amusing incidents in terms of its popularizing intention (see above, n. 216) and is delighted to note the special attention paid to the natives (loc. cit., *Storia universale*, CLXXX, 219, 225–26). Note that in the same issue of the *Antologia* two other works by Compagnoni are reviewed, or rather castigated, by a critic signing himself K.X.Y., who is of course Niccoló Tommaseo: the *Storia dell'Impero Ottomano* (pp. 134–37), from which the reviewer quotes an extract littered with blunders of style and thought, and the *Dell'arte della parola* (pp. 143–44), which since it concerns Tommaseo more immediately moves him to conclude savagely: "The most remarkable characteristic of the Chevalier Compagnoni's writings is their boldness" — "boldness" which in the context is quite clearly a synonym for "impudence." In his *Dictionary of Synonyms* in fact Tommaseo is at pains to explain that "boldness can be without true strength, when it comes from stupidity, or from insane audacity, or from desperate fury . . . boldness is the term we apply to the person who unblushingly accepts blame or deserved infamy . . . there can be a stupid or criminal boldness . . . the dull-witted speaker, the charlatan, the unrepentant criminal sometimes show themselves bolder than the innocent person" (nos. 1767, 3449). And again in the

as 1823, apparently, it was occasionally mentioned in some North American journal; we are also told that a translation was published in the United States "with typographical luxury."[269] But even if all these details turned out to be true, the fact remains that the good Giuseppe Compagnoni's greatest work was quickly and completely forgotten. More than a century was to pass before Morandi rediscovered it and drew it to the attention of the pupils of the Scuola Normale di Pisa (1939), and to the forgetful exhumer of certain *Viejas polémicas sobre el Nuevo Mundo.* So that confronted with the row of Stella's twenty-nine slim volumes one really feels very much as the good Stella himself felt the morning of 30 December 1833, when having received the news of Compagnoni's death he betook himself to the cathedral, as he tells us, to join "the vast throng of mourners that had doubtless gathered to present the country's gratitude at the exequies of such a well-deserving man." In the whole quintuple lofty vaulted nave of Milan Cathedral there was not a soul to be seen. "I found the church deserted! . . . a plain coffin lay unwatched before a chapel."[270]

---

late (1863) memoirs *Di Giampietro Vieusseux e dell'andamento della civiltà italiana in un quarto di secolo* (in *Ricordi storici intorno a Giampietro Vieusseux* [Florence, 1869], p. 112), thirty years after Compagnoni's death, the implacable Dalmatian returns to the attack with redoubled venom, denouncing his victim as "another priest escaped from church . . . as facile a writer as Giordani is difficult, as inelegant as the most inelegant in Italy, as light as the lightest in France; a mishmash of Porcacchi and Chiari."

269. Letter of T. Dandolo to Luigi Stella, 1834, placed in preface to Compagnoni's translation of Photius's *Bibliotheca* (Milan: Silvestri, 1836), I, viii. I have found no confirmation of the fact, even in the recent and lengthy volume by H. R. Marraro, *Relazioni fra l'Italia e gli Stati Uniti* (Rome, 1954).

270. Letter of Luigi Stella to T. Dandolo, ibid., I, xvi.

Bibliography of Works Cited

Suggestions for Further Research

Index

Bibliography of Works Cited

Acosta, Joseph de. *Historia natural y moral de las Indias.* 3d ed. Madrid: Alonso Martín, 1608.
———. *Historia natural y moral de las Indias.* Introduction by Edmundo O'Gorman. Mexico: Fondo de Cultura Económica, 1940.
Adams, Abigail. *Letters of Mrs. Adams, the Wife of John Adams.* Boston: C. C. Little and J. Brown, 1840.
Adams, John. *A Defence of the Constitutions of Government of the United States of America, against the Attack of M. Turgot, in His Letter to Dr. Price, Dated the Twenty-second Day of March, 1778.* In *The Works of John Adams, Second President of the United States,* vol. 4. Boston: Little, Brown and Company, 1850–56.
Adams, Percy G. *Travelers and Travel Liars, 1660–1800.* Berkeley and Los Angeles: University of California Press, 1962.
Adickes, Erich. *Kant als Naturforscher.* 2 vols. Berlin: W. de Gruyter & Co., 1924–25.
———. *Kants Ansichten über Geschichte und Bau der Erde.* Tübingen: Mohr, 1911.
Aleardi, Aleardo, *Le prime storie,* 2d ed. Verona: Libreria alla Minerva, 1858.
Algarotti, Francesco. *Pensieri diversi.* In *Opere.* 8 vols. Livorno: Coltellini, 1764.
———. *Saggio sopra l'impero degli Incas.* In *Opere varie.* Venice, 1757. Also in *Opere.* 8 vols. Livorno: Coltellini, 1764.
Allen, Don Cameron. "The Degeneration of Man and Renaissance Pessimism." *Studies in Philology,* 35 (1938), pp. 202–27.
———. "Donne among the Giants." *Modern Language Notes,* 61 (1946), pp. 257–60.
———. *The Legend of Noah: Renaissance Rationalism in Art, Science, and Letters.* Urbana: University of Illinois Press, 1949.
Allen, Hervey. *Israfel: The Life and Times of Edgar Allan Poe.* New York: George H. Doran, 1926.
Alvarez López, E. "La filosofía natural en el P. José de Acosta." *Revista de Indias,* 4 (1943), pp. 305–22.
American Reader, An. See Rascoe.
American Writer, The. See Denny.
Ampère, Jean Jacques. *Promenade en Amérique.* 2 vols. Paris: Michel Lévy, 1856.
Amunátegui, Miguel Luis. *Don Manuel de Salas.* Santiago de Chile: Imprenta Nacional, 1895.
———. *Los precursores de la independencia de Chile: Memoria histórica presentada a la Universidad de Chile en cumplimiento del artículo 28 de la lei de 19 de noviembre de 1842.* 3 vols. Santiago de Chile: Imprenta de J. Núñez, 1870–72.
Annoni, Ada. *L'Europa nel pensiero italiano del Settecento.* Milan: Marzorati, 1959.
Armstrong, Elizabeth. *Ronsard and the Age of Gold.* Cambridge: Cambridge University Press, 1968.
Arndt, Karl J. "The Effect of America on Lenau's Life and Work." *The Germanic Review,* 33, no. 1 (February 1958), pp. 125–42.
Arnold, Matthew. *Five Uncollected Essays.* Edited by Kenneth Allott. Liverpool: University Press, 1953.
———. *The Portable Matthew Arnold.* Edited by Lionel Trilling. New York: The Viking Press, 1949.
Arnoldsson, Sverker. *La conquista española de América según el juicio de la posteridad: Vestigios de la leyenda negra.* Madrid: Insula, 1960.
———. *La leyenda negra: Estudios sobre sus orígenes.* Gothenburg: Acta universitatis gothoburgensis, 1960.
Atkinson, Geoffroy. *Les relations de voyages du XVIIᵉ siècle et l'évolution des idées.* Paris: Champion, n.d.
Bacon, Francis. *Essays, or Counsels Civil and Moral, with Other Writings.* London: George Newnes, 1902.
Baker, Paul R. *The Fortunate Pilgrims: Americans in Italy, 1800–1860.* Cambridge, Mass.: Harvard University Press, 1964.

Baldensperger, Fernand. *Le mouvement des idées dans l'émigration française, 1789–1815.* Paris: Plon-Nourrit, 1924.

―――. "Le séjour de Talleyrand aux États-Unis." *Revue de Paris,* 31 (1924), pp. 364–87.

Baldini, Gabriele. *Melville, o le ambiguità.* Milan and Naples: R. Ricciardi, 1952.

Ballanche, Pierre Simon. *Oeuvres.* 6 vols. Paris: Bureau de l'Encyclopédie des Connaissances Utiles, 1833.

―――. *Palingénésie sociale: Prolégomènes.* In *Oeuvres.* Paris and Geneva: Barbezat, 1830.

Barlow, Nora, ed. *Charles Darwin and the Voyage of the Beagle.* New York: Philosophical Library, 1946.

Barros Arana, Diego. *Notas para una bibliografía de obras anónimas y seudónimas sobre la historia, geografía y la literatura de América* (1882). In *Obras completas,* vol. 6. Santiago de Chile: Imprenta Cervantes, 1909.

Bartoli, Daniello. *La Ricreazione del Savio* (1659). In *Trattatisti e narratori del Seicento,* edited by Ezio Raimondi. Milan and Naples: R. Ricciardi, 1960.

Batllori, Miguel, S. I. *El abate Viscardo: Historia y mito de la intervención de los jesuitas en la independencia de Hispanoamérica.* Caracas: Instituto Panamericano de Geografía e Historia, 1953.

―――. "L'interesse americanista nell'Italia del Settecento: Il contributo spagnolo e portoghese." *Quaderni Ibero-Americani,* 12 (1952), pp. 166–71.

Baudet, Henri. *Paradise on Earth: Some Thoughts on European Images of Non-European Man.* New Haven and London: Yale University Press, 1965.

Baudin, Louis. *L'empire socialiste des Inka.* Travaux et mémoires de l'Institut d'Ethnologie de l'Université de Paris, vol. 5. Paris: Institut d'Ethnologie, 1928.

Bayard, Ferdinand Marie. *Voyage dans l'intérieur des Etats-Unis, à Bath, Winchester, dans la vallée de Shenandoah, . . . pendant l'été de 1791.* 2d ed. Paris: Batilliot frères, 1798.

Bazin, Christian. *Chateaubriand en Amérique.* Paris: La Table Ronde, 1969.

Beard, Charles A., and Mary R. *The American Spirit: A Study of the Idea of Civilization in the United States.* The Rise of American Civilization, vol. 4. New York: Macmillan, 1942.

Belin, J.-P. *Le mouvement philosophique de 1748 à 1789.* Paris, 1913.

Beltrami, Giacomo Costantino. *Alle sorgenti del Mississippi.* Edited by Luciano Gallina. Novara: Istituto Geografico De Agostini, 1965. (French edition: *La découverte des sources du Mississippi.* New Orleans, 1824.)

―――. *Notizie e lettere.* Published on behalf of the Municipio di Bergamo and dedicated to the Minnesota Historical Society. Bergamo, 1865.

Berkeley, George. *A Miscellany, Containing Several Tracts on Various Subjects, by the Bishop of Cloyne.* London: J. and R. Tonson, 1752.

Bernard, Claude. *Introduction à l'étude de la médecine expérimentale.* Paris, 1865.

―――. *Leçons sur les effets des substances toxiques et médicamenteuses.* Paris: J. B. Baillière; Orléans: P. Jacob, 1883.

―――. *Leçons sur les phénomènes de la vie communs aux animaux et aux végétaux.* 2 vols. Paris: J. B. Baillière et fils, 1878–79.

Bernardin, Édith. *Les idées religieuses de Madame Roland.* Publications de la Faculté des Lettres de Strasbourg, 2d ser., vol. 11. Paris: Société d'Edition "Les Belles Lettres," 1933.

Bernardin de Saint-Pierre, Jacques-Henri. *Harmonies de la nature* (1796). In *Oeuvres posthumes de Bernardin de Saint-Pierre.* Paris: Firmin Didot, 1833.

Bernheimer, R. *Wild Men in the Middle Ages: A Study in Art, Sentiment, and Demonology.* Cambridge, Mass.: Harvard University Press, 1952.

Bernstein, Harry. "Anthropology and Early Inter-American Relations." *Transactions of the New York Academy of Sciences,* 2d ser., vol. 10, no. 1 (November 1947), pp. 2–17.

―――. *Origins of Inter-American Interest, 1700–1812.* Philadelphia: University of Pennsylvania Press, 1945.

―――. "Some Inter-American Aspects of the Enlightenment." In *Latin America and the Enlightenment,* edited by Arthur P. Whitaker. The Appleton-Century Historical Essays. New York and London: Appleton-Century, 1942.

Bertin, L., et al. *Buffon.* Collection Les grands naturalistes français, edited by R. Heim. Paris: Muséum National d'Histoire Naturelle, 1952.

Berveiller, M. *Mirages et visages du Pérou.* Paris, 1959.

Beutler, Ernst. *Essays um Goethe.* Leipzig: Dieterich, 1941.

Beyerhaus, Gisbert. "Abbé de Pauw und Friedrich der Grosse: Eine Abrechnung mit Voltaire." *Historische Zeitschrift,* 134 (1926), pp. 465–93.

Bielschowsky, Albert. *Goethe, sein Leben und seine Werke.* Munich: C. H. Beck, 1918.

Bigland, Eileen. *The Indomitable Mrs. Trollope.* London: James Barrie, 1953.

Blake, William. *America.* In *Poetry and Prose,* edited by Geoffrey Keynes. Bloomsbury: Nonesuch Press, 1932.

Blanke, Gustav H. *Amerika im englischen Schrifttum des 16. und 17. Jahrhunderts.* Bochum-Langen-dreer: Heinrich Poppinghaus, 1962.

Blumbach, Johann Friedrich. *De generis humani varietate nativa liber.* Göttingen: Vandenhoeck, 1775.

Boas, George. *The Happy Beast in French Thought of the Seventeenth Century.* Contributions to the History of Primitivism. Baltimore: Johns Hopkins Press, 1933.

Boas, George, and Lovejoy, Arthur O. *Primitivism and Related Ideas in Antiquity.* The Johns Hopkins University Documentary History of Primitivism and Related Ideas, vol. 1. Baltimore: Johns Hopkins Press, 1935.

Boccage, Marie Anne Lepage du. *La Colombiade.* In *Recueil des oeuvres de Madame du Boccage, des Académies de Padoue, Bologne, Rome, Lyon et Rouen,* vol. 3. Lyon: Frères Perisse, 1770.

―――. *La Colombiade di Madame du Boccage.* Translated by several people, with a preface by Paolo Frisi. Milan: Mavelli, 1771.

Bode, Carl. *The Anatomy of American Popular Culture, 1840–1861.* Berkeley and Los Angeles: University of California Press, 1959.

Bodin, Jean. *La méthode de l'histoire.* Translated and introduced by Pierre Mesnard. Publications de la Faculté des Lettres d'Alger. Paris: Société d'édition "Les Belles Lettres," 1941 (Original edition: *Methodus ad facilem historiarum cognitionem,* 1566).

Bolton, Herbert Eugene. "The Epic of Greater America." *American Historical Review,* 38 (1933), pp. 448–74.

Bolton, Herbert Eugene, and De Gandia, Enrique. *Do the Americas Have a Common History? A Critique of the Bolton Theory.* Edited by Lewis Hanke. New York: Knopf, 1964.

Bonar, J. *A Catalogue of the Library of Adam Smith.* 2d ed. London, 1932.

Bonneville, Z. de Pazzi. *Les Lyonnaises protectrices des états souverains et conservatrices du genre humain, ou traité d'une découverte importante et nouvelle sur la science militaire et politique.* Amsterdam: Marc-Michel Rey, 1771.

Boorstin, Daniel J. *The Americans: The Colonial Experience.* New York: Random House, 1966.

―――. *The Americans: The National Experience.* London: Weidenfeld & Nicholson, 1966.

―――. *The Genius of American Politics.* Chicago University Charles R. Walgreen Foundation Lectures. Chicago: University of Chicago Press, 1953.

Bossi, Luigi. *Elogio storico del conte commendatore Gian Rinaldo Carli.* Venezia. Stamperia C. Palese, 1797.

Boswell, James. *Boswell in Holland, 1763–1764, Including his Correspondence with Belle de Zuylen (Aélide).* Edited by Frederick A. Pottle. Yale Edition of the Private Papers of James Boswell, vol. 2. New York: McGraw-Hill, 1952.

―――. *Boswell on the Grand Tour: Germany and Switzerland, 1764.* Edited by Frederick A. Pottle. Yale Edition of the Private Papers of James Boswell, vol. 4. New York: McGraw-Hill, 1953.

―――. *Boswell's Journal of a Tour to the Hebrides with Samuel Johnson, LL.D.* Edited by Frederick A. Pottle and Charles H. Bennett. New York: The Viking Press, 1936.

―――. *The Life of Samuel Johnson, LL.D., by James Boswell, Esq.* Everyman's Library, Biography, vols. 1 and 2. London: J. M. Dent; New York: E. P. Dutton, 1906.

―――. *London Journal, 1762–63.* Edited by Frederick A. Pottle. Yale Edition of the Private Papers of James Boswell, vol. 1. London, 1951.

Bowers, David F. *Foreign Influences in American Life: Essays and Critical Bibliographies.* Princeton Studies in American Civilization. Princeton: Princeton University Press, 1944.

Bremer, Frederika. *La vie de famille dans le Nouveau Monde: Lettres écrites pendant un séjour de deux années dans l'Amérique du Sud et à Cuba par Mme Frederika Bremer* (1853). Translated by R. de Puguet. 3 vols. Paris: Librarie de l'Association pour la propagation et la publication de bons livres, n.d. (ca. 1855).

Brie, Friedrich. "Die Anfänge des Amerikanismus." *Historisches Jahrbuch,* 59 (1939), pp. 352–87.

Briggs, Harold E. "Keats, Robertson and 'that most hateful land'." *PMLA,* 59 (1944), pp. 184–99.

Brissot de Warville, Jean-Pierre. *Mémoires de Brissot . . . sur ses contemporains et la Révolution française.* With notes by M. F. de Montrol. Brussels, 1830.

―――. *Nouveau voyage dans les États-Unis de l'Amérique septentrionale, fait en 1788, par J. P. Brissot.* 3 vols. Paris: Buisson, 1791.

―――. *Recherches philosophiques sur le droit de propriété et sur le vol.* Paris, 1782.

Broglie, Charles Louis Victor de, and Ségur, Louis Philippe. *Deux Français aux États-Unis et dans la Nouvelle Espagne en 1782: Journal de voyage du prince de Broglie et lettres du comte de Ségur.* With a foreword and notes by the Duc de Broglie. Mélanges publiés par la Société des Bibliophiles Français. Paris: Imprimerie Lahure, 1903.

Brooks, Van Wyck. *The Dream of Arcadia: American Writers and Artists in Italy, 1760–1915.* New York, 1958.

―――. *The Flowering of New England, 1815–1865.* With an introduction by M. A. DeWolfe Howe and illustrations by R. J. Holden. Boston: Merrymount Press, 1941.

———. *The Life of Emerson*. New York: E. P. Dutton, 1932.

———. *The Times of Melville and Whitman*. London: J. M. Dent, 1948.

Bruhns, Karl. *Alexander von Humboldt: Eine wissenschaftliche Biographie*. 3 vols. (Vol. 1: *Seine Jugend und ersten Mannesjahre; sein Reiseleben in Amerika und Asien*, by Julius Löwenberg). Leipzig: F. A. Brockhaus, 1872.

Buffon, George Louis Leclerc, Comte de. *Correspondance inédite de Buffon, à laquelle ont été réunies les lettres publiées jusqu'à ce jour*. 2 vols. Assembled and annotated by M. Henri Nadault de Buffon. Paris: L. Hachette, 1860.

———. *Morceaux choisis de Buffon*. Paris: Dabo-Butschert, 1829.

———. *Oeuvres complètes de Buffon*. 32 vols. Paris: Baudoin frères (and later Delangle frères), 1824–28.

Burckhardt, Jacob. *Weltgeschichtliche Betrachtungen*. Edited by Rudolf Marx. Leipzig: A. Kröner, 1935.

Burney, Charles. *An Eighteenth Century Musical Tour in France and in Italy* (1773). Edited by Percy A. Scholes. London: Oxford University Press, 1959.

Bury, John Bagnell. *The Idea of Progress: An Inquiry into Its Origin and Growth*. London: Macmillan, 1924.

Byron, George, Lord. *His Very Self and Voice: Collected Conversations of Lord Byron*. Edited by Ernest J. Lovell, Jr. New York: Macmillan, 1954.

———. *The Works of Lord Byron, with His Letters and Journals, and His Life by Thomas Moore, Esq.* 17 vols. London: J. Murray, 1832–36.

Caldas, Francisco José de. *Obras de Caldas*. Edited by Eduardo Posada. Biblioteca de historia nacional, vol. 9. Bogotá: Imprenta Nacional, 1912.

———. *Semanario de la Nueva Granada: Miscelánea de ciencias, literatura, artes e industria, publicada por una sociedad de patriotas granadinos bajo la dirección de Francisco José de Caldas* (1808–1810). Paris: Lasserre, 1849.

Calderón de la Barca, Frances. *Life in Mexico* (1842). Garden City, N.Y., n.d.

Canby, Henry Seidel. *Walt Whitman, an American: A Study in Biography*. Boston and New York: Houghton Mifflin, 1943.

Canby, Henry Seidel. See Thoreau, *Natural History*.

Carbia, Rómulo D. *La Crónica oficial de las Indias occidentales: Estudio histórico y crítico acerca de la historiografía mayor de Hispanoamérica en los siglos XVI a XVIII, con una introducción sobre la crónica oficial en Castilla*. Biblioteca Humanidades, vol. 14. La Plata, 1934.

———. *Historia de la leyenda negra hispano-americana*. Buenos Aires: Ediciones Orientación Española, 1943.

Carli, Gian Rinaldo. *Delle lettere americane*. 2 vols. Cosmopoli [Florence], 1780.

———. *Trecentosessantasei lettere di Gian Rinaldo Carli, capodistriano*. Annotated by Baccio Ziliotto. N.p., n.d. (but Trieste, 1909).

Cassarà, Salvatore. *La politica di Giacomo Leopardi nei "Paralipomeni." Esposizione e note*. Palermo: Giannone & Lamantia, 1886.

Cassirer, Ernst. *Goethe und die geschichtliche Welt: Drei Aufsätze*. Berlin: Bruno Cassirer, 1932.

Cassirer, Ernst. See Kant, *Werke*.

Castiglioni, Luigi. *Viaggio negli Stati Uniti dell'America settentrionale fatto negli anni 1785, 1786 e 1787 da Luigi Castiglioni: Con alcune osservazioni sui vegetabili più utili di quel paese*. 2 vols. Milan: Stamperia di G. Marelli, 1790.

Castle, Eduard. *Der grosse Unbekannte: Das Leben von Charles Sealsfield*. Vienna: Wulf Stratowa Verlag, 1952.

Castle, Eduard. See Lenau.

Cather, Thomas. *Journal of a Voyage to America in 1836*. London: Rodale Press, 1955.

Cattaneo, Carlo. *Opere edite ed inedite di Carlo Cattaneo*. 7 vols. Assembled and arranged by Agostino Bertani. Florence: Successori Le Monnier, 1881–92.

Cellier, Léon. *Fabre d'Olivet: Contribution à l'étude des aspects religieux du romantisme*. Paris: Nizet, 1953.

Chabod, Federico. "L'idea di Europa." *Rassegna d'Italia*, 2, no. 4 (April 1947), pp. 3–17; no. 5 (May 1947), pp. 25–37.

———. *Storia della politica estera italiana dal 1870 al 1896*. Vol. 1, *Le premesse*. Bari: Laterza, 1951.

Chasles, Philarète. *Études sur la littérature et les moeurs des Anglo-Américains au XIX* siècle. Paris: Amyot, 1851.

Chastellux, François-Jean, Marquis de. *De la félicité publique, ou Considérations sur le sort des hommes dans les différentes époques de l'histoire* (1772). New edition, corrected and enlarged by the author. 2 vols. Bouillon: Imprimerie de la Société typographique, 1776.

———. *Voyages de M. le Marquis de Chastellux dans l'Amérique septentrionale dans les années 1780, 1781 & 1782*. 2d ed. 2 vols. Paris: Prault, imprimeur du Roi, 1788–91.

Chateaubriand, François-René, Vicomte de. *Génie du christianisme* (1802). New edition, with foreword and notes. 2 vols. Paris: Berche & Tralin, 1877.

_____. *Itinéraire de Paris à Jérusalem* (1811). Preceded by *Notes sur la Grèce* and followed by *Voyages en Italie et en France*. 2 vols. Paris: Firmin Didot, 1854.

_____. *Mémoires d'outre-tombe*. Centenary edition, prepared by Maurice Levaillant. 2d ed., revised and corrected. 4 vols. Paris: Flammarion, 1949–50.

_____. *Oeuvres complètes*. 30 vols. Paris: Fain, 1826. (This edition cited for *Essai historique sur les révolutions* [1797], vols. 1–2, and *Les Natchez* [1801–26], vols. 19–20.)

_____. *Voyage en Amérique*. Critical edition, prepared by Richard Switzer. Paris: Marcel Didier, 1964.

_____. *Voyages en Amérique, en Italie, au Mont-Blanc: Mélanges littéraires*. Paris: Garnier, 1859.

Chaunu, Pierre. *L'Amérique et les Amériques*. Paris: Armand Colin, 1965.

Chénier, André. *Oeuvres complètes*. Edited by Gérard Walter. Bibliothèque de la Pléiade. Paris: Nouvelle Revue Française, 1940.

Chevalier, Michel. *Lettres sur l'Amérique du Nord*. 2 vols. Paris: C. Gosselin, 1836.

Chinard, Gilbert. *L'Amérique et le rêve exotique dans la littérature française au XVIIe et au XVIIIe siècle*. Paris: Hachette, 1913.

_____. "Eighteenth-Century Theories on America as a Human Habitat." *Proceedings of the American Philosophical Society*, 91 (1947), pp. 25–57.

_____. "L'esprit national dans la poésie américaine." *Revue de synthèse historique*, 29 (1919), pp. 161–79.

_____. *L'exotisme américain dans la littérature française au XVIe siècle d'après Rabelais, Ronsard, Montaigne, etc*. Paris: Hachette, 1911.

_____. *L'exotisme américain dans l'oeuvre de Chateaubriand*. Semicentennial Publications of the University of California, 1868–1918. Paris: Hachette, 1918.

_____. *L'homme contre la nature: Essais d'histoire de l'Amérique*. Actualités scientifiques et industrielles, no. 1070. Paris: Hermann, 1949.

_____. *Les réfugiés huguenots en Amérique: Avec une introduction sur le Mirage Américain*. Paris: Société d'édition "Les Belles Lettres," 1925.

_____. *Thomas Jefferson, the Apostle of Americanism*. Boston: Little, Brown & Company, 1944.

Chinard, Gilbert, ed. See Lahontan.

Chinchilla Aguilar, Ernesto. *La Inquisición en Guatemala*. Guatemala: Instituto de Antropologia e Historia de Guatemala, 1953 (review by Rafael Heliodoro Valle in *Revista de Historia de America*, 35–36 [1953], pp. 246–48).

Christie, John Aldrich. *Thoreau As World Traveler*. New York: Columbia University Press, 1965.

Church, Henry Ward. "Corneille de Pauw and the Controversy over His *Recherches philosophiques sur les Américains*." *PMLA*, 51 (1936), pp. 178–206.

Ciampini, Raffaele. See Mazzei, *Lettere*.

Clavigero, Francesco Saverio. *Storia antica del Messico, cavata da' migliori storici spagnuoli, e da' manoscritti e dalle pitture antiche degl'Indiani: Divisa in dieci libri, e corredata di carte geografiche e di varie figure, e Dissertazioni sulla terra, sugli animali e sugli abitatori del Messico*. 4 vols. Cesena: Gregorio Biasini, 1780–81. (Spanish versions: *Historia antigua de México*. 1st ed. of the original written in Castilian by the author. Introduction by Mariano Cuevas. 4 vols. Colección de escritores mexicanos, nos. 7–10. Mexico: Porrúa, 1945; *Historia antigua de México*. Translated by José Joaquin de Mora [1st ed., London, 1826]. 2 vols. Preface by J. Le Riverend Brusone. Biographical study by Rafael Garcia Granados. Mexico: Delfin, 1944.)

_____. *Storia della California*. Spanish translation by Garcia de San Vicente. Mexico, 1852.

Cobo, Bernabé. *Historia del Nuevo Mundo* (1653). Edited by D. Marcos Jiménez de la Espada. 4 vols. Publicaciones de la Sociedad de Bibliófilos Andaluces. Seville: E. Rasco, 1890–93.

Codazzi, Agostino. *Memórie inedite di Agostino Codazzi sui suoi viaggi per l'Europa e nelle Americhe, 1816–1822*. Edited by Mario Longhena. Milan: Alpes, 1930.

Collingwood, Robin George. *The Idea of History*. Oxford: Clarendon Press, 1946.

_____. *The Idea of Nature*. Oxford: Clarendon Press, 1945.

_____. *The New Leviathan; Or, Man, Society, Civilization and Barbarism*. Oxford: Clarendon Press, 1942.

Compagnoni, Giuseppe. *La chimica per le donne*. Venice: A Curti, 1797.

_____. *Dell'arte della parola considerata nei varii modi della sua espressione, sia che si legga, sia che in qualunque maniera si reciti: Lettere ad E. R., giovinetto di 14 anni*. Milan: Stella, 1827.

_____. *Lettere a tre giovani sulla morale pubblica*. Milan: Sonzogno, 1824.

_____. *Memorie autobiografiche di Giuseppe Compagnoni*. Edited by Angelo Ottolini. Milan: Treves, 1927.

_____. *Orazione sulla pace* [*di Lunéville*], *per ordine del Governo Cisalpino*. Milan: Stamperia Italiana e Francese, yr. 10 (1800).

_____. *Prospetto politico dell'anno 1790*. Venice: Graziosi, 1791.

_____. *Storia dei Tartari, compilata dal sig. Giuseppe Belloni* [*Compagnoni*], *antico militare italiano, e pubblicata in continuazione al Compendio della storia universale del sig. Conte di Ségur*. 7 vols. Compendio della storia universale antica e moderna, vols. 115–121. Milan: Stella, 1825.

————. *Storia dell'America, in continuazione del Compendio della storia universale del sig. Conte di Ségur.* 28 vols. and general index. Compendio della storia universale antica e moderna, vols. 26–53. Milan: Fusi, Stella e Compagni, 1820–23.

————. *Vita ed imprese di Bibì uomo del suo tempo.* In Demetrio Diamilla Müller. *Biografie autografe ed inedite di illustri italiani di questo secolo.* Turin: Pomba, 1853.

————. *Vita letteraria del cavaliere Giuseppe Compagnoni, scritta da lui medesimo.* Milan: Stella, 1834.

Compagnoni, Giuseppe, and Albergati Capacelli, F. *Lettere piacevoli, se piaceranno.* Modena: Società Tipografica, 1791.

Comte, Auguste. *Auguste Comte méconnu. Auguste Comte, conservateur. Extraits de son oeuvre finale (1851–1857).* Preface by Léon Kun. Paris: H. Le Soudier, 1898.

————. *Cours de philosophie positive.* 2d ed., with preface by Ed. Littré. 6 vols. Paris: Corbeil, Crété, 1864.

Concolorcorvo [Calixto Bustamante Carlos Inca]. *El Lazarillo de ciegos caminantes desde Buenos Aires hasta Lima* (1773). Introduction by Ventura García Calderón. Biblioteca de cultura peruana, vol. 6. Paris: Desclée, de Brouwer, 1938.

Condemarín, José Dávila. *Bosquejo histórico de la fundación (y progresos) de la insigne Universidad Mayor de San Marcos de Lima y matrícula de los SS. que componen su muy ilustre Claustro en 6 de setiembre de 1854.* Lima, 1854.

Contribuciones para el estudio de la historia de América. See Furt, Jorge M.

Cook, Capt. James. *The Voyages of Captain James Cook round the World.* Selected from his Journals and edited by Christopher Lloyd. New York: Chanticleer Press; London: Cresset Press, 1949.

Cook, Capt. James. See Forster, *Voyage round the World.*

Cordier, Henri. *Histoire générale de la Chine et de ses relations avec les pays étrangers depuis les temps les plus anciens jusqu'à la chute de la dynastie mandschoue.* 4 vols. Paris: P. Geuthner, 1920.

Correspondance littéraire, philosophique et critique par Grimm, Diderot, Raynal, Meister, etc. 16 vols. Paris: Garnier frères, 1877–82.

Crèvecoeur, Hector Saint-John de. *Letters from an American Farmer.* Garden City: Dolphin Books, 1782.

Croce, Benedetto. *Aneddoti di varia letteratura.* Naples: R. Ricciardi, 1942.

————. *Bibliografia vichiana.* Enlarged and elaborated by Fausto Nicolini. 2 vols. Milan and Naples: R. Ricciardi, 1947–48.

————. *Il carattere della filosofia moderna.* Saggi filosofici, vol. 10. Bari: Laterza, 1941.

————. *Conversazioni critiche.* Ser. 5. Scritti di storia letteraria e politica, vol. 32. Bari: Laterza, 1939.

————. *Discorsi di varia filosofia.* 2 vols. Saggi filosofici, vols. 11–12. Bari: Laterza, 1945.

————. *Estetica come scienza dell'espressione e linguistica generale.* 5th rev. ed. Filosofia dello spirito, vol. 1. Bari: Laterza, 1922.

————. *La filosofia di Giambattista Vico.* 2d rev. ed. Saggi filosofici, vol. 2. Bari: Laterza, 1922.

————. *Goethe.* 4th enlarged ed. Scritti di storia letteraria e politica, vol. 12. Bari: Laterza, 1946.

————. *La letteratura del Settecento: Note critiche.* Scritti di storia letteraria e politica, vol. 37. Bari: Laterza, 1949.

————. *Problemi di estetica e contributi alla storia dell'estetica italiana.* 2d rev. ed. Saggi filosofici, vol. 1. Bari: Laterza, 1923.

————. *Saggio sullo Hegel, seguito da altri scritti di storia della filosofia.* Saggi filosofici, vol. 3. Bari: Laterza, 1913.

————. *Ultimi saggi.* Saggi filosofici, vol. 7. Bari: Laterza, 1935.

————. *Uomini e cose della vecchia Italia.* 1st ser. Scritti di storia letteraria e politica, vol. 20. Bari: Laterza, 1927.

————. *Varietà di storia letteraria e civile.* 1st ser. Scritti di storia letteraria e politica, vol. 29. Bari: Laterza, 1935.

Cunliffe, Marcus. *The Literature of the United States.* London: Oxford University Press, 1954.

————. *The Nation Takes Shape: 1789–1837.* Chicago: Chicago University Press, 1959.

Curcio, Carlo. *Europa: Storia di un'idea.* 2 vols. Florence: Vallecchi, 1958.

Curti, Merle. *Probing Our Past.* New York: Harper & Brothers, 1954.

————. *The Roots of American Loyalty.* New York: Columbia University Press, 1946.

Curtius, Ernst Robert. *Kritische Essays zur europäischen Literatur.* Berne: A. Francke Verlag, 1950.

Cuvier, Georges. *Discours sur les révolutions du globe, avec des notes et un appendice d'après les travaux récents de MM. de Humboldt, Flourens, Lyell, Lindley, etc.* (1825). Edited by Dr. Hoefer. Paris: Firmin Didot, 1867.

Darwin, Charles. *Journal of Researches into the Natural History and Geology of the Countries Visited during the Voyage of H.M.S. Beagle round the World, under the Command of Capt. Fitz Roy, R.N. (Voyage of a Naturalist round the World.)* New York: D. Appleton, 1871.

————. *The Origin of Species by Means of Natural Selection; Or, The Preservation of Favored Races in the Struggle for Life and The Descent of Man and Selection in Relation to Sex* (*1859*). New York: Modern Library, n.d. (but 1936).

Daudin, Henri. *De Linné à Jussieu: Méthodes de la classification et idée de série en botanique et en zoologie* (*1740–1790*). Études d'histoire des sciences naturelles, vol. 1. Paris: F. Alcan, 1926.

Dávalos, José Manuel. *De morbis nonnullis Limae grassantibus ipsorumque therapeia*. Montpellier: J.-F. Picot, 1787.

Defourneaux, Marcelin. *L'Inquisition espagnole et les livres français au XVIIIᵉ siècle*. Paris; Presses Universitaires de France, 1963.

De Gandia, Enrique. *Historia crítica de los mitos de la conquista americana*. Madrid: J. Roldán, 1929.

———. "El panamericanismo en la historia." *Boletín de la Academia Nacional de la Historia*, 15 (1941), pp. 383–93.

Delacroix, Jacques-Vincent. *Mémoires d'un Américain, avec une description de la Prusse et de l'isle de Saint-Domingue, par l'auteur des Lettres d'Affi à Zurac, & de celles d'un philosophe sensible*. 2 vols. Lausanne and Paris, 1771.

D'Elia, Donald J. "Dr. Benjamin Rush and the Negro." *Journal of the History of Ideas*, 30, no. 3 (1969), pp. 413–22.

Delisle de Sales, Jean-Baptiste Claude Isoard. *De la philosophie de la Nature, ou Traité de morale pour le genre humain, tiré de la philosophie et fondé sur la nature*. 6 vols. Amsterdam: Arkstée & Merkus, 1770–74.

———. *Histoire philosophique du monde primitif, par l'auteur de la Philosophie de la Nature* (1780). 4th ed. 7 vols. + atlas. Paris: Barrois aîné, 1793–95.

De Maillet, Benoît. *Telliamed, ou Entretiens d'un philosophe indien . . . sur la diminution de la mer* (1735). 2d ed., 1755.

De Maistre, Joseph. *Considérations sur la France* (1796). Lyon and Paris: Pélagaud & Roblot, 1873.

———. *Oeuvres inédites du comte Joseph de Maistre* (*Mélanges*). Published by Count Charles de Maistre. Paris: Vaton frères, 1870.

———. *Soirées de Saint-Pétersbourg, ou Entretiens sur le gouvernement temporel de la Providence, suivies d'un Traité sur les sacrifices*. Paris: Garnier frères, 1922.

Denina, Carlo. *La Prusse littéraire sous Frédéric II*. 3 vols. Berlin: Rottmann, 1790–91.

Denny, Margaret, and Gilman, William H., eds. *The American Writer and the European Tradition*. Published for the University of Rochester. Minneapolis: University of Minnesota Press, 1950.

De Pauw, Corneille. "Amérique." In *Supplément à l'Encyclopédie, ou Dictionnaire raisonné des sciences, des arts et des métiers*, vol. 1, pp. 343–54. Amsterdam: M. M. Rey, 1776–77.

———. *Défense des Recherches philosophiques sur les Américains*. Berlin, 1770; Berlin, 1771. (Citations of this work refer to the 1770 ed. unless otherwise stated.)

———. *Recherches philosophiques sur les Américains, ou Mémoires intéressants pour servir à l'histoire de l'espèce humaine, par Mr. de P.****. 2 vols. Berlin: G. J. Decker, Imp. du Roi, 1768–69.

———. *Recherches philosophiques sur les Égyptiens et les Chinois* (1773). *Oeuvres philosophiques de Pauw*, vols. 4–5. Paris: J.-F. Bastien, 1794–95.

———. *Recherches philosophiques sur les Grecs*. 2 vols. Berlin: G. J. Decker & fils, 1788.

De Sanctis, Francesco. *Giacomo Leopardi*. Edited by Walter Binni. *Opere*, vol. 8. Bari: Laterza, 1953.

De Stefano, Francesco. *Gian Rinaldo Carli* (*1720–1795*): *Contributo alla storia delle origini del Risorgimento italiano*. Collezione storica del Risorgimento italiano, 1st ser., vol. 30. Modena: Società Tipografica Modenese, 1942.

De Tipaldo, Emilio. *Biografia degli Italiani illustri nelle scienze, lettere ed arti del secolo XVIII, e de' contemporanei*. 10 vols. Venice: Tipografia di Alvisopoli, 1834–35.

Dickens, Charles. *American Notes and Pictures from Italy*. Everyman's Library. London: J. M. Dent; New York: E. P. Dutton, 1907. (1st ed.: *American Notes for General Circulation*. London, 1842.)

———. *Letters from Charles Dickens to Angela Burdett-Coutts, 1841–1865*. Selected and edited from the collection in the Pierpont-Morgan Library, with a critical and biographical introduction by Edgar Johnson. London: Jonathan Cape, 1953.

———. *The Life and Adventures of Martin Chuzzlewit*. The Oxford India Paper Dickens, 17 vols. London: Chapman & Hall, Humphrey Milford, n.d.

Diderot, Denis. *Oeuvres*. Text established and annotated by André Billy. Bibliothèque de la Pléiade. Paris: Gallimard, 1946.

———. *Pensées sur l'interprétation de la nature*. N.p., 1754.

Diderot, Denis. See *Correspondance littéraire*.

Dilthey, Wilhelm. *Hegel y el idealismo*. Translated by Eugenio Ímaz. Mexico: Fondo de Cultura Económica, 1944.

Dingwall, Eric John. *The American Woman: A Historical Study*. London: Gerald Duckworth, 1956.

Doll, Eugene Edgar. *American History as Interpreted by German Historians from 1770 to 1815*. Philadelphia: American Philosophical Society, 1949. (*Transactions of the American Philosophical Society*, new ser., vol. 38 [1948], pt. 5).

Donoso, Ricardo. *Fuentes documentales para la historia de la independencia de América*, vol. 1: *Misión de investigación en los archivos europeos.* Mexico: Instituto panamericano de geografía e historia, 1960.

Doyon, René-Louis. "Stendhal: Notes sur l'Angleterre et l'Amérique." *Table-Ronde*, 72 (December 1953), pp. 9–28.

Drouin de Bercy, Léon. *L'Europe et l'Amérique comparées.* 2 vols. Paris: Rosa, 1818.

Dumoland, Henry. "Stendhal et la politique." In *Annales de l'Université de Grenoble, Section Lettres-Droit*, 6, no. 2 (1929).

Echeverria, Durand. *Mirage in the West: A History of the French Image of American Society to 1815.* Foreword by Gilbert Chinard. Princeton: Princeton University Press, 1957.

———. "Roubaud and the Theory of American Degeneration." *French-American Review*, 3 (1950), pp. 24–33.

Eckermann, Johann Peter. *Gespräche mit Goethe in den letzten Jahren seines Lebens.* Edited and introduced by Ernst Beutler. Gedenkausgabe, vol. 24. Zurich: Artemis-Verlag, 1948.

Eguiara y Eguren, Juan José de. *Prólogos a la Biblioteca mexicana.* Foreword by Frederico Gómez de Orozco. Spanish translation, annotated, with biographical study and bibliography of the author, by Agustín Millares Carlo. Biblioteca americana de obras latinas. Mexico: Fondo de Cultura Económica, 1944. (1st ed.: *Bibliotheca mexicana, tomus primus.* Mexico, 1755.)

Elton, Oliver. *A Survey of English Literature, 1730–1780.* 2 vols. London: Edward Arnold, 1928.

———. *A Survey of English Literature, 1830–1880.* 2 vols. London: Edward Arnold, 1920.

Emerson, Ralph Waldo. *The Complete Works of Ralph Waldo Emerson.* With a biographical introduction by Edward Waldo Emerson. Centenary edition. 12 vols. Boston and New York: Houghton, Mifflin, 1903–04.

———. *Journals of Ralph Waldo Emerson.* Edited by Edward Waldo Emerson, and Waldo Emerson Forbes. 10 vols. Boston and New York: Houghton, Mifflin, 1909–14.

———. *Selected Essays of Ralph Waldo Emerson.* London, Edinburgh, Dublin and New York: Thomas Nelson & Sons, n.d.

Encina, Francisco Antonio. "Gestación de la Independencia." *Revista Chilena de Historia y Geografía*, 89 (1940), pp. 5–56.

Epinay, Mme Louise d'. *Gli ultimi anni della Signora d'Épinay: Lettere inedite all'abate Galiani (1773–82).* Edited by Fausto Nicolini. Biblioteca di cultura moderna, vol. 242. Bari: Laterza, 1933.

———. *La Signora d'Épinay e l'abate Galiani: Lettere inedite (1769–72).* With introduction and notes by Fausto Nicolini. Biblioteca di cultura moderna, vol. 169. Bari: Laterza, 1929.

Errante, Vincenzo. *Lenau: Storia di un martire della poesia.* Pubblicazioni della R. Università di Milano, Facoltà di Lettere e Filosofia. Messina and Milan: G. Principato, 1935.

Ezquerra, Ramón. "La critica española sobre América en el siglo XVIII." *Revista de Indias*, 87–88 (January–June 1962), pp. 159–289.

Fabian, Bernard. *Alexis de Tocquevilles Amerikabild: Genetische Untersuchungen über Zusammenhänge mit der Zeitgenössischen, insbesondere der englischen Amerika-Interpretation.* Beihefte zum Jahrbuch für Amerikastudien, no. 1. Heidelberg: Carl Winter, 1957.

Fabre d'Olivet, Antoine. *Histoire philosophique du genre humain; ou, l'homme considéré sous ses rapports religieux et politiques dans l'état social, à toutes les époques et chez les différents peuples de la terre.* New (3d) ed., enlarged with bio-bibliography by Sédir. 2 vols. Paris: Bibliothèque Chacornac, 1910. (1st ed.: *De l'état social de l'homme*, 1822; 2d ed.: *Histoire philosophique*, 1824.)

———. *La langue hébraïque restituée, et le véritable sens des mots hébreux rétabli et prouvé par leur analyse radicale . . .* 2 vols. Paris: Chez l'auteur, 1815–16.

———. *Les Vers dorés de Pythagore, expliqués et traduits pour la première fois en vers eumolpiques français: Précédés d'un Discours sur l'essence et la forme de la poésie chez les principaux peuples de la terre . . .* Paris: Treuttel & Würtz, 1813.

Faguet, Émile. *Dix-huitième siècle: Études littéraires.* 13th ed. Nouvelle bibliothèque littéraire. Paris: Lecène, Oudin, 1894.

———. *Politiques et moralistes du dix-neuvième siècle.* 16th ed. 3 vols. Nouvelle bibliothèque littéraire. Paris: Boivin, n.d. (ca. 1930).

Fairchild, Hoxie Neale. *The Noble Savage: A Study in Romantic Naturalism.* New York: Columbia University Press, 1928.

Falco, Giorgio. *La polemica sul Medio Evo.* Biblioteca della Società Storica Subalpina, new ser., vol. 143. Turin: Fedetto, 1933.

Faner, Robert Dunn. *Walt Whitman and Opera.* Philadelphia: University of Pennsylvania Press, 1951.

Faugère, M. L. See Roland, Mme, *Mémoires écrits.*

Fay, Bernard. *Bibliographie critique des ouvrages français relatifs aux États-Unis (1770–1800).* Bibliothèque de la Revue de littérature comparée, 7, pt. 2. Paris: E. Champion, 1925.

———. *Civilisation américaine.* Paris: Sagittaire, 1939.

———. *L'esprit révolutionnaire en France et aux États-Unis à la fin du XVIIIe siècle.* Bibliothèque de la Revue de littérature comparée, 7, pt. 1. Paris: E. Champion, 1925.

Febvre, Lucien. *Civilisation: Le mot et l'idée. Exposés par . . . Émile Tonnelat, Marcel Mauss, Alfredo Niceforo et Louis Weber.* Première Semaine internationale de Synthèse, pt. 2. Paris: Alcan, 1930.

Feijóo y Montenegro, Fray Benito Jerónimo. *Obras escogidas.* With biography and criticism of his writings by Don Vicente de la Fuente. Biblioteca de autores españoles, vol. 56. Madrid: M. Rivadeneyra, 1863.

Feugère, Anatole. "Raynal, Diderot et quelques autres historiens des deux Indes." *Revue d'histoire littéraire de la France,* 20 (1913) pp. 343–78; 22 (1915) pp. 408–52.

Fischer, Jürgen. *Oriens-Occidens-Europa: Begriff und Gedanke "Europa" in der späten Antike und im frühen Mittelalter.* Wiesbaden: F. Steiner, 1957.

Flagg, Edmund. *The Far-West; or, A Tour beyond the Mountains, Embracing Outlines of Western Life and Scenery, Sketches of the Prairies, Rivers, Ancient Mounds, Early Settlements of the French, etc.* (1838). In W. S. Tryon, ed., *A Mirror for Americans,* q.v.

Flourens, Pierre. *Buffon: Histoire de ses travaux et de ses idées.* 2d ed. Paris: Paulin, 1850.

Fonticelli, Antonio. *Americologia; ossia, Osservazioni storiche e fisiologiche sopra gli Americani, con un breve ragguaglio delle ultime scoperte fatte dai Russi nel Mar Pacifico.* Genoa: Eredi di A. Scionico, 1790.

Forster, George. *A Voyage round the World in His Britannic Majesty's Sloop Resolution, Commanded by Capt. James Cook, during the Years 1772, 3, 4, and 5.* 2 vols. London: B. White, 1777.

———. *Werke.* 4 vols. Edited by Gerhard Steiner. Frankfurt: Insel Verlag, 1967–1970.

Franck, A. *La philosophie mystique en France à la fin du XVIIIe siècle.* Paris, 1866.

Franz, Eckhart G. *Das Amerikabild der deutschen Revolution von 1848/9: Zum Problem der Übertragung gewachsener Verfassungsformen.* Heidelberg: Carl Winter, 1958.

Frisi, Paolo. See Boccage, *La Colombiade* (Milan).

Fueter, Eduard. *Geschichte der neueren Historiographie.* 3d ed., edited by Dietrich Gerhard and Paul Sattler. Handbuch der mittelalterlichen und neueren Geschichte, pt. 1. Munich and Berlin: R. Oldenbourg, 1936.

Furt, Jorge M. "De arte histórica." In R. R. Caillet-Bois et al., *Contribuciones para el estudio de la historia de América: Homenaje al Doctor Ravignani.* Buenos Aires: Peuser, 1941.

Galiani, Ferdinand. *Correspondance avec Madame d'Epinay, Madame Necker, Madame Geoffrin, etc.* With a study of the life and works of Galiani, by Lucien Perey and Gaston Maugras. 2d ed. 2 vols. Paris: C. Lévy, 1881.

Galiani, Ferdinand. See Epinay, and Nicolini, *Amici,* "G. Vico," "Intorno a F. Galiani."

Galinsky, Hans. "*Naturae Cursus:* Der Weg einer antiken kosmologischen Metapher von der Alten in die Neue Welt; Ein Beitrag zu einer historischen Metaphorik Weltliteratur." In *Arcadia, Zeitschrift für vergleichende Literaturwissenschaft,* 1 (1966), pp. 277–311; 2 (1967), pp. 11–78, 139–72. (Republished in abbreviated form in Galinsky, Hans, *Amerika und Europa: Sprachliche und sprachkünstlerische Wechselbeziehungen in amerikanischer Sicht.* Munich: Langenscheidt Verlag, 1968.)

Garcilaso de la Vega, el Inca. *Comentarios reales de los Incas.* Edited by Ángel Rosenblat. 2 vols. Buenos Aires: Emecé, 1943.

Garlick, Richard Cecil, Jr. *Philip Mazzei, Friend of Jefferson: His Life and Letters.* The Johns Hopkins Studies in Romance Literatures and Languages, extra vol. 7. Baltimore: Johns Hopkins Press; London: Oxford University Press, 1933.

Gaulmier, J. *Volney.* Paris: Hachette, 1959.

Gerbi, Antonello. "Diego de León Pinelo contra Justo Lipsio." *Fénix,* 2–3 (1945–46).

———. *Il peccato di Adamo ed Eva: Storia della ipotesi di Beverland.* Milan: La Cultura, 1933.

———. *La politica del Romanticismo: Le origini.* Biblioteca di cultura moderna, vol. 220. Bari: Laterza, 1932.

———. *La politica del Settecento: Storia di un'idea.* Biblioteca di cultura moderna, vol. 158. Bari: Laterza, 1928.

———. *Viejas polémicas sobre el Nuevo Mundo: En el umbral de una conciencia americana.* 3d ed. Lima: Banco de Crédito del Perú, 1946. (1st ed.: suppl. to *Historia,* 1, Lima, 1943; 2d ed.: Lima, 1944.)

Gervinus, Georg Gottfried. *Geschichte des neunzehnten Jahrhunderts seit den Wiener Verträgen.* 8 vols. Vol. 3 (1858): *Die Revolution der romanischen Staaten in Südeuropa und America.* Leipzig: Wilhelm Engelmann, 1855–66.

———. *J. G. Forster.* In *Schriften zur Literatur,* edited by Gotthard Erler. Berlin, 1962.

Gidney, Lucy M. *L'Influence des Etats-Unis d'Amérique sur Brissot, Condorcet et Mme Roland.* Paris: Rieder, 1930.

Gilij, Filippo Salvatore. *Saggio di storia americana; o sia, Storia naturale, civile e sacra de' regni e delle provincie spagnuole di Terra-ferma nell' America meridionale.* 4 vols. Rome: L. Perego erede Salvioni, 1780–84.

Gini, Corrado. "Le migrazioni nella preistoria e nella storia e il popolamento del continente americano." *Rivista di storia economica,* 52, no. 11 (November 1962), pp. 1403–04.

Gioberti, Vincenzo. *Del rinnovamento civile d'Italia* (1851). Edited by F. Nicolini. Bari: Laterza, 1911.

Gittings, Robert. *John Keats: The Living Year*. London: William Heinemann, 1954.
Gobineau, Joseph-Arthur. *Essai sur l'inégalité des races humaines* (1854). 4th ed. Paris: Firmin-Didot, n.d.
Goethe, Johann Wolfgang. *Autobiographische Schriften*. Edited by Kurt Jahn. Leipzig: Insel-Verlag, 1910.
──────. *Belagerung von Mainz: Kampagne in Frankreich*. In *Goethe's Werke*, edited by Ernst Hermann, vols. 25 (*Reisen*) and 26 (*Skizzen, Fragmente und Uebersetzungen*). Berlin: G. Grote, 1873.
──────. *Briefe an Charlotte von Stein*. Edited by Jonas Fränkel. 3 vols. Jena: Eugen Diederichs, 1908.
──────. *Dichtung und Wahrheit*. Edited by Kurt Jahn. Leipzig: Insel-Verlag, 1922.
──────. *Gespräche*. Edited and introduced by Wolfgang Pfeifer-Belli. 2 vols. Zurich: Artemis-Verlag, 1949. (Memorial edition, edited by Ernst Beutler, vols. 22–23).
──────. *Italienische Reise*. Edited by Hans Timotheus Kroeber. 2 vols. Leipzig: Insel-Verlag, 1913.
Goez, Werner. *Translatio Imperii: Ein Beitrag zur Geschichte des Geschichtsdenken und der politischen Theorien im Mittelalter und in der frühen Neuzeit*. Tübingen, 1958.
Goldsmith, Oliver. *A History of the Earth and Animated Nature* (1774). 2 vols. London and Edinburgh: A. Fullarton & Co., n.d.
Gollwitzer, Heinz. *Europabild und Europagedanke*. Munich: C. H. Baeck, 1951.
Greene, John C. "The American Debate on the Negro's Place in Nature, 1780–1815." *Journal of the History of Ideas*, 15 (1954), pp. 384–96.
Grimm, Jakob. See *Correspondance littéraire*.
Guerrazzi, Francesco D. *Il secolo che muore*. Rome, 1885.
Guillemin, Henri. *À vrai dire*. 6th ed. Paris: Gallimard, 1956.
Guyénot, Émile. *L'évolution de la pensée scientifique: Les sciences de la vie aux XVIIᵉ et XVIIIᵉ siècles; L'idée d'évolution. L'évolution de l'humanité*, sec. 3, vol. 68. Paris: Albin Michel, 1941.
Haldane, John. *Possible Worlds and Other Essays*. London: Chatto & Windus, 1932.
Halévy, Élie. *La formation du radicalisme philosophique*. Vol. 1: *La jeunesse de Bentham;* vol. 2: *L'évolution de la doctrine utilitaire de 1789 à 1815;* vol. 3: *Le radicalisme philosophique*. Paris: F. Alcan, 1901–04.
Hall, Basil. *Travels in North America in the years 1827 and 1828*. Including a new preface by Ferdinand Anders. Graz: Akademische Druck- und Verlagsanstalt, 1965. (French translation: *Voyage dans les États-Unis de l'Amérique du Nord, et dans le Haut et le Bas-Canada*. Introduction by Philarète Chasles. 2 vols. Brussels: H. Dumont, 1835.)
Hall, Max. *Benjamin Franklin and Polly Baker: The History of a Literary Deception*. Williamsburg, Va.: University of North Carolina Press, 1960.
Hamann, Johann Georg. *Briefwechsel*. Edited by W. Ziesemer and A. Henkel. 7 vols. Leipzig: Insel-Verlag, 1955–57.
──────. *Sämtliche Werke*. Edited by J. Nadler. 6 vols. Vienna: Thomas-Morus-Presse, 1949–57.
Hamilton, Thomas. *Men and Manners in America*. 2 vols. Edinburgh: W. Blackwood, n.d. (1833).
Handlin, Oscar, ed. *This Was America*. Cambridge, Mass.: Harvard University Press, 1949.
Hanke, Lewis. *Aristotle and the American Indians: A Study in Race Prejudice in the Modern World*. London: Hollis & Carter, 1959.
──────. "Bartolomé de las Casas: An Essay in Hagiography and Historiography." *Hispanic American Historical Review*, 33 (1953), pp. 136–51.
──────. *Bartolomé de las Casas, pensador político, historiador, antropólogo*. Translated by Antonio Hernández Travieso. Prologue by Fernando Ortiz. Sociedad Económica de Amigos del País, Ediciones de su biblioteca pública, vol. 5. Havana, 1949.
──────. "Pope Paul III and the American Indians." *Harvard Theological Review*, 30 (1937), pp. 65–102.
──────. "The *requerimiento* and Its Interpreters." *Revista de Historia de América*, 1, no. 1 (March 1938), pp. 25–34.
Hanke, Lewis, ed. *Do the Americas have a Common History? A Critique of the Bolton Theory*. New York: Knopf, 1964. (Spanish translation: *¿Tienen las Américas una historia común? Una crítica de la teoria de Bolton*. Mexico: Editorial Diana, 1966.)
Hanks, Lesley. *Buffon avant l'"Histoire naturelle."* Paris: Presses Universitaires de France, 1966.
Harris, Victor Irvin. *All Coherence Gone*. Chicago: University of Chicago Press, 1949.
Hartmann, Nicolai. *Die Philosophie des deutschen Idealismus*. Vol. 2: *Hegel*. Geschichte der Philosophie, vol. 8. Berlin and Leipzig: W. de Gruyter, 1929.
Hauser, Henri. *La modernité du XVIᵉ siècle*. Bibliothèque de la Revue Historique. Paris: F. Alcan, 1930.
Hausrath, Adolf. "J. V. von Scheffel und Anselm Feuerbach." *Deutsche Rundschau*, 52 (July–September 1887), pp. 97–122.
Hawthorne, Nathaniel. *The Scarlet Letter*. The World's Popular Classics. New York: Books Inc., n.d.
Hazard, Lucy Lockwood. *The Frontier in American Literature*. New York: Barnes & Noble, 1941.

Hazard, Paul. *La pensée européenne au XVIIIe siècle, de Montesquieu à Lessing.* 3 vols. Paris: Boivin, 1946.

Hegel, Georg Wilhelm Friedrich. *Die Phänomenologie des Geistes.* Edited by Georg Lasson. 2d ed. Philosophische Bibliothek, vol. 114. Leipzig: Felix Meiner, 1921.

———. *La scienza della logica.* Edited by Arturo Moni. 3 vols. Classici della filosofia moderna, vol. 25. Bari: Laterza, 1925.

———. *Vorlesungen über die Philosophie der Geschichte.* With introduction and notes by F. Brunstäd. Universal-Bibliothek, vols. 4881-4885a. Leipzig: Philipp Reclam, n.d. (ca. 1907).

———. *Vorlesungen über die Philosophie der Weltgeschichte.* Edited by Georg Lasson. 2 vols. Leipzig: Felix Meiner, 1920.

———. *Werke.* Berlin: Duncker und Humblot, 1832-45. (This edition used for the following works: *Ueber das Verhältniss der Naturphilosophie zur Philosophie uberhaupt* [1802] and *Ueber die wissenschaftlichen Behandlungsarten des Naturrechts* [1802-03], vol. 1; *Enzyklopädie der philosophischen Wissenschaften im Grundrisse,* vols. 6-7; *Vorlesungen über die Aesthetik,* vol. 10; *Vorlesungen über die Philosophie der Religion,* vol. 11; *Wie der gemeine Menschenverstand die Philosophie nehme,* vol. 16; *Vorrede zu Hinrichs' Religionsphilosophie,* vol. 17; and *Philosophische Propedeutik,* vol. 18.)

Heine, Heinrich. *Sämtliche Werke.* Edited by O. Walzel. 10 vols. Leipzig: Insel-Verlag, 1911-15.

Henríquez Ureña, Pedro. *Literary Currents in Hispanic America.* The Charles Eliot Norton Lectures, 1940-41. Cambridge, Mass.: Harvard University Press, 1941. (Spanish translation: *Las corrientes literarias en la América hispánica.* Translated by Joaquín Díez-Canedo. Biblioteca americana, vol. 9. Mexico and Buenos Aires: Fondo de Cultura Económica, 1949.)

Hérault de Séchelles, Jean-Marie. *Voyage à Montbard* (1785). With preface and notes by F. A. Aulard. Les chef-d'oeuvres inconnus. Paris: Librairie des Bibliophiles (Jouaust), 1890.

Herder, Johann Gottfried von. *Briefe zur Beförderung der Humanität.* Frankfurt and Leipzig, 1793-98.

———. *Idées sur la philosophie de l'histoire de l'humanité.* Translated by Émile Tandel. 3 vols. Paris, 1874; *idem,* translated by E. Quinet. Paris: Levrault, 1877-78.

———. *Sämtliche Werke.* Edited by Bernhard Ludwig Suphan. 33 vols. Berlin: Weidmann, 1877-1913.

Hernández Luna, Juan. "Antonio Caso y el porvenir de América Latina." *Cuadernos Americanos,* 6, no. 3 (1947), pp. 123-30.

Herr, Richard. *The Eighteenth Century Revolution in Spain.* Princeton: Princeton University Press, 1958.

Hilliard d'Auberteuil, Michel-René. *Essais historiques et politiques sur les Anglo-Américains.* 2 vols. Brussels, 1781-82.

Hofe, Harold von. "Friedrich Schlegel and the New World." *PMLA,* 76, no. 1 (1961), pp. 63-67.

———. "Jacobi, Wieland and the New World." *Monatshefte, A Journal Devoted to the Study of German Language and Literature,* 49, no. 4 (May 1957), pp. 187-92.

Höffner, Joseph. *Christentum und Menschenwürde: Das Anliegen der spanischen Kolonialethik im goldenen Zeitalter.* Trier: Paulinus-Verlag, 1947.

Horn, Georg. *Arca Noae; sive Historia imperiorum et regnorum à condito orbe ad nostra tempora.* Ex Officina Hackiana, Lugduni Batavorum et Roterodami, 1666.

Humboldt, Alexander von. *Ansichten der Natur, mit wissenschaftlichen Erläuterungen.* 3d ed. 2 vols. Stuttgart and Tübingen: J. G. Cotta, 1849.

———. *Correspondance de Alexandre de Humboldt avec Varnhagen von Ense.* Translated from the German by Max Sulzberger. Paris: Bohné; Brussels: Fr. van Meenen, 1860.

———. *Essai politique sur le royaume de la Nouvelle-Espagne.* 5 vols. Paris: F. Schoell, 1811.

———. *Essai politique sur l'île de Cuba.* 2 vols. Paris: J. Smith, 1826.

———. *Examen critique de l'histoire de la géographie du nouveau continent, et des progrès de l'astronomie nautique aus XVe et XVIe siècles.* 5 vols. Paris: Gide, 1835-39.

———. *Kosmos: Entwurf einer physischen Weltbeschreibung.* 5 vols. Stuttgart and Tübingen: J. G. Cotta, 1845-62.

———. *Lettres américaines d'Alexandre de Humboldt* (1798-1807). With introduction and notes by E. T. Hamy. Paris: E. Guilmoto, n.d. (but 1904).

———. *Lettres de Alexandre de Humboldt à Varnhagen von Ense* (1827-1858). French translation by C.-F. Girard. Geneva: L. Held; Paris: Hachette, 1860.

———. *Reise in die Aequinoctial-Gegenden des neuen Continents.* Stuttgart: Cotta, 1859-60. (Spanish edition: *Viaje a las regiones equinocciales del nuevo continente, hecho en 1799 hasta 1804.* 5 vols. Paris: Rosa, 1826.)

———. *Vues des Cordillères, et monuments des peuples indigènes de l'Amérique.* Paris: Grecque-Latine-Allemande, n.d. (1816).

Hume, David. *Essays Moral, Political and Literary.* London and Edinburgh: Henry Frowde, 1904.

———. *The Letters of David Hume.* Edited by J. Y. T. Greig. 2 vols. Oxford: Clarendon Press, 1932.

_____. *New Letters.* Edited by Raymond Klibansky and Ernest C. Mossner. Oxford: Thomas Nelson & Sons, 1954.

Humphreys, Robin A. *William Robertson and His "History of America."* London: Hispanic and Luso-Brazilian Councils, 1954.

Ilchester, Giles Stephen Holland Fox Strangways, Earl of. *Chronicles of Holland House, 1820–1900.* London: J. Murray, 1937.

Irving, Washington. *The Sketch-Book of Geoffrey Crayon, Esq.* (1819). Paris: Baudry's European Library, 1846.

Iturri, Francisco. *Carta crítica sobre la Historia de América del señor don Juan Bautista Muñoz.* Madrid: Oficina del Gobierno, 1798.

Jacquemont, Victor. *Correspondance avec sa famille et plusieurs de ses amis pendant son voyage dans l'Inde, 1828–1832.* 2 vols. Paris: Fournier, 1833.

_____. *Correspondance inédite avec sa famille et ses amis, 1824–1832.* 2 vols. Paris: Michel Levy, 1867.

_____. *Lettres à Jean de Charpentier.* 2d ed. Paris: Muséum National d'Histoire Naturelle, 1933.

_____. *Lettres à Stendhal.* Edited by Pierre Maes. Paris: Poursin, 1933.

Jacquemont. Collection Les grands naturalistes français, edited by R. Heim. Paris: Muséum National d'Histoire Naturelle, 1959.

James, Henry. *The American Scene.* London: Chapman and Hall, 1907.

_____. *Hawthorne.* London: Macmillan, 1879.

Jameson, John Franklin. *The American Revolution Considered as a Social Movement.* Princeton: Princeton University Press, 1940.

Jefferson, Thomas. *The Life and Selected Writings of Thomas Jefferson.* Edited, with an introduction, by Adrienne Koch and William Peden. New York: The Modern Library, 1944.

_____. *Notes on the State of Virginia.* Edited, with an introduction and notes, by William Peden. Publications of the Institute of Early American History and Culture. Chapel Hill: University of North Carolina Press, 1955.

_____. *Notes on Virginia.* (1st ed. dated Paris, 1782, in fact, 1784) In *Works,* edited by P. L. Ford (see below), vol. 3, pp. 349–517.

_____. *The Papers of Thomas Jefferson.* Edited by Julian P. Boyd. 60 vols (17 vols. published to date). Princeton: Princeton University Press, 1950–.

_____. *The Works of Thomas Jefferson.* Collected and edited by Paul Leicester Ford. 12 vols. New York and London: G. P. Putnam's Sons, 1904–05.

Jefferson, Thomas. *Catalogue of the Library.* See Sowerby.

Johnson, Edgar. *Charles Dickens: His Tragedy and Triumph.* 2 vols. London: Victor Gollancz, 1953.

Johnson, Edgar. See Dickens, *Letters.*

Jolis, Giuseppe. *Saggio sulla storia naturale della provincia del Gran Chaco, e sulle pratiche, e su' costumi dei popoli che l'abitano, insieme con tre giornali di altrettanti viaggi fatti alle interne contrade di que' Barbari.* Faenza: Lodovico Genestri, 1789.

Jones, Howard Mumford. *America and French Culture, 1750–1848.* Chapel Hill: University of North Carolina Press; London: Oxford University Press, 1927.

_____. *Ideas in America.* Cambridge, Mass.: Harvard University Press, 1944.

_____. *O Strange New World: American Culture, the Formative Years.* New York: Viking Press, 1964.

_____. *The Pursuit of Happiness.* Michigan University William W. Cook Foundation Lectures. Cambridge, Mass.: Harvard University Press, 1952.

_____. *Theory of American Literature.* Cornell University Messenger Lectures on the Evolution of Civilization, 1947. Ithaca: Cornell University Press, 1948.

Juan, Jorge, and Ulloa, Antonio de. *Noticias secretas de América sobre el estado naval, militar y político de los reynos del Perú y provincias de Quito, costas de Nueva Granada y Chile . . .* (ca. 1750). 2 vols. London: R. Taylor, 1826.

_____. *Relación histórica del viage a la América meridional hecho de orden de Su Magestad para medir algunos grados de meridiano terrestre. . . .* 4 vols. Madrid: Antonio Marín, 1748.

Kalm, Pehr. *En resa til Norra Amerika.* 3 vols. Stockholm: L. Salvii kostnad, 1753–61.

Kames, Henry Home, Lord. *Sketches of the History of Man* (1774). 3d ed. 2 vols. Dublin: James Williams, 1779.

Kant, Immanuel. *Briefwechsel von Immanuel Kant.* Edited by H. E. Fischer. 3 vols. Bibliothek der Philosophen, vols. 1, 6, 7. Munich: Georg Müller, 1912–13.

_____. *Kritik der Urteilskraft.* In *Immanuel Kant's Sämtliche Werke,* vol. 6. Leipzig: Insel-Verlag, 1921.

_____. *Menschenkunde oder philosophische Anthropologie.* Edited by F. C. Starke. Leipzig: Die Expedition des europäschen Aufsehers, 1831.

_____. *Werke.* Edited by Ernst Cassirer. 10 vols. and suppl. Berlin: Bruno Cassirer, 1912–22.

Keats, John. *The Letters.* Edited by Maurice Buxton Forman. 3d rev. ed. London and New York: Oxford University Press, 1948.
———. *The Poetical Works of John Keats.* Edited with an introduction and textual notes by H. Buxton Forman. London: Oxford University Press, 1934.
Kennedy, John Hopkins. *Jesuit and Savage in New France.* Yale Historical Publications. New Haven: Yale University Press, 1950.
Kersten, Kurt. *Der Weltumsegler: Johann Georg Adam Forster, 1754–1794.* Berne: A. Francke Verlag, 1957.
Keyserling, Hermann von. *Südamerikanische Meditationen.* 2d ed. Stuttgart and Berlin: Deutsche Verlags-Anstalt, 1933.
King, Henry Stafford. *Echoes of the American Revolution in German Literature.* University of California Publications in Modern Philology, 14, no. 2. Berkeley: University of California Press, 1929.
Knight, William Angus. *Lord Monboddo and Some of His Contemporaries.* London: J. Murray, 1900.
Konetzke, Richard. "Alexander von Humboldt als Geschichtsschreiber Amerikas." *Historische Zeitschrift,* 188, no. 3 (December 1959), pp. 526–65.
Kratz, Guglielmo, S. I. "Gesuiti italiani nelle missioni spagnuole al tempo dell'espulsione (1767–1768)." *Archivum Historicum Societatis Iesu,* 11 (1942), pp. 27–68.
Kraus, Michael, *The Atlantic Civilization: Eighteenth-Century Origins.* Published for the American Historical Association. Ithaca: Cornell University Press, 1949.
———. *A History of American History.* New York: Farrar & Rinehart, 1937.
Krieg, H. "Tiergeographische und ökologische Beobachtungen und Probleme in Südamerika." In *Tier und Umwelt in Südamerika.* Ibero-Amerikanische Studien des Ibero-Amerikanischen Instituts Hamburg. Hamburg: Conrad Behre, 1940.
Kubrin, David. "Newton and the Cyclical Cosmos: Providence and the Mechanical Philosophy." *Journal of the History of Ideas,* 28, no. 3 (July–September 1967), pp. 325–46.
Kuhn, Helmut. "Amerika-Vision und Wirklichkeit." *Anglia,* 73 (1955), pp. 467–83.
Kühnemann, Eugen. *Goethe.* 2 vols. Leipzig: Insel Verlag, 1930.
Kürnberger, Fredinand. *Der Amerikamüde: Amerikanisches Kulturbild* (1855). Berlin, Leipzig and Dresden: Die Brücke, n.d. (ca. 1925).
La Condamine, Charles Marie de. *Journal du voyage fait pour ordre du Roi, à l'Équateur, servant d'introduction historique à la mesure des trois premiers dégrés du Méridien.* 3 vols. Paris: Imprimerie Royale, 1751–52.
———. *Relation abrégée d'un voyage fait dans l'intérieur de l'Amérique méridionale, depuis la Côte de la Mer du Sud, jusque aux Côtes du Brésil et de la Guiane, en descendant la rivière des Amazones.* In *Histoire de l'Académie Royale des Sciences, Année 1745.* Paris: Imprimerie Royale, 1749, pp. 391–492.
La Douceur (pseudonym). *De l'Amérique et des Américains, ou Observations curieuses du philosophe La Douceur, qui a parcouru cet hémisphère pendant la dernière guerre, en faisant le noble métier de tuer des hommes sans les manger.* Berlin: S. Pitra, 1771.
Lahontan, Louis-Armand, Baron de. *Dialogues curieux entre l'auteur et un sauvage de bon sens qui a voyagé, et Mémoires de l'Amérique septentrionale.* Edited by Gilbert Chinard. Baltimore: Johns Hopkins Press; Paris: A. Margraff, 1931.
Langdon-Davies, John. *Sex, Sin and Sanctity.* London: Gollancz, 1954.
Lanson, Gustave. *Histoire de la littérature française.* 3d ed. Paris: Hachette, 1895.
Lapp, John C. "The New World in French Poetry of the Sixteenth Century." *Studies in Philology,* 45, no. 2 (April 1948), pp. 151–64.
Larkin, Oliver Waterman. *Art and Life in America.* New York: Rinehart & Company, 1949.
Lasaulx, Ernst von. *Neuer Versuch einer alten, auf die Wahrheit der Tatsachen gegruendeten Philosophie der Geschichte* (1856). Edited by Eugen Thurnher. Munich: Oldenbourg, 1952.
Las Casas, Fray Bartolomé de. *Doctrina.* Prologue and selection by Agustín Yáñez. Biblioteca del estudiante universitario, vol. 22. Mexico: Ediciones de la Universidad Nacional Autónoma, 1941.
Lasson, Georg. See Hegel, *Die Phänomenologie, Vorlesungen . . . Weltgeschichte.*
Lastres, Juan B. "El doctor José Manuel Dávalos (1758–1821)." *Documentos* (Lima), 3, no. 1 (1951–55), pp. 155–82.
Lavergne, Léonce de. *Les économistes français au XVIIIᵉ siècle.* Économistes et publicistes contemporains. Paris: Guillaumin, 1870.
Lawrence, T. E. *The Letters.* Edited by David Garnett. London and Toronto: J. Cape, 1938.
Lebègue, Raymond. "Réalités et résultats du voyage de Chateaubriand en Amérique." *Revue d'histoire littéraire de la France,* 68, no. 6 (1968), pp. 905–34.
———. "Structure et but du *Voyage en Amérique* de Chateaubriand." In *Connaissance de l'étranger: Mélanges offerts à la mémoire de J. M. Carré.* Paris: M. Didier, 1964.
Lenau, Nikolas. *Sämtliche Werke und Briefe.* Critical text, edited by Eduard Castle. 6 vols. Leipzig: Insel-Verlag, 1910–23.

Leopardi, Giacomo. *Opere: Canti. Operette morali. Pensieri. Bruto Minore e Teofrasto. Volgarizzamenti. Martirio de' Santi Padri. Paralipomeni della Batracomiomachia. Saggi giovanili ed altri scritti non compresi nelle Opere. Carte napoletane con giunte inedite o poco note.* Edited by Riccardo Bacchelli and Gino Scarpa. Milan: Officina Tipografica Gregoriana, 1935.

———. *Puerili e abbozzi vari.* Edited by Alessandro Donati. Scrittori d'Italia, vol. 91. Bari: Laterza, 1924.

———. *Saggio sopra gli errori popolari degli antichi.* Edited by Prospero Viani. Vol. 4 of the *Opere complete,* in 16 vols. Florence: Le Monnier, 1859.

———. *Zibaldone di pensieri.* 2 vols. Tutte le opere di Giacomo Leopardi, edited by Francesco Flora, vols. 1–2. Milan: Mondadori, 1937–38.

Le Riverend Brusone, Julio. See Clavigero, *Storia antica.*

Lespinasse, Julie de. *Lettres de Mademoiselle de Lespinasse, suivies de ses autres oeuvres et de lettres de Madame du Deffand, de Turgot, de Bernardin de Saint-Pierre.* Paris: Charpentier, 1876.

Lesser, Friedrich Christian. *Théologie des insectes, ou Démonstration des perfections de Dieu dans tout ce qui concerne les insectes.* With notes by P. Lyonnet. 2 vols. The Hague: Jean Swart, 1742. (Original edition: *Insecto-theologia,* Frankfurt and Leipzig, 1738.)

Leturia, Pedro. "Maior y Vitoria ante la conquista de América." *Estudios Eclesiásticos,* 11, no. 41 (January 1932), pp. 44–82.

Lévi-Strauss, Claude. *Tristes tropiques.* Paris: Union Générale d'Edition, 1955.

Lewis, Richard Warrington Baldwin. *The American Adam: Innocence, Tragedy and Tradition in the Nineteenth Century.* Chicago: University of Chicago Press, 1955.

Liancourt, François Alexandre Frédéric de la Rochefoucauld, duc de. *Journal de voyage en Amérique et d'un séjour a Philadelphie, 1 octobre 1794 à 18 avril 1795.* Edited by Jean Marchand. Institut Français de Washington, Historical Documents, bk. 12. Paris and Baltimore: E. Droz, 1940.

Lillibridge, George D. *Beacon of Freedom: The Impact of American Democracy upon Great Britain, 1830–1870.* Philadelphia: University of Pennsylvania Press, 1955.

Lloyd, Christopher. See Cook, *Voyages.*

Lopez, Claude-Anne. *Mon Cher Papa: Franklin and the Ladies of Paris.* New Haven and London: Yale University Press, 1966.

Losacco, M. *Indagini leopardiane.* Lanciano, 1937.

Lovejoy, Arthur Oncken. *Essays in the History of Ideas.* Baltimore: Johns Hopkins Press, 1948.

———. "Goldsmith and the Chain of Being." *Journal of the History of Ideas,* 7 (1946), pp. 91–98.

———. *The Great Chain of Being: A Study of the History of an Idea.* Cambridge, Mass.: Harvard University Press, 1942.

Lovejoy, Arthur, and Boas, George. See Boas and Lovejoy.

Lovell, Ernest J. See Byron, *His Very Self.*

Lowell, James Russell. *A Fable for Critics* (1848). In Rascoe, *An American Reader,* q.v.

Löwenberg, Julius. See Bruhns.

Löwenstern, Isidore. *Les Etats-Unis et la Havane: Souvenirs d'un voyageur.* Paris: Bertrand; Leipzig: Michelsen, 1842.

Lowie, Robert Harry. *The History of Ethnological Theory.* New York: Farrar & Rinehart, 1937.

Löwith, Karl. *Von Hegel zu Nietzsche.* Zurich and New York: Europa Verlag, 1941.

Lynskey, Winifred. "Goldsmith and the Chain of Being." *Journal of the History of Ideas,* 6 (1945), pp. 363–74.

———. "The Scientific Sources of Goldsmith's *Animated Nature.*" *Studies in Philology,* 40 (1943), pp. 33–57.

Macaulay, Thomas Babington. *Essays and Lays of Ancient Rome.* London: Longmans, Green, 1902.

McDermott, John Francis. *Private Libraries in Creole Saint Louis.* Baltimore: Johns Hopkins Press, 1938.

Mackie, John Milton. *From Cape Cod to Dixie and the Tropics* (1864). In Tryon, *A Mirror for Americans,* q.v.

Madariaga, Salvador de. *Cuadro histórico de las Indias: Introducción a Bolívar.* Buenos Aires: Editorial Sudamericana, 1950.

Maes, Pierre. *Un ami de Stendhal: Victor Jacquemont.* Paris: Desclée and de Brouwer, 1934.

Mandeville, Bernard. *The Fable of the Bees, or Private Vices, Public Benefits.* Edited by F. B. Kaye. 2 vols. Oxford: Clarendon Press, 1924.

Maneiro, Juan Luis. *De vitis aliquot Mexicanorum, aliorumque qui sive virtute, sive litteris Mexici imprimis floruerunt.* 3 vols. Bononiae: Ex Typ. Laelii a Vulpe, 1791–92.

Marion, Seraphim. *Relations des voyageurs Français en Nouvelle France au XVIIᵉ siècle.* Paris: Presses Universitaires de France, 1923.

Marmontel, Jean François. *Les Incas, ou La destruction de l'empire du Pérou* (1770). 2 vols. Paris, 1777.

———. *Mémoires de Marmontel, secrétaire perpétuel de l'Académie française.* Edited by Jean-Maurice

Tourneux. With an introduction by M. F. Barrière. Bibliothèque des mémoires relatifs à l'histoire de France pendant le XVIII^r siècle, vol. 5. Paris: Firmin-Didot, 1891.

Marquez, Pietro. *Due antichi monumenti di architettura messicana.* Rome: Salomoni, 1804.

Marraro, Howard Rosario. *Relazioni fra l'Italia e gli Stati Uniti.* Quaderni del Risorgimento, vol. 6. Rome: Edizioni dell'Ateneo, 1954.

Marraro, Howard Rosario. See Mazzei, *Memorie.*

Marryat, Frederick. *A Diary in America, with Remarks on Its Institutions.* 2 vols. Paris: Baudry, 1839.

———. *Life and Letters of Captain Marryat.* By Florence Marryat. Leipzig: Tauchnitz, 1872.

Martin, Edwin Thomas. *Thomas Jefferson: Scientist.* New York: Henry Schuman, 1952.

Martineau, Harriet. *Biographical Sketches.* London: Macmillan, 1869.

———. *Retrospect of Western Travel.* 2 vols. London: Saunders and Otley, 1838.

———. *Society in America.* London, 1837. (French translation: *De la société américaine.* Translated by Benjamin Laroche. 3 vols. Brussels: Société Belge de Librairie, 1838. German translation: *Die Gesellschaft und das sociale Leben in Amerika.* Kassel, 1838; Quedlinburg, 1846.)

Martire di Anghiera, Pietro. *Décadas del Nuevo Mundo.* Translated from the Latin by Dr. D. Joaquín Torres Asensio. Buenos Aires: Editorial Bajel, 1944.

Matthiessen, Francis Otto. *American Renaissance: Art and Expression in the Age of Emerson and Whitman.* London and New York: Oxford University Press, 1941.

Maugras, Gaston. See Galiani.

Maurois, André. *Chateaubriand.* Paris: B. Grasset, 1938.

May, Henry F. *The End of American Innocence: A Study of the First Years of Our Own Time, 1912–1917.* London: Jonathan Cape, 1960.

Mazzei, Filippo. *Lettere di Filippo Mazzei alla corte di Polonia (1788–1792).* Edited by Raffaele Ciampini. Vol. 1: July 1788–March 1790. Fonti per la storia d'Italia, vol. 2. Bologna: Zanichelli, 1937.

———. *Memorie della vita e delle peregrinazioni del fiorentino Filippo Mazzei, con documenti storici sulle sue missioni politiche come agente degli Stati Uniti d'America, e del re Stanislao di Polonia.* 2 vols. Lugano: Tipografia della Svizzera Italiana, 1845–46. (English translation: *Memoirs of the Life and Peregrinations of the Florentine, Philip Mazzei, 1730–1816.* Translated by Howard R. Marraro. New York: Columbia University Press, 1942.)

———. *Philip Mazzei, Virginia's Agent in Europe: The Story of His Mission as Related in His Own Dispatches and Other Documents.* Edited by Howard R. Marraro. New York: New York Public Library, 1935. (Reprinted from the *Bulletin of the New York Public Library* [March–April, June–July, 1934].)

———. *Recherches historiques et politiques sur les États-Unis de l'Amérique septentrionale.* 4 vols. Colle [Paris]: Froullé, 1788.

Meinecke, Friedrich. *Die Entstehung des Historismus.* 2 vols. Munich and Berlin: R. Oldenbourg, 1936.

Melville, Herman. *The Complete Stories.* Edited with an introduction and notes by Jay Leida. New York: Random House, 1949.

———. *The Confidence-Man.* With an introduction by Roy Fuller. Chiltern Library, no. 19. New York: United Book Guild; London: John Lehmann, 1948.

———. *Moby Dick.* Edited by Luther S. Mansfield and Howard P. Vincent. New York: Farrar, Strauss, & Young, 1952.

———. *Moby Dick; Or, The Whale.* Illustrated by Rockwell Kent. New York: The Modern Library, 1944.

———. *Romances of Herman Melville: Typee, Omoo, Mardi, Moby Dick, White Jacket, Israel Potter, Redburn.* New York: Tudor Publishing Co., 1931.

Mencken, Henry Louis. *The American Language: Supplement One.* New York: A. A. Knopf, 1945; *Supplement Two, idem,* 1948.

Méndez Plancarte, Gabriel, ed. *Humanistas del siglo XVIII.* Biblioteca del estudiante universitario, vol. 24. Mexico: Ediciones de la Universidad Nacional Autónoma, 1941.

Mendiburu, Manuel de. *Diccionario histórico-biográfico del Perú.* 2d ed., with additions and bibliographical notes by Evaristo San Cristóbal. 11 vols. Lima: Imprenta "Enrique Palacios," 1931–34.

Menéndez Pelayo, Marcelino. *Estudios y discursos de crítica histórica y literaria.* Edited by Enrique Sanchez Reyes. Obras completas, vols. 6–12. Santander: Consejo Superior de Investigaciones Científicas, 1942.

———. *Historia de los heterodoxos españoles.* 8 vols. Biblioteca Emecé de obras universales. Buenos Aires: Editorial Emecé, 1945.

Mérimée, Prosper. *Correspondance générale.* 17 vols. Paris: Le Divan; Toulouse: Privat, 1941–64.

Mesnard, Pierre. *L'essor de la philosophie politique au XVI^r siècle.* Paris: Boivin, 1936.

Mesnard, Pierre. See Bodin.

Millares Carlo, Agustín. "Feijóo en America." *Cuadernos Americanos,* 3, no. 3 (1944), pp. 157–59.

Miller, Perry. *Errand into the Wilderness.* Cambridge, Mass.: Harvard University Press, Belknap Press, 1956.

Minguet, Charles. *Alexandre de Humboldt, historien et géographe de l'Amérique espagnole (1799–1804).* Paris: Faculté des lettres et sciences humaines, 1969.

Molina, Giovanni Ignazio. *Memorie di storia naturale lette in Bologna nelle adunanze dell'Istituto.* 2 vols. Bologna: Tipografia Marsigli, 1821.

――――. *Saggio sulla storia civile del Chili.* Bologna: Stamperia di S. Tommaso d'Aquino, 1787.

――――. *Saggio sulla storia naturale del Chili.* Bologna: Stamperia di S. Tommaso d'Aquino, 1782.

――――. *Saggio sulla storia naturale del Chili.* 2d enlarged ed. Bologna: Tipografia de' fratelli Masi, 1810.

Mommsen, Wilhelm. *Die politischen Anschauungen Goethes.* Stuttgart: Deutsche Verlags-Anstalt, 1948.

Monge, Carlos. "Aclimatación en los Andes: Confirmaciones históricas sobre la agresión climática en el desenvolvimiento de las sociedades de América." *Anales de la Facultad de Ciencias Médicas de Lima,* 28 (1945), pp. 307–83.

――――. "Aclimatación en los Andes: Influencia biológica del Altiplano en las guerras de América." *Revista de Historia de América,* 25 (1948), pp. 1–25.

――――. *Influencia biológica del Altiplano en el individuo, la raza, las sociedades y la historia de América.* Lima: Editorial Minerva, n.d. (1940).

――――. "Política sanitaria indiana y colonial en el Tahuantinsuyo." *Anales de la Facultad de Ciencias Médicas de Lima,* 17 (1935), pp. 231–76.

Monglond, André. *Le préromantisme français.* Paris: Librairie José Corti, 1966.

Montaigne, Michel de. *Essais.* Edited by Albert Thibaudet. Bibliothèque de la Pléiade. Paris: Nouvelle Revue Française, 1937.

Monti, Vincenzo. *Epistolario.* Edited by A. Bertoldi. 6 vols. Florence: Le Monnier, 1928–31.

Moore, John Robert. "Goldsmith's Degenerate Song-Birds: An Eighteenth-Century Fallacy in Ornithology." *Isis,* 34 (1942–43), pp. 324–27.

Moore, Thomas. *Poems Relating to America* (1806). In *The Poetical Works of Thomas Moore, Complete.* London: Longman, Green, 1865.

Moore, Thomas. See Byron, *Works.*

Moorehead, Allen. *Darwin and the Beagle,* London: Hamish Hamilton, 1969.

Morandi, Carlo. "Giuseppe Compagnoni e la storia dell'America." *Annali della R. Scuola Normale Superiore di Pisa: Lettere, Storia e Filosofia,* 2d ser., vol. 8, no. 3 (1939), pp. 252–61.

――――. *L'idea dell'unità politica d'Europa nel XIX e XX secolo.* Milan: Marzorati, 1948.

――――. *Problemi storici italiani ed europei del XVIII e XIX secolo.* Milan: Istituto di Studi di Politica Internazionale, 1937.

Moras, Joachim. *Ursprung und Entwicklung des Begriffs der Zivilisation in Frankreich (1756–1830).* Hamburger Studien zu Volkstum und Kultur der Romanen, vol. 6. Hamburg: Seminar für Romanische Sprachen und Kultur, 1930.

Moreau de Saint-Méry, Médéric Louis Elie. *Voyage aux États-Unis de l'Amérique.* Edited with an introduction and notes by Stewart L. Mims. Yale Historical Publications. Manuscripts and Edited Texts, vol. 2. New Haven: Yale University Press, 1913.

Mornet, Daniel. *Les sciences de la nature en France au XVIIIᵉ siècle: Un chapitre de l'histoire des idées.* Paris: Armand Colin, 1911.

Morse, Jedidiah. See Pictet.

Mossner, Ernest Campbell. *The Life of David Hume.* Austin: University of Texas Press, 1954.

Moxó, Benito María de. *Cartas mejicanas escritas por D. Benito María de Moxó en 1805.* Presented by Andrés Herrero. Genoa: Tipografia Pellas, n.d. (1837–38).

――――. *Cartas mejicanas escritas por D. Benito María de Moxó, año de 1805.* 2d ed., corrected and amended. Genoa: Tipografia Pellas, n.d.

Mumford, Lewis. *Herman Melville.* New York: Literary Guild of America, 1929.

Muñoz, Juan Bautista. *Historia del Nuevo-Mundo.* Vol. 1 (only one published). Madrid: Viuda de Ibarra, 1793.

Muratori, Lodovico Antonio. *Il cristianesimo felice nelle missioni de' Padri della Compagnia di Gesù nel Paraguai.* Venice: Giambattista Pasquali, 1752.

Muthmann, Friedrich. *Alexander von Humboldt und sein Naturbild im Spiegel der Goethezeit.* Zurich and Stuttgart: Artemis-Verlag, 1955.

Nevins, Allan, and Commager, Henry Steele. *America: The Story of a Free People.* Oxford: Clarendon Press, 1943.

Nicolini, Fausto. *Amici e corrispondenti francesi dell'abate Galiani: Notizie, lettere, documenti.* Biblioteca del Bollettino dell'Archivio Storico, vol. 1. Naples: Banco di Napoli, 1954.

――――. "Giambattista Vico e Ferdinando Galiani." *Giornale storico della letteratura italiana,* 71 (1918). (Also in *Bollettino dell'Archivio Storico del Banco di Napoli,* 4 [31 December 1951], pp. 49–123.)

_____. *La giovinezza di Giambattista Vico (1668–1700): Saggio biografico.* 2d rev. ed. Biblioteca di cultura moderna, no. 216. Bari: Laterza, 1932.

_____. "Intorno a Ferdinando Galiani, a proposito d'una pubblicazione recente." *Giornale storico della letteratura italiana,* vol. 52, pp. 1–55.

_____. *La religiosità di Giambattista Vico: Quattro saggi.* Biblioteca di cultura moderna, no. 467. Bari: Laterza, 1949.

Nicolini, Fausto, ed. See Croce, *Bibliografia;* Epinay; Vico.

Niebuhr, Barthold Georg. *Lebensnachrichten über Barthold Georg Niebuhr, aus Briefen desselben und aus Erinnerungen seiner nächsten Freunde.* 3 vols. Hamburg: Perthes, 1838–39.

Niebuhr, Reinhold. *The Irony of American History.* New York: Charles Scribner; London: James Nisbet, 1952.

Niggli, P. "Goethes Schriften zur Mineralogie und Geologie von 1812–1832." *Neue Zürcher Zeitung,* 7 and 10 October 1950.

Nordenskiöld, Erik. *The History of Biology: A Survey.* Translated from the Swedish by Leonard Bucknall Eyre. New York: Tudor Publishing Co., 1936.

Nuix, Giovanni. *Riflessioni imparziali sopra l'umanità degli Spagnuoli nell'Indie, contro pretesi filosofi e politici, per servire di lume alle storie dei signori Raynal e Robertson.* Venice: F. Pezzana, 1780. (Spanish translation: *Reflexiones imparciales sobre la humanidad de los españoles en las Indias, contra los pretendidos filósofos y políticos, para ilustrar las historias de M. M. Raynal y Robertson.* Translated and annotated by Pedro Varela y Ulloa. Madrid: Joaquín Ibarra, 1782.)

O'Gorman, Edmundo. *Fundamentos de la historia de América.* Mexico: Imprenta Universitaria, 1942.

_____. "Sobre la naturaleza bestial del indio americano." *Filosofía y Letras,* 1 (1941), pp. 141–58 and 305–15.

O'Gorman, Edmundo, ed. See Acosta, *Historia* (1940); Teresa de Mier, *Escritos y memorias.*

Olschki, Leonardo. *Storia letteraria delle scoperte geografiche: Studi e ricerche.* Florence: L. S. Olschki, 1937.

Onis, José de. "The Letter of Francisco Iturri, S. J. (1789): Its Importance for Hispanic-American Historiography." *The Americas,* 8 (1951), pp. 85–90.

Ortega y Gasset, José. *Obras.* 3d ed., corrected and enlarged. 2 vols. Madrid: Espasa-Calpe, 1943.

Ortiz, Fernando. See Hanke, *Bartolomé de las Casas, pensador político.*

Oviedo y Valdés, Gonzalo Fernandez de. *Historia general y natural de las Indias, islas y tierra firme del Mar Oceano, por el capitan Gonzalo Fernández de Oviedo y Valdés, primer cronista del Nuevo Mundo.* Edited by José Amador de los Ríos. 4 vols. Madrid: Imprenta de la Real Academia de la Historia, 1851–55.

_____. *Sumario de la natural historia de las Indias* (1526). Edited, introduced, and annotated by José Miranda. Biblioteca americana, vol. 13. Mexico and Buenos Aires: Fondo de Cultura Económica, 1950.

Pace, Antonio. *Benjamin Franklin and Italy.* Philadelphia: American Philosophical Society, 1958.

Paine, Thomas. *Representative Selections.* With introduction, bibliography, and notes, by Henry Hayden Clark. New York: American Book Company, 1944.

Pallain, G. See Talleyrand, *Correspondance.*

Palmer, Robert R. *Catholics and Unbelievers in Eighteenth-Century France.* Princeton: Princeton University Press, 1939.

Parker, F. D. "José Cecilio del Valle: Scholar and Patriot." *The Hispanic American Historical Review,* 32 (1952), pp. 516–39.

Parrington, Vernon Louis. *Main Currents in American Thought: An Interpretation of American Literature from the Beginnings to 1920.* New York: Harcourt, Brace and Company, 1930.

Paupe, Adolphe. "Lettres inédites de Victor Jacquemont à Sutton Sharpe." *Revue d'histoire littéraire de la France,* 14 (1907), pp. 696–711.

Pearce, Roy Harvey. "Hawthorne and the Sense of the Past, Or, The Immortality of Major Molineux." *English Literary History,* 21 (December 1954), pp. 327–49.

_____. *The Savages of America: A Study of the Indian and the Idea of Civilization.* Baltimore: Johns Hopkins Press, 1953.

_____. "The Significance of the Captivity Narrative." *American Literature,* 19, no. 1 (March 1947), pp. 1–20.

Peden, William. See Jefferson, *Life, Notes on the State of Virginia.*

Peramas, José Manuel. *De vita et moribus sex sacerdotum Paraguaycorum.* Faenza: Archii, 1791.

_____. *De vita et moribus tredecim virorum Paraguaycorum.* Faenza: Archii, 1793. (Spanish translation of the introduction to this work: *La República de Platón y los guaraníes.* Translation and notes by Juan Cortés del Pino. Prologue by Guillermo Furlong. Buenos Aires: Emecé, 1946.)

Perey, Lucien. See Galiani.

Pérez-Marchand, Monelisa Lina. *Dos etapas ideológicas del siglo XVIII en México a través de los papeles de la Inquisición.* Mexico: El Colegio de México, 1945.

Pernety, Antoine-Joseph. *Dissertation sur l'Amérique et les Américains, contre les Recherches philoso-phiques de Mr. de P.****. Berlin: G. J. Decker, 1770.
_____. *Examen des Recherches philosophiques sur l'Amérique et les Américains et de la Défense de cet ouvrage.* 2 vols. Berlin: G. J. Decker, 1771.
_____. *Histoire d'un voyage aux Iles Malouines, fait en 1763 & 1764, avec des observations sur le détroit de Magellan et sur les Patagons.* New and enlarged edition, with preface by Delisle de Sales. 2 vols. Paris: Saillant & Nyon, 1770.
Perrier, Edmond. *La philosophie zoologique avant Darwin.* Bibliothèque scientifique internationale, vol. 45. Paris: Germer Baillière, 1884.
Perrin du Lac, F.-M. *Voyage dans les deux Louisianes et chez les nations sauvages du Missouri, par les États-Unis, l'Ohio et les provinces qui le bordent, en 1801, 1802 et 1803; avec un aperçu des moeurs, des usages, du caractère et des coutumes religieuses et civiles des peuples de ces diverses contrées.* Paris: Capelle & Renand, 1805.
Perroud, Claude. See Roland, *Lettres, Mémoires de Mme Roland.*
Peterson, Merrill D. *The Jefferson Image in the American Mind.* New York: Oxford University Press, 1960.
Peyton, John Lewis. *Over the Alleghanies, and across the Prairies: Personal Recollections of the Far West, One and Twenty Years Ago* (1870). In Tryon, *A Mirror for Americans,* q.v.
Picavet, F. *Les Idéologues.* Paris: Alcan, 1891.
Pictet, C. *Tableau de la situation actuelle des États-Unis d'Amérique d'après Jedidiah Morse et les meilleurs auteurs américains.* 2 vols. Paris: Du Pont, 1795.
Pierson, George Wilson. *Tocqueville and Beaumont in America.* New York: Oxford University Press, 1938.
Pitman, James Hall. *Goldsmith's "Animated Nature": A Study of Goldsmith.* Yale Studies in English, vol. 66. New Haven: Yale University Press, 1924.
Poe, Edgar Allen. *Works.* 8 vols. London: J. Schiells; Philadelphia: J. B. Lippincott, 1895.
Poniatowski, Michel. *Talleyrand aux États-Unis, 1794–1796.* Paris: Presses de la Cité, 1967.
Pope-Hennessy, Una. *Charles Dickens, 1812–1870.* London: Chatto & Windus, 1945.
_____. *Three English Women in America.* London: E. Benn, 1929.
Porras Barrenechea, Raúl. *Las relaciones primitivas de la conquista del Perú.* Cuadernos de historia del Perú, vol. 2. Paris: Les Presses Modernes, 1937.
Prescott, William Hickling. *History of the Conquest of Mexico, and History of the Conquest of Peru.* New York: Modern Library, 1936.
Proudhon, Pierre Joseph. *La guerre et la paix* (1861). Brussels, n.d.
Quérard, Joseph-Marie. *La France littéraire, ou Dictionnaire bibliographique des savants, historiens et gens de lettres de la France.* 12 vols. Paris: Firmin Didot, 1827–64.
Quinet, Edgar. *La Création.* In *Oeuvres complètes,* vols. 22–23. Paris, n.d.
Raimondi, E., ed. *Trattatisti e narratori del Seicento.* Milan and Naples: R. Ricciardi, 1960.
Raleigh, John Henry. *Matthew Arnold and American Culture.* Berkeley and Los Angeles: University of California Press, 1961.
Rascoe, Burton, ed. *An American Reader: A Centennial Collection of American Writings Published since 1838.* New York: G. P. Putnam, 1938.
Raynal, Guillaume Thomas François. *Histoire philosophique et politique des établissements des Eu-ropéens dans les deux Indes.* Corrected and enlarged edition. Introduction by M. A. Jay. Supplement by M. Peuchet. 12 vols. and atlas. Paris: Amable, Coste, 1820–21.
Reed, E. E. "The Ignoble Savage." *Modern Language Review,* 59 (January 1964), pp. 53–64.
Remond, René. *Les États-Unis devant l'opinion française, 1815–1852.* 2 vols. Paris: A. Colin, 1962.
Reyes, Alfonso. *Obras completas,* vol. 3. Colección Letras mexicanas. Mexico: Fondo de Cultura Económica, 1956.
_____. *Última Tule.* Mexico: Imprenta Universitaria, 1942.
Reyes, Alfonso. See Teresa de Mier, *Memorias.*
Reynolds, Reginald. *Beds: With Many Noteworthy Instances of Lying on, under or about Them.* New York and London: Doubleday, 1952.
Rice, Howard C., Jr. "Jefferson's Gift of Fossils to the Museum of Natural History in Paris." *Proceedings of the American Philosophical Society,* 95, no. 6 (1951).
Riley, Thomas A. "Goethe and Parker Cleaveland." *PMLA,* 57 (1952), pp. 350–74.
Robertson, William. *The History of America.* 2 vols. London: W. Strahan, 1777–78.
Robertson, William Spence. *La vida de Miranda.* Translated by Julio E. Payró. Buenos Aires: Academia Nacional de la Historia, 1938.
Robin, Charles C. (abbé). *Nouveau voyage dans l'Amérique septentrionale, en l'année 1781; et Campagne de l'armée de M. le comte de Rochambeau.* Philadelphia and Paris: Moutard, 1782.
Robin, Claude C. *Voyages dans l'intérieur de la Louisiane.* Paris, 1807.
Roger, Jacques. *Les sciences de la vie dans la pensée française du XVIIIe siècle.* Paris: A. Colin, 1963.

Roland, Mme Jeanne Marie (Mlle Phlipon). *Lettres*. Edited by Claude Perroud, assisted by Mme Marthe Conor. New ser., 1767–1780. 2 vols. Collection de documents inédits sur l'histoire de France, publiée par les soins du Ministre de l'Instruction publique, 4th ser., no. 73. Paris: Imprimerie Nationale, 1913–15.

———. *Lettres en partie inédites de Madame Roland (Mademoiselle Phlipon) aux demoiselles Cannet*. With introduction and notes by Charles-Aimé Dauban. 2 vols. Paris: H. Plon, 1867.

———. *Mémoires de Madame Roland*. New critical edition, by Claude Perroud. 2 vols. Paris: Plon-Nourrit, 1905.

———. *Mémoires écrits durant la captivité*. 2 vols. New edition, by M. L. Faugère. Paris: Lahure, 1864.

Romeo, Rosario. *Le scoperte americane nella coscienza italiana del Cinquecento*. Milan and Naples: R. Ricciardi, 1954.

Rosa, Gabriele. *Storia generale delle storie*. 2d ed., revised and corrected. Milan: Hoepli, 1873.

Rosenblat, Ángel. *La población indigena de América desde 1492 hasta la actualidad*. Buenos Aires: Institución Cultural Española, 1945.

Rosenblat, Ángel. See Garcilaso.

Rothschild, Salomon de. *A Casual View of America: The Home Letters of Salomon de Rothschild, 1859–1861*. Edited by S. Diamond. London: The Cresset Press, 1962.

Roubaud, Pierre Joseph André. *Histoire générale de l'Asie, de l'Afrique et de l'Amérique*. 15 vols. Paris: Chez Des Ventes de la Doué, 1770–75.

Rouché, M. *La philosophie de l'histoire de Herder*. Publications de la Faculté des Lettres de l'Université de Strasbourg, vol. 93. Paris: Société d'édition "Les Belles Lettres," 1940.

Rousseau, Jean-Jacques. *Discours sur l'origine et les fondements de l'inégalité parmi les hommes* (1754). With an introduction by F. C. Green. Cambridge: The University Press, 1944.

Rowse, A. L. *The Elizabethans and America*. London: Macmillan, 1959.

Rush, Benjamin. *Autobiography*. Edited by G. W. Corner. Princeton: Princeton University Press, 1948.

Sadleir, Michael, *Trollope: A Commentary*. London: Constable, 1947.

Sadleir, Michael. See Trollope, Anthony, *Autobiography*.

Sainte-Beuve, Charles Augustin. *Causeries du lundi*. Paris: Garnier frères, n.d.

———. *Portraits littéraires*. New edition, revised and corrected. 3 vols. Paris: Garnier frères, 1862–64.

Saint-Priest, Alexis de. *Histoire de la chute des jésuites au XVIIIᵉ siècle (1750–1782)*. Paris: Librairie d'Amyot, 1844.

Salas, Manuel de. *Escritos de don Manuel de Salas y documentos relativos a él y a su familia*. 3 vols. Santiago de Chile: Imprenta Cervantes, 1910–14.

Santillana, G. de. *Processo a Galileo*. Milan: Mondadori, 1960.

Sarrailh, Jean. *L'Espagne éclairée de la seconde moitié du XVIIIᵉ siècle*. Paris: Imprimerie Nationale, 1954.

Schachner, Nathan. *Thomas Jefferson*. New York: Appleton, Century, Crofts, 1951.

Scheffel, Joseph Viktor von. *Werke*. Edited by K. Siegen and M. Mendheim. 6 vols. Stuttgart: Bong, 1918.

Schlegel, Friedrich von. "Fragmente aus dem Nachlass." Edited by Alois Dempf. *Merkur, Deutsche Zeitschrift für europäisches Denken*, 10 (1956), pp. 1175–81.

———. *The Philosophy of History*. Translated from the German by James Burton Robertson. 7th rev. ed. London: Bell & Daldy, 1873.

———. *The Philosophy of Life, and Philosophy of Language*. Translated from the German by the Rev. A. J. W. Morrison. New York: Harper & Brothers, 1848.

———. *Vorlesungen über Universalgeschichte, 1805–6*. Edited by J. J. Anstett. In *Kritische Ausgabe*, vol. 14. Paderborn: Schöningh, 1960.

Schopenhauer, Arthur. *Sämtliche Werke*. 5 vols.: vols. 1–2, *Die Welt als Wille und Vorstellung*; vol. 3, *Kleinere Schriften*; vols. 4–5, *Parerga und Paralipomena*. Edited by Eduard Grisebach and Hans Henning. Leipzig: Insel-Verlag, 1916.

Schulin, Ernst. *Die weltgeschichtliche Erfassung des Orients bei Hegel und Ranke*. Göttingen, 1958.

Sells, Arthur Lytton. *Les sources françaises de Goldsmith*. Bibliothèque de la Revue de littérature comparée, vol. 12. Paris: E. Champion, 1924.

Sepúlveda, Juan Ginés de. *Tratado sobre las justas causas de la guerra contra los indios*. With a foreword by Marcelino Menéndez y Pelayo and critical study by Manuel García-Pelayo. Mexico: Fondo de Cultura Económica, 1941. (Original Latin version: *Democrates alter*, 1547.)

Serban, Nicolas. *Leopardi et la France: Essai de littérature comparée*. Paris: E. Champion, 1913.

Sestan, Ernesto. *Europa settecentesca ed altri saggi*. Milan and Naples: R. Ricciardi, 1951.

Seybold, Ethel. *Thoreau: The Quest and the Classics*. Yale Studies in English, vol. 116. New Haven: Yale University Press, 1951.

Siegfried, André. *Tableau des États-Unis*. Paris, 1954.

Smalley, Donald. See Trollope, Anthony, *North America* (1951); Trollope, Frances, *Domestic Manners*.

Smallwood, William Martin. *Natural History and the American Mind.* Columbia Studies in American Culture, vol. 8. In collaboration with Mabel Sarah Coon Smallwood. New York: Columbia University Press, 1941.

Smith, Bernard. *European Vision and the South Pacific, 1768–1850: A Study in the History of Art and Ideas.* Oxford: Clarendon Press, 1960.

Smith, Henry Nash. "Origins of a Native American Literary Tradition." In Denny and Gilman, *The American Writer,* q.v.

———. *Virgin Land: The American West as Symbol and Myth.* Cambridge, Mass.: Harvard University Press, 1950.

Smith, J. F. D. *Voyage dans les États-Unis de l'Amérique, fait en 1784 par J. F. D. Smith.* Translated from the English by Barantin de Montchal. 2 vols. Paris: Buisson, 1791.

Solórzano y Pereyra, Juan de. *Política indiana.* Madrid: Imprenta Real de la Gazeta, 1776. (Original Latin version, *De Indiarum jure,* 1629–39. Spanish translation, by the author, first published in 1648.)

Sommervogel, Carlos, S.I. *Bibliothèque de la Compagnie de Jésus.* New ed. 11 vols. Brussels: Oscar Schepens; Paris: Alphonse Picard, 1890–1932.

Soret, Frédéric-Jacob. *Zehn Jahre bei Goethe: Erinnerungen an Weimars klassische Zeit, 1822–1832.* Edited by H. H. Houben. Leipzig: F. A. Brockhaus, 1929.

Sowerby, E. Millicent. *Catalogue of the Library of Thomas Jefferson.* 5 vols. Washington, D.C.: Library of Congress, 1952–59.

Spell, Jefferson R. *Rousseau in the Spanish World before 1833: A Study in Franco-Spanish Literary Relations.* Austin: University of Texas Press, 1938.

Spencer, Terence. *Fair Greece Sad Relic: Literary Philhellenism from Shakespeare to Byron.* London: Weidenfeld & Nicholson, 1954.

Spoerri, William Theodor. *The Old World and the New: A Synopsis of Current European Views on American Civilization.* Schweizer Anglistische Arbeiten, no. 3. Zurich and Leipzig: M. Niehan, 1937.

Stark, Werner. *America, Ideal and Reality: The United States of 1776 in Contemporary European Philosophy.* International Library of Sociology and Social Reconstruction. London: Kegan Paul, 1947.

Stathers, Madison. *Chateaubriand et l'Amérique.* Grenoble: Allier frères, 1905.

Stebbins, L. P. and R. P. *The Trollopes.* New York: Columbia University Press, 1945.

Stendhal. *Correspondance.* 3 vols. Paris: Pléiade, 1962–68.

———. *De l'amour.* 2 vols. Lyon: Lardanchet, 1922.

———. *Histoire de la peinture en Italie.* Paris: Le Divan, n.d.

———. *Mélanges de littérature.* Paris: Le Divan, n.d.

———. *Promenades dans Rome.* 3 vols. Paris: Le Divan, 1931.

———. *Le rouge et le noir.* 2 vols. Paris: Le Divan, 1927.

———. *Souvenir d'egotisme.* Paris: Le Divan, 1927.

———. *Vie de Rossini.* 2 vols. Paris: Le Divan, 1929.

Stone, Harry. "Dickens' Use of His American Experiences in *Martin Chuzzlewit.*" *PMLA,* 72, no. 3 (June 1957), pp. 464–78.

Strich, Fritz. *Goethe und die Weltliteratur.* Berne: A. Francke Verlag, 1946.

Strout, Cushing. *The American Image of the Old World.* New York: Harper & Row, 1963.

Sumner, Charles. *Prophetic Voices Concerning America: A Monograph.* Boston and New York: Lee and Shepard, 1874.

Talleyrand, Charles Maurice de. *Correspondance diplomatique de Talleyrand; La mission de Talleyrand à Londres en 1792; Correspondance inédite de Talleyrand avec le Département des affaires étrangères, le général Biron, etc; Ses lettres d'Amérique à Lord Lansdowne.* With an introduction and notes by G. Pallain. Paris: E. Plon, Nourrit, 1889.

———. *Talleyrand in America as a Financial Promoter, 1794–96: Unpublished Letters and Memoirs.* Translated and edited by Hans Huth and Wilma J. Pugh. Annual Report of the American Historical Association for the year 1941, vol. 2. Washington, D.C.: United States Government Printing Office, 1942.

Tanner, André, ed. *Gnostiques de la Révolution.* 2 vols. Vol. 1: *Claude de Saint-Martin;* vol. 2: *Fabre d'Olivet.* Le Cri de la France, collection dirigée par Pierre Courthion, vols. 27–28. Paris: Egloff, 1946.

Tasso, Torquato. *Gerusalemme liberata.* Edited by Luigi Bonfigli. Scrittori d'Italia, vol. 130. Bari: Laterza, 1930.

———. *Il mondo creato.* Edited by G. Petrocchi. Florence: Le Monnier, 1951.

Taylor, Gordon Rattray. *Sex in History.* Past in the Present Series. London: Thames & Hudson, 1953.

Teggart, Frederick John. *Theory and Processes of History.* Berkeley and Los Angeles: University of California Press, 1941.

Temple, Edmund. *Travels in Various Parts of Peru, Including a Year's Residence in Potosi.* 2 vols. Philadelphia, 1833.

Teresa de Mier, Fray Servando. *Escritos inéditos.* Selection, introduction and notes by José María Miquel i Vergés and Hugo Díaz-Thomé. Mexico: Centro de Estudios Históricos, El Colegio de México, 1944.

――――. *Escritos y memorias.* Selection and introduction by Edmundo O'Gorman. Biblioteca del estudiante universitario, vol. 56. Mexico: Universidad Nacional Autónoma, 1945.

――――. *Historia de la revolución de Nueva España.* 2 vols. London: G. Glindon, 1813.

――――. *Memorias de fray Servando Teresa de Mier, del convento de Santo Domingo de México.* Introduction by Alfonso Reyes. Biblioteca Ayacucho, vol. 17. Madrid: Editorial América, n.d. (1917?).

Thierry, Augustin. *Dix ans d'études historiques.* Brussels: Méline, 1835.

Thistlewaite, Frank. *The Great Experiment.* Cambridge: Cambridge University Press, 1955.

Thompson, G. A. *Narrative of an Official Visit to Guatemala from Mexico.* London: John Murray, 1829.

Thoreau, Henry David. *Journal.* Edited by Bradford Torrey and Francis H. Allen, with a foreword by Henry Seidel Canby. Boston: Houghton, Mifflin, 1949.

――――. *The Natural History of Massachusetts.* In *The Works of Henry David Thoreau,* selected and edited by Henry Seidel Canby. Cambridge Edition of the Poets. Boston: Houghton, Mifflin, 1946.

――――. *Walden and Other Writings.* Edited, with an introduction, by Brooks Atkinson. New York: Modern Library, 1937.

Ticknor, George. *Life, Letters and Journals.* 2 vols. Boston and New York: Houghton, Mifflin, 1909.

Tier und Umwelt in Südamerika. See Krieg.

Tocqueville, Alexis de. *De la démocratie en Amérique.* Introduction by Harold J. Laski. 2 vols. Paris: Gallimard, 1951.

――――. *Oeuvres et correspondance inédites d'Alexis de Tocqueville.* Edited by Gustave de Beaumont. 2 vols. Paris: Michel Lévy frères, 1861.

――――. *Voyages en Sicile et aux États Unis.* Edited by J. P. Mayer. Complete works, vol. 5, pt. 1. Paris: Gallimard, 1957.

Tognetti Burigana, Sara. *Tra riformismo illuminato e dispotismo napoleonico: Esperienze del "cittadino americano" Filippo Mazzei.* Rome: Storia e Letteratura, 1965.

Tomani, Silvana. *I manoscritti filosofici di Paolo Frisi.* Pubblicazioni della Facoltà di Lettere e Filosofia dell'Università di Milano, 44. Florence: La Nuova Italia, 1968.

Torrielli, Andrew J. *Italian Opinion on America, as Revealed by Italian Travelers, 1850–1900.* Harvard Studies in Romance Languages, vol. 15. Cambridge, Mass.: Harvard University Press, 1941.

Toynbee, Arnold Joseph. *A Study of History.* 6 vols. London: Oxford University Press, 1935–39.

Trahard, Pierre. *La jeunesse de Prosper Mérimée.* Paris: Champion, 1925.

Trattatisti e narratori del Seicento. See Raimondi.

Trollope, Anthony. *An Autobiography.* With an introduction by Michael Sadleir. London: Oxford University Press, 1924.

――――. *North America.* 3 vols. Tauchnitz Collection of British Authors, vols. 606–608. Leipzig: Bernhard Tauchnitz, 1862.

――――. *North America.* Edited with introduction, notes and new materials by Donald Smalley and Bradford Allen Booth. New York: Alfred A. Knopf, 1951.

Trollope, Mrs. Frances. *Domestic Manners of the Americans* (1832). Edited, with a history of Mrs. Trollope's adventures in America, by Donald Smalley. New York: Alfred A. Knopf, 1949.

――――. *The Life and Adventures of Jonathan Jefferson Whitlaw; or, Scenes on the Mississippi.* Paris: Baudry's European Library, 1836.

――――. *Vienna and the Austrians: With Some Account of a Journey through Swabia, Bavaria, the Tyrol, and the Salzbourg.* 2 vols. London: R. Bentley, 1837.

Tryon, Warren S., ed. *A Mirror for Americans: Life and Manners in the United States, 1790–1870, as Recorded by American Travelers.* 3 vols. Chicago: University of Chicago Press, 1952.

Turner, Ernest Sackville. *A History of Courting.* London: Michael Joseph, 1954.

Turner, Frederick Jackson. *The Frontier in American History.* New York: H. Holland, 1935.

Tuveson, Ernest Lee. *Millennium and Utopia: A Study in the Background of the Idea of Progress.* Los Angeles: University of California Press, 1949.

Ulloa, Antonio de. *Noticias americanas: Entretenimientos fisico-históricos sobre la América meridional y la septentrional oriental* (1772). Madrid: Imprenta Real, 1792.

Unánue, Doctor José Hipólito. *Obras científicas y literarias.* 3 vols. Barcelona: Tipografía La Academia, de Serra Hnos. y Russell, 1914.

Untermeyer, Louis. See Whitman.

Urzidil, Johannes. *Das Glück der Gegenwart: Goethes Amerikabild.* Goethes-Schriften in Artemis-Verlag, vol. 6. Zurich: Artemis-Verlag, 1957.

652   *Bibliography of Works Cited*

Vail, Eugène A. *De la littérature et des hommes de lettres des Etats-Unis d'Amérique.* Paris: Gosselin, 1841.
Valdizán, H. *Apuntes para la bibliografía médica peruana.* Lima, 1928.
_____. *La Escuela de Medicina.* In Unánue, *Obras científicas,* q.v.
Valle, José Cecilio del. *Obras.* Compiled by José del Valle and Jorge del Valle Matheu. 2 vols. Guatemala: Tip. Sánchez & de Guise, 1929–30.
Vargas Ugarte, Rubén, S.I. *La "Carta a los españoles americanos" de don Juan Pablo Vizcardo y Guzmán.* Lima: Editorial del C.I.M.P., 1955.
_____. *Don Benito María de Moxó y de Francolí, arzobispo de Charcas.* Publicaciones del Instituto de Investigaciones Históricas, no. 56. Buenos Aires: Imprenta de la Universidad, Facultad de Filosofía y Letras, 1931.
_____. *Jesuitas peruanos desterrados a Italia.* Lima: La Prensa, 1934.
Varnum, Fanny. *Un philosophe cosmopolite du XVIII siècle, le Chevalier de Chastellux.* Paris: Librairie Rodstein, 1936.
Vauvenargues, Luc de Clapiers, Marquis de. *Oeuvres morales.* 3 vols. Paris: E. Plon, 1874.
Venturi, Franco. *L'antichità svelata e l'idea del progresso in N. A. Boulanger.* Bari: Laterza, 1947.
_____. *La jeunesse de Diderot.* Paris: Skira, 1939.
Venturi, Franco, ed. *Illuministi italiani,* vol. 3. Milan and Naples: R. Ricciardi, 1958.
Viatte, Auguste. *Les sources occultes du romantisme: Illuminisme, théosophie, 1770–1820.* 2 vols. Bibliothèque de la Revue de littérature comparée, vols. 46–47. Paris: Champion, 1928.
Vico, Giambattista. *La scienza nuova.* Edited by Fausto Nicolini. 2 vols. Scrittori d'Italia, vols. 112–113. Bari: Laterza, 1911–16.
[Vidaurre, Felipe Gomez de?]. *Compendio della storia geografica, naturale e civile del regno del Chile.* Bologna, 1776.
Vidaurre, Manuel de. *Suplemento a las Cartas americanas.* Lima, 1827.
Viëtor, Karl. *Goethe: Dichtung, Wissenschaft, Weltbild.* Berne: A. Francke Verlag, 1949.
Villard, Léonie. *La France et les États-Unis: Échanges et rencontres (1524–1800).* Lyon: Les Éditions de Lyon, 1952.
Violo, A. *Relazioni tra l'Italia e gli Stati Uniti durante il Settecento.* Rome, 1950–51. (Unpublished thesis.)
Visconti, Dante. *Le origini degli Stati Uniti d'America e l'Italia.* Pubblicazioni del Centro Italiano di Studi Americani, Roma, 2d ser., vol. 1. Padua, 1940.
Volney, Constantin-François. *Tableau du climat et du sol des États Unis* (1803). In *Oeuvres complètes de Volney.* Paris: Firmin Didot frères, 1846.
Voltaire, François Marie Arouet de. *Candide.* In *Romans et contes.* Text established and annotated by René Groos. Bibliothèque de la Pléiade. Paris: Gallimard, 1932.
_____. *Collection complète des oeuvres.* New revised, corrected, and enlarged edition. London, 1770–79. (No publisher is given, and the indication "à Londres" is missing in the early volumes. This edition used particularly for vols. 1–6, containing the *Essai sur les moeurs* [the "Discours préliminaire" occupies 256 pp. of vol. 1] and 40–47, containing the *Questions sur l'Encyclopédie.*)
_____. *Oeuvres complètes.* New edition, prepared by Louis Moland. 52 vols. Paris: Garnier, 1877–85. (This edition used especially for vols. 17–20 [*Dictionnaire philosophique*], 27–29 [*Mélanges . . .*] and 49 [*Correspondance*].)
Vorzimmer, Peter. "Darwin, Malthus and the Theory of Natural Selection." *Journal of the History of Ideas,* 30, no. 4 (October–December 1969).
Walpole, Horace, 4th Earl of Oxford. *The Letters.* Edited by Peter Cunningham. 9 vols. Edinburgh: John Grant, 1906.
Walzel, Oskar. *Vom Geistesleben des 18. und 19. Jahrhunderts.* Leipzig: Insel-Verlag, 1911.
Webb, Daniel. *Selections from les Recherches philosophiques sur les Américains of M. Pauw.* Bath, 1789.
_____. *Selections from M. Pauw, with Additions.* Bath, 1795.
Wegelin, Christof. *The Image of Europe in Henry James.* Dallas: Southern Methodist University Press, 1958.
Weinberg, Albert K. *Manifest Destiny: A Study of Nationalist Expansion in American History.* Chicago: Quadrangle Books, 1963.
Wheatley, Vera. *The Life and Work of Harriet Martineau.* London: Secker & Warburg, 1957.
Whitaker, A. P. "The Americas in the Atlantic Triangle." In Hanke, *Do the Americas have a Common History?,* q.v.
_____. *The Western Hemisphere Idea: Its Rise and Decline.* Ithaca: Cornell University Press, 1954.
Whitaker, A. P., ed. *Latin America and the Enlightenment.* The Appleton Century Historical Essays. New York and London: Appleton Century, 1942.
Whitman, Walt. *Poetry and Prose.* With a biographical introduction and edited by Louis Untermeyer. Inner Sanctum Library of Living Literature. New York: Simon & Schuster, 1949.

Wieland, C. M. *Beyträge zur geheimen Geschichte der Menschheit.* In *Sämmtliche Werke,* vol. 14. Leipzig: Göschen, 1796.

———. "Koxkox und Kikequetzel, eine Mexikanische Geschichte" (1769–1770). In *Sämmtliche Werke,* vol. 14. Leipzig: Göschen, 1796.

Williams, Stanley Thomas. "Cosmopolitanism in American Literature before 1880." In Denny and Gilman, *The American Writer,* q.v.

Williamson, G. "Mutability, Decay and Seventeenth-Century Melancholy." *English Literary History,* 2 (1935), pp. 121–50.

Willson, Lawrence. "The Transcendentalist View of the West." *Western Humanities Review,* 14 (1960), pp. 183–91.

Wilson, Edmund. *Apologies to the Iroquois.* London: Allen, 1960.

Wish, Harvey. *Society and Thought in America.* Vol. 1: *Society and Thought in Early America: A Social and Intellectual History of the American People through 1865;* vol. 2: *Society and Thought in Modern America.* New York: Longmans, Green, 1950, 1952.

Wolpe, Hans. *Raynal et sa machine de guerre.* Paris: Génin, 1956.

Wolper, Roy S. "The Rhetoric of Gunpowder and the Idea of Progress." *Journal of the History of Ideas,* 31, no. 4 (October–December 1970), pp. 589–98.

Wright, Frances. *Views of Society and Manners in America during the years 1818-19-20.* London, 1821. (French translation: *Voyage aux États Unis d'Amérique, ou Observations sur la société, les moeurs, les usages et le gouvernement de ce pays, recueillies en 1818, 1819 et 1820.* Translated by J. T. Parisot. 2 vols. Paris: Béchet aîné, 1822.)

Wright, L. B. *Culture on the Moving Frontier.* Bloomington: Indiana University Press, 1955.

Wright, L. B., ed. *The Elizabethans' America.* London, 1965.

Zavala, Silvio. *América en el espíritu francés del siglo XVIII.* Biblioteca de El Colegio Nacional, vol. 11. Mexico: El Colegio Nacional, 1949.

———. *La filosofía política en la conquista de América.* Colección Tierra firme, vol. 27. Mexico and Buenos Aires: Fondo de Cultura Económica, 1947.

———. *Las instituciones jurídicas en la conquista de América.* Madrid: Junta para Ampliación de Estudios e Investigaciones Científicas, Centro de estudios históricos, Sección hispanoamericana, 1935.

———. "Las Casas ante la doctrina de la servidumbre natural." *Revista de la Universidad de Buenos Aires,* 3d ser., vol. 2 (1944), pp. 45–58.

———. *Servidumbre natural y libertad cristiana según los tratadistas españoles de los siglos XVI y XVII.* Publicaciones del Instituto de Investigaciones Históricas de la Universidad de Buenos Aires, no. 87. Buenos Aires: Peuser, 1944.

Ziliotto, Baccio. See Carli, *Trecentosessantasei lettere.*

Zimmermann, Eberhard August Wilhelm. *Specimen zoologiae geographicae, quadrupedum domicilia et migrationes sistens.* Leyden: Theod. Haak et socios, 1777.

Zumbini, Bonaventura. *Studi sul Leopardi.* 2d ed. 2 vols. Florence: Barbera, 1909.

Suggestions for Further Research

Quid juvat in tantis cervellum perdere libris?
Magister Stopinus

THE books I have used in my own research are mentioned in the footnotes on the appropriate pages; those cited on more than one occasion are also listed in the Bibliography of Works Cited. It goes without saying that these references, as also the rare biographical annotations, are inversely proportionate to the notoriety of the person under discussion. It did not seem necessary to outline the life of Byron or Jefferson, Leopardi or Hegel, and even less desirable to attempt to apprise the reader of the infinite bibliography concerning them. It did seem useful, on the other hand, to be somewhat more liberal with facts regarding a Filippo Mazzei or a Father Gilij, a Lord Kames or a Delisle de Sales.

I have also had to conclude, after a tentative effort, that a chronological survey of the principal works of the polemic would be somewhat superfluous too; such an outline can be gleaned from the text or, for the reader in haste, from the index, and in any case the temporal successivity it would reveal does not always imply an ideological dependence or descent.

More useful, it seemed to me, might be a list of the works I had *not* seen, but which, to judge from citations or catalog listings, or the mere promise of the title, appeared to contain material that would serve to enrich and develop some area of the history of the polemic. It may well be that some of these writings will prove to be useless, repetitious, or even completely extraneous to the argument. But a confession of ignorance is the basis of every research program.

On the overseas expansion of Europe and overall verdicts pronounced by the Europeans on the Americas:

Adams, Ephraim Douglas. "The Point of View of the British Traveller in America." *Political Science Quarterly*, 29, no. 2 (June 1914), pp. 244–64.
Allen, Walter, ed. *Transatlantic Crossing*. London, 1971.
Amaral, L. *As Américas antes dos europeos*. São Paulo, 1946.
Athearn, Robert G. *Westward the Briton*. London, 1953.
Baudin, L. "L'Empire des Incas d'après quelques écrivains français des XVI, XVII et XVIIIᵉ siècles." *Revue de l'Amérique Latine*, 21 (1921), pp. 22–29.
Berger, Max. *The British Traveller in America, 1836–1860*. New York, 1943.
Brodersen, Arvid. "Themes in the Interpretation of America by Prominent Visitors from Abroad." *The Annals* (of the American Academy of Political and Social Science), 295 (1954), pp. 21–32. (This volume of the *Annals* is entitled *America through Foreign Eyes*.)
Brooks, John Graham. *As Others See Us: A Study of Progress in the U.S.* New York, 1910.

Cawley, R. R. *Unpathed Waters: Studies in the Influence of the Voyagers on Elizabethan Literature.* Princeton, 1940.

Cohen, Bernard. "The New World as a Source of Science for Europe." *Actes du IXme Congrès International d'Histoire des Sciences.* Barcelona-Madrid, 1959, pp. 95–130.

Cook, Mercer. *French Travellers in the U.S., 1840–70.* Ph.D. dissertation, Brown University, 1936.

Desjardins, Simon. "L'Amérique au XVIIIe siècle, vue par un Français." *La vie des peuples,* 7 (1922), pp. 399–425.

Enkvist, N. E. *Caricatures of Americans on the English Stage Prior to 1870.* Societas Scientiarum Finnica. Commentationes Humanarum Litterarum, 18, no. 1. Copenhagen, 1951.

Fess, Gilbert Malcolm. *The American Revolution in Creative French Literature (1775–1937).* Columbia, Mo., 1941.

Ford, Guy Stanton. "Two German Publicists on the American Revolution." *Journal of English and Germanic Philology,* 8 (1909), pp. 144–76.

Franco, Angel. *El tema de América en los autores españoles del siglo de oro.* Madrid, 1954.

Franzen, Erich. "Europa blickt auf America." *Der Monat,* 50 (November 1952), pp. 129–41.

Gillespie, J. E. *The Influence of Oversea Expansion on England to 1700.* New York, 1920.

Golino, Carlo L. "On the Italian 'Myth' of America." *Italian Quarterly,* 3, no. 9 (Spring 1959), pp. 19–33.

Hatfield, James Taft, and Hochbaum, Elfrieda. "The Influence of the American Revolution upon German Literature." *Americana Germanica,* 3 (1899–1900), p. 334.

Heilman, Robert B. *America in English Fiction, 1760–1800.* Baton Rouge, 1937.

Heindel, Richard H. *The American Impact on Great Britain, 1898–1914.* Philadelphia, 1940.

————. *American Influences Abroad: An Exploration.* New York, 1950.

Hubbard, Geneviève G. *French Travelers in America, 1775–1840: A Study of Their Observations.* Ph.D. dissertation, American University, 1936.

Jones, Howard M. "The Image of the New World." In *Elizabethan Studies and Other Essays, in Honor of G. F. Reynolds.* Boulder, Col., 1945.

Lasky, Melvin J. "Amerika blickt auf Europa." *Der Monat,* 50 (November 1952), pp. 180–94.

Lillibridge, G. D. "American Images in Great Britain, 1820–40." Master's thesis, University of Wisconsin, 1948.

Mahieu, Robert G. *Les enquêteurs français aux Etats-Unis de 1830 à 1837.* Paris, 1934.

Masterson, J. R. "Records of Travel in North America 1700–1776." Ph.D. dissertation, Harvard University, 1938.

Mathews, M. McLeod. "Notes and Comments Made by British Travellers and Observers upon American English." Ph.D. dissertation, Harvard University, 1936.

Mereness, Newton D., ed. *Travels in the American Colonies.* New York, 1916.

Mesick, Jane Louise. *The English Traveler in America, 1785–1835.* Columbia University Studies in English and Comparative Literature. New York, 1922.

Miller, Ralph Norman. "The Historians Discover America: A Study of American Historical Writing in the Eighteenth Century." Dissertation, Northwestern University, 1946.

Monaghan, Frank. *French Travellers in the United States, 1765–1932: A Bibliography.* New York, 1933.

Nevins, Allen. *American Social History as Recorded by British Travellers.* London, 1923. 2d rev. ed., *America through British Eyes.* London, 1948.

O'Gorman, Edmundo. *La idea del descubrimiento de América.* Mexico, 1951.

Parrington, Vernon Louis, Jr. *American Dreams: A Study of American Utopias.* 2d ed. New York, 1964.

Pauling, J. K. *The United States and England.* New York, 1815.

————. *A Sketch of Old England by a New England Man.* New York, 1822.

————. *John Bull in America.* London, 1825.

Pedro, Valentín de. *América en las letras españolas del siglo de oro.* Buenos Aires, 1954.

Pope-Hennessy, Una, ed. *The Aristocratic Journey: Being the Outspoken Letters of Mrs. Basil Hall.* New York and London, 1931.

Rapson, Richard L. *Britons View America, 1860–1935.* Seattle and London, 1971.

Rein, A. "Ueber die Bedeutung der überseeischen Ausdehnung für das europäische Staatensystem." *Historische Zeitschrift,* 137 (1927), pp. 44–71.

————. *Das Problem der europäische Expansion in der Geschichtsschreibung.* Hamburg, 1929.

————. *Die europäische Ausbreitung über die Erde.* Potsdam, 1931.

Reyes, A. "América desde Europa." In *Marginalia,* 1st ser. Mexico, 1952, pp. 101–05.

Richards, P. *Amerika durch die Lupe der Karikatur.* Leipzig, 1913.

Rodrigue, Elisabeth M. "Les voyageurs français aux Etats-Unis pendant la première moitié du XIXe siècle." Ph.D. dissertation, Radcliffe, 1946.

Rossi, Joseph. *America's Image in Mazzini's Writings.* Madison, Wis., 1954.

——. "The American Myth in the Italian Risorgimento: The *Lettere* from America of Carlo Vidua." *Italica*, 38, no. 3 (September 1961), pp. 227–35.

Sherman, Stuart. *The Emotional Discovery of America*. American Academy of Arts and Letters, Academy Publications no. 54 (1926).

Sherrill, Charles H. *French Memories of Eighteenth Century America*. New York, 1915.

Silva. J. *Viajeros franceses en México*. Mexico, 1946.

Spiller, Robert E. *The American in England during the First Half Century of Independence*. New York, 1926.

Stuart, James. *Three Years in North America*. Edinburgh, 1833.

Trent, William P., et al. *The Cambridge History of American Literature*. Vol. 1. Cambridge, 1965.

Tuckermann, Henry T. *America and Her Commentators: With a Critical Sketch of Travel in the United States*. New York, 1864.

Tudisco, Anthony. "América en la literatura española del siglo XVIII." *Anuario de Estudios Americanos* (Seville), 11 (1954), pp. 565–85.

Villaverde. Juan. "América en el pensamiento de Vico." *Philosophia* (Cuyo, Argentina), 2, nos. 2–3 (1945).

Walz, John A. "The American Revolution and German Literature." *Modern Language Notes*, 16 (1901), pp. 336–51, 411–18, 449–62.

Ware, Mrs. "English Travellers of Rank in America." *North American Review*, 74 (1852), pp. 197–98.

Wheeler, Paul M. *America Through British Eyes: A Study of the Attitude of the Edinburgh Review toward the United States of America from 1802 to 1861*. Rock Hill, S.C., 1935.

Wittke, Carl. "The American Theme in Continental European Literature." *Mississippi Valley Historical Review*, 28 (June 1941), pp. 3–26.

More specifically, for the opinions expressed on the American native, see all the abundant bibliography on the state of nature and the "noble savage," among which one might mention the following:

Barba, P. A. "The American Indian in German Fiction." *German-American Annals*, n.s. 11 (1913).

Bissell, Benjamin. *The American Indian in English Literature of the Eighteenth Century*. New Haven, 1925.

Clerc, Charley. "Le Voyage de Jean de Léry et la découverte du 'bon sauvage'." *Revue de l'Institut de Sociologie*, Fondation Solvay, Brussels (1927), pp. 305–28.

Foreman, Carolyn Thomas. *Indians Abroad, 1493–1938*. Norman, Okla., 1943.

Gallotti, Jean. "Le Bon Sauvage avant Jean-Jacques Rousseau." *Le monde français*, 4 (1946), pp. 380–92.

Hodgen, Margaret T. *Early Anthropology in the Sixteenth and Seventeenth Century*. Philadelphia, 1964.

Lee, Sidney. "The American Indian in Elizabethan England." In *Elizabethan and Other Essays*, edited by F. S. Boas. Oxford, 1929.

Lopez Jimenez, Miguel. *Le degeneración de las razas americanas*.

Myres, J. L. *The Influence of Anthropology on the Course of Political Science*. London, 1914.

Ogden, H. V. S. "The State of Nature and the Decline of Lockian Political Theory in England, 1760–1800." *American Historical Review*, 46, no. 1 (1940), pp. 21–44.

Pearce, Roy Harvey. "The Eighteenth Century Scottish Primitivists: Some Reconsiderations." *E.L.H.*, 12 (1945), pp. 203–20.

Rowe, John H. "Ethnography and Ethnology in the Sixteenth Century." *The Kroeber Anthropological Society Papers*, 30 (1964), pp. 1–19.

Van Tieghem, P. "L'Homme Primitif et ses vertus dans le préromantisme européen." *Bulletin de la Société d'Histoire Moderne* (June 1922).

Vasquez, Josefina Zoraida. "El Indio Americano y su circunstancia en la obra de Fernández de Oviedo." *Revista de Indias*, 17, nos. 69–70 (1957), pp. 483–519.

Weber, Paul C. *The American Indian in Imaginative German Literature in the First Half of the Nineteenth Century*. New York, 1926.

And on the savage as seen by the Americans themselves:

Driver, David Miller. *The Indian in Brazilian Literature*. New York, 1942.

Keiser, Albert. *The Indian in American Literature*. New York, 1933.

On the influence of European ideas in the Americas:

Barbagelata, Hugo D. *L'influence des idées françaises dans la révolution et dans l'évolution de l'Amérique Espagnole*. Paris, 1917.

Baron, S. W. *People and Americans: A Memoir of Transatlantic Tourists*. London, 1953.

Battistessa, Angel J. "Cadalso y Montesquieu." *Hispania* (Buenos Aires), 10, no. 114 (1937).

Chinard, Gilbert. "The American Dream." In *Literary History of the United States.* Rev. ed. New York, 1953.

Effelberger, Hans. "Amerikanische Geschichtsauffassung (Geschichtsphilosophie)." *Die Neueren Sprachen,* 46 (1938), pp. 51–61.

Fischer, Walter. "Über einige Beziehungen der Literaturgeschichte der Vereinigten Staaten zur amerikanischen Kulturgeschichte." *Die Neueren Sprachen,* 31 (1923), pp. 38–57.

Hatfield, J. T. *German Culture in the United States.* Evanston, Ill., 1936.

Henriquez Ureña, P. *Historia de la cultura en la América Hispánica.* Mexico, 1947.

Jantz, H. S. "German Thought and Literature in New England, 1620–1820." *Journal of English and Germanic Philology,* 41 (1942), pp. 1–45.

Jones, Howard Mumford. "Importation of French Literature in New York City, 1750–1800." *Studies in Philology,* 28 (1931), pp. 235–51.

———. "Importation of French Books in Philadelphia, 1750–1800." *Modern Philology,* 32 (1934), pp. 157–77.

Pfeffer, Karl Heinz. "England im Urteil des amerikanischen Literatur vor dem Bürgerkrieg." *Palaestra* (Leipzig), 177 (1931).

Spurlin, Paul M. *Montesquieu in America, 1760–1801.* New York, 1969.

Vossler, O. *Die amerikanischen Revolutionsideale in ihrem Verhältniss zu den europäischen, untersucht an Th. Jefferson.* Munich and Berlin, 1929.

Zea, L. *América como conciencia.* Madrid, 1953.

CHAPTER 1: BUFFON AND THE INFERIORITY OF THE ANIMAL SPECIES OF AMERICA

On the immediate precedents of the Buffonian theses and on these theses themselves:

Collier, K. B. *Cosmogonies of Our Fathers: Some Theories of the Seventeenth and Eighteenth Centuries.* New York, 1934.

Cunningham, D. J. "Anthropology in the Seventeenth Century." *Journal of the Royal Anthropological Institute of Great Britain and Ireland,* 38 (1908), pp. 14–23.

Febvre, Lucien. "Un chapitre d'histoire de l'esprit humain: Les sciences naturelles de Linné à Lamarck et à Georges Cuvier." *Revue de synthèse historique,* 43 (1927).

Hervé, Georges. "Les débuts de l'ethnographie au XVIII⁰ siècle (1701–65)." *Revue de l'École d'Anthropologie de Paris,* 19 (1909), pp. 345–66, 381–401.

Kiernan, Colm. *Science and the Enlightenment in Eighteenth Century France.* Studies on Voltaire and the Enlightenment, vol. 59. Geneva, 1968.

Lovejoy, A. O. "Buffon and the Problem of Species." *Popular Science Monthly,* 79 (1911), pp. 464–73, 554–67.

Pei Wen-Chung. "On the Problem of the Change of Body Size in Quaternary Mammals." *Scientia Sinica,* 12, no. 2 (1962), pp. 231–35.

Roule, Louis. *L'histoire de la nature vivante d'après l'oeuvre des grands naturalistes français.* Paris, 1924.

Thienemann, A. "Die Stufenfolge der Dinge: Der Versuch eines natürlichen Systems der Naturkörper aus dem XVIII Jahrhundert." *Zoologische Annalen,* 3 (1910), pp. 185–275.

Tinker, Chauncey B. *Nature's Simple Plan: A Phase of Radical Thought in the Mid-Eighteenth Century.* Princeton, 1932.

Vyverberg, Henry. *Historical Pessimism in the French Enlightenment.* Cambridge, Mass., 1958.

Whitney, Louis. *Primitivism and the Idea of Progress in English Popular Literature of the Eighteenth Century.* Baltimore, 1934.

CHAPTER 2: SOME FIGURES OF THE ENLIGHTENMENT

On the theory of climates:

Garosci, A. *J. Bodin: Politica e diritto nel Rinascimento francese.* Milan, 1934.

Heiberg, J. L. "Théories antiques sur l'influence morale du climat." *Scientia,* 27 (1920), pp. 453–64.

Missenard, André. *L'homme et le climat.* Paris, 1937.

Smith, Samuel Stanhope. *An Essay on the Causes of Variety of Complexion and Figure in the Human Species.* 2d ed. New Brunswick [N.J.] and New York, 1810.

Tooley, M. J. "Bodin and the Medieval Theory of Climate." *Speculum,* 28 (1953), pp. 64–83.

On Voltaire:

Baldensperger F. "Voltaire et les affaires sud-américaines." *Revue de Littérature Comparée*, 11, no. 1 (1931), pp. 581–606.
David, Jean. "Voltaire et les Indiens d'Amérique." *Modern Language Quarterly*, 9, no. 1 (1948), pp. 90–103.
De Salvio, Alfonso. "Voltaire and Spain." *Hispania* (Stanford, Calif.), 7 (1924), pp. 69–110, 156–64.

On Raynal:

Feugère, Anatole, *Un précurseur de la Révolution Française: Raynal*. Angoulême, 1922.
Irvine, Dallas D. "The Abbé Raynal and British Humanitarianism." *The Journal of Modern History*, 3, no. 4 (1931), pp. 564–77.
Liedike, Kurt. "Die Darstellung Amerikas durch den Abbé Raynal und damit verbundene Zeitprobleme." Dissertation, Erlangen, 1954.

CHAPTER 3: DE PAUW AND THE INFERIORITY OF THE MEN OF AMERICA

De Pauw's biography has yet to be written. A fair number of sources are indicated in the studies by Beyerhaus and Church (see Bibliography of Works Cited). But neither of them used, for example, the memoirs of Dieudonné Thiebault, which contain curious details on Pernety's summons to Berlin, apparently the result of a mistake (Dieudonné Thiebault, *Mes souvenirs de vingt ans de séjour à Berlin, ou Frédéric le Grand* [Paris, 1804], V, 86–101; in the abridged version [Paris, 1860], II, 295–303), and a lively portrait of de Pauw, which I think merits transcription, if for no other reason than to interrupt the monotony of the present inventory:

Quintus [Colonel Guichard], although of French origin, did not like the French; he said everything bad of them that came to his mind and did them every disservice which lay within his power. One day I found the abbé de Paw with him and there was a sort of contest between the two men to see which of them would treat our nation the worst. Quintus considered us from the political viewpoint and reviewing all the past centuries from the Gallic migrations and the Sicilian Vespers down to the present maintained that always and everywhere we began by beguiling and finished by making ourselves detested. I raised some objections to which he paid no heed. The abbé de Paw reduced our literature to a few bits of frippery and asserted that if the worst philosophy student in the meanest school in Germany was not capable of making a better classification of our knowledge than d'Alembert's, in the introduction to the *Encyclopédie*, he would be thrown out of the window. At this I turned toward Favra and asked: "Captain, do you think I should reply?" "No," he told me, laughing. "They are raving. Just don't answer."

This abbé de Paw, who at that time had just published his work on America and the Americans, had been so lauded by Quintus and some others that Frederick had conceived the idea of having him with him [Denina mentions this too: "His old friend Colonel Quintus or Guichard introduced him to Frederick II" (*La Prusse littéraire sous Frédéric II* [Berlin, 1790–91], III, 144; cited by Burney)]. De Paw came and stayed several months at both Berlin and Potsdam. But he was sharp-tongued and harsh; he was inclined to peremptory judgments; in a word, he possessed to a very high degree that arrogant and conceited attitude that has been only too common in our modern philosophers and has consequently been adopted too generally by our youth, to the detriment of the refinement and virtue which once characterized our manners. Now Frederick set great store by this refinement in all those he dealt with, so that once he had spent some time in de Paw's company and seen how crude and scathing his manner was, he realized that the man did not suit him at all, and neglected him; whereupon the latter felt in his turn that he would do well to withdraw, and departed.

His work on America had also brought him some vexations. Dom Pernety, the King's librarian in Berlin, published a refutation of it which though long and very tedious amassed much incontestable proof of the falsity of the fundamental principle advanced by the canon of Gueldre. A French officer who had formerly been aide-de-camp to the Maréchal de Saxe, and who spent the rest of his days at Spandau, also refuted it, in a pamphlet containing a witty phrase that caught on everywhere: "Chapter one: how that, in order to be able to say that a thing has degenerated, one must first of all prove that it has been better."

Now abbé de Paw was no more a man to suffer contradiction than to correct himself; whence one may judge with what disdain and indignation he was to flee before this jest.

Quintus thus lost a support he had relied upon. He was left with nothing but his own merit. (*Souvenirs*, V, 390–92; abridged edition, II, 416–17. There are slight differences between the two texts; the final allusion is to the "philosophe La Douceur," whom Thiébault evidently identifies with Zaccaria de Pazzi de Bonneville: see above, chap. 4, sec. 7. On the [anti-Frederick] alterations made to the original text, see Général Baron [Paul] Thiébault, *Mémoires*, ed. F. Calmettes [Paris, 1894–95], V, 14–16)

On the "natural" slavery of the natives and the corresponding disputes:

Carro, V. D. *La teología y los teólogos-juristas españoles ante la conquista de América*. Madrid, 1944.

Wish, Harvey. "Aristotle, Plato, and the Mason-Dixon Line." *Journal of the History of Ideas*, 10 (1949), pp. 254–66.
Zavala, Silvio. "La evangelización y la conquista de las Indias según Fray Juan de Silva, o. f. m." *Caravelle*, 12 (1969), pp. 82–114.

CHAPTER 4: EUROPEAN REACTIONS TO DE PAUW

It is here that a methodical exploration would probably give the best results. Cited among the very earliest antagonists of de Pauw are a certain abbé Croizier, Father Lorenzo Hervás y Panduro (*Historia de la vida del hombre*), and the Jesuit Father François Para du Phanjas (*Principes de la saine philosophie* [Paris, 1774], vol. 1); among his admirers, Sébastien Mercier (*Tableau de Paris*).

As far as reviews or at least mentions of the *Recherches* are concerned the following periodicals should be examined:

Journal historique et littéraire (Luxembourg): December 1770, p. 394; September 1773, p. 159; February 1784, p. 176.
Allgemeine Deutsche Bibliothek (Berlin), 12, no. 1 (1770), pp. 114–39 (referring to the German translation of the *Recherches*, Berlin, 1769). *Lettre d'un Anonyme à l'Auteur de la Gazette Littéraire de Berlin*, feuille 296 (ca. 1770).
Allgemeine Deutsche Bibliothek (Berlin), 22, no. 1 (1774), pp. 366–82.
Journal des Sçavans, 73 (May 1774); no. 1, pp. 63–127, no. 2, pp. 361–89.
Histoire de l'Académie Royale des Inscriptions et Belles-Lettres, 40 (1780), *Mémoires* (24 January 1775, 10 July and 19 November 1776).
Mecure de France, 5 August 1786 (artícle entitled "Observations sur une opinion de M. de Pauw," which according to Echeverria, *Mirage in the West*, p. 139, contains "the most important refutation" of the climatic theory).

And judging from the title or the name of the author, or from allusions in other works, I suspect one might find something in:

Barton, Benjamin Smith. *Observations on Some Parts of Natural History*. Vol. 1 (only one published). London, 1787.
Bougainville, Louis Antoine de. *Voyage autour du monde en 1766, 67, 68 et 69*. Neuchâtel, 1772.
Bourdon, L. G. *Voyage d'Amérique*. London and Paris, 1786.
Crome, A. F. W. *Ueber die Grösse, Clima und Fruchtbarkeit des nordamerikanischen Freystaats*. Dessau and Leipzig. 1783.
Demeu[s]nier, Jean Nicholas. "Etats-Unis"; article in *Encyclopédie méthodique*. 4 vols. Paris, 1784–88. Reprinted separately as *Essai sur les Etats-Unis*. Paris, 1786.
Essai sur l'histoire naturelle d'Amérique, 1777 (see Mornet, op. cit., p. 23).
Liancourt, François de la Rochefoucauld, duc de. *Voyage dans les Etats-Unis de l'Amérique fait en 1795, 1796 et 1797*. 8 vols. Paris, yr. VII.
Renelle, Mme L. E. B. *Nouvelle Géographie à l'usage des instituts et des gouvernantes françaises*. Berlin, 1786–89 (esp. pp, iii, 7–10, 49–75; excellent people in a terrible country).
[Roux?]. *Le Nouveau Mississippi, ou Les Dangers d'habiter les bords du Scioto, par un patriote voyageur*. Paris, 1790.

A belated follower of de Pauw in terming the American man degenerate seems to be discernible in the famous doctor (and disciple of Buffon?) Robert Knox (*The Races of Man* [Edinburgh, 1849; London, 1862]).

On Galiani I have not seen:

Weigand, Wilhelm. *Der Abbé Galiani: Ein Freund des Europäer*. Bonn, 1949.

With the thesis of the westward march of history the field of inquiry obviously expands immeasurably; even limiting oneself to the corollary of the happy destiny of the New World there is an overabundance of texts. Merely by way of example one might mention:

Baritz, Loren. "The Idea of the West." *American Historical Review*, 46, no. 3 (April 1941), pp. 617–40.
Benz, Ernst. "Ost und West in der christlichen Geschichtsschreibung." *Die Welt als Geschichte*, 1 (1935), pp. 488–513.
Cochrane, R. C. "Bishop Berkeley and the Progress of Arts and Learning: Notes on a Literary Convention." *Huntington Library Quarterly*, 17, no. 3 (May 1954), pp. 229–49.
Crocker, Lester G. "Linguet's Prognostication for the American Colonies." *French-American Review*, 2 (1949), pp. 45–52.

Kliger, S. "The Gothic Revival and the German 'Translatio imperii ad Teutonicos'." *Modern Philology*, 45 (1947), pp. 73–103.

On Mme Roland one should study the Perroud edition of the letters of her later years (2 vols, Paris, 1900–03), the articles by Perroud in the *Révolution Française* (1896–99) and, here again, among the multitude of books and articles, at least the following:

Bader, C. *Mme Roland, d'après des lettres et des manuscrits inédits.* Paris, 1892.
Dobson, Austin. *Four Frenchwomen.* London, 1890.

CHAPTER 5: THE SECOND PHASE OF THE DISPUTE

On Father Feijóo:

Almoina, José. "El padre Feijóo y América." *La Nación* (Ciudad Trujillo), 14 and 20 September 1944.
Palacio Atard, V. "Feijóo y los americanos." *América Española* (Cartegena, Colombia), 13 (1957), pp. 335–49.

For some years now the ideas of the American Jesuits have been the object of renewed curiosity, especially in Mexico:

Gonzales y Gonzales, Luis. "El optimismo nacionalista como factor de la independencia de México." In *Estudios de historiografia americana.* Mexico, 1948.
Hernandez Luna, J. "El pensamiento racionalista francés en el siglo XVIII mexicano." *Filosofia y Letras* (Mexico), 12 (1947), pp. 233–50.
Navarro, B. "Los Jesuitas y la Independencia." *Abside* (Mexico), 16, no. 1 (1952), pp. 43–62.

At the center of this attention, of course, is Father Clavigero, who has been studied by Ramón Iglesia, Rubén Garcia, and Gonzales Obregón, as well as the learned:

Millares Carlo, A. "Sobre una traducción de la 'Historia de Méjico' de Clavigero." *Filosofia y Letras* (Mexico), 9 (1945), pp. 97–100.

See also:

Burrus, Ernest J. "Clavigero and the Lost Sigüenza y Góngora Manuscripts." *Estudios de Cultura Nacionál*, Mexico (Universidad Nacional Autónoma, Instituto de Historia), I, pp. 59–90.
———. "Hispanic Americana in the Manuscripts of Bologna, Italy." *Manuscripts*, 3 (1959), pp. 131–47.
Castañon, R. J. "Francisco Javier Clavigero." *Boletín Bibliográfico de la Secretaría de Hacienda y Crédito Publico* (Mexico), 33, no. 1.
Rico Gonzales, V. *Historiadores mexicanos del siglo XVIII.* Mexico, 1949.
Ronan, Charles, S. J. *Francisco Javier Mariano Clavigero: A Study in Mexican Historiography.* Ph.D. dissertation, University of Texas, 1958.

Father Molina has been less fortunate, but he too has been the object of some recent studies:

Diaz Arrieta, H. "La literatura chilena durante el siglo XVIII." *Boletín de la Academia Chilena de la Historia*, 49 (1953), pp. 43–56 (deals only with Molina and Lacunza).
Donoso, Ricardo. "El abate Molina en los paises sajones." In *Miscellanea Paul Rivet.* Mexico, 1958.
Espinosa, Januario. *El abate Molina.* Santiago, 1946.
Eyzaguirre, J. "Correspondencia de los jesuitas expulsos chilenos con el gobierno espanõl." *Boletín de la Academia Chilena de la Historia*, 58 (1958), pp. 89–101.

I have already mentioned that I was not able to see the main work by Father Velasco:

Velasco, Juan de. *Historia del Reino de Quito.* 1844.

Brandin (see below, p. 664) was supposed to publish it in 1788–89; Ternaux-Compans obtained (1840) only the second part of it for his collection; the complete edition, in three parts, was published in Quito in 1841–44. The first volume was reprinted in Quito in 1940, edited by R. Reyes. See also I. J. Barrera, "El padre Juan de Velasco," *Missionalia Hispanica* (Madrid), 10, no. 31 (1958), pp. 21–37.

On Gilij, "rediscovered" by Father Abel Salazar, see:

Gilij, Felipe Salvador. *Ensayo de Historia Americana.* Foreword and introductory study by Antonio Tovar. Biblioteca de la Academia Nacional de Historia, vols. 71–73 (translation of the first part, devoted to the Orenoco valley). Caracas, 1965.

Giraldo Jaramillo, G. "Notas biográficas sobre el padre F. S. Gilij y su Saggio di storia americana." In *Presencia de América en el pensamiento europeo*. Bogotà, 1954.

In general:

Grajales, G. *Nacionalismo incipiente en los historiadores Coloniales, Estudio historiográfico*. Mexico, 1961.

On the early North American reactions, one could perhaps find something in:

Chinard, G. "The American Philosophical Society and the World of Science, 1768–1800." *Proceedings of the American Philosophical Society*, 77 (1943), pp. 1–11.
Clark, Harry H. "The Influence of Science on American Ideas, 1775 to 1809." *Wisconsin Academy of Sciences and Letters, Transactions*, 35 (1944).
Haraszti, Zoltan. *John Adams and the Prophets of Progress*. New York, 1964.
Streit, Robert. *Bibliotheca Missionum*. Vols. 2–3. Aachen, 1924–27.

While the following ought to shed some light on the genesis and diffusion of Jefferson's ideas:

Browne, Charles A. "Thomas Jefferson and the Scientific Trends of His Time." *Chronica Botanica* (Waltham, Mass.), 8, no. 3 (1944), pp. 363–423.
Chinard, G. "An American Philosopher in the World of Nations." *Virginia Quarterly Review*, 19 (1943), pp. 189–203.
――――. "Jefferson among the Philosophers." *Ethics*, 53 (1943), pp. 255–68.
――――. "Jefferson's Influence abroad." *Mississippi Valley Historical Review*, 30 (1943), pp. 171–86.
Clark, Austin H. "Thomas Jefferson and Science." *Washington Academy of Sciences Journal*, 33 (July 1943), pp. 193–203.
Henline, Ruth. "A Study of 'Notes on the State of Virginia' as an Evidence of Jefferson's Reaction against the Theories of French Naturalists." *The Virginia Magazine of History and Biography*, 55 (July 1947), pp. 233–46.
Kinball, Marie. *Jefferson: The Scene of Europe, 1784 to 1789*. New York, 1950.
Seeber, Edmund D. "Critical Views on Logan's Speech." *Journal of American Folklore*, 60 (1947), pp. 130–46.
Shapley, Harlow. "Notes on Thomas Jefferson as a Natural Philosopher." *Proceedings of the American Philosophical Society*, 87, no. 3 (1943), pp. 234–37.

But almost all these works are mentioned and probably absorbed in the volume by Edwin T. Martin (see Bibliography of Works Cited).

On the ideas of Mazzei:

Marraro, H. R., ed. "Philip Mazzei on American Political, Social and Economic Problems." *The Journal of Southern History*, 15 (1949), pp. 354–78.

And see also:

"'Colle', the Residence of Philip Mazzie [*sic*]." *Virginia Magazine of History and Biography* (Richmond), 9 (1901–02), p. 163.

On Moreau de Saint-Méry, see the new edition of his fundamental work, *Description topographique, physique, civile, politique et historique de la partie française de l'Isle de Saint-Domingue* (1797), edited by Blanche Maurel and Etienne Taillemite, 3 vols. (Paris, 1958).

Tantet, V. *Les refugiés politiques en Amérique: Moreau de Saint-Méry, libraire à Philadelphie*. Paris, 1905 (offprint).

Finally on the genesis and diffusion of Herder's ideas one should consult:

Grundmann, Johannes (Karl Friedrich Johannes). *Die geographische und völkerkundliche Quellen und Anschauungen in Herder's Ideen*. Berlin, 1900.
Learned, M. D. "Herder and America." *German-American Annals*, 2, no. 9 (September 1904), pp. 536–70.
Sauter, E. *Herder und Buffon*. Rixheim, 1910.
Tronchon, H. *La fortune intellectuelle d'Herder en France: Bibliographie critique*. Paris, 1920.

On the questions and authors discussed in chap. 9, sec. 5, "The Quakers, the Marquis, and the Girondist," but relating to this chapter, see also:

Ellery, E. *Brissot.* Cambridge, Mass., 1915.
Philips, Edith. *The Good Quaker in French Legend.* Philadelphia, 1932.
Sicot, Lucien. *Le marquis de Chastellux (1734–1788).* Paris, 1902.

And the abundant sources cited by Howard C. Rice, Jr. in his monumental edition of Chastellux's *Voyages* (Chapel Hill, N.C., 1963).

CHAPTER 6: THE REACTION TO DE PAUW IN SPANISH AMERICA

This section is certainly the one in which one would expect the most curious discoveries. But the bibliographical material is exceedingly scattered and most of the reactions to the European calumnies are found in works dealing with politics or medicine, or in autobiographical writings, rather than in works on natural history or philosophy (which are in any case almost nonexistent). As for Portuguese America, is it really possible that no Brazilian writer sided with or against Buffon? It can only be my own fault or misfortune that I have not succeeded in finding any. Nor have I found anything at all in:

Hamilton, Charles Granville. "English-speaking Travelers in Brazil, 1851–87." *Hispanic American Historical Review,* 40, no. 4 (November 1960), pp. 533–47.

This seems to be one more of the many peculiarities that distinguish Brazil from the rest of Latin America (see L. Hanke, *Common History,* pp. 32–33, 157–58, 306–07).

For the "prehistory" of these disputes, or rather the beginnings of a Latin American geographical awareness, I would like to see:

Lopetegui, L. *El padre J. de Acosta S. I. y las misiones.* Madrid, 1942.

As far as the individual authors are concerned some, such as Mier and Valle, have considerable bibliographies, although these are almost exclusively biographical, and in Mier's case fictional too (Arenas, Reynaldo, *El mundo alucinante,* Mexico, 1969; English trans: *Hallucinations,* New York, 1971); thus I will limit myself to a few random indications:

On Dávalos (and Unánue, Valdés, etc.):

Lastres, Juan B. *La cultura peruana y la obra de los médicos en la emancipación.* Lima, 1954.

On Salas:

Eyzaguirre, Jaime. "D. Manuel de Salas procesado por la Inquisición." *Boletín de la Academia Chilena de la Historia,* 57, no. 2 (1957), pp. 32–46.

On Unánue:

Paz Soldan, C. E. *Himnos a Hipólito Unánue.* Lima, 1955.
Salazar Bondy, Augusto. "H. Unánue en la polémica sobre América." *Documenta* (Lima), 2, no. 1 (1949–50), pp. 395–413.

On Iturri and Muñoz:

Catálogo de la Colección de don Juan Bautista Muñoz. Vol. 1. Prologue by A. Ballesteros Beretta. Madrid, 1954.
Furlong, Guillermo, S.I. "El santafecino Francisco Iturri y el ecuatoriano Antonio de Alcedo." *Historia* (Buenos Aires), 8 (1957), pp. 87–92.
Muro Orejón, A. J. B. M. "Las fuentes bibliográficas de la Historia del Nuevo Mundo." *Anuario de Estudios Americanos* (Seville), 10 (1953), pp. 265–337.

On a presumed collaborator of Iturri:

Furlong, Guillermo, S. J. *Gaspar Juarez, S. I., y sus Noticias Filologicas (1789).* Buenos Aires, 1954.

Another Jesuit expelled from the Plata was:

Falkner, Thomas. *A Description of Patagonia and the Adjoining Parts of South America.* Hereford, 1774 (rpt. in facsimile, with notes by A. E. S. Neumann, Chicago, 1935; brief comments on this work can be found in Samuel S. Trifilo, "British Travel Accounts on Argentina before 1818," *Journal of Inter-American Studies,* 2, no. 3 [July 1960], pp. 246–48).

On Moxó:

Razquin Febregat, F. "El dr. D. Benito de Moxó y de Francolí, último arzobispo de Charcas." *Ilerda* (Lérida), 3 (1945), pp. 7-50.

The ideas contained in a work dedicated to Unánue and written by one of his followers could well prove interesting, but I have not seen:

Brandin, Abel Victorino. *De la influencia de los diferentes climas del Universo sobre el Hombre y en particular de la influencia de los climas de la América Meridional.* Lima, 1826.

The following deal with Caldas:

Bateman, A. D. *F. J. de Caldas.* Hojas de Cultura Popular Colombiana, no. 50. Bogotà, 1955.
Bubach, E. "El influjo del ambiente en don Francisco Caldas y su transcendencia." *Revista de la Universidad del Cauca* (Popayan), 22 (1955), pp. 63-76.
Murillo, L. M. "La Patria, la sabiduria y el sacrificio de Fr. J. de Caldas." *Boletín de Historia y Antigüedades* (Bogotá), 37 (1950), pp. 421-31.

And on Mier one should see at least what Alfonso Reyes has to say in his *Reloj de Sol* (and in his *Obras completas,* III, 433-42), the articles in the *Hispanic American Historical Review* (1932), and the *Cuadernos Americanos* (September–October 1943), in addition to the anthology edited by Edmundo O'Gorman (1945), the essay dealing with Mier by O'Gorman again in his *Seis estudios históricos de tema mexicano* (Universidad Veracruzana, Biblioteca de la Facultad de Filosofia y Letras, no. 7; Xalopa, Mexico, 1960), and:

Hadley, Bedford K. "The Enigmatic Padre Mier." Dissertation, University of Texas, ca. 1955.
La Maza, Francisco de. *El guadalupanismo mexicano.* Mexico, 1953.
Lombardi, John V. *The Political Ideology of Fray Servando Teresa Mier, Propagandist for Independence.* Cuernavaca, 1968.
Mendirachaga Cueva. "Apellidos de Nueva León: Guerra, apellido materno de Fray Servando." *Abside,* 22, no. 4 (1958), pp. 417-38.

On the influence of Jean-Jacques Rousseau in Argentina:

Ruiz Güinazú, E. *Epifania de la Libertad: Documentos secretos de la Revolución de Mayo.* Buenos Aires, 1952.

On Cecilio del Valle the following seem to offer some promise:

Baumgartner, Louis E. *José del Valle of Central America.* Durham, N.C., 1963.
Guandique, J. S. "J. C. del Valle, precursor de la sociologia centro-americana." *Estudios Centroamericanos* (San Salvador), 2 (1947), pp. 11-16.
Lavin, Pablo F. "J. C. del Valle, un panamericanista." *Americas* (Washington, D.C.), 17, no 9 (September 1965), pp. 7-9.
Parker, Franklin Dallas. *J. C. del Valle and the Establishment of the Central American Confederation.* Tegucigalpa, 1954.
Peraza, J. Antonio. *Luz y espíritu de d. J. C. del Valle.* San José de Costa Rica, 1954.
Perez Cadalso, Eliseo. *J. C. del Valle, apóstol de América.* Tegucigalpa, 1954.
Picado, T. "Valle y el sistema americano." *Novedades* (Managua), 4 March 1950.
Reina Valenzuela, J. "Actualidad de J. C. del Valle." *La Pajarita de Papel* (Tegucigalpa), 2, pp. 7-8.
——. *José Cecilio del Valle y las ciencias naturales.* Tegucigalpa, 1946.
Valle, Rafael Heliodoro. *Cartas de Bentham a J. C. del Valle.* Mexico, 1942.

CHAPTER 7: HEGEL AND HIS CONTEMPORARIES

Among the really innumerable works dealing with the authors in this chapter I will mention only those few which I think touch on at least some of the points I have treated.

On the repercussions of the American Revolution in Italy:

Goggio, E. "Italy and the American War of Independence." *Romanic Review,* 20 (1929), pp. 25-34.
Procacci, G. "La storiografia italiana sulla rivoluzione americana nel corso del Risorgimento." Paper read to the 22nd National Congress on the History of the Risorgimento, Florence, 9-12 September, 1953.

On the (literary) repercussions in Germany there are a dozen articles listed by Henry S. King, op. cit., pp. v-vi, who used almost all of them in his modest review.

On Kant:

Adickes, E. *Untersuchungen zu Kants Physische Geographie.* Tübingen, 1911.
Laing, B. M. "Kant and Natural Science." *Philosophy,* 19 (1944), pp. 216–32.

On French emigration to America:

Carré, Henri. *Les émigrés français en Amérique, 1789–93.* Paris, 1898.
Child, Frances S. "French Refugee Life in the United States, 1790–1800." Dissertation, Columbia University, 1940.

On Volney:

Chinard, Gilbert. *Volney et l'Amérique.* Paris, 1924.

On Chateaubriand:

Butor, Michel. "Chateaubriand et l'ancienne Amérique." In *Répertoire II,* Paris.
Le Hir, Y. "Chateaubriand et la langue des Hurons." *Revue de littérature comparée,* 42, no. 1 (January–March 1968), pp. 103–04.
Moreau, Pierre. "Chateaubriand en Amérique." *Revue des Cours et Conférences,* 25, no. 2 (1924), pp. 408–16, 568–74.

On an author we have not considered:

Baldensperger, Fernand. "Les Etats-Unis d'Amérique dans la vie et les idées de Vigny." *Revue de littérature comparée,* 3 (1923), pp. 616–35.

On Goethe's interest in America and, reciprocally, America's interest in Goethe, there is a profusion of studies; but most of them, fortunately, appear to be included in or superseded by such recent works as I have been able to read:

Grueningen, J. P. von. "Goethe in American Periodicals, 1860–1900." *PMLA,* 50 (1935), pp. 1155–64.
Hellersberg-Wendriner, Anna. "America in the World View of the Aged Goethe." *Germanic Review,* 14 (1939), pp. 270–76.
Klenze C. von. "Das amerikanische Goethebild." *Mitteilungen der deutschen Akademie* (1933), pp. 184–210.
Mackall, L. L. "Briefwechsel zwischen Goethe und Amerikanern." *Goethe Jahrbuch,* 25 (1904).
Mühlberger, Josef. "Goethe und Amerika." *Welt und Wort,* 4, no. 1 (January 1949), pp. 1–7.
Schönemann, F. "Goethe in Amerika." *Zeitschrift für französischen und englischen Unterricht,* 31 (1932).
Schreiber, Carl F. "Goethe und Amerika." *Jahrbuch der Goethegesellschaft,* 15 (1929), pp. 233 ff.
Sell, Friedrich E. "American Influence upon Goethe." *American-German Review,* 9, no. 4 (April 1943), pp. 15–17.
Wadepuhl, Walter. "Goethe und Amerika." *Deutsch-amerikanische Geschichtsblätter* (Chicago), 22–23 (1924).
———. "Amerika, du hast es besser." *Germanic Review,* 7 (1932), pp. 186–91.
———. *Goethe's Interest in the New World.* Jena, 1934.
White, Horatio S. "Goethe und Amerika." *Goethe Jahrbuch,* 5 (1884).
Wukadinovic, Spiridion. *Goethes Novelle, "Der Schauplatz," Coopersche Einfluss.* Halle, 1909.

On Lenau my shortcomings are certainly more serious. I have not seen either certain writings dealing specifically with Lenau and America, such as:

Baker. "Lenau and Young Germany in America." Dissertation, Baltimore, 1897.
Blankenagel, J. C. "Deeds to Lenau's Property in Ohio." *Germanic Review,* 2 (1927), pp. 202–12.
Knortz, Karl. *Die Christliche Kommunistiche Kolonie der Rappisten in Pennsylvanien und neue Mittheilungen über Lenaus Aufenthalt unter den Rappisten.* Leipzig, 1892.
Mulfinger, G. A. "Lenau in America." *Americana-Germanica,* 1, nos. 1–2 (1897), pp. 1–61.
Roustan, L. "Le séjour de Lenau en Amérique." *Revue de littérature comparée,* 8 (1928), pp. 62–86.

nor others, which might well prove useful for a better understanding of his attitudes:

Klenze, C. von. *The Treatment of Nature in the Works of Lenau.* Chicago, 1902.
Korr, A. *Lenau's Stellung zur Naturphilosophie.* Münster, 1932.

nor, finally, others which discuss Kürnberger's novel, inspired (supposedly) by Lenau's American experience:

Kohlschmidt, W. "Kürnberger's Lenauroman *Der Amerikamüde.*" *Zeitschrift für deutsche Bildung,* 19 (1943).
Meyer, Hildegard. *Nord-Amerika im Urteil des deutschen Schrifttums bis zur Mitte des 19 Jahrhunderts: Eine Untersuchung über Kürnbergers "Amerikamüden" mit einer Bibliographie.* Hamburg, 1929.
Mulfinger, G. A. *Kürnberger's Roman "Der Amerikamüde."* Philadelphia, 1903 (first published in *German-American Annals,* n.s. 1, nos. 6–7, with the title: "F. Kürnberger's Roman '*Der Amerikamüde,*' dessen Quellen und Verhältnis zu Lenau's Amerikareise").

Nor is this all. The literature on the German emigration to America is considerable and would certainly offer interesting research possibilities (see, for example, for the period 1815–50, Gollwitzer, op. cit., pp. 335–37). More generally I am conscious of having somewhat neglected the reflections of the New World in German literature. I have not seen:

Barba, P. A. "Emigration to America Reflected in German Fiction." *German-American Annals,* 12.
Breffka, C. *Amerika in der deutschen Literatur.* Cologne, 1917.
Desczyk, Gerhard. *Amerika in der Phantasie deutscher Dichter.* Chicago, 1925.
Efroymson, Clarence W. "An Austrian Diplomat in America, 1840." *American Historical Review,* 41 (1935–36), pp. 503–14.
Goebel, J. "Amerika in der deutschen Dichtung." In *Forschungen zur deutschen Philologie: Festgabe für R. Hildebrand.* Leipzig, 1894.
———. "Amerika in der Phantasie deutscher Dichter." *Jahrbuch der deutsch-amerikanische Gesellschaft* (Illinois), 1924–25.
Grundt, J. *Die Aristokratie in Amerika.*
Jones, Howard Mumford. "The Colonial Impulse: An Analysis of the "Promotion" Literature of Colonization." *Proceedings of the American Philosophical Society,* 90 (1946), pp. 131–61.
Julius, Nicolaus Heinrich. *Verzeichnis einer während 40 Jahren in Europa und Amerika zusammengebrachten Bibliothek.* Berlin, 1850.
Kapp, Friedrich. "Zur deutschen wissenschaftlichen Literatur über die Vereinigten Staaten von Amerika." *Historische Zeitschrift,* 31 (1874), pp. 241–88.
Kohn, Maximilian. "Amerika im Spiegel deutscher Dichtung." *Zeitgeist,* 32 (1905).
Pochmann, Henry A. *German Culture in America: Philosophical and Literary Influences, 1600–1900.* Madison, Wis., 1957.
Schroeder, Samuel. "Amerika in der deutschen Dichtung von 1850–90." Dissertation, Heidelberg, 1936.
Weber, Paul. C. *America in Imaginative German Literature in the First Half of the Nineteenth Century.* New York, 1926.

Nor, on immigrants into the United States:

Curti, M, and Birr, K. "The Immigrant and the American Image in Europe, 1860–1914." *The Mississippi Valley Historical Review,* 37 (1950), pp. 203–20.
Thwaites, Reuben G., ed. *Early Western Travels, 1784–1846.* Cleveland, 1904–07.

And I have seen very little of other German authors who, like Kürnberger, dealt with American themes. On Karl Postl, better known under the pseudonym of Charles Sealsfield, these would seem to be of some interest:

Dallman, W. P. "The Spirit of America as Interpreted in the Works of Sealsfield." Dissertation, St. Louis, 1937.
Djordjewitsch, M. *Sealsfield's Auffassung des Amerikanertums und seine literarhistorische Stellung.* Weimar, 1931.

Other references can very easily be extracted from the monumental work of Eduard Castle (see Bibliography of Works Cited).

On May one should see at least:

May, Klara. *Mit Karl May durch Amerika.* Radebuhl, 1932.

And on Gerstäcker:

O'Donnell, G. H. R. "Gerstäcker in America, 1837–43." *PMLA,* 42 (1927), pp. 1036–43.
Prahl, A. J. "America in the Works of Gerstäcker." *Modern Language Quarterly* (Seattle), 4, no. 2 (June 1943), pp. 213–24.

But it would certainly be more profitable to delve further into the reactions of the North American scientists around 1800, looking at the original texts, such as:

Clinton, De Witt. *Introductory Discourse, Delivered Before the Literary and Philosophical Society of New York, on the 4th of May, 1814.* New York, 1814.
Williamson, Hugh. *Observations on the Climate in Different Parts of America.* New York, 1811.

in addition to the works of Barton (see above, p. 403) and Samuel Stanhope Smith (p. 245).

On Humboldt there is an article with a promising title which I have not seen:

Humboldt, A. von. "Über die Urvölker von Amerika." *Neue Berlinische Monatsschrift,* 15 (1806).

Nor have I read an old book on Hegel:

Barth, Paul. *Die Geschichtsphilosophie Hegels und der Hegelianer.* Leipzig, 1890.

nor the recent study:

O'Gorman, Edmundo. "Hegel y el moderno panamericanismo." *Revista de la Universidad de la Habana,* 22 (1939) (rpt. in *Letras de México,* 2, no. 8).

But with regard to Hegel, is it really worth mentioning a mere couple of the innumerable omissions?

CHAPTER 8: THE DISPUTE'S TRIVIALIZATION AND OBSTINATE VITALITY

This field too is boundless. I can only list some useful or necessary "complements" to the bibliography cited.

On Scheffel:

Burfila, Herm. J. V. von Scheffel als Politiker. 1925.
Krieger, Bogdan. *Scheffel als Student.* Stuttgart, 1926.

On Comte:

Hawkins, Richmond L. *Auguste Comte and the United States (1816-1853).* Cambridge, Mass., 1936.

On Stendhal:

Brown, Gordon. *Les idées politiques et religieuses de Stendhal.* Paris, 1939.
Brussaly, Manuel. *The Political Ideas of Stendhal.* New York, 1933.
Dumolard, Henry. "Stendhal et la politique." *Annales de l'Université de Grenoble,* 1929, no. 2, pp. 123-67.
Leroy, Maxime. *Stendhal politique.* Paris, 1929.
Marshall, James F. *Stendhal and America.* Ph.D. dissertation, University of Illinois, 1948. Summarized in *French-American Review,* 10-12 (1949), pp. 240-67.
Siler, James H. "Stendhal et l'Amérique." *Le Divan,* 39 (1947), pp. 131-34.

On Captain Hall:

Chinard, Gilbert. "Alexis de Tocqueville et le capitaine Basil Hall." *Bulletin de l'Institut Français de Washington,* 15 (December 1946), pp. 9-18.

On the Trollopes, mother and son, see the copious bibliography cited in the Smalley edition of *Domestic Manners,* pp. 444-53, and the Smalley-Booth edition of *North America* (see Bibliography of Works Cited), together with:

Griffin, R. A. "Mrs. Trollope and the Queen City." *The Mississippi Valley Historical Review,* 37 (1950), pp. 289-302.
Harlow, A. *The Serene Cincinnatians.* Society in America Series. New York, 1950.
Thorp, Willard, and Drinker, Henry S. *Two Addresses Delivered to Members of the Grolier Club* ("Trollope's America" and "The Lawyers of A. Trollope.") New York, 1950.

And perhaps, for possible comparisons and parallels:

Abdy, E. S. *Journal of a Residence and Tour in the United States of North America, from April, 1833, to October, 1834.* London, 1835.

On Miss Martineau:

Lipset, Seymour Martin. *Revolution and Counterrevolution.* London, 1969.
Petzold, Gertrud von. *Harriet Martineau und ihre sittlich-religiöse Weltschau.* Bochum-Langendreer, 1941.
Webb, R. K. *Harriet Martineau.* London, 1960.

On Dickens:

Cairo Guide. Compiled and written by FWP (Federal Writers Project). Cairo, Ill., 1938.
Lansden, John M. *A History of the City of Cairo, Ill.* Chicago, 1910.
Wilkins, William Glyde, ed. *Dickens in America.* London, 1911.

On Emerson:

Anzilotti, Rolando. "Emerson in Italia." *Rivista di letterature moderne e comparate,* 11, no. 1 (March 1958), pp. 3–14.

On Melville:

Sealts, Merton M., Jr. "Melville's Reading: A Checklist of Books Owned and Borrowed" (Pt. III, cont.). *Harvard Library Bulletin,* 3, no. 2 (Spring 1949), pp. 268–77.

On Thoreau I would like to see:

Keiser, Albert. "Thoreau's Manuscript on the Indians." *Journal of English and Germanic Philology,* 27 (1928), pp. 183–99.

And on Whitman:

Boatright, Mody C. "Whitman and Hegel." *University of Texas Studies in English,* 9 (1929).
Falk, R. P. "Walt Whitman and German Thought." *Journal of English and Germanic Philology,* 40 (July 1941), pp. 315–30.
Fulghum, W. B., Jr. "Whitman's Debt to Joseph Gostwick." *American Literature,* 12 (January 1941), pp. 491–97.
Muirhead, J. H. "How Hegel came to America." *Philosophical Review,* 37 (1928), pp. 226–40.
Schyberg, Frederik. *Walt Whitman.* Copenhagen, 1933.
Sussman, Herbert L. *Victorians and the Machine: The Literary Response to Technology.* Cambridge, Mass., 1968.
"W. Whitman and the Germans." *German-American Annals,* 1906.

and the "definitive" biography by Gay Wilson Allen, *The Solitary Singer: A Critical Biography of Walt Whitman* (New York, 1955).

On James the bibliography is boundless: my curiosity has been aroused by the title and a review of Peter Buitenhuis, *The Grasping Imagination: The American Writings of Henry James* (Toronto, 1970). And one should also perhaps examine:

Clark, Harry H. *The Idea of Progress in American Literature.* New York, 1951.
Ekirch, Arthur Alphonse, Jr. *The Idea of Progress in America.* New York, 1944.

The latest manifestations of de Pauwism and of anti-de Pauwism could be documented and illustrated with hundreds, indeed thousands of newspaper cuttings and periodical articles. I will make do with mentioning, since I discussed Papini, the rejoinder of the Columbian humanist:

Sanín Cano, B. "G. Papini y la cultura latinoamericana." *Revista de La Habana,* 5 (1947), pp. 403–10.

The silence in Donald Heiney's *America in Modern Italian Literature,* New Brunswick, N.J., 1965, furnishes convincing if negative proof of the complete oblivion suffered by the Buffon-de Pauwian theses in our own times (a single reference to the landscape of the United States being "without savor, without mountains, without surprise," in Giuseppe Cassari: ibid., p. 144).

But the theme of the ideological relations between the two worlds has in fact never been so alive as it is today. Suffice it to indicate, among the recent discussions:

Baron, S. W. *People and Americans: A Memoir of Transatlantic Tourists.* London, 1953.
Burnham, J., ed. *What Europe Thinks of America.* New York, 1953.

and to recall that almost all the frequent congresses of the last few years that have been devoted to the relations between the two worlds have produced fragments of de Pauwian themes and distorted echoes of ancient rejoinders, borne on the current or swept up in the polemic vortex of more recent but no less fatuous boasts, reciprocal fears, and contrite (if not hypocritical) self-searchings.

CHAPTER 9: SUPPLEMENTS AND DIGRESSIONS

In section one, before considering Father Acosta and Father Cobo, one should examine the ideas of Las Casas, on whom see:

Alvarez Lopez, E. "El saber de la naturaleza en el Padre Las Casas." *Boletin de la Real Academia de la Historia* (Madrid), 132 (1953), pp. 201–29.

On the attempts to explain how the Americas were populated, and the existence of certain animal and vegetable species there, see Carroll L. Riley et al., eds., *Man Across the Sea: Problems of Pre-Columbian Contacts*, Austin, Texas, 1971.

Section two might profit from a glance at:

Bates, Marston. *Where Winter Never Comes: A Study of Man and Nature in the Tropics*. New York, 1952.
Cilento, Raphael. *The White Man in the Tropics*. Melbourne, 1925.

Index

671